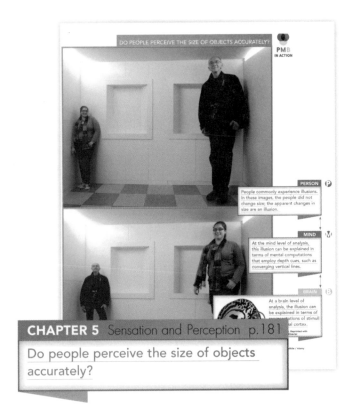

DO PEOPLE PERCEIVE THE SIZE OF OBJECTS ACCURATELY?

PM B IN ACTION

PERSON (P)

People commonly experience illusions. In these images, the people did not change size; the apparent changes in size are an illusion.

MIND (M)

At the mind level of analysis, this illusion can be explained in terms of mental computations that employ depth cues, such as converging vertical lines.

BRAIN (B)

At a brain level of analysis, the illusion can be explained in terms of representations of stimuli in the visual cortex.

CHAPTER 5 Sensation and Perception p.181

Do people perceive the size of objects accurately?

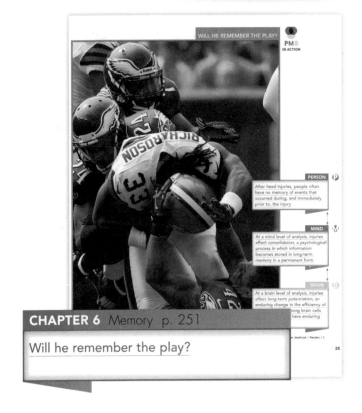

WILL HE REMEMBER THE PLAY?

PM B IN ACTION

PERSON (P)

After head injuries, people often have no memory of events that occurred during, and immediately prior to, the injury.

MIND (M)

At a mind level of analysis, injuries affect consolidation, a psychological process in which information becomes stored in long-term memory in a permanent form.

BRAIN (B)

At a brain level of analysis, injuries affect long-term potentiation, an enduring change in the efficiency of connections among brain cells that may have enduring.

CHAPTER 6 Memory p. 251

Will he remember the play?

25

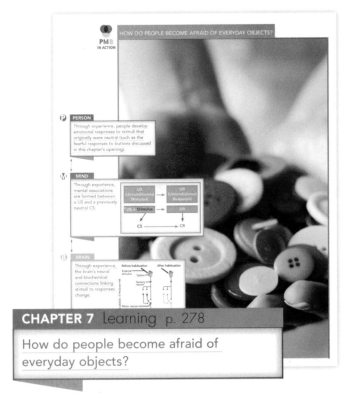

HOW DO PEOPLE BECOME AFRAID OF EVERYDAY OBJECTS?

PM B IN ACTION

(P) **PERSON**

Through experience, people develop emotional responses to stimuli that originally were neutral (such as the fearful responses to buttons discussed in this chapter's opening).

(M) **MIND**

Through experience, mental associations are formed between a US and a previously neutral CS.

US (Unconditioned Stimulus) → UR (Unconditioned Response)

US + Stimulus → UR

CS → CR

(B) **BRAIN**

Through experience, the brain's neural and biochemical connections linking stimuli to responses change.

CHAPTER 7 Learning p. 278

How do people become afraid of everyday objects?

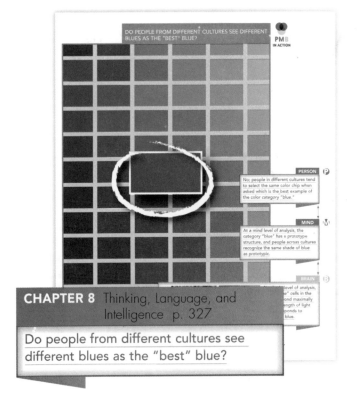

DO PEOPLE FROM DIFFERENT CULTURES SEE DIFFERENT BLUES AS THE "BEST" BLUE?

PM B IN ACTION

PERSON (P)

No; people in different cultures tend to select the same color chip when asked which is the best example of the color category "blue."

MIND (M)

At a mind level of analysis, the category "blue" has a prototype-structure, and people across cultures recognize the same shade of blue as prototypic.

BRAIN (B)

At a brain level of analysis, "blue" cells in the brain respond maximally to the wavelength of light that corresponds to the best blue.

CHAPTER 8 Thinking, Language, and Intelligence p. 327

Do people from different cultures see different blues as the "best" blue?

PMB In Action Figures

CHAPTER 9 Consciousness p. 377

What is conscious experience like?

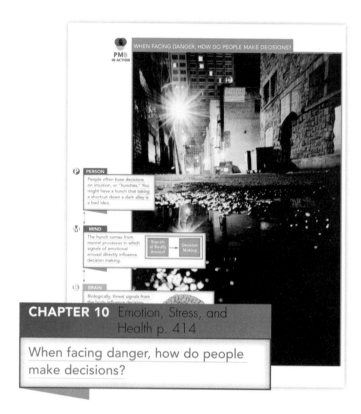

CHAPTER 10 Emotion, Stress, and Health p. 414

When facing danger, how do people make decisions?

CHAPTER 11 Motivation p. 498

Do environmental stimuli control people's motivation?

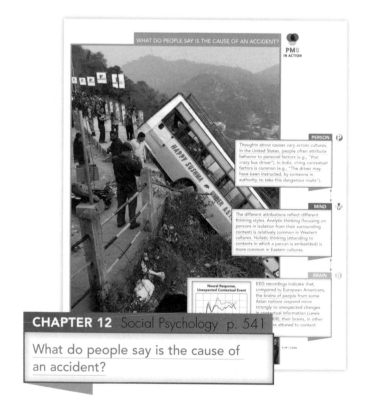

CHAPTER 12 Social Psychology p. 541

What do people say is the cause of an accident?

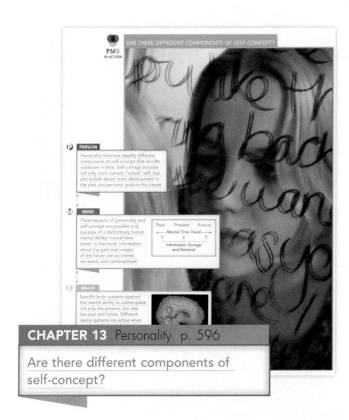

PMB IN ACTION

PERSON

Personality theorists identify different components of self-concept that involve variations in time. Self-concept includes not only one's current, "actual" self, but also beliefs about one's development in the past and personal goals in the future.

MIND

These aspects of personality and self-concept are possible only because of a distinctively human mental ability: mental time-travel. In the mind, information about the past and images of the future can be stored, retrieved, and contemplated.

Past   Present   Future
|←— Mental Time Travel —→|
Information Storage and Retrieval

BRAIN

Specific brain systems support the mental ability to contemplate not only the present, but also the past and future. Different neural systems are active when

CHAPTER 13 Personality p. 596

Are there different components of self-concept?

PMB IN ACTION

PERSON

At a person level of analysis, self-control is an ability to work toward goals, avoid distractions, and suppress unwanted emotional reactions. It first develops in childhood. Individual differences in childhood self-control abilities predict self-control abilities in later life.

MIND

At a mind level of analysis, self-control ability reflects the workings of interconnected mental systems that are concerned with attention and executive control.

Attention
Which Stimuli Are Important

Executive Control
What Are My Goals
What Can I Do To Reach Them

BRAIN

At a brain level of analysis, the abilities reflect interconnections (in red circle) between brain regions, which grow stronger across development.

CHAPTER 14 Development p. 617

How do people develop control over their own behavior?

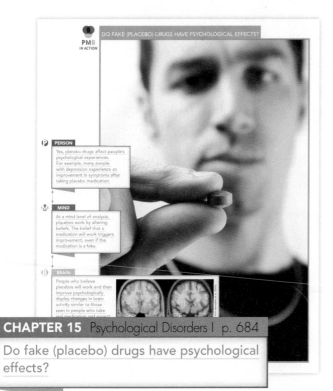

PMB IN ACTION

PERSON

Yes, placebo drugs affect people's psychological experiences. For example, many people with depression experience an improvement in symptoms after taking placebo medication.

MIND

At a mind level of analysis, placebos work by altering beliefs. The belief that a medication will work triggers improvement, even if the medication is a fake.

BRAIN

People who believe placebos will work and then improve psychologically display changes in brain activity similar to those seen in people who take

CHAPTER 15 Psychological Disorders I p. 684

Do fake (placebo) drugs have psychological effects?

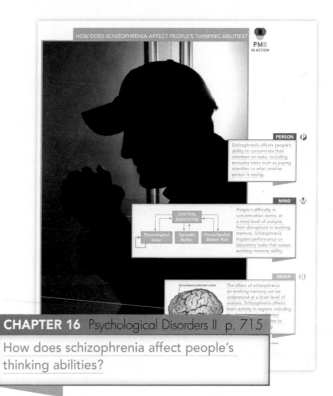

PMB IN ACTION

PERSON

Schizophrenia affects people's ability to concentrate their attention on tasks, including everyday tasks such as paying attention to what another person is saying.

MIND

People's difficulty in concentration stems, at a mind level of analysis, from disruptions in working memory. Schizophrenia impairs performance on laboratory tasks that assess working memory ability.

CENTRAL EXECUTIVE
Phonological Loop   Episodic Buffer   Visuo-Spatial Sketch Pad

BRAIN

Dorsolateral prefrontal cortex

The effect of schizophrenia on working memory can be understood at a brain level of analysis. Schizophrenia affects brain activity in regions including the dorsolateral prefrontal cortex, a brain region central to

CHAPTER 16 Psychological Disorders II p. 715

How does schizophrenia affect people's thinking abilities?

The woman in our cover image, a drawing by Spanish artist Juan Francisco Casas, is intent; she perceives with a purpose—to learn, one might guess, about the social world and her place in it. Casas's creation vividly illustrates three features of *Psychology: The Science of Person, Mind, and Brain:*

The Target of Study: As British psychologist Hans Eysenck put it, psychology is about people: thinking, feeling, self-aware individuals whose minds and brains give them the power to keenly observe the world—and themselves.

The Scientific Strategy: Psychology is built on scientific observation. The first step in constructing the science is not to speculate idly about human nature; it is to carefully observe people. Advice from the great Austrian philosopher Ludwig Wittgenstein sums up the strategy: "Don't think, but look!"

Our Invitation to the Reader: You are a keen observer of the social world. You have important insights about the topics addressed in this book. Use them! Join us, the author team and the global community of psychological scientists, as we look into the powers of brain and mind and the complexities of persons' lives: the phenomena that make psychology the most compelling of twenty-first-century sciences.

Psychology
The Science of Person, Mind, and Brain

Daniel Cervone
University of Illinois at Chicago

Tracy L. Caldwell
Dominican University, pedagogical author

WORTH
PUBLISHERS

A Macmillan Education Imprint
New York

Publisher: Rachel Losh
Senior Acquisitions Editor: Daniel DeBonis
Development Editors: Cathy Crow, Mimi Melek
Assistant Editor: Nadina Persaud
Editorial Assistant: Katie Pachnos
Marketing Manager: Katherine Nurre
Marketing Assistant: Allison Greco
Executive Media Editor: Rachel Comerford
Director of Editing, Design, and Media Production
    for the Sciences and Social Sciences Tracey Kuehn
Managing Editor: Lisa Kinne
Senior Production Editor: Vivien Weiss
Production Manager: Sarah Segal
Photo Editor: Bianca Moscatelli
Photo Research: Elyse Rieder; Rona Tuccillo
Art Director: Diana Blume
Interior and Cover Designer: Babs Reingold
Art Manager: Matthew McAdams
Illustrations: Evelyn Pence; Raised Media
Composition: TSI evolve
Printing and Binding: RR Donnelley
Cover Art: Juan Francisco Casas

Library of Congress Preassigned Control Number: 2014952936

ISBN-10: 1-4292-2083-X
ISBN-13: 978-1-4292-2083-5

Printed in the United States of America

First printing

Worth Publishers
41 Madison Avenue
New York, NY 10010
www.worthpublishers.com

Prepared with TLC for the future of psychology:
The Intro Psych student

Macmillan Education Archive

DANIEL CERVONE is Professor of Psychology at the University of Illinois at Chicago. He earned his BA at Oberlin College and his PhD from Stanford University, where he was a student of Albert Bandura. He has held visiting faculty positions at the University of Washington and the University of Rome "La Sapienza," and has been a Fellow at the Center for Advanced Study in the Behavioral Sciences.

In addition to introductory psychology, Dan teaches courses in personality psychology, social cognition, and research methods to the diverse student body at UIC. He is graduate advisor to students in both social/personality and clinical psychology in UIC's doctoral program in psychology, and serves as a Fellow in UIC's undergraduate Honors College.

Dan is the author of a graduate-level and undergraduate texts in personality, and co-editor of four volumes in personality science. He has published numerous scientific articles, primarily in the study of social-cognitive processes and personality. He has also served as the Program Chairperson of the annual convention of the Association for Psychological Science on three occasions and is the U.S.-based Chairperson of the inaugural International Convention of Psychological Science.

Macmillan Education Archive

TRACY L. CALDWELL (Pedagogical Author) is Associate Professor of Psychology at Dominican University, where she was recently appointed a Diversity Fellow. She earned her BA at The College of New Jersey and her PhD in personality and social psychology from the University of Illinois at Chicago. Tracy teaches introductory psychology, as well as personality psychology, social psychology, the psychology of gender, and research methods and statistics. She has also taught seminars in social cognition and the psychology of romantic relationships. She is the faculty advisor for Dominican University's Psychology Club and Dominican University's chapter of Psi Chi, the International Honors Society in Psychology.

Tracy has published articles on a variety of topics, including how stereotypes are formed, how people with a repressive coping style process threat, and how to best assess humor styles. She currently conducts research on the scholarship of teaching and learning, sex differences in the attractiveness of humor in romantic relationships, and the efficacy of accommodating learning styles.

Contents in Brief

An Alternative Contents in Brief

The *Brain, Mind,* and *Person* parts of this book are modular; the parts, and the individual chapters within them, do not depend on information introduced beyond Chapters 1 and 2 and thus can be covered in any order. This gives instructors the option of taking alternative approaches to the course, such as the *Person, Mind,* and *Brain* organization suggested below.

Contents

Gallery Stock

Gallery Stock

S4M / Getty Images

Gallery Stock

Chapter 7   Learning   259

Gallery Stock

Chapter 8   Thinking, Language, and Intelligence   307

Gallery Stock

Loyall Sewall / Gallery Stock

Maya Almeida / Gallery Stock

Gallery Stock

H&D Zielske / Gallery Stock

Chapter 13 Personality   549

Michael Prince / Gallery Stock

Hugh Arnold / Gallery Stock

Amani Willett / Gallery Stock

Chapter 16 Psychological Disorders II: Schizophrenia, Personality Disorders, and Dissociative Disorders   703

Erin Mulvehill

Preface

A CONVERSATION WITH A COLLEAGUE LAUNCHED THIS BOOK. She said that, a couple weeks into the semester, a student in her introductory psychology class had asked, "Why are we learning about biology? I signed up for a psychology course."

This, we realized, was a very good question.

The student understood the biology. But he couldn't relate the biological facts—about brain cells, biochemicals, neural pathways, genetic mechanisms, and so forth—to psychological ones. How could he? He had hardly learned any psychology yet.

Introductory psychology does not have to be like this. Students do not have to study genetic mechanisms before understanding the psychological qualities that people may inherit. They don't have to memorize brain structures before learning about the psychological phenomena that researchers try to understand more deeply by studying the brain. Most important, they do not have to wait until their book's closing chapters to encounter the topic of greatest interest to them: the experiences of *people,* living in a social world—a world of families, friends, relationships, ethnic groups, socioeconomic settings, and cultural practices. Fully functioning, socially embedded people need not be cordoned off into the closing chapters of an introductory psychology textbook. They could appear, front-and-center, in every chapter. Their appearance, we quickly realized, would open the door to a novel pedagogical strategy—one capable of solving numerous practical problems faced by introductory psychology instructors and their students.

Our Pedagogical Strategy

Psychology: The Science of Person, Mind, and Brain was written to execute this strategy, and thereby to improve students' learning experiences in introductory psychology. The strategy itself is relatively simple; it consists of two steps.

Levels of Analysis

The first step is a **levels-of-analysis** approach. As others have noted (e.g., Harré, 2002, Mischel, 2009), psychological scientists today work at different levels of analysis that complement one another. Much of the field is organized by three analytical levels:

1. *Person:* The whole individual, who develops as a member of groups, a society, and a culture
2. *Mind:* Mental representations, cognitive processes, and affective processes with which the cognitive processes interact
3. *Brain:* The massively interconnected neural systems that make it possible for us to have minds and to be persons

Programs of theory and research conducted at person, mind, and brain levels of analysis are not "competing perspectives." They are mutually complementary routes to scientific understanding. In combination, they make today's psychology a multifaceted yet integrated science.

A levels-of-analysis framework has two big advantages. In addition to being accurate (as a reflection of today's field), it also is intuitive. Even before taking an introductory psychology course, people (1) discuss the psychological lives of persons, (2) are familiar with the capabilities of the mind (remembering, learning, etc.), and (3) know that the biological brain is what enables them to have a mind and to be a person. *Psychology: The Science of Person, Mind, and Brain* capitalizes on people's intuitive knowledge when presenting scientific theory and research.

A "Person-First" Approach

With three levels of analysis, one has to decide where to start—the conceptual level at which to introduce topics. Many books start "at the bottom." Writers cover the anatomy and physiology of neurons before discussing the thought and feelings of persons, or detail neural pathways from the eye to the brain before describing the range of perceptual information that people acquire as they interact with the environment.

Psychology: The Science of Person, Mind, and Brain consistently starts "at the top." We introduce a *person-first* approach to introductory psychology. Individual chapters first present phenomena at a *person* level of analysis: scientific theory and research focused on the lives of persons in sociocultural contexts. Subsequent material deepens readers' understanding by exploring those phenomena more deeply, at the levels of *mind* (cognitive and affective processes) and *brain* (neural and biochemical systems). Each chapter—even the early ones, such as the chapters on the brain and nervous system, sensation and perception, and memory—executes the person-first mission.

Solving Pedagogical Problems

This two-part strategy is designed to solve practical pedagogical problems. The problems were evident to us when we first discussed the student who wondered why he was "learning about biology." They became even more evident, and more pressing, across the years during which *Psychology: The Science of Person, Mind, and Brain* was developed. In focus groups, surveys, and chapter reviews, scores of instructors throughout North America repeatedly cited the following five vexing challenges. If you're a seasoned intro psych instructor, they will be familiar to you. If you're a student about to embark on the introductory course, rest assured that these are the challenges we have worked to overcome!

(1) Enhancing Student Engagement. Students look forward to introductory psychology; it sounds like one of the most interesting courses in the curriculum. But they often come away disappointed. They hope to learn about human experiences but instead find themselves slogging through technical topics they cannot directly relate to questions about people. Many thus become less engaged.

I was one of them. When I took the course in college, I learned relatively little about what I had thought was the field's main target of investigation: people. It wasn't just that the research subjects frequently were pigeons, rats, or dogs. The larger problem was that, even when humans came into view, they were so dissected into parts—brain structures; information-processing boxes; isolated attitudes, motives, and traits—that it was difficult to glimpse the whole. The psychology of whole persons seemed like an afterthought. I, too, became less engaged.

Our person-first strategy overcomes this problem. Its unique format lets readers see, from the outset, how theories and findings throughout psychology bear on inherently intriguing questions about people. The person-first strategy is executed from the start—literally from Chapter 1, page 1, which discusses social stereotypes and their effects on students' academic performance.

Greater student engagement, in turn, enhances learning. "Interest," one researcher explains, "motivates learning about something new and complex. . . . New knowledge, in turn, enables more things to be interesting" (Silvia, 2008, p. 59). A person-first pedagogical strategy can boost both interest and achievement.

(2) Maximizing Student Comprehension. Comprehension is highest when readers possess an intellectual framework into which they can "place" new material (Kintsch, 1994). In traditional introductory psychology textbooks, students lack this intellectual framework when encountering some of the field's most technical content. The course instructor knows, for example, how neurotransmitter functioning bears on emotional experience and how neural interconnections enable conscious experience. The instructor thus can easily place biological facts into a psychological framework. But the student usually cannot. This may impede comprehension and recall of the biological facts.

Comprehension could be enhanced if introductory textbooks revisited the "lower-level" details after presenting "higher-level" findings about psychological experience and social behavior. But, in practice, this occurs infrequently; most information about the brain is confined to an early chapter of the book. As a result, students not only may be baffled by biological material at the outset of the course, but they also may never come to see how research on neural, biochemical, and genetic mechanisms deepens the understanding of psychological experience.

Psychology: The Science of Person, Mind, and Brain addresses this problem directly. Our person-first approach consistently foregrounds questions about human experience and social behavior. In chapters with substantial biological content (e.g., Chapter 3: The Brain and the Nervous System; Chapter 4: Nature, Nurture, and Their Interaction; and Chapter 5: Sensation and Perception), we begin by discussing research on the experiences of people living in a social world. This coverage provides readers with a readily comprehensible framework that facilitates their learning of subsequent material on biological mechanisms. In chapters that focus on mental processes, personal experience, or social behavior, relevant brain research is placed near the chapter's conclusion. Again, readers possess an intellectual framework that enhances their comprehension of the biologically grounded research.

(3) Coverage That Is Integrated. A third benefit of our person-first approach involves a particularly challenging goal: conveying an integrated view of psychological science as a whole. In disciplines outside of psychology, introductory courses commonly achieve this goal; I still recall how intro courses I took in college explained a field's "big picture"—its main intellectual challenges and strategies of investigation. Unfortunately, introductory psychology was an exception. There, I couldn't tell if there *was* a "big picture." Some psychologists did research with animals, others with people, and some did no research at all. In one chapter, I learned that social influences cause behavior. In another, it was elements of the mind. Elsewhere, genes, neurons, or biochemicals were the cause. No overarching conceptual framework connected the various theories and findings. Psychology seemed like a hodge-podge.

I now understand that psychology is not, in reality, a hodge-podge. Today's field is highly integrated; advances in different branches of the field commonly complement one another. The challenge is to show this to readers.

Our levels-of-analysis strategy meets this challenge. By covering a given phenomenon at each of three analytical levels, we show how diverse scientific findings converge and, in total, provide an integrated understanding of human behavior. Visual features (detailed below) complement the text by enabling readers to see, at a glance, the integrated nature of psychological science.

(4) Critical Thinking. We all want our students to think critically—not merely to absorb facts, but to acquire skills that make them critical consumers of scientific information. How can one foster critical thinking from the very outset of an introductory psychology course?

A person-first strategy promotes this goal—especially in comparison to alternative strategies. Students struggle to think critically about brain anatomy and biochemistry; when they encounter such material, they have few intuitions and are challenged merely to comprehend the basic facts. By comparison, however, students have strong intuitions about persons. By starting all chapters at a person level of analysis, *Psychology: The Science of Person, Mind, and Brain* enables instructors to engage their students in critical thinking about psychological science from the very start.

(5) Coverage That Is Up-to-Date. Finally, the person-first format facilitates coverage of psychological science that is fully up-to-date. To see this, consider a major development in the contemporary field. Back in the twentieth century, some suggested that progress in brain science would eliminate the need for psychology; neuroscientific explanations might replace psychological ones (see McCauley, 1986). Today, however, many recognize that psychological findings guide brain research. As Nobel Laureate Eric Kandel explains, "You can't understand the brain unless you understand psychology. . . . You can't do meaningful biology, particularly of the human mind, without having a good psychological background" (Kandel, 2013). Multiple subfields illustrate Kandel's point. For example, to identify brain systems underlying memory, one must first identify, at a psychological level of analysis, the different forms of memory that exist. To identify biological bases of depression, one must distinguish among psychologically distinct types of depression.

Today's hybrid fields—cognitive neuroscience, social neuroscience, affective neuroscience, cultural neuroscience—show how psychological findings guide brain research. In these fields, researchers revisit, at a *brain* level of analysis, phenomena that were first established at *person* and *mind* levels. An optimal way to teach students about these research programs is to mimic the scientific field itself: First present the psychological findings, and then revisit them through the lens of brain research. This is the essence of our person-first strategy.

Another up-to-date aspect of *Psychology: The Science of Person, Mind, and Brain* is our coverage of psychological disorders. In contemporary clinical science, investigators develop focused therapies that target particular disorders; "the overwhelming majority of randomized clinical trials in psychotherapy compare the efficacy of specific treatments for specific disorders" (Norcross & Wampold, 2011, p. 127). In the professional field, the study of therapies and the analysis of disorders thus are closely linked. However, in most introductory psychology textbooks, they are separated; books commonly review disorders and therapies in separate chapters. This separation may have been appropriate decades ago, but it is not optimal for representing the discipline today. In our coverage of psychological disorders in Chapters 15 and 16, we integrate coverage of disorders and their treatment. This enables readers to see how contemporary psychologists devise and evaluate treatments that target specific types of psychological distress.

In sum, thanks to our person-first approach, educational goals that once conflicted become complementary. Should a textbook be maximally comprehensible to students or maximally up-to-date scientifically? It can be both; the pedagogical strategy that enhances comprehension dovetails with the scientific strategy that guides today's research. Should a book aim to integrate the science or to engage student interest? Again, it can do both. By organizing coverage around levels of analysis, one can simultaneously integrate psychological science and engage students in questions about people—the inherently interesting questions that motivated them to enroll in our course in the first place.

Executing the Person-First Mission

The primary means through which *Psychology: The Science of Person, Mind, and Brain* executes its pedagogical strategy is through its novel organization of material within chapters.

Organization of Within-Chapter Coverage

Our levels-of-analysis approach shapes the organization of individual chapters in two ways.

1. Chapters that focus primarily at a *mind* or *brain* level of analysis (e.g., Chapter 6: Memory, or Chapter 3: The Brain and the Nervous System) nonetheless begin at a *person* level. Individual case studies and person-level research findings provide an introduction to material that is readily understandable and that illustrates the personal and social significance of the information-processing and biological mechanisms covered later in the chapter.

2. Chapters that focus at a *person* or *mind* level include coverage of the brain. (*Psychology: The Science of Person, Mind, and Brain* does not confine its coverage of neural systems to one chapter of the text.) The *brain* level of analysis, however, is introduced only after the psychological principals are established— which enables readers to comprehend the psychological significance of the brain research. Furthermore, the brain-level coverage reinforces the learning of psychological-level material presented previously.

Let's preview a few chapters to see how the strategy is executed:

> *Chapter 3: The Brain and the Nervous System* Most brain chapters begin with the smallest unit of analysis: the individual neuron. Unfortunately, the introductory student rarely can fathom how the functioning of a neuron relates to the psychological experiences of a person. By contrast, we begin with person-focused examples that illustrate two features of the brain as a whole: *networks* (i.e., interconnections within the brain) and *plasticity* (experience-driven changes in brain matter). Both are the focus of contemporary, cutting-edge research. Yet both make it *easier* for students to comprehend the brain and its relation to psychology, because they relate directly to everyday psychological experience. Up-to-date coverage thus goes hand-in-hand with student comprehension and engagement.

> *Chapter 4: Nature, Nurture, and Their Interaction* Chapters on nature, nurture, and genetics commonly begin by reviewing the gene's molecular structure. For many students, this is a rehash of high school biology that appears unrelated to questions about psychological experience and social behavior. We begin instead with a study of gene-by-environment interaction that shows how genes and socioeconomic settings both contribute to a well-known personal quality, intelligence. This person-focused example is scientifically up-to-date yet easily comprehensible. Students quickly grasp the psychological significance of the material in the chapter ahead.

> *Chapter 11: Motivation* All introductory psychology textbooks review motivation and basic biological needs (e.g., hunger). But much of today's science of motivation encompasses social needs, as well as socially acquired thinking processes through which people can influence their own motivational states. Our person-level focus brings the full range of motivational processes into view. This simultaneously enhances student interest (everybody is interested in influencing their own level of motivation) and yields coverage that is fully up-to-date.

> *Chapter 14: Development* Some chapters on developmental begin with biological content: the biology of conception, fetal development, and brain development in prenatal, childhood, and adolescent periods. In this format, students have difficulty connecting the biological facts to developmental *psychology* (which they haven't learned about yet). By contrast, we begin with the psychology, covering cognitive development and the brain only *after* the psychological principles are established. As a result, the chapter begins with a psychological topic of inherent interest to students; the significance of the subsequent biological material is more readily apparent to them; and material in different sections of the chapter is integrated.

The opening two chapters of *Psychology: The Science of Person, Mind, and Brain* also advance the book's unique pedagogical strategy. In Chapter 1, students see how a socially relevant problem (gender stereotypes and math performance) can be addressed at complementary person, mind, and brain levels of analysis. Chapter 2, Research Methods, covers techniques used to study the social behavior of people, the workings of the mind, and the neural and biochemical mechanisms of the brain.

Finally, *opening vignettes* are one more organizational feature that promotes the person-first mission. Unlike those of some texts, our chapter-opening vignettes are not designed merely to capture readers' attention. They serve a deeper pedagogical purpose: to introduce the chapters' main substantive themes. For example, a theme of Chapter 3, The Brain and the Nervous System, is that the brain must be understood as a network whose distinct parts are massively interconnected. The opening vignette, the story of a patient with Capgras syndrome, introduces this theme by portraying the psychological costs incurred when one of the network's connections is broken. A theme of Chapter 4, Nature, Nurture, and Their Interaction, is that biological mechanisms and environmental experience interact—so much so that even people with the same genetic makeup can differ significantly. The opening vignette introduces this theme through a story of identical triplets, one of whom differs markedly from his siblings in personality and sexual orientation. In all cases, the opening stories introduce a chapter's theme at a person level through stories of individuals or groups. The opening content is revisited within the chapter, where students see how scientific findings resolve puzzles presented in the vignette.

Chapter 1's opening vignette introduces the theme of the book. It shows students how a compelling social phenomenon, stereotype threat, can be understood at person, mind, and brain levels of analysis. As promised, students do not have to wait to encounter the lives of people living in the social world.

Modular Organization

A second means of promoting a person-first approach to introductory psychology involves the organization of the book as a whole.

The chapters of *Psychology: The Science of Person, Mind, and Brain* are arranged into four parts. After Introduction (Chapters 1 and 2), they correspond to our three levels of analysis: Brain (Chapters 3–5), Mind (Chapters 6–11), and Person (Chapters 12–16). Chapters in each part review subfields of psychology whose primary research focus is at the given level of analysis.

The parts are modular; after the completion of Chapters 1 and 2, they can be read in any order. Modularity provides flexibility—which, we find, many instructors want.

A key to the book's modularity is found in Chapter 2, Research Methods. The chapter introduces not only research designs but also methods of data collection, including methods used in cognitive science and in brain research. This coverage provides readers with background sufficient to understand phenomena and research findings presented in all later chapters of the book.

Visualizing Person, Mind, and Brain Levels of Analysis

Two features visually reinforce our levels-of-analysis approach. Both show readers how theory and research conducted at different levels of analysis—person, mind, brain (PMB)—interconnect. The features are called **PMB in Action** and **PMB Connections.**

PMB in Action integrates material found *within* each chapter of the text. This full-page feature shows how a question central to the given chapter can be understood at each of our three levels of analysis. PMB in Action synthesizes material that readers have encountered at earlier points in the chapter; earlier ideas and illustrations are brought together in one place, allowing the reader to see how research on the mind and brain deepens one's understanding of questions about people.

PMB Connections integrates material *between* chapters. Readers see how a topic addressed at a given level of analysis in one chapter is also addressed, at different levels of analysis, in other chapters. For example, in our chapter on social psychology, a PMB Connections visual highlights the personal experience of cognitive dissonance and then points to research on memory (the dissonant ideas must be stored and associated) and the brain (neural systems involved in memory and emotion must be connected) that bears on the person-level social psychological finding. Most chapters of *Psychology: The Science of Person, Mind, and Brain* contain multiple PMB Connections features; readers recurringly see how topics in different parts of the book interconnect.

Enrichment Features

Each chapter contains enrichment features that expose readers to key topics in psychological science. These features are not "boxed" and thereby segregated from the flow of text, where they may be skipped by readers. Instead, they are integrated into the narrative and placed at points where they deepen readers' understanding of overall chapter material. Our three enrichment features are *Research Toolkit, Cultural Opportunities,* and *This Just In.*

Research Toolkit

In each subfield of psychology, researchers employ specialized data-collection tools. Personality psychologists, for example, overcome limits of self-report measures via implicit measures of individual differences. Cognitive psychologists map the mental representations used in problem solving through think-aloud verbal protocols. Teaching students about such research tools is part of our educational mission. The question is, "Where should a textbook introduce these methods?"

⊕ RESEARCH TOOLKIT

Experience Sampling Methods

Psychologists often study motivation in the lab. There, they can manipulate variables experimentally to determine their impact on motivation. However, psychologists aren't fundamentally interested in motivation in laboratories. They want to know about motivation in everyday life. They thus need a research tool to measure experiences of motivation—and lack of motivation—that occur when people encounter the activities that make up their day.

A problem is that there are so many activi

In principle, researchers might videotape e a few days, assess motivation-related thoughts a complete motivational record. But this is ir research participants, and it leaves the resear information that would take ages to analyze f

What's the solution? *Hint:* You read abou

◎ CULTURAL OPPORTUNITIES

Arithmetic and the Brain

"3 + 4 = ____?" It's not a hard one; every educated person can answer the question. In fact, people almost everywhere can answer the question when it's written using these exact symbols. Arabic numerals (the written digits 0, 1, 2, 3, . . .) are used the world over.

ce the answer "7"? rrywhere. Numerals e in all cultures. So ume in all cultures,

e different parts of o groups of people, ile they were in an ng brain images to active when people

⏻ THIS JUST IN

Big Data

Suppose you want to answer the following question: *Do media reports (e.g., major stories reported in the news) affect people's everyday behavior? If, for example, the media reports on an environmental disaster, do people subsequently spend more time learning about the environment?*

A researcher's first challenge is to figure out how one could possibly answer that question. Some traditional methods are limited. For example, responses to a survey that asks people, "Does the media affect your behavior?" might not be accurate. The media might have more (or less) effect on behavior than people realize.

Making matters more difficult, the question concerns people *in general*: the tens or hundreds of millions of people who might hear the media report. How could you learn how all of them responded after hearing a piece of news?

You could do it with *big data*. "Big data" refers to the wealth of information that exists in digital records, that is, computer-based records that automatically record Internet browsing, financial transactions (e.g., shopping), and patterns of electronic communication. These "digital records of the people we call, the places we go, the things

Some textbooks compartmentalize research methods, with all discussion of methodology appearing in one early chapter. The drawback is plain to see. Early in the semester, students are unfamiliar with the substantive scientific questions that the methods are designed to answer.

Rather than compartmentalizing methods coverage, *Psychology: The Science of Person, Mind, and Brain* distributes it throughout the text. In addition to a foundational research methods chapter (Chapter 2), each subsequent chapter of the text presents a research technique germane to that chapter's topic. This is done in a **Research Toolkit** feature. Each Research Toolkit describes a scientific challenge, encourages students to think critically about it, and presents a research tool that provides a solution. The Research Toolkit thus covers methods where they can best be understood: within the context of the substantive psychological questions.

⊕ RESEARCH TOOLKIT

Cultural Opportunities

Some textbooks discuss culture in only one section of the book (e.g., within a social psychology chapter). This compartmentalization conflicts with the findings of today's psychological science. Cultural beliefs and practices shape the developing person, the mind, and the brain—and the body as a whole, as made evident by findings on nature–nurture interactions.

In order to capture these scientific advances, each chapter of *Psychology: The Science of Person, Mind, and Brain* contains an enrichment feature called **Cultural Opportunities.** It showcases findings from the study of psychology and culture that address fundamental questions in psychological science.

◎ CULTURAL OPPORTUNITIES

This Just In

We're bombarded daily—by journals, scientific organizations, and the popular press—with news of novel findings in psychological science. Many of these are incremental advances that need not be covered in introductory psychology. But some are breakthroughs that fundamentally reshape scientific understanding. We cover these breakthroughs in an enrichment feature called **This Just In.** Each chapter of the text exposes students to "just in" findings that are cutting-edge yet readily comprehensible.

In addition to providing information about recent findings, This Just In teaches a more general lesson. The introductory student needs to understand not only that psychology is a science, but also that it is a rapidly evolving one. Advances in theory and research—including the invention of novel data-collection methodologies that were entirely unavailable a generation ago—produce new knowledge at a fast pace. There is no better way of teaching this lesson than by exposing students not only to classic research paradigms of the past, but also to the methods and findings that drive today's science forward.

◖ THIS JUST IN

Integrated Media: Try This!

Psychology: The Science of Person, Mind, and Brain uniquely integrates the textbook experience with research experience. Readers take part in the methods of psychological science thanks to a feature called **Try This!**

In each chapter, readers are directed to our Web site, www.pmbpsychology.com, where they are invited to take part in a Try This! research experience. The Web site provides feedback on users' own results and compares those results with published research findings. After readers return to the text, they learn more about the research experience in their subsequent reading.

Try This! creates a uniquely active textbook experience. Readers learn—not only by reading, but also by "doing"—that psychology is a science built on a firm foundation of research results.

TRY THIS!

Research on the hippocampus and memory for spatial locations illustrates the close connection between mind and brain. Performing the specific task of spatial memory requires the use of a specialized biological tool in your brain, the hippocampus. This chapter's Try This! exercise introduces a different mental activity (one not involving memory) that also illustrates this connection. Try it now! Go to www.pmbpsychology.com. A little later on, we will discuss the activity and detail the parts of your brain that were most active when you did the exercise. ◉

Pedagogical Program

In some textbooks, the pedagogical program is literally an afterthought—an element added after the main text is written. In *Psychology: The Science of Person, Mind, and Brain,* the pedagogical program has been integrated into the text from the start by our pedagogical author, Tracy L. Caldwell. Dr. Caldwell's pedagogy is designed to enhance student engagement, to deepen readers' understanding of material, and to challenge readers to find out for themselves how much they have learned from the main text.

The pedagogy is designed around Bloom's Taxonomy of Educational Objectives, a systematic enumeration of learning objectives developed by the educational psychologist Benjamin Bloom and revised subsequently by psychologists and education researchers (Krathwohl, 2002; Munzenmaier & Rubin, 2013). The objectives move far beyond the simple first goal of retaining *knowledge* of basic facts. As Bloom's Taxonomy recognizes, course instructors want students to acquire deeper intellectual skills: *comprehending* material (interpreting its meaning and extrapolating beyond information provided), *applying* knowledge (e.g., using a concept to solve problems), *analyzing* information (breaking down complex phenomena into constituent parts), *synthesizing* material (generating a novel intellectual product by relating ideas to one another), and *evaluating* concepts and findings (judging their relative worth). These learning objectives—knowledge, comprehension, application, analysis, synthesis, and evaluation—constitute the six levels of Bloom's system (which we pursue without assuming that they comprise a strict hierarchy in which, for example, evaluation is necessarily more complex than synthesis).

Readers benefit from a range of pedagogical features that pursue various levels in this set of educational objectives:

> *Preview Questions* placed before major chapter subsections pose questions that are answered in the reading. The questions highlight for readers upcoming points that are particularly important for study and comprehension.

> *Chapter Summaries* repeat those questions and provide a set of answers that serve as a synopsis of each chapter as a whole.

> *Think About It* asks students to pause and reflect on topics from the perspective of a psychological scientist—to question theoretical claims, interpretations of research, and the generalizability of research findings across social settings and cultures.

> *In Your Life* questions that appear throughout each chapter help students identify applications of scientific material to their everyday lives. This feature reinforces the book's consistent aim of showing readers the relevance of psychological science to everyday life.

> *What Do You Know?* assessments, which appear at the end of each section, give students an opportunity to immediately test their own learning. What Do You Know? questions typically target the knowledge and comprehension levels and occasionally the analysis level of Bloom's Taxonomy of Educational Objectives.

> *Questions for Discussion* found in end-of-chapter material support the achievement of higher levels of Bloom's taxonomy—up through Level 6, Evaluation. The broad, open-ended Questions for Discussion, which can form the basis for class discussion, are a natural springboard to application, analysis, synthesis, and evaluation—the critical thinking skills that comprise higher levels of Bloom's Taxonomy.

> An end-of-chapter *Self-Test,* consisting of 15 multiple-choice questions, is designed to challenge students through the first four Bloom's Taxonomy levels.

Left/Right Organization

Preview Questions

> What is the relation between the left and right sides of the brain?
> For what functions are the left and right sides of the brain specialized?
> If the left and right sides of the brain were cut off from each other, would you have two brains? How do we know?

THINK ABOUT IT

What was the experimental design in the Little Albert experiment? Was there, in fact, an experimental design? A control group? Might Albert have started crying just from the stress of being in a lengthy experiment with two strangers and loud noises?

In your own semantic network, what is the distance between the concepts *psychology* and *fascinating*?

WHAT DO YOU KNOW?...

23. Match the personality structure on the left with the quote that exemplifies it on the right.
1. Self-efficacy belief   a. "I'd like to do some volunteer work this summer."
2. Goal   b. "Watching videos of kittens on the Internet is a poor use of my time."
3. Standard   c. "I think I'd be really good at tutoring kids in math."
24. List a few examples of how thoughts can influence feelings and of how feelings can influence thoughts.

Summary of Pedagogical Features According to Bloom's Taxonomy

	Questions for Discussion	Self-Test	What Do You Know?	Think About it	In Your Life	Preview Questions
Evaulation	■					
Synthesis	■					
Analysis		■	■			
Application						
Comprehension	■	■	■	■	■	■
Knowledge	■	■	■	■	■	■

Alignment with APA Guidelines and MCAT 2015

APA Learning Guidelines 2.0

In order to support students' undergraduate experience in psychology as well as career development, the content in *Psychology: The Science of Person, Mind, and Brain* is aligned with *The APA Guidelines for the Undergraduate Psychology Major 2.0*. These guidelines present a rigorous standard for what students should gain from foundational courses as well as the complete major. A full concordance to the APA guidelines is posted in the Resources area of LaunchPad at www.macmillanhighered.com/launchpad/Cervone1e. The Test Bank is also aligned to these guidelines, and instructors can sort questions by APA learning goal.

Goal 1: Knowledge Base in Psychology

American Psychological Association Learning Goals	Cervone, *Psychology: The Science of Person, Mind, and Brain 1e* Learning Objectives/Content
1.1 Describe key concepts, principles, and overarching themes in psychology	Ch 1
	Ch 2
	Ch 3
1.2 Develop a working knowledge of psychology's content domains	Ch 4
	Ch 5
	Ch 6
1.3 Describe applications of psychology	Ch 7
	Ch 8
	Ch 9
	Ch 10
	Ch 11
	Ch 12
	Ch 13
	Ch 14
	Ch 15
	Ch 16
	What Do You Know? features in each chapter.
	Try This! features in each chapter.
	This Just In features in Chapters 2–16.
	What Do You Know, Preview Questions assessments in each chapter.
	Self-Test assessments at end of each chapter.

Goal 2: Scientific Inquiry and Critical Thinking

American Psychological Association Learning Goals

2.1 Use scientific reasoning to interpret psychological phenomena

2.2 Demonstrate psychology information literacy

2.3 Engage in innovative and integrative thinking and problem solving

2.4 Interpret, design, and conduct basic psychological research

2.5 Incorporate sociocultural factors in scientific inquiry

Cervone, *Psychology: The Science of Person, Mind, and Brain 1e* Learning Objectives/Substantive Content

Ch 1: Today's Psychological Science: The Unity of Psychology; Scientific and Nonscientific Questions About Human Behavior; Thinking Critically About Psychological Science. Psychology as a Science of Person, Mind, and Brain. Psychology's History: Schools of Thought.

Ch 2: The Challenge of Research Methods. Research Goals and Research Designs. Data: Quantitative and Qualitative. Obtaining Scientific Evidence: Psychological and Biological. Scientific Explanation.

Ch 3: Brain and Behavior: General Principles. Zooming In on the Brain.

Ch 4: Thinking About Nature and Nurture: Two Tales. Nature, Nurture, and Individual Differences. Genes and Individual Development. Evolution and Psychology. Nature, Nurture, and the Brain.

Ch 5: Perceptual Systems. The Visual System. The Auditory System. The Olfactory System. The Gustatory System. The Haptic System. Sensation and Perception in a Social World. Attention.

Ch 6: Learning from AJ and HM. Levels of Analysis: Memory and Mind; A Three-Stage Model of Memory. Models of Knowledge Representation. Memory: Imperfect But Improvable. Memory and the Brain.

Ch 7: Classical Conditioning. Operant Conditioning. Observational Learning.

Ch 8: Categorization. Language. Language and Thought. Reasoning, Judgment, and Decision Making. Problem Solving. Mental Imagery. Intelligence.

Ch 9: Consciousness Studies in the History of Psychology. The "What" and "Who" of Consciousness. The Psychology of Consciousness. Sleep. Dreams. Altered States of Consciousness.

Ch 10: Defining Emotion and Mood. Emotion. Mood. Emotion and the Brain. Stress and Health.

Ch 11: The Variety of Motives. Biological Needs and Motivation. Achievement Needs. Social Needs. Cognition and Motivation. Motivation in Groups. Motivation and the Brain.

Ch 12: Social Behavior. Social Cognition. Culture. Social Cognition and the Brain.

Ch 13: What Is Personality? Personality Theories. Freud's Psychoanalytic Theory. Humanistic Theory. Trait Theory. Social-Cognitive Theory. Personality and the Brain.

Ch 14: Cognitive Development. Social Development: Biological and Social Foundations. Social Development Across the Life Span. Older Adulthood. Moral Development.

Ch 15: Psychological Disorders. What "Counts" as a Psychological Disorder? Therapy. Depressive Disorders. Anxiety Disorders. Obsessive-Compulsive Disorder.

Ch 16: Psychotic Disorders and Schizophrenia. Personality Disorders. Dissociative and Conversion Disorders.

Research Toolkit features in each chapter.

What Do You Know, Preview Questions assessments in each chapter.

Self-Test assessments at end of each chapter.

Goal 3: Ethical and Social Responsibility in a Diverse World

American Psychological Association Learning Objectives

3.1 Apply ethical standards to evaluate psychological science and practice

3.2 Build and enhance interpersonal relationships

3.3 Adopt values that build community at local, national, and global levels

Cervone, *Psychology: The Science of Person, Mind, and Brain 1e* Learning Objectives

Ch 1: Cultural Opportunities: Psychology Goes Global.

Ch 2: Cultural Opportunities: Back Translation. The Ethics of Research.

Ch 3: Cultural Opportunities: Arithmetic and the Brain.

Ch 4: Thinking About Nature and Nurture: Two Tales: Genes, Intelligence, Poverty, and Wealth; Cultural Practices and Biological Evolution. Cultural Opportunities: Nature, Nurture, and Cultural Beliefs.

Ch 5: Cultural Opportunities: Perceiving Absolute and Relative Size.

Ch 6: Cultural Opportunities: Autobiographical Memory.

Ch 7: Cultural Opportunities: Learning to Like Food.

Ch 8: Cultural Opportunities: Adjectives, Verbs, and Patterns of Thought. Language and Thought. This Just In: Poverty and Performance on Intelligence Tests.

Ch 9: Cultural Opportunities: Eastern Analyses of Conscious Experience.

Ch 10: Cultural Opportunities: Culturally Specific Emotions.

Ch 11: Cultural Opportunities: Choice and Motivation.

Ch 12: Social Behavior. Social Cognition. Culture. Cultural Opportunities: Social Psychology.

Ch 13: Cultural Opportunities: Self-Esteem.

Ch 14: Cultural Opportunities: Ethnic and Racial Identity.

Ch 15: What "Counts" as a Psychological Disorder: Psychological Disorder or Normal Reaction to the Environment? Therapy. Cultural Opportunities: Diagnosing Disorders.

Ch 16: Cultural Opportunities: Latah.

Goal 4: Communication

American Psychological Association Learning Objectives

4.1 Demonstrate effective writing for different purposes

4.2 Exhibit effective presentation skills for different purposes

4.3 Interact effectively with others

Cervone, *Psychology: The Science of Person, Mind, and Brain 1e* Learning Objectives

Ch 2: Research Goals and Research Designs. **Data:** Quantitative and Qualitative.

Ch 8: Language. Language and Thought.

Ch 11: Social Needs. Cognition and Motivation. Motivation in Groups. Motivation and the Brain.

Ch 12: Social Behavior. Social Cognition.

Ch 15: Therapy.

What Do You Know?, Preview Questions in each chapter.

Self-Test assessments at end of each chapter.

Goal 5: Professional Development

American Psychological Association Learning Objectives	Cervone, *Psychology: The Science of Person, Mind, and Brain 1e* Learning Objectives
5.1 Apply psychological content and skills to career goals	**Ch 1:** Today's Psychological Science: Six Contemporary Psychologists; The Diversity of Psychology.
	Ch 2: The Challenge of Research Methods. Research Goals and Research Designs. Obtaining Scientific Evidence: Psychological and Biological. The Ethics of Research.
5.2 Exhibit self-efficacy and self-regulation	**Ch 4:** Thinking About Nature and Nurture: Two Tales. Nature, Nurture, and Individual Differences.
5.3 Refine project-management skills	**Ch 6:** Learning from AJ and HM. Memory: Imperfect But Improvable.
5.4 Enhance teamwork capacity	**Ch 7:** Classical Conditioning. Operant Conditioning. Observational Learning.
	Ch 8: Language and Thought. Reasoning, Judgment, and Decision Making. Problem Solving. Intelligence.
5.5 Develop meaningful professional direction for life after graduation	**Ch 9:** The "What" and "Who" of Consciousness. Sleep. Dreams. Altered States of Consciousness.
	Ch 10: Emotion. Mood. Stress and Health.
	Ch 11: Biological Needs and Motivation. Achievement Needs. Social Needs. Cognition and Motivation. Motivation in Groups. Motivation and the Brain.
	Ch 13: What Is Personality? Personality Theories. Freud's Psychoanalytic Theory. Humanistic Theory. Trait Theory. Social-Cognitive Theory.
	Ch 14: Cognitive Development. Social Development: Biological and Social Foundations. Social Development Across the Life Span. Older Adulthood. Moral Development.
	Ch 15: Psychological Disorders. What "Counts" as a Psychological Disorder? Therapy. Depressive Disorders. Anxiety Disorders. Obsessive-Compulsive Disorder.
	Ch 16: Psychotic Disorders and Schizophrenia. Personality Disorders. Dissociative and Conversion Disorders.
	Research Toolkit features in each chapter.
	This Just In features in Chapters 2–16.

Psychology and MCAT 2015

The Medical College Admission Test (MCAT) began including test items assessing knowledge of psychology in 2015. One-fourth of the test's questions pertain to the "Psychological, Social, and Biological Foundations of Behavior," and the majority of those items address material covered in the typical introductory psychology course. The table below shows how topics covered in *Psychology: The Science of Person, Mind, and Brain* correspond to the topics enumerated in the MCAT *Preview Guide*. A complete listing of the correspondence between MCAT psychology topics and this book's contents is available for download from the Resources area of LaunchPad at www.macmillanhighered.com/launchpad/Cervone1e.

MCAT 2015 Correlation for Cervone, *Psychology: The Science of Person, Mind, and Brain* 1e

MCAT 2015 Category Content Category 6A: Sensing the environment	Cervone 1e, Correlations Section Title or Topic	Page Number
Sensory Processing		
Sensation	Chapter 5: Sensation and Perception	159–209
• Thresholds	Haptic Perception	198–199
• Weber's Law (PSY)	Haptic Perception	198
• Signal detection theory (PSY)	Perceptual Systems	161
• Sensory adaptation	Gustatory Perception	194–195
	From Skin to Brain: Biological Bases of Haptic Perception	200–201
Sensory receptors	Receptor Cells	162
• Sensory pathways	From Eye to Brain: Biological Bases of Visual Perception	179
	From Mouth to Brain: Biological Bases of Gustation	196
	The Experience of Pain	202
• Types of sensory receptors	From Eye to Brain: Biological Bases of Visual Perception	176–177
	From Nose to Brain: Biological Bases of Olfaction	192–193
	From Mouth to Brain: Biological Bases of Gustation	196
	From Skin to Brain: Biological Bases of Haptic Perception	200
	The Experience of Pain	202
Vision		
Structure and function of the eye	From Eye to Brain: Biological Bases of Visual Perception	175–179
Visual processing	From Eye to Brain: Biological Bases of Visual Perception	179–182
• Visual pathways in the brain	From Eye to Brain: Biological Bases of Visual Perception	178
• Parallel processing (PSY)	Visual Perception	165–166
• Feature detection (PSY)	Visual Perception	180–182
Hearing		
Auditory processing	From Ear to Brain: Biological Bases of Auditory Perception	187–189
• Auditory pathways in the brain	From Ear to Brain: Biological Bases of Auditory Perception	187–189
Sensory reception by hair cells (PSY)	From Ear to Brain: Biological Bases of Auditory Perception	188
Other Senses (PSY, BIO)		
Somatosensation	Gustatory Perception	194–195
• Pain perception (PSY)	The Experience of Pain	202
Taste	The Gustatory System	193–197
• Taste buds/chemoreceptors that detect specific chemicals	From Mouth to Brain: Biological Bases of Gustation	196
Smell	The Olfactory System	189–193
• Olfactory cells/chemoreceptors that detect specific chemicals	Perceiving Odors	191
• Pheromones (BIO)	Perceiving Odors	190–191
• Olfactory pathways in the brain (BIO)	From Nose to Brain: Biological Bases of Olfaction	192
Kinesthetic sense	The Kinesthetic System	201
Vestibular sense	The Kinesthetic System	201

MCAT 2015 Correlation for Cervone, *Psychology: The Science of Person, Mind, and Brain* 1e (cont'd)		
MCAT 2015 Category **Content Category 6A: Sensing the environment**	**Cervone 1e, Correlations** **Section Title or Topic**	**Page Number**
Perception		
Perception	Chapter 5: Sensation and Perception	159–209
• Bottom-up/Top-down processing	The Experience of Pain	202
• Perceptual organization (e.g., depth, form, motion, constancy)	Visual Perception	163–171
• Gestalt principles	Visual Perception Shape	170

Thanks!

I once thought I'd employ the phrase "It takes a village" in this thank-you section of the preface. But "village" now seems too small a population unit. A remarkably large number of people has contributed, directly and indirectly, to this book's production.

Jenny DeGroot and Nicholas DeGroot Cervone observed years of oddities. Most people don't bring their work computer on "vacation." Other parents were not typing rapidly during time-outs at grade school basketball games. Thanks for putting up with all that!

Thanks also to family in Florida for kindly asking, "How is your book going?" at every holiday season. On a much more serious note, during the course of the writing, our family suffered a tragic loss that was attributable to a psychological disorder. Nothing can lessen the pain of such events. But they do motivate the author to craft a textbook that might inspire some readers to enter into and eventually advance this field in a way that may improve treatments for psychological distress (a motivation reflected in this book's dedication).

Numerous individuals provided information to the author throughout the years of writing. Colleagues at the Department of Psychology at the University of Illinois at Chicago generously shared their knowledge of topics ranging from neurotransmitters to cognitive science to communities and cultures. Friends outside psychology have kept me up-to-date on relevant developments in the world of science and the world at large; in this regard, I particularly thank my professorial pal, Mr. Aninda Roy.

My experience teaching introductory psychology at UIC has greatly benefited the present work. Undergraduates' moments of comprehension and puzzlement, interest and occasional boredom provided clues as to how best to structure material. Remarkably skilled graduate teaching assistants at UIC frequently shared insights into ways of enhancing undergraduate students' engagement in, and comprehension of, psychological science.

I'd like also to acknowledge earlier academic experiences that placed me in a position to write this book. The faculty at Oberlin College provided an extraordinarily hands-on, active undergraduate experience. The Department of Psychology at Stanford University, where I earned my PhD, was a veritable Psychology Hall of Fame—except that the hall-of-famers were there, still playing, and still in their prime. It was inspiring.

Four colleagues deserve special thanks. During our years of co-authoring a graduate-level personality psychology textbook, Gian Vittorio Caprara provided me with an educational experience rivaled only by my years in college. Larry Pervin's invitation to co-author his classic undergraduate personality text presented an opportunity that proved invaluable both personally and professionally. I deeply appreciate the support, throughout the writing of this book, of Walter Mischel, whose call for an integrative science of the person is echoed throughout its pages. Finally, I had the incredible good fortune of working, in graduate school, with Albert Bandura. The essential feature of Bandura's psychology is a call for psychology to center its attention on the cognitive capabilities that make humans unique and the psychosocial experiences that are the foundation of these capabilities. Had the field paid greater attention to this message when Bandura first sounded it, a person-first intro psych textbook would not be such a novelty today.

Throughout the preparation of this book, we benefited from the insights of a large team of chapter reviewers and focus group attendees.

Carol Lynn Anderson
Bellevue College

Jessyca Arthur-Cameselle
Manhattanville College

Josh Avera
De Anza College

Jeffrey Baker
Monroe Community College

Cynthia Barkley
California State University, East Bay

Dave Baskind
Delta College

Rinad Beidas
Temple University

Joseph Benz
University of Nebraska at Kearney

Garrett Berman
Roger Williams University

Matthew Blankenship
Western Illinois University

John Broida
University of Southern Maine

Michelle Renae Byrd
Eastern Michigan University

Jessica Cail
Pepperdine University

Kevin M. Chun
University of San Francisco

Sheree Conrad
University of Massachusetts

Kristi Cordell-McNulty
Angelo State University

Ginean Crawford
Rowan University

Deanna DeGidio
Cuyahoga Community College
Eastern Campus

Christopher Dehon
Monroe Community College

Daneen Deptula
Fitchburg State University

Nick Dominello
Penn State University

Dale Doty
Monroe Community College

Curtis Dunkel
Western Illinois University

Frederick Elias
California State University, Northridge

Renee Engeln
Northwestern University

Staussa C. Ervin
Tarrant County College, South

Todd Farris
Los Angeles Valley College

Dan Fawaz
Georgia Perimeter College

Diane Feibel
University of Cincinnati—Blue Ash
College

Adam Fingerhut
Loyola Marymount University

Donna Fisher Thompson
Niagara University

Claire Ford
Bridgewater State University

Alan Fridlund
University of California, Santa Barbara

Erica Gannon
Clayton State University

Marilyn Gibbons-Arhelger
Southwest Texas State University

Bryan Gibson
Central Michigan University

Jennifer Gibson
Tarleton State University

Jamie Lynn Goldenberg
University of South Florida

Jennifer Gonder
Farmingdale State College, SUNY

Chris Goode
Georgia State University

Wind Goodfriend
Buena Vista University

Jeffrey Goodman
University of Wisconsin-Eau Claire

Cameron L. Gordon
University of North Carolina
Wilmington

Ray Gordon
Bristol Community College

Jonathan Gore
Eastern Kentucky University

Raymond J. Green
Texas A&M University-Commerce

LaShonda Greene-Burley
La Salle University

Sheila Greenlee
Christopher Newport University

Robert Guttentag
University of North Carolina at
Greensboro

Shawn Haake
Iowa Central Community College

Meara Habashi
University of Iowa

Justin David Hackett
University of Houston-Downtown

Sowon Hahn
University of Oklahoma

Carrie Hall
Miami University (OH)

Deletha Hardin
The University of Tampa

Christian L. Hart
Texas Woman's University

Mark Hauber
Hunter College

Erin Henshaw
Eastern Michigan University

Julie Hernandez
Rock Valley College

Sachi Horback
Bucks County Community College

Allen Huffcutt
Bradley University

Charles Huffman
James Madison University

Jack Kahn
Curry College

Donald Kates
College of DuPage

Julie Kiotas
Pasadena City College

Laura Kirsch
Curry College

Laura Knight
Indiana University of Pennsylvania

Tim Koeltzow
Bradley University

Gordon D. Lamb
Sam Houston State University

Mark Laumakis
San Diego State University

Natalie Lawrence
James Madison University

Marlene Leeper
Tarrant County College, Northeast

Kenneth J. Leising
Texas Christian University

Fabio Leite
The Ohio State University at Lima

Barbara Lewis
Susquehanna University

Christine Lofgren
University of California, Irvine

Nicolette Lopez
University of Texas at Arlington

Ben Lovett
Elmira College

Martha Low
Winston-Salem State University

Pamela Ludemann
Framingham State University

Margaret Lynch
San Francisco State University

Amy Lyndon
East Carolina University

Jason Lyons
Tarleton State University

Lynda Mae
Arizona State University

Thomas Malloy
Rhode Island College

Michael Mangan
University of New Hampshire

Karen Marsh
University of Minnesota Duluth

Man'Dee Kameron Mason
Tarleton State University

Dawn McBride
Illinois State University

Todd J. McCallum
Case Western Reserve University

Yvonne McCoy
Tarrant County College, Northeast

Ticily Medley
Tarrant County College, South

Ronald Mehiel
Shippensburg University

Diana Milillo
Nassau Community College

Dan Miller
Indiana University—Purdue
University Fort Wayne

Dennis Miller
University of Missouri

Robin Morgan
Indiana University Southeast

Laura Naumann
Sonoma State University

Bryan Neighbors
Southwestern University

Todd Nelson
California State University, Stanislaus

Glenda G. Nichols
Tarrant County College, South

Arthur Olguin
Santa Barbara City College

Lynn Olzak
Miami University (OH)

Charles Thomas Overstreet, Jr.
Tarrant County College, South

John Pierce
Villanova University

Thomas G. Plante
Santa Clara University

Laura Ramsey
Bridgewater State University

Heather J. Rice
Washington University in St. Louis

Vicki Ritts
St. Louis Community College, Meramec

Ronald Ruiz
Riverside City College

Shannon Rich Scott
Texas Woman's University

Sandra Sego
American International College

Gregory Shelley
Kutztown University

Teow-Chong Sim
Sam Houston State University

Jesse Tauriac
Lasell College

Paul Thibodeau
Oberlin College

Felicia Thomas
California State Polytechnic
University, Pomona

Donna Thompson
Midland College

Michelle Tomaszycki
Wayne State University

Jan Tornick
University of New Hampshire

Jose Velarde
Tarrant County College, Southeast

Jeffrey Wagman
Illinois State University

Nancy Woehrle
Wittenberg University

Brandy Young
Cypress College

Ryan Zayac
University of North Alabama

Zane Zheng
Lasell College

A huge thank-you to all of you; your efforts greatly strengthened the final product. Thanks also to Glenn and Meg Turner, Cathy Crow, and Brad Rivenburgh of Burrston House, who organized and synthesized the extensive review processes.

A remarkable team of professionals at Worth Publishers is responsible for this book's production. The energy and creativity of Senior Acquisitions Editor Dan DeBonis were crucial in bringing the project to fruition. Worth Publisher Rachel Losh, Assistant Editor Nadina Persaud, Editorial Assistant Katie Pachnos, and Managing Editor Lisa Kinne provided additional key support. The production process has also benefited from the work of Worth's Director of Editing, Design, and Media Production for the Sciences and Social Sciences, Tracey Kuehn; Executive Media Editor, Rachel Comerford; and Production Manager, Sarah Segal. Preparation of the manuscript was speeded by the reference-list-creation wizardry of UIC's Lara Mercurio. The tireless efforts of Photo Editor Bianca Moscatelli and Photo Researchers Elyse Rieder and Rona Tuccillo contributed substantially to the book's visual appearance, as did the work of Art Director Diana Blume and Art Manager Matthew McAdams. We had the great good fortune of having, as our Interior and Cover Designer, the brilliant artist Babs Reingold. Special thanks to Senior Production Editor Vivien Weiss for somehow piecing together the project's many parts.

The writing has benefited from the skills of two exceptional Developmental Editors. Mimi Melek provided critical instructive feedback throughout the book's early development. The subsequent contributions of Cathy Crow were so extensive, so constructive, and executed so efficiently that I cannot help but wonder if, in reality, a team of professionals was working under the pen name "Cathy Crow."

Finally, thanks to two Worth professionals without whom we would not be here. Catherine Woods's confidence in the project at its outset is deeply appreciated. Once under way, the work was nurtured for years by the wisdom and warmth of Kevin Feyen, who contributed immeasurably to the final product.

Acknowledgments

Although the main text of this book is sole-authored, *Psychology: The Science of Person, Mind, and Brain* has been a collaboration from start to finish. The project would never have come into being were it not for the intellectual insights of my infinitely valued colleague, Dr. Tracy L. Caldwell of Dominican University. The student quoted at the start of this preface was a student of Tracy's. Her recognition that this student's—and all students'—experiences in introductory psychology could be fundamentally improved sparked the conversation (and subsequent flurry of emails) that established the person-first, levels-of-analysis framework executed here.

These communications occurred shortly before Dr. Caldwell joined the faculty at Dominican. Because the assistant-professor years are not the time to write a textbook, I took on the authorship role. Yet Dr. Caldwell's input is felt on every page. She authored the book's pedagogical features: Preview Questions, Chapter Summaries and Answers (Appendix B), In Your Life questions, What Do You Know? assessments, Questions for Discussion, and end-of-chapter Self-Tests. Tracy crafted, with me, a key media piece: the Try This! activities. She independently authored a major instructional item: the Statistics appendix (Appendix A). Yet this list, extensive as it is, substantially underestimates Dr. Caldwell's actual impact. All throughout the many years of writing, she was central to the discussions in which the book's features were formulated and refined. This project not only began with a conversation; it also continued as one. We have always thought of this as "our book," and you should, too.

We jointly thank Worth Publishers for their incredible professionalism and support.

University of Illinois at Chicago

Daniel Cervone

Multimedia to Support Teaching and Learning

LaunchPad with LearningCurve Quizzing

A comprehensive Web resource for teaching and learning psychology, LaunchPad combines Worth Publishers' award-winning media with an innovative platform for easy navigation. For students, it is the ultimate online study guide with rich interactive tutorials, videos, e-Book, and the LearningCurve adaptive quizzing system. For instructors, LaunchPad is a full-course space where class documents can be posted, quizzes are easily assigned and graded, and students' progress can be assessed and recorded. Whether you are looking for the most effective study tools or a robust platform for an online course, LaunchPad is a powerful way to enhance your class.

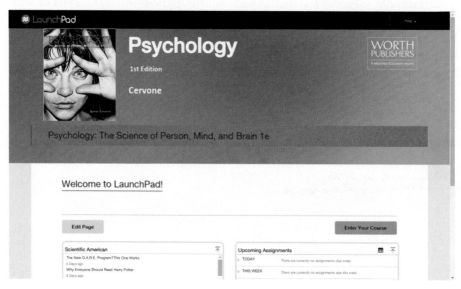

LaunchPad to Accompany *Psychology* can be previewed as well as purchased at www.macmillanhighered.com/launchpad/Cervone1e.

> *Psychology* and LaunchPad can be ordered together with
> ISBN-10: 1-319-01707-X / ISBN-13: 978-1-319-01707-1

LaunchPad for *Psychology* includes all the following resources:

> The **LearningCurve** quizzing system was designed based on the latest findings from learning and memory research. It combines adaptive question selection, immediate and valuable feedback, and a game-like interface to engage students in a learning experience that is unique to them. Each LearningCurve quiz is fully integrated with other resources in LaunchPad through the Personalized Study Plan, so students will be able to review with Worth's extensive library of videos and activities. And state-of-the-art question analysis reports allow instructors to track the progress of individual students as well as their class as a whole.

> **An interactive e-Book** allows students to highlight, bookmark, and make their own notes, just as they would with a printed textbook.

> **Concept Practice**, created by award-winning multimedia author Thomas Ludwig (Hope College) and John Krantz (Hanover College), helps students solidify their understanding of key concepts. With these in-depth tutorials, students explore a variety of important topics, often in an experimental context in the role of either researcher or subject. Tutorials combine animations, video, illustrations, and self-assessment.

> **Video Activities** include more than 100 engaging video modules that instructors can easily assign and customize for student assessment. Videos cover classic experiments, current news footage, and cutting-edge research, all of which are sure to spark discussion and encourage critical thinking.

> **Labs** offer an interactive experience that fortifies the most important concepts and content of introductory psychology. In these activities, students participate in classic and contemporary experiments, generating real data and reviewing the broader implications of those findings. A virtual host makes this a truly interactive experience.

> **The *Scientific American* Newsfeed** delivers weekly articles, podcasts, and news briefs on the very latest developments in psychology from the first name in popular science journalism.

> **Deep integration** is available between LaunchPad products and Blackboard, Brightspace by D2L, and Canvas. These deep integrations offer educators single sign-on and gradebook sync now with auto-refresh. Also, these best-in-class integrations offer deep linking to all Macmillan digital content at the chapter and asset level, giving professors ultimate flexibility and customization capability within their LMS.

Additional Student Supplements

> The **CourseSmart e-Book** offers the complete text of *Psychology* in an easy-to-use format. Students can choose to purchase the CourseSmart e-Book as an online subscription or download it to a personal computer or a portable media player, such as a smartphone or iPad. The CourseSmart e-Book for *Psychology* can be previewed and purchased at www.coursesmart.com.

> *The Horse That Won't Go Away* by Thomas E. Heinzen, Scott O. Lilienfeld, and Susan A. Nolan is an engaging and accessible introduction to the need for psychological science. Starting with the strange case of Clever Hans, the horse that could count and do math, the authors take the reader on a tour of cases where science triumphed over self-deception.

> *Pursuing Human Strengths: A Positive Psychology Guide* by Martin Bolt of Calvin College is a perfect way to introduce students to the amazing field of positive psychology as well as their own personal strengths.

> *Psychology and the Real World: Essays Illustrating Fundamental Contributions to Society,* **Second Edition,** is a superb collection of essays by major researchers that describe their landmark studies. Published in association with the not-for-profit FABBS Foundation, the new edition of this engaging reader includes Alan Kazdin's reflections

on his research on treating children with severe aggressive behavior, Adam Grant's look at work and motivation, and Steven Hayes's thoughts on mindfulness and acceptance and commitment therapy. A portion of all proceeds is donated to FABBS to support societies of cognitive, psychological, behavioral, and brain sciences.

Take advantage of our most popular supplements!

Worth Publishers is pleased to offer cost-saving packages of *Psychology: The Science of Person, Mind, and Brain* with our most popular supplements. Below is a list of some of the most popular combinations available for order through your local bookstore.

Psychology & LaunchPad Access Card
ISBN-10: 1-319-01707-X / ISBN-13: 978-1-319-01707-1

Psychology & i>Clicker
ISBN-10: 1-319-02221-9 / ISBN-13: 978-1-319-02221-1

Psychology & *Psychology and the Real World,* Second Edition
ISBN-10: 1-319-02222-7 / ISBN-13: 978-1-319-02222-8

Course Management

> Worth Publishers supports multiple Course Management Systems with enhanced cartridges for upload into Blackboard, Angel, Desire2Learn, Sakai, and Moodle. Cartridges are provided free upon adoption of *Psychology* and can be downloaded from Worth's online catalog at www.worthpublishers.com. Deep integration is also available between LaunchPad products and Blackboard, Brightspace by D2L, and Canvas. These deep integrations offer educators single sign-on and gradebook sync now with autorefresh.

Assessment

> The **Computerized Test Bank** powered by Diploma includes a full assortment of questions totaling over 2500 items. This includes an array of multiple-choice and essay questions written to test students at specific levels of Bloom's Taxonomy: knowledge, comprehension, application, analysis, synthesis, and evaluation. All the questions are matched to the outcomes recommended in the 2013 APA Guidelines for the Undergraduate Psychology Major. The accompanying gradebook software makes it easy to record students' grades throughout a course, sort student records, view detailed analyses of test items, curve tests, generate reports, and add weights to grades.

> The **i>Clicker Classroom Response System** is a versatile polling system developed by educators for educators that makes class time more efficient and interactive. i>Clicker allows you to ask questions and instantly record your students' responses, take attendance, and gauge students' understanding and opinions. i>Clicker is available at a 10% discount when packaged with *Psychology.*

Presentation

> **Interactive Presentation Slides** are another great way to introduce Worth's dynamic media into the classroom without lots of advance preparation. Each presentation covers a major topic in psychology and integrates Worth's high-quality videos and animations for an engaging teaching and learning experience. These interactive presentations are complimentary to adopters of *Psychology* and are perfect for technology novices and experts alike.

> The **Instructor's Resource Manual** features a variety of materials that are valuable to new and veteran teachers alike. In addition to background on the chapter reading and suggestions for in-class lectures, the manual is rich with activities to engage students in different modes of learning. The Instructor's Resources can be downloaded at www.macmillanhighered.com/launchpad/Cervone1e.

> **The Video Anthology for Introductory Psychology** includes over 150 unique video clips to bring lectures to life. Provided complimentary to adopters of *Psychology*, this rich collection includes clinical footage, interviews, animations, and news segments that vividly illustrate topics across the psychology curriculum.

> **Faculty Lounge** is an online forum provided by Worth Publishers where teachers can find and share favorite teaching ideas and materials, including videos, animations, images, PowerPoint slides, news stories, articles, Web links, and lecture activities. Sign up to browse the site or upload your favorite materials for teaching psychology at www.worthpublishers.com/facultylounge.

For scientific purposes, treat people as if they were human beings.

– Harré & Secord

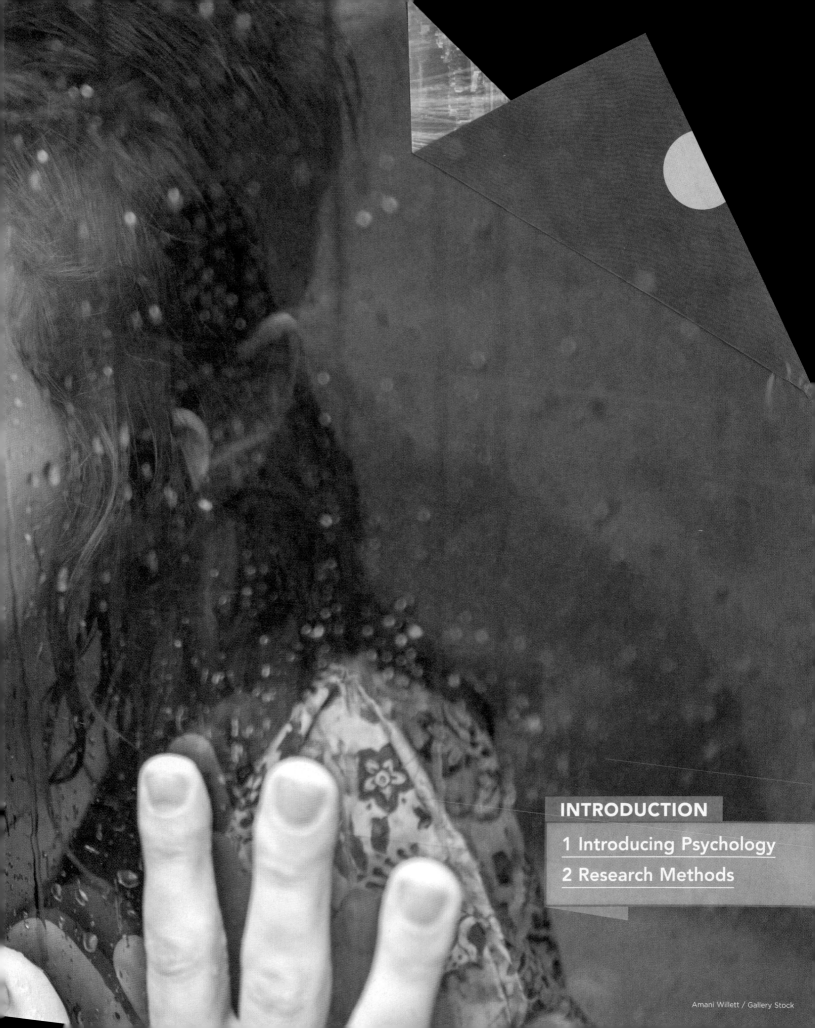

INTRODUCTION

Introducing Psychology 1

CLAUDE, AN AFRICAN AMERICAN CHILD GROWING UP in Chicago in the 1950s, was puzzled. He learned that he could swim in the local municipal pool, but only on Wednesdays. He could skate at the neighborhood roller rink, but only on Thursdays. These were the rules for "Black" kids. "We could be regular people," he said to himself, "but only in the middle of the week?"

Where, he wondered, did the rules come from? How many were there? Why did they apply to some people but not others?

Years later, a psychologist analyzed the dilemma faced by this child and millions more. He explains that, from experiences like this, children learn two lessons. They learn they are not merely individuals but members of a group—in this case, Blacks. Then, they learn what society thinks of their group: "We have a pretty good idea," the psychologist explains, "of what other members of our society think about lots of things, including the major groups . . . in society." In particular, we come to know society's *stereotypes:* simplistic beliefs about what group members are like.

The psychologist then had an idea. He thought that stereotypes might affect people's performance at school. If people are reminded of a negative stereotype about their group just before taking a math test, for example, the stereotype might distract them, make them anxious, and lower their test scores.

Then the psychologist and his colleagues did something important: They tested his idea through scientific research. Their experiments show that:

> Stereotypes affect *people:* When reminded of a stereotype about their group, people tend, on average, to perform less well.

> Stereotypes affect the *mind:* They create mental distractions and feelings of anxiety that interfere with the thinking processes needed to perform well on tests.

> Stereotypes affect the *brain:* They activate brain regions that generate emotional reactions, rather than brain regions that contribute to good test performance.

Jaimie Duplass / Getty Images

Jasper James / Getty Images

iStock / 360 / Getty Images

Psychologist Claude Steele grew up in Chicago in the 1950s, where his experience of segregation motivated his later research on the psychological effects of stereotypes.

Here you see the psychologist's journey: from ideas about human experience to research on people, the mind, and the brain that puts those ideas to the test.

It was the child's journey, too—for the child, Claude, *is* the psychologist: Professor Claude Steele, who experienced discrimination as a youth in Chicago in the 1950s and 1960s, and later became one of America's preeminent psychological scientists (Steele, 2010).

It will be your journey, too. Test your own ideas about the human experience as you learn about psychology: the science of person, mind, and brain. ◉

Preview Question

> What is psychology?

WELCOME TO PSYCHOLOGY. Our opening story about stereotypes and their effects on people, the mind, and the brain shows you what this field is about. **Psychology** is the scientific study of:

> *Persons*: people and their behavior, including behavior in social and cultural settings
> The *mind*: mental activity, including feelings and thoughts, in humans and other species
> The *brain*: the biological basis of the abilities to behave, feel, and think

Psychology is, in short, the science of person, mind, and brain.

This chapter introduces the science of psychology. It first presents the job activities of six contemporary psychologists. Their work displays not only psychology's diversity, but also one of the field's unifying themes. As you will see, that theme involves scientific methods. Psychologists do not rely merely on intuitions when studying people, the mind, and the brain; they rely on evidence gathered through scientific research.

Next, we present some psychological research. You will see how three types of research—studies of (1) people's behavior, (2) the mind's emotional and thinking processes, and (3) the brain's biological systems—complement one another.

Finally, we'll look back at psychology's history. Ancient scholars posed some of the questions that are pursued in psychology today. The big difference between the present and the past is today's scientific methods, which enable psychologists to provide novel, data-based answers to timeless questions about human nature.

Today's Psychological Science

Tens of thousands of people, worldwide, are engaged in the science of psychology. Six have described what they do for a living, to introduce you to their field. Let's meet them.

Six Contemporary Psychologists

Preview Question

> What are some examples of the diversity characterizing the field of psychology?

If you dropped in on our six psychologists at work, here is what you would find.

What image comes to mind when you think of a psychologist?

psychology The scientific study of persons, the mind, and the brain.

PAULINE MAKI *If you walk into my research laboratory, you might see me giving someone this instruction:*

After I say a word, come up with as many words as you can that rhyme with it. You'll have one minute. Ready? The word is "name." Go.

Why would a psychologist ask anybody to do this? The task measures mental performance. Researchers in psychology explore

Macmillan Education Archive

factors that affect how well people perform on tasks. There are many. Some are expected: how tired you are, how much effort you put into the task. But others are surprising. It turns out that, on average, women produce more words on this task than men do and that their performance can depend on the level, in their bodies, of the body chemical estrogen. Estrogen, which plays an important role in pregnancy, also affects mental abilities. Our research linking estrogen levels to thinking shows a tight connection between biology and the mind.

Body–mind connections are important for a number of reasons. Women with breast cancer take medications that lower their estrogen levels. Does the medication impair their mental abilities? The topic also is important for men. For example, treatments for prostate cancer affect their body chemistry in ways that might affect mental performance.

So that's my job. I'm a scientist who studies how body chemistry affects the mind. We hope to better understand how the body's inner chemistry, as well as the medications people take, impact mental abilities.

Pauline Maki, whose research on body chemistry and mental performance advances a major goal of psychological science: relating the workings of the mind to the biological mechanisms of the brain.

Courtesy Ed Cutrell

ED CUTRELL When you envision a psychologist, you probably don't imagine somebody who spends one week talking to farmers in rural India about composting, another talking with urban sex workers in Bangalore about how they use mobile phones, and another working with software engineers to design technologies. But that's not unusual for me. I'm a psychologist at Microsoft Research India.

I try to understand how computing systems can improve life in developing communities. Although there are nearly 5 billion mobile phones worldwide, technology's benefits remain out of reach for many. Some countries struggle to provide electricity and connectivity to all citizens, and some businesses and families can't afford hardware. But finances aren't the whole story. Limited education and literacy; political, gender, or religious prohibitions on technology use; and differences in cognitive models—how people organize information mentally—also pose obstacles. Overcoming them requires understanding not only technology, but also people. I study how people in diverse communities think, feel, and relate to each other and then connect this to the design of technological solutions.

Ed Cutrell, on the job in Bangalore, India. He is learning about life in Indian communities in order to design information technologies that meet the unique needs of their citizens.

Our group has designed systems to help farmers share sustainable farming techniques; to help children share PCs in low-resource schools; and to improve nonliterate women's access to microfinance in rural India. Each technology was designed for people living in a context very different from my own, and most likely yours. My psychology training helps me understand their life contexts, aspirations, and needs, and helps to shape technology for them.

Macmillan Education Archive

LYNNE OWENS MOCK When I tell people I'm a psychologist, they assume I have a leather couch where people lie down and tell me their troubles. However, I spend most of my time in communities in Chicago. I direct the research division of a community mental health center. In this job, I have a wide range of duties:

❯ When community service organizations run programs, somebody has to figure out if they work. I do this. For example, I recently evaluated a voter registration rally and a program to develop leadership skills in young women. My psychological training helps

Macmillan Education Archive

Lynne Mock, who puts principles of psychological science to work in urban communities. By employing the research methods described in Chapter 2, Dr. Mock is able to evaluate scientifically the effectiveness of community programs.

me to learn what community leaders think, and to analyze and report scientific evidence that shows whether programs are working.

> I coordinate a committee to monitor research ethics, in other words, whether it's acceptable to conduct research in a certain way. This activity is common for psychologists; all our research follows ethical principles that protect people's rights.

> I run a support group for grandparents raising grandchildren. We discuss challenges such as substance abuse and raising boys to manhood. My psychology training taught me how to listen carefully and ask questions to help the group discuss experiences that are personal and sometimes painful. It also helps me update grandparents' knowledge of child development, based on current research.

On top of this, I teach university courses, including *African American Psychology*. Real-life examples from the community are key to the success of my classes—and my career.

Gloria Balague, sports psychologist, working with athletes. Sports psychologists help athletes develop psychological skills that enable them to remain calm, confident, and focused during competition.

Macmillan Education Archive

GLORIA BALAGUE *I am watching the team at practice; tomorrow I will be watching the game. I am working; I am the team's sport psychologist.*

I study psychological factors that affect athletic performance, for example:

> Working together as a group. *Even in individual sports (e.g., swimming), athletes train in groups. Interactions among team members can affect everybody's performance.*

> Decision making: *Athletes have to focus attention on key information, make quick decisions, and refocus quickly after a mistake or distraction.*

> Confidence: *Athletes have to maintain confidence, even after a loss.*

> Controlling emotion: *Athletes sometimes "choke," losing control of their emotions and performing below their abilities. Controlling emotion is a skill people can learn.*

Macmillan Education Archive

When working with athletes, I draw on my training in clinical psychology. As in clinical work, sports psychologists teach people various skills to cope with difficulties. If someone—a client in therapy or an athlete—is very anxious, we may teach that person to replace anxiety-related thoughts (e.g., "Everyone will think that I am incompetent") with thoughts that help people remain calm (e.g., "Others may think that I am nervous, which is true, but I still know what I'm doing"). These strategies help athletes to remain composed and focused.

The bottom line is that psychological skills, just like physical ones, are trainable. Everyone can improve mentally if they work at it. I guess I could be called a "head" coach.

Practice doesn't always make perfect When the competition starts, anxiety can cause athletes to slip up. Some psychologists work with athletes, teaching them strategies to control their emotions.

AP Photo / The Canadian Press, Robert Skinner

Dominican University

ROBERT CALIN-JAGEMAN *When I tell somebody that I'm a psychologist, they'll often ask what type of people I work with. Then I have to explain that I don't work with people; I study Aplysia californica, a large sea slug that lives in the ocean. Usually, this is confusing enough to bring the conversation to a screeching halt. So I'll introduce my work this way.*

I am interested in how memories are formed. We constantly encounter information, some of which we remember permanently. I try to understand how the brain, a biological organ, can store and access memories.

What does this have to do with sea slugs? They provide an amazing opportunity to see how the brain stores memories. Like all animals, Aplysia form memories. But unlike most, they do it with an extremely simple nervous system: only 20,000 brain cells (by comparison, a honeybee has 1 million and humans have 100 billion). With so few cells, we can trace the cell-by-cell formation of memories by implanting electrodes into cells while Aplysia learn new information.

Although sea slugs are a somewhat unusual topic of study, my day is typical for a research psychologist and college professor. In the morning, I check in with students in my lab, make sure the Aplysia are fed and comfortable, and then I'm off to teach classes. In the afternoon, it's back to the lab. In the evening, I try to digest the day's research results.

Jason Geil

Robert Calin-Jageman, who explores the biological basis of memory by studying cell-to-cell communications in an organism with a simple nervous system, *Aplysia californica* (a large sea slug).

Macmillan Education Archive

LEE L. MADDEN *Dropping by my office, you may see me talking with one person, or two, or even five. Depending on the patient(s) in the room and the topic discussed, there may be tears, laughter, hollering, or even silence. It's what you don't see that makes me a clinical psychologist.*

Inside my head I am schema building. I am creating a knowledge base about the patient, testing my hypotheses, then crafting interventions to figure out exactly where the individual is stuck and how to help.

Psychology researchers, like those described earlier, garner scientific information that I need to assess the combination of psychological factors existing in each of my patients. The scientific findings help me to teach a patient lessons that are necessary for better self-understanding and then to work with the strengths of the patient to reach his or her goals. As a clinical psychologist, I need to understand how patients regulate emotions; organize information and make decisions; perform on the job, socially, and within the family; and understand the world and their place in it. I need to discover the person's level of confidence and motivation, and how well the individual understands the physiology of the body including the nervous system. Does the person understand that he or she lives in a specific culture? Is the person living in the present, ruminating about the past, or projecting him- or herself into the future in ways that cause distress? Answers to these questions are my data.

Macmillan Education Archive

Lee Madden, a clinical psychologist, works with individuals and groups in therapy. She uses findings from psychological science to understand her patients and to help them understand themselves.

Building an understanding of patients and interventions for them—while maintaining a relationship of trust, privacy, and ethical behavior—is the totality of my work. Useful work it is, in part thanks to knowledge gained from the psychological research you are soon to learn about in this book.

The Diversity of Psychology

Our six psychologists provide your first look at today's field of psychology. What did you observe? One can't help but notice how much their jobs differ from one another. They work in laboratories, communities, athletic fields, and information-technology offices. They work with individuals, groups, and communities. And sea slugs! Some aim to create new scientific knowledge. Others apply existing knowledge to help people.

Additional biographies would reveal more diversity. Psychologists work in hospitals, schools, businesses, and governments (Figure 1.1). They study people ranging in age from fetuses (to discover the earliest age of consciousness, Chapter 9) to older adults (to understand the wisdom of old age, Chapter 14). They explore the inner mental life of individuals (e.g., when conducting therapy, Chapters 15 and 16), interactions among hundreds or thousands of individuals (in social psychology, Chapter 12), and "virtual" interactions among millions (in research conducted on social networking sites, Chapter 2). Some focus on the person as a whole, others on specific aspects of mental life, and yet others on biological mechanisms within the brain.

There is, then, no one type of job that encompasses "being a psychologist." Psychologists bring a wide range of skills to a wide range of challenges.

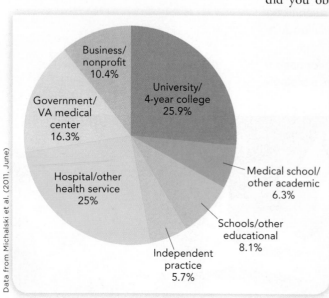

Data from Michalski et al. (2011, June)

figure 1.1

Where psychologists work There is no one place where psychologists work. You can find members of the profession in colleges and universities, in hospitals and medical schools, in businesses, in government, and in private practice.

🔧 WHAT DO YOU KNOW?...

1. In this section, you read that some psychologists "aim to create new scientific knowledge," whereas "others apply existing knowledge to help people." Describe how the work of community psychologist Lynne Owens Mock supports both aims.

See Appendix B for answers to What Do You Know? questions.

The Unity of Psychology

Preview Questions

› What's so bad about intuition?
› What's a good alternative to intuition?

All this diversity raises a question. What common threads tie together psychologists' activities? Sure, their work is diverse. But does it have anything in common?

A key common thread is a commitment to the methods of science. This commitment helps to unify psychology and also to distinguish it from other fields. Novelists, journalists, poets, playwrights, and philosophers provide valuable ideas about human nature, just as psychologists do. But psychologists—unlike professionals in these other fields—test their ideas scientifically. They know that even their favorite ideas about people might be wrong, and they seek scientific evidence to evaluate those ideas.

Other sciences—biology, chemistry, physics—of course share psychology's commitment to scientific methods. What makes psychology unique is its application of rigorous scientific methods to questions about behavior, emotions, thinking processes, and therapies to reduce psychological distress.

> What image comes to mind when you think of a scientist?

In a moment, we will say more about scientific methods. But first, let's look at intuition. The limits of intuition motivate psychologists to employ the methods of science.

INTUITION AND ITS LIMITS. In psychology, are scientific methods really needed? The question arises due to the unique role of intuition—spontaneous insights and "hunches"—in the field of psychology, as compared to other sciences.

When you take your first class in biology, chemistry, or physics, you have few intuitions about how things work. How do elements combine into chemical compounds? How do subatomic particles interact? Before taking the class, you haven't the foggiest idea; you have no intuitions. But in psychology, you have many intuitions before class begins. Suppose that, on the first day of psychology class, your instructor asks, "What are the main ways that people's personalities differ?" You probably have lots of intuitions about the answer. Your intuitions seem correct to you. And, in many cases, they might actually be correct (see Oltmanns & Turkheimer, 2009).

Your good intuitions could prompt you to ask, "In psychology, do we even need scientific research?" Maybe the field's questions are "no brainers": trivially easy to answer through intuition alone. If this is what you're thinking, consider the psychological intuitions quoted in the right margin, expressed by various wise individuals.

> How many of the arguments you've experienced happened because you and someone else had different intuitions about the same question?

Well, which is it? Does power corrupt or not? Are people evil or good? Do people want a just ruler or freedom? One thing's for sure: We're not going to find out by relying on intuitions. Intuitions are all over the map.

SCIENTIFIC METHODS. Psychology cannot live on intuition alone. It needs methods that are so convincing that everybody, no matter what their original intuitions, will recognize the value of the information they provide.

Fortunately, these methods already exist. They have been known for centuries as *scientific methods.*

The term **scientific methods** refers to a broad array of procedures through which scientists obtain information about the world. Scientific methods involve three key steps:

1. *Collect evidence.* Scientists do not just sit back and think about what the world might be like. They go out into the world and observe it. These observations provide the evidence on which they base their conclusions.

2. *Record observations systematically.* Scientists keep careful, precise accounts of what they observe, and summarize observations systematically (e.g., in tables and graphs). This gives them accurate records that can be communicated easily to other scientists.

3. *Record* how *observations were made.* Scientists don't merely tell you what they observed. They also record exactly how they observed it: the equipment they used and steps they took to obtain the evidence. These records enable other scientists to engage in *replication,* that is, to repeat the procedures in order to verify the original results.

When psychologists take these three steps to obtain information, they usually try to get a *lot* of information. Here's an example involving the question "Are women more talkative than men?" In everyday life, you might answer based on a small amount of information from personal experience: "Yeah, sure they are. My friend Mark is really quiet, but Charlene is always talking up a storm." Psychologists, by comparison, obtain a vast amount of information that goes far beyond personal experience. Two psychologists answered this question by analyzing results from 63 prior studies of talkativeness conducted between the years 1968 and 2004 (Leaper & Ayres, 2007). In each of the prior studies, researchers used the three steps above (collect evidence,

> Power tends to corrupt, and absolute power corrupts absolutely.
>
> —Lord Acton (British historian and political theorist)
>
> It is said that power corrupts, but actually it's more true that power attracts the corruptible.
>
> —David Brin (Author)
>
> In spite of everything, I still believe that people are really good at heart.
>
> —Anne Frank (Diarist and Holocaust victim)
>
> All that is necessary for the triumph of evil is that good men do nothing.
>
> —Edmund Burke (Political theorist and philosopher)
>
> God has planted in every human heart the desire to live in freedom.
>
> —George W. Bush (U.S. president)
>
> Few men desire liberty: The majority are satisfied with a just master.
>
> —Sallust (Roman historian and politician)

Bettmann / CORBIS

Scientific methods The English philosopher and scientist Sir Francis Bacon, who explained the virtues of scientific methods more than 400 years ago. History reports that, unfortunately, he was so enamored of scientific methods that, to answer a question on how cold temperatures affect the preservation of meat products, he conducted an experiment in freezing cold weather, caught pneumonia, and died.

scientific methods A broad array of procedures through which scientists obtain information about the world. Scientific methods involve three key steps: collect evidence, record observations systematically, and record *how* observations were made.

record observations, and record how observations were made) to observe many men and women. Altogether, in the 63 studies combined, 4,385 people were observed. That's a lot of information! It yielded a surprise: on average, men were slightly more talkative than women.

In addition to scientific observations, there is room in science for intuition. Scientists may rely on intuitions when first formulating their ideas (as you saw in the case of Claude Steele, in this chapter's opening story). But to evaluate their ideas, they rely on evidence gathered through scientific methods.

TRY THIS!

In *Psychology: The Science of Person, Mind, and Brain,* you not only will learn about the results of psychologists' research, you will also get to experience their research methods firsthand, thanks to a feature called Try This! Get on the Internet and enter the Web address www.pmbpsychology.com to find Try This! research experiences for each chapter of the book.

Do the exercise for Chapter 1 now; it's a test of your memory ability. We will discuss the results of this test later in the chapter.

And, speaking of memory, don't forget to come back to read the rest of this chapter once you're done. ◉

Scientific methods are used throughout psychology—even where you might not expect it. It is no surprise that psychologists use scientific methods to learn how body chemistry affects mental performance (see Pauline Maki's work, described earlier) or how neurons form the basis of memory (see Robert Calin-Jageman's work). But they are no less scientific when working on real-world problems. Lynne Mock, as you saw, does not just "cross her fingers" and hope that community service programs work. She evaluates their effectiveness with scientific methods.

Chapter 2 reviews scientific methods that psychologists use to answer questions. Here, let's examine the questions themselves.

🌀 WHAT DO YOU KNOW?●●●

2. Though relying on _____ may be useful when we first formulate ideas, psychologists evaluate those ideas using _____ methods.

3. Why is it important for researchers to not only record their observations systematically, but also record how they made those observations?

Scientific and Nonscientific Questions About Human Behavior

Preview Question

> What makes a question "scientific"?

Psychologists use scientific methods to answer questions—but not just any type of questions. Scientific methods answer *scientific* questions. Learning to distinguish scientific from nonscientific questions in psychology will help you to understand the scope of the field.

Scientific questions are ones that can be answered by gathering evidence through the scientific methods we just described. If a question is a scientific one, then evidence is required to answer the question convincingly. In other words, scientific questions are *empirical;* an empirical question is one that can be answered by making observations of the world that provide evidence.

scientific questions Questions that can be answered by gathering evidence through scientific methods.

Let's experience scientific questions through an exercise. For each of the following questions about human behavior, ask yourself whether it is a scientific question (based on the definition above):

1A. Is it okay to break into a drug store and steal medicine if you're extremely ill, desperately need the medicine, and can't afford it?

1B. Do men and women differ in the degree to which they think it is okay to break into a drug store and steal medicine to help a person who is extremely ill, needs it, and can't afford it?

2A. Are there really angels and, if so, how many are there?

2B. Why do so many people believe that there really are angels, when angels cannot be seen?

3A. Are all bachelors unmarried?

3B. Are married people happier or less happy than people who are single?

You surely noticed that the "A" and "B" questions differed. For the B questions, you could imagine evidence that would answer the question definitively. Sometimes getting the evidence would be easy; for example, you could ask men and women what they think about the drug store question (1B). Sometimes it would be difficult; it might be hard to answer 2B thoroughly (see, e.g., Boyer, 2001). Nonetheless, for all the B questions, you could gather evidence that would answer the question, and without evidence you cannot answer it convincingly. The questions are scientific.

The A questions are not like this; they cannot be answered by gathering evidence. They represent three other types of questions: normative questions, questions of faith, and questions of logic.

1. *Normative questions* ask how a person *should* act. (A *norm* is a rule or standard of excellence representing desirable or socially acceptable behavior.) If you ask yourself, "Should I lie to the guy I'm dating about why I want to break up, since it will be easier than telling the truth?" you're asking a normative question. "Thou shalt not kill" answers a normative question ("Is killing acceptable?"). Normative questions are not answered by gathering evidence, but by appealing to accepted rules of conduct. No scientific evidence is even relevant to a norm such as "Thou shalt not kill."

2. *Questions of faith.* Question 2A might sound like a scientific question, but it's not. It is a question of faith, that is, one which rests on religious beliefs that cannot be proven through scientific facts. Religious beliefs address the *supernatural* world—a realm beyond the world of nature studied by the sciences.

3. *Questions of logic.* Like 2A, 3A also might look like a scientific question. Maybe you could gather evidence by asking a number of men two questions—"Are you a bachelor?" and "Are you married?"—and determining whether answers to the questions go together. But don't do that. Question 2A can be answered based solely on *logic,* that is, rules for drawing conclusions from statements. Because bachelor means "a man who is not married," you do not need scientific evidence to answer Question 3B.

Now that you know what scientific questions are, it is important to recognize that they are not all the same; scientists ask different types of questions. When they are just starting to acquire knowledge, their scientific questions tend to be very general; they ask, in essence, "What is the world like?" For example, in Chapter 14 you will learn about a psychologist (Jean Piaget) who began his studies of children by giving them problems they had never seen before and asking, "Can they solve them? If so, how?" Later, scientists' questions usually become more specific; they ask exactly how one factor influences another. You saw this in our opening story, where a psychologist

Forensic psychology Psychologists in the field of forensic psychology provide information to the legal system. For example, if the perpetrator of a crime is unknown, they create psychological profiles of potential suspects (Canter, 2011), or if a defendant pleads innocent due to insanity, they assess the defendant's mental state. Work in forensic psychology also illustrates the distinction between scientific and nonscientific questions. A question such as "What psychological factors predict criminal behavior?" is a scientific question; one can collect scientific evidence to answer it. However, the question of whether or *not* a given type of behavior (e.g., assault, theft, gambling, drug use) is a crime is not a scientific question; it is a normative question involving social rules that dictate acceptable and unacceptable forms of behavior.

Steven Robertson / Getty Images

What are some things you believe, even if no scientific evidence exists to support your belief?

predicted that a specific social factor (stereotypes) would have a specific effect on school performance (lower test scores). Chapter 2 presents the research methods psychologists use to answer different types of scientific questions.

> ### ✪ WHAT DO YOU KNOW?...
>
> 4. "Is our God a loving god?" is an example of a question of _____, whereas "Is it okay to watch pirated movies?" is an example of a _____ question. Neither these nor questions of logic are _____ because they cannot be answered by gathering _____.

Thinking Critically About Psychological Science

> The key to understanding anything is a combination of observation, especially the quantitative kind of observation we call measurement, and the systematic way of thinking we call logic.
>
> —Peter Atkins (2003, p. 276)

Our analysis of scientific and nonscientific questions teaches a general lesson. Psychology requires *critical thinking* skills. **Critical thinking** is the ability to think logically, to question assumptions, to evaluate evidence, and, more generally, to be open-minded yet skeptical about information you hear (see the Research Toolkit). People who think critically do not merely "absorb" ideas passively. They evaluate t hem actively. When learning about a scientific theory, they scrutinize its claims. When learning about research findings, they look for flaws or limitations in research methods and ask whether similar results would be obtained if the study were run with a different group of participants, at a different point in time, in a different society or culture. Progress in psychology—or any science—rests not only on scientific observation but also on critical thinking skills, which are needed to interpret and explain whatever has been observed.

We'll try to build your critical thinking skills as we make our way through this book. Ideally, you not only will learn some facts about psychology; you'll become a "critical consumer" of psychological science.

One method we will use to promote critical thinking is a Think About It feature that you will find throughout the book. It will raise critical questions of the sort a professional psychologist would ask when scrutinizing theory and research. On the left is an example.

> ### ◯ THINK ABOUT IT
>
> Earlier in this chapter, you read about research showing that, on average, men are slightly more talkative than women. Is that still true? Some of the studies the researchers reviewed were conducted decades ago (recall that the studies took place between 1968 and 2004). Maybe contemporary social changes, such as women's greater participation in higher education and expanded leadership roles in government and business, have changed the pattern of gender differences observed previously.

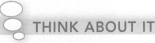

critical thinking Thinking skills that include the ability to think logically, to question assumptions, to evaluate evidence, and, generally, to be open-minded yet skeptical.

⊕RESEARCH TOOLKIT

Open-Minded Skepticism

Research in psychology requires specialized tools. Each chapter of this book will highlight one such tool and present it in depth, in a feature called Research Toolkit.

In subsequent chapters, the tool presented in the Research Toolkit will match the specific topic of the chapter. Here in Chapter 1, our topic is psychology as a whole. We'll thus present a tool that psychologists use no matter what topic they are studying. It is an intellectual tool—a way of thinking—that we'll call *open-minded skepticism.*

Like the phrase "jumbo shrimp," "open-minded skepticism" sounds like an oxymoron (a phrase containing a contradiction). Someone who is open-minded is receptive to unusual ideas; a skeptic doubts them. But in good science, open-mindedness and skepticism combine. A scientist must be receptive to new ideas yet also skeptical about them, accepting them only if substantial research supports them. Let's see how open-mindedness and skepticism combine on a topic about which you should be skeptical: ESP.

ESP, or extra-sensory perception, refers to an ability to perceive things (i.e., to detect information in the environment) without relying on normal physical and biological mechanisms of perception. If a fortune-teller could literally "look into your future," it would be a case of ESP.

Is ESP real? The vast majority of psychologists don't think so. But a good scientist is open-minded. It *could* be real, and the only way to find out is to conduct research.

One psychologist recently did this. Daryl Bem, of Cornell University, conducted experiments to see whether people could foretell the future (Bem, 2011). For example, in one study he asked participants to predict whether each of five types of pictures—negative images, positive images, emotionally neutral pictures, erotic pictures, and romantic but not erotic pictures—would soon appear on the left or the right side of a computer screen. For the erotic photos (but not the other pictures), participants guessed accurately *more than* half the time. According to Bem, this meant they could foretell the future; they had powers of ESP (Bem, 2011).

Upon learning of Bem's results, most psychologists were skeptical. They still doubted that ESP exists. Being scientists, they did not merely sit around doubting. Their skepticism motivated them to carry out research of their own.

One research team in the United Kingdom tried three times to replicate the results of one of Bem's experiments, but couldn't; their "results failed to provide any evidence" supporting Bem's ESP claims (Ritchie, Wiseman, & French, 2012, p. 3). A team of researchers in the United States ran seven experiments using Bem's method and "found no evidence supporting [ESP's] existence" (Galak et al., 2012). Researchers in the Netherlands reanalyzed Bem's data (i.e., the numerical summaries of his results) and concluded that his studies never showed that ESP exists in the first place (Wagenmakers et al., 2011). They detected a problem that you, too, may have noticed. Sure, participants seemed to have ESP when it came to the erotic pictures. But what about the *other four types of pictures*? On those, they showed no sign of ESP at all. When one examines the overall pattern of results—in the studies by Bem and the other researchers—there is essentially no evidence that ESP exists.

That may be bad news for members of the American Association of Psychics (an actual organization), but the overall set of events is good for psychological science. The combination of open-mindedness and skepticism enabled psychologists to produce a body of ESP research findings that, in the long run, was consistent and convincing—and negative.

✪ WHAT DO YOU KNOW?...

5. Open-minded _____ may sound like an oxymoron, but it is possible to achieve.

Psychology as a Science of Person, Mind, and Brain

This chapter's opening story showed you that psychologists address questions in three ways: by studying (1) persons, (2) the mind, and (3) the brain. Let's now examine this idea in depth. We will explore the notion of levels of analysis, and then present person, mind, and brain analyses of the same phenomenon: gender differences in performance on math tests.

Levels of Analysis

Preview Question

› What characterizes the "levels-of-analysis" approach to explaining psychological phenomena?

Research on persons, the mind, and the brain represents different *levels of analysis* in psychological science. In any science, **levels of analysis** are different ways of describing and explaining an object or event. A concrete example clarifies the idea.

Suppose you see an iPhone on which someone is playing a game—let's say, Angry Birds. How would you describe what you are seeing? You could say:

A. The phone is displaying Angry Birds.
B. An information-processing device is carrying out a large series of computer-programming commands.
C. An electronic device is executing electronic input/output operations at a speed of 800 MHz at its central processing unit (CPU).

These three statements reflect different levels of analysis. The level of analysis of Statement A is the phone as a whole (viewed from the perspective of a person using it). The level of analysis of Statement B is computer software; the statement refers to the steps of information processing that take place according to commands in a computer program. The level of analysis of Statement C is electronic hardware; electrons are racing around in the phone's CPU.

The levels differ considerably. Answers to the question "How does it work?" illustrate how big the differences are. At the level of hardware, the answer is "a silicon chip electronically processes digitized instructions." At the level of software, the answer is "a series of programming steps displays screen images that are partly based on input from a user." At the highest level (Statement A), the answer is, "You fling birds with a slingshot and they land on pigs."

Notice three facts about the levels of analysis:

1. Each one is correct. You should not be asking, "Which one is the right description of what the phone is doing?" They are all right, in their own way, and complement one another.

levels of analysis Different ways of describing and explaining any given object or event. Psychological phenomena can be studied at three levels—person, mind, and brain.

2. As you move down a level (from A to B, or B to C), the lower level deepens your understanding of the higher level. How can the phone display Angry Birds (level A)? By executing software programming steps (level B). How can the phone execute all these programming steps (level B)? It is thanks to the device's fast-running electronic central processing unit (level C).

3. If you want to understand the phone as a whole, it is best to start "at the top" (the highest level of analysis, A above). If you started at the bottom—that is, if, hypothetically, you could shrink yourself, climb into the CPU, and see electrons whirring about—you wouldn't even know, from the electrical activity alone, that the phone was playing Angry Birds.

Levels of analysis in psychology are similar to the levels of analysis in the Angry Birds example:

> Person, mind, and brain explanations complement one another; they can each be correct in their own way.

> As you move down a level (from person to mind, or mind to brain), the lower level deepens your understanding of the higher level.

> It generally is best to start "at the top," at the person level of analysis. If you started at the bottom—observing bits of electrical activity at a spot within the brain—you wouldn't know, from the electrical activity alone, what a person was doing.

Let's see how levels of analysis work in psychology through an example.

What's happening here? Are electrons buzzing about in electronic hardware? Is information processing occurring in computer software? Is a game being played? All three things are happening. The smartphone's activity can be described at three different levels of analysis: electronic hardware, computer software, and the game as a whole, as experienced by a user. Similarly, psychological issues can be addressed at each of three levels of analysis: that of the physical brain, the thinking processes of the mind, and the experiences of persons.

Ian Dagnall / Alamy

🐦 WHAT DO YOU KNOW?...

6. Different levels of _____ complement each other and deepen our understanding of a phenomenon. Of person, mind, and brain levels, if one's goal is to understand complex psychological phenomena, it is typically best to start at the _____ level of analysis.

A Levels-of-Analysis Example: Gender, Stereotypes, and Math Performance

Preview Question

> How can gender differences in math performance be explained at the person, mind, and brain levels?

Our example involves performance on math tests. Research shows that when men and women take math tests that are important to them, fewer women than men attain the highest test scores (Cole, 1997). Gender differences are not always found. Instead, they occur in a specific setting: when people take "high-stakes" tests, that is, tests that are highly personally significant (e.g., a college entrance exam). The scientific question, then, is: Why do relatively few women get the highest-level scores on high-stakes math tests?

EXPLANATION AT PERSON, MIND, AND BRAIN LEVELS OF ANALYSIS. This question can be answered in three different ways:

Answer 1: One stereotype in our society is that women are not good at math. All women—even those who are brilliant mathematicians—will be aware of this stereotype. If they think of the stereotype when taking an important math test, it will distract them, lowering their performance. The impact of social stereotypes on women's performance thus explains the gender difference.

Once we've got a good psychological theory, then it makes sense to ask how the brain does it. . . . The psychological level of analysis . . . provides a framework for interpreting the neuroscientific data. Otherwise, it's all just pixels.

—John Kihlstrom (2006)

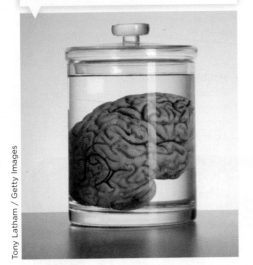

It's an intact human brain But it's not thinking anything. Thinking and other activities of the mind are not done "by brains" but by people *using* their brains.

Tony Latham / Getty Images

Answer 2: Good performance on math tests requires not only knowledge of math, but also a calm state of mind. Distressing emotions, such as anxiety, can interfere with the thinking processes (memory, concentration) needed to solve math problems. If women experience more anxiety than men during important math tests, then the influence of emotion on thinking explains the gender difference.

Answer 3: The brain is very complex; different parts of the brain do different things. If parts of the brain that are *not* useful for solving math problems are highly active during a math test, their activity can interfere with regions of the brain needed for math. This can hurt performance. If women's brain activity during math tests differs from men's, then brain activity explains the gender difference in math test performance.

The answers refer to three different aspects of the same phenomenon: *people* (who experience stereotypes), the *mind* (in which emotions influence thinking processes), and the *brain* (and its many subparts). The person, mind, and brain explanations may each be correct and can complement one another. As you move down a level, you get a deeper understanding of the higher level. Why are people affected by stereotypes? It is because, at the level of mental processes, emotions influence thinking. Why do emotions influence thinking? It is because, at the level of the brain, a part of the brain that generates emotions is connected to parts of the brain involved in the logical thinking needed to do math.

Note that the three levels of analysis, although complementary, are not identical. Person and mind differ. People have minds, but the mind is not identical to the person as a whole; there is more to you than just your thinking processes. Mind and brain differ. If you poke around in a human brain, you won't literally see any thoughts in there, and a brain removed from a body won't, by itself, be able to do any thinking.

Had you ever considered that the mind and the brain differ?

You (a person) think (a mental, or mind, activity) using your brain (the biological tool needed for thinking). The three answers about women and math tests, then, illustrate distinct *person*, *mind*, and *brain* levels of analysis.

RESEARCH AT PERSON, MIND, AND BRAIN LEVELS OF ANALYSIS. In addition to proposing explanations at different levels of analysis, psychologists also conduct research at each of the three levels—*person, mind,* and *brain*—to see whether their explanations are correct. Here is an example.

At a person level, two psychologists (Quinn & Spencer, 2001) ran the following study. They asked men and women to come to a psychology laboratory and take a math test. Some of the men and women simply sat down and took the test. Others first received this information: "Prior use of these problems has shown them to be gender-fair—that is, men and women perform equally well on these problems" (Quinn & Spencer, 2001, p. 64). The researchers found that when men and women just sat down and took the test, men outperformed women. But when participants first were told that the tests were gender-fair, women and men performed equally. The gender-fair instructions reduced *stereotype threat* (Steele, 1997), that is, negative thoughts and feelings that occur when people think they may confirm a negative stereotype about their group (as you saw in this chapter's opening story). The elimination of stereotype threat eliminated male–female differences in performance (Quinn & Spencer, 2001). The findings, then, supported a *person-level* explanation: Women are affected by stereotypes that lower their performance.

In research conducted at a mind level of analysis, psychologists explored the relationship between anxiety and thinking processes (Ashcraft & Kirk, 2001). They expected that, within the minds of all persons, anxiety can impair thinking. To test this, they asked a group of research participants (1) to report how much anxiety they experience when thinking about math and (2) to try to remember a list of words and numbers. When the researchers related levels of anxiety to accuracy of memory, they found that *higher* anxiety was associated with *worse* memory (Ashcraft & Kirk, 2001). Because memory is needed to perform well in math (you have to keep track of the numbers and words in a math problem), high anxiety thus could reduce math performance. This fact about the mind (anxiety can impair memory and thinking) deepens our understanding of the previous fact about people. Why do stereotypes affect people's scores on math tests? The stereotypes may increase anxiety, which impairs thinking.

At our third level of analysis, a team of psychologists (Krendl et al., 2008) studied women's brain activity during math tests by using *brain-imaging* methods, which depict activity in the brain while people perform tasks. In their study, some women, but not others, were told that prior research shows that men and women differ in math ability; this information was expected to increase the impact of stereotypes. All women—whether they heard this stereotype-relevant information or not—then took a math test.

> On what kinds of tasks might you experience heightened anxiety and reduced memory capacity?

The study produced two findings. First, stereotypes influenced performance; women who heard the stereotype-relevant information performed less well. Second, stereotypes influenced the brain. Women who heard the stereotype-related information showed increased activity in a brain region involved in the production of emotional experiences. Among women who did *not* hear the stereotype information, the most active brain regions were those useful for solving math problems (Krendl et al., 2008). This finding further deepens our understanding. Stereotypes activate different brain regions; the brain activity contributes (at the level of the mind) to different patterns of emotion and thought; and the brain and mental activity contribute (at the level of persons) to gender differences in test scores (Figure 1.2).

Factors in addition to stereotypes can affect math performance and contribute to gender differences. Men and women may differ in their level of interest in math, in specific mental abilities (including abilities that enable people to succeed in nonmathematical fields), and in brain structure and functioning (Ceci, Williams, & Barnett, 2009; Stoet & Geary, 2012). Most psychological phenomena are affected by many factors, and math performance is no exception. Nonetheless, research on how stereotypes can affect persons, the mind, and the brain shows how different levels of explanation can combine to provide multilevel understanding in psychological science.

😊 WHAT DO YOU KNOW?...

7. Research at the _____ level of analysis deepens our understanding of the effect of gender stereotypes on math performance by showing that anxiety impairs _____. Research at the _____ level deepens our understanding further by demonstrating that stereotypes activate brain regions associated with _____, rather than those useful for math processing.

Earlier in this chapter, you tried our first Try This! exercise. If you didn't, do it now; it's at www.pmbpsychology.com. Let's review what you learned.

Our first Try This! teaches a valuable lesson about the power of scientific methods, which can provide knowledge that exceeds what one knows from intuition alone.

lightpoet / Shutterstock

Stereotype threat Women's performance on math tests can be affected by stereotypes. Why? It can be understood at three different levels of analysis: (1) The individual *person* is affected by social stereotypes; (2) processes in the *mind* that are needed for memory are impaired by anxiety; and (3) the activation of *brain* systems involved in emotional arousal can interfere with the activity of brain systems required for mathematical reasoning.

The Virginian-Pilot file photo

Negative stereotypes This student in Norfolk, Virginia, was, in 1958, one of the first Black students to attend a previously all-White school. Among the many challenges such students faced were social stereotypes. Psychological research shows that stereotypes can affect people's behavior, thinking processes, and brain activity.

figure 1.2

PMB IN ACTION

HOW DO GENDER STEREOTYPES AFFECT TEST PERFORMANCE?

Each chapter of this book contains a PMB in Action feature like this one. PMB in Action shows you how a given question (in this case, "How do gender stereotypes affect test performance?") can be answered at each of three levels of analysis: person, mind, and brain.

(P) PERSON

Gender stereotypes about math performance can affect people, causing women to experience negative thoughts and feelings known as stereotype threat that, in turn, lower test performance.

(M) MIND

Gender stereotypes can affect mental processes, increasing anxiety which, in turn, impairs memory. Impaired memory ability can lower test performance.

Emotional Arousal: **INCREASED ANXIETY** → Thinking Ability: **IMPAIRED MEMORY**

(B) BRAIN

Stereotypes can affect the brain, increasing activity in a lower region of the brain involved in producing emotions, rather than higher-level brain regions that are useful for solving math problems.

Gallery Stock

Intuitively, you probably thought that the only way in which memory could be flawed is that you might forget information you saw previously. But thanks to Try This!, you learn of the existence of another type of flaw: "remembering" information you did *not* see previously. When trying to remember words presented on a list, many people have the experience of recalling a word that was not actually present. The carefully constructed research methods of the Try This! exercise (Roediger & McDermott, 1995) convincingly demonstrate this fascinating and surprising fact about memory.

At this point in your reading, you also should be able to identify the level of analysis at which the Try This! exercise was conducted. It was at a *mind* level of analysis; the study reveals a property of the mind, namely, a memory error. You will learn more about the mind, and its powers—and errors—of memory, in Chapter 6.

Psychology: The Science of Person, Mind, and Brain: An Overview

You will encounter person, mind, and brain analyses throughout this book; this is why it is titled *Psychology: The Science of Person, Mind, and Brain*. The book's organization reflects activity in the twenty-first-century science of psychology. After psychologists learn an interesting fact about the behavior of people, they often try to "dig deeper" to understand it at the level of the mind's structures and processes. Once they accomplish that, they dig deeper still, to understand the brain activity that enables the mind to function as it does. You'll do the same thing, as you encounter research findings at the levels of person, mind, and brain.

This book reflects psychology's multilevel nature in two ways:

1. *Individual chapters:* Each chapter begins with a story about the behavior and experiences of a person. Our effort, in each chapter, is to introduce you first to the human experiences that motivate psychologists to study the material covered in that chapter. Once we do this, we'll move down to mind and brain levels of analysis, to see how research on mental systems and brain mechanisms deepens the scientific understanding of people. Coverage of the brain generally is found in the later sections of any given chapter. You'll thus be learning about brain research only after first learning about the psychological phenomena that researchers are trying to understand by studying the brain.

2. The book as a whole. This book has four parts. Here in the initial part, the current chapter introduces the field and Chapter 2 acquaints you with its main research methods. The other three parts of the book—Brain, Mind, and Person—cover parts of the field in which research at brain, mind, and person levels of analysis predominates. Individual chapters within each part focus on specific topics in psychological science: for example, how we perceive the world; factors that affect our level of motivation; how individuals develop psychologically from childhood through adulthood; and how therapy can help people who are experiencing psychological disorders. The brain, mind, and person parts can be read in any order; Chapters 1 and 2 provide enough background that you can move directly to any of the other parts of the book.

Learning that your psychology book has separate parts, each with chapters on separate topics, can create a false impression. It might appear that psychology is a collection of isolated subfields that have little to do with one another. This is not the case. Especially in recent years, psychology has become a highly integrated science, with different parts of the field informing one another. The levels of analysis we have discussed are key to this integration. Researchers in different branches of the field commonly explore, at different levels, the same psychological phenomenon. Their research results thus inform one another. Consider this example.

TRY THIS!

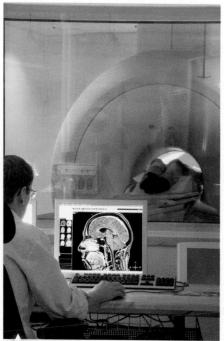

Deco / Alamy

Brain imaging When studying the brain, a key source of evidence is brain imaging. Brain-imaging methods enable researchers to see which parts of a person's brain are most active when the person is engaged in different types of mental activities. The methods, then, help researchers to connect across levels of analysis, from *brain* to *mind* and *person*.

Psychologists are interested in *self-control*, people's ability to regulate their emotions and behavior. If you feel like ordering a big dessert but then give yourself contrary instructions (e.g., "Don't forget how fattening desserts are!" or "Don't even look at the dessert menu!"), you are exerting self-control. Self-control is explored in different branches of the field, at different levels of analysis:

> At a person level, personality psychologists identify individual differences in self-control abilities that are evident early in life and persist into adolescence and adulthood (Chapter 13).

> At a mind level, memory researchers find there is a mental system with "executive" abilities that can control the flow of thoughts and emotions (Chapter 6).

> At a brain level, researchers find that interconnected brain regions are active when self-control is exerted (Chapter 3); one brain region regulates activity in another.

Research in these different areas combines to yield a coherent portrait of how the brain and mind enable people to exert self-control. Such examples of integration abound in psychology today, as you'll see in the chapters ahead.

Throughout this book, we will highlight these interconnections among different branches of psychology. A PMB Connections feature will show you how research studies conducted at one level of analysis connect to studies conducted at other levels of analysis, which are presented elsewhere in the text.

Psychology's History

Thus far in this chapter, we have focused on the present: today's psychological science. Now let's look back in time. Understanding psychology's past can enrich your understanding of the contemporary science.

When reviewing psychology's history, it is hard to know where to start. Humans have been asking psychological questions about humans—"Can this person be trusted?" "Is that person a good leader?" "Do these people like me?"—throughout our species' history (Heyes, 2012). The dawn of humanity, however, is too far back to begin. We want to start with the first systematic psychological theories, that is, the first organized frameworks for understanding people and the human mind.

"The way this works is that you say the first thing that comes to your mind…"

Joseph Farris / Cartoonstock.com

Psychologists in the Ancient World: Aristotle and the Buddha

Preview Question

> How were Aristotle and the Buddha like and not like modern psychologists?

The first systematic psychological theories are ancient. Psychology's history began more than 2400 years ago.

ARISTOTLE. Many foundations of Western civilization were established in a relatively short period of time by the people of a relatively small city—fifth-century BCE Athens and its population of less than 100,000 citizens. Their accomplishments are nearly beyond belief: unsurpassed architecture and sculpture; philosophical analyses that stood for centuries as the greatest intellectual achievements of the Western world;

the invention of novel forms of literature and entertainment, such as dramatic theater; and political systems that form the basis of democratic government.

The Athenians also explored *psyche*—in Greek, "the soul or mind." Athens's greatest "psyche-ologist" was Aristotle.

Aristotle was not a psychologist in the contemporary sense of the word. He didn't answer questions by using scientific methods—but who can blame him? They weren't invented until 2000 years after he lived. Yet he formulated ideas about the mind, and the relation between mind and body (Bolton, 1978), in the careful, logical, systematic manner of a scientific theory.

Aristotle was interested in classification. To *classify* something is to identify it as a member of a category. For instance, if Fido strolls by and you call him a "dog," you've classified him, placing him into the category "dog." Aristotle classified different types of mental capacities, that is, the variety of things that the human mind is able to do. Remarkably, his ancient classification scheme seems modern; it resembles classifications found in twenty-first-century psychology. Aristotle's categories included:

> *Perception:* The ability of people and animals to become aware of objects in the environment.

> *Memory:* Aristotle not only classified memory as a distinct ability, but also recognized variations among different types of memory. Some memories, he noted, "pop" into mind (e.g., while reading this, you might suddenly think of something a friend said recently), whereas others come to mind only with effort (e.g., during an exam, it might take effort to remember the name of the ancient Greek who classified different mental abilities).

> *Desire, rational thought, and action:* Aristotle discussed differences between humans and animals. Both, he said, have desires that motivate behavior. But unlike animals, humans also have rational thought, that is, careful, logical thinking. Human action, then, has two distinct causes that frequently conflict: desire and rational thinking.

We'll say more about Aristotle in a moment. But first, let's look at the ideas of someone who lived at about the same time as Aristotle, but in a different part of the world.

The Greek scholar Aristotle, who developed sophisticated ideas about the mind more than 2300 years ago but lacked the scientific methods needed to put those ideas to the test.

When was the last time rational thinking conflicted with desire in determining your behavior?

THE BUDDHA. In northern India, in the sixth to fifth century BCE, the son of a wealthy ruler decided to seek wisdom rather than wealth. History tells us that he found it. He became known as the Buddha.

You may think of the Buddha as a religious figure, which certainly is correct. Yet he posed questions that were purely psychological. In particular, he asked about the causes of emotion: Why, despite their intelligence, are people so prone to experiencing negative emotions—anger, jealousy, disappointment, envy? The Buddha proposed that two thoughts combined to create emotional suffering: People (1) believe they are separate from the world (as opposed to being part of the world of nature), and (2) believe they will be happier if they acquire more worldly possessions (more money, a nicer home, higher-status friends, etc.). Rather than happiness, however, these thoughts cause suffering. People inevitably want more and more things. They become stuck in a cycle of desire, disappointment, envy, and more desire.

Do you think the Buddha was correct in his belief concerning the cause of suffering?

The Buddha suggested a cure for suffering; in contemporary psychological language, he proposed a "therapy" to reduce negative emotion. It was meditation. Meditating on the nature of self and the causes of suffering, he said, could bring insight that eliminates emotional distress.

He who dies with the most toys, WINS!

t_kimura / Getty Images

This is just the sort of thinking that the Buddha warned against.

Like Aristotle, the Buddha did not employ scientific methods; he was not a psychologist in the contemporary sense of the term. Yet his *ideas* seem contemporary. Researchers today, like the Buddha, study how thinking processes create emotional distress (Chapters 10 and 14). They also explore the effects of meditation on brain functioning (Chapter 9).

LEARNING FROM THE ANCIENTS. Our look at Aristotle and the Buddha teaches us two lessons. The first concerns the question of what is, and is not, "new" in contemporary psychological science.

Although many questions asked in contemporary psychology are new, what is striking is that so many have been asked for ages. Ancient questions—such as how one can classify different types of mental activity and how thoughts and emotions interact—remain current today. Aristotle would be surprised by contemporary research methods, but would find many of the questions being addressed in twenty-first-century psychology familiar. Today's psychology provides novel, research-based answers to timeless questions about human nature.

The second lesson concerns the goals of psychology, that is, the aims of all this thinking about people, the mind, and the brain. Aristotle's and the Buddha's goals differed. Aristotle pursued knowledge for knowledge's sake: "He wished to understand men for the sake of that understanding" (Watson, 1963, p. 44). The Buddha pursued a practical goal: He was "not motivated by theoretical curiosity" but by "the overriding practical aim . . . of deliverance from suffering" (Bodhi, 1993, p. 4); he wanted to help people live happier lives (Dalai Lama & Cutler, 1998). The differences mirror those found in psychology today. Many psychologists are researchers whose goal is to expand scientific knowledge about people, the mind, and the brain. But thousands of others, like the Buddha, work on a practical goal. They apply psychological knowledge—in schools, communities, businesses, and one-on-one therapy encounters—to improve people's well-being.

What do you think is the value of seeking knowledge for knowledge's sake?

🌐 WHAT DO YOU KNOW?...

8. In what way(s) was Aristotle like a modern psychologist? Which statements in the following list apply?
   a. He systematically formulated ideas about the mind–body connection.
   b. He answered questions using scientific methods.
   c. He was interested in classification.
   d. He was interested in the causes of emotional suffering.
   e. He proposed a therapeutic technique for reducing emotional suffering.
9. In what way(s) was the Buddha like a modern psychologist? Which statements in the preceding (same) list apply?

Jumping Ahead 2000 Years: Locke, Kant, and "Nature Versus Nurture"

Preview Question

> How did the philosophers Locke and Kant believe that humans acquire knowledge?

We're now going to jump ahead by two millennia from the time of Aristotle and the Buddha. It's quite a jump—yet we are still hundreds of years in the past. You will meet two people who were philosophers, not psychological scientists; they did not answer questions using scientific methods. But they did raise questions that remain current today. Foremost among these is the nature–nurture question.

"NATURE VERSUS NURTURE." The distinction between *nature* and *nurture* pertains to the origin of psychological characteristics. Where did our beliefs, our abilities, and our likes and dislikes come from? Two possibilities are:

1. **Nature:** Nature (used in this context) refers to a biological origin of psychological characteristics. Characteristics that you have thanks to nature are ones you inherit; they are part of your genetic makeup. Colloquially, one says that they are "hard wired."

2. **Nurture:** Nurture, which means "to educate or bring up" (think "nursery school"), refers to the development of abilities through experiences in the world. Abilities that come from nurture are those you learn rather than inherit.

Nature undoubtedly is the source of some behaviors: coughing, sneezing, putting your hand out in a fraction of a second to break your fall if you slip on ice. Nobody had to teach you these things. Nurture clearly is the source of other actions: driving, cooking, riding a bicycle. You acquired these skills through experience. But many other cases are less clear. The relative significance of nature and nurture has been debated since the seventeenth century, when it was explored by John Locke.

> What are some things you're engaged in right now that could only have been learned by experience (nurture)? Which ones are "hard wired" (by nature)?

LOCKE. John Locke was a British philosopher who produced his major work in the late 1600s, a remarkable time in world history. In the prior two centuries, Europe had experienced an intellectual rebirth—a "renaissance." Scholars abandoned the ancient practice of relying on the authority of Aristotle or the Church for answers to scientific questions. Instead, they looked for their own answers. When, for example, the Italian scientist Galileo Galilei asked questions about the universe, he didn't look to the Bible for answers. He took out his telescope and looked to the skies. Renaissance scholars launched modern scientific methods.

By the time of Locke, scholars became optimistic that their era could unravel not only the mysteries of the physical world, but also the mysteries of the human mind. Locke took up the question "Where do people get their ideas; that is, what is the origin of concepts in the mind?"

Locke said that we get our ideas from experience; he argued for nurture, not nature. Ideas, he claimed, originate in our perceptions of the world. When we experience events, vision, hearing, and other senses bring information from the world into our minds. This experience-based information is the source of our ideas. We repeatedly experience, for example, that we can plunge our hand into a bucket of water but not into a tree, a rock, or a brick wall. From such experiences, we develop the concepts of "liquid" and "solid."

At birth, one hasn't yet had any experiences in the world. According to Locke, then, the mind at birth is a "blank slate": a blackboard on which nothing has yet been written. It has the capacity to be written upon; nature provides the ability to learn. But nurture—experience—provides all the ideas.

This conception of how we acquire ideas seems so obvious that you might wonder if anyone would question it. Someone did: a philosopher in eighteenth-century Germany named Immanuel Kant.

Red Images, LLC / Alamy

Speaking and writing The ability to speak and to understand others' spoken words is shaped significantly by nature. Throughout human history, people have communicated through spoken language. As a result, you inherited mental abilities that enabled you to speak fluently even before you went to school. But the ability to write is a product of nurture. Although biologically modern humans have been around for tens of thousands of years, the first writing system was not invented until about 3000 years ago, and you needed time in the classroom to learn how to write.

nature In psychology, a biological origin of psychological characteristics. Characteristics that come from nature are those that are inherited.

nurture The development of abilities through experiences in the world. Abilities that come from nurture are those that are learned rather than inherited.

KANT. Kant knew that people learned from experience. But he did not think of the mind as a blank slate. Some ideas, he believed, are present in the mind from birth, thanks to nature.

Kant would acknowledge that, yes, experience teaches that if you decide to plunge your hand into a space occupied by a brick wall, your decision will cause pain a short time later. But, Kant would ask, how did you learn the concept of "time," and the idea that some things happen "after" (later in time than) others? You can't *see* time. It's unlikely that, in childhood, your parents gave you a lecture on the nature of time. Yet concepts of time, and "before" and "after," seem to be part of the mind at an early age.

Similarly, Kant would ask, where did you learn the concept of "space"—that objects are located in three-dimensional physical space, with one object being behind, in front, above, or below another? Or the concept of causality—that one event can cause another? Again, children seem to know these concepts without being taught them explicitly.

Kant claimed that ideas such as space, time, and causality are innate: products of nature, not nurture. Kant, then, thought Locke got it wrong. The mind is not a blank slate. It contains some ideas at birth.

> Had you ever before considered that the concept of time is innate?

Today, scientists continue to debate the nature–nurture questions anticipated by Locke and Kant (Elman et al., 1996; Goldhaber, 2012; Pinker, 2002; Shea, 2012). You will see these questions in later chapters, especially Chapter 4, "Nature, Nurture, and Their Interaction."

ⓦ WHAT DO YOU KNOW?...

10. When speaking of his son's pitching talent, Steve brags he was "born with a golden arm." Is Steve's thinking more in line with Locke or with Kant?

Moving Into the Modern Era: Wundt and James

Preview Question

> › Why are Wundt and James considered the founders of scientific psychology?

When discussing Aristotle, the Buddha, Locke, and Kant, we said that each was not a psychologist, in the contemporary sense of the term. Now let's turn to the genuine article: psychological scientists.

WUNDT. Scientific psychology has a definitive starting point: 1875, when Wilhelm Wundt arrived at the University of Leipzig as a professor and started the experimental research laboratory that was formalized as the Institute of Experimental Psychology in 1879 (Bringmann & Ungerer, 1980; Harper, 1950).

As a student, Wundt studied biology and earned a medical degree. But three factors turned his attention to psychology. One was sheer interest; studying the mind, he thought, was more interesting than treating patients (Wertheimer, 1970). A second was his knowledge of technical advances in science and medicine. Wundt recognized that newly invented devices for observing parts of the body (e.g., the interior of the eye, the vocal cords) could be used to study psychological functions (seeing, speaking). The third was Wundt's knowledge of advances in the study of the nervous system. German scientists had developed experimental methods to study how the cells of the body's nervous system work. Because, as Wundt knew, the brain and nervous system are the biological bases of the mind, the advances in biology held the promise of a successful experimental psychology (Watson, 1963).

Wundt, then, initiated this new field. To do so, he took two critical steps. He wrote *Principles of Physiological Psychology,* a book that combined biological knowledge with analyses of the mind. In particular, he explored the mind's capacity for *consciousness,* that is, the capacity to perceive events in the world and to have feelings (Chapter 9). His second big step was to open his laboratory at the University of Leipzig (Harper, 1950). In his laboratory work, Wundt established procedures that would become standard throughout experimental psychology. He systematically varied the circumstances in which people performed tasks. He precisely measured aspects of their performance, such as the length of time it took them to solve problems (Robinson, 2002). In so doing, he pioneered the experimental methods we'll discuss in Chapter 2.

Wundt's lab attracted students from both Europe and the United States. When they returned home with their degrees, they spread knowledge of the new science of psychology. Wundt, deservedly called "the father of experimental psychology," thus planted the seeds of today's global psychological science community.

The father of experimental psychology, Wilhelm Wundt (seated), with his laboratory assistants in Leipzig.

JAMES. Wundt was not the only person to open a psychological laboratory in 1875. Another opened in the United States, at Harvard University (Boring, 1929; Harper, 1950). In terms of research activities, it was more modest in scope. But its director was an intellectual giant: William James.

James suffered from a problem that plagues few of us. He had such a wide range of talents that he had trouble deciding what to do for a living. In the 1860s, he switched "from science to painting to science to painting again, then to chemistry, anatomy, natural history, and finally medicine" (Menand, 2001, p. 75). After earning his medical degree, he switched to psychology and began writing an introductory psychology book. (After finishing it, he changed fields again and became one of America's greatest philosophers.)

James began his introductory psychology book in 1878. He thought he would finish it by 1880, but was off by a decade (Watson, 1963). The book grew "to a length," James remarked, "which no one can regret more than the writer himself" (James, 1890, p. xiii). When published in 1890, it proved worth the wait. Many view James's *The Principles of Psychology* as the greatest comprehensive volume in the history of the field (see Austin, 2013).

James's book not only introduced the field, but *defined* it. In 1890 psychology's scope was unclear; people didn't know exactly what the field was, or could be. By perceptively analyzing a vast range of topics—consciousness, self-concept, thought, emotion, instinct, social behavior, will power, hypnotism—James made each a part of the new field. His breadth of vision contributed significantly to the breadth of topics you will encounter in this book.

In his book's final chapter, James addressed nature, nurture, and the views of Locke and Kant. He sided with Kant more than Locke, concluding that the mind at

It must have been a good conference Third from the left in the front row, attending a conference at Clark University in 1909, is William James. Fourth from the right in the front row is another conference attendee, Sigmund Freud, whose psychoanalytic school of thought is introduced in the next section.

Clark University Archives

birth has a "native structure" (James, 1890, p. 889). Of particular importance, however, is not the content of James's conclusion but how he reached it. James explained that the way to resolve the age-old Locke/Kant philosophical debate was *not* by engaging in more philosophical debate. What was needed, instead, was scientific evidence. This intellectual move—from philosophical debate to scientific data—is the critical step that established psychology as a science.

⚡ WHAT DO YOU KNOW?

11. Wundt's practice of systematically varying the circumstances in which people performed tasks and precisely measuring their outcomes marked him as the "father of _____ psychology." James's agreement with Kant on the nature–nurture debate was grounded in _____ evidence.

◎ CULTURAL OPPORTUNITIES

Psychology Goes Global

In its early days, scientific psychology was a European and North American enterprise; the first laboratories and academic departments were established in western Europe and the United States. The field's nineteenth-century founders, however, had global goals, and held the first international psychology convention in Paris in 1889.

It turned out not to be quite as global as one might have hoped. Of the approximately 400 people in attendance, three were from the United States, four from England, and three from Germany; the vast majority were from the home country of France (Benjamin & Baker, 2012). The early twentieth century saw greater interaction among American and European psychologists. However, the field was slow to expand beyond its European and North American base; psychology's largest international convention, the International Congress of Psychology, was not held outside of Europe and the United States until 1972. Throughout much of its history, scientific psychology was not well informed by the scholars and cultural traditions of Asia, Africa, South America, and the Pacific (Berry, 2013).

Fortunately, matters have substantially changed in the twenty-first century. Psychology is now a global endeavor: The largest international association of psychology has 74 member nations (Benjamin & Baker, 2012), researchers collaborate across continents, and scientific journals have global scope. For instance, journals published by the Association for Psychological Science, an organization founded in the United States, included articles authored by scientists from 36 different nations in one recent two-year period (Cervone, 2012).

This global scope brings great opportunities—*cultural* opportunities. In the past, psychologists conducted research almost solely with people in their home country. They thus could not know whether a study's results would differ if it were conducted in a different culture. But today's psychologists often conduct research in multiple countries, with different cultures, to determine culture's impact (Gelfand, Chiu, & Hong, 2013). Cross-cultural evidence advances all branches of psychological science.

You will see these advances throughout this book, most notably in each chapter's Cultural Opportunities feature.

⚡ WHAT DO YOU KNOW?

12. What are two cultural opportunities afforded by an increase in the global scope of psychological science?

Schools of Thought

Preview Question

> What characterizes six of the most prominent schools of thought in psychology?

Most scientific activity in psychology today is problem-focused. Researchers try to solve specific scientific problems in the study of people, the mind, and the brain. But in the field's early days, they had another task: figuring out how, in general, the field should conduct itself. What should psychology's main focus of study be? How should psychologists formulate theories and conduct research?

Psychologists provided diverse answers to these questions. The field thus contained alternative *schools of thought,* that is, general approaches to building a psychological science. Let's review six of them. The first two, which we will consider together, are *structuralism* and *functionalism.*

STRUCTURALISM AND FUNCTIONALISM. The distinction between structuralism and functionalism in psychology is best understood through an analogy to biology (Titchener, 1898). Biologists can study the body in either of two ways. Dissection reveals the body's structures (bones, soft tissue, fluids). Study of the body *in action* reveals its functions, that is, what it does (digestion, respiration, and so forth). A similar distinction can be drawn in psychology.

Structuralism is a school of thought that emphasized study of the mind's basic components, or structures. Structuralists said that complex mental experiences were made up of simple, elementary components of the mind (Titchener, 1898). Like ingredients combined in a cake recipe, components of the mind combine to form an overall mental experience. Suppose, for example, that you look at a painting. You have one overall mental experience ("Hey, I like that weird smile on Mona Lisa"). This experience, structuralists would say, combines basic mental elements such as perception (you perceive patterns of light and color) and feelings (you like the picture). Perception and feeling, then, would be basic structures of the mind.

Functionalism emphasizes study of the mind in action. Functionalists were interested in what the mind *does*—what it's good for—rather than what components it contains. Functionalists tried to identify the mental activities that occur (e.g., learning, memory) as organisms adapt to their environment. They highlighted the relation between the mind and the body—in the language of this book, they related mind and brain levels of analysis—because mental functions evolved only if they were successful in promoting physical survival (Angell, 1906).

Proponents of structuralism and functionalism recognized that both schools of thought would contribute to psychology's growth (Watson, 1963). Their differences, then, were merely differences in emphasis. People disagreed on where psychologists should devote most of their efforts when forging the new field.

PSYCHOANALYSIS. Structuralism and functionalism developed in psychology departments in European and American universities. A third school of thought developed in the late nineteenth century outside of academia—in the offices of a physician in Vienna, Austria.

Sigmund Freud developed a school of thought known as *psychoanalysis.* As we detail in Chapter 13, psychoanalysis claims that the mind contains different parts (Freud, 1900, 1923). The parts are in conflict with one another. For example, one part contains sexual impulses, whereas another contains social rules that prohibit people from acting on their sexual impulses. Freud claimed that people are not fully aware of these conflicts; much of mental life occurs outside of awareness, or is *unconscious.*

Paul Signac / The Bridgeman Art Library / Getty Images

Elementary structures This painting can be analyzed in terms of its elementary structures. A pointillist painting by Frenchman Paul Signac, it consists of a series of individual dots of colored paint. The elementary structures, the dots, combine to form the overall portrait of a woman by a lamp. According to structural psychologists, the mind can be similarly analyzed in terms of elementary parts that combine to form an overall mental experience.

structuralism A school of thought focusing on the mind's basic components, or structures, and how they come together to create complex mental experiences.

functionalism A school of thought focusing on the mental activity of the mind rather than on its structure, as it interacts with the body and adapts to the environment.

Freud developed a theory of human nature and a therapy for treating psychological disorders, both of which had enormous impact on society. Yet within the science of psychology, Freud's work was—and, to the present day, is—sharply criticized. Researchers considered psychoanalysis too speculative; many of its claims could not even be tested. They looked for a firmer basis for building a science. One place they found it was the school of thought known as *behaviorism.*

Matt Meadows / Getty Images

Rat, mind, and brain? Psychologists in a school of thought known as behaviorism often conducted research on the behavior of laboratory animals, such as rats learning to navigate through mazes. This kind of research had a key advantage: It allowed for accurate scientific measurement of observable behavior. However, psychologists in other schools of thought, such as *humanistic psychology,* noted that it also had a big disadvantage: Research on rats deflected attention from the scientific study of psychological experiences unique to humans. In today's psychology, research with animals remains important in many branches of the field, but the large majority of research studies are conducted with people.

behaviorism A school of thought focusing solely on the prediction and control of behavior, by studying how the environment shapes observable actions.

humanistic psychology An intellectual movement which argues that everyday personal experiences—thoughts, feelings, hopes, fears, sense of self—should be psychologists' main target of study.

BEHAVIORISM. Behaviorism differed strikingly from structuralist, functionalist, and psychoanalytic approaches to studying the mind. The big difference was that, according to behaviorism's founder, John Watson, psychologists shouldn't study the mind at all. Watson (1913) declared **behaviorism** to be a school of thought whose sole focus is the "prediction and control of behavior" (p. 158). By behavior, Watson meant observable actions—visible movements of an organism that could be observed and accurately recorded by an experimenter. The contents of mind, by contrast, cannot be directly observed. Because observation is key to successful science, Watson reasoned that the study of mind could not be part of a scientific psychology. Psychology should focus exclusively on behavior.

The psychologist B. F. Skinner (1953) developed a slightly different version of behaviorism. Like Watson, Skinner emphasized the study of behavior, but he defined "behavior" to include thinking and feeling. Skinner's behaviorism thus analyzed the full range of psychological experiences. In Skinner's analysis, the ultimate cause of all behavior—all bodily movements, thoughts, and feelings—is the environment; environmental influences gradually shape behavior over the course of an organism's life. Psychology's primary task, then, is to study the impact of the environment on behavior. Chapter 7 details the psychological system Skinner developed.

Behaviorists believed that the processes through which the environment shapes behavior are universal—the same for all organisms. This theoretical claim had a major implication for conducting research: It meant that researchers could study any organism they wished. Most behaviorists chose to study animals that were easy to maintain in a laboratory, such as rats. When behaviorism dominated American psychology, in the 1920s through 1950s, the "rat lab" was where psychology students spent most of their time.

Behaviorism added scientific rigor to psychology. But many felt it had a second influence that was detrimental: By studying rats, behaviorism deflected attention from the unique qualities of human beings. This critique motivated a school of thought known as *humanistic psychology.*

HUMANISTIC PSYCHOLOGY. **Humanistic psychology** is an intellectual movement which argues that the everyday personal experiences of human beings—their thoughts, feelings, hopes, fears, and personal beliefs about who they are and what they wish to become—must be psychologists' main target of study (Smith, 1990). Humanistic psychologists direct the field's attention to the person as a whole, rather than to isolated psychological structures and processes considered one at a time.

To you, early in your first course in psychology, this point might seem obvious. Aren't all psychologists interested in people's experiences? But when humanistic psychologists surveyed psychology in the mid-twentieth century, they judged that human experience was being shortchanged. Behaviorists experimented on rats. Psychoanalysts discussed mental conflicts of which people were not even aware. "Neither of these two versions of psychology dealt with human beings as human. Nor did they deal with real problems of life," said Rollo May, a leading humanistic psychologist of the time (quoted in Smith, 1990, p. 8).

Humanistic psychologists addressed multiple challenges. Carl Rogers developed a humanistic theory of personality that centered on people's experiences of themselves, or self-concept (Chapter 13), as well as a method of therapy that provided a major alternative to psychoanalysis (Chapter 15). Abraham Maslow analyzed motivation, identifying human motivational needs ranging from food and safety to the need to mature and grow psychologically (Chapter 11). In this work, humanistic psychologists emphasized human strengths, especially people's inherent capacities to understand themselves and the world around them and to grow toward psychological maturity.

An intellectual movement in the twenty-first century parallels the earlier humanistic school of thought. **Positive psychology** argues that psychologists have devoted excessive attention to human frailties, and instead should focus on "positive individual traits" (Seligman & Csikszentmihalyi, 2000, p. 5) such as love, courage, forgiveness, and spirituality. These traits are strengths that enable people to cope with difficult circumstances, to bounce back from setbacks, and to gain wisdom from their experiences (Aspinwall & Staudinger, 2002; Gable & Haidt, 2005; Keyes, Fredrickson, & Park, 2012). Some worry that the positive psychology movement, though well intentioned, is insufficiently complex; most psychological characteristics—even those labeled "positive"—can have either positive or negative effects on well-being, depending on the situation a person is in (McNulty & Fincham, 2012). Nonetheless, positive psychology remains influential today, as it advances themes sounded originally by the humanistic psychologists of the past century.

Humanistic psychology is consistent with something else you can find in psychology today: this book. Humanistic psychologists argued that the experiences of people, who live complex lives and contemplate the lives they live, are psychology's ultimate target of investigation. They were right. Throughout this book, we strive to show how each of the diverse areas of psychological science illuminates the lives and experiences of people. Our primary tool to accomplish this is the book's *person-first* approach: We introduce topics, whenever possible, at a person level of analysis. This lets you see how each of the field's diverse topics sheds light on the human experience.

The latter decades of the twentieth century witnessed scientific advances that enabled psychologists to combine knowledge of people with information about the workings of the mind and brain. Many of these advances were spurred by the final school of thought to be discussed here, information-processing psychology and the cognitive revolution.

INFORMATION PROCESSING AND THE COGNITIVE REVOLUTION.

Behaviorists cautioned against studying the mind. They asserted that any analysis of thinking processes—how the mind retains knowledge, how one thought leads to another—would inevitably be speculative and thus unscientific. But this argument lost ground once a new piece of machinery appeared on the scene: computers. Computers store knowledge. One "thought" in the computer leads to another. These activities in

AP Photo / Disney-ABC Domestic Television, Ida Mae Astute

"I love life. It's a beautiful thing . . . even more so now." Surprising words from someone who recently lost her hands, feet, and one leg to flesh-eating bacteria. Yet those were the words of Aimee Copeland, interviewed here by Katie Couric. Her ability to bounce back from tragedy is a testament to her personal spirit, as well as an example of a human capacity highlighted by the positive psychology movement: the capacity to draw on personal strengths and grow as an individual, despite setbacks in life.

positive psychology An intellectual movement that emphasizes positive individual traits such as love, courage, and forgiveness rather than human frailties.

CORBIS

Where's the touchscreen? These women are programming ENIAC, the first general-purpose computer. By today's standards, it's a dinosaur: huge and slow. Yet it was key to the development of not only computer science, but also psychology. The ability of computers to execute tasks that resembled human thinking led many psychologists to view the human mind as an information-processing system.

> The computer is a member of an important family of artifacts called symbol systems. . . . Another important member of the family is the human mind and brain.
>
> —Herbert Simon (1996, p. 21)

cognitive revolution A school of thought focusing on the mind as an information-processing system; in so doing, it introduced novel forms of theory and research into psychological science.

information-processing system A device that can acquire, store, and manipulate symbols to transform information.

the computer are fully understood by science (computer science). If we can understand thinking in computers, many reasoned, why not in humans?

This reasoning launched an intellectual revolution in psychology in the late 1950s (McCorduck, 2004; Miller, 2003). The **cognitive revolution** argued that the mind's ability to acquire, retain, and draw on knowledge could, and should, be central to psychological science.

But how, exactly, could the mind be studied? Many researchers during the cognitive revolution studied the mind by treating it as an *information-processing system* (Simon, 1969). An **information-processing system** is any device that can acquire, store, and manipulate symbols (e.g., words and numbers). The symbols represent information and instructions for transforming information. Consider the calculator program in your computer. If you enter 2 and 3 and press the addition button, it produces 5. This means the calculator stored symbols representing 2 and 3, and instructions for addition that transformed the combination of 2, 3, and a + sign into 5. The key point for psychology was the following: Because you, too, can add 2 and 3 and get 5 in your mind, your mind may be thought of as an information-processing system that stores and manipulates symbols. Principles of information processing thus could guide the study of the human mind (Simon, 1979).

Today, psychologists recognize that the human mind and brain do not work exactly like a computer. For example, the physical brain changes when you repeatedly practice a thinking skill (Chapter 3), but the physical electronics of your computer do not change when you repeatedly run the same computer program. Nonetheless, the information-processing approach and the overall cognitive revolution were a boon to psychological science. As you'll see later in this book (especially in the chapters on the mind), they produced novel answers to questions about the mind that have intrigued psychologists since the time of Wundt and James.

🐾 WHAT DO YOU KNOW?

13. Match the school of thought with its major idea or area of interest.

1. Structuralism	a. Psychologists should focus on the mind's hidden conflicts.
2. Functionalism	b. Psychologists should study what the mind does, rather than its isolated parts.
3. Psychoanalysis	c. The mind should be understood as an information-processing system.
4. Behaviorism	d. Psychologists should study how different components of the mind come together to form mental experiences.
5. Humanistic psychology	e. Psychology should be built on the study of observable behaviors.
6. Cognitive revolution	f. Psychologists should study the person as a whole.

⟲ Looking Back and Looking Ahead

In this chapter, you've learned what psychology is and where it came from. Today's field is diverse, yet unified by a commitment to scientific research as the means of answering questions. Studies conducted at each of three levels of analysis—person, mind, and brain—inform one another, with mind and brain research deepening our understanding of phenomena first discovered by studying people in the social world. The success of the contemporary field rests on a long series of past achievements, especially the development of scientific methods.

Our next chapter describes research methods—strategies of research and methods of gathering evidence—that are used by today's psychological scientists. These methods achieve the potential first glimpsed by Wundt: the possibility of a truly scientific psychology.

Chapter Review

Now that you have completed this chapter, be sure to turn to Appendix B, where you will find a **Chapter Summary** that is useful for reviewing what you have learned in this introduction to psychology.

Key Terms

behaviorism (p. 28)
cognitive revolution (p. 30)
critical thinking (p. 12)
functionalism (p. 27)
humanistic psychology (p. 28)

information-processing system (p. 30)
levels of analysis (p. 14)
nature (p. 23)
nurture (p. 23)
positive psychology (p. 29)

psychology (p. 4)
scientific methods (p. 9)
scientific questions (p. 10)
structuralism (p. 27)

Questions for Discussion

1. In spite of the superiority of scientific methods over intuition, many of us prefer to rely on intuition to ponder scientific questions. Why do you suppose this is so? [Analyze]

2. The question "Is steak delicious?" is *not* an example of a scientific question. Why not? What are other examples of *non*scientific questions? [Analyze]

3. How can you rewrite the "steak" question above so that it is scientific? [Apply]

4. "How many clowns can fit in a Honda Civic?" is an example of a scientific question. Why? What are other examples of scientific questions? [Analyze]

5. How can you rewrite the "clowns" question above so that it is *not* scientific? [Apply]

6. Psychologists have examined whether first-borns are more successful than later-borns. To study this question scientifically, they had to define *success* so empirical evidence could be gathered. How might they have done so? What are the challenges of defining success? [Analyze]

7. Some psychologists study individual differences in appetite and eating behavior—that is, they seek to understand why some people love to eat and why others can hardly be bothered with food. What kinds of questions would they ask if they were to study this question at each of the three levels of analysis—person, mind, and brain? [Apply]

8. In terms of explaining how humans acquire knowledge, do you side with the "blank slate" view of Locke or with Kant's view that some knowledge is innate? What evidence do you find compelling for either side? Can both views be correct? [Evaluate]

9. You learned that some people fault positive psychology for being too simplistic, citing the fact that even some positive behaviors may have negative consequences in certain situations. What is an example of this idea? Do you agree with the claim that positive psychology may be too simplistic? [Evaluate]

Self-Test

1. The field of psychology encompasses a broad array of areas of study and of activities. One thing that unites the field, though, is that most psychologists
   a. have training in therapeutic techniques.
   b. believe the mind is a "blank slate."
   c. prefer scientific methods.
   d. have experienced psychoanalysis.

2. Lia wants to know whether the people who take Mr. Mekenian's 8:00 A.M. math class enjoy math more than those who take his 3:00 P.M. class, so she speaks with a couple of students in each class and forms an impression that they equally like math, which she then reports. What might Lia have done to better adhere to scientific methods?
   a. She could have recorded her observations more precisely, perhaps by handing out a scale.
   b. She could have described how she made her observations.
   c. She could have posed a question that was more scientific.
   d. Both a and b are correct.

3. "Do programs designed to help people quit smoking work?" is a scientific question because
   a. it would be useful to know the answer.
   b. it can only be answered by collecting evidence.
   c. it can only be answered by scientists.
   d. None of the above. This is not a scientific question.

4. Which of the following quotes best exemplifies the open-minded yet skeptical stance in science?
   a. "Maybe we can communicate with the dead, but I need to see scientific evidence."
   b. "I know we can communicate with the dead, because I myself have experienced it."
   c. "Maybe we can communicate with the dead, but I need to hear what an expert says."
   d. "There is no evidence that could convince me that we can communicate with the dead."

5. An examination of cultural differences in self-esteem is at the _____ level of analysis, whereas an examination of how these differences influence thinking processes occurs at the _____ level of analysis.
   a. mind; brain
   b. person; brain
   c. mind; person
   d. person; mind

6. The thalamus is a brain structure that acts as a kind of "switchboard," relaying incoming information to several areas of the brain and then integrating that information to help people form coherent perceptions. When people are anesthetized, activity in the thalamus greatly decreases. This finding has deepened psychologists' understanding of consciousness, such that research at the _____ level of analysis increased understanding at the _____ level of analysis.
   a. brain; person
   b. mind; person
   c. brain; mind
   d. mind; brain

7. The fact that phenomena such as consciousness, self-control, and math performance can be studied at different levels of analysis suggests that
   a. different levels of analysis are complementary.
   b. psychology is slowly becoming more scientific.
   c. we are social, psychological, and biological creatures.
   d. Both a and c are correct.

8. Aristotle may be counted as a psychologist on the basis that he
   a. was interested in classifying different mental activities.
   b. tried to understand the cause of human suffering.
   c. was the first to conduct psychotherapy.
   d. invented scientific methods.

9. The Buddha's explanation of the cause of human emotions is remarkable for its
   a. scientific validity.
   b. modernity.
   c. ignorance.
   d. audacity.

10. _____ would have a hard time explaining why babies have a sucking reflex.
    a. Kant
    b. James
    c. Locke
    d. Wundt

11. _____ would be most likely to agree with the evolutionary psychologists, who claim that sex differences in the kinds of features people look for in mates are rooted in our evolutionary past.
   a. Kant
   b. James
   c. Locke
   d. Wundt

12. _____ was among the first to use experimental methods to understand mental functioning, earning him the nickname "the father of experimental psychology."
   a. Kant
   b. James
   c. Locke
   d. Wundt

13. Humanistic psychologists and behaviorists would likely disagree on which of the following statements?
   a. People may be motivated by other people.
   b. Behaviors are largely shaped by the environment.
   c. People can be studied using scientific methods.
   d. Human thoughts and feelings should be the psychologist's focus.

14. The cognitive revolution was largely a reaction to the claims of
   a. structuralists.
   b. functionalists.
   c. behaviorists.
   d. psychoanalysts.

15. Locke's argument that we acquire knowledge through our experiences in the environment is most consonant with the focus of the
   a. structuralists.
   b. functionalists.
   c. behaviorists.
   d. evolutionists.

Answers

You can check your answers to the preceding Self-Test and the chapter's What Do You Know? questions in Appendix B.

Research Methods

2

IF YOU'RE GOING ON A FIRST DATE, WHAT SHOULD you plan to do? Perhaps something relaxing: a romantic movie; a walk in the park; a quiet, candlelit dinner where you can talk? Here's some advice from a dating Web site:

Try including an activity that will get the blood pumping! Find out if your date has always had an unfulfilled desire to go sky-diving or parasailing. Or maybe scary movies . . . [or] beach volleyball or a pickup game of flag football are a great way to [get] a good dose of physical arousal. . . . What makes the heart beat can also make the heart melt.

Sky-diving? Scary movies? Well, it could be; maybe physically arousing activities, including frightening ones, do trigger sexual attraction. To find out, two psychologists ran a study.

The participants were men walking across either of two pedestrian bridges that crossed a river in a mountainous region of Canada. One was a heavy, wide, solid cedar bridge that passed 10 feet above the water. The other was scary and arousing: a narrow bridge of wooden boards attached to wire cables, suspended 230 feet above the river. It tilted and swayed when anyone crossed.

The study's procedures were simple. A female experimenter approached unaccompanied men as they crossed the bridges, showed them a drawing of a woman, and asked them to write a dramatic story about her. When they finished, she gave each man her phone number and invited him to call, if he wanted. Afterward, researchers coded the amount of sexual imagery in the stories and recorded the number of men who called (calling was a sign of possible sexual attraction to the experimenter). They then compared the two groups: (1) men on the scary bridge who were physically aroused, and (2) men on the low, solid bridge who were relatively calm.

The results? The groups differed. Men walking on the frightening, arousing bridge displayed higher levels of sexual attraction. Compared with men on the low, solid bridge, they:

> wrote stories with more sexual content, and

> were 4 times more likely to call the experimenter.

The results were exactly what the dating Web site would have predicted!

Lawren / Getty Images

Do these research results convince you that frightening, physically arousing activities can increase sexual attraction? They shouldn't! Even the psychologists who ran the study were not convinced by the findings. Can you tell why not? You'll be able to once you read this chapter on research methods. ◉

EVERYBODY TRIES TO explain behavior. You probably do it all the time. Why did your roommate get so angry? "She's just in a bad mood." Why did that guy not return your message? "Bad memory; he must have forgotten." Why did you only get a C– on an exam? "I'm anxious when taking tests."

When psychologists try to explain behavior, they have a special burden: acquiring scientific evidence that puts their explanation to the test. This chapter presents the *research methods* they use to obtain that evidence.

When you signed up for a psychology class, you probably wanted to learn about people, not research methods. But it's hard to do one without the other; you need knowledge of research methods to appreciate what psychology teaches you about people, the mind, and the brain. Without that knowledge, your understanding of psychology would be superficial; you would know conclusions psychologists have reached while having no idea how they reached them.

Once you learn about research methods, you will have not only new information but also new abilities. You will be able to critique research, asking not just, "What did the psychologists find?" but "Was their research done well?" You will be able to identify different *types* of research, asking, "What *kind* of research was it, and what are the strengths and limits of that research method?" You might even start thinking about research of your own, asking not just, "How did those psychologists run their study?" but "How could I do it better?"

We will begin this chapter on research methods with an exercise in critical thinking. We'll present a research method with flaws, and you can see if you can detect them.

Next, three main sections of the chapter cover each of the three main elements of research methods:

1. *Research design:* The plan for a research project
2. *Data:* The information acquired in research
3. *Obtaining scientific evidence:* The procedures and scientific equipment psychologists use to obtain data about people, the mind, and the brain

Finally, we conclude with discussions of *scientific theories* and *research ethics*.

Experimental research in psychology In laboratories throughout the world, participants take part in psychology experiments. The research findings provide the evidence that psychological scientists use to develop and test their ideas about people, the mind, and the brain. In this study, a research participant is making judgments about the emotion expressed in faces that appear rapidly on a computer screen.

Macmillan Education Archive

The Challenge of Research Methods

When it comes to research, one critical thinking skill is paramount: detecting flaws. Few research plans are perfect. Many contain defects that compromise their value. Identifying and eliminating flaws in research is a critical skill for the psychologist—and one that you can develop.

Learning About People: A Flawed Strategy

Preview Question

› What are some flaws that can reduce the value of a study in psychology?

Here is a research plan with flaws. Spot them.

A FLAWED STRATEGY. A student who recently has moved into a college dorm wonders whether the other dorm residents like him. Being scientifically minded, he decides to conduct research and executes the following method.

The student walks down the hall, knocks on the first door he sees, and asks, "Do you like me, or what?" The person answers, "Uh, yeah, sure."

He continues to the next door. Nobody answers. He tries a few more, finds someone who is in, and asks, "Hey, do you like me?"

"Not really" is the reply.

He finds three more people:

> "Do you like me?" / "Well, I don't know, I guess."

> "You like me, don't you?" / "I don't, no."

> "You like me, right?"/ "Hey, come in, we're having a party! Sure, we like you!"

Confident in his plan, the student continues, eventually getting 20 responses. He then returns to his room, tries to remember what everybody said, and writes a summary of his results.

Want to find out what other people think about you? Don't just knock on doors and ask whoever happens to be home; your results could give you a flawed picture of people's actual opinions. You can get better information by following the research methods you will learn about in this chapter.

Macmillan Education Archive

THE FLAWS. As a plan for research, the student's efforts were far from perfect. But what, precisely, were the problems? Here are seven:

1. *People might not have answered honestly.* Residents who didn't like the student may not have wanted to admit that to his face, and thus may not have answered honestly.

When was the last time you engaged in some dishonesty to spare someone's feelings?

2. *The research procedure might have altered people's feelings.* Some residents may have liked the student before he did something as ridiculous as knocking on the door and asking, "Do you like me, or what?" Because the student was trying to *find out* if people liked him, not *alter* people's feelings about him, this, too, is a research flaw.

3. *People might have answered differently at a different time.* For example, the fifth person was enthusiastic, but maybe that was because a party was going on when the student knocked and asked his question.

4. *Other people's opinions might have differed.* The residents who weren't in their rooms might have had different opinions than those who were at home, but the student never talked to them.

5. *The varied phrasing of the question may have affected the answers.* The student phrased his question differently from one person to the next, and different phrasings may have prompted different responses.

6. *Some responses were difficult to interpret.* What, for example, was the real opinion of the person who said, "Well, I don't know, I guess"? The difficulty of interpreting the responses adds ambiguity to the research results.

Corbis / SuperStock

Her mouth can't be quite that big The picture is distorted; that is, the image in the photograph does not correspond to the structure of the real world. The same thing can happen in research. Flaws in the research process can produce a "picture" that does not correspond to the actual structure of the world. Research methods are designed to minimize distortions, so the researcher obtains an accurate portrait of human nature.

7. *The summary of people's responses may have been inaccurate.* When the student sat down to summarize what people said, he may have forgotten some of their statements. His summary thus may not have been accurate.

That's a lot of flaws. And they add up, with each contributing to one big overall problem: The research may have produced a picture of the world that is distorted. Like a camera with a damaged lens, research with flaws produces a "picture"—but one that portrays the world inaccurately. The student might conclude that most residents like him even if they don't, or that most don't like him even if they really do.

THINK ABOUT IT

Fix the flaws in the dorm study. Figure out ways to overcome the problems in its research methods.

Fixing the Flaws

Preview Question

> Who is capable of thinking critically about problems in psychological research?

Even now, at the start of this chapter, you can figure out how to fix many, if not all, of these seven research flaws. Consider a couple.

> How to fix #5: *"The varied phrasing of the question may have affected the answers."* It's easy. Have the student write down and memorize one phrasing of the question and ask it in exactly the same way to all people.

> How to fix #6: *"Some responses were difficult to interpret."* You could ask people to pick from among various multiple-choice answers. Their response could then be interpreted unambiguously.

Among the other flaws, some are easy to fix and others hard. But either way, you can imagine ways to fix them. You have the ability to think critically about problems in psychological research. You can detect and repair research flaws by applying critical thinking skills you use in everyday life to questions about research methods. And the research flaws you were just thinking about were realistic, even though our example was made up. The dorm study's flaws exemplify the sorts of problems psychologists must overcome when conducting research.

Let's now turn from our hypothetical example to the real thing: the research strategies of psychological science. Psychologists reduce research flaws by employing carefully planned research *designs*.

Research Goals and Research Designs

Professionals often begin their work with a design: an outline or sketch of the job to be done. Architects sketch designs for buildings. Fashion designers outline the cut and style of apparel. Psychologists design research. **Research designs** are plans for the execution of scientific research projects.

When conducting research, psychologists choose designs that achieve specific research goals. Let's first look at three goals for research, and then examine the research designs that enable psychologists to achieve them.

Research Goals

Preview Question

> What are the three goals of scientific research?

research design Plans for the execution of scientific research projects.

In psychology, or any science, a researcher usually has one of three goals: description, prediction, or causal explanation.

DESCRIPTION. When researchers begin to study a topic, they seek careful, systematic descriptions. Descriptions establish basic facts about the topic under study. These facts, once obtained, guide subsequent theory and research.

As an example, suppose your research topic is social anxiety, which is the tendency to become highly apprehensive, worried, and self-conscious in social settings. To get started, you need basic descriptive information; your overall goal is to establish facts about social anxiety. Those facts might be answers to questions such as:

› What percentage of people experience social anxiety?

› What are the typical thoughts and feelings of people who experience social anxiety?

› How early in life does social anxiety first develop?

These facts alone do not enable you to accomplish much; you cannot tell who is likely to become anxious, or why, or how to help alleviate their anxiety. Nonetheless, descriptive information that answers these questions would provide a foundation for future research.

PREDICTION. When pursuing the second goal, prediction, scientists try to forecast the occurrence of events. They want to know if information available at one point in time can be used to estimate an outcome that occurs later.

When studying something, there are two types of predictions: (1) What predicts its occurrence, and (2) once it occurs, what does it, in turn, predict. We will illustrate with the social anxiety example. Two types of prediction questions are:

1. What factors predict social anxiety? For example:

   › Does lower self-confidence predict higher levels of social anxiety?

   › Does the experience of warm, supportive parenting predict lower levels of social anxiety?

   › Are people who are biologically similar (e.g., identical twins) likely to have similar levels of social anxiety? (In other words, do biological factors predict social anxiety?)

2. What outcomes does social anxiety predict?

   › Do higher levels of social anxiety predict lower levels of professional success?

   › Do higher levels of social anxiety predict higher levels of courtesy toward others?

   › Do higher levels of social anxiety in childhood predict higher levels of social anxiety in adulthood? (In other words, are individual differences in social anxiety consistent across years of life?)

High anxiety Research shows that people who experience relatively high levels of anxiety in childhood are more likely than others to become highly anxious adults (Copeland et al., 2014). Such research fulfills one of the three goals of research, namely, prediction: Childhood anxiety predicts adulthood anxiety.

CAUSAL EXPLANATION. The third research goal is the ultimate goal of science: explanation (Salmon, 1989). Scientists try to explain *why* things happen: Why do solids melt at high temperatures? Why do offspring resemble their parents? Why do people experience social anxiety?

To answer *why* questions, scientists seek causal explanations. Causal explanations identify factors that directly influence outcomes; they show "how an outcome depends on other variables or factors" (Woodward, 2003, p. 6). Consider some possibilities in the case of social anxiety (i.e., where the "outcomes" are people's varying levels of social anxiety):

› Do certain types of thoughts (e.g., "I am going to embarrass myself") cause people to become socially anxious?

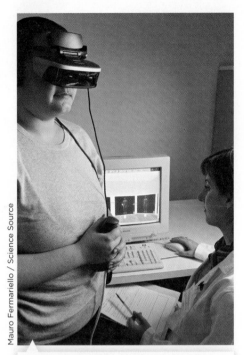

Experimenting with therapy The woman with the funny-looking eyewear is a client in virtual reality therapy, in which computer-generated imagery is used to expose clients, in a safe manner, to situations that make them anxious (see Chapter 15). If a researcher manipulated an aspect of therapy—for example, by assigning one group of clients to virtual reality therapy and another group to therapy that lacked the technology—and then compared the two groups, to see which type of therapy was more effective, the researcher would be running an *experiment*.

> Does training in relaxation skills cause people to experience less social anxiety?
> Do antianxiety medications work; that is, do they cause people to have less anxiety? If so, why; that is, what is the cause of their effectiveness?

A key aspect of causal explanation is manipulation. If a factor is manipulated and, as a result, an outcome varies, then the manipulated factor causally influenced the outcome (Woodward, 2003).

Causal explanations are valuable for two reasons. First, they advance the central goal of science: understanding of how the world works. Second, they open the door to practical applications. If you know, for example, that certain types of thoughts cause people to become anxious, then you can apply that knowledge to psychological therapy. Therapists can help people to eliminate those thoughts and replace them with ones that are less anxiety-inducing.

Importantly, prediction does *not* accomplish the goal of causal explanation. If, for instance, on a sunny summer day, you see people living near a beach putting boards over the windows of their homes and businesses, you can make a prediction: There is likely to be a tropical storm or hurricane. The people's behavior predicts the storm but, of course, does not cause it. (We return to the distinction between prediction and causal explanation later in the chapter, when discussing *correlational designs*.)

Now that you have learned about the three goals for research, let's turn to three research designs. The matching number is no coincidence. Each of the three designs—*surveys, correlational studies,* and *experiments*—accomplishes one of the three research goals: description, prediction, and explanation.

> **WHAT DO YOU KNOW?...**

3. Match the goal of research on the left with the set of questions that exemplifies it on the right. In this context, we are trying to understand test anxiety.

1. Description	a. "What factors cause test anxiety? If I were to manipulate whether someone succeeded or failed on a test this week, would I observe differences in test anxiety on next week's test?"
2. Prediction	b. "What are the basic facts about test anxiety? For example, what proportion of people experience it?"
3. Explanation	c. "What factors forecast test anxiety? For example, if I know how much self-esteem a person has, could I forecast whether he or she will experience test anxiety?"

Survey Methods

Preview Questions

> What is the survey method?
> How do samples differ from populations? Why do researchers collect data from samples rather than from whole populations?
> Why does random sampling increase the representativeness of a sample?

Researchers often want information about a large group of people. Before a national election, for example, they want to know the political opinions of voters. Getting the information might seem easy enough: Just ask the voters their opinions. But the problem is that there are so many voters. Who has time to talk to all of them?

It turns out that you don't need to talk to all of them. Instead, you can use the *survey method*. A **survey method** is a research design in which researchers obtain descriptive information about a large group of people by getting information from

survey method A research design in which researchers obtain descriptive information about a large group of people by studying a select subgroup of them.

a select subgroup of them (Groves et al., 2009). By selecting the subgroup carefully (as we explain below), one can be confident that the subgroup's views are similar to those of the group as a whole.

Surveys can be used to collect various types of evidence (Punch, 2003); you could, for instance, survey a subgroup of people and collect biological information (e.g., their height, weight, or blood pressure). In practice, however, most survey research presents people with simple yes/no or multiple-choice questions known as *survey items*. A survey (i.e., the full set of items) can address any topic and be of almost any length. The "5000 Question Survey" contains a vast array of items, including the question, "When you aren't filling out 5000 question surveys like this one, what are you doing?" (http://5000questionsur.livejournal.com/483.html). A survey designed to measure people's satisfaction with their life contains only one item: "I would describe my satisfaction with my overall life as _____" (Seligson, Huebner, & Valois, 2003).

◉ CULTURAL OPPORTUNITIES

Back Translation

Have you ever seen bad translations—messages that were well-intentioned but comically flawed? The Internet reports these examples:

> In a French hotel: *Please leave your values at the front desk.*
> In an elevator in Germany: *Do not enter the lift backwards, and only when lit up.*
> At a dry cleaners in Thailand: *Drop your trousers here for best results.*

These funny errors highlight a serious issue for psychological research. In today's psychological science, many researchers conduct studies cross-culturally; they run the same study in different parts of the world, to see whether results are consistent from one culture to another. There are two reasons that results may vary. One is important: Psychological processes may be culturally shaped and thus vary in different parts of the world. The other is a nuisance: When translating research materials from one language to another, errors in translation may affect research results. Psychologists thus must avoid, completely, the sorts of mistakes in translation that you just read. How do they do this?

A key research method for accomplishing this goal is *back translation*. **Back translation** is a method in which research materials—instructions to participants, survey items, experimental stimuli—are translated twice: (1) from the original, first language to a second language; and then (2) from the second language back to the first. The two translations are done by two different bilingual individuals, working independently. At the end of the process, the second translation is compared with the original experimental materials. If they match, the researcher can be confident that the translation into the second language was accurate (Brislin, 1970).

Back translation cannot solve all the problems encountered when conducting research cross-culturally, however. For example, in cross-cultural research on emotional experience, in-depth interviews with people from different cultures reveal emotional qualities not detected by standard back-translation techniques (Barger, Nabi, & Yu Hong, 2010). Nonetheless, for most research purposes, back translation is a critical tool for researchers studying how cultures shape the development of people, the mind, and brain.

back translation A method to assure the accuracy of translation by having the research materials translated twice (by different individuals)—first into the second language, and then from the second language back into the first.

☻ WHAT DO YOU KNOW?...

4. What problem is back translation designed to avoid?

Population

Sample

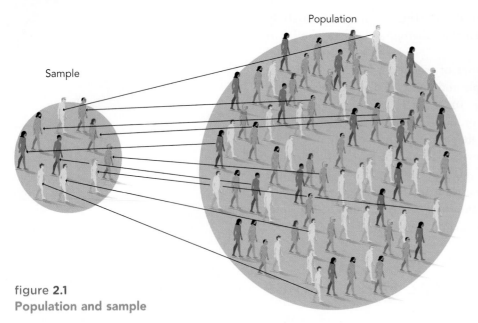

figure **2.1**
Population and sample

POPULATION AND SAMPLE. When survey researchers conduct a study, the overall, large group of people of interest to them is the study's **population.** In our earlier example, the nation's entire group of eligible voters is the population.

The select subgroup of people contacted by the researcher is called the **sample** (Figure 2.1). Researchers use information from the sample to draw conclusions about the population as a whole.

In many surveys, the sample is only a small fraction of the population. Nonetheless, information from the sample proves to describe the population accurately. For instance, in presidential elections, pollsters commonly sample only a couple thousand people from a voting population of 125 million. Yet, in the last two elections, the samples predicted the outcomes precisely (Graefe et al., 2013; Panagopoulos, 2009). The key to this precision is the selection of the sample.

Percent chance of winning

Romney
● 90
● 80
● 70
● 60
○ 50
○ 60
○ 70
○ 80
● 90
Obama

State-by-State Prediction and Result

538 Prediction

Actual

Random sampling By relying on random samples, pollsters can predict elections accurately. In the 2012 U.S. presidential election, pollster Nate Silver predicted state-by-state election outcomes with almost perfect accuracy.

population The overall, large group of people of interest to a researcher conducting a study.

sample The select subgroup of people contacted by a researcher, who uses information from the sample to draw conclusions about the population as a whole.

random sample A sample in which each individual's inclusion, or not, is determined by a chance process.

representative sample A sample in which the qualities of the individuals included match those of the overall population.

RANDOM SAMPLES. How do researchers decide which people from the population go into the sample? Hint: It's a trick question.

Researchers do not personally decide who goes into a sample. Instead, the sample is chosen randomly. In a **random sample,** each individual's presence in (or absence from) the sample is determined by a chance process (similar to flipping a coin or rolling dice). The chance process usually gives every member of the population an equal chance of being in the sample. For instance, to obtain a random sample of 100 of the 5000 students at a college, you would employ a chance process that gives each person a 1-in-50 chance of being selected.

Random sampling helps researchers obtain a sample that is *representative*. A **representative sample** is one whose qualities (gender, ethnicity, income, attitudes, personalities, etc.) match those of the overall population. If, for example, you are surveying students at your college where 13% are Latin American, 12% are African American, and 12% are Asian American, then a representative sample would contain approximately 13% Latin Americans, 12% African Americans, and 12% Asian Americans. A sample that is chosen randomly generally will be representative of the overall population from which it is drawn.

Even a large sample may produce inaccurate results if it is not chosen randomly. Suppose your instructor gives out a course evaluation on a day when 80 of 100 students enrolled in the course are in attendance. The sample is relatively large

Amy E. Price / Getty Images for SXSW

(80% of the population of 100 students) but is not random. The results thus may misrepresent the opinions of the class as a whole. For instance, the 20 students not in attendance might not like the course as much as the others (maybe that's why they skipped class), but none of them are in the sample. The sample results thus could be biased; they might overestimate the population's opinions of the course. The bias could be eliminated by sampling students randomly from the population of 100. (Among its many problems, the dorm study presented earlier failed to sample randomly.)

Survey research describes a population at a given point in time, thus achieving the first of the three goals for research. But to achieve the second goal, prediction, one needs a second research strategy: correlational designs.

THINK ABOUT IT

Do people always answer survey questions accurately? How common do you think inaccurate answers are? Here's a strange fact to consider: In one recent survey conducted in the United States, 1 out of 200 women reported becoming pregnant while being virgins (Herring et al., 2013).

⚡ WHAT DO YOU KNOW?...

5. In survey research, researchers collect information about a large group of people (a _____) by selecting a subgroup (a _____). Ideally, the researcher selects the subgroup through _____ sampling, to ensure that it is as _____ of the large group as possible.

Correlational Studies

Preview Questions

› What is a correlational study?
› What scientific goal does a correlational study help psychologists to achieve?
› What is a scatterplot and how is it interpreted?
› What is a positive correlation? A negative correlation?
› What is a correlation coefficient? What are examples of strong and weak positive and negative correlation coefficients?
› What is the major limitation of correlational designs?

In a **correlational study** (or a *correlational design*), researchers measure two or more quantities and determine whether higher (or lower) levels of one are associated with higher (or lower) levels of another. The measured quantities are called *variables*. A **variable** is any property that fluctuates. The property may fluctuate from person to person or from one time to another for any given person (e.g., your mood varies at different times of day). The results of a correlational study indicate the degree to which two or more variables are related.

Correlational studies commonly are conducted with large numbers of people. Researchers measure two or more variables in each individual and then ask whether, in the group as a whole, the variables are correlated. Sometimes the two variables are measured at the same point in time; for example, a researcher might measure people's current (1) annual income and (2) level of happiness in life to see whether the two are correlated (Diener, Tay, & Oishi, 2013). In other studies, the variables are measured at different time points; for example, researchers have correlated (1) personality qualities measured in childhood with (2) professional and personal success achieved in adulthood (Shiner & Masten, 2012). (Note that, in practice, most correlational studies are *not* conducted with participants chosen randomly from a large population, as in survey research.)

Psychologists achieve the scientific goal of prediction, discussed earlier, through the use of correlational designs. By measuring two variables, they can determine whether one variable predicts the other. Recall the prediction question "Do higher levels of

Time & Life Pictures / Getty Images

Stop the presses! Shown is the newly reelected President Harry Truman, with a newspaper headline announcing—erroneously—that he had lost. How could the newspaper have made such a mistake? They failed to use random sampling. Researchers polled voters by calling them on the phone. But, in 1948, not everyone had a phone, and Truman supporters were less likely to own phones than were supporters of his opponent. The poll's sample, then, was not representative of the population, and the unrepresentative sample incorrectly predicted the election outcome.

---

correlational study A research design whose aim is to determine the relation between two or more measured variables.

variable Any property that fluctuates, such as from person to person or from time to time.

Wealth and happiness She looks happy with her new car—and she's not alone. Correlational studies that relate one variable, wealth, to another variable, happiness, find that increases in wealth allowing people to make major new purchases are correlated with increases in levels of happiness (Deiner et al., 2013).

social anxiety in childhood predict higher levels of social anxiety in adulthood?" When answering this question in a correlational study, the two variables would be:

1. Variable 1: levels of social anxiety in childhood
2. Variable 2: levels of social anxiety in adulthood

A researcher would measure social anxiety in a group of children and then measure social anxiety again in those same people when they reach adulthood. At that point, the research would determine whether the two variables are related, that is, if Variable 1 predicts Variable 2.

Now the question is how, exactly, to determine whether two variables are related. One option is to draw a graph. A **scatterplot** is a graph that displays the relation between two variables. Data points representing the measurements of the two variables "scatter" about the visual display.

Figure 2.2 shows a scatterplot for two variables: amount of rainfall and percentage of people using umbrellas. In this hypothetical study, a researcher measured both variables on each of 20 days. Each point represents the measurement of the two variables on a given day.

figure 2.2
Rain scatterplot Scatterplots let researchers see the relation between two variables. In this case, the strong relation between rainfall and umbrella use can be seen at a glance.

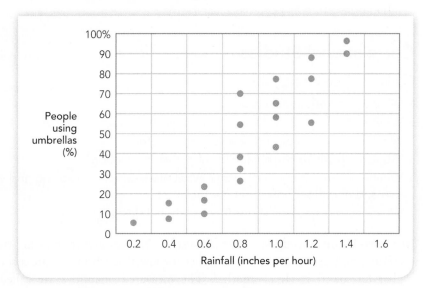

scatterplot A graph that displays the relation between two variables. Data points representing the measurements of the two variables "scatter" about the visual display.

positive correlation A correlation (statistical relation between two variables) in which higher levels of one variable co-occur with *higher* levels of the other variable.

negative correlation A correlation in which higher levels of one variable co-occur with *lower* levels of the other variable.

correlation coefficient (correlation) A numerical value that represents the strength of a correlation between any two variables.

POSITIVE AND NEGATIVE CORRELATIONS. If you look at the graph (Figure 2.2), the results are clear. When there's more rain, more people use umbrellas. This type of relation, in which higher levels of one variable co-occur with higher levels of the other variable, is called a **positive correlation.** Relations that go in the opposite direction, with higher amounts of one variable co-occurring with *lower* amounts of the other, are called **negative correlations.** You would expect, for example, that rainfall and the use of sunscreen would be correlated negatively. If the points in a scatterplot do not systematically go up or down—for instance, if they roughly form a circle—then the two variables are *uncorrelated*, that is, neither positively nor negatively correlated with each other.

The second option for determining whether two variables are related is to compute a number that summarizes the relation between them. The **correlation coefficient** (or simply **correlation**) is a numerical value that represents the strength of the relation between any two variables. It usually is symbolized with the letter *r*. The correlation is based on a formula (which can be found in this book's Statistics Appendix) that limits the minimum and maximum correlation to −1.0 and +1.0. Correlations above zero are called *positive correlations* and those below zero are called *negative correlations*. Let's illustrate what these numbers mean using some examples:

> A correlation of zero ($r = .00$) indicates that two variables don't go together at all. Higher levels of one are not systematically associated with either higher or lower levels of the other. For example, the correlation between (1) performance on skilled technical jobs (e.g., technician, accountant, computer programmer) and (2) the personality trait of extroversion is zero (Hurtz & Donovan, 2000). The personality trait refers to outgoing social behaviors that have nothing to do with technical skills.

> Strong positive correlations (i.e., near $+1.0$) indicate that high levels of one variable frequently co-occur with high levels of the other. For example, in one study the correlation between (1) perceived self-efficacy (i.e., confidence in one's abilities) and (2) behavior (specifically, the ability to behave effectively in situations that create a lot of fear) was $+.84$. Higher levels of self-efficacy were associated with higher levels of effective behavior (Bandura, Adams, & Beyer, 1977).

> Strong negative correlations (i.e., near -1.0) indicate that high levels of one variable frequently co-occur with *low* levels of the other. For example, when researchers correlated (1) the degree of unacceptable delays in customer service (e.g., delays occurring because "the employees are all sending text messages to their friends") with (2) people's liking of stores, the correlation was $-.73$ (Houston, Bettencourt, & Wenger, 1998). More unacceptable delays co-occurred with less liking.

Figure 2.3 displays some scatterplots and the correlation coefficients associated with each. In our rainfall and umbrellas example from Figure 2.2, the correlation is $+.91$. That number confirms the impression you got from the graph: Precipitation and umbrella use are strongly positively correlated.

CORRELATION . . . AND CAUSATION? Does a positive correlation between two variables prove that one variable caused the other? No. In fact, "No, no, a thousand times no." There could be other reasons for the correlation—such as coincidence. Here's an example.

In California, the average amount of rainfall in a given month correlates positively with the number of letters in the name of the month (Figure 2.4). Short-letter months get less rain. Yet neither letters nor rainfall causes one another; the correlation is sheer coincidence. California rainfall is less common in spring and summer than fall and winter, and the spring and summer month names (e.g., May, June) happen to be shorter.

Creativa / Shutterstock

Smoking kills How do we know? The evidence is primarily correlational. Since it is unethical to run an experiment in which non-smokers are forced to smoke, the critical data documenting the negative impact of smoking on health were correlations between smoking rates and mortality.

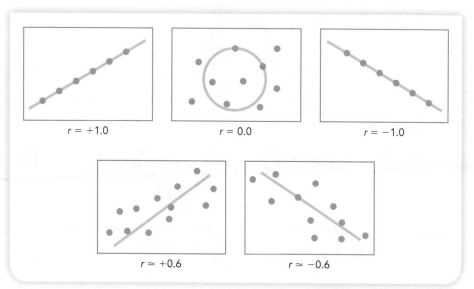

$r = +1.0$ $r = 0.0$ $r = -1.0$

$r \approx +0.6$ $r \approx -0.6$

figure 2.3
Scatterplots and correlations The correlation coefficient r indicates the strength and direction of the relation between two variables. The correlation coefficient summarizes information displayed visually in a scatterplot.

figure 2.4

Precipitation in Eureka, California
In Eureka, California, there is little rain in all three of the months with the shortest names. A lot of rainfall occurs in two of the three months with the longest names. The two variables thus are correlated positively. But neither variable causes the other; the graph illustrates the principle that correlation does not imply causation.

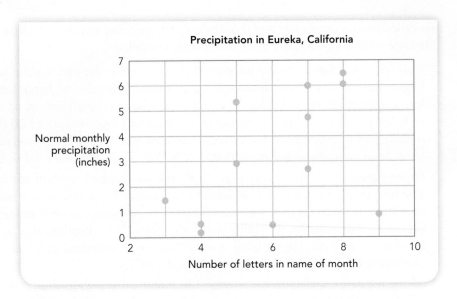

In our example, the conclusion is obvious; names of months can't cause rainfall. But often the question of causality is trickier. Consider these two examples:

1. Levels of poverty are positively correlated with rates of mental illness. Does poverty, however, cause mental illness? The question is difficult to answer, and it remains a point of debate (Sen, 2012). It is possible that the causal relationship runs in the opposite direction; mental illness would cause poverty if people with severe mental illness are less able to get good jobs.

2. Higher levels of education are positively correlated with levels of wealth in adulthood. Does that mean education causes greater wealth? Maybe not. Perhaps wealthy families send their children to school for longer and pass on their wealth to these children through inheritance, with education having no causal effect on wealth in adulthood.

In general, when two variables X and Y are correlated, there are four possibilities: (1) X causes Y; (2) Y causes X; (3) some third variable affects both X and Y, and thus neither X nor Y is a cause; (4) the relation between X and Y is sheer coincidence (Figure 2.5). A correlational research design can't distinguish one possibility from another. For this, one needs an experiment.

figure 2.5

Correlation and causation If one variable X is correlated with another variable Y, it is possible that X causally influences Y. But there are three other possibilities: Y causally influences X; some other variable (Z) influences both X and Y; or the relation between X and Y is sheer coincidence (as in Figure 2.6).

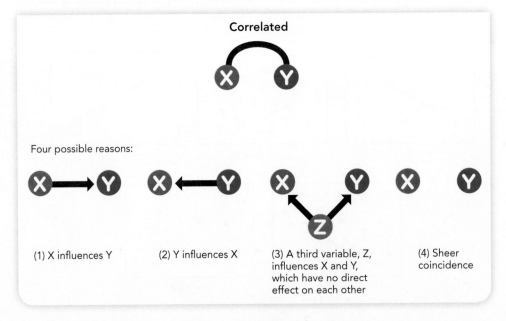

Experimental Designs

Preview Questions

> What scientific goal is achieved through experimental designs?
> How does an independent variable differ from a dependent variable?
> What is a hypothesis?
> What is a control group?
> What are the two defining characteristics of an experiment?
> How does random assignment enable researchers to establish a causal effect between independent and dependent variables?

When psychologists want to identify the causes of events, they conduct *experiments.* In everyday language, to "experiment" means to try something new. In psychology, however, the word has a more specific meaning. An **experiment** is a research design in which a variable is manipulated.

Earlier, we said that manipulation is key to causal explanation (Woodward, 2003). Experiments, which manipulate variables, thus are the psychologist's tool for achieving the goal of causal explanation.

In experiments, a researcher manipulates one or more variables to determine whether the manipulation affects other variables. The researcher's plan for manipulating variables is the **experimental design.**

EXPERIMENTAL DESIGN BASICS. In the terminology of experimental design, there are two types of variables: *independent* and *dependent* variables. It's important to remember which is which:

> *Independent variable:* Any variable that the experimenter manipulates is called an **independent variable.** If, for example, an experimenter studying memory gives some people one minute to memorize a list of words and gives other people two minutes, the manipulated variable, amount of time, is the independent variable.
> *Dependent variable:* The variable that is potentially influenced by the manipulated independent variable is called the **dependent variable.** Psychologists measure the dependent variable to see whether it was affected by the independent variable. In our memory example above, the experimenter would give people a memory test and measure the number of words they remember. The number of words remembered would be the dependent variable. The term *dependent* means that the level of this variable may be influenced by—or may "depend" on—the independent variable.

experiment A research design in which a variable is manipulated, with a goal of identifying the causes of events.

experimental design The researcher's plan for manipulating one or more variables in an experiment.

independent variable In an experimental design, any variable that the experimenter manipulates in order to see its effect on another variable.

dependent variable In an experimental design, the variable that is potentially influenced by the manipulation of the independent variable.

table **2.1**

Research Goals and Research Designs	
Research Goal	**Research Design**
Description: Establish basic facts about the topic under study.	*Survey method:* Use information from a sample to describe the characteristics of a population.
Prediction: Forecast the occurrence of events.	*Correlational study:* Determine the degree to which one variable predicts another variable.
Causal explanation: Identify factors that directly influence outcomes.	*Experimental design:* Manipulate independent variables to determine their causal impact on a dependent variable.

To manipulate the independent variable, the researcher creates different settings in which the dependent variable is observed. The settings are identical in all ways but one: the level of the independent variable changes. These different settings, which contain different levels of the independent variable, are called the study's **experimental conditions.** Memorization times of one minute and two minutes, in our example above, would be that study's two experimental conditions. (Table 2.1 summarizes the three research goals and three research designs we have discussed.)

The purpose of an experiment usually is to test a hypothesis. A **hypothesis** is a prediction about the result of a study. In our example, the researcher might predict that the number of words remembered will be higher in the two-minute memorization time condition than the one-minute condition. This prediction is the experimenter's hypothesis.

Many experiments contain one experimental condition that receives a special name: the *control group*. A **control group** is an experimental condition that eliminates the factor or factors that vary in the other experimental conditions. In other words, the control group brings the level of the independent variable down to zero: It eliminates it.

That was a lot of terminology: *independent variable, dependent variable, experimental conditions, hypothesis, control group.* Let's make these terms concrete with another example. Imagine you are interested in therapies for depression. In particular, you think that the frequency of therapy sessions (or the "intensity" of therapy; Moos & Moos, 2003) influences therapy's effectiveness; you expect that more frequent meetings will increase effectiveness. To test your idea, you plan a study in which different people receive therapy at different frequencies—for example, once every two weeks, once a week, and twice a week. Now let's phrase this in the terminology you just learned (Figure 2.6):

> The idea that more frequent sessions increase therapy effectiveness is your *hypothesis*.

> The frequency of meetings is your *independent variable*.

> Each level of frequency (one, two, or three times per week) is an *experimental condition*.

> The different experimental conditions manipulate the independent variable, frequency of meetings.

> A measure of depression would be your *dependent variable*.

If you are tracking the details, you're now asking, "What about the control group?" As a control group, you could create a fourth condition in which the level of the independent variable is brought down to zero: People receive no therapy. To see its value, imagine that you had run only the other three conditions and people in all three had displayed similar levels of depression at the end of therapy. What could you conclude?

experimental conditions The different settings in a research design, which contain different levels of the independent variable.

hypothesis A prediction about the result of a study.

control group An experimental condition that does not receive the experimental treatment.

Maybe all three therapies were very effective, but to the same degree. Or maybe none of the three therapies worked at all. Without the control group, there is no way of knowing. But with the control group, you can see whether therapy, in general, had any effect.

THE POWER OF RANDOM ASSIGNMENT.

Suppose you did conduct the depression study we just described. How would you decide which participant is assigned to which condition?

The answer is the same as that for random sampling: You wouldn't decide. *Nobody* would decide. Each participant would be allocated to an experimental condition through a random procedure. **Random assignment** is a process in which participants are allocated to conditions of an experiment on an entirely chance basis.

An experiment, then, has two defining characteristics: (1) more than one experimental condition, and (2) the random assignment of research participants to experimental conditions.

Random assignment serves a critical function. It reduces the possibility of a potential experimental **confound,** a factor other than the independent variable that might create differences between experimental conditions. One potential confound is differences between people. If different types of people are assigned to the different conditions of an experiment, one cannot determine the true cause of differences between the conditions, which may have resulted from (a) the experimental conditions or (b) *the people assigned to* the experimental conditions (see Research Toolkit). Random assignment solves this problem. It assures that, on average, the characteristics of the people assigned to the different conditions of an experiment will not differ at the outset of the study.

To see how this works, imagine running an experiment on memory with three experimental conditions and 90 participants. Some of the 90 might have exceptionally good memory and others might have unusually poor memory. Will these differences between people affect your results? If you use random assignment, they probably won't. By chance—thanks to random assignment—a few of the people with exceptionally good and poor memory are likely to end up in each of your three experimental conditions. As a result, *on average,* the three experimental groups will not differ at the outset of the study. If the groups differ at the end of the study, when the dependent variable is measured, you thus can be confident that the differences are due to your experimental manipulation.

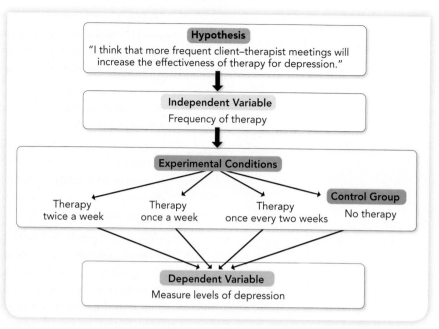

figure 2.6
Experimental design terminology

⊕RESEARCH TOOLKIT

Truly Random Assignment

You've learned that a key tool in the research psychologist's toolkit is *random assignment.* Let's examine it more closely.

In everyday language, *random* means "haphazard." But in science, its meaning is different. When researchers assign research participants to conditions of an experiment, they do not do so haphazardly. They use a formal procedure. A coin flip, a roll of dice, or a table of random numbers specifies the conditions to which each participant is assigned.

"Does this make any difference?" you might be asking. "Couldn't one just assign participants haphazardly?" As it turns out, yes, it makes a difference. A rare case of failing to assign participants randomly shows how much of a difference it can make.

random assignment A process in which participants are allocated to conditions of an experiment on an entirely chance basis.

confound A factor other than the independent variable that might create differences between experimental conditions.

A researcher wanted to study the stress of decision making—the sort of stress experienced by business executives making decisions that affect the lives of their employees. To do so, he ran an experiment—with monkeys (Brady et al., 1958). Rhesus monkeys were assigned to one of two experimental conditions:

> *"Executive monkey" condition:* Monkeys decided whether, and when, to press a lever placed in front them. If they didn't press it within 20 seconds, the monkeys received a brief electric shock.

> *Control condition:* Monkeys did not make decisions. Although a lever was placed in front of them, it was inactive; it didn't affect the occurrence of shocks. However, whenever an executive monkey (i.e., a monkey in the "executive monkey" condition) received a shock as a result of failing to press the lever, a control-group monkey got shocked, too. The two groups thus received the same amount of shock.

What happened? Bad news for the executive monkeys: After a few weeks on the job, they developed gastrointestinal ulcers and died. The researchers concluded that the stress of deciding when to press the lever impaired their health. But good news for the control group: Despite receiving the same number of shocks as the executive monkeys, no control-group monkeys died or developed ulcers. The message seemed clear: It appeared that having "executive control" increased stress, impaired health, and brought about the executives' demise.

Subsequently, more researchers studied the impact of having control over stress. Time and time again, they obtained findings *opposite* to the executive monkeys study: *Not* having control increased stress and impaired health (Lefcourt, 1973). A recent study of real-world leaders in business and government confirms that people in leadership positions tend to experience less stress thanks to their ability to make decisions that control outcomes (Sherman et al., 2012). The original executive monkey findings were contradicted so frequently that its conclusion about executive decision making increasing stress is today considered a "myth" (Overmeir & Murison, 2000, p. 162).

Why were the original executive monkey results so unusual? The researchers neglected random assignment. They assigned to the "executive monkey" condition those monkeys who had learned the lever-pressing task particularly quickly (presumably to speed completion of the study) and assigned slow-learning monkeys to the control group. The groups thus differed systematically *before* the lever-pressing task and shocks even occurred. These preexisting differences, and not the experimental manipulation, thus may have explained their later stress and death. The subsequent researchers who obtained different results wisely used random assignment (e.g., Weiss, 1971).

Today, essentially all researchers assign participants to conditions randomly. In the annals of psychology, the research-methods error in the executive monkey experiment is exceedingly rare. Yet it illustrates a critical point: The value of the information obtained from experiments hinges on the use of random assignment.

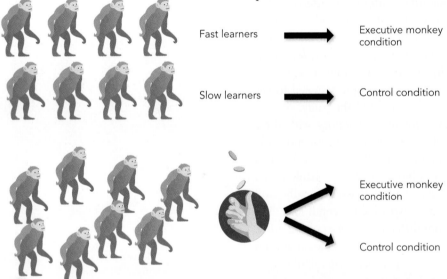

Fast learners → Executive monkey condition

Slow learners → Control condition

Executive monkey condition

Control condition

Executive monkey study

🌐 WHAT DO YOU KNOW?...

9. The following statement is incorrect. Explain why: "Random assignment increases the chances that any observed differences between experimental and control conditions are due to preexisting differences rather than to the manipulation of variables."

Now that you have learned about random assignment and the elimination of confounds, you can answer the question in this chapter's opening story. Recall that men walking on a frightening, physically arousing bridge showed more sexual attraction toward a woman than did men walking on a safe, solid bridge. Yet the researchers did not find the results to be convincing. Why not? They knew their study lacked random assignment and thus might have a confound. The men had not been randomly assigned to one bridge or the other; they had personally chosen to walk across a particular bridge. As a result, the variable (type of bridge) may have been confounded with men's personality styles. For example, men who opted for the frightening bridge may have been more bold, adventurous, and thrill-seeking—and maybe that is why they differed from others in sexual imagery and the tendency to call the female experimenter. Subsequent studies using random assignment (Dutton & Aron, 1974; Meston & Frohlich, 2003) demonstrated that fearful arousal can, in fact, increase sexual attraction. Those studies were much more convincing than research findings from a study lacking random assignment.

🌀 WHAT DO YOU KNOW?...

10. Suppose you wanted to test whether studying a little bit at a time over several days would lead to better test performance than cramming the night before. Match each of the components of such a study with its correct label in the list below.

1. Method for controlling for preexisting differences, such as test-taking ability	a. Hypothesis
2. Third condition that receives no instruction on how to study	b. Independent variable
3. Study instructions (study a little bit at a time vs. cram all at once)	c. Dependent variable
4. Uncontrolled variable, such as test-taking ability	d. Control group
5. "Studying a little bit at a time will lead to better test performance than cramming."	e. Confound
6. Test performance	f. Random assignment

Data: Quantitative and Qualitative

Research designs are plans for collecting scientific evidence. Now let's look at the evidence that is collected.

When psychologists gather scientific evidence, they call it "data." **Data** are any type of information obtained in a scientific study. There are two kinds: *quantitative* and *qualitative*.

Quantitative data are numerical. In **quantitative research methods,** participants' responses are described in terms of numbers. A psychologist who computes people's scores on an intelligence test, or records heart rate when workers with a tight job deadline are stressed, or times the number of seconds it takes people to perform a task, or counts the number of men who call a female experimenter (from our opening story) is collecting quantitative data. Most studies in psychology employ quantitative methods.

Qualitative data are sources of scientific information that are *not* converted into numbers. **Qualitative research methods,** then, are any of a wide range of methods in which researchers observe, record, and summarize behavior using words rather than numbers.

Let's begin our coverage of data in psychology with quantitative data.

data Any type of information obtained in a scientific study.

quantitative data Numerical data, that is, data in which scientific observations are recorded using numbers.

quantitative research methods Scientific methods in which participants' responses are described in terms of numbers.

qualitative data Sources of scientific information that are not converted into numbers, but reported in words.

qualitative research methods Any of a wide range of methods in which researchers observe, record, and summarize behavior using words rather than numbers.

Quantitative Data

Preview Questions

> What is measurement? What are three examples of measurement in psychology?
> What is an operational definition?
> In the measurement of variables, what are reliability and validity?
> What are some potential advantages and disadvantages of quantitative methods?
> What does it mean to say that a study's outcomes are statistically significant?

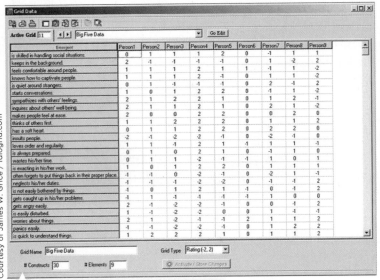

Courtesy of James W. Grice / Idiogrid.com

Want to be a psychology researcher? Here's what you'd be looking at during much of your working day; most research in psychology involves the collection and analysis of quantitative data. Yet the researcher's job is more exciting than it may appear. "How," one psychologist asks, "does one discover a new phenomenon? . . . Have a brilliant insight into behavior? Create a new theory? [By] exploring the data" (Bem, 1987, p. 172).

measurement Any procedure in which numbers are assigned to objects or events.

operational definition The specification of a procedure that can be used to measure a variable.

One of the biggest surprises of introductory psychology is all the numbers involved. Before taking the course, you might expect that words would suffice. When you contemplate the thoughts in your mind, you mostly encounter words, not numbers. When you experience complex, "mixed" emotions—the sort of feeling you might have if a boyfriend you want to stop seeing calls you to break up—you struggle to put your feelings into words, not numbers. But psychologists studying thoughts and emotions use numbers aplenty: graphs, charts, numerical tables, and the statistical analyses that produce them. Where do all these numbers come from?

MEASUREMENT. Psychologists get their numbers through a process called **measurement,** which is any technique that assigns numbers to information about objects or events (Stevens, 1948). (Later we'll present the specialized scientific equipment used to get this information, in the section "Obtaining Scientific Evidence." Here, we focus on the process of measurement itself.)

When it comes to physical properties, measurement is familiar. You measure length with a ruler and temperature with a thermometer. In doing so, you assign numbers (in centimeters and degrees, respectively) to physical properties (the distance from one end of a pencil to the other; the warmth of a room).

But what about *psychological* properties? People's thoughts, feelings, abilities, attitudes, and personality characteristics don't have length, width, or mass. So how can we measure them? The key step is to operationally define the psychological characteristics.

An **operational definition** specifies a procedure through which a property can be measured. The result of the procedure is, by definition, a measurement of the property. Here are examples of operational definitions for three psychological properties: (1) *intelligence,* (2) *self-esteem,* and (3) *fearful reactions*—in particular, among infants:

> *Intelligence:* You could ask people difficult questions and count how many they answered correctly. The result of the measurement procedure, the number of correct answers, would be, by definition, a measure of intelligence.

> *Self-esteem:* Present people with a series of statements that refer to oneself (e.g., "I feel that I have a number of good qualities") and ask them to indicate agreement or disagreement with each statement. Their average level of agreement or disagreement is an index of self-esteem (Rosenberg, 1965).

> *Fearful reactions among infants:* Because the participants in this case are infants, your procedures cannot include words (e.g., instructions or test questions). However, you are able to measure infants' *behavior.* For example, you could (1) stage surprising, potentially startling events in the infants' vicinity (e.g., a puppet head suddenly pops up behind a screen); (2) record their reactions on

What, beyond intelligence, do your final grades measure?

Measurement procedures Some of the first measurements of psychological characteristics were performed in the laboratory of the British scientist Sir Francis Galton in the late nineteenth century (Galton, 1883). Galton's term *anthropometric* is no longer used, but the principles he adopted—careful measurement and statistical analysis of quantitative data—were widely embraced (Boring, 1950).

video; and (3) code the footage, measuring the degree to which each infant cries or displays other physical signs of agitation (Kagan & Snidman, 1991).

Sometimes researchers employ different operational definitions of the same property. One may operationally define fear, for example, in terms of behavioral reactions, whereas another might operationally define it with a questionnaire that asks people to describe their tendency to become fearful. These differences can cause substantial problems when one tries to interpret research findings (Kagan, 1988). The different procedures might produce conflicting results. Consider what would happen in the case of studying fear if some people who, behaviorally, experience a lot of fear describe themselves on the questionnaire as calm and fearless (Myers, 2010). (They might say this to impress others or to convince themselves that they are not so afraid.) Research using a behavioral definition would indicate that those people are "high in fear," whereas research using a questionnaire-based definition would indicate that they are "low in fear."

Measuring emotion How could you measure fans' emotional reactions after watching yet another loss? They might not be in the mood to fill out a questionnaire that asks how they feel, and even if they do complete one, they might not want to admit their disappointment. So you need a different procedure—a different *operational definition* of emotion. One possibility, as you will learn in detail in Chapter 6, is to measure facial expressions. Particular movements of facial muscles can be measured directly and can reveal people's emotional states.

RELIABILITY AND VALIDITY. Once you decide on a measurement procedure, how do you know it is a good one? Measures should have two properties: *reliability* and *validity*.

> *Reliability:* A measure possesses **reliability** if it measures a psychological property consistently. Consider the cases above. When people take intelligence tests on two different occasions, their scores usually are consistent, even when testing sessions are years apart (Watkins & Smith, 2013). Similarly, people's self-esteem scores generally are consistent across years of life (Trzesniewski, Donnellan, & Robins, 2003). Both measures thus possess reliability. If, hypothetically, many people obtained a low score on one testing occasion and a high score on another, the test would lack reliability.

> *Validity:* A measure possesses **validity** if it measures what it is supposed to measure. Timing people in the 100-meter dash would be an *in*valid indicator of intelligence because a measure of running speed does not measure what you are supposed to be measuring, intelligence. Recent advances in the study of measurement provide a more precise definition of the concept. A measure is valid if "variations in the attribute [being measured] causally produce variations in the outcomes of the measurement procedure" (Borsboom, Mellenbergh, & van Heerden, 2004, p. 1061). For instance, when people step on a bathroom scale, variations in their weight (the attribute being measured) produce variations in the numbers the scale displays (the outcome of the measurement procedure). Thus, we know that the bathroom scale validly measures what it is supposed to measure, weight.

It is possible for a measure to be reliable without being valid. Revisiting the 100-meter dash example, the measure itself might be reliable—that is, people's times might be consistent from one running of the race to another. But no matter how reliable that information is, it still would not be a valid measure of intelligence.

THE ADVANTAGES OF NUMBERS. Measurement, then, is the answer to "Where are all these numbers coming from?" There's another question, however: *Why* do we want numbers, or what are the advantages of quantitative data?

There are three advantages, involving comparison, conciseness, and precision.

> *Comparison:* Psychologists often want to compare the actions or experiences of different people. Numbers make comparisons easy. Let's say you want to compare the degree to which two people are experiencing psychological depression. Without quantitative data, the comparison would be difficult. If one person says, "I've been feeling really down lately—sad and with little energy," and another remarks, "I don't seem to be interested in doing much these days; I can hardly get myself out of bed," it is impossible to tell which of the two is more severely depressed. But a quantitative measure of depression (e.g., Beck, Steer, & Brown, 1996)—that is, one that produces a value indicating the level of depression people are experiencing—yields numbers that can be compared easily.

> *Conciseness:* Psychologists need to communicate information concisely. They often must report the results of studies with large numbers of people in the limited space available for research reports in scientific journals. Numbers can be summarized concisely through statistical methods (discussed below and in the Statistics Appendix) and graphs (Figure 2.7). By comparison, words—for example, transcriptions of interviews—are difficult to summarize concisely (although methods to create such summaries have been developed; Grbich, 2009).

> *Precision:* Science needs precision. Throughout the history of science, precise measurements have fueled theoretical advances. Words—such as "The moon is really far away" or "Objects accelerate quite quickly when you drop them"—are imprecise. Numbers—such as "The moon is 239,000 miles away" or "Objects accelerate at 9.8 meters per second squared when you drop them"—possess the precision that science needs.

reliability An attribute of a measure; specifically, a measure possesses "reliability" if it produces results that are consistent from one measurement occasion to another.

validity An attribute of a measure; specifically, a measure possesses "validity" if it measures what it is supposed to measure.

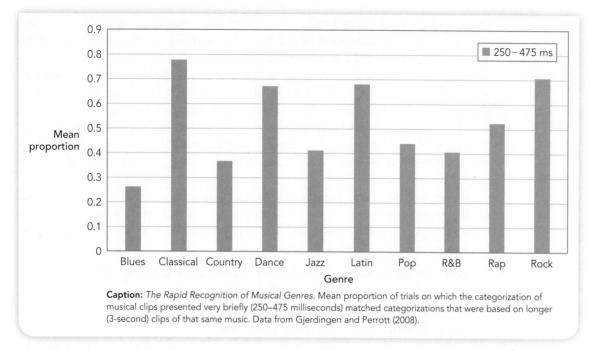

Caption: *The Rapid Recognition of Musical Genres.* Mean proportion of trials on which the categorization of musical clips presented very briefly (250–475 milliseconds) matched categorizations that were based on longer (3-second) clips of that same music. Data from Gjerdingen and Perrott (2008).

figure 2.7

How to read a graph Quantitative data can be presented concisely in graphs. Here's a tip for reading them: Read graphs *from the outside in.* Read the caption and the labels (the outside) first, and only then look at the bars, lines, and other data reports (the inside). If you do this carefully, you often can learn a lot about a study from the graph alone.

Let's try this with the graph above. From the outside (the caption and the labels) you learn that:

1. Researchers played clips of pieces of music for (a) a small fraction of a second (250–475 milliseconds) and (b) 3 seconds.
2. The clips represented various musical genres (blues, classical, etc.).
3. After hearing each clip, participants categorized its genre.
4. Researchers determined whether participants' categorizations of the short and long clips of a given piece of music matched.

Now look inside the graph, at the columns. You see a remarkable result. Even though the short clips were extremely short—blips of sound as brief as a quarter of a second—participants could recognize them. For classical and rock music, a mere quarter-second of sound was sufficient for participants to categorize the music in a manner that matched the categorization of the long clips. People can recognize music quickly! And people can learn a lot from a graph.

 **THIS JUST IN**

Big Data

Suppose you want to answer the following question: *Do media reports (e.g., major stories reported in the news) affect people's everyday behavior? If, for example, the media reports on an environmental disaster, do people subsequently spend more time learning about the environment?*

A researcher's first challenge is to figure out how one could possibly answer that question. Some traditional methods are limited. For example, responses to a survey that asks people, "Does the media affect your behavior?" might not be accurate. The media might have more (or less) effect on behavior than people realize.

Making matters more difficult, the question concerns people *in general:* the tens or hundreds of millions of people who might hear the media report. How could you learn how all of them responded after hearing a piece of news?

You could do it with *big data.* "Big data" refers to the wealth of information that exists in digital records, that is, computer-based records that automatically record Internet browsing, financial transactions (e.g., shopping), and patterns of electronic communication. These "digital records of the people we call, the places we go, the things we eat, and the products we buy," which "record our behavior as it actually happened," may "tell a more accurate story of our lives than anything we choose to reveal about ourselves" (Pentland, 2013, p. 80).

Researchers use novel methods to analyze big data. One is *data-mining* methods, which are numerical techniques for identifying patterns in very large data sets (Han, Kamber, & Pei, 2012). Rather than collecting new data, data-mining researchers look for informative patterns in existing sets of data. These data sets may come, for example, from large Internet firms (e.g., Google) that keep records of Internet browsing or shopping activity. The records may include hundreds of millions of observations of behavior on the Internet. Here is an example.

A team of researchers interested in science education wanted to know whether media coverage of science news leads people to seek out more information about scientific topics (Segev & Baram-Tsabari, 2012). To find out, they mined big data by accessing two types of Google databases:

1. *News coverage* of science—the amount of coverage of scientific topics in Internet news sources at any given time period, and

2. *Search queries* on scientific topics—the number of Google Internet searches for science-related information at any given time.

By accessing records across a five-year period, the researchers could determine whether variations in amounts of news coverage were related to the variations in the volume of search queries. Indeed, they were. People—that is, millions upon millions of Internet users—were more likely to search the Internet for scientific information after news coverage of major science-related events (e.g., the outbreak of a fast-spreading virus or news of an environmental disaster). Interestingly, the data mining also revealed a relation between Internet search and time of year. Science searches were much more common when schools were in session than during summer or midwinter academic breaks (Segev & Baram-Tsabari, 2012). Just as one would hope, educational systems prompt people to learn about science.

This particular *big data* research result is correlational; the volume of Internet searches correlated with news coverage and time of year. As you know, though, correlation does not prove causation; to establish causation, an experiment is needed. Fortunately, big Internet-based data sets can help here, too. Researchers have experimentally manipulated information on the social networking site Facebook to determine whether the information affects everyday behavior (Bond et al., 2012). On the day of a U.S. congressional election, some Facebook users saw an "informational" message (top image) indicating that it was Election Day and providing information about where to vote. Others saw a "social" message (bottom image) containing the election information and also pictures of Facebook "friends" who had already voted. Because this was done on Facebook, the experiment involved a big set of people: 61 million participants!

The social message proved to be influential. An analysis of public voting records showed that people who received the social message were significantly more likely to vote than were those who received only the informational message (Bond et al., 2012).

With its unique ability to provide information about the actual behavior of millions of people, big data will likely have a big future in psychological science.

Election Day polling Two versions of an "informational" message posted on Facebook. Those who saw the version showing their Facebook "friends" who had already voted were more likely to vote.

11. Everything we do on the Internet leaves a digital record and this entire data set, referred to as "big _____," can be analyzed using data-_____ techniques. In one such study, researchers demonstrated there is a correlation between Internet news coverage and the volume of search queries. Correlation does not prove _____, but other experimental research confirms that a link exists between the information we run across on the Internet and our everyday behavior.

MEASUREMENT PRINCIPLES IN PRACTICE. Now let's see how measurement works in practice. We'll look at two examples, the first of which involves political attitudes.

Suppose you want to study attitudes about a political question: *Should the government allow companies to drill for oil in wilderness areas?* If you ask people to express their attitudes in words, you will get information that is neither concise nor precise ("Well, I don't know, I guess I'm sort of against it, but the nation does need a lot of energy"). So you need numbers. To get them, take the two steps described earlier:

1. *Operationally define the variable:* You could ask people, "Are you in favor of, or opposed to, the government allowing companies to drill for oil in wilderness areas?" Then ask them to respond on a scale ranging from "in favor of" to "opposed to." The scale could look like this:

Opposed to allowing drilling in wilderness areas   In favor of allowing drilling in wilderness areas

2. *Assign numbers to observed variations:* In this case, assigning numbers is easy; simply number the scale.

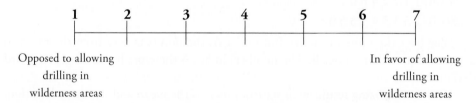

Opposed to allowing drilling in wilderness areas   In favor of allowing drilling in wilderness areas

Researchers would ask precisely the same question to all participants, each of whom would respond using the same easy-to-interpret scale. Note that this procedure overcomes two problems in the dorm study you read about earlier—varied phrasing of the question may have affected the answers, and some responses were hard to interpret.

Our second example is a little more complex. Psychologists who study performance in mathematics may ask whether any two math problems—let's call them Problem A and Problem B—differ systematically in the number of steps of thinking required to solve them. The variable of interest, then, is *amount of thinking*. How can one measure amount of thinking?

1. *Operationally define the variable:* Operationally defining this variable is tricky. There's no reliable way to ask people, "How much thinking did you do?" because they can't keep track of all the thoughts running though their heads—especially while they're concentrating on math problems. But here's something you can do: Time how long it takes people to solve the problem (Menon, 2012; Posner, 1978). Like any activity, thinking takes time. More thinking takes more time. Because additional steps of thinking require additional time, greater *amount of thinking* can be defined operationally as greater amount of time taken to solve the problem.

2. *Assign numbers to observed variations:* Again, in this case, assigning numbers is easy—simply count time in seconds. To determine whether more thinking was required to solve Problem A or Problem B, count the number of seconds it takes each participant to solve each problem and calculate whether, on average, it took longer to solve Problem A or Problem B.

SUMMARIZING AND ANALYZING NUMBERS: STATISTICS. Suppose you were measuring a variable discussed earlier, attitudes about oil drilling in wilderness areas. After you've collected 100 people's responses, someone asks, "What were people's attitudes like?" There are two ways to answer. You could list all 100 responses, one by one: "The first person indicated a 5 on my 7-point scale. The second person indicated 3. The third person was another 5—hey, what a coincidence, just like the first person! And then the fourth person. . . ." But that method would be terribly inconvenient. The second, better option is to use statistics.

Statistics are mathematical procedures for summarizing sets of numbers. Some of the procedures, called *descriptive statistics,* describe what, in general, the numbers are like. Others, called *inferential statistics,* help scientists draw conclusions about the numbers (to conclude whether one group of numbers differs from a second group). This book's Statistics Appendix presents descriptive and inferential statistics in detail. Here, we provide a brief overview.

When describing a set of numbers, one commonly wants to know what the numbers are like, on average. You can probably tell intuitively that answering the question "What were people's attitudes like?" requires knowing the average attitude score. You can determine the average by computing the statistical **mean,** the value obtained by adding up all the scores and dividing by the number of scores that there were. (For our attitude example, you would add up the scores and divide by 100.)

A second descriptive statistic is the **standard deviation,** which describes the degree to which numbers vary (or "deviate") from the mean. Consider two sets of numbers:

Set A: 1 1 2 2 4 6 6 7 7

Set B: 3 3 3 3 4 5 5 5 5

They have the same mean (4). But in Set A, the numbers vary from the mean to a greater degree than in Set B. The numbers in Set A therefore have a larger standard deviation.

After summarizing results with statistics such as the mean and standard deviation, psychologists often want to know whether the results differ from chance. The concept of differing from chance can be illustrated with a simple example. A flipped coin is expected to come up heads half the time and tails half the time. If you flip it 100 times, and it comes up heads 52 times instead of 50, you *don't* think, "Unbelievable! Two more heads than the expected 50!" You know this small difference, 52 instead of 50, can occur just by chance. But now imagine that instead of 52 heads, you got 92. That would be bizarre! It would differ so much from what was expected—that is, so much from the chance result—that you would suspect the coin had been "rigged" to come up heads more than half the time.

Statistical procedures can determine whether observed outcomes differ from the outcome expected by chance. Observed outcomes that differ from what would be expected by chance are called **statistically significant.** In our example above, 92 heads out of 100 would be a statistically significant outcome, whereas 52 out of 100 would not. The inferential statistics used to determine whether results vary from chance are called *significance tests.* (Principles of statistical significance are detailed in our Statistics Appendix.)

A common application of significance tests is determining whether two or more groups of numbers—such as mean scores of different groups of people in an experiment—differ from one another. For example, back in Chapter 1, you read about

statistics Mathematical procedures for summarizing sets of numbers.

mean The average score in a distribution.

standard deviation A statistic that describes the degree to which numbers vary, or deviate, from the mean.

statistically significant An experimental result is said to be statistically significant if observed outcomes vary from what would be expected by chance.

a study in which men and women differed in their performance on a math test, in part due to stereotype threat. Before saying that the groups "differed," the researchers conducted a significance test to find out whether the mean score in the different groups exceeded anything one would expect by chance alone.

Researchers usually analyze data from one study at a time. However, they sometimes summarize results from multiple studies. **Meta-analysis** is a statistical technique for combining results from multiple studies in order to identify overall patterns in the studies as a whole (Cooper, Hedges, & Valentine, 2009). So, in future chapters, when you read that researchers conducted a "meta-analysis," it merely means that they summarized results from numerous prior studies.

De Agostini / Getty Images

LIMITATIONS OF QUANTITATIVE DATA. Quantitative data are the bread-and-butter of psychological science: the source of information that fuels most of the field's growth. Yet some forms of quantitative data have limitations. Keep them in mind as you think critically about psychological research.

One shortcoming is that quantitative measures may fail to reveal information that could be detected in qualitative research (discussed below). In many quantitative studies, researchers construct a survey or questionnaire that is administered, in the same form, to all research participants. But participants might have important thoughts, feelings, and personal experiences not included in the survey. Suppose you wanted to survey college freshmen's thoughts about factors that had "the biggest impact" on their past education. You might ask them to rate, on 7-point scales, factors such as the quality of their teachers, the support of parents, and the amount they studied. Thanks to the Internet, you could send your survey to people around the world. Some of them, though, might want to report information that you didn't include in the survey. For instance, if asked about "the biggest impact" on their past education, students in Indonesia might want to say "the tsunami." (A tsunami late in the year 2004 destroyed hundreds of Indonesian school buildings.) But your quantitative measure didn't ask about that.

Another limitation is that numbers may fail to represent the complexity of some psychological characteristics. Consider people's personalities. Many personality tests assign to individuals scores on personality traits such as being warm-hearted, organized, or a procrastinator (see Chapter 13). But when people describe themselves in words, their

Does Mozart make people significantly smarter? Many people have speculated about a "Mozart effect"—the possibility that listening to music by the classical composer stimulates the brain, thereby raising people's performance on a variety of intellectual tasks. So is there really a Mozart effect? Specifically, is there a *statistically significant* effect—a difference between people who listen to Mozart and others that is greater than what would be expected by chance? To find out, researchers asked one group of people to listen to Mozart and another group to listen to a short story. Both groups then attempted some intelligence test items. A statistical test revealed *no* significant difference between the groups (Nantais & Schellenberg, 1999); on average, people who listened to Mozart did not perform significantly better or worse than others. This reveals an important virtue of statistical tests: They sometimes show that expected differences between groups are not statistically significant.

Quantitative research How might you explore people's beliefs about children and childcare? In quantitative research, you might develop a fixed set of survey items designed to measure beliefs. A limitation, however, is that people living in cultures other than your own might hold beliefs that you failed to include in your survey. In Bali, home to this grandmother and child, people believe that children are reincarnated from divine ancestors (Gerdin, 1981). Would you have included reincarnation questions in your quantitative survey? In cases such as this, qualitative methods are advantageous. Qualitative methods that allow people to describe their lives in their own terms can reveal beliefs and experiences that are surprising to the researcher.

Paul Souders / DanitaDelimont.com

Do you prefer quantitative multiple-choice exam questions or qualitative essay questions? Does it depend on how well you know the material?

meta-analysis A statistical technique for combining results from multiple studies in order to identify overall patterns in the studies as a whole.

descriptions sometimes reveal personality characteristics that are more complex than the trait scores suggest. For example, in one study (Orom & Cervone, 2009), four people described themselves as follows:

1. "I have a very welcoming personality that greets people with a smile or a nice joke or even a nice little hug, [but] another aspect of my personality is my mean side."

2. "I'm nice, helpful, kind, sweet . . . I'm easy to get along with [but] I have a quick and bad temper. I get jealous easily . . . very moody . . . bossy."

3. "[I am] organized for the most part [but] very rushed and messy at home."

4. "I like to be on time or early for a scheduled event [but] on things that I am less interested in doing I put off until close to deadline time."

No single "procrastination score" could, for example, describe the fourth person's tendency to procrastinate, which varies from one situation to another. A single quantitative "procrastination score," then, would not do a good job of describing that person. With such concerns in mind, some researchers opt for qualitative data.

🐾 WHAT DO YOU KNOW?...

12. For each of the "answers" below, provide the question. The first one is done for you.

   a. *Answer:* Using scores on a final exam to indicate understanding of course content would be an example of this kind of definition.
   Question: What is an operational definition?

   b. *Answer:* A conscientiousness questionnaire that accurately measures conscientiousness would possess this quality.

   c. *Answer:* This statistic tells us how much our scores deviate from the average score, or mean.

Qualitative Data

Preview Questions

› What are qualitative research methods? What are three examples of research that obtains qualitative data?

› What are three advantages of qualitative data? What are some reasons most psychologists prefer quantitative to qualitative data?

Qualitative data, as we noted above, are sources of scientific information that are *not* converted into numbers. Words are the main type of qualitative data. Psychologists conducting qualitative research may ask participants to describe, in their own words, their experiences and life circumstances. They then summarize and interpret participants' statements in words, rather than numbers.

The biggest source of qualitative information in psychology is interviews (Potter & Hepburn, 2005). Other information sources, such as observation of behavior in naturally occurring situations, also can provide qualitative research evidence. But interviews are most common. Let's look at an example involving efforts to halt the spread of HIV/AIDS in sub-Saharan Africa.

HIV/AIDS efforts hold promise and have achieved much success already, yet they present a puzzle. Drugs can now stop the disease from progressing, and in sub-Saharan nations, they often are available for free. The puzzle is that a great many patients drop out of treatment; they skip the necessary trips to medical clinics to get their free drugs. Why would people fail to make these clinic visits, which are critical to their health?

A team of researchers knew the reasons could be complex; simple quantitative survey items might not uncover them. So they conducted a qualitative study. They interviewed patients in Nigeria, Tanzania, and Uganda who had missed treatment for three months or more (Ware et al., 2013). The patients discussed circumstances associated with their missed appointments, as well as their experiences at the medical clinics. Analysis of the study's qualitative data indicated that patient dropout often resulted from "complex chains of events" (Ware et al., 2013, p. 6) involving both the challenges of life in sub-Saharan Africa and problems at the clinics. One man reported the following:

> When you go to look for money for [a motorcycle taxi] you find you do not have it. So . . . you miss your appointment and go to clinic on another day, [and the provider] starts quarreling with you about not having come on the appointed day. And when you tell that person you got problems, he tells you, "You should spend the night on the road." How can I spend the night on the road? Here I am, having failed to get money for taking me to the hospital and then I'm supposed to get money to spend the night somewhere and feed myself? These are some of the problems I have in going to the clinic.
>
> —Ware et al. (2013, p. 6)*

Such complex, culturally situated reasons might never have been uncovered in a traditional quantitative study.

ADVANTAGES OF QUALITATIVE DATA. Three considerations motivate psychologists to obtain qualitative, rather than quantitative, data: the desire to (1) understand personal meaning, (2) reflect the storylike quality of lives, and (3) obtain evidence that is naturalistic. Let's consider them.

The *personal meaning* of an event is its significance for the individual who is experiencing it. Personal meaning is hard to capture in numbers (Polkinghorne, 2005). Suppose a friend says, "I'm fed up with you." You're puzzled and want more information. But the information you want is not a number ("Exactly how fed up are you, on a scale from 1 to 7?") Instead, you want to know exactly what the statement means—the reasons for, and behind, the statement. To understand the meaning of people's statements, you generally need to let them speak in their own terms rather than handing them a fixed measurement scale (Kelly, 1955).

People's understanding of their own lives often has a storylike structure—a narrative that unfolds over time (McAdams, 2006). Words, rather than numbers, are the best way to represent the information in life stories. Similarly, scholars note that life is like a play (Goffman, 1959; Scheibe, 2000). People in your life play different roles (friends, parents, teachers, romantic partners, etc.), and your behavior toward them, as well as theirs toward you, can be understood only by taking these roles into account. Comprehending the "theatrical" aspects of psychological experience may require qualitative methods that capture the meaning of behavior as it occurs in social contexts (Harré, 2000).

Naturalistic evidence is true-to-life information about the actual state of the world. Such evidence is what the psychologist desires, but sometimes quantitative methods make it hard to get. The procedures needed to obtain quantitative data may interfere with the natural flow of events. For example, suppose that, to measure the state of calm concentration that people sometimes experience while at work, you interrupt workers and ask them, "On a 7-point scale, to what extent are you experiencing a state of calm concentration right now?" Your intrusive quantitative procedure will interfere with people's naturally occurring feelings. They might, for example, have been calmly concentrating *until* you interrupted them. Qualitative research strategies can avoid such intrusions. Qualitative researchers might, for example, observe ongoing events without interfering with them, or study preexisting written materials that provide information about people's experiences (Denzin & Lincoln, 2011).

THREE TYPES OF QUALITATIVE STUDIES. Let's look at three types of qualitative studies: (1) clinical case studies, (2) qualitative observational studies, and (3) qualitative community-participation studies.

Getty Images

All the world's a stage? Playwrights and social scientists have suggested that human affairs off the stage can be understood through a stage metaphor: You, and the people around you, play roles in the drama of life. Qualitative, rather than quantitative, data may be best suited to portray these dramas.

* © 2013 Ware et al. (2013). Toward an understanding of disengagement from HIV treatment and care in sub-Saharan Africa: A qualitative study. *PLoS Medicine, 10,* e1001369, doi: 10.1371/journal.pmed.1001469

The famed psychologist Sigmund Freud did not collect numerical data. He saw patients in therapy and prepared written reports describing their cases. Shown are Freud's notes on one of his cases.

THINK ABOUT IT

The observational study of the fate of cars parked in urban and suburban neighborhoods was conducted many years ago. Do you think you would observe similar differences between urban and suburban neighborhoods today?

case study A detailed analysis of one particular person or group of people; the person or group is the "case."

clinical case study In psychology, an analysis of someone receiving psychological therapy; generally a written summary of a case.

observational study A type of research in which researchers observe people's behavior from a distance without interacting with them.

community-participation study A type of research in which researchers collaborate with community residents to determine a study's goals and research procedures.

A **case study** is a detailed analysis of one particular person or group of people; the person or group is the "case." In psychology, a **clinical case study** is an analysis of someone receiving psychological therapy, which often is provided in a health center or clinic. Psychologists generally describe their cases in written summaries; clinical case studies, then, typically produce qualitative data.

A second type of research that can produce qualitative data is an **observational study,** in which researchers observe people's behavior from a distance without interacting with them. A researcher might, for example, sit inconspicuously in a school playground and observe friendly and aggressive behavior among schoolchildren (Ostrov & Keating, 2004). Although the results of an observational study can include numerical data (such as number of aggressive incidents), researchers commonly summarize their observations in written reports, yielding qualitative data (Polkinghorne, 2005).

> Do you think you might ever have unknowingly participated in an observational study?

In one observational study, a researcher provided compelling evidence of differences between rich and poor neighborhoods (Zimbardo, 1970). He parked two similar cars in different locations—an inner-city neighborhood and a wealthy suburb—and then observed what happened. In the suburban community, there wasn't much to observe; for five days, residents just passed the car by. But in the city, people began vandalizing the vehicle *within 10 minutes* of the study's start. They removed everything of value within two days. The researcher speculated that the sense of anonymity that pervades large urban neighborhoods was the primary reason vandalism occurred. In suburban neighborhoods, by comparison, residents are less anonymous and thus share a sense of personal responsibility for community property. The researcher's written report of his observations powerfully illustrated differences in social life from one neighborhood to another.

In an observational study, the psychologist does not interact with the research participants. However, in a different type of qualitative study, called a **community-participation study,** researchers collaborate with community residents to determine a study's goals and research procedures (Allison & Rootman, 1996; Kelly, 2004). The psychologist's aim is to understand community life and to help residents achieve social changes they desire. Because the residents are the experts on their community's experiences and goals, the psychologist works closely with them in designing research.

The data in community-based studies generally are qualitative. Psychologists listen closely to residents' reports about their lives, in order to understand the challenges they face in the community and how they cope with them. For example, in a study of how homeless mothers cope with the stresses of child care while living in poverty (Banyard, 1995), a psychologist interviewed 64 women living in emergency shelters in cities in the U.S. Midwest.

They didn't even know they were in an experiment Vehicle being vandalized during an observational study of vandalism conducted in urban and suburban neighborhoods.

An analysis of the qualitative data identified themes in the research participants' statements. The most common theme was the need to confront problems directly—to cope by seeking solutions rather than just worrying about problems. "When one deal doesn't work out," one woman reported, when discussing her search for housing for herself and her child, "I swallow my pride and I call somebody else. . . . You just can't give up" (Banyard, 1995, p. 881). These qualitative data provided a rich, emotionally meaningful understanding of homeless mothers' lives that might not have been obtained if the psychologist had used numerical data instead.

DISADVANTAGES OF QUALITATIVE DATA. Despite their virtues, qualitative methods have drawbacks. Disadvantages lie in precisely those areas where numerical methods are advantageous.

With qualitative data, comparison is difficult. Suppose you read two case studies by a therapist and want to compare the people; you might ask, "Which of the two experienced more severe psychological distress?" Qualitative case studies provide no simple answer of the sort you would get from a quantitative measure.

Qualitative methods also are not concise. For example, an American psychologist once studied an individual's personality qualitatively, by analyzing letters written by the person over a period of more than a decade (Allport, 1965). Interesting though it may have been, the resulting qualitative personality analysis was not concise: a book of more than 200 pages, describing only one individual. In addition, gathering such qualitative evidence is such a slow and labor-intensive process that qualitative methods inherently do not speed the path of scientific progress.

Because words are open to interpretation, qualitative methods also lack precision. Different speakers, with different personal and cultural backgrounds, may assign different meanings to the same word or phrase. In contrast, numbers are a "universal language" whose meaning is understood precisely.

Finally, qualitative data leave open the possibility of bias. When conducting a study, researchers commonly hope that the results are consistent with their own theoretical ideas. If the data are quantitative, researchers face unambiguous numerical facts that may disconfirm their hypotheses. But when the data are qualitative, they need to be interpreted, and the researcher's hopes may bias the interpretation. One of the most famous sets of investigations in the history of psychology has been criticized on these grounds. Sigmund Freud (1923) developed a theory of personality (see Chapter 13) based entirely on qualitative case-study evidence. Critics note that the person who interpreted the case studies was Freud himself; the interpretations thus may have been biased by Freud's desire to obtain evidence that supported his theory (Crews, 1998).

These disadvantages are substantial. As a result, most psychologists opt for quantitative rather than qualitative evidence. As we now turn to questions of research design, the studies we discuss will almost exclusively involve quantitative data.

☝ WHAT DO YOU KNOW?...

13. Which of the following statements are true of qualitative research methods or evidence? Check all that apply.

___ a. It is motivated, in part, by a desire to understand the personal meaning of an event.

___ b. A clinical case study is an example.

___ c. An observational study, such as a community-participation study, is an example.

___ d. It enables easy comparison of people.

___ e. Its resulting analyses are concise.

TRY THIS!

The next section of this chapter discusses research procedures that psychologists use to obtain their scientific evidence. Before reading about these procedures, experience one for yourself. Go to www.pmbpsychology.com and try your hand at the Try This! activity for Chapter 2. Do it now! We'll discuss the activity a little later in this chapter. ◉

Obtaining Scientific Evidence: Psychological and Biological

So far, you have learned about two main topics: data (qualitative and quantitative) and research designs (surveys, correlational studies, and experiments). We're not done yet. Recall that the purpose of research is to obtain scientific evidence. To get it, scientists need specialized tools and procedures. A biologist needs a microscope and a procedure for obtaining permanent images of what it reveals. A subatomic physicist needs a particle accelerator and a way of detecting the particles that it produces.

What are the specialized tools and procedures of the psychologist? The answer depends on the type of evidence the psychologist is pursuing. We'll review the ways in which psychologists obtain *psychological evidence* and *biological evidence*.

Psychological Evidence

Preview Questions

> What are three forms of psychological evidence that researchers obtain to study people's thoughts, feelings, and behaviors?
> What are two limitations of self-reports as a source of evidence about people's behavior?

Psychological evidence is information about people's thoughts, feelings, and behaviors. One source of such evidence is reports from the people themselves.

PARTICIPANTS AS INFORMANTS: SELF-REPORTS AND OBSERVER REPORTS. How might someone learn how you're feeling about your relationships or what you're planning to do next summer? One option is to just ask. **Self-report** methods are research techniques in which researchers ask participants to provide information about themselves.

The most common self-report method is a **questionnaire,** a set of questions or statements to which participants respond by choosing response options that best characterize their own thoughts. The survey question you saw earlier in this chapter, asking about oil drilling, is a typical self-report questionnaire item (see Table 2.2).

Sometimes people might not be able or willing to report accurately about themselves. This problem can be overcome by using **observer reports,** in which people describe the psychological characteristics of individuals they know. Parents, for example, might be asked to report on their children. College students might be asked to report on the personalities of their roommates. Research shows that observer reports can provide unique information not obtained merely by asking people to describe themselves (Oltmanns & Turkheimer, 2009).

PARTICIPANTS OBSERVED: DIRECT OBSERVATIONS OF BEHAVIOR. Some argue that psychology's reliance on self-report and observer-report methods is an *over*reliance (Kagan, 2002). These sources of evidence are inherently limited. People's reports about behavior—their own or someone else's—may be inaccurate for multiple

self-report Research techniques in which researchers ask participants to provide information about themselves.

questionnaire A set of questions or statements to which participants respond by choosing response options that best characterize their own thoughts.

observer report A research method in which researchers learn about various characteristics of a given individual by obtaining reports from other people who know that person.

table 2.2

Thought Record

Date/ Time	Situation	Automatic Thought(s)	Emotion(s)	Adaptive Response	Outcome
	1. What actual event or stream of thought(s), or daydreams or recollection led to the unpleasant emotion? 2. What (if any) distressing physical sensations did you have?	1. What thought(s) and/or images went through your mind? 2. How much did you believe each one at the time?	1. What emotion(s) (sad/ anxious/ angry, etc.) did you feel at the time? 2. How intense (0–100%) was the emotion?	1. (optional) What cognitive distortion did you make? 2. Use questions at the bottom to compose a response to the automatic thoughts. 3. How much do you believe each response?	1. How much do you believe each automatic thought? 2. What emotion(s) do you feel now? How intense (0–100%) is the emotion? 3. What will you do (or did you do)?
4/28	Stepped on the scale and it read 210; I have been trying to diet to get it down to 190.	I am unattractive. 80%	Sad 40%	Selective abstraction	Unattractive 40%
5:12 p.m.	Sinking feeling in my stomach, tension in my shoulders	I really want to lose the weight, but it isn't working. 95%	Frustrated 30%	Although I am a little overweight, there are still attractive things about me. 95%	Sad 20%
		I should be able to lose this weight. What's wrong with me? 60%	Ashamed 50%	Childish fantasy	I really want to 90% true, but relevance 10%
				Weight loss is about the control of calories and exercise and not about how much I want it. 90%	Frustrated 10%
				Thinking in "shoulds"	I should 10%
				Weight loss is hard and it takes time to develop a plan that works and that you can stick to. 95%	Ashamed 5% *Plan:* Revise my diet and increase exercise by going to the gym three days a week.

From © J. Beck, 2011. Adapted from *Cognitive Behavior Therapy: Basics and Beyond*, 2nd edition, and used with permission.

The Thought Record is an example of a self-report questionnaire. People are asked to report thoughts that popped into their minds ("automatic thoughts") and thoughts they devised to cope with negative emotions ("adaptive responses").

Direct observation When directly observing behavior, psychologists often use electronic coding systems to record behavior efficiently and relatively unobtrusively.

TRY THIS!

direct observation A research method in which researchers view the actions of research participants firsthand and record the behaviors they observe, often by counting specific behaviors.

Can you remember what you did in the past week?

reasons (e.g., faulty memory; motivations to make a good impression). Psychologists thus need alternative sources of evidence.

One alternative is **direct observation** of behavior, a form of evidence in which researchers view the actions of research participants firsthand and record the behaviors they observe. Typically, researchers develop a system for counting specific types of behavior that may occur when participants are observed. They then use this counting system to record participants' behavior during the course of a study. For example, in the study described in our opening story, researchers directly observed, recorded, and counted the behaviors of men who had walked across a safe or frightening bridge.

Direct observation of behavior may reveal facts not unearthed in self-reports. For example, in a study of conscientiousness among college students (Mischel & Peake, 1982), researchers observed behaviors such as conscientiously attending lectures, taking neat lecture notes, and submitting assignments on time. They also asked students to complete self-reports of the consistency with which they perform these conscientious acts. The direct observations and the self-reports often did not agree; students commonly reported that they were consistently conscientious, whereas direct observations of behavior revealed they were not.

PROBING THE MIND: LABORATORY TASKS THAT REVEAL MENTAL PROCESSES. As we discussed in Chapter 1, one aim of psychology is to understand the workings of the mind: the mental processes involved in memory, thought, and emotion. When searching for evidence about the mind, researchers face two challenges: Mental processes often cannot be observed (1) in someone else (if you look at a person, you can't see what she is thinking about) or (2) in oneself (an idea might "pop into mind" without your being able to identify how it got there). A new form of evidence—something other than self-reports or observer reports and direct observation—is needed.

This third form of evidence is laboratory tasks that reveal mental processes. Researchers devise novel tasks on which performance requires a specific mental skill. They give these tasks to participants in controlled laboratory settings (i.e., settings in which participants are not distracted by everyday activities). By recording people's performance on these tasks, researchers can gain insight into the workings of the mind. Here's an example.

Many psychologists believe there are two different types of thinking processes, "fast" and "slow" (Kahneman, 2011). Fast thinking occurs automatically; you cannot stop it from happening. Slow thinking requires deliberate effort. How can one test this idea, given that thinking processes cannot be directly observed? If you attempted this chapter's Try This! activity, you already know of one way to do so.

Earlier, we asked you to experience this chapter's Try This! activity. If you didn't do it then, try it now; it is on the Internet at www.pmbpsychology.com.

The Try This! activity was a specialized laboratory task called the *Stroop Task* (MacLeod & MacDonald, 2000; Stroop, 1935). As you saw, in the Stroop Task people are shown color names printed in different colors of ink (Figure 2.8). Sometimes the ink color and the named color correspond, but sometimes they do not. Participants must say, as quickly as possible, the color of the ink.

When the ink color and printed color name correspond, the task is easy. But when they conflict—for example, when the color name "blue" is printed in yellow—it is nearly impossible to stop yourself from reading "blue" when you want to say "yellow." Reading occurs so quickly that you can't stop it.

Now that you have tried the Stroop Task, ask yourself, "What does it say about how the mind works?" The Stroop Task shows that the mental processes involved in reading occur more quickly than the mental processes needed to name colors. This means that the mind works at different speeds, fast and slow.

Red	Blue
Yellow	**Green**
Blue	**Yellow**
Green	Red
Green	**Green**
Yellow	**Blue**
Blue	Red

Biological Evidence

Preview Question

> What are two main targets for research in studies of psychology and biology, and how do scientists learn about them?

In the past, the scientific evidence obtained in most areas of psychology was exclusively psychological. *Biological* evidence—information about the brain and the bodily systems it regulates—was pursued primarily in one corner of the field, where research focused on brain–behavior relationships. But today, things have changed dramatically. Researchers in practically every branch of psychology study brain–behavior relationships. You will encounter biological evidence in every chapter of this book.

Why the big change? It was fueled by technological advances in *neuroscience,* the scientific field that studies the brain and nervous system (see Chapter 3). Only 20 years ago, neuroscientists "lamented science's lack of even a basic understanding of human neuroanatomy," but today, "novel technologies and automation . . . map neural circuitry with unparalleled resolution and completeness" (Perkel, 2013, p. 250). These advances have enabled psychologists to pursue a goal we discussed in Chapter 1: deepening their understanding of people and the mind by conducting research at the level of analysis of the brain. Here, we'll briefly overview the equipment and procedures they use to do this.

EVIDENCE ABOUT THE BRAIN: EEG AND FMRI. Two types of activity occur in the brain. One is electrical and the other is chemical. Scientific evidence about the brain thus comes in two main varieties: electrical and chemical.

The brain's electrical activity is generated by its individual cells, called *neurons.* Electrical impulses travel from one end of the neuron to the other. Electrical activity within the brain thus can be recorded by scientific equipment that is sensitive to electrical activity. **Electroencephalography,** or **EEG,** is a technique for recording the brain's electrical activity by placing electrodes on the scalp. Each electrode records the amount of electrical activity occurring in the region of the brain nearest to it. The resulting recordings of electrical activity provide evidence of the amount of neural activity in different brain regions.

A second source of information about the brain's electrical activity is indirect. Rather than recording electrical signals, researchers record blood flow. Like other cells in the body, the brain's neurons need energy. Neurons that are more active—that is, more frequently generate electrical signals—need more energy. They get it from oxygen carried in the bloodstream. Blood flow, then, provides a clue to neuronal activity. An increase in blood flow to any given region of the brain indicates that activity in that brain region has increased. Researchers record blood flow during psychological activities using **functional magnetic resonance imaging (fMRI),** a technology for producing pictures, called *brain scans,* which reveal areas of the brain that were most active during the activity. Figure 2.9 shows an fMRI result: brain regions that are particularly active when people play and listen to music.

The brain's chemical activities involve its *neurotransmitters,* which are biochemical substances that travel from one neuron to another. When a neurotransmitter released by one neuron reaches a second neuron, it affects the activity of the second neuron.

figure 2.8
Stroop Task Naming colors does not sound like a hard task—unless you're trying to name the colors on the right! This simple procedure, called the Stroop Task, shows that reading occurs so quickly that you cannot stop it from happening and from interfering with the task of naming colors.

Science Photo Library / Getty Images

Bad hair day, but a good day for research The electrodes produce an electroencephalogram, a recording of brain activity. In addition, electrodes on a research participant's face can record muscular movements that are associated with facial expressions of emotion.

electroencephalography (EEG)
A technique for recording and visually depicting electrical activity within the brain in which electrodes on the scalp record neural activity in underlying brain regions. The record of electrical activity through this method is called an *electroencephalogram.*

functional magnetic resonance imaging (fMRI) A brain-scanning method that depicts activity in specific regions of the brain as people engage in psychological activities.

figure 2.9

Brain imaging Researchers use brain-imaging methods to study regions of the brain that are most active during different activities. In the study whose results are shown here, pianists and nonmusicians either listened to piano music (Listening condition) or pressed keys on a piano keyboard (Playing condition). Colored areas show brain regions that were more active among pianists when listening and when playing. Images in the Combined condition show regions that were more active among pianists during *both* listening and playing. As you can see, although all participants performed the same musical tasks, the pianists used more "brain power" when performing them.

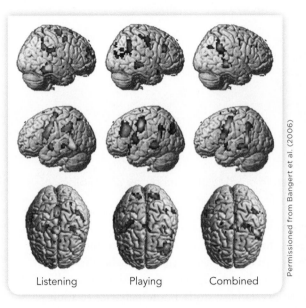

Permissioned from Bangert et al. (2006)

Listening   Playing   Combined

Colin Anderson / Getty Images

Skin conductance response The electrodes on the research participant's left hand record skin conductance response, a physiological response that indicates a person's level of anxiety. In this particular study, skin conductance is recorded while participants play the game YetiSports JungleSwing.

---

psychophysiology A field of study that provides scientific information about the relation between physiological reactions and psychological experiences.

skin conductance response (SCR) A measure of electrical resistance at the skin that uses the activity of sweat glands to provide a physiological measure of anxiety.

Neurons are thus said to "communicate" through neurotransmitters. Thanks to neurotransmitter activity, the brain contains networks of interconnected neurons that are in continuous communication.

In research, neurotransmitter activity can be manipulated by use of *psychoactive substances,* which are any chemical substances that affect psychological processes (e.g., perception, thinking, or emotion). Psychoactive substances exert their effects by altering the normal communications between neurons. In addition to their research use, psychoactive substances are widely used in therapies for people suffering from psychological disorders involving mood and emotion (see Chapter 15), as well as disorders involving severe alterations in the ability to accurately perceive and understand reality (see Chapter 16).

EVIDENCE ABOUT THE BODY: PSYCHOPHYSIOLOGY. If you're about to give a public speech, your whole body reacts: You sweat, your heart beats faster, and you feel "worked up." **Psychophysiology** is a field of study that provides scientific information about the relation between such physiological reactions and psychological experiences (Andreassi, 2007).

Psychophysiologists use specialized tools to record the activity levels of bodily systems. One is **skin conductance response (SCR),** a measure of electrical resistance at the skin (see photo). Skin conductance changes when sweat glands are active, which occurs when people are anxious. SCR thus provides a physiological measure of anxiety.

Another physiological measure is heart rate. Recordings made using heart rate monitors can detect changes in heart rate that occur as people perform different types of tasks.

Psychophysiological measures can yield information that goes beyond the information obtained in self-reports. Consider research on a *repressive coping style,* that is, a tendency to deal with stress by not thinking about information that is anxiety-provoking (e.g., Mund & Mitte, 2012). (A person who said, "Everything's fine" while actually experiencing a lot of stress would be displaying a repressive coping style.) In one study (Weinberger, Schwartz, & Davidson, 1979), researchers obtained information about people with a repressive coping style—or "repressors"—in two ways:

1. *Self-report measures:* Researchers asked participants to describe their typical level of anxiety in a self-report questionnaire.

2. *Physiological measures:* Researchers obtained SCR and heart rate measures while participants performed a mildly stressful task in which they heard a phrase that was potentially anxiety provoking (e.g., "His roommate kicked him in the stomach") and had to think of another phrase to complete the thought as quickly as possible.

On the self-report measures, repressors looked as if they were not anxious; they reported levels of anxiety no higher than those of most other people. But the psychophysiological measures told a different story. The skin conductance and heart rate measures revealed that, when performing the stressful task, repressors experienced much *higher* levels of anxious arousal than other individuals. Psychophysiological measures thus yielded information that went beyond what was available through self-reports.

Interestingly, the researchers also measured how long it took participants to generate the phrases. Repressors, they found, took more time (Weinberger et al., 1979). Why would that be? One possibility is that, during the experimental task, repressors engaged

figure 2.10

MIGHT PEOPLE WHO LOOK CALM REALLY BE ANXIOUS?

PM B
IN ACTION

PERSON **P**

Some people display a repressive coping style; they say they are calm when they actually are experiencing high levels of stress.

MIND **M**

Think of ways to respond to the environment
↓
Monitor one's own thoughts for anxiety-provoking content
↓
Suppress anxiety-provoking thoughts

Research methods that time people's responses suggest that repressors may take time to monitor and suppress their own anxiety-provoking thoughts.

BRAIN **B**

Psychophysiological research methods reveal that repressors experience high levels of anxiety arousal even when they say they are not anxious.

Tek Image / Science Source

Gallery Stock

69

in an extra step of information processing; they not only (1) thought of phrases to complete the idea they heard but, unlike others, also (2) monitored their own responses for

What would an SCR reveal about your levels of anxiety right now?

potential anxiety-provoking content and suppressed responses that were emotionally threatening (see Erdelyi, 1985). That second step of information processing would have taken additional time. The research methods thus provided both biological-level and mind-level evidence about people with a repressive coping style (Figure 2.10).

🔥 WHAT DO YOU KNOW?...

15. Neurons emit electrical activity, which can be detected with a technique called _____ or EEG. Active neurons need more energy, which they get from oxygen in the blood; a technology that tracks blood flow in the brain, _____, can thus track neural activity. Neural activity can also be studied by manipulating neural communication via _____ substances. The psychophysiological tool that measures _____ _____ _____ (SCR) provides an operational definition of anxiety that does not rely on self-report.

Scientific Explanation

At the start of this chapter, we noted the purpose of research. Research fuels explanation, which is the ultimate goal of science (Salmon, 1989). Evidence from research provides the information needed to develop, test, and improve scientific explanations. In psychology, the purpose of research is to provide information that psychologists can use in explaining the behavior and experiences of people, the workings of the mind, and the functioning of the brain. Now that we've learned about psychology's data, research designs, and forms of scientific evidence, let's see how psychologists formulate scientific explanations.

Theories in Science

Preview Question

> What is a scientific theory?

Scientific theory When scientists say they have "a theory," they are *not* like the theorist in the cartoon. A scientific theory is not a casual speculation; it is a systematic explanation of phenomena that is based on a large body of scientific evidence.

© Benita Epstein
www.benitaepstein.com

THEORIES EXPOUNDED

scientific theory In science, a systematic, data-based explanation for a phenomenon or set of phenomena.

Scientists explain phenomena by developing sets of ideas known as scientific theories. What is a *theory* in science? A committee formed by the U.S. National Academy of Science has provided a particularly clear definition:

> In everyday usage, "theory" often refers to a hunch or a speculation. When people say, "I have a theory about why that happened," they are often drawing a conclusion based on fragmentary or inconclusive evidence.

> The formal scientific definition of theory is quite different from the everyday meaning of the word. It refers to a comprehensive explanation of some aspect of nature that is supported by a vast body of evidence.

—National Academy of Sciences (2008, p. 11)

When scientists say they have a theory, it does *not* mean that they're just speculating. A **scientific theory** is a systematic, data-based explanation for a phenomenon or set of phenomena. When you read in this book

How do you suppose a theory differs from a hypothesis?

that psychologists have a theory that, for example, self-confidence boosts personal achievement, or children's thinking develops through a set of distinct stages, or pessimistic thinking styles cause people to become depressed, it means the psychologists have systematic explanations that are grounded in scientific evidence.

A theory may be broad or narrow in scope. Sigmund Freud (1900, 1930), for example, developed a theory of remarkable breadth; it was meant to explain the overall structure of mind, the development of children, psychological distress and personality differences among adults, and the relation between the individual and society. In contemporary psychological science, John Anderson and his colleagues have developed a theory designed to explain perception, memory, problem solving, and the development of skills (Anderson et al., 2004). Yet often, theories are narrowly focused. For example, one famous theory of the experience of pain (Melzack & Wall, 1965; see Chapter 5) is just that: a theory about one and only one psychological experience, pain.

✿ WHAT DO YOU KNOW?...

16. True or False? When a scientist says, "I have a theory," he or she is saying, "I have a loose, hunch-based explanation for a phenomenon or a set of phenomena."

The Relation Between Theory and Evidence

Preview Question

> What is the relation between theory and evidence?

Scientific theories and scientific evidence are connected by a two-way street. Sometimes the direction of travel is from theory to evidence. The scientist formulates a theory, develops a specific hypothesis based on that theory, and then designs research to test that hypothesis. You learned this in Chapter 1: A theory about how stereotypes affect performance generated a specific hypothesis about when *stereotype threat* effects would occur. Research conducted at person, mind, and brain levels of analysis tested that hypothesis.

The results of research determine scientists' level of confidence in their theories. If a theory generates hypotheses that repeatedly are confirmed, confidence in the theory grows. However, if a theory's hypotheses are disconfirmed by evidence, the theory needs to be either modified or abandoned.

In this "direction of travel," from theory to evidence, theory comes first and data are collected after a theoretical prediction is made. In practice, however, this sequence is less common than you might think. Science often proceeds in the opposite direction: Investigators (1) gather scientific data and then (2) try to devise a theory that explains important patterns in the collected data.

When traveling in this direction—from evidence to theory—psychologists are engaged in the process of discovery. By collecting and analyzing data carefully, they might discover interesting phenomena that need to be explained. Patterns in the data motivate and guide the subsequent development of theory. As one psychologist put it:

> Become intimately familiar with . . . the data. Examine them from every angle. . . . If a datum suggests a new hypothesis, try to find additional evidence for it elsewhere in the data. If you see dim traces of interesting patterns, try to reorganize the data to bring them into bolder relief. . . . [Look for] something—anything—interesting . . . . How does one discover a new phenomenon? Smell a good idea? Have a brilliant insight into behavior? Create a new theory? [By] exploring the data.

> —Bem (1987, p. 172)

> When you run onto something interesting, drop everything else and study it.
>
> —B. F. Skinner (1956, p. 223)

You will see throughout this book that both directions of travel between theory and research have advanced the science of psychology.

The Ethics of Research

When you got your driver's license, you were told that driving "is a privilege, not a right." When psychologists get their "research license"—the education and credentials that enable them to do research—they're told the same thing. Conducting research is a privilege. The rights that need to be protected are those of the research participants.

Ethical Review of Research

Preview Question

> How are decisions about the ethics of a research proposal made?

The Tuskegee study In 1997 U.S. President Bill Clinton publicly apologized, on behalf of the U.S. government, for the ethical lapses that, decades earlier, had plagued the Tuskegee study of syphilis. Clinton and Vice President Al Gore are shown with Herman Shaw, who had taken part in the study and was one of many individuals not properly informed of the nature of the research.

AP Photo / Doug Mills

All research in psychology, whether conducted with people or animals, is evaluated by an **Institutional Review Board (IRB),** a group of professionals who assess the ethics of a proposed research study. The IRB determines whether planned research is acceptable according to the principles and moral beliefs of society as a whole. All institutions that conduct research—universities, hospitals, and so forth—maintain an IRB.

Prior to conducting any study, researchers submit detailed plans for that study to their IRB. It decides whether the study can be run by weighing the study's benefits (the scientific knowledge gained) against its costs (the inconvenience and potential risk to participants).

IRBs in the United States function according to principles spelled out in the *Belmont Report* (National Commission for the Protection of Human Subjects of Biomedical and Behavioral Research, 1979), a document that guides the conduct of all research involving human beings. The report, and the nation's overall system for reviewing research ethics, developed in response to historical events, the most significant of which was the Tuskegee Study.

The Tuskegee Study was research, sponsored by the U.S. government, on syphilis, a bacterial disease spread by sexual contact. Researchers wanted to learn how the disease develops and maintains itself in the body in the absence of treatment. To find out, in 1932 they began a long-term study of a group of African American

Institutional Review Board (IRB)
A group of professionals who assess the ethics of a proposed research study.

men in Tuskegee, Alabama, who were diagnosed with the disease. In a gross violation of ethics, the researchers did not inform the participants that they had the disease. Furthermore, they did not offer the participants penicillin, an effective treatment for syphilis, when it became available some years after the study began. These egregious ethical violations fueled a distrust of the research process among African Americans that has lasted into the twenty-first century (Shavers, Lynch, & Burmeister, 2000).

WHAT DO YOU KNOW?...

18. The Belmont Report, a document that guides ethical conduct of all research using human beings, was developed in response to the _____ _____, a study in which the benefits of research on syphilis were not weighed against the _____ to the African American men recruited for the study.

Ethical Principles in Research

Preview Question

> What three principles guide ethical research in psychology?

The ethical principles that govern research are designed to avoid ethical horrors such as those of the Tuskegee experiment. Three principles are particularly important guides to research in psychology:

1. *Research participation must be voluntary.* People cannot be forced or coerced into taking part in research. People running a company cannot order employees to participate in research. People running a prison cannot force the prisoners to become participants in experiments. Researchers also cannot provide incentives so large that people find it hard to decline experimental participation.

2. *Participants must be informed.* People must receive information about the main procedures of a study before they formally decide to take part. To convey this information, researchers conduct a **consent procedure,** a process in which they describe a study's procedures and determine whether participants agree to take part.

3. *Participants must be able to withdraw.* Even after agreeing to take part during the consent procedure, participants may withdraw from a study at any point. They must be able to withdraw without penalty (e.g., without the loss of income or credit that participants receive when completing an experimental session).

Picture Partners / Alamy

Parental consent Children can take part in psychology experiments, too. Of course, they will not understand the consent procedure. Ethical review processes, then, call for *parental* consent. In all research with people under 18 years of age, parents must give permission for their children to participate.

consent procedure A process in which researchers describe a study's procedures and determine whether participants agree to take part.

Finally, at the conclusion of a study, a *debriefing* procedure conducted by the experimenter fully informs participants about the research in which they have taken part. Debriefing is particularly critical when experimenters cannot inform participants about all aspects of a study at its start because that information would invalidate the study's procedures. Experimenters must ensure that participants fully understand the procedures and purposes of the research.

Ethical principles also govern research with animals. Researchers must minimize distress or pain suffered by animals used in studies, as well as the number of animals used. Studies of animals constitute only a small percentage of psychology's overall research effort. Nonetheless, they have proven to be of great value not only to basic science, but also to applications that benefit human welfare. Many effective treatments for physical and mental health problems have been based on research conducted originally with animals (Miller, 1985).

In the United States, formal procedures for evaluating the ethics of research have been in place since the 1970s. They are part of U.S. law. Virtually every study you read about in the chapters ahead, therefore, exemplifies not only the scientific principles you learned throughout this chapter, but also the ethical principles enforced by an IRB.

🕊 WHAT DO YOU KNOW?...

19. True or False?
   a. According to the principle of voluntary participation, your teacher cannot force you to participate in a study he or she is running.
   b. Once you agree to participate in a study, you must continue to participate until the very end, to avoid penalty.

↩↪ Looking Back and Looking Ahead

In Chapter 1, you learned that psychologists are committed to the methods of science. They do not just speculate about people, the mind, and the brain. They try to ground their ideas in scientific evidence.

This chapter has shown you the methods through which psychologists obtain that evidence. The methods are diverse—as is inevitable in a field whose subject matter is as diverse as psychological science. But, despite the diversity, you learned that psychology's research methods are anchored in a relatively small set of research designs (survey methods, correlational studies, and experiments), types of data (quantitative and qualitative), and types of evidence (psychological and biological).

You will encounter these research methods over and over in the chapters ahead. Furthermore, no matter which chapter you turn to next, you will find a diverse *mix* of methods. In today's psychological science, researchers in every branch of the field bring to bear a range of methods on questions about persons, the mind, and the brain.

Chapter Review

Now that you have completed this chapter, be sure to turn to Appendix B, where you will find a **Chapter Summary** that is useful for reviewing what you have learned about research methods.

Key Terms

back translation (p. 41)
case study (p. 62)
clinical case study (p. 62)
community-participation study (p. 62)
confound (p. 49)
consent procedure (p. 73)
control group (p. 48)
correlation coefficient (correlation) (p. 44)
correlational study (p. 43)
data (p. 51)
dependent variable (p. 47)
direct observation (p. 66)
electroencephalography (EEG) (p. 67)
experiment (p. 47)
experimental conditions (p. 48)
experimental design (p. 47)
functional magnetic resonance imaging (fMRI) (p. 67)

hypothesis (p. 48)
independent variable (p. 47)
Institutional Review Board (IRB) (p. 72)
mean (p. 58)
measurement (p. 52)
meta-analysis (p. 59)
negative correlation (p. 44)
observational study (p. 62)
observer report (p. 64)
operational definition (p. 52)
population (p. 42)
positive correlation (p. 44)
psychophysiology (p. 68)
qualitative data (p. 51)
qualitative research methods (p. 51)
quantitative data (p. 51)
quantitative research methods (p. 51)
questionnaire (p. 64)

random assignment (p. 49)
random sample (p. 42)
reliability (p. 54)
representative sample (p. 42)
research design (p. 38)
sample (p. 42)
scatterplot (p. 44)
scientific theory (p. 70)
self-report (p. 64)
skin conductance response (SCR) (p. 68)
standard deviation (p. 58)
statistically significant (p. 58)
statistics (p. 58)
survey method (p. 40)
validity (p. 54)
variable (p. 43)

Questions for Discussion

1. People seem to love urban legends—those stories of questionable truthfulness that are often circulated via email. (A current popular one warns readers that Facebook will begin charging subscription fees.) Are your friends fooled by them? Take this opportunity to do a quantitative study to describe the beliefs of your friends. Go to the Web site snopes.com and choose five urban legends that you find particularly intriguing. Design a survey question to measure the believability of each one. Ask at least 10 friends or classmates to fill out your survey. Calculate and report the proportion of people who found each urban legend believable. Does this study primarily serve the purpose of description, prediction, or explanation? [Apply, Comprehend]

2. You can easily turn the above study into one whose goal is to *predict* who will find urban legends believable. Take a moment to think of a variable that could help predict who would be a believer. You might ask people how strongly they believe in astrology, for example. Design a survey including two questions, one about the believability of the urban legend, and one for the variable you choose, making sure to include a numerical scale for

each. Ask at least 10 friends or classmates to fill out your survey. Plot your data in a scatterplot. Does there appear to be a relation between the two variables? What do you estimate the correlation coefficient to be? [Synthesize]

3. Now let's focus on features of the urban legend itself that could increase its believability. Perhaps the source of the information about the legend might *explain* why we believe some urban legends and not others. We can easily *manipulate* this variable experimentally. Try it yourself! Create two versions of an urban legend—one that cites a legitimate authority (e.g., a sheriff) and one that doesn't. Randomly assign different groups of people to the conditions and ask them to evaluate its believability (using the survey item described above). Calculate the mean believability score for each of your conditions. Was your hypothesis supported? [Synthesize]

4. For your experiment above, consider the importance of random assignment. Identify a personality variable that could influence people's ratings of believability. How does random assignment help control for the effects of this variable? [Analyze]

Chapter Review

5. The items above walked you through two different methods for answering questions about interesting phenomena (survey research and experimentation). The appropriateness of these methods may be determined by a critical feature of the predictor: whether it can be manipulated or measured. If the predictor can be manipulated, as was the case with our legitimacy of authority variable, we can do experimentation. If the predictor can only be measured, as was the case with our belief in astrology variable, we do survey research. What predictor would you like to investigate? Can it be manipulated? What method will be most appropriate for testing its effects? [Analyze]

6. If you were applying for a job, would you prefer that your potential employer use qualitative or quantitative methods to assess your qualifications? Would you prefer a mix of both? Explain your answer. [Analyze]

7. Assume for the moment that it is true women tend to go to public restrooms in groups. Design a *qualitative* study to find out why. Which method will you use and why? A clinical case study? Observational study? Community-participation study? [Synthesize]

8. Suppose you want to find out whether there is any truth to your observation that women tend to go to public restrooms in groups. Design a *quantitative* study to investigate. What will be your population of interest? What steps will you take to make sure the sample you observe is representative of this population? What questions will you ask to help explain your observation? [Synthesize]

9. A *Los Angeles Times* headline reads "Popular Kids More Likely to Smoke, Research Says" (MacVean, 2012). Considering that these data were likely to have come from a correlational study, identify some potential third variables that could simultaneously cause kids to become more popular and to smoke. [Analyze]

10. We've asked questions about women's tendency to travel to public restrooms in groups and about people's beliefs in urban legends. What qualifies these questions as scientific? (You may wish to review the definition of *scientific* presented in Chapter 1.) [Analyze]

Self-Test

1. Shaun posts a sign-up sheet to her college's psychology department bulletin board advertising a survey she is conducting. Her population of interest is all undergraduates at her college. This recruitment technique
   a. is a good example of random sampling.
   b. assures that everyone in the population has an equal chance of being in the sample.
   c. is likely to produce a representative sample.
   d. is not likely to produce a representative sample because psychology students are likely to be overrepresented.

2. Which of the following pairs of variables is likely to be negatively correlated?
   a. Hours spent studying and exam score
   b. Days absent from class and final course grade
   c. Servings of caffeine and hours spent awake
   d. Hours per week spent at the gym and cardiovascular fitness

3. Cellie computes the correlation coefficient for the relation between inches of daily precipitation (rain and snow) in Chicago during December and number of daily on-time flights out of O'Hare International Airport (in Chicago) during December. Which of the following is the most likely value of this correlation coefficient?
   a. −3.43
   b. −.64

   c. .00
   d. .90

4. Even though ice cream sales and crime are correlated, we cannot claim that ice cream causes crime because
   a. crime probably causes ice cream sales to increase.
   b. summer heat is the likely cause of increases in both ice cream sales and crime.
   c. crime cannot be operationally defined.
   d. All of the above

5. Researchers (Damisch, Stoberock, & Mussweiler, 2010) manipulated what people were told about a golf ball before they were asked to sink as many putts out of 10 as possible. Half were told that the ball was lucky and the other half were simply told that this was the ball they had been using all day. The researchers measured the number of putts the participants were able to sink. In this study, the independent variable was _____ and the dependent variable was _____.
   a. the people who were told the ball was lucky; the people who were told this was the ball they had used all day
   b. number of putts; what people were told
   c. the people who were told this was the ball they had used all day; the people who were told the ball was lucky
   d. what people were told; number of putts

6. Random _____ is used to increase the representativeness of one's sample, whereas random _____ is used to help eliminate a potential confound: differences between people.
   a. sampling; selection
   b. assignment; selection
   c. sampling; assignment
   d. assignment; sampling

7. Asking people to fill out a self-esteem questionnaire would be an example of _____ research, whereas asking people to describe, in words, how positively they regard themselves would be an example of _____ research.
   a. correlational; qualitative
   b. correlational; quantitative
   c. quantitative; qualitative
   d. qualitative; quantitative

8. Ramon fills out a personality questionnaire designed to assess self-esteem and gets a mean score of 4 on a scale of 1 to 5. A month later, he fills it out again and gets the same score. At the very least, what quality can we be certain this questionnaire possesses?
   a. Validity
   b. Reliability
   c. Accuracy
   d. Variability

9. What was the operational definition of self-esteem in the above question?
   a. Ramon's mean score on the questionnaire
   b. The discrepancy between Ramon's score at each testing period
   c. How long it took Ramon to fill out the questionnaire
   d. Ramon's willingness to fill out the questionnaire

10. On your last exam, most students earned 75% of the available points. The ease with which you can now compare your own performance is a clear advantage of using
    a. words to quantify variables.
    b. the correlational method.
    c. numbers to quantify variables.
    d. the scientific method.

11. Yvonne compared the math skills of 8-year-old boys and girls and found that the girls outscored the boys, but that the mean difference was not statistically significant. What does this mean?
    a. This is a difference we would expect by chance.
    b. This is a much larger difference than we would expect by chance.
    c. This is not a difference we would expect by chance.
    d. There is a 1% probability that this finding was due to chance.

12. Which of the following research methods would be *least* useful for obtaining naturalistic evidence?
    a. Case study
    b. Observational study
    c. Community-participation study
    d. Laboratory experimental study

13. Chaya prides herself on her willingness to try new things and scored very high on this trait on a personality questionnaire she completed. However, direct observations of her behaviors this past week revealed that she was quick to shoot down novel ideas, she refused to go to the Ethiopian restaurant that her friends suggested, and she watched the same TV shows over and over. This discrepancy illustrates the limitations of
    a. observer reports.
    b. direct observation.
    c. self-reports.
    d. experimentation.

14. In science, a theory can be described according to all of the following qualities below, except which one?
    a. It is merely speculative.
    b. It is systematic.
    c. It is evidence-based.
    d. It can be broad or narrow in scope.

15. Bernie signed an informed consent form and got about halfway through the experiment when he started to feel uncomfortable. What is one of his rights as a research participant?
    a. He may request permission to withdraw from the study.
    b. He may withdraw from the study without penalty.
    c. He may withdraw from the study, with only a minor penalty.
    d. His rights will differ depending on where in the United States the study is run.

Answers

You can check your answers to the preceding Self-Test and the chapter's What Do You Know? questions in Appendix B.

Once we've got a good psychological theory, then it makes sense to ask how the brain does it. . . . Neuro-scientific evidence only makes sense if you already have a theory of structure and function, well worked out at the psychological level of analysis. . . . Otherwise, it's all just pixels.

– John Kihlstrom

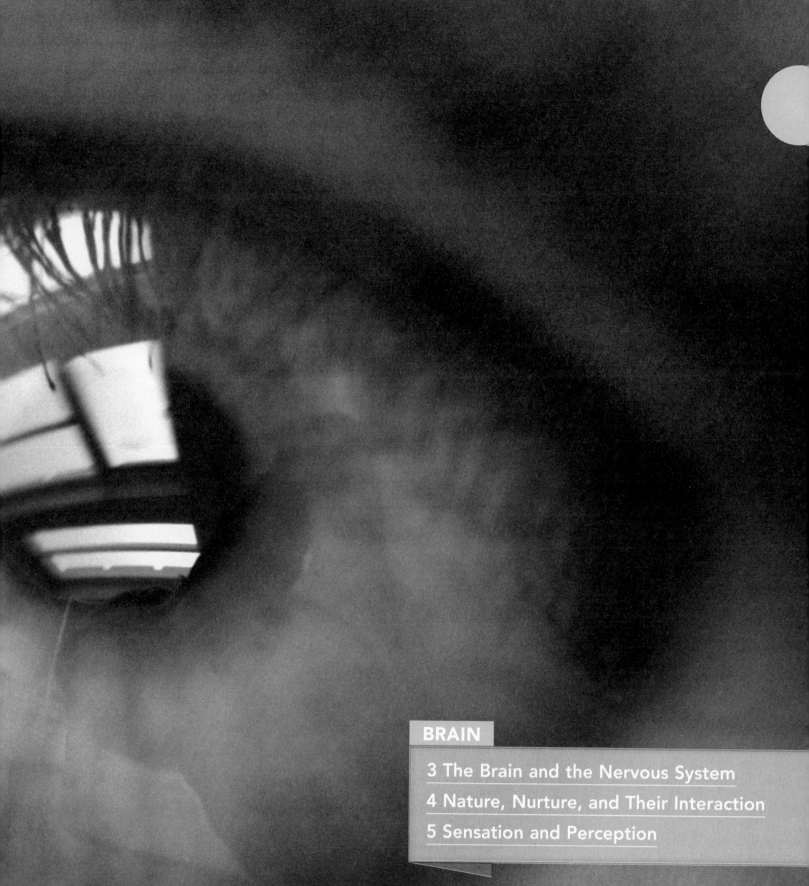

The Brain and the Nervous System

3

The patient was looking at his father, yet thought he was looking at an imposter. "He looks exactly like my father but he really isn't. He's a nice guy, but he isn't my father, Doctor."

"But why," the doctor asked, "was this man pretending to be your father?"

"That is what is so surprising, Doctor—why should anyone want to pretend to be my father? Maybe my father employed him to take care of me."

—Hirstein & Ramachandran (1997, p. 438)

THE CASE WAS MYSTIFYING. FOR YEARS, THE PATIENT'S RELATIONSHIP with his father was normal. But now, he didn't even recognize him! What do you think was wrong?

Maybe the patient had amnesia and couldn't remember his father. But that wasn't it. When he talked to his father on the phone, everything was normal: He recognized his father's voice, remembered their relationship, and they conversed as always. Problems arose only when he saw his father in person.

Maybe a part of the patient's brain that detects faces was damaged and he couldn't recognize anybody. But that wasn't it, either. He easily recognized *other* people: neighbors, casual friends, and the like. Yet his father was unrecognizable to him.

As it turns out, all the individual parts of the patient's brain were working properly. Yet something was broken: a connection *between* parts (Hirstein & Ramachandran, 1997).

Everyone's brain contains one region that detects faces and another that generates emotions. In most brains, they are interconnected. When a loved one comes into view, both brain regions are activated; the interconnection combines their activity, and the result is a "warm glow of recognition." You see and *feel as if* you're seeing your loved one.

In the patient's brain, the connection had become severed. Once this happened, he no longer experienced the "warm glow"; upon seeing his father, he didn't feel as if he was looking at his father. His brain damage—the broken connection—then caused his mind to play a trick on him. Without the feeling

Jose Luis Pelaez, Inc. / Blend Images / Corbis

that usually occurred when he looked at his father, the patient concluded that the man was an imposter.

Capgras syndrome, the patient's disorder, is rare. But the lesson it teaches is broadly important. When it comes to the brain, connections are key.

The brain is like the Internet. The Internet's power comes from connections among vast numbers of computers. The brain's power derives from connections among vast numbers of brain cells. Without the Internet connections, you couldn't email friends, watch YouTube videos, or play interactive games. Without the brain connections, you couldn't sing a song, read this book, or recognize your father. ◎

WHAT IS THE BRAIN LIKE? It seems so mysterious: a collection of biological cells packed under the skull that, somehow, gives you extraordinary powers—to create works of art; to feel the warmth of the sun; to imagine yourself traveling in a spaceship; and, even more remarkably, to *think about the fact that* you are creating art, feeling the sun's warmth, and imagining yourself in a spaceship.

This chapter begins with some general principles that help to explain the brain's workings. Next, we'll "zoom in" on the brain by reviewing its overall organization and then its individual cells. Finally, you'll learn about two communications systems that run throughout the body: the nervous system and the endocrine system.

Brain and Behavior: General Principles

The question "What is the brain like?" is not new. Scholars have speculated about it for thousands of years.

Ideas About the Brain Through the Ages

Preview Question

> What analogies have been used to describe the brain through the ages?

Throughout history, scholars contemplating the brain have proposed analogies (Hampden-Turner, 1981). The mysterious brain, they have said, might be analogous to some less mysterious object. The similarity might shed light on how the brain works.

> In ancient Rome, inventors devised pumps for propelling water into the city's fountains. Romans who contemplated the brain judged that it, too, is a pump (Daugman, 2001). A physician, Galen, said that the brain controlled bodily movements by pumping "animal spirits" through the body's nerves, which he claimed were like pipes (Vartanian, 1973).

> By the start of the eighteenth century, European inventors had devised complex new machines (e.g., mechanical clocks), and Isaac Newton had explained that the universe functions according to physical laws, like a machine. Scholars of the eighteenth century judged that the brain and the body of which it is a part work like a machine. The analogy was made most explicit in a book by the French physician Julien La Mettrie, entitled *L'homme Machine* ("Man a Machine," 1748; Wellman, 1992).

> In the nineteenth century, physicists formulated laws of energy, inventors harnessed energy for industrial use, and Sigmund Freud said that the brain is an energy system (Breuer & Freud, 1895). According to Freud, different parts of the brain store mental energy and use it to power behavior. Just as too much pent-up energy in a steam engine can cause mechanical problems, too much pent-up mental energy in the brain can cause psychological problems.

What is the brain like? In the ancient world, fountains that pumped water into the city of Rome were high-tech. Scholars, inspired by the technology, suggested that the brain works like a pump, circulating fluids around the body.

Mim Friday / Alamy

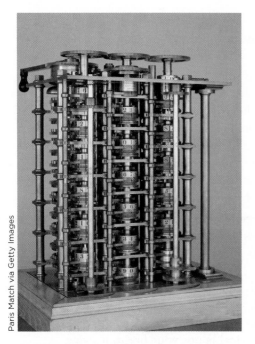

Babbage difference engine On the left is the first mechanical tool that seemed to "think": the *difference engine* devised by the British mathematician Charles Babbage. It could compute solutions to complex mathematical formulas. The power of machines such as the difference engine inspired students of the brain to propose that the brain could be understood as a mechanical device—a thinking machine in your head. On the right is the biological tool that Babbage used to invent the difference engine; Babbage's own brain is preserved in a science museum in London.

> In the second half of the twentieth century, society's new technological toy was the computer, and its favorite brain analogy was that—you guessed it—the brain is like a computer. The physical brain was analogous to computer hardware and the mind's beliefs and skills were akin to computer software (Simon, 1969). Interestingly, this analogy also worked in reverse: Computers, like brains or minds, are "machines who think" (McCorduck, 2004).

Our opening story introduced another analogy: The brain is like the Internet. The power of both comes from interconnections among large numbers of parts.

Each analogy—pump, machine, energy system, computer, and Internet—tells us something about the brain. Some (computer and Internet) are better than others (water pump; the Romans were better at plumbing than brain science). None is perfect, yet each is useful. The human brain is so massively complex that analogies are, in fact, a valuable first step toward understanding. So let's look at two more, both of which you should keep in mind throughout this chapter. The brain is like (1) a tool and (2) a muscle.

🔥 WHAT DO YOU KNOW?...

1. With changes in technology come changes in the _____ used to describe the brain.

See Appendix B for answers to What Do You Know? questions.

How the Brain Is Like a Tool

Preview Question

> What valuable points are highlighted by a brain-as-tool analogy?

The philosopher Rom Harré (2002, 2012) emphasizes that the brain is like a tool. People use their brains to do the jobs of everyday life. The brain/tool analogy highlights two valuable points:

1. You can use any tool for a variety of jobs, including those tasks for which it was not originally designed (Heyes, 2012). A screwdriver, for example, can serve not only as a screw turner, but also as a paint can opener, ice pick, or weapon.

Similarly, although your brain was originally designed to solve problems encountered in the evolutionary past, you can use it to perform contemporary tasks—reading, writing, driving—for which it was not designed originally.

2. When you use a tool to perform a job, it is you—not the tool—that is responsible for executing the job. You don't say, "My shovel cleared the snow off the sidewalk." You say that you did it, using a tool (the shovel). Similarly, you don't say, "My hands typed my paper" or "My legs ran 2 miles in under 11 minutes." *You* did those things, using biological tools—your hands and legs. Likewise, when solving a math problem, answering a trivia question, or learning a second language, it's you—not your brain—that's doing the problem solving, answering, or learning (Bennet & Hacker, 2003). You need your brain to do these jobs, but you, not your brain, did them.

The brain/tool analogy helps to avoid confusions that can occur when discussing the brain and people's psychological experience. It is not the brain having the experiences; it's the people. Although some writers talk about the "emotional brain" (Ecker, Ticic, & Hulley, 2012), "spiritual brain" (Beauregard & O'Leary, 2008), and "political brain" (Westen, 2007), the being who is emotional, spiritual, and political is not your brain; it's you.

> Why do you suppose people speak of the brain as if it's the one that is emotional?

WHAT DO YOU KNOW?...

2. The following statement is incorrect. Explain why: "The brain-as-tool analogy reminds us that it is the brain that performs tasks, not the person using the brain."

How the Brain Is Like Muscle

Preview Question

> How have researchers demonstrated that the brain is like muscle?

When you use a muscle repeatedly, it grows. As a result, you gain strength and are better able to perform physical tasks using that muscle.

Like a muscle, the brain also changes when you perform a task repeatedly. The changes make it easier for you to do that task in the future. Evidence of this comes from a study of juggling (Draganski et al., 2004).

Researchers invited to a lab 24 participants who did not know how to juggle and took pictures of their brains using neuroimaging methods (see Research Toolkit). Half the participants then spent three months learning how to juggle. The other half did not learn juggling. Afterward, brain images were taken again. By comparing the two sets of images, the researchers could see whether people's brains had changed during the three-month period.

They found that jugglers' brains did change. The changes occurred in an area of the brain critical to processing visual motion, as you might expect because juggling requires close visual attention to multiple moving objects (Figure 3.1). This brain region expanded among people who learned how to juggle; there was a greater volume of brain cells in this area after juggling. No changes occurred in the brains of nonjugglers (Draganski et al., 2004).

> Had you ever before considered the plasticity of your own brain?

The point of this research is not that juggling, per se, enhances the brain. It is more general: Experiences alter brain anatomy. Brain structures are not fixed and unchangeable. Instead, like muscle, they grow with experience. This feature of the brain is called **plasticity,** which is the brain's capacity to change physically as a result of experience (Zatorre, Fields, & Johansen-Berg, 2013).

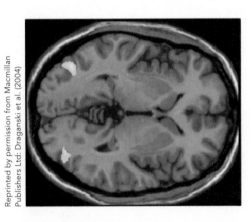

Reprinted by permission from Macmillan Publishers Ltd: Draganski et al. (2004)

figure 3.1

Your brain on juggling The brain areas shown in yellow are those that changed as a result of people learning how to juggle. Repeated juggling promoted the development of cells in these brain regions, which are key to processing visual motion. In this image, the brain is shown from the top, with the front of the brain on the right.

plasticity The brain's capacity to change physically as a result of experience.

Note how plasticity makes the brain *un*like a computer. If you run your favorite software application repeatedly, your computer's hardware does not change. But if you yourself perform the same task repeatedly, the biological "hardware" of your brain *does* change.

> ### 🐾 WHAT DO YOU KNOW? ...
>
> 3. How is the concept of plasticity related to the idea that the brain is like muscle?

Different Parts of the Brain Do Different Things

Preview Question

> › What can brain damage tell us about the structure and function of the brain?

The human brain looks a bit like a cauliflower: roundish, off-white, with ridges and bumps on the surface. Yet "the brain is like a cauliflower" is not a good analogy. Of the many ways in which the brain is *not* like a cauliflower, one is particularly noteworthy. All parts of a cauliflower are essentially the same. Plant tissue is *undifferentiated;* there are no significant biological differences between one part of the cauliflower and another. Brains are *not* like this. They are highly differentiated; distinct parts of the brain vary structurally and are involved in different types of mental activity.

BRAIN DAMAGE EVIDENCE. How do we know that the brain is differentiated? Cases of brain damage provide convincing evidence.

Whether through injury or illness, people sometimes incur damage to one part of the brain. When this happens, there are, in principle, three possible outcomes for the mind:

1. *No mental ability:* The person won't have any thoughts or feelings. It might be that every part of the brain must function normally in order to provide the capacity for thought.

2. *All mental abilities are intact but impaired:* The person will be able to think, but thinking will be less quick and intelligent. It might be that each part of the brain contributes equally to its overall speed and power.

3. *Selective loss of specific mental abilities:* Some thinking abilities will remain completely intact, but other abilities will be lost. This would indicate that the brain is differentiated and that the specific part that was damaged is needed for the specific mental ability that was lost.

What usually happens? Commonly it is #3. Brain damage often causes people to lose a specific mental ability. A case of brain damage from a century-and-a-half ago vividly illustrates the point.

PHINEAS GAGE. The damaged brain was that of Phineas Gage, a railroad construction worker in Vermont (Damasio et al., 1994). Gage's job was to supervise explosions designed to level land for laying track. Explosive force was supposed to go down into rock that was standing in the way of the railroad tracks. Unfortunately for Gage (but fortunately for science), an on-the-job error caused an explosion to go in the other direction—up toward Gage's head, propelling an iron rod up from the ground, into Gage's face, and straight through part of his brain. The rod then exited the top of Gage's skull (Figure 3.2).

What happened to Gage? As the *Boston Post* (September 13, 1848) reported, "The most singular circumstance connected with this affair is that he was alive . . . and in full possession of his reason." Most of Gage's mental abilities were intact. He could control the movements of his body, his speech was normal, and his memory was so good that he could even remember what happened to him in the accident. Gage seemed no less intelligent than before the accident occurred (Damasio et al., 1994).

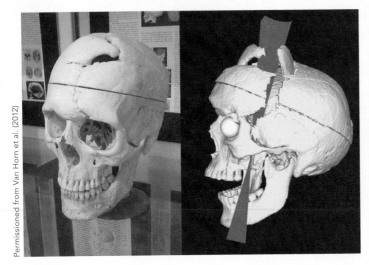

Permissioned from Van Horn et al. (2012)

Collection of Jack and Beverly Wilgus

figure 3.2
Phineas Gage The images above show where a metal rod went through the brain of Phineas Gage. The picture on the right shows Gage himself, holding the rod—a souvenir of the most famous accident in the history of brain science.

CONNECTING TO EXECUTIVE THINKING PROCESSES AND SELF-CONTROL

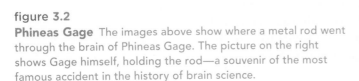

Ⓟ PERSON

Chapter 14: Children's ability to control impulsive behavior and emotional reactions increases as the frontal lobes, and executive thinking abilities, develop.

Ⓜ MIND

Chapter 6: The mind contains "central executive" thinking abilities. These are impaired when frontal regions of the brain are damaged.

Ⓑ BRAIN

Here, we focus on the brain and the effects of damage to a region in the front of the brain.

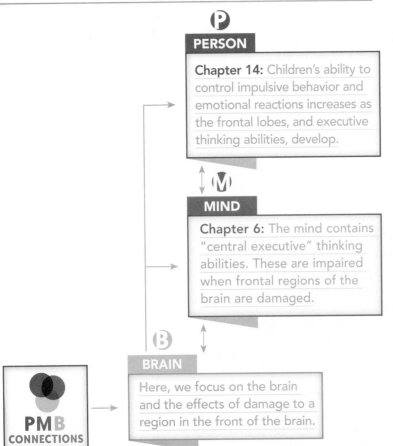

PMB CONNECTIONS

Gage's case, then, contradicts possibilities #1 and #2 above. Despite brain damage, he still could think, and just as quickly and intelligently as before.

Yet, in one specific way, Gage changed profoundly. Before the accident, he was well mannered. Afterward, he used profane language that offended friends and coworkers. Before, he had been industrious and responsible. After, he was so irresponsible that his employer had to fire him. Gage no longer could control his social behavior. He was unable to adhere to the rules, conventions, and responsibilities of society. His physician, John M. Harlow, summarized the change as follows:

> Previous to his injury . . . he possessed a well-balanced mind, and was looked upon by those who knew him as a shrewd, smart businessman, very energetic and persistent in executing all his plans of operation. In this regard his mind was radically changed, so decidedly that his friends and acquaintances said he was "no longer Gage." [After the accident, Gage was] fitful, irreverent, indulging at times in the grossest profanity (which was not previously his custom), manifesting but little deference for his fellows, impatient of restraint or advice when it conflicts with his desires, at times pertinaciously obstinate, yet capricious and vacillating, devising many plans of future operations, which are no sooner arranged than they are abandoned in turn for others appearing more feasible.

—quoted in Macmillan (2000, pp. 92–93)

The case of Phineas Gage shows that even major damage to the brain may not eliminate a person's ability to think, or even slow his or her thinking. Instead, brain damage is selective. It can cause people to lose one type of ability—in Gage's case, the ability to align one's behavior with social rules and responsibilities—while leaving others intact. This means that different parts of the brain are specialized. A given part of the brain may be critical to some mental activities, and irrelevant to others.

In summary, you've already learned a few lessons about the brain. It's a biological tool that we use to perform the tasks of life. It's a special kind of tool that becomes stronger the more it is used, like a muscle. It's a complex tool, with lots of specialized parts. Finally, as you learned in this chapter's opening story about a patient suffering from Capgras syndrome, even more complexity is involved: The various parts of the brain are highly interconnected. Even simple, everyday tasks require coordination among multiple brain regions.

Let's now look at this remarkable biological tool in detail, to find out how it gets its jobs done.

🌀 WHAT DO YOU KNOW?...

4. How might Phineas Gage have been affected by his accident if the parts of the brain were not specialized?

Zooming In on the Brain

We'll begin our tour of the brain by examining the big picture: the brain's overall structure and major subparts. Next, we'll "zoom in" a bit to look at the communications networks that connect these subparts to one another. We then will zoom in even more, to examine the brain's individual cells, or *neurons,* and how they communicate with one another.

Bottom-to-Top Organization

Preview Questions

> How does Aristotle's model of the brain compare to more recent conceptualizations of the brain?
> What did MacLean mean when he said that we have "three brains in one"?
> What are the structures of the lowest level of the brain and their functions?
> What are the structures of the middle level of the brain and their functions?
> What are the structures of the highest level of the brain and their functions?

Scholars studying the brain have long noted that its overall structure consists of three main parts. The first such brain model is more than 2000 years old, yet looks remarkably modern.

Aristotle, the greatest scientist of ancient Athens, suggested that the mind and brain have a three-part structure, with some parts being conceptually "high-level" structures that contribute to distinctly human thinking processes. In Aristotle's model, the lowest level is a vegetative mind responsible for growth and reproduction. One level up is an animal mind responsible for feelings of pleasure and pain. Finally, on top, a rational mind enables people to engage in logical thought (Aristotle, trans. 2010).

When formulating his model, Aristotle completely lacked contemporary scientific knowledge of brain structures. Nonetheless, his work has a contemporary ring to it. The twentieth century's most renowned conceptual model of the brain, proposed by the neuroscientist Paul MacLean (1990), similarly identifies a three-part, bottom-to-top organization of brain structures.

MacLean's model is known as the *triune brain.* "Triune" means "three in one." The **triune brain** model, then, suggests that the overall human brain consists of three main parts, each of which is a distinct functioning brain that carries out its own unique

triune brain Conceptual model of brain structure distinguishing among three main parts of the human brain that evolved at different points and perform distinct functions.

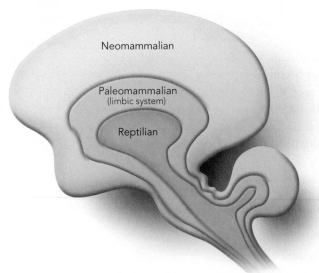

figure 3.3
Triune brain MacLean's triune brain model indicates that humans have three brains in one: a reptilian brain, a paleomammalian brain (also known as the limbic system), and a neomammalian brain. As species evolved, they retained the older brain systems and added new brain matter on top of it.

activities. You have, in essence, three brains in one. As in Aristotle's model, some parts of the brain are more advanced, and at a higher level, than others.

MacLean contended that the three levels of brain emerged at different points in the evolution of Earth's species (Figure 3.3):

1. The *reptilian brain,* the lowest level of the three brain regions, is evolutionarily ancient. It has existed since the evolution of reptiles.

2. The *paleomammalian* (ancient mammal) *brain,* the midlevel brain system, is newer, yet still quite old. It reached its full development with the evolution of mammals, more than 100 million years ago.

3. The *neomammalian* (new mammal) *brain* is the newest and highest-level brain system. It reached its fullest development in our species, *Homo sapiens,* somewhere between 50,000 and 200,000 years ago (Mithen, 1996).

According to MacLean, then, you possess not only the unique brain systems of a modern human, but also, tucked underneath, the brain of a nonhuman mammal and, beneath that, the brain of a reptile.

At first, "three brains in one" sounds weird. But consider the following three facts:

› Some of your experiences—which are products of your brain—are easy to put into words. You could, right now, say that "I'm reading my psych textbook" or "I plan to finish the brain chapter by tomorrow."

› Other experiences—still products of your brain—are strongly felt, yet very difficult to put into words. You may experience "mixed emotions" that you can't easily describe (e.g., a mix of happiness, sadness, and envy if a close friend announces that she's been offered a great new job that will cause her to move to a different town).

› Yet other activities of the brain are not "experiences" at all; you aren't even aware that the brain is doing them. Right now, your brain is regulating your body temperature and breathing rate, but you can't feel your brain doing so.

MacLean's triune brain model explains that these different experiences reflect the actions of different levels of brain. When you put experiences into words, you are using your neomammalian brain. Emotions, by contrast, are produced by the paleomammalian brain. It is not capable of producing language (so nonhuman animals aren't speaking to one another), which helps to explain why the emotions it produces sometimes can't easily be put into words. Finally, the reptilian brain executes simple functions like regulating body temperature and breathing. By itself, this brain system cannot produce consciously experienced feelings, so you don't feel your brain at work on the task of regulating internal physiological states. The three parts of the triune brain are connected to one another, and their activities thus can be coordinated. Nonetheless, their functions are distinct.

MacLean first proposed the triune brain model in 1969 (Newman & Harris, 2009). Although enormous scientific advances have been made since that time, MacLean's three-part, bottom-to-top organization remains a valuable overview of brain structures. So let's now look at these "three brains" in detail. In doing this, we'll use their standard contemporary biological names: (1) the *brain stem* (MacLean's reptilian brain), (2) the *limbic system* (the paleomammalian brain), and (3) the *cerebrum* (the neomammalian brain) and its outermost layer, the *cerebral cortex.*

brain stem The lowest region of the brain; its structures regulate bodily activities critical to survival.

BRAIN STEM. The lowest region of the brain is the **brain stem,** which sits at the top of the spinal cord. Three main structures of the brain stem—the *medulla,* the *pons,* and the *midbrain*—regulate bodily activities critical to survival (Figure 3.4).

The **medulla** plays a major role in *homeostasis,* which is the body's maintenance of a stable, consistent inner physical state. It contributes to homeostasis by regulating rates of physiological activity, such as heart rate and blood pressure. The medulla also is the key pathway from the brain to the rest of the body; communications between the spinal cord and higher regions of the brain run through the medulla. In addition, the medulla controls the "gag reflex," the contraction of the throat that prevents choking (Urban & Caplan, 2011).

The **pons** is a region of the brain stem located just above the medulla. It performs a number of functions and contains structures that control your rate of breathing. It also generates a distinctive stage of sleeping (REM sleep; see Chapter 9) in which the brain is highly active, generating dreams, but the body is essentially paralyzed. Studies show that if the pons is damaged, an animal, while asleep and dreaming, will move around and attack imaginary prey (Siegel, 2005). The pons also functions as a relay station, conveying signals among other brain regions (which you'll learn about below).

The third main brain stem structure is the **midbrain,** a small yet complex structure that contributes to an organism's survival in a number of ways. One region of the midbrain protects the organism by generating defensive reactions to threatening events. Evidence of this comes from studies in which researchers activate the key region of the midbrain artificially. When the midbrain is activated, animals display defensive responses even when no threat is present. For example, when researchers stimulated the midbrain of a rat, it became highly alert, its heart rate increased, and it began to flee—even though there was nothing in the environment to flee from (Brandaõ et al., 2005).

In addition to these three main structures (the medulla, pons, and midbrain), the brain stem houses a network of brain cells that you're relying on right now to keep you awake and alert as you read this chapter. This network is the **reticular formation,** a brain system that influences an organism's overall level of arousal (Gupta et al., 2010). This function of the reticular formation was discovered in studies with cats (Moruzzi & Magoun, 1949). Researchers stimulated the reticular formation, a low-level brain system, while recording activity in the cortex (discussed below), a high-level brain region. When they stimulated the reticular formation, activity in the cortex increased. The reticular formation, then, regulated the arousal level of other parts of the brain. Damage to the reticular formation can cause a *coma,* a state in which a person is alive but motionless, unaware of events, and unable to be awakened (Gupta et al., 2010).

> How active is your reticular formation right now?

Before we move up from the brain's lowest-level region, the brain stem, we note a significant brain structure located just behind it. The **cerebellum,** which looks like a miniature brain tucked under the back of the brain, regulates motor movement. With a damaged cerebellum, you would still be able to move your body, but those movements wouldn't be as coordinated and precise. Your posture might be altered and your stride less smooth, and you wouldn't be able to accurately perform tasks such as tracing an image on a piece of paper (Daum et al., 1993). The cerebellum is also needed to perform a task that a doctor may have asked you to do during a physical exam: Close your eyes and quickly touch your index finger to your nose (Ito, 2002). The doctor's test assesses your cerebellar functioning.

Controlling motor movements is not the cerebellum's only job. Like most parts of the brain, the cerebellum is connected to many other brain regions. Thanks to these connections, the cerebellum also is active in the control of emotion and thinking, including the accurate perception of passages of time (Strick, Dum, & Fiez, 2009). Compared to others, people with cerebellar damage are less accurate in

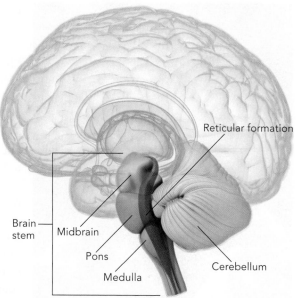

figure 3.4
The brain stem and the cerebellum
The brain stem (which contains the medulla, the pons, the midbrain, and the reticular formation) and the cerebellum.

---

medulla A structure in the brain stem that contributes to homeostasis by regulating rates of physiological activity and that serves as the communications pathway from the brain to the rest of the body.

pons A structure of the brain stem that carries out biological functions, including the control of breathing rate and generation of REM sleep.

midbrain A structure of the brain stem that contributes to survival in several ways, such as by generating defensive reactions to threatening events.

reticular formation A network of cells in the brain stem that influences bodily arousal.

cerebellum A brain structure located behind the brain stem that regulates motor movement and also contributes to emotion and thinking.

That's using the old cerebellum To perform the feats of a gymnast, you need your cerebellum, a part of the brain that enables people to make movements that are coordinated, smooth, and precise.

perceiving small variations in time intervals and in tapping out timed musical rhythms (Ivry & Keele, 1989).

LIMBIC SYSTEM. If all you had were a brain stem, you wouldn't have much psychological life. The brain stem would maintain your basic bodily functions, but you would lack feelings and emotions. For this, you need more brain.

Fortunately, evolution has provided you with more brain. All mammals possess a **limbic system,** which is a set of brain structures that resides above the brain stem but below higher brain regions (Figure 3.5). The limbic system enables mammals to have emotional lives.

MacLean first recognized that these different structures, located in different parts of the brain, should be thought of as a "system," that is, as a set of parts that work together (Newman & Harris, 2009). Later work confirmed MacLean's intuition; research shows that the limbic system's different parts are highly inter-connected. Mammals thus possess an interconnected system of brain structures that substantially expands their mental abilities, as compared to evolutionarily older organisms (Reep, Finlay, & Darlington, 2007). Let's look at the most significant structures in this system.

> What would your life be like without emotions?

The **hypothalamus** is a limbic system structure that is small yet critical to survival. It plays a key role in maintaining internal bodily states, such as body temperature. The hypothalamus also triggers behaviors that have been important throughout evolution, such as eating, drinking, and sexual response (King, 2006). The hypothalamus can perform these tasks thanks, in part, to its connections to the nearby *pituitary gland*, which is part of the body's *endocrine system* (discussed later in this chapter). The hypothalamus sends signals directly to the pituitary, which in turn

limbic system A set of brain structures just above the brain stem, including the hypothalamus, hippocampus, and amygdala, that give mammals the capacity to experience emotional reactions.

hypothalamus A limbic system structure key to the regulation of bodily states and behaviors such as eating, drinking, and sexual response.

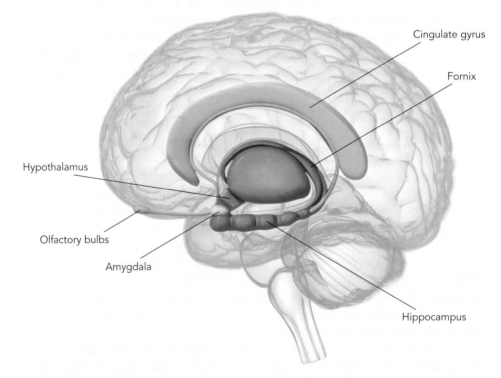

figure 3.5

The limbic system The limbic system and its most significant structures: the hypothalamus, the hippocampus, the amygdala, the fornix, the olfactory bulbs, and the cingulate gyrus.

communicates to the rest of the body. The hypothalamus is located just underneath the *thalamus,* a brain structure we'll revisit later. (*Hypo* means "under," so the name *hypothalamus* indicates its location.)

Startling research results obtained in the 1950s showed that the hypothalamus also is key to motivation (Olds, 1958; Olds & Milner, 1954). Researchers surgically implanted electrodes directly into the hypothalamus of rats. They connected the electrode to a lever that the rat could press, thereby delivering current to the electrode. By pressing the lever, then, the rat could stimulate its own hypothalamus (Figure 3.6). Would a rat really want to do that? Sure it would! Rats pressed the lever more than 5000 times an hour (Olds, 1958). In later research, rats consistently chose the stimulation even over food, starving themselves to death (Bozarth, 1994).

The brain stimulation was rewarding because the hypothalamus is part of a *reward circuit,* that is, a set of interconnected brain structures that normally becomes active when an organism pursues a rewarding stimulus or experience, such as food or sex (Haber & Knutson, 2010). Amazingly, even when there is no rewarding stimulus in the environment, activation of the circuit is highly rewarding (see Chapter 7). Although the anatomical details differ across species, contemporary neuroimaging research shows that a reward circuit similar to the one first identified in rats also exists in primates, including humans (Haber & Knutson, 2010).

The **hippocampus** is a curved, roughly banana-shaped structure in the limbic system that participates in two major tasks of everyday life. One of those tasks is remembering. The creation of permanent memories is carried out, in part, in the hippocampus (Bliss & Collingridge, 1993; Nadel & Moscovitch, 1997). If this biological tool is damaged, permanent memories of experiences cannot be formed (also see Chapter 6). Evidence of the hippocampus's role in memory comes from cases of *Alzheimer's disease,* a medical condition that generally strikes people in older adulthood. The hippocampus atrophies (i.e., becomes reduced in size) in Alzheimer's patients (Barnes et al., 2009), who lose their normal ability to remember events.

A second task the hippocampus helps to accomplish is *spatial memory,* the recall of geographic layouts and the location of items within them (Nadel, 1991). Have you ever parked your car in a large parking lot (e.g., at a shopping center or sports stadium) and later wandered around trying to find it? It's good you didn't leave your hippocampus in the car—you need it to remember where you parked. Evidence that the hippocampus contributes to spatial memory comes from research on a group of people who rely heavily on spatial skills: taxi drivers in London (Woollett, Spiers, & Maguire, 2009).

Prior to obtaining their taxi driver's license, London cabbies undergo extensive training to learn the location of thousands of city streets and how they interconnect. Researchers hypothesized that, as a result, cabbies' brains would differ from those of ordinary drivers. To test that idea, they asked taxi drivers and a control group of regular drivers to play a virtual reality video game in which players navigate a car through London streets. While participants played, their brain activity was recorded using fMRI (see Research Toolkit). When researchers compared the brains of the two groups of participants, they found that the hippocampus of taxi drivers was more highly developed. Taxi drivers had a greater volume of brain cells in the rear region of their hippocampus (Woollett et al., 2009).

This finding should remind you of the lesson about plasticity from the beginning of this chapter. The brain has specialized parts that strengthen with use. Just as athletes who exercise their muscles develop more muscle, taxi drivers who exercise their hippocampus develop more hippocampus.

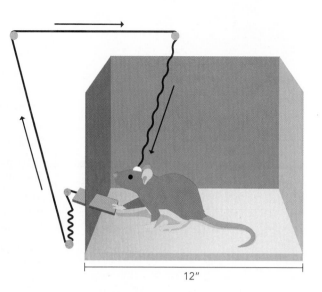

figure 3.6
Olds and Milner experiment In the research depicted here, rats could press a lever that sent electrical stimulation to their hypothalamus. The stimulation was enormously rewarding; rats would press the lever thousands of times an hour.

12"

hippocampus A limbic system structure needed for forming permanent memories and central to spatial memory (the recall of geographic layouts).

THINK ABOUT IT

If the hippocampus of taxi drivers is more highly developed than that of others, it could mean that learning and navigating complex streets increases brain development. *Or* it could mean that people with more highly developed hippocampi become taxi drivers. Which is it? (By analogy, tall people are more likely to become basketball players, but playing does not increase their height.) Recent research that (1) measured people's brain volume before and after taxi-driver training and (2) compared them with others who did not have that training indicates that the experience of learning complex roadways does, in fact, causally influence brain development (Woollett & Maguire, 2011). If you are thinking critically about psychological research, you will realize that these extra two research steps were necessary to reach this conclusion.

TRY THIS!

Research on the hippocampus and memory for spatial locations illustrates the close connection between mind and brain. Performing the specific task of spatial memory requires the use of a specialized biological tool in your brain, the hippocampus. This chapter's Try This! exercise introduces a different mental activity (one not involving memory) that also illustrates this connection. Try it now! Go to www.pmbpsychology.com. A little later on, we will discuss the activity and detail the parts of your brain that were most active when you did the exercise. ◉

figure 3.7
Amygdala and fear response Thanks to your amygdala, you can respond to threatening objects, such as a snake, before higher-level areas in your brain even recognize that a threat exists. Information goes from your eyes through a central brain region (the visual thalamus) and then right to the amygdala, which can generate an emotional response.

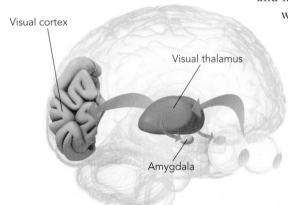

Visual cortex

Visual thalamus

Amygdala

The **amygdala** is a small structure shaped roughly like an almond (from which it gets its name: *amygdala* is the Greek word for "almond"). Like most brain structures, the amygdala is connected to numerous other structures in the brain; as a result, it is active during a variety of psychological processes (Labar, 2007). Yet one psychological process in which its role is particularly central is the detection of threat. Suppose you're walking in the woods and notice a snake slithering on the ground (Figure 3.7). Before you know it—that is, before you even say to yourself, "Geez, look at that, a snake!"—your body responds: You instantly experience fear and move out of harm's way. That quick response was generated by the amygdala, which receives inputs from your eyes and rapidly signals other brain mechanisms that, in turn, generate emotional arousal and halt your walking toward the snake (LeDoux, 1994). The amygdala response is so rapid that your body reacts before the rest of your brain has time to create a conscious experience of the snake.

The amygdala is not limited to the processing of information about threats that involve physical harm, however. Another type of threat that it processes is financial. In one study, two research participants with damaged amygdalas played a gambling game (De Martino, Camerer, & Adolphs, 2010). They chose whether to bet on coin flips with varying monetary payoffs. Most players are *loss averse,* that is, they avoid gambles that pose a good chance of losing

(Kahneman & Tversky, 1982). For example, you would probably refuse if someone offered to flip a coin, saying, "Heads, you win $50; tails, you lose—you give me $50." The thought of losing $50 is aversive, so you avoid the game. But if your amygdala were damaged, you might take the bet. The two participants with amygdala damage *accepted* bets that most other people avoided; specifically, they accepted bets that posed a significant chance of losing. They understood the gambling game and played it intelligently, but felt much less threatened by possible monetary loss (De Martino et al., 2010).

Let's conclude our discussion of the limbic system by noting three other structures. The *fornix* (Latin for "arch") is a curving structure that provides a connection between the hippocampus and the hypothalamus, thus helping these structures of the brain to interact and work as a system. The *olfactory bulbs* are brain structures required for a sense of smell. They receive information from the nasal cavity and transmit it to other parts of the brain. The *cingulate gyrus,* which wraps around the top of the limbic system, contributes to people's ability to stop themsselves from doing one thing and switch to doing something else. For example, suppose you are asked to name the color of the letters in the following word: ORANGE. You have to stop yourself from saying "orange," which springs to mind immediately, and switch to saying "blue." Brain imaging studies show that a region of the cingulate gyrus is particularly active when people perform such switching tasks (Carter et al., 1998).

⊕RESEARCH TOOLKIT

fMRI

Different physical activities—jogging, typing, eating, throwing a ball—use different parts of your body. Similarly, different mental activities—singing a song to yourself, adding numbers in your head, imagining what a friend looks like, worrying about an exam—use different parts of your brain. But which ones? Relating mental functions to brain functions is one of the great challenges of psychological science.

Meeting this challenge is particularly difficult because, when it comes to the brain, it is so hard to see what is going on. The brain is buried under the skull, and thus cannot be seen directly unless one performs neurosurgery. And even when one *can* see it, it's difficult to know what to look for. For some bodily organs, movement reveals the organ's function; for instance, movements of the heart show that it is pumping blood. But there are no movements of cells in the brain that correspond to psychological functions such as thinking or emotion. So what should you look for to link the activity of the mind to activity in the brain?

A major technique for studying the brain examines changes in blood flow. The technique, called *functional magnetic resonance imaging,* or *fMRI,* is a method for depicting the brain regions that are particularly active when people perform mental tasks. fMRI capitalizes on two facts about the body and brain (Cacioppo et al., 2003; Hunt & Thomas, 2008):

› When you use a part of your body intensively, blood flow to that area increases. The body automatically increases blood flow in order to supply that body part with extra oxygen to fuel its increased activity. Sometimes you can even see this happening; for example, when lifting weights, veins in your arm stand out. In the brain, the same principle holds. The flow of oxygenated blood increases in regions of the brain that are most active. (Oxygenated blood carries oxygen from the lungs to the rest of the body. By contrast, deoxygenated blood cells are those that have released oxygen but have not yet returned to the lungs for a new oxygen supply.)

amygdala A limbic system structure that contributes to the processing of threatening stimuli.

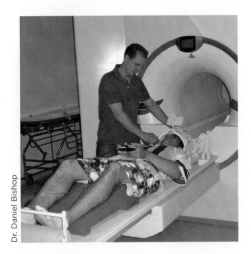

Dr. Daniel Bishop

figure 3.8
fMRI scan The research participant is about to enter an fMRI scanner. The participant can see information that is displayed on a video screen and can respond to it by using hand-held controls. The scanner creates images of the person's brain activity while doing so.

cerebral cortex A layer of cells on the brain's outer surface that is key to the human capacity for complex conceptual thought.

> Blood cells have magnetic properties that differ, depending on whether the cells are oxygenated or deoxygenated. Researchers observing blood flow under a strong magnetic field thus can identify those parts of the body and brain that are receiving relatively high levels of oxygenated blood.

Combining these two points yields the basic principle of fMRI methods: To link brain activity to activity of the mind, researchers can ask participants to engage in a mental task while they are under a strong magnetic field, and obtain images of the brain regions that receive an increased flow of oxygenated blood during this task.

The device that produces the brain images, the *scanner,* contains a magnet that produces the necessary magnetic field (Figure 3.8). The scanner's magnets are *extremely* powerful; many produce magnetic fields more than 50,000 times as powerful as the magnetic field of Earth (the force that moves the needle of a compass). Research participants must be careful to remove watches and other metallic objects before coming near the fMRI magnet—or it will remove the items itself.

fMRI research consists of a sequence of steps. After a participant enters the scanner, the researcher first collects baseline measures, that is, measures of cerebral blood flow that are taken before participants perform the specific mental task that is the focus of the study. Next, the participant is directed to engage in a mental task, and blood flow is measured again. Statistical methods then are used to compare the baseline to task-performance levels of oxygenated blood flow. These methods yield the fMRI brain images in this chapter and throughout this book.

However, fMRI cannot answer all questions of brain science. For example, it only indicates that activity in a brain region is *correlated with* performance of a task; thus, it cannot, by itself, establish that the brain region has a causal impact on performance. Nonetheless, researchers recognize its unique value in answering fundamental questions about the link between mind and brain (Mather, Cacioppo, & Kanwisher, 2013).

WHAT DO YOU KNOW?...

5. _____ magnetic resonance imaging, or fMRI, is a technique for measuring brain activity that uses magnetic fields to track changes in cerebral _____ flow before and after a participant engages in a mental activity.

CEREBRAL CORTEX. The last step up in our bottom-to-top voyage through the brain takes us all the way to the top, to the **cerebral cortex,** a layer of cells on the outer, top surface of the brain that is only a few millimeters thick. Although thin, it is powerful. This network of brain cells is the biological tool that enables people to have human thinking powers: to contemplate ourselves, our past, and our future; to communicate using language; to create works of art; and to gain some control over the impulses and emotions generated in lower regions of our brains.

When looking at the outer surface of a brain—at its cerebral cortex—the first thing you notice is that it's folded. The brain contains numerous ridges and grooves, and the cerebral cortex wraps its way around them. These folds in the brain's outer surface have a big advantage: They allow room for more brain—or, more specifically, for more cortical surface area. Just as folding a large item of clothing helps fit it into a small piece of luggage, the folds in the brain's surface allow a relatively large cerebral cortex to fit into your relatively small skull. (By way of comparison, you have a lot more brain power than an elephant, yet a much smaller skull.) The surface area of your cerebral cortex is about 2.5 square feet (Kolb & Whishaw, 1990), but thanks to the folds, your head does not have to be greater than 1.5 feet wide and 1.5 feet long to fit it all in there.

The next thing you would notice is that some of the grooves in the brain's surface are particularly deep. These are *fissures* that divide the cortex into a number of distinct parts, known as cerebral *lobes.* Let's now look at the brain's various lobes and the psychological activities in which they take part (Figure 3.9). But first, a reminder. As you learned in this chapter's opening, the parts of the brain are highly interconnected. When you perform almost any complex task, the brain's communication networks automatically coordinate activity in multiple lobes of the brain (Sporns, 2011).

Let's start our survey of the lobes of the cerebral cortex at the back of the brain. At the brain's rear is the **occipital lobe.** This region is heavily involved in the processing of visual information—in fact, it is commonly called the *visual cortex.* To see clearly, then, you need not only your eyes, but also your occipital lobe. Evidence of this comes from medical cases in which patients experience seizures (periods of abnormal brain activity) in their visual cortex. Although their eyes are working properly, their visual experience is distorted; they see things that aren't there and, in some cases, experience temporary blindness (Panayiotopoulos, 1999).

In addition to processing visual information coming in from the eyes, the occipital lobe is active when you generate visual information in your head—in other words, when you engage in mental imagery (see Chapter 8). Researchers find that when people are asked to close their eyes and think of specific images, their visual cortex becomes highly active (Kosslyn et al., 1996). Furthermore, patients whose occipital cortex is damaged may have difficulty generating mental imagery (Farah, 1984). Thus, even though seeing and imagining are two different types of activity—one being a detection of stimuli out in the world, the other an act of fantasy in your head—both activities employ the same biological tool: the brain's occipital lobe.

Moving from the occipital lobe toward the front and top of the brain, we next reach the **parietal lobes.** The parietal lobes contain brain matter needed for *somatosensory* information processing (Andersen et al., 1997), that is, the processing of information that relates features of your body (or *soma*) to features of the environment (which you detect through sensory systems). When do you use your somatosensory system? All the time! Imagine a simple activity: picking up a paper cup filled with water. This action seems so routine that you don't even give it a thought. Yet it's actually quite complex. To pick up the cup, there's a lot of information to take into account: (1) the exact location of the cup, (2) the amount of force required to pick it up without crushing it, (3) the location of your arm and hand, and (4) the amount of force exerted by your hand when you grasp the cup. The first two pieces of information come into the brain from a sensory system—your visual system, which lets you see where the cup is and what it's made of. The second two pieces of information come from your soma, or body—your

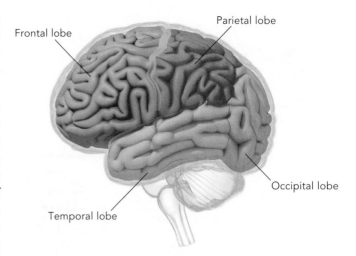

figure **3.9**
The lobes of the cerebral cortex
Fissures divide the cortex into a number of distinct parts, known as cerebral *lobes.*

No need to leave him a tip HERB, the Home Exploring Robot Butler, performs everyday tasks such as serving people food and beverages— that is, if things go well. After years of research and millions of dollars of technological investment, these jobs are still a challenge for HERB. In a recent demonstration for reporters, he did manage to grasp a bottle, but then held it upside down instead of right side up, and soon dropped it. It's difficult to design a robot that can perform sensorimotor tasks that are trivially easy for humans, thanks to the power of the parietal lobe of our brains.

occipital lobe The region of the cerebral cortex heavily involved in the processing of visual information and mental imagery; commonly called the visual cortex.

parietal lobes The region of the cerebral cortex that processes somatosensory information (i.e., relating the body to the environment).

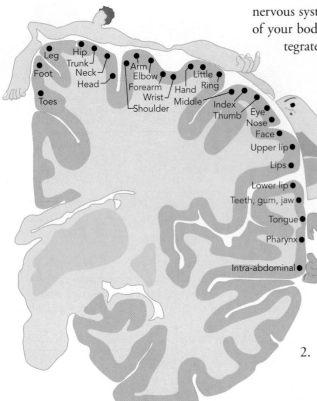

figure 3.10

Sensory cortex The different parts of your body send signals to different parts of the sensory cortex, which contains a "map" of the body as a whole.

nervous system provides your brain with information about the location and motions of your body. These two streams of information, sensory and somatic, have to be integrated somewhere. This happens in the parietal lobe (Andersen et al., 1997).

At the front of the parietal cortex is the **sensory cortex,** a strip of brain matter that receives information from all parts of the body. By processing this information, the sensory cortex lets you know that your back is itchy, your foot's "fallen asleep," or your arm is extended straight up in the air (something you can feel, without having to look to see where it is).

Nature has given the sensory cortex a remarkably systematic design. The sensory cortex represents each of the various parts of the body; body parts are "mapped" into the cortex (Figure 3.10). Sensory input from your foot goes to one part of the cortex, input from your knee goes to another, and so forth. This body-to-brain mapping has two notable features:

1. Adjacent body parts are mapped into adjacent areas of the cortex. For example, the part of your sensory cortex that processes information from your lips is next to the part that processes information from your nose. The cortex processes signals from your hand in a region adjacent to where it processes signals from your fingers.

2. The amount of space devoted to a body part in the brain is *not* proportional to the physical size of the body part. Instead, the amount of space in the cortex devoted to a body part relates directly to the sensitivity of that part of the body. Parts of your body that are highly sensitive (e.g., lips, fingers) receive more space in the somatosensory cortex than less sensitive parts (e.g., your elbow or back).

Normally, the sensory cortex is activated by input from parts of the body. But what would happen if it was activated directly—that is, if scientists reached right into the brain and electrically stimulated it? Wilder Penfield, a physician performing surgery on a patient with epilepsy, was the first person to do this (Costandi, 2008; Penfield & Boldrey, 1937). During surgery, the patient was awake. This is possible because there are no sensory receptors in the brain itself, so patients do not feel pain during brain surgery. When Penfield applied a mild electric stimulus to one region of the sensory cortex, the patient felt numbness in his tongue. When a nearby region was stimulated, he felt numbness in a different part of his tongue. When a different region was stimulated, he felt a tingling in his knee (Figure 3.11). By stimulating various regions and noting the sensations produced, Penfield was able to discover the mapping between the brain's sensory cortex and the rest of the body (Penfield & Boldrey, 1937).

Below the parietal lobes, its location and shape akin to a thumb on a mitten or baseball catcher's glove, is the **temporal lobe** (see Figure 3.9). Two psychological tasks that rely on the temporal lobe are hearing and remembering. Hearing is accomplished thanks to a region in the upper surface of the temporal lobe known as the **auditory cortex.** This part of the temporal lobe is active whenever you listen to sounds, detecting their pitch, volume, and timing in relation to one another. Listening to both spoken words and music requires use of your auditory cortex (Zatorre, Belin, & Penhune, 2002). As for memory, certain regions in the temporal lobe are key to organizing the multiple brain systems that become active when you remember facts and experiences (McClelland & Rogers, 2003). Damage to the temporal lobe causes people to forget even the names of common objects. For example, one patient with temporal lobe damage, when shown pictures of 24 different animals, was able to name only three correctly: cat, dog, and horse (McClelland & Rogers, 2003).

Finally, moving forward from the parietal lobes, you reach the **frontal lobes.** In humans, as well as in our evolutionary cousins, the great apes, the frontal lobes are the largest region of the brain, comprising about 35% of its total volume (Semendeferi et al., 2002).

sensory cortex A region of the parietal cortex that receives sensory information from all parts of the body.

temporal lobe The region of the cerebral cortex crucial to psychological functions, including hearing and memory.

auditory cortex A region of the temporal lobes that contributes to the processing of sounds and also is key to remembering facts and experiences.

frontal lobes A part of the cerebral cortex that is particularly large in humans and enables distinctive human mental abilities such as self-reflection (i.e., thinking about oneself).

Yet human frontal lobes have a number of unique features. These include especially rich interconnections among regions of the frontal lobes and similarly rich connections between the frontal lobes and other parts of the brain. These unique biological features underlie humans' most distinctive mental abilities (Semendeferi et al., 2002; Wood & Grafman, 2003): to think about ourselves; to set goals for ourselves and stick to them; to control our emotions; to recognize ourselves as social beings who are evaluated by others; in short, to live as members of civilized society. As you saw in the case of Phineas Gage, frontal lobe damage reduces the ability to control one's behavior according to the rules of society.

The frontal lobes also contain brain matter that is needed to control body movements. At the rear of the frontal lobes, in the area closest to the parietal lobe, is a region of the brain known as the **motor cortex.** This cortical region sends out signals that move the body's muscles; as we discuss in more detail below, the signals are sent to the spinal cord, where they are relayed to muscles in the body's extremities.

Studies by Penfield and colleagues provided early evidence of the functions carried out by the motor cortex (just as they did for the sensory cortex, as described above). Penfield found that electrical stimulation in different areas of the motor cortex triggers different types of motor movement. If you stimulate one area of the motor cortex, the patient's hand moves; stimulate another area, and an arm moves; and so forth (Penfield & Boldrey, 1937).

Penfield's findings seemed to suggest that the motor cortex, like the sensory cortex, contains a "map" of body parts, with different parts each controlling a different muscle of the body. Recent research, however, has shown that this idea is inaccurate (Graziano, 2010). Individual parts of the motor cortex do not control individual muscles. Instead,

> What coordinated movements are you engaging in right now?

a given part of the motor cortex commonly triggers coordinated activity in a number of *different* muscles. The activity generally is a meaningful action that, over the course of evolution, was adaptive for organisms of the given species. Stimulating different parts of a monkey's motor cortex, for example, produces movements such as reaching out to grasp an object, placing the hand to the mouth, or climbing or leaping movements (Graziano et al., 2002; Figure 3.12).

In front of the motor cortex are regions of the frontal lobe containing **association areas** of the cerebral cortex. Association areas receive sensory input that has been processed by other regions of the brain. They connect these inputs to memories and stored knowledge of the world (Pandya & Seltzer, 1982; Schmitz & Johnson, 2007). These connections between sensory input and stored knowledge enable people to have experiences that are psychologically meaningful. For example, you perceive not just a slowly moving human figure with a hand extended, but an old acquaintance who appears ready to apologize for a past wrongdoing. Your sensory system delivers the sound of a human voice coming through a small speaker, but association areas enable you to hear the loving tones of a parent calling to see how you're doing at college.

In front of the association areas is the **prefrontal cortex.** In terms of location, this is the part of the brain that resides immediately behind your forehead. The prefrontal cortex is a complex piece of biological machinery that contains many specialized subsections that contribute to a variety of mental functions. Two types of mental activities, however, stand out as particular specialties of the prefrontal cortex.

One is the ability to keep information in mind—to concentrate on facts, focus your attention, and manipulate information in your mind (Levy & Goldman-Rakic, 2000). The prefrontal cortex gives you a mental "workspace" (Dehaene & Naccache, 2001) where you can combine and manipulate information, whether it is coming in through your sensory systems or stored in memory. This ability enormously increases your mental powers. Without it, the flow

> How many separate pieces of information do you have in your mental "workspace" now?

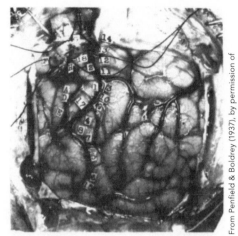

From Penfield & Boldrey (1937), by permission of Oxford University Press

14. Tingling from the knee down to the right foot.
13. Numbness all down the right leg, excluding the foot.
4. Felt like a shock and numbness in all four fingers but not in the thumb.
8. Felt sensation of movement in the thumb.
7. Same as 8.
5. Numbness in the right side of the tongue.
6. Tingling feeling in the right side of the tongue, more at the lip.
15. Tingling in the tongue, associated with up and down vibratory movements.

figure 3.11
Penfield brain stimulation The photo shows the top of the patient's brain during surgery. The numbers specify areas of the sensory cortex that were electrically stimulated by the surgeon. The text indicates the sensation that the patient felt when a given area of the cortex was stimulated.

---

motor cortex A region of the cerebral cortex that sends out signals controlling the body's muscular movements.

association areas Areas of the cerebral cortex that receive sensory information from other regions of the brain and connect it to memories and stored knowledge, enabling psychologically meaningful experiences.

prefrontal cortex The area of the brain immediately behind the forehead; a complex area that contributes to the ability to concentrate on facts, focus attention, manipulate information, and align behavior with social rules.

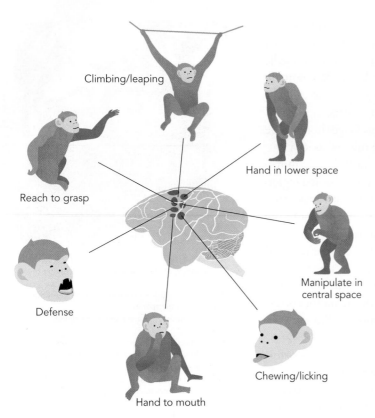

Climbing/leaping

Reach to grasp

Hand in lower space

Defense

Manipulate in central space

Hand to mouth

Chewing/licking

figure 3.12

Motor cortex stimulation Stimulation of different areas of a monkey's motor cortex produces meaningful patterns of action that involve multiple muscles, such as reaching out to grasp an object, or climbing and leaping (Graziano, 2010).

of your thoughts would be determined almost entirely by stimuli in the environment. Every sight, smell, and sound would pull your thoughts in one direction or another. The prefrontal cortex, however, gives you the "executive" abilities (Posner & Rothbart, 2007) to concentrate your thoughts on people, objects, and events that are not present in your current environment. You can even think about things that happened long ago or that might happen in the distant future; the prefrontal cortex enables humans, unlike other species, to engage in "mental time travel" (Suddendorf & Corballis, 2007).

The second function of the prefrontal cortex is the one lost by Phineas Gage: the ability to align your behavior with social rules and conventions. Why does frontal lobe damage impair this ability? The explanation involves both thoughts and emotions. Frontal lobe damage breaks the normal connections between (1) thoughts about the social world, which are generated in the cortex, and (2) feelings about the social world, which are generated in lower regions of the brain. As a result, people with frontal lobe damage may fail to experience emotions that normally keep our behavior in line with others' expectations. These include feelings of embarrassment over not fitting in with a crowd and anxiety about the possibility that others will think poorly of them (Bechara, Damasio, & Damasio, 2000). Frontal lobe damage also reduces *empathy* (Stuss, 2011; Wood & Williams, 2008), which is the ability to personally feel the emotions experienced by others with whom you interact (Agosta, 2010). This lack of empathy may explain the behavior of psychopathic criminals, that is, people who commit violent criminal acts without experiencing guilt, remorse, or empathy for their victims (Shamay-Tsoory et al., 2010).

In summary, you've seen that the brain has a bottom-to-top organization. Low-level structures in the brain stem regulate bodily states and serve basic survival-related needs. Middle-level structures of the limbic system enable organisms to have feelings and to form memories. And the high-level structures of the cerebrum, especially the cerebral cortex, enable people to engage in complex, creative, rational thought.

This might already seem like a lot of organization for one bodily organ. Yet there's more: The brain also has a left/right organization.

🧠 WHAT DO YOU KNOW?...

6. Match the brain structures on the left with the functions they regulate on the right.

1. Medulla, pons, and midbrain
2. Reticular formation
3. Cerebellum
4. Hypothalamus
5. Hippocampus

6. Amygdala
7. Cingulate gyrus
8. Occipital lobe
9. Parietal lobe
10. Temporal lobe

11. Frontal lobe

a. Task switching
b. Memory formation, spatial memory
c. Threat detection
d. Thinking about the self, goal-setting
e. Bodily activities critical to survival (e.g., breathing)
f. Arousal
g. Somatosensory information processing
h. Bodily states such as temperature
i. Motor movement
j. Hearing, remembering facts and experiences
k. Processing visual information

Left/Right Organization

Preview Questions

> What is the relation between the left and right sides of the brain?
> For what functions are the left and right sides of the brain specialized?
> If the left and right sides of the brain were cut off from each other, would you have two brains? How do we know?

You've got two legs, one on the left and one on the right. Same with your arms, hands, eyes, ears, kidneys, and many other body parts—you've got two of them, left and right.

CEREBRAL HEMISPHERES. The same is true, in a sense, for the brain. Although humans have only one brain, it has two parts, on the left and right, which are separated by a deep groove. The two sides are known as the brain's two **cerebral hemispheres** (Figure 3.13).

The relation between the left/right organization of the brain and the left/right organization of the body is surprising. When going from body to brain, signals cross. Information from the left side of the body reaches the right side of the brain, and information from the body's right side reaches the brain's left. Similarly, commands sent out from the brain to the body switch sides. The right side of the motor cortex, for example, controls the left side of the body. Even signals from parts of the body located very close to the brain switch sides. Information from your left eye, for example, reaches the right side of your brain. Research suggests that this crossing benefits the complex "wiring" of the brain that occurs early in the development of an organism (Shinbrot & Young, 2008).

The left and right hemispheres are connected through the **corpus callosum,** a structure containing more than 200 million cells that transmit signals from one side of the brain to the other. The corpus callosum extends from the front to the rear of the brain and thus connects the left and right sides of the frontal, parietal, and occipital lobes. Thanks to these connections, your left and right generally are in synchrony. Your two-handed tennis backhand is a coordinated movement, despite the fact that different sides of you0r brain control your left and right arms. You experience a coherent stream of music from the sounds coming out of your headphones, even though different sides of your brain process sounds from the earphones on the left and right.

SPECIALIZATION OF THE HEMISPHERES. The left and right hemispheres of a person's brain look quite similar, but "you can't tell a brain by its cover." Despite similar appearance, the hemispheres are specialized to perform different types of psychological activities. Some tasks primarily draw on the left side of the brain, whereas others primarily use the right.

The left hemisphere specializes in language. About 97% of right-handed individuals understand and produce language by using their left hemisphere; among left-handers, the percentage is still high, about 70% (Toga & Thompson, 2003). Two nineteenth-century physicians—Frenchman Paul Broca and German Carl Wernicke—discovered this in studies of people with impaired language ability, or *aphasia*.

Broca's insight came from a patient who was nicknamed "Tan" because "tan" was the only word he could speak. After a disease in early adulthood, he experienced an aphasia in which he could understand other people when they spoke, but could not produce words himself—other than, mysteriously, "tan" (Schiller, 1992). After the patient died, Broca examined the man's brain and found damage in a region of the left hemisphere that has become known as Broca's area (Figure 3.14). Normal functioning in this area is required for a person to produce words.

Some years later, Wernicke saw patients who had lost the ability to *understand* language. They could hear the sound of words, but could not determine what those

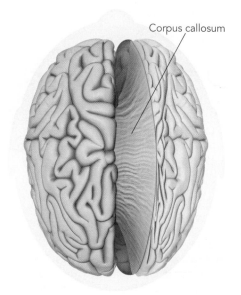

Corpus callosum

figure 3.13
Cerebral hemispheres and corpus callosum The left and right cerebral hemispheres are densely interconnected through the corpus callosum. The image shows what the brain would look like if the right hemisphere were pushed to the side in order to reveal the corpus callosum's connections between hemispheres.

cerebral hemispheres The two sides of the brain; the left hemisphere specializes in analytical tasks including math and language, while the right hemisphere is specialized for spatial thinking, the ability to create and think about images.

corpus callosum A brain structure that connects the two hemispheres of the brain, enabling them to work in synchrony.

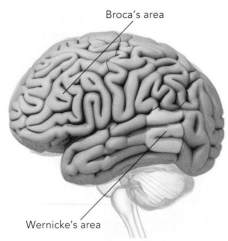

figure 3.14
Broca's and Wernicke's areas Two areas of the brain that are critical to language are (1) Broca's area, which contributes to people's ability to produce words, and (2) Wernicke's area, which is needed for the proper understanding of spoken language.

TRY THIS!

ORIENTATION

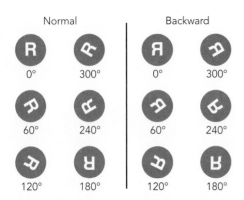

figure 3.15
Letters printed at an odd angle
Researchers ask participants a simple question: Are the letters printed in their regular orientation or backward? To answer the question, participants first have to rotate the mental image in their minds. This mental rotation task makes use of the right hemisphere of the brain, which specializes in spatial thinking (Milivojevic et al., 2009b).

sounds meant (Geschwind, 1970). Again, post-mortem examinations revealed brain damage. But this time, the damage was found in a different area of the brain than was seen in Tan's brain. This new area, which is needed for the comprehension of spoken language, is now known as Wernicke's area (Figure 3.14).

Both Broca's and Wernicke's areas are in the left hemisphere. Although later research (e.g., Sperry, 1982) showed that the right hemisphere has more involvement in language comprehension than Wernicke had thought, contemporary findings nonetheless confirm that, among the large majority of people, the predominant hemisphere in language production and understanding is the left (Josse & Tzourio-Mazoyer, 2004).

Language isn't the left hemisphere's only specialty. Another one is arithmetic. Images of people's brain activity while they multiply numbers "in their head" reveal that the left hemisphere is significantly more active than the right (Chochon et al., 1999).

Language and arithmetic have a lot in common. In both, individual symbols (words, numbers) are combined in a specific order according to various rules (of grammar or arithmetic). If the symbols are out of order, the result is meaningless; neither "2 2 4 + =" nor "Dog her ran Jane spot after" make sense. Activities that require one to combine symbols or objects in a step-by-step manner, according to specified rules, are called *analytical* tasks. On analytical tasks, the left hemisphere predominates. Interestingly, the two analytical tasks we just discussed, language and arithmetic, are so similar that the regions of the left hemisphere active during the tasks overlap (Baldo & Dronkers, 2007).

What is *not* considered an analytical task? *Spatial* activities differ from analytical ones. In spatial thinking, you create images in your mind. Suppose you were asked

> How many windows *are* there in the home in which you grew up?

how many windows were in the front of the home in which you grew up? You would first picture your home in your mind and then mentally count the windows you see. Mentally picturing the home is an example of spatial thinking.

Can you think of another mental activity that involves spatial thinking? You worked on one in this chapter's Try This! experiment.

Our Try This! activity was a *mental rotation* experiment. In mental rotation, people form an image in their minds and then try to imagine what that image would look like from a different visual angle. In our experiment, you saw the letter R printed at odd angles and had to rotate it in your mind until it was upright (see Figure 3.15). Mental rotation tasks of this sort are a form of spatial thinking because they involve thinking about images rather than logical relations among words or numbers.

Mental rotation experiments yield two fascinating results. You experienced one of them for yourself: It takes longer to rotate an image through a larger visual angle than a smaller one. Rotating a mental image thus is somewhat like rotating a physical object; just as it takes longer to rotate an object 180 degrees than 90 degrees, it takes longer to rotate an image in your head 180 degrees than 90 degrees (also see Chapter 8).

The second result involves the brain. Findings indicate that spatial thinking such as mental rotation is a specialty of the *right* hemisphere. Evidence comes from a study in which brain images were taken while participants performed the same task you encountered in our Try This! activity. While people performed the task, the right hemisphere of their brains was most active (Milivojevic, Hamm, & Corballis, 2009a). A big advantage of the right hemisphere during mental rotation tasks is speed; regions in the right hemisphere become active more quickly than do left-hemisphere regions when people try to rotate mental images as fast as they can (Milivojevic, Hamm, & Corballis, 2009b).

SPLIT BRAIN SYNDROME. The brain's two hemispheres, then, are like two teams of workers who specialize in different jobs. Thanks to the corpus callosum, they're in constant communication, so their overall activities are coordinated.

What if the lines of communication were broken? What would happen if the corpus callosum were cut? You wouldn't have "two brains" functioning in ignorance of each other, would you?

Incredibly, you would. Without the corpus callosum, the left and right hemispheres do, in fact, function as if they are "two separate brains" (Sperry, 1961, p. 1749)—like two groups of workers laboring on their specialized tasks unaware of the other's activities. Evidence of this comes from **split brain** experiments, which are studies of people or animals whose corpus callosum is cut, rendering it unable to transmit information between the hemispheres. Split brain research was pioneered by the neuroscientist Roger Sperry, who won a Nobel Prize in 1981 for his work.

Early research by Sperry and his students was done with cats. Like most animals, cats learn new responses in reaction to specific environmental stimuli (see Chapter 7). Sperry and colleagues taught cats a new response that was triggered by a stimulus displayed to only one eye of the cat; thus, that reached only one side of the cat's brain. Later, researchers displayed the information to the cat's other eye, to see whether the response the cat had learned would generalize from one eye—and from one side of the brain—to the other. Among normal cats (i.e., those whose corpus callosum was intact), the learning transferred. However, among cats whose corpus callosum was cut surgically, it did not. Split brain cats could perform the task using one side of their brain, but not the other (Sperry, 1961). The hemispheres therefore were ignorant of each other's learning if the corpus callosum had been cut.

Later research showed how splitting the corpus callosum affects the psychological experience of humans (Sperry, 1982; Sperry, Gazzaniga, & Bogen, 1969). Some people have their corpus callosum cut for medical reasons; the surgical procedure stops epileptic seizures from spreading from one side of the brain to the other. After surgery, patients seem remarkably normal; based on their everyday behavior, cutting the corpus callosum seems to have little effect. In everyday life, however, any given piece of information reaches both of the person's eyes or ears and thus is sent directly to both sides of the brain. What happens when information reaches only one side of the human brain?

Sperry and colleagues devised a clever procedure to find out. They placed patients in front of a projection screen, asked them to concentrate on a dot in the middle of the screen, and then briefly flashed words, simultaneously, on the screen's left and right sides (Figure 3.16). The word on the left thus reached only the brain's right hemisphere, while the word on the right reached only the brain's left side. When split brain patients were asked what word or words they saw, they inevitably named only the word on the right ("Ring" in the example shown in the image). You might think, then, that the patient was completely unaware of the fact that the other word ("Key" in the example) had even been shown. This, however, is not the case (Sperry et al., 1969).

Patients were unable to *name* "Key," but that's merely because the word reached their right hemisphere, which is unable to produce language. When given an opportunity, with their *left* hand (which is controlled by the right hemisphere), to reach behind the screen and pick up an object corresponding to the word that had been displayed, the patient did pick up a key. Thus, the right hemisphere saw and understood the word "key," but was unable to put the idea of "Key" into words. If, before revealing the key from behind the screen, the person was asked what he or she picked up, the patient would say "a ring." The answer to the question was being given by the left hemisphere, which was completely unaware of what the right hemisphere was doing.

Specialized testing therefore reveals the unique psychological experience of the split brain patient. Without such testing, the patient appears quite normal. The left hemisphere

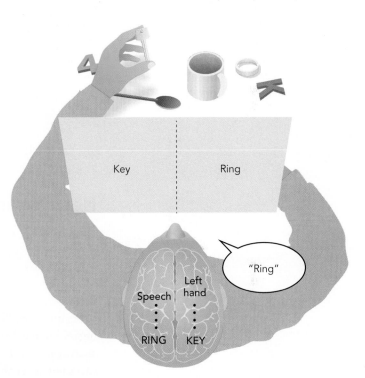

figure **3.16**
Split brain research paradigm In split brain syndrome, one side of the brain doesn't know what the other side is doing. The left hemisphere sees the word *ring* and the subject says "ring." The right hemisphere sees the word *key*, but the subject cannot say "key" because language capacities are located on the left side of the brain. Yet the left hand reaches out and picks up the key.

> Each brain half [seems] to have its own largely separate cognitive domain with its own private perceptual, learning, and memory experiences, all of which [are] seemingly oblivious to corresponding events in the other hemisphere.
>
> —Roger Sperry (1982, p. 1224)

split brain A surgical procedure in which the corpus callosum is cut. The resulting disruption of information transmission between cerebral hemispheres alters conscious experience.

has such a range of capabilities that it "does not miss" (Gazzaniga & Miller, 2009, p. 261) the right hemisphere from which it has been disconnected; patients seem not to be much bothered by occasional experiences in which they cannot name an object appearing briefly in their left visual field. In fact, people can live a relatively normal life with just the left side of their brain. In 2007, surgeons removed the entire right hemisphere of 6-year-old Cameron Mott, to stop violent seizures that she had been experiencing daily (Celizic, 2010). A few years after the surgery, Cameron was back in school and a good student. When a journalist asked "if she had any lingering effects from the surgery," she replied, "No. None at all" (Celizic, 2010). (People have more difficulty living with removal of the brain's *left* hemisphere, which is required for some complex language abilities; Bayard & Lassonde, 2001.)

✔ WHAT DO YOU KNOW?...

7. For each of the "answers" below, provide the question. The first one is done for you.
   a. Answer: The hemisphere in which the sensation of touch on your left arm would be processed.
      Question: What is the right hemisphere?
   b. Answer: The structure that connects the left and right hemispheres.
   c. Answer: For most people, the hemisphere that specializes in speaking and understanding language and in arithmetic.
   d. Answer: The hemisphere that specializes in spatial thinking.
   e. Answer: The field of vision where you would show a split brain patient an object so that she could name it. *Hint*: Think about where language is processed.

Networks in the Brain

Preview Question

> How does the architecture of our brains enable us to process large amounts of information simultaneously?

In addition to its bottom-to-top and left/right arrangement, the brain has yet a third type of organization. We'll introduce it with an analogy. Imagine a large apartment building. Its organization is both bottom-to-top (e.g., 40 floors atop one another) and left-to-right (e.g., apartments on the east and west sides of each floor might have different floor plans). Yet that's not all. A third type of organization connects people living in different parts of the building. Communications networks link residents on different floors and different sides of the building. For example, the tenants in apartments 38B, 19D, 21C, 4A, and 6E may be "friends" on a social networking site—as might the residents of 38C, 19A, 17C, 3B, and 8E, and numerous other combinations of residences. The network enables each group of friends to exchange information frequently and rapidly among themselves, despite their residing in different locations. These communications networks, then, are a third form of organization—one that cuts across floors and sides of the apartment building.

The brain works similarly. It has a third type of organization based on communications links that cut across the higher, lower, left, and right sides of the brain (Figure 3.13). These "networks in the brain" connect different regions to one another, enabling rapid communication among them (Bullmore & Sporns, 2009; Sporns, 2011, 2012). Thanks to these communications, brain activity in the different regions is coordinated. Like friends in a social network, the brain regions can share information, integrate knowledge, and synchronize their activities.

SYNCHRONIZING REGIONS OF THE BRAIN. Almost any complex thinking task draws on multiple brain regions that are networked. Consider an everyday example, such as a recent argument. In your mind, you can "relive" the event: You can picture where you were, feel the emotions you experienced when arguing, and remember words and sentences that were said. Importantly, you can do all of this *simultaneously*; you can bring the images, emotions, and words into your mind all at once. How—at the level of analysis of the brain—can we explain the ability of the mind to relive the argument?

To explain it, we need to refer to two aspects of the brain's biology:

1. *Specialized regions of the brain:* As you learned earlier in this chapter, different parts of the brain are specialized for different types of mental activities. Distinct brain regions contribute to the ability to "picture" things in the mind (i.e., form mental images), to generate emotions, and to understand and produce the words and sentences of language. We therefore must refer to each of these specialized regions of the brain to explain how you can relive the argument in your mind.

2. *Brain networks:* Referring to the individual regions of the brain is not enough, however, because we need to explain not only which parts were active but also how they managed to work in an integrated, synchronized way. For this, we need to refer to brain networks: the communications links that integrate activity in different brain regions. It's thanks to the connections among different parts of the brain—in left and right hemispheres, front and rear areas of the cortex, and lower and upper brain regions—that your mental experience consists of complex, coordinated combinations of images, sounds, and emotions. The networked activity of multiple brain regions, then, is what enables you to relive the argument.

What, biologically, are these networks that enable different parts of the brain to work in synchrony? The networks consist of large numbers of nerve cells in the brain. As we'll discuss in more detail below, many of these cells are thin and long—so long that they can transmit information from one part of the brain to another.

Many of these transmissions run through a brain structure known as the **thalamus,** which is located near the center of the brain. The thalamus serves as a kind of "relay station" for connections among brain regions (Figure 3.17; Izhikevich & Edelman, 2008). Connections into and out of the thalamus are made so rapidly that the brain as a whole can integrate activity in its higher and lower regions, as well as its left and right sides.

VISUALIZING BRAIN NETWORKS. Researchers recently have developed novel methods for visualizing the nerve fibers that connect regions of the brain (Le Bihan et al., 2001). Unlike fMRI methods that reveal activation in a specific brain region (see Research Toolkit), these new methods yield three-dimensional portraits of information networks that cross from one area of the brain to another. Color codings in these images indicate bundles of nerve fibers that travel in the same direction, taking information from one brain region to another.

These methods yield remarkable images of networks in the brain (Figure 3.18). The images immediately transform our understanding of the biological machinery that underlies our ability to think and feel. Beneath the cerebral cortex is an immensely complex web of interconnections that provide much of the brain's power.

The brain's power, then, is analogous to that of the World Wide Web. Your computer or smart phone enables you to do a lot of things: communicate with friends, get travel directions, shop, get weather reports, watch live sports events. These abilities are based not just on the machine in your hand, but on the fact that it's networked, that is, linked into a system that contains hundreds of millions of other computers. Similarly, most of your mental abilities are based not on activity in just one part of your brain, but on the coordinated activity of numerous brain regions that are networked.

Research on brain networks is still at an early stage of development. The major effort in the United States to study these networks was launched only in 2009

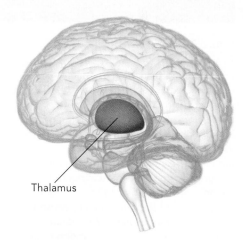

Thalamus

figure 3.17
Thalamus The thalamus, located centrally within the brain, serves as a "relay station" for communications among brain regions.

How does the idea that your mental abilities are made possible by networks jibe with your early understanding of how the brain works?

thalamus A structure near the center of the brain that serves as a "relay station" for rapid connections among brain regions.

figure 3.18

Brain networks Recently developed brain imaging technologies enable researchers to see the networks that connect brain regions to one another. (The colors, added in the imaging process, identify fibers that connect similar brain regions.) As you can see, the connections are immensely complex. The structures of the brain are densely interconnected. Such images cause scientists to rethink earlier conceptions of the brain, which focused on the role of individual brain regions rather than the connections among them. "We've never really seen the brain," said one. "It's been hiding in plain sight."

(National Institutes of Health, 2009). The long-term goal of this research is to map the entire **connectome,** the complete network of neural connections in the brain and overall nervous system of an organism (Sporns, Tononi, & Kötter, 2005). (The term *connectome,* a map of an organism's neural connections, is analogous to the word *genome,* a map of an organism's genetic information.)

Our discussion of brain networks should remind you of this chapter's opening story. You learned there that Capgras syndrome results from a breakdown in connections among different regions of the brain (also see Thiel et al., 2014). When this breakdown occurs, people recognize that the face of a loved one is a face, but lack the feelings required to judge that the face is familiar. Your own ability to recognize that, for example, Mom is actually Mom, and not some imposter, thus rests on the complex communications systems that are the "networks" in your brain (Figure 3.19).

👓 WHAT DO YOU KNOW?...

8.   a. What feature of the brain's organization enables its structures to share information, integrate knowledge, and synchronize activities?
     b. What structure of the brain acts as a "relay station" for multiple inputs from different areas of the brain?

◎ CULTURAL OPPORTUNITIES

Arithmetic and the Brain

"3 + 4 = _____?" It's not a hard one; every educated person can answer the question. In fact, people almost everywhere can answer the question when it's written using these exact symbols. Arabic numerals (the written digits 0, 1, 2, 3, . . .) are used the world over.

What parts of the brain are most active when people produce the answer "7"? Whatever parts they are, you'd expect them to be the *same parts* everywhere. Numerals are the same in all cultures. The concept of addition is the same in all cultures. So the parts of the brain that people use to add numerals are the same in all cultures, too, right?

Wrong. Research shows that people in different cultures use different parts of their brains when doing addition. Tang and colleagues asked two groups of people, native speakers of English and of Chinese, to add numbers while they were in an fMRI scanner (Tang et al., 2006). They examined the resulting brain images to identify the interconnected systems within the brain that were active when people performed arithmetic.

There were some commonalities among Chinese and English speakers. For both, the addition task activated an area of the brain that is also known to be active when people look at visual images and think about how objects relate to each other in space. Recall that when you learned about numbers, they were on a line—a one-dimensional space on which the numbers were arrayed. For all people, remembering facts about math (such as 3 + 4 equals 7) activates visual–spatial regions of the brain.

connectome The complete network of neural connections in the brain and overall nervous system of an organism.

figure **3.19**

ZOOMING IN ON THE BRAIN ••• **105**

WHY MIGHT A PERSON NOT RECOGNIZE THE FACE OF A LOVED ONE?

PMB
IN ACTION

PERSON Ⓟ

In Capgras syndrome (see this chapter's opening story), people have a strange experience: not recognizing the face of a familiar loved one.

MIND Ⓜ

It's a face

Is it familiar?
Exactly who is this?

Does it feel like I know this person?

The syndrome reflects a failure in coordination among mental systems: The person recognizes the face but lacks the feelings associated with it.

BRAIN Ⓑ

At a brain level of analysis, the syndrome reflects a breakdown in the communication between two parts of the brain: the fusiform face processing area responsible for facial recognition (shown in blue) and the amygdala (shown in red), part of the limbic system that produces the emotions that normally confirm you're looking at a loved one.

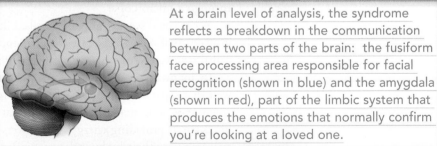

Gallery Stock

This woman does not have Capgras syndrome.

Visual learners Research shows that, when doing arithmetic, schoolchildren in China are more likely to use visual processing areas of their brains.

So that's how the cultural groups were the same. Here's how they differed: In the brains of English speakers, the addition task activated not only the visual–spatial region, but also Broca's area, the brain region used in processing language (described earlier). For English speakers, then, arithmetic resembles language; the language processing area of the brain is active during both activities. However, among Chinese speakers, Broca's area was almost entirely *in*active during arithmetic. Furthermore, visual processing areas of the brain were more active than they were among English speakers (Tang et al., 2006). The same task, presented with the same symbols, activated different brain regions in people from different cultures.

Why did Chinese speakers rely more on visual processing regions of the brain than did English speakers? Scientists do not know for sure, but one possibility suggested by the researchers involves the Chinese culture's educational practices in language and arithmetic (Tang et al., 2006). In school, children's language learning is visual; they need to learn the precise locations of the multiple strokes that make up Chinese language characters, which are more complex visually than are the letters of English. Furthermore, Chinese students commonly learn arithmetic by using an abacus, a device that explicitly represents numbers and calculations in terms of movements of objects in space (usually the movement of beads on a string). These cultural experiences with visually oriented materials may shape the development of the brain.

WHAT DO YOU KNOW?...

9. The following statement is incorrect. Explain why: "Research indicates that when native speakers of either English or Chinese solved an arithmetic problem, both Broca's area and visual–spatial processing regions of the brain were active, indicating that cultural experiences do not shape brain development."

Neurons

Preview Questions

> What distinguishes nerve cells from other cells of the body?
> How do neurons communicate electrochemically?
> How do neurons send signals from the axon terminal of one neuron to the dendrites of another?
> What determines whether a neuron will fire?
> How do neurons stay in place?

Let's continue zooming in on the brain. So far, we've discussed parts of the brain that you could see with the naked eye if you were to open up someone's skull and start looking around. But what would you see if, instead of the naked eye, you looked through a microscope?

What you'd see are individual cells. Like every other structure in the body, the brain is made up of cells. In the case of the brain, there are about 100 billion cells, and they are called *neurons*. **Neurons**—also called nerve cells—are the building blocks of the brain.

In many respects, neurons are like any other cell of the body. Each has a cell wall that separates the inside of the cell from its outside environment, a nucleus that contains genetic material, and additional structures that perform basic functions of life, such as providing energy that powers the cell. However, two features of neurons' anatomy (i.e., their biological structure) distinguish them from the body's other cells (Kuffler & Nicholls, 1976). The first is their shape, which is unique due to the presence of *dendrites* and *axons*. The second is their ability to communicate with one another, due to specialized structures found at *synapses*. Let's now look at these features of neurons in detail.

neurons Brain cells, also called nerve cells, distinguished by their unique shape and ability to communicate with one another.

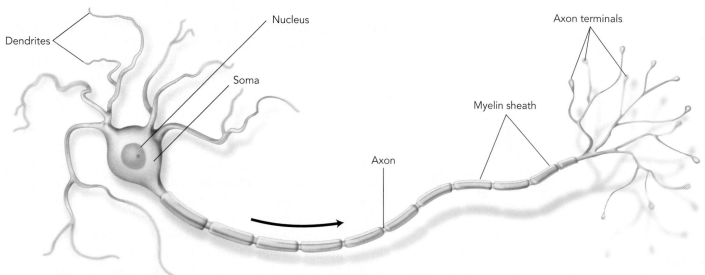

figure 3.20
Dendrites, soma, and axon The brain's neurons are cells that have three primary parts: (1) the main body of the cell, or the *soma*; (2) *dendrites*, which receive incoming signals from other neurons; and the neuron's (3) *axon*, a long, thin projection from the cell body along which signals are sent to other neurons. The axon is surrounded by a myelin sheath, a fatty substance that increases the speed with which signals travel along the axon.

DENDRITES AND AXONS. If you were asked to imagine a biological cell, you would probably picture something with a round or oval shape. Many cells indeed are shaped like that, but neurons are not. Two specialized structures give neurons a shape that is unique.

The first is **dendrites,** which are projections that branch out from the main body of the neuron, known as the soma. Like branches on a tree, the dendrites become thinner as they reach out farther from the soma (Figure 3.20).

The dendrites receive incoming signals from other neurons. They are like microphones, listening for signals from the neurons in their vicinity. Large numbers of dendrites can project out from the soma of any neuron, which means that any one neuron listens for, and can receive, incoming signals from many other neurons.

Neurons' second specialized structure is a thin and long projection known as an **axon.** Every neuron has one axon, which sends information out to other neurons. You could think of the axon as being analogous to a loudspeaker, broadcasting messages that might be heard by the "microphones"—the dendrites of nearby neurons.

Axons can be very long—as long as about 1 meter in human beings (Maday & Holzbaur, 2012). This means that a neuron can send information across relatively long distances, from one part of the brain to another or from the brain to a different part of the body. The "networks" that connect one brain region to another, which you read about earlier in this chapter, consist of axons that reach across brain regions.

At its far end, the axon branches into a large number of *axon terminals*. It is at the axon terminals that a neuron transmits its signals to other neurons. We discuss these transmissions below, in the section on synapses and neurotransmitters.

ACTION POTENTIALS. Sometimes neurons are at rest, "just sitting around," engaging in the same internal biochemical processes that you might see in any other cell of the body. But, periodically, neurons spring to life. They generate **action potentials** (also known as *nerve impulses* or *spikes*), which are electrochemical events in which an electrical current travels down the length of the axon, from the soma to the axon terminals (Bean, 2007). The word "electrochemical" indicates that the electricity generated during the action potential comes from chemical substances that have an electric charge.

Action potentials follow an "all or none" principle (Rieke et al., 1997). The neuron is either "firing" (generating an action potential) or not. There is no "in between," no small firings or half firings.

dendrites Projections that branch out from the main body of a neuron, receiving incoming signals from other neurons.

axon The thin and long projection from a neuron that sends outgoing signals to other neurons.

action potentials Nerve impulses (or spikes); electrochemical events in which an electrical current travels down the length of an axon.

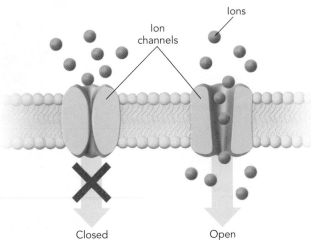

Ions

Ion channels

Closed   Open

figure 3.21
Ion channels Charged particles, or ions, move in and out of neurons through channels in the cell wall. These movements generate the electrical activity known as an action potential.

Image Source RF / Justin Lewis / Getty Images

Here's lookin' at you, squid
Scientists first learned about the electrical properties of neurons by studying squid (Hodgkin & Katz, 1949). Why squid? The axons that send signals to the wall of their body, or mantle, are exceptionally large—so large that scientists could insert electrodes directly into them. Electrical recordings revealed fluctuations in the electrical potential in the axon that, as scientists realized, could only have been caused by electrically charged particles flowing in and out of the cell.

Action potentials are remarkably powerful. The neurons of electric eels, for example, generate hundreds of volts of electricity—enough to shock a human being to death (Ornstein & Thompson, 1984). In humans, the electrical power of action potentials is so large that scientists can record brain activity by using electrodes attached to the *outside* of the head (see Chapter 2); in other words, the brain's electrical current is easily detectable through the skull.

The basis of this power is the electrical charges of chemical substances on the inside and outside of the neuron. When at rest, the neuron's interior mostly contains substances that are charged negatively. On the outside of the cell are sodium ions, which are charged positively. During an action potential, the sodium ions briefly enter the neuron through channels in the neuron's cell wall. This flow of charged particles generates an electric impulse in the vicinity of the channel (Figure 3.21).

Like lightning shooting from a thundercloud to Earth, the action potential shoots its way from the neuron's soma to its axon terminals. The electrical impulse moves down the length of the axon because electrical activity at one channel in the cell membrane acts as a switch that causes the next channel to pop open. When sodium ions rush in there, this electrical activity causes the *next* set of gates to open. In this way, the nerve impulse rushes down the length of the axon.

And it does rush! Although the process is complex, it's also quick; nerve impulses can travel down neurons at speeds in excess of 100 meters per second. They are speeded along by the **myelin sheath,** a fatty substance that surrounds the axon and acts as an electrical insulator. Myelin happens to differ in color from neurons; neurons are grey, whereas myelin is white. Areas of the brain that contain mostly neuron cell bodies and dendrites, which are not covered by myelin, thus are called the brain's *grey matter.* Bundles of myelin-covered axons traveling from one region to another are referred to as the brain's *white matter.*

This high speed of movement of any one action potential enables the neuron to generate a large number of action potentials in a small amount of time. Neurons can fire more than 100 times a second. The neuron's firing rate is the key piece of information in the signals that it sends to other neurons (Gabbiani & Midtgaard, 2001).

SYNAPSES AND NEUROTRANSMITTERS. Exactly how does a neuron send signals to other neurons? Scientists once believed that neuron-to-neuron communications were direct. They thought the axon terminals of one neuron were connected to the dendrites of another, like strings that are tied together. Activating one neuron thus would activate the other directly.

But then they discovered *synapses.* A **synapse** is a small gap that separates any two neurons. Although it is *very* small—about 20 nanometers, that is, 20 billionths of a meter (Thompson, 2000)—neurons still must communicate across the synaptic gap; neurons are not connected to one another directly. How do they communicate?

Neurons communicate chemically. A sending neuron—that is, a neuron transmitting a signal to a second neuron—releases **neurotransmitters,** which are chemical substances that travel across synapses. When neurotransmitter molecules are released into a synapse, some make their way across the synaptic gap and reach a receiving neuron, that is, a neuron that is receiving a signal from the sending neuron. This chemical connection from sending neuron to receiving neuron is the primary way that neurons communicate. (However, it is not the only way; see This Just In.) Let's examine the neurotransmitter's voyage across the synapse in detail (Figure 3.22).

The sending neuron stores neurotransmitters in small sacs known as **synaptic vesicles.** Synaptic vesicles are like tiny bubbles, each of which contains a small amount of neurotransmitter. The synaptic vesicles move within the neuron, down the length of the axon. When they reach the end of the axon and "dock" with the outer edge of the axon terminal (Hammarlund et al., 2007), they are able to release their contents, the neurotransmitters, into the synaptic gap.

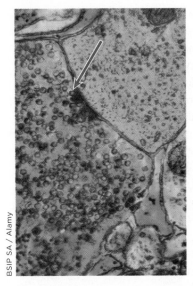

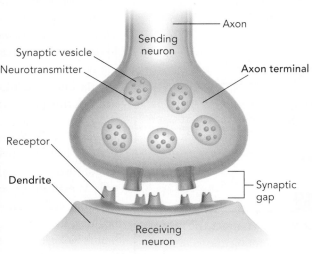

Axon

Sending neuron

Synaptic vesicle

Neurotransmitter

Axon terminal

Receptor

Dendrite

Synaptic gap

Receiving neuron

figure 3.22

Mind the gap To communicate with one another, neurons must send messages across a small gap known as a *synapse*. The diagram on the right shows the axon terminal of a sending neuron, the dendrite of a receiving neuron, and the synapse. On the left is an electron microscope image of actual sending and receiving neurons. The red arrow indicates a location at which one of the sending neuron's synaptic vesicles is reaching the end of the axon terminal, where it can release neurotransmitters into the synapse.

Some of the neurotransmitter molecules released from the sending neuron reach *receptors* on the dendrites of receiving neurons. Neurotransmitter **receptors** are sites to which neurotransmitters can attach. Chemically, the receptors are molecules to which neurotransmitter molecules can bind; the molecular shape of the neurotransmitter molecule determines whether it can bind to a given receptor. When a neurotransmitter from the sending neuron binds to the receptor of a receiving neuron, one bit of communication between neurons is complete.

The brain contains a number of different neurotransmitters. A variety of molecules, in other words, take part in the chemical communications between neurons. Some of them are listed in Table 3.1. As shown, different neurotransmitters are found in high concentrations in different parts of the brain and body.

What is the purpose of these chemical communications—that is to say, what is accomplished by the neurotransmitters that travel from the sending neuron to the receiving neuron? Their key function is to affect the receiving neuron's firing rate. Some neurotransmitters bind

myelin sheath A fatty substance that surrounds axons and acts as an electrical insulator.

synapse The small gap that separates any two neurons; chemical signals between neurons must bridge this microscopic gap.

neurotransmitters Chemical substances that travel across synapses between neurons; the primary way that neurons communicate.

synaptic vesicles Small sacs that store and transport neurotransmitters within neurons and release neurotransmitters into synapses.

receptors Sites on the dendrites of receiving neurons to which neurotransmitters can attach; chemically, molecules to which specific types of neurotransmitters can bind.

table 3.1

Major Neurotransmitters in the Body	
Neurotransmitter	**Role in the body**
Acetylcholine	A neurotransmitter used by spinal cord neurons to control muscles and by many neurons in the brain to regulate memory. In most instances, acetylcholine is excitatory.
Dopamine	The neurotransmitter that produces feelings of pleasure when released by the brain reward system. Dopamine has multiple functions, depending on where in the brain it acts. It is usually inhibitory.
GABA (gamma-aminobutyric acid)	The major inhibitory neurotransmitter in the brain.
Glutamate	The most common excitatory neurotransmitter in the brain.
Glycine	A neurotransmitter used mainly by neurons in the spinal cord. It probably always acts as an inhibitory neurotransmitter.
Norepinephrine	Acts as a neurotransmitter and a hormone. In the peripheral nervous system, it is part of the fight-or-flight response. In the brain, it acts as a neurotransmitter regulating normal brain processes. Norepinephrine is usually excitatory, but is inhibitory in a few brain areas.
Serotonin	A neurotransmitter involved in many functions including mood, appetite, and sensory perception. In the spinal cord, serotonin is inhibitory in pain pathways.

BSIP SA / Alamy

CONNECTING TO CONSCIOUS EXPERIENCE, PSYCHOLOGICAL DISORDERS, AND DRUG EFFECTS

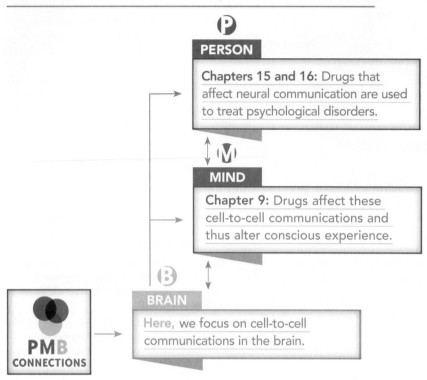

PERSON

Chapters 15 and 16: Drugs that affect neural communication are used to treat psychological disorders.

MIND

Chapter 9: Drugs affect these cell-to-cell communications and thus alter conscious experience.

BRAIN

Here, we focus on cell-to-cell communications in the brain.

PMB CONNECTIONS

to *excitatory* receptors, which increase the likelihood that the receiving neuron will generate an action potential. Others bind to *inhibitory* receptors, which decrease the likelihood that the receiving neuron will fire. The receiving neuron integrates inputs from its various receptors, and the integrated information determines the receiving neuron's firing rate (Gabbiani & Midtgaard, 2001).

GLIAL CELLS. Neurons are not the only cells in the brain. They have neighbors, called *glial cells*—and lots of them. The brain contains about as many glial cells as neurons (Azevado et al., 2009).

Glial cells support the biological functioning of neurons, by supplying nutrients and disposing of the brain's biological waste matter. They also hold neurons in place, which is what gives them their name; *glia* is the Greek word for "glue."

Glia differ from neurons anatomically. Unlike neurons, they do not have axons or dendrites, and do not generate action potentials. Thus, people had thought that glia do nothing other than provide support to neurons. However, recent research suggests that glia may have been underestimated. For example, glia change anatomically as a result of an organism's experiences, just as interconnections among neurons do (Fields, 2008), and they appear to influence the amount of communication that occurs in networks of connected neurons (Araque & Navarette, 2010; Werner & Mitterauer, 2013). Many scientists expect that future research will reveal unexpected ways in which glia contribute to mental life.

🐢 WHAT DO YOU KNOW?...

10. Match the structures on the left with the features and functions on the right.

1. Dendrites	a. Chemical substances that travel across the synapse
2. Axons	b. Increase the likelihood that the receiving neuron will fire
3. Myelin sheath	c. Branchlike projections that receive signals from other neurons
4. Synaptic vesicles	d. Gap that separates neurons
5. Synapse	e. Supplies neurons with nutrients and disposes of waste
6. Neurotransmitters	f. Decreases the likelihood that the receiving neuron will fire
7. Excitatory receptors	g. Thin, long projection that sends out signals to other neurons
8. Inhibitory receptors	h. Small sacs in which neurotransmitters of the sending neuron are stored
9. Glial cells	i. Fatty substance surrounding the axon that speeds neural transmission

---

glial cells Cells that hold neurons in place and also support their biological functioning, supplying nutrients to neurons and disposing of the brain's biological waste matter.

nervous system The complete collection of neurons that transmits signals among the parts of the body.

central nervous system The part of the nervous system found in the center of the body; its two main parts are the brain and the spinal cord.

spinal cord A bundle of neurons and glial cells that extends from the brain stem down to the bottom of the spine; it participates in two-way communications between the brain and the body.

sensory neurons Nerve cells that respond to external stimuli and send messages about the environment to the spinal cord.

⏻THIS JUST IN

Neural Communication

As far as we know, neurons communicate only through synaptic connections.

—Ornstein & Thompson (1984, p. 68)

In the twentieth century, scientists discovered that neurons communicate by sending messages across synapses. Once that was established, many naturally concluded that it was the *only* way neurons could communicate. The standard belief was that axon terminals are the one-and-only place where neurons emit neurotransmitters, and synapses the only place to which neurotransmitters are sent. But then, Douglas Fields, a researcher at the U.S. National Institutes of Health, noticed something.

While peering at a neuron through a high-powered microscope, Fields saw it move. It "twitched," as he put it (Hamilton, 2010). The neuron didn't move very far; in fact, its movement was barely detectable (Fields & Ni, 2010). But move it did, with movement occurring all along the axon, not merely at the axon terminals.

Fields and colleagues knew that the movement could only have been caused by a flow of chemical substance into, and out of, the neuron. What were these substances?

Research on the chemistry of the nervous system provided the answer: The twitching axon was releasing neurotransmitters along the length of its axon. These neurotransmitters were signals being sent to other cells in the brain—particularly to glial cells. This recently discovered signaling system appears to support neuron–glia communication that, in turn, maintains the brain's normal ability to transfer information rapidly through brain networks (Lohr, Thyssen, & Hirnet, 2011).

The remarkable new finding was that neural communication was occurring outside of the synapse. Unlike what scientists previously had believed, neurons engage in "nonsynaptic" communication, in addition to the synaptic communication that had been discovered many decades earlier.

◔ WHAT DO YOU KNOW?...

11. Douglas Fields observed that neural communication can occur outside of the _____, contrary to what was previously thought.

The Nervous System

Your psychological life depends on not only your brain, but also communications systems that link your brain to the rest of your body. The body's primary communication system is the **nervous system,** the complete collection of neurons that transmits signals among the parts of the body.

The brain, our focus so far in this chapter, is one part of the overall nervous system. Let's learn about the rest of the nervous system by examining its two main parts, the *central* and *peripheral* nervous systems.

Central Nervous System

Preview Question

> What are the structures of the central nervous system and their functions?

The **central nervous system** gets its name from its location; it is found in the center of the body. The central nervous system consists of two main parts, the brain and the spinal cord. We have already discussed the brain, so let's look at the spinal cord.

The **spinal cord** is a bundle of neurons and glial cells that extends from the brain stem down to the bottom of the spine. These cells run through the bones of the spine, which protects them from damage (Figure 3.23).

The spinal cord participates in two-way communications between the brain and body:

> In one direction, information from the environment is directed into the spinal cord, where it is then passed on to the brain. Specifically, **sensory neurons,** which respond to external stimuli, send messages about the environment into the spinal cord.

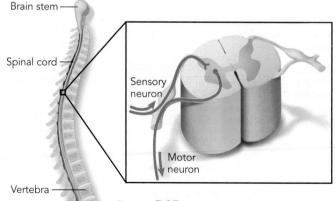

figure **3.23**
The spinal cord and central nervous system The spinal cord, which extends from the brain stem to the bottom of the spine, is key to the nervous system's two-way communications between the brain and body.

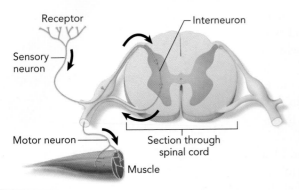

figure 3.24
Reflex Simple reflexes can be carried out by the spinal cord. Interneurons receive information from sensory neurons and send information directly to nerves that contact muscles.

> In the other direction, the brain's instructions for the body are sent through the spinal cord. After outgoing messages from the brain reach the spinal cord, **motor neurons** send out signals to the body's muscles. These signals enable the brain to control bodily movement.

Some bodily actions do not require signals that are sent to the brain. People possess **reflexes,** which are automatic, involuntary responses to external stimulation (Figure 3.24). For example, the leg movement that occurs when a doctor taps you on the knee during a physical examination is a reflex. (By comparison, play-acting that same leg movement is not a reflex.) Reflex actions are executed by neurons in the spinal cord. Sensory information reaches an *interneuron,* which is a neuron that relays information to a motor neuron that, in turn, puts the body into action.

⚡ WHAT DO YOU KNOW?...

12. For each of the "answers" below, provide the question.
   a. Answer: These neurons relay information about external stimuli from the spinal cord to the brain.
   b. Answer: The brain directs the body to move via these neurons in the spinal cord.
   c. Answer: These movements don't require input from the brain.

Peripheral Nervous System

Preview Question

> What are the structures of the peripheral nervous system and their functions?

The **peripheral nervous system** is found, as the name suggests, in the periphery of the body—that is, away from the body's center. All neurons outside of the central nervous system are part of the peripheral nervous system.

There are two ways of classifying the various parts of the peripheral nervous system. One method is by their physical location. **Cranial nerves** are those parts of the peripheral nervous system found in the head. These nerves extend out from the bottom of the brain and connect to structures in the head, such as the eyes, nose, and tongue. **Spinal nerves** extend from the spinal cord to the body's neck, torso, and limbs (Figure 3.25).

The second way of classifying the nerves of the peripheral nervous system is functionally, that is, in terms of what they do. The **somatic nervous system** provides the brain-to-periphery communications that enable you to control your bodily movement. For instance, when deciding to pass a soccer ball to your teammate rather than shooting on goal, the messages from your brain that adjust the movements of your leg and foot to get the ball to your teammate are carried along the somatic nervous system. The **autonomic nervous system,** on the other hand, provides the communications that control bodily functions that generally are *not* under your control; they occur without your even thinking about them. As you rush upfield deciding whether to pass or shoot, your heart beats faster than when you are at rest, your sweat glands are more active, your breathing is faster, and the pupils of your eyes are wider. But you don't make conscious decisions about altering your heart rate, breathing, sweating, and pupil dilation; these changes occur automatically, through signals carried by the autonomic nervous system.

The autonomic nervous system contains two divisions, that is, two subsystems that perform different tasks. The **sympathetic nervous system** prepares you for action. It activates the biological systems required for rapid activity, such as increased heart rate. This activation enables "fight" or "flight" responses—actions to confront a threat or to flee from it. Revisiting the soccer example above, the sympathetic nervous system was responsible for activating biological systems as you rushed up the field.

motor neurons Nerve cells that send out signals from the spinal cord to the body's muscles, enabling the brain to control bodily movement.

reflexes Automatic, involuntary responses to external stimulation.

peripheral nervous system That part of the nervous system found in the periphery of the body, outside of the central nervous system; it consists of the somatic nervous system and the autonomic nervous system.

cranial nerves Those parts of the peripheral nervous system found in the head; nerves that extend from the bottom of the brain to structures in the head such as eyes, nose, and tongue.

spinal nerves Those parts of the peripheral nervous system that extend from the spinal cord to the body's neck, torso, and limbs.

somatic nervous system Functionally, the part of the peripheral nervous system that provides the brain-to-periphery communications that allow(s) you to control your bodily movement.

autonomic nervous system Functionally, the part of the peripheral nervous system that provides the communications controlling bodily functions that generally are not under your control, such as breathing.

sympathetic nervous system A component of the autonomic nervous system that prepares organisms or action by activating biological systems required for "fight or flight" responses.

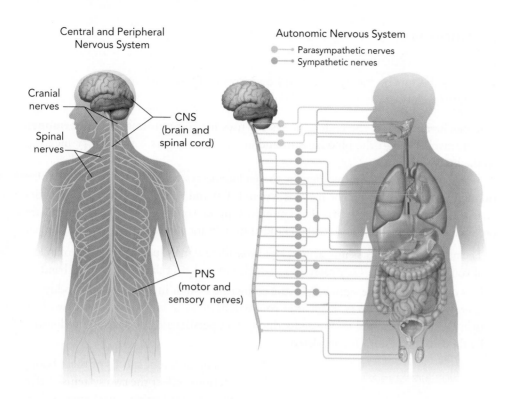

Central and Peripheral
Nervous System

Cranial nerves

Spinal nerves

CNS
(brain and
spinal cord)

PNS
(motor and
sensory nerves)

Autonomic Nervous System
Parasympathetic nerves
Sympathetic nerves

figure **3.25**
Peripheral nervous system The peripheral nervous system consists of all neurons that are outside of the central nervous system, extending throughout the body. Its parts can be classified by location (cranial or spinal) or by function (somatic or autonomic). The autonomic nervous system is further divided into the sympathetic and parasympathetic nervous systems.

But imagine what happens after you pass to your teammate: She scores, the game ends, your team wins, and now your body responds differently. You relax, rest, and may find that you need a bathroom break. Your body's *parasympathetic nervous system* is swinging into action. The **parasympathetic nervous system** is the part of the autonomic nervous system that maintains normal functioning of the body when you are *not* under threat or stress. It activates "basic housekeeping" functions such as digestion and elimination of bodily waste, and reduces heart rate and blood pressure to low, baseline levels of activity.

> When was the last time your sympathetic nervous system was activated? What did its activation feel like?

The different roles of the sympathetic and parasympathetic nervous systems explain everyday examples in which psychological factors influence physical functioning. For instance, the demands of travel can be stressful, and travelers often experience "traveler's constipation." During the stress of travel, the sympathetic nervous system is relatively more active than usual—and the parasympathetic system less active, which interferes with normal digestive system functioning.

🌐 WHAT DO YOU KNOW?...

13. The division of the peripheral nervous system that enables you to control your body's movements is the _____ nervous system. The autonomic nervous system is divided into two subsystems: the _____ nervous system, which, when activated, enables "fight or flight" responses, and the _____ nervous system, which restores normal functioning when a threat is no longer present.

The Endocrine System

The nervous system is not the only communication system within the body. A second is the **endocrine system,** which conveys signals from one part of the body to another using biochemicals. The biochemical signals affect activity in the body's organs.

As you'll see, the body's two communication systems are linked; brain activity affects endocrine activity. This link is an important connection between mind and body.

parasympathetic nervous system
A component of the autonomic nervous system that maintains normal functioning of the body when one is not under threat or stress by activating digestion and waste elimination and restoring baseline heart rate and blood pressure.

endocrine system A collection of glands that produce and secrete hormones, which carry messages from the brain to organs via the bloodstream.

Hormones

Preview Question

> What is the endocrine system and how does it differ from the nervous system?

The biochemicals that the endocrine system uses for communication are **hormones,** which travel through the bloodstream and act as "messengers." They carry messages to the body's organs.

Hormone-based communication in the endocrine system differs from communication in the nervous system. The nervous system is fast and specific, whereas the endocrine system is slower and less specific. For example, suppose you're on a playing field and see, out of the corner of your eye, a football headed straight for your head. Two things happen:

> The nervous system leaps into action, rapidly sending signals specifically to the muscles of your neck and arm. They cause you to duck and to deflect the ball with your hand.

> Less quickly, hormone signaling by the endocrine system increases overall bodily energy. This effect lingers. Even after you've deflected the football, you feel "worked up"; the arousal created by the endocrine system persists after the action produced by the nervous system is completed.

Have you ever experienced the delayed effects of the endocrine system?

The different speeds of these bodily reactions reflect the two systems' different communications mechanisms. The nervous system, as you learned, communicates electrically: Action potentials zip along axons. The endocrine system communicates chemically: Hormones float through the bloodstream. Electrical "zipping" is faster than chemical "floating."

Why would your body need the slow endocrine system if it's got the fast nervous system? Sometimes the brain needs to send signals that are widespread and long-lasting. If that flying football in our example were an opening kickoff and you were one of the players, you would want to arouse multiple biological systems that prepared you for prolonged physical activity. Because hormones spread throughout the body, they are well equipped for the job of increasing the supply of energy to multiple muscles.

💋 WHAT DO YOU KNOW?...

14. Describe the differences between the nervous system and the endocrine system in speed and in method of communication.

Glands

Preview Question

> What are the major endocrine glands and their functions?

Hormones are produced by *glands,* which are bodily organs that produce and secrete chemicals. The glands of the endocrine system are located throughout the body (Figure 3.26).

Ever wake up in the middle of the night to use the bathroom, then find yourself too awake to fall back to sleep? Perhaps the lights you turned on decreased your melatonin levels!

Two are in the brain. The **pineal gland** (so named because its shape resembles that of a pine cone) produces a hormone called *melatonin* that influences patterns of sleeping and wakefulness. The amount of melatonin released is affected not only by signals from the brain, but also by environmental factors. Darkness increases melatonin release that, in turn, induces drowsiness. If people are exposed to bright lights, their melatonin levels decrease (Lewy et al., 1980).

hormones Chemicals that the endocrine system uses for communication; they travel through the bloodstream and carry messages to the body's organs.

pineal gland An endocrine gland that produces a hormone called melatonin that influences patterns of sleeping and wakefulness.

The brain also houses the **pituitary gland,** an endocrine gland that is tiny (about the size of a pea) but powerful. In fact, it is so powerful that it is commonly called the "master gland" of the endocrine system. Its power derives from the fact that the pituitary gland releases hormones that influence biological activity in other glands. These include glands that respond to stress, contribute to reproduction, and regulate the body's use of energy. In addition, the pituitary is the point of contact between the nervous system and the endocrine system. Specifically, the brain's hypothalamus releases chemical substances that affect pituitary gland activity. Through this chain of influence—from hypothalamus to "master gland" pituitary to additional glands—the brain can influence endocrine activity throughout the body.

The body's other glands are located below the head, as shown in Figure 3.26:

> The **thyroid gland** releases hormones that regulate the body's metabolic rate, that is, the rate at which the body burns energy. The body's rate of burning energy influences a person's weight. Variations in thyroid functioning thus are correlated with variations in rates of obesity (Knudsen et al., 2005).

> The **thymus** produces hormones that influence the development and functioning of the immune system, and thus is important to overall health.

> The **adrenal glands,** which sit on top of the kidneys, produce hormones that respond to stress, as well as sex hormones, which are produced also by the gonads.

> The **pancreas** releases hormones that include insulin, which regulates the level of sugar in the bloodstream.

> The **gonads** are the organs that produce reproductive cells; the **ovaries** in women produce ova (eggs) and the **testes** in men produce sperm. In addition to eggs and sperm, the gonads also produce hormones. The ovaries produce *estrogens,* which stimulate the body to develop female sex characteristics such as breasts, and *progesterone,* which regulates the menstrual cycle. In men, the testes produce *testosterone,* which stimulates the development of male adult sex characteristics (e.g., deep voice, bone and muscle mass).

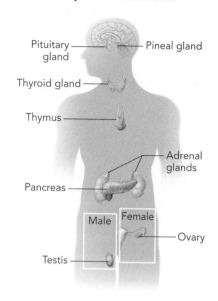

Major Endocrine Glands

figure 3.26
Major glands of the endocrine system

🌐 WHAT DO YOU KNOW?...

15. Match the structures on the left with their features and functions on the right.

1. Pineal gland	a. Produces hormones that respond to stress
2. Pituitary gland	b. Produces the hormone melatonin, which induces drowsiness
3. Thyroid gland	c. Produces reproductive cells and hormones including estrogen, progesterone, and testosterone
4. Thymus	d. "Master gland" that controls other glands and is the point of contact between the nervous and endocrine systems
5. Adrenal glands	e. Releases insulin
6. Pancreas	f. Releases hormones that influence the development and functioning of the immune system
7. Gonads	g. Releases hormones that regulate metabolism

Psychological Effects of Hormones: Estrogens

Preview Question

> How does estrogen affect memory and behavior?

Hormones clearly are central to biological functioning. What, though, is their psychological relevance? Why discuss them in a psychology textbook?

Hormones impact psychological functioning; they influence people's moods, motives, and mental abilities. Particularly clear evidence of this comes from research

pituitary gland The "master gland" of the endocrine system; it releases hormones that influence biological activity in several other glands, including those that regulate stress response, reproduction, and metabolic rate.

thyroid gland An endocrine gland that releases hormones regulating the body's metabolic rate.

thymus An endocrine gland that produces hormones influencing the development and functioning of the immune system.

adrenal glands Endocrine glands that produce hormones that respond to stress, as well as sex hormones.

pancreas The organ that releases hormones including insulin, which regulates the level of sugar in the bloodstream.

gonads The organs that produce reproductive cells—ovaries in women produce ova and testes in men produce sperm.

ovaries The reproductive cells in women that produce ova (eggs).

testes The reproductive cells in men that produce sperm.

on women's hormone levels and psychological functioning. Levels of ovarian hormones vary across the menstrual cycle. If psychological functioning similarly varies across the menstrual cycle, in tandem with hormone levels, this would provide evidence that hormones influence psychology. Let's look at two examples.

A research team (Maki, Rich, & Rosenbaum, 2002) knew that estrogen can influence the growth of brain cells in areas of the brain needed for memory. They thus predicted that estrogen levels and memory performance would be linked. To test their prediction, they studied women at two time points: early in the menstrual cycle, when estrogen levels are low, and later in the cycle, when levels are high. At both times, women read a list of words and later performed a task that measured whether they retained information from the word list in memory. Women's memory was found to vary across the menstrual cycle. As predicted, when estrogen levels were high, memory was superior (Maki et al., 2002).

The second example involves estrogen levels and styles of dressing and personal care. Researchers reasoned that, over the course of evolution, it was adaptive for women to appear attractive to mates during a particular time of the month: when they were most biologically fertile. During low-fertility periods, by contrast, it was adaptive to devote time to activities other than mating. The researchers hypothesized that, because we inherit psychological traces of the ancestral past, women today would still tend to pursue mates during biologically fertile periods, with this pursuit revealed in their styles of clothing and personal care. To test this hypothesis, the researchers took photos of women on both low- and high-fertility days in the given woman's menstrual cycle. Afterward, raters were asked to judge, for each pair of photos (i.e., photos from the high- and low-fertility period for each woman), "In which photo is the person trying to look more attractive?" (Haselton et al., 2007, p. 42). The judges, of course, did not know which photo was taken during the high-fertility period.

In which photo were women trying to look more attractive? As predicted, it was the photo from the high-fertility period; to a significant degree, judges rated this photo as the one in which women were choosing fashion items to enhance their attractiveness (Haselton et al., 2007). Ratings indicated that, during high-fertility periods, women wore more fashionable clothes that showed more skin (Table 3.2).

As with studies of the nervous system, then, research on the endocrine system reveals interconnections between biological mechanisms that evolved in the past and psychological experiences in the contemporary social world.

Research shows that women dress differently during high- and low-fertility times in their menstrual cycles. Women more often wear fashionable and revealing clothing during high-fertility times of the month.

table **3.2**

Women's Clothing Choices		
Judgment (percent concordance of judges' codes)	**High fertility**	**Low fertility**
Wearing "more fashionable clothes" (70%)	18	8
Wearing "nicer clothes" (77%)	17	8
Showing more skin (upper body) (77%)	11	6
Showing more skin (lower body) (93%)	7	5
Wearing "sexier clothes" (70%)	6	7
Wearing more "accessories" (63%)	6	7
Wearing a skirt in one session but not the other (100%)	3	0
Wearing a lacy top (87%)	3	1

Reprinted from *Hormones and Behavior*, 51:40–45, Haselton et al., Ovulatory shifts in human female ornamentation: Near ovulation, women dress to impress, © 2007, with permission from Elsevier

16. Estrogen has been found to influence both memory and how _____ women chose to dress.

⟲ Looking Back and Looking Ahead

In this chapter, you've learned a lot of details about the brain: its bottom-to-top and left/right organization; networks that connect its distinct regions; the functioning of its individual cells; and the brain's connections to the peripheral nervous system and endocrine system. But don't focus only on the details. Recall the reason for learning all these brain facts.

In psychology, brain research is important because it enhances our understanding of people: their thoughts, feelings, and actions. Every chapter in this book contains information about the brain. In every branch of psychology, researchers try to deepen their understanding of people's experiences and the mind's powers by learning more about the brain's neural and biochemical systems. By learning more about what the brain is like, we learn more about what people are like, too.

Chapter Review

Now that you have completed this chapter, be sure to turn to Appendix B (available at www.pmbpsychology.com), where you will find a **Chapter Summary** that is useful for reviewing what you have learned about the brain and the nervous system.

Key Terms

action potential (p. 107)
adrenal glands (p. 115)
amygdala (p. 92)
association areas (p. 97)
auditory cortex (p. 96)
autonomic nervous system (p. 112)
axon (p. 107)
brain stem (p. 88)
central nervous system (p. 111)
cerebellum (p. 89)
cerebral cortex (p. 94)
cerebral hemispheres (p. 99)
connectome (p. 104)
corpus callosum (p. 99)
cranial nerves (p. 112)
dendrites (p. 107)
endocrine system (p. 113)
frontal lobes (p. 96)
glial cells (p. 110)
gonads (p. 115)
hippocampus (p. 91)

hormones (p. 114)
hypothalamus (p. 90)
limbic system (p. 90)
medulla (p. 89)
midbrain (p. 89)
motor cortex (p. 97)
motor neurons (p. 112)
myelin sheath (p. 108)
nervous system (p. 111)
neurons (p. 106)
neurotransmitters (p. 108)
occipital lobe (p. 95)
ovaries (p. 115)
pancreas (p. 115)
parasympathetic nervous system
   (p. 113)
parietal lobe (p. 95)
peripheral nervous system (p. 112)
pineal gland (p. 114)
pituitary gland (p. 115)
plasticity (p. 84)

pons (p. 89)
prefrontal cortex (p. 97)
receptors (p. 109)
reflexes (p. 112)
reticular formation (p. 89)
sensory cortex (p. 96)
sensory neurons (p. 111)
somatic nervous system (p. 112)
spinal cord (p. 111)
spinal nerves (p. 112)
split brain (p. 101)
sympathetic nervous system (p. 112)
synapse (p. 108)
synaptic vesicles (p. 108)
temporal lobe (p. 96)
testes (p. 115)
thalamus (p. 103)
thymus (p. 115)
thyroid gland (p. 115)
triune brain (p. 87)

Chapter Review

Questions for Discussion

1. You learned that across time, when scholars described the brain, they typically chose some recently developed technology. Currently, we describe our brains as being computerlike or even Internetlike. What are some limitations of these analogies? What, if any, other technologies do you foresee taking their place? [Analyze]

2. As noted in the chapter, we can conceptualize the brain as a tool—one we use for thinking, among other things. This highlights the idea that our brains do not do our thinking for us; rather, *we* are the ones who use our brains to think. Do you think this suggests that our minds and our brains are separate? How do you conceptualize the relationship between the brain and the person using the brain? [Analyze]

3. A popular myth suggests we use only 10% of our brains. Is such a claim true? Explore the answer by specifying the areas of the brain likely to be active when you have a conversation with someone right before lunch. Is this proportion greater than or less than 10%? [Comprehend]

4. MacLean's triune brain is a model that suggests we have three brains in one: a reptilian brain, a paleomammalian brain, and a neomammalian brain. What behaviors and capabilities would be affected if any of these three levels were removed from the individual? Would we still be human if the neomammalian brain were removed? What about the paleomammalian brain? [Analyze]

5. *Mnemonics* are techniques used to organize information in memory so that it is easier to retrieve later. What mnemonics can you use to memorize the structures of the brain and their functions? How might MacLean's triune brain model help you organize this information? [Comprehend]

6. Name a part of the body whose sensory processing takes up a lot of "real estate" in the sensory cortex. Why might this particular body part take up so much space in the sensory cortex? [Analyze]

7. Name a part of the body whose motor processing takes up a lot of "real estate" in the sensory cortex. Why might this particular body part take up so much space in the motor cortex? [Analyze]

Self-Test

1. The hippocampus of London taxi drivers is larger than that of the average driver. What feature of the brain does this best illustrate?
   a. Its stability
   b. Its myelination
   c. Its plasticity
   d. Its reflexivity

2. The effects of Phineas Gage's accident on his intellect and personality illustrated which of the following about the brain?
   a. We use only 10% of it.
   b. Its parts are specialized.
   c. It is highly plastic.
   d. It can repair itself.

3. Which part of MacLean's triune brain is responsible for regulating bodily functions critical to survival?
   a. Neomammalian
   b. Paleomammalian
   c. Reptilian
   d. Vegetative mind

4. Damage to which of the following areas would cause your movements to become uncoordinated, even clumsy?
   a. Pons
   b. Midbrain
   c. Cerebellum
   d. Reticular formation

5. Of the following, which structure of the limbic system would be most active if you were to walk into your most challenging class and notice students clearing their desks, as if preparing to take a test (one for which you aren't prepared!)?
   a. Hippocampus
   b. Amygdala
   c. Fornix
   d. Cingulate gyrus

6. On which of the following properties of the body does fMRI capitalize to produce images?
   a. Radioactive substances are absorbed by organs.
   b. Blood flows to the areas of the body that are in use.
   c. The electricity of action potentials is very powerful.
   d. Skin conductance changes when sweat glands are active.

7. Damage to which of the following lobes would make it difficult for you to touch your finger to your nose with your eyes closed?
   a. Parietal
   b. Temporal
   c. Occipital
   d. Frontal

8. The rich interconnections between _____ lobes and other areas of the brain enable us to possess uniquely human capabilities, including the ability to think about ourselves and consider how others view us.
   a. parietal
   b. temporal
   c. occipital
   d. frontal

9. This area of the frontal lobes enables you to concentrate on taking this self-test, while simultaneously blocking out irrelevant stimuli.
   a. Motor cortex
   b. Association areas
   c. Sensory cortex
   d. Prefrontal cortex

10. That we're able to coordinate complex activities is due largely to the fact that the brain is
    a. plastic.
    b. specialized.
    c. networked.
    d. hemispheric.

11. Which of the following was not a finding in research comparing brain activation among English and Chinese speakers doing arithmetic?
    a. For both, the visual–spatial regions of the brain were activated.
    b. Among the English speakers, Broca's area was activated.

c. Among Chinese speakers, visual processing areas of the brain were activated.
d. Patterns of brain activation were nearly identical among English and Chinese speakers.

12. Which particular structure of the neuron can be as long as a meter (a little over 3 feet), allowing neurons to send information across relatively long distances?
    a. Axon
    b. Dendrite
    c. Synapse
    d. Glial cell

13. The incredible speed with which action potentials are able to rush down the length of an axon is enhanced by which of the following structures?
    a. Myelin sheaths
    b. Glial cells
    c. Synaptic gaps
    d. Dendrites

14. When used by neurons in the spinal cord, this neurotransmitter controls muscles, and when used by neurons in the brain, it regulates memory.
    a. Serotonin
    b. Norepinephrine
    c. Dopamine
    d. Acetylcholine

15. Unexplained weight gain would most likely be related to a decrease in the functioning of which of the following glands?
    a. Gonads
    b. Adrenal glands
    c. Thymus
    d. Thyroid gland

Answers

You can check your answers to the preceding Self-Test and the chapter's What Do You Know? questions in Appendix B.

Nature, Nurture, and Their Interaction

4

THE THREE BROTHERS—CALLED HM, HT1, AND HT2 in the scientific literature, to maintain their anonymity—were close. They grew up together; attended the same grade school, high school, and college; and hung out together as adults. Did spending all this time together, in the same neighborhoods and schools, cause them to develop similar personalities?

HT1 and HT2 did resemble one another psychologically. In childhood, HT1 was seen as stubborn and strong-willed, and HT2 was athletic and cocky. It was easy to see the resemblance. HM, however, differed from them. The parents described HM as delicate, sensitive, and artistic. An old home video supports their description: HT2 is seen boxing with an older relative, then HT1 starts boxing with HM. But HM so detests fighting that, rather than starting to box, he starts to cry.

Once they reached their teen years, HT1 and HT2 became interested in girls. When they grew older, their sexual partners were women. Again, HM differed. One day during his childhood, in a restroom at a baseball stadium, he noticed how much he enjoyed looking at men's genitals. In high school, he became sexually attracted to a male teacher. By his late teen years, HM knew he was gay.

The brothers' similarities and differences raise questions we address in this chapter on nature, nurture, and their interaction. Are psychological characteristics such as personality style and sexual orientation inherited—part of your genetically determined biological *nature?* Or are they learned—a result of the family, community, and culture in which you are *nurtured?*

What's your guess? Why, for example, do you think the brothers HT1 and HT2 were similar? Perhaps the cause was nature, that is, similar genes. If that's what you are thinking, it's a good guess; HT1 and HT2 are identical twins, and thus have the same genes. Their genetic similarity might explain their similar personalities and sexual orientation.

Why do you think HM differed? It doesn't seem as if the cause was nurture, because HM and his brothers grew up in the same environment. So maybe, again, it is nature: Perhaps genetic differences between HM and his identical-twin brothers produced their psychological differences. But if that's your guess, you're in for a

All images: Gallery Stock

surprise: HM had *the exact same* genes as HT1 and HT2—the three brothers are genetically identical *triplets* (Hershberger & Segal, 2004)! HM's personality and sexual orientation differed from that of his brothers, even though he had the very same genes as them and was raised in the very same household.

Are psychological qualities thus a product of nature? Or nurture? Or what? The chapter ahead will provide some clues. ◉

IMAGINE THAT YOU had different *genes,* the molecular material in the cells of your body that is the basis of biological inheritance. Instead of the genes you inherited from your parents, suppose you had genes from some other parents, yet were raised in the same household where you actually grew up. Do you think that, psychologically, you would be the same *you*—with the same thoughts and feelings, abilities and potentials, hopes and fantasies?

Now imagine that instead of having different genes, you were raised in an entirely different environment: a hunter-gatherer society with no stores, schools, or mass communication; or a Buddhist monastery, isolated from the outside world, where you meditated for hours a day. Do you think you would be the same *you*—with the same thoughts, feelings, abilities, potentials, hopes, and fantasies?

Likely your answers are "no" and "no." Even before reading this chapter, you know intuitively that your psychological makeup is influenced by your biological *nature*—qualities you inherited

The diversity of human environments Psychologists study how both biological and environmental factors—nature and nurture—shape people's beliefs, emotions, and behavior. The environmental factor can vary enormously. You may have grown up in an industrialized world, with twenty-first-century communications and commerce, but some people still live in hunter-gatherer societies where they obtain food from plants and animals in the wild and live without clocks and calendars. Shown here are women from such a society, the Hadza culture of Tanzania, in East Africa (Kaare & Woodburn, 1999). How do you think you'd differ from your current self if you had been raised there?

genetically. You also know that your psychology is shaped by *nurture*—the ongoing stream of experiences you have had since your birth.

"So," you may be asking yourself, "if I *already* know that nature and nurture are important, what am I going to learn from this textbook chapter on nature and nurture?" In a nutshell, you're going to learn how to *think like a psychologist* about nature and nurture. Two tales about nature and nurture will show you exactly what that means.

Thinking About Nature and Nurture: Two Tales

The first tale concerns a familiar psychological quality: intelligence. Consider this question:

Which is the more important cause of individual differences in intelligence: (1) inheritance (nature) or (2) experience (nurture)?

Once you learn to think like a psychologist about nature and nurture, you won't answer simply "#1" or "#2." Here's a study that shows why.

Genes, Intelligence, Poverty, and Wealth

Preview Question

> What explains intelligence? Nature? Nurture? Both?

In 2003, a team of psychologists (Turkheimer et al., 2003) studied intelligence in a large population of twins. They measured intelligence in pairs of (1) identical or **monozygotic (MZ) twins,** who have the same genes, and (2) fraternal or **dizygotic**

monozygotic (MZ) twins Siblings who, at conception, develop from a single fertilized cell that splits; identical twins.

dizygotic (DZ) twins Siblings produced during the same pregnancy who are conceived from two separately fertilized cells; fraternal twins.

Nature, nurture, and intelligence If Einstein had gone to the school on the right, would he have turned out to be Einstein? Though all children deserve to attend a good school, they don't all have that opportunity. Some benefit from computers and other technologies that boost learning, whereas others—like the children on the right, who live in a poor neighborhood in Haiti—may attend schools that lack electricity. As the chapter explains, the relative influence of nature and nurture on intelligence depends on which type of environment children grow up in.

(DZ) twins, who share only half their genes. By comparing MZ and DZ twins, they could determine the degree to which genes influence intelligence. (We'll explain later exactly how this comparison is done.)

In addition, the researchers measured each twin pair family's *socioeconomic status* (*SES*), which is an index of family wealth, parents' level of education, and the quality of jobs held by the parents. Because socioeconomic status shapes the environment twins experience once they are born, it is an aspect of nurture.

Why did the psychologists measure SES? They did so thanks to a critical insight into the question stated above; they realized that the question "Which is more important, nature or nurture?" might not be a good one. Its wording suggests that there is a single correct answer that applies to all people, in all places. But there may be no single correct answer; rather, genes might be more important in some environments and less important in others.

To find out, the researchers calculated the effects of genes on intelligence among people living at each of various SES levels (Figure 4.1). In high-SES environments, genes were the primary cause of individual differences in intelligence. But in economically poor environments, genes explained hardly anything at all. "In the most impoverished families," the genetic effect was "essentially zero" (Turkheimer et al., 2003, p. 626).

> What features of your school or home environment enabled you to develop your intelligence or other skills?

In this case, "thinking like a psychologist" means recognizing that nature and nurture are *not* independent forces, each with a fixed size. It means recognizing, instead, that nature and nurture are interdependent; that is, the effect of one may depend on the other (Ridley, 2003; Russell, 2011). Our simple question above—"Which is more important?"—is simplistic; it's not a good question.

You'll learn a similar lesson in our second tale of nature and nurture.

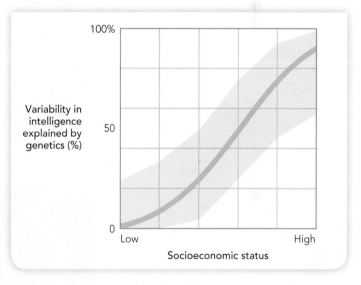

figure 4.1
Genes, intelligence, and SES
Do genes determine people's levels of intelligence? It depends where the people live. Researchers found that among families in relatively wealthy environments—that is, high-SES families—genes have a big impact. But among low-SES families, genes had hardly any influence at all.

💡 WHAT DO YOU KNOW?…

1. For people who are very poor, genes played almost no role in shaping intelligence, whereas for people in high-SES environments, they played a large role. Which statement does this finding best support?
   a. Nature and nurture are independent of each other.
   b. Nature and nurture are interdependent.

   See Appendix B for answers to What Do You Know? questions.

Cultural Practices and Biological Evolution

Preview Question

> What can lactose intolerance tell us about whether biology or culture came first?

"Which came first, the chicken or the egg?" That's a tricky question. But here's one that sounds easier: Which came first, human biology or human culture?

Most people would say biology. The biology of all present-day species is a product of *evolution*, the process through which species change across generations (as we discuss below). You might expect that our biological features evolved as ancestral humans adapted to Earth's *physical* challenges: the various floods, famines, droughts, diseases, predators, and ice ages that threatened the survival of our species. Then, *after* our biological nature was in place, humans began to develop the social practices and beliefs that make up human culture (Figure 4.2). In this conception, people's biological nature develops first, and then, later in human history, it runs into culture's newfangled rules and practices.

Evidence suggests, however, that this conception is wrong. Biology did not evolve first, prior to culture. Rather, biology and culture evolved together, or *coevolved*. **Coevolution** refers to processes through which biology and culture interacted in the course of human evolution (Durham, 1991; Figure 4.2). In coevolutionary processes, human biology evolves, in part, in response to the cultural practices that generation after generation of humans encounter.

Coevolution is evident in a behavior common to many—but not all—of us: drinking milk. To many people, drinking milk seems as natural as breathing air. Shouldn't almost everyone be able to digest the nutrients in milk, especially its key sugar molecule, *lactose*? Take a look at the map in Figure 4.3. In some parts of the

figure 4.2

Coevolution of biology and culture Some people expect that, as depicted in the upper panel, human biology evolved in response to the physical environment, and that human culture developed only after modern humans had fully evolved. However, much evidence suggests that the actual connections among biology and culture are as depicted in the lower panel. Culture and biology coevolved, influencing one another as human groups adapted to the challenges and opportunities of the physical environment.

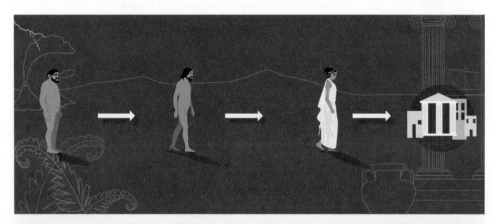

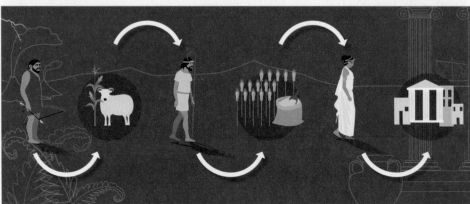

coevolution Processes through which biology and culture interact in the course of human evolution.

figure 4.3

Lactose intolerance map Rates of lactose intolerance vary enormously from one part of the world to another. In some regions, virtually everyone can digest lactose; in others, virtually everyone cannot. Lactose tolerance is common only in parts of the world where drinking milk was a common cultural practice. In those regions, humans evolved biologically in response to the cultural practice of drinking milk.

world, more than 9 out of 10 people can digest lactose, as you might expect. But in others, more than 9 out of 10 people cannot! In fact, in East Africa, where humans originally evolved, almost everyone is lactose intolerant; that is, they cannot digest lactose (Bloom & Sherman, 2005; Durham, 1991). Although people in all regions of the world can digest lactose in infancy, in a great many regions, most people lose that biological ability later in life.

At a biological level, genes explain variations in lactose tolerance (Laland, Odling-Smee, & Myles, 2010). To digest lactose, people need genes that produce a protein required for its digestion. In some parts of the world, most people possess these genes; in other parts, most do not.

What accounts for this biological difference of having the genes or not? Culture! Cultural differences created the differences in biology (Durham, 1991; Laland et al., 2010). Here's how it worked. Across thousands of years of evolution, different cultures developed different ways of producing and preparing food. One major difference involved milk, for which there were three main cultural practices:

1. *Raise dairy cows and serve milk.* In some cultures (e.g., in Northern Europe), people raised dairy cows, milked them, and encouraged the drinking of milk.

2. *Raise dairy cows and serve cheese.* In other cultures (e.g., in Southern Europe), people raised and milked cows, but turned much of the milk into cheese, which contains less lactose than raw milk.

3. *Don't raise dairy cows.* In yet other cultures (e.g., those of East Africa), people did not raise dairy cows. This was a wise choice; in hot, moist climates, dairy cows attract insects that carry disease, so raising them can be detrimental to human health. In these cultures, milk was not part of the diet.

In regions of the world with cultural practice #1, people who could digest lactose had an evolutionary advantage. They got nutrients from milk, grew stronger, and

Milk has been around for ages The lactose in milk provides nutrients. Why, then, is there any need for lactose-free milk? Shouldn't all humans, thanks to evolution by natural selection, have adapted to the environment and evolved the ability to digest lactose? Variations in lactose tolerance show that biology and culture interacted across the course of evolution.

thus were more likely to survive and reproduce. Across generations, the population contained more and more people who were lactose tolerant (because more and more of them were surviving and reproducing). Today, almost everyone is lactose tolerant in those regions of the world.

In regions with cultural practice #2, the ability to digest lactose was less of an advantage. People who had trouble digesting milk could still get nutrition from cheese. Today, in these areas of the world, about 50% of people are lactose tolerant.

In regions with cultural practice #3, the ability to digest lactose had no evolutionary advantage (because there was no milk). As a result, that biological ability did not evolve. Today, only a very small number of people in these parts of the world are lactose tolerant.

We see, then, that in the course of human evolution, neither biology nor culture "came first." Biology and culture were intertwined. Biology evolved, in part, in response to cultural practices.

Once again, "thinking like a psychologist" does not mean settling on one versus another answer to our question ("Which came first, human biology or human culture?"). It means rejecting the question as simplistic. As you learn about the way genes and environments interact, you'll learn to ask smarter, more sophisticated questions about nature and nurture. You, too, will learn to think like a psychologist.

> ### ✸ WHAT DO YOU KNOW?...
>
> 2. In what cultural context would the ability to digest lactose be an evolutionary advantage? How does this illustrate the idea that biology and culture are intertwined?

The Moral of the Stories: Nature and Nurture Interact

Preview Question

> › What does it mean to say that nature is dependent on nurture?

These two stories, about intelligence and lactose tolerance, have the same moral: Nature and nurture interact. People's psychological and biological characteristics reflect a combination of the two. Although we haven't yet analyzed genetic mechanisms at a detailed biological level (that happens later in this chapter), you can already see what that analysis has to explain: the interaction of genes and environmental influences.

Before we return to the psychology of humans, we note that gene–environment interactions are evident in simpler organisms, such as plants. The plants shown in Figure 4.4 are seven sets of genetically identical triplets. For each set of triplets, researchers planted one plant at each of three elevations: high, medium, and low.

Which was more important to plant growth, nature or nurture? Looking at the plants, that question hardly makes sense. Different environments (nurture) made little difference to some plants (e.g., #4) but greatly affected others (e.g., #1). Some genetically based differences seen in low elevation (e.g., plant #3 taller than #6) reverse at high elevation (#6 taller than #3). At both low and high elevations, plant #1 was the tallest of the seven, but at medium elevations, it was the second *shortest*. To predict the height of the plants, you need to know about their genes and their environments.

For some characteristics, genetic influences are predominant and environmental influence is negligible. Eye color, for instance, is determined overwhelmingly by genes (Zhu et al., 2004). For other characteristics, the reverse is true. As you saw earlier, among people living in poverty, environmental effects on individual differences in intelligence are large and genetic effects are small (Turkheimer et al., 2003). Yet, in general, both nature and nurture are influential and, to understand their influence, must be considered together.

The nature–nurture dichotomy, which has dominated discussions of behavior for decades, is largely a false one—all characteristics of all organisms are truly a result of the simultaneous influences of both.

—Paul Ehrlich (2000, p. 10)

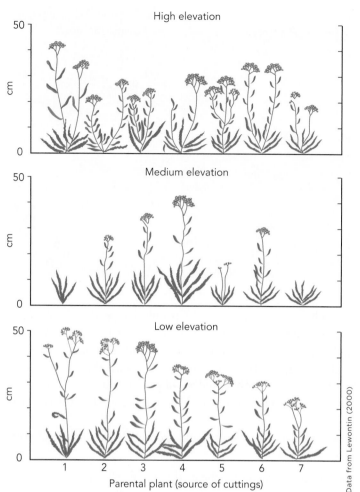

figure 4.4

Plant growth What determines which plants are bigger than others, nature (genetics) or nurture (environmental conditions)? As you can see from the plants, it's a combination of the two. Plant #1, for example, is much taller than #7 when the plants are grown at high or low elevation, but not when they're grown in a different environment, a medium elevation. The interaction of nature and nurture is a basic fact of biological life.

Data from Lewontin (2000)

With that lesson in place, let's look at nature, nurture, and individual differences in psychological characteristics.

WHAT DO YOU KNOW?...

3. Some traits, such as eye color, are determined overwhelmingly by _____. However, for other traits, such as intelligence, the effect of genes largely depends on the _____ in which one is raised.

Nature, Nurture, and Individual Differences

Why do people differ so much? Some are outgoing and others shy, some are intelligent and others less so, some are politically conservative and others liberal. One possible explanation is inheritance. In the field of **behavior genetics** (Kim, 2009), researchers try to determine the degree to which individual differences in the behavior of animals (including humans) are inherited—that is to say, are due to genes. Key to these efforts is the study of twins.

Twins and the Twin Method

Preview Question

› How can identical and fraternal twins' data be used to tell us about the influence of genes?

behavior genetics Field of study that investigates the degree to which psychological variations are inherited.

figure 4.5
MZ and DZ twins at conception
At conception, a sperm cell fuses with an egg cell to form a zygote, the initial cell capable of developing into a complete organism. On rare occasions (less than 1 in 200 conceptions), the zygote splits, forming two embryos that are genetically identical (left panel). When these embryos develop, they become MZ twins—two individuals who originate from one ("mono") zygote. Since they developed from the same original zygote, MZ twins share 100% of their genes. Fraternal (dizygotic) twins develop from two separate zygotes. They thus are no more or less similar than ordinary siblings.

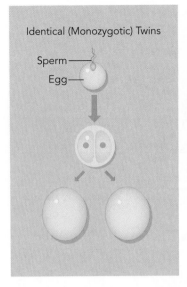

Identical (Monozygotic) Twins

Sperm
Egg

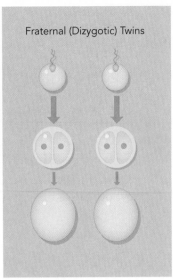

Fraternal (Dizygotic) Twins

North News and Pictures

They don't have to throw as many birthday parties Twins are rare—but not all that rare, as British parents Tracey and Davood Bagedan could tell you. Mrs. Bagedan gave birth to identical-twin sons in 2008, and identical-twin daughters in 2011. What's really rare is that all four twins share the same birthday date, February 27.

twin method A procedure for determining the degree to which genes account for individual differences by comparing degrees of similarity among MZ and DZ twins.

Twins are just what the behavior geneticist needs: people whose degree of genetic overlap is known. Humans share most genes, yet we all differ from one another a little bit; you aren't exactly the same, genetically, as your friends and neighbors. Finding out exactly how much your genes that can vary overlap with these other people would require a lot of work: time-consuming analysis of genetic material. With twins, however, the degree of overlap is known: 100% for MZ twins, and 50% for DZ twins (but see This Just In).

MZ and DZ twins' varying genetic overlap results from differing biological events at the point of conception (Figure 4.5):

› Monozygotic twins are produced when one *zygote,* the initial cell capable of developing into a complete organism, splits and forms two embryos.

› Dizygotic twins develop when, through fertilization, two *separate* zygotes are formed.

Knowing the degree of genetic overlap makes life easy for the scientist. Through a relatively simple procedure known as the **twin method,** researchers can compute the degree to which genes account for individual differences. Let's see how the twin method works.

The study of twins is similar—not identical, but similar—to an experiment. In an experiment, one factor varies (the level of the independent variable in one condition versus another) and others are controlled. In the twin method:

› One factor varies: the degree of genetic similarity in MZ and DZ twins.

› Other factors are controlled: For any given twin pair, MZ or DZ, the two twins are born at the same historical period; have parents of the same age and parenting skill; experience the same environmental settings—schools, neighborhoods, SES, and so forth. (This is true except in rare cases in which twins are adopted and raised separately.)

In an experiment, the researcher manipulates the independent variable. In a twin study, the variation of course occurs naturally. But in both cases, a researcher can determine whether the varying factor influences the outcome of the study, that is, its dependent variable.

In a twin study, the key outcome is the degree to which the co-twins resemble one another psychologically. If MZ twins are more similar to one another than DZ twins, genes are the likely cause.

Do you know any identical twins? How similar are they psychologically? Are they equally intelligent? Do they have the same exact personality traits?

In the twin method, researchers determine the degree to which genes contribute to individual differences by following a three-step procedure:

1. *Measure a psychological characteristic in a group of MZ twins and a group of DZ twins.* You could measure any characteristic discussed anywhere in this book: intelligence, personality, social attitudes, depression, eyesight, and so forth.

2. *Compute two correlations, one for the MZ twins and one for the DZ twins.* The correlations (see Chapter 2) are a numerical index of the MZ twins' and the DZ twins' degree of psychological similarity on the characteristics measured in Step 1.

3. *Compare the MZ correlation with the DZ correlation.* If the MZ correlation is larger than the DZ correlation, this means that genetics had an effect: The greater genetic overlap of the MZ twins caused them to be more similar to one another psychologically.

The difference between the MZ and DZ correlations indicates the degree of *heritability* of the psychological characteristic that was measured. **Heritability** is the degree to which individual differences in a characteristic—that is, the overall degree of person-to-person variation on that characteristic—are explained by genetic factors. If individual differences are caused entirely by genes, heritability is 100%. If genes have no effect—that is, if nurture, rather than nature, creates individual differences— then the psychological quality is not heritable, which is to say, heritability is 0%.

Let's see what heritability actually turns out to be by examining some research results.

🖤 WHAT DO YOU KNOW?...

4. If MZ twins are more similar to each other in intelligence than are DZ twins, what must we conclude is the likely cause?

The Heritability of Psychological Characteristics

Preview Question

> What do twin studies tell us about the heritability of personality, psychological disorders, and intelligence?

A great many psychological qualities are heritable. Twin studies commonly find that identical twins are more similar psychologically than are fraternal twins. Examples come from research on (1) personality traits, (2) psychological disorders, and (3) social and political attitudes.

PERSONALITY TRAITS. Genes contribute to individual differences in personality traits, that is, people's typical styles of behavior and emotion (see Chapter 13). Within some populations and for some traits, heritability is about 50%; roughly half of the person-to-person variability in personality traits is explained by genetics (Goldsmith, 1983).

Consider a study with an extraordinarily large population: 12,898 pairs of twins. They were part of a national twin registry in the nation of Sweden (Floderus-Myrhed, Pederson, & Rasmuson, 1980). The twins filled out questionnaires measuring two common personality traits: (1) *extraversion,* the degree to which a person is outgoing and sociable, and (2) *neuroticism,* a person's tendency to be anxious and to experience mood swings. When researchers executed the three-step twin method described above, they found that, for both extraversion and neuroticism, the MZ correlations were about twice as large as the DZ correlations. Overall, genetics accounted for half of the variation in personality.

heritability The degree to which genetic factors explain individual differences in a characteristic.

Identical twins raised separately Paula Bernstein and Elyse Schein are identical twins who were given up for adoption and raised in separate families. Not until adulthood did they even realize they had a twin sibling. When they met, they discovered surprising similarities; for example, both Ms. Bernstein and Ms. Schien were editors of their high school newspapers and studied film in graduate school. Yet they also differed as a result of their life experiences. Ms. Schein, who had experienced the loss of close relatives including her adoptive mother, writes that "despite all the twin studies, which point to genetics, I realize how my environment has required me to develop a shell of resilience. Circumstances have spared Paula from death, and I can't imagine her confronting this tragedy [a recent death in the family]" (Schein & Bernstein, 2007, p. 216).

© 2014 by Elena Seibert

 THINK ABOUT IT

The average income of people living in Sweden is among the highest in the world. Rates of poverty and violent crime are both low. Do you think the results of the twin study conducted in Sweden would be the same in all other nations?

In this large twin study, virtually all of the twins were raised together in the same household. What happens if they are raised separately? Researchers at the University of Minnesota (Bouchard, Lykken, & McGue, 1990) have studied more than 100 sets of twins who, due to adoption, were raised by different parents. If genes had no effect on personality, these twins might turn out to be no more similar than unrelated people. But findings show that they *are* similar, even though they were not raised together. On various personality measures, the correlation between the scores of identical twins raised apart was approximately $r = .5$—about as large as the correlation for identical twins raised together (Bouchard et al., 1990). Some studies have found that twins raised together are more similar than those raised apart; nonetheless, even if raised in different households, identical twins are far more similar to one another than are unrelated individuals (Pederson et al., 1988).

The heritability of personality, then, is much greater than 0%. However, it's also much *less* than 100%. Identical twins raised in the same household are far from psychologically identical; the correlation between their personalities rarely exceeds $r = .5$ (by comparison, the identical-twin correlation for height exceeds .9; Silventoinen et al., 2008). This means that, in addition to genes, environments also profoundly affect personality. Specifically, environmental factors can cause siblings in the same household to differ from one another (Plomin & Daniels, 1987).

Have you ever known two siblings who differ so much that you can hardly believe they are from the same family? Such differences are common. Different peer groups, different perceptions of the parents, and different parental behavior toward individual children all contribute to differences between siblings. For example, one study showed that mothers of identical twins do not always treat the twins identically; they sometimes respond in more negative, punitive ways to one twin than to the other. These differences in mothers' style of punishment predict differences in the twins. Twins whose mothers are less punitive tend to experience more positive emotional states (Deater-Deckard et al., 2001).

Thomas Hoebbel Photography

Same household, different personalities Eric, on the left, is a financial advisor who dresses formally and attends church regularly. Tom, on the right, is an artist who dresses informally and does not attend any religious institution. Yet they are brothers who grew up in the same household. Different experiences within a household can cause siblings to have different psychological qualities.

Does it surprise you that mothers of twins do not always treat their twins identically?

PSYCHOLOGICAL DISORDERS. Genes affect not only everyday personality traits. They also contribute to psychological disorders, that is, prolonged experiences of psychological distress that interfere with a person's everyday life (see Chapter 15). Let's consider a particularly severe disorder, *schizophrenia*.

Schizophrenia is a mental illness that creates severe disturbances in thinking and emotion (National Institute of Mental Health [NIMH], 2009). People with schizophrenia lose the normal capacity to understand the world of reality; they may experience visual hallucinations or hear voices. Often, their emotional life is disturbed (see Chapter 16).

Twin studies reveal that schizophrenia is highly heritable. More than 80% of the overall individual differences in schizophrenia (i.e., variation in whether or not a person is suffering from the disease) is caused by genetic factors (Pogue-Geile & Yokley, 2010). The effects of genes are seen by comparing the chances of developing schizophrenia among DZ and MZ twins. If one twin in a DZ twin pair has schizophrenia, there is only about a 1-in-6 chance that the other DZ twin will have the disease. But if one twin in an MZ twin pair suffers from schizophrenia, there is about a 1-in-2 chance—a 50% chance—that the other twin also will develop schizophrenia.

One way that genes are linked to schizophrenia is through *working memory,* a mental system used to store and manipulate information (Chapter 6). (If you multiply two numbers in your head, you are using your working memory system.) Genetic variations are related to variations in working memory ability (Goldberg et al., 2003). Low working memory ability, in turn, is common among people with schizophrenia.

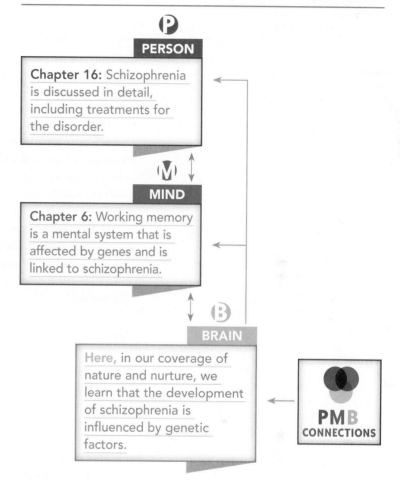

CONNECTING TO WORKING MEMORY AND SCHIZOPHRENIA

PERSON

Chapter 16: Schizophrenia is discussed in detail, including treatments for the disorder.

MIND

Chapter 6: Working memory is a mental system that is affected by genes and is linked to schizophrenia.

BRAIN

Here, in our coverage of nature and nurture, we learn that the development of schizophrenia is influenced by genetic factors.

PMB CONNECTIONS

SOCIAL AND POLITICAL ATTITUDES. Our third psychological characteristic, social and political attitudes, sounds like a product of nurture, not nature. Your attitudes are shaped by friends, neighbors, schools, religious institutions, community leaders, and even campaign ads. Does genetics have any influence?

It turns out that genetics does play a role. People who are more similar genetically tend to have more similar attitudes (Smith et al., 2012). In one study (Eaves et al., 1999), MZ and DZ twins reported their attitudes about social and political issues such as abortion, foreign aid, school prayer, and socialism. MZ twins were more similar than DZ twins; attitudes were heritable. Genes have less of an effect on attitudes than on personality or schizophrenia, and the environmental effects on attitudes are substantial (Eaves et al., 1999). Nonetheless, this study and others (Hatemi et al., 2009) reveal that attitudes are partly heritable.

In some ways, this result is puzzling. Most of the evolution of human genes occurred tens of thousands of years ago, before there were complex societies or political institutions. How could relatively ancient genes affect contemporary political and social attitudes?

The answer is that genes do not affect social attitudes directly. They do so through indirect routes, one of which involves physical sensitivity to threatening noises and images. Researchers (Oxley et al., 2008) compared participants with strong "conservative" political views (e.g., in favor of greater military spending and the use of the death penalty, and support for U.S. actions in the Iraq War) to those with "liberal" views

THINK ABOUT IT

Were it not for your experiences in society—your nurturing—you would not have any social or political attitudes. So how could attitudes be a product of inherited biology?

figure 4.6
Genes and political attitudes

figure 4.6
Genes and political attitudes
How can genes, which evolved before contemporary political parties, debates, and issues even existed, influence political attitudes? The effect is indirect. Research shows that people who display different emotional reactions to threats tend to have different political attitudes. Genes that affect the brain systems that influence emotional response thus could contribute to individual differences in political views.

(opposing the same policies). They measured participants' physiological reactions while exposing them to loud noises and to pictures displaying physical threats (e.g., a picture of a large spider on someone's face). People with different political views responded differently. Conservatives responded more strongly to the threatening images and noises than did liberals (Oxley et al., 2008).

Many factors other than genetics also shape political attitudes. Nonetheless, these results help to resolve the puzzle of how genes have any influence. Genetic variations can create individual differences in neural systems in the brain that are active when people respond to threat. These brain-system differences, in turn, contribute to individual differences in emotional response to threat. The differences in emotional response then affect political attitudes; people who respond strongly to threats are more likely to take actions (e.g., going to war) to combat them and thus are more likely to express political views labeled as "conservative" (Figure 4.6).

> How politically conservative or liberal are you? Do you think you are physiologically reactive in the way that is predicted by this research?

🌍 WHAT DO YOU KNOW?...

5. Which of the following statements about heritability are true? Check all that apply.
   ___ a. The greater psychological similarity of MZ twins compared with DZ twins can be taken as evidence of the environment's effect on personality.
   ___ b. MZ twins are not psychologically identical, due in part to the influence of different parental behavior toward the twins, among other environmental differences.
   ___ c. The mental illness schizophrenia is highly heritable, partly as a result of the heritability of working memory.
   ___ d. Social and political attitudes are at least in part heritable, largely due to the heritability of physical sensitivity to threat.

What Heritability Results Do, and Do Not, Mean

Preview Question

› What false conclusions should we avoid making when interpreting the results of twin studies?

You've just seen that a range of psychological qualities are at least partly heritable. People who are more similar genetically are more similar psychologically. But what, exactly, do these results mean—and *not* mean?

What heritability results *do* mean is that we can reject a "blank slate" argument (Pinker, 2002; see Chapter 1). The idea that, at birth, the mind has no inborn characteristics or tendencies is contradicted by twin-study results. Whether raised together or apart, identical twins resemble one another psychologically to a significant degree. Their identical genes contribute to their similar psychological styles.

However, here are three conclusions that *cannot* validly be drawn from twin-study results:

False Conclusion #1: Since psychological characteristics are heritable, they cannot change. A person's characteristics can change enormously, even if individual differences are heritable. Heritability and changeability can go hand in hand—for example, weight is highly heritable. MZ twins are more similar in weight than are unrelated people. But if you diet and exercise—or sit on a couch and eat doughnuts—your weight changes.

False Conclusion #2: 50% heritability for a trait means that half of each individual's trait is inherited. Statements about heritability are statements about individual differences in the *population*. Heritability percentages do not describe individual people. For instance, personality is 50% heritable, but that does not mean "half of one's personality is inherited." The word "half" does not refer to anything in an individual person, but to differences among people in the population at large. In general, numbers that describe a population of people do not also describe each individual person in that population. For example, the average height of students in your intro psych class might be 5′6″, but it's possible that no individual person is actually 5′6″ tall.

False Conclusion #3: If heritability within two groups is high, and the groups differ, then the differences between the groups are due to genes. Heritability describes the influence of genes *within a group*. Even if heritability is high, differences between groups may be due to the environment, not inherited biology. Consider physical height among citizens of South Korea and North Korea. Within each population, 80 to 90% of the variation in height is heritable. People in one population (South Korean) are much taller than in the other. But the difference between the populations is not caused by genes. It can't be; no fundamental genetic difference exists between the populations, both of which are of Korean ancestry (Johnson et al., 2009). Group differences are caused by an environmental factor: Nutrition and overall living conditions are poor in North Korea compared with South Korea.

AP Photo / Peter Smerdon, World Food Programme

Environments and differences *between* populations Even if a biological or psychological quality is highly heritable within populations, differences between two populations could be environmentally caused. Despite similar genetic background, people in North Korea are shorter than citizens of South Korea due to food shortages in the North.

🌐 WHAT DO YOU KNOW?...

6. Which of the following statements about the meaning of heritability are true? Check all that apply.

___ a. Even if a trait is highly heritable, it can still change.

___ b. Learning that heritability for a trait is 75% means that three-quarters of your personality is inherited.

___ c. Even if heritability for a trait is high, two groups could differ on that trait because of environmental factors.

💭 THINK ABOUT IT

Beware the *fallacy of division*, an error in which statements about a population (i.e., a large group of persons or things) are thought to apply to each of the individuals in the population. In reality, a population-level statement might not apply to individuals. For instance, the statement "Music CDs are disappearing" correctly applies to the overall population of CDs (there are fewer today than in the past) but not to any individual CD (i.e., if you see a CD, it will not disappear in front of your eyes). The point holds when it comes to heredity. Consider the statement that "the heritability of weight is 80%" (see Pietiläinen et al., 1999). It correctly applies to the population: About 80% of the person-to-person variability in weight in the population is explained by genetic influences; 20% is not. But the statement does not apply to individuals; it is *not* true that 80% of your body was created by genes and 20% by the environment. Rather, at the level of the individual case, genetic and environmental influences are inextricably mixed.

Genes and Individual Development

Thus far, we primarily have examined research on psychological characteristics: personality, psychological disorders, social attitudes, intelligence. Results reveal three facts about nature, nurture, and the psychology of people:

1. *Genetic similarity contributes to psychological similarity.* Identical twins, with their identical genes, are particularly similar to one another psychologically.
2. *Environments are influential.* People who are genetically identical often differ psychologically.
3. *Genes and environments interact.* You learned at the beginning of this chapter, for example, that the effect of genes on intelligence differed among people living in wealthy or poor environments.

If you're thinking like a scientist, the question you're asking is "why?" If we shift from a psychological to a biological level of analysis, can we explain why people's psychological qualities are affected by nature, nurture, and nature–nurture interactions?

Yes, we can, thanks to research on genes and gene expression.

Chromosomes, Genes, and Gene Expression

Preview Questions

> What is the relation between chromosomes, DNA, genes, and the genome?
> How do we get from DNA to protein building?

Your body's cells are, in some ways, like books. Books contain a chemical substance: ink. The ink, thanks to its arrangement on the page, conveys information—stories, facts, instructions. Your body's cells contain a chemical substance called **deoxyribonucleic acid,** or **DNA.** The DNA, thanks to its physical arrangement, contains information—the information needed to build the various parts of your body.

DNA AND GENES. The main ingredient needed to build body parts is protein molecules. Your body assembles protein molecules by following instructions encoded into DNA. This information is contained in the long sequence of chemical elements that make up the DNA molecule.

Any section of DNA that provides the full information needed to produce a protein is called a **gene.** Genes thus are the basic units of inheritance: the instructions used to build the body's parts. The entire set of genes—the complete hereditary information—possessed by an organism is called the **genome.**

In the cells of the body, genes are contained within **chromosomes,** biological structures that consist of highly organized, tightly packed strings of molecules (Figure 4.7). The cells of your body contain 46 chromosomes, which are located in the nucleus of the cells. Chromosomes are so small that 46 of them easily fit within a cell's nucleus. Yet they are so tightly packed that if you unwound any one chromosome and stretched it end to end, it would be roughly 6 feet long (National Institutes of General Medical Sciences, 2006).

We truly are a single human family; the genome is extremely similar from one person to the next. More than 99% of the sequences of biological molecules in DNA are the same in all persons, in all cultures of the world (National Institutes of General Medical Sciences, 2006). Yet there are variations. A given gene can come in different varieties, known as **alleles.** Different alleles produce different versions of a characteristic. For example, a gene that produces a chemical affecting bodily coloration comes in different alleles that are responsible for blue versus brown eye color (Sturm et al., 2008). Allelic variations in other genes are responsible for different human blood types.

deoxyribonucleic acid (DNA) The molecule found in chromosomes that encodes the instructions for building an organism.

gene Any section of DNA that provides the full information needed to produce a protein.

genome The entire set of genes possessed by an organism.

chromosomes Biological structures within the nucleus of cells that contain genetic information (DNA).

alleles Variations in specific genes that produce different versions of a characteristic, such as eye color or blood type.

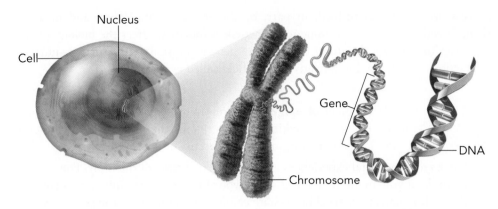

figure 4.7
Chromosomes and DNA DNA, the molecular material that is the basis of genetic inheritance, is found in chromosomes in the nuclei of your cells.

GENE EXPRESSION. There is a second way in which your body's cells are like books. The information in a book has no effect unless the book is opened, read, and acted upon. A cookbook with a cake recipe will not, by itself, produce any cakes; for that, ingredients must be assembled according to the recipe's instructions. Similarly, when the body wants to build a protein, the "recipe"—the information in DNA—cannot, by itself, do the job of producing protein molecules. The information in DNA needs to be read, ingredients must be gathered, and the ingredients must be assembled according to the DNA's instructions (Slavich & Cole, 2013).

This assembly process—the set of steps from DNA recipe to the production of a protein molecule—is known as **gene expression** (Vogel & Motulsky, 1997). Here's how it works:

> A molecule in the nucleus of a cell reads the information in DNA and creates another molecule, *ribonucleic acid* (*RNA*), which contains a copy of the DNA protein-building recipe.

> RNA is transported from one location in the cell to another, where there is biochemical machinery needed to build proteins (Nakielny et al., 1997).

> Cellular machinery reads the information in RNA, gathers molecules needed to build a protein, and assembles them according to the instructions that originally came from the DNA.

🧠 WHAT DO YOU KNOW?...

7. Your body's cells are to books what the arrangement of the ink on their pages is to _____. Within the nucleus of your body's cells are 46 chromosomes that contain _____, which are sections of DNA that contain information needed to produce a protein. Variations in genes are called _____. The process by which the "instructions" contained in DNA produce protein molecules is referred to as _____ expression.

Environmental Experience: Nurture Affects Nature

Preview Question

> How do our experiences affect gene expression? In other words, how does nurture influence nature?

What does the biology of gene expression have to do with the *psychology* of nature and nurture? Quite a lot! The timing of gene expression—that is, *when* the gene expression

gene expression A biological process in which information in DNA becomes active in the process of producing protein molecules.

process occurs—is determined, in part, by the environment. Nature and nurture, then, directly interact. Environmental experiences (nurture) affect the biology of the organism (its biological nature) by affecting gene expression. These nature–nurture interactions are explored in a relatively new field called *epigenetics.*

EPIGENETICS. In the field of **epigenetics,** researchers study how environmental experience "switches on" genes, making them active in the production of proteins (Masterpasqua, 2009). The switching-on process occurs in two steps:

1. Some environmental experiences alter the internal state of the body. For example, if you are under a lot of stress, your body may feel different to you; this feeling reflects internal body-state changes brought on by the stress (see Chapter 10).

2. The body-state changes affect biochemical activity occurring within the nucleus of cells. This biochemical activity can alter gene expression—the "switching on" of genes—because the cell nucleus is where chromosomes and, thus, genes reside.

As a result of this two-step process, nurture (environmental experience) affects biological nature (the biological structure of the organism).

Epigenetic principles have a fascinating implication: People with identical DNA may differ biologically if they experience environments that prompt different types of gene expression. You can see this in the accompanying photo. The two men differ physically; one is markedly taller and heavier. The difference might lead you to guess they are unrelated. But, in reality, they're identical twins. After being separated at birth, the man on the right was raised in a normal caring environment, whereas the man on the left was raised by "a neurotic and cruel relative" (Tanner, 1978, p. 121) who failed to provide adequate nutrition. The result was biological differences despite identical genes.

This example should remind you of HT1, HT2, and HM, the triplets described in this chapter's opening story. HM differed in behavioral style and sexual orientation from his brothers. Epigenetic processes could have caused the differences. Although HM had the same DNA as his brothers, environmental experiences could have "switched on" his genes in a way that differed from gene activation in HT1 and HT2.

The lesson? DNA is not destiny. Genes alone do not determine biological outcomes. Instead, in the development of the organism, genetic and environmental influences combine through epigenetic processes. Let's see some examples of epigenetics in action.

Epigenetic research has identified numerous factors that influence gene expression. For instance, stress, poor nutrition, loneliness, and parenting styles can affect whether, and when, cells use the information in DNA to produce proteins (Cole, 2009; Gottlieb, 1998; McEwen et al., 2012). One major focus of such research has been social relationships and physical health.

Researchers have long known that social factors influence physical health (Uchino, Cacioppo, & Kiecolt-Glaser, 1996). Social isolation impairs health. Conversely, people with many close personal relationships tend to have fewer diseases and to live longer. Why? To find out, researchers (Cole et al., 2007) obtained two key pieces of information from a group of research participants: (1) level of social isolation, as measured by a self-report survey in which people indicated whether they felt isolated from others and lacking in companionship, and (2) gene expression, as measured through a molecular genetic analysis of biological samples obtained from each participant. Data analysis revealed a strong association between social isolation and gene expression. Specifically, socially isolated individuals differed from others in the activity of genes that

Vladimir Godnik / Getty Images

Loneliness is bad not only psychologically, but also physically. Social isolation affects the inner state of the body, influencing gene expression and the functioning of the immune system. As a result, social isolation impairs physical health.

epigenetics The study of how environmental experience "switches on" genes, making them active in the production of proteins.

influence the *immune system,* the body's inner biological defense system; social isolation impaired the functioning of their immune systems, putting them at risk for poorer health.

Research on parenting (Champagne & Curley, 2009) provides another example of how experiences can affect gene expression and biological structure. The parents studied in this work were not human but rodent; laboratory rats, like people, have offspring that require care, and basic principles discovered in one species may generalize to another. When starting their work, the researchers knew that not all rat mothers are alike. Some attend closely to their infant pups, frequently licking and grooming them, whereas others spend much less time physically interacting with their offspring. The researchers also knew that the mothers' actions could predict the rat pups' later behavior; offspring of mothers who do a lot of licking and grooming tend to develop into adult rats that are relatively less fearful than others. Through what process, the researchers asked, could licking and grooming in infancy affect emotions and behaviors in adulthood? The answer turned out to be gene expression (Weaver, Meaney, & Szyf, 2006). Frequent grooming and licking during the first week of life altered chemical processes in cells. These alterations affected gene expression. The altered levels of gene expression, in turn, affected the biological and behavioral development of the baby rats.

THINK ABOUT IT

Research on social isolation, gene expression, and human health is correlational; social isolation is correlated with gene expression and health outcomes. But correlation does not prove causation. These findings thus do not provide evidence of a causal impact of social isolation on genetic mechanisms and health. However, other research, conducted with nonhuman animals, *does* provide such evidence. Experimentally manipulated levels of social isolation produce variations in animals' gene expression and immune system functioning (Slavich & Cole, 2013).

Joe Blossom / Alamy

Importance of maternal interaction Being licked by a rat might not sound like a good time to you—but if you were a baby rat, you'd love it! Research shows that the mother rat's behavior affects the baby rat's biological development. Mother affects baby through epigenetic processes. Interacting with the mother activates the babies' genes in a manner that benefits their biological and behavioral development.

 RESEARCH TOOLKIT

Molecular Genetic Methods

A generation ago, psychology's main tool for studying nature and nurture was the twin method. It succeeded in answering—with a resounding yes—the question, "Do genes contribute to individual differences in psychological characteristics?"

With that question answered, new ones arise: Which genes influence which psychological characteristics? How do they do it? How do environmental factors affect the process? These new questions require a new tool: *molecular genetic methods.*

Molecular genetic methods are biological techniques for studying specific genes and variations in those genes. Researchers analyze the molecular material in DNA (something not done in traditional twin studies). By identifying different alleles of a gene, they can relate those specific genetic variations to specific types of behavior.

Molecular genetic methods require biological material, such as a small blood sample from participants or cells collected from inside the mouth using a cotton swab. Researchers then analyze this material biologically, separating the DNA from other biochemical matter in the cells and then scrutinizing the genetic material (Association of Genetic Technologists, 2008).

Sometimes researchers know exactly what they're looking for in the DNA. They may wish, for example, to determine which of two different alleles of a specific gene is possessed by an individual. If so, they will scrutinize the genome at the specific location at which the gene of interest can be found.

However, sometimes there is no specific search plan. Researchers know that, somewhere in the genome, there must be genes associated with a psychological variable of interest, but they don't know where these genes are located along the lengthy strand

molecular genetic methods Biological techniques for studying specific genes and variations in those genes; researchers relate this genetic information to variations in behavior.

Human Genome Project In 2000 then-President Bill Clinton announced the achievements of the Human Genome Project, accompanied by J. Craig Venter (left) and Francis Collins (right), scientists who led private sector and governmental efforts to map the complete sequence of human genes.

DNA. They thus conduct a *genome-wide association study,* a method that relates the psychological variable to hundreds or thousands of genetic variations at once (Feero, Guttmacher, & Collins, 2010). For example, scientists studying genes and schizophrenia (see Chapter 16) examined variations in thousands of genes among a population of tens of thousands of research participants, and identified seven genetic variations that were significantly related to the occurrence of the psychological disorder (Schizophrenia Psychiatric GWAS Consortium, 2011).

Molecular genetic methods capitalize on knowledge gained through the **Human Genome Project,** an international effort to map the entire sequence of molecular material in the human genetic code. The project, begun in 1990, was completed in 2003 (National Human Genome Research Institute, 2003). Ever since, when researchers explore the genome, they do so with the benefit of a detailed map.

🐷 WHAT DO YOU KNOW?...

8. In molecular genetic methods, researchers analyze the molecular material found in DNA to identify _____ that may be at least partly responsible for certain behaviors.

GENE–ENVIRONMENT INTERACTION AND DEPRESSION. Since you're probably more interested in people than rat pups, let's see how interactions among genes and the environment affect psychological development in our species. Evidence comes from a remarkable, long-term investigation involving more than a thousand people in New Zealand who were studied from early childhood through early adulthood (Caspi et al., 2003). A main branch of this research project explored nature, nurture, and the development of depression.

The researchers measured two factors that might predict the development of depression, one genetic and the other environmental. The genetic factor was variation in—that is, different alleles of—a gene that affects the activity of the brain chemical *serotonin.* Serotonin is one of the many biochemicals that brain cells use to communicate with one another (see Chapter 3). The environmental factor involved life stress. The researchers measured the number of highly stressful life events (e.g., breakup of a significant relationship; loss of a job; homelessness) each research participant experienced.

Key to this study was that, as in other studies reviewed earlier in this chapter, the researchers did not ask the simple question, "Nature versus nurture: Which is more important?" Instead, they explored how genes and environments work together in helping people avoid depression or, alternatively, in contributing to the development of depressive symptoms.

Figure 4.8 shows how genetic and environmental effects combined to predict the development of one symptom of severe depression, suicidal behaviors and thoughts (Caspi et al., 2003). Were genes influential? Sometimes yes, and sometimes no. Among people who experienced few stressful life events, genetic variations hardly made any difference. In low-stress environments, few people contemplate suicide. Was the environment influential? Again, sometimes yes, and sometimes no. People with one type of genetic makeup rarely contemplated suicide, no matter how much stress they experienced; their genetic makeup seemed to protect them against developing depression. What was most influential was a *combination* of genetic background and environmental experience. Specifically, people whose (1) biological nature included a particular genetic allele (the short/short allele) and whose (2) nurturing included larger numbers of stressful events were far more likely than others to become depressed and to consider suicide (Caspi et al., 2003).

The findings, which have been replicated by others (Karg et al., 2011), show how nature and nurture combine in the development of depression. People who experience

Human Genome Project An international effort to map the entire sequence of molecular material in the human genetic code; initiated in 1990, the project was completed in 2003.

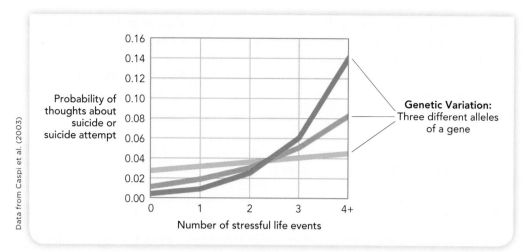

figure **4.8**

Genes, environmental experiences, and depression How do genes and environmental experiences affect depression and one of its symptoms, the risk of suicide? Genes and environments interact; the effect of genes depends on the environment, and the effect of the environment depends on genes. A genetic background that placed people at risk if they experienced a large number of stressful life events (blue line) had no effect if people experienced a small number of stressful life events.

high levels of environmental stress *and* who, due to genes that affect serotonin levels, are biologically inclined to react strongly to stressors are at greatest risk.

In summary, contemporary research shows not only that genes are important, but also that their importance, and basic workings, are best understood by looking at how genetic and environmental factors combine in the psychological development of the individual.

✋ WHAT DO YOU KNOW?...

9. Describe the concept of epigenetics. How would an epigenetics researcher respond to the question, "Which is more important, nature or nurture?"

ⓘ THIS JUST IN

"Identical" Twins

Monozygotic (MZ) twins originate from the splitting of one zygote. We call the twins "identical" and, for years, textbooks have taught that their genes are exactly the same, all along the genome. But this just in . . .

"Identical" twins are not always genetically identical after all. They are extremely similar; their genomes overlap enormously. Yet they aren't necessarily identical, and the differences can be significant.

Initial evidence of genetic variation in MZ twins came from a study of 19 MZ twin pairs (Bruder et al., 2008). When analyzing their genomes, researchers noticed differences; twins sometimes differed in the number of copies of a given gene that they possessed. Thanks to fluctuating biochemical processes occurring inside cells, sometimes one twin would be missing a gene, or have two or more copies of a gene, instead of having one copy of the gene like his or her co-twin. In the case of one twin pair, a twin was missing genes that put him at risk of leukemia, a disease he had contracted (Casselman, 2008). His twin, who was not missing the gene, did not develop the disease. Thus, the identical twins differed in the presence of the disease due to variations in genetics—despite the fact that they were "identical" twins!

Another study examined the genetic makeup of identical twins who varied in schizophrenia, that is, one had the mental disorder and the other did not. Again, the identical twins differed genetically, which might explain the difference in their schizophrenic symptoms (Maiti et al., 2011).

These new findings have big implications for the study of nature and nurture. In the past, when identical twins have differed in their behavior, emotion, or patterns of thinking, researchers have attributed the differences to nurture. Because the twins were identical biologically, scientists reasoned, differences between them must be due to environmental experience. But now, scientists know that, in at least some cases, behavioral differences between identical twins can be caused by differences in genetics.

Does this remind you of HM, HT1, and HT2, from our opening story? HM differed from his "genetically identical" brothers. It's possible that he was not, in fact, genetically identical!

🌀 WHAT DO YOU KNOW?...

10. When MZ twins do differ genetically, it is because one twin may differ from the other in the number of copies of a _____ he or she possesses.

TRY THIS!

It is now time to switch from reading about psychology research to experiencing it. Go to www.pmbpsychology.com to find the Try This! activity for Chapter 4, where you will be asked to solve some problems. As you try them, ask yourself what these problems might have to do with the topic of this chapter, nature and nurture. We will discuss the activity later on in this chapter. ◉

Evolution and Psychology

From your perspective, the combining of genes from your mother and father at the moment of your conception is the start of a story. But from your genes' perspective, it's only the latest page in a story that began long ago. Your genes are the product of **evolution,** the biological process through which species develop and change across generations.

Let's look at how evolution works. Then we'll explore the implications of evolutionary processes for psychology.

Natural Selection

Preview Question

> How do characteristics—psychological and otherwise—evolve?

The great British biologist Charles Darwin had a simple idea. When it came to questions of evolution, Darwin said, Earth was like a giant, long-running livestock farm (Wright, 1978). On an actual farm, farmers select animals for breeding. If, for example, they want cattle that are large, they select the largest cattle currently on the farm and allow them to mate. In the next generation, they do the same thing: Select the largest cattle, and allow *them* to mate. After a few generations of selection and mating, the farmer ends up with a population of cattle that are larger than the ones he originally owned. Across generations, the cattle evolve.

Evolution on a contemporary farm differs in one main way from evolutionary processes that occurred on Earth millions of years ago. Back then, there were no farmers; no individuals intentionally selected organisms for breeding. Instead, nature—that is, features of the natural environment—did the selection.

As Darwin explained, in any naturally occurring environment some of an organism's features are more *adaptive* than others—that is, the features help the organism survive and reproduce in that environment. A long neck is adaptive if the environment contains food hanging on branches of tall trees. Bright feathers are adaptive if they attract mates. Across generations, features that are adaptive become more frequent; the reproducing organisms pass them down to their offspring via genetic inheritance. Just as large cattle became more common across generations on the farm environment, long-necked or brightly colored organisms (in our example) became more common

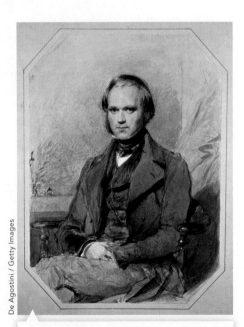

De Agostini / Getty Images

Charles Darwin in 1840, not long after he first formulated the principle of evolution through natural selection.

evolution The biological process through which species develop and change across generations.

across generations in certain natural environments. Through this simple process, species evolve.

When you examine evolved species in their natural habitats, it often seems as if they had been "designed" to fit the environment. However—and this point is key to Darwin's explanation of how species evolve—there is no "designer" (Dennett, 1995). There merely is nature itself. **Natural selection** is the process by which, across generations, features of a population of organisms change, depending on whether those features are adaptive in a given environment.

EVOLVED MECHANISMS. The long-term goal of any organism is survival and reproduction. To achieve that goal, organisms have to overcome many short-term obstacles: avoiding a predator, recovering from an injury, detecting a food source, and so forth. Because organisms face specific problems, evolutionary processes tend to equip them with problem-specific **evolved mechanisms,** that is, inherited biological subsystems that evolved due to their success in solving a specific problem faced repeatedly during the evolution of a species.

An example of a biological evolved mechanism is calluses (DeKay & Buss, 1992). Repeated friction on your hands or feet causes calluses to develop. You don't have to learn to produce calluses; the callus-producing mechanism is "built in" as part of your evolutionary heritage. This evolved mechanism must have been advantageous over the course of evolution, enabling people, for example, to work longer hours on manual tasks without injuring their hands.

Note, however, that this evolved mechanism does not, by itself, cause you to break out in calluses. If you lead a life of leisure, with no manual labor, your hands won't have any calluses at all. Calluses only develop in a specific circumstance, namely, one in which you repeatedly experience friction on the skin. Thus, the observed characteristic (the callus) results from a *combination* of nature (the evolved mechanism) and nurture (the activity that causes the friction on the skin that activates the callus-producing mechanism).

PROXIMAL AND DISTAL CAUSES. The example of calluses highlights another aspect of evolution-based explanations: the distinction between *proximal* and *distal* causes. In an evolutionary analysis, **proximal causes** are events and mechanisms that are present at the time an organism reacts to the environment, whereas **distal causes** are factors in the distant past that caused a biological mechanism to evolve.

The question "Why did you get that callus?" has two types of answers. One is proximal: Your skin cells reacted to friction on your skin. The other is distal: Across millions of years of primate evolution, organisms that could form calluses were better adapted to their environments, causing the callus-producing mechanism to evolve.

Jose Luis Pelaez / Getty Images

Proximal and distal causes What caused this person's skin to tan? The proximal cause is that she recently was sitting out in the sun. The distal cause is that, as a result of evolution, her skin contains a tanning mechanism; this evolved mechanism was beneficial to humans because it protected against the harmful effects of overexposure to sunlight.

> **natural selection** The process whereby features of a population of organisms change, across generations, depending on the degree to which those features are adaptive (i.e., help organisms to survive and reproduce in a given environment).

> **evolved mechanisms** Biological systems that developed over the course of evolution, thanks to their success in solving a specific problem faced repeatedly by members of a given species.

> **proximal causes** In an evolutionary analysis, events and mechanisms in the present environment that determine an organism's responses.

> **distal causes** In an evolutionary analysis, factors in the distant past that caused a biological mechanism to evolve.

WHAT DO YOU KNOW?...

11. Explain why sweating is an evolved mechanism, making sure to note what problem we repeatedly faced in the past that it solved. Describe how sweating, like calluses, results from a combination of nature and nurture.

Evolutionary Psychology

Preview Questions

› According to evolutionary psychologists, how did the mind evolve to produce our contemporary mental abilities, desires, and preferences?

› What are three limitations of evolutionary explanations of the modern mind?

CONNECTING TO PROBLEM SOLVING AND PERSONALITY

P
PERSON
Chapter 13: The study of personality may be informed by evolutionary principles.

M
MIND
Chapter 8: Evolutionary principles are related to a specific mental ability: problem solving.

B
BRAIN
Here, we see how, in general, evolution shaped the modern human brain and mental abilities.

PMB CONNECTIONS

Principles of evolution are important not only to biology, but also to psychology. Many of the problems faced in the evolutionary past were psychological in nature. To hunt animals or build shelters, people had to organize themselves into coordinated teams. To get help from others when sick or injured, they had to establish social bonds with the people who could provide the help. To reproduce, they had to attract mates. To avoid losing offspring, they needed to be effective parents. The ability to interact socially with others, therefore, was critical to survival and reproduction.

This suggests that evolutionary pressures shaped not only physical characteristics, but also mental ones. People with mental abilities that were adaptive—who could organize groups, establish friendships, attract mates, and parent effectively—were more likely to survive, reproduce, and have offspring who survived and reproduced. These mental abilities, then, were shaped by evolution.

This insight has given rise to a subfield of psychology known as **evolutionary psychology,** in which researchers explore the evolutionary foundations of contemporary human mental abilities, preferences, and desires (Buss, 1991; Caporeal, 2001).

All evolutionary psychologists agree that Darwinian natural selection produced the contemporary human mind that we possess today. But they do not all agree on the exact nature of that mind and the exact role of evolution in shaping it. Let's now turn to two views of evolution and psychology. The first is the *inherited mental modules* perspective.

INHERITED MENTAL MODULES. One popular view is that, thanks to evolution, the human mind consists of numerous *mental modules*. A **mental module** is a subsystem of the mind and nervous system that performs a specific task in response to a specific type of environmental input (Fodor, 1983). The retina, at the back of the eye, is an example. It performs one task and one task only: responding to light that enters the eye. It won't respond to sound. It can't tell if it's warm or cold. Because it is specialized to become active only in response to a specific type of input (light), it is considered modular. All psychologists agree that evolutionary processes created the modular mechanism that is the retina.

Some evolutionary psychologists propose that, over the course of evolution, the human mind acquired a large number of additional modules, each of which, like the retina, responds to a type of environmental input faced repeatedly by our evolutionary ancestors (Buss, 1991; Pinker, 1997). Consider a few examples throughout evolution:

> People had to be effective parents. Thus, a module for parenting could have evolved.

> People had to attract mates. Thus, a mate-attraction module could have evolved.

> People had to avoid being cheated when exchanging goods (e.g., trading products in a marketplace). Thus, a cheating-detection module could have evolved (Cosmides, 1989; also see Chapter 8).

The list could go on and on. There could be hundreds of such modules, each of which evolved hundreds of thousands of years ago.

evolutionary psychology Field of study that explores the evolutionary foundations of contemporary human mental abilities, preferences, and desires.

mental module A proposed subsystem of the mind and nervous system that performs a specific task in response to a specific type of environmental input.

Earlier, in our Try This! activity, you attempted to solve two kinds of problems. (If you didn't, go to www.pmbpsychology.com and try them now.) You probably found one of them to be difficult—the problem involving a clerical job and the categorizing of documents. The other problem, involving a crackdown against underage drinking, was relatively easy.

Why was one problem easier than the other? In their basic structure, the problems were identical: They both presented a rule to be tested ("If a person has a D rating, then his documents must be marked Code 3"; "If a person is drinking beer, then he or she must be over 20 years old") and four cards to turn over to see whether the rule was broken.

The psychologist Leda Cosmides (1989; Cosmides & Tooby, 2013) explains that the underage drinking problem was easy because of human's evolved biological nature. Throughout evolution, people exchanged goods: food, drink, livestock, and so forth. The goods were necessary to survival, so it was important not to be cheated out of them. People who were able to detect cheating attempts were more likely to retain their goods, survive, and reproduce. Through natural selection, therefore, a mental module to detect cheating evolved. The underage drinking problem activated this mental module because it contained a case of potential cheating (underage drinking). The module, in turn, made problem solving easy.

The clerical problem, on the other hand, did *not* activate an evolved mental module. Over the course of evolution, our ancient ancestors did not spend any time filing documents; thus, there is no "document-filing module" in the human brain to activate. With no specialized mental module to help you, the clerical problem was more difficult—despite its having the same overall structure as the underage drinking problem. The different types of problems thus reveal the role of nature in the structure and functioning of the human mind.

According to evolutionary psychologists, mental modules solve problems by producing preferences. Preferences that evolved in the evolutionary past shape your present likes and dislikes. For instance, why do you like pie, cake, and milkshakes when they can make you fat? During periods of evolutionary history when food was scarce, it was adaptive for humans to prefer high-calorie foods; those who didn't like those foods were more likely to starve. Today, we inherit that ancient preference. Why do homeowners spend time and money planting flowers and arranging backyard garden landscapes, when they could spend those resources on food and clothing for themselves? Throughout evolutionary history, flowers indicated that food was near. People who were attracted to flowers encountered more food and were more likely to survive and reproduce. Today, we inherit the evolved liking of flowers (Joye, 2007).

In this view, mental modules are specified in your genes (Lickliter & Honeycutt, 2003). Just as genes contain information to build body parts such as a heart and lungs, they contain information used to build neural systems that correspond to each mental module. These genetically specified mental modules are thought to be universal, that is, possessed in basically the same way by humans everywhere (Tooby & Cosmides, 2005). Just as people around the world have the same bodily organs, they have the same "mental organs" (Pinker, 1997).

This viewpoint makes a startling claim. Thoughts and preferences that you think you learned from modern society are, in reality, inherited—"wired in" by evolutionary processes that occurred hundreds of thousands of years ago. Here are two examples.

When men evaluate the physical attractiveness of female figures, they rate "curvy" figures with a low waist-to-hip ratio (relatively thin waist and wide hips) as more attractive (Singh, 1993). Are these preferences learned through social experience? Evolutionary psychology says no; they instead are inherited due to evolution. Throughout evolutionary history, wide hips signaled that a woman possessed body fat that could be used as energy during pregnancy. Preferring wide hips thus was adaptive

TRY THIS!

Lisa Romerein / Getty Images

Bouquet for Mom $200

Sure, Mom's great, but $200 flowers? Why do people spend money—funds they could use for necessities of life, such as clothes and food—on flowers? Our tendency to like flowers may be a product of our species' evolutionary past, when the presence of flowers in natural environments was associated with the presence of food sources.

Does it give you comfort to know that your preference for high-calorie foods is shaped by evolution?

THINK ABOUT IT

Evolutionary psychologists claim that contemporary humans have a "stone age mind" (Cosmides & Tooby, 1997) that was adapted to the environment experienced hundreds of thousands of years ago, when people hunted animals and gathered food growing in the wild. Today, we live in a very different environment of supermarkets, mass transit, smart phones. . . . Humans are handling this environment quite well; we have longer life spans and higher standards of living than ever before (Morris, 2010). How come? If our minds really are adapted to a stone-age environment, why are we so good at using modern technology?

because it enhanced reproductive success. As a result, the evolutionary psychologist argues, contemporary men inherit a mental module that predisposes them to prefer a small waist-to-hip ratio (Singh, 1993).

An evolutionary psychologist (Buss, 1989) found that men and women differed in their desires for a mate (i.e., a serious romantic partner). Women emphasized wealth; men's financial resources, as reflected in job status or the ability to pay for dinner at a nice restaurant, were important to them. Men emphasized looks; they were attracted mostly to women's physical attributes. Evolutionary psychology claims these preferences are not learned, but inherited (Buss, 1989). Throughout evolution, women have borne the physical burden of pregnancy. It was adaptive for them to seek men with status and resources, who could provide food and shelter during pregnancy and after childbirth. Men, in contrast, were free from the physical burdens of pregnancy and thus had less need for mates who could take care of them. Men's preference for young, fit women also is said to have an evolutionary basis, because women who are young and fit

> Does this sex difference in mate preferences characterize you and your friends?

are more likely to have a successful pregnancy (Buss, 1989). Men who preferred such women thus would have more offspring, and future generations of men would inherit the preference.

Who's paying the bill? Evolutionary psychologists believe that men inherit a tendency to pay the dinner bill because, throughout the course of evolution, displaying resources (status, money, etc.) was a good way to attract potential mates.

THE INHERITED-MODULES HYPOTHESIS: THREE LIMITATIONS. The inherited-mental-modules approach to evolutionary psychology has been promoted with extraordinary zeal in recent decades. Proponents have touted it as not only "a new paradigm for psychology science" (Buss, 1995, p. 1), but also potentially "a fundamental advance for our species" that would benefit from "a true, natural science of humanity" (Tooby & Cosmides, 2005, p. 63). The idea has had great impact in not only psychology, but also society at large. "I seemed to encounter it everywhere I turned," one writer reports:

> During almost every wait in the supermarket checkout line, I would find reference to the evolutionary psychology of human mating on the covers of . . . magazines. [In newspapers] I would often find articles . . . about the evolutionary psychology of mating, parent–child relationships, or status seeking. And it seemed to be all over television, and not just on "high-brow" channels like PBS.

> —Buller (2005, p. 3)

A main proponent of the mental-modules perspective, Harvard University psychologist Steven Pinker is one of the few psychologists to appear on *TIME* magazine's annual list of the most influential people in the world (Wright, 2004).

Acclaim, however, does not imply correctness. In recent years, many scientists have questioned evolutionary psychologists' claims (e.g., Heyes, 2012). No one doubts the significance of evolution to human behavior, yet the exact ways in which evolution did, or did not, shape contemporary humans' abilities and preferences is a point of debate. Three factors raise questions about the inherited-modules perspective:

1. *Subsequent research findings failed to confirm some original findings.* Sometimes attractiveness is *un*related to waist-to-hip ratio, in contrast to evolutionary-psychology explanations. Men's judgments of attractiveness are more affected by

women's overall weight than by the ratio of waist size to hip size (Tassinary & Hansen, 1998). Sometimes men and women do *not* differ very much in their mate preferences. In nations where the gender difference in personal income is relatively small, the gender difference in mate preference is relatively small, too (Eagly & Wood, 1999). This implies that women may prefer men with wealth not merely because of factors in the evolutionary past but due to factors in the contemporary present: Being economically disadvantaged, they need more financial support.

2. *The mind cannot consist merely of mental modules.* Even if the mind contains modules that solve specific problems, it has to contain *more than* just those modules (Dehaene & Naccache, 2001; Mithen, 1996). Suppose a single parent is deciding, one evening, whether to spend time with her child or call a babysitter to go on a date. Even if her mind contains a module devoted to dating problems and another module devoted to parenting problems, it must contain something more: a general-purpose-thinking system that can combine information about parenting and dating, weigh one against the other, and make a decision. Researchers studying the mind recognize that mental modules are, at best, only a subset of the overall mechanisms of the mind (Dehaene & Naccache, 2001).

3. *Genes don't, by themselves, determine the nature of an organism.* This third point is one you've already learned. Organisms—including people—develop through dynamic interactions between nature and nurture. Genetic information by itself does not produce an organism, as you saw in our coverage of epigenetics. Many scholars (e.g., Elman et al., 1996; Fodor & Piatelli-Palmarini, 2010; Lewontin, 2000; Lickliter & Honeycutt, 2013) question the inherited-modules hypothesis because it overestimates the role of inheritance and underestimates interactions between biology and the environment, that is, between nature and nurture.

These three limitations are significant, suggesting that an alternative perspective—a refashioned evolutionary psychology—may be needed. To meet this need, researchers have introduced "new thinking" (Heyes, 2012, p. 2091) into evolutionary psychology. Two thoughts are central to these advances. One is that evolution has produced not only mental modules that solve specific problems, but also "general-purpose" mechanisms that help solve a wide variety of problems. Just as your hand is a general-purpose physical tool—that is, a tool you use on an enormous variety of tasks—some elements of the mind are general-purpose mental tools (Heyes, 2012). Consider the mental ability to learn new skills by observing others (see Chapter 7). It is general-purpose, not problem-specific; you can learn to solve an unlimited variety of problems (fixing a household appliance; changing a baby's diaper; fitting in at a social event) by observing others.

The second idea is one we have discussed earlier in this chapter, namely, that inheritance and experience *combine* to shape the brain and mind of the individual (Caporeal, 2001; Heyes, 2003, 2012). Increasingly, psychological scientists recognize that psychological abilities are not all "wired in" by evolution. Instead, they develop gradually as people interact with the environment (Karmiloff-Smith, 2009).

Ineke Oostveen

The nations of the world differ in gender equality, that is, the degree to which men and women are equal in financial and social power. Contrary to the predictions of evolutionary psychology, preferences in mate selection vary in countries with varying degrees of gender equality. An example of such a country is the Netherlands, which leads the world in gender equality according to a United Nations survey (United Nations Development Programme, 2012). Illustrating this equality is Pauline van der Meer Mohr, a former senior executive in banking and now president of the Executive Board of Erasmus University Rotterdam, in the Netherlands.

🌐 WHAT DO YOU KNOW?...

12. True or False?

   a. An example of a mental module is our preference for fatty foods.

   b. Evolutionary psychologists assume mental modules are universal.

   c. According to the text, in explaining behavior, a strength of the inherited-modules perspective is that it carefully addresses the interactions between nature and nurture.

⊙ CULTURAL OPPORTUNITIES

Nature, Nurture, and Cultural Beliefs

The cultures of the world differ. Some differences, such as varying languages, clothing, and food, are obvious. Another variation, however, is more subtle: Cultures differ in their beliefs about the relation between individuals and society. *Individualistic* cultures promote the importance of individual rights. They value the needs of the individual over those of society and allow people to express themselves freely, even if their self-expressions might seem odd to others. *Collectivistic* cultures, by contrast, highlight the rights of groups: families, societies, nations. They promote the belief that the individual's primary responsibility is to promote group welfare, and they foster conformity to traditional group practices. The culture of the United States is commonly seen as individualistic, whereas cultural patterns in Japan are a classic case of collectivism (Kitayama & Markus, 1999).

Where do these cultural variations come from? Is it just random chance that some parts of the world end up with individualistic cultures and others are collectivistic, or is there a systematic cause?

Evidence indicates that cultural variations in individualism–collectivism arose through the process emphasized throughout this chapter: the interaction between nature and nurture. When presented with a biological challenge (a challenge in nature), societies respond by adapting culturally (an adaptation in nurturing).

One example of culture adapting to biology involves pathogens (germs that make people sick). Some cultural practices shield people against pathogens and illness. In particular, collectivist cultures prompt people to bond closely with their own group and avoid contact with outsiders, thereby avoiding foreign germs (Fincher et al., 2008). This suggests an interesting hypothesis: Groups that encounter higher levels of biological pathogens should be more likely to adopt collectivistic cultural practices, to protect themselves from the germs. Correlational research confirms the hypothesis. When measures are taken in different parts of the globe, regions with higher levels of biological pathogens are found to have higher levels of collectivist beliefs (Figure 4.9; Fincher et al., 2008).

A second example of biology shaping culture involves depression. Collectivist cultures promote social harmony—getting along with others—and, in so doing, reduce everyday levels of stress (Chiao & Blizinsky, 2010). Stress, in turn, can trigger bouts of depression; as we've seen, this is particularly true among people who are genetically predisposed to become depressed in stressful environments. This idea, too, suggests an interesting hypothesis: Genes that promote stress and collectivism should be positively correlated. A population with a high level of depression-inducing genes should be more likely to embrace collectivist beliefs that protect against depression. Again, this is exactly what researchers have found (Figure 4.10 on the facing page; Chiao & Blizinsky, 2010).

This research shows how biology could shape culture. But the route from biology to culture is a two-way street: Cultural practices also shape biology. This is particularly true for cultural practices involving marriage, as shown by research on three populations in the Caucasus region (Marchani et al., 2008). The Caucasus Mountains, which bridge Europe and Asia, have been home to multiple flows of immigration throughout human history. The genetic makeup of twenty-first-century residents thus may combine material from diverse immigrant groups of the past.

figure **4.9**
Pathogens and culture Research on pathogens and cultural beliefs demonstrates one type of relation between biology and culture. Areas of the world with higher levels of biological pathogens are more likely to have collectivist social beliefs, which can encourage people to bond closely with their own group, avoid outsiders, and thus avoid picking up foreign germs (Fincher et al., 2008).

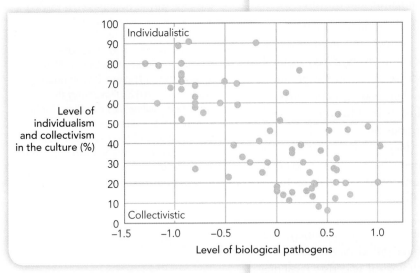

In the research, investigators measured *genetic diversity,* the degree of variation in the genome among members of a given population, within each of three cultural groups in the Caucasus. Because all three groups had been living, for generation upon generation, in the same general area of the world, you might expect them to have roughly the same degree of genetic diversity. But, instead, one group displayed much *less* genetic variability than the others. Why? The cause was culture. Historically, the group with less genetic diversity had adopted two distinctive cultural practices: (1) Group members were encouraged to marry only members of their own local group; and (2) married couples lived with the husband's parents, which reduces people's tendency to stray from home. Thanks to these cultural practices, this group had less social contact, and thus less sexual mixing, with the various immigrant groups that had passed through their area of the world. As a result, they are less genetically diverse today (Marchani et al., 2008).

The lesson from the Caucasus is that not only do genes contribute to variations in culture, but culture contributes to variation in the human genome.

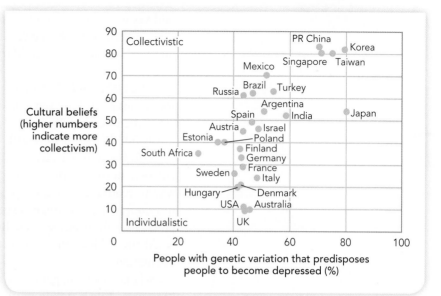

figure 4.10
Genetic variability and culture
Cultures vary in the percentage of people who possess a genetic variation that predisposes individuals to depression. As shown, cultures in which this genetic variation is common have more collectivist beliefs. These beliefs promote social harmony which, in turn, can help reduce stress and depression (Chiao & Blizinsky, 2010).

🔰 WHAT DO YOU KNOW?...

13. How can an increase in pathogens shape collectivist cultural practices?

Nature, Nurture, and Diversity: The Case of Sexual Orientation

Preview Questions

> Can evolutionary theory explain homosexuality?
> What does research suggest concerning the genetic basis of homosexuality?

In the course of evolution, the "bottom-line" marker of success is reproduction. If members of a species fail to reproduce, the species dies out. You might expect, then, that evolution would have produced a desire to engage in sexual activity that is universal—shared by all human adults.

But that's not what happened. Instead, people exhibit different **sexual orientations,** the primary form of a person's sexual and romantic attraction. People with a *heterosexual* orientation are attracted to members of the opposite sex, those with a *homosexual* orientation are attracted to members of their same sex, and *bisexual* individuals are attracted to both men and women.

This three-part classification, however, does not capture the full range of variation in sexual orientation. For example, a recent study found many women who reported being "mostly" heterosexual: attracted to men romantically and sexually, but experiencing some degree of sexual attraction to women as well (Thompson & Morgan, 2008).

Surveys (e.g., Kinsey, Pomeroy, & Martin, 1948) provide estimates of how common the different sexual orientations are. It's difficult to specify precise numbers, however, because survey responses vary depending on the exact question asked. In surveys in the United States and the United Kingdom, about 1.5% of men reported same-sex sexual activity within the past year. But a larger number (greater than 6%)

sexual orientation A person's primary form of sexual and romantic attachment, whether to the opposite sex (heterosexual), the same sex (homosexual), or both (bisexual).

said yes when survey items asked men if they had ever had same-sex activity at any time in their lives. Women's rates of homosexuality in these surveys were lower than men's (Dawood, Bailey, & Martin, 2009).

EVOLUTION AND SEXUAL ORIENTATION. Although these numbers may sound small, in some ways they are big. If the 6% estimate is correct for the world at large, then nearly 300 million people have engaged in same-sex activity (there being nearly 5 billion adults overall).

This big number raises a big challenge for evolutionary theory. Homosexual orientation impairs reproduction because, of course, heterosexual pairing is the only way to reproduce. Because people who are exclusively homosexual do not leave behind offspring, you might expect that evolution would have eliminated homosexual preferences from our species. But that hasn't happened, as nearly 300 million people could attest. How, then, can evolutionary theory explain the existence of homosexual orientation?

Scholars have suggested a range of answers to this question (Bailey & Zuk, 2009). One interesting possibility is that some genes have different effects in men and women. In men, they increase the likelihood of homosexuality. In women, the same genes increase the likelihood of childbirth; that is, they boost women's biological capacity to have offspring. Initial evidence supporting this possibility came from a study in Italy (Camperio-Ciani, Corna, & Capiluppi, 2004). Homosexual and heterosexual men filled out surveys indicating the number of children borne by women in their family (their mother, aunts, etc.). Female relatives of homosexual men were found to have more children, on average, than relatives of heterosexual men. A follow-up study yielded the same result: larger numbers of children among women who are relatives of homosexual men (Iemmola & Camperio-Ciani, 2009).

This result can explain how homosexuality may have evolved. The explanation is that homosexuality *per se* did not evolve. Instead, what evolved is a particular gene that, for human reproduction, has both benefits and costs. The benefit is that it increases childbearing among many women; the cost is that it reduces reproduction among some men (those who are homosexual). In the course of evolution, the benefits outweighed the costs.

The large size of gay rights rallies is a reminder that large numbers of men and women are homosexual, despite the fact that homosexual orientation may be disadvantageous from an evolutionary perspective.

AP Photo / Darryl Bush

GENETICS AND INDIVIDUAL DIFFERENCES IN SEXUAL ORIENTATION. Another source of evidence about the roots of sexual orientation is one discussed earlier in this chapter: twin studies. Researchers compare MZ to DZ twins to determine whether genetic factors contribute to individual differences in sexual orientation.

You learned earlier that genetics influences a wide range of psychological tendencies. Sexual orientation is no exception. MZ twin pairs are more similar in sexual orientation than are DZ twin pairs. In one study that focused on twins and homosexuality, researchers recruited homosexual research participants who had a twin and then determined the sexual orientation of the other member of the twin pair. Among women, 48% of MZ co-twins were homosexual or bisexual, compared with 16% for DZ twins. Likewise, among men, the MZ percentage of 52% was higher than that among DZ twins, 22% (Dawood, Bailey, & Martin, 2009).

A study of thousands of twins in Sweden similarly indicated a role for genetics (Långström et al., 2010). By comparing MZ to DZ twins, researchers found that genetics explains slightly more than one-third of the overall variability in sexual orientation. Shared environmental factors—having the same parents, the same socioeconomic status (SES), living in the same neighborhood—had no effect at all.

Genetic effects thus are significant to sexual orientation. But one-third of the variance—the finding in the Swedish study—still leaves two-thirds of the variability in sexual orientation *un*explained. What other factors could be influential? Research has uncovered a surprising possibility, as you'll see next.

> Is this information about homosexuality consistent with your opinions and beliefs?

PRENATAL ENVIRONMENT AND SEXUAL ORIENTATION. When people discuss nature and nurture, they usually compare genetic influences (nature) to environmental influences that people experience after they are born (nurture). There's something else to consider, though: the **prenatal environment,** that is, the biological environment experienced *before* a person is born. Findings indicate that prenatal factors influence sexual orientation.

One clue to this influence is that men with larger numbers of older brothers are more likely to be homosexual. Each older brother increases the odds of homosexuality by about 33% (e.g., a .06 chance would rise to .08; Dawood et al., 2009). You might expect the increase to be caused by nurture, not nature; maybe spending time with older male siblings increases attraction to males. But research reveals something else: an impact of the prenatal environment. Key evidence comes from studies of adopted children (Bogaert, 2006). To see their value to research, imagine two types of male children who experience the following environments:

1. No biological older siblings, but adopted into a household with older siblings
2. One or more older biological brothers, but adopted and not raised with them

Findings show that children of the second, but not the first, type are more likely to be homosexual. Having older siblings increases rates of homosexuality even if siblings are not raised together (Bogaert, 2006). How can this be? One explanation is *maternal immune response* (Bogaert, 2006). The maternal, female immune system recognizes a male child as biologically "foreign" and produces antibodies. With more male children, there are more antibodies, which may affect fetal brain development in a way that influences sexual orientation.

Additional evidence that the prenatal environment influences sexual orientation comes from an unlikely source: finger length. The link between finger length and sexual orientation involves hormones called *androgens* (*hormones* are biochemicals that travel through the body and influence bodily organs; see Chapter 3). In the prenatal environment, androgens stimulate the development of male sexual characteristics and

prenatal environment The biological environment experienced before a person is born.

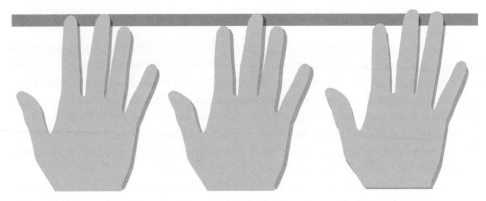

High 2D:4D
Index finger longer
than ring finger

Equal 2D:4D
Index and ring fingers
of equal length

Low 2D:4D
Index finger shorter
than ring finger

figure **4.11**
2D:4D ratio How long is your second digit compared to your fourth? Some research suggests that the 2D:4D ratio is related to sexual orientation.

also affect the development of the hand (Hines, 2010). Men and women thus differ in relative finger length as follows:

> Among men, the fourth digit of the hand (the ring finger) tends to be longer than the second digit (the index or pointer finger); in other words, men's **2D:4D ratio**— the length of the second digit divided by that of the fourth digit—tends to be low.

> Among women, whose androgen levels are lower, the second digit tends to be as long as or longer than the fourth; women tend to have a high 2D:4D ratio (Figure 4.11).

The effect of androgens on both sexual characteristics and finger length leads to an interesting hypothesis: 2D:4D ratio may predict sexual orientation. To test it, researchers conducted a meta-analysis of studies involving thousands of people in Europe and North America (Grimbos et al. 2010). They found that women with a higher (more typically female) 2D:4D ratio were more likely to be heterosexual. Among men, 2D:4D ratio and sexual orientation were not linked in this study. However, research in Japan has not only confirmed the relation between 2D:4D ratio and sexual orientation among women, it has also provided evidence of a link among men (Hiraishi et al., 2012). Overall, findings to date indicate that the "nature and nurture" of sexual orientation may include a causal factor beyond genetics and the social environment: androgens in the biological environment in which the fetus develops.

2D:4D ratio A relation between two finger lengths (the second and fourth digit of the hand) that is related to variations in sexual orientation.

> ### 🐦 WHAT DO YOU KNOW?...
>
> 14. True or False?
>   a. The gene that increases the probability of childbearing in women may increase the likelihood of homosexuality in men.
>   b. Twin studies suggest that genes account for a majority of the overall variability in sexual orientation.
>   c. Men who have a large number of older brothers are more likely to be homosexual.
>   d. Research suggests that maternal immune response, a feature of the prenatal environment, may play a role in shaping sexual orientation.

Nature, Nurture, and the Brain

Thus far in this chapter, we've primarily focused on two of the three levels of analysis in psychology: the person and the mind (see Chapter 1). You first saw how nature and nurture affect qualities of people, such as their intelligence, personality, social attitudes, and experience of psychological disorders. You then saw two analyses of mind: "mental-modules" evolutionary psychology and "new thinking" in evolutionary psychology, which emphasizes that the mind contains flexible, general-purpose mental systems. Let's now move to the third level of analysis, that of the brain.

Genes and Brain Structure

Preview Question

> How do genes shape brain development?

You have a human brain because you have human genes. The brain, like other structures of the body, requires the genetic code of DNA for its development. Yet the story of how the brain develops is not a story of genes alone. A little bit of counting shows why.

The total number of genes in the human genome is surprisingly small: not millions of genes, but about 25,000 of them (Pennisi, 2005). The total number of neural interconnections in the brain is astronomically large: not millions or even billions of connections, but *trillions* of them. The human brain contains about 100 billion neurons, and a typical neuron might connect to a thousand other neurons (Penn & Shatz, 1999), resulting in trillions of points at which one brain cell signals another.

Now compare the numbers. Genes can't possibly determine exactly which neurons connect to which other neurons; there isn't enough information in the genetic code. The big puzzle in the study of nature, nurture, and the brain is the question of how the brain gets "wired up." What determines which neurons connect to which other ones, forming the network of brain communications that enable us to think and feel?

Genes are key to the first stage of the brain's wiring process. Genetic information causes neurons to connect from one general region of the brain to another; for example, from a region that receives information from the eyes to a region in the rear of the brain that processes visual information. However, these region-to-region connections are not precise enough for the brain to function properly (Penn & Shatz, 1999). The brain requires a second step of development in which the exact neuron-to-neuron connections are formed. This second step requires experience.

✎ WHAT DO YOU KNOW?...

15. Why can't genes entirely determine which neurons connect with which other neurons?

Environmental Experience and Brain Structure

Preview Question

> How does environmental experience shape brain development?

The brain needs stimulation from the outside world. Experience—interactions between the person and the external environment—is necessary for its proper development (Zhang & Poo, 2001). But exactly how does external experience affect the inner workings of the brain? There are two types of effects; environmental stimulation influences (1) connections among brain cells and (2) genes.

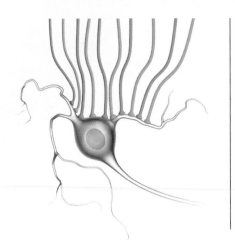
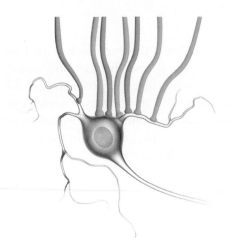
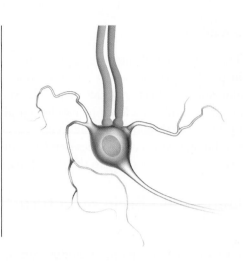

figure **4.12**
Neural pruning The images show neural connections within the visual system of a mammalian brain soon after birth (top), after a few days of visual experience (middle), and later in life, after a large amount of visual experience (bottom). With experience, neural pruning occurs; connections are fewer in number, which makes the neural system as a whole more efficient.

EXPERIENCE AND CONNECTIONS AMONG BRAIN CELLS. Environmental stimulation activates neurons, the cells of the brain. This activation alters the way in which neurons connect to one another. The principle guiding the development of these connections is expressed in a simple phrase: "Neurons that fire together, wire together" (Edelman & Tononi, 2000, p. 83). When environmental stimulation causes a group of neurons to fire at the same time, the interconnections among those neurons grow stronger.

What about neurons that don't fire together? Their connections grow *weaker*. The brain "prunes" connections among brain cells that are not needed (Ruthazer & Aizenman, 2010); through **neural pruning,** unneeded connections among brain cells are eliminated. (The process is called "pruning" because it's similar to how a gardener might prune away unwanted branches of a plant.) By strengthening connections that are used as the organism interacts with the environment, and by pruning away connections that are not used, the brain adapts to the environment (Schwartz, Schohl, & Ruthazer, 2011). Brain connections, then, are not fully specified in the genes. They are sculpted through experience.

The process of neural pruning has a surprising implication. The time of your life at which you have the most interconnections among the cells of your brain is when you are born. With experience, unused connections are pruned away (Kanamori et al., 2013; Low & Cheng, 2006; Figure 4.12), leaving you with a brain that more effectively and efficiently processes information from the environments you experience frequently.

What happens when the developing brain is not sufficiently stimulated? Connections among brain cells do not form at a normal rate. As a result, a person's abilities to think and act are impaired. The brain *needs* environmental interaction to develop properly. Cases of childhood neglect show what happens if these interactions are lacking. Babies who spend most of their time by themselves in cribs, with little interaction with others, develop more slowly. They fail even to perform simple behaviors, such as sitting up and walking, in the same manner as children who experience more stimulating environments (Shatz, 1992).

What kind of environmental interaction do you suppose is optimal for proper development? Does television provide enough stimulation?

Experimental research confirms that the brain needs experience. Classic research explored the development of the brain's visual system, that is, the brain region that processes information coming into the brain through the eyes. Researchers performed a surgical procedure in which they closed one eyelid of a young monkey (Weisel, 1981), preventing the monkey from receiving normal environmental stimulation to that eye. A few months later, they surgically opened the eyelid. The eye itself was unharmed by this procedure, yet the monkey could not see out of the eye. Why not? Although the monkey's *eye* was biologically normal, its *brain* was not. Without environmental

neural pruning Elimination of connections among neurons that occurs when the connections are not needed for an organism's functioning.

stimulation, the region of the brain that processes signals from the eye did not get properly wired up. To develop properly, the brain needs to experience the world.

The brain's need for environmental experience also is evident in the development of a specific human visual ability, facial recognition. People are remarkably good at recognizing faces (see Chapter 5); for instance, you would recognize an old friend instantly, even if you had not seen him or her for years. In part, this ability is a product of evolved biological nature; over the course of evolution, the ability to distinguish friends and family from strangers was important to survival. Yet the ability also is shaped by nurture. For it to develop, a person must interact visually with the social world during infancy. People lacking these interactions do not develop normal face perception; in particular, they do not developed accurate "configural" facial perception, that is, perception of the relations among facial features (e.g., distance between eyes) that distinguish one face from another (Borjon & Ghazanfar, 2013; Maurere, Le Grand, & Mondloch, 2002).

Brain research confirms that environmental experience impacts the ability to perceive faces. Researchers recorded electrical activity in the brain while participants looked at images of four types: faces, houses, visually scrambled faces, and visually scrambled houses (Röder et al., 2013). The participants included groups whose visual experiences during infancy were either (1) normal or (2) disrupted due to cataracts (a medical condition that impairs vision) that were surgically corrected later in life. Brain activity in the groups differed. Among individuals with normal experience during infancy, brain activity in response to faces was distinctive, that is, it differed from activity when houses or scrambled faces were viewed. But among people whose visual experiences in infancy had been disrupted, brain activity in response to faces was *not* distinctive; their brains reacted in the same manner to faces as to houses (Figure 4.13). Early-life visual experience thus is necessary to later-life face recognition.

EXPERIENCE, GENE EXPRESSION, AND BRAIN DEVELOPMENT. Recent research reveals the biological steps through which experience influences the connections among brain cells. What do you think those steps might be? *Hint:* You learned about a key step earlier in this chapter.

Environmental experience affects neural connections by influencing *gene expression,* the process in which instructions encoded into DNA are put into action to produce proteins. As you learned, environmental experiences can determine when gene expression occurs; experiences can "switch on" genes. When the "switching on" occurs within brain cells, environmental experience can alter the cells' connections with one another. Let's see how this works in the brain's visual system.

Researchers have found that visual stimulation affects gene expression within brain cells that process visual information (Ruthazer & Aizenman, 2010). Thanks to powerful microscopes, you literally can see how this works. Look at the images in Figure 4.14 on page 155, which show the same brain cell before, and after, a mouse received visual stimulation. Stimulation from the environment affects the inner chemistry of the cell. When the eyes opened, this stimulated a key brain chemical that moved into the main body of the brain cell (the glowing part of the image on the right) and altered gene expression. The altered gene expression, in turn, contributes to the "pruning" of neural connections; connections that are not required for good vision are pruned away. As a result, the animal's vision improves (Schwartz et al., 2011).

Radius Images / Alamy

Explore the world, develop the brain Research shows that when babies interact with the world outside the crib, their brains develop more quickly.

🐸 WHAT DO YOU KNOW?...

16. The phrase "Neurons that fire together, _____ together" refers to the idea that when environmental experience causes neurons to fire simultaneously, their interconnections strengthen. Without sufficient environmental experience, neurons may be eliminated in a process called neural _____. Environmental experience influences brain development via _____ expression.

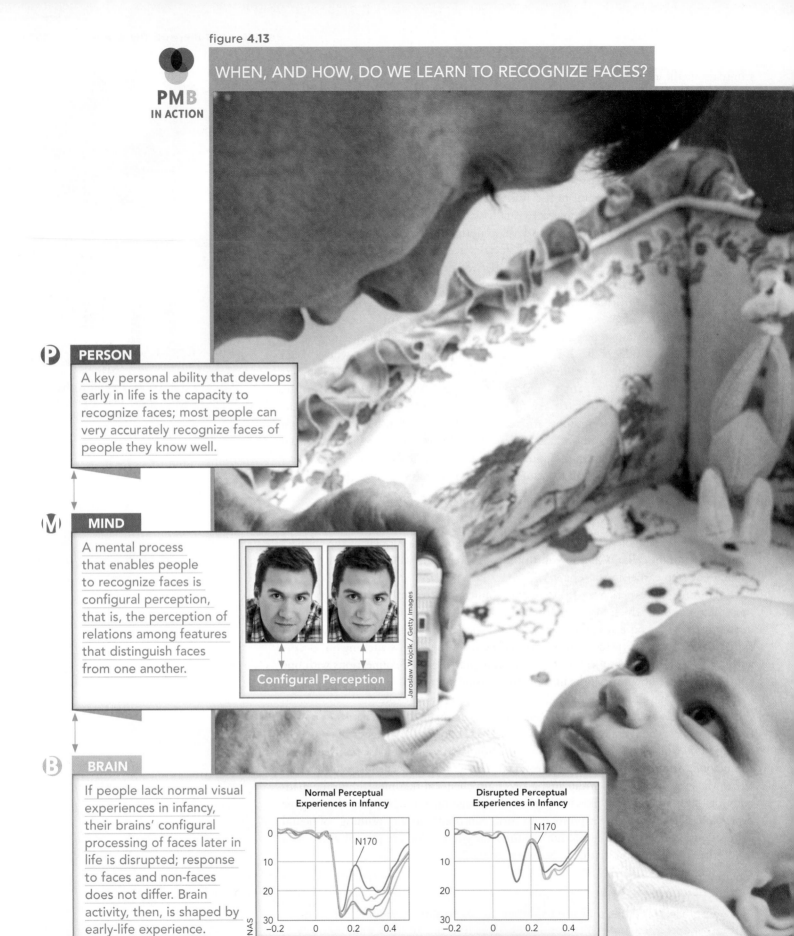

figure **4.13**

WHEN, AND HOW, DO WE LEARN TO RECOGNIZE FACES?

P **PERSON**

A key personal ability that develops early in life is the capacity to recognize faces; most people can very accurately recognize faces of people they know well.

M **MIND**

A mental process that enables people to recognize faces is configural perception, that is, the perception of relations among features that distinguish faces from one another.

Configural Perception

Jaroslaw Wojcik / Getty Images

B **BRAIN**

If people lack normal visual experiences in infancy, their brains' configural processing of faces later in life is disrupted; response to faces and non-faces does not differ. Brain activity, then, is shaped by early-life experience.

Normal Perceptual Experiences in Infancy

N170

Disrupted Perceptual Experiences in Infancy

N170

PNAS

Eric O'Connell / Gallery Stock

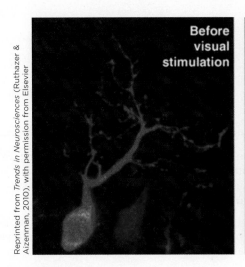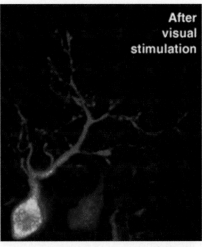

Reprinted from *Trends in Neurosciences* (Ruthazer & Aizenman, 2010), with permission from Elsevier

figure **4.14**
Experience, genes, and the brain
Microscopic images enable us to see how experience affects neurons. Visual stimulation altered the inner chemistry of the neuron shown here, as indicated by the glowing area in the image on the right.

⟲⟳ Looking Back and Looking Ahead

Our last topic—the story of visual stimulation, genes, and brain cells—illustrates a theme that you saw throughout this chapter: Biological and environmental factors interact. Research on (1) people and the social contexts in which they live, and on (2) genes, neurons, and the whole organism in which they function, leads to the same conclusion: Biology and the environment—nature and nurture—are not competing forces, fighting for control over an organism. They are partners. They need each other. This is the major lesson of contemporary research on nature and nurture.

You will see this lesson again and again in other chapters of this book, for example, as we explore the ways in which nature and nurture combine to shape emotional experience and health (Chapter 6), thinking processes (Chapter 9), personality (Chapter 13), psychological development (Chapter 14), and the experience of psychological disorders (Chapters 15 and 16).

Chapter Review

Now that you have completed this chapter, be sure to turn to Appendix B, where you will find a **Chapter Summary** that is useful for reviewing what you have learned about nature, nurture, and their interaction.

Key Terms

2D:4D ratio (p. 150)
alleles (p. 134)
behavior genetics (p. 127)
chromosomes (p. 134)
coevolution (p. 124)
deoxyribonucleic acid (DNA) (p. 134)
distal causes (p. 141)
dizygotic (DZ) twins (p. 122)
epigenetics (p. 136)

evolution (p. 140)
evolutionary psychology (p. 142)
evolved mechanisms (p. 141)
gene (p. 134)
gene expression (p. 135)
genome (p. 134)
heritability (p. 129)
Human Genome Project (p. 138)
mental module (p. 142)

molecular genetic methods (p. 137)
monozygotic (MZ) twins (p. 122)
natural selection (p. 141)
neural pruning (p. 152)
prenatal environment (p. 149)
proximal causes (p. 141)
sexual orientation (p. 147)
twin method (p. 128)

Chapter Review

Questions for Discussion

1. You learned that among people who possessed the allele that could have predisposed them for depression, only those who experienced many stressful life events developed suicidal thoughts and behaviors. That is, it was only in a particular kind of environment that gene expression took place; genes and environment interacted. Consider the possibility that genes and environment interact to produce variations in extraversion. Among those who possess the allele that predisposes them to be extraverted, what kinds of environments do you suppose would interact with those genes to cause people to be more or less extraverted? That is, in what contexts might the extraversion gene be more likely to get expressed? [Analyze]

2. It's obvious to us that physical characteristics such as height and hair color are genetically determined. But how might the environment influence the expression of the genes that produce these characteristics? Can you think of characteristics—physical or psychological—that could *not* be influenced by the environment? Can you think of characteristics—physical or psychological—that could *not* be influenced by genes? [Analyze]

3. What is your opinion of evolutionary psychologists' explanation of homosexuality (i.e., the idea that homosexuality per se didn't evolve, but that a gene evolved that is expressed differently in men and women. In women, it increases childbirth; in men, it increases the probability of homosexuality)? [Evaluate]

4. How would an evolutionary psychologist explain why we help one another? That is, how is helping behavior an adaptive feature that would enable an individual to survive and reproduce? [Analyze]

5. Knowing what you know about how environmental experiences shape brain development, what recommendations would you make to new parents? [Apply]

6. More and more evidence indicates that homosexuality is, at least in part, genetically determined and that the prenatal environment may also play a role in its development. Do you think that the accumulation of this evidence will help to decrease homophobia? [Analyze]

7. You learned that even twins growing up in the same household are not psychologically identical; they have different personalities, at least in part because of differences in the way their parents treat them. What other environmental differences might they experience? How are your environment and those of your siblings different? What effects has this had? [Analyze]

8. In 1998 a young Lindsay Lohan starred in the movie *The Parent Trap*, which depicted the reunion between separated-at-birth identical twins. In the movie, the twins were physically identical, differing only in their attire and accents. They did differ psychologically, however. Given your understanding of epigenetics, what features of this depiction were accurate? Which were inaccurate? What recommendations would you offer to the filmmakers if accuracy was their goal? [Analyze]

Self-Test

1. Research by Turkheimer and colleagues (2003) indicated that genes had a small influence on intelligence in poor environments but a large effect in high-SES environments. What does this suggest about the relative effects of nurture and nature?
   a. Nature has a stronger influence on intelligence.
   b. Nurture has a stronger influence on intelligence.
   c. Nature and nurture interact to influence intelligence.
   d. Neither nature nor nurture influences intelligence.

2. Among cultures that encourage the drinking of milk, nature selects for the gene that enables members of that culture to digest lactose. Among cultures for which milk is not important, few people possess this gene. These facts support which of the following ideas about the relation between biology and culture?
   a. Culture precedes biology.
   b. Biology and culture coevolve.
   c. Biology precedes culture.
   d. Culture and biology do not interact.

3. Which of the following traits is likely to be the most heritable?
   a. Height
   b. Sense of humor
   c. Intelligence
   d. Open-mindedness

4. If the only difference between MZ and DZ twin pairs is their genetic similarity, then the difference in the degree to which the two twin types resemble each other psychologically must be caused by
   a. shared environmental factors.
   b. genes.
   c. the interaction between genes and environment.
   d. nonshared environmental factors (e.g., being treated differently by parents).

5. Based on research by Bouchard and colleagues (1990) on the psychological similarity of twins raised apart, we would estimate that the correlation for twins raised apart on the trait of conscientiousness would be approximately
   a. −.5.
   b. .5.
   c. −.05.
   d. .05.

6. Based on twin studies, we know that the heritability of personality traits is not 1.00. This leaves room for what other kind of influences?
   a. The influence of shared environmental factors
   b. The influence of genes
   c. The influence of nonshared environmental factors (e.g., differential treatment by parents)
   d. Both a and c

7. Heritability studies indicate that variations in genes do account, in part, for variations in personality. Which of the following would be reasonable to conclude based on this finding?
   a. If heritability is high within two groups, and the groups differ, then the difference must be genetically based.
   b. If the heritability for a trait is 50%, then half of that trait was inherited by each person in the population.
   c. If a trait is highly heritable, then it will never change.
   d. Humans are not born as "blank slates."

8. Using the metaphor of books to describe your body's cells, what part of the book represents DNA?
   a. The words, which provide instruction
   b. The spine, which provides support
   c. The page, which provides a surface
   d. The glue, which holds everything together

9. In molecular genetic methods, sometimes researchers know exactly what allele they are interested in. At other times, they conduct a(n) _____ to identify the genetic basis of a behavior of interest.
   a. genome-wide association study
   b. epigenetic analysis
   c. behavior genetic study
   d. zygotic analysis

10. Recent advances in molecular genetic analyses of monozygotic twins indicate that identical twins
    a. are not always genetically identical.
    b. are rarely genetically identical.
    c. are no more genetically identical than dizygotic twins.
    d. are no more genetically identical than any two people.

11. The process of natural selection is *incompatible* with which of the following ideas?
    a. Features possessed by an organism may be adaptive in one environment but not another.
    b. Inherited biology, not environmental experience, fully explains observed differences between organisms of a given species.
    c. Features that are adaptive become more frequent because they get passed down from one generation to another.
    d. If an environment changes, some species may become extinct.

12. Which of the following patterns of preferences for mates should we expect to observe, according to evolutionary psychologists?
    a. Men should prefer curvy women to skinny women because their shape signals their ability to provide financial resources.
    b. Men should prefer curvy women to skinny women because their shape signals their reproductive capability.
    c. Men should prefer skinny women to curvy women because their shape signals their ability to provide financial resources.
    d. Men should prefer skinny women to curvy women because their shape signals their reproductive capability.

13. Which of the following would *not* be supportive of the mental-modules hypothesis?
    a. Research indicating that women prefer men who can provide resources
    b. Research indicating that men prefer curvy women
    c. Research indicating that sex differences in mate preferences are not universal
    d. Research indicating that people solve problems better when cast in terms of exchanging goods (e.g., trading products in a marketplace)

14. In an interesting illustration of culture's influence on biology, researchers found that among people living in the Caucasus Mountains, there was little genetic diversity because of the
    a. cultural practice of marrying within one's local group.
    b. cultural practice of living with the husband's parents.
    c. disproportionately high rates of monozygotic twins.
    d. Both a and b

15. Although shared family environments account for none of the variability in sexual orientation, one theory is that variations in which of the following types of environment may be influential?
    a. Prenatal
    b. Military
    c. School
    d. Work

Answers

You can check your answers to the preceding Self-Test and the chapter's What Do You Know? questions in Appendix B.

Sensation and Perception 5

HUBERT DOLEZAL, A 29-YEAR-OLD AMERICAN, kept a diary while visiting St. John's of Kissos, a small seaside village on the rocky coastline of Greece. Here are some of his entries:

Day 1 (early in day): The first few steps I took . . . tremendously shaky. These steps were awkward, difficult. Any task requiring . . . precise performatory coordination is horrendously strenuous.

Day 1 (later in the day): I notice a substantial improvement in my ability to walk a straight line after walking only 40 feet.

Day 2: For the first time, I was able to walk down 6–8 steps without help. The most serious difficulty now is [on] such relatively trivial tasks as operating my portable tape recorder.

Day 3: This is the first time I've been able to walk upstairs alternating steps (i.e., one footstep per step).

Day 5: I've abandoned the use of my walking stick.

Day 6: I'm more sure-footed than ever before. For the first time, I've successfully alternated feet going down the last 6 of the 50 stairs. This was unthinkable even yesterday; yet this morning I did it fairly naturally and briskly.

Jaroslaw Wojcik / Getty Images

Nicole Blade / Getty Images

Day 9: For the first time, it's relatively easy to change batteries in the portable tape recorder.

Day 11: Carrying heavy suitcases up and down wet and slippery mule trails poses no problem.

What a rapid recovery! But from what? On Day 1, it sounded as if our visitor to Greece had sustained major injuries to his legs. Yet on Day 2, he was walking down stairs. On Day 2, he couldn't operate a simple electronic device. Maybe his hands were injured? A few days later, though, he operated the device easily.

Here's what actually happened. What Hubert Dolezal "recovered" from was not an injury, but dramatic alteration in perception. As part of an experiment, on Day 1 he donned upside-down glasses, that is, glasses with special prisms that turned his entire field of vision upside down.

He had been seeing right side up for a lifetime. Yet within days, Dolezal adapted to seeing upside down. How could the visual system—a primary topic in this chapter on sensation and perception—have adapted so quickly to images of a world turned upside down?

Before we delve into the chapter, here's a quick fact about vision. Due to the curvature of the front of your eye, images of the world reverse—left to right, and up to down—before reaching the back of your eye. This raises another question: How did *you* adapt to images of a world turned upside down? ◉

IMAGINE YOU ARE an organism—any creature, great or small—crawling around in the world. What is your most fundamental challenge? Finding food? Avoiding predators? Or maybe it is staying warm or getting rest if you're injured.

Each of these is important. Yet they all rely on something even more fundamental: accurate sensation and perception. To find food, you've got to be able to see or smell it. To avoid predators, you have to see, smell, or hear them. Avoiding cold and recovering from injury require that you sense the inner environment of your body, to know that you're cold or injured. Survival requires sensation and perception, our focus in this chapter.

Perceptual Systems

Preview Question

> What is the difference between sensation and perception?

People can sense events and perceive the world thanks to their **perceptual systems,** which are interconnected parts of the body that deliver sensory and perceptual information (Gibson, 1966; Withagen & Michaels, 2005). As you will learn in this chapter, humans have six perceptual systems:

1. The **visual system,** which enables you to perceive information that comes in the form of light

2. The **auditory system,** which enables you to get information about the environment in the form of sound waves

3. The **gustatory system,** which is sensitive to chemical substances and provides the sense of taste

4. The **olfactory system,** which detects airborne chemical substances and provides the sense of smell

5. The **haptic system,** through which you gain information about objects by touching them

6. The **kinesthetic system,** which detects information about the location of body parts (e.g., whether your arm is at your side or sticking up in the air) and the relation of your body as a whole to the force of gravity (e.g., whether you're right side up or upside down)

We will present each perceptual system in two steps. First, we examine the psychology of the system: the information it delivers and the psychological principles through which it works. Next, we'll explore the system's biology: the neural mechanisms that enable it to do its job. We will, in other words, focus first at person and mind levels of analysis (see Chapter 1) and then at the level of the nervous system and brain.

Next in the chapter, we examine three phenomena in which social factors influence sensory and perceptual experience: (1) the experience of pain; (2) the perception of faces; and (3) motivated perception, that is, the influence of motivational states on

---

perceptual systems Interconnected parts of the body that deliver sensory and perceptual information; humans have six perceptual systems.

visual system The perceptual system detecting environmental information that reaches the body in the form of light.

auditory system The perceptual system detecting environmental information that consists of sound waves.

gustatory system The perceptual system that is sensitive to chemical substances and provides the sense of taste.

olfactory system The perceptual system that detects airborne chemical substances and provides the sense of smell.

haptic system The perceptual system through which people acquire information about objects by touching them.

kinesthetic system The perceptual system that detects information about the location of body parts.

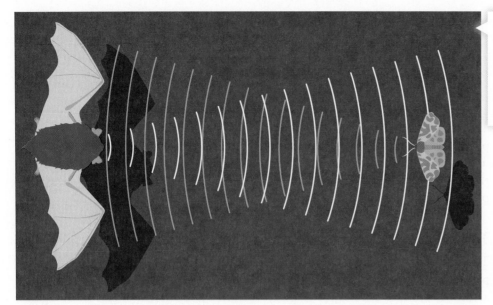

Bat echolocation The six perceptual systems discussed in the text are not the only possible perceptual systems—they're just the six that humans have. Bats, for example, have one we don't: echolocation. They perceive the location of objects in space by sending out sound waves that bounce off the objects, back to them.

perceptual experience. We conclude with *selective attention,* in which you "zoom in" on streams of information in the environment, focusing on one while avoiding distraction from others.

Before we begin, here is a word on defining *sensation* and *perception.* One approach to defining them refers to biological processes. **Sensation** occurs when cells at the periphery of the body detect physical stimuli; **perception** occurs when systems in the brain process these signals and produce conscious awareness of sensory inputs. These definitions accurately portray steps of biological processing, but present two problems when one turns to psychological experiences. First, sensory experiences result from activity in the brain, not merely in the periphery of the body; Chapter 3 explains that activating a brain region known as the *sensory cortex* causes people to experience bodily sensations. Second, perception can occur *without* conscious awareness. In studies of *unconscious perception* (also called *subliminal perception*), researchers present information so briefly that participants are not aware of its content. Nonetheless, the participants are affected by the information, which means they must have perceived it (see, e.g., Marcel, 1983; Siegel et al., 2013).

A different approach to defining sensation and perception is psychological. Two everyday examples illustrate the difference in psychological experiences that this approach captures: (1) If you bump your knee, say, "Ow, it hurts!" and someone asks, "Where does it hurt?" you point to your knee. (2) If you see a traffic accident, say, "Wow, an accident!" and someone says, "Where do you see it?" you do not point to your eye. Case #1 is an example of *sensation,* a feeling that is located at a point in the body, whereas #2 is an example of *perception,* a psychological process in which people acquire information about objects and events in the environment (Hacker, 2004, 2010).

🦇 WHAT DO YOU KNOW?...

1. The biological process that occurs when cells at the periphery of the body detect physical stimuli is called _____. The biological process in which systems in the brain process incoming signals and produce conscious awareness of sensory inputs is _____.

See Appendix B for answers to What Do You Know? questions.

sensation The biological process occurring when cells at the periphery of the body detect physical stimuli.

perception The biological process occurring when systems in the brain process sensory signals and produce awareness of sensory inputs.

From Physical Stimulus to Psychological Experience

Preview Question

› How are physical events translated into psychological events?

The main scientific challenge in the study of sensation and perception is to relate the physical world to the psychological world. The environment contains physical stimuli: light waves, sound waves, heat sources, and so forth. When people encounter them, they have psychological experiences: sights, sounds, feelings of warmth. How are the physical events translated into psychological events?

Transduction

The translation from physical to psychological begins with **transduction,** a biological process in which physical stimuli activate cells in the body's nervous system. Once activated, the cells send nerve impulses toward the brain that function as signals, telling the brain that physical stimulation has occurred. Processing of the signals in the brain itself gives rise to perceptual and sensory experience.

Transduction does not fully determine a person's sensory and perceptual experiences. Other factors—especially the setting in which the stimulation occurs and the person's state of mind when it occurs—also are influential. But transduction is the critical first step.

Receptor Cells

The cells in the nervous system that transduce physical stimuli are called **receptor cells.** Different types of receptor cells are sensitive to different types of physical stimulation from the environment. When stimulated, they send signals to the brain.

In general, any one type of receptor cell is sensitive to one type of stimulation. For example, receptor cells in the eye, called **photoreceptors,** are sensitive to stimulation by light. A variety of receptor cells located just under the surface of the skin are sensitive to physical pressure. Receptors in the ear are stimulated by sound waves. By using these impulses, the perceptual system as a whole can gather information about the outside world.

Let's see exactly how perceptual systems acquire this information by exploring the visual system.

🐾 WHAT DO YOU KNOW?...

2. Transduction begins when physical stimuli activate _____ cells.

The Visual System

"I saw it with my own eyes!" "Seeing is believing." "I'm from Missouri, the Show Me State." When we need reliable information, in vision, we trust.

Visual Perception

Preview Questions

› How are we able to perceive depth even with one eye closed?
› What are the advantages of having two eyes?
› How does the visual system enable us to perceive motion?
› How do past experiences and current context influence perception of shape?

What were you expecting on top of the pyramid, a nose? Since the days of ancient Egypt, humankind has chosen to symbolize its belief in a watchful God with an eye—a choice reflecting the paramount role of visual perception in human experience.

James E. Knopf / Shutterstock

---

transduction A biological process in which physical stimuli activate cells in the nervous system, which then send nerve impulses to the brain, where processing gives rise to perceptual and sensory experience.

receptor cells Nervous system cells that are sensitive to specific types of physical stimulation from the environment and send signals to the brain when stimulated.

photoreceptors Receptor cells in the eye that are sensitive to stimulation by light.

> What does it take for us to notice whether someone dimmed the lights?

> How does our attention to the overall environment enable us to experience color?

> Do colors have opposites?

Ciao Hollywood / Splash News / Corbis

The visual system delivers four different types of information, namely, information about (1) distance and size; (2) motion; (3) shape; and (4) brightness and color.

Think a one-eyed monster has no depth perception? Think again. Thanks to monocular cues to depth, Mike Wazowski of *Monsters, Inc.* actually has little trouble perceiving depth.

DISTANCE AND SIZE. Stop reading for a moment and look around your environment. (But don't forget to return to the reading!) No matter where you are, you'll immediately notice that some objects are closer than others. Your phone is nearby. A car seen through a window is farther away. The window is closer than the car but farther than the phone. The perception of distance—called **depth perception,** because you are judging how deep into three-dimensional space an object lies in relation to you—is so easy that, until you take a psychology course, you might not even think about it. But how do you do it?

Before we answer this question, note how distance relates to perceptual information about another feature of the world: objects' size. Judgments about size are *not* determined solely by the amount of space an object takes up in your *visual field,* which is the range of the potentially observable world that can be perceived at any point in time. If you make a circle with your thumb and forefinger and look through it at the moon, your fingers take up more space in your visual field than the moon. However, you perceive the moon as bigger because you also perceive it as very distant.

To judge distance and size, your visual system uses **cues to depth,** which are sources of information that enable organisms to judge the distance between themselves and the objects they perceive. There are two types of depth cues:

What are two ways your life would be different if judgments of size *were* determined by the amount of space objects took up in your visual field?

1. **Monocular cues** are available to an organism even if it is using only one eye.

2. **Binocular cues** are depth cues that require two eyes.

To experience the power of monocular cues, look around your environment again—but this time, cover one of your eyes. Do you still perceive depth? Sure you do! Numerous monocular cues provide distance information. Two examples are shown in Figure 5.1.

At first glance, the two people appear to be of different sizes: A big one behind a little one. But how different are they? If you measure them, you'll find that their physical size on the page is identical. Yet you perceive that the monster on top is farther away and bigger. This perception is caused by your visual system's use of two monocular cues:

> **Converging vertical lines:** Vertically oriented lines that get closer to one another, or converge, create the perception of depth. This perception is based on our experience of the physical world. If you look down a roadway or railroad track, the two edges of the road or rails of the track converge visually as you look into the distance. Even when converging lines appear on a printed page, your visual system automatically conveys the perception of depth.

figure **5.1**
Two binocular cues to depth
Converging vertical lines and variations in texture make the gentleman on top look much larger than the one on the bottom.

depth perception The perception of distance.

cues to depth Sources of information that enable us to judge the distance between ourselves and the objects we perceive.

monocular cues Depth cues that are available even when we use only one eye.

binocular cues Depth cues that require two eyes.

converging vertical lines A monocular depth cue consisting of vertically oriented lines that get closer to one another, creating the perception of depth.

Culture Club / Getty Images

Leonardo DaVinci's *The Last Supper* uses the perceptual cue of converging vertical lines to create a sense of depth.

figure 5.2
Occlusion Thanks to occlusion, a monocular cue to depth, the figure on the bottom appears closer to you than the one on the top.

> **Texture:** Variations in visual *texture,* the various markings on the surface of objects in a visual scene, are a second monocular cue to depth. Imagine seeing a rough surface that extends into the distance—for example, the rocks on which a railroad track sits. Looking at the rocks nearby, you can see the individual features and spaces between them. As you look into the distance, the rocks become indistinguishable "dots" and blur together. Figure 5.1 incorporates such variations in texture in the marks that portray the texture of the bricks. These contribute to the perception of depth.

In your elementary school art class, which monocular cues did you use to create the illusion of distance?

A third monocular distance cue is **occlusion,** a visual phenomenon in which one object partly blocks another from view. The blocking indicates that the first object is in front of the other—in other words, that it is closer to you. Occlusion alone is sufficient to indicate distance. Figure 5.2 eliminates converging verticals and texture yet, due to occlusion, one runner still appears closer than the other.

Another monocular distance cue is **shading,** which is the presence within a visual image of a relatively dark area that appears to have been created by blocking a source of light. Objects can appear closer to or farther from you based solely on how they are shaded. Look at Figure 5.3. Some of the circles seem to rise up above the square, and thus to be closer to you than is the square itself. Other circles seem to sink into the square, away from you. But none are actually closer or farther away—they're all just sitting there on the page. The figure's shading creates the perception of distance.

Another monocular cue to depth is an object's **clarity,** which is the degree of distinctness, as opposed to fuzziness, of a visual image. Clearer objects appear to be closer.

texture A monocular depth cue based on markings on the surface of objects in a visual scene.

occlusion A monocular depth cue in which one object in the field of vision partly blocks another from view.

shading A monocular depth cue based on the presence within a visual image of a relatively dark area that appears to have been created by blocking a source of light.

clarity The degree of distinctness, as opposed to fuzziness, of a visual image; a monocular depth cue.

figure 5.3
Shading Shading is an important cue to depth. The figure's shading creates the perception that some of the circles seem to rise up above the square, and thus are closer to you than is the square itself, whereas other circles seem to sink into the square, away from you.

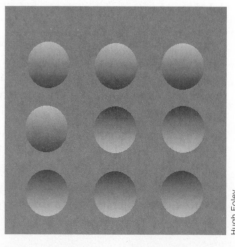

Hugh Foley

In general, they are; you usually can see objects right next to you more clearly than those that are farther away. However, sometimes clarity varies while actual distance remains constant. If so, the variations in clarity can create an illusory perception of change in distance that is startling. If you live in an area with fog, mist, or smog, a mountain range can appear far in the distance. But if the atmosphere clears up, the mountain suddenly appears to have jumped forward closer to you.

Finally, the perception of objects' distance and size is affected by environmental context, that is, the overall set of visual cues in the environment in which the object is placed. The role of context is illustrated by the odd-looking group of people in Figure 5.4.

It turns out that the oddity is not the people but the room; it is an **Ames room,** an apparatus for studying the perception of size. Its key feature is that it is not cubic. As you can see in Figure 5.5, the wall slants back, away from the viewer. In addition, the floor and ceiling are not parallel; the ceiling height is higher on the left than the right. The room is designed so that it's impossible to detect these deviations from a room's typical cubic shape. Your visual system (1) assumes that a room (the context in which the people are viewed) is cubic and (2) interprets people's height in light of this assumption (O'Reilly, Jbabdi, & Behrens, 2012). The only interpretation that fits the assumption is that the people on the right are big.

Clarity as a distance cue The artist heightens the sense of the mountains' distance by reducing their clarity.

figure **5.4**
Ames room That woman—no, that man—is huge! Or are they?

Ames room An apparatus for studying the perception of size; the room is not cubic, contrary to the visual system's assumption, and this creates perceptual illusion involving size.

figure **5.5**
Ames room explained The woman and man in Figure 5.4 on the preceding page are not huge. They are in an Ames room, which creates illusions of size. As shown here, the walls of an Ames room are not at right angles, and the ceiling is not parallel to the floor.

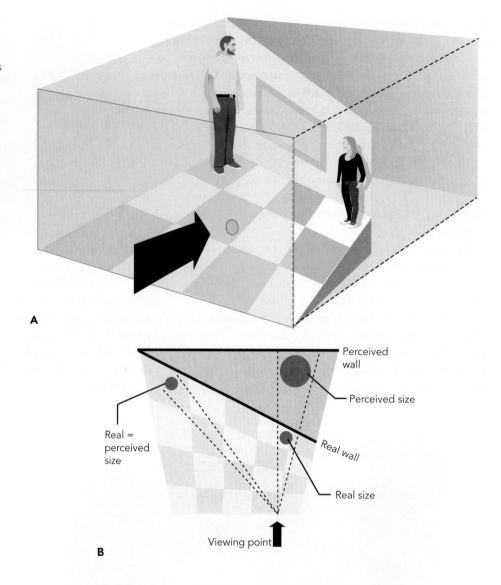

figure **5.6**
View Master View Masters create the perception of three-dimensional space through stereopsis. They present slightly different images to your left and right eyes.

Dorling Kindersley / Getty Images

With all these monocular cues to depth, you might wonder why we evolved to have two eyes. Binocularity has its advantages. With two eyes, organisms have a "spare"; vision is maintained even if one eye is injured. Two eyes also provide a wider visual field; organisms can take in more information with two eyes than one. In addition, binocular vision provides more accurate depth perception (Bingham & Pagano, 1998), thanks to two binocular cues to depth: *stereopsis* and *convergence*.

Stereopsis is the perception of three-dimensional space produced by the fact that the images reaching your two eyes are not identical (Figure 5.6). The images vary because your eyes are a couple of inches apart. You can see the effect this has by holding your hand in front of your face, with your thumb right near your nose and palm facing to the left, and closing one eye and then the other. Your hand appears to "jump" because your eyes are receiving different images. When you look at distant objects, the difference between the images is tiny. But when you look nearby, it is large. The degree

stereopsis The perception of three-dimensional space produced by the fact that images reaching your two eyes vary slightly because your eyes are a few inches apart; a binocular depth cue.

of difference between the two images thus is a binocular cue that provides information about distance.

Convergence is a depth cue that involves the muscles that move your eyes. When you look at close objects (e.g., a few inches from your face), your eye muscles must exert effort to focus your eyes on it. If the object gets ever closer, more muscular effort is required to make your eyes converge. Feedback from these muscles to your brain provides an extra source of information about the distance of objects (Wexler & van Boxtel, 2005).

People who have trouble turning their eyes toward each other may suffer from *convergence insufficiency*, a treatable disorder of the binocular vision system.

You've learned about a wide range of cues to depth. Table 5.1 summarizes them for you.

table **5.1**

Cues to Depth	
Monocular Cues	**Binocular Cues**
Converging vertical lines	Stereopsis
Texture	Convergence
Occlusion	
Shading	
Clarity	
Environmental context	

◉ CULTURAL OPPORTUNITIES

Perceiving Absolute and Relative Size

Here's a simple perceptual task. You're shown the design labeled "Original"—a square with a vertical line in it (Figure 5.7). This image is removed, and you then see a square of a different size than the original square. It has no line in it. The task is to draw one of two

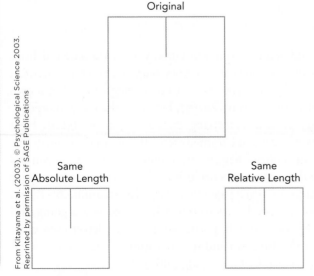

From Kitayama et al. (2003). © Psychological Science 2003. Reprinted by permission of SAGE Publications

Original

Same Absolute Length

Same Relative Length

figure **5.7**
Studying perception and culture Stimulus materials used in research on cultural factors in perception. Participants were first shown the "Original" image and were then shown a square (with no line in it) of a different size than the original square. Next, participants were asked to draw a line whose *absolute* length was the same as the original line, or one whose *relative* length was the same as the original. (The lower two images show lines drawn accurately under these two instructional conditions.)

convergence A binocular depth cue based on the effort eye muscles must exert to look at objects very close to the face.

types of lines: one whose (1) *absolute* length is the same as the original, or whose (2) *relative* length (i.e., relative to the size of the square) is the same as the original. (The lower two images show lines drawn accurately under these two instructional conditions.) Now here's a question for you: What's this task doing in a textbook feature about culture?

It turns out that people in different cultures perform differently on the task. The graph shows the average magnitude of error (the difference between the line drawn and the correct line length) for two groups of college students: Japanese students at Kyoto University, in Kyoto, Japan, and American college students at the University of Chicago in Illinois. Japanese students made smaller errors—that is, did better—on the relative length task than the absolute length task. But U.S. students found the relative length task more difficult; they performed better on the absolute length task than the relative length task (Figure 5.8; Kitayama et al., 2003).

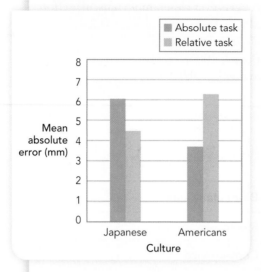

figure 5.8
Cultural variation on a perceptual task The graph shows the average magnitude of error in lines drawn by college students in Japan and in the United States. Japanese students' errors were smaller (i.e., their performance was better) on the relative length task than on the absolute length task. U.S. students showed the opposite result, performing more accurately on the absolute length task (Kitayama et al., 2003). The results reflect cultural difference in analytic and holistic perception.

These differences in perception and performance reflect a more general cultural difference in "analytic" versus "holistic" perception (Nisbett et al., 2001). Cultural practices in North America promote analytic thinking in which objects are examined in terms of their distinct parts. U.S. students, having grown up with these cultural practices, are particularly good at isolating a distinct part of a figure—in this case, the vertical line—and reproducing it. Asian cultures promote holistic patterns of perception in which objects are viewed in relation to their overall context—in this case, the context for the vertical line being the square. Japanese students, therefore, are better able to perceive and reproduce the relation between context and part (square and line), and perform better on the relative task.

The results show how the mental process of perception can be fully understood only by considering the person who's doing the perceiving, and the culture in which that person lives.

WHAT DO YOU KNOW?...

3. Why does holistic thinking improve the ability to estimate the relative length of a line, whereas analytic thinking fosters absolute estimates? Who engages in holistic and analytic processing?

PERCEIVING MOTION. In addition to size and distance, your visual system delivers information about motion. This information is of two types: relating to (1) the movement of objects in the environment (with respect to you, who are not moving), and (2) your own movement through an environment (which is stationary). Let's consider them in order.

People are very good at perceiving the movement of objects. Even slight movements are detected immediately. If you were to hold this book in front of you at arms' length, the amount of movement required for you to notice that motion occurred is no larger than the tiny space between two letters on this page (Sekuler, Watamaniuk, & Blake, 2002). People also are good at detecting where objects are going and how fast. In perception research, participants rapidly detect even quite small variations in the direction and speed of stimuli, such as dots moving on a computer screen (Sekuler et al., 2002).

THINK ABOUT IT

Do you think you perceive motion when images on your retina (the back of your eye) move? How can that be? If you move your head while looking around a room, the images of the room on your retina move, but you do not perceive that the room is moving.

The visual system is so inclined to detect motion that we sometimes perceive it even when it's not occurring. In the **phi phenomenon,** observers view two (or more) objects that are stationary but flash in an alternating sequence. What they perceive is not stationary flashing objects, but motion; the display appears to viewers to consist of one object that moves from one location to another.

Motion also conveys information about the type of object that is moving—especially if it is a living being. Swedish psychologist Gunnar Johansson conducted research (reviewed in Cutting, 2012) in which light sources were attached to the limbs of people who were filmed while they walked around in a dark room. The resulting film depicted merely a collection of moving dots: white points of light on a black background (Figure 5.9). Yet viewers immediately recognized that they were looking at human beings. Movement, in the absence of any other visual cues (faces, clothing, etc.), instantly indicates that the moving object is a person. From the motion of dots alone, research participants often can identify people's sex and even their emotional state (the actors being filmed were asked to move as if they were experiencing various emotions; Atkinson et al., 2004; Gold et al., 2008).

Now imagine a different case: The objects in your view are stationary, but you are moving—for example, you are jogging through a wooded park. What is your perceptual experience like? There are two facts to note:

> *The images that reach your eyes are in motion, yet the environment appears stable.* Every time you take a step, the images that reach your retina—for instance, images of nearby trees—jump around, as a result of your body's movement. Yet you don't think, "Man, look at those trees go!" Your visual system correctly tells you that the environmental objects are stable, even though their images on your retina are moving. This means there is no one-to-one correspondence between movement of light at your retina and your perception that objects in the environment have moved.

For centuries we have thought of the retinal image as a picture projected and focused on a screen, the image being mobile and the screen fixed. The image is supposed to be freely transposable over the retina. But actually it is the other way round. The image is perfectly stationary, being anchored to the world, and the retina moves relative to the image.

—James J. Gibson (1968; pp. 337–338)

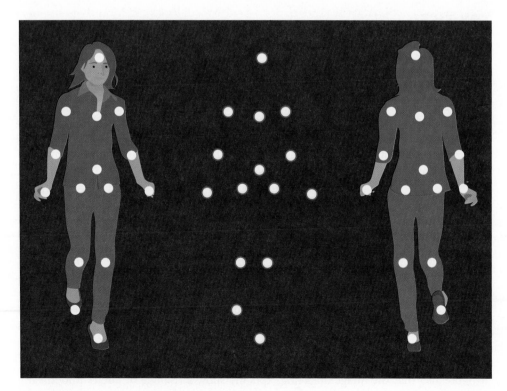

figure **5.9**
Biological motion dot figures If you look at the dots in the middle of this image, they merely seem to form a random geometric shape. But in motion, they look like a person.

phi phenomenon An illusory perception of visual motion that occurs when stationary objects flash in an alternating sequence and are perceived as a single object moving back and forth.

figure **5.10**
Optical flow Even video games with relatively simple graphics can produce a compelling experience of motion, thanks to optical flow. Nearby objects such as the red and white signs along the side of the road go zipping by, whereas the city in the distance stays relatively stable.

> *When you move through the environment, you experience a systematic flow of visual images.* As you jog, images of objects change at different rates of speed. Images of nearby objects (e.g., the ground below you) flow past rapidly, whereas images in other regions of your field of view (a hill in the distance) change much more slowly. The psychologist James J. Gibson emphasized that this **optical flow,** the continuous change in visual images that moving organisms encounter, provides visual information about their movement. Video game designers capitalize on optical flow to create illusions of motion and depth (Figure 5.10).

TRY THIS!

Now that you have learned about the perception of smotion, it is time to take part in an experiment. Go to www.pmbpsychology.com for this chapter's Try This! activity. We'll discuss the experiment later in the chapter—but be sure to do it now, so you see the procedures, and your results, before getting to this later section of the reading. ◉

SHAPE. In addition to distance and motion, your visual system also provides information about shape, that is, the outline or contour of objects. In fact, the visual system is so inclined to detect shape that you end up seeing shapes that aren't really present. Look at Figure 5.11, which depicts a Kanizsa triangle, devised by Italian psychologist Gaetano Kanizsa (1976). You perceive a bright white triangle in the center, on top of another triangle and three black circles. But in the open area in the center, no lines exist; in other words, there is no bright white triangle—a shape formed by three continuous lines—on the page. In fact, if you focus intently on one of those open, line-free areas, your perception of a white triangle will fade away. But if you shift your attention back to the image as a whole, the bright white triangle returns.

figure **5.11**
Kanizsa figure The image is a Kanizsa triangle. People perceive a white triangle in the center, atop another triangle and three black circles, even though the figure contains no set of continuous lines forming a triangle. The human visual system is so inclined to detect shapes that people see continuous geometric shapes even when they do not exist.

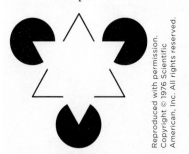

Note also that the image does not explicitly show a triangle or circles underneath the bright white triangle. The drawing merely depicts three V-shaped lines and three "Pac-Man" images. Yet the tendency to experience familiar geometric shapes causes you to perceive triangles and circles.

optical flow The continuous change in visual images that occurs when organisms move through the environment.

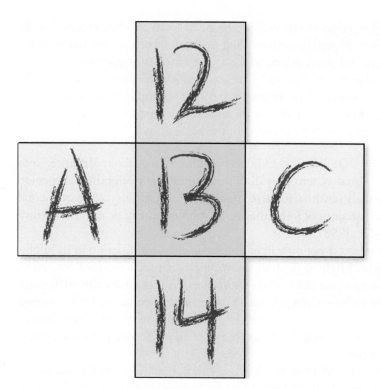

figure **5.12**
B or 13? Read up-and-down, and the center image is a 13. Read left-to-right, and it's a B. Perception of a stimulus is influenced by the context in which the stimulus occurs.

Your visual system's interpretation of shapes depends on the context in which they occur. The middle box in Figure 5.12 displays a vertical line next to a curved "m" shape on its side. What do you see? If you read up-and-down, the context is numbers and the shape in the middle is perceived as a 13. If you read left-to-right, the context is letters and the shape suddenly is a "B." The idea that context guides the perception of any object is often called a *Gestalt* principle of perception, named for a nearly century-old school of thought, Gestalt psychology, which emphasized the perception of whole, organized structures (Wagemans et al., 2012). Figure 5.13 illustrates a number of Gestalt principles.

Sometimes your visual system does not know precisely "what to do with" shapes and their contours. Some figures, in other words, are open to two interpretations, and the visual system "flips" back and forth between them as it struggles to make sense

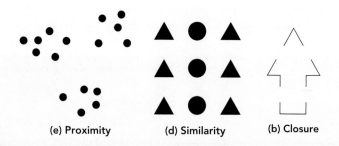

(e) Proximity   (d) Similarity   (b) Closure

figure **5.13**
Gestalt principles When you perceive a collection of objects, you spontaneously group some of them together. *Gestalt principles* describe basic ways in which this grouping occurs. **(a)** According to the principle of *proximity*, items that are near each other (i.e., proximal) are grouped together. You thus perceive three groups of dots in the image in part (a). **(b)** The principle of *similarity* says that physically similar items are grouped together in perception. This creates the perception of columns (rather than rows) in image (b). **(c)** The principle of *closure* suggests that people tend to perceive complete forms, so you see an arrow in image (c), even though the shape itself is incomplete.

SSPL via Getty Images

figure 5.14
Figure-ground perception The vase illustrates the principle of figure-ground perception—as do the profiles that are also visible. The appearance of the scene varies depending on which part is viewed as the figure and which part is the background.

of the environment. The edges of the vase in Figure 5.14 can also be perceived as the outline of a human face in profile. Your varying perceptions of the vase illustrate the principle of **figure-ground perception,** which is the visual system's tendency to divide a scene into (1) objects, or "figures," that are the focus of attention, and (2) the background context in which these figures occur. For example, when you look at Figure 5.14 and see profiles, they move to the foreground, and the white area of the vase temporarily appears to be behind them, in the background.

BRIGHTNESS AND COLOR. In addition to information about distance, motion, and shape, your visual system provides information about brightness and color. Human vision is extremely sensitive to these visual qualities. Cells in your eyes respond to the smallest possible amount of light, that is, one photon (the basic elementary unit of light; Rieke & Baylor, 1998).

Your visual system detects not only light's presence, but also variation in its brightness (e.g., if room lights brighten or dim). How much change is required for you to notice? This is a question about *just noticeable differences.* A **just noticeable difference (JND)** is the minimal variation in a physical stimulus (light, sound, etc.) that a person can detect. JNDs have been explored since the nineteenth century by researchers in **psychophysics,** a branch of psychology that studies relations between physical stimuli and psychological reactions.

What, then, is the answer? How much change in light is required for you to notice? It turns out that there is no one fixed answer. Instead, it depends. With a bit of thinking, you can figure out for yourself what the answer depends on. Compare these two circumstances:

1. You're in a room illumined by only one candle, and someone standing behind you lights a second candle. Will you notice the change in illumination?
2. You're outdoors on a bright sunny day, and someone standing behind you lights a candle. Will you notice the change in illumination?

In both cases, the amount of change is the same: the light of one candle. But in #1 you notice the change and in #2 you don't. In other words, in #1 the light of one candle exceeds the JND and in #2 that same light is less than the JND. The lesson is that the JND is not constant; its value depends on how much light is already in the environment. If a lot of light is present, then a bigger change in illumination is needed for you to notice the change in brightness.

Your perception of an object's brightness depends on not only light coming from that object, but also light coming from *nearby* objects. The visual system responds to the contrast between brightness in different areas of the visual field. Figure 5.15 illustrates this. It appears to display a dark gray

> In what way could your current context be affecting perception of a nearby object?

figure-ground perception The visual system's tendency to divide a scene into objects, or "figures," that are the focus of attention and the background context.

just noticeable difference (JND) The minimal variation in a physical stimulus such as light or sound that a person can detect.

psychophysics A branch of psychology that studies relations between physical stimuli and psychological reactions.

figure 5.15
Brightness The two squares on the left and right are identical. You perceive them differently because of their surrounding context.

square on the left and a light gray square on the right. But those two squares are identical! The perception of their difference is caused by their contexts: The left square is much darker than its surrounding context and thus is perceived as darker than the square on the right.

Now let's consider the perception of color. We need to begin with the physics of light. Visible light is one little sliver of the overall *electromagnetic spectrum,* which is the full range of physical energy that is made up of electricity and magnetism. Electromagnetic energy exists in the form of physical waves. The waves vary in wavelength (Figure 5.16). Many long (e.g., radio waves) and short (e.g., x-rays) wavelengths cannot be detected by the visual system, which is sensitive to one sliver of the spectrum—the region of visible light.

Within that region, variations in wavelength correspond to variations in color. The shortest detectable wavelengths appear violet, and the longest are experienced as red. Note that the color is not present in the light itself; light energy is not literally "colored." Color is a psychological experience that occurs when the visual system is activated by light energy.

Wavelength does not entirely determine the psychological experience of color. We know this because wavelengths and color may fail to correspond in two ways: (1) Sometimes different wavelengths of light are experienced as the same color; and (2) sometimes the same wavelength of light produces, in different circumstances, different color experiences. Both phenomena are shown in Figure 5.17.

In panels (a) and (b), the apples look roughly the same: a few red apples nestled between some yellow and green fruits. The light reaching your eye from panels (a) and (b) differs considerably, though, due to a bluish filter placed over the image in panel (b). You thus have the same color experience, red, despite varying wavelengths of light. The tendency for a given object to be perceived as having the same color despite changes in illumination is called **color constancy.**

In panels (b) and (c), the apples look different. The apples in (c) are strange-looking: of a blue-purple variety. They appear quite unlike the normal red apples in (b). Yet the apple images in panels (b) and (c) are identical. You thus experience different colors of apple when looking at (b) and (c), despite the fact that the wavelengths of light reaching your eyes from the apples are the same.

The lesson here is that your visual system does not respond to individual points of color but to the visual environment as a whole (Shevell & Kingdom, 2008). This makes sense evolutionarily. The ability to perceive colors—like other abilities—evolved because it contributed to organisms' survival and reproduction. This biological success requires organisms to be attuned to their overall environment. Figure 5.18 shows how color perception aids an organism's survival. If you're a bee, you need to find flowers. Without color vision, it's difficult to find them; they blend into the background of a

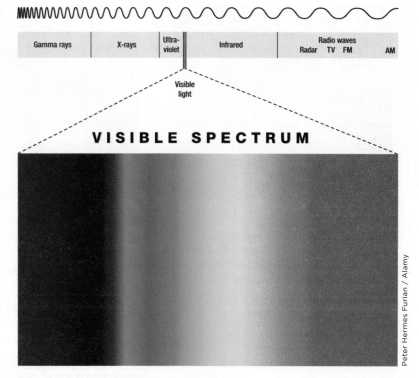

VISIBLE SPECTRUM

figure **5.16**
Electromagnetic spectrum Visible light is a narrow section of the overall electromagnetic spectrum.

Peter Hermes Furian / Alamy

A   B   C

tatnki / iStock / 360 / Getty Images

figure **5.17**
Color constancy The images illustrate the principle of color constancy. The light reflecting off the apples in parts (a) and (b) differs considerably, yet you see them both as being red. The wavelengths of light from the apples in part (b) actually match those of the apples in part (c).

color constancy The tendency for a given object to be perceived as having the same color, despite changes in illumination.

figure 5.18
Bees need color, too A colorblind bee would have difficulty finding the flowers. Color perception aids organisms' ability to survive in their environments.

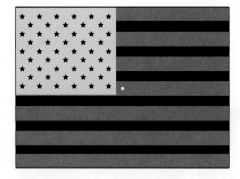

figure 5.19
Opponent processes in color perception In color perception, yellow–blue and green–red are opposing color pairs. You can experience this opposition by staring at the dot in the middle of this flag for a full 30 seconds, and then directing your attention to a blank white wall and blinking your eyes. When you blink, you'll see a flag of familiar colors.

plant's leaves (see the left panel of the figure). But with color vision, they "pop" right out from the environmental background (the right panel). It is not surprising, then, that bees have been able to perceive color for hundreds of millions of years (Chittka, 1996).

One last key fact about color perception is that colors have opposites. You can imagine a reddish brown but not a reddish green. Red and green are opposites. It's easy to imagine a yellowish green but not a yellowish blue. Blue and yellow are opposites. *Opponent processes* in perception create visual experiences featuring two opposing color pairs: red-green and yellow-blue (Hurvich & Jameson, 1957). In special circumstances, you can experience these opposites at play. Look at Figure 5.19 and follow its instructions. You'll find that the colors (green, yellow) will jump rapidly to their opposites (red, blue) in the *afterimage*, the image you see after looking at the depicted image. Why? Although more than one biological mechanism is involved, one key process involves biochemicals in cells within the eye that respond to color (Ritschel & Eisemann, 2012). When you stare at one color for a long time, biochemicals which react to that color become temporarily depleted. When you then look at a blank wall, the chemical that responds to an *opposite* color is abundant, and it dominates your perceptual experience.

Let's now look more deeply at the biology of perception.

⚡ WHAT DO YOU KNOW?...

4. Match the cues to distance and size on the left with the information about them on the right.

1. Converging vertical lines	a. A monocular cue; objects in the foreground appear highly detailed, whereas those in the distance appear less detailed.
2. Texture	b. A monocular cue; an object's placement in front of another indicates its distance.
3. Occlusion	c. A binocular cue; the difference in images received by our two eyes is greater for nearby objects than it is for far-away objects.
4. Clarity	d. A monocular cue; the appearance of railroad tracks coming together in the distance is one example.
5. Stereopsis	e. A binocular cue; it takes more muscular effort for your eyes to focus on a nearby object relative to a far-away object.
6. Convergence	f. A monocular cue; a mountain appearing farther away on a foggy day is one example.

5. The visual system is excellent at perceiving movement and _____ —so good, in fact, that in the Kanizsa triangle, we perceive lines depicting triangles that aren't there. The amount of change in light required for you to detect a change, also known as the _____ _____ _____, depends, in part, on the amount of light already in the environment. Thanks to _____ _____, you can accurately identify colors in varying amounts of light. If you were to stare at a green image for a while, then stare at a white wall, you'd likely see green's opposite, _____.

From Eye to Brain: Biological Bases of Visual Perception

Preview Questions

› Through what biological process are we able to convert light energy into information that is sent to the brain?

› How is visual information processed once it reaches the brain?

› Given the complexity of visual information, how are we able to perceive objects accurately?

The first piece of biological machinery that enables you to see is, of course, the eye.

THE EYE. Four biological mechanisms near the front of the eye (Figure 5.20a) begin the work of visual perception: the *cornea,* the *pupil,* the *iris,* and the *lens.* The **cornea** is the transparent material at the eye's very front. Its curvature begins the process of focusing light, to produce a sharp image of the outside world. The **pupil** is the opening through which light passes (Figure 5.20b). The size

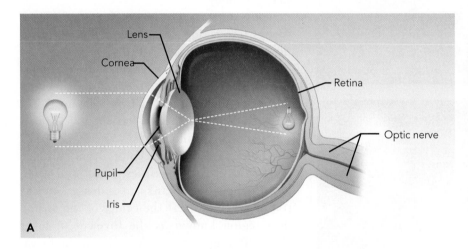

A

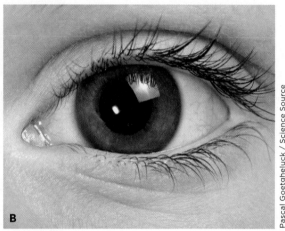

B

Pascal Goetgheluck / Science Source

figure **5.20**

Eye Light from the environment passes through a series of structures in the front of the eye: the cornea, pupil, and lens. Sensory receptors are in the eye's retina. As you can see from the light bulb, images appear upside down (and left–right reversed) on the retina—yet you see them right side up (a). The size of the pupil opening is controlled by the iris (b).

of the opening is controlled by the **iris,** the colorful structure that surrounds the pupil. The iris *dilates* the pupil (i.e., widens the opening) in dim light and constricts it in bright light. Finally, the **lens** is a second transparent biological mechanism that focuses incoming light. Unlike the cornea, the lens's focusing mechanism is adjustable. Muscles in the eye adjust the flexible lens to sharpen images of objects at different distances. With age, the lens loses some of its flexibility, causing people to need supplementary lenses—that is, eyeglasses—to see both near and far objects clearly.

The inner volume of the eye is filled with a transparent fluid. Light passes through this fluid and reaches the **retina,** the rear wall of the eye, which contains a system of nerve cells that respond to light and send signals toward the brain.

As we noted in this chapter's opening story about upside-down glasses, the image that reaches the retina is upside down; due to the curvature of the lens, the image "flips." So why don't you see the world upside down when you look at the image on the retina? Or why didn't the man who wore upside-down glasses see the world upside down when he looked at the image on his retina? It's because people *don't* literally "look at the image on the retina." People look at the world outside themselves. The retina is merely one of a series of biological tools that enable you to perceive information about

cornea The transparent material at the very front of the eye; its curvature begins the process of focusing light.

pupil The opening in the eye through which light passes.

iris The colorful eye structure that surrounds the pupil and responds to low and high light levels by dilating or constricting the pupil.

lens An adjustable, transparent mechanism in the eye that focuses incoming light.

retina The rear wall of the eye containing nerve cells that respond to light and send signals to the brain.

figure **5.21**
Upside-down reading What was it like for that man in Greece (from our opening story) to wear upside-down glasses? It was a little like your experience reading the text above. Whether the image on your retina is right side up or upside down, you can still use the biological tools of your visual system to acquire information about the environment.

Hey, this material in my textbook is upside down! But, come to think of it, with a little effort I still can pick up the information in the text.

figure **5.22**
Rods and cones In this colorized image, taken with a powerful microscope, the retina's rods are shown in green and cones in blue.

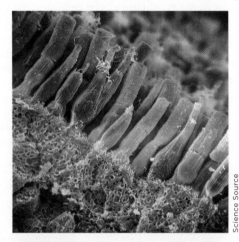

Science Source

figure **5.23**
Fovea In this image of the retina, the darker red area is the fovea, which contains a dense concentration of cone cells.

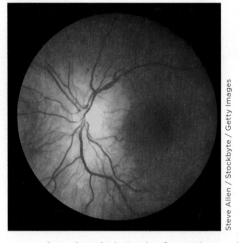

Steve Allen / Stockbyte / Getty Images

the world that arrives in the form of light. If something alters the usual way that light strikes the retina—as when you put on upside-down glasses; or stand on your head; or try reading the material in Figure 5.21—you still can, with a little practice, accurately pick up information about the world.

Once light reaches the retina, the body's nervous system swings into action. The nerve cells that transduce light energy are called *photoreceptors,* as noted earlier in this chapter. The retina contains two types of photoreceptors, whose names reflect their shapes: *cones* and *rods* (Figure 5.22). An average human retina has about 5 million cones and 100 million rods (Winkler, 2013).

Cones are photoreceptors that provide two critical visual qualities: *detail* and *color.* Detail is possible thanks to a dense concentration of cones near the center of the retina, in a region known as the **fovea** (Curcio et al., 1990; Figure 5.23). You rely on the fovea, and its concentration of cones, when focusing attention to get a sharp, detailed look at an object. When you focus on any one object, you'll notice that others, in the periphery of your visual field, appear blurrier and less detailed. Light from these objects falls outside of the fovea, where there are fewer cones.

Cone cells also enable us to see in color. Different types of cone cells are sensitive to different wavelengths of light—that is, to wavelengths we perceive as differently colored. The combination of these sensitivities gives us color perception. Amazingly, although we can identify a huge number of different colors, there is *not* a huge number of different cone types. There are just three: cones that are maximally sensitive to wavelengths of light corresponding to (1) blue, (2) green, and (3) red (Figure 5.24). They combine to provide the full spectrum of color experiences (Sharpe et al., 1999). (A TV similarly combines red, green, and blue beams of light to produce a spectrum of colors.)

Due to genetic variations, some people lack normal functioning in certain cone types. The result is **color blindness,** an insensitivity to one or more of the colors red, green, or blue (Sharpe et al., 1999). If all of your color-sensitivity cones are working

> Have you ever had to use any of your "biological tools" differently, perhaps in response to a strain, sprain, or broken bone? How quickly were you able to adapt?

cones Photoreceptors that are concentrated near the center of the retina and that provide visual detail and color.

fovea A region near the center of the retina that features a dense concentration of cones.

color blindness An insensitivity to one or more of the colors red, green, or blue.

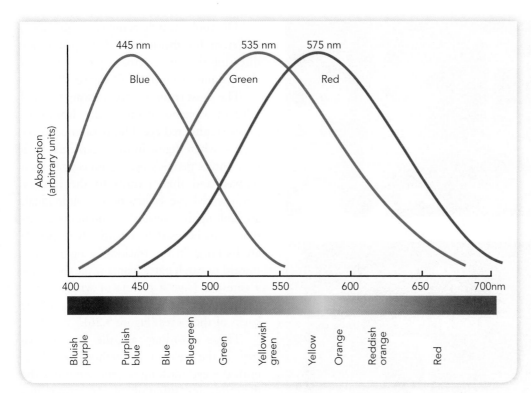

properly, you'll see the number 74 in Figure 5.25. If they aren't, you may see nothing but dots.

Rods are photoreceptors that enable you to see in low illumination. They are the receptors that, as noted earlier, can respond to as little as one photon of light; a cone cell, by comparison, requires about 100 times as many photons to become active. Thanks to the sensitivity of rods, you can see outdoors after the sun sets, or indoors when only a small light is on.

Although rods allow people to see in low illumination, they do not enable us to see color. Unlike cones, rods are not color sensitive. They do not respond at all to long wavelengths of light in the red range. You experience this at night; when the sun sets, the environment looks not only darker, but also less colorful, and red objects appear black. You do not, however, entirely lose your color vision at night. Research shows that, even if only rods are active, the visual system as a whole provides some experience of color, in part by making "educated guesses" about the color of familiar objects based on past experience of them in bright light (Pokorny et al., 2006).

The retina picks up most of its visual information during **visual fixations,** periods when a person's gaze is held in one location. Fixations occur between **saccades,** which are rapid movements of the eyes from one position to another. A challenge for researchers is to track the rapid movements and fixations of a perceiver (see Research Toolkit).

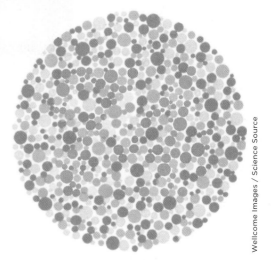

figure **5.25**
The color-blindness test People who do not have normal human color vision may not see the number 74 embedded within this figure.

⊕RESEARCH TOOLKIT

Eye Tracking

People rarely just stare at one spot. Whether looking at a room, a face, or a landscape, people's gaze shifts from place to place. The fovea takes in visual details during the fixations between shifts. This means that by measuring eye movements and fixations, researchers can learn how people interact visually with the world. But how do they measure eye movements and visual fixations?

rods Photoreceptors that enable vision in low illumination.

visual fixations Periods when a person's gaze is held in one location, when most visual information is picked up.

saccades Rapid movements of the eyes from one position to another.

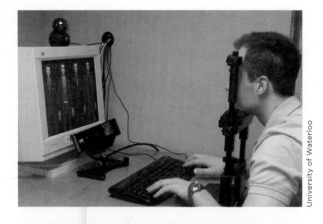

figure 5.26
Eye tracking The participant is taking part in research using eye tracking methods, which record eye movements and the direction of participants' gaze during the course of an experiment.

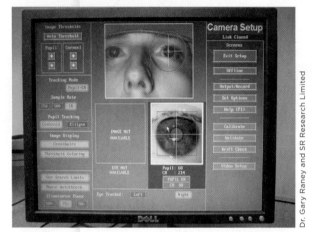

figure 5.27
Tracking eye movements The monitor shows the video display researchers see during an eye-tracking experiment. The cross hairs over the eye in the two images indicate the center of the eye's pupil, and thus the direction in which the individual is looking at that moment.

The tool researchers use is an *eye tracker,* a system for measuring where people are directing their gaze across a given period of time (Raney, Campbell, & Bovee, 2014).

The most common eye tracking method relies on a phenomenon familiar from flash photography: red eye. Photographic red eye occurs when light from a camera's flash unit enters people's eyes, bounces off their retinas, and then returns to the camera. Because red eye occurs only if individuals are looking directly at the camera, its occurrence can be used to record where people are looking. In eye tracking, a light shines toward research participants while they view a stimulus (e.g., a picture or written text), and a camera records light bouncing off the backs of their eyes (Figure 5.26).

These recordings are the first of two steps in the eye tracking method. In the second, the eye-tracking system computes the direction and duration of eye movements and fixations, and then delivers to the researcher a summary of that information, usually in a computer display (Figure 5.27).

In addition to their value in basic research, eye tracking methods can be used to answer practical questions. For example, Web designers want to know how people interact with information on Web pages: how long they look around, where they look first, where their eyes move next, and so forth (Cutrell & Guan, 2007). Eye tracking during Internet browsing provides this information. In Figure 5.28, the magenta coloring shows places on a Web page where users spent the most time directing their gaze.

figure 5.28
Eye tracking of Web browsing Researchers have used eye tracking methods to find out where people direct their gaze when looking at Web pages. In the image, the magenta coloration indicates places where Internet users directed their gaze for relatively long periods of time.

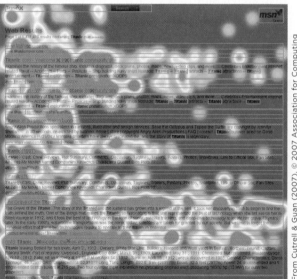

☄ WHAT DO YOU KNOW?...

6. In the first step of the eye tracking method, the eye tracker's camera records light that is bounced off the eyes' _____. In the second step, the tracker computes the direction and _____ of eye movements during fixations.

Once its cones and rods are stimulated, the eye's job is to send visual information to the brain. Key to this information flow are **ganglion cells,** which receive information from the retina and transmit it into the brain. The long fibers of the ganglion cells, along which these signals travel, form the **optic nerve** (see Figure 5.20a). There are far fewer ganglion cells than there are rods and cones; each ganglion cell, then, receives and integrates information from multiple photoreceptors.

At the spot along the retina at which the optic nerve exits the eye, there are no photoreceptors. Light striking that spot thus creates no visual experience. It's the **blind spot**—the location in the visual field at which nothing is seen. This might seem odd to you because, when you look around, you seem to see everything; you don't usually experience a blind spot. Your brain normally "fills in" the blind spot, providing you with a continuous visual experience. But you *can* experience it—see Figure 5.29.

FROM EYE TO BRAIN. The route along which signals travel from the eye into the brain contains three major steps. The first two involve the *optic chiasm* and the *lateral geniculate nucleus.*

❯ At the **optic chiasm,** visual signals carried by the optic nerves cross (Figure 5.30). Information from the left eye crosses over to the right side of the brain, and vice versa. (This crossing is a general property of brain wiring; see Chapter 3.)

figure 5.29
Blind spot If you close your left eye, look at the cross with your right eye, and vary the distance between yourself and the image, at one point the black dot will disappear. This happens when light from the dot hits your retina's blind spot.

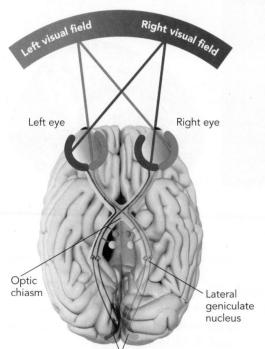

Left visual field | Right visual field
Left eye | Right eye
Optic chiasm
Lateral geniculate nucleus
Visual cortex

figure 5.30
The visual pathways in the brain Information makes its way from eye to brain in a series of steps. Signals switch sides, from one hemisphere of the brain to another, at the optic chiasm. Computations on the incoming signals are performed at the lateral geniculate nucleus. Signals are then sent to the visual cortex for additional visual information processing.

ganglion cells Cells that form the optic nerve and pass visual information from the retina to the brain.

optic nerve The biological pathway along which information leaves the eye and moves toward the brain, formed by the long fibers of ganglion cells.

blind spot The location in the visual field at which nothing is seen because light from that location projects to an area of the retina in which there are no photoreceptors; this is the retinal area where the optic nerve exits the eye.

optic chiasm The location in the brain where visual signals carried by the optic nerves cross, sending information from the left eye to the right side of the brain, and vice versa.

figure **5.31**
Visual cortex mapping Stimulation on the retina is mapped to activity in the visual cortex. When the visual image on the left was shown to a monkey and thus activated corresponding areas in the monkey's retina, corresponding activation was found in the monkey's visual cortex, as shown on the right.

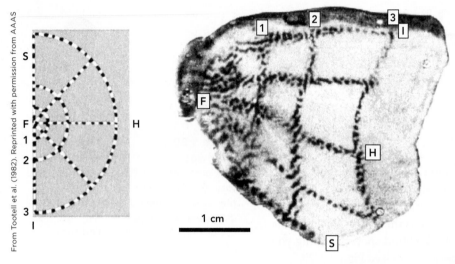

❯ Cells in the **lateral geniculate nucleus** receive visual signals and perform "computations" on them. Some computations, for example, compare the amount of red-wavelength light to green-wavelength light reaching the retina and thus produce the opponent process discussed earlier in the chapter (Shapley & Hawken, 2011).

The third step of processing, which we'll consider in detail, occurs in the *visual cortex.*

THE VISUAL CORTEX. Signals from the lateral geniculate nucleus reach the **visual cortex,** a region in the rear of the brain devoted to processing visual information (Belliveau et al., 1991). The biological processing required for the perception of visual features discussed earlier (size, shape, motion, etc.) occurs in the visual cortex.

The visual cortex contains layers of cells that progressively integrate signals coming from multiple photoreceptors in the eyes. The first layer of processing maps retinal activation into visual cortex activation (Tootell et al., 1982). In this mapping, adjacent areas of the retina are represented in adjacent areas of the cortex (Figure 5.31).

These mappings from retina to visual cortex provide insight into visual illusions. Earlier in this chapter, you saw a size illusion: Sometimes two identical objects appear to differ in size (see Figure 5.1). It turns out that, during this visual illusion, cortical activation corresponds to their *perceived* size, not their actual size (Figure 5.32).

figure **5.32**
Visual illusion in the brain The ring on top appears larger than the one on the bottom, although they are actually the same size. It also generates different activity in the visual cortex. The ring on the bottom produces the pattern of activation shown in green, which differs from the red pattern of activation produced by the ring on top.

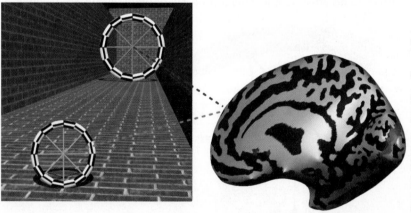

From Huk (2008). Reprinted from *Current Biology, 18,* with permission from Elsevier

lateral geniculate nucleus Cells that receive visual signals and perform "computations" on them before transmitting the same signals to the visual cortex.

visual cortex A region in the rear of the brain devoted to processing visual information.

Objects of the same actual size that appear larger/smaller have larger/smaller activation patterns in the cortex (Huk, 2008).

This result provides a link between levels of analysis (Figure 5.33). People experience illusions. The visual system's processing of cues such as texture and converging vertical lines explains the illusions in terms of the workings of the mind. Research on the visual cortex shows what happens at the level of the brain.

figure 5.33

PMB
IN ACTION

PERSON P

People commonly experience illusions. In these images, the people did not change size; the apparent changes in size are an illusion.

MIND M

At the mind level of analysis, this illusion can be explained in terms of mental computations that employ depth cues, such as converging vertical lines.

BRAIN B

At a brain level of analysis, the illusion can be explained in terms of representations of stimuli in the visual cortex.

From Huk (2008). Reprinted with permission from Elsevier

Michael Doolittle / Alamy

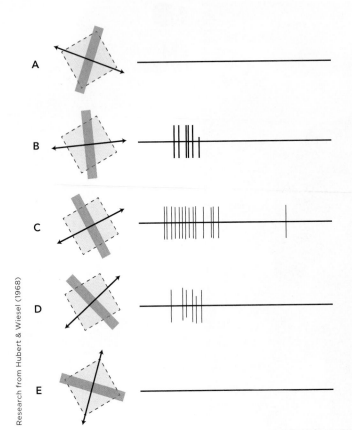

Research from Hubert & Wiesel (1968)

figure 5.34
Hubel and Wiesel line On the left are lines, at different angles, shown to a monkey. On the right is a recording of activity by one cell in that monkey's visual cortex; the vertical lines indicate activity in the cell. As you can see, the cell responded maximally to a line at a particular angle (the angle in image C).

More than a half-century ago, neuroscientists David Hubel and Torsten Wiesel conducted Nobel Prize–winning work on exactly how the visual cortex does its job (Hubel, 1963). They discovered individual cells in the cortex that are "feature detectors." The cells respond to specific visual features such as size, shape, and motion. For example, a cortical cell may respond maximally to lines that appear at a specific angle (Figure 5.34).

More recent research on the visual cortex highlights the ways in which the cortex combines the processing of different types of information. Visual properties such as the shape, brightness, texture, and color of objects influence one another, due to complex information processing in the cortex that integrates information about these perceptual features (Shapley & Hawken, 2011). This integration produces more accurate perception of objects. If you view, for example, a blue car that's partly in the shade, partly in the sun, and partly dented, the physical light that reaches your retina varies from one part of the car to another. Yet you do not perceive a multicolored car. You perceive, accurately, a car that is of a continuous shade of blue, as a result of your cortex's ability to integrate multiple visual features.

> Did this blue car example remind you of the earlier demonstration (Figure 5.17) of color constancy with an apple in a bowl of fruit? The same principle is at work.

WHAT DO YOU KNOW?...

7. Match each structure on the left with its feature on the right.

1. Rods	a. The first brain structure to do any "computations" on visual information
2. Cones	b. Where information from the right eye crosses over to the left side of the brain (and vice versa)
3. Fovea	c. Where the optic nerve exits the eye; an area absent of photoreceptors
4. Ganglion cells	d. Photoreceptors that detect detail and color
5. Optic nerve	e. Formed by the long fibers of the ganglion cells
6. Blind spot	f. Cells that receive information from the retina and transmit it to the brain
7. Optic chiasm	g. Photoreceptors that are very sensitive to light
8. Lateral geniculate nucleus	h. Area on the retina with a dense concentration of cones

The Auditory System

"Huh? What?"

The top 10 most commonly occurring words in English are "the," "of," "and," "a," "to," "in," "is," "you," "that," and "it" (Burch, 2000). Yet, if you listen to people conversing—above the sounds of music, traffic, video games, washing machines, and other people conversing—it may seem like the most common words are "huh" and "what." People often struggle to make themselves heard.

It's remarkable that we can hear any meaningful sounds at all. The physical stimuli that reach your ears are sound waves. **Sound waves** are variations in pressure that travel through some substance, such as the air. Your auditory system can convert these variations in air pressure into signals that provide information about the world.

sound waves Variations in pressure that reach the ears and are converted by the auditory system into signals.

The auditory system can create meaning from air pressure even when multiple sound waves occur simultaneously. So you shouldn't always need to say, "Huh?"

From an evolutionary perspective, auditory perception has great advantages. The visual system is sufficient to detect friends and foes, predators and prey—as long as they're not hiding! The capacity to detect environmental threats and opportunities that are out of sight enhances organisms' chances of survival.

Let's look at the types of information the auditory system delivers. Then we'll examine the biological mechanisms that make auditory perception possible.

Train track listening Sound waves generally travel through the air. But they also can travel through a solid medium, such as a railroad track.

Auditory Perception

Preview Questions

> What are the qualities of sound?
> How do we know where a sound is coming from?
> What psychological processes enable you to not only hear sounds, but also recognize them?

When you listen, you perceive meaningful sources of sound: a friend's hello; a fire truck's siren; the rhythmic thump of a bass line. Yet psychologists who study perception generally focus not on the perception of specific sound sources, but on auditory qualities that accompany any source of sound (McLachlan & Wilson, 2010). We'll look at four such qualities: loudness, pitch, timbre, and location of the sound source. Then we will examine psychological processes that enable you to identify what you're listening to.

LOUDNESS. Sometimes you can hear a pin drop. Sometimes you can't hear yourself think. Auditory experiences differ in **loudness,** the intensity, or strength, of an auditory experience. Loudness thus refers to something subjective: the degree to which a perceiver experiences a sound as intense (Plack & Carlyon, 1995).

Your psychological experience of loudness is determined primarily by the physical properties of sound waves. Sound waves with more physical energy are perceived as louder. Scientists measure the physical intensity of sound waves in *decibels* (dB); in other words, just as one measures physical length in meters, one measures the physical intensity of sound waves in decibels. Figure 5.35 shows the number of decibels associated with a range of sounds. On a decibel scale, a sound of 10 dB is 10 times louder than a 0-dB sound; a 20-dB sound has 10 times the intensity of 10 dB or 100 times the intensity of 0 dB; and so forth. (In the figure, the car, at 70 dB, thus is 10 times louder than the 60-dB conversation.)

Although the physical intensity of sound waves and perceptions of loudness are closely related, it is not an exact relationship. Two research findings show that physical intensity and psychological experience do not correspond precisely:

1. *Variations in the intensity of a sound wave do not correspond to variations in perceived loudness.* An increase in physical intensity of 10 dB—that is, a 10× increase—doubles perceived loudness (Stevens, 1955); it does not produce a 10× increase in loudness.

2. *People experience loudness illusions.* When people hear sequences of tones with different patterns of rise and fall in volume, followed by a final tone that is always of the same physical intensity, their perceptions of the loudness of the final tone differ (Jesteadt, Green, & Weir, 1978; Reinhardt-Rutland, 1998). Because the final tones are identical, the perception that they differ is illusory.

loudness The subjective experience of the intensity, or strength, of an auditory experience.

figure **5.35**
The decibel scale The measuring unit that scientists use to measure the physical intensity of sound waves is *decibels* (dB). On a decibel scale, a sound of 10 dB is 10 times louder than one of 0 dB; a 20-dB sound has 10 times the intensity of a 10-dB sound; and so forth. Zero decibels is the physical intensity required for the experience of hearing.

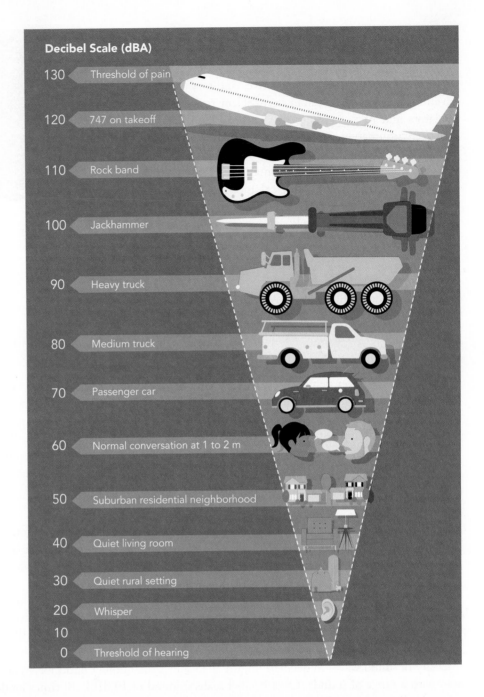

Decibel Scale (dBA)

130	Threshold of pain
120	747 on takeoff
110	Rock band
100	Jackhammer
90	Heavy truck
80	Medium truck
70	Passenger car
60	Normal conversation at 1 to 2 m
50	Suburban residential neighborhood
40	Quiet living room
30	Quiet rural setting
20	Whisper
10	
0	Threshold of hearing

PITCH. A second property of sounds is their **pitch,** the sound experience that we usually describe with the words "low" and "high." The keys on the far left of a musical keyboard produce a "low-pitched" sound; as you move to the right side of the keyboard, the tone becomes increasingly higher in pitch.

The physical property of sound waves that produces variations in pitch is their *frequency*. The **frequency** of a sound wave is the number of vibrations that occur during any fixed period of time. As shown in Figure 5.36, waves of higher frequency produce the perception of higher pitch.

As with loudness, pitch is a psychological experience that is not determined solely by the physical sound waves reaching the ear. A perceptual illusion again illustrates how physical stimuli and psychological experience can diverge. The psychologist Roger Shepard (1964) created a series of tones—now known as *Shepard Tones*—that produce a bizarre psychological experience. When listening to these tones, people experience an infinitely rising scale; one after another, the tones appear to go up and up, each one higher

pitch The sound experience that we usually describe with the words "low" or "high" (such as a musical note or voice).

frequency The physical property of sound waves that produces variations in pitch, based on the number of vibrations that occur during any fixed period of time.

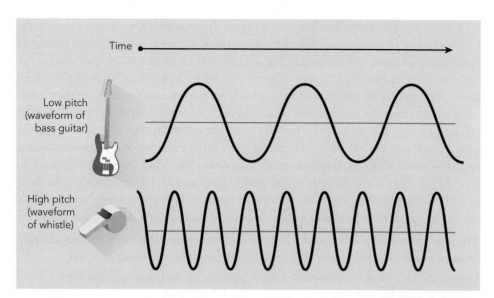

figure 5.36
Sound wave frequency and pitch Sound waves of higher frequency (more vibration during any given unit of time) have a higher pitch.

than the last. Yet, physically, the sound waves do not become infinitely more frequent. Instead, the physical stimuli "circle back" on themselves, rather like—in the visual domain—the stairs in an M. C. Escher drawing that appear to go up and up and yet circle back to where they started (see the accompanying image).

TIMBRE. A third sound quality is apparent if you compare the sound of a flute with the sound of a violin. Even when played at the same pitch and loudness, their sounds differ. You might say that the violin's sound is "richer."

This richness is part of the violin's timbre (pronounced *TAM-ber*). **Timbre** is the "signature" of a sound that enables you to distinguish it from other sounds, even when they have the same pitch or loudness. Variations in timbre generally reflect variations in the complexity of physical sound waves. The sound quality of a violin is richer than that of a flute because the sound waves emanating from the violin are more complex (Rasch & Plomp, 1999).

In the everyday environment, timbre is critical to auditory perception (Menon et al., 2002). Consider your ability to recognize voices. In person and even on the phone, you can instantly recognize the voices of numerous friends and family members. The recognition is not based solely on loudness and pitch. Your phone is designed to deliver different voices at similar levels of loudness. Different friends may have voices whose pitch is similarly high or low, yet the quality of their voices—the voices' timbre—differs, and this enables you to recognize them.

LOCATION. An animal in its natural environment that hears a predator wonders first and foremost, "Where is it?" Organisms need to hear not only the qualities of sounds—loudness, pitch, timbre—but also *where* those sounds are coming from. They need, in other words, to *localize* sounds: to identify the location of the sound source.

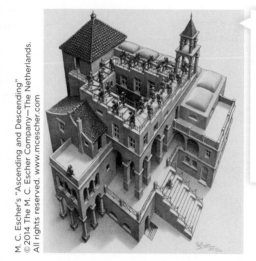

Escher steps The steps at the top of this M. C. Escher drawing seem to go continuously up (or down, depending on your direction of travel). The visual phenomenon is similar to an auditory phenomenon known as *Shepard Tones*, in which tones appear to form a scale that infinitely rises from one tone to the next.

Stradivarius This Stradivarius violin sold at auction for $3.5 million. And it wasn't because of its loudness or pitch! The auditory quality that makes such instruments unique is timbre.

timbre The distinctive "signature" of a sound, based on variations in the complexity of sound waves.

To understand auditory localization, we must distinguish between two dimensions: (1) left/right and (2) up/down. [The third dimension, distance, is determined primarily by loudness (Coleman, 1963); sounds that are less loud are perceived as more distant.] A bit of reflection on human anatomy suggests that left/right localization might be easier because your ears are on the left and right sides—not the top and bottom—of your head.

If a sound comes from your left, and then another from your right, you'll usually be able to localize the sounds. To provide left/right information, the auditory system capitalizes on an obvious fact: Your ears are on different sides of your head. Sound waves thus travel different routes to reach one versus the other ear (Middlebrooks & Green, 1991). They travel directly to the ear on the near side, but must also make their way around your head to reach the ear on the far side. Two cues to localization result from the layout of your head and ears: *timing* and *pressure*. For a sound from your left:

> **Timing:** The sound reaches your left ear before your right ear because it takes a small amount of time for sound waves to travel around your head to your right ear.

> **Pressure:** The sound wave produces more pressure on your left ear than right ear because it loses pressure while traveling around your head.

CONNECTING TO MEMORY AND TO PSYCHOLOGICAL DISORDERS

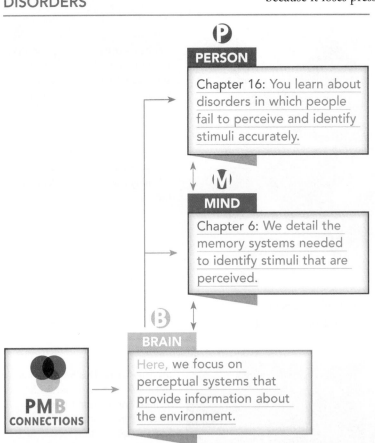

Your auditory system automatically processes and combines these cues, which makes left/right sound localization easy.

The same cues, however, can make another type of sound localization difficult: front/back localization. Suppose two identical sounds come from two locations—directly in front and in back of you. The sounds have the same location on the left/right dimension (in the middle). Their timing and the air pressure they exert are the same at your left and right ears. When people hear such sounds, they often experience *front/back confusions:* They think a sound came from in back of them when, in reality, it came from in front (or vice versa; Middlebrooks & Green, 1991). You may have experienced this when driving and hearing the distant sound of a siren (e.g., from an ambulance or fire truck); it can be hard to tell if the sound is coming from in front of you or behind.

What about up/down sound localization? Suppose that two sounds come from straight in front of you, one from up in the air and the other from down on the ground. It might seem impossible to distinguish them, since their timing and pressure at the two ears are identical. Yet people often can make up/down distinctions accurately (Middlebrooks & Green, 1991). How? The key factor is the shape of the ear, which affects the physical signals that make their way into your nervous system. This effect differs, depending on whether sound waves enter the ear from above or below, because your ear is not symmetrical from top to bottom; that is, the shape of the top and bottom parts of your ear do not match. Sound waves thus "bounce around" the ear in different manners, depending on whether they enter from the bottom or the top. Such differences can enable people to perceive whether a sound came from above or below.

WHAT'S MAKING THE SOUND? In addition to loudness, pitch, timbre, and location, you want to know what's actually making the sound. Was that cry from a baby or a cat? Was the rumble thunder or an explosion? These are questions of *auditory recognition,* the identification of a sound's source.

---

timing In the study of auditory perception, a cue to the location of a sound source that is based on the difference in time it takes a sound coming from your side to reach each ear.

pressure In the study of auditory perception, a cue to the location of a sound source that is based on the difference in pressure on left and right ears produced by a sound wave coming from one side.

In general, people are quite good at auditory recognition. In one study (Gygi, Kidd, & Watson, 2004), participants heard 70 sounds ranging from A (airplane flying) to Z (a zipper). Each sound was presented for just a few seconds. Many were uncommon (e.g., the sound of a helicopter). Yet participants recognized stimuli accurately the majority of the time.

To recognize sounds, people need preexisting knowledge. Without it, recognition is impossible; if you aren't already familiar with the Indian Purple Frog (which sounds a bit like a chicken), you won't be able to identify it no matter how loudly it croaks. To recognize a sound, people must maintain the sound in short-term memory, activate knowledge of sound stored in long-term memory (see Chapter 6), and compare the two (McLachlan & Wilson, 2010).

> What sounds would you have difficulty identifying?

👣 WHAT DO YOU KNOW?...

8. For each of the "answers" below, provide the question. The first one has been completed for you.
   a. Answer: This feature of sound waves determines loudness.
      Question: What is intensity?
   b. Answer: This feature of sound waves determines pitch.
   c. Answer: This sound quality enables you to distinguish between the sounds of electric versus acoustic guitars.
   d. Answer: This type of localization is made difficult by the fact that when a sound comes straight at you (or straight at your back), the timing and pressure of the sound are identical.
   e. Answer: This type of localization is made possible by the fact that the tops and bottoms of our ears are asymmetrical.

From Ear to Brain: Biological Bases of Auditory Perception

Preview Question

> Through what biological process are we able to convert sound waves into meaningful information?

Now let's look at the biological machinery that makes auditory perception possible. You won't be surprised to hear that the story begins at the ear.

AUDITORY PROCESSING IN THE EAR. In everyday language, "ear" refers to those visible structures appended to the sides of your head. But in the study of auditory processing (Moore & Linthicum, 2004), the term **ear** refers to a complex biological mechanism with three overall sections: an *outer ear, middle ear,* and *inner ear* (Figure 5.37).

Sound waves first reach the *pinna,* the portion of outer ear that captures sound waves and directs them down the *auditory canal* to the *eardrum.* The **eardrum** is a thin membrane that vibrates when struck by sound waves. Sound waves of different intensity and magnitude create different patterns of vibration at the eardrum.

The eardrum's movement activates mechanisms in the middle ear. Specifically, vibrations of the eardrum cause motion in an interconnected series of small bones in the middle ear called *ossicles.* Motion of the ossicles, in turn, creates activity in the inner ear, where transduction—the conversion of sound wave vibrations into neural signals—occurs.

ear A biological mechanism for hearing with three overall parts: an outer ear, middle ear, and inner ear.

eardrum A thin membrane within the ear that vibrates when struck by sound waves.

figure 5.37
Structure of the ear In order for you to detect sound waves, they have to travel down the auditory canal to the eardrum, whose vibrations activate mechanisms in the middle ear. Those mechanisms, in turn, create activity in the inner ear, where sound wave vibrations are converted to neural signals.

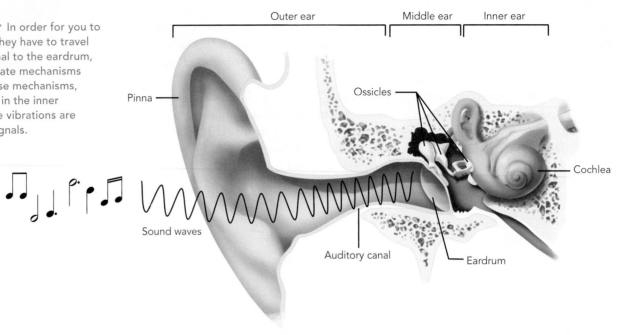

Transduction occurs within a spiral-shaped, fluid-filled body in the inner ear called the *cochlea*. The cochlea contains auditory **hair cells,** which are the auditory receptor cells responsible for transduction (Gillespie & Müller, 2009). The hair cells get their name from their shape (Figure 5.38). Motion of the ossicles causes vibration of the cochlea's fluid, which in turn causes the hair cells to move. Finally, the movement of the hair cells sets off neural impulses that travel to the brain.

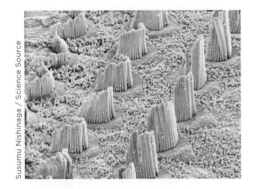

figure 5.38
Hair cells of the inner ear This extreme close-up shows the hair cells of the inner ear—the receptor cells of the auditory system.

Loud noises—such as those experienced at a rock concert— can damage the hair cells of the ear and produce *noise-induced hearing loss.* The hearing loss may be accompanied by a continual buzzing sound in the ear known as tinnitus (NIDCD, 2013). Shown on the left is Chris Martin of the British band Coldplay, who suffers from tinnitus and campaigns to raise awareness of the risks surrounding noise exposure. On the right is his well-protected daughter, Apple, in the arms of her mother, Gwyneth Paltrow.

hair cells Auditory receptor cells in the inner ear that are responsible for transduction of sound waves.

THE AUDITORY CORTEX. Auditory signals leave the inner ear along the **auditory nerve,** a bundle of thousands of nervous system cells that originates at the cochlea and carries auditory information to the brain. As with the optic nerve, there is a crossing of nerve fibers, with signals from the left ear reaching the right side of the brain, and vice versa.

The high-level processing required to make sense of signals from the cochlea is done in the *auditory cortex.* The auditory cortex is a brain region located on the temporal lobe (see Chapter 3) that is primarily devoted to the processing of auditory information. It takes up about one-eighth of the overall cortical surface of the brain (Woods & Alain, 2009).

Auditory cortex

figure 5.39
Auditory cortex The brain processes auditory signals in the auditory cortex, which contains tens of millions of neurons to contribute to your experience of sound.

The auditory cortex is therefore a substantial brain region. It contains tens of millions of neurons. Does this brain matter have any overall organization? Recall that the visual cortex is organized systematically; physical stimuli that strike neighboring areas of the retina are processed by neighboring areas of the visual cortex (Figure 5.31). The auditory cortex is similar, except that the organization is based on pitch (Wessinger et al., 1997). Sounds that are similar in pitch—that is, sounds whose waves have similar frequency (Figure 5.36)—are processed in neighboring areas of the auditory cortex (Figure 5.39). Sounds that differ greatly in pitch are processed in locations farther apart (Woods & Alain, 2009).

The auditory cortex deals with other information in addition to pitch. Brain-imaging studies with human and nonhuman primates have identified specialized regions of the cortex that process information about (1) the location of sounds, (2) the identification of the source of a sound, and (3) vocalizations by members of one's own species (Rauschecker & Tian, 2000).

👀 WHAT DO YOU KNOW?...

9. Like an actual drum, the _____ vibrates when struck by sound waves. These vibrations, in turn, move small bones of the inner ear called _____. Transduction occurs when these vibrations cause the _____'s fluid to vibrate, thereby causing the _____ cells to move and to send neural impulses to the _____ cortex via the auditory _____. Sounds that are similar in pitch are processed in _____ areas of the brain.

The Olfactory System

If you walk into a department store, among the first items you see—placed right up front because they're so profitable—are perfumes. Consumers shell out big bucks for little bottles of scent. The prices and purchases attest to the power of *olfaction*, the perception of airborne chemical substances—or, more simply, the sense of smell.

Perceiving Odors

Preview Question

› What are some types of stimuli we can smell?

Olfaction provides a range of information. It not only tells you *that* something smells. It also provides information about (1) *intensity*, or how strong the smell is, and (2) *pleasantness,*

You'd be joyful, too, if you could afford this Jean Patou product. It costs about $400 an ounce.

Sam Granado / KRT / Newscom

auditory nerve A bundle of nerve cells that carries auditory information from the inner ear to the brain.

Passing the smell test Dogs, including those trained to sniff out explosives, rely on olfaction more than vision.

whether the **odorant**—the thing that smells—smells good or bad (Moskowitz, Dravnieks, & Klarman, 1976). These two dimensions are distinct; different parts of the brain process information about pleasantness and intensity (Anderson et al., 2003).

Olfaction also detects a range of different odorants, including (1) foods, (2) *pheromones,* and (3) chemical signals of cell damage and disease, as you'll see immediately ahead.

In our discussion of olfaction, we'll focus primarily on olfaction by humans. Yet smell is even more important to other species. Consider the dog. In a study of dogs that had been trained to detect bombs, their detection ability was found to be equally good whether containers of explosive material were brightly or very dimly lit. The dogs relied so heavily on olfaction that impaired vision made no difference to them. Furthermore, if an explosive was moved around a room and then placed in plain sight, the dogs did not walk directly to it, as would an organism relying primarily on vision. Instead, they traced a path to the explosive that followed its past movements, which left a scent (Gazit & Terkel, 2003). Among dogs, then, olfaction dominates vision in the guidance of behavior. They trust their sense of smell more than their sense of sight. Humans, by comparison, "don't trust their nose" (Sela & Sobel, 2010, p. 13) as much as their vision. This psychological difference is accompanied by a biological one: About 12.5% of dogs' brain mass is devoted to olfaction, as compared with less than 1% for humans (Williams, 2011).

> Does this information explain any seemingly bizarre canine behavior you've ever witnessed?

FOOD ODORS. One class of stimuli that you perceive olfactorily is food. The ability to detect food odors was critical over the course of evolution, for two reasons. One, of course, is that it enabled organisms to find food. The other is that it enabled them to avoid spoiled food, which can be dangerous to eat. Mammals have a keen ability to smell the spoilage and thus avoid the danger (Takahashi, Nagayama, & Mori, 2004).

When presented with good (not spoiled) foods, how accurately can people identify them by their odors? Intuitively, it seems that sometimes we can identify odors accurately, yet other times we can't tell what a smell might be. Research is consistent with this intuition; accuracy varies considerably. In one study (Cain, 1979), participants presented with common odorants (e.g., chocolate, cinnamon, peanut butter) correctly identified them only 45% of the time. However, days later, participants returned to the lab and were asked to identify the odors again, using the labels they generated on the first day. After some practice, participants applied their original label consistently 77% of the time (Cain, 1979). Even if a label was inaccurate (e.g., they smelled nutmeg and labeled it "cloves"), participants used the label ("cloves") consistently when smelling the substance, which means that their ability to recognize the smell was very good.

> How accurate are you at recognizing odor? The last time you walked into a home where dinner was cooking, were you able to identify it olfactorily?

If you're young, enjoy your food aromas now. Your ability to make subtle distinctions among foods by your sense of smell is likely to decline with age. One study presented food odors to two groups of people: young adults in their early twenties and older adults in their seventies. The younger adults were better able to classify different types of foods based on their smell (Schiffman & Pasternak, 1979).

PHEROMONES. Another class of stimuli detected by the olfactory system is *pheromones.* **Pheromones** are chemical signals that are produced within the body of one organism, secreted by that organism, and then detected by another organism of the

odorant Anything that smells; odorants include a variety of substances such as foods, pheromones, and chemical signals of cell damage and disease.

pheromones Chemical signals produced and secreted by one organism and detected by another organism of the same species, triggering a distinctive reaction.

same species. When detected, the pheromone triggers a distinctive reaction in the organism that receives it. Female fish, for example, secrete sex pheromones when they are ready to spawn; the pheromones, once detected by male fish, trigger reproductive behavior in the male (Wyatt, 2009).

Pheromones are detected primarily by the olfactory system. The olfactory system, then, has evolved to be highly sensitive to the odors of pheromones. In fact, many mammals (but not humans) have a second olfactory system designed specifically to aid in the detection of pheromones (Firestein, 2001).

The precise chemical substances that function as pheromones have been identified in other species, but not in humans (Wyatt, 2009). This has led some to question whether communication by pheromones is important to our species. Yet some evidence supports that it is important. Researchers find that women living in close quarters, such as a college dorm, may develop menstrual cycles that are synchronous (i.e., they coincide). The cause appears to be pheromones detected by the olfactory system. Women naturally secrete different biological compounds (e.g., through sweat glands) at different stages in the menstrual cycle. Some of the compounds affect the length of other women's menstrual cycles. As a result, over time, menstrual cycles tend to synchronize (Stern & McClintock, 1998).

CELL DAMAGE AND DISEASE. Researchers recently have discovered a third class of stimuli perceived through olfaction: chemicals associated with cell damage and disease (Munger, 2009).

Cellular damage and inflammation caused by disease create distinctive molecular activity in the body. Researchers have identified the exact molecular changes, and then have looked within the olfactory system to see whether organisms detect them. Indeed, they do (Rivière et al., 2009). Thanks to receptors in their olfactory systems, mammals are able to detect molecular markers of illness. This ability has practical implications for human health. Cancer can be detected in early stages of its development by dogs that recognize signs of cancer in patients' breath (Sonoda et al., 2011).

The ability to detect cell damage and disease must have been an advantage throughout the course of evolution. To remain healthy themselves, organisms would benefit from avoiding others who are ill. When seeking mates for reproduction, organisms benefit from finding a mate healthy enough to reproduce. The struggle for survival, then, relies in part on the olfactory system.

❧ WHAT DO YOU KNOW?...

10. True or False?
    a. Research indicates that although humans may not be terribly accurate at detecting food odors, we are fairly consistent.
    b. The ability to detect pheromones is important enough to humans that they have evolved a second olfactory system just for detecting them.
    c. One practical application of mammals' ability to detect cell damage and disease is that dogs can detect cancer in its early stages by smelling patients' breath.

From Nose to Brain: Biological Bases of Olfaction

Preview Questions

› Through what biological process are we able to convert airborne chemical signals into information that is sent to the brain?
› Why are some people more sensitive to odors than others?

You don't need to take a psychology class to know that olfaction begins at the nose. When you sniff, airborne substances enter your nasal cavity. Let's look at what happens next: the biological processes that produce the sense of smell.

figure 5.40

From nose to brain A series of processing steps leads from nose to brain, that is, from odorants entering the nose to the experience of smell that results from neural processing in the brain. Sensory receptors that are activated by odorants (1) send signals to the olfactory bulbs (2), which in turn send signals to the olfactory cortex (3). The olfactory cortex is interconnected with the thamalus (4), a "relay station" for information processing near the center of the brain. Both through the thalamus, and directly, the olfactory cortex is connected with regions near the front of the brain for further processing (5).

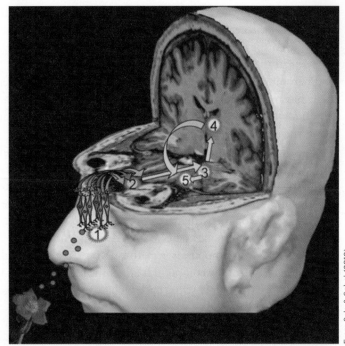

From Sela & Sobel (2010)

FROM NOSE TO BRAIN. The biological bases of olfaction involve a three-step process (Sela & Sobel, 2010; Figure 5.40):

1. *Receptor cells.* Both of your nostrils contain more than 10 million receptor cells that are activated by odorants, pheromones, and disease-related molecules in the air. Different types of receptor cells are sensitive to different molecular signals. The receptor cells convert chemical signals into electrical signals that eventually reach the brain.

2. *Olfactory bulbs.* Signals from receptor cells are sent to the **olfactory bulbs,** collections of cells near the front of the brain. After the signals are received, cells in the olfactory bulbs begin the process of identifying odors; different patterns of activity in the olfactory bulbs' cells are associated with different odors (Sela & Sobel, 2010).

3. *Olfactory cortex.* Signals from the olfactory bulbs are sent to the **olfactory cortex,** a neural system in a lower region of the brain known as the limbic system (see Chapter 3). Neural processing in the olfactory cortex completes the processes through which smells are recognized. Exactly how this processing is conducted is not fully understood; however, evidence suggests that the *duration* of neural activity in the olfactory cortex is significant. Rather than there being specific sets of cells that correspond to particular smells, different smells—which variously linger over time—are associated with different durations of nerve cell activity over time (Poo & Isaacson, 2009).

INDIVIDUAL DIFFERENCES AND GENETICS. People differ considerably in the sensitivity of their olfactory system. Consider a study in which researchers (Cain & Gent, 1991) presented low levels of four odorants—chemicals that smelled like wood, gas, flowers, and pears—and determined the minimum chemical concentration of each odor that participants could detect. In a study with this design, there are two possible results:

1. People's ability to detect odors may vary from one odor to another; that is, one person might be good at detecting wood smells and not flower smells, and another might be good at detecting flowers but not wood.

2. People's ability to detect odors may be consistent from one odor to the next, but some people may have consistently better odor detection than others.

olfactory bulbs Collections of cells near the front of the brain that receive signals from olfactory receptor cells and begin the process of identifying odors.

olfactory cortex A neural system that completes the biological processing needed to recognize smells.

The researchers obtained result #2: Some people had better odor detection than others. But the sensitivity of odor detection for any individual was consistent across various odors.

Genetic variations explain much of the variation in olfactory ability. Genes that encode instructions for the olfactory system's receptor cells are key (Hasin-Brumshtein, Lancet, & Olender, 2009). Genetic variations create differences in the number and diversity of olfactory receptors that people possess. Differences in receptors, in turn, produce person-to-person differences in the sense of smell.

🕊 WHAT DO YOU KNOW?...

11. Molecular signals activate _____ cells in the nostrils, which then relay those signals to the _____ _____. These signals are sent to the _____ cortex in the _____ system. The _____ of nerve cell activity in the brain seems to be associated with recognition of odors. Individual differences in the ability to detect odors are largely explained by _____ variations.

The Gustatory System

Victory is *sweet*. Defeat is *bitter*. When the salesman tried to trick you into paying too much for a used car, the experience left a *bad taste* in your mouth. When your relationship broke up and your ex said, "I never really cared about you anyway," it was just *sour* grapes. The psychological experience of taste, which is produced by the *gustatory system,* is so central to human experience that we use tastes as metaphors for discussing life's ups and downs.

Taste, in fact, may be necessary to life itself. People who lose their sense of taste have trouble getting themselves to eat, despite needing nutrition to live. One such person, who lost gustatory ability after radiation therapy for cancer, said that, without taste, being served a meal is like "being presented with a piled-high plate of charcoal biscuits by a menacing giant who says 'Eat it up, it will do you good.'" As one doctor described such a loss:

> If, by a mighty effort, the "cinders" are forced down with copious fluid, the consequences are acute indigestion or vomiting. . . . [I]f there is anything objectionable to feel (such as gristle in [meat]) a sort of panic nausea may be the next reaction. . . . The patient is not hungry anyway, and it is easier to starve.

> —MacCarthy-Leventhal (1959, p. 1138)

We need tastes. The *gustatory system* gives them to us by responding to the chemical properties of foods and sending these responses to the brain.

Gustatory Perception

Preview Questions

> Besides salty and sweet, what are the other types of tastes we can detect? What the heck is *umami*?
> Why don't all salty foods taste the same?
> What is the difference between flavor and taste?
> What is a supertaster?

When you try different foods, your perceptions of them differ in two ways:

1. *Qualities:* You notice different *qualities*; that is, different foods have entirely different types of tastes.
2. *Dimensions:* Taste experiences differ along a number of dimensions. For example, some tastes are more intense than others.

Foodcollection / Getty Images

Expensive taste Just as people spend money for olfactory experiences, they spend for taste experiences. A black truffle—a form of mushroom used for flavoring in European cuisine—like this one often sells for more than $100 an ounce.

Let's review these two aspects of taste perception and then discuss *flavor*, an experience that combines taste and smell.

TASTE QUALITIES. Humans perceive five distinct taste qualities. Even complex food tastes—the robust flavors of a spicy Chinese stir-fry or the subtlety of French haute cuisine—are blends of these five simple, basic types of taste (Breslin & Spector, 2008):

1. *Sweet:* Most people—in fact, most mammals—are attracted to sweet tastes. This makes sense when one considers evolutionary processes. Foods that taste sweet are high in simple carbohydrates, which provide energy the body needs. The ability to detect these sweet, high-carbohydrate foods thus was adaptive over the course of evolution.

2. *Salty:* Salty tastes come from foods and flavorings containing the chemical *sodium.* (Salt itself is, chemically, sodium chloride.) Organisms need sodium to maintain normal bodily functioning. Again, our liking for saltiness makes sense evolutionarily; across evolution, it was essential for organisms to develop the ability to obtain sodium, through the taste experience of saltiness.

3. *Bitter:* Many potentially edible substances in the natural world that are poisonous taste bitter. The gustatory perception of bitterness, then, appears to have evolved as a "warning signal." It protects organisms against edible dangers.

4. *Sour:* Sour tastes are triggered by foods that, chemically, are acids. Lemons, for example, contain a high level of citric acid. The ability to detect sour tastes may have evolved because sourness signals the degree of ripeness of fruits, which change in acidity during the ripening process.

5. *Umami:* Scientists only recently discovered and named a fifth taste: **umami,** which corresponds to the taste we usually call "savory" (Li et al., 2002). The rich flavor of a beef stew includes the taste umami. A refreshing fruit salad or a chewy marshmallow do not. Umami is triggered by high levels of protein in food. This taste experience thus may have evolved to help organisms identify and ingest the protein they needed for bodily growth.

> When was the last time you experienced umami?

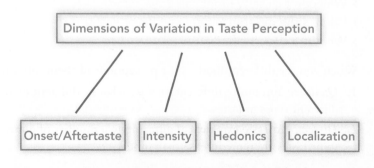

ZUMA Press, Inc. / Alamy

Umami Burger This place sounds great—after you learn about gustatory perception.

DIMENSIONS OF GUSTATORY EXPERIENCE. All salty tastes are not the same. Neither are all sour tastes, nor gustatory experiences of the other taste categories. Tastes also differ along a number of taste dimensions.

Four taste dimensions describe variations in gustatory experience (Figure 5.41). *Onset/aftertaste* describes taste experience across time. For example, some tastes linger, whereas others "vanish" soon after a food is swallowed. *Intensity* describes the strength of the gustatory experience. Two foods might both be sour, but one could have a much greater intensity of sourness than the other. *Hedonics* refers to how much you like the taste. Hedonics and intensity are often

figure **5.41**
Variations in taste experience

Dimensions of Variation in Taste Perception

Onset/Aftertaste Intensity Hedonics Localization

umami A taste sensation that is "savory," triggered by high protein levels in food.

related; you might like salty potato chips—unless they're *too* salty (i.e., unless the saltiness is too intense). Finally, *localization* is perception of where within the mouth a taste is experienced. The gustatory system's taste receptors provide information about whether a taste occurs on the left or right side of the tongue (Shikata, McMahon, & Breslin, 2000).

FLAVOR. We have been considering perceptual systems one at a time, but sometimes they work together. A prime case of this is the perception of food.

Imagine that you're trying to guess the seasonings in some food (e.g., "What's in that tomato sauce?"). Some of the perceptual information you gather comes from taste. But, some of it comes from smell—that is, from the olfactory system. The combination of two perceptual systems—gustation and olfaction—contributes to the overall perceptual experience of the food, or its *flavor*.

In the experience of flavor, your perceptual systems integrate information about taste and smell to produce a coherent perceptual experience (Auvray & Spence, 2008). You don't have two separate experiences of a food product, one olfactory and one gustatory ("Hmm, I smell some garlic somewhere"; "Oh, and I taste some garlic in my mouth"). You have one integrated perceptual experience of the food ("There's garlic in that soup").

Both everyday observation and scientific findings show how smell and taste interact. If you have a stuffy nose from a cold, or just hold your nose when eating, you cannot perceive the flavor of food as keenly as normal. Research shows that smells influence tastes. For example, a food's odor can influence how sweet it tastes (Auvray & Spence, 2008).

SUPERTASTERS. Not everyone's experience of foods is the same. Some of us are **supertasters:** people who have greater sensitivity to tastes than others.

Supertasters were discovered in research by psychologist Linda Bartoshuk and her colleagues (Bartoshuk, 2000). In their studies, participants were asked to rate, on a measurement scale, the intensity of their experiences when tasting various substances. A subset of individuals provided extremely high ratings of intensity. There were two possible interpretations of this result: (1) These people were more sensitive to tastes than others; or (2) they were no more sensitive to tastes than others, but merely tended to make more extreme ratings when filling out measurement scales during psychology experiments.

To determine which interpretation was correct, the researchers devised a clever new measurement procedure (Bohannon, 2010). They asked people to rate the most intense sensation (e.g., an intense pain) they ever experienced, and then to rate the intensity of taste experiences. The use of two ratings allowed the researchers to control for people's general tendency to make low- or high-intensity ratings when completing scales. The results confirmed that supertasters were "super": They made uniquely high ratings of sensory intensity specifically when tasting food.

> Are you a picky eater? Perhaps you are a supertaster! Supertaster tests can be found easily on the Internet.

🐾 WHAT DO YOU KNOW?...

12. Four of the five basic types of tastes are sweet, salty, sour, and bitter. Name the fifth and explain why it would be evolutionarily adaptive to detect it. The experience of flavor combines which two perceptual systems?

From Mouth to Brain: Biological Bases of Gustation

Preview Question

> Through what biological process are we able to convert gustatory information from our mouths to our brains?

supertasters People who have greater sensitivity to tastes than others.

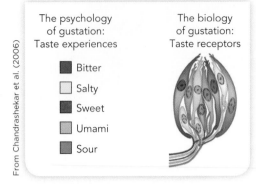

The psychology of gustation: Taste experiences

The biology of gustation: Taste receptors

■ Bitter
□ Salty
■ Sweet
▨ Umami
■ Sour

figure 5.42

Taste receptors Research on gustation can link findings at two levels of analysis. At the level of the mind, taste includes five types of experiences. At the level of the brain, there are five corresponding taste receptors.

figure 5.43

Supertaster tongue Supertasters have more of the bumps on the tongue that contain taste buds than do other people.

taste receptors Cells that are stimulated by chemical substances in food, whose activation begins the process of transmitting gustatory information to the brain.

taste buds Bundles of taste receptors, found primarily on the tongue but also on the roof of the mouth and throat.

gustatory cortex The brain region in the parietal lobe that completes the processing of perceptual signals of taste.

In taste perception, connecting psychological phenomena to biological mechanisms is straightforward. The biology of gustation directly explains many of the psychological phenomena you just learned about.

The first step in getting gustatory information from mouth to brain involves **taste receptors,** which are cells that are stimulated by chemical substances in food. When stimulated, taste receptors release neurotransmitters that begin the process of transmitting gustatory information to the brain (Smith & Margolskee, 2001). Taste receptors are bundled together in **taste buds,** each of which contains about 50 to 100 receptor cells. Taste buds are found primarily on the tongue, but also on the roof of the mouth and throat (Breslin & Spector, 2008).

Evidence indicates that there are five types of taste receptors. The good news—if you're trying to connect psychological and biological levels of analysis—is that these receptor types correspond to the five taste qualities we just reviewed. Different types of receptor cells are "tuned" to detect each of the five taste qualities: sweet, salty, bitter, sour, and umami (Chandrashekar et al., 2006; Figure 5.42). Contrary to what was once thought, receptors of each type are found in multiple areas of the tongue; it is *not* the case that any one large region of the tongue is responsive only to one taste quality.

Biological analyses of the gustatory system also reveal individual differences. Supertasters have more of the bumps on the tongue that contain taste buds. They thus have more taste receptors and superior gustatory perception (Figure 5.43).

Signals from taste receptors travel along neural pathways to a lower region of the brain known as the brain stem (see Chapter 3), and then to an upper region known as the gustatory cortex. The **gustatory cortex,** a region in the brain's parietal lobe, completes the processing of perceptual signals involving taste (Kobayakawa et al., 2005). It is highly connected to other regions of the brain, which means that taste perception is affected by other sensory inputs and the overall state of the body (de Araujo & Simon, 2009). Scientists are just starting to learn how information about taste is represented in this brain region (see This Just In).

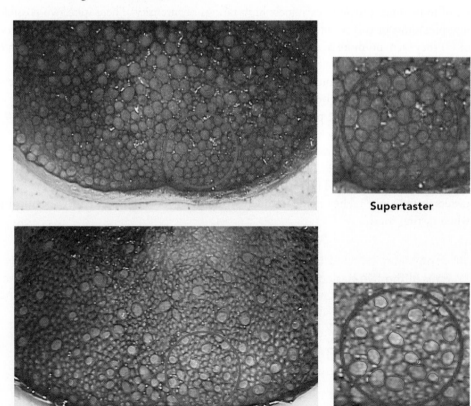

Supertaster

Non-Supertaster

🐦 WHAT DO YOU KNOW?...

13. Taste buds consist of taste _____ that convey signals to the brain stem, then to the _____ cortex of the _____ lobe.

🌑 THIS JUST IN

Taste Maps in the Brain

In our coverage of visual perception, you learned that there is a mapping—a direct spatial correspondence—between activity in the retina and activity in the visual cortex (Figure 5.31). Might there be a similar cortical mapping for taste, that is, for gustatory perception?

For quite a while, people didn't think so. By way of comparison, there is no such map for the sense of smell. When any given odorant is processed in the brain, the processing is done by neurons in different locations; there is no single location in the brain for the processing of each distinct type of smell (Chen et al., 2011). Maybe the processing of taste, researchers had reasoned, is similar to the processing of smell.

However, recent research advances (Chen et al., 2011) have led to a surprising discovery: There *is* a "gustotopic map" in the cortex. Five distinct regions of the cortex process each of the five types of gustatory signals: sweet, salty, bitter, sour, and umami.

The discovery required painstaking research. Researchers had to present different tastes to organisms (mice) while recording the activity of large numbers of individual cells in the cortex. This enabled them to establish the exact locations in which each taste sensation is processed. The accompanying image shows the result for the taste sensation of bitter. As you can see, bitter tastes were processed in the same region of the cortex in each mouse.

The researchers found locations like this for each of the five taste sensations, establishing yet another link from biological mechanisms to psychological experience.

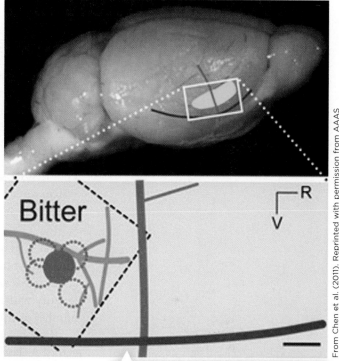

From Chen et al. (2011). Reprinted with permission from AAAS

Gustatory processing in the brain The top photo shows a mouse's brain, with the yellow area indicating the location in the cortex in which gustatory processing occurs. The bottom image is an enlarged diagram of this location in the mouse's brain. In the diagram, the solid red circle and four dotted-line circles indicate the neural regions, in the brains of each of five mice, that were sensitive to bitter tastes.

🐦 WHAT DO YOU KNOW?...

14. What does it mean to say there is a "gustatopic map" in the cortex?

The Haptic System

Try this. Close your eyes and ask a friend to hand you an everyday object. What can you learn about the object without even looking at it (or listening to or smelling it)? A lot! You'll quickly acquire a wealth of information: its size . . . its shape . . . what it's made of. You might even be able to identify exactly what the object is.

This information comes through your *haptic system,* the perceptual system through which people acquire information about objects by touching them (Lederman & Klatzky, 2009). (The word *haptic* comes from the Greek word for "touch.")

Not all types of touch are the same. As James J. Gibson (1962) pointed out, there are two types:

1. *Active touching:* Sometimes you touch an object. You purposefully explore it to learn about its properties.
2. *Being touched:* Sometimes objects touch you. They variously bump, scratch, or rest gently upon the surface of your skin.

The two types of touch differ psychologically. Through active touching, you perceive physical properties of objects in the environment—for example, whether they are smooth, rough, warm, or cold (Turvey & Carello, 2011). When being touched, your psychological experience centers on a point of your body; for example, if the object is a bowling ball that touches you by landing on your foot, you feel pain in your foot.

In this section of the chapter, we'll first look at the types of information you acquire by using your haptic system. After reviewing these psychological processes, we'll move down to a biological level of analysis, to learn about the nervous-system mechanisms that make haptic information gathering possible.

Haptic Perception

Preview Questions

> On what parts of the body is touch perceived most accurately?
> How do hand and finger movements deliver information about texture, temperature, and hardness?
> How do we detect mass?

Let's first look at the precision, or *acuity,* of the haptic system. We'll then see how this system reveals information about (1) the surfaces of objects (their texture, temperature, and hardness), and (2) objects' size and shape.

ACUITY. If somebody taps you, you can locate the tap: It was felt on your arm, or shoulder, or head, or back. How precisely can you locate it, though? This is a question about the *acuity* of the haptic system, that is, the accuracy with which the system can identify whether it has been stimulated, where the stimulation has occurred, and the number of stimulations that occurred.

Researchers have developed psychophysical procedures to measure haptic system acuity. A classic method is the *two-point procedure,* developed by the nineteenth-century German scientist Ernst Weber. In the **two-point procedure,** researchers touch the skin of a research participant with two stimuli (e.g., two pencil points). The space between the stimuli varies across experimental trials. Sometimes they are spaced well apart, but other times they are so close that people can't even tell there are two stimuli; it feels as if there is just one. On each trial, then, participants are asked whether they experience one point touching their skin or two. The smallest distance at which they can detect two different stimuli touching their skin is called the two-point *threshold.* This distance indicates the acuity of the haptic system; a smaller distance (i.e., a lower threshold) means greater acuity (a greater ability to distinguish between stimuli).

Two-point sensitivity

Two-point procedure The two-point procedure for measuring haptic system acuity.

> Have you ever had trouble finding an itch on your back?

A key finding is that the two-point threshold distance varies across different parts of the body. At some regions of the body, the distance is quite small; the haptic system has excellent acuity. At other parts, acuity is relatively poor; that is, the two-point threshold is large. The differences between regions of the body are considerable (Figure 5.44); some two-point thresholds are more than 10 times larger than others. The greatest acuity is found at the fingers. The lowest is at the shoulder, back, and various areas of the leg.

two-point procedure A method to measure haptic system acuity that assesses the smallest distance at the skin at which people can perceive two separate stimuli rather than one.

SURFACES: TEXTURE, TEMPERATURE, AND HARDNESS. The haptic system delivers information about the surfaces of objects. The type of information

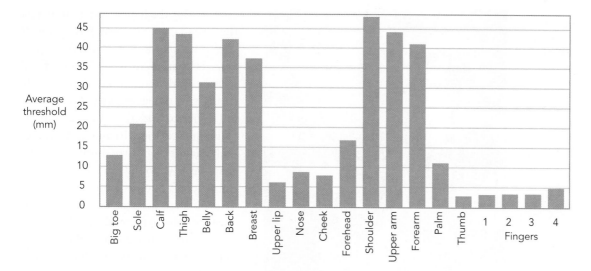

figure **5.44**
Two-point threshold results Research using the two-point threshold method shows that the haptic system has different levels of sensitivity in different parts of the body. Haptic sensitivity is particularly high (i.e., the threshold for detection of differences, graphed on the vertical axis, is low) at the face and fingertips.

received depends on how you explore the surface. Different types of hand and finger movements deliver different types of information (Figure 5.45).

When you move your fingertips back and forth across the surface of an object, you acquire information about texture—whether the surface is rough or smooth. The physical property that has the greatest influence on your perception of roughness is the distance between raised areas on the surface. Whether you move your finger across the surface quickly or slowly, a surface with gaps between raised areas will feel rough (Lederman & Klatzky, 2009).

Touch also provides information about temperature. When holding your fingers still on an object's surface, you usually find that the object feels slightly cool. The surface temperature of your skin is similar to the inner temperature of your body, which is warmer than most indoor and outdoor environmental temperatures, so the object in the environment feels cool.

The temperature of objects can affect other judgments. When people touch two objects and try to identify whether they are made of different materials, the objects' temperatures affect people's identification. It is harder to identify differences between materials if they are heated to the same temperature (Lederman & Klatzky, 2009).

A third surface property you perceive haptically is hardness. Pressing against an object's surface—such as a melon to judge its ripeness or a bicycle tire to judge whether it needs air—tells you how hard it is. Research reveals that people are very good at perceiving the stiffness of materials. When presented with objects made from materials that varied systematically in physical stiffness, participants could judge hardness accurately based on haptic perception of the degree to which the surface of the object deformed (changed shape) under the pressure of their fingers (Tiest & Kappers, 2009).

SIZE AND SHAPE. The haptic system also delivers information about an object's size and shape. Exploring an object by touch with your eyes closed, you can identify its approximate length and width. By holding the object and moving it around, you can estimate its mass (weight).

A principle you learned earlier, in the section on the visual system and brightness, applies also to the haptic system and perception of mass. You can apply that principle here to answer the following question: How big a difference in physical mass is

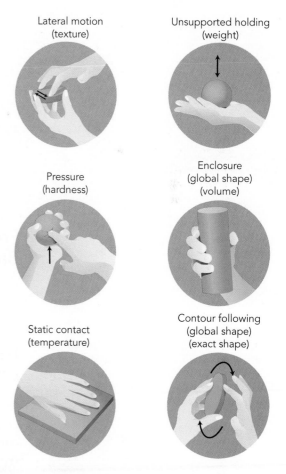

Lateral motion (texture)

Unsupported holding (weight)

Pressure (hardness)

Enclosure (global shape) (volume)

Static contact (temperature)

Contour following (global shape) (exact shape)

figure **5.45**
Types of touching Touching objects in different ways provides different types of haptic perception.

Big Cheese Photo LLC / Alamy

If the box were smaller, this woman would probably think it was heavier. Holding mass constant, larger objects are perceived as being lighter.

Are you surprised that people will judge the smaller of two equal-weight objects to be the heavier one?

required for the haptic system to detect that the mass of an object has changed? The principle of *just noticeable differences* is that there is no single, fixed answer to that question. If somebody hands you two envelopes, one weighing 1 ounce and the other 2 ounces, you'll notice the difference. If somebody hands you two dumbbells, one weighing 24 pounds, 15 ounces, and the other 25 pounds, you won't notice. The smallest detectable difference increases as the mass of objects increases.

Like other perceptions, the perception of mass is subject to illusions. For example, when judging the weight of two objects that weigh the same but are of different sizes, size influences weight judgments: Larger objects are perceived as lighter. Even with practice lifting the objects, people judge that smaller objects are heavier than larger ones when the objects are, in reality, the same weight (Flanagan & Beltzner, 2000).

🌀 WHAT DO YOU KNOW?...

15. True or False?
   a. Using the two-point procedure, scientists have learned that the greatest haptic acuity is found at the back.
   b. As the mass of two objects increases, it becomes more difficult to detect small differences in weight between them.

From Skin to Brain: Biological Bases of Haptic Perception

Preview Question

> Through what biological process are we able to convert haptic information from our skin to our brains?

Let's now look under the skin—literally—to examine the biological bases of haptic perception.

The body contains, underneath the skin, **cutaneous receptors,** which are receptor cells that convert physical stimulation into nervous-system impulses (Iggo & Andres, 1982). For example, you feel a tap on your leg because the tap activates cutaneous receptors, which send impulses that travel to your spinal cord and then to your brain. There are different types of cutaneous receptors, and their response to stimuli differs in two main ways:

1. *Breadth:* Some receptors (such as those in the fingertips) respond to stimulation in a specific narrow area of the skin's surface, whereas others respond to a broader area of stimulation.

2. *Speed of adaptation:* After the skin is stimulated, some receptors return quickly, and others more slowly, to their original firing rate (Lederman & Klatzky, 2009).

These differences produce different types of sensory experience. Pricking your finger with a pin feels different from pressing on the side of your hand because the two types of stimulation activate different types of receptors.

cutaneous receptors Receptor cells under the skin that convert physical stimulation into nervous-system impulses.

One distinct type of cutaneous receptor responds to changes in temperature. It transduces physical temperature into neural signals that lead to the experience of hot and cold.

16. We have different types of _____ receptors, which respond to stimuli in two different ways. Some receptors have greater or lesser _____ of response, referring to how much of the skin needs to be stimulated, and some have greater or lesser _____ of adaptation, referring to how long it takes for the receptors to return to their original firing rate.

The Kinesthetic System

Preview Question

› What is our sixth sense?

Imagine you're playing the game Twister, all twisted up after a few moves. Now imagine that the only lamp in the room falls over and hits you on the head, plunging you into darkness and causing you temporarily to lose memory of the fact that you're playing Twister. Even though you can't see your arms and legs, and don't remember moving your hands and feet to the various colored circles, you still know you're twisted up. You can feel it.

This feeling comes from your *kinesthetic system,* the perceptual system that delivers information about the orientation of your body and its various parts. A key source of these signals is nervous system inputs coming from your muscles. Even when signals from the skin and bones are blocked (e.g., through anesthesia), people are aware of the position of their limbs thanks to information coming from the muscular system (Matthews, 1982). This indicates that kinesthetic feedback from muscles is a unique perceptual system.

Brain-imaging studies also indicate that the kinesthetic system is a distinct perception system (Guillot et al., 2009). Research participants were asked to imagine (1) visual imagery: what it would look like if they performed various muscle movements; and (2) kinesthetic imagery: what it would *feel* like to perform the movements. Visual and kinesthetic imagery activated different regions of participants' brains. This further shows that the kinesthetic system is a distinct, sixth system of perception.

In addition to nervous system input from muscles, another biological mechanism that contributes to kinesthetic abilities is the *vestibular system,* found within the inner ear. The vestibular system contains small fluid-filled structures. When you tilt or rotate your head, the fluid moves. The movement triggers receptor cells that provide information to the brain—information needed for proper balance. If the vestibular system is not functioning properly, people experience vertigo, a sense of dizziness and spinning when their head changes position (Bhattacharyya et al., 2008).

Twister—a feast for the kinesthetic senses.

Tony Hopewell / Getty Images

THINK ABOUT IT

Ever since grade school, you probably have been taught that there are "five senses": sight, hearing, taste, touch, and smell. But are there only five? What if you were weightless, in outer space? You'd immediately know you were weightless. What "sense" would tell you that?

With your eyes closed, can you touch your finger to your nose? You have your kinesthetic sense to thank.

17. Upon waking up, even before opening your eyes, you know exactly how your body is positioned because of processing in the _____ system.

Sensation and Perception in a Social World

Now that you've learned about each of the six perceptual systems, let's look at three examples in which social factors shape perceptual experience. The first is the experience of pain.

The Experience of Pain

Preview Question

› What explains pain?

Pain is a signal. It tells you that something is wrong: Some part of your body has been, or is being, damaged. The experience of pain alerts an organism to the existence of damage and the need to take action to protect itself from further harm.

Specialized cells, called **nociceptors,** are the body's pain receptors; they send electrical signals to the brain when activated by harmful stimuli, such as a cut or burn (Apkarian et al., 2005). Nociceptors send signals of two types: fast and slow. The fast signals produce the sudden, sharp pain you experience when injured, whereas the slow signals produce the prolonged, dull pain that lingers after an injury.

Pain sensation might sound purely biological: Activate some nociceptors and you feel pain. But consider the case of Lewis Coulbert, a British soldier in Afghanistan. A bullet struck him in the arm when his platoon came under attack from the Taliban. The bullet surely activated plenty of nociceptors, yet, in the midst of the fighting, he didn't even realize he had been shot. "It was not until the end of the contact that I noticed my arm was covered in blood," said Coulbert, who reported that he "pulled out the bullet . . . and carried on" (Crick, 2009).

Have you had an experience similar to the soldier's? What "high-level" thinking processes were responsible?

The case is heroic, but not unique. The experience of pain is determined by not only physical factors, but also social and psychological influences. A classic theory explains how this works. According to the **gate control theory of pain** (Melzack & Wall, 1965), the spinal cord contains a biological mechanism that acts like a gate. Sometimes it is open, letting pain signals through to the brain, but sometimes it is closed. When it's closed, pain signals cannot get past the spinal cord to the brain and, as a result, people do not experience pain when nociceptors fire. A critical insight of the theory is that thinking processes—or, at a brain level of analysis, signals from the cortex—travel down to the spinal cord and determine whether the gate is open. Thus, there is "top-down" control of pain; "high-level" thinking processes directly influence "low-level" mechanisms in the spinal cord. In the soldier's case, his mental concentration on the demands of battle likely was a top-down influence that closed the spinal cord gate.

Knowledge about the brain has advanced dramatically in the decades since the gate control theory was proposed. Yet the theory has held up well. Contemporary findings confirm that people experience different levels of pain in different social contexts, and neural pathways running from the brain down to the spinal cord are responsible for this influence of social settings on pain perception (Fitzgerald, 2010).

The experience of pain also is influenced by biochemicals known as *endorphins* (Sprouse-Blum et al., 2010). Endorphins reduce pain by blocking pain signals that otherwise would pass from the body's periphery, through the spinal cord, to the brain. Intense, prolonged exercise increases the release of endorphins, reducing pain experience (Scheef et al., 2012).

Just days before the 2010 Winter Olympics, U.S. skier Lindsey Vonn crashed in practice and suffered a painful injury that threatened to keep her out of the games. But instead of withdrawing, she competed—and won. Vonn was the gold medalist in the Olympic downhill event. Athletes sometimes can perform at high levels despite injury thanks to "top-down" control of pain.

AP Photo / Frank Gunn, CP

nociceptors Specialized pain receptors that are activated by harmful stimuli such as a cut or burn.

gate control theory of pain The theory that the spinal cord contains a biological mechanism that acts like a gate; when closed, pain signals do not reach the brain, resulting in no experience of pain even though there is pain receptor activity.

✪ WHAT DO YOU KNOW?...

18. According to the gate control theory of pain, stimulating nociceptors does not guarantee the experience of pain. Why not?

The Perception of Faces

Preview Question

> Why are we so good at recognizing faces?

If you played with a cat for 10 minutes and, at some point in the future, were shown 10 cats—the one you played with and 9 others of the same color and species—you would have a hard time picking out the original cat from the group. If you looked at a tree for 10 minutes and, later, were shown 10 trees, you again would have difficulty picking out the original. But if you meet someone, speak with her for 10 minutes, and then are shown this person and 9 strangers, you'll have little trouble picking her out.

People are extraordinarily good at facial recognition. We can recognize—at a glance and at a distance—lots of people, even if we haven't seen them for a long time.

Where did this ability originate? From an evolutionary perspective, it would be costly *not* to recognize people—to confuse friend with foe, family member with stranger, your child with someone else's child. The ability to recognize others would have been critical to survival, reproduction, and the survival of offspring across evolutionary history. Natural selection thus would have favored the evolution of this ability.

Much evidence suggests that evolution also has provided a specific neural mechanism that is devoted to the processing of faces. A region of the brain known as the *fusiform gyrus* (Figure 5.46) is active when people look at human faces, and more active during face-recognition tasks than during other perceptual activities (Kanwisher, 2000).

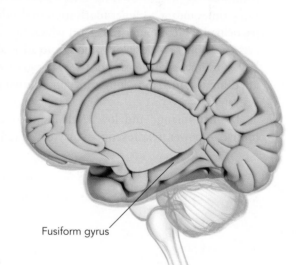

Fusiform gyrus

figure **5.46**
Fusiform gyrus Evidence suggests that the fusiform gyrus is a part of the brain that is specialized to enable quick, accurate recognition of human faces.

Humans' ability to detect faces is apparent from the beginning of life. In research, newborns have been shown cartoon images of either normal faces or faces in which the features have been scrambled (e.g., a cartoon with an eye where the mouth should be). Newborns pay more attention to the normal faces, which suggests that they are biologically inclined to perceive faces (McKone, Crookes, & Kanwisher, 2009).

✪ WHAT DO YOU KNOW?...

19. Humans' excellent ability to recognize faces was likely shaped by natural _____.

Motivated Perception

Preview Question

> Does motivation—one's goals and desires—influence perception?

Motivated perception research suggests that this man is in for quite a disappointment. When people are extremely thirsty, a bottle of water appears larger than when they are not thirsty.

Throughout this chapter, we have discussed what people perceive, but not what they *want* to perceive. Let's now look at the influence of motivations on perceptions.

Initial evidence that a person's motivations can influence his or her perceptions came from a study in which children estimated the size of either of two objects: (1) coins or (2) cardboard disks of the same size as coins (Bruner & Goodman, 1947). The children judged that the coins—a desired object—were larger than the disks. When the researchers examined two subgroups of participants in this study—namely, children from rich and poor neighborhoods—they found that poor children were especially likely to overestimate the coins' size.

More recent evidence of motivational influences comes from a study featuring a simple task: estimating the size of a glass of water (Veltkamp, Aarts, & Custers, 2008). The researchers measured the length of time since each participant had last consumed a beverage. Long times meant a higher motivation to drink. The researchers also showed, to some participants, a computer screen on which the words "drinking" and "thirst" appeared extremely briefly—just long enough to mentally activate thoughts of drinking. The largest estimates of the size of the water glass were made by students who hadn't had anything to drink for a long time, and for whom thoughts of drinking were mentally activated.

If small change and low levels of thirst can have these effects, more powerful motives—power, sex, revenge—may have even more influence on perception.

✋ WHAT DO YOU KNOW?...

20. Our current _____ (e.g., for money or for water) can shape our perceptions.

Attention

Wherever you are at the moment, there are a lot of objects to see, but you're only looking at one of them. There are probably a lot of sounds, too—the soft buzz of a neon light; the whirr of an overhead fan—that you hadn't even noticed. There are pressures on your skin from your clothes or the chair in which you're sitting that entirely escaped your attention. You perceive only a small slice of the world—that slice to which you pay *attention*. **Attention** is the process of bringing an idea or an external stimulus into conscious awareness.

Attention takes effort (Kahneman, 2011). Although some occurrences (e.g., a sudden loud noise) do "grab" your attention, often you have to exert effort to keep your mind from wandering. Even when you want to, it can be difficult to fix your attention on a rambling anecdote, a classroom lecture, or the pages of a textbook.

However, when you do exert effort, you find that you've got a mental power: *selective attention*. **Selective attention** is the capacity to choose the flow of information that enters conscious awareness, when more than one flow of information exists in the environment. Thanks to selective attention, if there are 3 people talking at once, or 8 people out on a dance floor, or 22 people running around a football field, you can "zoom in" mentally on any one of them. Researchers have explored people's ability to attend selectively to sounds (*auditory selective attention*) and sights (*visual selective attention*), as we'll see in the closing sections of this chapter.

> What features of the environment are competing for your attention right now?

attention The process of bringing an idea or an external stimulus into conscious awareness.

selective attention The capacity to choose the flow of information that enters conscious awareness.

The Power of Forever Photography / Getty Images

Auditory Selective Attention

Preview Question

> Do people hear only what they want to hear?

To study auditory selective attention, researchers ask participants to wear headphones that project different sounds—for example, speakers reading different passages of text—to the left and right ears. Participants are instructed to ignore the sounds in one ear while attending to the other. To ensure that they attend to the correct message, participants are asked to "shadow" it, that is, to repeat the material out loud. This simple experimental procedure produces three key research findings (Neisser, 1976; Treisman, 1969):

3. *Selective attention.* Most people find the task to be easy. They have little trouble tracking the sounds coming into one ear, despite the potential confusion of a different sound stream entering the other ear.

4. *Unawareness of unattended information.* People usually pick up very little, if any, of the information entering the unattended ear. Although the sounds enter the ear, they are not deeply processed by the brain. People may not even notice if the spoken language in the unattended ear changes. Auditory selective attention thus enables people to pick up one flow of sounds while largely ignoring another.

5. *Some unattended information does enter awareness.* If you are listening to the information in your right ear and your own name is spoken in your left ear, you will notice it. Some personally significant information, such as your name, appears to "pop out" from the stream of unattended sound. This implies that some mental processing occurs automatically (Treisman & Gelade, 1980). Even if you are not intentionally searching for the sound of your name, you automatically will hear it.

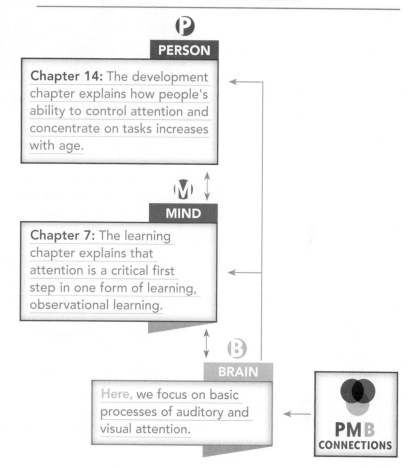

CONNECTING TO OBSERVATIONAL LEARNING AND TO PSYCHOLOGICAL DEVELOPMENT

PERSON

Chapter 14: The development chapter explains how people's ability to control attention and concentrate on tasks increases with age.

MIND

Chapter 7: The learning chapter explains that attention is a critical first step in one form of learning, observational learning.

BRAIN

Here, we focus on basic processes of auditory and visual attention.

PMB CONNECTIONS

✿ WHAT DO YOU KNOW?...

21. In research on auditory selective attention, what finding led researchers to conclude that some mental processing occurs automatically?

Visual Selective Attention

Preview Question

> Do people see only what they want to see?

The study of visual selective attention began with a research paradigm devised by psychologist Ulric Neisser and his associates (Becklen & Cervone, 1983; Neisser & Becklen, 1975). A video displayed two overlapping events: two groups of visually overlapping basketball players running, dribbling, and passing basketballs. Participants had to attend to one team, counting the number of times its team members passed the ball. At one point in the film, an unexpected event occurred: A woman carrying an umbrella walked straight across the screen. Surprisingly, hardly anyone noticed her. Although her image on the screen—and thus on participants' retinas—was prominent, she went unnoticed by the large majority of participants (see, e.g., Becklen & Cervone, 1983).

Does anyone see a woman with an umbrella? Research on visual selective attention shows that people fail to notice visually prominent, unexpected events when they are concentrating on other events in a scene.

Later researchers obtained similar results with an event even more unexpected: the intrusion of a gorilla (Simons & Chabris, 1999). While two teams of basketballers played, a gorilla—well, a research assistant dressed in a gorilla suit—walked directly across the screen while participants counted passes. Again, most people didn't even notice.

Do these selective attention experiments sound familiar to you?

TRY THIS! They should—they are exactly the sort of research experience you had in our Try This! experiment, introduced earlier in this chapter. As you see now, that experiment was not designed merely to see if you could follow motion in a fast-moving event. It was designed to show how little information people pick up from a *second* event when attending to the first one—even though the second event is passing right before their eyes!

How could people miss a woman with an umbrella? Or a gorilla? Neisser (1976) explains that perception is guided by anticipations. People actively anticipate certain types of information. They search for the anticipated information and, if it's there, pick it up. Unexpected information simply isn't picked up.

Neisser's argument underscores a general point about the material in this chapter. Perception is an active psychological activity. Your perceptions of the world reveal information about the world, and yourself.

⚡ WHAT DO YOU KNOW?•••

22. True or False?
    a. Visual selective attention is so good that in one study, participants who watched a video of people playing with a basketball failed to notice a woman carrying an umbrella walk across the screen.
    b. Visual selective attention is so good that, in one study, participants who watched a video of people playing with a basketball failed to notice a gorilla walk across the screen.

⟳ Looking Back and Looking Ahead

All of your knowledge of the world—its sights, sounds, and smells; its people, places, and things—comes to you through your perceptual systems. In this chapter, you have seen how perceptual systems bring you this information and have learned about the biological tools they use to do it.

What can you do with information once you perceive it? You can use it in the future, if you remember it, thanks to your powers of memory. If the information you perceive serves as the basis for acquiring new skills, you experience learning. Some of the information you perceive (the sight of someone waving happily at you) stirs your emotions. Other perceptions (the smell of a fresh-baked pie) increase your motivation (to eat). Babies need perception for psychological development. Adults need it to navigate the social world. For everyone, perception and sensation comprise much of one's conscious experience. Throughout this book—particularly in chapters on memory, learning, emotion, motivation, development, social psychology, and consciousness—we encounter phenomena whose foundation lies in the wondrous abilities of our perceptual systems.

Chapter Review

Now that you have completed this chapter, be sure to turn to Appendix B, where you will find a **Chapter Summary** that is useful for reviewing what you have learned about sensation and perception.

Key Terms

Ames room (p. 165)
attention (p. 204)
auditory nerve (p. 189)
auditory system (p. 160)
binocular cues (p. 163)
blind spot (p. 179)
clarity (p. 164)
color blindness (p. 176)
color constancy (p. 173)
cones (p. 176)
convergence (p. 167)
converging vertical lines (p. 163)
cornea (p. 175)
cues to depth (p. 163)
cutaneous receptors (p. 200)
depth perception (p. 163)
ear (p. 187)
eardrum (p. 187)
figure-ground perception (p. 172)
fovea (p. 176)
frequency (p. 184)
ganglion cells (p. 179)
gate control theory of pain (p. 202)
gustatory cortex (p. 196)
gustatory system (p. 160)

hair cells (p. 188)
haptic system (p. 160)
iris (p. 175)
just noticeable difference (JND) (p. 172)
kinesthetic system (p. 160)
lateral geniculate nucleus (p. 180)
lens (p. 175)
loudness (p. 183)
monocular cues (p. 163)
nociceptors (p. 202)
occlusion (p. 164)
odorant (p. 190)
olfactory bulbs (p. 192)
olfactory cortex (p. 192)
olfactory system (p. 160)
optic chiasm (p. 179)
optic nerve (p. 179)
optical flow (p. 170)
perception (p. 161)
perceptual systems (p. 160)
pheromones (p. 190)
phi phenomenon (p. 169)
photoreceptors (p. 162)
pitch (p. 184)

pressure (p. 186)
psychophysics (p. 172)
pupil (p. 175)
receptor cells (p. 162)
retina (p. 175)
rods (p. 177)
saccades (p. 177)
selective attention (p. 204)
sensation (p. 161)
shading (p. 164)
sound waves (p. 182)
stereopsis (p. 166)
supertasters (p. 195)
taste buds (p. 196)
taste receptors (p. 196)
texture (p. 164)
timbre (p. 185)
timing (p. 186)
transduction (p. 162)
two-point procedure (p. 198)
umami (p. 194)
visual cortex (p. 180)
visual fixations (p. 177)
visual system (p. 160)

Questions for Discussion

1. One theme of this chapter is summarized by the last two sentences: "Perception is an active psychological activity. Your perceptions of the world reveal information about the world, and yourself." What is revealed about individuals who see the Virgin Mary in their potato chips or toast? Why doesn't everyone see these images? [Analyze]

2. Piggybacking off of question #1, what are other examples of how our perceptions of ambiguous objects (i.e., objects that can be interpreted in more than one way) reveal information about ourselves? [Comprehend]

3. Why can't we tickle ourselves? That is, how can the same stimulus—fingers wiggling on your skin—cause you to feel "tickled" when applied by others but not when you do it to yourself? [Analyze]

4. Prosopagnosia is a rare disorder in which individuals are unable to recognize faces. Congenital insensitivity to pain with anhidrosis (CIPA) is a rare genetic disorder in which individuals are unable to feel pain. How can an evolutionary perspective help us to understand why these disorders are so rare? [Synthesize]

Chapter Review

5. You were probably not terribly surprised to learn of the monocular cues we use to perceive distance. For example: We know, based on years of experience, that when we look down the street, the sidewalks appear to converge, and we use this convergence information to perceive how far away a distant object is. Why, then, when asked to draw landscapes for the first time in elementary school, do you suppose children have such difficulty creating the proper perspective? Why must we be taught how to draw what we literally see? [Analyze]

6. Would you want to be a supertaster? What foods would you be likely to avoid? What might be the health consequences of this avoidance? [Comprehend]

7. Why do we need greater haptic acuity at the fingers and less at the back? [Analyze]

8. Are there individual differences in haptic acuity? Use the two-point procedure to test for yourself! What might explain the pattern of results you found? [Apply, Analyze]

9. Now that you understand the normal biology of visual processing, think about what could go wrong at any point in the process. Using what you've learned about the individual functions of the following structures, consider how damage to each one might affect vision: cornea, pupil, lens, retina (rods and cones), ganglion cells, optic nerve, optic chiasm, lateral geniculate nucleus, visual cortex. [Analyze]

10. Now that you understand the normal biology of auditory processing, think about what could go wrong at any point in the process. Using what you've learned about the individual functions of the following structures, consider how damage to each one might affect hearing: pinna, eardrum, ossicles, hair cells of the cochlea, auditory nerve, auditory cortex. [Analyze]

Self-Test

1. Which of the following is based on information obtained through the haptic system?
   a. Experiencing a stabbing pain in one's side
   b. Judging that a roommate's perfume is too strong
   c. Enjoying the savoriness of a French onion soup
   d. Concluding that one versus another object is heavier

2. Which of the following cues to depth would be *least relevant* if you wanted to create a two-dimensional painting that appeared three-dimensional?
   a. Converging vertical lines
   b. Shading
   c. Occlusion
   d. Stereopsis

3. If you were to stare at a red and yellow image for a long time, then look at a blank page, what colors would appear in the image you see?
   a. Green and blue
   b. Green and yellow
   c. Red and blue
   d. Red and yellow

4. Choose the sequence below that correctly orders the process through which visual information is transferred from visual stimuli to the brain.
   a. Pupil, lens, retina (rods and cones), cornea, ganglion cells, optic nerve, optic chiasm, visual cortex, lateral geniculate nucleus
   b. Retina (rods and cones), cornea, pupil, lens, ganglion cells, optic nerve, optic chiasm, lateral geniculate nucleus, visual cortex
   c. Cornea, pupil, lens, ganglion cells, optic nerve, retina (rods and cones), optic chiasm, lateral geniculate nucleus, visual cortex
   d. Cornea, pupil, lens, retina (rods and cones), ganglion cells, optic nerve, optic chiasm, lateral geniculate nucleus, visual cortex

5. Two identical gray circles are depicted on two different backgrounds: one light and one dark. How will they be perceived?
   a. They are identical and so they will appear as such.
   b. The one on the light background will appear darker than the one on the dark background.
   c. The one on the dark background will appear darker than the one on the light background.
   d. The one on the dark background will appear smaller than the one on the light background.

6. We experience front/back confusions in localizing sounds because
   a. sound reaches the right and left side at the same time.
   b. pressure from sound waves is equal on the right and left side.
   c. the shape of the ear is asymmetrical.
   d. Both a and b are correct.

7. Choose the sequence below that correctly orders the process through which auditory information is transferred from auditory stimuli to the brain.
   a. Ossicles, eardrum, hair cells of the cochlea, auditory nerve, auditory cortex
   b. Eardrum, ossicles, auditory nerve, hair cells of the cochlea, auditory cortex
   c. Eardrum, ossicles, hair cells of the cochlea, auditory nerve, auditory cortex
   d. Hair cells of the cochlea, eardrum, ossicles, auditory nerve, auditory cortex

8. Some people are better than others at detecting odors, and these differences are explained by genetic variations that cause some people to have
   a. more olfactory receptors.
   b. larger olfactory bulbs.
   c. a more complex olfactory cortex.
   d. larger nostrils.

9. Choose the sequence below that correctly orders the process through which gustatory information is transferred from food chemicals to the brain.
   a. Taste receptors (in taste buds), gustatory cortex, brain stem
   b. Brain stem, gustatory cortex, taste receptors (in taste buds)
   c. Taste receptors (in taste buds), brain stem, gustatory cortex
   d. Gustatory cortex, taste receptors (in taste buds), brain stem

10. Supertasters experience taste more intensely than do others, owing to
    a. more time spent training in taste perception.
    b. the greater number of taste receptors they have.
    c. the greater size of their gustatory cortexes.
    d. the greater size of their brain stems.

11. The distance measured in the two-point threshold is most similar to which of the following concepts related to a different sense?
    a. Just noticeable difference
    b. Color constancy
    c. Figure-ground perception
    d. Selective attention

12. Of two objects of the same weight, but differing size, which will be judged as heavier and why?
    a. The larger, because we expected it to be lighter.
    b. The smaller, because we expected it to be lighter.
    c. Neither, because prior experiences with mass do not influence our judgments.
    d. Neither, because prior experiences with weight do not influence our judgments.

13. According to the gate control theory of pain, what can you do to avoid experiencing pain?
    a. Meditate
    b. Sing a distracting song
    c. Focus on other features of the environment
    d. All of the above

14. Of the following, who is most likely to overestimate the size of an ice cream cone?
    a. Someone who dislikes ice cream
    b. Someone who dislikes ice cream and isn't hungry
    c. Someone who loves ice cream
    d. Someone who loves ice cream and is hungry

15. All of the following are valid conclusions to draw, based on the experiments involving the woman with the umbrella and the gorilla, except which one?
    a. People can be so selective in their attention that they miss obvious stimuli.
    b. Perception is an active psychological activity.
    c. As long as there is retinal activity, perception occurs.
    d. We often don't perceive unexpected information.

Answers

You can check your answers to the preceding Self-Test and the chapter's What Do You Know? questions in Appendix B.

If we are to understand consciousness—the fact we think and feel and that a world shows up for us—we need to look at the ways in which each of us carries on the processes of living in and with and in response to the world around us.

— Alva Noë

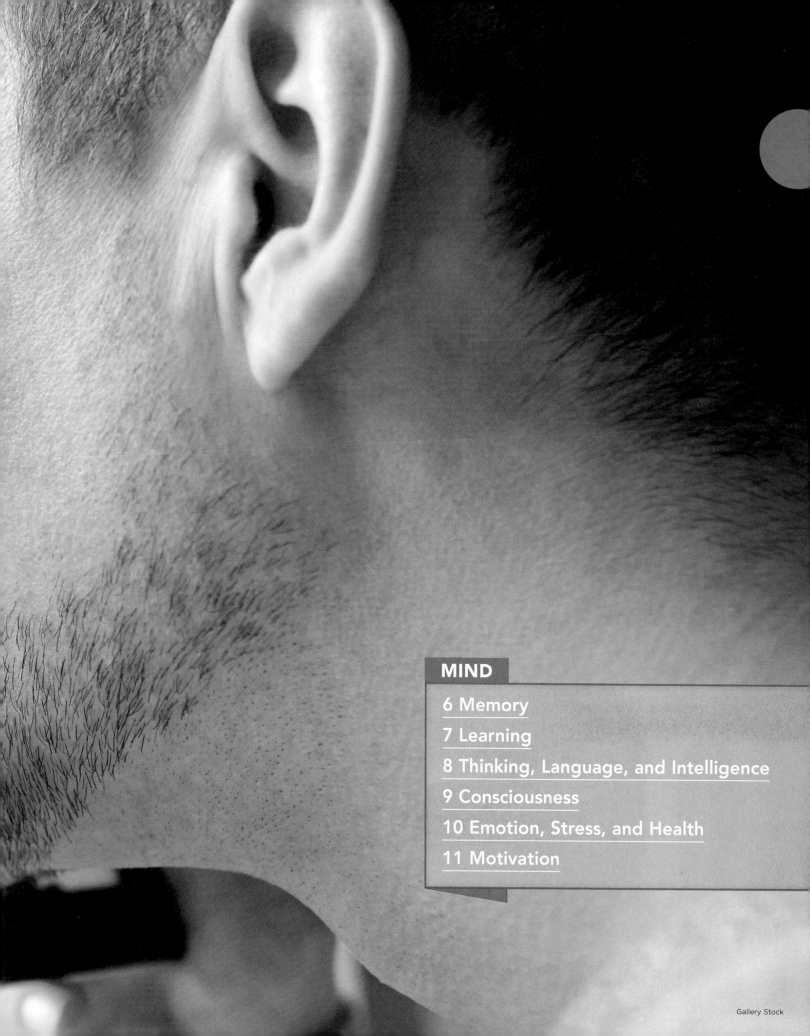

Memory

6

AJ WROTE TO A PSYCHOLOGIST FOR HELP. Her problem? Too much memory. "I remember everything," AJ reported. "I'm talking to you and in my head I'm thinking about something that happened to me in December 1982" (Parker, Cahill, & McGaugh, 2006, p. 35).

The psychologist was skeptical. Was AJ's memory really exceptional? To find out, he gave AJ random dates and asked her to report her memories of each day (Parker et al., 2006):

July 1, 1986: "I see it all, that day, that month, that summer. Tuesday. Went with (friend's name) to (restaurant name)."

October 3, 1987: "That was a Saturday. Hung out at the apartment all weekend, wearing a sling—hurt my elbow."

April 27, 1994: "That was Wednesday. . . . I was down in Florida. I was summoned to come down and to say goodbye to my Grandmother who they all thought was dying but she ended up living. My Dad and my Mom went to New York for a wedding. Then my Mom went to Baltimore to see her family. . . . This was also the weekend that Nixon died."

When psychologists checked her memories against written records, time after time, AJ's memory was right on the mark: "highly reliable . . . accurate . . . phenomenal" (Parker et al., 2006, p. 46).

Now consider a second case: HM. In 1953, at age 27, HM underwent brain surgery to treat epileptic seizures. After the surgery, he lost the ability to remember new information; if asked what he had been doing a week, a day, or even a few minutes earlier, he could not recall (Corkin, 2002). He could remember events from his childhood (Scoville & Milner, 1957) but nothing since his surgery, which "trapped him in a mental time warp where TV is always a new invention and Truman is forever president" (Schaffhausen, 2011).

HM's memory loss created deep personal problems. He could not establish friendships because he couldn't recall having met a person previously. He was frequently confused—understandable when

December 1982: "I'm talking to you and in my head I'm thinking about something that happened to me. . . ."

July 1, 1986: "I see it all, that day, that month, ..."

October 3, 1987: "That was a Saturday. Hung out at the apartment . . . ."

April 27, 1994: "That was a Wednesday. . . . I was down in Florida. I was summoned to come down and. . . ."

Pride—and memory People couldn't experience feelings of pride—or other feelings, such as regret or nostalgia—were it not for the powers of memory. Our ability to remember relationships with others and experiences in our past enriches emotional life.

a person thinks he's 27 but sees an elderly man in the mirror. HM "[relived] his grief over the death of his mother every time he [heard] about it" (Schaffhausen, 2011).

The cases of AJ and HM are unusual. Yet they teach us lessons that apply to everyone, as you'll see in this chapter on memory.

If you want to learn how the mind works, begin with the study of memory. It underpins so much of mental life. To speak, you have to remember the meanings of words. To solve a math problem, you need to remember rules of algebra. To motivate yourself to study, you must remember your goal of getting good grades. To experience emotions such as pride or regret, you have to remember your past behavior and your relationships to other people. Memory, our focus in this chapter, is the cornerstone of mental life. ◉

Learning from AJ and HM

Our opening story introduced two people whose memory was exceptional—AJ's was exceptionally good, and HM's exceptionally bad. Their cases teach two lessons beyond the obvious point that people's memory abilities differ. The first lesson concerns the role of memory in the life of a person as a whole.

The Role of Memory in the Lives of Persons

Preview Question

› What are some examples of everyday experiences that rely on the ability to remember?

Intellectually, AJ is a perfectly ordinary person (Parker et al., 2006). Her intelligence test scores are average and her school grades were mostly Bs and Cs. Exceptional memory is her sole distinctive mental quality—yet it dominates her life. One memory triggers another and another, bringing a "non-stop, uncontrollable" flood of memories that is "totally exhausting . . . I run my entire life through my head every day and it drives me crazy!" (Parker et al., 2006, p. 35).

HM, too, was ordinary in many respects (Corkin, 2002). A pleasant man with a sense of humor, he had good powers of concentration and could participate in conversations (Squire, 2009). He remembered how to perform routine tasks and could navigate around his house. He lost only the capacity to form permanent memories of facts and experiences after his surgery. Yet this one loss shattered his life. Without normal memory, he could not maintain a sense of personal identity—an understanding of his personal qualities, values, and goals, and how his life had unfolded over the years.

What were you doing on August 26, 2008? You probably don't remember. But the woman in the photo does. She is Jill Price—known in the scientific literature as "AJ." If you could ask her what she was doing then, she would immediately be able to tell you that she was having her picture taken while sitting on her couch during a sunny day in Los Angeles.

The first lesson learned from AJ and HM, then, is that memory is more important than one might think. You need it not only to answer questions when taking a test or playing a trivia game. You need it to be a fully human *person*—a being with knowledge of your past, your strengths and flaws, your roles in society, and your aspirations for the future. When memory is lost—as occurred with HM, and as occurs in Alzheimer's disease—a person's normal sense of self is lost, too (Cohen & Eisdorfer, 2001).

Memory is needed not only by individuals, but also by whole societies. Throughout human history, many societies have been oral cultures, that is, cultures lacking written forms of communication. Can these societies

John Birdsall / AgeFotostock

Storytelling creates shared memories Memory is important to not only the lives of individuals, but also the lives of cultures. In many cultures, storytelling creates shared memories that maintain cultural traditions and enable them to be shared with people from other cultures. Shown here is Dr. Oluseyi Ogunjobi, a storyteller from Nigeria, which has long had a rich cultural tradition of storytelling (Omotoso, 1978).

maintain, across generations, their cultural traditions—religious beliefs; holidays and associated ceremonies; epic stories, poems, and songs—when they cannot write anything down? Indeed, they can, by storing the cultural information in the individual memory systems of members of the society (Rubin, 1995).

The Varieties of Remembering

Preview Question

> What is memory, and what do the cases of AJ and HM teach us about the varieties of remembering?

The second lesson AJ and HM teach is that there are *different types* of memory. We will define "memory" and then explore this point in detail.

Memory is the capacity to retain knowledge. If at one point in time you know something, and at some later point you still know it, then you have remembered it.

AJ and HM show us that there are varieties of memory. Consider two questions:

> Did AJ have exceptionally good memory?
> Did HM lose his memory?

These questions are tricky. AJ's memory for life events she experienced personally was exceptionally good. Yet she had "great difficulty with rote memorization" (Parker et al., 2006, p. 36), which contributed to her merely average grades in school. HM lost his ability to recall facts and experiences after his surgery, yet consider what he did *not* lose. HM could still participate in conversations, which means he remembered thousands of words and grammatical rules for forming sentences. He was friendly and had a sense of humor, which means he remembered social rules for interacting with people. HM also remembered how to perform everyday activities such as sitting in chairs, opening doors, and eating with utensils. He even remembered how to do crossword puzzles (Schaffhausen, 2011). For somebody who lost his memory, HM remembered quite a lot!

What activities are you engaged in now that require "how to" memory?

The fact that AJ's and HM's memories were exceptional in some ways and ordinary in others teaches us that there are *different types* of memory. A person can lose one type while retaining another.

Both: Jiri Rezac / Polaris Images

The varieties of remembering are revealed by rare cases in which people lose some memory abilities due to brain damage, but retain others. A rare virus caused Clive Wearing to lose the ability to form new memories. As his diary entries reveal, he concludes, over and over again, that he has just awoken for the first time in years. Yet Wearing, who was an accomplished professional musician, remembers how to play the piano expertly.

🐾 WHAT DO YOU KNOW?...

1. If someone can remember the personal events of her life but isn't terribly good at rote memorization, what does that tell us about memory types?

See Appendix B for answers to What Do You Know? questions.

memory The capacity to retain knowledge.

CONNECTING TO THE BRAIN, PERSONALITY, AND SOCIAL BEHAVIOR

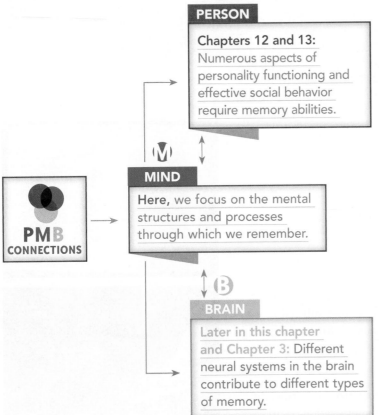

P

PERSON

Chapters 12 and 13: Numerous aspects of personality functioning and effective social behavior require memory abilities.

M

MIND

Here, we focus on the mental structures and processes through which we remember.

PMB CONNECTIONS

B

BRAIN

Later in this chapter and Chapter 3: Different neural systems in the brain contribute to different types of memory.

Levels of Analysis: Memory and Mind

How can psychology explain people's ability to remember information? You learned in Chapter 1 that psychologists formulate scientific explanations at three levels of analysis: person, mind, and brain. Let's see how each might help to explain the following simple example.

One day in class, your psychology instructor briefly flashes up on screen the following: **"Exam: Next Tuesday. Textbook Coverage: Chapters 7, 8, and 9."**

A few days later, you think to yourself: "They said something in class about a psych exam, didn't they? Maybe I should have put it in my calendar. Hmm, what was it?" After some mental effort, you remember "Tuesday" and "Chapters, 7, 8, and 9." How can psychology explain this ability to remember?

> A *person* level of analysis might identify personality factors or social influences that affect memory. For example, if you are highly motivated to excel in the class, you might tend to remember the information. If you were distracted (e.g., by a text message) when the information appeared, you might not remember it.

> A *brain* level of analysis would refer to neural systems you use when remembering information. Researchers would try to identify biological mechanisms whose functioning is required in order for people to remember anything.

Person and brain levels of analysis are informative; but when it comes to the study of memory, they are incomplete. The person level does not explain how memory works: the processes and structures that enable a person to remember material. The brain level provides biological information, but may fail to provide the psychological information needed to fully understand memory. Consider the results when one research team obtained brain images during a memory task (Miller et al., 2002). The brain activity of participants varied substantially from one person to another—even though they were all performing the exact same task! Based on the biological information alone, one couldn't even tell that the participants were engaged in the same psychological activity. This suggests the need for another level of analysis: the mind.

Explanations at a *mind* level of analysis refer to processes of thinking and to information that people acquire, retain, and draw upon when they think. Psychologists working at a mind level of analysis try to answer questions such as the following: How do people detect information in the environment (e.g., information such as "Exam, Tuesday, Chapters 7, 8, and 9")? Where and how do they store information after they detect it? How long does information remain in memory once it is stored? How do people retrieve stored information when they need it? Such questions are at the heart of mind-level analyses of memory.

Historically, research at a *mind* level of analysis was inspired by developments in computer science. Psychologists drew an analogy between computers and the human mind (Newell & Simon, 1961). A computer is built of electronic hardware but runs software—programs or "apps." You can understand the software without understanding the hardware. You know, for example, that your smartphone directed you to the nearest Starbucks by (1) identifying your location; (2) accessing a map; and

(3) using that map, determining the shortest route from your location to a Starbucks. You know this even if you lack knowledge of the electronic components inside your phone; you can understand the flow of information without understanding the electronics. Similarly, *cognitive psychologists*—those who specialize in the study of mental processes, especially memory, reasoning, learning, and problem solving—judged that they could study flows of information in the human mind (the software) without fully understanding how the brain (the hardware) works (Simon, 1992).

In the rest of this chapter, we will follow their lead. We first will focus on memory and the mind: mental processes that enable you to retain information. Then, at the end of the chapter, we'll explore memory and the brain.

THINK ABOUT IT

The analogy between (1) the human mind and (2) a computer was valuable to cognitive psychologists studying memory. But no analogy is perfect. Are there some ways in which the human mind is *not* like a computer? Does your computer get emotional? Does it know it's a computer?

WHAT DO YOU KNOW?...

2. It is possible to understand memory by studying processes at the _____ level of analysis even if we do not yet understand those processes at the _____ level of analysis.

A Three-Stage Model of Memory

To explain events, scientists often propose explanatory *models*. A model is a depiction of structures and processes that caused an event to happen (Harré, 2002).

In the study of memory, the key event is that people retain information; they remember material presented previously. To explain this, psychologists propose explanatory models that depict mental structures and processes that enable people to remember material. One major model is the **three-stage memory model** (Atkinson & Shiffrin, 1968).

In the three-stage memory model, information makes its way from the environment to your permanent memory in three steps, or stages: (1) *sensory memory*, (2) *short-term memory*, and (3) *long-term memory* (Figure 6.1). Let's examine each stage in detail.

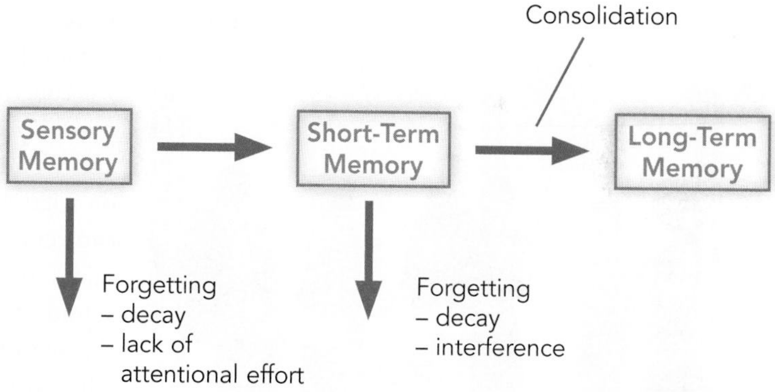

Sensory Memory

Preview Question

> What is sensory memory and what are two types of sensory memory?

Sensory memory is memory that is based on the workings of sensory systems, that is, the psychological systems that enable you to see, hear, and feel the world (see Chapter 5). You usually think of these systems as being involved only in perception, such as the perception of light (vision) or sound (hearing). But they contribute to memory, too. Different perceptual systems (e.g., vision, hearing, touch) produce different forms of sensory memory. Let's first look at **iconic memory,** which is sensory memory of visual images.

BRIEF MEMORY FOR IMAGES: ICONIC MEMORY. In psychology's first demonstration of iconic memory, George Sperling (1960) showed participants three rows of four letters for a very brief period: 50 milliseconds (1/20th of a second). The

figure 6.1

Three-stage model of memory How does information in the world make it into your long-term memory system? In the three-stage model of memory, information enters sensory memory, is transferred to short-term memory, and then (if not forgotten) enters long-term memory.

---

three-stage memory model A conceptual depiction of the memory system in which information is said to be stored in any of three storage systems: sensory memory, short-term memory, or long-term memory.

sensory memory Memory that is based on the workings of sensory systems.

iconic memory Sensory memory of visual images.

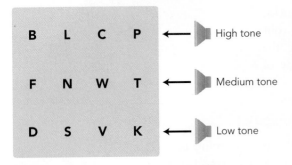

B L C P ← High tone

F N W T ← Medium tone

D S V K ← Low tone

figure 6.2

Sperling's iconic memory paradigm In a study of the capacity of sensory memory, Sperling showed participants a series of letters for a very brief period of time. Immediately afterward, he sounded a tone that indicated which row of letters the participant should try to recall. Participants could recall most of the letters in the row, which showed that their sensory memory, for a brief amount of time, contained a large amount of information.

presentation was so brief that participants had no time to think about the material; if they subsequently could recall any letters, it would be thanks to iconic memory.

Participants did not do very well on this task; when asked to recall the 12 letters, they reported only about one-third, that is, four letters. What does this mean? Sperling recognized that there are two possibilities:

1. The capacity of sensory memory is small—about four items.
2. The capacity of sensory memory is large, but information fades so quickly that as participants report the initial letters ("I saw a B, and an L . . ."), others fade away.

Sperling devised a clever test of these possibilities. After presenting the letters, he immediately sounded a tone indicating which row of letters participants should report (Figure 6.2). In this situation, participants performed excellently; they recalled *most* of the indicated information. Because participants did not know which row of letters would be signaled by the tone, their excellent performance meant that most of the letters were in iconic memory when the tone sounded. Sperling thus discovered that the capacity of iconic memory is large, but the duration for which it can store information is brief.

More recently, researchers have sought the biological basis of iconic memory. You might think it would be in the eye. However, findings indicate that the biological basis of iconic memory is a network of neural systems in the brain (Saneyoshi et al., 2011).

BRIEF MEMORY FOR SOUNDS: ECHOIC MEMORY. Iconic memory is not the only type of sensory memory. People also possess **echoic memory,** which is sensory memory for sound.

You are probably already familiar with echoic memory from the so-called *cocktail party effect:* At a party, you overhear someone mention your name and wonder, "What was he saying about me?" If you quickly concentrate on what you heard, you usually can remember what the person said 1 to 2 seconds earlier; the sound is very briefly stored in the sensory system of hearing. This brief storage system is your echoic memory.

> Thanks to echoic memory, we're often able to parrot back what someone has been saying to us when we've been accused of not listening!

Sensory memory, then, is the first stage in getting information such as "the exam is next Tuesday" from the classroom projection screen into your mind. The second stage is short-term memory.

Frederic Cirou / Getty Images

Echoic memory If you overhear someone mention your name at a crowded party, you often can retrieve a memory of what that person said in the previous few seconds, before the mention of your name attracted your attention. You're retrieving the information from echoic memory, which stores sound for brief periods of time.

WHAT DO YOU KNOW?...

3. Sperling sounded a tone *after* presenting participants with rows of letters to indicate which row they should report. How did this help him to determine whether the capacity of iconic memory was large or small?

TRY THIS!

You have just read about some memory experiments. Now, it's time to participate in one—this chapter's Try This! activity. Go to www.pmbpsychology.com and try your hand at an experiment that tests your memory ability. We'll discuss your results just ahead in the chapter—so do it now! ◉

echoic memory Sensory memory for sound.

Short-Term (Working) Memory

Preview Questions

> What are short-term memory and encoding? What is the capacity of short-term memory?
> Why do we forget information soon after it reaches short-term memory? What strategies can we use to reduce forgetting?
> How does working memory differ from short-term memory? What are its three components?

The second stage in the three-stage model of memory is **short-term memory,** which is a memory system that enables people to keep a limited amount of information actively in mind for brief periods of time (Jonides et al., 2008).

You already have some intuitive knowledge of how short-term memory works. If someone says that his phone number is 312-555-2368 and you want to remember it, you know three things:

1. You'd better enter the number into your cell phone soon, or you'll forget it. The information might fade from your memory in a matter of seconds.

2. You can keep the information alive in memory by repeating it to yourself over and over again ("312-555-2368," "312-555-2368," . . .) until you write it down.

3. If the number had been much longer—for example, 312-555-2368-82695873—you would never have been able to remember it.

You know intuitively, then, that (1) you possess a mental system that holds information for only a limited amount of time; (2) you can increase the retention time by repeating information to yourself; yet (3) there is a size limitation; even repetition does not work if there is too much information. This system is short-term memory. Psychologists have explored four main questions about short-term memory:

> How does information get into short-term memory?
> How much information can short-term memory hold?
> What causes much information in short-term memory to quickly be forgotten?
> What can you do to retain information in short-term memory?

GETTING INFORMATION INTO SHORT-TERM MEMORY: ENCODING. Much of the information that reaches sensory memory fades rapidly and can never be recalled, as you learned earlier. But some of it makes its way from sensory to short-term memory. The process of getting information from sensory memory to short-term memory is called *encoding*.

Encoding is any process that transforms information from one format to another. Recall that in sensory memory, the information format is physical stimulation (e.g., light waves that reach the eye; sound waves at the ear). The contents of short-term memory, though, are generally not physical sensations. They are ideas. In our exam-next-Tuesday example, you didn't remember physical stimuli, such as "a dark vertical line with a horizontal bar on top" (the letter T in "Tuesday"). You remembered ideas: The exam is on Tuesday and the chapters to study are 7 through 9. This means that your mind encoded the physical input, converting it into ideas that are meaningful.

What information is encoded into short-term memory? There are two types: information to which we devote *attentional effort* and information that "leaps into mind" without effort because we are biologically attuned to it.

Attentional effort is a focusing of attention on something in the environment that is relevant to a goal you are trying to achieve (Sarter, Gehring, & Kozak, 2006). In everyday terms, it's called "concentrating." If, right now, you look up from your

---

short-term memory A memory system that enables people to keep a limited amount of information actively in mind for brief periods of time.

encoding The process through which information is transferred from sensory memory to short-term memory and, in the transfer, converted from physical stimulation to conceptual information (i.e., ideas).

attentional effort Focusing attention on a stimulus in the environment; concentration.

John Lund, Blend Images / Getty Images

Do you see a light bulb? If you scan the picture, and scan some more, eventually you will find an image of a light bulb. The simple game teaches a lesson about how information gets into short-term memory. Finding the light bulb requires attentional effort. Once you do find it, an image of the light bulb makes its way to your short-term memory. Images of most of the *other* people, animals, and objects—the ones you scanned past when looking for the light bulb—will *not* be in your short-term memory, because you did not devote attentional effort to them. Stimuli to which you devote attentional effort thus are those most likely to move from sensory memory to short-term memory.

Washington Stock Photo / Alamy

Grabbing attention There's a lot to see: branches, twigs, leaves, rocks. But you can't miss that snake! Information about the snake moves quickly from iconic to short-term memory.

reading and glance around the room, many objects are in view: walls, furniture, books, an old poster, scraps of paper, candy wrappers, a roommate, and so on. You might think all this information would be overwhelming, but it isn't. What normally happens is that you concentrate, or focus your attention, on one item at a time. If your goal is to clean your room, you might focus on the candy wrapper. If you want to redecorate, you might focus on the poster. Sometimes focusing attention requires effort; if there's a big stack of books and papers on your desk, you might have to concentrate to notice some scattered candy wrappers. Similarly, if you're surrounded by a variety of sounds—people talking, a radio playing, cars outside your window, other people chatting—you can "pick out" one stream of sound by exerting a bit of concentrated effort. This is attentional effort (Kahneman, 1973).

> What information are you blocking out right now to devote attentional effort to reading this?

Information receiving attentional effort is the information most likely to move from sensory memory to short-term memory. This is what Sperling's experiments demonstrated. When participants heard a tone, they directed attentional effort to a specific row of letters. Those letters then were the ones encoded into short-term memory.

Attention, therefore, determines which information is encoded into short-term memory from sensory memory. Interestingly, this path from attentional effort to short-term memory is a two-way street. The contents of short-term memory influence what you pay attention to. If you were thinking about some object in the recent past, that object is more likely to grab your attention if it appears in the present environment (Downing, 2000).

Although attentional effort is needed often, sometimes objects simply grab your attention. For instance, if you're on a hike and encounter a long, thin object slithering on the ground, you would notice it immediately, even if you had not been focusing attentional effort on snakes. If there is a burning smell in your home, you would notice it, even if you hadn't been concentrating on the possibility of a fire. Or if a particularly attractive person walks by, you would notice automatically (Maner, DeWall, & Gailliot, 2008).

These examples illustrate a second type of information we encode into short-term memory: information about objects that grab our attention automatically. These objects usually have evolutionary significance; they have been relevant to survival and reproduction throughout human history. People who failed to notice them—who didn't automatically pay attention to a threatening animal, a fire, or an attractive member of the opposite sex—were less likely to survive and reproduce. The human mind, then, has evolved to automatically notice these evolutionarily significant people, objects, and events (Öhman & Mineka, 2001; Schaller, Park, & Kenrick, 2007). Evidence of this comes from research on the speed with which information fades from iconic memory. Emotionally threatening stimuli (e.g., a scorpion, a weapon) fade relatively slowly (Kuhbandner, Spitzer, & Pekrun, 2011), which raises their chances of being transferred from iconic to short-term storage.

In sum, information goes from sensory memory to short-term memory in two ways: (1) through attentional effort and (2) automatically. Now let's turn to our second question about short-term memory: its capacity.

THE SPACE LIMITS OF SHORT-TERM MEMORY: CAPACITY. What is the capacity of short-term memory; that is, how many pieces of information does it hold? More than a half-century ago, George Miller summarized existing research and concluded that the answer is "seven, plus or minus two" (Miller, 1956, p. 81). This number was found across a variety of tasks:

> When research participants heard different sounds (simple tones that varied in pitch), they couldn't accurately remember them all if they heard more than seven.

> When participants tasted substances varying in saltiness, they couldn't keep track of more than seven different tastes.

> When listening to numbers, letters, or words read aloud at a rate of one per second, they rarely could remember more than seven of them.

Miller therefore concluded that the best estimate of the capacity of short-term memory was seven pieces of information.

Not long after Miller's work, other psychologists began to recognize that his classic estimate was an overestimate (Cowan, 2001). It turned out that, in some of the research Miller reviewed, participants likely had time, during the experiment, to transfer some information from short-term memory into *long*-term memory. The estimate of seven thus overestimated the capacity of short-term memory per se (Jonides et al., 2008). Contemporary evidence suggests that the classic estimate of seven is merely a "legend" (Cowan, Morey, & Chen, 2007, p. 45) and that short-term memory's capacity is actually only four pieces of information (Cowan, 2001).

Four pieces of information may not seem like much. Yet if you try to think of more than four different things at a time, you'll realize that it's a lot. Try to think simultaneously about: (1) a fact about psychology (e.g., the capacity of short-term memory), (2) a fact about history (e.g., the *Magna Carta* was written in 1215); (3) an upcoming social plan ("We're going to see *High School Musical IX* on Saturday"); (4) a mathematical formula (e.g., the area of a circle); (5) a fact about the solar system (Jupiter has the largest number of moons); plus . . . . "Hey, wait a minute," you might be thinking, "Once I got to #5, I forgot the date of the *Magna Carta*." Keeping your attention focused on more than four things at once is extraordinarily difficult.

> **THINK ABOUT IT**
>
> When psychologists first estimated the capacity of short-term memory, they assumed that its capacity was independent of the *type* of information people were trying to remember. But might some kinds of information be more difficult to keep track of in short-term memory than others? (*Hint:* Research on "working memory," reviewed below, provides an answer.)

> What strategies do you use to keep information running in your short-term memory?

FORGETTING INFORMATION IN SHORT-TERM MEMORY: DECAY AND INTERFERENCE. Let's again follow the fate of our psych exam information: *Day of exam is Tuesday; Chapters on exam are 7, 8, and 9.* "Tuesday," "7," "8," and "9" are four pieces of information, so all of it should fit into short-term memory. But even if you paid attention in class and all the information was encoded in short-term memory at the time, you still might forget it. Why? Two factors contribute to forgetting: *decay* and *interference*.

Decay is the fading of information from memory. Like a skywriter's message on a windy day, the contents of short-term memory decay rapidly. How rapidly? In other words, what is the rate at which information in short-term memory decays?

Answering this question is difficult; a seemingly attractive research strategy is limited. To measure decay, one could (1) present information to participants, (2) wait for varying periods of time, and then (3) ask them to recall it. But there's a problem: During the waiting period, some people might devise strategies for enhancing their memory (e.g., if the information included the three-letter sequence KFJ, they might note that the letters are the initials of a famous U.S. president, only backward). These strategies would counteract the natural effects of decay.

Fading fast Like information from a skywriter on a windy day, information in short-term memory decays rapidly.

Mark Sunderland / Alamy

decay The fading of information from short-term memory.

Can you think of a way to determine how rapidly information decays from short-term memory *in the absence of* memory-enhancement strategies? One approach is to give participants a task to perform during the waiting period, such as counting backward by 3s from a large number (Brown, 1958; Peterson & Peterson, 1959). The task is hard enough that people cannot do it while also devising memory strategies.

What proportion of material would you guess an individual forgets after 18 seconds?

Research using this method shows that information in short-term memory decays quite rapidly. On average, people forget about 90% of the information they learn after only 18 seconds of counting backward (Peterson & Peterson, 1959). That's a lot of forgetting! Information decays so rapidly that, in less than half a minute, most of it fades away.

After discovering this rapid decay of information, psychologists performed more research that revealed something interesting: Some information does *not* decay rapidly (Neath, 1998). Information presented in the first few trials of the task decays slowly (Keppel & Underwood, 1962). In fact, on the very first trial, there is no evidence of short-term memory decay at all; even after counting backward for 18 seconds, people remember information presented on the first trial (Figure 6.3). Why would this be so?

The explanation is interference. **Interference** is a failure to retain information in short-term memory that occurs when material learned earlier or later prevents its retention. There are two types of interference: proactive and retroactive. **Proactive interference** occurs when material learned earlier impairs memory for material learned later. Conversely, **retroactive interference** occurs when material learned later impairs memory for material learned earlier.

As an example of these two types of interference, imagine that you sign up for a class in which 20 people are enrolled, and on the first day everyone introduces themselves in class. What would your memory of the 20 names be like? You'd probably remember the names of the first few people because when you heard them, no other names were yet stored in your short-term memory—there was no proactive interference. By the time the fifth or sixth person is introduced, however, your head is so full of names that it's hard to remember any more. Proactive interference from the first few names impairs memory for the later ones.

Results shown in Figure 6.3 demonstrate this process. On the first few trials of a task, people's memory is excellent because there is no proactive interference. On later trials, proactive interference begins, and information decays rapidly.

This example also illustrates retroactive interference. When the last few people (i.e., the 18th, 19th, and 20th classmates) introduce themselves, you probably would remember their names. Because there are no further introductions after these people, there is no retroactive interference. You'd be more likely to forget the names of the students introduced just prior to that (e.g., the 15th, 16th, and 17th classmates to speak). Retroactive interference created by the names of the last few students interferes with memory for the names that preceded them.

Combining what you've learned about proactive and retroactive interference, you can make some predictions about memory performance. Whenever people try to recall a list of items, there is:

> A *primacy effect:* Items at the beginning of the list are not affected by proactive interference (because no items came before them) and thus are remembered well.

> A *recency effect:* Items at the very end of the list are not affected by retroactive interference (because no items came after them) and thus are remembered well.

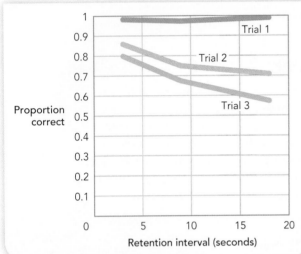

figure 6.3
Short-term memory decay Memory decays rapidly from short-term memory. On the second and third trials of a task in which people try to remember a series of letters or numbers, information significantly decays within 20 seconds. However, on the first trial of a memory experiment, information is retained—there is no decay in 20 seconds. This indicates that forgetting results from not only decay, but also proactive interference. At the start of a study, when no prior information has been learned, there is no proactive interference, and memory performance is excellent.

interference Failure to retain information in short-term memory that occurs when material learned earlier or later prevents its retention.

proactive interference A short-term memory impairment that occurs when material learned earlier impairs memory for material learned later.

retroactive interference A short-term memory impairment that occurs when material learned later impairs memory for material learned earlier.

Items in the middle of the list are subject to both proactive and retroactive interference. Memory for those items thus should be relatively poor.

This discussion of primacy and recency effects should remind you of something: the Try This! activity you attempted earlier in this chapter.

The activity tested your memory for a long list of words. Importantly, it didn't report merely the overall number of words you remembered; instead, you learned the number of words you remembered from different parts of the list—beginning, middle, and end.

If you were like most people, you remembered relatively few words from the middle of the list. In that part of the list, memory can be impaired by both proactive and retroactive interference.

Figure 6.4 shows the results obtained when researchers run the Try This! experiment with a large group of participants and plot results for each word position. The finding is known as the **serial position effect,** which is people's tendency to display better recall for items positioned at the beginning or end of a list than in the middle.

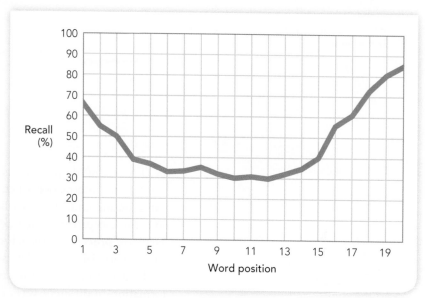

figure **6.4**
The serial position effect When people try to remember a list of words, the words presented at the beginning and end of the list are remembered best. Proactive and reactive interference decrease memory for words in the middle. The pattern of results, in which memory varies depending on a word's position in the list, is called the serial position effect.

RETAINING INFORMATION THAT IS IN SHORT-TERM MEMORY: REHEARSAL AND DEEP PROCESSING. You have seen how information in short-term memory may be forgotten. Forgetting, though, is not your goal; if "Exam next Tuesday, Chapters 7, 8, and 9" is announced, you want to remember it. What mental strategies might help you retain the information in short-term memory?

One strategy is to repeat the information to yourself over and over. This strategy is similar to rehearsing lines for a performance—where the "performance" is correctly recalling information a few days later—and therefore is called *rehearsal.* **Rehearsal** is the strategy of repeating information to retain it in short-term memory (Atkinson & Shiffrin, 1968).

Rehearsal does maintain information in short-term memory; as long as you keep repeating the information, it will be retained there. Yet, as a memory strategy, rehearsal has two big limitations. One is obvious: It's inconvenient. You surely have things to do other than repeating "Tuesday, Chapters 7, 8, and 9" until you can find someplace to write it down.

The other limitation is that merely repeating information is not particularly effective. Psychologists have explored the effectiveness of rehearsal by varying the amount of time that people rehearsed items prior to a memory test. After rehearsal times of varying lengths, they asked participants to recall the words. What did they find? In a sense, nothing. Repeating a word for a longer time period had no effect on later memory for it (Craik & Watkins, 1973).

Because rehearsal is not as effective a strategy as one might like, if you want to remember information, you need another strategy. One is to process information "deeply."

REX USA / Everett Collection

Rehearsal You can prevent information in short-term memory from decaying by repeating it over and over, or *rehearsing* it, in the way that an actress—in this case, Kate Hudson—rehearses lines for a performance.

serial position effect The tendency to display superior recall for items positioned at the beginning or end of a list rather than in the middle.

rehearsal The strategy of repeating information to retain it in short-term memory.

figure 6.5
Depth of processing In a depth-of-processing study, participants are presented with a word—in this case, "TIGER"—and in different experimental conditions are asked questions that prompt them to think about the word in a shallow or deep manner (Craik & Tulving, 1975). Deeper processing enhances memory.

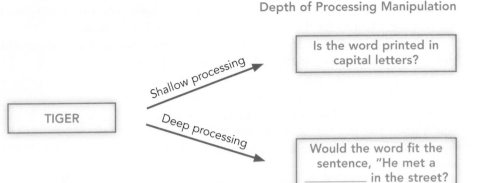

Depth of Processing Manipulation

The idea of "deep"—versus "shallow"—processing describes variations in how people think about information when it is presented. Deep processing is thinking about something meaningful, such as what a word means. Shallow processing is thinking about something superficial, such as the color or case (upper or lower) of the printed word. **Depth of processing,** then, is the degree to which people think about meaningful rather than superficial aspects of presented information (Craik & Tulving, 1975).

In depth of processing studies, researchers ask participants to think about information in different ways (Figure 6.5). They find that deeper thinking improves memory. Fergus Craik and Endel Tulving (1975) found that the ability to recall information is more than four times greater when information is processed in a deep, rather than shallow, manner.

> If you have used flashcards to study for tests, have you found that they promote deep processing?

🕛 THIS JUST IN

Sources of Information and Short-Term Memory

People obtain information from different sources. Sometimes we hear information (e.g., when someone tells us something), sometimes we see it (e.g., when reading a book), and sometimes we rely on touch (e.g., to find out whether water from a shower is warm). Does the information source—sound, sight, touch—affect the way short-term memory works?

Traditional theories of short-term memory would suggest "no"; as you have seen, those theories discuss information in general, irrespective of how it was obtained. New research findings, however, may prompt psychologists to revise their theories.

Researchers conducted a study that, in some respects, was similar to traditional research on short-term memory decay: They presented information, waited varying lengths of time (different retention intervals), and then asked people to recall the information (Bigelow & Poremba, 2014). A critical difference, however, was that the researchers presented information of three different types:

1. *Auditory:* Participants heard tones presented for 1 second each.
2. *Visual:* Participants saw geometric figures presented for 1 second each.
3. *Tactile:* Participants felt a metal bar that vibrated for 1 second.

After retention intervals that varied from 1 to 32 seconds, another stimulus was presented (another tone, figure, or vibration), and participants had to judge whether it was the same as the previous one. The accuracy of their judgments was the measure of the retention of information in short-term memory; if the stimulus was still in memory, then participants could judge accurately. The key research question was

depth of processing The degree to which people think about meaningful rather than superficial aspects of presented information.

whether stimuli of different types, each presented for 1 second, would be remembered equally well.

As it turns out, they were *not*. As you can see in Figure 6.6, people's memory for auditory information was substantially less good than their memory for visual or tactile information. People displayed what the researchers called an "Achilles ear": weaker short-term memory when the information source was sound.

The findings have significant implications for theoretical models of memory. They suggest that, rather than there being one short-term memory system, people possess different memory subsystems that handle different types of information and that each contributes to people's short-term memory abilities.

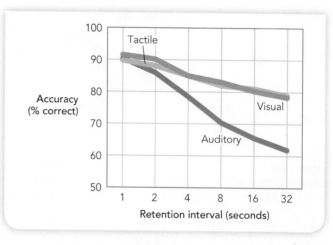

figure **6.6**
Memory for different kinds of information

✊ WHAT DO YOU KNOW?•••

4. True or False?
   According to Figure 6.6, people were better at retaining auditory information in short-term memory than they were at retaining tactile or visual information.

FROM "SHORT-TERM MEMORY" TO "WORKING MEMORY." You've just read that short-term memory is a limited-capacity memory system from which information is lost due to interference and decay, and in which information can be retained through rehearsal and deep processing. There are two more things to learn about short-term memory. They are so significant that they expand the conception of this memory system from *short-term memory* to something psychologists call *working memory*.

1. There are two sets of letters below. Cover up one, look at the other for 30 seconds, then look away from the page and try to remember it. Then do the same thing with the other set of letters.

TGVCDPB   XYRWHKQ

2. Which set of letters was easier to remember? Based on what you've learned about short-term memory so far, they should be equally easy or hard, because they contain the same number of letters. But most people find that they differ. The first series, in which all the letters sound similar, is harder to remember than the second, whose letters sound different (Baddeley, 2003). Why should the sound of the letters make a difference?

3. You've learned about different strategies people can use to remember information: exerting attentional effort, rehearsing, processing information deeply. The existence of these different strategies raises a question not answered by the original three-stage memory model (Atkinson & Shiffrin, 1968; Figure 6.1): What system of mind is involved in selecting and executing strategies for task performance? In the original three-stage model, short-term memory was merely a "container" for holding information, not a system that selected among task strategies.

To answer these questions, psychologists expanded the original conception of short-term memory. In the new conception, rather than short-term memory, psychologists propose **working memory,** which is a set of interrelated systems that both store and manipulate information (Baddeley, 2003; Baddeley & Hitch, 1974; Repovš & Baddeley, 2006). Working memory has three components (Figure 6.7):

> The *phonological loop* is a limited-capacity memory system that encodes information according to its sound. It is active when you are "talking to yourself," whether the talk involves an inner conversation ("I wonder what I should do for fun tonight?")

working memory A set of interrelated systems that both store and manipulate information; its three components are the phonological loop, visuospatial sketchpad, and central executive.

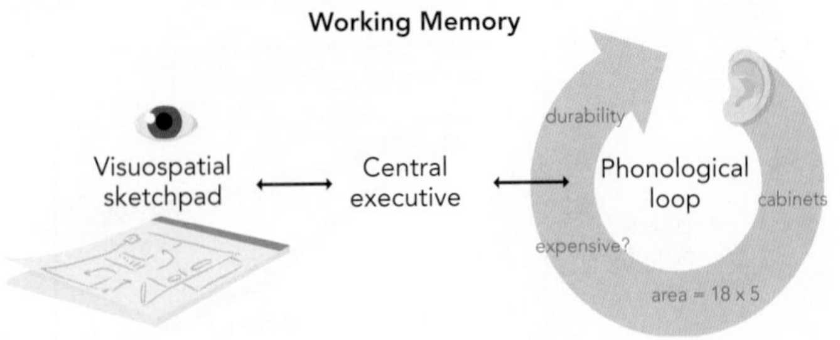

Working Memory

figure 6.7
Working memory Psychologists conceive of working memory as consisting of three systems: a *visuospatial sketchpad* that processes visual imagery; a *phonological loop* that is active when your thinking involves words, sentences, or arithmetic problems; and a *central executive* that controls the attention focus of the system as a whole.

CONNECTING TO THE BRAIN AND TO SELF-CONTROL

Ⓟ **PERSON**

Chapters 12 and 14: Working memory contributes to people's capacity for self-control and to the development of this capacity in childhood.

Ⓜ **MIND**

Here, we focus on the interrelated mental systems that make up working memory.

Ⓑ **BRAIN**

Later in this chapter and Chapter 3: The brain's frontal lobes are key biological tools underlying the mind's working memory system.

PMB CONNECTIONS

or solving an arithmetic problem (e.g., 14 × 3 = 42, then dividing 42 by the square root of 36, which is 6, and concluding the answer is 7; Lee & Kang, 2002). Because it deals with sounds, the phonological loop may have difficulties working with different pieces of information that sound similar. Recall that TGVCDPB was harder to remember than XYRWHKQ; the similar sounds in TGVCDPB created phonological loop interference.

> The *visuospatial sketchpad* is a limited-capacity memory system that processes visual images. The sketchpad enables people to create and manipulate images in their mind, as occurs when an artist or architect is at work. As its name suggests, the visuospatial sketchpad processes (1) visual information (e.g., memory for the appearance of objects you have recently seen around you) and (2) spatial information (memory of the location of the objects and their movement in the environment; Baddeley, 2003).

> The *central executive* is a mental "workspace" with "the capacity . . . to manipulate and create new representations" (Baddeley, 2003, p. 836). It is not a passive container for holding information, but an active system that focuses attention on tasks and can switch attention from one task to another. Information from both the visuospatial sketchpad and the phonological loop reaches the central executive, which thus can make decisions based on a wide range of information. The central executive can also work at different speeds. Sometimes it is slow and deliberate; for example, you might concentrate for long periods on a difficult math problem. But sometimes it acts quickly and automatically, with little conscious deliberation. For example, when driving, your mind responds so automatically to traffic that, after you've arrived at your destination, you may hardly remember the experience of driving the car.

What's the most complex type of math problem you can solve using your working memory before you have to break out a pencil and paper or calculator?

Like the phonological loop and visuospatial sketchpad, the central executive's capacity is limited. In practice, this means that your ability to concentrate can be frustratingly small. Even if you have to finish this chapter right now to prepare for an upcoming exam, you may find your mind "wandering" (Feng, D'Mello, & Graesser, 2013); you become distracted rather than focusing on your reading. People's ability to control their thoughts, emotions, and behavior relies on working-memory capacity (Hofmann et al., 2008). Physical and mental fatigue can reduce capacity, making self-control more difficult (Muraven & Baumeister, 2000).

When working on complex tasks, people combine information from different systems into one mental workspace. An architect, for example, might design a structure using her visuospatial sketchpad but simultaneously evaluate it and consider alternatives using her phonological loop (thinking, "It might be better if we knock out this wall"). A person can make decisions, then, based on a combination of visuospatial and verbal information.

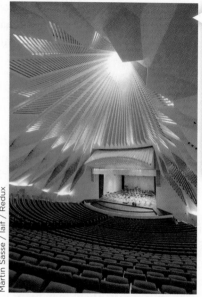

Using the visuospatial sketchpad Designing a concert hall requires thinking simultaneously about visual information (what will it look like?), auditory information (what will it sound like?), and technical information about the engineering of structures (will it fall over?). Architects can bring this information together in their minds, thanks to a system in working memory called the visuospatial sketchpad. Shown is Spanish architect Santiago Calatrava and the interior of the auditorium he designed in Santa Cruz de Tenerife, in the Canary Islands.

💧 WHAT DO YOU KNOW?...

5. True or False?
   a. Some information takes quite a bit of attentional effort to encode, whereas information that has evolutionary significance (e.g., a fire) grabs our attention automatically.
   b. Miller's estimate of the capacity of short-term memory, seven plus or minus two, may be an underestimate, and 11 pieces of information may be more accurate.
   c. When research participants are presented with information to be remembered over several trials, information from the first few trials is less likely to decay than information presented later.
   d. When research participants are presented with information to be remembered over several trials, the later-learned material may be lost due to retroactive interference.
   e. Of shallow or deep processing, rote memorization would be considered deep processing.
   f. According to the concept of working memory, we actively process information with the help of a phonological loop, a visuospatial sketchpad, and a central executive.

Long-Term Memory

Preview Questions

> What is long-term memory? How long does it last? How much can it hold? What are different types of long-term memory?
> Once information enters long term-memory, does it automatically become unforgettable?
> What two factors enable us to retrieve information from long-term memory?

So far, you've seen how information travels from sensory memory to short-term or working memory. (In practice, psychologists often use the terms *short-term memory* and *working memory* interchangeably.) You've also learned about factors that influence whether that information is remembered for long periods of time, so you can use it later. If it is remembered, where does that information go? It gets stored in **long-term memory,**

long-term memory The mental system that stores knowledge for extended periods of time.

Even if you don't ride a bike for decades, you'll always be able to hop on and pedal away. Memories for many motor skills last a lifetime.

Doesn't the conductor need sheet music, too? Expert orchestral conductors, such as Alan Gilbert of the New York Philharmonic, commonly lead their orchestras without even looking at the sheet music. They've got it in their heads—a testament to the virtually infinite capacity of long-term memory.

semantic memory Memory for factual information.

which is the mental system that stores knowledge for extended periods of time. When, in an example above, deeply processed material was remembered for a long period of time, the depth of processing caused the information to be stored in long-term memory.

LONG-TERM MEMORY BASICS: DURATION, CAPACITY, AND TYPES OF MEMORY. One question about long-term memory that psychological science wants to answer is "How long does a long-term memory last?"

Think back to your childhood: a favorite teacher; a day when you got a great present; a "bad day" when you did something embarrassing. It's not hard to remember them, despite the passage of time. Memories of some experiences last a lifetime.

Another type of memory that lasts is memory for how to *do* things. Even if you haven't ridden a bike for years, you can hop on now and pedal away. If you hadn't read anything for years, you would still be able to read material instantly if somebody put a book in front of you. Similarly, memories for many facts do not fade away. You won't forget the name of the first U.S. president or the number of sides of a triangle. They are stored in your memory, permanently.

Long-term memory, then, may never fade away. Information in long-term memory can reside there permanently.

A second question concerns long-term memory's capacity. You're storing lots of information in long-term memory during your college years. Will you eventually "run out of space"?

No, you won't—long-term memory has no space limitation. Consider two historical examples. Some Jewish scholars of the Talmud, an ancient work of law and ethics that is thousands of pages long, have been able to remember not only the entire text but where, on each printed page, each passage of text appears (all editions include the same number of pages and the same material on each page; Stratton, 1917). The Italian symphony conductor Arturo Toscanini had such an exceptional memory for musical works that he knew "every note of every instrument of about 250 symphonic works and the words and music of about 100 operas" (Marek, 1975, p. 414).

How can long-term memory be infinite? It's puzzling if you think that memories are "stored" in long-term memory. The idea of "storage" makes it sound as if memory is a container that eventually will fill up. But this isn't the only way to think about long-term memory. Some theorists argue that we should think of remembering as an activity (e.g., Stern, 1991). To remember something is to *do* something. A person "remembers the year World War II ended" when she does something: She says "1945." A person "remembers a personal experience" when he does something: He forms a mental image that corresponds to the event. Because there is no limit to the number of things we can do using our minds, there is no limit to long-term memory.

A third question about long-term memory concerns the different types of information people recall. Consider some of the examples above: remembering the name of a U.S. president, a personal experience from childhood, and how to ride a bike. Each one of these examples is a different type of long-term memory (Tulving, 1972): semantic memory, episodic memory, and procedural memory, respectively.

> **Semantic memory** is memory for factual information. This information includes abstract concepts (e.g., a dog is a mammal) and concrete factual information (e.g., the capital of Kansas is Topeka). You might not be able to recall the time or place where you learned a given fact (e.g., where you learned that Topeka is the capital of Kansas), yet you still retain the factual information in semantic memory.

> **Episodic memory** is memory for events that you have experienced. Autobiographical memories—of your first date, high school graduation, or the birth of a younger sibling—are all examples of episodic memory. Episodic memory differs from semantic memory in two ways. First, you have a memory for being there: a firsthand experience of the event, including its sights, sounds, and smells. Second, episodic memory has a temporal sequence to it. Things happen one after another, and remembering one event sometimes triggers memories of what happened next. AJ, whom you read about in the chapter opening, had exceptional memory of this type.

> **Procedural memory** is memory of how to do things, such as ride a bike, drive a car, tie your shoes, and use a fork and knife. Before taking this psychology course, you may not have thought of these types of activities as aspects of "memory." Yet they are; they are cases in which you are able to do something at one point in time because you have acquired and retained knowledge from earlier experiences. An interesting aspect of procedural memory is that you often remember how to do something (the procedural memory) without recalling either the experience of learning it (episodic memory) or the factual description of how to do it (semantic memory). For instance, if you're like most people, you know how to tie your shoes, but you don't remember the childhood experience in which you first learned how and can't describe the exact steps of shoe-tying. Tying your shoes is a procedural memory, not an episodic or semantic memory.

Ethan Miller / Getty Images

Procedural memory "Bunny ears, bunny ears, playing by a tree. Criss-crossed the tree, trying to catch me." These basketball players might not remember childhood rhymes that helped them learn how to tie their shoes. And they might not remember the first time they tied their shoes correctly. But they do remember how to tie them. When it comes to shoe-tying, they have procedural memory, but probably not semantic or episodic memory.

This shoe-tying example raises another way of classifying memories; some are *explicit* and others *implicit* (Schacter, 1987). **Explicit memory** is conscious recall of previously encountered information or experience. **Implicit memory** is task performance that is affected by previous information or experience, even if that prior material is not explicitly remembered. The case of HM, presented in this chapter's opening, illustrates the distinction clearly. Researchers taught HM a difficult mirror-tracing task, in which one traces an image using a pencil while being able to see his hand only in a mirror. With practice, HM improved on the task. Yet, being HM, he could not remember any of the occasions on which he had practiced. HM thus had implicit memory from his practice sessions—an improvement in performance—while not having any conscious, explicit memory of the experiences.

Mirror-tracing task HM could remember how to perform a mirror-tracing task, such as the one shown here, but could not remember the experiences during which he learned and practiced the task. He retained implicit memory of those experiences, but no explicit memory of them.

Sahid L. Rosado Lausell

Have you ever tried to explain to someone how to ride a bike? Tough, right? What are some other implicit memories that are difficult to make explicit?

The different types of memory are distinct, yet they influence one another. Consider semantic and episodic memory. Evidence at both *mind* and *brain* levels of analysis supports the distinction between them. Research, however, also shows that if you have more of one type of memory, you are likely to acquire more of the other (Greenberg & Verfaellie, 2010). Increased semantic memory, for example, can enhance episodic memory. If you read a book about a travel location, you will acquire semantic knowledge. If you then visit the location, the increased semantic memory will tend to increase the detail and richness of the episodic memories you form.

GETTING INFORMATION INTO LONG-TERM MEMORY PERMANENTLY: CONSOLIDATION. Earlier, we said that psychologists have compared the mind to a computer. In many ways, the comparison is apt; for example, the mind's short-term and long-term memory are like a computer's random access memory and its

episodic memory Memory for events you have experienced.

procedural memory Memory for how to perform behaviors.

explicit memory Conscious recall of previously encountered information or experience.

implicit memory Task performance that is affected by previous information or experience, even if the prior material is not explicitly remembered.

permanent, hard-drive storage. However, minds and computers differ when it comes to the process of storing information permanently.

In a computer, permanent storage takes only a fraction of a second: the time needed to save information onto a hard drive. But in the mind, it can take hours or days. Information in long-term memory gradually *consolidates*. **Consolidation** is a process in which information in long-term memory changes from a fragile state, in which the information can be lost, to a fixed state in which it is available relatively permanently (McGaugh, 2000).

Cases of head trauma—for instance, people hitting their heads in a traffic accident or a sports injury—can disrupt the process of consolidation. You might expect that a surprising and painful accident would be unforgettable. But, instead, people often do not remember the accident at all. A head injury can disrupt biological processes in the brain that are required in order for a memory to consolidate (McAlister, 2011). As a result, people might not remember what they were doing before the accident occurred. (We'll explore biological processes in consolidation later in this chapter, in a section on memory and the brain.)

Injury disrupts memory consolidation "I don't remember the exact play. Once I came off the field, I didn't really know I had scored. I can't really remember what happened." Those were the words of Pittsburgh Steelers running back Le'Veon Bell, who sustained a blow to the head sufficient to knock off his helmet on his way to scoring a touchdown. His memory—or lack of it—illustrates the principle of consolidation. Before the play started, he had in mind information about the play (where to line up, when the ball would be snapped, where he should run, etc.). During the play, he concentrated intently, but afterward, he didn't remember what happened. The head injury disrupted the consolidation process needed for the experiences to enter into memory permanently.

Consolidation processes occur not only when people acquire a new memory, but also when they are reminded of an old one. Reminders trigger a period of *re*consolidation during which memories are once again temporarily fragile and unstable, as they were when being consolidated originally (Lee, 2009). During the reconsolidation period, the unstable long-term memories can be substantially altered; in fact, in some cases, they can be erased. In one study conducted across a three-day period, researchers first presented a geometric figure along with a mild electric shock across a series of experimental trials (Schiller et al., 2010). On Day 2, they conducted two key experimental conditions:

1. Repeated presentation of the geometric figure with no shock

2. A reconsolidation period triggered by reminding participants about the geometric figure, and then repeated presentation of the figure with no shock

On Day 3, the researchers presented the geometric figure again and measured participants' reactions. In the first experimental condition, participants reacted fearfully; their reactions showed that they remembered that the geometric figure had been paired with shock. In the second condition, participants did not react at all; their reactions suggested that they had completely forgotten the connection between the figure and shock, even though information about the connection previously existed in long-term memory. Memory thus was significantly altered during the previous day's reconsolidation period.

The findings illustrate that activating a memory is *not* like opening a book on a shelf, where the information in the book remains unchanged. Instead, during a reconsolidation period, activating a memory is more like opening a word-processing file *in edit mode*, where information can be altered.

RETRIEVING INFORMATION FROM LONG-TERM MEMORY: CUES AND CONTEXT. Information held in long-term memory is not useful unless you can get it out of there. You need to retrieve the information ("Hmm, when was that exam?") from long-term memory and transfer it back into working memory ("Aha, I remember: Tuesday!"), where you can use it. The process of accessing information stored in long-term memory is called **retrieval.**

Two factors can help you retrieve information from long-term memory. One is *retrieval cues,* which are environmental stimuli related to the information you are trying to recall. When you encounter a cue, its relation to information stored in memory helps you remember that information. Suppose you are strolling about town and someone

consolidation A transformation of information in long-term memory from a fragile state, in which information can be lost, to a more fixed state in which it is available relatively permanently.

retrieval The access of information that has been stored in long-term memory.

AP Photo / Gail Burton

asks you to name one of the three highest-grossing films of all time, and you happen to walk past a travel agency with cruise ship posters. Bingo! *Titanic* springs to mind. The posters are retrieval cues that helped you recall *Titanic*.

The second factor is *context,* that is, the overall situation or environment you are in when learning information and then trying to recall it. If the contexts at the time of learning and recall match, memory is better. A study of deep-sea divers illustrates the point. Divers learned lists of words in one of two contexts: on dry land or under water (Godden & Baddeley, 1975). Later, when they tried to recall the information in each of the two contexts, divers' memory was better when the contexts matched (e.g., learned under water and recalled under water) than when they mismatched (e.g., learned under water and recalled on dry land). Later research tested divers' memory for information in decompression tables, which indicate how to avoid adverse effects from changing depth under water. Again, memory was impaired when the learning and recall contexts differed (Martin & Aggleton, 1993).

You may think of the word "context" as referring to external conditions, such as a classroom or coffee shop. However, people's emotional states also are contexts that affect memory. People's memory is better when their emotional state at recall matches their emotional state at the time they encoded the information. Gordon Bower (1981) put research participants into either a happy or sad mood and then gave them some information to learn. Later, he again induced a happy or sad mood and asked them to recall the information. Bower's experimental design thus included four conditions: learn when happy/recall when sad; learn when happy/recall when happy; learn when sad/recall when sad; learn when sad/recall when happy. The participants' memory was best when the recall context matched the learning context (Figure 6.8), that is, in the learn-when-happy/recall-when-happy and learn-when-sad/recall-when-sad conditions (Bower, 1981). Mood, then, is a contextual cue that can enhance memory.

In summary, retrieval cues and context help you retrieve information from long-term memory. And, once you've retrieved it, where does it go? Having concluded our coverage of the three-stage memory model (sensory, short-term or working, and long-term), answering this question should be easy. The information goes back to your working-memory system, where you can use it to answer questions, make decisions, and solve problems.

Ernest Manewal / Lonely Planet Images / Getty Images

Not a bad study strategy—if you're a diver Memory is superior when the context in which you try to remember information matches the context in which you learned it. So if you're a diver who needs to remember information when you are under water, that's the place to study it.

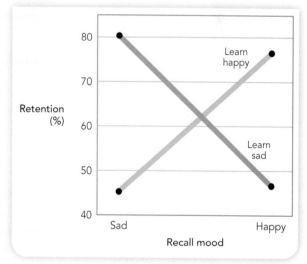

figure **6.8**
Mood and memory Participants learned information when in either a sad or happy mood, and then tried to recall it when in either a sad or happy mood. Recall was best when the learning and recall moods matched, indicating that mood is a contextual cue that can influence memory.

⚡ WHAT DO YOU KNOW?...

6. Some theorists suggest it's more useful to think of memory as an activity, rather than as something we _____ in containers. Knowing that long-term memory has a limitless capacity is an example of _____ memory, whereas your ability to read is an example of _____ memory. You don't have to remember learning how to read to be able to read, which means reading is also an example of a(n) _____ memory. Research on context effects suggest that if you are learning this material while in a happy mood, your retrieval of it will be best when you are in a(n) _____ mood.

Models of Knowledge Representation

Have you ever watched a quiz show and wondered how the winner knew so much? The famous American on the hundred dollar bill, the names of the Three Musketeers, the director of the 2014 Oscar winner for Best Picture. . . . But it's not just quiz show winners who possess a huge amount of knowledge. You do, too. You easily can recall zillions of facts: the name of your high school, whether Mexico is south or north of the United States, the approximate price of a gallon of milk. You also can remember how to do a zillion things: scramble an egg, drive a car, ride a bike, speak in grammatically correct sentences. Now that we've seen how information makes its way from sensory to short-term to long-term memory, our next question is how your long-term memory can retain such vast amounts of information.

Psychologists address this question by studying **knowledge representation,** which refers to the form in which we retain knowledge in long-term memory and connect different pieces of knowledge to one another. Let's introduce the topic with an analogy.

Instead of asking how knowledge is represented in the human mind, suppose you asked, "How is knowledge represented in libraries?" (Let's put aside digital storage and Internet access and imagine a traditional library with hard-copy books.) The answer would have a few parts: (1) Knowledge is stored using symbols (e.g., words) printed on paper; (2) large numbers of symbols, usually representing knowledge of a particular topic, are gathered together into books; and (3) the books are organized by a cataloguing system (e.g., the Library of Congress system) that enables people to retrieve any book relatively quickly. This answer says nothing about which specific books are in any particular library. Instead, it addresses a broader question: How, in general, is knowledge represented?

Psychologists ask this question about the mind. To answer it, they have proposed three main theoretical models, each of which contributes to our scientific understanding of memory and mind: *semantic network, parallel distributed processing,* and *embodied cognition* models.

Semantic Network Models

Preview Questions

> What is a network?
> In a semantic network model of memory, what determines how closely any two concepts in the mind are related?
> Are people generally aware of when ideas in their minds have been primed?

To introduce the idea of semantic networks, let's first look at the idea of a *network,* which is any collection of interconnected elements. The Internet, for example, is a communications network in which the elements that are interconnected are computers. In any network, elements in the network vary in how closely they are connected to one another. Two computers in a science laboratory might be closely connected, through a local network that serves the lab, and distantly connected, through the Internet, to a computer on the other side of the world.

In many networks, if two elements have a close connection, activating one of them will strongly influence the other. As an example, imagine a physical network, such as a fishing net. The knots represent the elements of the network. They are connected by cords running from one knot to another. If you shake one knot, the knots closer to it will move a lot, but knots farther away may move only a little.

Now, let's use these ideas to understand the mind. A **semantic network model** is a conceptual model of long-term memory in which memory consists of a large set of

knowledge representation The format in which knowledge in long-term memory is retained, and in which elements of that knowledge are interconnected.

semantic network model A conceptual model of knowledge representation in which long-term memory consists of a large set of individual concepts connected to one another.

individual concepts that are connected to one another. Any one concept (e.g., "spring break") is linked to another ("vacation") and another ("get a tan"). The interconnections create a network of concepts.

What determines how closely any two concepts are related in the mind? In principle, it could be anything: size (maybe concepts of whales and passenger planes will be closely related), color (licorice and bowling balls), or sound (actors and tractors). However, what usually connects two concepts is semantics. *Semantics* refers to the meaning of words, sentences, or other communications. "Cold" and "snow" are semantically similar because they are both related in meaning to the idea of winter weather. "Vacation" and "tan" are related in meaning to "spring break."

In the semantic network model shown in Figure 6.9, the mind processes one concept at a time (Collins & Loftus, 1975). In this network, you may be thinking about fire engines at one moment, and at the next, ambulances. The distance between two concepts—represented, in the model, by the length of the line between them—determines the likelihood that thinking of one will lead you to think of the other. Notice that the distance between some concepts, such as "car" and "truck," is shorter than between others, such as "red" and "sunrises." So, according to this network model, you would be more likely to think of "truck" when you think of "car," than you would to think of "sunrises" when you think of "red."

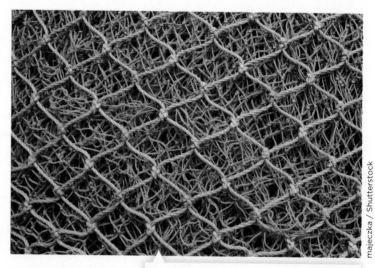

Like knots linked in a fishing net, concepts are linked together in the mind in a semantic network.

majeczka / Shutterstock

In your own semantic network, what is the distance between the concepts *psychology* and *fascinating*?

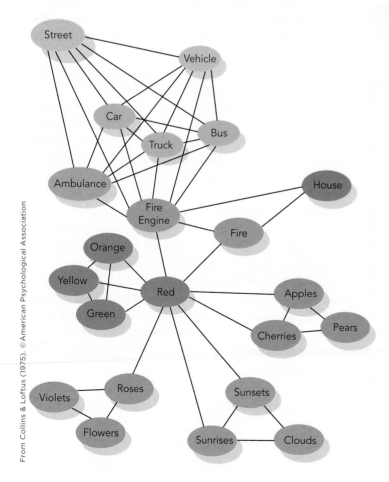

From Collins & Loftus (1975). © American Psychological Association

figure 6.9

A semantic network model Semantic network models represent knowledge as a network of associations among concepts in the mind. Concepts that are closer in meaning (e.g., car and truck) are linked more closely within the model than those whose meanings are unrelated (e.g., car and clouds). Activating one concept will activate others to which it is linked.

Priming

How do psychologists know that ideas in the mind are associated with one another? A key research tool for demonstrating these mental connections is priming. **Priming** occurs when exposure to information activates a concept in your mind that you use in your subsequent thinking. The information is said to "prime" the concept.

Here is a simple example. Pronounce these three words as you read them:

bait
hook
bass

Now pronounce these three:

drums
guitar
bass

Your pronunciation of "b-a-s-s" likely differed from one reading to another due to priming. "Bait" and "hook" primed the concept of fishing. This, in turn, caused you to pronounce "b-a-s-s" in the way that corresponds to a type of fish. "Drums" and "guitar" primed the concept of music, which caused you to pronounce "b-a-s-s" as the name of an instrument.

How does priming work? According to semantic network models, concepts have a certain amount of activation at any given time (Collins & Loftus, 1975). *Activation* is the ease with which a concept comes to mind at any given time (Bruner, 1957).

In the example above, "drums" and "guitar" increased the activation level of the concept "music." Once this happened, the concept affected your thoughts about the letters "b-a-s-s."

Even very brief priming can activate concepts in memory. For example, in one experiment (Gillath et al., 2008), researchers presented erotic photographs extremely briefly: for 30 milliseconds (less than 1/30th of a second). In another condition, they presented nonerotic photos for the same duration. The researchers then asked participants, all of whom were in romantic relationships, how willing they would be to sacrifice other parts of their lives (time spent on hobbies or with friends) to spend more time with their romantic partners. Compared with those who saw neutral photos, participants briefly primed with erotic photos were more willing to make such sacrifices (Gillath et al., 2008). Why would viewing erotic photos for 1/30th of a second have this effect? The photos prime erotic concepts that, in turn, activate concepts about romantic relationships, which are closely linked in people's semantic networks. The activation of romantic concepts then influences people's thinking when they are asked if they would make sacrifices to spend more time with romantic partners.

Chris Fitzgerald / CandidatePhotos / The Image Works

Priming in advertising Advertisers sometimes try to influence your thoughts by pairing an image with a single word that primes concepts in your semantic memory.

priming The presentation of information (a "prime") that activates a concept stored in memory.

👀 WHAT DO YOU KNOW?...

7. True or False?
   Priming is a research tool that can be used to demonstrate that concepts are related to one another in a semantic network.

Concepts can become active in memory without your even knowing it. People often are not aware of how concepts are connected in their memory or how activation spreads throughout their semantic network. They sometimes aren't even aware of the events that prime concepts; in the priming study described in the Research Toolkit, photos were presented so briefly that the participants weren't even aware of their content. Nonetheless, priming affected their thinking.

> What are the external events in your current environment? What concepts could they be priming?

This lack of awareness has important implications for everyday behavior. People's behavior can be affected by social factors of which they aren't even aware. Briefly presented information—for example, words or pictures in an advertisement—can spread so rapidly through semantic networks that people are not even aware of their effects. As a result, social information can influence your thoughts and feelings without your even knowing it (Wilson & Dunn, 2004; see Chapter 12).

In sum, semantic network models have proven valuable for understanding how knowledge is represented in the mind. By modeling knowledge as a network of linked concepts, psychologists can explain how ideas trigger one another, and how social influences affect thinking. Yet, as the study of mind advanced in the latter decades of the twentieth century, psychologists identified limitations to the semantic network approach and sought alternatives.

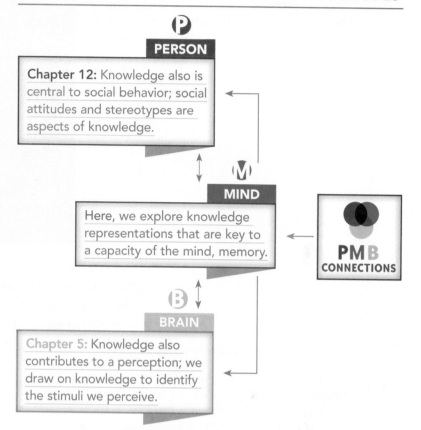

CONNECTING TO PERCEPTION AND SOCIAL ATTITUDES

PERSON
Chapter 12: Knowledge also is central to social behavior; social attitudes and stereotypes are aspects of knowledge.

MIND
Here, we explore knowledge representations that are key to a capacity of the mind, memory.

PMB CONNECTIONS

BRAIN
Chapter 5: Knowledge also contributes to a perception; we draw on knowledge to identify the stimuli we perceive.

🐦 WHAT DO YOU KNOW?...

8. According to semantic network models of long-term memory, what are some concepts that would be activated if you were getting ready to relocate from one dwelling to another?

Parallel Distributed Processing Models

Preview Question

> What are the basic elements in a parallel distributed processing model of mind?

An alternative to semantic network models is **parallel distributed processing** models of knowledge representation, or **PDP** models, for short (McClelland & Rogers, 2003; Rogers & McClelland, 2004; Rumelhart, McClelland, & the PDP Research Group, 1986). The PDP approach differs from semantic network models in the following manner.

In semantic network models, the simplest elements were individual concepts; concepts such as cars, trucks, and vehicles (Figure 6.9) were interconnected in the network. In PDP models, the basic elements are much simpler: processing units that do nothing other than turn on or off. No individual processing unit represents a concept. Rather, concepts are represented by patterns of activation in large numbers of units.

An analogy helps explain this. Imagine an electronic sign made up of numerous individual light bulbs; let's say it's a sign that displays scrolling news headlines, and the headline at the moment is "John Kerry visits Russia." Now answer two questions: (1) Which light bulb represents the concept "John Kerry"? (2) Which light bulb is scrolling? Obviously, no individual light bulb represents the concept and no light

parallel distributed processing (PDP) A conceptual model of knowledge representation in which long-term memory consists of simple processing units that turn on and off; concepts are represented by patterns of activation in large numbers of units.

Scrolling signs, such as these by the conceptual artist Jenny Holzer, represent information through a system of light bulbs. Yet no individual bulb, by itself, represents any single piece of information. Similarly, PDP models represent knowledge by a system of individual processing units that merely turn on and off.

bulbs are scrolling. The information represented in the sign is contained in the sign *as a whole*. PDP models are like this. Many individual units take part in representing any piece of knowledge; the knowledge thus is "distributed" across the units.

An appealing feature of the simple units in PDP models is that they resemble, in their simplicity, the units contained in the brain: neurons, or brain cells (Chapter 3). Neurons turn on and off; that is, they fire ("on") or are in a resting state ("off"). Similarly, the units of a PDP model either turn on or off. Inputs from other neurons determine whether a given neuron fires. Similarly, inputs from other processing units determine whether a given PDP processing unit turns on. The resemblance between PDP models and brain processes is an advantage in pursuing the long-term goal of relating processes of the mind to activities in the brain.

THINK ABOUT IT

Are there some aspects of memory that semantic network and PDP models do *not* explain? When you remember an experience that was personally embarrassing, you do not merely recall the information. You also relive the embarrassment; you have a "whole body" feeling that accompanies your memory. How can psychologists start to explain these bodily feelings that occur during some memories? (*Hint:* See the section on embodied cognition below.)

WHAT DO YOU KNOW?...

9. Contrast the simplest elements of the semantic network model with those of the parallel distributed processing (PDP) model. What do the PDP's simplest elements resemble, at the level of the brain?

Embodied Cognition

Preview Question

› How does an embodied cognition approach to memory differ from semantic network and PDP models?

Our first two models of knowledge representation, semantic networks and parallel distributed processing, were the primary theories informing research on memory and mind in the last quarter of the twentieth century. Here in the twenty-first century, scientific understanding has been expanded by a new theoretical model: *embodied cognition*.

The central question embodied cognition theorists address is, "When you think, what part of your mind do you use?" The question might seem silly; it's the "thinking part"—some part of mind devoted to memory, reasoning, and other types of complex thought—isn't it? You might expect so; but consider these research findings:

1. *Bodily movements can affect concentration.* When participants took four steps (a) forward, (b) backward, or (c) sideways before performing a task that required concentration, their performance was better after stepping backward (Koch et al., 2009).

2. *The physical warmth of a held object can influence thoughts about other people.* When participants held hot coffee before rating someone's interpersonal "warmth," their ratings were higher than if they had held iced coffee (Williams & Bargh, 2008).

3. *Perceptual variables influence the speed of conceptual thinking.* When participants judged, as quickly as possible, whether blenders are "loud" (i.e., whether the concept "blender" is associated with the property "loud"), they answered more quickly if they previously had been asked whether leaves rustle than whether cranberries are tart (Barsalou et al., 2003).

From the perspective of semantic network and PDP models, these findings are weird. Why would bodily movements affect concentration or physical warmth affect thoughts about other people? Why would thinking about leaves speed thinking about blenders—particularly odd since leaves and blenders are not semantically linked? The answer, according to embodied cognition, is that perceptual and motor systems take part in thinking processes (Anderson, 2003; Lakoff, 2012; Wilson, 2002). In **embodied cognition,** parts of the mind that previously were thought to participate only in relatively simple perceptual and motor-movement tasks also contribute to complex thought. This happens even when the thoughts are not, in any literal way, related to perception or physical movement.

Here's how embodied cognition explains the three findings above:

1. Moving backward is associated with avoiding objects. Avoidance movements usually occur in potentially harmful situations that require concentration (to avoid the harm). The part of mind that causes you to step backward thus increases concentration.

2. Judgments of interpersonal warmth are made using the same perceptual systems that are used to judge physical warmth. "Warming up" that system with hot coffee thus influences the interpersonal judgments.

3. Even if there is no loud blender in their vicinity, people use their auditory system (the perceptual system that detects sound; Chapter 5) to judge whether blenders are loud. The question about rustling leaves activates the auditory system, so it is ready to use, speeding judgments, when people think about the loudness of blenders.

In each case, a part of the mind that normally carries out perception or bodily movement—an "embodied" part of mind—also contributes to thinking.

Figure 6.10 contrasts semantic network and embodied cognition approaches to memory (Barsalou et al., 2003). In a semantic network model, perceptual systems play no role in remembering; they are active only when people first experience an event. In embodied cognition, by contrast, the visual system is active both when people experience an event *and* when they remember it. People remember information by reactivating their original perceptual experience, essentially "replaying" events in their mind.

Embodied cognition is consistent with evolutionary principles (Glenberg, 2010). In the distant past, survival required keen perception (e.g., to spot prey) and good motor skills (to evade predators and create tools; Mithen, 1996). Human perceptual and motor systems evolved to meet these needs. Once they evolved, these same systems were used for thinking; the evolved brain systems got "recycled" (Dehaene, 2004). Parts of

embodied cognition A conceptual model of knowledge representation in which parts of the mind previously thought to participate only in relatively simple mental activities, such as perceiving an event, also contribute to complex thought and memory.

figure **6.10**
Embodied cognition compared to semantic network In a semantic network model of memory (top panel), people remember experiences by retrieving information from storage in a semantic network. The semantic network is separate from the visual system, which plays no role in remembering the event. In an embodied cognition model (bottom panel), the visual system takes part in both perceiving the original experience and remembering it. People remember the experience by reactivating areas of the visual system that were active when the event originally was seen.

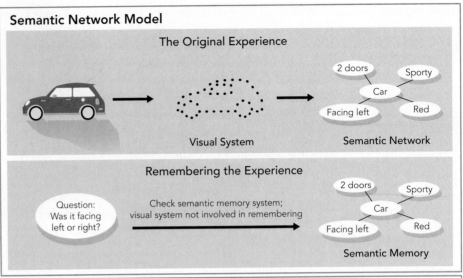

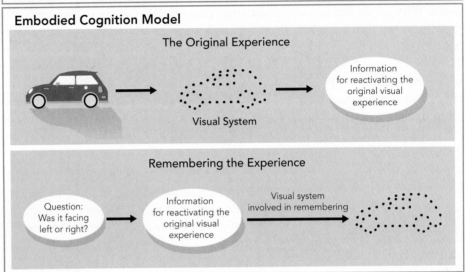

From Barsalou et al. (2003). © 2003 Elsevier

the mind and brain that evolved to perform one function (e.g., perception, movement) were reused for others (e.g., thinking, memory).

An aspect of everyday thinking that embodied cognition can explain is people's frequent use of metaphors. Metaphors are figures of speech in which one thing is described in terms of something else to which it is not directly related. If you say a friend is in "the depths" of depression or an athlete is at "the height" of her career, you are using physical metaphors (depth, height) to describe emotion and achievements. Why are such physical metaphors so common? Semantic network and PDP models don't tell us, but embodied cognition does. Our visual system, which evolved to detect the presence and location of physical objects, takes part in thinking. When it does, it brings its physical framework with it, which fosters physical metaphors when thinking (Lakoff & Johnson, 1999).

Whom do you "look up" to? In coming to admire this person, were there occasions when you literally looked up to him or her?

🌐 WHAT DO YOU KNOW?...

10. According to _____ cognition, bodily metaphors may have their origins in physical experiences. For example, getting a "cold shoulder" from someone may cause us to literally feel _____.

Memory: Imperfect But Improvable

When analyzing something, scientists ask two types of questions: "How does it work?" and "How well does it work?" So far in this chapter on memory, you've read about *how* it works: Information enters memory through a series of stages (sensory, short-term, and long-term memory) and is retained in long-term memory in ways that can be understood by semantic network, PDP, or embodied cognition models.

Let's now turn to questions about *how well* memory works. How accurate are our memories? What can you do to improve your memory?

Errors of Memory

Preview Question

> How do errors of memory show that human memory processes differ substantially from memory storage in an electronic device, such as a computer's memory system?

Memory is imperfect. People forget things: names, song lyrics, answers to exam questions. The imperfection in these cases is our failure to remember something seen or heard earlier.

This type of memory failure isn't surprising. Many of the psychological processes you learned about in this chapter—a lack of attentional effort, a confusion of similar sounds, a failure to process information deeply—can cause you to forget material that you have seen. Another type of memory imperfection, however, is surprising: false memory, or memory for things you have *not* seen.

FALSE MEMORY. **False memory** occurs when people "remember" events that never happened in the first place. They recall a personal experience—seeing something occur, being in a particular place at a particular time—but history shows that the experience never actually happened.

In a simple demonstration of false memory (Roediger & McDermott, 1995; see Chapter 1's Try This!), participants first heard a list of words that were semantically related, for example:

sour	honey
candy	soda
sugar	chocolate
bitter	heart
good	cake
taste	tart
tooth	pie
nice	

Next, they saw a new set of words. Some of the new words were on the original list and others were not. Participants tried to remember which new words had been seen previously, on the original list.

You can envision how it felt to participate in this experiment through a simple exercise. Cover up the list of words above. Now try to answer the following questions:

> Was "radio" on the list?
> Was "pie" on the list?
> Was "shoe" on the list?
> Was "sweet" on the list?

false memory The experience of "remembering" an event that, in reality, never occurred.

If you're like most of the participants in this study, you remembered that the list did not contain the words "radio" or "shoe" and that it did contain the word "pie." And, like most participants, you probably remembered that the list contained the word "sweet." But look back at the list now and try to find "sweet." It's not there! The researchers found that words like "sweet"—words similar in meaning to the original words but *not* actually presented—were remembered "at about the same level as items actually presented in the middle of the list" (Roediger & McDermott, 1995, p. 806; recall from earlier in the chapter that there is a serial position effect in memory for lists). When trying to remember words from these lists, participants experienced false memory, just as you probably did right now. They remembered something that hadn't actually occurred.

This research finding shows that human memory processes differ substantially from memory storage in an electronic device, such as the hard drive of your computer. In electronic systems, memory is passive. The electronic device merely records information that is entered into it, places the information into a permanent storage system, and retrieves it when instructed to do so. The process is so simple that the computer couldn't experience false memory. Human memory processes, however, involve active thinking. When you "input" information (in this case, read a list of words to be remembered), you do not merely store the information that is presented. You think about words and images that go beyond the information given. Being presented with words like "sugar," "chocolate," and "tooth" activates additional concepts in your semantic network, such as "sweet" (and perhaps also "dentist"). This capacity for active thought makes us more creative than computers. However, it also makes us prone to memory errors because, when we try to recall the information, a synonym or another word related to those on the list may come to mind.

People exhibit false memory not only for simple information, such as words on a list, but also for personal experiences. Elizabeth Loftus asked adult research participants whether they could remember details from four childhood events (Loftus, 1997). Three of the episodes she presented were real events that actually had happened in the participants' lives. The fourth, however, was fictional; it was a story that involved the participant getting lost in a shopping mall at age 5. After presenting each episode, Loftus asked participants if they could recall experiencing the event.

If human memory were error-free, the participants would remember the real events and report no memory for the false one. As it turns out, the participants did remember

Elizabeth Loftus, cognitive psychologist and false memory expert, shown testifying in court about the accuracy of eyewitnesses' memory of an alleged crime.

Jodi Hilton / Getty Images

real events most of the time; 68% of participants reported remembering some details about the events that had actually occurred. Surprisingly, more than one-fourth of the participants also reported that they "remembered" experiencing the fictional event (Loftus, 1997).

> Think about an event from your childhood you have described over and over to friends. How surprised would you be to learn that some of the memories you described were false?

How could human memory be prone to this error? Loftus explains that if someone suggests to you that an event happened (or merely that it might have happened), your imagination goes to work. You form a mental image of the event and imagine your thoughts and feelings in this situation. Even if the event never occurred, this "act of imagination . . . makes the event seem more familiar and that familiarity is mistakenly related to childhood memories rather than to the act of imagination" (Loftus, 1997, p. 74).

Loftus's findings have substantial implications not only for psychology, but also for legal proceedings. As an example, in 1994 a 30-year-old man, Steven Cook, charged that 17 years earlier he had been sexually molested by Cardinal Joseph Bernardin of Chicago. The evidence Cook presented in court was his memories. He reported that, while in therapy, he had suddenly recalled the abuse experience after repressing it for more than a decade and a half. Members of a jury might think that this memory proved the cardinal was guilty. Loftus's research, however, raises the possibility that the memory was false, even if Cook honestly believed that his report was true. In this case, the plaintiff himself came to doubt the accuracy of his own memory. Cook eventually withdrew his case against the cardinal, concluding that his memory was not reliable (Nolan, 1994).

BIASES IN EYEWITNESS MEMORY. A second form of memory error also is relevant to legal proceedings. It is **eyewitness memory,** which is memory for events that we personally observe (as opposed to events we merely hear about). If you observe a car accident and report the details to police, or witness a crime and pick the perpetrator out of a line-up of suspects, you're relying on eyewitness memory.

We often believe that eyewitness memories can't be wrong. "I saw it with my own eyes!" people say to express this belief. But, in fact, these memories *can* be wrong.

> Approaching my sixtieth birthday, I started to experience . . . memories, especially of my boyhood in London before World War II . . . [I remembered that] one night, a thousand-pound bomb fell into the garden next to ours, but fortunately it failed to explode. . . . On another occasion, an incendiary bomb, a thermite bomb, fell behind our house and burned with a terrible, white-hot heat.
>
> [Later] I spoke of these bombing incidents to my brother Michael . . . five years my senior. My brother immediately confirmed the first bombing incident . . . but regarding the second bombing, he said, "You never saw it. You weren't there. . . . We were both away at Braefield at the time. But David [our older brother] wrote us a letter about it. A very vivid, dramatic letter. You were enthralled by it."
>
> Clearly, I had not only been enthralled, but must have constructed the scene in my mind, from David's words, and then appropriated it, and taken it for a memory of my own.
>
> —Oliver Sacks (2013)

Paul Cates, Innocence Project

Victim of memory error In 1995 a crime victim identified Sedrick Courtney, of Tulsa, Oklahoma, as the perpetrator of an assault and burglary. In 1996 the victim's memory of Mr. Courtney's role in the crime contributed to his conviction. In 2012, after Mr. Courtney had spent many years in prison, DNA testing showed that the victim's memory was inaccurate; Mr. Courtney was innocent of the crime and the charges against him were dismissed. When wrongful convictions occur in criminal cases, memory errors are a primary cause (Innocence Project, 2012).

eyewitness memory Memory for events that are personally observed (rather than being learned of second-hand, through conversation or reading).

Paul Cates, Innocence Project

figure 6.11
Wrongful conviction DNA evidence has led to the review of many legal cases in which individuals convicted of a crime were actually innocent. Research on these cases reveals that the most common cause of any wrongful convictions was inaccurate memory! In more than three-fourths of the cases studied, inaccurate eyewitness memory contributed to the accused person being convicted wrongfully.

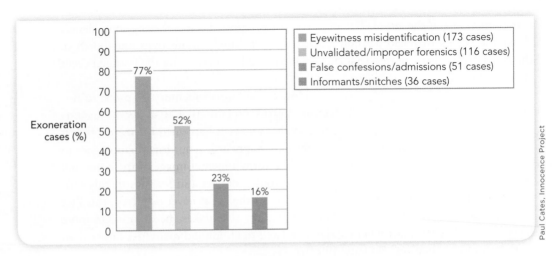

After witnessing an event, people may hear information that distorts their eyewitness memory (Figure 6.11). Research by Loftus shows how this can work.

In one study, Loftus showed participants a film with eight political demonstrators disrupting instruction in a classroom (Loftus, 1975). Afterward, participants were asked one of two questions: "Was the leader of the four demonstrators who entered the classroom a male?" or "Was the leader of the 12 demonstrators who entered the classroom a male?" Later, the participants were asked to recall how many demonstrators took part in the protest. The questions affected people's eyewitness memory. Although everyone had seen 8 demonstrators, people who had been asked the question mentioning 12 demonstrators remembered that the number of demonstrators was approximately 9. Those who had been asked the question mentioning 4 demonstrators remembered that there were about 6 of them.

> Is it unethical to use leading questions to influence someone's recall of an event?

In related research, participants saw a film of a traffic accident and later were asked how fast the cars in the accident had been going (Loftus, 2003). In different experimental conditions, Loftus varied the phrasing of the question about the cars' speed at impact. She asked some participants how fast the cars were going when they "hit" each other, and others how fast they were going when they "smashed into" each other. Again, the language used in the question altered people's eyewitness memory (Loftus, 2003). Participants who heard the words "smashed into" as opposed to "hit" remembered the cars as going faster.

THE ACCURACY OF FLASHBULB MEMORY. A third type of memory error involves **flashbulb memory,** which is vivid memory of unexpected, highly emotional, and significant events. Every once in a while, as a society, we experience an unexpected and emotionally stimulating event: a political assassination, a terrorist attack, or a sudden natural disaster. When people first hear of the event, their emotions are aroused and senses heightened. When people look back on the event, they often feel they can see perfectly, in their mind, not only the event but also where they were when they first heard about it, almost as if a flashbulb had gone off originally and imprinted an indelible image onto their memory.

> For what event—big or small—do you have a flashbulb memory?

Fantastic Rabbit / Alamy

How fast were they going when they hit? Even if you has witnessed it first-hand, your memory for the accident could be affected by the words people use, after the fact, to describe it. When asked how fast the cars were going when they "smashed into" (rather than "hit") each other, people remembered the cars as going faster. The way events are described can affect eyewitness memory.

flashbulb memory Vivid memory of unexpected, highly emotional, and significant events.

Because they are so vivid, flashbulb memories seem like a form of memory that is not prone to error. You might expect that they are more accurate than ordinary memories of everyday events. But are they?

To find out, researchers began a study of memory immediately after a major "flashbulb" event: the 9/11 terrorist attacks. On September 12, 2001, they asked participants to report their experiences in detail—where they were, whom they were with, what they were doing—when they first heard of the attacks. They also asked participants how confident they were that their memories of the events were accurate. To compare flashbulb memory with ordinary memory, participants also answered these questions with respect to a second event, namely, an everyday activity that had occurred recently.

The researchers then asked participants these same questions 7, 18, and 224 days later (Talarico & Rubin, 2003). This enabled them to study changes in both the accuracy of flashbulb and regular memories, and people's confidence in that accuracy. Accuracy was measured in terms of the consistency between the original memory and the memory at a later time; if memory at a later time is not consistent with memory only one day after the event, then the later memory is inaccurate.

Flashbulb memories An emotionally arousing event, such as a terrorist attack, in unforgettable. Yet people often are confident that they can recall not only the event, but precisely where they were, and what they were doing, when first learning about it. Research suggests that such *flashbulb* memories are less accurate than people commonly think.

As you can see in Figure 6.12, over time people's confidence in their everyday memories declined, but their confidence in their *flashbulb* memories remained high.

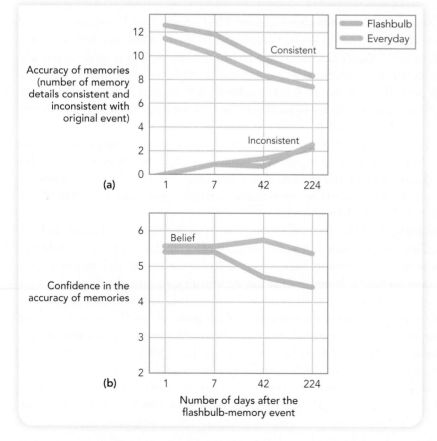

figure **6.12**

Confidence—and accuracy?—of flashbulb memory
People commonly are confident that their memory for "flashbulb" events is accurate. But frequently they're wrong. Research shows that people are more confident of the accuracy of flashbulb memories than everyday memories (b), even when the flashbulb memories are no more accurate than everyday memories (a).

Was their relatively high level of confidence in flashbulb memories matched by a high level of accuracy? No, people remembered "flashbulb" events with no greater accuracy than everyday events. Participants' perception that their flashbulb memories were more accurate than their memory for everyday events was false.

WHAT DO YOU KNOW?...

11. The following statement is incorrect. Explain why, referring to Elizabeth Loftus's "getting lost in a shopping mall" study: "Human memory is similar to electronic devices in its passivity. We record information about our experiences exactly as they are experienced, and retrieve those memories in the exact same form."

◎ CULTURAL OPPORTUNITIES

Autobiographical Memory

"I am smart."

"I'm beautiful."

"[I'm] a funny and hilarious person."

—European American children's self-descriptions,
from Wang (2004)

"I'm my mom and dad's child, my grandma and grandpa's grandson."

"I practice the piano every day."

"I play with my friend Yin-Yin at school."

—Chinese children's self-descriptions,
from Wang (2004)

What do you notice about the above quotes? They suggest that European American and Chinese children view themselves differently. In Western cultures, self-concept is individualistic (see Chapter 12). People tend to think of themselves in terms of physical characteristics and inner psychological qualities that highlight their individuality and distinguish them from others. In Eastern cultures, self-concept is more collectivistic. People's self-concepts include thoughts about their relationships to their family, friends, and members of the wider social community.

These different views of self may affect an aspect of memory: **autobiographical memory,** which is memory of experiences from one's own life. As we experience life events, we construct memories of them; we retain mental images and factual knowledge of events and develop a storyline, or personal narrative, about our lives (McAdams, 2001; Nelson & Fivush, 2004).

The psychologist Qi Wang (2006) explains how people from individualistic and collectivistic cultures might form different types of autobiographical memory. An individualistic culture draws attention to one's own contributions to events and thus may cause people to dwell on their personal feelings during activities. As a result, people may have more detailed, rich autobiographical memory. A collectivistic perspective, by comparison, leads people to pay attention to the experiences of the group of which they are a part and the environment in which the group's experience occurs. As a result, people with collectivistic self-concepts should have *less* detailed memory of their own actions and experiences.

In a study with preschool children, kindergarteners, and second graders from the United States and China, children were asked to recall events from their lives (e.g., "how you spent your last birthday," "a time when your mom or dad scolded you for something"). Their memories were coded to identify variations in specificity. A memory such as, "Once I said a bad word at home, then they got mad at me" would be

autobiographical memory Your memory of facts and experiences from your own life.

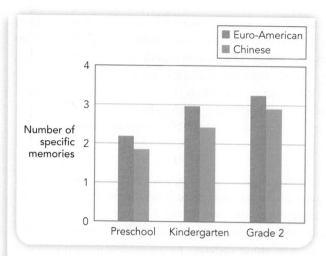

figure 6.13
Autobiographical memory across cultures Does culture influence memory? To find out, researchers studied autobiographical memory among two groups of children: European American children and children in China. They conducted their study with preschoolers, kindergarteners, and second graders. American children were found to have more specific memories of events from their lives than were Chinese children. The cultural difference reflects the distinct individualistic and collectivistic cultures in which American and Chinese children, respectively, are raised (Wang, 2004).

more specific than a general recollection such as "My mom told me stories every night" (Wang, 2004). The autobiographical memories of children from the United States and China were found to differ (Figure 6.13). American children's memories were more specific; they centered on "detailed, one-moment-in-time events and contained rich spontaneous references to emotions" (Wang, 2004, p. 11). Chinese children's memories were more general, featuring "relatively skeletal accounts of past experiences that tended to center on daily routines and had fewer emotional expressions" (p. 11). Culture thus shaped autobiographical memory.

The research findings should remind you of a broader lesson about psychology that you learned in Chapter 1: Different levels of analysis in psychological science inform one another. Wang was interested in the workings of the mind, specifically, the cognitive processes through which autobiographical memories are created. Yet her research was informed by research on persons and the cultural settings in which they live. Research on culture provided clues about the mental processes by which autobiographical memories develop.

🌀 WHAT DO YOU KNOW?...

12. The following statement is incorrect. Explain why:
"When asked to recall memories of events in their lives, the recollections of children from China and the United States were equally specific, indicating how little a role culture plays in autobiographical memory."

Improving Your Memory

Preview Questions

› What is chunking and how does it increase the amount of information a person can store in short-term memory?

› What are mnemonics and how do they improve memory?

Much of this chapter has concerned memory's limitations: Storage in sensory memory is brief; the capacity of short-term memory is limited; some long-term "memories" are not accurate—the memories are false. After learning of the limitations, you might be asking, "Is there anything I can do to improve my memory?"

People have asked this question for thousands of years. In fact, the need to improve memory was greater in the past than today (Danziger, 2008). Before the invention of the printing press, copies of documents, even important ones such as sacred texts and legal proclamations, were scarce. People who needed to know the information in these documents had to memorize it. The demand for memory skills was so high that in ancient Rome, for example, training in memory was part of a formal education.

Today, technology does much of our memory work for us. We can access facts and figures on the Internet, so we don't need to memorize them. Yet we often still do need that "old-fashioned" memory device, the human mind; whether you're trying to remember a formula during a math exam or someone's name at a party, you need memory skills. So let's look at two strategies for enhancing them. The first, *chunking,* is a technique for packing more information into short-term memory. The second, *mnemonics,* is a set of techniques for organizing information in long-term memory in a way that makes it easier to retrieve.

CHUNKING. As you'll recall from earlier in this chapter, short-term memory can hold only a few pieces of information. If somebody reads you a list of 15 names, numbers, or words, you're likely to remember only about a half-dozen of them.

Chunking is a strategy for increasing the amount of information you can retain in short-term memory. The strategy is to group different pieces of information into one memorable piece, or "chunk" of information. As an example, quickly read the line of letters below, then cover up the line, and see how many you can remember:

A L J F K G W B B H O

If you're like most people, you remembered a couple letters at the beginning (A, L) due to primacy effects and some at the end (H, O) due to recency effects, but you couldn't remember half or more of the letters.

Now read the letters again, while trying to group together some letters. Here's a hint: presidents of the United States. Let's group them so that the virtue of the hint becomes obvious:

A L   J F K   G W B   B H O

There are four chunks of information. Each one contains the initials of an American president: Abraham Lincoln, John F. Kennedy, George W. Bush, and Barack H. Obama. Each chunk packs two or three pieces of information into one memorable group. By remembering the four chunks, which is easy, you're able to remember 11 individual letters, which was hard.

An even more effective example of the benefits of chunking involves the following list of numbers. Read it quickly and try to recall the numbers:

1 4 9 1 6 2 5 3 6 4 9 6 4 8 1

Again, you probably recalled just a few, from the beginning and end of the list—unless you noticed the sequence: 1^2, 2^2, 3^2, 4^2, 5^2, 6^2, 7^2, 8^2, 9^2. Once you notice that, the original 15 pieces of information (the 15 numbers) are reduced to one chunk; all you have to do is remember the single fact that the string of numbers is the result of listing the square of integers starting with 1.

Chunking doesn't expand the storage capacity of short-term memory; your memory holds the same number of "packages" of information. Chunking simply stuffs more information into each package.

The second memory enhancement tool works on a different principle. It enhances memory by providing memorable methods of organizing the information you need to recall.

MNEMONICS. Memory can be enhanced by **mnemonics,** which are strategies for organizing information in memory. Mnemonic strategies usually add a small amount of information to material that you need to remember; the additional information increases the organization of information, making it easier to recall the material you need (Higbee, 1996). Just as a library cataloging system is useful for finding books in a library, mnemonics are useful for locating information in memory.

One simple type of mnemonic uses acronyms (abbreviations formed from the initial parts of other words). In a trigonometry class, you may have needed to remember that the sine of an angle equals the opposite side of a triangle divided by

---

chunking A strategy for increasing the amount of information retained in short-term memory in which distinct pieces of information are grouped into "chunks."

mnemonics Strategies for enhancing memory, in particular by organizing information in a manner that aids recall.

the hypotenuse, the cosine is the adjacent side divided by the hypotenuse, and the tangent is the opposite side divided by the adjacent side. How are you going to remember all that? You can use the acronym SOHCAHTOA (Sine Opposite Hypotenuse, etc.). The acronym is an extra piece of information to remember, but it's useful: It organizes information that you otherwise might forget.

SOHCAHTOA only helps in trig classes, however. Other mnemonic strategies boost recall of diverse types of information (Higbee, 1996). For example:

> In the *peg system,* information people need to recall is associated with other information that is easy to remember. The easy-to-remember pieces of information are like pegs on which pieces of hard-to-remember information are "hung." In one version of the system, the pegs are simple rhymes (One is a Bun, Two is a Shoe, Three is a Tree, Four is a Door, Five is a Hive). If you need to remember a set of grocery items—say, aspirin, milk, dog food, butter, ground beef—you "hang" them on the pegs. For example, you might imagine biting into a bun filled with aspirins, stepping into shoes filled with milk, seeing bags of dog food hanging from a tree with dogs jumping up to reach the food, and so forth. The weird-but-memorable images make the items easier to remember.

> In the *method of loci,* familiar locations are used to organize information in memory (Roediger, 1980). To recall items, one thinks of a familiar setting (e.g., your bedroom) and associates each item to be recalled with a specific location in that setting. Using our earlier grocery list, you might imagine placing aspirin on your bed where the pillow usually goes, putting a gallon of milk in front of your TV, and stuffing a drawer full of dog food. To remember the items, one "walks around the room," inspecting the familiar locations to find each item (Figure 6.14). The method of

Memory champion Johannes Mallow, a winner of the World Memory Championships, can perform incredible feats of memory, including remembering sequences of 500 random digits and 350 playing cards after studying them for only 5 to 10 minutes. Was he born with a "really big brain"? No. He learned mnemonic strategies, which helped turn him into a memory champion.

Peter Foerster / EPA / Newscom

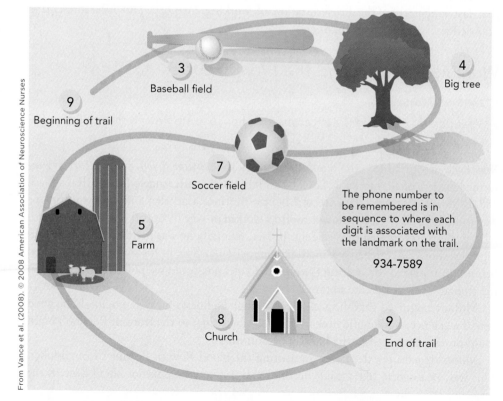

From Vance et al. (2008). © 2008 American Association of Neuroscience Nurses

figure 6.14
Method of loci How can you remember a long list of items? One strategy is the method of loci. You think of some location with which you're familiar, and then mentally "place" the items you need to recall in different spots within that location. When you have to remember the items, you can mentally "find" the objects right where you left them.

loci can powerfully boost memory; "results are often striking and dramatic, [with people] using loci frequently recalling two to seven times as much as control subjects" (Bower, 1970, p. 499).

🕹 WHAT DO YOU KNOW?...

13. Match the memory improvement technique on the left with its example to the right.

1. Chunking	a. Associating items on your shopping list with places in your living room
2. Peg system	b. Using ROY G. BIV to remember the colors of the rainbow
3. Method of loci	c. Adding easily imagined phrases (e.g., "One is a Bun") to pieces of information that need to be remembered.

Memory and the Brain

This chapter has so far been psychological rather than biological. We have explored psychological processes through which people achieve a mental ability: memory. But memory also rests on a piece of physical hardware: the brain. Let's now move down a level of explanation, from mind to brain, and learn about the neural systems that underpin the psychological skills of memory.

Which part of the brain do you think is responsible for memory? Recall that the mind contains different memory systems (e.g., short-term, long-term) and retains different types of knowledge (semantic memory, episodic memory, procedural memory). This fact about the mind is relevant to our question about the brain. No *one* part of the brain is solely responsible for memory. Rather, different types of memory draw on different brain systems (Squire & Wixted, 2011).

Let's look at brain systems underlying three memory abilities: (1) maintaining information in working memory; (2) forming permanent memories, that is, memories that last longer than the brief duration of working memory; and (3) representing knowledge in a permanent manner.

Working Memory and the Frontal Lobes

Preview Question

› What part of the brain is active when we concentrate on and manipulate information?

Way back in April 1881, the book review section of *Brain: A Journal of Neurology* informed readers of a remarkable book by an Italian scientist, Angelo Mosso (Rabagliati, 1881). Mosso described the case of Michele Bertino, a gentleman whose misfortune was to be located 45 feet below a rooftop workman who dropped a brick. As Mosso related, Bertino survived the accident; in fact, mentally he was perfectly fine. The falling brick, however, created a 1-inch-diameter circular hole in his skull, just above and behind his forehead. By peering through the hole, one could see pulsations of blood in the frontal lobes of Bertino's brain.

Mosso recognized that the accident, although bad news for Bertino, might be good news for science. Systematic observations of blood flow to the front of Bertino's brain could provide insight into the biology of thinking.

Mosso rigged up a device for measuring the blood flow in Bertino's frontal lobes. This was, in essence, like taking Bertino's pulse—but the pulse of blood flow in the

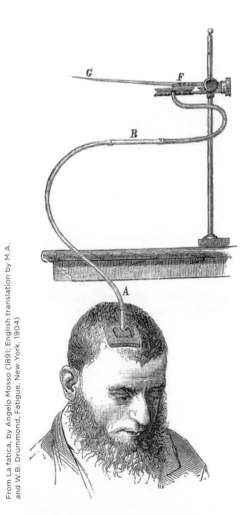

From La fatica, by Angelo Mosso (1891; English translation by M.A. and W.B. Drummond, Fatigue, New York, 1904)

figure 6.15
Angelo Mosso's apparatus for measuring blood flow in Michele Bertino's brain.

brain rather than at the wrist (Figure 6.15). Mosso observed that when Bertino concentrated on information, blood flow increased. When he solved an arithmetic problem, or was criticized for making an error, or was suddenly reminded of some activity he was supposed to be engaged in, more blood flowed to his frontal lobes. Mosso's analysis provided unique evidence that the frontal lobes are involved in thinking.

In contemporary scientific language, what Mosso observed is that the frontal lobes underpin working memory, the mental system that enables us to concentrate on, and consciously manipulate, small amounts of information. Contemporary evidence supports Mosso's observation. In one study, researchers obtained brain images while research participants performed two tasks. One task was so easy that it required little working-memory activity: Participants simply counted the numbers 1 through 10, in order. The other task required more working-memory action: They were asked to generate random orderings of the digits 1 through 10, being careful not to repeat a digit. When the researchers compared brain activity during the two tasks (Petrides et al., 1993), they found that working-memory activity was associated with activation in the frontal lobes.

✤ WHAT DO YOU KNOW?...

14. Contemporary research corroborates Mosso's observation that thinking—in particular, working-memory activity—is associated with increased activity in the frontal _____.

The Hippocampus and the Formation of Permanent Memories

Preview Questions

> What brain systems are critical for the formation of more permanent memories? How can they be enhanced?
> What brain system is critical for our ability to make cognitive maps?

Information in working memory does not stay there for long. In the working-memory experiment we just reviewed, participants likely forget any given string of random numbers they had generated within a minute or less. What brain systems enable you to form more permanent memories?

The key systems are found in the temporal lobes, the large sections of brain matter on the right and left sides of the brain, located under the skull just above the ears. Scientists have known since 1953 that the temporal lobe is needed for forming permanent memories—that's the year HM had his surgery and lost his memory, as you might recall from this chapter's opening story. That surgery damaged brain matter in HM's temporal lobe. Later in HM's life, newly developed technologies enabled researchers to create images of his brain; those images confirmed the existence of long-term temporal lobe damage (Corkin et al., 1997)—a conclusion further confirmed by postmortem dissections of HM's brain (Worth & Annese, 2012).

Within each temporal lobe is a structure that contributes directly to the formation of permanent memories: the *hippocampus* (Figure 6.16). Research on the hippocampus provides insight, at a brain level of analysis, into a mental process you learned about earlier: consolidation, or the transformation of memories that are fragile into ones that are permanent (Squire, 1992). Consolidation occurs thanks to a biological process in the hippocampus known as long-term potentiation. **Long-term potentiation** is an enduring increase in the efficiency of communication between brain cells (Bliss & Collingridge, 1993). Cell-to-cell communications become more efficient, due to changes in the biochemical processes through which brain cells

---

long-term potentiation An enduring increase in the efficiency of communication between brain cells.

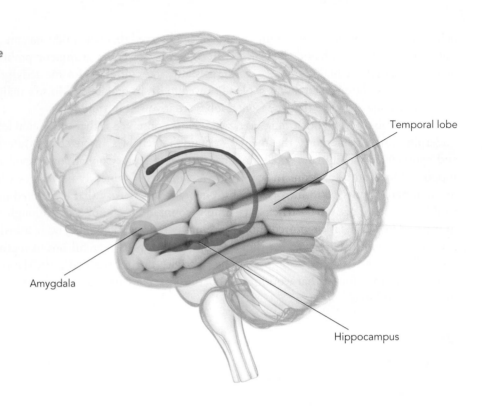

figure **6.16**
Hippocampus and temporal lobe

Temporal lobe

Amygdala

Hippocampus

influence one another's firing (McIntyre, McGaugh, & Williams, 2012). These long-lasting changes in the brain enable organisms to have long-lasting memories. The biological changes occur only gradually, which is why the psychological process of consolidation is gradual.

Long-term potentiation helps explain the effects of head injuries on memory (discussed earlier). Head injuries, such as those that occur in contact sports, can disrupt the biochemical processes required for long-term potentiation to occur (De Beaumont et al., 2012). As a result, the formation of long-term memories is disrupted (Figure 6.17).

Changes in the hippocampus across the life span produce changes in memory ability. The hippocampus often shrinks in size in older adulthood, and older adults with smaller hippocampus volume have relatively poor semantic memory (Zimmerman et al., 2008). Conversely, increases in hippocampus size improve memory. In one study, older adults participated in a year-long program of aerobic exercise, that is, exercise that moderately increases heart rate for extended periods of time. Compared with a group that did not exercise aerobically, aerobic exercisers had a larger hippocampus and better memory (Erickson et al., 2011).

> How much aerobic activity do you engage in during a given week?

Get that hippocampus going!
Research shows that exercise classes can increase the size of the hippocampus, as well as memory ability, among older adults.

Kali Nine LLC / Getty Images

spatial memory The ability to recall the layout of one's physical environment.

One form of memory for which the hippocampus is particularly critical is **spatial memory,** which is the ability to recall the layout of one's physical environment. Complex mammals have good spatial memory, thanks to their ability to create *cognitive maps* (Tolman, 1948). Cognitive maps are mental representations of a physical layout.

figure 6.17

PMB
IN ACTION

PERSON Ⓟ

After head injuries, people often have no memory of events that occurred during, and immediately prior to, the injury.

MIND Ⓜ

At a mind level of analysis, injuries affect *consolidation*, a psychological process in which information becomes stored in long-term memory in a permanent form.

BRAIN Ⓑ

At a brain level of analysis, injuries affect *long-term potentiation*, an enduring change in the efficiency of communication among brain cells that enables us to have enduring memories.

© Aaron Josefczyk / Reuters / Corbis

The hippocampus is key to cognitive map making (Nadel, 1991). Evidence of its role comes from research in which the hippocampus is damaged. Consider research with homing pigeons, a species that has excellent spatial memory. If a young pigeon's hippocampus is damaged, its ability to find its way home—or anywhere else—is substantially impaired (Nadel, 1991).

The hippocampus is not the only brain system that contributes to the formation of enduring memories. Another is the amygdala, which is located very close to the hippocampus (see Figure 6.16) and which also takes part in creating permanent memories (Bermudez-Rattoni, 2010). It appears to play a larger role in memory formation when people do not think deeply about material—that is, when they engage in shallow processing (Figure 6.5). Thanks to amygdala activation, people may remember emotionally significant material even when their initial processing of the material was shallow (Ritchey, LaBar, & Cabeza, 2011).

🐦 WHAT DO YOU KNOW?...

15. HM, who could not form permanent memories, suffered from damage to the hippocampus, a structure located in the _____ lobe. The hippocampus is particularly important to consolidation, which occurs as a result of the biological process of long-term _____, whereby cell-to-cell communication is made more efficient due to biochemical changes. The hippocampus is particularly important to the formation of _____ memory, the ability to recall the layout of one's physical environment. The _____, which is near the hippocampus, also aids in the formation of permanent memories.

The Distributed Representation of Knowledge

Preview Question

> Does the way information is stored in the brain resemble the way a book is stored in a library?

The hippocampus is key to the formation of permanent memories, that is, the process in which a given memory becomes permanently stored. But once that permanent storage occurs, the hippocampus's role is less important. Other brain regions take part in permanent memory storage—especially regions of the brain's outermost layer of cells, the cerebral cortex (Squire & Wixted, 2011; see Chapter 3).

How is any given memory stored in the cerebral cortex? There are two possibilities. One is that the brain works like a library. Your brain retains information, and libraries store information—for example, the information in a book. In a library, any given book is stored in a particular location. In other words, the whole book—every word and picture—is stored in one given place. Does your brain work like this, storing all your memory about a person, place, or experience in one biological spot under the skull?

In a word, no. Instead, the brain primarily works according to a second principle of information storage: *distributed* storage. When you remember an experience—its sights and sounds, how it felt, and factual information identifying the people and places you experienced—you activate multiple regions in the brain. The overall pattern of brain activation provides the memory (Schacter, 1996). The knowledge you retain about the experience, then, is distributed across multiple parts of the brain.

Psychologists who have advanced parallel distributed processing models of memory (discussed above) have shown how and where this psychological processing can occur in the brain (McClelland & Rogers, 2003). Their model (Figure 6.18)

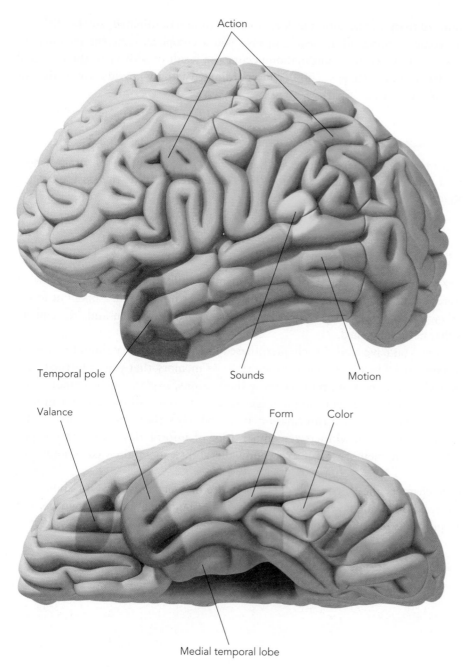

Action

Temporal pole

Sounds

Motion

Valance

Form

Color

Medial temporal lobe

figure 6.18

Distributed brain systems Memories are not stored in one location in the brain. They are distributed across different brain regions. In this model of memory and the brain (McClelland & Rogers, 2003), neural activity in the temporal lobe coordinates activity in other brain regions that process the sights, sounds, and actions that come to mind when you remember your experiences.

identifies multiple parts of the brain that become active when you try to remember something.

Suppose you're trying to remember something about a movie; perhaps someone asks you, "How did you like Johnny Depp in *Pirates of the Caribbean*?" and you're trying to activate a memory of his performance to answer the question. There is no one spot—no single location—in your brain that contains the "memory of Johnny Depp in *Pirates of the Caribbean*." Instead, memories of what he looked like, how he sounded, how he moved, and so forth are represented in different locations of the brain. Activity in the different locations has to be coordinated, so the different features come to mind all at once and give you a complete, coherent memory. In this theoretical model, the coordination occurs as a result of activity in the temporal cortex (McClelland & Rogers, 2003). The coordinated activity provides you with your memory of Captain Jack Sparrow.

✔ WHAT DO YOU KNOW?...

16. If our memory of an experience activates multiple regions in the brain, why aren't our memories more disjointed? In other words, what makes them coherent?

⟳⟲ Looking Back and Looking Ahead

Memory might seem like a mystery. People remember childhood events yet forget what they were talking about a minute ago. They remember how to ride a bike but forget when they learned how. They forget events that happened to them and "remember" events that never happened.

Now that you have read this chapter, these facts about memory should no longer seem mysterious. The distinctions among types of memory that you've learned, and the research and theory supporting these distinctions, explain such memory successes and failures. Sure, you might forget what you were talking about a minute ago—but it's not just you. Information in everybody's short-term memory fades quickly. Yes, quiz show winners remember a lot of information—but it's not just them. Long-term memory gives everybody the ability to retain vast amounts of information.

In the chapters ahead, you will continue to see memory at work. Our abilities to recognize and think about everyday objects, to understand and produce language, and to solve problems rely on our memory.

Chapter Review

Now that you have completed this chapter, be sure to turn to Appendix B, where you will find a **Chapter Summary** that is useful for reviewing what you have learned about memory.

Key Terms

attentional effort (p. 219)
autobiographical memory (p. 244)
chunking (p. 246)
consolidation (p. 230)
decay (p. 221)
depth of processing (p. 224)
echoic memory (p. 218)
embodied cognition (p. 237)
encoding (p. 219)
episodic memory (p. 229)
explicit memory (p. 229)
eyewitness memory (p. 241)
false memory (p. 239)

flashbulb memory (p. 242)
iconic memory (p. 217)
implicit memory (p. 229)
interference (p. 222)
knowledge representation (p. 232)
long-term memory (p. 227)
long-term potentiation (p. 249)
memory (p. 215)
mnemonics (p. 246)
parallel distributed processing (PDP)
  (p. 235)
priming (p. 234)
proactive interference (p. 222)

procedural memory (p. 229)
rehearsal (p. 223)
retrieval (p. 230)
retroactive interference (p. 222)
semantic memory (p. 228)
semantic network model (p. 232)
sensory memory (p. 217)
serial position effect (p. 223)
short-term memory (p. 219)
spatial memory (p. 250)
three-stage memory model (p. 217)
working memory (p. 225)

Questions for Discussion

1. One might argue that echoic memory has been keeping friendships and marriages together for years. Case in point: Have you ever half-listened to someone else's chatter, only to have that person complain that you weren't even listening? How does echoic memory "save" you? Dramatize this concept for the class, then explain the role of echoic memory. [Apply]

2. Researchers Randolph-Seng and Nielsen (2007) found that individuals who had been primed with religious words (e.g., baptism, commandments) were less likely to cheat on a visuospatial task than were those who had been primed with sports-related or neutral words. That is, subtly exposing individuals to some versus other words influenced their moral behavior. Look around your classroom. Are there objects or words now present that could be priming your thoughts, feelings, and/or behaviors? Explain. [Comprehend]

3. In the section on embodied cognition, there was a discussion about two metaphors that involve the physical body: "height of her career" and "depths of depression." Can you think of other metaphors that include these up/down directions? [Comprehend]

4. Below are several examples of metaphors that involve the physical body. Are they each examples of embodied cognition? That is, when we use them, are we referring to our physical bodies to help us think about our experiences? What do you think is the origin of these metaphors? [Analyze]

   a big mouth
   to cost an arm and a leg

   to have a sweet tooth
   a pain in the neck
   to pull someone's leg
   to put one's foot in one's mouth
   to see eye to eye

5. Recall Loftus's (1975) study in which she showed individuals a film depicting eight demonstrators and was able to influence individuals' recall of how many individuals were in the movie by asking different types of leading questions. What does this study suggest about the role of post-movie conversation in forming a memory of that movie? When does our memory for a film stop changing? [Analyze]

6. Given the fallibility of memory demonstrated by Loftus and her colleagues, what is your stance concerning whether we should rely on eyewitness memory in trials? [Evaluate]

7. Describe, in writing, as many details as you can of a personal flashbulb memory. Now check the accuracy of the details by comparing your notes to those of several reliable sources (think carefully about what is considered a reliable source!). How much correspondence was there between your version and that of your reliable source(s)? Why do you suppose we are so confident in the accuracy of our flashbulb memories? [Apply, Analyze]

8. How does chunking as an aid to memory relate to the semantic network model of memory? [Analyze]

Chapter Review

9. You learned that a mnemonic is a technique for adding a small amount of information to material you need to remember. Adding this information enables you to better organize the information (e.g., the method of loci, whereby you organize to-be-remembered items by associating them with a walk through several different rooms). What is it about *organizing* the information that helps you retain it better? What would the alternative be? [Analyze]

10. Given what you have learned in this chapter, what are three pieces of advice you would give to a friend who wanted to do well on an upcoming exam and why? [Synthesize]

Self-Test

1. In the context of levels of analysis, hardware is to software as
   a. mind is to brain.
   b. person is to mind.
   c. person is to brain.
   d. brain is to mind.

2. What did George Sperling's study on sensory memory indicate about the properties of iconic memory?
   a. Its capacity is large and its duration is brief.
   b. Its capacity is large and its duration is long.
   c. Its capacity is small and its duration is brief.
   d. Its capacity is small and its duration is long.

3. The importance of memory-enhancing strategies is made apparent by the rate at which information in short-term memory decays, which is
   a. about 90% of information in about 18 seconds.
   b. about 90% of information in about 36 seconds.
   c. about 18% of information in about 90 seconds.
   d. about 18% of information in about 36 seconds.

4. Tasha, after having taken ballet lessons for years, decides it's time to try modern dance. She has trouble remembering the new dance moves, often reverting to the ballet style. What type of interference is she experiencing and why?
   a. Retroactive interference, because new knowledge is interfering with old knowledge
   b. Retroactive interference, because old knowledge is interfering with new knowledge
   c. Proactive interference, because new knowledge is interfering with old knowledge
   d. Proactive interference, because old knowledge is interfering with new knowledge

5. You want to permanently encode the concept of retroactive interference into your long-term memory. Which of the following is the best example of deep processing of the concept?
   a. Repeat the definition of retroactive interference several times until it "sticks."
   b. Write down the definition of retroactive interference at least 10 times.

   c. Generate several examples of retroactive interference from your own life.
   d. Pay special attention to how "retroactive interference" sounds when you say it aloud.

6. Short-term memory and working memory differ in all of the following ways except which?
   a. Working memory is an active system; short-term memory is a passive storage system.
   b. Working memory expands on short-term memory by including a phonological loop.
   c. Working memory is enacted outside of conscious awareness; short-term memory is entirely under our control.
   d. Working memory expands on short-term memory by including a visuospatial sketchpad.

7. That you can't perfectly remember all the lessons that shaped your ability to read (and yet you still can read) supports which of the following statements?
   a. Reading is a semantic memory that is also an explicit memory.
   b. Reading is a procedural memory that is also an implicit memory.
   c. Reading is a semantic memory that is also an implicit memory.
   d. Reading is a procedural memory that is also an explicit memory.

8. Ravi memorized the definitions of all of his vocabulary words in preparation for the upcoming quiz, but was surprised to find that his teacher used slightly different versions of the definitions on that quiz. Which of the following is true of Ravi's study strategy?
   a. He encoded the words using only one retrieval cue.
   b. He encoded the words using several retrieval cues.
   c. He encoded the words deeply, thinking carefully about their meanings.
   d. He encoded the words using too many retrieval cues.

9. A researcher primed her participants with a concept, then recorded how long it took them to interrupt a second researcher. According to the semantic network model of knowledge representation, what concept was most likely primed?
   a. Ageism
   b. Rudeness
   c. Achievement
   d. Thrift

10. In embodied cognition, we use our bodies to encode our experiences and then replay those experiences to help us retrieve information. Accordingly, under which of the following circumstances would it be easiest for an individual to give someone directions to get from the college library to the dining hall? Suggest that the person giving directions
    a. picture an aerial map of campus.
    b. imagine walking from the library to the dining hall.
    c. think about how the books are shelved at the library.
    d. imagine the sounds of the dining hall.

11. A researcher reads the following words to participants: "bed," "rest," "nap," "slumber," "dream," "blanket." According to research on false memory, what word are they likely to *misremember* having been on the list?
    a. "Needle," because it's a noun.
    b. "Heart," because it ends in a consonant.
    c. "Sleep," because it's semantically similar.
    d. "List," because the words are in a list.

12. What is the cautionary tale told by the research on individuals' flashbulb memories of the 9/11 terrorist attacks?
    a. Do not confuse your confidence in a memory with its accuracy.
    b. Pay more attention to the details of everyday memories.
    c. Seek out as many emotionally stimulating experiences as possible.
    d. Do not let post-event information create false memories for that event.

13. What would be the best technique for memorizing the following sequence of letters? CBSABCNBCTBSUSATNT
    a. Rehearsal
    b. Method of loci
    c. Peg system
    d. Chunking

14. According to recent research, to increase the size of the hippocampus, and thus improve semantic memory, what can one do?
    a. Take up yoga
    b. Join a Pilates class
    c. Find an aerobics class
    d. Do crossword puzzles

15. Which of the following is true of how the memory of an event, such as learning how to solve a math problem, is stored?
    a. It's only an example of a procedural memory, so it's stored in the hippocampus.
    b. It's only an example of a semantic memory, so it's stored in the hippocampus.
    c. It's only an example of an episodic memory, so it's stored in the hippocampus.
    d. It is a complex memory whose components are represented in several different parts of the brain.

Answers

You can check your answers to the preceding Self-Test and the chapter's What Do You Know? questions in Appendix B.

Learning

"I HAVE ALWAYS BEEN FEARFUL OF BUTTONS. For me, touching a button would be like touching a cockroach. It feels dirty, nasty, and wrong."

Buttons???

"When I was younger," the woman continued, "my brother used to tease me by opening my mum's button tin. I hid in my bedroom until he put them away."

"My cousin was wearing a button necklace one day. . . . I could not stand being in the same room as her" (Saavedra & Silverman, 2002).

The woman's button fear sounds so bizarre that you might guess her case is unique. But it's not. Consider this 9-year-old boy: At home, he had trouble getting dressed because he didn't want to touch his clothes' buttons. In class, his efforts to avoid touching the buttons on his school uniform continually distracted him from his work. At play, his main goal was to avoid contact with buttons on the clothes of his friends.

To learn more about this boy, psychologists conducted research in which they measured his reactions to buttons of different types. They found that he was moderately afraid of metal buttons, more afraid of large plastic buttons, and most afraid of plastic buttons that were small.

Why? Why would anybody be afraid of any buttons at all? An earlier event in the boy's life provides a clue. At age 5, he had a startling, frightening experience that happened to involve buttons. While working on a school art project that used plastic buttons, he ran out of them. He went to his teacher's desk for more, reached up to get some from a large bowl, slipped, knocked over the bowl, and a sea of buttons crashed down on his head. His natural fear of being hit on the head by falling objects somehow transferred to a fear of the objects themselves: buttons—and not just the particular buttons at school, but buttons in general (Wheeler, 2008).

In one respect, the cases are unusual. Button fears are rare. But in another, they are commonplace: The psychological processes involved are pervasive, affecting many aspects of all people's lives. You'll find out about them in this chapter on learning. ◉

Getty Images, clockwise from top buttons: Elizabeth Livermore; Davies and Starr; Dorling Kindersley; Lucia Brusetti Photography

White House learns Bollywood
Thanks to principles of learning, people can pick up an endless variety of skills—even ones that, in the past, were unknown in their culture.

VIRTUALLY EVERYONE YOU know can read and write, multiply and divide, make a phone call, and ride a bike. These abilities are so common that, if you didn't know better, you might think they were innate—"hardwired" aspects of people's inherited biology. But they're not; they are learned.

Learning is any relatively long-lasting change in behavioral abilities or emotional reactions that results from experience. It is only thanks to learning that people can write, read, do arithmetic, make a phone call, and ride a bike. In fact, most everyday activities—getting dressed, sending text messages, driving a car, preparing a meal, making a good impression on others—require skills that are acquired through learning. Learning, the topic of this chapter, thus provides the basis of most of your everyday behavior.

Learning teaches you not only how to perform behaviors, but also *where, when,* and *how much* to perform them. You learn not only how to play a musical instrument, but where and when to play it (at a time and place that doesn't drive your neighbors batty). You learn not only how to tell entertaining jokes, but how much to do it (enough to be entertaining, but not annoying). Through learning, you adapt to outcomes in the environment: people's attention, approval, disapproval, or boredom. Psychologists who study learning believe these adaptations to environmental rewards and punishments explain much of psychological life.

Psychologists have discovered different ways in which people learn. This chapter will present three of them: *classical conditioning, operant conditioning,* and *observational learning.* We will review the basic psychological principles involved in each, as well as the biological mechanisms that underlie the psychological capacity to learn.

Classical Conditioning

As you experience the world, one event often signals the occurrence of another. A flashing light in your rearview mirror signals that a police officer may pull you over. A ringing phone in the middle of the night signals that there may be a family emergency. Once you learn the connection between the first event and the second, your reaction to the first one changes. You may react anxiously to the flashing light and the ringing phone—even though the first time you ever saw a light flash or heard a phone ring, you were perfectly calm. The change in responding to one stimulus, after you learn its connection to a second one, is called learning through **classical conditioning.**

Classical Conditioning in Everyday Life

Preview Question

› What is an example of classical conditioning in everyday life?

You're already familiar with classical conditioning from everyday life. You've seen people's reaction to a stimulus change once they learn that it predicts a second stimulus. Here are some examples.

Suppose a child hears a parent address her by her full name rather than a nickname—for instance, "Elizabeth" rather than "Lizzy"—and, immediately afterward, the parent scolds the child. If this happens a few times, the child learns that

learning Any relatively long-lasting change in behavioral abilities or emotional reactions that results from experience.

classical conditioning A form of learning that occurs when an organism encounters a stimulus that repeatedly signals the occurrence of a second stimulus.

when she hears her full name, scolding will follow. She learns, in other words, that one stimulus (full name) predicts another (scolding). Once she learns this, her emotional response to the first stimulus will change. Through classical conditioning, she'll become fearful when hearing her full name.

Classical conditioning also can produce positive emotions. Imagine that you hear a musical jingle in the distance outside your window. Soon afterward, an ice cream truck, the source of the jingle, pulls up in front of your house. Once you learn to associate the distant jingle with the subsequent arrival of ice cream, you will (if you're an ice cream lover) come to like the jingle.

Classical conditioning can change your reactions not only to specific sights and sounds (e.g., the jingle), but also to *types of* people and places. Suppose you once experienced the breakup of a relationship while visiting an amusement park. In the future, you might find amusement parks less amusing than you used to because you associate them with the breakup. Your emotional reaction to a type of situation, amusement parks, changes as a result of learning through classical conditioning. In this chapter's opening story, you saw how a boy's reactions to a type of object, buttons, changed after a frightening experience. That change was a case of classical conditioning.

How, exactly, does classical conditioning work? As you've seen elsewhere in this book, the question can be answered at different levels of analysis. Let's first look at psychological processes in classical conditioning. Then we'll move to a biological level of analysis, examining brain mechanisms that underlie this form of learning.

Hooray for the red, bleached white, and blue This advertisement employs a main principle of classical conditioning. It pairs bleach (a relatively neutral stimulus) with the stars and stripes of the American flag (which can trigger positive feelings) in the hope that viewers, through conditioning, will learn to pledge allegiance to Tide.

WHAT DO YOU KNOW?...

1. If you were to learn that the sound of a dentist drill predicted pain, your _____ to the sound of that drill would change.

See Appendix B for answers to What Do You Know? questions.

Pavlov and the Psychology of Classical Conditioning

Preview Question

> In classical conditioning, what is the association that an animal learns?

The Russian biologist Ivan Pavlov (1849–1936) initiated research on psychological processes in classical conditioning. He did so only after an earlier line of research that was purely biological. In studies of the digestive system, Pavlov placed different stimuli in a dog's mouth and recorded the amounts of salivation produced. He found, for example, that food triggers salivation, which contributes to the chemical processing of food, but that marbles do not because the dog can spit out marbles without needing extra saliva (Pavlov, 1928). (Pavlov's research on the digestive system earned him a Nobel Prize in 1904.) This connection between food and salivation is a biologically determined *reflex,* that is, an involuntary reaction that occurs automatically, without learning.

"Pavlov? Sure, I knew him . . ." This dog, as preserved by a taxidermist, resides in the Pavlov Museum of Ryazan, Russia, a city southwest of Moscow. When alive, the dog was a subject in Pavlov's research on classical conditioning. (The device in its mouth collects saliva.)

Robert K. Lawton

Ivan Pavlov, in white beard and hat, playing a game with colleagues. (The game is *gorodki*, a Russian folk sport similar to bowling, in which pins are knocked down by throwing a bat rather than rolling a ball.) Pavlov was an avid athlete, believing that "physical lustiness is the necessary condition for powerful mental activity."

RIA Novosti / Alamy

unconditioned stimulus (US)
A stimulus that elicits a reaction in an organism prior to any learning.

unconditioned response (UR)
A reaction to an unconditioned stimulus that occurs automatically, prior to any learning.

conditioned stimulus (CS) An event that elicits a response from an organism only after the organism learns to associate it with another stimulus that already evokes a response.

conditioned response (CR)
A response to a conditioned stimulus that occurs as a result of learning through classical conditioning.

PHYSIOLOGICAL REACTIONS TO PSYCHOLOGICAL STIMULI. While studying this biological process, Pavlov noticed something of psychological interest. Sometimes dogs salivated when *no* physical stimuli were in their mouths. After a few days in the lab, a dog might salivate when it heard the footsteps of a laboratory assistant who previously had brought it food.

Pavlov knew that no natural, inherited connection existed between the sound of footsteps and salivation. There was, however, a *learned* connection. The dogs learned that the sound of footsteps predicted the arrival of food. Once they did so, they began responding reflexively to the sound, which triggered the physiological response, salivation.

If you're a pet owner, you probably have noticed this sort of learning yourself. Your dog may react excitedly not only when it sees dog food, but when it sees you open the cabinet door where you store her food. If so, your dog has learned that the open door signals that soon she'll be dining.

Pavlov devised a research procedure to discover the exact processes through which animals learn to associate different types of stimuli. Let's examine his classic procedures in detail.

STIMULUS–RESPONSE CONNECTIONS. Pavlov recognized that the essence of classical conditioning is a learned connection between two types of stimuli: (1) an unconditioned stimulus and (2) a conditioned stimulus.

An **unconditioned stimulus (US)** is one that elicits a reaction in an organism prior to any learning. The reaction it elicits is called an **unconditioned response (UR).** For example, if a sudden and very loud noise occurs in front of you, you will startle: Your head will jerk back and your hands will move up in the air. You do not have to learn to startle; the startle response occurs the first time you ever encounter the loud noise (Quevedo et al., 2010). The noise, then, is an unconditioned stimulus (US) and the startle response is an unconditioned response (UR). In his main experiments, the US Pavlov used was food and the UR was salivation.

The second type of stimulus, the **conditioned stimulus (CS),** is one that elicits a response from an organism *only after* the organism learns to associate it with an unconditioned stimulus. At first, the conditioned stimulus is neutral; it does not elicit any response. But once an organism (person or animal) learns that the neutral stimulus predicts an unconditioned stimulus, its reaction changes: The previously neutral stimulus becomes a CS that elicits a response, usually of the same general type as was elicited by the US. For instance, if, on a number of occasions, you experienced a flashing light and then a loud startling noise, you would learn that such a light predicts the noise and the light would elicit a startle response. Returning to an earlier example, once Lizzy learned that "Elizabeth" predicts scolding, the name "Elizabeth" elicited a fear response. In the terminology of classical conditioning, the response that is triggered by a conditioned stimulus is called a **conditioned response (CR).**

Let's use the terminology you just learned—US, UR, CS, CR—to reexamine what Pavlov originally observed in his lab. Food was a US that elicited a UR, salivation. The sound of footsteps originally was a neutral stimulus. However, after the dogs learned that footsteps predict food, footsteps became a CS that produced the CR of salivation.

Pavlov developed formal research procedures (Figure 7.1) in which he substituted the sound of a bell for the experimenter's footsteps. Pavlov rang the bell (the CS), gave the dog food (the US), and collected saliva to measure the dog's response. He later determined whether the dog salivated upon hearing the bell. Inevitably, it did. All dogs learn through classical conditioning.

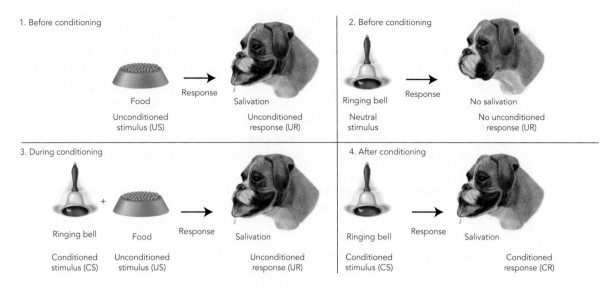

1. Before conditioning

Food
Unconditioned stimulus (US)

→ Response

Salivation
Unconditioned response (UR)

2. Before conditioning

Ringing bell
Neutral stimulus

→ Response

No salivation
No unconditioned response (UR)

3. During conditioning

Ringing bell
Conditioned stimulus (CS)

+ Food
Unconditioned stimulus (US)

→ Response

Salivation
Unconditioned response (UR)

4. After conditioning

Ringing bell
Conditioned stimulus (CS)

→ Response

Salivation
Conditioned response (CR)

figure 7.1
Pavlov's classical conditioning paradigm Before conditioning, unconditioned stimuli trigger unconditioned responses. During conditioning, a previously neutral stimulus, such as a ringing bell, is paired with the unconditioned stimulus. After conditioning, the stimulus is no longer neutral; it now is a conditioned stimulus that elicits a conditioned response.

🐾 WHAT DO YOU KNOW?...

2. Marnie had a toy called a "jack-in-the-box" that she played with often. She would turn a crank, which then activated the tune "Pop Goes the Weasel." The crank also caused a surprise: A clown would pop out of the box at an unpredictable moment. This would startle her every time. Now every time Marnie hears this tune, she startles. For this example, identify the US, UR, CS, and CR.

Classical Conditioning Across the Animal Kingdom

Preview Questions

› What types of organisms learn through classical conditioning?
› Why did a research participant known as Little Albert become afraid of a small white rat during the course of a psychology experiment, when the rat itself did nothing to make Albert afraid?

It's not just dogs who learn through classical conditioning. All members of the animal kingdom do it. In principle, *any* organism might learn *any* association between *any* conditioned stimulus and *any* unconditioned stimulus. Let's look at classical conditioning in simple organisms.

CLASSICAL CONDITIONING IN SIMPLE ORGANISMS. Even fruit flies can learn through classical conditioning. In research, fruit flies have been placed in containers with two different odors. In one of the containers, the flies receive a mild electric shock, whereas in the other container, they receive no shock. Later, researchers put the flies in a third container that has one of the odors on one end, and the other odor on the other end. What happens? They fly away from the odor previously paired with shock (Dudai, 1988). This means that this simple organism, a fruit fly, learned to associate the CS, odor, with the US, shock.

Another simple organism that learns through conditioning is the honeybee (Bitterman, 2006). Researchers placed honeybees in an area containing dishes of two different colors. Initially, the colors were neutral; honeybees didn't prefer one to the other. The researchers then put a neutral stimulus (plain water) on one dish and an attractive US (a solution of water and sugar) on the other, and allowed the honeybees to fly to both dishes to learn what they contained. Later, researchers placed the honeybees in an area with empty dishes of the same two colors. Which color dish did the bees fly to first? They consistently flew to the color of dish that previously had contained the sugar solution. In other words, they learned that color, the CS, predicts sugar, the US.

What about more complex organisms? Let's look at classical conditioning in organisms with the most complex brains of all: human beings.

CLASSICAL CONDITIONING IN HUMANS: EMOTION. Early in the twentieth century, an American psychologist, John Watson, read about Pavlov's experiments and became intrigued. Could Pavlov's research with dogs be extended to humans? To find out, he and a colleague, Rosalie Rayner, ran an experiment on the classical conditioning of human emotions. The emotion they studied was fear, and the human was an 11-month-old named Little Albert. (The guidelines for ethical treatment of research participants that you read about in Chapter 2 were not yet in place when they ran the study in 1920.)

Watson and Rayner's experiment featured two key items, in addition to Little Albert himself: a white rat, which served as a conditioned stimulus, and a steel bar that made a loud noise—the unconditioned stimulus—when struck with a hammer. At the outset of the study, Little Albert seemed to like the rat, watching it closely and displaying no fear. However, he was quite afraid of the noise. Whenever Watson struck the bar with the hammer, the noise caused Little Albert to startle and cry (an unconditioned response).

After observing Little Albert's reactions to the two stimuli, the rat and the noise, Watson and Rayner combined the two. They took the rat out of a basket and banged on the steel bar just as they showed the rat to Albert. Albert startled and fell over (Watson & Rayner, 1920). Watson and Rayner then repeated the pairing of the CS and US (the rat and the noise) six more times. Each time, Little Albert startled, fell over, or cried.

Next came the critical trial. Watson and Rayner showed the rat to Little Albert *without* banging on the bar. What do you think happened? Now Albert was afraid of the rat. When he saw it, he cried, fell over, and crawled away from it as fast as he could (Watson & Rayner, 1920). Through classical conditioning, Little Albert had learned a new emotional reaction—fear of the rat. Further tests indicated that Little Albert eventually developed fears of many objects that were in some way similar to the rat: a rabbit, a fur coat, and even a Santa Claus mask (Figure 7.2).

Note that Little Albert's fear did not result from anything the rat did. Its behavior didn't change. What changed is that Albert learned a CS–US association: He learned that the rat was a CS that predicted the noise, a US. Upon learning this, Little Albert became afraid of the rat. Watson and Rayner's finding demonstrated that human emotions could be shaped by classical conditioning.

> ○ **THINK ABOUT IT**
>
> What was the experimental design in the Little Albert experiment? Was there, in fact, an experimental design? A control group? Might Albert have started crying just from the stress of being in a lengthy experiment with two strangers and loud noises?

Which of your fears might have been classically conditioned?

figure 7.2

Little Albert Rosalie Raynor, Little Albert, and John Watson (with mask), the experimenters and participant in the first study of the classical conditioning of emotions in a human being. Watson showed a variety of stimuli, such as this mask, to Little Albert to determine which of them elicited fear before and after conditioning. Today, psychologists question both the ethics and the substance of Watson's study (Fridlund et al., 2012), as well as the identity of the child known as Little Albert (Powell et al., 2014). Nevertheless, historically, it was a highly influential report on the power of classical conditioning to shape human emotional reactions.

CLASSICAL CONDITIONING IN HUMANS: SELF-ESTEEM AND SEXUAL RESPONSE. The effects of classical conditioning are not limited to simple responses, such as fear, or to young children, such as Little Albert. Conditioning can influence the complex responses of adults. Conditioning, for example, can affect people's overall feelings about themselves, or their *self-esteem*.

In one self-esteem study, experimenters first asked participants to provide information about themselves (e.g., their first name and birthday). Next, classical conditioning trials paired this personal information with different types of facial expressions shown on a computer screen. In one experimental condition, all the faces were smiling. In another, they were mixed: smiling, frowning, and neutral. Afterward, the experimenters measured participants' self-esteem. Conditioning influenced people's feelings about themselves. The trials in which personal information consistently was paired with smiling faces distinctively increased self-esteem (Baccus, Baldwin, & Packer, 2004).

Another adult response that can be shaped by classical conditioning is sexual arousal. Conditioning can convert neutral stimuli into sexually arousing ones. In a study conducted with heterosexual men and women, the CS was a non-arousing photo of a person of the opposite gender, and the US was an arousing 30-second film of heterosexual activity. In the conditioning trials, the experimenters displayed the photo and then, immediately afterward, the film clip. They then measured participants' sexual response to the photo, using physiological equipment that records arousal in the genitals. Classical conditioning altered sexual response. After conditioning, the photo alone aroused sexual response (Hoffmann, Janssen, & Turner, 2004).

> How do you feel about the possibility that conditioning can explain why you're attracted to someone?

Here's the key point about these studies of flies, honeybees, Little Albert, self-esteem, and sexual arousal: Classical conditioning can be found everywhere. All complex organisms can learn when a CS predicts a US; afterward, their response to the CS changes.

> **Red light district** There is nothing inherently arousing about neon lights or the words "red light district." But their repeated association with sex can cause a stimulus that otherwise would be emotionally neutral to become sexually arousing.

Five Basic Classical Conditioning Processes

Preview Questions

> If you want to teach an animal to associate a conditioned stimulus with an unconditioned stimulus, about how long should you wait, after the conditioned stimulus, before presenting the unconditioned stimulus?

> In classical conditioning, if you slightly alter the conditioned stimulus that an animal previously has learned to associate with an unconditioned stimulus, what happens?

> In classical conditioning, what is extinction?

> What happens when a stimulus that normally produces a response in an organism is presented over and over again?

> How does research on compensatory responses explain some cases of drug overdose?

You've learned the basic fact of classical conditioning: Once organisms associate a conditioned stimulus with an unconditioned stimulus, the previously neutral CS evokes the same type of response as did the US. Yet there's more to learn. Pavlov and later researchers investigated five key aspects of the learning process: *acquisition, generalization, extinction, habituation,* and *compensatory responses.*

ACQUISITION. In the study of learning, **acquisition** is attaining the ability to perform a new response; after learning, the organism is said to have "acquired" the response. When Pavlov's dogs first salivated (the CR) upon hearing a bell (the CS), or Lizzy first responded fearfully (the CR) when hearing the name "Elizabeth" (the CS), the CR had been acquired.

Research has answered three basic questions about the acquisition of conditioned responses. The first is, if you want an organism to quickly acquire a CR, how long should you wait after presenting the CS, before presenting the US?

Try to answer this for yourself. Imagine Pavlov's lab: To get an animal to learn, you ring the bell (the CS) and then wait—how long?—before presenting the food (the US).

If you answered, "not long at all," you're right! You should present the food almost immediately after ringing the bell. If you wait longer—that is, ring the bell but don't present the food until a few minutes later—the dog might not recognize the connection between the bell and food. Research confirms that the amount of time elapsing between the presentation of the CS and US strongly affects learning. Animals learn most quickly when the gap between the CS and US is only a fraction of a second (Figure 7.3).

A second finding in the study of acquisition shows that animals have a keen sense of time. They learn not only that the CS predicts the US, but also the amount of time that transpires between the two (Savastano & Miller, 1998). Animals learn to respond to the CS at exactly the point in time in which the US is most likely to appear. For example, when the CS is a tone, the US is a puff of air to the eye, the UR is an eyeblink (caused by the air puff), and the duration between the CS and US

Pavlovian gaming Would you rather be playing a game than learning about psychology? It turns out that you can do both. The committee that awards Nobel Prizes has created an online game that teaches the principles of classical conditioning. You can play it yourself at http://nobelprize.org/educational_games/medicine/pavlov/pavlov.html. Good luck!

acquisition In the psychology of learning, attaining the ability to perform a new response; "acquiring" a response.

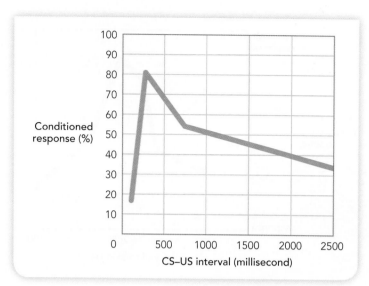

figure 7.3
Timing the CS and US The degree of classical conditioning that occurs when a CS is paired with a US varies according to the CS–US interval, that is, the interval of time separating the CS and US. Conditioning occurs most strongly when the interval is brief.

is half a second, animals will learn to close their eyes precisely half a second after they hear the tone (Gluck, Mercado, & Myers, 2008).

A third question is whether animals learn to associate the CS and US gradually or suddenly. If an animal learned gradually, it might respond slightly to a CS after 10–20 pairings of the CS and US, moderately after another 10–20 pairings, and fully after 50 or more CS–US pairings. If it acquires the CS–US connection suddenly, the animal might abruptly "get it" and quickly transition to a state at which it responds strongly to the CS.

Research shows that animals suddenly "get it." Within just a few trials, they change abruptly from a state in which they do not respond to the CS to one in which they respond to it strongly and consistently (Gallistel, Fairhurst, & Balsam, 2004). Although psychologists have been studying learning for more than a century, only relatively recently have they come to appreciate the sudden manner in which organisms acquire a new response.

In summary, research on acquisition shows that (1) organisms will best acquire the ability to respond to a CS if the duration between CS and US is brief; (2) they will learn to respond precisely when the US is most likely to occur; and (3) they will learn all this quickly, rapidly transitioning from no response to a full response to the CS.

GENERALIZATION. In Pavlov's experiments, dogs learned to salivate when a bell rang. What do you think would have happened if Pavlov changed bells—that is, switched to a bigger bell with a deeper tone or a smaller one with a higher pitch?

It turns out that when you change bells—or vary any other aspect of the conditioned stimulus—organisms still respond, but not quite as strongly. Psychologists call this *generalization*. **Generalization** is a learning process in which conditioned responses are elicited by stimuli that vary from the conditioned stimulus that originally was paired with the unconditioned stimulus.

You've already seen two cases of generalization. Little Albert's fear generalized: He became afraid not only of the white rat, but also of other white or furry objects—stimuli that varied from, yet in some ways were similar to, the rat. The button fear described in our opening story generalized, too. The 9-year-old boy was afraid of not only the buttons at school, but also buttons in general.

Generalization occurs systematically. Stimuli that vary more and more from the original CS elicit less and less of a CR (Bower & Hilgard, 1981; Figure 7.4). You saw this, too, in the opening story; the boy was less fearful of metal buttons than

generalization A learning process in which responses are elicited by stimuli that vary slightly from the stimuli encountered during acquisition of a response.

figure 7.4

Generalization In generalization, an organism responds to a stimulus that is similar to a CS to which it previously had learned to respond. In this study, goldfish had learned an association between a US, which was an electric shock, and a CS, which was a 200-Hertz tone (200 Hertz is roughly equal, in tone, to the G below middle C on a piano keyboard). When the goldfish heard tones higher or lower than 200 Hertz, they responded to them; their response generalized from the 200-Hertz tone to others.

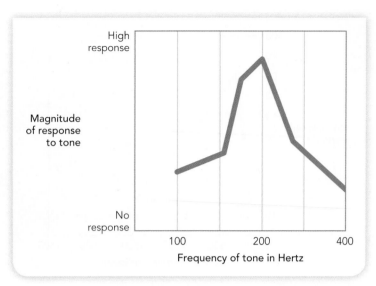

plastic ones. Laboratory experiments document generalization. In one study (Lissek et al., 2008), conditioning trials paired pictures of geometric rings (neutral stimuli) with uncomfortable electric shocks (USs). Participants later viewed pictures of other rings whose sizes varied systematically from the rings that were shown originally. Classically conditioned fear generalized to rings of other sizes. And as the depicted rings increasingly departed in size from the original ones, participants' physiological responses became weaker.

Generalization explains experiences that otherwise would be puzzling. Consider the case of Pearson Brack, a bombardier in World War II. After a series of successful flights, Brack developed a strange symptom. When he saw from the plane's altimeter that he had ascended to 9000 feet, he started to become uncontrollably anxious: He trembled, turned pale, and started breathing rapidly. Once the plane descended a few hundred feet, he was fine. But if it ascended again, he became anxious again, with the anxiety increasing as it reached 10,000 feet, at which point Brack would faint. What was the cause? It couldn't be the altitude itself; other crew members felt fine and Brack previously had flown at these altitudes.

A psychological analysis suggested that the cause was classical conditioning (Mischel, 1968). The reading of 10,000 feet had become a conditioned stimulus that triggered panic. Lower altitudes triggered lower levels of anxiety, due to generalization. Key evidence for this conclusion was that, on the mission before his symptoms began, enemy fighters attacked Brack's plane. It rolled, dove uncontrollably, and almost crashed. Brack sustained an injury in the turmoil. The attack likely occurred while Brack's plane was flying at exactly 10,000 feet. That altitude, then, was paired with a US (the attack) and thus became a powerful CS, with effects that generalized to nearby altitudes.

Responses do not generalize to all stimuli. Organisms discriminate between stimuli. **Discrimination** in classical conditioning is a learning process in which organisms respond to one stimulus but not another. If, for example, Pavlov had trained a dog using a bell as a CS and then had switched stimuli—say, from Pavlov ringing a bell to Pavlov singing a song—the dog likely would not respond to the singing in the same way that it responded to the ringing. It would discriminate between the two stimuli.

○ ○
○ **THINK ABOUT IT**
○

Does Pavlov's classical conditioning approach explain Pearson Brack's fear? Or might there be additional relevant psychological processes—memories of past missions, confidence in his ability—in the case of a human being?

Think of an object to which you have a classically conditioned fear response. To what other objects might you generalize this response?

discrimination In the study of learning, a process in which organisms distinguish between stimuli, responding to one stimulus but not another.

EXTINCTION. What do you think would happen, after conditioning, if a researcher kept ringing the bell, but there was never another trial in which the dog received food? Would the dog salivate to the bell, trial after trial, forever? No, it wouldn't. What actually happens is *extinction*. In classical conditioning, **extinction** is a gradual lessening of a conditioned response when a CS is presented repeatedly without any presentations of the US. When a CS occurs repeatedly but the US does not follow, organisms gradually display less and less of the conditioned response. Eventually, they stop responding altogether; the CR becomes extinct. Your dog eventually would stop salivating when you rang the bell if there was no more food. Little Albert's fear would eventually have extinguished if Watson and Rayner had repeatedly presented the rat without ever again banging on the steel bar.

Dionne McGill / Alamy

Interestingly, when extinction occurs, it does not mean that an organism has completely forgotten the CS–US connection. If, after extinction in a traditional Pavlovian experiment, you wait a day and then start ringing the bell again, the dog will salivate again the first few times it is rung. The dog will exhibit **spontaneous recovery,** the reappearance of an extinguished CR after a period of delay following extinction (Rescorla, 2004; Figure 7.5).

> What is a classically conditioned response you *wish* would become extinct?

Humans, too, exhibit spontaneous recovery. A study of fear conditioning among college students shows how this works (Huff et al., 2009). The study had three main steps:

1. Conditioning trials paired an electric shock, a US, with pictures of snakes or spiders, the CS. After this conditioning, but not before, students reacted fearfully to the pictures.

2. Next, extinction trials presented the CS without the US; that is, the photos were shown, but there was no electric shock. These extinction trials eliminated students' fearful reactions to the pictures.

Exposure and extinction Therapists use the classical conditioning principle of extinction to reduce people's fears. To reduce extreme fear of height, a therapist might expose a client to a setting that combines great height with physical safety. Since no harm (i.e., no US) occurs in the presence of height (the CS), the person's fear (the CR) gradually extinguishes.

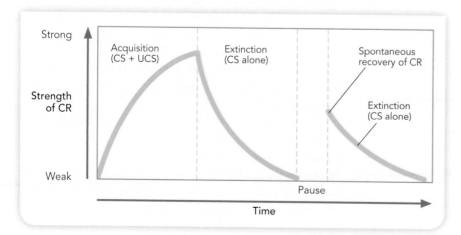

figure 7.5
Spontaneous recovery In spontaneous recovery, a conditioned response reappears after a gap in time (a "pause") following extinction. This implies that, even after extinction trials, a trace of the original learning experience (the acquisition trials) remains.

extinction In the study of learning, a gradual lessening of a response that occurs when a stimulus is presented repeatedly without any presentations of an unconditioned stimulus (in classical conditioning) or reinforcer (in operant conditioning).

spontaneous recovery The reappearance of an extinguished conditioned response after a period of delay following extinction.

Habituation If you lived here, trains would rumble right past your apartment from five in the morning until after midnight. How do residents get any sleep? When a rumbling train—or any other stimulus—is presented repeatedly, people habituate to the stimulus; their response to it gradually lessens. Thanks to habituation, residents of this apartment building can get a good night's sleep.

Justin Kase zsixz / Alamy

3. Finally, the next day students returned to the lab and were shown the snake or spider pictures again. Their fearful reactions returned; they reacted fearfully to the pictures despite the previous day's extinction trials. The students exhibited spontaneous recovery (Huff et al., 2009).

CONNECTING TO THE BRAIN AND TO PSYCHOTHERAPY

Ⓟ

PERSON

Chapter 15: Psychologists use principles of learning to help people change their behavior in therapy.

Ⓜ

MIND

Here, you're learning about the mind's ability to form new connections.

Ⓑ

BRAIN

Later in this chapter: We discuss how research on the brain provides insight into the biological basis of classical conditioning.

PMB CONNECTIONS

HABITUATION. The fourth conditioning process, habituation, differs from the previous three (acquisition, generalization, and extinction) in that it does not involve pairing a CS and US. Instead, **habituation** is a change in behavior that occurs when one stimulus, which normally evokes a response in an organism, merely is presented repeatedly. The organism's response to the stimulus gradually lessens; in colloquial terms, it "gets used to" the stimulus.

Habituation occurs all the time. On a cold winter day when you first put on a coat, it may feel heavy. Not long afterward, you barely notice that you're wearing it; you habituate to the coat's weight. If you're in a room with a noisy air conditioning or heating system, you might notice the noise at first, but eventually you become unaware of it. You habituate to the sound. If you move from a rural area to a city, you may at first be bothered by the around-the-clock lights and sounds, but soon you habituate to them.

In summary, research on acquisition, generalization, extinction, and habituation yielded consistent results. Pavlov's research findings meant that a wide range of responses (in a wide range of organisms, and in both the laboratory and everyday life) could be understood in terms of a small set of learning principles.

COMPENSATORY RESPONSES AND DRUG TOLERANCE. Besides learning that a CS predicts a US, animals also do something else. They learn to *prepare for* the anticipated effects of the US. Once they learn that a CS signals an imminent US that will affect them physiologically, their bodies automatically respond in a manner that prepares them for this effect. This preparation is called a *compensatory response*.

habituation A lessening in response that occurs when a stimulus that normally evokes a reaction in an organism is presented repeatedly.

Compensatory responses are biological reactions that are the opposite of the effects of a stimulus and thereby attempt to counterbalance those effects (Siegel, 2005; Siegel & Ramos, 2002).

In their research, Pavlov's colleagues gave dogs injections of adrenalin, a drug that increases heart rate. When they did this repeatedly, they found that the drug gradually had less and less of an effect on heart rates. The dogs, it appeared, had developed physiological reactions that counteracted the effects of the drug. To test this idea, researchers placed the dogs in an area of the lab where they usually received the adrenalin injections, but gave them an injection of a neutral substance rather than adrenalin. In response, the dogs' heart rates *de*creased. When the dogs experienced the conditioned stimuli (the area of the lab, the injection needle) that normally signaled the presentation of a drug that increased heart rate, they automatically reduced their heart rate to compensate for the anticipated effects of the drug (Siegel & Ramos, 2002).

This conditioning research on dogs is directly relevant to humans. People exhibit drug tolerance, reacting less and less to a fixed amount of a drug. The compensatory response discovered by researchers directly contributes to this reduction in drug effects (Siegel, 2005). When people take a drug repeatedly, their bodies automatically produce biological responses that counteract the drug's effects. As a result, they need higher amounts of the drug to obtain a given level of drug effectiveness.

Compensatory responses are situation-specific. They occur in situations in which an organism (nonhuman animal or person) has experienced a drug previously. This pairing of situation and drug turns the situation into a conditioned stimulus that triggers the compensatory response. Other situations, in which a drug has not been used previously, do not trigger compensatory responses. This means that the same person will respond differently to the same drug in different situations (Siegel, 2005).

The situation-specificity of drug tolerance explains tragic cases of overdose in the use of illegal drugs. Heroin users sometimes suffer fatal overdoses even when postmortem exams reveal that the level of the drug in their bloodstream was not excessively high (Siegel, 2001). Such overdoses usually occur when users take the drug in a new situation. In familiar situations, their bodies produce a compensatory response. But in the unfamiliar situations, they don't. Users' tolerance of the drug thus is lower, and overdose is more likely.

Such overdoses can even occur with prescription drugs. Siegel and Ellsworth (1986) report the case of a cancer patient taking morphine for pain relief. He usually received the drug in the same situation: his dimly lit bedroom. One day, he happened to take the same amount of the drug in a different setting—a brightly lit living room—and died of a drug overdose.

In summary, organisms can tolerate different amounts of a drug in different situations. A drug may produce modest effects in one situation, but large effects in another.

River Phoenix Deaths from drug overdose often occur when users take a drug in an unfamiliar environment where their bodies do not automatically produce compensatory responses that lessen drug effects. The actor River Phoenix died of an overdose after taking an illegal drug in a nightclub restroom.

Nancy Schiff / Getty Images

🐾 WHAT DO YOU KNOW?...

4. Match the key aspect of the learning process on the left with its description to the right. In this context, imagine you had acquired a classically conditioned fear of German Shepherds when you were bitten by one owned by your neighbor.

1. Generalization	a. Several years have passed and you have not been harmed by German Shepherds, so walking by your neighbor's dog no longer elicits fear (though the fear could spontaneously recover).
2. Extinction	b. Your neighbor's German Shepherd barks all day and you grow so accustomed to hearing the barking, you lose your fear of him.
3. Habituation	c. You fear other large dogs as well, especially ones that look like German Shepherds.

compensatory response A biological reaction to a conditioned stimulus that is the opposite of the effects of the stimulus and therefore partially counteracts its effects.

◎ CULTURAL OPPORTUNITIES

Learning to Like Food

How do the following dishes sound?

> *Duck blood soup* (main ingredient: the blood of a freshly killed duck)
> *Deku Delight* (main ingredient: smoked and pan-fried rats)
> *Chipotle-Mescal salsa with roasted locusts* (instructions: "Garnish the salsa with locusts and serve with nacho chips")

Maybe they don't sound so good to you. But food preferences vary across cultures. What is tasty home cooking in one culture is disgusting and inedible in another. Sure, you might not eat duck blood soup. But people from other cultures may hesitate to eat a breakfast of grain products drenched in yellow 5, yellow 6, red 40, and blue 1 (food dyes common in U.S. breakfast cereals).

How, then, do people learn to eat such a wide variety of foods? They do so, at least in part, through classical conditioning. The conditioning process creates a learned connection between foods' (1) nutrients and (2) appearance and flavor.

When people are hungry, the nutrients in food are unconditioned stimuli (USs). Automatically, without any learning, the nutrients reduce hunger and increase energy. Hunger reduction and energy increase thus are unconditioned responses (URs) triggered by the US.

Foods have not only nutritional value, but also appearance and flavor. When people eat a food, its appearance and flavor are paired with its nutritional value, the US, and thus become conditioned stimuli (CSs). Thanks to this pairing of flavor/appearance with nutrition, people learn to like a food's appearance and flavor—even if it looks and tastes like a roasted locust (Mobini, Chambers, & Yeomans, 2007).

This classical conditioning analysis makes an interesting prediction. If people eat a new food when they are *not* hungry, then they should not develop a liking for that food. This is because, when one is not hungry, eating will not trigger the UR (needed energy increase and reduced hunger).

Researchers have tested this prediction with a cleverly designed experiment (Appleton, Gentry, & Shepherd, 2006). First, they combined plain yogurt with exotic spices to create four yogurts with unusual flavors that research participants had never tasted before. They then asked participants to try two of the yogurts at specific times during the day, when their body had high energy requirements (just before lunch and dinner, when participants were hungry), and to sample the other two at a time of low energy requirements (just *after* breakfast or lunch). Later, participants indicated which yogurts they liked best. People liked the yogurts they had eaten when they were hungry better than those they had eaten when they were not hungry (Appleton et al., 2006). The results were exactly as predicted by the classical conditioning analysis. Participants developed a preference for flavors (CSs) that were associated with the body receiving needed energy (a UR).

Tony McNicol / Alamy

Mmm, bug sushi! Maybe it doesn't look tasty to you—but if you had been raised in a different culture, it might, thanks to classical conditioning.

🐾 WHAT DO YOU KNOW?...

5. People who do not live in New Jersey may have trouble understanding the appeal of Taylor Ham (a.k.a. pork roll), a salty and fatty breakfast meat often enjoyed on a hard roll with cheese. Many from New Jersey, however, have developed a classically conditioned preference for it. For this example, identify the US, UR, CS, and CR.

Beyond Pavlov in the Study of Classical Conditioning

Preview Questions

> What is blocking and how did the discovery of blocking alter psychologists' understanding of the processes involved in classical conditioning?

> What happens when animals learn that they cannot control unpleasant outcomes they wish to avoid?

> How does conditioned taste aversion (the Garcia effect) provide information about the role of evolution and biology in classical conditioning?

> Through what research strategy have scientists succeeded in identifying the biological bases of classical conditioning?

Pavlov's work did have limitations. Later researchers sometimes made discoveries that were inconsistent with Pavlov's original findings. Let's look at three of them—blocking, learned helplessness, and the Garcia effect.

ACQUIRING NEW INFORMATION. Pavlov believed that if a CS is paired with a US, animals always will learn to associate the two. It turns out, however, that sometimes they don't. They only learn to associate a CS with a US if that CS provides *new* information about a US, that is, information the animal did not have previously.

We know this from research on *blocking*. In **blocking,** animals fail to learn that a CS predicts a US if they *already* can predict the US based on other cues (Rescorla, 1988). Their prior knowledge blocks the learning of new CS–US associations.

In blocking research (Kamin, 1968), researchers first exposed animals to a series of trials in which one CS, a sound, predicted the occurrence of the US, a shock. Next, animals experienced a second set of trials in which two stimuli, the sound plus a light, predicted the same US. Researchers then examined whether animals would respond when only the second stimulus, the light, was presented. Pavlov thought they would—but they didn't! Although the light had been paired repeatedly with the shock, animals never learned to associate the two. Their prior knowledge of the sound–shock association link blocked their learning of the light–shock association (Kamin, 1968).

Blocking research shows that classical conditioning is more complex than Pavlov thought. Animals don't merely learn simple associations between two stimuli. They acquire information about their environment as a whole (Rescorla, 1988). When they already have enough information—that is, when they already can predict the occurrence of a US—they don't bother to pick up more information that is redundant. This finding prompted psychologists to develop new theories of learning that emphasize animals' overall knowledge of environmental cues that predict biologically significant events (Rescorla & Wagner, 1972).

LEARNED HELPLESSNESS. Pavlov showed that animals learn when two events (the occurrence of a CS and a US) are related. Later research showed that animals also can learn when two events are *not* related. When they learn that (1) aversive outcomes are not related to (2) their own behavior—in other words, that their behavior cannot control the aversive occurrence—they experience a severe reduction in motivation known as **learned helplessness.**

In classic learned helplessness research (Maier & Seligman, 1976; Figure 7.6), dogs were placed in a box with two sides separated by a barrier that they could easily jump over. Experimenters placed a dog in one side of the box and then administered an electric shock to that side. Dogs quickly escaped the shock by jumping over the barrier. In so doing, they learned that their behavior (jumping over the barrier) could control the outcome (avoid the shock).

---

blocking A failure to learn an association between a conditioned stimulus and an unconditioned stimulus that occurs if other environmental stimuli already predict occurrences of the unconditioned stimulus.

learned helplessness A severe reduction in motivation that occurs when animals learn that their own behavior cannot control unpleasant outcomes.

Dog with *no* prior experience
of unavoidable shocks

Dog *with* prior experience
of unavoidable shocks

figure **7.6**

Learned helplessness If dogs experience an electric shock that they can avoid, they normally take action to escape it (left panel). But if dogs first encounter *un*avoidable shocks and subsequently encounter shocks they can avoid, they experience learned helplessness: a state of reduced motivation in which they do not try to escape the shocks.

Then, with a different group of dogs, the experimenters introduced an additional procedure at the outset of the experiment. Before entering the box, these dogs experienced a series of electric shocks that they could *not* avoid. Next, they entered the box and received the shocks that were easily avoidable by jumping over the barrier. Unlike the first group of dogs, this second group never figured out how to avoid the shocks. Instead of running around and trying to jump over the barrier when the shocks were administered, as the first group of dogs did, this second group just gave up. They lay down passively on the floor while the shocks were administered.

The second group of dogs experienced learned helplessness. The researchers concluded that the dogs' experience with uncontrollable shocks caused them to expect that shocks and their own behavior were *un*related. This, in turn, caused them to respond helplessly: to not even try to escape the later shocks, which they easily could have avoided (Maier & Seligman, 1976).

> In what situations does it seem like you can't do anything to control your outcomes?

Though conducted with dogs, this research has profound implications for humans. Life often seems like it can't be controlled. You try to lose weight, but fail. You ask people out on a date, and they say no. You apply for jobs, and don't get them. When this happens, there's a risk: You might *wrongly* conclude that *nothing* you can do will work—that all attempts will always fail. If you draw this conclusion, you might experience learned helplessness, give up, and thus fail to try out some new strategies that could succeed.

Psychologists have developed interventions to combat this risk. One was designed for first-year college students (Wilson & Linville, 1985), a group at risk of concluding, falsely, that good grades at college are beyond their control. In the intervention, people were informed that many students get lower grades than they expect when they first start college, but that in future semesters these same students earn much higher grades. The intervention emphasized that the transition from low to higher grades was normal. Therefore, low grades at first did *not* mean that academic success was beyond one's control.

This simple intervention worked. Compared with students in a control group who did not receive it, students who received the anti-learned-helplessness intervention earned higher grades the next semester (Wilson & Linville, 1985).

BIOLOGICALLY RELEVANT STIMULI AND CONDITIONED TASTE AVERSION. Another finding that moves beyond Pavlov's work involves **conditioned taste aversion,** the rapid learning of a connection between food (specifically, the taste of a food) and illness that occurs after consuming that food (Garcia & Koelling, 1966). Organisms learn very speedily that the food is a CS that signals the UR, illness. Conditioned taste aversion is also called the **Garcia effect,** in honor of the researcher who discovered it, John Garcia.

Have you ever eaten some unusual dish, gotten sick, and then decided never to eat it again? (This happened to your author once in college; I haven't eaten moussaka, a Greek casserole dish, ever since.) It sounds like a simple case of classical conditioning: Sickness is the UR, the unusual food is the CS, and you learn to associate the two. In some ways, conditioned taste aversion is similar to other cases of classical conditioning; for example, as in other forms of conditioning, the CR generalizes (from the food flavor with which conditioning occurred to similar flavors; Richardson, Williams, & Riccio, 1984). Yet the example of conditioned taste aversion does not fit the traditional Pavlovian conditioning paradigm in three respects:

1. You associated food and illness after only one learning trial, unlike the usual Pavlovian paradigm, where multiple trials are required for an organism to learn a new response.

2. You learn the connection even though a significant period of time separates the CS (the food) and the UR (the sickness). In typical conditioning experiments, the US must rapidly follow the CS (see Figure 7.3).

3. You avoid the food, but, unlike what Pavlov might have predicted, you don't avoid other stimuli that also predicted illness, such as the fork you used to eat the food or the location you were in when you first began to feel sick. (Your author did not forever avoid the college cafeteria after eating the moussaka.)

What's different about the association of food and sickness? Garcia recognized that the difference lies in organisms' evolution. Across the course of evolution, some CS–US connections have been biologically relevant, whereas others have not. The connection between food and illness has been biologically relevant; throughout evolutionary history, organisms that failed to learn this connection would repeatedly become ill and thus would be less likely to survive and reproduce. Compare this to the CS used by Pavlov: a bell. It is biologically irrelevant; over the course of their evolution, dogs rarely if ever encountered ringing bells that signaled the presence of food. The Garcia effect, then, shows that organisms learn biologically relevant associations much more rapidly than Pavlovian theory would have anticipated.

Garcia's findings opened the door to research on how a species' evolutionary past affects its ability to learn in the present (Domjan & Galef, 1983). Seligman (1970) has suggested that the link between the evolutionary past and contemporary learning can be understood with the concept of *preparedness*. **Preparedness** refers to the ease with which an organism can learn to associate a stimulus and response. Thanks to evolutionary pressures, some stimulus–response connections (e.g., food and illness) are easy to learn; they are highly prepared. Others, which were not important during the course of evolution (e.g., bell ringing and food), are low in preparedness and therefore more difficult to learn.

In sum, contemporary research has moved beyond Pavlov in a number of ways. Researchers now understand that organisms acquire information about the overall nature of their environment, that this information includes cases in which stimuli

conditioned taste aversion (Garcia effect) The rapid learning of a connection between the taste of a food and illness that occurs after consuming that food.

preparedness The ease with which associations between a stimulus and a response can be learned; as a result of a species' experiences over the course of evolution, some stimulus–response connections are "prepared," that is, are easy to learn.

Preparedness Every year in the United States, more than 30,000 people die in traffic accidents. Only about 10 people a year die from snake bites. Yet many people are highly fearful of snakes (Öhman & Mineka, 2001) and few are fearful of cars. Why? Snake fears are biologically prepared because snakes have been a threat across the course of human evolution. Cars, of course, did not exist during the course of evolution, so people are not biologically predisposed to fear them.

Stockbyte / Getty Images

and responses are *un*connected, and that some links between stimuli and responses are easier to learn than others, thanks to predispositions that organisms acquired over the course of evolution.

These advances are important, but they do not overturn basic foundations laid by Pavlov more than a century ago. Through the psychological processes of classical conditioning, a wide spectrum of organisms learns new responses to the environment when encountering stimuli that predict one another. These psychological findings prompt contemporary researchers to seek the biological bases of conditioning processes, as you'll see now.

🐌 WHAT DO YOU KNOW?...

6. True or False?
   a. If you failed to notice that a loud fire alarm was accompanied by a flickering light, you might be experiencing blocking because the CS (alarm) would be enough to predict the US (fire).
   b. Learned helplessness is at work when we learn that the only thing that can control outcomes is our own behavior.
   c. The Garcia effect runs counter to traditional Pavlovian conditioning because, in it, conditioning can occur even after one pairing of the CS and US; and even though you don't learn to avoid other stimuli, that also could predict the US.

Biological Bases of Classical Conditioning

Preview Question

> What happens at the level of the nervous system when an animal experiences habituation?

Eric Kandel In 2000 Kandel won a Nobel Prize for his research on the biological bases of learning.

© EPA European Pressphoto Agency b.v. / Alamy

The human brain contains billions of neurons (see Chapter 2). Each one of them communicates to a large number of other neurons through neurotransmitters—chemical substances that travel from one neuron to another. Because the brain is the biological basis of behavior, whenever your emotions or behavior change as a result of classical conditioning, a change must have occurred somewhere in this soupy sea of nerve cells and biochemicals. But where? With so many neurons to search through, how could a researcher ever locate the changes that constitute the biological basis of learning?

One way is to study a simpler nervous system possessed by an organism with far fewer neurons than a human being. The neuroscientist Eric Kandel (2006) has identified biological bases of learning by studying a very simple animal, *Aplysia*.

Aplysia are sea slugs—big ones, commonly more than a foot long. To scientists, these creatures have three valuable characteristics: (1) Their nervous system has only about 20,000 neurons; (2) the individual neurons are quite large, and thus easy to study; (3) *Aplysia* can learn through conditioning, despite being such simple organisms. Kandel's insight, then, was that he could identify the biological bases of classical conditioning by studying these simple creatures.

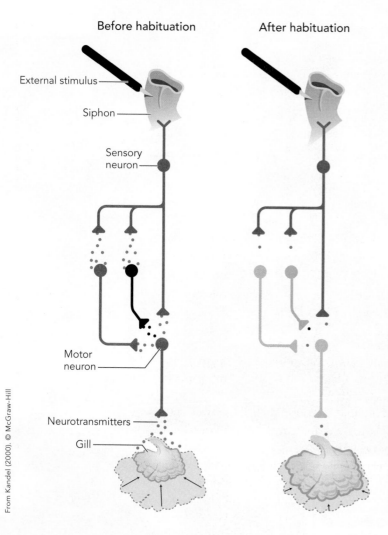

Before habituation

After habituation

External stimulus

Siphon

Sensory neuron

Motor neuron

Neurotransmitters

Gill

From Kandel (2000). © McGraw-Hill

figure **7.7**

The biology of habituation Research with a simple organism, *Aplysia*, reveals the precise biological mechanism that underlies the behavioral change known as habituation. When an external stimulus first makes contact with a part of the *Aplysia* (its siphon), the *Aplysia* strongly withdraws its gill. After repeated presentations of the stimulus, it withdraws its gill only slightly. A reduction in the amount of neurotransmitter released by a motor neuron explains this change in behavior.

In one line of research (reviewed in Kandel, Schwartz, & Jessell, 2000), Kandel and colleagues identified the nervous-system changes that occur in habituation. They did this by studying a simple reflex: When touched by an object, an *Aplysia* reflexively retracts its gill (the organ it uses to breathe). If the *Aplysia* is touched repeatedly, it habituates to the stimulus and gradually stops withdrawing the gill. Kandel discovered the exact biological change responsible for habituation. It involves communication between one neuron, which detects the stimulus, and another neuron, which controls gill movement. When the stimulus strikes the *Aplysia* repeatedly, the neuron that detects this stimulus gradually sends lesser amounts of neurotransmitters to the neuron that controls motor movement. When this latter neuron receives less neurotransmitters, it is less likely to fire and thus to cause the gill to retract (Figure 7.7). The changes that occur when *Aplysia* learn to associate a CS and US are similar, but they involve activity in a combination of neurons that converge on the neuron that controls gill movement (Kandel, 1991).

Kandel's research fulfills the promise formulated by Pavlov. The great Russian scientist anticipated that the psychology of learning could be explained in terms of the biology of the nervous system. By discovering biological mechanisms of classical conditioning in the *Aplysia,* Kandel has taken a critical step toward achieving this goal. More research is needed; it is a large step from the nervous system of sea slugs to the brains of humans. Nonetheless, Kandel's research begins to provide psychology with a complete, three-level—person, mind, and brain—picture of classical conditioning (Figure 7.8).

figure 7.8

PMB
IN ACTION

HOW DO PEOPLE BECOME AFRAID OF EVERYDAY OBJECTS?

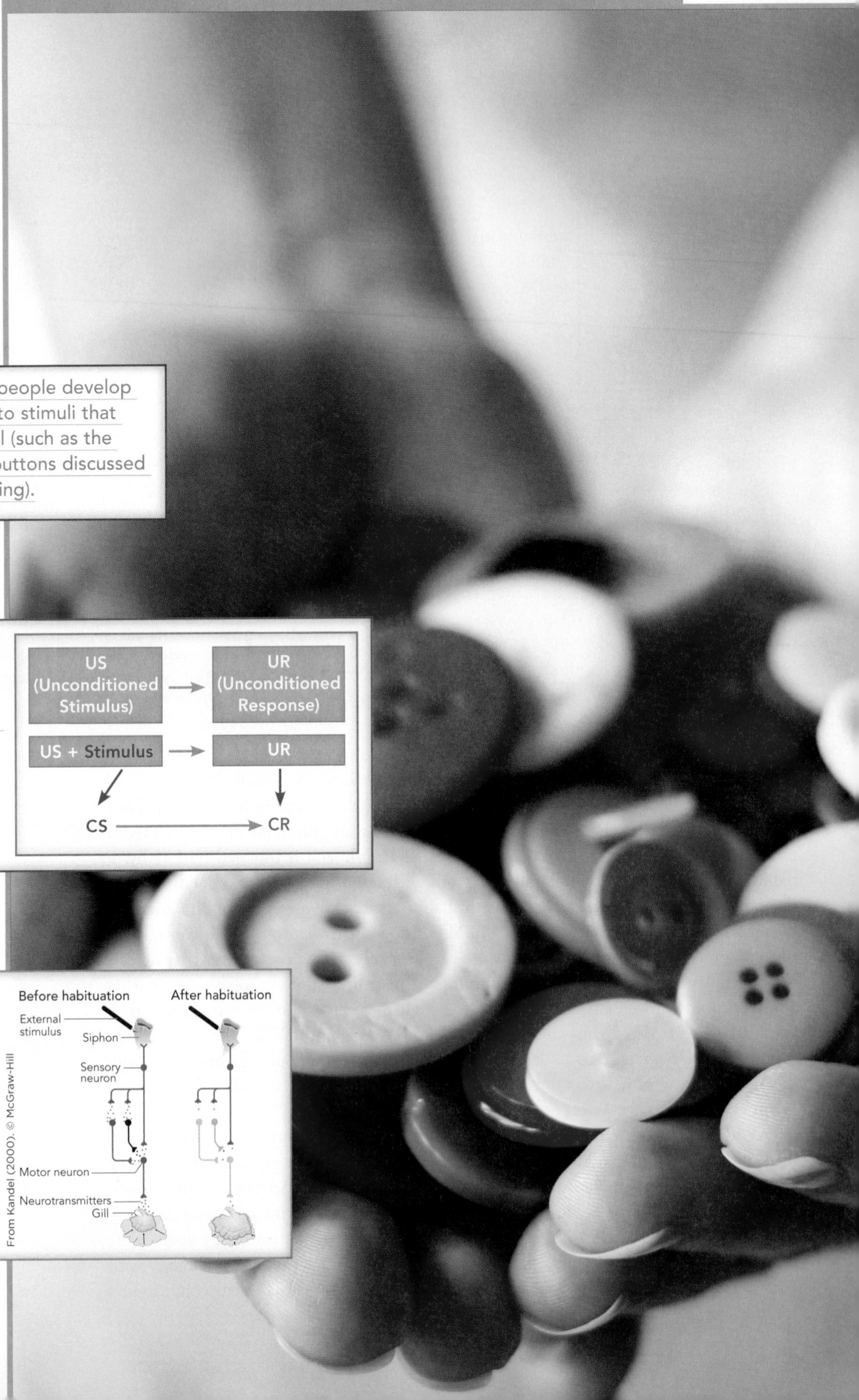

(P) PERSON

Through experience, people develop emotional responses to stimuli that originally were neutral (such as the fearful responses to buttons discussed in this chapter's opening).

(M) MIND

Through experience, mental associations are formed between a US and a previously neutral CS.

(B) BRAIN

Through experience, the brain's neural and biochemical connections linking stimuli to responses change.

From Kandel (2000). © McGraw-Hill

Solidcolours / Getty Images

✋ WHAT DO YOU KNOW?...

7. An *Aplysia* will reflexively withdraw its gill in response to a stimulus. However, if an object touches the gill repeatedly, the *Aplysia* habituates, or "gets used to," the stimulus and stops retracting its gill. What is the stimulus-detecting neuron doing to cause gill withdrawal to stop?

TRY THIS!

Before you read about a second form of learning, operant conditioning, see it in action. Go to www.pmbpsychology.com and try your hand at this chapter's Try This! activity. It tests your skill in teaching an animal to learn through operant conditioning. When you're finished, come back to the chapter, where you will learn about the scientific principles that are built into the activity. ◉

Operant Conditioning

Classical conditioning is just one form of learning. A second is **operant conditioning**, in which behavior is modified by its consequences.

The core idea behind operant conditioning is that the consequences that follow any bit of behavior alter the likelihood that the behavior will be performed in the future. This, in principle, is true for virtually any behavior by any organism. For instance, if your dog sits up and there is a positive consequence (a dog treat), it will be more likely to sit up in the future. If you party the night before an exam and there is a negative consequence (you fail), you will be less likely to party pre-exam in the future. The environmental consequences shape future behavior. This is the essence of operant conditioning.

> What positive consequence would you like to experience as a result of reading this chapter?

Operant Conditioning in Everyday Life

Preview Question

> What is an example of operant conditioning in everyday life?

Examples of operant conditioning are abundant in everyday life. Suppose that you see a parent arguing with a small child and eventually giving in to the child's demands. You may realize that the child, as a result, is more likely to argue in the future. The parent's giving in is a positive consequence that raises the likelihood of the child repeating the behavior.

Alternatively, imagine you have a friend you'd like to know better. You hope the person will "open up" by talking more about personal thoughts and feelings. You know that, for this to occur, you need to pay attention and display interest whenever your friend shows the slightest sign of discussing personal topics. Your attention and interest are consequences that raise the likelihood that he or she will continue to open up. If, instead, you yawn and look at your watch, these consequences will make that behavior less likely.

Consequences alter behavior. The challenge for psychological science is to understand the exact processes through which learning from consequences occurs.

✋ WHAT DO YOU KNOW?...

8. True or False?

   According to the concept of operant conditioning, behaviors followed by negative consequences are likely to recur.

operant conditioning A form of learning in which the future likelihood of performing a type of behavior is modified by consequences that follow performance of the behavior.

Comparing Classical Conditioning to Operant Conditioning

Preview Question

> What are the two main differences between classical conditioning and operant conditioning?

Operant conditioning and classical conditioning differ in two main ways: (1) the order of the stimulus and the behavior, and (2) the type of behavior that is learned.

1. *Order of stimulus and behavior:* In classical conditioning, a stimulus comes first and triggers a response, that is, some behavior. For example, a bell rings (the stimulus) and then the dog salivates (the behavior). In operant conditioning, this order is reversed: A stimulus *follows* a behavior. You buy a raffle ticket (the behavior) and then you win a TV (a desired stimulus). You try a new strategy in a video game (the behavior) and your video game character is blown to bits (an undesired stimulus). Because the stimuli follow responses, they are called response *consequences.* Operant conditioning researchers examine how different types of consequences affect the tendency to perform behaviors again in the future.

2. *Type of behavior learned:* In classical conditioning, researchers study behaviors that are immediately triggered by an environmental stimulus. A bell rings, and it triggers salivation in Pavlov's dog. The rat appears, and it triggers fear in Little Albert. In operant conditioning, researchers study actions that appear to be "spontaneous"; that is, they occur even when no triggering stimulus is in sight. You may suddenly decide to text a friend—even though she is not there asking you to send a text. Or you may spontaneously turn off a TV and start writing a paper for class—even though your professor is not standing around reminding you to work on the paper. Importantly, these behaviors affect the external world (including other people). The text to your friend causes her to cheer up. The work you put into the paper causes your professor to be impressed by your writing and to grade the paper as an A. Most behaviors influence, or "operate on," the environment; this is why these behaviors are called *operants* and why the process through which people learn them is called operant conditioning (Skinner, 1953).

In what ways have you "operated on" the environment today?

Operant conditioning research, then, greatly expands the scope of learning processes beyond those studied by Pavlov. Let's now look, in detail, at psychological processes in operant conditioning.

🐾 WHAT DO YOU KNOW?...

9. Which of the following is an example of learning via classical conditioning and which is an example of learning via operant conditioning?
   a. You help your boss out of a jam and get a bonus.
   b. After receiving the bonus and otherwise being treated well by your boss, you feel happy whenever you see her.

Thorndike's Puzzle Box

Preview Questions

> What was the main research result in Thorndike's studies of how animals learn to escape from puzzle boxes?
> What is the law of effect?

Research on operant conditioning has a long history in psychology. It can be traced to work by an American psychologist named Edward L. Thorndike (1874–1949).

figure 7.9
Thorndike puzzle box Edward Thorndike placed cats in puzzle boxes and studied how long it took them to escape, a task that required pulling the string to open the door.

At about the same time that Pavlov began to study classical conditioning in Russia, Thorndike started experiments on a different type of learning at Columbia University in New York. He placed cats in *puzzle boxes,* enclosures the cat could escape from by performing a relatively simple behavior (Figure 7.9). For example, the puzzle box might have a door to which a string was attached; the cat could escape by pulling the string, which opened the door. To provide the cats with an incentive to escape, Thorndike put them in the puzzle boxes when they were hungry and placed some food outside the puzzle box (Chance, 1999).

TRIAL-BY-TRIAL LEARNING. Once the cat figured out how to escape, the experiment was not over. Thorndike would put the cat back in the puzzle box, from which it would have to escape once again. This would happen repeatedly. On each trial—that is, each return to the puzzle box—Thorndike recorded how long it took the cat to figure out how to escape.

Thorndike discovered that the cats gradually escaped more quickly (Figure 7.10). Initially, it would take them a couple of minutes. They would waste time on behaviors that didn't help them to get out of the box, such as clawing at the wall. But after a few trials, their behavior became more focused. They spent almost all their time performing actions (such as trying to pull the string connected to the door) that, on previous trials, had enabled them to escape. Eventually, they escaped the puzzle box in just a matter of seconds.

Thorndike found, then, that the cats rapidly learned. Their behavior changed as a result of their experience in the puzzle box. Over time, they learned to perform only those behaviors that, in the past, had been followed by successful escape.

figure 7.10
Thorndike results The cats that Thorndike placed into puzzle boxes escaped more and more quickly with practice. At first, it took them a long time to escape. But gradually, they learned to perform only those behaviors that freed them from the box and thus escaped quickly.

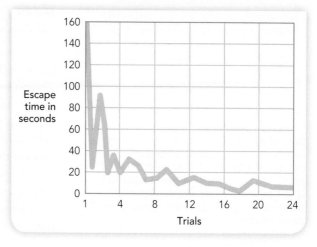

THE LAW OF EFFECT. Thorndike realized that his discovery did not pertain merely to cats in boxes. He had discovered a general principle of learning that he called the *law of effect*. The law describes relations among (1) the *situation* the animal is in, (2) a *behavior* it performs, and (3) an *outcome* that follows the behavior. The **law of effect** states that when an organism performs a behavior that leads to a satisfying outcome in a given situation (i.e., an outcome that is pleasurable or beneficial), it will be more likely to perform that behavior when it encounters the same situation in the future. The likelihood of the behavior, then, goes up when the response consequence—the event that follows the behavior—is positive.

The law of effect explains the cat's behavior. Each time the cat escapes the box, this satisfying outcome strengthens the connection between the stimulus (the puzzle box with its door closed) and the behavior that enabled the cat to escape (pulling the string attached to the door). When placed back in the puzzle box, the cat is thus likely to perform the behavior again.

> ### THINK ABOUT IT
>
> If you play a video game, you adapt your strategies, doing more of what works best. The law of effect explains this: Behavior that leads to good outcomes becomes more frequent. But if you so excel at the game that it becomes easy, you grow bored with it and *stop* playing. Can the law of effect explain this change?

> ### ⓦ WHAT DO YOU KNOW?...
>
> 10. The following information is incorrect. Explain why: "Thorndike's work with cats in puzzle boxes led him to conclude that cats, like most organisms, cannot learn through their experiences. This led him to formulate the law of effect, which states that the likelihood of a behavior is not tied to consequences."

Skinner and Operant Conditioning

Preview Questions

> ❯ In Skinner's analysis of operant conditioning, what is a reinforcer?
> ❯ What is the difference between positive and negative reinforcement?
> ❯ How does reinforcement differ from punishment?

After Thorndike, many psychologists explored how animals learn from experience (Bower & Hilgard, 1981); indeed, the study of learning came to dominate American psychology from the 1920s through the early 1960s. Among these many researchers, one became the most eminent psychologist of the twentieth century: B. F. Skinner (Haggbloom et al., 2002).

Skinner (1904–1990) began his career in psychology as a student at Harvard University, where he later served on the faculty. As a student, he developed a new research method (detailed below) for studying how environmental events shape behavior (Skinner, 1938). He continued this basic research on learning throughout his career, while also writing scientific books (Skinner, 1953, 1974) and even a novel, *Walden II* (Skinner, 1948), that explained to the public the principles of learning he had discovered and their implications for society.

CONSEQUENCES SHAPE BEHAVIOR. Skinner's central insight was the same as Thorndike's: Behavior is shaped by its consequences. When you do something, a consequence usually follows. Use a GPS, and you find the place you're looking for. Tell dirty jokes to socially conservative friends, and you find they are not amused. These consequences not only influence your emotional reactions, as Pavlov noted; they also determine whether you perform these behaviors again in the future. Thanks to the positive consequence, finding your desired location, you start using your GPS more. Due to the negative consequence, the displeasure of your conservative friends, you tell them dirty jokes less often.

Although Skinner's insight was the same as Thorndike's, his overall contributions were far broader. Skinner not only generated experimental results showing

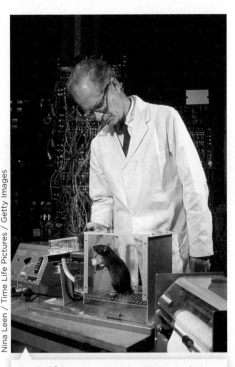

Nina Leen / Time Life Pictures / Getty Images

B. F. Skinner in his lab. Skinner, who had quite a head for science, devised the research technology shown here, which records the rat's lever presses as the experimenter administers reinforcements.

law of effect A principle of learning which states that when an organism performs a behavior that leads to a satisfying outcome in a given situation, it will be more likely to perform that behavior when it again encounters the same situation.

table **7.1**

Reinforcement and Punishment		
	Effects on Behavior	
	Increase frequency of behavior	**Decrease frequency of behavior**
Present stimulus	Positive reinforcement	Positive punishment
Remove stimulus	Negative reinforcement	Negative punishment

Psychologists distinguish among four types of response consequences that affect the frequency with which people perform behaviors. The frequency of behavior is increased by two types of reinforcement: positive (a reinforcing stimulus is presented) and negative (an aversive stimulus is removed). The frequency of behavior is decreased by two types of punishment: positive (an aversive stimulus is presented) and negative (a desired stimulus is taken away).

that consequences influence behavior, but he also developed a new technology for conducting research on these influences (see Research Toolkit) that was widely adopted in psychology laboratories around the world. Furthermore, he advanced an entire school of thought, called *behaviorism,* which argues that all actions and experiences of all organisms must be explained by referring to the environmental influences that a given organism has encountered (Skinner, 1974). Skinner forcefully argued that behaviorism and the principles of operant conditioning could explain most of the phenomena in the field of psychology because most of psychology is concerned with behaviors that are followed by response consequences.

Central to Skinner's theoretical system was his analysis of how two types of response consequences, *reinforcers* and *punishments,* shape behavior. Let's examine these now.

REINFORCEMENT. In operant conditioning, the stimulus of central interest is called a *reinforcer.* A **reinforcer** is any stimulus that occurs after a response and *raises* the future probability of that response. Skinner's research analyzed how reinforcers raise the probability that a reinforced behavior will occur again, thereby shaping behavior.

Skinner identified two types of reinforcement—positive and negative (Table 7.1). In **positive reinforcement,** the occurrence of a stimulus increases the likelihood that a given type of behavior occurs. If you diet, exercise, and lose weight and then friends say, "Wow, you look great!" their comments may serve as positive reinforcements that increase the future likelihood of you dieting and exercising. In **negative reinforcement,** the removal of a stimulus increases the likelihood that a given type of behavior occurs. If you take two aspirin for a headache and your headache goes away, then the removal of the headache is a negative reinforcer; its removal raises the probability that you'll take aspirin the next time you have a headache.

Here's another example; see if you can tell whether it's a positive or negative reinforcer. Imagine that you have a neighbor who plays music too loudly. You yell, "Quiet!" and the neighbor turns the music off. What kind of reinforcer was the cessation of music? It was a negative reinforcer that makes it more likely that, the next time the music is too loud, you will yell "quiet" again.

> What particular reinforcer would make it more likely that you would leave your residence early enough to get to school on time? Is this a positive or negative reinforcer?

Craig Swanson © www.perspicuity.com

Notice that "reinforcer" is defined in terms of the effects of a stimulus on the probability of behavior, *not* in terms of whether people like, or enjoy, the stimulus. Some stimuli that people do not like are effective positive reinforcers. Suppose you live in a region that periodically is struck with natural disasters (e.g., hurricanes or earthquakes). You don't like the disasters, yet they are positive reinforcers. Their occasional occurrence powerfully raises the probability of some behaviors, such as purchasing electrical generators and stocking up on emergency water supplies.

reinforcer In operant conditioning, any stimulus that occurs after a response and raises the future probability of that response.

positive reinforcement A stimulus whose occurrence following a behavior raises the future likelihood of that behavior.

negative reinforcement A stimulus whose removal following a behavior raises the future likelihood of that behavior.

Time-out Do you still remember when you got a time-out for misbehaving? *Time-out* procedures are, in the language of learning theory, a negative punishment. The punishment is the withdrawal of a desired stimulus: play time with other children.

Digital Vision / Getty Images

PUNISHMENT. Skinner recognized that behavior is affected by not only reinforcement but also punishment. A **punishment** is a stimulus that *lowers* the future likelihood of behavior. Scolding a misbehaving child, ticketing a speeding driver, and booing an athlete who fails to hustle are all cases of punishment; these response consequences tend to lower the likelihood of the behavior they follow.

As with reinforcement, one can identify "positive" and "negative" versions of punishment. *Positive punishment* is the presentation of an aversive stimulus, and *negative punishment* is the taking away of a desired stimulus. Table 7.1 summarizes the two types of reinforcement and punishment.

An everyday setting that illustrates the distinction between positive and negative punishment occurs in child care. When a child misbehaves, a caretaker could opt for positive punishment by presenting an aversive stimulus (e.g., scolding the child). There is, however, a popular negative-punishment alternative: the *time-out*. As you might remember from your own childhood, children in time-out are socially isolated. They lose access to desired stimuli such as toys and playmates. Research indicates that this negative punishment can effectively increase children's compliance with adults' requests (Everett et al., 2007).

> What memorable positive and negative punishments did you experience as a child?

Punishment can get results. Yet Skinner devoted almost all his research efforts to the study of reinforcement rather than punishment. He did so for two reasons, involving effectiveness and ethics. While punishment works, he regarded it as an ineffective way to change behavior because people may act against someone who is punishing them. Second, Skinner judged that rewarding desirable behavior is ethically superior to punishing undesirable action (e.g., Skinner 1948). Let's follow Skinner's lead and focus in detail on reinforcement processes.

❀ WHAT DO YOU KNOW?...

11. Match the example of operant conditioning on the left with its correct label in the middle and its explanation on the right.

This situation:	**is an example of this kind of operant conditioning:**	**because:**
1. Your car stopped making an annoying sound after you put on your seatbelt.	a. Positive punishment	e. Applying an aversive stimulus decreased the likelihood of your repeating that behavior.
2. Your teacher yelled at you for being late to class.	b. Negative reinforcement	f. Removing a desirable stimulus decreased the likelihood of your repeating that behavior.
3. Your friend took you out to lunch in appreciation of your listening attentively to her problems.	c. Negative punishment	g. Removing an aversive stimulus increased the likelihood of your repeating that behavior.
4. Your cell phone was taken away because you missed curfew.	d. Positive reinforcement	h. Applying a desirable stimulus increased the likelihood of your repeating that behavior.

punishment In operant conditioning, a stimulus that *lowers* the future likelihood of a given behavior.

A Skinnerian community
In his novel *Walden II*, B. F. Skinner depicted a community built on his principles of learning—a community in which desirable behaviors were so consistently reinforced that people lived in harmony and there was no need for elaborate systems of punishment (e.g., jails). Some have acted on his message. These signs are posted at Los Horcones, a community in Mexico that was established in 1973 according to principles outlined in Skinner's book. The community is still in existence today.

Four Basic Operant Conditioning Processes

Preview Questions

› What is a schedule of reinforcement?
› How do different reinforcement schedules affect behavior?
› What is a discriminative stimulus?
› How does research on discriminative stimuli explain people's tendency to act differently in different situations?
› How can organisms learn complex behaviors through operant conditioning?

Skinner discovered a number of systematic, and sometimes surprising, relations between reinforcement and behavior. As you'll see in this section, the discoveries involved four basic operant conditioning processes: *schedules of reinforcement, extinction, discriminative stimuli,* and the *shaping of complex behavior*.

Skinner believed that his research on each process was highly relevant to human behavior (Skinner, 1953). Note, however, that his studies were conducted on animals. Why animals? According to Skinner, just as principles of physics apply to all physical objects, principles of learning apply to all organisms. Thus, for ease of conducting research, he studied relatively simple organisms (especially pigeons and rats) in a relatively simple experimental setting, a *Skinner box* (see Research Toolkit).

⊕RESEARCH TOOLKIT

The Skinner Box

When scientists conduct research, they often isolate their object of study from the surrounding environment. Chemists put chemical substances into a test tube. Biologists put cell cultures into a Petri dish. This isolation is required to discover lawful scientific processes. Suppose you left a cell culture sitting out in the environment, instead of protected by a Petri dish. Dust, germs, and other objects would then become mixed together with the biological material, contaminating your experiment.

Like other scientists, psychologists who study learning need to isolate their object of study from environmental variables that could contaminate their experiments.

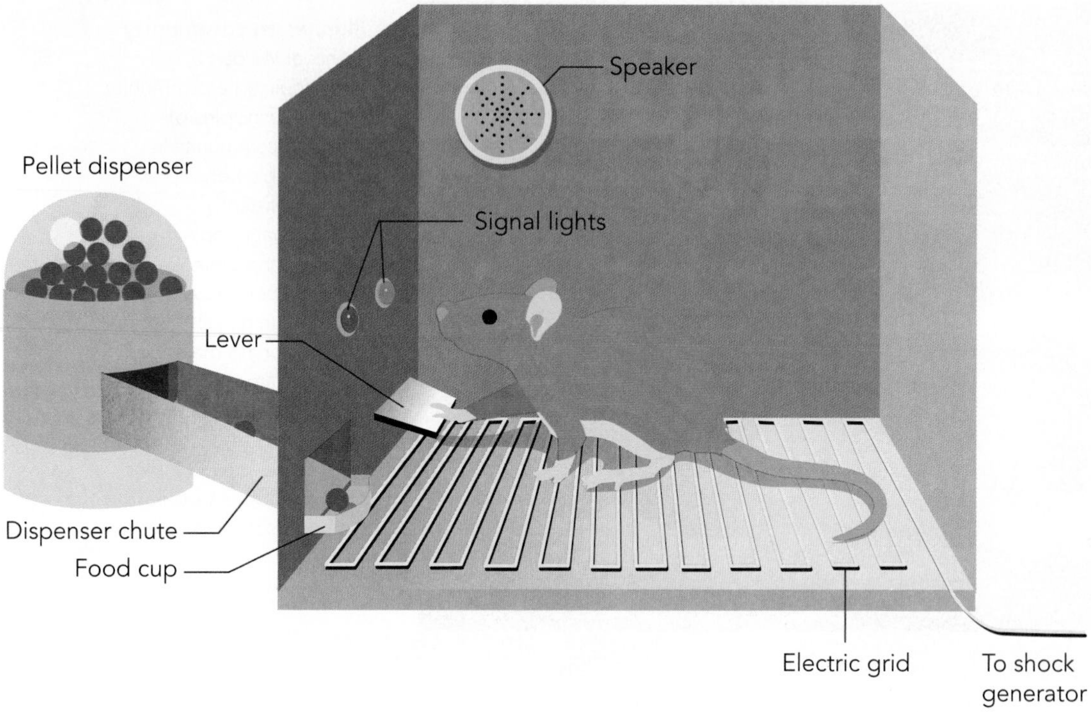

figure **7.11**
Skinner box A Skinner box, the primary research tool used by operant conditioning researchers to identify the relation between reinforcements and behavior.

What they need is a controlled environment in which an animal can roam freely while the researchers control variables that might influence its behavior. This is what B. F. Skinner provided by inventing the Skinner box (which he referred to as an "operant conditioning chamber").

The **Skinner box** is a piece of laboratory apparatus that is used in the study of operant conditioning. Its main virtue is simplicity. It has only three main elements (Figure 7.11):

1. *A device that the animal can act upon.* If the Skinner box is designed for research with rats, this device is usually a lever that the rat can press. For research with pigeons, it is a small disk on a wall that the pigeon can peck. The device records the number of times the animal responds (i.e., the number of lever presses or pecks).

2. *A mechanism for delivering reinforcers.* This is usually a small opening through which food or water can be delivered. For studies on the effects of punishment, rather than reinforcement, the box might also contain an electric grid that delivers shocks that punish the animal's behavior.

3. *A signal that can serve as a discriminative stimulus.* This is usually a light that turns on or off. Sometimes it is a speaker that delivers a tone.

Because the Skinner box is so simple, the experimenter can control *all* the variables in the animal's environment. The experimenter can decide whether to reinforce the animal's behavior, how frequently to deliver reinforcements, and whether to provide the animal with a signal (e.g., a light) indicating whether a behavior will be reinforced. And that's it—these are all the variables in the environment that the animal experiences.

By controlling all the variables in the environment, Skinner was able to obtain remarkably powerful experimental results. Skinner box studies produce results that are so reliable that the basic pattern of findings (discussed in the next section) is replicated, time and time again, with essentially every individual animal that is placed into the box.

Skinner box The primary laboratory apparatus in the study of operant conditioning; it includes a device for animals to act upon (e.g., a lever to press) and a mechanism for delivering reinforcers.

🕹 WHAT DO YOU KNOW?...

12. The simplicity of the operant conditioning chamber gave Skinner control. Control, in turn, increased his ability to _____ his findings.

SCHEDULES OF REINFORCEMENT. In both the laboratory and everyday life, the relation between behaviors and reinforcers varies. Sometimes reinforcers occur consistently and predictably. Every time you pay the cashier at a grocery store, the behavior is reinforced (you get a bag of food). Other times, however, reinforcers are sporadic and unpredictable. You always root, root, root for your home team, but often the behavior is *not* reinforced (sometimes they lose).

> **THINK ABOUT IT**
>
> Do reinforcers affect behavior in the same way in humans as in animals (e.g., laboratory rats)? What about the role of expectations? Humans daydream about reinforcers they might experience in the future. Rats do not. Might some psychological processes in reinforcement be unique to humans?

Skinner recognized that different *schedules of reinforcement* exist. A **schedule of reinforcement** is a timetable that indicates when reinforcers occur, in relation to the occurrence of behavior. Different schedules of reinforcement produce different patterns of behavior (Ferster & Skinner, 1957). Schedules of reinforcement differ in two ways: (1) the consistency of the reinforcement schedule and (2) whether time is a factor in the delivery of reinforcers (see Figure 7.12).

	Ratio Reinforcement after a specified number of responses	Interval Reinforcement after a specified period of time
Fixed Schedule consistent from one trial to the next	**FR** (fixed ratio)	**FI** (fixed interval)
Variable Schedule changes from one trial to the next	**VR** (variable ratio)	**VI** (variable interval)

figure 7.12
Reinforcement schedules Skinner explained that reinforcement schedules differ in two ways: first, whether the presentation of reinforcers depends on time (interval schedules) or the number of responses performed (ratio schedules) and, second, whether their presentation is consistent (fixed schedules) or varies unpredictably (variable schedules).

Regarding consistency, sometimes the schedule with which reinforcers are delivered remains the same, or is "fixed," from one trial to the next. (A trial in Skinner's experiments is any sequence in which a behavior or series of behaviors is followed by a reinforcer.) In **fixed schedules of reinforcement,** the delivery of reinforcers is consistent across trials. In **variable schedules of reinforcement,** the delivery of reinforcers is inconsistent; it changes unpredictably from one trial to the next.

Regarding time, sometimes an organism must wait for a period of time before a reinforcer is delivered. In **interval schedules of reinforcement,** a reinforcer is delivered subsequent to the first response the organism makes after a specific period of time elapses. There is nothing the organism can do to make the reinforcement occur more quickly. In another pattern, however, time is not a determining factor in the scheduling of reinforcements. In **ratio schedules of reinforcement,** the organism gets a reinforcer after performing a certain *number of* responses. If it responds faster, it is reinforced sooner.

> On which schedule of reinforcement is your texting reinforced?

As shown in Figure 7.12, these two distinctions combine to create four types of reinforcement schedules: fixed interval (FI), variable interval (VI), fixed ratio (FR), and variable ratio (VR). Let's look at each one, examining both Skinner's laboratory results and their relevance to everyday life.

In a *fixed interval* (FI) schedule, reinforcers occur after a consistent period of time has elapsed from one trial to the next. For example, suppose a rat is pressing a lever under an FI schedule, and the interval is 1 minute. This means that, once the rat presses the lever and is given a reinforcer, it cannot get another one for 60 seconds. After the full minute elapses, the first time the rat presses the lever, it receives another reinforcer.

FI schedules produce relatively low rates of behavior (Figure 7.13). Once a reinforcer is presented, an animal tends not to respond for awhile. The animal generally exhibits high rates of response only in the few seconds before the end of the interval. As a result, the animal's overall level of behavior is low in comparison to that of animals reinforced under any of the other three reinforcement schedules.

FI schedules are common in everyday life. One example of a reinforcer that often occurs on an FI schedule is classroom exams; you might be in a class that has exams

schedule of reinforcement In operant conditioning research, a timetable that indicates when reinforcements occur, in relation to the occurrence of behavior.

fixed schedule of reinforcement In operant conditioning research, a timetable for reinforcement that is consistent across trials.

variable schedule of reinforcement In operant conditioning research, a timetable for reinforcement that is inconsistent across trials; the delivery of reinforcers changes unpredictably.

interval schedule of reinforcement In operant conditioning research, a timetable for reinforcement in which the reinforcer is delivered subsequent to the first response an organism makes after a specific period of time elapses.

ratio schedule of reinforcement In operant conditioning research, a timetable for reinforcement in which a reinforcer is administered only after an organism performs a certain number of responses.

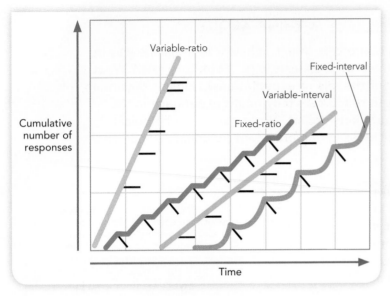

figure 7.13
Schedules of reinforcement results
Different schedules of reinforcement produce different rates of response, with the highest response rates being produced by variable ratio schedules. The short black lines protruding from the lines and curves indicate when a reinforcer was delivered.

on a fixed schedule, maybe once every four weeks. (Exams are reinforcers; they reinforce studying. If there were no exams, most people would study less than they do in classes with exams.) So exams in your class are reinforcers that occur on a predictable, fixed schedule. What, then, would Skinner's theory predict about the behavior of students in a course with regularly scheduled exams?

Because the exams occur on an FI schedule, Skinner would predict that students' frequency of studying for the course would vary across time, just like the behavior of a rat in a Skinner box (see Figure 7.13). He would expect that, after one exam occurs, students would not do much studying for awhile. Rather, they would exhibit high rates of studying only in the few days and hours just prior to the next exam. Of course, for many students, this is exactly what occurs— it's called cramming. Skinner would say that there's nothing unique about this; it has nothing to do, specifically, with exams, or students, or even human beings. Cramming for a test is simply one example of the general pattern of behavior that occurs under an FI schedule of reinforcement.

In a *variable interval* (VI) schedule, reinforcements occur after a period of time that is unpredictable to the organism in the Skinner box. For example, the interval might be set to 1 minute on average, but could vary from 10 seconds to 110 seconds from one trial to the next. VI schedules produce patterns of behavior that occur at a higher rate, and more consistently, than behavior under an FI schedule (see Figure 7.13). A simple change in our cramming example above shows how this works in everyday life. Suppose you had pop quizzes in a course, instead of scheduled exams. You likely would study at a relatively consistent rate, always keeping up on readings and reviewing lecture notes, so that you'd always be ready for an exam. This type of consistency in behavior is exactly what occurs in Skinner boxes, under VI schedules.

The ratio schedules of reinforcement yield higher rates of response than either of the interval schedules (see Figure 7.13). In the *fixed ratio* (FR) schedule, a reinforcer is delivered after an organism performs a certain number of responses, and that number stays consistent from one trial to the next. For instance, a rat might be reinforced after every 20th lever press. With an FR schedule, the reinforcement occurs after a certain number of responses no matter how long, or short, a period of time the animal takes to perform these responses. Under an FR schedule, organisms get more reinforcements if they respond more quickly (unlike the FI schedule).

To see the power of an FR schedule, imagine two types of jobs: one in which you get paid by the hour, and the other—the FR job—in which you get paid more if you speedily accomplish more work. You would get paid by the hour, for example, in a fast-food restaurant. If you service more diners, you do *not* earn more money. On the other hand, you would be paid according to an FR schedule if you sold magazine subscriptions over the phone and were paid according to how many you sold. As business managers know (Lazear, 1986), the FR schedule of the magazine-sales job is likely to be more motivating. People are less likely to "slack off" when working under the ratio schedule of reinforcement.

In a *variable ratio* (VR) schedule, reinforcements are delivered after an organism performs a certain number of responses *on average*. The exact number of responses required on a given trial varies unpredictably from one trial to the next. For example, a rat's lever-pressing behavior might be reinforced after 20 lever presses on average, but the rat might press the lever only 10 times before it is reinforced on one trial, then press the lever 30 times on the next trial.

Under a VR schedule, animals get reinforced only sporadically. An animal might, on some trials, have to press the lever 50 times or more just to receive one reinforcer.

Eric Raptosh Photography / Getty Images

Photo Researchers / Getty Images

Variable ratio schedules of reinforcement A VR schedule in a Skinner box is identical to the schedule of reinforcement on a slot machine. The reinforcement schedule is addicting to people and rats alike.

You might expect these schedules to produce low rates of response. But instead, the opposite occurs! VR schedules produce the highest response rates (see Figure 7.13). A remarkable finding from Skinner's lab is that, while getting very few reinforcements, animals on a VR schedule will exhibit very high rates of response.

The power of the VR schedule explains the power of gambling devices, such as slot machines. Slot machines reinforce a sequence of behavior: putting money in the machine and pulling a lever (an action that, ironically, looks quite like the behavior of a rat pressing a lever in a Skinner box). Critically, they reinforce the behavior only sporadically, on a variable ratio schedule. Large payouts do occur, but only once every few hundred or thousand plays. Despite the low frequency of reinforcement, the device is addictive. Whether you're a pigeon in a Skinner box or a human in a casino, the VR schedule can seize control of your behavior and cause you to lose your nest egg.

EXTINCTION. Earlier in this chapter, you learned about extinction in classical conditioning. In operant conditioning, *extinction* refers to the pattern of behavior that results when a behavior that previously was reinforced is no longer followed by any reinforcers. For instance, suppose an experimenter had reinforced the lever-pressing behavior of a rat, giving it a small piece of food every time it pressed on the lever. If the experimenter suddenly stopped reinforcing that behavior, that would be a case of extinction.

What happens to the animal's behavior during extinction? The pattern of extinction depends on the schedule of reinforcement that the animal had experienced previously. If its behavior had been reinforced consistently (e.g., on an FR schedule with a reinforcement occurring after every few responses), extinction is rapid. Animals quickly stop responding when reinforcers cease. However, if the behavior had been reinforced on an irregular, random schedule (e.g., on a VR schedule with large numbers of behaviors sometimes being required to obtain one reinforcer), extinction is very slow. An animal might perform a large number of behaviors while receiving no reinforcement at all.

Extinction, then, is fast if an animal has been reinforced consistently but slow if an animal has been reinforced only intermittently. Compare the following two human cases in terms of extinction:

> You put money into a vending machine, press a button indicating your selection, but there is no reinforcer: The machine fails to deliver your snack.

> You buy a lottery ticket at a local convenience store, but there is no reinforcer: You do not win the lottery.

In the vending machine example, one trial in which you don't get a reinforcer is enough: You stop putting money into that machine. In the lottery

Don't reinforce that behavior on a variable ratio schedule! Parents faced with a whining child occasionally "give in"; to stop the whining, they buy the toy. Skinner's research on schedules of reinforcement shows that giving in only makes matters worse. If parents give in occasionally, they reinforce the whining behavior on a variable ratio schedule—which can make the behavior more frequent and extremely persistent.

Mika / Corbis

ticket example, one trial in which you don't get a reinforcer has hardly any effect: Lottery players often buy tickets repeatedly, for months or years, without winning. The properly functioning vending machine reinforces behavior on an FR schedule, whereas the lottery reinforces behavior on a VR schedule, and—whether in the Skinner lab or in everyday life—VR schedules produce behavior that extinguishes very slowly.

DISCRIMINATIVE STIMULI. Your behavior commonly changes from one situation to the next. You're talkative with friends, yet quiet in class or in a church. You work hard on some courses, but "blow off" others. You speak formally to your professor and casually to your roommate. Operant conditioning explains these variations in behavior in terms of discriminative stimuli. A **discriminative stimulus** is one that provides information about the type of consequences that are likely to follow a given type of behavior. Discriminative stimuli may signal that, in one situation, a behavior likely will be reinforced, whereas in another situation, that same behavior may be punished.

An example of a discriminative stimulus in social interactions is a "shhh" signal (see photo). The gesture indicates that the typical consequences of talking do not hold. Typically, if you talk about some topic, your behavior is reinforced by the attention of the people listening to you. The "shhh" signal indicates that, instead, this same behavior is likely to be punished; something in the typical environment has changed (e.g., someone nearby, who shouldn't hear your conversation, is listening in), and the behavior will result in negative consequences.

Many of the everyday situations you encounter contain discriminative stimuli—signals indicating the type of behavior that is or is not acceptable. If you walk into a room in which everyone is quiet, their behavior is a discriminative stimulus telling you that loud, lively behavior will not be reinforced here. If you walk into a loud, lively party, the behavior of other people is a discriminative stimulus indicating that quiet, studious behavior will not be reinforced. Discriminative stimuli, then, explain why a person's behavior can vary so much from one situation to another.

> Have you ever failed to notice a discriminative stimulus? At what cost?

Hola Images / Corbis

Looks like talking will not be reinforced In the language of operant conditioning, this gesture is a discriminative stimulus. "Shhhh" indicates that the behavior of talking will not be followed by a reinforcer.

discriminative stimulus Any stimulus that provides information about the type of consequences that are likely to follow a given type of behavior in particular situations.

 **THIS JUST IN**

Reinforcing Pain Behavior

"Ouch."

"What's wrong? Are you OK?"

"Ouch. Ow. It hurts. Ow."

Pain is internal. It's an inner feeling created by receptors within your body that detect harmful stimuli, such as cuts or burns (see Chapter 5). But *expressions* of pain—saying, "ouch," or showing pain on your face—are external. People out there, in the external environment, hear, see, and respond to your pain expressions.

A major lesson of this chapter is that the external environment shapes behavior. Some environmental stimuli, called reinforcers, increase the frequency of the behavior that precedes them. Classic research by Skinner shows that when rats press a lever, reinforcers increase the frequency of their lever-pressing behavior. Research "just in" suggests that the same principle holds when it comes to pain behavior: Reinforcers can increase the frequency of people's expressions of pain. This might happen even when the reinforcers are kind, caring responses ("What's wrong? Are you OK?") meant to decrease, rather than increase, pain experience.

A recent operant learning theory of pain behavior outlines four steps through which this happens (Figure 7.14; Gatzounis et al., 2012). After experiencing pain (Step 1), people may exhibit a pain behavior (Step 2). That pain behavior brings attention from

Experience of pain	Expression of pain	Attention from others	Probability of pain expression increases
	Ow!	Can I help?	Ow! Ow!

figure **7.14**
Stages of pain

other people (Step 3). The extra attention can reinforce the pain behavior, making it more frequent in the future (Step 4).

Research supports the theory (Kunz, Rainville, & Lautenbacher, 2011). Research participants experienced, across a series of trials, a very warm stimulus that was painful (but not harmful). In different experimental conditions, the researchers reinforced different types of reactions to the painful stimulus. On some trials, participants received a reinforcer whenever they displayed a *neutral* facial expression during the stimulation. On other trials, they received a reinforcer whenever they displayed a *painful* facial expression. The study produced two key results:

› *Reinforcers increased expressions of pain.* Researchers observed that participants appeared to be in greater pain during the trials in which pain expressions were reinforced.

› *Pain expressions were positively correlated with pain experiences.* When the researchers asked participants how much pain they actually were experiencing, people who had displayed more pain on their face also reported experiencing more pain.

What does this mean for your everyday experiences? Imagine you're with someone experiencing minor pain—perhaps a friend recovering from a small injury. Whenever they grimace, say, "ow," or talk about their pain, your natural reaction is to comfort them: to say kind words and attend to their needs. In many ways, comfort is good. Yet in one way, it might backfire. Your attention can reinforce their pain behavior, increasing their grimacing, "ow"-ing, and talking. If it does, they, in turn, might pay more attention to their injury—and, as a result, experience higher levels of pain. Your intentions were good, but the principles of reinforcement can trump good intentions.

Nicole S. Young / Getty Images

Does comforting pain reinforce pain? It's natural to comfort someone in pain. But that comforting might have an unintended side effect: reinforcing expressions of pain, and thus increasing pain experience.

💧 WHAT DO YOU KNOW?...

13. Name something a well-intentioned person might say to someone in pain that can inadvertently reinforce pain behavior and thereby cause more pain.

THE SHAPING OF COMPLEX BEHAVIOR. A rat placed in a Skinner box does not immediately start pressing the lever. Lever pressing, from the rat's perspective, is a somewhat complex behavior. It has to locate the lever, balance to reach it, and learn to press down with sufficient force. How can one teach the rat to do this complex act?

In operant conditioning, organisms learn complex behaviors through *shaping*. **Shaping** is a step-by-step learning process in which psychologists reinforce behavior

shaping In operant conditioning, the learning of complex behavior through a step-by-step process in which behaviors that successively approximate a desired, final behavior are reinforced.

Dave Stamboulis / Alamy

Even bird-brained organisms can learn complex actions if you shape their behavior with reinforcements.

that approximates some desired behavior. The approximations become closer and closer to the target behavior over a series of learning trials.

Did you ever wonder how animal trainers teach lions to jump through hoops, seals to balance balls on their noses, and parrots to ride bicycles? They do it by shaping the animals' behavior through operant conditioning. Suppose you want to train a parrot to ride a bicycle. You can't just sit around waiting for your parrot to hop on the bike and start pedaling, and only then give it a reinforcer. That's never going to happen. Instead, you have to begin with something simple. You might at first reinforce the bird merely when it walks in the direction of the bike. Next, you might reinforce it only when it gets closer to the bike, then only when it touches the bike, and so forth. After a potentially painstaking series of shaping experiences, your parrot eventually will become a cyclist.

Much human learning also is shaped gradually. When, as a child, you learned proper manners for eating, adults first reinforced simple actions, such as picking up and using a fork. They didn't wait until you made it through a formal meal, complete with proper use of salad fork and butter knife, before reinforcing your behavior. Similarly, in a foreign language class, the instructor's goal is to teach you how to converse in complete sentences. But first, she reinforces something much simpler: the speaking of simple words and phrases. In both cases, behavior is gradually shaped. Over time, the behavior that is reinforced becomes more complex.

THINK ABOUT IT

Much human behavior is learned by shaping. But is all of it? What about driving? When you learned to drive, did you at first make a lot of mistakes— say, put your foot on the radio button? Drive straight ahead into the garage wall? Or did you get the behavior mostly right the first time, before you had ever been reinforced for good driving?

✪ WHAT DO YOU KNOW?...

14. Of ratio and interval schedules of reinforcement, _____ schedules yield higher rates of response because the reinforcements depend on the organism doing something. Of fixed and variable ratio schedules, _____ ratio schedules produce the highest rates of response, surprisingly. Behaviors reinforced on a _____ ratio schedule tend to extinguish slowly, especially if the behavior itself was reinforced very intermittently, as in gambling. A discriminative stimulus indicates whether a given behavior will be reinforced or _____ in a given situation. Simple organisms can learn complex responses by being _____ for behaviors that approximate a desired behavior.

TRY THIS!

Earlier, in this chapter's Try This! Activity, you attempted to teach a pigeon to peck on a wall. Try it again. Now that you have learned the principles of operant conditioning, you should be able to get a higher score than you did previously. In particular, apply what you have learned about schedules of reinforcement and how they can increase rates of response, to improve your score.

Beyond Skinner in the Study of Operant Conditioning

Preview Questions

> What does it mean to say that there are "biological constraints on learning"?

> Do research findings in the study of biological constraints on learning confirm, or call into question, the principles of learning developed by Skinner?

> Why might rewards sometimes lower people's tendency to engage in an activity?

Skinner believed that his principles of operant conditioning would be comprehensive. In theory, they would explain all operant behavior, by all organisms, in all environments. Skinner made this claim explicitly. His first book (Skinner, 1938) was *The Behavior of Organisms*—a title that conveyed his belief that principles of learning discovered by studying rats in Skinner boxes would apply to all organisms and all forms of operant behavior.

Research has shown, however, that Skinner's claim is not correct. His principles of learning are sometimes insufficient. Skinner failed to attend to some factors that have proven important to learning and behavior. Two such factors are (1) biological constraints on learning that are based in the evolutionary history of the species being studied, and (2) the way in which rewards alter not only people's actions, but also their thoughts about their actions.

BIOLOGICAL CONSTRAINTS ON OPERANT CONDITIONING. Why did Skinner choose to conduct experiments on the lever-pressing behavior of rats and the pecking of pigeons? Convenience. It is relatively easy to maintain a lab full of rats or pigeons and to measure lever pressing and pecking. Skinner presumed the choice of organism and behavior wouldn't matter; principles of learning, he thought, should apply across all species.

On this point, Skinner turned out to be wrong. The choice of organism and behavior sometimes does make a difference. The differences reflect animals' innate biology, which produces *biological constraints* on learning (Domjan & Galef, 1983; Öhman & Mineka, 2001). A **biological constraint** on learning is an evolved predisposition that makes it difficult, if not impossible, for a given species to learn a certain type of behavior when reinforced with a certain type of reward.

Consider two operant conditioning experiments with a pigeon:

1. A pigeon is reinforced with food whenever it pecks a particular spot on a wall.
2. A pigeon is reinforced with food whenever it flaps its wings.

Skinner would have predicted that the two experiments should work the same way; the reinforcer, food, would raise the probability of responding. However, the experiments actually turn out differently (Rachlin, 1976). The pecking experiment works as Skinner expected, but the flapping experiment does not. Food reinforcers do not raise the probability of wing flapping. Why not?

The answer lies in the pigeons' biological predispositions. For a pigeon, pecking and food naturally are biologically connected. Wing flapping and food, however, are not. In fact, wing flapping and eating were usually *disconnected* during pigeons' evolution. For a pigeon in the presence of food, flapping its wings is a bad idea: It flies away and gets no food. Pigeons' evolutionary history, then, constrains learning; they find it difficult to learn the connection between the behavior, wing flapping, and the reinforcer, food.

This is only one of many cases in which a species' evolutionary past constrains its ability to learn through operant conditioning. In another (Breland & Breland, 1961), researchers reinforced a raccoon for picking up two coins and dropping them in a box. The raccoon picked up the coins. But instead of dropping them in the box, it rubbed them together, dipped them into the box, pulled them out, rubbed them some more, and never let go. The researchers had never reinforced these behaviors. Yet the raccoon performed them repeatedly. Why? Its actions were a case of *instinctual drift,* in which animals exhibit behavior that reflects their species' evolved biological predispositions, rather than their individual learning experiences. Raccoons instinctively moisten their paws and food, and rub their food before eating, and in the experiment the raccoon instinctively did the same thing with the coins, in the absence of reinforcement.

Why is this raccoon moistening its food? Not because somebody reinforced the behavior. Rather, this behavior reflects the evolution of the species; raccoons are biologically predisposed to moistening their food before eating it.

McDonald Wildlife Photog. / AnimalsAnimals

biological constraint An evolved predisposition that makes it difficult or impossible for a given species to learn a certain type of behavior when reinforced with a certain type of reward.

Evolution also plays a role in human learning. Consider language. Shaping through operant conditioning cannot explain human language learning (Chomsky, 1959). Young children quickly learn not only the words of their language, but also the language's syntax, that is, the rules through which sentences are formed. They do so despite the fact that parents rarely provide explicit reinforcements for syntax use (Brown, 1973). Humans are biologically predisposed to learn language; we inherit capabilities that make it easy for us to learn to understand and produce sentences (Pinker, 1994).

REWARDS AND PERSONAL INTEREST IN ACTIVITIES. Skinner thought that the effects of reinforcement on behavior were the same for all species. No matter who you are—rat, pigeon, or human—reinforcers are supposed to raise the probability of future behavior.

Yet there is a complicating factor to which Skinner gave little thought. Rats and pigeons do not think about themselves and the causes of their behavior. ("Am I really the sort of rat who should be stuck in a box pressing a lever all day long?") People, on the other hand, think about themselves incessantly. Sometimes their thoughts can cause rewards to "backfire"—decreasing rather than increasing behavior.

In a classic study, researchers tested the effects of rewards on preschool children who were intrinsically interested in drawing, that is, who naturally liked to draw (Lepper, Greene, & Nisbett, 1973). In one experimental condition, the children were asked to draw pictures for a chance to win a "Good Player Award." After they finished, the children received the award. In a second condition, children were asked to draw pictures but with no mention of an award. A few days later, there was a free period during which the children could do anything they wanted, including drawing. Did the Good Player Awards increase the probability of drawing during this period, as Skinner would have predicted? No. The very opposite occurred: Children in the *no*-award condition spent *more* time drawing. Why?

The rewards changed children's thoughts about their behavior (Lepper, Greene, & Nisbett, 1973). At the start of the study, the children were interested in drawing; they knew they drew pictures out of personal interest. But the Good Player Awards caused them to think that they drew pictures to get external rewards. As a result, the children became less interested in drawing when no rewards were available.

> What activities do you engage in that you find intrinsically interesting? When have you been rewarded for doing something you already enjoy?

A summary of more than 100 studies confirms that rewards can reduce children's interest in activities (Deci, Koestner, & Ryan, 1999). The research shows that rewards can backfire—a result not anticipated by Skinner's analysis of operant conditioning.

In summary, these two scientific findings—biological constraints on learning and the reduction of intrinsic interest in activities that is caused by external rewards—move beyond the understanding of reinforcement and behavior provided by Skinner.

💡 WHAT DO YOU KNOW?...

15. Both statements below are incorrect. Explain why:
    a. "The fact that it's just as easy to teach a pigeon to peck as it is to flap its wings indicates that our evolutionary history has no effect on our ability to learn through operant conditioning."
    b. "Just as Skinner would have predicted, rewards always increase the likelihood of a behavior, even when people are intrinsically motivated to do something."

Biological Bases of Operant Conditioning

Preview Question

> How do psychologists know that the brain contains a "reward center"?

Now that we've learned about psychological processes in operant learning, we can move to a biological level of analysis. What brain mechanisms allow organisms to learn through operant conditioning?

A first step in answering this question was taken more than a half-century ago, when researchers (Olds & Milner, 1954) discovered that the brain contains a *reward center*, a neural region whose stimulation is pleasurable to organisms. In this classic research, investigators implanted an electrode in a rat's brain that allowed them to stimulate the limbic system electrically. The researchers then placed the rat in a Skinner box and stimulated its brain whenever the rat pressed the box's lever (Figure 7.15). The consequence that followed the rat's behavior was electrical stimulation, which was pleasurable and proved to be reinforcing. The rats repeatedly pressed the lever in order to gain stimulation of their reward center (Olds & Milner, 1954). The results showed, then, that the brain contains a region dedicated to producing pleasurable experiences.

Research has advanced considerably from these early days. Rather than identifying a general area of the brain that is involved in reward, researchers now search for specific neurons that are responsible for operant conditioning. This operant conditioning research has progressed, thanks to study of a simple organism you learned about earlier, *Aplysia* (Rankin, 2002). *Aplysia* eat by biting. Researchers (Brembs et al., 2002) reinforced biting by electrically stimulating a reward area of the *Aplysia* nervous system. This reinforcer changed the *Aplysia*'s behavior; it increased their frequency of biting. The researchers then explored neuron-to-neuron connections in the *Aplysia* nervous system to identify the exact biological change responsible for the change in behavior. They discovered that, when the behavior changed, so did a specific neuron in *Aplysia* that controls the motor movement of biting. After reinforcement, this neuron became more excitable, in other words, more likely to fire (Brembs et al., 2002). The change in nerve cell firing, then, was responsible for the change in behavior.

Further research with *Aplysia* has shown that the precise cellular changes that occur in operant conditioning differ from those that occur in classical conditioning

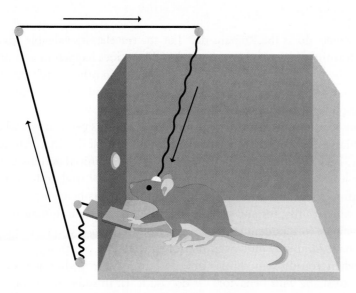

figure **7.15**

Reward center Instead of reinforcing a rat with an external reward, such as food or water, you can reinforce it with internal stimulation. The rat will press a lever repeatedly in order to gain electrical stimulation of a pleasure center in its brain.

(Lorenzetti et al., 2006). This means that classical conditioning and operant conditioning, which differ psychologically, also differ biologically.

In more complex organisms, the situation is more complicated. In humans, for instance, rewards have a number of effects—including changing behavior, altering thoughts, and altering emotional states—each of which has different biological underpinnings. Different biological systems contribute, for example, to the experience of wanting a reward that may occur in the future, as opposed to experiencing a reward one has just received (Berridge & Robinson, 2003).

Despite this greater complexity, research conducted with animals (e.g., laboratory rats) has identified a biological substance in mammals that is key to their ability to learn through rewards: *dopamine,* one of the brain's neurotransmitters. Different types of findings suggest that dopamine is central to reward processes. The presentation of rewarding stimuli (e.g., food, water, or opportunities for sex) increases levels of dopamine in the brain (Schultz, 2006; Wise, 2004). Furthermore, when the normal functioning of dopamine is blocked, rewards no longer control animals' behavior.

In one study (Wise et al., 1978), rats were reinforced by food for lever pressing. After learning to press the lever, they were assigned to different experimental conditions. In one, reinforcement for lever pressing ceased; as you might expect, these rats gradually stopped pressing the lever. In a second condition, reinforcement continued; these rats kept pressing. Finally, the key experimental condition combined two features: (1) Lever pressing was reinforced, but (2) rats received an injection of a drug that blocks the neurotransmitter effects of dopamine. These rats *stopped* pressing the lever. Their behavior resembled that of the rats in the no-reinforcement condition. The results suggest, then, that at a biological level of analysis, reinforcers influence behavior through their effect on the dopamine system.

✪ WHAT DO YOU KNOW?...

16. Research with *Aplysia* indicates that operant and classical conditioning, which are psychologically different, are also _____ different. The neurotransmitter _____ is central to reward processes.

Observational Learning

"When in Rome, do as the Romans do." For the traveler, it's valuable advice. For the student of learning, it's something to ponder. What does happen in an unfamiliar environment where you don't know the local customs—in other words, an environment where you don't know which behaviors are reinforced and which are punished? How exactly do you learn how to do as the Romans do?

Operant conditioning provides one answer. From this perspective, when entering an unfamiliar cultural setting, you're like a rat on its first day in a Skinner box. The rat, at first, hasn't the foggiest idea how to behave. Its initial actions are essentially random. It learns how to act only due to a slow process of trial-and-error learning in which reinforcements or punishments gradually shape its behavior.

Is this what it's like for you when you enter a novel environment—for example, if you participate in a student exchange program that sends you to a foreign culture? Do you behave randomly and await reinforcements and punishments—smiles from strangers when you do something right, and angry stares when you do something insulting—to shape your behavior? Or do you learn in some other way?

Most people learn to "do as the Romans" by *watching* the Romans. In unfamiliar settings, we often observe how others act, gain information about appropriate and inappropriate types of behavior from our observations, and then base our behavior on what we observed. This human ability to learn by observation enables us, quickly and easily, to fit in with the group rather than stick out from the crowd.

Psychological Processes in Observational Learning

Preview Questions

› How do the results of Bandura's Bobo doll experiment contradict the expectations of operant conditioning analyses of learning?

› What psychological processes are involved in observational learning, that is, what processes are required for a person to learn to perform a behavior displayed by a psychological model?

Curiously, this human capacity for learning by observation received little attention from psychologists studying operant conditioning. The psychologist Albert Bandura, however, paid it a lot of attention and pioneered research on *observational learning*. (Bandura used his findings about observational learning as a foundation for his theory of personality; see Chapter 13.)

In **observational learning,** people acquire new knowledge and skills merely by observing the behavior of other people (Bandura, 1965; 1986). Those other people are called *psychological models,* and observational learning thus is also referred to as **modeling.** In practice, the terms *observational learning* and *modeling* are used interchangeably.

LEARNING WITHOUT REINFORCEMENT. Observational learning is efficient. Through observational learning, people can acquire complex skills all at once, without tedious trial-and-error shaping processes.

Bandura (1965) documented the power of observational learning in research (also discussed in Chapter 4). He showed children a short film in which an adult acted aggressively toward an inflated clown doll, or "Bobo doll." The adult performed specific behaviors (such as hitting the doll in the nose with a hammer) that the children were unlikely to have performed before. Later, when the children were observed in a playroom, Bandura found that the children spontaneously performed many of the same behaviors they had seen in the film (see photos).

Albert Bandura

Observational learning of aggression In Bandura's research on observational learning, children saw an adult pummeling a clown doll. Later, in a playroom, the children did the very same thing. They learned the aggressive behavior that was displayed by the model, even though they never were reinforced for it.

Note that the children performed these behaviors even though they never had been reinforced for performing them. There was no trial-and-error learning in which the children's behavior gradually was shaped by its consequences, like that of a rat in a Skinner box. Instead, instantaneous learning occurred: Children correctly performed the behavior—they hit the clown doll right in the nose with the hammer—the very first time they had a chance. They learned this behavior merely by watching it on film. As Bandura emphasized, this result shows that people have a capacity to learn that is not explained by the principles of operant conditioning. Observational learning is thus a third type of learning, distinct from operant and classical conditioning.

SUBPROCESSES IN OBSERVATIONAL LEARNING. Bandura recognized that his experiment had revealed a distinct form of learning that had been largely overlooked by operant conditioning researchers: To a much greater extent than the

observational learning (modeling)
A form of learning in which knowledge and skills are acquired by observing others.

Model's
Behavior

Observer's
Behavior

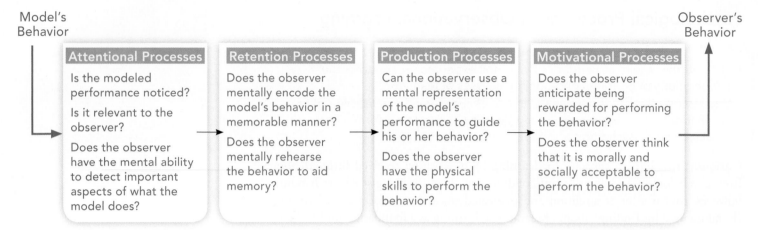

Attentional Processes

Is the modeled performance noticed?

Is it relevant to the observer?

Does the observer have the mental ability to detect important aspects of what the model does?

Retention Processes

Does the observer mentally encode the model's behavior in a memorable manner?

Does the observer mentally rehearse the behavior to aid memory?

Production Processes

Can the observer use a mental representation of the model's performance to guide his or her behavior?

Does the observer have the physical skills to perform the behavior?

Motivational Processes

Does the observer anticipate being rewarded for performing the behavior?

Does the observer think that it is morally and socially acceptable to perform the behavior?

figure **7.16**

Subprocesses in observational learning Bandura outlined the series of psychological steps, or subprocesses, required for an observer to perform an action modeled by someone else. The processes are attending to the model, retaining memory of the model's behavior, being able to produce the observed behavior, and being motivated to do so.

CONNECTING TO PERSONALITY DEVELOPMENT AND THE BRAIN

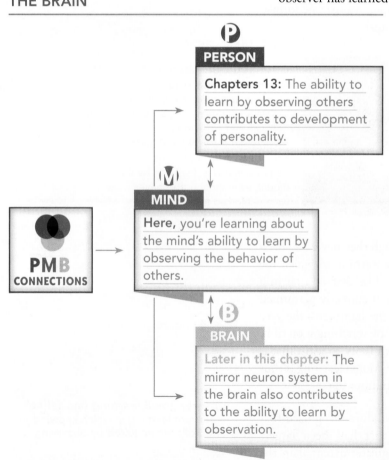

P

PERSON

Chapters 13: The ability to learn by observing others contributes to development of personality.

M

MIND

Here, you're learning about the mind's ability to learn by observing the behavior of others.

B

BRAIN

Later in this chapter: The mirror neuron system in the brain also contributes to the ability to learn by observation.

PMB CONNECTIONS

rats and pigeons in a Skinner lab, humans have the ability to learn complex acts through observation. To explain this ability, Bandura (1986) analyzed subprocesses in observational learning—in other words, the psychological processes that are required for a person to get from the performance of a behavior by a model to the performance of a similar behavior by an observer. He identified four subprocesses (Figure 7.16):

1. *Attention:* The observer must pay close attention to the model's behavior.
2. *Retention:* The observer must create, and retain, memory for the model's actions.
3. *Production:* The observer must be able to draw on a mental representation of the model's behavior and must have the basic motor skills necessary to produce the remembered action.
4. *Motivation:* The observer must be motivated to perform the behavior. Even if the observer has learned the action, he or she still might decide not to perform it.

The fourth step in Bandura's analysis, motivational processes, underscores a point that received relatively little attention from Skinner. It is the distinction between *acquisition* and *performance*. To *perform* a behavior is to engage in that behavior. To *acquire* a behavior is to have the *potential* to engage in a behavior. As Bandura emphasized, people can acquire the skill to perform a behavior, yet not be motivated to do it. By watching a crime show on TV, you might learn ways to commit a criminal act. Nonetheless, you likely choose (wisely) not to perform those behaviors. Learning, then, cannot be measured solely by studying what individuals *do* because they may have learned actions that they choose not to perform.

In summary, research on observational learning substantially expanded psychology's understanding of learning in two main ways. First, it highlighted a phenomenon that had received little attention from previous learning theorists (i.e., Pavlov, Thorndike, Skinner): people's ability to learn behaviors rapidly through observation alone. Second, it explained that phenomenon through a novel set of conceptual tools. Rather than referring merely to simple stimulus–response mechanisms, Bandura explained human learning by referring to complex processes carried out in the mind: attention to models, retention of memory of their behavior, and the use of that memory to guide behavior.

🌣 WHAT DO YOU KNOW?...

17. What would Skinner have predicted about the behavior of the children in Bandura's Bobo doll study?

18. A friend of yours misunderstands Bandura's observational learning and asks, "Does Bandura really think that I'm going to hit someone just because I watched someone else do it?" Explain to your friend the distinction Bandura made between *acquisition* and *performance*.

Comparing Operant Conditioning and Observational Learning Predictions

Preview Questions

> Can spanking increase aggression in children?
> Does research on the effects of spanking support theoretical predictions made by operant conditioning or observational learning analyses?

Sometimes models send contradictory messages. They model one type of behavior, but tell others that this behavior is not allowed. An example of this is spanking by parents who are trying to control their children's unruly, aggressive behavior. The spanking is intended as a punishment. An operant conditioning analysis would thus suggest that the spanking would make children less unruly. Yet the parent who is spanking is providing a role model of aggressive behavior; the spanking itself is an act of physical aggression toward the child.

What is the effect of spanking? To find out, researchers conducted a large-scale, long-term study with more than 2000 families (Taylor et al., 2010). When children were 3 years of age, researchers asked mothers to report whether, and how frequently, they spanked their child. Parents differed: About 45% reported no use of spanking; about one-fourth said they spanked one or two times a month; and one-fourth reported a higher spanking frequency. The researchers also measured the children's level of aggression, specifically, whether each child was defiant, had angry moods, and hit others. Then, two years later, mothers reported their 5-year-old child's current level of aggressiveness, measured in terms of arguing, bullying, meanness to others, and fighting. With the age 3 and age 5 measures, the researchers could relate earlier spanking to later levels of aggressiveness.

The results suggest that spanking increases children's aggressiveness (Taylor et al., 2010). Mothers who spanked their children more frequently at age 3 produced children who, at age 5, were more aggressive. This surely wasn't their goal; mothers who spanked were trying to establish a strict household that produced children who were well behaved. But their efforts backfired. Note that spanking predicted age 5 aggressiveness even after the effects of age 3 aggressiveness were accounted for statistically. The results, then, could *not* be explained in terms of the child's personality trait of aggressiveness alone. Instead, they strongly suggest that parental behavior affected the child. Psychological modeling (children saw their parents acting aggressively) was more powerful, in this case, than operant conditioning via response consequences (being spanked for unruly behavior)—just as Bandura would have predicted.

🌣 WHAT DO YOU KNOW?...

19. If punishment (operant conditioning) were more powerful than observational learning, what would be the long-term effects of spanking on children's unruly behavior and aggressiveness?

20. What are the long-term effects of spanking on aggressiveness?

Observing a Virtual Self

Preview Question

> › What is one way in which modern computer technology can enhance the power of modeling?

People are exposed to a wider range of psychological models in contemporary society than they were in the past. Centuries ago, people in rural villages learned social behaviors and professional skills by observing others who lived in their town (Braudel, 1992). By the mid-twentieth century, most people in rich countries observed people who lived all over the world, thanks to TV. Today, the Internet provides access to an unending stream of expert models on instructional videos. At any time of day or night, you can see a model changing a spark plug, riding a skateboard, or making a cheese soufflé.

Thanks to contemporary digital technology, researchers can overcome a problem that, in the past, limited the effects of psychological models—that expert models sometimes have minimal impact on individuals because the expert seems to differ so much from them. "Sure, Tony Hawk can skateboard," you might think, after watching an instructional video, "But that's because he's Tony Hawk. *I* could never do it." How can psychologists provide people with psychological models who seem similar to them?

One way to do this is through *virtual representations of the self* (VRSs; Fox & Bailenson, 2009). A VRS is a modeling display in which people observe an image that looks just like them. Here's how it's done. If you participate in a VRS study, psychologists first take a digital photo of you. They then enter the image into computer software that creates a three-dimensional visual image that looks like you. This image is displayed within a larger computer-generated environment. The image, then, is a "virtual" self. You watch this virtual self expertly engaging in actions within the computer-generated environment. This solves the problem; the expert actions are modeled by someone who looks highly similar to you: your virtual self.

In one study (Fox & Bailenson, 2009), VRSs were used to help people to improve their health by getting more exercise. Participants were assigned to one of three modeling conditions. In one, they watched a computer-based display showing someone else running on a treadmill for 5 minutes. In another condition, participants saw a virtual representation of themselves running on the treadmill for 5 minutes. In a third condition, which controlled for exposure to a VRS, participants saw a VRS just standing around for 5 minutes. (The second and third conditions are displayed in Figures 7.17a and 7.17b.) The experimenters measured the amount of exercise participants did in a 24-hour period subsequent to these video displays. They found that people who saw their VRS exercising engaged in more exercise themselves—spending more time running, playing sports, or working out in gyms (Fox & Bailenson, 2009).

figure 7.17

The self as model To provide learners with models who are similar to themselves, researchers use virtual representations of the self (VRSs). In research by Fox and Bailenson (2009), participants who saw their VRS jogging on a treadmill subsequently got more exercise than those who saw their VRS just standing around doing nothing.

What would it be like to watch a virtual version of yourself exercising?

🌀 WHAT DO YOU KNOW?...

21. One way to be your own best model would be to participate in a VRS (_____ _____ of the _____) study because watching a VRS can be highly motivating.

Biological Bases of Imitation

Preview Question

› What neural system directly contributes to organisms' tendency to imitate the behavior of others?

People's ability to learn by observing others' behavior can be explained not only at a psychological level of analysis, but also at a biological level. Our brains contain **mirror neurons,** which are cells in the brain that fire when an organism takes action and also when it observes another organism take that action (Rizzolatti, Fogassi, & Gallese, 2001). Their firing contributes to the imitation of the other organism's behavior.

Mirror neurons are located in the brain's motor cortex, which contains neural systems that control the movement of the body (see Chapter 3). Whenever you make a movement—for example, when you reach out to pick up a can of soda—neurons in the motor cortex become active and send signals to the relevant body parts. Surprisingly, some of these same motor neurons—the mirror neurons—also become active merely when you observe *someone else* make that same movement. Their activity provides the brain with an automatic "copying" mechanism (Iacoboni et al., 1999). When you observe someone else perform a motor movement, mirror neurons automatically prepare your body to make that same movement.

Mirror neurons originally were discovered in research with monkeys (Rizzolatti et al., 2001). Experimenters recorded neural activity in monkeys' brains during two activities: (1) when they themselves picked up a piece of food, and (2) when they observed someone else (either a human or another monkey) pick up a piece of food. The activities—taking action oneself and observing someone else perform that action—are quite different. Yet, remarkably, researchers discovered that a set of neurons—the mirror neurons—fire in the same manner during *both* activities (Figure 7.18).

Importantly, these mirror neurons did *not* fire when the monkeys merely observed a piece of food, or observed a hand making a grasping movement when there was no food in sight, or when they observed a piece of food being picked up with pliers instead of by hand. The mirror neurons were highly selective. They fired only when the monkey observed the action of a hand picking up the food. This shows that mirror neurons are highly specialized. Each mirror neuron is designed to mirror a particular motor movement (in this case, the picking up of an object with one's hand).

Further research revealed mirror neurons at work in humans (Iacoboni et al., 2009). Researchers observed people's brain activity while they performed a simple task: lifting their index finger. They told participants exactly when to lift their finger by showing either of two displays on a video screen: (1) a hand in motion, lifting one of its fingers, or (2) a symbol (a letter X) that appeared on a static picture of a hand (Figure 7.19).

Although the task that participants performed in the two conditions was the same (raising a finger), brain activity in the two conditions differed. Brain activity was higher when participants moved their finger while observing a moving hand than when they looked at a static picture of a hand (Iacoboni et al., 2009). Observing a motor movement by someone else (the hand lifting one of its fingers) automatically activated the participants' mirror neuron system. This result thus showed that there is a system in the brain, the mirror neuron system, specifically dedicated to copying observed actions.

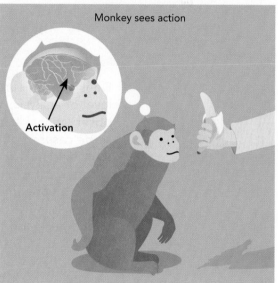

figure 7.18

Mirror neuron system The same neural system in the monkey's brain—the mirror neuron system—is active when the monkey grasps a banana or when the monkey observes someone else grasp a banana. Thanks to the mirror neuron system, it is easy for the monkey to imitate someone else's actions.

mirror neurons Neurons in the motor cortex that fire not only when an organism engages in an action, but also when it observes another organism engaging in that same action.

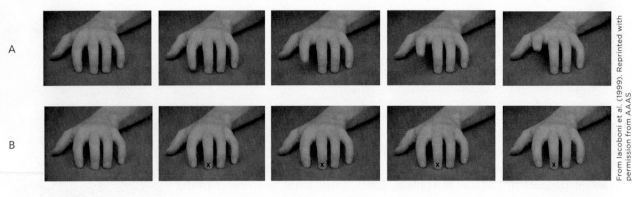

A

B

From Iacoboni et al. (1999). Reprinted with permission from AAAS

figure **7.19**

Mirror neuron research Participants in research on mirror neurons saw these pictures. Sometimes they were instructed to lift their finger after seeing someone else's finger lifted (i.e, when viewing the images shown in Row A). Other times, they were to lift their finger when a small letter X indicated which finger they should lift (Row B). In both cases, then, they (1) received an instruction and (2) lifted their finger. So you might expect that, in both cases, their brain activity would be the same. But it differed: The photos in Row A, which display movement by another person, uniquely activated the participants' mirror neuron system.

Mirror neurons may explain a variety of common, and sometimes puzzling, behaviors in animals and people. Why do birds instantly fly away when observing one bird taking flight? Why do people yawn when they observe someone else yawn? In these and innumerable other cases, observing an action may automatically activate neurons that mirror the action being observed.

THINK ABOUT IT

Does mirror neuron research explain, at a brain level of analysis, earlier research findings on observational learning? Or does it only explain *some cases* of observational learning? Recall that Bandura's analysis of observation learning included complex mental processes (storing, and drawing upon, mental representations of behavior observed in the past) that seem to go beyond the phenomena addressed in mirror neuron research.

WHAT DO YOU KNOW?...

22. When you observe someone else perform a motor movement, the _____ neurons in your brain automatically prepare your body to make that same movement.

↩↪ Looking Back and Looking Ahead

The psychology of learning illustrates a main theme of our book. A recent advance in the field, as you've seen, is that researchers can identify the biological bases of learning in the brain. But to achieve this biological advance, they first needed *psychological* advances. Pavlov's earlier discovery of classical conditioning, Skinner's explorations of operant conditioning, and Bandura's research on observational learning established principles of learning that were psychological. Only after these principles were in place could researchers move down a level of analysis, to the biology. Once they did so, their efforts produced an integrative, multilevel understanding of how organisms, including people, learn.

You'll see the fruits of their efforts elsewhere in this book. Basic researchers and applied psychologists use learning principles to motivate people (Chapter 11). Personality psychologists use them to understand how personality develops (Chapter 13). Therapists employ those principles to foster psychological change (Chapter 15). Because most everyday activities involve learning, the implications of the psychology of learning are far-reaching.

Chapter Review

Now that you have completed this chapter, be sure to turn to Appendix B, where you will find a **Chapter Summary** that is useful for reviewing what you have learned about learning.

Key Terms

acquisition (p. 266)
biological constraint (p. 293)
blocking (p. 273)
classical conditioning (p. 260)
compensatory response (p. 271)
conditioned response (CR) (p. 262)
conditioned stimulus (CS) (p. 262)
conditioned taste aversion
    (Garcia effect) (p. 275)
discrimination (p. 268)
discriminative stimulus (p. 290)
extinction (p. 269)
fixed schedule of reinforcement (p. 287)

generalization (p. 267)
habituation (p. 270)
interval schedule of reinforcement
    (p. 287)
law of effect (p. 282)
learned helplessness (p. 273)
learning (p. 260)
mirror neurons (p. 301)
negative reinforcement (p. 283)
observational learning (modeling)
    (p. 297)
operant conditioning (p. 279)
positive reinforcement (p. 283)

preparedness (p. 275)
punishment (p. 284)
ratio schedule of reinforcement
    (p. 287)
reinforcer (p. 283)
schedule of reinforcement (p. 287)
shaping (p. 291)
Skinner box (p. 286)
spontaneous recovery (p. 269)
unconditioned response (UR) (p. 262)
unconditioned stimulus (US) (p. 262)
variable schedule of reinforcement
    (p. 287)

Questions for Discussion

1. Classical conditioning occurs when a CS helps us predict the occurrence of a US. Name a CS that would help you predict each of the following: a fire, the loud noise of an explosion, the burn of a slap across your face. Given these examples, what might be the evolutionary adaptiveness of classical conditioning? [Comprehend, Apply, Analyze]

2. Have you ever noticed that beer advertisements rarely make reference to qualities of the beer itself? Instead, they use classical conditioning to make you feel positively about their products. Explain how the ads do this by identifying the US, UR, CS, and CR for a typical beer ad (or come up with one of your own). [Comprehend, Apply]

3. Imagine that, as a child, you had been attacked by a Rottweiler so that you now have a classically conditioned fear of all Rottweilers (alternately, if you have had a similar experience, think about it). To what other stimuli might you generalize this fear? What might be adaptive about this generalization? What would cause your fear to become extinct? What might be adaptive about this extinction? [Comprehend, Apply]

4. The Garcia effect occurs when we come to associate a food with sickness, so that we never want to eat that food again. But why must the food be unusual? Why can't it be some food for which we have many existing experiences? [Analyze]

5. In your own words, what distinguishes classical from operant conditioning? [Analyze]

6. Recall that in Maier and Seligman's (1976) research on learned helplessness, one group of dogs quickly learned to avoid electric shock by jumping from one side of a box to another, whereas the other group had earlier learned they were helpless to avoid the shock and so did nothing. For the non-helpless group of dogs, specify the US, UR, CS, and CR. [Comprehend, Analyze]

7. People often confuse the terms negative reinforcement and punishment. What can you do to avoid this confusion? What examples can you draw on for help? [Comprehend, Analyze]

8. Identify two discriminative stimuli you have experienced so far today. What behavior-reinforcement contingencies did they signal? Did they work? (What does "work" mean in this context?) [Comprehend, Apply]

9. In this chapter, you've learned about three processes through which individuals learn: classical conditioning, operant conditioning, and observational learning. Of these three, is there one in particular that can best explain your particular music preferences? Is some combination of the three useful? Explain. [Apply, Analyze, Evaluate]

Chapter Review

Self-Test

1. Which of the following could be an unconditioned stimulus for fear?
   a. An electric shock
   b. A snake
   c. A spider
   d. A rat

2. Which of the following concepts or studies can best explain how individuals may acquire phobias?
   a. Bandura's "Bobo doll" study
   b. Conditioned taste aversion (the Garcia effect)
   c. Watson and Rayner's Little Albert study
   d. Kandel's work with *Aplysia*

3. In the process of classical conditioning, the conditioned response is often the same as the unconditioned response. What changes now is that the CR is _____.
   a. triggered by the CS
   b. triggered by the US
   c. followed by the CS
   d. followed by the US

4. According to Garcia and Koelling's research on conditioned taste aversion, you could be conditioned to dislike a given food (CS), even if it were paired with a US
   a. only once.
   b. after a delay.
   c. repeatedly.
   d. Both a and b are correct.

5. You learned pottery by watching your teacher, which is an example of _____. As you practiced, you derived immense satisfaction from improvements in your pots and consequently, you got quite good at it, which is an example of _____.
   a. operant conditioning; observational learning
   b. observational learning; operant conditioning
   c. classical conditioning; operant conditioning
   d. operant conditioning; classical conditioning

6. Punishment is to _____ a behavior as reinforcement is to _____ a behavior.
   a. modifying; altering
   b. continuing; discontinuing
   c. modifying; discontinuing
   d. discontinuing; continuing

7. You opened an umbrella when it started to rain because, when you've done so in the past, the rain stopped falling on you. This is an example of _____.
   a. positive punishment
   b. negative reinforcement
   c. positive reinforcement
   d. negative punishment

8. Bringing an umbrella with you every day is a behavior that is reinforced on which of the following schedules?
   a. Variable interval
   b. Variable ratio
   c. Fixed interval
   d. Fixed ratio

9. Redeeming coupons is a behavior that is reinforced on which of the following schedules?
   a. Variable interval
   b. Variable ratio
   c. Fixed interval
   d. Fixed ratio

10. You would like to continue to foster a love of reading in your 9-year-old cousin. She is already an avid reader. What should you do?
    a. Leave her alone; she is intrinsically motivated.
    b. Give her a reward for every book she reads.
    c. Leave her alone; she is extrinsically motivated.
    d. Give her a reward for every third book she reads.

11. You walked into the family den on Thanksgiving to find everyone staring at the football game on television, so you waited until a commercial before starting a conversation. In this scenario, your decision to remain quiet was signaled by a
    a. conditioned stimulus.
    b. discriminative stimulus.
    c. negative reinforcer.
    d. positive reinforcer.

12. Jonah would be much happier if his roommate would learn to put his dishes in the sink. According to research described in this chapter, what technique will be most effective in this regard?
    a. Any sort of punishment; teach him what *not* to do.
    b. Observational learning; just keep modeling the appropriate behavior.
    c. Shaping; reward him for getting successively closer to the goal.
    d. Classical conditioning; teach him to fear dirty dishes.

13. If Skinner had been right, after the children in Bandura's (1965) Bobo doll studies observed the model interact with Bobo, what behaviors would they have engaged in?
    a. Whatever behaviors they found personally reinforcing
    b. The same as those of the model, but only if she had been reinforced
    c. Whatever behaviors they found personally punishing
    d. The same as those of the model, but only if she had been punished

14. Which of the following findings contradict what Skinner would have predicted?
    a. There are biological constraints on learning.
    b. Reinforced behaviors tend to recur.
    c. Children who are spanked later become more aggressive.
    d. Both a and c contradict Skinner's predictions.

15. Which of the following findings, if true, would support the idea that mirror neurons are highly specialized? Neural activity in monkeys' brains was similar when they picked up a piece of food and when they
    a. observed a hand making a grasping movement when there was no food in sight.
    b. observed another monkey pick up a piece of food.
    c. observed a piece of food being picked up by pliers instead of a hand.
    d. merely observed a piece of food

Answers

You can check your answers to the preceding Self-Test and the chapter's What Do You Know? questions in Appendix B.

Thinking, Language, and Intelligence

IN CHITA, A CITY IN EASTERN SIBERIA, RUSSIA, a young child grew up without normal human contact. Natasha, as the girl was known, was raised in isolation in one room of an apartment. Adults living in other rooms had no contact with her except to drop off food. Her only companions were some cats and dogs. When police discovered her at the age of 5 in 2009, Natasha "had the clear attributes of an animal" (Halpin & Booth, 2009). She jumped at people and lapped up food from plates. She could understand Russian but could not speak it. Having grown up with dogs, she "tried to communicate through barking instead."

In 1922 the Irish novelist James Joyce began the work that he considered his greatest. Joyce already had mastered English literature; his recently completed novel *Ulysses* had been hailed as "a work of high genius" (Wilson, 1922). Indeed, Joyce had so mastered the English language that, for his next book, he decided to do the seemingly impossible: invent a new language—an idiosyncratic language, or *idioglossia*. After years of effort, he completed *Finnegans Wake* in a language of his own creation:

What clashes here of wills gen wonts, oystrygods gaggin fishy-gods! Brékkek Kékkek Kékkek Kékkek! Kóax Kóax Kóax! Ualu Ualu Ualu! Quaouauh! Where the Baddelaries partisans are still out to mathmaster Malachus Micgranes and the Verdons cata-pelting the camibalistics out of the Whoyteboyce of Hoodie Head.

In San Diego, California, in the 1970s, a pair of infant twins was raised in relative isolation. Their grandmother provided for their physical needs, but did not interact with them socially. The twins had no contact with other children. Their low intelligence test scores at age 5 caused some to conclude that they were mentally impaired. Like Natasha, the twins had not learned to speak their native language. But like Joyce, they invented an entirely new language of their own—an idioglossia. Seemingly without effort, they conversed with each another in this language of their own creation:

"Pinit, putahtraletungay."
"Nis, Poto?"
"Liba Cabingoat, it."

Quaouauh! Where the Baddelaries partisans are still out to mathmaster. . . .
What clashes here of wills gen wonts, oystrygods gaggin
Brékkek Kékkek Kékkek Kékkek! Kóax Kóax Kóax! Ualu Ualu. . . ."

"Pinit, putahtraletungay."
"Nis, Poto?"
"Liba Cabingoat, it."
"La moa, Poto?
"Ya" . . . ."
"Finish, potato salad hungry."
"This, Poto?"
"Dear Cabengo, eat."
"Here more, Poto?"
"Yeah."

"La moa, Poto?"

"Ya."

The children, who called each other Poto and Cabengo, were conversing while eating potato salad. Translated, they said ("Education," 1979):

"Finish, potato salad hungry."

"This, Poto?"

"Dear Cabengo, eat."

"Here more, Poto?"

"Yeah."

Why did Natasha, who possessed a biologically normal human brain, not have normal human abilities to think and use language? Why were the twins—who were uneducated and socially isolated—so *un*like Natasha and, instead, more like Joyce? What do these cases teach us about the powers of the mind and the role of social experience in the development of these powers? These are the sorts of questions you will encounter in this chapter on thinking, language, and intelligence. ◎

LET'S BEGIN THIS CHAPTER with an exercise. Look away from this page and stop thinking; try not to think about anything for as long as you can. When a thought pops into your mind, return to the reading. Good luck.

Welcome back. I suspect you weren't away for long. It's hard to stop thinking! Some thought or another—even if it was just the thought that "I'm not supposed to be thinking"—probably came to mind soon after you tried to stop.

In this chapter, we'll discuss the ever-present phenomenon of thinking. We'll do so by exploring different types of thinking: *categories* people use to identify what they're thinking about; *language,* the tool we use for so much of our thinking; the *reasoning, judgment, and decision making* that occur when we choose among options; *problem solving* when we seek solutions to difficult challenges; and thinking in pictures, or *mental imagery.* Finally, we'll address the nature of human intelligence.

Most of this chapter is devoted to the mind—specifically, to mental processes in thinking, language, and intelligence. But we'll also move down to a brain-level analysis, so you can see how people's ability to think can be understood at the levels of mind and brain. In particular, we will discuss language and the brain, and the biology of intelligence.

Categorization

If your psychology instructor held in her hand a thin rectangular metal object with a video screen and it suddenly started to ring, you wouldn't think, "Hey, look at that, a ringing piece of metal with a video screen." You'd think it's her "smartphone." If she was carrying 500 sheets of paper bound together with some cardboard on the top, bottom, and one side, you wouldn't think, "Look at all that paper and cardboard." You'd think it's "a book." If she was accompanied by a short-legged, midsize, mixed-breed Labrador/basset hound, your first thought probably would not be "It's a mammal" or "It's a short-legged, midsize, mixed-breed Labrador/basset hound." You'd think it is "a dog."

All this might sound kind of obvious. Yet these simple examples illustrate a critical fact about thinking: People *categorize* objects and events. To **categorize** something is to see it as a *type* of thing, that is, as a member of a group. Almost every time you

Deep in thought Rodin's *The Thinker* looks like he can hardly stop himself from thinking about something. That doesn't make him unusual, though; it's hard for anybody to stop thinking.

ClassicStock / Alamy

Scattergories Categorization is so much fun, they made a game about it!

The Photo Works

categorize To classify an item as a *type* of thing, that is, a member of a group.

see anything—a person, plant, animal, object, or event—you recognize it as a member of a category. Even in those rare cases when you can't immediately categorize an object (see photo), the rarity tells you that 9999 times out of 10,000, categorization is easy.

Let's explore two ways in which categories differ: (1) category *level* and (2) category *structure*.

Hard to categorize A science fiction creature? A weird fungus? It's actually a star-nosed mole, a small mammal that lives in Canada and the northeastern United States. Sometimes you don't know how to categorize something. But that experience is very rare. Usually, we confidently and quickly categorize the people, places, events—and animals—of daily life.

Todd Pusser / Nature Picture Library

Category Levels

Preview Question

> What categories are most natural to use?

Consider three categories we just mentioned: (1) mammal, (2) dog, and (3) mixed-breed Labrador/basset hound. "Dog" is a higher-level category than "mixed-breed Labrador/basset hound" because all mixed-breed Labrador/basset hounds are dogs. Similarly, "mammal" is a higher-level category than "dog" because all dogs are mammals. Categories 1–3 are ordered from highest to lowest.

Category level thus refers to a relation between categories in which low-level categories are contained within (i.e., are subsets of) higher-level ones (Rosch, 1978). Compared to higher-level categories, lower-level categories are relatively narrow and specific, and they contain fewer members. Among the animals of the world, far fewer are "mixed-breed Labrador/basset hounds" than "dogs" or "mammals."

> What did you have for dinner last night? How would you describe it if you used too high-level a category?

The psychologist Eleanor Rosch (1978) explained that some category levels seem more natural to us than others. Some, in other words, come to mind spontaneously, whereas others are rarely used. Suppose a friend purchases a new item—the one in the photo. You probably would not say, "Hey, you got a new vehicle." The category "vehicle" is unnaturally high. You also are unlikely to say, "Hey, you got an all new 2015 black Honda Fit with alloy wheels." That category is unnaturally low. You would probably use a middle-level category, saying, "Hey, you got a new car."

Middle-level categories that we use naturally are called *basic-level categories*. **Basic-level categories** are moderately abstract categories that combine two qualities: informativeness and efficiency (Rosch, 1978). You call your friend's vehicle a "car" and (returning to an earlier example) your professor's animal a "dog" because the basic-level categories "car" and "dog" efficiently provide enough information for most purposes.

Max Herman / Alamy Live News

New car One could call it "a vehicle." A Honda engineer might call it a "Honda Fit with 1.5 liter 16-valve engine." But if a friend pulled up driving this, you would likely describe it by using the basic-level category "car." For most purposes, basic-level categories provide sufficient information in an efficient manner.

🐦 WHAT DO YOU KNOW?...

1. Place the following three items in order of higher- to lower-level categories: chair, furniture, and stool.
2. Of the above items, which is at the basic level?

See Appendix B for answers to What Do You Know? questions.

category level A relation between categories; one category is of a lower level than another when all members of the former category are contained within the latter, higher-level category.

basic-level categories Categories that are informative and efficient, and that thus are used most commonly to categorize items.

Categorization is not to be taken lightly. There is nothing more basic than categorization to our thought, perception, action, and speech. Every time we see something as a *kind* of thing . . . whenever we intentionally perform any *kind* of action . . . and any time we either produce or understand any utterance of any reasonable length, we are employing . . . categories. Without the ability to categorize, we could not function at all.

—George Lakoff (1987, pp. 5–6)

Category Structure

Preview Question

> What is the structure of categories?

How do we know if an item fits into a category? **Category structure** refers to the rules that determine category membership. Different categories have different structures, that is, different types of rules. You can see this with a simple exercise. Perform these two tasks:

Task #1: Categorize the following numbers into the categories "odd" or "even":

17

44

100

53

9

Task #2: Categorize the following into the categories "educational" or "entertaining":

a calculus lecture

The Simpsons

a documentary movie

a trip to an art museum

a Rachael Ray cooking show

The instructions were the same, yet the tasks differed. In #1, categorizations were clear-cut; every item fit unambiguously into one category or the other. In #2, some items were clear-cut—calculus is educational; *The Simpsons* is pure entertainment—but others were ambiguous. Rachael Ray is entertaining, but you learn a little something, too.

The categories "odd" and "educational" (or "even" and "entertaining") have different types of structure. "Odd" has a clear-cut boundary; there are no ambiguous cases. "Educational" does *not* have a clear-cut boundary; rather, experiences vary in the degree to which they are educational, and sometimes it is hard to tell whether an example belongs in the category or not. Let's look at three types of category structure: *classical, fuzzy,* and *ad hoc.*

CLASSICAL CATEGORIES. **Classical categories** have rules that determine membership unambiguously. There are no "in-between" cases; items clearly fit into a category or not. This category structure is called "classical" because it has been discussed since the classical era of ancient Greece by writers such as Aristotle (1963 CE/350 BCE).

"Odd" and "even" are classical categories. The defining feature for "even," for example, is "a whole number that, when divided by 2, results in a whole number." If a number has that feature, it is even; if not, it is not. Another example is "bachelor." If you are a man and not married, you are a bachelor; otherwise, you're not. There are no in-between cases. Examples discussed in the classical era by Aristotle include location (if you are "in the market," you cannot be anywhere else) and time (e.g., "yesterday" identifies a clear-cut time period).

FUZZY CATEGORIES. The boundaries of many everyday categories are "fuzzy" rather than clear-cut. **Fuzzy categories** have boundaries that are ambiguous; it can be difficult to tell whether an item is a member of the category or not.

You've already seen a fuzzy category: "educational." Was the Rachael Ray show educational? Maybe no (it's not as educational as calculus), but maybe yes (you do

category structure The rules that determine category membership.

classical categories Categories whose boundaries are unambiguous due to clear-cut rules for determining category membership.

fuzzy categories Categories whose boundaries are ambiguous.

learn something). Another example is the category "athletes." Soccer players are athletes. But what about race car drivers? Pool players?

A philosopher, Ludwig Wittgenstein (1953), first explained how categories violate the classical structure. When looking closely at how people actually use categories, he explained, you rarely see explicit rules and sharp boundaries like those that define even/odd or bachelor. Instead, rules are subtle, ambiguous, and used flexibly. He gave the example of the category "game." What defines the category? It's hard to say. Checkers and Monopoly are games—but so are the strategic military exercises known as "war games." Politics, romance, and life itself could be said to be games. The category structure has no sharp boundaries.

Wittgenstein suggested that categories have a **family resemblance** structure: Category members share many features, but no single feature is absolutely necessary for membership in the category. Category members are like members of a family (Figure 8.1); they are similar without necessarily sharing any one feature. The category "game" is like this. There is no one thing an activity must have to be a member of the category—not pieces, or a board, or a ball, or competitors you play against (solitaire is a game). Yet "games" have enough shared features that we can immediately tell that some things are games (football, Monopoly) and others are not (coughing, dreaming).

> Have you ever tried to define what art is? Do you think this a category for which the concept of *family resemblance* is useful?

Eleanor Rosch proposed a related idea: *prototype* structure. In a **prototype structure,** a category is defined by its most typical, central member. That member is the **prototype,** the "clearest case of category membership" (Rosch, 1978, p. 36). Individual items are closer or farther from the category's center, depending on their resemblance to the prototype.

A category with prototype structure is "chair." A wooden chair, of the sort you might find at a kitchen table, is a prototypical chair; it's at the center of the category. A large vinyl bag filled with small pieces of foam also is a member of the category "chair"—it's a "bean bag" chair—but it is far from the category's center; it is low in prototypicality.

> What does the prototypical dog look like?

figure 8.1

Family resemblance In many everyday categories, category members resemble one another, but there is no one quality that items absolutely must have to be in the category. In this case, the category is literally a family; the people resemble each other, though there is no one feature (nose size, hair color, glasses, ear size, or mustache) that they all possess.

> **Eleanor Rosch,** who developed a highly influential prototype analysis of category structure.

family resemblance A category structure in which category members share many features but no single feature is absolutely necessary for membership.

prototype structure A category structure in which category membership is defined according to the resemblance of items to a central, most typical member (the prototype).

prototype The most typical, central member of a category.

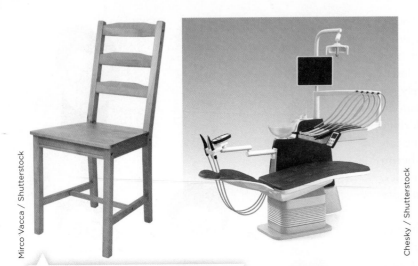

Mirco Vacca / Shutterstock

Chesky / Shutterstock

A chair and . . . um . . . a chair Both objects belong to the category "chair." But the chair on the left is prototypical of the category, while the dental chair on the right resides in the category's fuzzy periphery. People more quickly identify the one on the left as belonging to the category "chair."

Prototypical pop star Aimi Eguchi, the "ultimate love bomb," was a member of the Japanese pop group AKB48. She sang, appeared in magazines and TV commercials, and was gaining popularity—until it was revealed that she didn't exist (http://abcnews.go.com/Technology/fake-japanese-pop-star-surprises-fans/story?id=13926819). Aimi was a prototype. She was a computer-generated image with facial features that were based on each of six real people in the group, making her the group's most prototypical member.

The Photo Works

ad hoc categories Categories whose structure is defined according to the relevance of items to a goal; items in the category are useful for some common purpose.

When you think about categories, your thoughts reflect the prototypicality of its members (Rosch, 1978). Think of a bird. Now think of another. And another. If you're like most people, the first one that came to mind was a prototypical bird (e.g., a robin). If you thought of one low in prototypicality (penguin, ostrich), it probably wasn't until the second or third bird. When listing examples of a category, people tend to mention prototypical members first.

Prototypicality also influences the speed of thinking. When judging whether items belong to a category, people make judgments about prototypical items more quickly. Consider the category "sex." People more quickly judge that prototypical items (lust, arousal) are category members than less prototypical items (candles, bed). Response speed also reveals individual differences; people with a stronger heterosexual orientation more quickly judge that "reproduction" is a member of the category (Schwarz, Hassebrauck, & Dörfler, 2010).

Prototypes also affect emotions. People like prototypical members more. This is true even for abstract categories. When participants viewed random patterns of dots, they liked the patterns that were similar to the most typical, average dot pattern—the prototype (Winkielman et al., 2006).

Prototypes can vary across cultures. Consider, for example, the category "good person." To find out if its prototype structure varies, researchers asked people from a variety of countries to list the qualities they associate with a "good person" (Smith, Smith, & Christopher, 2007). Ethical and moral qualities such as honesty, kindness, and caring for others were part of the prototype universally. Yet there were also cultural differences. For example, in Taiwan but not in the United States, being self-directed and achievement-oriented was central to the category "good person."

AD HOC CATEGORIES. Not all categories have classical or fuzzy structures. **Ad hoc categories** are groupings of items that go together because they relate to a goal that people have in a specific situation (Barsalou, 2010). The phrase *ad hoc* means "for this"; ad hoc categories thus contain items that are all useful for some common purpose.

The following example (from Little, Lewandowsky, & Heit, 2006) shows why ad hoc categories need to be included among the types of category structures. Consider these items:

Pictures

Cats

Children

Jewelry

Money

Documents

Do these items strike you as members of any one category? They would if a house caught fire. They are members of the category "things to save from a burning house." This ad hoc category has a meaningful structure, but it isn't classical or fuzzy; there are no clear-cut classical boundaries and no prototypical item. Ad hoc categories, then, are unique—distinctive ways in which people group together people, places, and things on specific occasions.

You may have noticed that the categories we have discussed—"bachelors," "birds," "chairs," "things to save from a burning house"—were identified using words; they were language-based. Not all categories use language. For instance, you can categorize the sounds of musical instruments without being able to describe them in words. (If asked what a guitar sounds like, you wouldn't have much to say except, "Um, like a guitar.") But most of the time, categorization and language are intertwined. Let's turn, then, to the psychology of language.

PhotoStock-Israel / Alamy

Ad hoc category These items don't fit into any standard category. They have no family resemblance, and there is no single prototype that they resemble. Yet they are members of a category—the ad hoc category "things to take on a camping trip."

THINK ABOUT IT

Most categories involve words. So which do you think came first: the category or the word? Do you first formulate an idea and then learn a word for it, or do you first learn a word and then its meaning (the category of things to which it refers)? (We'll talk about this later in the chapter, in the section on language and thought.)

WHAT DO YOU KNOW?...

3. Match the category on the left with its corresponding type on the right.

1. Sculpture   a. Classical
2. Pregnant   b. Fuzzy
3. Items in a salad   c. Ad hoc

4. For the category you labeled as fuzzy, what is an example of its prototype?

Language

In everyday speaking, a "language" is a system of communication used by people from a specific region or culture. Mandarin, Hindi, Spanish, and English, for example, are languages—the four with the most native speakers.

What Do We Mean by "Language"?

Preview Question

> Do dogs use language?

In psychology, however, the word "language" usually does not refer to a specific language, but to language in general: the ability to communicate using the words and rules of a language. **Language** is a communication system in which sounds, or non-auditory symbols such as hand gestures, have meaning (Hauser, Chomsky, & Fitch, 2002). In psychology, the branch of the field that studies how people communicate meaningfully through the use of language is known as *psycholinguistics*.

Language is not the only way that organisms communicate. Bacteria communicate by sending chemical signals (Pai & You, 2009). Animals communicate about their personal territory by leaving scents; that's what your dog is doing when stopping at every tree in the neighborhood. However, these are not examples of

language A communication system in which sounds have meaning and rules govern the way in which linguistic units (e.g., words) can be combined.

Two ways to communicate Both signs communicate the same information, but only the one on the left uses language. It conveys the same information as the sign on the right, but does so through a set of marks that look nothing like a person slipping and falling.

Keith Bell / Alamy

A. Aleksii / Shutterstock

language, which has two properties that distinguish it from these other forms of communication:

1. *Arbitrary relation between words and things:* The relation between the sounds of words and the objects to which they refer is often arbitrary (Brown, 1958). Consider "cat" and "dog." The words don't sound like the sounds made by cats and dogs. In print, they don't look anything like a cat or dog. Yet they refer to these animals.

2. *Generativity:* A language's rules are **generative,** which means that they can be used to produce (or "generate") an infinite number of sentences—including sentences

> The exception to this arbitrariness is onomatopoeia: when words sound like the concepts they're meant to convey, such as "giggle" and "hiccup."

that no one has ever uttered before. For example, not only is "The big dog chased the cat" a sentence, but so are "The big dog chased the cat who had chased the mouse," "The big dog chased the cat who had chased the mouse that had eaten the cheese," "The big dog chased the cat who had chased the mouse that had eaten the cheese that belonged to a man," "The big dog chased the cat who had chased the mouse who had eaten the cheese that belonged to a man who owned a small dog that chased another cat who chased another mouse that had eaten cheese owned by another man," and so forth. The list of potential sentences is endless.

Now let's see how this unique mechanism of communication, language, is organized.

> **☾ WHAT DO YOU KNOW?...**
>
> 5. The idioglossia between the isolated twins, described in the chapter opening, is an example of language because of the arbitrariness of the relation between the _____ of the words and objects to which they refer and because they could use the words to generate sentences that no one had ever heard before, a concept called _____.

The Structure of Language

Preview Questions

› How is language organized?
› What do the rules of syntax do?

generative A characteristic of language referring to the fact that linguistic rules enable speakers to produce (or "generate") an infinite number of sentences.

Language is highly structured. You can't make any sounds you want and expect to be understood. You must follow language's rules—and there are a lot of them, at multiple levels of organization. This sounds hard, yet it turns out to be easy. One of our mind's most amazing powers—one you probably took for granted before now—is the ability to effortlessly follow multiple rules, at multiple levels of language organization, simultaneously. Once you consider these levels of organization, you will more deeply appreciate the power of the human mind.

LEVELS OF ORGANIZATION. Suppose you want to talk about your experiences in psychology (Figure 8.2). At the highest level of organization of language, you're engaged in a *conversation*. Conversations have rules (Grice, 1975). If a friend says, "I have been feeling really depressed lately," and you reply, "Don't you love my new hat!" then you are violating a rule—the implicit rule that people should cooperate with each other when conversing.

Conversations are structured by different points of view, or conversational "positions," that people adopt (Harré & van Langenhove, 1999). At one moment, you may provide information to someone. A moment later, you may ask a question; your position shifts from "information provider" to "question asker." Different positions bring different obligations, such as to provide information or to listen carefully.

In any conversation, the meaning of statements depends on the setting in which they occur (Austin, 1962). Suppose, at a dinner table, you say, "Salt." Its meaning depends on the setting. It could be a command (to pass the salt), comment (that the food's too salty), or answer (if someone has asked what you just added to your food).

Moving down one level (Figure 8.2), language is organized into sentences. Sentences bring remarkable power. With them, you can communicate about not only your immediate environment, but also those millions of miles ("It must be cold on Pluto") and billions of years away ("The Big Bang must have been really loud"). Sentences can even refer to things that never existed ("When conversing, how do unicorns avoid poking each other's eyes out?").

At the next level down are the main parts of sentences, which are phrases. The **syntax** of a language is the set of rules that determine whether a particular series of phrases forms a sentence that is grammatically correct. Some arrangements of phrases are correct ("Psych professors tell the funniest jokes," "Psych professors wonder why people differ"), whereas others are not ("Psych professors wonder the funniest jokes"). We discuss syntax in detail below.

One more level down, phrases are made up of words. Individual words can convey meaning by themselves: "No," "Eureka."

Moving down another level, words contain parts that convey meaning. "Funniest," for example, contains two parts: "funny" plus "est," which conveys extremity. "Unhappiest" contains three parts: the emotion (happy), extremity ("est"), and a reversal of the emotional state ("un"). These parts are *morphemes*. A **morpheme** is the smallest part of a language that conveys meaning. Morphemes can be as small as a single letter—for example, the letter "s" after "professor" (Figure 8.2) conveys plurality.

Finally, at the lowest level of analysis, language consists of sounds. *Phonemes* are the smallest units of sound that convey meaning in a language. Here, too, language is organized; some sounds patterns are common in a language, whereas others are not. Different languages use different sounds. Hawaiian does not contain some sounds found in English (e.g., the sounds of the letters B or Z). The Chinese language Mandarin uses pitch (how high or low your tone of voice is) to convey meaning to a much greater extent than does English (e.g., Klein et al., 2001).

Let's now focus on one of these levels: syntax.

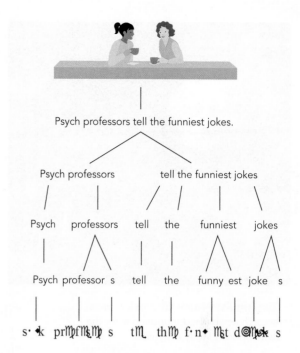

figure 8.2
Levels of organization of language
Talking is easy, yet language is highly complex. It is organized at multiple levels, ranging from conversations to speech sounds. Amazingly, your mind automatically and simultaneously keeps track of the rules that govern language at each of these levels whenever you have a conversation.

syntax The set of rules determining whether a series of phrases form a sentence that is grammatically correct.

morpheme The smallest unit of a language that itself conveys meaning; words contain one or more morphemes.

The linguist Noam Chomsky, whose research established foundations for the contemporary study of syntax.

SYNTAX AND SENTENCES. Consider this sentence: "Colorless green ideas sleep furiously." Odd though it may seem, this statement is a sentence. "Furiously green sleep ideas colorless" is not a sentence, but "Colorless green ideas sleep furiously" is.

Noam Chomsky, a linguist at the Massachusetts Institute of Technology, composed the sentence to show how syntax works. Syntactic rules, Chomsky explained, are like rules of mathematics. In a mathematical formula, you can plug in any numbers and obtain a valid answer; the area of a circle is $\pi \times radius^2$ for circles of any size. Similarly, with syntactic rules, you can plug in any noun and verb phrases and get a syntactically valid sentence. If "Crotchety old Ida sleeps fitfully" is a sentence, so is "Colorless green ideas sleep furiously."

Chomsky set out to discover the rules of syntax, that is, the rules that govern the grammatical correctness of sentences. The following sentences give you a sense of these rules:

"Psych professors tell the funniest jokes."

"The funniest jokes are told by psych professors."

"Jokes—the funniest ones—are told by professors of psych."

"It's psych professors who tell the jokes that are the funniest."

The sentences differ in their wording. Yet, at a deeper level, they're the same; they express the same concept. The first sentence says it most simply, with a *noun phrase* ("psych professors") followed by a *verb phrase* ("tell the funniest jokes"). The other sentences simply shift these components around; in the second sentence, for example, the noun phrase shifts from the sentence's beginning to its end. In the study of language, these shifts are called *transformations.*

You now can see what rules of syntax do. They specify how a core sentence such as "Psych professors tell the funniest jokes" can be transformed. A **transformational grammar** is the set of rules governing how components of a sentence can be shifted around to create other sentences that are grammatically correct. (The words "syntax" and "grammar" have overlapping meanings. Both refer to rules that govern language use. "Grammar" includes rules of syntax that determine whether a series of words is a correct sentence, as well as rules of style such as "do not split infinitives.")

These are facts about language. Here's an amazing fact about psychology: All native speakers of a language know how to use its rules of transformational grammar, *even if they cannot say what those rules are.* You know "Psych professors tell the funniest jokes" is a sentence and "Psych professors wonder the funniest jokes" is not, even if you can't identify the grammatical rule that the latter sentence violates. Furthermore, you used grammatical rules correctly at an early age, before you ever took a course on English grammar. How did you learn the syntax of your native language? This is a question of language acquisition.

---

transformational grammar The set of rules governing how components of a sentence can be shifted to create other sentences that are grammatically correct.

🐦 WHAT DO YOU KNOW?...

6. Match the examples on the left with their corresponding labels on the right.

1. -ing
2. Raising your voice at the end of a sentence to indicate you're asking a question
3. Responding to "How are you?" by saying "Do you know where my keys are?"
4. "Best book ever read this is I."

a. Violation of a rule of conversation
b. Violation of a rule of syntax
c. Morpheme
d. Phoneme

Language Acquisition

Preview Question

› How do children acquire language?

Everybody acquires language—and fast! Children know about 13,000 words before they start school (Pinker, 1999). They also can understand and produce sentences in active and passive voice, and present and past tense, before they learn what

> What do you find most difficult about learning another language?

"voice" or "tense" mean. Three types of theories have been proposed to explain how children acquire language skills.

REWARDS. The first theory is famous for being more wrong than right. The learning psychologist B. F. Skinner (1957; see Chapter 7) believed that children learn language by experiencing environmental rewards. If a child looks at a cookie and says, "Cookie," the behavior is rewarded: Adults praise the child (and may give her the cookie). Because people tend to repeat behaviors that, in their experience, have been rewarded, rewards could drive language acquisition.

But there's a problem with Skinner's theory: It cannot explain how children learn grammar even when they are *not* rewarded for doing so (Chomsky, 1959)—and they usually are not. Parents rarely reward grammar use; "in general," researchers find, "parents [seem] to pay no attention to bad syntax" (Brown, 1973, p. 412). They reward statements that are factually correct, even if grammatically flawed. Yet children learn grammar.

INNATE MECHANISMS. In a second type of theory, Chomsky (1965, 1980; Hauser et al., 2002) argued that language ability is innate. We don't "learn" grammar any more than we "learn" breathing or digestion; each is done automatically by evolved biological mechanisms (see Chapter 4). Chomsky proposed, specifically, that people inherit a mental mechanism—a "language-acquisition device" (Chomsky, 1965, p. 32)—dedicated to processing the syntax of language. Without any instructions from parents, as in the case of the isolated twins in our chapter opening, children's language mechanism extracts meaning from the speech sounds they hear.

There, of course, is some role for learning as well—children learn the specific language spoken in their society. But, in Chomsky's theory, the overall capacity to acquire language is inherited. Language, then, is an **instinct** (Pinker, 1994), that is, a behavioral tendency people possess due to biological inheritance. Birds fly, fish swim, and people talk. Even a brief experience with other speakers—a "triggering experience" (Anderson & Lightfoot, 1999, p. 698)—will switch on the inherited language mechanism.

According to Chomsky, humans' inherited language mechanism contains a **universal grammar,** which is a set of rules that enable people to understand and produce sentences. It is "universal" in that all human beings possess the grammatical ability. Chomsky therefore predicts that all human languages will have common features, including sentences containing noun and verb phrases.

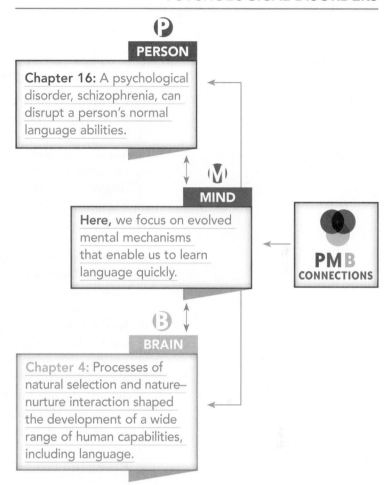

CONNECTING TO EVOLUTION AND TO PSYCHOLOGICAL DISORDERS

P PERSON

Chapter 16: A psychological disorder, schizophrenia, can disrupt a person's normal language abilities.

M MIND

Here, we focus on evolved mental mechanisms that enable us to learn language quickly.

PMB CONNECTIONS

B BRAIN

Chapter 4: Processes of natural selection and nature–nurture interaction shaped the development of a wide range of human capabilities, including language.

THINK ABOUT IT

Suppose you study a number of languages—Mandarin, Spanish, English, Arabic, French, Hindi—and find that they have grammatical features in common. Does this *prove* the hypothesis of a universal grammar (the idea that all human languages have common features)? No! There could always be some other language you haven't studied yet that does *not* have these grammatical features.

instinct A behavioral tendency possessed by an animal due to its biological inheritance.

universal grammar A set of linguistic rules that, according to Chomsky, are possessed by all humans and that enable people to understand and produce sentences.

Chomsky's proposal has been accepted widely, but not universally (see This Just In). In a third type of theory, learning plays a larger role than Chomsky envisioned, but the learning is more complex than the reward process Skinner proposed.

↻ THIS JUST IN

Universal Grammar?

By the late twentieth century, Noam Chomsky's claim that all people possess a universal grammar—"a plan common to the grammars of all languages"—was said to be "a discovery that fills linguists with awe" (Pinker, 1994, pp. 9, 14). Here in the twenty-first century, some are no longer awestruck. Evans and Levinson (2009) argue that universals are not a discovery but a "myth." They note that the world contains many languages—by one count, 6909 (http://www.ethnologue.com/)—and that neither Chomsky nor his followers checked every one of them to see if, in fact, the grammar spoken by people around the world is universal.

Evans and Levinson find variations in language grammars that are unpredicted by Chomsky. Some languages lack adverbs. Others lack adjectives. Still others appear to lack the distinction between noun and verb; for example, rather than having the verb "sing" and the noun "singers," a language may have just one word that gets embedded into surrounding phrases such as "the ones who sing" (Evans & Levinson, 2009). Furthermore, some languages have word types not found in English, that is, types of words other than nouns, verbs, adjectives, adverbs, and prepositions.

The exact structure of the world's languages is a question to be resolved by linguists, not psychologists. Yet these findings are a cautionary tale for psychology. Before looking into the mind or brain for the source of universal human tendencies, one has to be sure that they really are universal—that all the world's people, living in the world's diverse cultures, actually display the same tendencies.

☝ WHAT DO YOU KNOW?...

7. Grammar may not be as _____ as Chomsky believed. Some languages, for example, lack adjectives.

STATISTICAL LANGUAGE LEARNING. The third approach to the study of language acquisition is called **statistical language learning** (Rebuschat & Williams, 2012; Romberg & Saffran, 2010). It proposes that children acquire language by learning patterns of sounds and words they hear frequently, in other words, that are statistically common. According to statistical learning theory, then, the key mental mechanism in language learning is a general ability to distinguish between frequent and rare events.

Here's the type of question statistical language learning theory can answer. If you say "pretty baby" to a baby, how does the child know you said "pretty baby" and not "pri tee-bay bee" (i.e., three words, the second of which is formed by the letters "tyba"). The explanation, according to statistical language learning theory, is that the baby hears some sounds more frequently than others. In English, "pre" occurs at the beginning of words far more often than "tyba," and "pre" is always followed by at least one syllable to form a word. The child's mind thus automatically guesses that "pre" and "ty" go together—merely because they have gone together so frequently in the past (Saffran, 2003). Evidence suggests that not only individual words, but also grammatical rules, can be learned through experiences (Elman, 1991; Rebuschat & Williams, 2012).

statistical language learning
A theory of language acquisition proposing that people acquire language by learning patterns of sounds and words that they hear frequently, that is, that are statistically common.

Do you enjoy word jumbles? If so, your success at them is due, in part, to statistical language learning.

Statistical language learning represents "a new view of language acquisition" (Kuhl, 2000). Like Skinner's approach, it emphasizes the role of experience in learning language. But unlike Skinner, it identifies an inherent mental ability that infants possess that enables them to learn language: the ability to identify the frequency with which various speech sounds are heard. Statistical language learning differs strikingly from the approach of Chomsky. Unlike Chomsky, who proposed that knowledge of grammatical structure is innate (i.e., an inherited product of human evolution), statistical language learning theorists propose that grammar is learned through experience. This emphasis on experience suggests that, in language acquisition, culture plays a substantial role. To acquire a language, you have to coordinate your behavior with that of others in your culture (Chater & Christiansen, 2010). To communicate, you have to communicate like them.

The cases of Natasha in Siberia and of the twins in San Diego, from this chapter's opening, can be addressed from either an innate or a statistical learning perspective. Chomsky would say that the twins, who developed their own language, provided each other with "triggering experiences" that turned on their innate language mechanisms. Statistical learning theorists would suggest that the twins learned to coordinate their communications with each other. Both perspectives would predict that the isolated Natasha would fail to develop human language. She lacked a triggering experience— communication with other people. And, sadly, growing up with dogs, she learned to coordinate her vocal sounds with theirs.

> ### ✺ WHAT DO YOU KNOW?...
>
> 8. According to one theory of language acquisition, language is a(n) _____, much like flying is to birds, and we rely on a universal _____ to help us communicate. Running counter to this idea is statistical language learning, a theory suggesting that we acquire language by noticing which sounds and words are most statistically _____, a practice that requires us to coordinate our behavior with others of our _____.

◎ CULTURAL OPPORTUNITIES

Adjectives, Verbs, and Patterns of Thought

People around the world communicate by linking noun phrases to verb phrases. Are there any significant cultural differences in *how* they do this?

Philosophers provide insight into this question. They note that language is a social activity; to communicate, you must coordinate your actions (speaking, writing) with those of others (Wittgenstein, 1953). Because different cultures have different social practices, language use may vary across cultures (Wierzbicka, 1999). Evidence of differences comes from a study conducted in one Western (Melbourne, Australia) and one Eastern (Seoul, South Korea) locale.

The study's methods were simple (Kashima et al., 2006). Participants wrote descriptions of various topics—for example, their own family and a friend's family. The researchers analyzed the *types of words* people used: nouns, adjectives, state verbs (verbs describing a person's feeling at a particular time and place, e.g., "likes," "hates," "prefers"), or action verbs (verbs describing behaviors, e.g., "hugs," "argues," "talks").

The cultures differed enormously in word use (Figure 8.3). Australians used a lot of adjectives. When describing family life, for instance, about two-thirds of their statements included adjectives describing the given family. South Koreans, by contrast, hardly ever used adjectives; they used state verbs instead. Rather than writing, "The family is talkative," they would write, "The family likes talking to one another" ("like" being a psychological state experienced while talking).

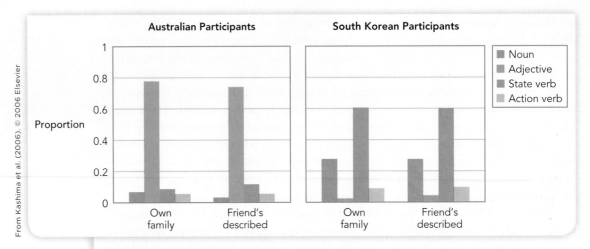

From Kashima et al. (2006). © 2006 Elsevier

figure 8.3

What's that family like? The words you use to answer that question depend on the culture in which you were raised. People from a nation with a Western culture, Australia, primarily used adjectives, which describe enduring inner traits a person possesses. People from a nation with an Eastern culture, South Korea, primarily used state verbs, which describe inner psychological states that change as people move from one situation to another (Kashima et al., 2006).

What could create these cultural differences? One possibility is cultural variations in overall patterns of thinking (Nisbett et al., 2001). In Western cultures, people tend to think about inner properties of objects that endure across time and place. When Westerners say "is talkative," they refer to an enduring inner trait of the family. In Eastern cultures, people tend to think about how people (or objects) relate to the environment in which they are located. State verbs capture these person–environment relations; to say that the family "likes" something is to describe their reaction to their circumstances.

When it comes to language use, then, culture makes a difference.

🌀 WHAT DO YOU KNOW?...

9. Given the above discussion on cultural variations in patterns of thinking and language, determine which of the sentences below was likely written by someone from a Western culture and which was likely written by someone from an Eastern culture.
   a. "My friend enjoys playing tennis with her family. Though she has doubts about her academic skills, she thinks it would be great if she could go to college nearby."
   b. "My friend is a great tennis player. She is not very confident about her academic skills, but has the goal of going to college nearby."

Language and the Brain

Preview Questions

› What did early discoveries in the study of language and the brain say about brain regions involved in producing and understanding language?
› How has contemporary brain-imaging evidence altered scientists' earlier beliefs about language and the brain?

Let's shift levels of analysis, from the mind to the brain. What parts of the brain are most involved in language use? We'll look at some early discoveries in this field of study, and then at recent brain-imaging evidence.

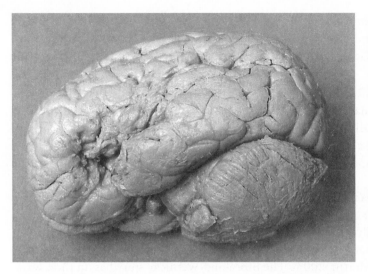

figure 8.4
Broca's patient's brain The photo on the left shows the left side of the brain of Broca's patient, Leborgne, who could understand speech but could not produce spoken words. The photo on the right is a close-up image of the brain damage, which occurred in a region that has come to be known as Broca's area.

EARLY DISCOVERIES. In the nineteenth century, French physician Paul Broca had an unusual patient. A man named LeBorgne had, Broca explained, "all the freedom of his intelligence and his movements . . . but he cannot speak" (Schiller, 1979, p. 174). He could *understand* speech; when asked a question, he gestured in ways that revealed his understanding. But he could not put his thoughts into words. LeBorgne suffered from **aphasia,** an impairment of language abilities that occurs while other mental abilities remain intact.

When LeBorgne died in 1861, Broca performed an autopsy and examined his brain (Schiller, 1979). There was disease-related damage in a region of the left frontal lobe (Figure 8.4) that, today, is known as **Broca's area.** Because the patient (1) could not speak and (2) had left-side frontal lobe damage, Broca concluded that this region of the brain is needed to produce speech (Rorden & Karnath, 2004). The study of subsequent patients confirmed his conclusion.

People with damage to Broca's area may be able to produce some meaningful speech, but their verbal output, produced with difficulty, consists only of individual words rather than grammatical sentences. When asked to describe the weather in a sentence, a patient might say merely, "Weather . . . sunny" (Geschwind, 1970).

Later in the nineteenth century, a German physician and researcher, Carl Wernicke, observed patients who could not *understand* language (Geschwind, 1970). Their hearing was intact, but words made no sense to them. Like Broca, Wernicke examined his patients' brains after their deaths. He found damage in an area different from the one identified by Broca: a region in the left temporal lobe, near the part of the brain that processes sound, which has come to be known as **Wernicke's area** (Figure 8.5).

Because patients with damage in Wernicke's area cannot understand language, they also cannot produce meaningful sentences. They are able to easily combine nouns and verbs according to rules of syntax, but their sentences are meaningless

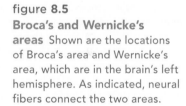

Broca's area

Left hemisphere

Wernicke's area

figure 8.5
Broca's and Wernicke's areas Shown are the locations of Broca's area and Wernicke's area, which are in the brain's left hemisphere. As indicated, neural fibers connect the two areas.

aphasia An impairment of language abilities that occurs while other mental abilities remain intact.

Broca's area A region of the frontal lobe in the left hemisphere of the brain needed to produce speech.

Wernicke's area A region in the temporal lobe of the left hemisphere of the brain needed to understand language and to produce meaningful sentences.

Think about how frustrating it is when you just don't *get* what someone is saying. Do you think this even comes close to the experience of someone with damage to Wernicke's area?

semantically. A patient might say, "I was over in the other one, and then after they had been in the department, I was in this one" (Geschwind, 1970, p. 941).

BRAIN-IMAGING EVIDENCE. These early studies of language and the brain told a simple story. The brain, it appeared, contained two specialized language devices: one that produced grammatical language (Broca's area) and one that understood it (Wernicke's area). Damage one area, and the corresponding language ability (production or understanding) is impaired.

However, brain damage is not the only relevant source of evidence. Another—unavailable in Broca's and Wernicke's day—is brain imaging. Brain images taken while people (primarily healthy volunteers with no brain damage) produce and listen to language reveals that the simple story about language and the brain was *too* simple (Bookheimer, 2002; Martin, 2003). The Broca-and-Wernicke story has, in three ways, "turned out to be wrong" (Fedorenko & Kanwisher, 2009, p. 2):

1. *Areas beyond Broca's and Wernicke's areas contribute to language.* Imaging studies reveal that a large number of interconnected brain regions, primarily in the frontal, temporal, and parietal lobes, contribute to people's ability to produce language (Bookheimer, 2002).

2. *Broca's and Wernicke's areas are involved in other mental activities in addition to language.* Contemporary evidence shows that these brain regions are not language specific; that is, they are not involved only in language understanding and production (Fedorenko & Kanwisher, 2009). For example, "language regions" of the brain are active when people perceive colors (Siok et al., 2009). When participants had to distinguish among colors presented in their right visual field, and that thus were processed on the left side of the brain (see Chapter 3), neural regions active in language processing were also active in the color perception task.

3. *Brains differ.* The Broca/Wernecke conception assumed that everybody was basically the same. Just as all people use eyes to see and ears to hear, maybe everybody uses the same anatomical areas of the brain for language. fMRI evidence, however, reveals "high levels of anatomical variability" (Fedorenko & Kanwisher, 2009, p. 2). People can differ in the exact areas of the brain that are active during language use. For example, when researchers presented sentences about hockey to people who varied in their knowledge of the sport, their patterns of brain activation differed (Beilock et al., 2008). Among expert players and long-time fans, an area of the brain involved in motor movement was also active during the processing of the sentences (Figure 8.6).

The original belief, that damage to Broca's and Wernicke's areas disrupts language, is correct. But the idea that these two brain regions are *uniquely responsible for* language is not. Broca's area and Wernicke's area are parts of the brain needed for normal language use, but they are not independently responsible for language.

figure 8.6
Expertise, language, and brain activation Researchers asked three types of people—expert hockey players, knowledgeable hockey fans, and novices unfamiliar with the game—to read sentences about actions occurring in a hockey game. Before and during reading, the researchers measured brain activity in the dorsal premotor cortex of the left hemisphere, an area of the brain involved in controlling bodily movements. Although all participants were reading the same material, their patterns of brain activation differed. Unlike novices, expert players and fans showed higher activation in the part of the brain that usually is used to control motor movements.

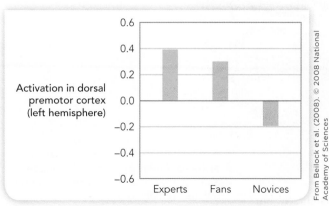

From Beilock et al. (2008). © 2008 National Academy of Sciences

b. Damage to Broca's area would only disrupt the ability to produce language.
c. Brain-imaging studies indicate that Broca's area and Wernicke's area are the only areas that contribute to language processing.
d. People differ from one another in patterns of brain activity during language use.

Animals' "Language"

Preview Question

> Why don't animals have language?

So far, we've discussed communication among human beings. What about our furry friends?

Animals definitely can communicate. Bees, for example, make movements that signal the presence of food to other bees. But is this language? Recall that language is a system in which the language-user can generate novel communications by combining symbols that are arbitrarily related to the objects to which they refer. Can animals do this?

If you observe animals, it doesn't look as if they are doing this. But maybe that's because they haven't been taught properly. The psychologist Herbert Terrace decided to find out what would happen if an animal received language training, as human do (Hess, 2008).

Terrace raised a newly born chimpanzee, which he named Nim Chimpsky (after Noam Chomsky), in a human setting: a New York City apartment populated by humans. Terrace's goal was to pit Chimpsky versus Chomsky. If Chimpsky learned language, he would disprove Chomsky's contention that language stems from a uniquely human innate brain mechanism.

Terrace knew Chimpsky would never speak like a human; chimps lack the physical ability to produce human speech sounds. But they do have manual dexterity. Terrace therefore tried to teach Nim sign language. A **sign language** is a language in which bodily movements, especially of the hands and fingers, are used to convey information. Nim was tutored in sign language day after day, year after year.

Herbert Terrace

Nim Chimpsky, who was raised in a human world. He never complained about washing dishes, but that might just be because he never learned human language.

What happened? After four years of instruction, Terrace concluded that Nim never developed true language use (Hess, 2008). He could imitate signs his teachers made. However, unlike a human child, Nim never generated *novel* combinations of signs to express ideas. Nim is not alone in the animal world; no animal has ever displayed true language use.

Human language abilities require a wide range of cognitive skills (Fitch, Hauser, & Chomsky, 2005; Pinker & Jackendoff, 2005), and Nim, and other animals, do possess *some* of them. For example, the skills of language acquisition include using symbols (words) to refer to objects in the world, remembering the meaning of the symbols, and combining them. Many animal species can perform some of these skills. A chimp named Washoe, for example, learned hand signals that symbolized "please"

sign language A language in which bodily movements, especially of the hands and fingers, are used to convey information.

Fetch Mickey Mouse After years of training, the dog Chaser learned the names of more than 1000 toys (Pilley & Reid, 2011). When commanded to get one—"goldfish," "chipmunk," "Mickey Mouse"—her ability to retrieve the correct item showed her knowledge of the words. Chaser's amazing abilities reveal that dogs can acquire one component of human language: associating names with objects in the world. But many other aspects of language are uniquely human. Human children not only learn the meanings of words; they also generate novel combinations of words that follow grammatical rules—an ability unseen in other species (Yang, 2013).

Sapir–Whorf hypothesis A conception of the relation between language and thought which claims that language shapes thinking; this hypothesis implies that people who speak different languages think differently about the world around them.

and "drink," and combined them into "please drink" (Gardner & Gardner, 1969). An African Grey Parrot learned speech sounds that referred not only to objects, but also to categories of objects (Pepperberg, 1991).

Remarkable as these animal abilities are, however, they are not the same as human language (Hauser et al., 2002). Animals fail to display language skills that are common among humans. For example, animals know which members in their pack are the dominant ones, but their vocalizations don't reflect this knowledge. They signal others with sounds but, when doing so, don't take into account the knowledge and goals of the animals to whom they're communicating, as humans do. Most important, animal communication is not generative; animals do not use rules of syntax to generate an indefinite variety of sentences, as even young human children do. "Nearly a century of intensive research" shows that "no species other than humans has a comparable capacity to recombine meaningful units into an unlimited variety of larger structures" (Hauser et al., 2002, p. 1576).

How do your pets communicate with you, if not through language?

🐾 WHAT DO YOU KNOW?...

11. Although it's true that chimps are capable of using symbols to refer to objects in the world and of combining those symbols, it is not true to say that they use language. Why?

Language and Thought

Some of the differences between languages are obvious. They sound different. Written words look different. Another difference, however, is more subtle. One language may not have a word that corresponds to a word in another language. Research on emotion words illustrates this (Wierzbicka, 1999). Tahitian contains no word that corresponds to the English word "sad." English has no word that corresponds to the Polish *przykro*, a negative emotion experienced when someone doesn't display an expected amount of affection. German does not contain a word that corresponds precisely to the English word "emotion."

These differences raise a big question: What is the relation between language and thought? When thinking about people's feelings, do speakers of Tahitian, English, Polish, and German have the same types of thoughts, or do they have fundamentally different thoughts because their languages differ? If your language doesn't contain a word corresponding to *przykro*, will you recognize the feelings of someone who did not receive an expected amount of affection?

The Sapir–Whorf Hypothesis

Preview Question

› Does language shape reality?

Two twentieth-century scholars who studied language and culture, Edward Sapir and his student Benjamin Whorf, believed that language determines the nature of thought. The **Sapir–Whorf hypothesis** (Whorf, 1956) claims that language shapes thinking, with the result that people who speak different languages think differently about the world around them. The effect of language on thinking primarily involves categorization. A language's words furnish categories that people use when they think;

therefore, speakers of different languages, which contain different words, have different thoughts. You cannot, for example, have the thought that some people are "nerds" unless you speak a language that contains the word "nerd."

If correct, this hypothesis is tremendously important for understanding human cultures. People who speak a different language than you may have a fundamentally different view of reality. Their perception of good and bad, right and wrong, may differ from yours.

Is the Sapir–Whorf hypothesis correct? Some evidence does support it. One supportive study explored how language affects the way people think about the locations of objects. In English, we say adjacent objects are to the "left" and "right" of each other. In a native Mesoamerican language spoken in Mexico, people say they are to the east and west of each other; this language employs geographic words instead of left and right. It turns out that the words affect people's interactions with objects. If you align objects, show them to people, turn the people around 180 degrees, and ask them to realign the objects, people who speak the Mesoamerican language will reverse the original left–right ordering in order to preserve their east–west ordering (Levinson, 1996). This impact of language on thought supports the Sapir–Whorf hypothesis.

Such support, however, is relatively rare (Bloom & Keil, 2001). Other evidence contradicts the Sapir–Whorf hypothesis, as we'll see now.

🐦 WHAT DO YOU KNOW?...

12. True or False?

    According to the Sapir–Whorf hypothesis, people who speak languages with a different number of color terms should think differently about colors.

Embodied Cognition

Preview Question

> What does research on the Sapir–Whorf hypothesis tell us about the effect of language on thinking?

Brent Berlin and Paul Kay tested the Sapir–Whorf hypothesis by studying people's thoughts about colors (Berlin & Kay, 1969; Kay et al., 1997). Languages vary in how many color terms they possess. A language spoken in New Guinea, for example, has only two color words: One refers to a range of greens, blues, and dark colors, and the other to white plus a range of reds, yellows, and orange (Foley, 1997). Other languages have as many as 11 color terms that all speakers use frequently. If language affects thought, people who speak languages with different numbers of color terms should think differently about colors.

> Do you know the names of every color in the room where you are now? Can you see the objects whose colors you can't name?

However, they don't. People who speak different languages think *similarly* about color. When Berlin and Kay showed participants color chips (Figure 8.7) and asked which were the best (i.e., the purest example of their general type of color), speakers of *different* languages identified the *same* colors. For example, speakers of a language with fewer than four color terms identified the same red, yellow, green, and blue chips as speakers of English. Later research confirmed these findings (Regier, Kay, & Cook, 2005). The results contradict the Sapir–Whorf hypothesis because language variations did not produce variations in thinking. Why not?

figure 8.7
Color chips Berlin and Kay showed color chips to people from different cultures who spoke languages containing different numbers of color words. Differences in language did *not* affect people's judgments about colors. The color chip that looks like the best, truest "blue" to you also tends to look best to people from other cultures who speak different languages.

The simplest explanation is that people's thoughts about color are influenced by the workings of the visual system. The human visual system responds to some shades of color more strongly than to others (see Chapter 5). The visual system is universal. As a result, there are universal tendencies in the ways in which people categorize colors (Figure 8.8).

Berlin and Kay's findings raise a broader point. Human thinking is *embodied* (see also Chapter 7). That is, when we think about abstract concepts, such as color, we use parts of the mind that evolved to relate our physical body to physical objects. Mental systems that originally evolved to help us perceive objects (to see and smell them) and to move our body toward or away from those objects are used in various forms of thinking (Barsalou, 1999; see also Chapter 6). Contrary to what Sapir and Whorf hypothesized, thinking is affected by more than just language.

🌀 WHAT DO YOU KNOW?...

13. Research indicates that people's thoughts about color are determined by the workings of the _____ system, not by language. This contradicts the _____–_____ hypothesis but supports the idea that our thinking is embodied.

Thought and Language

Preview Question

> How do we know that thought influences language?

Not only does language influence thought, but the opposite is also true: Thought influences language. People often formulate an idea that they have trouble putting into words. The idea thus exists *before* language to express the idea is formulated.

Evidence that thoughts can precede language comes from the study of gesture (McNeill, 2005). *Gestures* are bodily movements, such as motions involving the arms, hands, and fingers that convey meaning. Sometimes you may struggle to put into words a meaning that you already have communicated by gesturing; for example, if you are trying to describe the complex movements of a dancer, you might start moving your hands and arms like the dancer did before you can formulate a sentence that describes the dancer's movements in words. Some psychologists view the mind as engaged in back-and-forth dialogue between mental images and language (McNeill, 2005).

Both: Hill Street Studios / Getty Images

Communicating through gesture People communicate not only through words, but also through gestures. Sometimes the gestures convey ideas even before the words do. This suggests that some thoughts exist in the form of mental images that are then put into words.

figure 8.8

DO PEOPLE FROM DIFFERENT CULTURES SEE DIFFERENT BLUES AS THE "BEST" BLUE?

PMB IN ACTION

PERSON Ⓟ

No; people in different cultures tend to select the same color chip when asked which is the best example of the color category "blue."

MIND Ⓜ

At a mind level of analysis, the category "blue" has a prototype structure, and people across cultures recognize the same shade of blue as prototypic.

BRAIN Ⓑ

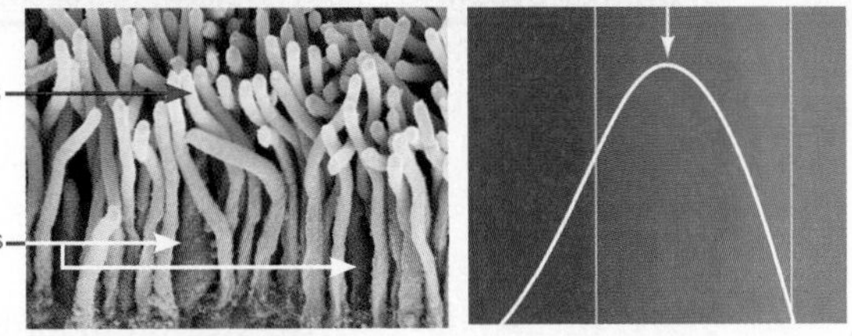

At a brain level of analysis, some "cone" cells in the retina respond maximally to a wavelength of light that corresponds to prototypic blue.

Rods
Cones

Science Photo Library / Alamy

⚡ WHAT DO YOU KNOW?...

14. Gestures are evidence that thought can precede language because (choose one):

___ a. You can use them to convey ideas even before you have the words to convey them.

___ b. You can use them to convey ideas even before your thoughts are organized enough.

TRY THIS!

The next section of this chapter discusses reasoning, judgment, and decision making. But before reading about these topics, experience some of them for yourself in this chapter's Try This! activity. It presents some of the actual problems that researchers have used to discover how people think and make decisions. Go to www.pmbpsychology. com and complete the Try This! activity for Chapter 8 now. We'll discuss it a little later in the chapter. ◉

Reasoning, Judgment, and Decision Making

As you've just seen, people are good at language. Even young children understand and produce sentences expertly. Now, however, we'll explore three types of thinking—reasoning, judgment, and decision making—in which even educated people make systematic mistakes.

Reasoning

Preview Questions

> What psychological processes get in the way of good logical reasoning?
> Do people always have difficulty with logical reasoning?

Do you read detective stories? If so, you can anticipate the climax. Before dazzled onlookers, the private eye reviews evidence, analyzes its implications logically, and draws conclusions so compelling that the criminal confesses on the spot.

The detective is engaged in **reasoning,** which is the process of drawing conclusions that are based on facts, beliefs, and experiences (Johnson-Laird, 1990). In reasoning, a person does not merely remember facts, but combines them to reach conclusions that go beyond the information that originally was perceived (Markman & Gentner, 2001).

Detective stories preview research findings in the psychology of reasoning. Notice not only the powers of the detective, but also the reactions of the onlookers: dazzled. In a good detective story, the facts are available to everyone—including the reader—but only the detective figures things out. Others are stumped. Detective stories suggest that most people aren't very good at reasoning.

Much psychological research suggests the same thing. A distinguished psychologist concluded that research on logical reasoning skills shows that people have only "a modicum of competence" (Johnson-Laird, 1999, p. 109). Why aren't we better at reasoning?

CONFIRMATION BIAS. Reasoning often is impaired by *confirmation bias.* **Confirmation bias** is the tendency to seek out information that is consistent with whatever initial conclusions you have drawn, and to disregard information that might contradict those conclusions.

> We had all listened with the deepest interest to this sketch of the night's doings, which Holmes had deduced from signs so subtle and minute that, even when he had pointed them out to us, we could scarcely follow him in his reasoning.
>
> —Arthur Conan Doyle,
> *The Treasury of Sherlock Holmes* (2007, p. 267)

---

reasoning The process of drawing conclusions that are based on facts, beliefs, and experiences, combining them to reach conclusions that go beyond the information originally perceived.

confirmation bias The tendency to seek out information that is consistent with one's initial conclusions, and to disregard information that might contradict those conclusions.

Confirmation bias can impair reasoning because your initial conclusion might be wrong. To find out for sure, you should seek out *dis*confirming evidence, that is, evidence that could disprove your guess. If you think "the man who committed the midnight murder in the hotel was the butler," you'd better be sure there's no evidence that the butler was somewhere *other than* the hotel at midnight. If you look only for confirming evidence ("the butler had a motive"), you might miss critical disconfirming evidence ("witnesses saw the butler asleep in a movie theatre at midnight").

You can see confirmation bias in action by trying an arithmetic problem (from Wason, 1960). Your job is to figure out the rule of arithmetic that generates sets of numbers. You first see three numbers that conform to the rule. You then need to suggest additional sets of three numbers that might help you determine what the rule is. After each set of three, you're told whether your numbers conform to the rule. When you think you know what the rule is, you can take a guess.

Here are the first three numbers:

2   4   6

What do you think the rule might be? And what new set of three numbers would you suggest to find out what it is?

Here's what a typical participant did. The participant would first think the rule is "a series of even numbers" and then suggest new sets of even numbers to see if they conform to the rule. "How about 8, 10, 12?" "14, 16, 18?" "20, 22, 24?" Each time, the participant learned that, yes, the numbers conform to the rule the experimenter had used. Yet the rule was *not* "a series of even numbers." The actual rule was "any three numbers arranged in order of increasing magnitude."

Participants thus displayed confirmation bias. They suggested numbers consistent with their initial guess, and failed to suggest other possibilities (e.g., 1, 3, 5) that could *dis*confirm their initial guess.

Confirmation bias is pervasive. Once people develop opinions and beliefs, they commonly seek out information that confirms their thinking (Nickerson, 1998). Social psychologists (see Chapter 12) propose, for example, that confirmation bias explains people's tendency to believe media reports are biased against their own political attitudes. When people with either pro-Israeli or pro-Arab opinions viewed identical media coverage of a conflict in the Middle East, both groups thought the coverage was biased against their point of view (Vallone, Ross, & Lepper, 1985). How could people perceive opposite biases—anti-Israeli, anti-Arab—in the same media coverage? Confirmation bias explains it. Before the broadcast began, people already expected the media coverage to be unfair. During the coverage, they attended closely to anything that confirmed this expectation. When the broadcast was over, they had better memory for this confirmatory information. Confirmation bias, then, caused everyone to conclude that the media coverage was unfair to their own point of view.

Was the media coverage fair and balanced? Research has shown that after hearing media coverage of a controversial issue, the Arab–Israeli conflict, people on both sides of the issue tended to judge that the coverage was slanted against their own views. This occurs due to confirmation bias; people notice and remember arguments that confirm their prior expectation of media bias, and thus conclude that media coverage is unfair. The same may occur in televised debates, as viewers judge whether the media is treating their favored candidate fairly.

Brendan Smialowski / AFP / Getty Images

Do you believe in ESP? What kind of information might you tend to notice and remember in support of this belief?

REASONING ABOUT EVOLUTIONARILY RELEVANT PROBLEMS.

Do people always find reasoning difficult? The psychologist Leda Cosmides doesn't think so. She notes that reasoning problems presented in research—identifying rules of arithmetic, evaluating media coverage—were not relevant during the course of human evolution. Contemporary humans might be better at reasoning when contemplating problems that their evolutionary ancestors faced.

One such problem is not getting cheated when exchanging goods (Cosmides, 1989). People have exchanged goods for thousands of years, either by trading or by using currency. In the past, they might have exchanged livestock for grain. Today, you exchange money for groceries. Throughout human history, it has been important to avoid being cheated. Evolution may have equipped people with the ability to reason accurately about problems that involve the possibility of cheating when goods are exchanged.

Cosmides tested this by presenting different problems with an identical logical structure—that is, the same relations among pieces of information. The problems, however, differed in substance, that is, in the topic being discussed:

> Some problems involved the detection of cheating in the exchange of goods. For example, one described a hypothetical cultural situation: "If a man eats cassava root, then he must have a tattoo on his face." (Participants were told that, in this culture, cassava root is an aphrodisiac and a tattoo is a sign of being married.) If you ate cassava root but had no tattoo, you would be cheating, that is, breaking the social rule of no sex outside of marriage.

> Other problems had nothing to do with cheating. For example, people checked, for a clerical job, whether documents followed this rule: "If a person has a D rating, then his documents must be marked code 'y.'"

Participants performed poorly on problems that had nothing to do with cheating (the document filing problem). However, they performed excellently when the problem involved potential cheating by the breaking of a social rule (the cassava root problem; Cosmides, 1989). On the latter task, they avoided confirmation bias.

Why are people good at solving cheating-detection problems? Cosmides suggests that evolution has produced an innate brain mechanism dedicated to the solution of problems involving the exchange of goods. Although this claim is controversial, it is consistent with a finding from brain research: Different parts of the brain are active when people reason about social exchange problems than when they reason about logically similar problems that do not involve the exchange of goods (Ermer et al., 2006).

Does Cosmides's idea sound familiar? It should. Her idea about the origins of a brain mechanism for solving problems is essentially the same as Chomsky's idea about the origins of a brain mechanism dedicated to processing grammar. Both claim that evolution gave rise to the brain mechanisms and associated mental abilities that people possess today (Buss, 2009).

🐾 WHAT DO YOU KNOW?...

15. Which of the following statements are true? Check all that apply.
   ___ a. Avoiding reading negative reviews of a cell phone you just purchased because you don't want to admit you made a poor choice is an example of confirmation bias.
   ___ b. Confirmation bias causes us to seek out all the available evidence needed to reach a conclusion, even disconfirming evidence.
   ___ c. One domain in which humans are especially good at avoiding confirmation bias is in the detection of cheating.
   ___ d. Leda Cosmides suggests that humans have evolved a brain mechanism that is responsible for reasoning about social exchange.

Judgment Under Uncertainty

Preview Question

> How do people judge the likelihood of uncertain events?

Life is full of guesses, big and small. "Will I like this new romantic comedy with computer-animated talking animals enough to spend $10 on a movie ticket?" "Will I get as good an education at moderately expensive State U as at super-expensive Private

College?" "Is the relationship I'm in 'just for now,' or really serious?" "Should I invest money in the stock market, or are stocks likely to lose value in the years ahead?" To answer each of these questions, you need to make a *judgment,* that is, you need to draw a conclusion based on an evaluation of evidence.

For each question, uncertainty exists. You don't know for sure how things will turn out. You don't even know the probability that things will turn out one way or the other: Are the chances that you'll enjoy the movie more like a 50-50 coin flip or a 100-to-1 long shot?

The question for psychology is how people make these guesses. What are the mental processes through which people make judgments under conditions of uncertainty? There are two general types of possibilities.

1. *Mind like a computer.* One possibility is that the mind works like a computer program that processes statistical information. Maybe people perform mental calculations in which their minds automatically combine large amounts of information to estimate the chances of different outcomes occurring, and their judgments are based on these calculations.

2. *Simplifying rules of thumb: Heuristics.* The second possibility is that people cannot perform computer-like calculations because of memory limitations. Human short-term memory holds only a small amount of information (see Chapter 7). It thus may be impossible for people to keep track of the large numbers of facts and figures needed to make computations in the way a computer does (Simon, 1983). Instead, people may rely on *heuristics* that simplify the task of predicting events.

A **heuristic** is a rule of thumb, that is, a simple way of accomplishing something that otherwise would be done through a more complex procedure. For example, if you are in a residential area of a big city and wish to go downtown, you could follow step-by-step directions from an Internet mapping service or you could use a heuristic: "Move toward the tallest buildings." The heuristic will get you downtown.

> What heuristic do you apply for figuring out what to order in a restaurant whose cuisine is new to you?

Judgmental heuristics are simple mental procedures for making judgments under conditions of uncertainty. Extraordinarily insightful research by Amos Tversky and Daniel Kahneman identified three judgmental heuristics that people use to make a wide variety of judgments: the availability, representativeness, and anchoring-and-adjustment heuristics (Tversky & Kahneman, 1974).

Kahneman and Tversky On the left, Daniel Kahneman in 2002 receives a Nobel Prize for his research on human judgment and decision making. Kahneman worked in collaboration with Amos Tverky, pictured on the right, who died in 1996, before the Nobel committee acknowledged their landmark contributions.

heuristic A rule of thumb, that is, a simple way of accomplishing something that otherwise would be done through a more complex procedure.

AVAILABILITY. In the **availability heuristic,** people base judgments on the ease with which information comes to mind. The rule of thumb—the heuristic—is that when information about a person, place, or thing comes to mind easily, the person, place, or thing is more common. Suppose someone asks, "Do more people have last names starting with S or Z?" You don't have to count up all the people in the world. You can instead base your judgments on availability. It's easy to think of people with *S* last names, but hard to think of many *Z* names, so the relative ease tells you that *S* names are more common.

In general, then, the availability heuristic works well. But sometimes it creates errors. This happens when factors other than actual frequency affect availability. Here's an example.

> What do you think is more common: words (of three or more letters) that start with the letter *k* or that have *k* as the third letter in the word? (Take a moment to guess.)

You probably thought something like this: "Hmm, first letter *k*; that's easy: kite, kitten, kayak, kazoo, keep, keeper, keeping, keepsake, knife, knifing, knit, knitting. . . . Geez, there's millions of 'em. *K* in third position . . . um . . . Bake, rake, make . . . um . . . ark." Words *starting* with *k* come to mind easily. Most people, relying on the availability heuristic, thus say that words starting with *k* are more common. But in reality, words with *k* as the third letter are more common. The fact that we organize our "mental dictionary" according to words' first letters makes them more available mentally, despite their being less frequent in reality.

REPRESENTATIVENESS. The **representativeness heuristic** is a psychological process that comes into play when people have to decide whether a person or thing is a member of a given category. When relying on representativeness, people base these judgments on the degree to which the person or object resembles the category. Suppose you meet a shy, middle-aged man wearing eyeglasses and a sweater. Do you think he is a librarian or a construction worker? If your stereotype of a librarian includes "glasses" and "sweater," you'll say "librarian." The man resembles, or is representative of, the category "librarian."

The representativeness heuristic often produces accurate judgments. However, like availability, it can cause people to make judgmental errors. Consider this example from Tversky and Kahneman (1983):

> Linda is 31 years old, single, outspoken, and very bright. She majored in philosophy. As a student, she was deeply concerned with issues of discrimination and social justice and also participated in anti-nuclear demonstrations. Which is more probable?
>
> (A) Linda is a bank teller.
> (B) Linda is a bank teller and is active in the feminist movement.

Did you say "B"? Six out of seven people did when Tversky and Kahneman asked them. But "B" is wrong because everyone who is "a bank teller and active in the feminist movement" also is "a bank teller." "B" therefore cannot be more probable than "A"; all "B"s *are* "A"s (all feminist bank tellers are bank tellers) and some "A"s are not "B"s (some bank tellers are not feminists). If the human mind worked like a statistical computer program, everyone would say "A." However, the mind instead relies on representativeness and, since Linda resembles people's conception of a feminist, most people say "B."

In general, the representativeness heuristic can produce errors when it distracts people from the *base rates* of categories, that is, the overall likelihood that any item would be in the category. Consider our librarian/construction worker example. There are 8 times more construction workers in the United States than there are librarians (www.bls.gov); the base rate of the category "construction worker" is much higher.

availability heuristic A psychological process in which people base judgments on the ease with which information comes to mind.

representativeness heuristic A psychological process in which people judge whether a person or thing belongs to a given category by evaluating the degree to which the person or object resembles the category.

So the man—even if he is wearing glasses and a sweater—may well be a construction worker.

These judgment problems should sound familiar to you; they were in this chapter's Try This! activity. If you haven't completed that yet, go to www.pmbpsychology.com and do it now.

TRY THIS!

ANCHORING AND ADJUSTMENT. The third judgmental heuristic, *anchoring and adjustment,* comes into play when people estimate an amount (e.g., "What GPA am I likely to earn next semester?" "How many people will show up at the party I'm planning?"). In the **anchoring-and-adjustment heuristic** (or just "anchoring"), people make estimates by formulating an initial guess (the "anchor") and adjusting it to reach a final judgment.

Anchoring can create judgmental errors. This happens when irrelevant anchor values bias people's judgments. Tversky and Kaheman asked participants to estimate the percentage of world nations that are African. Before participants made their estimates, the researchers spun a wheel of fortune containing numbers from 0 to 100 and asked participants to indicate whether the correct answer was more or less than the random value generated by the wheel. The anchor values were random—obviously irrelevant to the task. Yet they biased people's judgment. Participants adjusted their estimates up from low anchors and down from high ones, but the adjustments were insufficient. Those who saw a high random anchor thought that nearly twice as many of the world's nations were African as did people who first saw a low random number.

Random anchor values can affect important judgments, such as people's judgments about how much money to spend on a purchase. Just prior to an auction for an item whose value was less than $100, researchers asked bidders to write down the last two digits of their Social Security number. "Huh?"—you should be saying to yourself. "What difference would writing down a Social Security number make to an auction bid?" Due to anchoring effects, it made a big difference. People's bids were correlated with their Social Security numbers; people with higher Social Security numbers bid more money (Ariely, Loewenstein, & Prelec, 2004). The numbers came to mind, and served as anchors, when they asked themselves, "How much should I bid?"

Table 8.1 summarizes these three heuristics and reasons why reliance on heuristics can sometimes produce judgmental errors.

⚙ WHAT DO YOU KNOW?...

16. Match the examples on the left with their corresponding heuristic on the right.

1. Being willing to pay more for a shirt when it is purchased in a store with high-priced clothing than you would be willing to pay for it in a store with economy-priced clothing	a. Availability
2. Thinking you're more likely to die from a shark attack than from a vending machine falling on you because it's easier to conjure up examples of shark attacks	b. Representativeness
3. Shopping at a busy clothing store and deciding that the well-dressed, middle-aged man is a manager, even though the odds are that he is a salesperson	c. Anchoring and adjustment

anchoring-and-adjustment heuristic
A psychological process in which people formulate estimates by starting with an initial guess (an "anchor") and adjusting it to reach a final judgment.

table **8.1**

Judgmental Heuristics

Judgmental Heuristic	Question That People Typically Answer Using the Heuristic	Psychological Process	Source of Error
Availability	How frequently does it occur? (e.g., Do more words start with *k* or have *k* as the third letter?)	The ease with which information comes to mind.	Some factors that affect the ease with which information comes to mind are unrelated to frequency.
Representativeness	Is an item a member of a given category? (e.g., Is Linda a bank teller or a bank teller active in the feminist movement?)	The resemblance between the item and the category.	Representativeness can distract people from information about base rates—the overall likelihood that any item is in a given category.
Anchoring and Adjustment	How many are there? (e.g., What percentage of the world's nations is African?)	Adjustment from an initial guess.	Even irrelevant anchor values are influential, and adjustment away from them is often insufficient.

Decision Making

Preview Question

> How logically do we make decisions?

Cherry or blueberry pie? Rent a DVD or go to a movie theatre? Vacation in an exciting metropolis or a relaxing wilderness? Have surgery for your broken bone or put it in a cast and see if it heals by itself? Life presents decisions, large and small.

Decision making is the process of making a choice, that is, selecting among alternatives. Sometimes the benefits of the alternatives cannot be known for sure; you can't tell how well the broken bone will heal if put in a cast. Other times, the benefits *are* known with certainty, yet it's still difficult to decide. You know what cherry pie and blueberry pie taste like, yet it's hard to choose between them.

How do people make decisions? To understand the psychology of decision making, it's best first to consider a "standard model" of decision making and then to look at psychological factors that make the standard model inadequate. (The standard model was, for many years, the explanation of decision making in economics.)

The standard model of decision making has two components. One involves **subjective value,** the degree of personal worth that an individual places on an outcome. In the standard model of decision making, people choose the alternative available to them that has the highest subjective value. Note that subjective value can differ from objective value. Consider two cases: (1) Two people offer you a temporary one-day secretarial job; one will pay $50 and the other $75. (2) Two people offer you a three-month secretarial job; one will pay $6250 and the other $6275. In both cases, the objective difference between the offers is $25. But in #1, the difference feels big, whereas in #2, it feels small. The *subjective* value of $25 differs in the two cases.

The second component of the standard theory is that, when making decisions, people consider how their choices will affect their net worth (i.e., the overall monetary assets they possess). You might enjoy a city vacation more than a wilderness vacation. But if either vacation would wipe out your personal savings, you'll probably skip a vacation for this year.

In the standard model, people's choices are highly logical. The decision maker compares subjective values, evaluates personal worth, and calculates a logical, rational

decision making The process of making a choice, that is, selecting among alternatives.

subjective value The degree of personal worth that an individual places on an outcome.

decision. In reality, however, people aren't as logical and rational as the standard model suggests. Research by Kahneman and Tversky (1979, 1984) undermined the standard model of decision making.

FRAMING EFFECTS. A major blow to the standard model was Kahneman and Tversky's demonstration of framing effects. In a **framing effect,** decisions are influenced by the way alternative choices are described, or "framed." According to the standard model, different framings should be inconsequential, because they don't affect the actual value of alternatives. However, it turns out that framing has big effects. Consider the following two choices (from Kahneman & Tversky, 1984, p. 343):

Choice #1

Imagine that the United States is preparing for the outbreak of an unusual Asian disease, which is expected to kill 600 people. Two alternative programs to combat the disease have been proposed. Assume that the exact scientific estimates of the consequences of the programs are as follows:

- If Program A is adopted, 200 people will be saved.
- If Program B is adopted, there is a one-third probability that 600 people will be saved and a two-thirds probability that no people will be saved.

Which of the two programs would you favor, A or B?

Choice #2

Imagine the same circumstance as above (an unusual Asian disease is expected to kill 600 people) and consider the following two programs:

- If Program C is adopted, 400 people will die.
- If Program D is adopted, there is a one-third probability that nobody will die and a two-thirds probability that 600 people will die.

If you're like most people, you chose Programs A and D. A seems better than B; if 200 people can be saved for sure (A), why choose a program whose most likely outcome is that no one will be saved (B)? D seems better than C; if one program leaves 400 people sure to die (C), why not choose an alternative that might prevent the deaths of everyone (D)?

About 3 out of 4 people chose Program A over B, and Program D over C. This seems sensible—except that A is *identical* to C, B is *identical* to D, and thus Choice #1 is identical (in terms of costs and benefits of the programs) to Choice #2. This becomes obvious if you look back at the choices. For example, 200 saved (A) is identical to 400 die (C) because there are 600 people.

The standard model predicts that decisions would be the same in Choices #1 and 2, because the numbers of people saved are identical in both cases. But preferences actually *reverse:* People prefer the sure thing (save 200) in Choice #1, which is framed in terms of lives saved, and the risky option (maybe save 600, but a big chance of saving no one) in Choice #2, where choices are framed in terms of deaths. People think differently about gains and losses; framing reverses the preferences.

MENTAL ACCOUNTING. Kahneman and Tversky identified a second problem with the standard model. Recall an idea from that model: People base decisions on how alternative choices affect their net worth. This idea, too, fails to describe the way people actually make decisions. Consider the following choices (adapted from Kahneman & Tversky, 1984, p. 347):

Choice #1

Imagine that you have decided to see a play and paid the admission price of $20 per ticket. As you enter the theater, you discover that you have lost the ticket. The seat was not marked, and the ticket cannot be recovered. Would you pay $20 for another ticket?

Framing effects identified in basic research on decision making have been used to promote health. Rather than a positive framing that identifies the benefits of taking a health test, this poster incorporates a negative framing that highlights the risk of missing out on the test. Research shows that public health appeals that are framed negatively can remind people of their vulnerability to health problem and thus increase their likelihood of taking health-promoting actions (Meyerowitz & Chaiken, 1987).

NHS

You wouldn't miss picking up your kids from school

Don't miss having your cervical screening test.
It only takes a few minutes and it could save your life.

Three points to remember: 1. Get screened every 3 years (every 5 years if you're 50+)
2. Know the benefits 3. Tell your friends

Phone your GP to book an appointment **www.mphds.org**

Produced by Manchester Public Health Development Service MMHSCT April 2012

Manchester Mental Health and Social Care Trust. ©Health and Wellbeing Service.

framing effect A phenomenon in decision making in which people's decisions are affected by the way in which outcomes are described, or "framed."

Choice #2

Imagine that you have decided to see a play where admission is $20 per ticket. As you enter the theater, you discover that you have lost a $20 bill. Would you pay $20 for a ticket for the play?

In Choice #1, most people say no, they would not buy another ticket. In Choice #2, almost 9 out of 10 people say that, yes, they *would* buy one. Psychologically, then, the choices differ enormously. But in terms of how they affect net worth, they are identical. In both, if people see the play, they end up with $40 less net worth than when they started; $20 of that worth was lost and $20 was spent on the ticket to get in. Why, then, do people's choices differ?

As Kahneman and Tversky explain, when making decisions, people usually do not consider their overall net worth—the total value of all the bank accounts, investment accounts, property, and other assets they own. Instead, they engage in **mental accounting,** a thinking process in which people divide their assets and expenditures into distinct cognitive categories. For example, you might have a category for "amount of money I can spend on entertainment." If you buy a $20 ticket and lose it, then that $20 comes out of your entertainment mental account, and you're less likely to buy another ticket. If you lose a $20 bill, that $20 does not come out of your entertainment mental account; your entertainment mental account, then, still has as much money in it as it did before you lost the bill. So you buy a $20 ticket despite losing the $20 bill.

In summary, Tversky and Kahneman revolutionized science's understanding of judgment and decision making by humanizing it. Rather than performing calculations like a computer, people use simplifying strategies—heuristics, mental accounts—required by human beings with limited short-term memory capacity.

🐟 WHAT DO YOU KNOW?●●●

17. Consider the following. A hurricane is coming and you have to figure out which of two protocols to follow to convince the town's 3000 citizens to evacuate to safety. If they do not evacuate, they will die.

    › If Protocol 1 is followed, 2000 people will die.

    › If Protocol 2 is followed, there is a one-third probability that nobody will die and a two-thirds probability that 3000 people will die.

    According to Kahneman and Tversky's research on framing effects, and given that the choice is framed in terms of deaths (rather than lives saved), which of the protocols are most people likely to choose?

18. Consider the following two choices:

    › *Choice #1:* Imagine that you bought a voucher for $40 worth of food at a restaurant. When you get to the restaurant, you realize you have lost the voucher. Would you pay $40 for your meal?

    › *Choice #2:* Imagine that you go to a restaurant planning to spend about $40 for your meal. As you arrive, you realize you have lost two $20 bills. Would you still go to dinner as planned?

    According to Kahneman and Tversky's research on mental accounting, in which situation would more people be likely to answer yes?

Problem Solving

If you like puzzles and games, you may know the Tower of Hanoi problem (see photo). At the start, disks are stacked on one of three pegs. You have to move them to a different peg while following two rules: (1) Move only one disk at a time, and (2) never put a larger disk on a smaller one. The simple combination of disks, pegs, and rules produces a challenging puzzle.

When working on this sort of task, you're engaged in **problem solving,** a thinking process in which people try to reach a solution by working through a series of steps.

---

mental accounting A thinking process in which people divide their assets and expenditures into distinct cognitive categories, rather than thinking about their overall costs and net assets.

problem solving A thinking process in which people try to reach a solution by working through a series of steps.

Problem solving occurs not only when working on puzzles, but when tackling challenges in science, mathematics, or engineering, where you have to figure out how to work through a series of challenging steps to reach a solution.

The Problem Space and Heuristic Search

Preview Question

> How do people solve problems?

To solve a problem, you have to maneuver through its problem space. A **problem space** is the full set of steps it is possible to take when solving the problem. Suppose the problem is to form an English word out of the three letters *tca*. The problem space consists of the six possible arrangements of the letters: *tca, tac, atc, act, cta, cat.*

On simple problems—such as forming a word from *tca*—you can envision the entire problem space and simply select a solution. However, this is rare; the problem space usually is much bigger. In the Tower of Hanoi problem, there are many ways to move the disks. In a game of chess, the number of possible moves is enormous. You cannot envision the whole problem space; the amount of information exceeds the capacity of short-term memory (see Chapter 7).

How do people solve problems when they can't envision the entire problem space? As in judgment under uncertainty, heuristics come to the rescue. People use simple strategies, or *problem-solving heuristics,* to reach a solution.

One such heuristic is means–ends analysis (Newell & Simon, 1972). **Means–ends analysis** is a problem-solving strategy in which, at each step of a problem, people aim merely to reduce the distance between where they are now and where they want to end up (Simon, 1990). Rather than trying to determine a long series of steps that will lead to a problem solution, people merely look one step ahead; they select a "next step" that will bring them closer to their desired outcome. In the Tower of Hanoi problem, you might select any option that places a disk on the peg you want to reach. In the late stages of a chess game, you might choose any move that gets one of your pieces onto a square from which it can attack your opponent's king.

Dmitry Elagin / Shutterstock

Tower of Hanoi puzzle Can you move the disks on the left to the peg on the right, moving one disk at a time and never placing a larger disk on a smaller one? Problem-solving tasks such as the Tower of Hanoi puzzle are used in research to study the strategies through which people solve problems.

✪ WHAT DO YOU KNOW?...

19. When the _____ space is overwhelming, rather than working through every possible step, sometimes we simply do something that will get us at least a little bit closer to the solution, according to our own _____ analysis.

Problem Solving by People and by Computers

Preview Question

> How do computers solve problems?

Two types of evidence indicate that people use means–ends analysis to solve problems. The first comes from research in which psychologists ask people to think out loud while trying to solve problems (see Research Toolkit). Participants' statements often reveal that they are using means–ends analysis. They frequently mention their current state, desired

When devising study strategies, what does your means–ends analysis look like?

problem space The full set of steps it is possible to take when solving a problem.

means–ends analysis A strategy for solving complex problems in which, at each step toward a solution, people aim to reduce the distance between their current state of progress and the final problem-solving goal they want to achieve.

Herbert Simon, pioneer in the study of human problem solving—plus many other topics. Simon won a Nobel Prize in Economics for his studies of decision making in organizations. With colleagues at Carnegie Mellon University, he wrote some of the world's first "intelligent" computer programs, that is, programs that could solve problems rather than merely perform simple calculations.

Carnegie Mellon University

THINK ABOUT IT

In what ways might information processing by a computer be similar to human thinking? In what ways does it differ from human thinking?

end point, the difference between the two, and how they might take a step that reduces the difference (Simon, 1990).

The second source of evidence involves computers. Allen Newell and Herbert Simon (1961) wrote a computer program, the *General Problem Solver,* that solved a wide variety of problems. It did so through means–ends analysis, manipulating symbols until it reached desired end states. The steps through which the General Problem Solver accomplished tasks often resembled those taken by human problem solvers. "Protocols of human problem-solving behavior in a range of tasks—playing chess, solving puzzles, writing computer programs—contain many sequences of behavior . . . quite similar to the means-ends analysis of the General Problem Solver" (Newell & Simon, 1961, p. 2014). The convergence between human and computer problem solving suggests that people and the program solved problems in the same way: through means–ends analysis.

WHAT DO YOU KNOW?●●●

20. True or False? Newell and Simon's computer program, the General Problem Solver, solved problems using means–ends analysis, much like humans.

⊕RESEARCH TOOLKIT

Think-Aloud Protocol Analysis

If you watch people work on a problem—a mathematical proof, a chess game, a puzzle in a newspaper—it's hard to know what they're thinking. You know something's "going on in there"; after a while, a solution seems to pop right out. But what exactly were they thinking? And how could you find out?

Finding out is more difficult than it may sound. You could just ask people what they were thinking, but this solution isn't good enough. Because information in short-term memory decays quickly (Chapter 7), they might simply forget the exact strategy they used.

Fortunately for research on human thinking, psychologists have devised a research tool that overcomes this difficulty. **Think-aloud protocol analysis** (or "verbal protocol analysis") is a procedure in which participants verbalize their thoughts while solving a problem (Ericsson & Simon, 1984; Fox, Ericsson, & Best, 2011); that is, they say out loud all the ideas that run through their heads. The experimenter records and analyzes the statements to determine the problem-solving strategy used. Verbalizing thoughts is easy; we often think to ourselves when solving a problem ("$3 \times 19 =$ ___? Hmm, let's see. Three times nine is 27, so there must be a 7 in the ones place. . . ."), so all one needs to do is to give voice to such thinking. With only a bit of practice, verbalizing does not impair people's normal task performance (Fox et al., 2011).

You can see how this works from the transcription below—it's a think-aloud protocol recorded while a research participant attempted the Tower of Hanoi problem (from Anzai & Simon, 1979). In the problem, the disks are numbered (1, 2, 3. . .) and the pegs are identified by letters (A, B, C).

I'll take 2 from C, and place it on B.

And I'll take 1 and . . . place it from A to B.

think-aloud protocol analysis
A research method in which participants verbalize their thoughts while solving a problem, which enables experimenters to record and analyze the problem-solving strategies used.

So then, 4 will go from A to C.

And then . . ., um . . ., oh . . ., um . . .

I should have placed 2 on C. But that will take time. But I'll stay with this a little more.

I'll take 1 from B and place it on A.

Then I'll take 2 from B to C.

Oh, this won't do. . . .

I'll take 2 and place it from C to B again.

And then, I'll take 1, and from A. . . .

Oh no! If I do it this way, it won't work!

The protocol provides a window into the mind of the participant. You can see which strategies the person tried, and even his or her reaction when one of the strategies failed.

Protocol analysis has been applied widely. For example, to find out whether people were giving honest or "fake" answers on a personality test, researchers asked test takers to think out loud while answering test questions (Robie, Brown, & Beaty, 2007). Think-aloud protocols revealed that some participants weren't describing their actual personality at all; they were trying to figure out which answers would make the best impression on the person scoring the test. For example (from Robie et al., 2007, p. 500):

"I wonder what type of responses they want?"

[Reads item] "Generally yes, so I'll say probably yes because it's true and it looks good on the sheet."

"If I answer definitely yes to all of these, they'll think I'm lying."

[Reads item] "I don't remember reading anything about getting a commission. . . . However, if I say definitely yes, they are going to be thinking that I am going to be cutthroat."

Think-aloud protocol analysis, then, is a valuable tool for learning how people solve problems—including the problem of figuring out how to make a good impression on personality tests!

✥ WHAT DO YOU KNOW?•••

21. Which of the following statements is true? Check all that apply.

___ a. Think-aloud protocol analysis was designed to understand the strategies people use to solve problems.

___ b. Participants who engage in think-aloud protocol analysis find that even with practice, verbalizing their thoughts impairs their thinking.

___ c. Think-aloud protocol analysis is not very useful for understanding the thinking processes people use when solving the "problem" of how to answer items on a personality test.

Mental Imagery

Picture yourself in a building you know well, such as the house where you grew up. How many windows were on the front of the building?

Now consider this question: How did you figure out how many windows there were?

If you're like most people, you formed a picture of the building in your mind and counted the windows. If so, you relied on a distinct form of thinking called *mental imagery*. **Mental imagery** is thinking that involves pictures and spatial relationships (i.e., relationships involving location in space) rather than words, numbers, and logical rules. When thinking with mental imagery, you have the experience that you're "looking at a picture" in your mind. Let's consider two types of thinking that illustrate the power of mental imagery: (1) mental rotation and (2) contemplation of mental distance.

mental imagery Thinking that involves pictures and spatial relationships rather than words, numbers, and logical rules.

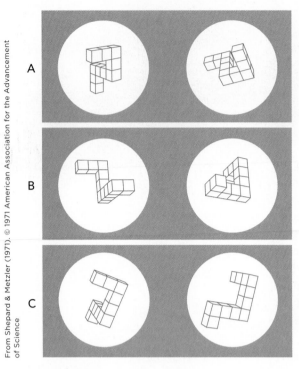

figure 8.9

Shepard blocks Are the blocks on the left the same as those on the right? Roger Shepard created these images to study mental rotation. He measured the time participants needed to determine whether the blocks on the left and right match up. (Parts A and B are the same when properly rotated; the two blocks in part C do not match up.)

Mental Rotation

Preview Question

› What determines how quickly we can rotate images in our head?

Much insight into mental imagery has come from research by Roger Shepard and colleagues on mental rotation. **Mental rotation** is the ability to turn an image in your mind, much as you would turn a physical object in the world.

In their research, Shepard and colleagues showed people pairs of abstract objects (Shepard & Metzler, 1971). Participants had to determine whether the objects were the same (i.e., had the same shape) if rotated. As shown in Figure 8.9, some pairs were the same; they could be matched up through rotation. Others did not match no matter how they were rotated. The study's dependent measure was the time it took participants to rotate the objects mentally, in other words, to determine whether the objects matched after rotation.

The study produced startlingly precise results. The time needed to rotate mental images correlates almost perfectly with the number of degrees through which the image has to be rotated (Figure 8.10). Compared to a 60° rotation, people take twice as long to rotate blocks 120° and three times as long to rotate them 180°. This is true whether blocks are rotated in the plane of the picture (Figure 8.9a) or in depth (Figure 8.9b). Either way, people mentally rotate objects at about 60° per second.

❤ WHAT DO YOU KNOW?...

22. True or False?

Compared with a 50° rotation, it would take you twice as long to rotate blocks 100° and three times as long to rotate them 150°.

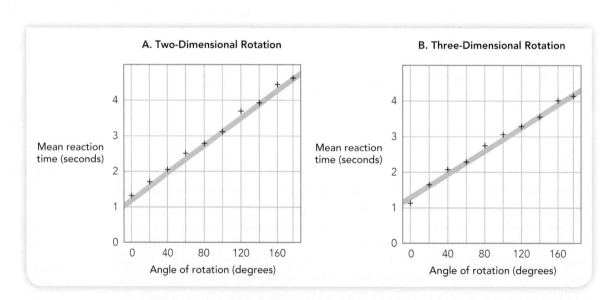

figure 8.10

Mental rotation results In their research on mental rotation, Roger Shepard and colleagues found that the amount of time participants needed to determine whether blocks (see Figure 8.9) matched was precisely related to the number of angular degrees that the blocks had to be rotated.

mental rotation The psychological process of turning an image in one's mind, much as a person might turn a physical object in the world.

Mental Distance

Preview Question

> What does research on mental distance suggest about how we use mental imagery?

Research by Stephen Kosslyn (1980) complements the mental imagery studies of Shepard. Kosslyn showed participants the pictures displayed in Figure 8.11. After participants formed a clear, accurate image of each one, Kosslyn took the pictures away and asked people questions about the objects that were pictured, for example, "Did the speedboat have an anchor?" Again, the time taken to answer was the dependent measure.

Before asking the questions, Kosslyn instructed participants to "mentally stare at" one end of their mental image (Kosslyn, 1980, p, 37). In different experimental conditions, they stared at either the left or right side of the boat, or the top or bottom of the clock tower. The instructions thus varied the "distance" between (1) where people stared and (2) the object about which they were asked a question—where "distance" is not an actual physical distance, but the distance between images in participants' minds. Kosslyn found that people took longer to answer if they had to cover more mental distance (Kosslyn, 1980). If, for instance, they had been staring at the top of the tower, they more quickly answered, "Was there a flag on top?" than if they had been staring at the bottom. People thus not only create images in their mind, but also mentally travel across them.

Some theories would have difficulty explaining Kosslyn's results. For example, semantic network models (Chapter 7) suggest that people store information by linking together facts that are represented verbally (e.g., facts such as "boats" have "anchors"). In a semantic network model, the instruction to stare at one versus another part of the boat wouldn't be expected to affect the links between stored facts. Kosslyn's finding, that the instruction did affect people's speed in answering questions, thus suggests that people were not relying on verbal facts alone, but on mental images.

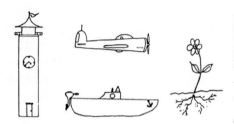

From Kosslyn (1973). © 1973, Psychonomic Society, Inc.

figure 8.11
Distance in mental imagery Research participants were asked to study these figures, and then to look away and answer questions such as whether there was a flag on the top of the clock tower. Kosslyn (1980) found that it took longer to answer these questions if the participants had to travel, in their minds, across longer distances in the mental image.

WHAT DO YOU KNOW?...

23. Imagine you were given a picture of a clown long enough to form an accurate image of it, then the picture was taken away. Next, you were asked to "mentally stare at" the top of the image. Will it take you longer to report the clown's hair color or her shoe color? Briefly explain.

Intelligence

You probably have a good sense of your level of intelligence. Most people have taken standardized intelligence tests and received scores ranking them in comparison to others. However, you may have less understanding of what, exactly, intelligence is. Is it something in your head—maybe a part of the brain? Or it is just a label that summarizes people's performance when answering the questions on intelligence tests?

If you've ever asked yourself what intelligence is, you're not alone. Psychologists puzzle over the question. Although researchers have developed measures of intelligence and identified factors that influence people's intelligence test scores, basic questions about the nature of intelligence are debated to the present day. Let's begin our study of intelligence, then, by examining definitions of the term.

Defining Intelligence

Preview Question

> What is—and isn't—intelligence?

We call people "intelligent" when we see them do something difficult that requires thinking. Whether it's learning a foreign language, solving a math problem, inventing the electric light bulb, developing a novel form of poetry, or just correctly answering lots of questions on an intelligence test, the accomplishment—the learning, the solving of problems, or the creation of something new—indicates the person's intelligence (Gardner, 1993, Sternberg, 1985). **Intelligence,** therefore, is the ability to acquire knowledge, to solve problems, and to use acquired knowledge to create new, valued products. To many psychologists, intelligence refers, more specifically, to a *general* ability to do these things—that is, an ability to comprehend information and respond effectively to problems that arise on different types of activities (Deary, Penke, & Johnson, 2010).

This definition indicates not only what intelligence is, but also what it is not. "Intelligence" does *not* refer to the following:

> *Personality traits:* Personality traits are motivational and emotional tendencies (see Chapter 13), not mental abilities.

> *Physical abilities:* You might be able to run a marathon or lift 200 pounds over your head, but these abilities, which require little knowledge, are not signs of intelligence.

> *Specific skills:* A person who, for example, has exceptional memory for baseball statistics or an unusually good sense of direction, but who does not display a broad ability to comprehend information, would not be said to be highly intelligent.

🐾 WHAT DO YOU KNOW?...

24. Check the items below that most psychologists would agree are indicators of intelligence.
    ___ a. ability to use knowledge to create new products
    ___ b. ability to solve problems
    ___ c. physical abilities
    ___ d. personality traits
    ___ e. ability to acquire knowledge

"General" Intelligence and Differences Between People

Preview Questions

> How has intelligence been measured?
> Is there a "general" intelligence?
> What cognitive processes contribute to individual differences in general intelligence?

Our definition of intelligence leaves some important questions unanswered. The most significant is whether there is one type of intelligence or multiple types, that is, distinct mental abilities, each of which is a type of intelligence. Let's look at the origins of intelligence testing, which focused on measuring one type of intelligence, known as *general intelligence.*

intelligence The ability to acquire knowledge, to solve problems, and to use acquired knowledge to create new, valued products.

ORIGINS OF INTELLIGENCE TESTING AND IQ. More than a century ago, psychologists began to measure differences in people's mental abilities (Brody, 1992; Fancher, 1979). A pioneer in the field was the French psychologist Alfred Binet. Binet reasoned that some children might have mental disabilities and thus would need extra help from teachers. To identify these children, Binet devised an intelligence test.

Before Binet, psychologists interested in intelligence had measured people's perceptual ability and memory capacity. Binet's test, however, was different. He measured logical reasoning, vocabulary use, and factual knowledge; children taking his test had to identify objects, explain the logical relation between ideas, and construct sentences using challenging vocabulary words. These test items tapped abilities that are important to school achievement. Binet's test thus was a success; test scores predicted classroom achievement. Today's intelligence tests, which employ items similar to those Binet developed, strongly predict school success (Greven et al., 2009).

> How well do you think scores on intelligence tests predict success outside of school, such as at work or in social situations?

In 1912 a German psychologist, William Stern, provided a valuable scoring system for intelligence tests (Wasserman & Tulsky, 2005). Stern capitalized on an insight from Binet, who recognized that, when assessing a child's intelligence, one should consider the child's age. Different children might develop the same ability at different ages. The child who develops the ability earlier is said to be more intelligent.

Stern included age in a formula for computing **intelligence quotient,** or **IQ,** which is a measure of overall intelligence that takes into account a person's age. It does so by

SSPL / The Image Works

Intelligence test for children
A 1937 version of the intelligence test created originally by Binet. The test uses objects, rather than written questions, so it can be administered to children who may not yet have learned to read.

The Image Works

Twists and turns in the early history of intelligence testing Alfred Binet (photo on left) developed intelligence testing early in the twentieth century as part of a French governmental effort to identify children who had "special needs" due to low intellectual performance and might "benefit from special education programs" (Nicolas & Levine, 2012, p. 323). Soon, however, the principles of intelligence testing turned in a different direction: from providing people with special opportunities to potentially denying them opportunities. At Ellis Island, the main point of immigration into the United States during the first half of the twentieth century, officials employed intelligence tests due to public concern that "the immigration authorities were failing to prevent mentally defective people from entering the country" (Richardson, 2003, p. 147). Officials eventually realized that many immigrants were obtaining low scores simple due to their lack of familiarity with the procedures and language of the tests being used.

IQ (intelligence quotient) A measure of overall intelligence that takes into account a person's age.

Marilyn vos Savant who, at age 10, correctly answered every question on an IQ test designed for adults. According to the scoring procedure, this gave her a mental age of 22 years, 11 months, and (by applying the IQ formula in the text) an IQ of 228—the highest IQ of any known person. Her IQ, remarkable though it is, raises questions about what one can achieve through IQ alone. Ms. Savant has made a career writing magazine columns about puzzles, games, and simple facts of science. "Look at Barack Obama, look at how he is applying his intelligence," one critic says. "It just sort of seems strange to me that instead of dealing with more complex problems, a lot of what she does is just answer riddles or simple research things, things that anybody could go to a library and look up the answer to" (Knight, 2009).

mental age A measure of a child's intelligence based on both the child's test responses and the responses of other children who have taken the same test. The child's mental age is equivalent to the average age of other children who perform as well as that child.

general intelligence (g) A measure of overall mental ability based on total performance across a number of different types of intellectual tests.

Wechsler Adult Intelligence Scale (WAIS) A popular test of intelligence that assesses verbal comprehension, perceptual reasoning, working memory, and mental processing speed.

relating any given child's test performance to the average age of children who perform similarly on that test. Here's an example.

> Suppose that a 7-year-old child takes an intelligence test with 60 items and answers 43 correctly.

> Suppose also that many other children of different ages have previously taken the test, and the average age at which they first were able to answer 43 questions was age 8.

The *mental age* of the 7-year-old who answered 43 questions correctly, then, is 8. A child's **mental age** is the average age of children who perform as well as he or she did on an intelligence test.

Stern included mental age in his formula for IQ:

$$IQ = (\text{mental age/chronological age}) \times 100$$

An average child—one whose mental age equals his or her chronological age—would have an IQ of 100. The 7-year-old with a mental age of 8 would have an IQ of 114 (8/7 × 100). When intelligence tests are given to adults, with age no longer being a relevant factor, the tests are scored so that the mean score in a population is 100 and the standard deviation (an index of the degree to which numbers spread, or vary, from the mean; see Chapter 2) is 15; about two-thirds of people, then, receive IQ scores between 85 and 115.

THE NATURE OF GENERAL INTELLIGENCE. Computing a person's IQ score is easy. But it leaves a difficult question unanswered: "What, exactly, does the IQ score measure?"

The first step in answering that question involves the following fact: Whenever people take tests measuring different mental abilities, those who get high scores on any one test (e.g., verbal skills) tend also to get high scores on others (e.g., math skills). Individual differences on the separate tests correlate positively (Deary, 2001). What explains the positive correlations? More than a century ago, the British psychologist Charles Spearman (1904) explained them by proposing the variable **general intelligence,** or **g.** People with high (low) *g* tend to perform well (poorly) on tests of mental ability.

IQ, then, measures *g*. IQ scores measure individual differences in general intelligence.

THINK ABOUT IT

Is general intelligence something that psychologists *discovered*? Or is it an idea that psychologists *invented*?

Let's see exactly how this works by examining one popular test of intelligence, the **Wechsler Adult Intelligence Scale,** or the **WAIS** (Wechsler, 2008). The WAIS includes measures of four aspects of mental ability:

1. *Verbal Comprehension:* The ability to comprehend words, verbally presented information, and the relations among pieces of verbal information

2. *Perceptual Reasoning:* The ability to remember, reason about, and solve problems involving pictures, shapes, and other visually presented material

3. *Working Memory:* The ability to retain and manipulate information in working memory

4. *Processing Speed:* The ability to respond rapidly to simple information, such as reading a letter on a page and writing it down as quickly as possible

Although these four abilities are distinct—comprehending words differs conceptually from solving problems involving shapes—the four WAIS abilities are correlated positively (Deary, 2001). People with relatively high Verbal Comprehension scores tend also to get relatively higher Perceptual Reasoning, Working Memory, and Processing Speed scores. The positive correlations among test scores can be summarized by g. In a hierarchical model, the four WAIS factors are linked to the high-level factor of general intelligence (Figure 8.12). To assess g, the tester combines a person's scores on the four measures.

Is g a single thing—for example, a single structure in your brain? No. If you look inside your brain, you won't find "a g." General intelligence is merely is a summary of some numbers: the positive correlations among test scores when a group of people take a number of different tests (Borsboom & Dolan, 2006; Deary, 2001). A wide variety of mechanisms in the brain could contribute to the correlations among test scores. But no single brain mechanism would correspond directly to g (van der Maas et al., 2006).

It might at first sound odd that the single variable g does not correspond to a single thing in the brain. An analogy makes it clear. Suppose you're running a theatre group, putting on a musical, and need people for the show. You develop tests for the needed talents: a singing test, a dancing test, a test for stage design ability, and a test for technical skills such as lighting the stage. People's scores on these tests might correlate positively. Even if they do, that doesn't mean people's brains contain a "General Theatre Ability." There are other explanations for the positive correlations. People who sing well in childhood might be more likely to appear in stage shows. Once in the shows, they receive dance lessons. Eventually, they hang out with people who do stage design and lighting. As a result of these experiences, they pick up diverse theatre-related knowledge and skills, and the four tests correlate positively. Analogously, people who have diverse classroom educational experiences may pick up the diverse knowledge and skills that go into g.

These skills are significant. People with higher scores on tests of general intelligence often achieve higher levels of academic and professional success. A study of tens of thousands of British schoolchildren showed that general intelligence scores at age 11 substantially predicted school achievement in math and English at age 16 (Deary et al., 2007). Research relating g to professional success indicates that higher levels of general intelligence predict higher levels of success in job-training programs and higher levels of on-the-job work performance (Ree & Earles, 1992).

GENERAL INTELLIGENCE AND WORKING MEMORY. The psychologist Raymond Cattell (1987) explained that, to identify cognitive processes that contribute to intelligence, you first have to distinguish between two forms of general intelligence: fluid and crystallized. *Fluid intelligence* refers to mental abilities that can benefit performance on almost any challenging task; these abilities have "the 'fluid' quality of being directable to almost any problem" (Cattell, 1987, p. 97). Thanks to fluid abilities, people can perform intelligently even on tasks they have never seen before (e.g., puzzles, logic problems, or detecting patterns in a series of geometric shapes). *Crystallized intelligence* refers to socially acquired knowledge. Someone who knows a lot of facts, or an unusually large number of vocabulary words, would be said to have high crystallized intelligence. In contrast to fluid intelligence, the knowledge that comprises crystallized intelligence is generally more helpful on some tasks than others; knowing words, for example, helps in solving verbal problems but not arithmetic problems.

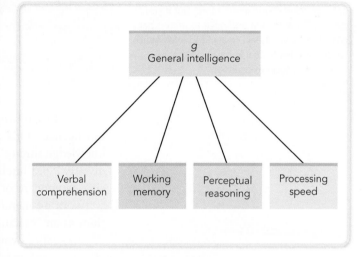

figure 8.12
WAIS abilities and g The Wechsler Adult Intelligence Scale (the WAIS) measures the four mental abilities depicted here. Scores on tests of these four abilities are correlated positively with one another. General intelligence, or g, summarizes such positive correlations among different aspects of mental ability.

Fluid and crystallized intelligence
The first time you play a logic game, such as Sudoku, you can solve it using your fluid intelligence, a form of intelligence that can be directed toward any challenging task, including one you have never seen before. But if you are playing Trivial Pursuit and have to remember bits of trivia, you need crystallized intelligence, which includes factual knowledge that you acquired through experience.

It is difficult to identify specific cognitive processes that contribute to crystallized intelligence. This aspect of knowledge is diverse—people acquire a wide range of knowledge through experiences—so the cognitive processes involved may be equally diverse. Fluid intelligence, however, is different. Many researchers suggest that a specific component of the mind is key to fluid intelligence: working memory.

Working memory (see Chapter 7) holds information for brief periods and functions as an "executive" that focuses a person's attention on tasks and helps people to avoid distraction. Individual differences in working memory capacity predict individual difference in fluid intelligence (Engle, 2002). For instance, when researchers measure people's ability to avoid distraction, those who are less distractible are found to have higher fluid intelligence (Engle et al., 1999) and higher scores on intelligence tests that combine fluid and crystallized intelligence abilities (Colom et al., 2004).

> Have you ever tried to train yourself to avoid distraction?

Individual differences in working memory capacity thus contribute to individual differences in fluid intelligence. This fact, however, leaves unanswered the following question: Why do people differ in working memory capacity and fluid intelligence? In other words, why are some people smarter than others?

🌀 WHAT DO YOU KNOW?...

25. What would your mental age be if you were 10 and you scored the same as the average 10-year-old on an intelligence test? What would be your IQ?

26. If you scored high on the WAIS Verbal Comprehension, Perceptual Reasoning, and Working Memory abilities, what can you predict about your score on the WAIS Processing Speed ability?

27. Of the following two characteristics, which is an example of fluid intelligence?
    a. Remembering that a *decathlon* is a competition consisting of 10 athletic events
    b. The ability to figure out how many events are in a decathlon by thinking about the similarity between the words "decathlon" and "decade"

28. If an individual scores high on tests of fluid intelligence, what can you predict about the capacity of his or her working memory?

Inherited Biology and Intelligence

Preview Question

› Is inherited biology the only determinant of intelligence?

One possible cause of individual differences in intelligence is biological inheritance. Just as people inherit genes that determine their eye color or height (see Chapter 4), they may inherit genes that determine their level of intelligence. Intelligence, then, may be a fixed, genetically determined quality that you couldn't alter even if you wanted to.

Over the years, some psychologists have made this claim. If intelligence is biologically determined, then society perhaps should not spend much money educating people with low IQ scores, because education won't boost their intellectual ability (Herrnstein & Murray, 1994; Jensen, 1969).

Do the facts support the controversial claim that intelligence is determined genetically? Let's look closely at this question by examining a biologically determined trait and then comparing it to intelligence.

Here are four facts about height, a biologically determined trait:

1. *There are few if any differences in the average level of the trait from one generation of humans to the next.* The genetic material possessed by any population changes only very slowly. If biology determines a trait, then the trait generally does not change rapidly across generations. For example, a generation or two ago, people were roughly the same height they are now; the genetic material that determines height hasn't changed much in only a few generations.

2. *An individual's social experiences have little influence on the trait.* If, for example, you go to a basketball camp, you might develop skills—they are socially acquired—but spending time at the camp will not cause you to grow taller.

3. *Individual differences in the trait will be stable.* If you are taller than most people this year, you won't be shorter than most people next year.

4. *Inheritance will explain individual differences* within *different socioeconomic groups in society.* Within wealthy communities and poorer communicates, children with tall (short) parents and grandparents will grow up to be relatively tall (short) adults. Within any population of people, individual differences in height are determined primarily by biology (Silventoinen et al., 2008).

These four facts are true, then, for biologically determined traits, such as height. Are they also true for intelligence? Let's look at the evidence.

CHANGES ACROSS GENERATIONS. Intelligence tests have been around for a long time. Test publishers use many of the same test items from one year to the next. Even when they add new items, they do so carefully, conducting statistical analyses to ensure that the tests don't vary in difficulty from one year to the next. This makes it possible to compare IQ scores across historical periods; researchers can thus see whether IQ changes from one generation to another.

Would you expect substantial changes? If biology completely determines intelligence, you shouldn't expect changes; the human genome doesn't vary much from one generation to the next. But research by the New Zealand psychologist James Flynn (1987, 1999) shows that IQ changes are substantial. Flynn analyzed IQ scores across decades of the twentieth century for different countries, one at a time. His results were startling. In each country, people became *more* intelligent across the decades of the second half of the twentieth century. IQ scores went up a lot (Figure 8.13). In England, for example, scores shifted by nearly 30 points (statistically, nearly 2 standard deviations) in only a half century, 1940 to 1990.

This increase in intelligence across generations has become known as the Flynn effect. The **Flynn effect** is the rise in a population's average IQ over time.

figure **8.13**
Flynn effect Maybe we're not so dumb after all. Research by James Flynn shows that IQ scores today are, on average, much higher than in the past. In the graph, the most recent IQ score average for a given nation is given the value 100. The standard deviation of IQ scores is 15. IQ scores, then, have increased at the astounding rate of about a full standard deviation per quarter century.

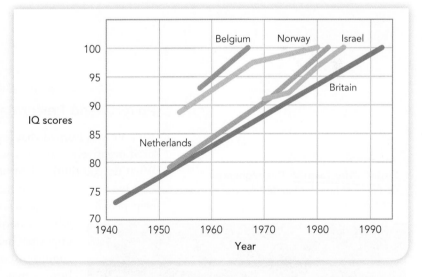

How does it feel to know that you may be more intelligent than previous generations of your family members?

Flynn effect Name given to the relatively rapid rise in intelligence test scores that is evident across generations.

The Flynn effect is so large that it couldn't possibly result from changes in human biology. By comparison, there are no proportional changes in human height. The standard deviation of height is about 3 inches; a comparable change, then, would be 5–6 inches in average height in a half-century. No such changes occurred during the twentieth century or any other comparable period in human history (Steckel, 1995). The Flynn effect therefore shows that factors *other than* biology must be influencing IQ scores.

It is difficult to know precisely what those factors are (Neisser, 1997). Rather than truly being more intelligent, people today might simply be better at taking tests; people might acquire test-taking skills by working on puzzles or video games, or by taking classes in which test-taking tips are taught. Alternatively, improvements in education might provide people today with more knowledge and skills, that is, more crystallized intelligence. So let's look at the effect of education on intelligence test scores.

THE EFFECTS OF A SOCIAL EXPERIENCE: EDUCATION. Does attending school increase your intelligence? Research evidence says yes. People who spend more time in school become more intelligent; they achieve higher scores on intelligence tests (Ceci, 1991).

Two sources of evidence support this conclusion. One is the correlation between years spent in school and IQ scores. Rather than being .00 (like the correlation between number of days in basketball camp and height), the correlation is large, about .80. The positive correlation is found even after accounting for other factors, such as the possibility that more intelligent kids start school early (Ceci, 1991). Education, then, is a social experience that increases intelligence.

The second source of evidence involves summer vacation. Summer vacation is great—the best part of the school year! But when it comes to intelligence, it's costly. IQ declines during the summer break; students' IQ scores are higher at the end of a school year than at the start of the next school year. This is particularly true among low-income children, who are less likely to engage in educationally enriching activities during the summer (Ceci, 1991; also see This Just In).

> What educationally enriching activities could you tolerate during the summer?

⏱ THIS JUST IN

Poverty and Performance on Intelligence Tests

Suppose you learned that levels of poverty and scores on intelligence tests were correlated negatively—in other words, that greater poverty was associated with a lower IQ. What do you think might be responsible for the correlation?

One possibility is that intelligence affects income. Higher levels of intelligence may help people to excel in school, obtain more education, and thus land higher-paying jobs (see Sorjonen et al., 2012). An additional possibility, though, is the opposite: Income may affect intelligence. Being poor—experiencing conditions of poverty, and the many burdens and challenges they bring—may lower people's ability to solve the sorts of problems found on intelligence tests.

Recent findings document this second possibility with a remarkable population: a group of people who are sometimes relatively rich and sometimes relatively poor (Mani et al., 2013). These research participants were sugar cane farmers in India. Prior to the annual harvest, the farmers have little money and face substantial economic burdens; many report pawning personal property and taking out loans in order to pay bills. But after they harvest and sell their crops, they are relatively wealthy and, for the next few months, have far fewer financial worries.

Sugar cane farmer This might not be the best time for him to take an intelligence test.

Amet Bhargava / Corbis

Researchers administered intelligence test items to the farmers at two different times of year, before and after the harvest. Farmers obtained substantially lower test scores before the harvest, when experiencing poverty (Figure 8.14). Their ability to solve intelligence test items was relatively higher *after* the harvest, when they had more money.

Why would poverty impair people's ability to solve problems presented on intelligence tests? The researchers explain that poverty is distracting. When poor, people "must manage sporadic income, juggle expenses, and make difficult tradeoffs. Even when not actually making a financial decision, these preoccupations can be present and distracting . . . [and people] lose their capacity to give other problems their full consideration" (Mani et al., 2013).

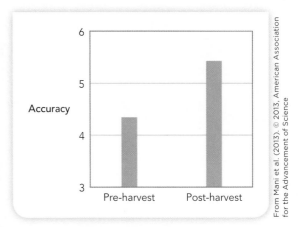

✔ WHAT DO YOU KNOW?...

29. True or False? Research comparing sugar cane farmers' scores on intelligence tests during times of relative wealth and poverty leads to the conclusion that intelligence affects income, not that income affects intelligence.

figure 8.14

Income and thinking abilities Sugar cane farmers solved intelligence test items more accurately after their annual harvest, when they had more money and thus were less distracted by worries about paying bills.

STABILITY OF INDIVIDUAL DIFFERENCES. Are individual differences in intelligence as stable as individual differences in height, with some people always being taller than others? To find out, researchers studied adolescents at two time periods: age 14 (on average) and three years later (Ramsden et al., 2011). They expected intelligence to be stable, like height. But "we were very surprised," the project leader reported. Many adolescents changed a lot. "We had individuals that changed from being in the 50th percentile, with an IQ of 100, [all] the way up to being in the (top) 3rd percentile, with an IQ of 127" (Aubrey, 2011). Scores also went down. One individual's verbal IQ score dropped by 20 points—a change that, by comparison with height, would be like becoming more than 3 inches shorter!

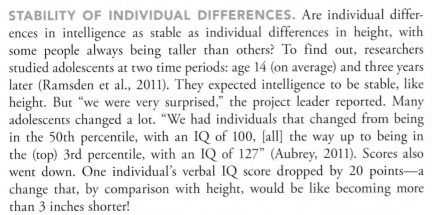

Changes in IQ scores turned out to be correlated with changes in the brain (Ramsden et al., 2011). Through brain-imaging evidence, the researchers found that changes in the verbal component of IQ scores correlated with changes in the density of neurons in a part of the brain needed for producing speech (Figure 8.15). This result means that the variations in IQ weren't due to "random" factors, such as test takers not trying as hard one of the two times they took the test. The changes were meaningful. People varied, across time, at the level of the mind (the ability to answer the test items) and the brain (neural density).

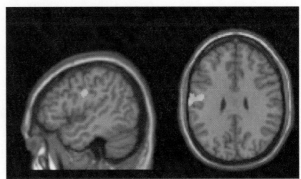

SOCIOECONOMIC STATUS. If intelligence were like height, then, within any of a variety of socioeconomic groups, rich or poor, genetic factors would be the major determinant of individual differences.

But it turns out that the impact of genes on intelligence is not like this. When it comes to intelligence, sometimes genetic effects are big and sometimes they're small. Critical evidence comes from a study of hundreds of pairs of identical and fraternal twins from families of diverse economic backgrounds (Turkeimer et al., 2003; reviewed in detail in Chapter 4). In wealthy populations, genetics explained the vast majority of individual differences in intelligence. But in poor populations, genetics explained only a very small percentage of the individual differences.

Why would genetic factors have only a small effect within populations of people who are poor? Children living in poverty may experience poor nutrition, inconsistent

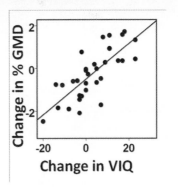

figure 8.15

IQ changes and the brain Researchers have found that adolescents' intelligence test scores can change substantially and that the changes correlate with changes in the brain. The scatterplot shows the relation between changes in verbal IQ (VIQ) and changes in grey matter density (GMD; the density of neurons) in areas of the brain shown above. These areas are known to be involved in producing speech.

Food for thought The Akshaya Patra Foundation, a nongovernmental organization, provides more than 1 million meals a day to poor schoolchildren in India. The foundation knows that performance in school is more than just inherited smarts; children need good nutrition to achieve their intellectual potential. Beneficiaries of the program know this, too. One man reported that, before the program started in his boyhood, he would sometimes faint from hunger at school and barely passed his courses. But once his nutrition improved, "My attention span went up. My concentration went up." He graduated, then graduated from college, and is now a software engineer (Vedantam, 2012).

"I don't even know where to begin. I have no material with the exception of a single textbook given to each child. . . . Very little education in the school would be considered academic in the suburbs." (p. 29)

[The physics teacher] shows me his lab. The six lab stations in the room have empty holes where pipes were once attached. "It would be great if we had water." (p. 27)

—Jonathan Kozol (1991),
quoting teachers at
East St. Louis High School, Illinois

parental care, and substandard school facilities. These environmental factors, not found in wealthy populations, can strongly affect children's intellectual development (Nisbett, 2009).

Do you live in an environment where genes can have an impact on the heritability of your intelligence?

We began this section of the chapter by asking whether intelligence is like height: determined almost entirely by inherited biology, and little affected by the environment. You've now seen that it is not. Thanks to today's research evidence, we can, as one scholar put it, "shake off the yoke of hereditarianism in . . . our thinking about intelligence" (Nisbett, 2009, p. 199) and recognize that both genetic and environmental factors shape a person's mental ability.

🐾 WHAT DO YOU KNOW?...

30. Which of the following findings are consistent with the claim that intelligence cannot only be biologically determined? Check as many that apply.
    ___ a. People's IQ scores have steadily increased across generations.
    ___ b. People's IQ scores decrease during the summer.
    ___ c. Adolescents' percentile scores on intelligence tests changed across two time periods; some increased and others decreased.
    ___ d. The effect of genes on intelligence is lower among the poor.

Multiple Intelligences

Preview Question

> Are there multiple types of intelligence?

Consider the following three people:

1. A Russian schoolboy who frequently cut class, received poor grades, and obtained a higher education only at the insistence of his father

2. An introverted boy in India who was a poor student, had trouble learning multiplication tables, and saw himself as intellectually "sluggish"

3. A child in Spain who had such difficulty learning to read, write, and do arithmetic that he almost didn't make it through grade school

These students don't sound like a very promising lot. But the three boys are (1) Igor Stravinsky, commonly considered the twentieth century's greatest composer of symphonic music; (2) Mohandas Gandhi, the revered Indian spiritual and political leader who led his nation to independence; and (3) Pablo Picasso, universally acknowledged as one of the greatest geniuses in the history of art (Gardner, 1993). They each displayed the highest possible level of brilliance in their fields.

Note two facts about Stravinsky, Gandhi, and Picasso:

> If they had been given intelligence tests in childhood, their scores would not have predicted their extraordinary achievements. Lots of other children would have had higher IQ scores but lesser achievements in adulthood.

> They each excelled in one domain of life—that is, one type of activity—and the domains differed considerably from one another. The political achievements of Gandhi required skills quite different from those needed for the musical achievements of Stravinsky or the visual-artistic achievements of Picasso. Picasso was the person to call if you wanted a work of visual art, but not if you needed a string quartet or a nonviolent political movement.

The fact that Stravinsky, Gandhi, and Picasso each displayed exceptional intellectual ability in one domain of life but not others raises an important question. Is the concept of general intelligence the right way to think about human mental abilities?

Howard Gardner (1993, 1999) thinks not. According to his **multiple intelligences theory,** people possess a number of different mental abilities. Each is a distinct form of intelligence; that is, they are not merely aspects of general intelligence. Gardner emphasizes that one can have a high degree of one intelligence and a low degree of another.

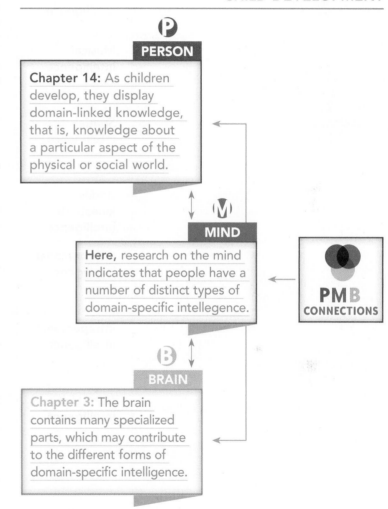

CONNECTING TO BRAIN SYSTEMS AND CHILD DEVELOPMENT

PERSON
Chapter 14: As children develop, they display domain-linked knowledge, that is, knowledge about a particular aspect of the physical or social world.

MIND
Here, research on the mind indicates that people have a number of distinct types of domain-specific intelligence.

PMB CONNECTIONS

BRAIN
Chapter 3: The brain contains many specialized parts, which may contribute to the different forms of domain-specific intelligence.

Charles Peterson / Getty Images

Art Tatum There's no question Art Tatum was a genius. But he possessed one particular *type* of genius: extraordinary musical intelligence. His abilities, then, were consistent with *multiple intelligences theory*, which explains that there are a variety of distinct mental abilities, any of which can be called "an intelligence."

multiple intelligences theory
A theory proposed by Gardner claiming that people possess a number of different mental abilities, each of which is a distinct form of intelligence.

Howard Gardner's multiple intelligences theory proposes that human intellect contains eight different forms of intelligence.

table **8.2**

Multiple Intelligences

Intelligence	Definition	Typical Professions of High Scorer
Linguistic intelligence	The ability to learn languages and to use language effectively in communication	Poets, professional writers, public speakers
Logical-mathematic intelligence	The ability to employ analytic, scientific reasoning and to understand and carry out mathematical operations	Mathematicians, computer programmers, scientists
Musical intelligence	The ability to appreciate, perform, and create musical forms, employing rhythm, melody, and chord structure	Musical performers, composers, and teachers
Spatial intelligence	The ability to visualize, and manipulate in one's mind, images of two- and three-dimensional space	Architects, artists, designers, mathematicians
Bodily-kinesthetic intelligence	The ability to use one's body to achieve goals and to express ideas and emotions	Athletes, dancers, actors
Interpersonal intelligence	The ability to understand the ideas and motives of other people, and to work with others effectively	Politicians, salespersons, community leaders
Intrapersonal intelligence	The ability to understand our own thoughts, motives, and emotions and to enhance one's well-being	Psychologists, writers, philosophers
Naturalistic intelligence	Sensitivity to the natural world and ability to discern differences among plant and animal species	Biologists, farmers, gardeners, conservationists

Gardner has proposed eight different types of mental ability—that is, eight different intelligences. Table 8.2 lists them, along with professions in which you might expect to find people with particularly high levels of the given intelligence.

How can we know these are distinct intelligences, rather than different aspects of one overall, general intelligence? Gardner (1993) cites a variety of evidence. One is **child prodigies,** children who exhibit exceptional mastery of a skill at a very early age. Prodigies usually are not "generalized geniuses" who excel at everything. Rather, they often excel in one form of intelligence. For example, a twentieth-century musical prodigy, the jazz pianist Art Tatum, taught himself piano at age 3. He soon could play complete songs after hearing them only once. By age 6, he was playing, by himself, pieces he heard that were written as duets,

child prodigies Children exhibiting exceptional mastery of a skill at a very early age.

apparently "unaware that there were supposed to be two players" (Art Tatum, n.d.). There is no evidence that Tatum was exceptionally skilled at the verbal, logical, or mathematical tasks included on the WAIS. But in musical intelligence, he was an off-the-charts genius.

Another form of evidence is **savant syndrome,** in which people who are mentally impaired in most areas of life display exceptional performance—an "island of genius" (Treffert, 2009, p. 1)—in one domain. Savant syndrome is sometimes seen among people with autism, a brain disorder whose symptoms include an impaired ability to interact socially with others. People with savant syndrome display exceptionally high levels of skill early in life in specific tasks, such as music, math, or art. The differences in their performance in different domains—impaired in some, exceptionally skilled in others—are consistent with Gardner's claim that the mind contains multiple intelligences that are distinct from one another.

In savant syndrome, then, exceptional skill accompanies mental impairment early in life. There are also cases where people develop exceptional intellectual abilities *late* in life, in the midst of declining overall mental capacity. Researchers (Miller et al., 1998) report five cases in which patients in their 50s and 60s developed artistic abilities while suffering from *dementia,* a progressive decline in mental functioning, due to an abnormal biological deterioration of the front of the brain. These patients' overall ability to think and act effectively grew worse and worse. But their artistic abilities improved!

The image shown in Figure 8.16 was painted by one of these patients, a woman in her mid-60s whose "speech became repetitive and rambling" (Miller et al., 1998, p. 979) due to the dementia, but whose artwork became remarkably skilled. The researchers suggest that the patients' dementia made them less emotionally inhibited than they previously had been, which in turn allowed them to express themselves more freely in their art.

This evidence, too, supports Gardner's multiple intelligences approach. If some mental abilities improve while others deteriorate, the pattern of changes cannot be explained in terms of general intelligence.

Gardner's theory has been criticized, however. Some argue that the evidence in support of it is still sparse (Waterhouse, 2006). Yet others see great virtue in Gardner's work. The people around you—even if they aren't Stravinskys, Gandhis, and Picassos—often possess distinctive skills and abilities that are not captured by traditional intelligence tests. Multiple intelligences theory helps us appreciate the rich range of mental abilities possessed by the world's diverse individuals.

Permissioned from Miller et al. (1998)

figure 8.16
Art despite dementia The artist was a woman in her 60s suffering from dementia. Although her ability to express ideas in words deteriorated as a result of the dementia, her artistic skills improved.

savant syndrome A syndrome characterized by mental impairment in most areas of life but exceptional performance in one domain.

Gardner's approach is not the only theory that moves beyond the traditional "general intelligence" approach. For example, Robert Sternberg's **triarchic theory of intelligence** proposes that intelligent behavior requires three distinct mental components:

1. A *knowledge-acquisition* component, through which people acquire the information needed to solve problems
2. *Executive* components, which people use to develop plans for solving problems and to assess how well their plans are working
3. *Performance* components, which carry out the plans formulated by the executive components

In Sternberg's model, the components of a person's intelligence might be more highly developed in one aspect of life than another; for instance, you might have a lot of intelligence when it comes to fixing a car (i.e., a lot of knowledge, executive-planning skills, and ability to carry out the plans), but less intelligence when it comes to planning a meal (or vice versa). As in Gardner's approach, then, intelligence is not a "general" ability. It is a collection of mental skills that enable you to solve problems in specific areas of life.

> Do you possess a distinctive skill that might not be measured by a traditional intelligence test?

🌀 WHAT DO YOU KNOW?...

31. Howard Gardner cited child _____, among other cases, as evidence of the existence of multiple intelligences. Others are more compelled by evidence indicating that intelligence is a _____ skill. Sternberg's _____ theory of intelligence includes a _____ component, through which we acquire the skills needed to solve problems; _____ components, which we use to develop plans and for measuring our success in achieving them; and _____ components, which enable us to carry out the plans.

The Neuroscience of g

Preview Questions

> Do people with big brains tend to be smarter?
> How are brain connections related to intelligence?

Let's conclude by focusing on a biological level of analysis and asking whether observed individual differences in overall intelligence, or *g*, can be explained in terms of underlying individual differences in nervous system structure or functioning (Deary et al., 2010).

BRAIN SIZE. If you see one cartoon character with a small head, and one with a large head, it's not hard to guess which is the smart one. But is there any truth to the stereotype? Are people with larger brains more intelligent?

It turns out that the answer is yes (Deary et al., 2010). The most convincing evidence comes from a meta-analysis, that is, a statistical summary of results of large numbers of studies. One meta-analysis summarized more than three dozen prior studies, with more than 1500 participants (McDaniel, 2005). Results revealed that IQ correlated positively with brain volume ($r = +.33$). Bigger-brained individuals got higher IQ scores.

The correlation, .33, is significantly greater than zero. Yet it is nowhere near a perfect correlation of 1.0. Many people with small brain volume have high IQ scores (and vice versa). For example, the brain of Walt Whitman, a genius of American

triarchic theory of intelligence A theory of intelligence proposed by Sternberg, which says that intelligent behavior requires three distinct mental components: knowledge acquisition, executive planning, and performance.

poetry, was below average in size (Gould, 1981). Brain size thus does not determine your level of intelligence; it merely predicts individual differences in intelligence to a moderate degree.

BRAIN CONNECTIONS. Intelligence does not reside in any one part of the brain. Intelligent behavior requires coordination among large numbers of brain regions (Bullmore & Sporns, 2009). Individual differences in intelligence thus might be grounded in the way these regions are interconnected.

People differ in the strength of interconnections in the brain. One person might have well-developed connections between any two brain regions, whereas, in another person's brain, these regions might be connected weakly. Evidence suggests that people with highly developed interconnections process information more efficiently and, as a result, get higher IQ scores (Deary et al., 2010). Just as a highway system is efficient if there are numerous roads connecting different places, a brain is efficient if it contains numerous connections among its different places.

In one study (Li et al., 2009), researchers measured brain interconnections among two groups of participants: people with (1) average to high IQ scores and (2) very high IQ scores (>120). Using images of the strength of these interconnections (Figure 8.17), they computed a measure of *brain efficiency,* the overall strength of interconnections in the person's brain. The average-to-high and very high IQ participants differed significantly in brain efficiency (Li et al., 2009). People who had stronger axon interconnections among the regions of their brains, and who thus were able to process information more efficiently, were more intelligent (Figure 8.18).

This research, conducted at a brain level of analysis, directly connects to research you learned about earlier that was conducted at a mind level of analysis. You saw that people's mental powers are significantly shaped by their environmental experiences.

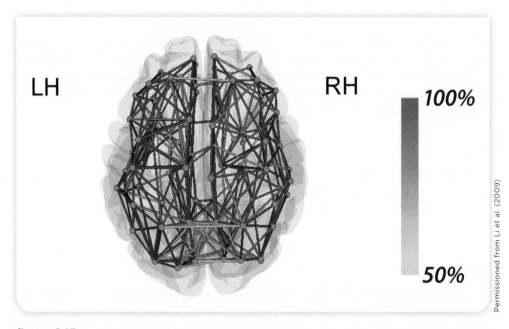

figure **8.17**

Brain connections In this brain image, the green dots indicate areas of the brain and the bars, which vary in color, indicate links among them. The color of the bar represents the percentage of people (in research by Li et al., 2009) who had a direct connection between any two areas. Some connections (red) were possessed by 100% of participants, whereas others (yellow) were present in about half the participants. People with more interconnections overall were found to have higher IQs. (LH and RH indicate right and left hemisphere as you look down on the brain from above.)

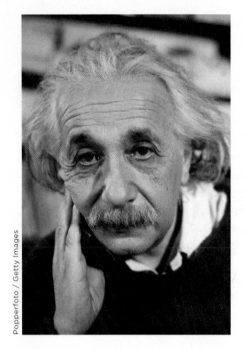

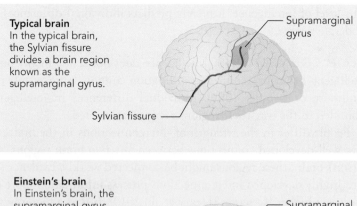

Typical brain
In the typical brain, the Sylvian fissure divides a brain region known as the supramarginal gyrus.

Supramarginal gyrus

Sylvian fissure

Einstein's brain
In Einstein's brain, the supramarginal gyrus was not divided by the Sylvian fissure.

Supramarginal gyrus

Sylvian fissure

figure 8.18
Einstein's brain After his death, the brain of the great physicist Albert Einstein was removed and analyzed to see whether there were any biological clues to his exceptional genius. Researchers found that Einstein lacked one of the grooves (the Sylvian fissure) that is normally found in the human brain (Witelson, Kigar, & Harvey, 1999). The researchers speculated that the absence of this groove may have enabled Einstein to develop an exceptionally dense network of interconnections among brain cells. This unique network of interconnections may have fueled his unique mental power.

Schooling, for example, boosts IQ. Environmental experiences affect brain connections, too; different experiences create different interconnections in the brain (Edelman & Tononi, 2000; see Chapter 3). Research on neural interconnections and intellectual ability thus can give us a brain-level understanding of how people's intelligence is shaped by their experiences in the world.

✪ WHAT DO YOU KNOW?...

32. Two features of the brain are related to IQ scores: (1) brain _____ (though the correlation between it and IQ is far from perfect) and (2) how well _____ different brain regions are to one another.

⟳ Looking Back and Looking Ahead

This chapter put on display the mind's powers: the abilities to categorize objects in an instant, create sentences that adhere to complex linguistic rules, and form mental images that we traverse as if the world had been recreated in our heads. Yet it also displayed the mind's limits. When making decisions about risky, uncertain options, our minds rely on simple rules of thumb that sometimes lead us astray.

The mind can do even more than you've seen in this chapter. It gives you the power not only to think, but also to be aware of the fact that you are thinking. You not only can solve problems like a computer; you can feel proud of your solutions—*un*like a computer. The abilities to be consciously aware of the world and yourself, and to feel as well as think, are explored in other chapters on the mind.

Chapter Review

Now that you have completed this chapter, be sure to turn to Appendix B, where you will find a **Chapter Summary** that is useful for reviewing what you have learned about thinking, language, and intelligence.

Key Terms

ad hoc categories (p. 312)
anchoring-and-adjustment heuristic (p. 333)
aphasia (p. 321)
availability heuristic (p. 332)
basic-level categories (p. 309)
Broca's area (p. 321)
categorize (p. 308)
category level (p. 309)
category structure (p. 310)
child prodigies (p. 352)
classical categories (p. 310)
confirmation bias (p. 328)
decision making (p. 334)
family resemblance (p. 311)
Flynn effect (p. 347)
framing effect (p. 335)
fuzzy categories (p. 310)

general intelligence (*g*) (p. 344)
generative (p. 314)
heuristic (p. 331)
instinct (p. 317)
intelligence (p. 342)
IQ (intelligence quotient) (p. 343)
language (p. 313)
means–ends analysis (p. 337)
mental accounting (p. 336)
mental age (p. 344)
mental imagery (p. 339)
mental rotation (p. 340)
morpheme (p. 315)
multiple intelligences theory (p. 351)
problem solving (p. 336)
problem space (p. 337)
prototype (p. 311)

prototype structure (p. 311)
reasoning (p. 328)
representativeness heuristic (p. 332)
Sapir–Whorf hypothesis (p. 324)
savant syndrome (p. 353)
sign language (p. 323)
statistical language learning (p. 318)
subjective value (p. 334)
syntax (p. 315)
think-aloud protocol analysis (p. 338)
transformational grammar (p. 316)
triarchic theory of intelligence (p. 354)
universal grammar (p. 317)
Wechsler Adult Intelligence Scale (WAIS) (p. 344)
Wernicke's area (p. 321)

Questions for Discussion

1. You learned that animals' communication is not considered language because animals don't use a sequence of symbols to generate novel sentences. Are there examples of communication in humans that, similarly, conveys information, but that would not be considered language? [Analyze]

2. We all know that first impressions are lasting impressions. How might confirmation bias explain this phenomenon? Have you ever been the "victim" of confirmation bias—that is, can you give an example of a time when someone may have been more attentive to negative information about you and less attentive to positive information? What are other real-world examples of confirmation bias? [Analyze, Comprehend]

3. In 2007 a cat named Oscar experienced mild fame. It seemed Oscar had an uncanny ability to predict the deaths of at least 50 patients at the nursing and rehabilitation home where he lived. As patients neared the end of their lives, Oscar would curl up in bed with them, seemingly to see them off. His "hit rate" was so good

that nurses used his visits as a signal that they should call in the family members of the soon-to-be-departed. Many have debated the true cause of his tendency to join people in their hospital beds hours before they died. What explanation does confirmation bias provide? [Analyze]

4. You learned about three judgmental heuristics: availability, representativeness, and anchoring and adjustment. In what way do they benefit our judgment making? Conversely, generate examples of instances when these heuristics may result in poor judgments (this may be accomplished most easily with representativeness and anchoring and adjustment). What seems to be the trade-off in applying heuristics? [Analyze, Comprehend]

5. You read about research by Shepard and Metzler (1971) in which the amount of time it took participants to answer a question about a rotated shape depended on how much they would have to mentally "unrotate" that shape. How is this an example of embodied cognition? [Analyze]

Chapter Review

6. What do you think explains the Flynn effect; that is, why has the average IQ increased so rapidly across time? Are you and your peers smarter than your parents or other childhood caregivers, or is something else at work? [Analyze]

7. How do you suppose Gardner determined that there were eight different types of intelligence? If you were to start from scratch to determine how many different kinds of intelligence existed, where would you begin? [Synthesize]

8. Come up with a definition for "street smarts." Which of Gardner's multiple intelligences is involved in street smarts? Are there skills inherent in street smarts that are not reflected in his list? Do the same for "book smarts." [Analyze]

9. This chapter's Cultural Opportunities feature presents information about research on the role of culture on language. In it, you learned that people in Western cultures are adjective users, whereas people from Eastern cultures use state verbs (e.g., "likes," "hates," "prefers"). This difference originates in differences in how people think; Westerners tend to think about the inner qualities of objects, whereas Easterners consider objects as being embedded in environments. What do you think are the implications of this for the kinds of attributions people make about others' behavior? For instance, what kinds of inferences would Westerners and Easterners make for someone who showed up late for class? For someone who brought cupcakes to class? [Analyze]

Self-Test

1. Of the following items, which is at the highest category level?
   a. Vessels
   b. Glasses
   c. Mugs
   d. Bowls

2. Which of the following is the best example of a fuzzy category?
   a. Even numbers
   b. Rock music
   c. Minerals
   d. Crimes

3. Which of the following could not be categorized as a morpheme of the English language?
   a. *anti*
   b. *dis*
   c. *un*
   d. *ris*

4. Which of the following sentences is syntactically incorrect?
   a. The yellow computer cried softly.
   b. A naked tree sings tunelessly.
   c. The hairy rake happily galloped.
   d. Hungry a man voraciously ate lunch.

5. Chomsky claimed that humans possess an evolved biological mechanism that enables them to acquire language and that they therefore inherit the universal rules of all languages. Which of the following recent findings is simultaneously true and argues against his claim?
   a. Psychologists have not identified any brain structures related to language processing.
   b. Linguists have found that the rules of grammar are, in fact, not universal.
   c. Psychologists have found that language is processed in several areas of the brain.
   d. Twins can create syntactically correct language with one another, even in the absence of rewards.

6. Here are four findings presented in the chapter. (1) Grammar is not as universal as Chomsky thought; (2) research indicates that Australians describe one another with more adjectives and fewer state verbs than do South Koreans; (3) we can learn at least some rules of grammar through rewards; and (4) we can also learn grammar through statistical language learning. Which of the following conclusions do these particular findings lead us to draw?
   a. The ability to acquire language is entirely innate.
   b. The environment plays a very small role in language acquisition.
   c. Culture plays a large role in shaping language.
   d. Skinner's theory of language acquisition is most useful.

7. How has brain-imaging evidence enhanced our understanding of the functioning of Broca's and Wernicke's areas?
   a. It suggested, among other things, that other brain areas are also responsible for language processing.
   b. It confirmed, among other things, the belief that these brain areas are only responsible for language processing.
   c. It suggested, among other things, that everyone's brains look the same when processing language.
   d. It confirmed, among other things, the belief that these brain areas are the only ones responsible for language processing.

8. On what basis did researchers claim that Nim Chimpsky's use of sign language was not an example of true language use?
   a. Nim lacked the physical ability to produce human sounds.
   b. Nim's manual dexterity was bad, so his signs were ambiguous in their meaning.
   c. Nim could not produce novel combinations of signs to convey meaning.
   d. Nim was not even able to imitate simple signs.

9. *Schadenfreude* is a German term that refers to the pleasure we derive from others' pain. For example, people may experience *schadenfreude* when their presidential candidate wins, especially if it means a bitter defeat for the other side. There is no term for this emotional experience in the English language, though it has become increasingly popular as a borrowed word. If the Sapir–Whorf hypothesis is true, which of the following would also be true?
   a. We've always had this emotional experience, but not the word to express it.
   b. Prior to our having learned of this term, we may not have experienced this emotion.
   c. Other English words do an inadequate job describing this emotion, but we still experience it.
   d. Our experience of this emotion will be much less extreme now that we have a word for it.

10. Your teacher tells you that she has an arithmetic rule in mind that characterizes a sequence of three numbers: 2, 4, and 6. You can test your theory of the rule by naming any three numbers and she will tell you whether you are correct. Your theory is that the rule is any three even numbers that ascend in order. If you let confirmation bias guide your theory-testing, which three numbers will you name?
    a. 1, 3, 5
    b. 6, 8, 10
    c. 6, 18, 30
    d. 5, 3, 1

11. Suppose you saw in a shopping mall a woman you had never seen before whose hair, nails, and clothing were black and who had several face and ear piercings and tattoos. You immediately figured that she was a tattoo artist, which is very rare, rather than a college student, which is much more common. What heuristic does this illustrate?
    a. Representativeness
    b. Availability
    c. Mental accounting
    d. Framing effects

12. An individual rejects an offer to go to the movies because she has already been twice that week and instead suggests she and her friend go to dinner, where she spends the same amount of money she would have spent if she had gone to the movies. Which of the following heuristics was she relying upon when she rejected the movie offer?
    a. Representativeness
    b. Availability
    c. Mental accounting
    d. Framing effects

13. What is the trade-off of allowing heuristics to guide our processing?
    a. On the one hand, they are an efficient way to make judgments; on the other, they may lead to errors.
    b. There is no trade-off; heuristics always lead us to make accurate judgments.
    c. On the one hand, they lack efficiency; on the other, they consistently lead to the best judgments.
    d. There is no trade-off; heuristics always lead us to make inaccurate judgments.

14. If there is such a thing as general intelligence, *g*, then how should scores on the four subscales of the Wechsler Adult Intelligence Scale (WAIS; Verbal Comprehension, Perceptual Reasoning, Working Memory, and Processing Speed) be related?
    a. Verbal Comprehension and Perceptual Reasoning should be positively correlated and Working Memory and Processing Speed negatively correlated.
    b. Verbal Comprehension and Working Memory should be positively correlated and Perceptual Reasoning and Processing Speed negatively correlated.
    c. All the scales should be positively correlated with one another except for Processing Speed, which should be uncorrelated with any subscale.
    d. All the scales should be positively correlated with one another.

15. Which of the following conclusions about the effects of genes and the environment on intelligence is supported by research described in this chapter?
    a. Intelligence is entirely shaped by heredity.
    b. Intelligence is entirely shaped by the environment.
    c. Intelligence is shaped by an interaction of genes and environment.
    d. We do not yet know what causes some people to have more intelligence than others.

Answers

You can check your answers to the preceding Self-Test and the chapter's What Do You Know? questions in Appendix B.

Consciousness

9

FIVE YEARS AGO, THE PATIENT WAS IN A CAR CRASH. The accident fractured his skull and damaged his brain. Since then, his mind has seemed devoid of thought. His eyes are open. But if you talk to him, he doesn't answer, and if you try to get his attention, he seems unaware of your presence. Except for simple reflexes such as opening his eyes and breathing, he doesn't even move. His diagnosis? "Persistent vegetative state." A team of medical specialists evaluated him for a month and could find no sign of human thought.

Then some other doctors had a different idea. They knew that, from the outside, his mind seemed blank. But how did things look "from the inside"? To find out, they put him in a brain imaging device. While taking pictures of his brain, they asked him to imagine two everyday activities: hitting some tennis balls and walking from room to room in his house. Next, they asked him simple yes/no questions—for example, "Do you have any brothers?"—and told him to think about tennis playing if the answer was "no" and to think about walking through his house if the answer was "yes."

If you had observed his doctors, their behavior would have looked futile. Why ask questions of a man who has seemed completely without human thought for five years? You would expect the brain images to be blank. But they weren't! When the man was asked to imagine playing tennis and walking through his house, his brain activity resembled that of perfectly normal, healthy people who had been asked to think about those same activities (Monti et al., 2010). When the doctors checked his answers to the yes/no questions, they found that he got them right. He was no vegetable. He could hear the doctors' voices, understand their questions, and answer them correctly.

His injuries had robbed this man of many abilities: walking and talking, smiling and frowning, even nodding or shaking his head. Yet there is something he still had: consciousness. 🎯

Gallery Stock

WHAT ARE YOU experiencing right now? You're thinking about the sentences on this page. You might be feeling the temperature of the room you're in (especially if it's too warm or too cold), the pressure of a chair against your skin (especially if it's uncomfortable), or the sound of some nearby music (especially if it's loud). You might be experiencing hunger, fatigue, sleepiness, or maybe a feeling of interest as you start a new chapter of this book.

These external stimuli and internal feelings—temperature, sound, fatigue, and so forth—are stimuli of which you are *conscious*. **Consciousness** is your awareness and personal experience of your surroundings and yourself.

Consciousness Studies in the History of Psychology

Preview Question

> What could have made consciousness an "unmentionable topic" by the 1980s?

The history of psychological studies of consciousness is long and somewhat odd. At the outset of scientific psychology, it was the field's #1 topic. Wilhelm Wundt and his associates, in psychology's first laboratory, studied the flow of thoughts and feelings that make up a person's conscious experiences (Blumenthal, 2001; see Chapter 1). Three decades of research culminated in the publication of the book *Experimental Analysis of the Phenomena of Consciousness,* by Wundt's main laboratory assistant (Wirth, 1908).

Wundt's efforts placed consciousness in the forefront of psychological science. Researchers in Europe and the United States explored the structure of conscious experience and the functions that consciousness serves. By 1911, a textbook writer could proclaim that "the generally accepted first problem in psychology is to determine the character of consciousness as we immediately experience it" (Pillsbury, 1911, p. 60).

But soon thereafter, everything changed. A school of thought known as *behaviorism* (see Chapter 7) contended that consciousness studies should be jettisoned from psychological science. The behaviorist argument was simple and, to many, compelling: Science progresses through careful observation and measurement; conscious states cannot be directly observed and measured; consciousness, therefore, cannot be a topic for scientific investigation in psychology. "The time seems to have come," a leading behaviorist declared in 1913, "when psychology must discard all reference to consciousness" (Watson, 1913/1994, p. 249).

In the early 1960s, psychology saw the emergence of a new school of thought. Researchers asserted that thinking processes—memory, reasoning, problem solving—could be understood by drawing analogies between human thinking and information processing in computers (Newell & Simon, 1961; see Chapter 6). The computer metaphor invigorated the study of many aspects of thinking. However, it did little for the study of consciousness. Computers can process a lot of information, but, as we discuss in detail below, they are not conscious; your word processor can fix your spelling mistakes, but it does not feel pride in its accomplishments. The computer metaphor thus did not spur consciousness research.

Thanks substantially to behaviorism and the computer metaphor, consciousness studies essentially dried up for three-quarters of a century. By the late 1980s, consciousness had become "an unmentionable topic in science" (Prinz, 2012, p. 3).

It's been going in and out of style Consciousness was a major focus of study among nineteenth-century founders of psychology, but was neglected during much of the twentieth century. In recent decades, scientists have again focused their attention on the topic—as illustrated by this poster, which celebrates the twentieth anniversary of an inaugural scientific conference on consciousness studies by depicting major figures in the field.

20th Anniversary Toward a Science of Consciousness, Tucson Conference, University of Arizona.

consciousness Awareness and personal experience of oneself and one's surroundings.

But then things changed dramatically again. In the past quarter-century, the study of consciousness has experienced a rebirth. Its sheer magnitude has been startling; nearly twice as many scientific papers on consciousness were published in one recent 15-year period as had been published in the previous 85 years put together (Prinz, 2012). Psychologists, philosophers, and neuroscientists have combined efforts to produce new answers to fundamental questions about consciousness. Let's begin our study of consciousness with two of these questions: *What is consciousness? Who has consciousness?*

✦ WHAT DO YOU KNOW?...

1. True or False?
   a. Behaviorists objected to the study of consciousness on the basis that because consciousness could not be objectively measured, it could not be scientifically investigated.
   b. The metaphor that emerged in the 1960s, that human thinking processes were similar to computer information processing, led to a resurgence of interest in the study of consciousness.

   See Appendix B for answers to What Do You Know? questions.

The "What" and "Who" of Consciousness

Step 1 in the study of consciousness is to identify what it is. This can be done by recognizing consciousness's defining features.

Consciousness: What Is It?

Preview Questions

> What does it mean to say that consciousness is "subjective"?
> What psychological quality must something have in order to say that it has "consciousness"?

Consciousness has two defining features: (1) It is *subjective,* and (2) it involves more than the mere detection of stimuli in the environment.

SUBJECTIVITY. Consciousness is personal. It exists, and must be assessed, from the perspective of the individual person—the "subject"—who is having the conscious experience. This is what it means to say that consciousness is "subjective" (Mandik, 2001). Only you can identify the contents of your conscious experience and what it is like to experience them.

In this respect, consciousness is relatively unique. Many other personal qualities are objective; that is, someone observing you can provide an independent, unbiased view of those qualities. This is not true for consciousness, however. An example illustrates the difference between subjective experience and objective facts.

Sometimes, as a result of injury or surgery, people lose a limb. More than 90% of these people experience **phantom limb syndrome,** the subjective conscious experience that the amputated limb is still attached to their body (Ramachandran & Hirstein, 1998). They often experience pain in the limb—despite its having been amputated. (The pain is produced within the brain, not the limb itself; see Chapter 3.)

The amputation is an objective fact. Someone other than the patient can assess whether the limb is still attached. If a patient claims, "Doctor, my limb is actually still attached," the doctor can check the true state of affairs and say, "Sorry, you're wrong; it turns out that it is not attached." The pain, however, is subjective. If the patient says, "Doctor, I'm in pain," there is nothing for the doctor to "check" to verify the

phantom limb syndrome The subjective conscious feeling that an amputated limb is still attached to one's body.

statement, and it would make no sense for the doctor to respond, "Sorry, you're wrong; it turns out that you are not in pain." The patient is the one-and-only expert on his or her own conscious experience of pain.

This is what it means for pain, and other conscious experiences, to be subjective. Such experiences occur, and can be verified, only from the point of view of the individual conscious subject.

MORE THAN MERE "DETECTION" OF THE ENVIRONMENT. The second feature of consciousness involves a distinction between (1) detecting and responding to events, and (2) feeling something after the event is detected.

Many organisms and human-made objects detect stimuli and respond to them. An "electric eye" detects you when you walk through a doorway into a store and responds by ringing a bell, alerting the storekeeper to your presence. A thermometer detects frigid temperature and responds by displaying "5°." A Venus Flytrap detects an insect on its surface and responds by closing its leaves, trapping the insect.

These objects detect and respond to events yet are *not* conscious. To see this, compare your experience on a cold day to that of the thermometer. Like the thermometer, you detect frigid temperature and say, "It's, like, 5 degrees out here!" But you do something the thermometer doesn't; you *experience* the cold. You feel what it "is like" to be out in the frigid temperature. That's not true for the thermometer. Except as a joke, you wouldn't say, "I wonder what it's like for my poor thermometer to be outside on such a cold day."

This simple example makes an important point. Consciousness involves more than just detecting and responding to events. It involves feelings. The scientific study of consciousness is the study of what it *feels* like to be a conscious being (Chalmers, 2010).

Now that we have learned what consciousness is, we can devote the remainder of this chapter to the main topics in the study of consciousness: the question of which beings have conscious experience; psychological and biological processes in consciousness; the dreamy alteration in conscious experience that is sleep; and alterations in conscious experience caused by meditation, hypnosis, and drugs.

> **"On days like this, I wish I were a real thermometer."** Real thermometers detect the temperature but do not feel cold; unlike our cartoon friend, real thermometers do not have conscious experiences. Consciousness thus involves more than merely detecting environmental stimuli.

© Mark A. Hicks

💧 WHAT DO YOU KNOW?...

2. Though amputation is an objective fact, the pain of _____ limb syndrome illustrates that pain (and consciousness) is a _____ experience.

3. Your bathroom scale detects and responds to your weight when you step on it. Why can it not be said to have consciousness?

Consciousness: Who Has It?

Preview Questions

> On what basis did the French philosopher René Descartes declare that consciousness is a basic fact of life?
> When, during development, do humans first experience consciousness?
> Do animals have consciousness? How do we know?
> Do animals have self-consciousness? How do we know?
> Why don't robots have consciousness?

Earth is home to billions of creatures. It also houses billions of man-made devices—computers, smartphones, robots—that process information. Which of these are conscious?

PEOPLE. The one being that you can be sure is conscious is yourself; you know that you experience the world. Your own consciousness is a basic fact of life.

The French philosopher René Descartes made this observation about 400 years ago. He was searching for a secure basis of knowledge—facts that he knew, for certain, were true. Descartes understood that some things that appear true could be false. For instance, the earth appears flat. The sun appears to turn red when it sets. But these are illusions, not facts. Was there anything he could know was true, for sure?

Descartes judged that the only fact of which he could be certain was the fact of his own existence and conscious experience. Even if he tried to doubt it—asking himself, "Hmm, do I, Descartes, even exist?"—the act of doubting, Descartes concluded, proved that he really did exist, because somebody had to be doing the doubting, and that person had to be Descartes himself. "I think," Descartes claimed, "therefore I am."

You can engage in the line of thinking Descartes pioneered and easily conclude that your own consciousness exists, too. You're likely not alone. One can entertain the thought that "I alone exist; everybody else is a figment of my imagination." But we will ignore that unlikely possibility and presume that all biologically normal humans possess consciousness. When asking, "Who has consciousness?" you confidently can answer, "people."

What is it like to have consciousness?

Human consciousness is pervasive; it occurs almost all the time. When awake, you're generally conscious of your surroundings, your feelings, and the thoughts running through your head. When asleep, you spend much of the time dreaming, which is a form of conscious experience; although not awake, you are experiencing the vivid, sometimes weird images and storylines of your dreams.

There is another sense in which consciousness is pervasive: It starts early in life and persists throughout the life span. Some evidence suggests that humans have conscious awareness before birth. Third-trimester fetuses, for example, are aware of sounds near the mother's abdomen (Eliot, 1999). They also appear to be aware of musical sounds. In a study, researchers used an ultrasound machine to observe the reactions of 27- and 35-week-old fetuses to the musical notes middle C and high C (Shahidullah & Hepper, 1994). All fetuses reacted by moving their arms and legs when middle C was played. When the researchers repeated middle C a number of times, all infants habituated to the sound, that is, they responded to it less and less. (Habituation occurs at all ages; see Chapter 7.) When the experimenters switched notes to high C, older fetuses, but not the 27-week-olds, responded once again by moving their arms and legs. This suggests that the older fetuses were consciously aware of not only the sound, but also the *difference* in sound; they were conscious of the fact that middle C and high C differed.

Studies of infants complement this research on fetuses. When adults become consciously aware of a stimulus, they display a distinctive pattern of brain activity. A similar pattern of brain activity in response to stimuli has been observed in infants as young as 5 months old (Kouider et al., 2013). This finding further suggests that conscious awareness is evident early in life.

This capacity for consciousness usually lasts a lifetime. However, people sometimes lose it. Injury or illness can extinguish conscious experience, as you saw in this chapter's opening story. Researchers did identify a person who had been diagnosed as

The philosopher René Descartes, depicted in discussion with Christina, Queen of Sweden. (Unfortunately, this was one of Descartes's last discussions; he died of pneumonia contracted during his wintertime visit to Sweden in 1649–1650.) To Descartes, the existence of conscious experience was the one fact about the world of which he could be certain.

THINK ABOUT IT

Descartes said, "I think, therefore I am" (i.e., "Therefore, I and my conscious mind exist"). But you could program a computer to say, "I think, therefore I am." Does that mean it would exist, with a conscious mind?

being in a persistently vegetative state—that is, a state lacking conscious awareness—yet whose brain activity indicated that he actually was consciously aware of the world. Unfortunately, many other patients in this study (Owen et al., 2006) were not. They showed no distinctive brain activity in response to the researchers' probing. Both behavioral and brain evidence indicated that these other patients, although alive, had lost the capacity for consciousness.

NONHUMAN ANIMALS. How do we know that nonhuman animals are conscious? They *appear* to be conscious; your dog seems excited when you arrive home and tired after she runs around in a park. But appearances could be deceiving. A motion-sensitive electronic device could appear conscious if programmed to excitedly shout "Hello!" when you pass by. What firm evidence is there, then, that animals have a conscious mind?

There are two types of evidence. One is behavioral. When animals perform tasks, they are distractible in much the same way that people are. Researchers observe that animals sometimes lose track of important information (e.g., the location of offspring) when engaged in an activity unrelated to that information (e.g., obtaining food for oneself; Baars, 2005). The parallel between human and animal distractibility suggests that both human and animal mental life consists of conscious experience of limited size. We and our furry friends can focus on only a small amount of information at any given time.

> How can you tell if an animal, such as a dog, is distracted?

The second source of evidence is biological. The brain systems needed for human consciousness (see below) exist, in quite similar form, in mammals other than humans. This cross-species similarity suggests that all mammals have conscious feelings (Baars, 2005).

When discussing animal consciousness, it is important to distinguish consciousness from *self-consciousness.* Consciousness, as you've learned, occurs when an organism has subjective experiences, or feelings. **Self-consciousness** is different; it refers to thinking *about* yourself. People are thinking self-consciously when they contemplate themselves, their experiences, and how they appear to others.

You can have conscious feelings without self-conscious thoughts. For instance, if you are injured, you immediately have a conscious feeling of pain. *Afterward,* you might have self-conscious thoughts such as "I'm hurt!" or "What happened to me?" The initial pain, before the thoughts, shows that conscious feelings can occur without self-conscious thinking.

Few animals show any sign of self-conscious thought. In fact, few seem even to recognize themselves. In a **mirror self-recognition test,** researchers first expose an animal to its image in a mirror. They then make an unusual mark on the animal and place it in front of the mirror again, to determine whether it recognizes that the mark is a mark on itself. (Rubbing the mark on its body, for example, would be a sign of recognition.) Only a few species other than humans—gorillas, chimpanzees, orangutans, and probably dolphins (Reiss & Marino, 2001; Suddendorf & Butler, 2013)—can pass the mirror recognition test. Household pets such as dogs and cats cannot.

Even nonhuman species that pass the mirror self-recognition test lack self-conscious thinking of the human variety. A central feature of human self-conscious thought is **mental time travel,** the ability to project yourself backward or forward in time in your mind (Suddendorf & Corballis, 2007). People commonly think about themselves in the past and the prospective future, dwelling on past events, how they could have acted differently, and how

> How often have you engaged in mental time travel today?

Self-recognition Dolphins can pass a "mirror self-recognition" test. If a triangular mark is applied to a dolphin and it then passes in front of a mirror, the dolphin will position itself in front of the mirror in a way that enables it to take a long look at the mark. This means that the dolphin recognizes that "the dolphin in the mirror" with a mark on its body is itself.

Diana Reiss

self-consciousness The *process* of thinking about oneself, that is, thinking about one's own experiences and how one appears to others.

mirror self-recognition test A method for evaluating an animal's capacity to recognize itself in which researchers determine whether the animal looking at itself in a mirror behaves in a manner indicating its recognition of a mark made on its body.

mental time travel The ability to project yourself backward or forward in time in your mind.

they will cope with events next time (Kahneman & Miller, 1986). There is no convincing evidence that animals do any of this. Humans appear to be unique in their ability to engage in mental time travel.

In sum, then, humans have a unique form of self-conscious mental life. But we are not unique in having conscious experiences. A vast number of animal species consciously experience pains and pleasures, desires and fears.

Not all animals have consciousness, however. Many simple organisms, such as insects or worms, lack the brain systems required for conscious experience. They detect and react to events in the environment, but scientific findings provide no firm grounds for concluding that they have conscious feelings. Some argue that even fish, a relatively complex class of organisms, lack the brain structures required for conscious feelings. Analyses of the nervous system of fish suggest that they merely react to the environment reflexively, experiencing neither pleasure nor pain (Rose, 2002).

ROBOTS? If you walk into a Honda office in Japan, ASIMO, the receptionist, will stroll up, say hello, shake your hand, and show you around the place. ASIMO will answer simple questions and, with some practice, may even learn to recognize you the next time you stop by.

This wouldn't be all that impressive for a flesh-and-blood receptionist. But—as you may have guessed from his wacky name—ASIMO is a robot.

Is ASIMO conscious? It certainly looks like it. If something walks up to you, shakes your hand, and answers your questions, it would be reasonable to guess that it is conscious. Yet ASIMO surely lacks consciousness. So do his electronic relatives: computers, smartphones, chess-playing software programs, robotic vacuum cleaners, and the like. These devices do process information. They encode incoming information into memory, combine it with stored information, and execute programs that manipulate the information. But they do not have feelings; they are no more conscious than a thermometer.

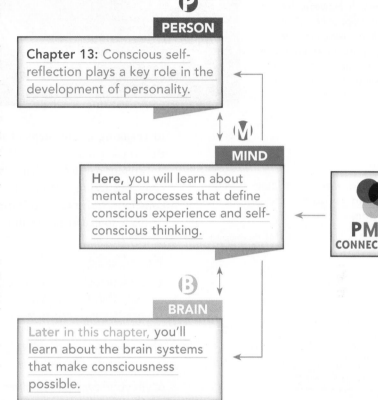

CONNECTING TO BRAIN SYSTEMS AND PERSONALITY PROCESSES

(P) PERSON

Chapter 13: Conscious self-reflection plays a key role in the development of personality.

(M) MIND

Here, you will learn about mental processes that define conscious experience and self-conscious thinking.

PMB CONNECTIONS

(B) BRAIN

Later in this chapter, you'll learn about the brain systems that make consciousness possible.

Larry Downing / Reuters / Newscom

"It only looks like I'm excited to meet the President."
On a trip to Japan, U.S. President Barack Obama met ASIMO the robot. ASIMO greeted the president; kicked a soccer ball to him; and walked, ran, and hopped around the stage. But none of this means that ASIMO is conscious. Robots detect and respond to stimuli without having the feelings that are the hallmark of consciousness.

No chest-thumping by the winner An IBM computer beat world chess champion Gary Kasparov on May 11, 1997. Kasparov was disappointed that he lost the chess match. However, his computer opponent, Deep Blue, didn't rejoice in victory. The computer program displays an exceptionally high level of chess-playing intelligence, but not consciousness.

> I'm afraid. I'm afraid, Dave. Dave, my mind is going. I can feel it. I can feel it.
>
> —HAL the computer,
> *2001: A Space Odyssey*

Information processing, by itself, is not sufficient to produce conscious experience (Chalmers, 1996; McGinn, 1999; Searle, 1980). Information processing is merely the manipulation of symbols (numbers or words) according to logical rules. Consciousness is different; it involves not only symbol manipulation, but also emotions, sensations, and other feelings. In fact, logical reasoning is not even necessary for conscious experience. An animal bitten by a predator experiences pain immediately, prior to engaging in any steps of information processing to determine, for example, who the attacker was.

Present-day robots (and other information-processing machines) thus do *not* have conscious feelings. What about robots of the future? Many believe they will never be conscious. Others are optimistic, suggesting that with extra circuits, today's robots can be made to experience feelings (Parisi & Petrosino, 2010). Stay tuned!

😮 WHAT DO YOU KNOW?...

4. Descartes's famous quote "I think, therefore I am" conveys the idea that the only thing about which we can be certain is our own _____. Consciousness exists even before we are _____, as illustrated by research with fetuses who could detect differences in sounds.

5. In your own words, describe why an animal's distractibility is evidence of its consciousness.

6. In your own words, describe why an animal's inability to recognize itself in the mirror is evidence of its lack of self-consciousness.

7. A robot can manipulate symbols according to logical rules, but because it doesn't experience _____, it cannot be said to possess consciousness.

The Psychology of Consciousness

Our discussion of people, nonhuman animals, and robots shows you what consciousness is: the ability to *feel* events—to suffer the pains and enjoy the pleasures of life. Now let's examine the psychological processes of consciousness in detail. We'll begin with a classic theory of conscious experience called *dualism*. As you'll see, dualism is intuitively appealing yet deeply flawed. Try to detect the flaws. Thinking critically about the drawbacks of dualism helps you to understand how the mind and brain do—and do not—work.

Dualism

Preview Question

> Is the mind separate from the body?

Dualism is a theory about the mind, the brain, and conscious experience. Dualism proposes that mind and body are two separate entities. The body is a physical, material object, whereas the mind is nonphysical—an immaterial "spirit." According to dualism, the physical brain does not produce consciousness. Consciousness is a property of

dualism The proposition that the mind and body are two separate entities, with consciousness being a property of the nonphysical mind.

Stan Honda / AFP / Getty Images

"And the Lord God formed man of the dust of the ground, and breathed into his nostrils the breath of life; and man became a living soul" (Genesis 2:7). Dualism is at least as old as the Old Testament. In the biblical story of humans' creation, as depicted here by Michelangelo, Adam consists of two parts: a material body ("formed . . . of the dust") and a nonmaterial soul (that is "breathed into" the body). The soul that makes Adam a thinking being, then, does not depend on the body for its existence. (It is also of interest that, in Michelangelo's depiction, God and his contingent are roughly the same shape as the human brain.)

the nonphysical mind. The brain is merely the location at which the conscious mind and physical body interact.

Dualism is an ancient belief. Buddhism, some philosophies in ancient Greece, and Christianity all posit a mind, or soul, that is distinct from the body and lives on after the body's death.

In later Western philosophy, the most famous dualistic view was developed by Descartes, whose ideas we discussed earlier in this chapter. He proposed that the mind and body interact at a specific spot within the brain: the pineal gland (Figure 9.1). Why the pineal gland? His reasoning combined two ideas:

> Descartes believed that there must be one spot—a single location—in the brain at which information from all perceptual organs (eyes, ears, etc.) comes together. This spot is like a "theatre" within the brain. For example, at a movie theatre, sounds and images must be projected to the same place, so you can experience them together. Analogously, Descartes thought the sounds and sights of the world are projected into one spot in the brain.

> Descartes knew the pineal gland is biologically unique. Other brain structures come in pairs, with parallel structures in the brain's left and right sides (see Chapter 3), but there is only one pineal gland. He thus concluded that information was projected there.

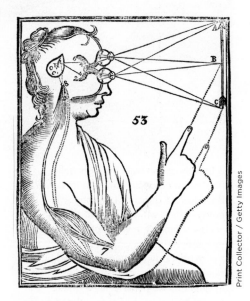

figure 9.1
In Descartes's theory of consciousness, the body displays information from the environment within the brain, at the pineal gland (shown, much larger than normal size, in the image within the skull, on the left). The mind—which has no physical existence, only a mental one—encounters this information at the pineal gland, resulting in conscious experience.

 THINK ABOUT IT

Is dualism testable? Or does its claim that consciousness is a property of a nonphysical mind—a spirit—make it an idea that cannot be tested scientifically?

In Descartes's dualism, the nonphysical mind views the images in the pineal gland, makes decisions, and directs the body's actions by affecting mechanisms in the brain.

🕊 WHAT DO YOU KNOW?•••

8. For each of the "answers" below, provide the question. The first one is done for you.
   a. Answer: A theory claiming that consciousness is a property of the non-physical mind and that the brain is where the mind and body interact.
   Question: What is dualism?
   b. Answer: The philosopher who is most associated with dualism.
   c. Answer: The particular area of the brain that Descartes identified as the site where sights and sounds of the world must be projected.

If this ghost can walk through walls, how can it hold something in its hand? Because the ghost is a nonphysical entity—that's why it can float through walls—shouldn't any object fall through its hands? This drawing illustrates the mind–body problem exhibited in dualistic theories of consciousness. In dualism, the mind is like a ghost: a nonphysical spirit. There is thus no way to explain how the mind can influence the body, which is a physical object.

A homunculus view of conscious experience. The problem is that one still has to explain why *the homunculus* is conscious.

mind–body problem A conceptual problem that arises within dualistic theories (see dualism), namely, that there is no way to explain how a nonphysical mind can influence the physical body without violating laws of science.

homunculus problem A problem in scientific explanation that arises if an organism's capacity for consciousness is explained by proposing that a structure in its mind or brain is conscious. The problem is the failure to explain how consciousness arises in the mind or brain structure.

Problems with Dualism

Preview Question

› What are some limitations of dualism?

Today, scholars recognize that dualism is deeply flawed (e.g., Dennett, 1991). Two problems stand out: the *mind–body problem* and the *homunculus problem*.

THE MIND–BODY PROBLEM. Dualism claims that the mind influences the body. The mind perceives information in the brain and then directs the body's action.

In saying this, dualism encounters the **mind–body problem.** The problem is that there is no way to explain how the mind influences the physical body without violating laws of science (Dennett, 1991). A basic principle of science is that only physical objects or forces (e.g., gravity or magnetism) can influence other physical objects. Since, according to dualism, the mind is *non*physical, it should be *un*able to influence the body.

THE HOMUNCULUS PROBLEM. The **homunculus problem** is a problem in scientific explanation (McMullen, 2001). It arises whenever a theory states that a structure in the mind or brain has conscious experiences. That structure is like a small conscious person-in-the-head: a homunculus. (*Homunculus* in Latin means "small human.") Descartes's theory worked like this. He said that the mind experiences information displayed in the brain. The mind thus was consciously aware of the information; it was a homunculus in the brain.

What's the problem with a homunculus? If a theory claims that people are conscious because a structure in the brain is conscious, it does not solve the problem of consciousness. It merely introduces a new problem to be solved: Why is the structure in the brain conscious? The cartoon here illustrates the problem. If Descartes says that "the person whose brain is shown has consciousness thanks to the homunculus, who consciously experiences sights and sounds displayed in the brain," then he has not explained why *the homunculus* has consciousness, and so has not provided an explanation of how consciousness occurs. Saying that "the homunculus has, in his brain, an even smaller homunculus" clearly does not offer any serious progress in explaining how consciousness works.

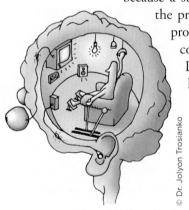

© Dr. Jolyon Trosianko

THINK ABOUT IT

When you hear a scientific explanation, think critically. Suppose someone says, "Water is wet because it is made of wet molecules." Once you think about it, you see that this is no explanation at all; it does not explain why *the molecules* are wet and thus does not explain wetness (see Hanson, 1961; Nozick, 1981). Similarly, saying that "people have consciousness because information in the brain is perceived by the conscious mind" does not explain why *the mind* is conscious and thus does not explain consciousness.

A challenge for psychology, then, is to build a theory of consciousness that does not run into the mind–body or homunculus problems.

WHAT DO YOU KNOW?...

9. Which is the better summary of the mind–body problem?
   a. If the mind is a nonphysical object, then it would violate a law of science to say that it can affect a physical object, the body.
   b. The science of mind–body relations is still unable to explain how the mind, a nonphysical object, can affect the body, a physical object.

10. Which is the better summary of the homunculus problem?
    a. To explain consciousness by claiming there is a structure in the brain (a homunculus) that experiences consciousness requires one to specify where that structure is.
    b. To explain consciousness by claiming there is a structure in the brain (a homunculus) that experiences consciousness, one introduces the problem of explaining how that structure is itself conscious.

Overcoming the Problems of Dualism

Preview Question

> How can one explain consciousness without proposing that the images of the outer world are reproduced within the brain?

One theory that avoids the problems of dualism has been proposed by the philosopher Daniel Dennett and his colleagues (Dennett, 1991; Dennett & Kinsbourne, 1992; Schnieder, 2007). The theory has three main features.

The first feature involves the distinction between two potential activities of the mind: *reproducing* a stimulus in the environment, and *detecting* a stimulus in the environment. In Descartes's theory, the brain reproduces stimuli; it essentially creates a picture of the world within the head. If a red arrow appears in front of someone's eyes, the person's brain reproduces the image (see Figure 9.1). Dennett realized, however, that to explain consciousness, you do not need to propose that the mind reproduces stimuli. Instead, it may primarily *detect* features of stimuli and, based on what it detects, make "educated guesses" about what is in the environment. If a red arrow is placed in front of you, different parts of your mind detect different features of this stimulus: its long shape, pointy top, color, orientation (pointing up), and so on. Once a few of these features are detected, you can infer—that is, make a good guess—that the stimulus is a red arrow, because a red arrow is just about the only thing that has all these features (long, pointy, etc.).

The second feature involves time. Dennett explains that different parts of the brain take different amounts of time to do their work. A brain mechanism that detects shape, for example, might work faster than one that detects color. This means there is no single place in the mind—no inner theatre—in which the world is reproduced at any one particular time. Instead, conscious experience is continually updated as different brain regions do their work (Dennett, 1991). Usually, this updating is so fast that you are not aware of it. But sometimes it unfolds slowly, and you can sense your brain at work. Look at Figure 9.2, which depicts a *Necker Cube*. After a second or two, your conscious experience changes, and then changes again; the cube periodically "flips" (sometimes the front appears to be in the lower right of the image, but sometimes it is in the upper left). There is no one fixed, static conscious experience of the image, as Descartes's theory would have suggested.

Finally, in Dennett's theory, there is no homunculus. No single part of the mind observes images and makes decisions. Rather, consciousness is based on the action of

"I understand that you believe the world rests upon the backs of four white elephants. Is that correct?"

"Indeed, this is so," replied a holyman.

"Now tell me, just what is it that stands beneath the great white elephants?"

"Under each of the four," the sage replied, "there stands another great white elephant."

"And what is beneath that set of elephants?"

"Why, four more elephants."

"And what is beneath that set. . ."

"No need to keep asking. It's elephants all the way down!"

—from "World-Elephants"
(based on an ancient Hindu myth)

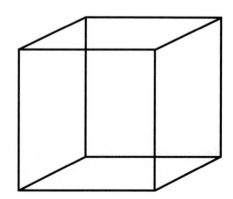

figure **9.2**
Necker Cube Although the Necker Cube does not change, your conscious experience of it does. Dennett's theory of consciousness would explain that your brain creates successive "drafts" of the information it receives.

large numbers of psychological processes that occur simultaneously, in fractions of a second. These multiple processes each contribute to interpretations of what is happening outside the mind, that is, to conscious experience of the world.

Dennett is not the only contemporary theorist to formulate a theory of consciousness. Others have proposed that consciousness consists of a "workspace" with connections to different regions of the mind that process information simultaneously. The connections enable the mind to combine information of different types (Dehaene & Naccache, 2001). Consciousness results from the overall pattern of connections, not from a single homunculus.

These contemporary theories have an interesting implication. They imply that when you shift levels of analysis from mind to brain, you should *not* expect to find any one brain structure that independently produces consciousness. Instead, Dennett's theory—unlike Descartes's—implies that large numbers of separate brain mechanisms will each play a role in constructing our conscious experiences. Let's now look at consciousness from a biological point of view.

🌐 WHAT DO YOU KNOW?...

11. Identify whether the statements below were more likely made by Descartes or by Dennett.
    a. "Our brains do not reproduce stimuli; rather, they detect stimuli and we make educated guesses about them."
    b. "There is one area in the brain, the pineal gland, that produces conscious experience."
    c. "Conscious experience is not a static experience; rather, it is continually updated."

🌀 CULTURAL OPPORTUNITIES

Eastern Analyses of Conscious Experience

Theories developed in "the West" (Europe and America) inspire most contemporary research on consciousness. Some of them were developed recently, whereas others, such as Descartes's, are centuries old. Yet all these Western conceptions are relative newcomers compared to theories of consciousness developed in the East. Particularly noteworthy are Buddhist and Hindu conceptions originating in South Asia (especially the region corresponding to the contemporary nation of India) more than 2000 years ago.

Like many current-day psychologists, classic Buddhist and Hindu scholars tried to characterize the nature of consciousness and to explain how conscious experiences occur. The traditional South Asian theories, however, differ from modern psychological theories in two important ways.

The first difference involves the role of the body and brain in consciousness. Virtually all modern theories presume that consciousness arises entirely from brain activity (Searle, 1998). Ancient South Asian scholars, however, judged that it reflected the activity of not only the physical brain but also "an extra-physical reality" (Dreyfus & Thompson, 2007, p. 90)—some mental quality that could not be explained in terms of biology. In Hinduism, this mental quality is a nonphysical self that is spiritual in nature and thus separate from the body. In Buddhism, the mind is nothing but an endless stream of mental events that do not depend on the physical body; the mind is merely "associated with the body during [a person's] lifetime" and lives on "after the [body's] death" (Dreyfus & Thompson, 2007). The Eastern theories thus are dualistic.

Second, Eastern theories recognize a wider variety of conscious experiences. Western theories tend to focus on a relatively small number of phenomena: conscious awareness, mental states during sleep, and perhaps variations in positive and negative mood or a small set of emotions (anger, sadness, happiness). Eastern scholars, however, distinguished among an enormous variety of conscious states. For example, the Buddhist Asanga, writing in the fourth century BCE, differentiated eight types of consciousness, variously based on sensory systems and personal knowledge (Dreyfus & Thompson, 2007). Other Buddhist texts identify negative states—for instance, lack of awareness of the causes and effects of one's own actions—that receive less attention in Western writing (Guenther & Kawamura, 1975). Hindu texts address mental states, such as awe and heroism (see Shweder, 1993), that have only recently received attention in Western psychology (Van Cappellen & Saroglou, 2012).

Finally, Eastern traditions are unique in identifying a series of *jhanas,* which are varying states of mental concentration that can be achieved through meditation (Goleman, 1988). At first, meditators experience sustained attention, awareness of bodily states, and a feeling of bliss. Gradually, they achieve a state of serenity in which there is no conscious awareness of bodily states and no feeling of pleasure or pain. Eventually, the meditator attains a jhana in which the mind is cleared of all normal conscious states.

Even though they were not scientific theories in the modern sense of the term, Eastern analyses of consciousness deserve attention. Through careful description of conscious experiences, Eastern scholars carried out a task that is critical to good science: describing the full range of phenomena that scientific theories ultimately must explain.

✪ WHAT DO YOU KNOW?

12. Which of the following statements about the differences between traditional South Asian theories and modern psychological theories of consciousness are accurate? Check all that apply.

_____ a. Traditional South Asian theories are not dualistic, whereas modern psychological theories are.

_____ b. Traditional South Asian theories view consciousness as arising from brain activity and an "extra-physical reality," whereas modern psychological theories regard consciousness as arising only from brain activity.

_____ c. Traditional South Asian theories describe a wider variety of conscious experiences than do modern psychological theories, including *jhanas,* states of consciousness acquired through meditation.

Consciousness East and West The Buddhist spiritual leader, the Dalai Lama of Tibet, is shown here meeting with psychologist Richard Davidson, of the University of Wisconsin.

University of Wisconsin at Madison

The Biology of Consciousness

Why is there consciousness? It is not necessary for biological survival. Insects, worms, fish, and many other simple organisms survive just fine without conscious feelings. In fact, they exhibit complex behavior. Salmon, for example, migrate from fresh water to oceans and then manage to find their way back to their original freshwater location to reproduce, all without consciously experiencing their trip.

Christian Aslund / Getty Images

Let's address this question by exploring the biology of consciousness. We'll first look to the past and ask why consciousness evolved. Then we'll turn to the present to see how activity in the contemporary human brain gives rise to conscious experience.

Zombies One creature of interest to students of consciousness is fictional: zombies. Zombies look like people (well, ones who have decayed a bit) and walk around, detect objects, and respond to them, as people do. Yet, according to the standard scholarly definition of "zombie" (Kirk, 2009), they lack conscious experience; there is nothing it "is like" to be a zombie. Interestingly, zombies seem as if they *could* exist; it is easy to imagine human-like beings that lack conscious feelings yet could survive and reproduce. This fact, in turn, raises a critical question: Why *do* we have consciousness? As two leading scholars put it, "Why aren't we just big bundles of unconscious zombie agents?" (Koch & Crick, 2001, p. 893).

Evolution and Consciousness

Preview Questions

> What is the evolutionary advantage of consciousness?
> How evolutionarily old is consciousness?

Ever since the insights of Charles Darwin, scientists have recognized that organisms evolve through natural selection. Characteristics that are advantageous in a given environment—in other words, that help organisms to survive and reproduce in that environment—become more frequent from one generation to the next. A Darwinian perspective, then, raises the question: What advantage is there to consciousness? How does it help organisms survive and reproduce?

THE EVOLUTIONARY ADVANTAGE CONSCIOUSNESS. One evolutionary advantage of consciousness involves decision making. Simple organisms lacking consciousness make simple decisions; they respond reflexively to specific stimuli that trigger specific responses. Organisms with consciousness, however, can do something more complex: combine different pieces of information and decide how to act based on this combination (Merker, 2005).

The ability to combine information promotes survival. Imagine an organism that has not eaten for some time and thus is low in bodily energy. Suppose it smells food in the vicinity but also hears a predator in the distance. What does it do? Ideally, the organism would combine two pieces of information, weighing one (presence of food) against another (possibility of predator). If it felt extremely hungry, the food was near, and the predator sounded far away, it would eat. If the predator sounded closer and the organism didn't feel too hungry, it would flee. To combine the information, the organism needs to bring the various sounds, smells, and feelings of hunger together in the same mental place (Merker, 2005). Consciousness is that place. Conscious organisms, then, can make intelligent decisions that combine multiple pieces of information.

THE ORIGINS OF CONSCIOUSNESS. Consciousness is old. Mammals have it, and they have existed for at least 100 million years (Baars, 2005). Evidence suggests that consciousness is even older than that—going back perhaps 300 million years (Cabanac, Cabanac, & Parent, 2009). Key evidence comes from research on lizards.

If you handle a lizard, its heart rate increases, which suggests that the lizard is consciously aware of the handling (Cabanac & Cabanac, 2000). A lizard's brain has a cortex, which is needed for conscious experience. Other organisms with an evolutionary history older than lizards (e.g., amphibians, such as frogs) lack a cortex and do *not* react physiologically when handled, which suggests that they lack consciousness (Cabanac et al., 2009). Lizards have existed for about 300 million years. This combination of facts suggests that consciousness is roughly that old.

Tony Spagnoli

"Sure, I'm conscious. What's the big deal?" Research suggests that lizards have conscious experiences, which means that consciousness has existed among animal species for hundreds of millions of years.

🐢 WHAT DO YOU KNOW?...

13. True or False?
    a. Consciousness enables us to combine information to make decisions, which surely aided in our survival.
    b. A lizard's brain has a cortex and its heart rate increases when handled, suggesting that it has consciousness.
    c. Consciousness is estimated to have existed for about 100 million years.

Consciousness and the Brain

Preview Question

> What subsystems of the brain are necessary for an organism to have conscious experience? How do we know?

Let's turn from the past to the present—from the evolution of consciousness to today's brain and how it creates conscious experience. How does activity in masses of cells in your head cause you to experience pleasure, pain, love, and hate?

FROM BRAIN MATTER TO CONSCIOUS EXPERIENCE. No question in science is more difficult to answer. In fact, it is so difficult that some argue it is unanswerable. *Mysterianism* is a theoretical claim that human beings lack the mental capacity to ever figure out how brain mechanisms produce conscious experience; it will always remain a mystery (McGinn, 1999).

The mystery lies in the stark difference between biological matter and conscious experience. If you look into the brain, you find cells and neurotransmitters. They function according to normal laws of physics. If you reflect on your conscious experience, you observe something completely different: thoughts and feelings that seem disconnected from ordinary physical matter. Consider these questions: How much does your current conscious experience weigh? About how big is it? These questions don't even make sense. Conscious experience exists, yet it lacks physical properties such as mass and size. This disconnect between physical brain matter and conscious experiences makes it difficult even to imagine how the physical action of brain cells could create consciousness.

BRAIN SYSTEMS REQUIRED FOR CONSCIOUSNESS. Scientists cannot, at present, fully answer the difficult question of exactly how brain functioning produces conscious experience. Nonetheless, they have made progress on a slightly easier question: What subsystems of the brain are necessary for an organism to have conscious experience? Research identifies two critical aspects of brain functioning (Alkire, Hudetz, & Tononi, 2008; Edelman & Tononi, 2000).

> *Integrated activity.* To have consciousness, organisms need a brain in which activity in different brain regions is coordinated, or "integrated." No one structure in the brain independently produces consciousness. Rather, consciousness arises only when activity in numerous interconnected brain structures is integrated.

> *Thalamo-cortical connections.* Two brain structures whose interconnections are key to consciousness are the thalamus and the cortex. The thalamus, located near the center of the brain (see Chapter 3), receives inputs from multiple sensory systems, sends information out to multiple areas of the cortex, and receives input back from these regions of the cortex. These back-and-forth connections between the thamalus and cortex, known as *thalamo-cortical circuits,* integrate activity in multiple brain regions and thus serve as a basis for consciousness (Figure 9.3).

A famous case of an individual who lost consciousness supports the conclusion that intact thalamo-cortical circuits are required for conscious experience. In 1975 Karen Ann Quinlan, a young woman in Pennsylvania, experienced respiratory-system failure after consuming a combination of alcohol and drugs. Subsequently, she lost

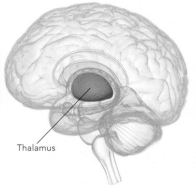

Thalamus

figure 9.3
Thalamo-cortical circuits The brain contains huge numbers of neural connections between the thalamus, located near the center of the brain, and the cortex. These connections are crucial for consciousness. The red, blue, and green images represent these thalamo-cortical connections, color-coded to indicate the region of the cortex to which the thalamus is connecting.

Karen Ann Quinlan, who experienced respiratory failure that caused her to lose consciousness—and never regain it. The respiratory failure damaged her thalamus, a brain structure that is key to conscious experience.

AP Photo / Ho

consciousness and never regained it, living in a vegetative state for a decade. (Her case became famous because it highlighted ethical questions involving the rights and care of patients in that state.) After her death, an autopsy revealed that the respiratory failure had caused damage to her thalamus; other parts of her brain were intact (Kinney et al., 1994). The loss of cortical connections through the thalamus thus appeared to be the cause of her permanent loss of consciousness. This autopsy, combined with contemporary research on brain mechanisms in consciousness, has an implication for the patient you read about in this chapter's opening story. It suggests that, despite the considerable brain damage he experienced, thalamo-cortical connections in his brain were relatively intact.

THALAMUS, CORTEX, AND CONSCIOUSNESS. How do scientists know that thalamo-cortical circuits are so important? Research with anesthetic drugs provides evidence. General anesthetics, of the sort used in surgical procedures, cause people to lose consciousness. By administering them while taking images of people's brains, researchers can identify brain changes that accompany the loss of consciousness.

Findings indicate that anesthetics induce unconsciousness by reducing activity in the thalamus. Consciousness ceases when thalamo-cortical circuits no longer integrate information that is processed at multiple sites in the cortex (Alkire, Haier, & Fallon, 2000). The fact that unconsciousness and reduction of activity in thalamo-cortical circuits occur simultaneously implies that these circuits are key to consciousness (Alkire et al., 2008).

Brain research thus shows that the integration of activity in large numbers of separate brain regions is needed for conscious experience. Interestingly, this biological fact is consistent with psychological experience. Psychologically, our experiences generally are coherent and unified. If a large green garbage truck whizzes past you, your sensory receptors receive different types of information: a flash of green light, a whiff of garbage, the sound of a truck engine, a breeze on your skin. Consciously, however, you experience one thing: a truck whizzing by. If someone asks, "What just happened?" you probably will not say, "There was a bright green light. I smelled some garbage. There was the sound of an internal combustion engine. And I felt a breeze." Instead, you'll report one coherent conscious experience: "A garbage truck."

At a biological level, then, thalamo-cortical circuits integrate activity in multiple brain regions (Edelman, 2003). At a psychological level of analysis, the conscious mind combines separate pieces of sensory and perceptual information. This enables people to have unified, coherent conscious experiences (Figure 9.4).

WHAT DO YOU KNOW?...

14. The following statement is incorrect. Explain why: "Just as Descartes had predicted, research in which general anesthetics are used to investigate consciousness indicates that the pineal gland is the sole key brain structure that gives rise to conscious experience."

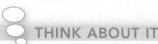 **THINK ABOUT IT**

Research shows that brain activity integrated by thalamo-cortical circuits is necessary for consciousness. But does this research fully explain how consciousness occurs? If the brain and its integrated circuits were not attached to the rest of the body, would the brain have conscious experience?

figure 9.4

WHAT IS CONSCIOUS EXPERIENCE LIKE?

PM B
IN ACTION

PERSON Ⓟ

People's conscious experiences are unified; although you have separate perceptual systems (e.g., vision, hearing, olfaction), you don't experience separate, disconnected colors and smells. You consciously experience one thing: flowers.

MIND Ⓜ

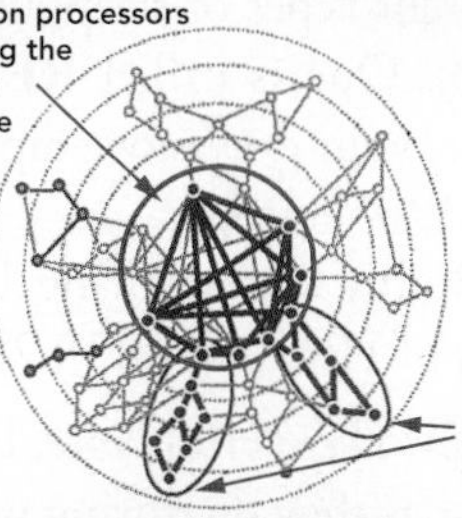

Information processors comprising the conscious workspace

processors mobilized into the conscious workspace

In the mind, multiple processes are active simultaneously, but only a subset is recruited into a "conscious workspace." There, they can be integrated.

From Dehaene & Naccache (2001). © 2001 Elsevier

BRAIN Ⓑ

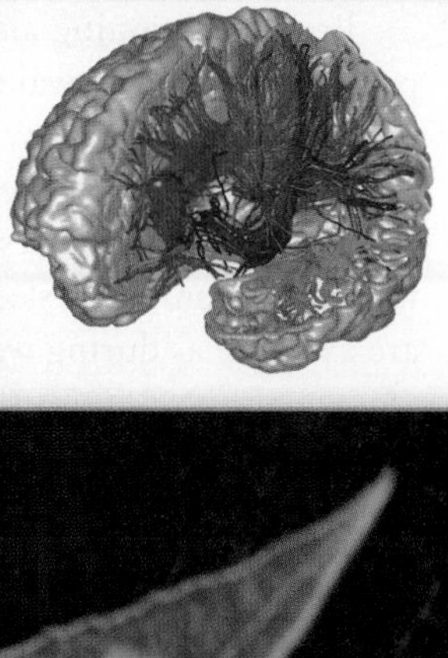

In the brain, neural connections running primarily through the thalamus integrate activity in different brain regions.

From Izhikevich & Edelman (2008). © 2008 by The National Academy of Sciences, USA

Gallery Stock

TRY THIS!

Now that you've learned about the psychology and biology of consciousness, it's time to experience the powers, and limits, of the conscious mind in this chapter's Try This! activity. Go to www.pmbpsychology now and complete the activity for Chapter 9: Consciousness. We'll discuss it later in this chapter. ◉

Sleep

Thus far in this chapter, you have learned about how you consciously experience the sights and sounds of the external world. Yet, during about a third of your life, you don't experience them. About a third of the time, if someone held a picture in front of your face, tapped you gently on the arm, or whispered in your ear, you wouldn't even notice. These are the times when you are asleep.

The Varieties of Sleep

Preview Questions

> What characterizes REM and non-REM sleep?
> Why, during REM sleep, do our eyes move rapidly but our muscles stay relatively still?
> What characterizes sleep stages?

The word "sleep" seems to refer to a single state. You may believe that when you fall asleep at night, your mind and body enter a resting state—the state of sleep—and that this state continues uninterrupted for about 8 hours, until you wake up. If this is how you think about sleep, you're in for a surprise.

TWO TYPES OF SLEEP. Sleep is not a single state. You alternate between two different types of sleep, usually about every 90 minutes, throughout the night (Siegel, 2003). One is called **REM (rapid eye movement) sleep** because, during this sleep phase, your eyes move rapidly back and forth. The other state is **non-REM** (sometimes "NREM") **sleep.**

Bodily states during REM and non-REM sleep differ markedly (National Institutes of Health [NIH], 2011; Biological Sciences Curriculum Study [BSCS], 2003):

> *REM sleep:* Heart rate, blood pressure, and breathing rate vary during REM sleep, just as they do during waking periods. Both men and women experience genital arousal (even if not having sexual dreams).

> *Non-REM sleep:* Heart rate and blood pressure are lower than during wakefulness and are very consistent throughout the non-REM period. Body temperature is lower than wakefulness, and breathing slows.

Brain functioning also differs in REM versus non-REM sleep. Unlike what happens when you are awake, adjacent neurons in the cortex fire at the same time during non-REM sleep. This synchronous activity produces distinctive brain waves that can be detected by EEG methods (see Research Toolkit). But during REM sleep, brain activity is different; it resembles brain activity during *waking* periods more than activity during non-REM sleep. In REM sleep, (1) brain cells in the cortex and brain stem are as active as during waking states, (2) the brain consumes as much energy as when you are awake, and (3) brain waves resemble those of wakefulness (Siegel, 2003).

Brain-imaging evidence reveals that REM-sleep eye movements are associated with activity in multiple brain regions (Hong et al., 2009). These include not only the visual

REM (rapid eye movement) sleep A sleep stage during which there is rapid eye movement, frequent dreams, and brain activity *resembling* that of waking periods.

non-REM sleep Sleep stage in which brain activity differs from that of waking states, and breathing rate, heart rate, blood pressure, and body temperature are relatively low.

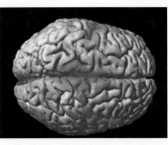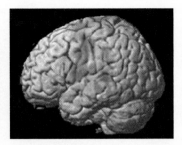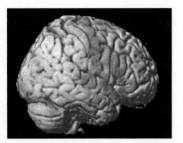

From Hong et al. (2009). © 2008 Wiley-Liss, Inc.

figure 9.5
You may be asleep, but your brain is hard at work The images show the numerous regions of the brain that are highly active during REM sleep.

cortex, but also nonvisual sensory areas, the motor cortex, regions of the brain that process language, and the thalamus (Hong et al., 2009). The brain's multiple systems that produce conscious experience thus are active during REM sleep (Figure 9.5).

People dream during both REM and non-REM sleep, but during REM sleep, dreams are more frequent and more vivid. When awakened during a REM period, people report having been in the midst of a dream more than 80% of the time, whereas during non-REM sleep periods, they report this only about one-third of the time (Stoerig, 2007). REM dreams commonly are more vivid than non-REM dreams, though people do sometimes report vivid dreams during non-REM periods (Solms, 2000).

What is the function of REM sleep's rapid eye movements? Brain-imaging evidence suggests some possibilities (Hong et al., 2009). One is that the eye movements are "scanning" the dream imagery. When awake, your eyes move frequently as you scan the environment (see Chapter 5). Similarly, when asleep, their movement may indicate your scanning of your dream world. Consistent with this idea, when people's eyes move more frequently, they report (when awakened) more vivid dream imagery (Hong et al., 1997). Another possibility is that the eye movements contribute to the production of dream images (Hong et al., 2009). Eye movements may be part of a mental system that retrieves, from memory, visual images that are incorporated into dreams.

With all the brain activity that occurs during REM sleep, you might wonder how you manage to stay asleep. As you learned, the motor cortex is active during REM sleep. Why, then, aren't you running around your bedroom while you are having a dream about running, or shouting out loud whenever you are shouting in your dreams?

During REM sleep, your body remains still because your brain "switches off" the body's main system for moving your muscles. It does this by altering brain chemistry. The brain changes the release of neurotransmitters that, during waking periods, activate cells that control motor movement (Siegel, 2003). As a result, during REM sleep, you are largely paralyzed; the muscles in your arms and legs do not move at all. (Other muscles, such as those that control the heart and eyes, function normally.) Sometimes this paralysis lasts for a brief period after people wake up, and they experience a potentially frightening state known as *sleep paralysis,* in which a person is awake but temporarily unable to move or talk (Hishikawa & Shimizu, 1995).

What would your life be like if, during REM sleep, you were not paralyzed?

Evidence of how the brain switches off muscle movements during dreams comes from a study in which researchers disabled the brain's switching-off mechanism. This was done in research with cats. Researchers intentionally damaged an area in the brain stem that is required to switch off muscle movement during sleep (Jouvet & Delorme, 1965). The cats fell asleep normally but, while sleeping, would walk, run, and sometimes even fight. The cats appeared to be acting out their dreams!

SLEEP STAGES. When during the night do these periods of non-REM and REM sleep occur? You might expect that it varies. Maybe different people experience non-REM and REM sleep at different times, or perhaps any given person experiences

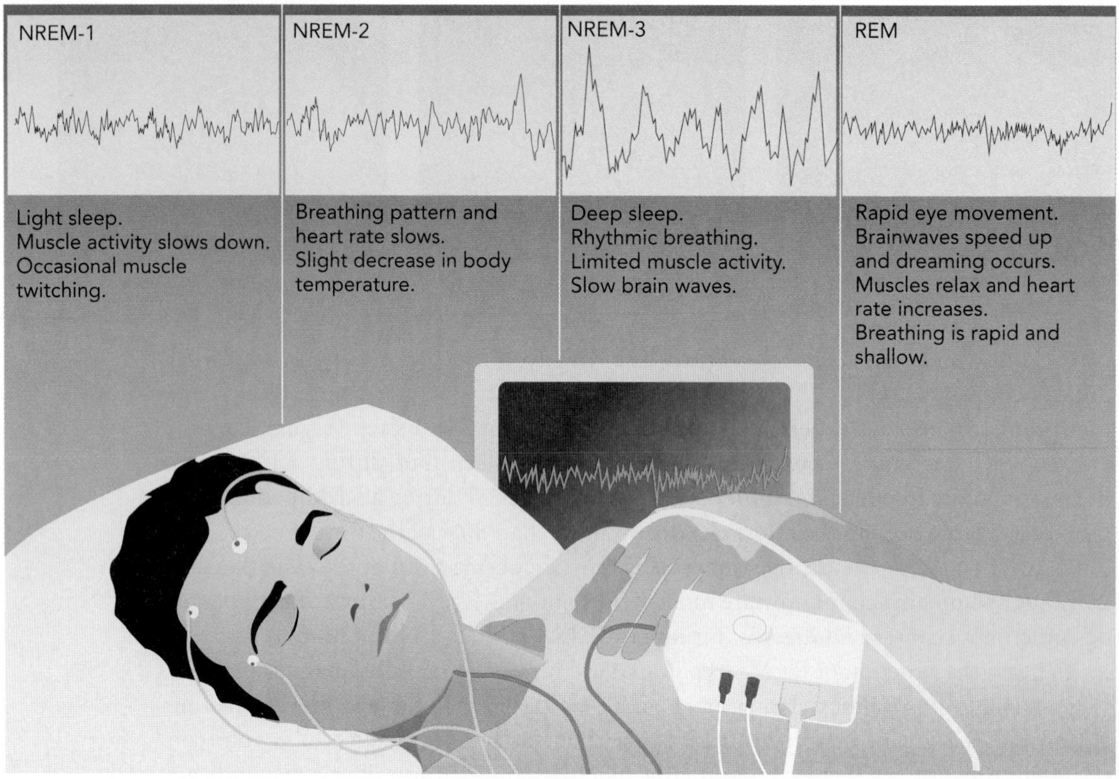

NREM-1	NREM-2	NREM-3	REM
Light sleep. Muscle activity slows down. Occasional muscle twitching.	Breathing pattern and heart rate slows. Slight decrease in body temperature.	Deep sleep. Rhythmic breathing. Limited muscle activity. Slow brain waves.	Rapid eye movement. Brainwaves speed up and dreaming occurs. Muscles relax and heart rate increases. Breathing is rapid and shallow.

figure 9.6

Sleep stages Recordings of brain activity obtained while people sleep reveal the existence of distinct sleep stages. There are three stages of non-REM (i.e., no rapid eye movement) sleep: NREM-1, NREM-2, and NREM-3. Each one, in order, is a progressively deeper stage of sleep. After NREM-3, people move into a stage of REM sleep. During REM sleep, the brain is highly active, much as it is when people are awake.

different sleep patterns from one night to the next. If this is what you expected, you are in for another surprise about sleep. Sequences of non-REM and REM sleep do not vary significantly from person to person, or from one night to the next. Rather, essentially every night, every person experiences the same **sleep stages,** that is, the same sequence of changes in REM and non-REM sleep (Silber et al., 2007).

During the first 90 minutes after you fall asleep, you experience a series of three non-REM sleep stages: NREM-1, NREM-2, and NREM-3 (Silber et al., 2007; Figure 9.6). Each one, in order, is a progressively deeper stage of sleep. Your heart rate and breathing slow from one stage to the next, and your brain waves look less and less like those that occur when you are awake. But after about 90 minutes, a remarkable thing happens. Instead of staying in deep, NREM-3 sleep, you emerge from it and experience your first period of REM sleep. This first REM period is relatively brief, and after it you head back down again, through the stages of non-REM sleep. This cycle repeats itself during the night, with the only change being that, as the night progresses, the REM periods become longer and you do not descend all the way down to the deepest stage of non-REM sleep.

Biochemical and neural processes are responsible for the transitions from non-REM to REM sleep (Dement, 1978). These biological processes cannot be altered; even experimental manipulations explicitly designed to alter them are ineffective. For example, researchers have found that, by applying a small electrical impulse to a certain region of cats' brains, they could induce REM sleep in the cats. However, if a sleeping cat had just emerged from a REM sleep cycle, this same manipulation had no effect (Dement, 1978). Once it completed one REM sleep cycle, the cat had to experience a non-REM sleep period before it could experience additional REM sleep.

Small sets of cells in lower regions of the brain control this sleep cycle. A group of neurons in the base of the forebrain known as "sleep-on" neurons induce sleep. Among the factors that activate these neurons is increased body heat (Siegel, 2003); it is not

sleep stages The sequence of changes in REM and non-REM sleep that everyone experiences in the same order.

surprising, then, that people become sleepy on a hot summer afternoon. A group of "REM on" neurons in the brain stem initiates REM sleep, which is terminated by a different set of brain-stem neurons known as "REM off" cells (Solms, 2000). Discovery of these brain mechanisms again shows that the sleep cycle is a thoroughly biologically determined process.

⊕RESEARCH TOOLKIT

EEG

People have been interested in the mysteries of sleep and dreams for thousands of years. Yet the most basic facts—that sleep occurs in stages, with dreams being most frequent during one of those stages, REM sleep—were unknown until only about a half-century ago. Their discovery required the invention of a research tool, the EEG. **EEG,** or **electroencephalography,** is a technique for visually depicting the electrical activity of the brain (Olejniczak, 2006).

The brain produces electrical activity whenever an action potential travels down the length of a neuron (see Chapter 3). Because there are billions and billions of neurons, a lot of electrical activity occurs—so much that electrodes placed on the scalp can easily record it.

The electrodes detect *brain waves,* which are cyclical patterns of activity in any given brain region. In other words, in any area of the brain, there are wave-like rises and falls in activity. These fluctuations are created by rhythmic patterns in the firing of neurons, especially those connecting the brain's thalamus and cortex (Lopes da Silva, 1991).

In EEG research, participants wear electrodes that are placed on specific regions of the scalp (and may be held in place there by a cap; see photo). The electrodes detect waves of activity in the area of the brain directly underneath them. The resulting brain wave recordings are then plotted on a graph.

EEG In EEG research methods, electrodes placed on the scalp detect electrical activity in the brain.

Stephanie Pilick / Newscom

Conveniently for sleep researchers, EEG recordings can be taken while a person is sleeping. The electrodes are not uncomfortable, so participants can doze off while wearing them.

Researchers began to use EEG to study sleep in the mid-twentieth century. Once they did so, they quickly noticed that brain waves change dramatically during the night (Dement, 1978). As you saw in Figure 9.6, from Stage 1 to 3 of NREM (non-REM) sleep, brain waves slow down and become larger in amplitude (the height of the wave). In the relatively deep sleep of Stage 3, brain waves are relatively slow; your mind is at rest. But then, during REM sleep, there is a burst of activity, with brain waves occurring much more rapidly. This graphical depiction of brain activity during sleep alerted scientists to the existence of sleep stages.

Like many good tools, EEG can be used for more than one purpose. In addition to sleep, researchers use EEG to study topics such as emotion, motivation, and individual differences in children's temperament. Researchers throughout psychology have "caught the EEG wave."

🗸 WHAT DO YOU KNOW?...

15. True or False?
    a. EEG is the abbreviation for electrocardiogram.
    b. According to EEG readings, brain waves are greater in amplitude during REM sleep than they are during non-REM sleep.

EEG (electroencephalography)
A technique for recording and visually depicting electrical activity within the brain in which electrodes on the scalp record neural activity in underlying brain regions. The record of electrical activity through this method is called an *electroencephalogram.*

16. Identify whether the items below characterize REM sleep or non-REM sleep.
    a. Muscles are largely paralyzed.
    b. Heart rate and blood pressure are consistent.
    c. Body temperature is lower than during wakefulness.
    d. Consists of three stages that are each progressively deeper.
    e. Brain activity is similar to that of wakefulness.
    f. Dreams are frequent and typically more vivid.
    g. Heart rate and blood pressure are lower than during wakefulness.
    h. Genital arousal occurs.

Studying Sleep

Preview Question

› How have sleep labs been used to study the timing of the body's internal clock?

Studying sleep scientifically is challenging. Scientists need to observe normal 8-hour nights of sleep, which people usually experience at home. Yet they need to record physiological activity during sleep, which requires equipment found only in a lab.

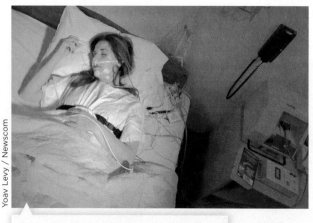

Sleeping for science This woman is participating in research in a sleep lab, where participants can spend the night in comfort while their bodily and brain activities are recorded.

SLEEP LABS. Researchers meet this challenge by conducting research in sleep labs. A **sleep laboratory** is a scientific facility for studying sleep that includes a hotel-like room in which research participants can spend the night, as well as equipment for monitoring participants' biological rhythms and brain activity while they are sleeping.

Sleep labs have two big advantages for research. First, researchers can monitor research participants' heart rates, brain waves, eye movements, and other aspects of physiology while they are sleeping. Second, they can control environmental factors that would be impossible to control in the home environment. This control enables experimental tests of competing theoretical explanations of sleep, waking, and internal biological states. Here's an example.

MANIPULATING LENGTH OF DAY. People (and other mammals) experience a **circadian rhythm,** an approximately 24-hour cycle of changes in internal bodily processes, including those involved in body temperature, hunger and feeding, and sleep and wakefulness. Why is the cycle 24 hours long? One possibility is biological. Internal physiological processes may produce and maintain the 24-hour cycle. A second possibility is environmental. People live in environments that shift according to 24-hour cycles: The sun sets and rises; alarm clocks ring; late-night talk shows are broadcast. These external cues, rather than internal biology, may explain the regularity of our circadian rhythms.

How could one find out which factor—inner biological or outer environmental cues—is most influential? An ideal study would create an "alternative world" in which all environmental cues, such as patterns of light and dark, were rescheduled. One could then see if shifts in the external environment change people's biological rhythms.

Researchers have created this alternative world in sleep labs. In one study (Czeisler et al., 1999), participants lived in a sleep lab for a month. They had no access to watches or clocks. Unbeknownst to the participants, the researchers created different light–dark schedules in the lab. For some participants, darkness and daytime light

sleep laboratory A scientific facility for studying sleep; research participants spend nights sleeping while their biological rhythms and brain activity are monitored.

circadian rhythm The approximately 24-hour cycle of changes in internal bodily processes.

repeated every 28 hours, instead of the normal 24. For others, the light–dark cycle repeated every 20 hours. Researchers recorded participants' physiological states (e.g., body temperature) throughout, to determine whether their normal 24-hour bodily rhythms shifted when living in 20- or 28-hour days.

> How likely would you be to volunteer for a month-long sleep study in which you didn't have access to watches or clocks?

Remarkably, the shifts in environmental cues had *no effect* on bodily rhythms. The circadian rhythms of people experiencing 20- and 28-hour days were 24.17 and 24.15 hours, respectively (Czeisler et al., 1999)—times that were essentially the same and that corresponded closely to the 24-hour period of a normal day. The body, then, has an internal clock that can maintain a 24-hour cycle of biological processes, even when environmental cues vary from this 24-hour period.

✌ WHAT DO YOU KNOW?...

17. By manipulating light–dark schedules in a _____ lab, scientists were able to demonstrate that environmental cues do not affect the 24-hour _____ rhythm.

 THINK ABOUT IT

The research participants in sleep lab studies tend to be healthy individuals who live in wealthy nations and thus do not experience severe conditions of life (malnourishment, untreated medical conditions, etc.). How do we know that their sleep patterns are similar to those of people who face more difficult living conditions?

Sleep Theories

Preview Question

> Why do we sleep?

It's possible to imagine a world in which animals did not sleep. They might rest, to save energy, yet not lapse into the states of unawareness that comprise sleep. From the perspective of any individual organism, this sleep-free world would seem advantageous. Sleep is dangerous. The sleeping animal is vulnerable to attack from one who is awake.

Yet, in the real world, all mammals sleep. In fact, all known mammals experience both non-REM and REM sleep (Capellini, Barton et al., 2008). Over the course of evolution, sleep must have possessed some advantage that outweighed its costs.

Identifying this advantage is difficult. Scientists have not reached complete agreement on the primary benefits of sleep. They have, however, identified some possibilities.

Non-REM sleep may help the body repair itself. During non-REM sleep, the body's rate of *metabolism*—that is, the rate of internal chemical reactions necessary to life—is lower. Lower metabolic rate gives the body time to repair damage that may have occurred during wakefulness (Siegel, 2003). But some evidence calls into question whether bodily repair explains the *need* for sleep. Consider animals that hibernate. In the period right after awaking from hibernation, animals need large amounts of non-REM sleep, rather than the small amounts you might expect if sleep were required for bodily repair and the body had been repairing itself during the hibernation period (Capellini, Nunn et al., 2008).

An alternative possibility is that sleep is needed not to repair the body as a whole, but to repair only one bodily organ in particular: the brain. When animals are awake, their bodies produce biochemical waste products that can build up in the brain and harm its functioning. Changes that occur within the brain when animals sleep make it easier for the brain to remove these waste products (Xie et al., 2013).

Other biological needs may contribute to sleep patterns. One possibility is food needs. Herbivores (animals that eat plants but not meat) need more time to forage for food than do carnivores (meat eaters). They also tend to get less REM and non-REM sleep than carnivorous species. Their need for extra foraging time may limit the time they have available to sleep (Capellini, Nunn et al., 2008). Another need involves the brain. Especially early in life, the brain must establish neural connections. The mental activity of REM sleep may aid this neural process, helping the brain to establish connections required for efficiently processing environmental stimuli when awake. In all mammalian species, REM sleep is more abundant early in life than in adulthood (Frank, 2011).

In summary, it is difficult to know exactly why animals need to sleep. But there is no question that they do need their daily shut-eye, as research on sleep deprivation illustrates.

🐦 WHAT DO YOU KNOW?...

18. Which of the following statements about sleep are accurate? Check all that apply.
    _____ a. The lower metabolic rate of non-REM sleep may be necessary for the brain to repair itself.
    _____ b. Herbivores, who require more time to forage for food, have less time available for sleep.
    _____ c. Non-REM sleep, which is more abundant early in life than in adulthood, helps to establish neural connections.

Sleep Disturbed

Preview Questions

> In what ways does sleep deprivation impair performance?
> What characterizes sleep disorders?

In 1959 a radio announcer named Peter Tripp staged a "wakeathon." While being observed by medical personnel, Tripp stayed awake for a record 201 consecutive hours. The record didn't last for long. In 1964, a high school student named Randy Gardner broke it by staying awake for 264 hours—11 consecutive days!

Wakeathon 1950s radio personality Peter Tripp, after almost 3 consecutive days of sleep deprivation.

In some jobs, there's no time to sleep
The U.S. military recognizes that a major threat to effective performance by military personnel is sleep deprivation (Williams et al., 2008). The Department of Defense trains soldiers in sleep-deprived states, to prepare them for battlefield experiences, and conducts research to identify the mental abilities that are most affected by a lack of sleep (e.g., Maddox et al., 2009).

sleep deprivation Going without adequate sleep, which not only makes you tired but also impairs normal conscious experiences.

SLEEP DEPRIVATION. What's it like to go for days without sleep, or to experience extreme **sleep deprivation?** Being sleep deprived does more than just make you tired. It impairs your normal conscious experiences. After about 4 days, both Tripp and Gardner started hallucinating. Tripp thought some spots on a table were insects. Gardner thought a street sign was a person. Soon after that, Gardner, who was white, had a delusional experience in which he thought he was a prominent black athlete (Coren, 1998).

Research in which participants are kept awake for extended periods confirms that sleep deprivation disrupts thinking. When

25 volunteers from the U.S. military were kept awake for 56 hours (Kahn-Greene et al., 2007), they experienced anxiety, depression, and paranoid thinking similar to that experienced by people with severe psychological disorders (see Chapter 16). When a group of medical students was kept awake for 65 hours, they took a long time to answer simple questions and, when answering, spoke with slurred speech (Kamphuisen et al., 1992). Even modest reductions in sleep across a series of days can create ill effects. When the sleeping of a group of adults was restricted to less than 6 hours a night for 14 consecutive days, their ability to think deteriorated; they were less able to pay attention to tasks, responded more slowly to events, and their memory was impaired (Van Dongen et al., 2003).

There's a lesson here. If you've got an exam coming up, be sure to get plenty of sleep! Inadequate sleep is "the performance killer" (Czeisler & Fryer, 2006). It reduces your alertness and ability to concentrate and solve problems. Even if sleep is merely reduced (e.g., to 5–6 hours) for a few nights in a row, your body seems to "remember" that you got inadequate amounts of sleep on previous nights and you can become as mentally impaired as if you "pulled an all-nighter," staying up for 24 hours in a row. For example, in a study conducted with a population of healthy young-adult participants, participants whose sleep was restricted to 6 hours a night performed significantly less well on measures of alertness and sustained attention than those who slept for more than 8 hours a night (Lo et al., 2012).

Inadequate sleep impairs performance not only on complex mental activities, such as taking a test, but also on simpler tasks that require sustained attention and quick reactions, such as driving. In the United States, drowsy drivers cause 20% of all automobile accidents (Czeisler & Fryer, 2006). One-fifth of accidents might thus be prevented if everyone got a good night's sleep!

> Think of a time when you were sleep deprived. Were the effects similar to those described here?

SLEEP DISORDERS. In the cases of sleep deprivation we just discussed, people who were medically healthy got inadequate amounts of sleep. This lessened sleep resulted from personal choices or social pressures, such as a busy work schedule. A second type of sleep disturbance is different; it results from a medical condition. A **sleep disorder** is any medical condition that disrupts normal patterns of sleep. A person suffering from a sleep disorder may have difficulty falling asleep or staying asleep, or may suddenly fall asleep at times when they need to stay awake. Let's look at four main kinds of sleep disorder (American Sleep Apnea Association, 2013; National Heart, Lung, and Blood Institute [NHLBI], n.d.).

Narcolepsy is a relatively rare disorder in which people experience sudden, extreme feelings of sleepiness during the day. Even if they have gotten 8 hours of sleep the night before, people with narcolepsy experience exhaustion, low energy, and mental "cloudiness" during the day. They have trouble staying alert in situations where they are not physically active (such as a classroom lecture). The recurring bouts of sleepiness can significantly interfere with their ability to function normally in school or at work.

Some people with narcolepsy not only feel exhausted, but also fall asleep suddenly and without control. These uncontrollable bouts of sleep tend to be brief "microsleeps" that may last only for a very brief period (Brooks & Kushida, 2002). They nonetheless can be dangerous if people are engaged in an activity such as driving when overcome by sleep.

Narcolepsy is caused by an abnormality in levels of a chemical in the brain that influences wakefulness. Unfortunately, the exact cause of this abnormality is not known and no sure-fire cure is available. Narcolepsy usually is treated by a combined drug and behavioral strategy. Patients may receive a stimulant drug (a drug that

sleep disorder Any medical condition that disrupts normal patterns of sleep.

narcolepsy A sleep disorder in which people experience sudden, extreme feelings of sleepiness during the day, even if they've had adequate sleep; sometimes accompanied by "microsleeps."

increases nervous system activity; see below) while also being instructed to take scheduled naps (Littner et al., 2001).

Sleep apnea is a disorder in which people suffer from brief pauses in breathing while they are asleep. (The word *apnea* comes from a Greek word meaning "without breathing.") Although there are different kinds of sleep apnea, in the most common variety the underlying cause is blockage of airways needed for breathing, especially the passageway at the rear of the throat. When people's breathing is interrupted, their brain briefly awakens them so that they can breathe normally. These awakenings are necessary to sustain life, yet costly when it comes to a good night's sleep.

Sleep apnea can have a variety of negative effects. Because their sleep is disturbed, people suffering from sleep apnea may experience the impaired ability to think that characterizes anyone who is sleep deprived, as discussed above. In addition, they are at risk for serious health problems such as heart failure. Sleep apnea disrupts the body's ability to maintain normal levels of oxygen in the bloodstream. This, in turn, can cause cardiovascular problems that lead to heart failure (Javaheri et al., 1998). Some evidence links the occurrence of sleep apnea to obesity and indicates that weight loss can reduce sleep apnea symptoms (Romero-Corral et al., 2010).

The third sleep disorder is **insomnia,** which is prolonged difficulty in falling asleep or staying asleep when you have an opportunity to sleep (with that difficulty not caused by one of the other three sleep disorders described above). Everyone has trouble falling asleep on occasion. But some people experience such difficulty night after night, for two weeks in a row or more. These are people suffering from insomnia, a disorder that affects about 10% of the population (Neubauer, 2004).

There are two types of insomnia. In one, disturbed sleep is a side effect of other medical conditions or medications taken to treat them. In the other, insomnia results directly from biological or psychological factors (e.g., stressful daily events). Some foods and drinks, such as caffeine consumed close to bedtime, also can make falling asleep difficult. Alcohol can make falling asleep easier, but causes sleep to be "lighter"; that is, it raises the chance of waking up during the night rather than getting a sound eight hours of sleep. Bedtime environments that are too warm or too noisy can also make sleep harder to achieve (Ohayon & Zulley, 2001).

One treatment for insomnia is sleeping pills, obtained either by prescription or over the counter. They can reduce the time it takes to fall asleep (Dzierzewski et al., 2010; Lemmer, 2007), but have significant drawbacks, including the fact that they can be addictive. Psychological therapies are a second treatment option. In sleep therapies, psychologists educate people about factors that interfere with sleep and teach them techniques that promote a state of relaxation before bedtime (Dzierzewski et al., 2010).

Everybody wants a good night's sleep, and everybody, at least on occasion, has

Jerry Garcia Sleep apnea is a common disease that has affected millions of Americans—including celebrities such as the late Jerry Garcia, leader of the legendary rock band The Grateful Dead. He died of a heart condition that was exacerbated by his sleep apnea.

AP Photo / Kristy McDonald, file

Kevin Mazur / AEG via Getty Images

Michael Jackson Jerry Garcia was not the only legendary musician to suffer from sleep problems. Michael Jackson suffered from persistent insomnia, for which he received a variety of drugs, including ones not normally prescribed for sleep disorder. A coroner's report indicated that these drugs directly contributed to his death in 2009.

sleep apnea A disorder in which people suffer from brief pauses in breathing while they are asleep, causing them to wake up.

insomnia A sleep disorder involving prolonged difficulty in falling asleep or staying asleep.

trouble getting it. Let's conclude this section on sleep with some sleep tips from the U.S. National Institute on Health (NIH, 2011). If you want a good night's sleep:

> **Establish a schedule, and stick to it.** It's helpful to go to bed, and get up, at about the same time every day.

> **Don't exercise late in the day.** Exercise is a great thing, but it can interfere with sleep if you exercise within a couple hours of bedtime.

> **Avoid caffeine, nicotine, alcohol, and large meals late at night.** Caffeine and nicotine are stimulants that can interfere with sleep. Alcohol makes sleep lighter, and large meals late at night can cause indigestion, which interferes with sleeping.

> **Relax before bedtime.** A relaxing activity, such as reading, can make it easier to fall asleep.

> **Create a good sleeping environment.** A TV or computer at your bedside can be a distraction that interferes with sleep. Try to establish a quiet sleeping area free from bright lights, noises, and electronic media.

How many of these tips do you follow? Which could you follow more closely?

WHAT DO YOU KNOW?...

19. Even mild sleep _____ (e.g., less than 6 hours a night for a couple of weeks) can impair memory and the ability to pay attention. This loss of the ability to pay attention can have dire consequences; in the United States, drowsy drivers account for _____% of automobile accidents. Many individuals suffering from _____ experience "microsleeps." The most common cause of _____ _____ is blockage of airways needed for breathing. Though many people experience bouts of sleeplessness, only 10% of the population experiences them to the extent that those suffering from _____ do.

Gio Barto / Getty Images

No wonder she can't get to sleep If you want a good night's sleep, you might not want to put your TV right above your bed. Sleep experts suggest that, if you want to fall asleep right away, you should eliminate distractions, bright lights, loud noises, and video screens from your bedroom environment (NIH, 2011).

Dreams

Quick: Name something complex and colorful that you created, but that you didn't intend to create and that you don't understand even though you made it yourself. *Hint:* When you created it, you were asleep.

Dreams are a puzzle. We all dream. But it's difficult to know why we dream, what our dreams mean, or even if there is any meaning hidden amidst the storylines and images we concoct while sleeping.

What Do People Dream About?

Preview Question

> How bizarre is the content of our dreams?

To understand dreams, a first step is to learn *what* people dream about. Psychologists have collected dream reports, often by waking people in sleep labs during REM sleep periods and asking them to report their dreams' contents. Researchers record the content of many people's dreams and identify common themes.

In one such study (reviewed in Domhoff, 2005), researchers analyzed more than 600 dream reports from 58 research participants. Dreams, they found, often are not as bizarre as you might expect. Although some feature fantastic dream landscapes, the vast majority of dreams took place in locations familiar to dreamers from their everyday life. Similarly, the most common activity in these dreams was routine: talking. Only about 1 out of 20 dream reports contained bizarre content completely unlike that of normal life.

A European researcher has conducted a statistical analysis of dream content (Schwartz, 2004). She analyzed the storylines of both her own dreams, recorded in a dream diary, and those of 100 college students whose dreams are part of a freely accessible Internet archive of dream reports (dreambank.net). The analysis revealed five types of dream content that were most common:

1. Conversations and work activities in school or a work environment
2. Interactions with either romantic partners or family members, generally in indoor settings
3. Sports activities
4. Flying, fighting, or war (men's dreams); or shopping or colors (women's dreams)
5. Motion, such as running or driving fast, combined with violence, threats, and fear

Again, most dreams were not particularly bizarre; many referred to everyday activities taking place in everyday locations.

One way in which dream content does differ from everyday life is that dreams contain a higher frequency of threats and potential personal harm. In everyday life, we rarely fall through space, run from attackers, or make emergency calls to 911. But in dreams, these sorts of things happen all the time. Analyses of dream content reveals that dreams contain more negative content (fear, threats, harm) than is generally found in everyday life (Valli et al., 2008).

> Why do you suppose dreams contain more negative content than is found in everyday life?

In sum, by analyzing dream diaries, psychologists have characterized the content of dreams. Yet this effort still leaves a major question unanswered: *Why* do people dream? Let's try to answer that question now.

💢 WHAT DO YOU KNOW?...

20. A recent statistical analysis reveals that _____ are not as bizarre as one might think. Compared to real life, however, they contain a _____ (higher or lower?) frequency of threats and potential personal harm.

Dream Theories

Preview Question

> Why do people dream?

There is no one answer to the question of why people dream, rather than spending their nights in dreamless sleep. Instead, psychologists have offered alternative theories of dreaming. Sigmund Freud developed the first of these dream theories.

WISH FULFILLMENT. In his classic work *The Interpretation of Dreams* (Freud, 1900), Freud proposed that we dream to protect our sleep. Without dreams, Freud believed, our minds' sexual and aggressive desires (see Chapter 13) would wake us repeatedly.

Specifically, Freud proposed that dreams release unconscious mental energy through wish fulfillment. According to his **wish-fulfillment theory,** dreams depict the fulfillment of unconscious wishes. By doing so, they drain off some pent-up mental energy, enabling you to stay asleep.

Freud knew that the storylines of dreams often do not *appear* to fulfill wishes. In fact, they frequently appear to depict just the opposite: something feared rather than something wished for. Freud thought, however, that the storylines of dreams hide their true meaning. If a psychologist, working with the dreamer, could analyze the dream's meaning fully, he or she inevitably would identify an unconscious wish hidden in the dream's storyline.

wish-fulfillment theory Freud's proposal that dreams help us stay asleep by depicting the fulfillment of unconscious wishes, thereby releasing pent-up mental energy.

Freud's theory was fascinating. However, his scientific evidence was weak. He relied on his own interpretations of people's dreams. Because Freud naturally had a "rooting interest" in his own theory, it's possible that his interpretations were biased by his desire to support his own theory. Others, recognizing this limitation in Freud's work, have developed alternative theories of dreams.

MAKING SENSE OF RANDOM BRAIN SIGNALS. In Freud's theory, the initial trigger for a dream is highly meaningful: an unconscious desire. In a second theory we will consider now, the initial trigger is psychologically meaningless.

J. Allan Hobson and colleagues (Hobson, 1988; Hobson & McCarley, 1977) have proposed an **activation-synthesis theory** of dreams. It claims that dreams are produced in two steps. The first is essentially random: During sleep, an area of the brain stem known as the *pons* (see Chapter 3) generates electrical signals randomly. In the second step, these signals are interpreted by higher regions of the brain that are involved in complex thought. Dreams, then, are simply the brain's attempt to make sense of random brain signals.

The activation-synthesis model explains one surprising feature of dreams—namely, that they sometimes are bizarre. Although many dreams depict mundane events, as we noted above, some are weird. A person might dream, for example, that "I had to play a game where I was a stealth bomber and I had to bomb a train. . . . I missed the train and I crashed. Then I appeared by the plane and I walked in with a police officer and we walked into a bedroom in the plane and Clint Eastwood was laying in the bed with one arm in a sling" (from dreambank.net). How could our minds produce such weird storylines? The activation-synthesis theory explains that the brain is trying to make sense of lower-level signals that are utterly meaningless. The brain does its best to create meaning. But, since the original neural signals don't make sense, the resulting storyline of the dream commonly makes little sense either.

> Why do you suppose our brains try to make sense of the meaningless electrical signals produced by the pons?

PREPARATION FOR THREAT. Antti Revonsuo, a researcher in Finland, proposes a third theory of dreams (Revonsuo, 2000). It is grounded in a question about evolution: What was the evolutionary function of dreaming—how might dreams have promoted survival and reproduction?

Dreaming, Revonsuo proposes, helps people prepare for everyday threats. In the ancient past, the environment was unrelentingly threatening; predators and harsh weather conditions abounded. The mind's capacity to create dreams evolved to help cope with the threats. Threats in dreams serve as mental simulations of threats in everyday life. Dreams, then, are a mental "rehearsal"; they activate mental and physical systems needed to cope with threats, including neural systems needed to escape threatening situations. The rehearsals enable people to respond more quickly and effectively to threats in waking life.

Elena Elisseeva / Shutterstock

Why so scary? Dreams often are threatening and frightening. Some psychologists believe that the scary content provides a clue to the puzzle of why people dream. Dreams may help prepare people for everyday threats by serving as mental simulations of potential harm that could occur in waking life.

activation-synthesis theory A theory about the processes through which dreams are generated, claiming that dreams are the brain's attempt to make sense of random brain signals.

Some evidence supports this theory. As you learned above, dreams often contain threats and feelings of fear. They can be extremely realistic; you feel as if you're really experiencing the threatening dream content. This realism contributes to the dream's ability to activate brain systems needed to cope with the real world. Research indicates that brain systems active when people respond quickly to real-life events are also active during REM sleep periods (Revonsuo, 2000).

You've just seen three different theories of dreams. The fact that psychology contains more than one theory means that questions about dream life are not entirely answered. Each theory might be partly correct. People experience a wide variety of dreams; different dreams may have different causes; and more than one theoretical idea may be needed to explain all aspects of dreaming.

⚫ WHAT DO YOU KNOW?...

21. Match the theory on the left to one of its features on the right.

    1. Freud's wish-fulfillment theory

    2. Activation-synthesis theory

    3. The evolutionary perspective

    a. Dreams are mental simulations of dangerous situations that enable us to practice defending against threats.

    b. Dreaming is a way of fulfilling our sexual and aggressive impulses so that they don't repeatedly awaken us.

    c. Dreams are the brain's way of making sense of random brain signals.

 **THIS JUST IN**

(Day)Dreaming

We have been discussing dreams—mental activity that occurs while you are asleep. How similar is this activity to the mental activity that occurs when you are awake?

Our everyday language suggests a point of similarity. Suppose that, while awake, you let your mind wander, allowing thoughts to drift across topics both real and imaginary. We call this mental activity a type of dreaming: *day*dreaming. The word suggests a fundamental similarity between sleeping and waking life. It implies that two activities—dreams when asleep, and daydreams while awake—might rely on similar mental processes and regions of the brain.

If you are thinking critically, like a scientist, you will realize that word similarity is not a good basis for drawing scientific conclusions. If you want to know whether dreaming and daydreaming are similar, you need scientific evidence. As it turns out, some such evidence is just in.

A team of researchers recently reviewed two large sets of published studies that investigated, through brain-imaging methods, brain activity while (1) dreaming and (2) daydreaming. They did so with a key question in mind: To what extent does brain activity during dreaming and daydreaming overlap? The answer, in brief, was "a lot." Among eight brain regions found to be particularly active during REM sleep, seven of them—all but one—also were highly active during daydreaming (Fox et al., 2013). So, in this case, the word similarity *was* an accurate sign; dreaming and daydreaming were highly similar when evaluated according to brain activity.

Dreaming and daydreaming are not identical, however. The researchers' review suggested one way in which they differ. During daydreams, thinking is less goal-directed—less focused on specific topics and aims—than during other forms of thought, such as trying to solve a problem. During nighttime dreams, thinking is even less goal-directed than during daydreams. Brain imaging supports this conclusion; frontal regions of the brain that control goal-directed thinking are less active during dreams than daydreams

(Fox et al., 2013). The researchers suggest that dreams are "intensified" daydreams, with the mind wandering even more freely at night than when you are just "spacing out" during the day.

22. Which of the following statements about daydreaming are true?

_____ a. Brain activity during daydreaming is identical to brain activity during REM sleep, when we typically dream.

_____ b. Thinking is more goal-directed during daydreaming than it is during sleep.

_____ c. Thinking is less goal-directed during problem solving than it is during daydreaming.

_____ d. The frontal regions of the brain are less active during daydreaming than during problem solving.

Altered States of Consciousness

Thus far in this chapter, we've discussed aspects of conscious experience that everyone normally experiences on a daily basis. Each day, you sometimes are awake and consciously experiencing the world; you sometimes are asleep and in mentally active REM sleep; and you sometimes are in the mentally quieter state of non-REM sleep.

In addition to these three mental states, people occasionally experience alterations in normal, everyday conscious experience. We'll conclude the chapter by looking at three alterations in conscious states that are produced by meditation, hypnosis, and psychoactive drugs.

Meditation

Preview Questions

› What is meditation designed to do and what are its two main techniques?

› How do we know that meditation improves mental abilities?

Try the following three-part exercise:

1. For a minute or so, pay attention to your conscious thoughts. What ideas run through your mind?

2. Now try that step again, while attempting to concentrate on just one idea or image. Let nothing other than that one image enter your mind.

3. Finally, try to think of nothing at all. Attempt, for a minute, to clear your mind of words and images.

If you're like most people, numerous thoughts flit in and out of your head. Even if you're trying to concentrate on just one thing, or to clear your mind of everything, ideas invade your conscious experience. The contents of your own mind can seem out of your control (Wegner, 1994).

You likely experienced difficulty controlling the contents of your conscious mind when you attempted our Try This! activity. You were asked to try not to think of a white bear. But when asked to indicate when one came to mind, you probably indicated that the bear frequently popped back into consciousness—even though you were trying to keep it out. The contents of your conscious mind thus were not entirely under your control.

Can you gain greater control? People who meditate say you can. **Meditation** is any practice in which people focus their attention for an extended period of time (Walsh & Shapiro, 2006). Meditative methods are designed to increase people's ability

"I can't stop thinking of white bears." It's not just white bears who can't stop thinking about them. As you learned firsthand in our Try This! activity, people can't stop thinking about them, either. If asked *not* to think about a vivid object, such as a white bear, thoughts about the object inevitably pop into consciousness (Wegner et al., 1987). The contents of your conscious mind thus are not entirely under your control.

Northern Canada. Wayne R. Bilenduke / Getty Images

TRY THIS!

meditation Any practice in which people focus their attention for an extended period of time, as a method for increasing their ability to concentrate.

to concentrate. With practice, meditators gain greater ability to focus their minds on thoughts of their own choosing. The world's cultures have produced numerous specific meditative techniques. Yet they can all be understood as one of two types (Goleman, 1988):

1. *Concentration on a single object or event.* In a meditation practice developed in the Himalayan region of South Asia, for example, meditators are instructed, during their first few months of meditative practice, to focus solely on the flow of their own breath (Rama, 1998). In other meditation traditions, practitioners may concentrate on a repeated word or phrase, known as a *mantra;* for example, "om" is a common mantra in South Asian meditative practice.

2. *Clear the mind of all thoughts.* A second meditative goal is to attain a state of emptiness—a mental void. The meditator tries to attain "non-conceptual experience" (Chodron, 1990), that is, an experience stripped of the concepts learned from society.

The significance of meditation differs for different people. For many, it is a religious practice. A Hindu may meditate on the qualities of a deity to better understand the spiritual world; an Islamic Sufi meditator may seek closer spiritual connection to the Prophet Muhammad and to Allah; and Buddhists may meditate to understand, accept, and alleviate suffering (Goleman, 1988). For many clinical psychologists, meditation is a therapy method (Walsh & Shapiro, 2006). Irrespective of their religious beliefs, they judge that meditative practice can help clients become aware of their thoughts and feelings and gain greater control over their emotional life (Baer, 2003).

> Do you think prayer can be considered a form of meditation?

In this chapter, we won't focus on either the religious or therapeutic purposes of meditation. Instead, we'll examine a third implication of meditative practice. Meditation can inform psychological science about the full spectrum of human conscious experiences. It potentially reveals a "fourth state" of consciousness that "has nothing in common with the [other] three" (wakeful consciousness, REM sleep, and non-REM sleep; Arya, 1978, p. 5). In scientific terms, then, meditative practice uniquely reveals a phenomenon that requires scientific explanation—a distinct psychological state that Western scientists otherwise might overlook.

You may be skeptical of this claim. Meditators seem to be just sitting there, doing nothing. Have they really attained a unique conscious experience, with superior power to focus their attention and control the contents of their minds? To find out, let's examine scientific evidence on the effects of meditation. We'll consider evidence at two levels of analysis: the influence of meditation on (1) psychological processes of the mind, and (2) biological mechanisms in the brain.

Cultura RM / Gary Latham / Getty Images

Buddhist monks in Cambodia, engaging in meditation Meditation has been a common practice in Eastern cultures for thousands of years.

MEDITATION AND PSYCHOLOGICAL PROCESSES. Eastern spiritual traditions have claimed, for millennia, that meditative practice enhances mental skills. It is only in recent years that scientific evidence has validated this claim (Tang & Posner, 2009).

In studying meditation, contemporary psychological scientists take two steps that were not previously taken by traditional practitioners of meditation. One involves measurement. Psychologists have devised tests to measure precisely the degree to which meditation improves people's ability to focus their attention. The other is the experimental comparison of groups. Researchers systematically compare individuals who have and have not meditated.

In one study, researchers used an "attentional blink" task to measure people's skill in concentrating attention (Slagter et al., 2007). Participants viewed a series of about 20 letters and numbers that appeared extremely rapidly (about 1/20 of a second) on a computer screen. On some trials, most of the stimuli were numbers, but some were letters. After these stimuli went zipping by, participants were asked to report the letters that appeared. This proved a difficult task. People's minds tended to wander after they saw the first letter—their attention "blinked"—and they then missed the next letter presented. When two groups of participants attempted this task—(1) meditators trained for three months in meditation that focuses attention, and (2) nonmeditators—meditators showed superior attentional ability. They were better able to sustain their attention to the rapidly presented stimuli, as indicated by their superior scores on the attentional blink task (Slagter et al., 2007). Scientific methods therefore confirmed ancient wisdom. Meditation improves people's ability to focus their attention.

> What would be some of the advantages of an increased ability to focus your attention?

MEDITATION AND BRAIN PROCESSES. Once you learn that meditation changes psychological abilities (specifically, the ability to focus attention), a new question arises: What brain mechanisms underlie these psychological changes? The psychological findings establish facts about the mind that can be explored at a biological level of analysis.

A clue to identifying the brain systems that meditation influences can be found in basic research on attention. Attention, the psychological process in which people focus their minds on an object or idea, has long been of interest to experimental psychologists (Kahneman, 1973; Triesman, 1964; see Chapter 5). Contemporary research explores attention at both psychological and biological levels of analysis and identifies parts of the brain that are particularly central to the focusing of attention (Posner & Rothbart, 2007). Here, then, is the clue: These brain systems may be the ones that change when people engage in meditative training (Lutz et al., 2008).

To find out, researchers conducted a brain-imaging study (Brefczynski-Lewis et al., 2007). Three groups of people participated: (1) novice meditators, with limited training in meditative techniques; (2) expert meditators with an average of 19,000 hours of meditation; and (3) *highly* practiced expert meditators, with an average of 44,000 hours of practice. (The latter two groups included people residing at meditative retreats, who meditate an average of 10 hours a day.) Participants in each group had their brains scanned during a meditation exercise in which they concentrated their attention on a small dot appearing on a video screen.

As predicted, the brain activity of expert meditators differed from that of nonmeditators. When regions of the brain known to support attention were examined, the brains of meditators with 19,000 hours of practice were more active than those of novice meditators; meditative training thus influenced brain processes. Interestingly, when the brains of meditators with 44,000 hours of practice were examined, they were *less* active. For this highly expert group, the concentration task was so easy that it required little mental effort (Brefczynski-Lewis et al., 2007). Other researchers similarly have found large differences in brain activation when comparing novice meditators with Buddhist monks who were expert in meditative practice (Manna et al., 2010).

Research on meditation and the brain reinforces a conclusion about how the brain works. Brain systems are "plastic" (see Chapter 3). Neural connections are not entirely determined by your genetic makeup. Instead, the brain's inner wiring changes as a result of your experience. Meditation is an experience that can significantly change the biology of the brain, and thus the mental abilities of the person.

> **THINK ABOUT IT**
> Research shows that the minds and brains of people who meditate differ from those of others. Why? Do meditators acquire specific mental skills? Or, thanks to hours spent in a calm meditative state, might they simply be more relaxed, with their emotional relaxation affecting the mind and brain?

> **Russell Simmons,** co-founder of Def Jam Recordings, is a meditator—and he's not alone. "Oprah. Jerry Seinfeld. Paul McCartney. Phil Jackson. Ellen DeGeneres. Forest Whitaker . . . they all meditate and credit the practice as one of the foundations of their success," he notes (Simmons, 2014, p. 5).

Terrence Jennings / Retna Ltd. / Corbis

23. Which of these statements about meditation are accurate? Check all that apply.
_____ a. One goal in meditation is to focus on a single object or event.
_____ b. Another goal in meditation is to clear the mind of all thoughts.
_____ c. Scientific evidence indicates that meditation reduces the ability to focus attention.
_____ d. In one study, activity in areas of the brain that support attention was greater during a concentration task in a group of expert meditators (those with 19,000 hours of training) compared to novice meditators.
_____ e. In the same study described above, the brain activity of highly expert meditators (those with 44,000 hours of training) was actually lower than those of novice meditators.

Hypnotic suggestions and brain activity Amir Raz of McGill University (left/rear), conducting research on the influence of hypnotic states on mind and brain. In the research shown here, a participant is performing a cognitive task you learned about in Chapter 2: the Stroop task. Findings show that hypnotic suggestions can influence information processing and brain activity during the task. Among highly hypnotizable persons, the suggestion that English language letters are actually "meaningless symbols" reduces activity in a brain system, the anterior cingulate cortex, that is active when people face conflicts between two responses—in this case, (1) saying the color of ink in which a word is written and (2) reading the word itself (Raz, Fan, & Posner, 2005).

Don Hogan Charles / The New York Times / Redux Pictures

Hypnosis

Preview Questions

> Is everyone hypnotizable?
> How is a hypnotic state induced?
> How do we know hypnosis works?

Most people learn something about hypnosis well before taking a psychology class. Popular culture—TV, movies—introduces us to the topic.

Here in a course on psychological science, you have to "unlearn" much of what popular culture has taught you. In the popular-culture story, hypnosis is a mysterious method of mind control. Stare at a watch for a few moments, and a hypnotist purportedly will have you in a trance, and soon you'll be barking like a dog, clucking like a chicken, or heading to Elmer's house to be turned into rabbit stew.

Research shows, however, that hypnosis does not really work this way. It is not a method of mind control (Raz & Shapiro, 2002). People who are hypnotized do not entirely lose conscious control of their thoughts and actions, although it is true that they may sometimes perform behaviors that, they report, occurred outside of their control. It also is not as mysterious as it may first appear. Recent advances suggest that hypnosis can be understood through normal methods of psychological science (Posner & Rothbart, 2011).

Hypnosis is an altered state of consciousness brought about through interaction between someone who makes suggestions to an individual (the "hypnotist") and a hypnotic subject. When hypnotized, the hypnotic subject becomes highly suggestible, that is, his or her behavior is unusually responsive to suggestions from the hypnotist, rather than being driven by personal goals and intentions.

Hypnosis, then, is not a method of mind control, yet it also is not mere myth. It is a genuine phenomenon with real psychological effects; as one expert summarized, "Hypnotized subjects can be oblivious to pain; they hear voices that aren't there and fail to see objects that are clearly in their field of vision; they are unable to remember the things that happened to them while they were hypnotized; and they carry out suggestions after hypnosis has been terminated" (Kihlstrom, 2007, p. 445). Let's look more closely at the questions of how hypnosis works and who can be hypnotized.

hypnosis An altered state of consciousness characterized by the subject's unusual responsiveness to suggestions made by the hypnotist.

hypnotic induction The process of inducing a state of hypnosis in a subject, usually through procedures combining relaxation and focused attention.

THE "HOW" AND "WHO" OF HYPNOSIS. Psychologists induce states of hypnosis through **hypnotic induction** procedures. A standard procedure, long in use, combines relaxation and focused attention (Weitzenhoffer & Hilgard, 1962). At the outset, the hypnotist informs participants that the process of hypnosis is up to them; they can achieve a hypnotic state only if they want to. (Note how this actual practice differs from the popular-culture myth that hypnotists can control the minds of unwitting victims.) Participants are encouraged to focus their attention on a specific target, such as a spot on a wall, while relaxing. The relaxation is very thorough; the hypnotist guides the process by suggesting that the participant's muscles are relaxing, body is feeling heavy and tired, and eyelids are feeling heavy and needing to close. Once the hypnotic subject's eyes close, the hypnotist instructs the subject to focus on the words of the hypnotist, and leads the person into a hypnotic state from which, the hypnotist suggests, the participant will not emerge until instructed to do so. Having reached this state, hypnotized people are highly suggestible. Their experiences are guided by the instructions of the hypnotist.

You might be thinking, "This would never work on me." If so, you may be right. Not everyone is hypnotizable. People differ considerably in their susceptibility to hypnosis.

Psychologists have developed procedures to identify who is, and is not, hypnotizable. In the Stanford Hypnotic Susceptibility Scale (Weitzenhoffer & Hilgard, 1962), the hypnotic subject undergoes an induction of the sort we just described and then receives suggestions regarding a series of tasks. Some are simple, such as the suggestion that one's eyelids are getting heavy and are closing. Others are more elaborate. For example, the psychologist places three boxes in front of the subject and suggests, "I have placed *two* boxes in front of you . . . just two boxes. Do you see them?" (Weitzenhoffer & Hilgard, 1962, p. 44). Then the participants are asked what they see. The overall degree to which the subject responds to the suggestions indicates the depth to which the person has become hypnotized (e.g., saying "I see two boxes" would indicate greater depth). Results suggest that people differ widely in their hypnotizability. Only about one in eight or nine show substantial hypnotic effects on the full range of tasks (Kihlstrom, 2007).

In summary, then, hypnotic procedures can powerfully affect people's psychological responses. But the strongest effects are seen in only a subset of highly hypnotizable people.

> Have you ever tried hypnosis? If so, how hypnotizable were you?

PSYCHOLOGICAL EVIDENCE OF HYPNOTIC EFFECTS. Why do hypnotic induction procedures affect people's responses? There are two possibilities:

3. *Unique hypnotic effect:* Hypnotic procedures create a unique mental state in which people's thoughts and actions are controlled, to a substantial degree, by the hypnotist's suggestions.

4. *Social role effect:* Hypnotic procedures cause people to *act as if* they are experiencing a unique mental state in which their thoughts and actions are controlled by the hypnotist's suggestions. They adopt the social role of "hypnotized person" (Sarbin, 1950; Spanos & Hewitt, 1980).

Many situations create social roles. At the doctor, you are expected to act in a manner consistent with the social role of "patient." In class, you are expected to act according to the role of "student." Possibility #2 suggests that, similarly, being in a hypnotic procedure causes people to act according to the role of "hypnotized person." They adopt the role, convince themselves that they are hypnotized, and interpret their own behavior accordingly.

Which possibility do you think is correct? Before you try to answer that question, consider some research by the eminent psychologist Ernest Hilgard and his colleagues (Hilgard, Morgan, & Macdonald, 1975). They hypnotized participants and then asked them to put one of their hands in painfully cold water. Prior to this chilly experience, the hypnotist made two suggestions to participants: (1) They would not *consciously* experience any pain when their hand was in the water, but (2) a "hidden part" of them would be aware of the pain. The researchers then measured pain in two ways: (1) Participants reported consciously, in words, on their experiences; and, (2) in a procedure designed to tap the "hidden part" of the individual, participants typed numbers onto a keypad to indicate their level of pain.

Hilgard and colleagues found that the conscious and "hidden" parts of hypnotized participants provided different pain reports (Hilgard et al., 1975). Consciously, hypnotized subjects reported little pain, despite having plunged a hand in frigid water. However, when typing numbers into a keypad, many participants reported that they *were* in pain.

The researchers interpreted this finding as evidence that hypnotized participants' minds contain two parts that, through hypnosis, become disconnected. The conscious part truly experiences no pain, as a result of hypnosis. The "hidden part," however, is aware of the pain.

Other research similarly shows the action of different parts of the mind. Hypnotized people have been shown information (e.g., a list of words) and then given a hypnotic suggestion for amnesia, that is, the suggestion that they will lose their memory of the material. Later, they are given tests of both explicit and implicit memory (Chapter 6). After the hypnotic suggestion, people lack explicit memory; they don't consciously remember the material. Yet they do have *implicit* memory; when performing a task that requires them to think of a word, they tend to think of one that was on the previous word list (Kihlstrom, 2007). The results thus suggest that the mind contains at least two different memory systems.

This conclusion—strange as it may sound at first—is consistent with other findings in psychology. The behavior of split-brain patients (Chapter 3) reveals that their minds contain two parts. One can consciously discuss the person's experiences, whereas the other can respond to stimuli but is unable to report on them consciously. Measures of "explicit" and "implicit" attitudes in social psychology often are poorly correlated with each other (Chapter 12), which suggests that people can be "of two minds" about a given topic.

What about the social role hypothesis? Some psychologists think that the findings of Hilgard and colleagues can be explained in terms of social roles (Spanos & Hewitt, 1980). Others, however, doubt this. They think it unlikely that the social role hypothesis can explain complex phenomena such as a participant's different levels of performance on tests of implicit and explicit memory. In general, then, research suggests that—at least for highly hypnotizable people—the psychological effects of hypnosis are real.

BIOLOGICAL EVIDENCE OF HYPNOTIC EFFECTS. You still might be skeptical about hypnosis. It's not impossible that the psychological evidence we just reviewed can be explained in terms of social roles. Biological evidence would be even more convincing. Since people generally cannot voluntarily control the activation of regions of their brains, any effects of hypnosis on brain functioning could not be explained by saying that people voluntarily adopted the social role of "hypnotized person."

Researchers have, in fact, obtained such evidence. Using a research procedure similar to that of Hilgard and colleagues, researchers examined the effects of hypnosis on the experience of pain (Vanhaudenhuyse et al., 2009). They added a procedure unavailable to Hilgard decades earlier: fMRI, which enabled them to study brain activity during a painful task.

Highly hypnotizable participants took part in research procedures on two different days, during which they either were or were not hypnotized. The painful stimuli on both days were brief pulses of a laser directed to the back of the left hand. (The laser stimulated pain receptors, thereby producing a sensation of pain.) Researchers recorded brain activity and also asked participants to rate the severity of the pain they experienced.

As in prior research, hypnosis reduced conscious pain. Participants reported less pain on the day they were hypnotized. In addition, hypnosis influenced brain activation. When participants were *not* hypnotized, the laser pulses caused activation in a wide variety of brain regions. However, when they *were* hypnotized, these same stimuli remarkably "failed to elicit any cerebral activation" (Vanhaudenhuyse et al., 2009, p. 1050; Figure 9.7). Hypnosis apparently caused high-level brain regions to influence lower-level regions of the brain that are directly involved in the experience of pain.

The key finding, then, is that identical stimuli had different effects on neural activity when participants were hypnotized. This should be enough to convince even the skeptic that hypnosis is a real phenomenon that influences both mind and brain.

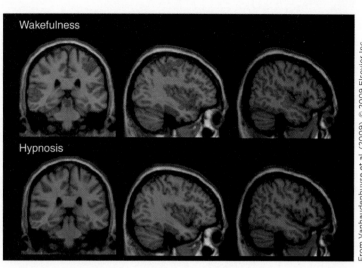

Wakefulness

Hypnosis

figure 9.7

Hypnosis and the brain In research, people experienced painful stimuli either when awake in the normal way, or after being hypnotized. Hypnosis reduces brain activity, as shown, in addition to reducing participants' conscious reports of pain.

WHAT DO YOU KNOW?...

24. A standard hypnotic _____ procedure involves relaxation and focused attention. Once hypnotized, people are highly _____; they are willing to be guided by the instructions of a hypnotist. Only about one in eight or nine people are able to be _____. Hilgard's research indicated that people's minds have two parts that become disconnected during hypnosis and that they map onto explicit and _____ memory. Experimental research suggests that hypnosis alters both the mind and _____.

Psychoactive Drugs

Preview Question

> What are the effects of hallucinogens, opioids, stimulants, and depressants and how do they work?

A while back, some residents of the Caribbean wanted to alter their conscious states. They did so the quick way: They took out their paraphernalia—bowls for burning and tubes for inhaling—and used drugs. Is their drug use a sign of the moral decay of modern society? Well, no; it was *quite* a while back. The drug paraphernalia, researchers determined, was about 2400 years old (Fitzpatrick et al., 2009). Study of prehistoric societies reveals signs of similar drug use in multiple regions of the world, including the Americas and Europe (Echeverría & Niemeyer, 2013; Rudgley, 1995).

Humans, then, have long used *psychoactive drugs*. A **psychoactive drug** is any chemical substance that affects the nervous system in a manner that alters conscious experience. Psychoactive drugs exert these effects by changing communications among cells in the nervous system.

Once people begin abusing drugs, it can be difficult for them to stop—even when they can see that it is harming their own health (Everitt et al., 2008). Such users suffer from **drug addiction,** a compulsive, habitual, uncontrollable use of a harmful chemical substance (National Institute on Drug Abuse [NIDA], 2010). Drug addiction is widespread. Researchers estimate that 25 million people worldwide are addicted to psychoactive drugs (United Nations Office on Drugs and Crime [UNODC], 2009).

Why are psychoactive drugs so addicting? It's primarily because they activate a reward center in the brain (Tan, Rudolph, & Lüscher, 2011). The brain's reward center normally produces pleasurable feelings when organisms engage in activities that are naturally rewarding, such as eating or sex. Drugs artificially activate this reward system and thereby directly create such feelings of pleasure. This makes them highly

psychoactive drug Any chemical substance that affects the nervous system in a manner that alters conscious experience.

drug addiction Compulsive, habitual, uncontrollable use of a harmful chemical substance.

addicting. (Chapter 11 discusses motivational processes and brain mechanisms that can cause people to become addicted to stimulant drugs.)

There are different types of psychoactive drugs. We'll examine four: *hallucinogens, opioids, stimulants,* and *depressants.*

HALLUCINOGENS. **Hallucinogens** are substances that profoundly alter consciousness, causing people to experience phenomena such as hallucinations and a loss of contact with reality. Hallucinogenic effects have long been experienced across the globe. Traditional cultures in Central America, South America, and South Asia have used hallucinogens in religious ceremonies for centuries (Nichols, 2004).

Traditional cultures discovered the effects of hallucinogenic substances that occur naturally. "Magic" mushrooms found in Mexico and South America, for example, produce hallucinogenic effects because they contain *psilocybin,* a chemical substance that powerfully alters mental experiences.

More recently, people have produced hallucinogens synthetically, that is, by combining chemicals in a laboratory. The first to do so was Albert Hoffman, a Swiss chemist working on drugs for migraine headaches. In 1943 he reported an unusual experience: "a not unpleasant intoxicated-like condition, characterized by an extremely stimulated imagination. In a dreamlike state . . . I perceived an uninterrupted stream of fantastic pictures, extraordinary shapes with intense, kaleidoscopic play of colors" (Hoffman, 1979, p. 47). Hoffman had been working on **LSD (lysergic acid diethylamide)** and guessed that a small amount of LSD must have been absorbed into his skin, causing the psychological effects. To test his idea, Hoffman next ingested 0.25 milligrams of the drug. It was more than enough:

> Everything in my field of vision wavered and was distorted as if seen in a curved mirror. . . . Everything in the room spun around, and the familiar objects and pieces of furniture assumed grotesque, threatening forms. . . . I was seized by the dreadful fear of going insane.

—Hoffman (1979, pp. 48–49)

Hoffman had experienced the first LSD "trip."

For two decades after Hoffman's discovery, few people in the United States experienced LSD trips. But the drug gained popularity in the 1960s, due largely to the efforts of two psychologists at Harvard University, Timothy Leary and Richard Alpert (Lattin, 2010). They first experienced hallucinogens when sampling magic mushrooms in Mexico. They then experimented with LSD and became convinced that it was beneficial, awakening users to new, enlightening conscious experiences. Leary and Alpert gave the drug to colleagues, writers, artists, and even their students. They launched a campaign to get people, as Leary put it, to "turn on, tune in, and drop out" of mainstream society by exploring LSD's mind-expanding powers.

Their campaign was remarkably successful. Hallucinogens became a staple of the 1960s counterculture. Popular music and art reflected, and contributed to, growth in the use of these drugs.

Today, hallucinogen use persists. About 1% of teens and 7% of young adults in the United States have tried LSD at least once (Substance Abuse and Mental Health Services Administration [SAMHSA], 2010). It persists despite legal sanctions: Possession of hallucinogens is illegal. It persists despite health risks: Hallucinogens can impair

CONNECTING TO NEUROTRANSMITTER SYSTEMS AND THERAPIES FOR PSYCHOLOGICAL DISORDERS

P

PERSON

Chapters 15 and 16: Therapists prescribe drugs in an effort to reduce psychological distress.

M

MIND

Here, we focus on the effects of psychoactive drugs on the mind.

B

BRAIN

Chapter 3: Drugs affect neurotransmitters in the brain that carry out communications among brain cells.

PMB CONNECTIONS

hallucinogens Substances that profoundly alter consciousness, causing people to experience phenomena such as hallucinations and a loss of contact with reality.

LSD (lysergic acid diethylamide) A synthetic chemical that affects the firing of neurons in the brain, thereby inducing widespread biological, and thus psychological, effects.

health through multiple routes. For example, some users feel that they have superhuman powers and attempt bizarre, dangerous activities such as trying to fly (Nichols, 2004). Another risk is psychological. Among people who are pre-disposed to psychological distress, the disturbing alterations of consciousness that hallucinogens create can trigger depression or psychosis, that is, a loss of the normal ability to understand the world of reality (Nichols, 2004).

Some readers of this text may be seeking an expansion of conscious experience. If so, compare pills to skills. As you learned above, the skills of meditation enhance conscious awareness—without the costs, legal jeopardy, and health risks of hallucinogens.

What biological processes explain LSD's psychological effects? The drug affects the actions of the neurotransmitter serotonin (Aghajanian & Marek, 1999; Nichols, 2004). When people take LSD, brain cells that are activated by serotonin—"serotonergic" neurons—fire abnormally. Serotonergic neurons are found in multiple regions of the brain. As a result, LSD has widespread biological, and thus psychological, effects.

Evidence indicates that hallucinogens may have additional biological effects (Fantegrossi, Murnane, & Reissig, 2008). Both LSD and the psilocybin found in magic mushrooms uniquely influence the inner workings of brain cells in the cortex (González-Maeso et al., 2007). The resulting combination of effects—on (1) a neurotransmitter (serotonin) used for communication *between* cells and on (2) biological activity *within* individual cells—may explain why hallucinogenic effects are so powerful.

The psychedelic era 1960s rocker Janis Joplin and her psychedelic Porsche—one of many hallucinogen-inspired symbols of the era.

OPIOIDS. Opioids are chemical substances whose primary psychoactive effect is the reduction of pain. They reduce pain by attaching themselves to nervous system cells that are involved in generating pain and related emotions (Holden, Jeong, & Forrest, 2005). Through such action, the drug morphine, for example, lessens the transmission of pain signals from the body to the brain, thereby lowering the conscious experience of pain.

Pain reduction is not the opioids' only psychoactive effect. Opioids can also produce powerful feelings of euphoria and ecstasy (van Ree, Gerrits, & Vanderschuren, 1999). This makes opioid drugs highly addictive. People crave the positive feelings they create and seek to avoid the withdrawal symptoms—agitation, insomnia, muscular aches—that occur when drug use is stopped. Opioid addiction is a significant health risk. For instance, opioids can cause fatal respiratory system failures, especially if used in combination with other drugs (NIDA, 2011).

You don't need to take drugs to experience the pain-relieving effects of opioids. You've got them in your system already. The body naturally produces *endogenous opioids* (*endogenous* means "originating within the body"). Just like opiate drugs that people ingest, the body's endogenous opioids lessen pain by reducing the transmission of pain signals from the spinal cord to the brain (Holden et al., 2005). Research shows that intense exercise increases levels, within the brain, of endogenous opioids—especially *endorphins,* one of the opioids produced endogenously (Landolfi, 2012; Scheef et al., 2012). As a result, athletes may perform at high levels despite seemingly painful injuries. The endogenous opioid system blunts their conscious experience of pain.

Considering his leg was broken, he ran a pretty good time In the 2012 London Olympics, Manteo Mitchell broke a bone in his leg while running in the 4 × 400 meter relay—yet he still finished. In fact, he ran an excellent time. How'd he do that? Although Mitchell experienced pain, he experienced *less* pain than would a sedentary person whose leg was broken. During intense exercise, the body's endogenous opioid system blunts the conscious experience of pain.

opioids Chemical substances whose primary psychoactive effect is the reduction of pain; can also induce feelings of euphoria and ecstasy.

Don't drink the whole can Moderate amounts of caffeine (e.g., a few cups of coffee a day) are not harmful to adults (Food and Drug Administration [FDA], 2007). But overdoses are. Extremely high caffeine intake can lead to high blood pressure and cardiovascular system failure (Kapur & Smith, 2009).

Anthony Collins / Alamy

stimulants Psychoactive drugs that increase nervous system activity and thus enhance alertness and energy.

caffeine A chemical compound found in coffee, tea, energy drinks, sodas, and chocolate that increases alertness.

nicotine A stimulant found in tobacco products that increases alertness while enhancing feelings of pleasure and emotional well-being.

attention-deficit hyperactivity disorder (ADHD) A condition marked by high distractibility, low ability to concentrate, and impulsive behavior such as fast and frequent moving and talking.

amphetamines Stimulants that strongly increase alertness and produce euphoric feelings.

cocaine A powerful stimulant that increases alertness and produces euphoric feelings, and thus is highly addictive.

ecstasy A recreational drug that can reduce anxiety and create feelings of intimacy and euphoria while raising body temperature; both a stimulant and a hallucinogen.

depressants Psychoactive drugs that reduce arousal in the central nervous system, lowering conscious experiences of excitability and anxiety.

benzodiazepines Psychoactive drugs prescribed for anxiety that reduce feelings of anxiety while also inducing muscular relaxation and sleepiness; may also produce pleasurable feelings.

STIMULANTS. **Stimulants** are psychoactive drugs that increase nervous system activity and thus enhance alertness and energy. Stimulants also can enhance people's sense of psychological well-being and self-esteem, as well as lower their inhibitions (Gawin & Ellinwood, 1988).

You might be in easy reach of the most commonly ingested stimulant drug right now: caffeine, a chemical compound found in coffee, tea, energy drinks, sodas, and chocolate. **Caffeine** increases alertness by interfering with naturally occurring biochemical processes that decrease brain activity (e.g., when you're sleepy; Ribeiro & Sebastião, 2010). Although caffeine's psychoactive effects are milder than those of some other stimulants, it still can be addicting. If regular users suddenly quit taking caffeine, they experience withdrawal symptoms such as headache and fatigue that are caused by changes in cerebral blood flow (Sigmon et al., 2009).

Another stimulant, **nicotine,** is found in tobacco products. Nicotine triggers the release of neurotransmitters that increase alertness, as well as a neurotransmitter, dopamine, that enhances feelings of pleasure and emotional well-being (see Chapter 7). Alertness and well-being might sound good. But getting them through the nicotine in tobacco products isn't worth the costs. Tobacco use is extraordinarily harmful to health. Smoking is estimated to have killed 100 million people in the twentieth century, and it is projected to kill many times that number in the twenty-first (NIDA, 2010), due to persistently high smoking rates worldwide (Giovino, 2012).

Ritalin is a stimulant drug that is sometimes prescribed to treat **attention-deficit hyperactivity disorder (ADHD),** a condition marked by high distractibility, low ability to concentrate, and impulsive behavior such as fast and frequent moving and talking (NIH, 2012). Ritalin lessens ADHD symptoms by affecting neural communication in the brain's frontal cortex, a region needed for sustained concentration and the control of behavior (Devilbiss & Berridge, 2008).

Amphetamines are powerful stimulants that increase alertness and produce euphoric feelings by affecting multiple neurotransmitters, including dopamine (Berman et al., 2009). Amphetamines have practical medical uses. However, both amphetamines and methamphetamines (a chemically similar stimulant) are used illegally as recreational drugs. More than half a million Americans at any given time use these drugs for the rush of energy and positive emotions they produce (SAMHSA, 2009). **Cocaine,** another simulant, has similar effects on conscious experience and thus is also highly addictive. Cocaine's effects are particularly powerful when the drug is processed into a form that can be smoked, known as *crack cocaine* (Schifano & Corkery, 2008).

A drug that has gained in popularity in recent years is **ecstasy,** which is both a stimulant and a hallucinogen. Ecstasy can reduce anxiety and create feelings of intimacy and euphoria—effects that have added to its popularity. However, ecstasy also harms physical health; for example, it can abnormally raise body temperature and thus induce heat stroke (Rogers et al., 2009).

DEPRESSANTS. **Depressants** are psychoactive drugs that reduce arousal in the central nervous system. In so doing, they can lower conscious experiences of excitability and anxiety. Depressants achieve these effects in part by increasing the effects of inhibitory neurotransmitters, that is, neurotransmitters that reduce activity in the brain (Julien, 2005).

One class of widely used depressants is **benzodiazepines,** psychoactive drugs that reduce feelings of anxiety while also inducing muscular relaxation and sleepiness (Tan et al., 2011). Because of these effects, benzodiazepines such as Valium, Xanax, and Ativan are prescribed frequently to treat anxiety disorders (see Chapter 15). In addition to reducing anxiety, benzodiazepines activate the brain's reward center and thus produce pleasurable feelings. This makes them particularly addicting.

The most commonly used depressant of all is **alcohol,** a chemical compound found in beer, wine, and spirits. Beverages containing alcohol, which enhances the action of inhibitory neurotransmitters in the brain and reduces the action of excitatory neurotransmitters (Valenzuela, 1997), have been part of human societies for millennia. Various 7000-year-old jars for holding wine have been found in Iran, and 9000-year-old containers for a beerlike brew have been found in China (Gately, 2008). Humans thus have long experienced the feelings of relaxation and the lessening of inhibitions that alcohol can produce. Of course, this means people have also experienced its negative effects. Drinking impairs decision making and performance. High levels of chronic alcohol use can damage areas of the brain needed for memory and the control of motor movements (NIDA, 2010).

How does alcohol affect behavior? It depends. Sometimes, a few drinks can make people warm and outgoing. At other times, drinking may cause those same individuals to become hostile and belligerent. Understanding these differences requires multiple levels of analysis: not just a brain level of analysis (the effects of alcohol on neural communication) but a mind level (analysis of the specific thinking processes that alcohol affects) and person level (in particular, consideration of the social setting in which the person is drinking).

At the level of the mind, alcohol has two notable effects: (1) reducing the amount of information in a situation that people can pay attention to and (2) impairing individuals' ability to think deeply about that information (Steele & Josephs, 1990). In short, drinking impairs thinking. This impact of alcohol on mental processes, in turn, helps to explain the impact of drinking on people's social behavior.

People who have been drinking are strongly affected by social cues. They are particularly influenced (before their attention is heavily impaired) by cues that happen to grab their attention. If they notice others who are pleasant, alcohol may increase their warmth and pleasantness. If they notice someone who they think is insulting them, alcohol may increase their belligerence. This is why the effects of alcohol on behavior "depend." They depend on cues in a person's immediate social environment.

Finally, let's conclude our discussion of psychoactive substances with the most frequently used illicit drug, **marijuana** (NIDA, 2014). Marijuana is a difficult drug to classify, for two reasons. First, it produces a wide range of effects; marijuana can influence both conscious feelings and thinking abilities. Second, its effects vary; the exact influence of the drug on any given occasion depends on the amount of marijuana consumed, as well as on individual differences in people's reaction to the drug (Ameri, 1999).

Despite these variations, there is a pattern of effects that occurs commonly. Users tend to experience feelings of euphoria accompanied by a relaxed, tranquil state (Ameri, 1999). These effects are caused by a chemical substance in marijuana, tetrahydrocannabinol (THC), that affects the activity of cells in the brain. Specifically, THC affects neural activity in parts of the brain that contribute not only to emotional states (e.g., pleasurable feelings), but also to cognition (memory, thinking, concentration). The widespread biological influence explains its wide range of psychological effects.

In the past, public health officials sometimes exaggerated the negative effects of marijuana use. Today, by contrast, users may enjoy the drug's psychological effects while giving little thought to its potential long-term costs. Yet costs exist. Consider research that compared (1) people who never used marijuana to (2) people who used marijuana consistently across a long span of life, from their late teenage years to their 30s (Meier et al., 2012). This study's key dependent variable was intelligence test scores; researchers examined participants' IQ scores (see Chapter 8) early and later in life. They found that, over time, persistent marijuana users became less intelligent. Persistent users lost about 6 IQ points, whereas the IQ scores of nonusers went up slightly across the course of the study.

Table 9.1 summarizes the psychoactive drugs we have reviewed, plus selected additional drugs whose use is relatively widespread.

It's relaxing. It induces euphoria. But it might be costing him IQ points. Research shows that persistent marijuana use, across years of life, can lower people's IQ scores.

Pablo Porciuncula / AFP / Getty Images

alcohol A depressant chemical compound found in beer, wine, and spirits that induces feelings of relaxation and a lessening of inhibitions.

marijuana A drug that produces a wide range of effects that commonly include both euphoria and a relaxed, tranquil state.

table 9.1

Psychoactive Drugs		
Drug	**Classification**	**Common Short-Term Effects on Conscious Experience***
Alcohol	Depressant	Relaxation, tension reduction, elevated mood
Amphetamine	Stimulant	Increased alertness, euphoric feelings
Benzodiazepine	Depressant	Reduced anxiety, relaxation, sleepiness
Caffeine	Stimulant	Enhanced alertness, arousal, attention
Cocaine	Stimulant	Euphoria, enhanced energy, alertness
Ecstasy	Hallucinogen, stimulant	Reduced anxiety, euphoria, visual hallucinations
Heroin	Opioid	Euphoric rush, "clouded" thinking, pain reduction
LSD	Hallucinogen	Distorted sensory and perceptual experiences, intense positive and negative emotions
Marijuana	Depressant, hallucinogen	Euphoria, calmness, distorted perception and impaired thinking, paranoia
Nicotine	Stimulant	Elevated mood, relaxation, improved concentration, appetite reduction
Psilocybin	Hallucinogen	Hallucinations, altered perception of time, intense emotional states
Ritalin	Stimulant	Increased attention and concentration, reduced distractibility

*The short-term effects of psychoactive drugs can vary from one person to another. In addition to short-term effects, many psychoactive drugs have major negative effects on psychological and physical health. The United States' National Institute on Drug Abuse estimates that alcohol abuse and illegal drug use contribute to more than 100,000 deaths annually and that tobacco use is linked to more than 4 times that number of annual deaths (NIDA, 2010).

💭 WHAT DO YOU KNOW?...

25. Hallucinogens such as lysergic acid diethylamide, or _____, cause people to hallucinate and to lose touch with reality. Opioids, such as the drug _____, reduce the transmission of pain signals from the body to the brain. Nicotine, a _____, triggers the release of the neurotransmitter _____, which enhances feelings of well-being. Ecstasy, which is both a stimulant and a _____, can reduce anxiety and create feelings of intimacy and euphoria but can abnormally raise body temperature. The most commonly used depressant, _____, works by enhancing the action of _____ neurotransmitters and reducing the action of _____ neurotransmitters.

↩ Looking Back and Looking Ahead

Consciousness once seemed like a complete mystery—its puzzles beyond the reach of science. But as you've seen in this chapter, things look different today. Researchers have made substantial progress in solving the scientific puzzles consciousness presents.

This progress comes from research conducted at different levels of analysis. Careful study of the mind is required to avoid the pitfalls of the homunculus problem. Cutting-edge brain-imaging methods are needed to identify the interconnected neural systems required for conscious experience.

Not all the puzzles of consciousness are solved, however. Science still lacks a complete understanding of how the physical matter of the brain gives rise to the subjective experiences of consciousness. For any of you considering a scientific career in this field, this gives you something challenging to work on!

Chapter Review

Now that you have completed this chapter, be sure to turn to Appendix B, where you will find a **Chapter Summary** that is useful for reviewing what you have learned about consciousness.

Key Terms

activation-synthesis theory (p. 389)

alcohol (p. 401)

amphetamines (p. 400)

attention-deficit hyperactivity disorder (ADHD) (p. 400)

benzodiazepines (p. 400)

caffeine (p. 400)

circadian rhythm (p. 382)

cocaine (p. 400)

consciousness (p. 362)

depressants (p. 400)

drug addiction (p. 397)

dualism (p. 368)

ecstasy (p. 400)

EEG (electroencephalography) (p. 381)

hallucinogens (p. 398)

homunculus problem (p. 370)

hypnosis (p. 394)

hypnotic induction (p. 394)

insomnia (p. 386)

LSD (lysergic acid diethylamide) (p. 398)

marijuana (p. 401)

meditation (p. 391)

mental time travel (p. 366)

mind–body problem (p. 370)

mirror self-recognition test (p. 366)

narcolepsy (p. 385)

nicotine (p. 400)

non-REM sleep (p. 378)

opioids (p. 399)

phantom limb syndrome (p. 363)

psychoactive drug (p. 397)

REM (rapid eye movement) sleep (p. 378)

self-consciousness (p. 366)

sleep apnea (p. 386)

sleep deprivation (p. 384)

sleep disorder (p. 385)

sleep laboratory (p. 382)

sleep stages (p. 380)

stimulants (p. 400)

wish-fulfillment theory (p. 388)

Questions for Discussion

1. According to the mirror recognition test, dogs do not have self-consciousness. But anyone who has ever seen a dog stumble or fall might argue that they do seem to experience our most self-conscious of emotions: embarrassment. Are they really experiencing embarrassment or are we anthropomorphizing them (i.e., assigning human characteristics where they are not warranted)? Explain. [Analyze]

2. If ASIMO was programmed to pass the mirror recognition test, would it possess self-consciousness? Explain. [Analyze]

3. Humans possess self-consciousness, whereas dogs and cats do not. Why, evolutionarily speaking, would it be necessary for us to have it, but not them? What uniquely human activities require self-consciousness? [Synthesize]

4. Recall that, according to dualism, the mind and body are two separate entities and consciousness is a property of the mind. Though the arguments against the validity of dualism are convincing, dualism can be said to have an *intuitive* appeal. Do you agree or disagree? Explain. [Evaluate]

5. Research by Hong and colleagues indicates that rapid eye movement is associated with more vivid dream imagery. However, the direction of this relationship is not clear: Do the vivid dreams cause us to move our eyes more, as if scanning the dream landscape; or does the eye movement itself somehow cause the vivid dreaming? How

could you design an experiment to establish the direction of the effect? [Synthesize]

6. We know that sleep deprivation impairs performance. What is your own personal operational definition of sleep deprivation? In other words, how much sleep do you need on a nightly basis for maximal performance and mood? Does everyone need the same amount of sleep? [Comprehend]

7. How's your sleep hygiene—that is, have you established habits that promote restful sleep? Check out the recommendations provided in the text for getting a good night's sleep. Of these, which are you currently practicing? What would it take for you to adopt all the recommendations? [Comprehend]

8. An evolutionary perspective of why we dream suggests that dreams serve as mental simulations that enable us to rehearse for real-life threats. Anecdotally speaking, does this ring true for your own experiences? How could you scientifically test the theory that dreams help us practice for real-life danger? What *particular* hypothesis would you test and how would you operationally define your variables? [Synthesize]

9. Meditation requires practice. Try it for yourself! What is particularly challenging about meditation? What does this challenge suggest about how the mind works? Connect this difficulty to the concept of short-term or working memory (if you've already read the memory chapter, Chapter 6). [Apply, Analyze]

10. What distinguishes meditation from hypnosis? [Analyze]

Chapter Review

1. Which of the following lacks consciousness?
   a. A lizard
   b. A Smartphone
   c. A puppy
   d. They all lack consciousness.

2. Daisy and Maisy are identical twins who report literally feeling each other's pain. For example, when Daisy cut her finger while chopping vegetables, across town, Maisy's finger stung. If their claim is valid, which of the following features of consciousness would it challenge?
   a. Its objectivity
   b. Its pervasiveness
   c. Its subjectivity
   d. Its innateness

3. A researcher affixes tape in the shape of an X to an elephant's left temple and leads her to a mirror. The elephant repeatedly swings her trunk up toward the X on her left temple, and not toward her right temple. What can we infer about the elephant?
   a. She has consciousness.
   b. She has self-consciousness.
   c. She can mentally time travel.
   d. Both "a" and "b" are correct.

4. The "mind–body" problem could be "solved" if
   a. nonphysical objects could influence physical objects.
   b. the pineal gland really was biologically unique.
   c. we assumed the mind was a nonphysical object.
   d. there really was a homunculus in the mind's "theatre."

5. According to Descartes's theory of conscious experience, if someone were to present you with an image of a rabbit, it would be processed in _____ area(s) of the brain. Dennett disagreed, citing evidence that stimuli are processed in _____ area(s) of the brain.
   a. multiple; one
   b. one; multiple
   c. multiple; limited
   d. one; limited

6. Relative to Western theories of consciousness, Eastern theories are
   a. more modern.
   b. more comprehensive.
   c. less dualistic.
   d. less sophisticated.

7. The evolutionary advantage of consciousness is that it enables us to combine information. Which of the following decisions most required this skill?
   a. "I was low on cash, so I bought generic."
   b. "I heard a loud noise, so I ran."
   c. "I was hungry, so I ate."
   d. "I fell, so I got up."

8. Under anesthesia, activity in the thalamo-cortical circuits decreases. Because these are the circuits associated with the ability to combine information, it would appear that the ability to combine information is
   a. integral to consciousness.
   b. antithetical to consciousness.
   c. irrelevant to consciousness.
   d. antagonistic to consciousness.

9. You are asleep. Your heart rate, breathing rate, and blood pressure are highly variable. You may even be experiencing sexual arousal. You are probably in which of the following stages of sleep?
   a. Stage 1
   b. Stage 2
   c. Stage 3
   d. REM

10. Researchers wishing to understand whether circadian rhythms are caused by the environment or by our biology brought participants into a lab and manipulated whether the day was 20 or 28 hours long. They found that both groups' bodily rhythms varied on a 24-hour cycle. On the basis of this study alone, what should they have concluded?
    a. Circadian rhythms were unaffected by the environment.
    b. Circadian rhythms were unaffected by biology.
    c. Circadian rhythms were caused by several factors.
    d. Circadian rhythms were caused by the environment and by biology.

11. You have been extraordinarily busy lately. To create more time in the day, you sacrifice two hours of sleep a night, so that you have been getting about six hours per night for the past two weeks. What will be the likely effect?
    a. Nothing. Your strategy for reducing sleep was sound.
    b. A slight decrease in performance, but nothing to be concerned about.
    c. You may become as impaired as if you had pulled an "all-nighter."
    d. You have already done irreversible damage to your thalamus.

12. Sleep apnea has been linked to heart failure and to obesity. Based on this, what can we conclude about the relationship between these three conditions?
    a. Sleep apnea simultaneously causes heart failure and obesity.
    b. Sleep apnea causes obesity, which causes heart failure.
    c. Obesity causes heart failure, which causes sleep apnea.
    d. More information is needed to establish causality.

13. Of the three dream theories discussed in the text, which is the least well equipped to explain why dreams sometimes are bizarre?
    a. Wish fulfillment
    b. Activation-synthesis
    c. Preparation for threat
    d. None of the above; all are well equipped to explain why dreams sometimes are bizarre.

14. Which of the following pieces of information most convincingly argues against the idea that a subject's behavior during hypnosis is due to the social role effect?
    a. Hypnosis may be used as a therapeutic tool.
    b. People retain implicit memories formed during hypnosis, but not explicit memories.
    c. There are individual differences in hypnotizability.
    d. People become very suggestible during hypnosis.

15. Which of the following substances can your body produce on its own, especially during exercise?
    a. Hallucinogens
    b. Opioids
    c. Stimulants
    d. Depressants

Answers

You can check your answers to the preceding Self-Test and the chapter's What Do You Know? questions in Appendix B.

Emotion, Stress, and Health 10

IN THE AIRPORT OF THE FUTURE, a computer at the security checkpoint will read your mind and determine whether you intend to commit a terrorist act.

Science fiction? The U.S. Department of Homeland Security (DHS) doesn't think so. In fact, it's been working on such a computer system for years. Project Hostile Intent, a DHS research program, aimed to identify passengers who might be trying to deceive security officers (Department of Homeland Security, 2008). This effort continues today with DHS's Future Attribute Screening Technology (FAST) project (DHS, 2011).

How does the program work? Homeland Security doesn't tell us, exactly, because "the specific behavioral indicators being measured are sensitive information and therefore are not . . . discussed" (DHS, 2008, p. 2). But you can take an educated guess—at least, once you read this chapter on emotion.

When you experience an emotion, it shows on your face. Even if you try to hide the emotion, it still shows for a very brief period of time. Fleeting facial-muscle movements, known as micro-expressions, reveal inner emotional states—such as the states of stress and fear that anyone would experience when trying to sneak illegal items past a security checkpoint.

An emotions researcher, Paul Ekman, has developed a way to detect micro-expressions. In his research, high-speed video cameras capture even brief facial-muscle movements. These muscle movements uncover emotions people are trying to conceal. Dr. Ekman also has served as a consultant to Project Hostile Intent (Johnson, 2009).

In Ekman's original research, videos of facial expressions were classified, or coded, by people—a time-consuming process. More recently, researchers have developed computer software that can code facial expressions accurately (Terzis, Moridis, & Economides, 2011). With such software in hand, Homeland Security may achieve its goal: "[a] computer [that] will analyze . . . behavior and identify indicators of deception" (DHS, 2008)—computerized mind-reading based on the psychology of emotion. ◎

Getty Images, clockwise from background: Image Source; drbimage; Peter Dazeley

Maya Almeida / Gallery Stock

407

"WHAT ARE YOU thinking about?"

People ask this all the time. Sometimes your honest answer is "Nothing; I wasn't thinking about anything." You were just spacing out.

"How are you feeling?"

People ask this all the time, too. But, the honest answer never is "nothing." You're always feeling *something:* tired, peppy, bored, intrigued, angry, grateful, calm, anxious. Feelings are ever-present (Russell, 2003).

This chapter begins by exploring two types of feelings: the rapidly occurring and sometimes intense experiences we call *emotions;* and the relatively long-lasting but typically less intense psychological states that we call *moods.* After analyzing emotion and mood psychologically, we'll move down a level of explanation to examine brain systems that contribute to these psychological experiences. Finally, we'll focus on the emotions that arise when people are under stress, the impact of stress on physical health, and strategies you can use to make life less stressful.

Defining Emotion and Mood

Let's begin by defining our terms—a particularly important task in the psychology of emotion and mood. Fortunately, the task is easy. We won't need strange new technical terms. Words you already use to discuss your feelings will prove useful (see Hacker, 2004).

Emotion

Preview Question

> What are the four key components of an emotion?

What is "emotion"? Let's see how people use the term. In English, "emotion" describes psychological experiences with three components: (1) a *feeling* (if you say that you're experiencing an emotion, you're inevitably feeling good or bad), (2) a *thought* (when experiencing an emotion, such as sadness or anger, you usually are thinking about the person or event that caused the emotional reaction to occur), and (3) *bodily arousal* (your physiological state is different than it was before the emotion occurred; Wierzbicka, 1999). Here's an example. Suppose a driver cuts you off in traffic and you experience an emotion: anger. The emotion includes the three components:

1. *Feeling:* Once your anger kicks in, you feel different than you did moments earlier.
2. *Thought:* You're thinking about the other driver; you're angry *at him* because he almost got you into an accident.
3. *Bodily arousal:* You're more aroused, physiologically, when angry. People may describe the physiology of anger with phrases such as "I was steamed" or "He got my blood boiling."

If one of these components were missing, you would not say that you were experiencing an emotion. For example, suppose #3, bodily arousal, had been absent; perhaps you responded calmly, merely uttering soft-spoken words such as "It is unfortunate how many poor drivers populate our roadways." Thanks to the calm state of your body, you would not say that you had "gotten emotional" (i.e., had experienced an emotion) when cut off.

In addition to these three key components—thought, feeling, bodily arousal—most emotions have a fourth component: facial expression (Ekman, 2003). You often can tell at a glance not only that a person is emotionally aroused, but also what emotion he or she is feeling (Figure 10.1).

He's emotional Emotions have three components. You can see them here on the face of Australian tennis star Lleyton Hewitt: (1) *feeling* (Hewitt obviously feels angry; you can tell from the expression on his face); (2) *thought* (he is angry *about* something—probably the officiating), and (3) *bodily arousal* (the muscular tension in his face and neck indicates that he is not in a relaxed bodily state).

Greg Wood / AFP / Getty Images

If someone were to see your face right now, what emotion would they detect?

figure **10.1**

What is she feeling? Can you match the faces to these emotions: anger, disgust, fear, happiness, sadness, and surprise? Sure you can. Each of these emotions is associated with a distinctive facial expression.

iStockphoto / Getty Images

Not all languages of the world use the word "emotion" in exactly the same way (Wierzbicka, 1999). Yet, for our purposes here, the way you naturally use "emotion" in English suffices to define the term. An **emotion** is a psychological state that combines feelings, thoughts, and bodily arousal and that often has a distinctive accompanying facial expression.

✋ WHAT DO YOU KNOW?

1. Imagine that while you were out walking one day, you witnessed an act of kindness: someone helping an elderly woman cross the road. You momentarily felt different than you had prior to seeing this and thought to yourself, with a smile, "I'm so glad there are helpful people in this world." What question do you need to ask to determine whether you experienced an emotion?

   See Appendix B for answers to What Do You Know? questions.

Mood

Preview Question

> How do moods differ from emotions?

You already know that moods differ from emotions—your everyday use of the words reveals your knowledge. If a relationship broke up and you started crying, you'd say that you "got emotional" not that you "became moody." If you've been feeling grouchy

---

emotion A psychological state that combines feelings, thoughts, and bodily arousal and that often has a distinctive accompanying facial expression.

and depressed all day, you would say you are "in a bad mood." "Emotion" and "mood" refer to different psychological states. Let's look at some differences.

> Moods last longer than emotions. Although emotions vary in duration, some lasting for seconds and others for hours (Verduyn, Van Mechelen, & Tuerlincx, 2011), they tend not to be as long-lasting as moods, which can last for many hours or days.

> Moods are not necessarily accompanied by a specific pattern of thinking (emotion component #2, above). You might be in a "bad mood" or "peppy mood" without knowing why; you can feel "moody" without being moody "at" or "about" something. By comparison, when you are emotional, your emotion is directed toward some person, object, or event (Helm, 2009). You're angry *at* someone, jealous *of* someone, or guilty *about* something.

> Moods are not strongly linked to facial expressions. People's moods may not show on their faces; you could be in a low mood without anyone realizing it when looking at you. Moods, unlike emotions, do not trigger the distinctive facial displays shown in Figure 10.1.

Mood can thus be defined as a prolonged, consistent feeling state, whether that state is positive (a "good mood") or negative (a "bad mood").

> How has your mood been lately?

With these definitions in place, let's now look in detail at the psychology of emotion.

😮 WHAT DO YOU KNOW?

2. Mood or emotion? Specify whether each of the following statements best describes a mood or an emotion.
   a. "Abbie always gets a little depressed during winter, though she can't really tell you why."
   b. "Barney's work colleagues remark that no matter how stressful things are at the office, he remains typically very upbeat."
   c. "Candida visibly blushed when realizing she had addressed a new acquaintance by the wrong name during the whole party."
   d. "Deshawn was overcome with joy at his surprise 21st birthday party, a joy that was clearly visible in his wide smile."

Emotion

The history of research on emotion is somewhat unusual. For much of the early and mid-twentieth century, emotion was essentially ignored. Psychologists focused on learning (Chapter 7) and questioned whether emotion was a scientifically useful concept (Duffy, 1934). The problem with studying emotion, they believed, was that it involved unobservable aspects of mind that could not be measured objectively.

Starting in the late 1950s, psychologists began to develop methods for studying the mind (Gardner, 1985). Yet emotion continued to receive little attention. Most psychologists of this era viewed the mind as an information-processing device, similar to a computer. Because computers do not experience emotions, the information-processing approach provided little insight into emotional experience.

Some psychologists bucked these trends. Silvan Tomkins (1962, 1963) developed a theory of emotion that drew on the evolutionary biology of Charles Darwin. Richard Lazarus analyzed ways in which people can control their emotional reactions (Lazarus & Alfert, 1964). But these were minority voices; emotion—a phenomenon central to human experience—received less attention than it deserved.

---

mood A prolonged, consistent feeling state, either positive or negative.

In the last quarter of the twentieth century, the scene shifted. A set of intriguing research findings drew psychologists' attention to emotion. Investigators found that emotions can directly influence thinking processes. Other researchers identified brain systems that give rise to emotional experience. Research on emotion and culture revealed that some emotions occur in all cultures, whereas others vary across the globe. In total, this diverse set of findings—which you'll learn about in this chapter—attracted the attention of a generation of researchers. Today, the study of emotions flourishes in psychology (Armony & Vuilleumier, 2013; Lewis, Haviland-Jones, & Barrett, 2008).

In fact, the field has become so large that organizing it is a challenge. We will do so by posing four key questions that today's researchers seek to answer. The first is "Why do we have emotions?"

TRY THIS!

Before you start reading the material on why we have emotions, experience for yourself one of the research tasks that researchers use when trying to answer this question. Go to www.pmbpsychology and take part in Chapter 10's Try This! activity. We'll discuss it in the upcoming section of this chapter—so do it now! ◉

Why Do We Have Emotions?

Preview Question

> What are four psychological activities that we can accomplish with the help of emotions?

Could life exist without emotions? You can imagine it. Science-fiction beings who think and act like you, yet who have no emotions, aren't hard to picture. But those beings are fictional; human beings lead emotional lives. Why do we have emotions?

Ever since Darwin, scientists have answered this question by looking to our evolutionary past (Nesse & Ellsworth, 2009). Throughout human evolution, emotions must have been advantageous; they must have promoted survival. Let's consider four psychological activities that have been important throughout human history and that

Emotionless characters like Data are the stuff of science fiction. But how would they have fared in real life, over the course of evolution? Contemporary psychologists suggest that emotions enhanced survival over the course of evolutionary history.

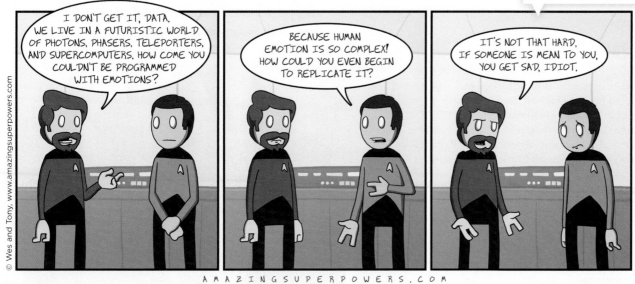

© Wes and Tony, www.amazingsuperpowers.com

AMAZINGSUPERPOWERS.COM

are influenced by emotional states: decision making, motivation, communication, and moral judgment.

CONNECTING TO NATURE AND NURTURE IN THE EVOLUTIONARY PAST AND TO CONTEMPORARY SOCIAL INTERACTION

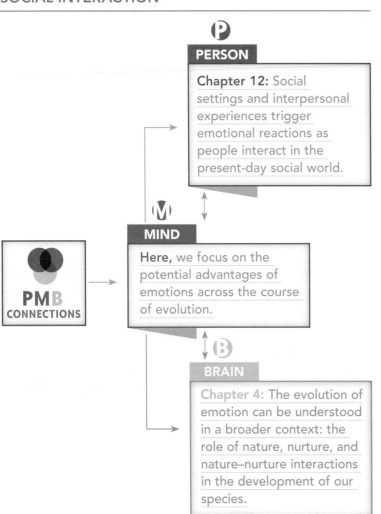

Ⓟ PERSON

Chapter 12: Social settings and interpersonal experiences trigger emotional reactions as people interact in the present-day social world.

Ⓜ MIND

Here, we focus on the potential advantages of emotions across the course of evolution.

PMB CONNECTIONS

Ⓑ BRAIN

Chapter 4: The evolution of emotion can be understood in a broader context: the role of nature, nurture, and nature–nurture interactions in the development of our species.

EMOTION AND DECISION MAKING. Suppose you have to make an important decision. What should be your frame of mind? Many suggest it's best to decide while in a calm, cold, unemotional state. Entire philosophies have been built around this idea. In ancient Greece and Rome, Stoic philosophers promoted a calm, unemotional lifestyle because they thought emotions impair sound judgment (Solomon, 1993).

Contemporary research contradicts the Stoics. People often make *good* decisions when they "go with their gut," that is, when they base decisions on feelings. Research employing the Iowa Gambling Task (Bechara et al., 2005) demonstrates this.

The **Iowa Gambling Task** is a method for studying the influence of emotions on decision making. Participants play a card game. On each of a long series of trials, they (1) pick a card from one of four decks and (2) win or lose money, depending on the card they picked. Cards from two of the decks turn out to yield consistent but modest winnings. Cards from the other two decks yield larger winnings on many trials but, on occasion, produce *very* large losses; in the long run, people lose money by picking cards from these decks. While people decide which card to choose, researchers record their nervous-system arousal, to measure emotional reactivity.

The Iowa Gambling Task yields a remarkable finding: Emotions *benefit* decision making (Bechara et al., 1994). To understand this result, one must distinguish among three types of experimental trials that occur during the task (Table 10.1).

1. *Early trials:* Initial card choices made at the beginning of the experiment
2. *Middle trials:* Card choices made after participants have experienced a limited number of successes and failures on the task
3. *Late trials:* Trials near the conclusion of the experiment, after participants have experienced a large number of trials, with success and failure, on the task

"To be moved by passion is not manly . . . [if] a man's mind is nearer to freedom from all passion . . . also is it nearer to strength" (Marcus Aurelius, *Meditation*, pp. 106–107). That, anyway, was the belief of Marcus Aurelius, ruler of the Roman Empire from 161 to 180 CE, and shown here as portrayed by Richard Harris in the movie *Gladiator*, with Russell Crowe. Marcus Aurelius was a Stoic philosopher who believed that emotions caused people to make poor decisions. Contemporary research suggests otherwise.

Dreamworks / Universal / The Kobal Collection / Buitendijk, Jaap

Iowa Gambling Task A method for studying, via a card game with monetary payoffs, the influence of emotions on decision making.

The research yields the following results. On early trials, participants are just guessing. They have not yet figured out the task; that is, they cannot say which decks are bad and which are good, and they do not have any intuitions about how best to play. During early trials, they are as likely to choose cards from the bad decks (those that produce occasional large losses) as the good ones (those that produce consistent modest winnings).

On late trials, participants *have* figured out the task. They can explain, in words, which decks are good and which are bad. They perform well, choosing cards from the good decks.

None of this is surprising. But here's the key result (Bechara et al., 1997). On middle trials, participants cannot explain in words which decks are bad and which are good; they have not yet played long enough to possess explicit knowledge about which cards to choose. Yet they perform well, choosing cards primarily from the good decks!

How can they have made good decisions without being able to say which decks were good or bad? They relied on their feelings. On the middle trials, whenever participants reached for a card from the bad deck, they tended to experience high levels of physiological arousal; their body's emotion systems sent a signal indicating that these decks were bad (Damasio, 1994). When they felt this signal, they avoided the bad decks and chose the good ones—before they even knew *why* they were choosing one deck over another. Their decisions were guided by intuition—an emotional "hunch"—that some decks were better (Bechara et al., 1997). Subsequent studies have confirmed that, by relying on their emotions, people choose good decision strategies even before they can say what those strategies are (Wagar & Dixon, 2006).

Have there been times when you should have gone with your gut but didn't? Were your emotions perhaps telling you something?

Research on patients with brain damage provides additional evidence of how emotion benefits decision making (Damasio, 1994). The brain damage, which affected the brain's frontal lobes, interfered with patients' emotional life but not their thinking abilities. Cognitively, the patients were normal, with more than enough intelligence to understand the task. But emotionally, they differed from others; when playing the Iowa Gambling task, the brain-damaged patients experienced no emotional arousal at all, even when losing money. To the Stoic philosopher, they would be ideal decision makers. So how did they do on the task? Terribly! On trial after trial, they chose as many cards from the bad deck as the good deck, and lost money (Bechara et al., 1997).

These results suggest one evolutionary advantage for emotions. If people with normal emotional arousal make good decisions, and brain-damaged patients lacking emotional arousal make poor decisions, then emotion benefits decision making (Figure 10.2).

Denis Tangney Jr. / Getty Images

Shortcut through the alley? How would you decide whether to take a shortcut down a dark alley? It is unlikely that you would look up crime statistics on the Internet and calculate the probability of your getting mugged. Instead, emotions would be your guide. When you look down the alley, you immediately experience emotional arousal—a sense of apprehension—that stops you before you head down the alley, and sends you along more well-lit streets.

table **10.1**

Iowa Gambling Task	Early Trials	Middle Trials	Late Trials
Cognition (Can participant explain which decks are good/bad?)	No	No	Yes
Emotion (Participant's physiological arousal when choosing card)	Low	High	High
Decision Making (Does participant choose cards from the good decks?)	No	Yes	Yes

During middle trials of the Iowa Gambling Task, participants' performance is unusual. They cannot explain which card decks are good and bad, yet they make good decisions anyway, choosing cards primarily from the good deck. Their emotional arousal guides their decision making.

PMB IN ACTION

figure 10.2

WHEN FACING DANGER, HOW DO PEOPLE MAKE DECISIONS?

P PERSON

People often base decisions on intuition, or "hunches." You might have a hunch that taking a shortcut down a dark alley is a bad idea.

M MIND

The hunch comes from mental processes in which signals of emotional arousal directly influence decision making.

| Signals of Bodily Arousal | → | Decision Making |

B BRAIN

Biologically, threat signals from the body influence decision-making processes in the brain. Frontal lobe damage (red area) can prevent the processing of these signals, causing people to make overly risky decisions.

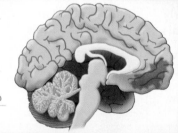

Peeter Viisimaa / Getty Images

Over the course of evolution, emotional experience may have helped organisms survive by fostering quick, intuitive decisions that promoted survival. Much recent research confirms that emotions influence decision making, while also revealing additional brain systems that underpin the relation between feelings and decisions (Wu, Sacchet, & Knutson, 2012). This body of research provides a rich, multilevel understanding of how emotions influence decision making.

EMOTION AND MOTIVATION. Throughout most of human history, survival was a lot of work. People had to hunt and gather food, build shelters, protect themselves from predators, and, once agriculture developed, grow, harvest, and store crops. To do all this, they needed to acquire skills that would enable them to be good hunters and gatherers, builders, and farmers. Where did they get the motivation to learn difficult behaviors and then engage in them, day after day, year after year?

Part of the answer involves thoughts about the future. People understood that if they didn't work today, there might not be enough food tomorrow. But, as you know from experience, sometimes thinking is not enough. People often think about future plans—to get more exercise, to quit smoking, to save more money—yet procrastinate. Thoughts alone are often insufficient to spur people into action. Here is where emotions help.

Emotions have motivational power (Lazarus, 1991). Anger motivates you to strike out at someone. Disgust motivates you to distance yourself from the disgusting stimulus. Even less intense emotions can motivate action. Consider the emotion of interest.

Interest is an emotion you experience when engaged in a task that, to you, is novel, complex, yet comprehensible (Silvia, 2008). If, for example, you are knowledgeable about modern art, an exhibit of new paintings is interesting; you are intrigued by its novelty and can comprehend its complexity. But if you do not follow modern art, the show might be incomprehensible and thus of no interest to you.

> Which of your current classes present material that is novel and complex, yet comprehensible?

Interest increases motivation. People who experience the emotion of interest when working on a task tend to spend more time on it and need less time to learn its complexities (Sansone & Thoman, 2005). This suggests an evolutionary advantage for the emotion of interest. Throughout human evolution, people who felt interest in activities may have been better at learning skills necessary for survival.

Similarly, other emotions may have been beneficial throughout evolution. Fear motivates people to avoid situations that are threatening, and thus may have helped our evolutionary ancestors to survive by avoiding threats. Guilt motivates people to treat others well and to adhere to social rules (Baumeister, Stillwell, & Heatherton, 1994). This behavior, in turn, could benefit group survival.

EMOTION AND COMMUNICATION. A third function served by emotion is communication. Emotions communicate information. When people are emotionally aroused, you can tell from their looks; their emotional expressions convey information about their psychological state.

A key source of emotional information, as noted above, is the face. Facial expressions can reveal the specific emotion a person is experiencing. Look back at Figure 10.1. You immediately can recognize each emotional state. Every facial expression, in other words, communicates information about emotion.

Darwin (1872) noted two key facts about emotional facial expressions. First, the ability to communicate through facial expression can improve an organism's chances of survival. Consider, for example, how facial expressions benefit infants. Although babies cannot communicate through language, they can communicate; their facial expressions indicate whether they are content or in need. Conversely, adults, through their facial expressions, can communicate with infants, who recognize smiling and frowning faces

Mychele Daniau / AFP / Getty Images

Poker face Facial expressions convey information to others. They are also difficult to control. Professional poker players know that the best "poker face" is one that is hidden from view.

> The chief expressive actions, exhibited by man and by the lower animals, are . . . innate. The young and the old of widely different races, both with man and animals, express the same state of mind by the same movements.
>
> —Darwin (1872, p. 191)

by 3 months of age (Barrera & Maurer, 1981). This two-way communication through facial expression enhances infants' well-being and survival. The ability to communicate through facial expression can also enable organisms to avoid physical conflict. If people are so angry that they feel like hitting someone, their facial expression communicates that anger. "Reading" the expression allows for time to defend oneself.

Second, Darwin noted that some human and animal facial expressions are similar. An angry man and an angry dog both lower their eyebrows and bare their teeth (see photos). This implies that the emotions evolved in mammals prior to the evolution of humans and that humans and animals possess essentially the same emotion-generating biology. Emotion, then, is like digestion or respiration: a biological system possessed by all mammals.

Corbis / Superstock

Classic Image / Alamy

Emotion and evolution Charles Darwin recognized that the similarity in these sneers is no coincidence. Some emotional reactions are a product of evolution.

You've just seen that emotions (1) enable communication and (2) are a product of evolution. Combining these facts yields a fascinating implication: People around the world should be able to communicate with one another through facial expression. Why is that? Human biology is universal; people in all parts of the globe share the same basic biological structures and functions (arms, legs, torso, and head; digestion, respiration, etc.). If evolution gave rise to emotions and emotional expressions, then they should be universal, too. People in different cultures should display similar facial expressions when experiencing the same emotion, as well as recognize emotional expressions displayed by people from other cultures.

In classic research, Ekman and Friesen (1971) tested this idea among members of an isolated group: the Fore people of New Guinea. Individuals in this culture had minimal contact with the outside world; they interacted almost exclusively with members of their own culture and had never

Show me what your face would look like if you were about to fight.

Show me what your face would look like if you learned your child had died.

Show me what your face would look like if you met friends.

Paul Ekman, Ph.D / Paul Ekman Group, LLC

figure **10.3**

Do these facial expressions look familiar? Researchers asked these men to "show me what your face would look like" in various circumstances. Although the people asked to pose the faces are from a culture different from yours, you can immediately recognize which face displays anger, which sadness, and which happiness. These facial expressions are essentially the same the world over.

seen a movie or TV show. Thus, they could not have learned, though social experience, how Westerners display emotions on their faces. Ekman and Friesen showed Fore individuals photographs of people of Western culture posing facial expressions of happiness, sadness, anger, surprise, disgust, and fear. Could the Fore recognize these emotions?

If facial expressions are like words—learned in one's own culture and variable across hundreds of languages around the world—then they wouldn't be able to. But it turned out that they could! Despite having no contact with Westerners, the Fore identified accurately—sometimes with perfect accuracy—facial expressions posed in the West (Ekman & Friesen, 1971). Conversely, when Fore individuals were asked to pose facial expressions of emotion, Westerners could recognize them with similar accuracy (Ekman, 1993; Figure 10.3).

Biological research on the anatomy of facial muscles likewise suggests that facial expressions are universal. A specific set of muscles produces facial expressions of emotion. Anatomical studies show that there is little person-to-person variation in these facial muscles (Waller, Cray, & Burrows, 2008). Facial muscles are therefore a universal biological mechanism enabling all people to communicate emotions to one another.

THINK ABOUT IT

Ekman's research suggests that a given facial expression is always associated with a given type of emotion. Is that always true? Or might emotional expressions differ from one situation to another? Consider the man shown in Figure 10.4a. He looks angry and hostile. But is that how he's really feeling? Turn to page 418 (Figure 10.4b) to find out.

Doug Mills / The New York Times / Redux Pictures

figure **10.4a**

Can you tell what he's feeling? Take a guess, then turn to page 418 to see if you're right.

In addition to expressing your feelings, facial expressions can influence the emotion that you feel. Research findings support the **facial feedback hypothesis,** which is the prediction that biological feedback from facial muscles directly influences emotional experience. To test the hypothesis, experimenters ask participants to perform simple tasks that move their facial muscles into positions that correspond to positive or negative emotions. They then measure people's emotional state. When participants are asked, for example, to hold a pencil in their teeth—an action that moves facial muscles into the shape of a smile—their emotional experience becomes more positive. When they are asked to move their eyebrows down and closer to one another—a movement that is part of the facial expression of sadness—their emotions become more negative (McIntosh, 1996).

facial feedback hypothesis The prediction that biological feedback from facial muscles directly influences emotional experience.

Doug Mills / The New York Times / Redux Pictures

figure 10.4b
He doesn't look so angry now Former United States Senator Jim Webb, shown here at a political rally, looks excited and enthused. But taken out of context, his facial features looked angry and hostile (see page 417). The meaning of emotional expressions can vary depending on the social setting in which you see them (Barrett, Lindquist, & Gendron, 2007).

Image Source / Getty Images

Is it the pencil? Research testing the facial feedback hypothesis suggests that this woman's apparently happy state could have been caused by the muscle movements involved in holding the pencil.

Other tests of the facial feedback hypothesis involve Botox, a cosmetic treatment that reduces wrinkles by lowering the activity of facial muscles. Two Botox-based findings support the hypothesis:

1. Botox slows people's understanding of written sentences containing emotional content (Havas et al., 2010). By limiting the facial muscle movement that occurs naturally as we read emotional content, Botox actually reduces the emotional feelings that can help people to rapidly understand emotion in text (Glenberg, 2010).

2. Botox reduces neural activity in regions of the brain that contribute to emotional experience (Hennenlotter et al., 2009). In both cases, the impact of Botox on emotion implies that facial muscles influence emotional experience.

Although biological factors contribute strongly to facial expressions, culture plays a role, too. The exact facial signals that people use to infer others' emotional states vary across cultures. Evidence of this comes from a study using digitized photos in which facial features in areas around the eyes, mouth, and eyebrows were systematically manipulated (Jack, Caldara, & Schyns, 2012). Researchers asked both Western Caucasian and East Asian participants to view the photos and judge the emotion each displayed. Through a statistical analysis, they then identified the facial features to which participants paid greatest attention. These features differed across cultures. Western Caucasians concentrated on the eyebrows and mouth when making judgments about emotion. People in East Asia paid more attention to direction of gaze, that is, where the person in the photo was looking (down, up, left, or right). The exact reason for the cultural difference is not known, but it may reflect differences in the way people express, as opposed to hide, their feelings in different cultures (Jack et al., 2012). Whatever the exact cause, the results argue against the notion that evolved biological factors completely determine the "language" of emotional expression.

Facial expression is not the only way people communicate emotions. Another is *nonverbal vocalizations,* that is, sounds that do not involve words. In the United States, people cheer when celebrating, growl when angry, laugh when amused, and scream when afraid. Do people in other cultures make these same sounds while expressing these emotions? To find out, researchers (Sauter et al., 2010) obtained recordings of these various sounds (people cheering, growling, etc.) among members of two cultures: one European and one African—specifically, an isolated subculture in the southern African nation of Namibia. In this Namibian culture, individuals receive no formal education and have no contact with members of Western culture, which makes them a particularly interesting point of comparison.

The researchers read stories with a variety of emotional content to people in both cultures, played for them sounds of emotion recorded in the *other* culture (i.e., Namibians heard the sounds made by Europeans and vice versa), and asked participants to match sounds to emotions. The responses of participants from both cultures were highly accurate (Sauter et al., 2010). For example, despite having no contact with Westerners, Namibians could recognize what Europeans sound like when angry, sad, and fearful. The results suggest that emotional vocalizations, just like emotional facial expressions, are substantially based in evolved biology. They are not learned "from scratch," but instead reflect an inherited system for communicating emotional states to others.

> What emotional vocalizations do you use most frequently?

⚕RESEARCH TOOLKIT

Facial Action Coding System (FACS)

To study emotions, you have to measure them. Researchers need a measurement tool to identify the emotion a person is feeling and how long it lasts. What tool will do the job?

One possible method is self-report: Just ask people if they are experiencing an emotion and, if so, which one. Self-report isn't good enough, though, for a number of reasons. For instance, people might not want to talk openly about their emotions; they may be more motivated to create a good impression of themselves than an honest one (Paulhus & Reid, 1991). Furthermore, people might not be able to report their emotions accurately; for example, emotional states might shift so rapidly from one emotion to another that people can't precisely identify the range of emotions they're experiencing. Finally, asking people to self-report might inadvertently *change* their emotional states by, for example, calling attention to their emotional experience (Gasper & Clore, 2000). This is undesired because the goal is to measure naturally occurring emotions, not to alter them. Imagine someone is feeling wistful while daydreaming about the past, and you run up and say, "Hey, could you fill out a questionnaire that measures your emotions?" The person won't be feeling wistful anymore. Your request will disrupt her flow of thoughts and alter her emotional experience. Psychology needs a better tool.

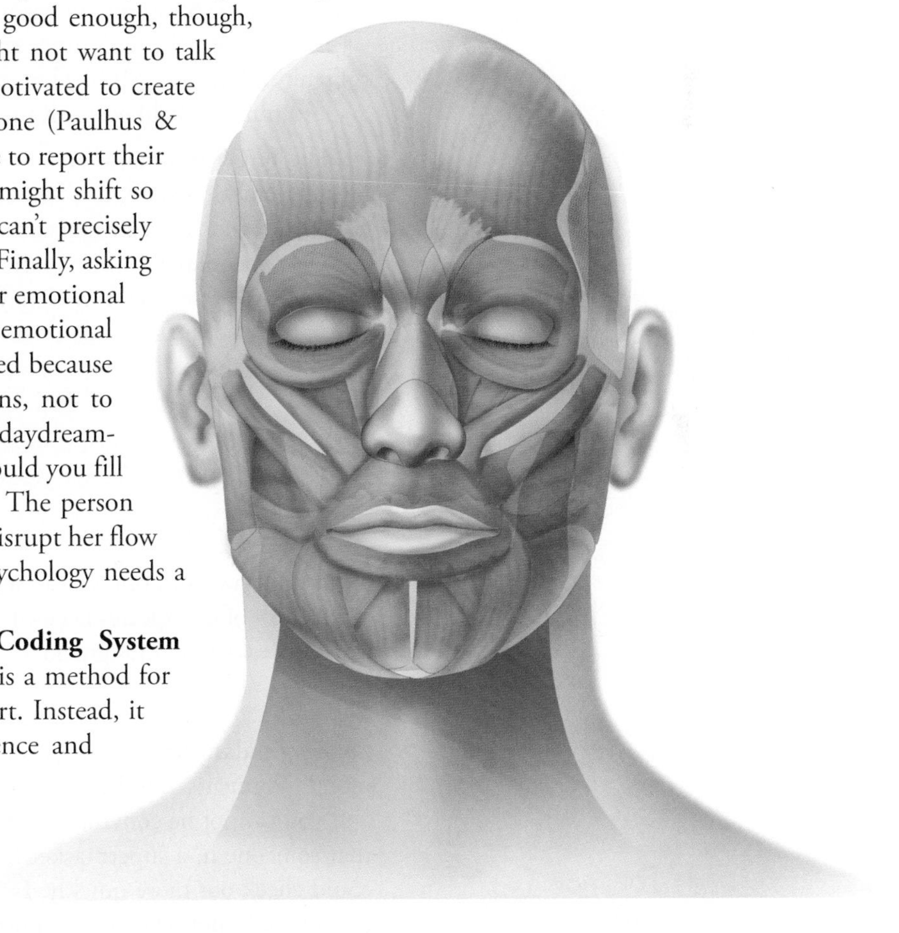

Fortunately, it has one: the **Facial Action Coding System** (**FACS**; Cohn, Ambadar, & Ekman, 2007). FACS is a method for measuring emotions that does not rely on self-report. Instead, it capitalizes on the link between emotional experience and facial expression.

As you learned from the main text of this chapter, different emotions are associated with different facial expressions. When a person starts to experience an emotion, there is a facial "action": movement of one or more parts of the person's face. By classifying, or coding, these actions, FACS provides a systematic method for measuring expressions of emotion.

The FACS method is based on an analysis of facial anatomy. Facial expressions employ a specific set of muscles (Figure 10.5), and the FACS coding scheme classifies their movements. Specifically, FACS provides coding for 9 movements in the upper face (e.g., movements of eyebrows), 18 in the lower face (e.g., various mouth

figure **10.5**
Psychology's FACS is a coding method based on biological knowledge, specifically, information about the exact facial muscles that are active when people express emotions.

Facial Action Coding System (FACS) A method for measuring emotions that capitalizes on the link between emotional experience and facial expression; in this system, researchers code muscular movements occurring in specific parts of the face.

movements), and a set of additional movements of the head as a whole (e.g., tilting the head). To code these movements accurately, researchers film people's faces using high-speed cameras that capture large numbers of frames per second, and then they view the films in slow motion (Polikovsky, Kameda, & Ohta, 2010). This process enables them to detect not only full-blown facial expressions, but also "micro-expressions" (Ekman, 2003), that is, slight, briefly occurring movements of facial musculature (e.g., a tightening of the lips or a movement of eyebrows), as discussed in the chapter's opening.

FACS has opened the door to a number of discoveries about emotions and facial expressions. Here are some examples:

> *Embarrassment:* There is a distinctive facial expression associated with feeling embarrassed (Keltner, 1995). Facial signs of embarrassment include a tight-lipped smile, eyes directed downward, and head turned slightly away from another person.

> *Genuine versus social smiles:* Genuine smiles differ from fake, "social" smiles (Ekman, 1993). Both involve movement of facial muscles to form a smile. But during genuine smiles, unlike fake ones, people move muscles that produce wrinkles ("crow's feet") in skin near the corners of the eyes.

> *Micro-expressions:* Skilled law enforcement officials are able to catch liars by detecting "micro-expressions" of emotion, that is, extremely brief emotional expressions that can reveal the liar's inner emotional state (Ekman, O'Sullivan, & Frank, 1999; Frank & Ekman, 1997). They are especially able to do so with the benefit of high-speed filming (Polikovsky, Kameda, & Ohta, 2010).

The FACS is a major advance in the measurement of emotion. Yet, as a measure of inner emotion state, it is imperfect. Factors other than inner feelings can influence facial expressions; for instance, the link between positive feelings and smiling is stronger when people are around others than when they are alone (Mauss & Robinson, 2009). FACS assessment thus may benefit from considering not only people's emotion states, but also the social contexts in which they experience and express them.

✿ WHAT DO YOU KNOW?...

3. In measuring an emotion—say, happiness—describe one problem you avoid when using the FACS instead of a self-report measure of emotion.

In sum, a wealth of research suggests that a third function served by emotion across the history of our species is communication of feelings and intentions. A fourth function concerns moral judgment.

EMOTION AND MORAL JUDGMENT. **Moral judgments** are decisions that involve fundamental questions of right and wrong. Compared with other judgments, moral judgments are ones in which you are certain that your belief is absolutely right and you cannot be convinced otherwise (Skitka, 2010). Suppose you hear in the news that someone in a supermarket line knocked a few other shoppers unconscious so he could check out more quickly. Is that OK? Of course not; it's immoral, you're sure of it, and could not be convinced otherwise.

How do people make moral judgments? Sometimes they rely on thinking—reasoning about social situations and the correctness of actions (Aquino et al., 2009; Kohlberg, 1969). Other times, though, they rely on emotions. Even when people can't think of any specific reason why a behavior is or is not morally accepted, they still are certain of their moral judgments. Emotions fuel intuitions about what is right and wrong (Haidt, 2001).

moral judgments Decisions that involve fundamental questions of right and wrong.

Research by Jonathon Haidt (2001) shows how emotion contributes to moral judgment. Participants read about hypothetical behaviors that (1) cause no harm to anyone, yet (2) feel morally wrong (e.g., eating a dead pet dog, or a brother and sister having sex). Participants were certain these behaviors are wrong. Yet they couldn't say why. Haidt found that, when trying to explain their judgments in such situations, people are "morally dumbfounded. . . . [They] stutter, laugh, and express surprise at their inability to find supporting reasons" (Haidt, 2001, p. 817). These moral judgments are explained by emotional reactions; people experience the emotion of disgust when thinking about such behaviors and thus judge them to be immoral.

> What is a behavior you think is morally wrong, even if you can't come up with any specific legal reason why it is wrong?

The experience of moral dumbfounding should be familiar to you; it is the experience you likely had when completing this chapter's Try This! activity. The second Try This! research task you worked on was used in the brain research on emotion and moral judgment that we will review now.

TRY THIS!

Brain research confirms that emotions contribute to moral judgment. In one study, brain images were taken as participants made judgments about different behaviors, some of which violated moral rules (Greene et al., 2001). When people were making moral judgments, regions of the brain involved in emotional experience were particularly active.

Trolley Dilemma People sometimes make moral judgments without knowing why they made them. An example is judgments made about the Trolley Dilemma, shown here. Imagine that a trolley car is headed toward six people. In the top version of the dilemma, you can flip a switch and divert the car so that it hits and kills only one person instead of six. Would you do this? In the bottom version, you can pick up one person and throw him in front of the car, so that it hits and kills only one person instead of six. Would you do that? Most people say yes to the first question but no to the second, even though both entail the same number of lives saved and lost. The action of physically moving a person against his or her will generates emotional reactions that are not produced by the action of flicking a switch, and these emotions contribute to the different moral judgments made in the two situations.

Again, the findings suggest that emotion was beneficial evolutionarily. Consider the case of sexual relations among siblings. During human evolution, such relations would have been very bad for survival; inbreeding increases the chances of birth defects, among other survival risks. The emotional reaction of disgust prevents the behavior and thus enhances survival of the species (Hauser, 2006).

So far in this chapter, we've discussed universals. All people, in all cultures, experience emotions that influence their decision making, motivation, communication, and moral judgment. But universals are not the whole story of emotion. When it comes to emotional life, people can differ.

🔥 WHAT DO YOU KNOW?...

4. Match each emotional experience on the left with the fact about emotion it illustrates on the right.

   1. Kelsie was so anxious about doing well on her upcoming exam that she studied every day for a week.

   2. Aaron followed his intuition to pick "a" instead of the equally good option "c" on the multiple-choice exam.

   3. When asked if it would be okay to serve the remains of a cat that had just died to the family who loved it, Bridget couldn't explain why she was repulsed.

   4. Abel could tell by the look on his mother's face that it was time to stop asking questions and start helping her prepare dinner.

   a. Emotions can aid in our decision making.

   b. Emotions have motivational power.

   c. Emotions communicate information.

   d. Emotions support moral judgments.

Why Do People Have Different Emotional Reactions to the Same Event?

Preview Questions

> How does our thinking affect our emotions?
> What kinds of thoughts influence emotional experience?

People confronting the same event can experience markedly different emotions. For instance, if two students get a D on a chemistry exam, one might be sad but the other anxious. If you tell a joke about lawyers to two people, one might be amused but the other angry. Why do people's emotions differ?

THE PERSONAL MEANING OF EVENTS. Environmental events, by themselves, do not produce emotions. Emotions result from the *meaning* that people give to events. The personal significance of an event—what the event means to an individual—is the immediate cause of his or her emotion. If a low exam score means "My parents will kill me," a student will feel anxious. If it means "I can't reach my professional dreams," she will feel sad (Higgins, 1987). If someone listening to your lawyer joke is thinking, "Hey, my mom's a lawyer; that's an insult!" then he will feel angry.

Individual differences in emotional experience therefore reflect the power of thinking. Thoughts shape emotional experience. When people's thoughts vary, emotional experiences vary, too (Lazarus, 1991; Scherer, Schorr, & Johnstone, 2001).

Thoughts so powerfully shape emotions that people can have a wide range of emotional reactions while merely sitting around by themselves. Even if nothing changes in the outer environment, changes within the mind can alter our emotional state (Nowak & Vallacher, 1998). Novelists capture this circumstance vividly. Consider the emotional life of a character created by Russian writer Leo Tolstoy. He begins in happy reverie, dreaming of the joys of married life as he sits in a hotel room just prior to his wedding. But then, look what happens:

> Happiness is only in loving and wishing her wishes, thinking her thoughts . . . that's happiness.
>
> "But do I know her ideas, her wishes, her feelings?" some voice suddenly whispered to him. The smile died away from his face, and he grew thoughtful. And suddenly a strange feeling came upon him. There came over him a dread and doubt—doubt of everything. "What if she does not love me? What if she's marrying me simply to be married?" . . . And strange, most evil thoughts of her began to come to him. He was jealous of [another man] . . . He suspected she had not told him everything.
>
> He jumped up quickly . . . with despair in his heart and bitter anger against all men, against himself, against her.
>
> —Tolstoy (*Anna Karenina*, 1886, p. 451)

His shifting thoughts about a highly meaningful event—his upcoming marriage—jolt him from one emotion to another and another, all in a matter of seconds.

APPRAISING EVENTS. The examples above have something in common. The thoughts that produce emotions are ideas about the relation between an event (the grade, the joke, a fiancée's feelings) and the self. "My parents will kill *me*"; "*My* mom's a lawyer"; "What if she does not love *me*?"

People react emotionally to events that they see as relevant to their own well-being (Lazarus, 1991). If someone says, "That's a great outfit you're wearing," you feel happy because the comment reflects on you (your appearance and your good taste in clothes). If someone watching TV says, "That's a great outfit Angelina Jolie is wearing," the statement has little emotional impact because it is not significant to your own self-concept (unless you are a huge Angelina Jolie fan). You experience emotions when you judge that an event is significant to your desires, goals, well-being, obligations, and individual rights.

Psychologists call these judgments *appraisals*. **Appraisals** are evaluations of the personal significance of ongoing and upcoming events (Ellsworth & Scherer, 2003; Lazarus, 1991; Moors, 2007).

It depends on how you appraise the situation If a coach singles you out, even angrily, there is a huge range of possibilities for how you might feel, ranging from, "He hates me and I'll never get any better at this" to "I'm the best player, so the coach is pointing to me."

APPRAISAL THEORIES OF EMOTION. According to **appraisal theories of emotion,** people continuously monitor the relation between themselves and the world around them. They pay attention to, and try to determine the meaning of, daily events from the large (a long, serious discussion) to the small (a quick, ambiguous glance). Appraisal theories of emotion explain that this process of making sense of events—appraising them—determines the emotion people experience.

The psychologist Richard Lazarus identified a small number of appraisals that can generate a wide variety of emotional experiences (Lazarus, 1991; Smith & Lazarus, 1990). In his appraisal theory of emotion, key appraisals include the following:

> *Motivational significance:* Is the event relevant to my concerns and goals?
> *Motivational congruence:* Does it facilitate my goals or hinder them?
> *Accountability:* Who is to blame (or who deserves credit) for an event?
> *Future expectancy:* Can things change (e.g., for the better)?

appraisals Evaluations of the personal significance of ongoing and upcoming events.

appraisal theories of emotion Theories claiming that emotions arise from a psychological process in which people continuously monitor the relation between themselves and the world around them, with these appraisals determining the emotion they experience.

figure **10.6**

Appraisals and emotion Suppose you heard someone say that he didn't think your relationship was working out. What emotions would you experience? It depends on what you're thinking. Cognitive appraisal theories of emotion explain that appraisals—thoughts about the incoming information—shape subsequent emotional experiences. As shown here, different types of appraisals tend to produce different types of emotions.

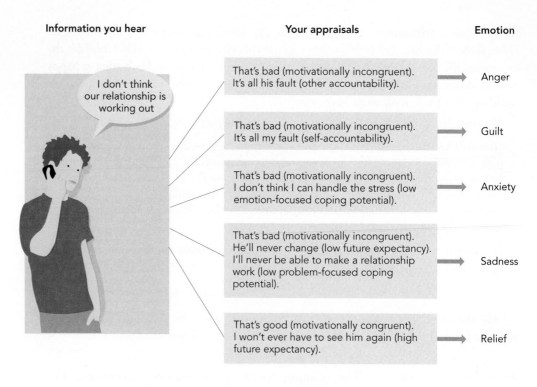

> There is nothing either good or bad, but thinking makes it so.
>
> —William Shakespeare, *Hamlet*, Act II, scene ii

> *Problem-focused coping potential:* Can I myself bring about change that solves a problem?

> *Emotion-focused coping potential:* Can I adjust, psychologically, to the event?

A simple example shows how these appraisals shape your emotions. Suppose your relationship partner tells you it's "not working out" (Figure 10.6). You could experience any of a number of different emotions when hearing the news. The exact emotion you experience will be determined by your appraisals—the thoughts that quickly run through your head at the time. If you think, "It's his fault that this didn't work," you'll tend to feel angry. If you think, "I'm incapable of ever being in a relationship that works out," you'll tend to feel sad or depressed. Research shows that individual differences in the appraisals people make predict the emotions they experience (Kuppens, Van Mechelen, & Rijmen, 2008).

Thus, there is a lot of thinking behind emotions. Without thoughts like "I'm to blame" or "Things might improve," you wouldn't experience emotions such as guilt or hope.

Despite all this thinking, emotions happen quickly (Barrett, Ochsner, & Gross, 2007). You can experience complex emotional reactions "in the blink of an eye" because your thinking is fast, too; people appraise events automatically, in a fraction of a second (Moors & De Houwer, 2001). If a boyfriend calls to say a relationship isn't working, multiple thoughts—"He's a jerk," "I'm a loser," "I'll never have to see him again"—rapidly come to mind.

🧠 WHAT DO YOU KNOW?...

5. Think of a time when you failed an exam or performed really poorly on an assignment. Describe the appraisals that shaped your emotional response. Consider the motivational significance, motivational congruence, accountability, and future expectancy of those appraisals. What problem-focused coping strategy could you engage in to overcome the failure?

◎ CULTURAL OPPORTUNITIES

Culturally Specific Emotion

Do people the world over experience the same emotions? Or might people in one culture experience emotions that don't even exist in another?

Appraisal theories of emotion suggest one answer. As you learned from the main text, appraisal theories explain that the emotions you experience are determined by the meaning you attach to events. Your appraisals—your interpretations of others' intentions and actions, and your beliefs about your capabilities, individual rights, and social obligations—shape your emotional experiences.

Research in cultural psychology reveals that different cultures teach people different lessons about individual rights and obligations (Markus & Kitayama, 1991). Therefore, people from different cultures may differ in the appraisals they make and the emotions they experience (Figure 10.7). Appraisal theories of emotion, then, suggest that emotional experience may vary across cultures. People might experience emotions that are unique to their cultural setting.

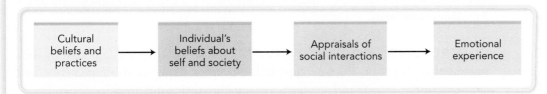

figure 10.7
Culture, appraisal, and emotion

Let's consider an example from the Hindu culture of northern India (Shweder, 2003; also see Parish, 1991). This culture is "collectivistic" (see Chapter 12). Compared to the culture of the United States, which emphasizes people's individual rights (and thus is "individualistic"), Hindu culture emphasizes the collective: the family, community, and society as a whole. Individuals who grow up in this culture repeatedly learn about their social obligations. They are taught lessons about how they should act in order to fulfill their duties to society.

Within this particular collectivistic culture, the social obligations of men and women differ. Cultural norms dictate that women should act in a modest, deferential manner. They are expected to be quiet, not to make a show of themselves, and to respect the wishes of others (Shweder, 2003). Thus, individual women who grow up in this Hindu culture believe that it is their personal obligation to uphold this cultural norm.

How does this affect emotions? These culturally grounded beliefs produce an emotion that is relatively unknown in the United States: *lajja*. Lajja is an emotion that people feel when they are "behaving in a civilized manner and in such a way that the social order and its norms are upheld" (Shweder, 2003, p. 160). Women feel lajja when they are acting in a shy, respectful manner toward others. In other words, rather than feeling bad because they seem shy and are not "standing out from the crowd," they feel good that their actions are consistent with their obligations to others.

Researchers who study this culture argue that lajja does not correspond directly to any emotion experienced in Western culture (Shweder, 2003). Lajja does not, for example, correspond to "pride." People feel proud when their personal achievements are outstanding and superior to others. But lajja does not involve any sense of superiority; just the opposite, it is a sense of "fitting in" to a social organization in which others are superior.

If you, the reader, are not from India, you may be thinking that you can't tell—you can't intuitively *feel*—exactly what lajja is like. If so, that's exactly the point! Because you don't possess the beliefs and experiences of a citizen of northern India, you don't have exactly the same emotional experiences.

Lajja This novel, by the Indian author Taslima Nasrin, uses as its title the name of an emotional state that is common in India, but relatively unknown in the United States.

Jean-Loup Gautreau / AFP / Getty Images

❤ WHAT DO YOU KNOW?...

6. The following statements are incorrect. Explain why.
   a. "Lajja is a universally shared emotion that women experience when they feel that their behavior is consistent with their societal obligations."
   b. "Appraisal theories of emotion are not particularly well suited to explaining cultural differences in emotional experience."

Can You Control or Predict Your Emotions?

Preview Questions

> What can we do to control our emotions? What shouldn't we do?
> How well can we predict the degree of our happiness if we win a lot of money?

Emotions sometimes seem unmanageable. Tragedies cause grief that can seem overwhelming. Insults can create anger that seems out of control. Can people control these emotional reactions?

CONTROLLING EMOTION BY CHANGING APPRAISALS. Appraisal theories suggest that they can. Because appraisals—people's thoughts about events—shape emotion, people can control emotions by changing their thinking.

> What upcoming event do you have planned? What are your anticipatory appraisals about it?

One way to change your thinking is to alter *anticipatory appraisals,* which are thoughts that people have prior to the occurrence of an event. If, before a trip to the dentist, you tell yourself, "This visit is going to be terrible!" then your thought is an anticipatory appraisal.

In one experiment on anticipatory appraisals, researchers (Lazarus & Alfert, 1964) manipulated appraisals prior to a film depicting a potentially emotionally arousing event: a ritual surgical procedure conducted on boys in a non-Western, nonindustrialized culture. In one condition, participants were told that the film depicted a positive, joyful cultural experience. In another condition, participants viewed the film with no prior appraisal-related instructions. Physiological measures of emotional arousal taken during the film showed that participants who watched the film with no prior instructions became highly emotionally aroused; for them, the film was disturbing. Participants who first heard the appraisal information were much less emotionally aroused despite seeing exactly the same film (Lazarus & Alfert, 1964; Figure 10.8).

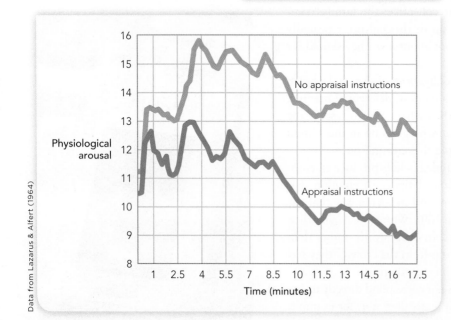

Data from Lazarus & Alfert (1964)

figure 10.8
Anticipatory appraisals When people watched a filmed surgical procedure without prior instructions (No Appraisal condition), they became emotionally aroused when the filmed operation started and remained aroused during the course of the film. But when, in a different experimental condition, people watched the same film after first receiving instructions that altered the way they thought about the depicted events (Appraisal Instructions), the participants were relatively calm, as indicated by their lower level of physiological arousal.

Through anticipatory appraisals, people also can gain control over impulsive emotions, specifically, impulsive desires to engage in a behavior that they are supposed to avoid. In research on *delay of gratification* (Chapter 13), children are asked not to eat a food treat that's set before them, such as a marshmallow. Most kids can't avoid it; they eat the treat even when instructed not to. However, children who are taught anticipatory appraisals—for example, to think of the marshmallow as a ball they can play with rather than a food—are able to refrain from eating it (Mischel, 1974). The anticipatory appraisals directly reduce children's level of impulsive emotional arousal (Metcalfe & Mischel, 1999).

SUPPRESSING SIGNS OF EMOTION. Sometimes it's too late for anticipatory appraisals. You're already emotional: angry, sad, fearful, disgusted. What can you do if you want to hide these emotions from others—to remain "cool as a cucumber" or to "keep a stiff upper lip"?

If you're already emotionally aroused and don't want it to show, you need to *suppress* your emotion. Emotion **suppression** is any conscious, intentional effort to prevent yourself from showing any visible sign of emotional arousal (Gross, 1998). If you are upset but try not to mention your feelings to others or let them show on your face, then you are engaged in emotion suppression.

A primary question about emotion suppression is its effects: Does suppressing an emotion reduce a person's emotional arousal? Or, does trying to appear calm "backfire," intensifying the emotional state instead? To find out, a researcher gave different instructions to three groups of participants prior to their viewing an emotionally stressful film (it depicted the medical amputation of a limb). In one condition, participants received anticipatory appraisal instructions similar to those in research discussed above; they were asked to appraise the film in a scientific manner, remaining emotionally detached while focusing on technical details of the surgery. In a second condition, participants received thought-suppression instructions; they were told that if they felt emotionally upset during the film, they should "try not to let those feelings show. . . . Try to behave in such a way that a person watching you would not know you were feeling anything" (Gross, 1998, pp. 227–228). Finally, a control group was provided neither instruction. The dependent variables included physiological measures of emotional arousal (heart rate, autonomic nervous system activity) during the film.

The two strategies for controlling emotion—anticipatory appraisal and suppression—had different effects. Anticipatory appraisal worked. People who focused on the film's technical details were less aroused than others. Thought suppression backfired, at least when it came to physiological arousal. People who tried to suppress outer signs of emotion were *more* aroused than participants in the other two groups (Gross, 1998). Subsequent studies confirm these results; efforts at suppressing emotion often increase, rather than decrease, emotional arousal (Roberts, Levenson, & Gross, 2008).

Other research links emotion suppression to a behavior many of us try to avoid: overeating (Butler, Young, & Randall, 2010). Every day for a week, people in heterosexual relationships indicated whether they (1) kept their emotions to themselves, rather than revealing them to their partner, and (2) ate more, less, or the same amount as usual that day. Among women who were overweight, but not among those who were underweight, thought suppression predicted overeating; on days when they suppressed their emotions, overweight women ate more than usual. Suppressing signs of emotion may have increased women's negative emotional experience and prompted them to eat more as a way of coping with their negative feelings.

Mary Evans / Ronald Grant / Everett Collection (10326560)

The power of anticipatory appraisals In real life, amputations are horrifying. But in comedies, people may react to them with laughter. How can that be? The context—the comedic film in which the amputation occurs—influences *anticipatory appraisals*, the thoughts people have just prior to an event. Appraisals, in turn, shape emotional reactions. In this image from *Monty Python and the Holy Grail*, King Arthur becomes annoyed with the Black Knight, who tries to continue the battle even after being disarmed.

Have your efforts to suppress an emotion ever had these kinds of ironic effects?

suppression Any conscious, intentional effort to prevent oneself from showing any visible sign of emotional arousal (or other such psychological states).

PREDICTING YOUR EMOTIONS. Controlling emotions, as you've just seen, is difficult. Once an emotion starts up, efforts to suppress it can backfire. Let's now consider something that seems like it should be easier: not controlling, but merely *predicting* your own emotional state.

How do you predict you would feel if you lost weight, started a new relationship, or won a lot of money? Or if you gained weight, experienced a breakup, or lost a lot of money? People usually predict that such events will have a big impact on their emotional life—but their predictions commonly are wrong. When predicting emotions, people make a systematic error: They overestimate the impact of life events on emotions. Good and bad events usually have less effect than people expect. In general, people often are poor at affective forecasting, that is, predicting the degree, and duration, of their emotional (or "affective") reactions to events (Wilson & Gilbert, 2003).

Enjoy the win while you can
Research shows that the impact of positive events on emotions does not last as long as people expect.

In one study (Wilson et al., 2000; Study 3), psychologists asked college football fans how happy they would be in the days following a big game if their team won. For each of a few days following the game (which the team did, in fact, win), these same participants completed a survey indicating how happy they actually were feeling. Fans overestimated the emotional impact of the win. The good news of the team's victory had less strong and less long-lasting effects on emotion than fans had predicted.

Overestimation is common. When predicting the effects of events—electoral outcomes, results of medical tests, interactions with friends and romantic partners, increases in personal wealth—on their emotions, people commonly overestimate (Kahneman et al., 2006; Wilson & Gilbert, 2003). They anticipate that bad events will be emotionally worse and good events more emotionally uplifting than they actually turn out to be (Figure 10.9).

These findings seem disheartening, implying that you can't do much to change your emotions. You might predict that you'll be happier if you break up with your current dating partner, transfer to a new school, or get a higher-paying job. But your prediction could be wrong. Some psychologists have suggested that people's sense of well-being—their overall happiness or unhappiness with their life—can't be changed. Your level of happiness, they suggest, is a stable personality trait; if something good happens in your life, you might feel better for a day or two, but then you quickly return to your typical emotional level (Lykken & Tellegen, 1996). Recent results, however, have shed new light on the question of life events and happiness (see This Just In).

figure **10.9**
Predicted and experienced emotional intensity People often expect that life events—good or bad—will have a big, long-lasting effect on their emotional life. They often are wrong. The emotional impact of events is frequently smaller and briefer than expected.

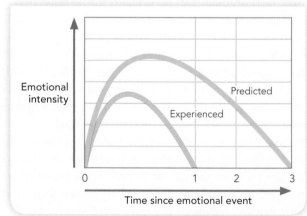

◑ THIS JUST IN

Making Yourself Happier

Can you make yourself happier? Many psychologists had thought the answer was no. They reached this conclusion primarily due to results from studies of twins.

Identical twins' reports of how happy they are with their lives are often quite similar; if one twin is happy (or unhappy), the other tends to be happy (or unhappy), too. Identical twins are more similar in their level of happiness than are nonidentical siblings, including fraternal twins—which means that genes contribute to individual differences in happiness (Lykken & Tellegen, 1996). But to what extent? Some psychologists have believed that the contribution of genes is so big that people cannot do anything to change their typical level of happiness: "Trying to be happier is as futile as trying to be taller" (Lykken & Tellegen, 1996, p. 189).

But eventually more data arrived, and conclusions changed. A remarkably large-scale study has shown that levels of happiness can, in fact, change, despite the influence of genetics (Headey, Muffels, & Wagner, 2010). Researchers in Germany studied more than 60,000 people, ranging from young adults in their 20s to older adults in their 60s. They studied them annually across a substantial time period, 1984 to 2008. The key measure was happiness, or overall satisfaction, with one's life, measured on an 11-point self-report scale (ranging from "totally dissatisfied" to "totally satisfied").

This exceptionally large set of data produced two keys facts contradicting the view that happiness is determined entirely by genetics:

> *Change across time:* Many people's level of happiness with their lives changed substantially during the course of the study. Between 1989 and 2004, a large number of people (38.1% of the overall sample) had experienced substantial changes in their level of life satisfaction (Figure 10.10). The idea that genetic factors produce a stable, life-long level of happiness was blatantly contradicted.

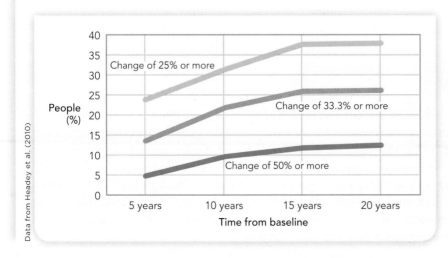

figure **10.10**

Change in life satisfaction To find out if people's satisfaction with life is stable or changes over time, researchers measured life satisfaction over a 20-year period starting in the mid-1980s and at 5-year intervals (Headey, Muffels, & Wagner 2010). At each time point, they determined each person's life satisfaction percentile, that is, his or her standing compared to others (the average person is at the 50th percentile). The graph shows the percentage of people whose percentile scores changed by 25%, 33.3%, and 50% over time. As you can see, there was a lot of change!

Volunteering helps everyone Engaging in altruistic volunteer activities not only helps others, it also increases the happiness of the volunteers. The volunteer, and the soon-to-be new homeowners (in green shirts), are participating in a homebuilding event in Oregon organized by Habitat for Humanity and the NBA's Portland Trailblazers.

Sam Forencich / NBAE via Getty Images

> *Social factors promote happiness:* A variety of life changes were found to promote happiness (Headey et al., 2010). One was the setting of goals for altruistic behavior, that is, activities that help others rather than merely benefiting oneself. People who committed themselves to altruistic life goals were found to experience higher levels of happiness with their lives; people whose primary goal was to acquire more material goods, by contrast, became *less* happy. A second life change affecting happiness was exercise. People who exercised frequently reported higher satisfaction with life.

So, there's some good news for those of you looking to make your life even happier.

🌀 WHAT DO YOU KNOW?●●●

8. Which of the following statements are true about happiness? Check all that apply.

___a. Genes contribute, in part, to individual differences in happiness.

___b. In a study conducted between 1989 and 2004, researchers found that none of the participants experienced change in their happiness levels.

___c. Setting altruistic life goals is associated with greater happiness.

___d. Focusing on the acquisition of material goods is associated with greater happiness.

___e. Exercise is associated with greater happiness.

Mood

How are you feeling right now? Decide which of the following words describes your current feelings. Are you feeling:

Relaxed?	Calm?
Gloomy?	Jittery?
Sleepy?	Depressed?
Excited?	Peppy?
Tense?	Contented?
Energetic?	Sluggish?

These words describe different aspects of mood (Russell, 2003; Thayer, 1996). *Mood* is your feeling state; the term refers to the feelings—of sluggishness, peppiness, contentment, depression, and so on—that are an ever-present part of your conscious experience. To be "in" a certain mood is to experience a consistent type of feeling for a prolonged period.

Sometimes you barely notice your mood; it's in the "background" of your mental life, unnoticed until someone asks, "How are you feeling?" Sometimes, though, your mood dominates your consciousness. If you're in a depressed mood, it can be hard to stop ruminating about how bad you're feeling.

The Structure of Mood

Preview Question

> What does it mean to say that we can describe any mood with two simple structures: valence and arousal?

Look back for a moment at the list of mood-related words above. If you think about them, you'll notice two things:

> *Similarities:* Some of the mood states described by the words are similar. "Tense" and "excited" are an example; the feeling of your body when you're tense and when you're excited is similar. Likewise, "gloomy" and "sluggish" are similar; if you're feeling gloomy, it's likely that you're also feeling sluggish.

> *Opposites:* Some of the mood states seem like opposites of the other. "Relaxed" and "tense" are an example. As you feel more tense, you simultaneously feel less relaxed; thus, they're opposites. The same is true for "peppy" and "sluggish."

Low and high arousal One major dimension of variation in mood is arousal, as illustrated by the low (left) and high (right) states of arousal of former U.S. Secretary of State Hillary Clinton.

MOOD DIMENSIONS. The similarities and opposites have an important implication. They suggest that the 12 mood terms in the list above may not refer to a dozen distinct, unrelated psychological states. Rather, there may be some underlying *dimensions of mood*. **Dimensions of mood (or mood dimensions)** are universal variations in feeling states, that is, variations that can describe the mood of any and all people.

An analogy will make the idea of mood dimensions clear. Instead of psychological mood, consider six terms we can use to describe the physical body: "skinny," "chubby," "thin," "plump," "emaciated," and "rotund." Although these six terms are separate words, they clearly do not refer to six separate, distinct physical qualities. Rather, they refer to *variations* in one underlying dimension: weight.

Similarly, although a large number of words can refer to mood, there may be a small number of basic mood dimensions. Mood terms that are opposites—relaxed/tense; peppy/sluggish—exist at different ends of the mood dimensions, just as "skinny" and "chubby" are at different ends of a bodily dimension of weight.

In the psychology of mood, the complete set of dimensions required to describe variations in mood experiences is called the *structure of mood.*

IDENTIFYING THE STRUCTURE OF MOOD. To identify the structure of mood, researchers rely on statistical tools. They statistically analyze survey responses in which people describe their moods on simple ratings scales. Research findings converge on a simple conclusion: There are two dimensions of mood (Russell, 2003; Watson & Tellegen, 1985). Although not all psychologists agree on the best labels for these dimensions, a popular approach identifies the dimensions *arousal* and *valence.*

> *Arousal* refers to the level of activation of the body and brain during the mood state. It ranges from low ("calm," "sluggish") to high ("peppy," "tense").

> *Valence* refers to the positivity or negativity of the mood, that is, the degree to which it is a "good" (e.g., contented) or "bad" (e.g., depressed) mood.

Psychologists combine these two dimensions to obtain a structure that can describe the spectrum of moods people experience (Figure 10.11). The structure functions like

mood dimensions Universal variations in feeling states; variations that can describe the mood of any and all people.

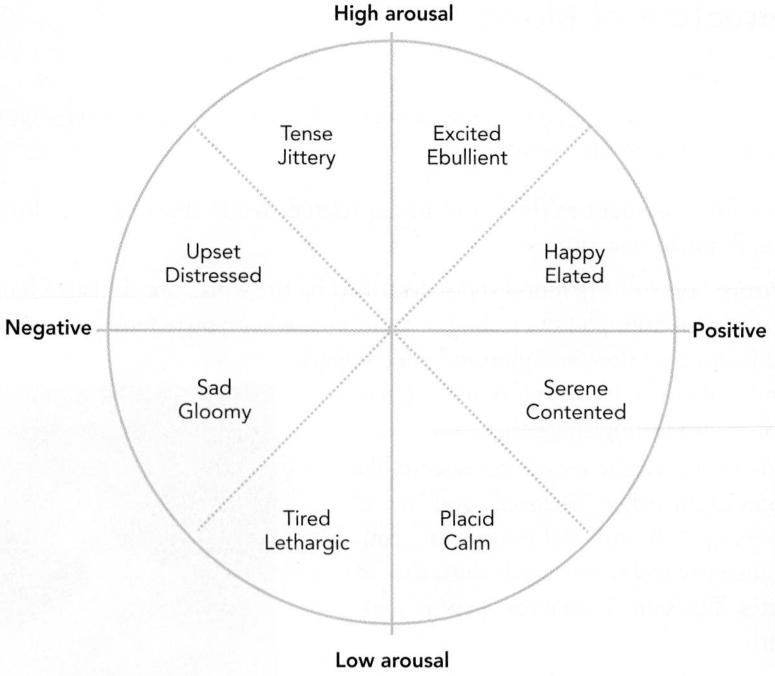

From Russell (2003). © 2003 American Psychological Association, Inc. Reprinted with permission

figure **10.11**

The structure of mood Everyday moods differ on two main dimensions: (1) *arousal* and (2) *valence* (the positivity or negativity of the mood). The variety of terms that we use to describe mood ("upset," "tense," "excited," etc.) can be located within this two-dimensional space.

> Where are you currently located on the "mood map"?

a map. No matter where you are on Earth, your location can be identified on a map defined by lines of longitude and latitude. No matter what your mood at any given time, it can be located somewhere in the "mood map," defined by lines of valence and arousal (Russell, 2003).

🐾 WHAT DO YOU KNOW?...

9. Where would each of these four mood adjectives be located in the "mood map": "sluggish," "peppy," "depressed," and "energetic"? Consider first whether they are of negative or positive valence, then whether they are of high or low arousal. Use Figure 10.11 to help answer the question.

Improving Your Mood

Preview Question

› What activities have been demonstrated to improve mood?

Just as a map describes your location but doesn't tell you how to get somewhere new, the two-dimensional structure of mood describes your mood but doesn't tell you how to change it. But change often is what you want. You're tired of feeling grouchy and sluggish. How can you move toward contented and peppy?

Many factors affect your mood. Some are life stresses—relationship problems, professional setbacks, death of a loved one—that make you tense and can affect your health, as we discuss later in this chapter. Others

⭕ THINK ABOUT IT

The two-dimensional model of mood says that, at any one time, you are located in one place in the mood map. But what about "mixed" feelings, of the sort you might experience if you won a competition but, simultaneously, your best friend lost? When experiencing mixed feelings, are you in two locations in the mood map at once?

are unexpected events that brighten your day: An old friend calls to say hello; people compliment you on your appearance; you win a contest. But you can't count on these unexpected events to occur, and their effects on mood may be short lived. Fortunately, you've got more options; some types of activities have been shown to reliably improve mood states.

PHYSICAL ACTIVITIES. One such activity is exercise (Thayer, 1996). Regular exercise can improve mood. Evidence of this comes from experimental studies that randomly assign people to experimental conditions in which they do or do not exercise regularly (Blumenthal et al., 1999). In a study of adults suffering from chronically depressed mood, one group of participants took 45-minute exercise classes 3 times a week for 4 months. In a second experimental condition, participants did not regularly exercise but took antidepressant medications. Participants in the exercise group experienced more positive mood—that is, they were much less depressed—after the four months of exercise than before. Furthermore, exercise improved depressed mood as effectively as did the antidepressant drugs. When researchers checked in with participants six months later, most of the participants were still exercising and remained in a more positive mood (Babyak et al., 2000).

The change in mood that resulted from exercise primarily was a shift along one of the two dimensions of the two-dimensional model of mood (see Figure 10.11): the positivity–negativity dimension. What about the other dimension, arousal? Some activities reliably lower high-arousal states of tension and stress. One is yoga.

In yoga, practitioners learn physical poses that build bodily strength and flexibility, while simultaneously focusing one's attention in a calm and concentrated manner. The skills of yoga may improve mood. To find out, researchers (Streeter et al., 2010) assigned participants to one of two groups. In one, participants engaged in 60-minute yoga sessions 3 times a week for 12 weeks. In the other, participants walked for 60 minutes 3 times a week for 12 weeks. Both groups thus got a similar amount of exercise. But yoga had a greater effect on mood. Yoga participants reported higher levels of positive mood and lower levels of anxious arousal; that is, they improved on both mood dimensions. This study also involved brain-level analyses. Through brain-imaging methods, the researchers found evidence that yoga may increase levels of a brain chemical that contributes to calm, low-arousal states of mind (Streeter et al., 2010). Other studies confirm that training in yoga can substantially reduce levels of stress (Michalsen et al., 2005).

Other physical interventions also have the power to reduce anxiety. In massage therapy, pressure is applied to the body in order to manipulate, and relax, muscles and other soft tissues of the body. A statistical analysis of more than three dozen studies shows that massage therapy influences mood (Moyer, Rounds, & Hannum, 2004). Even single sessions of massage therapy reduce feelings of anxious tension.

The effects of exercise, yoga, and massage therapy teach a general lesson about mood. Your mood reflects the overall state of your body (Thayer, 2003). Changes in the condition of the body, then, directly influence mood.

MUSIC. Another activity that can affect your mood is music. Intuitively, you know that music can alter your feelings. An upbeat song peps you up. Hearing your favorite band can brighten a dull or depressed mood. Research backs up your intuitions.

Laboratory experiments reveal that music and mood are systematically linked (Krumhansl, 2002). In this research, participants heard passages of symphonic music that varied in tempo, rhythm, and tone. They reported experiencing different emotions during the different musical passages. Furthermore, physiological recordings (heart

lightwavemedia / Shutterstock

It's as relaxing as it looks Research indicates that yoga reduces anxious moods.

Does your current exercise program benefit your mood?

rate, blood pressure) showed that their internal bodily states varied across musical passages, just as you would expect if the sound of music was altering their mood (Krumhansl, 1997).

Brain imaging confirms the effect of music on inner states of the body. Pleasant and inspiring music activates brain regions associated with the experience of pleasurable, rewarding stimuli (Blood & Zatorre, 2001; Koelsch et al., 2006).

Finally, singing may have unique effects on mood as well. In a survey of college choir members, the large majority reported that singing improves their mood (Clift & Hancox, 2001). In research comparing the effects of singing with merely listening to choral music, singing produced greater increases in positive mood, in addition to increased levels of a protein that is part of the body's immune system (Kreutz et al., 2004).

The effects of music on mood are puzzling, though. Why should a series of tones, patterned across time, affect people's feelings? Psychological science cannot answer this question definitively. However, theorists suggest an interesting possibility (Scherer, 2004). Music may automatically activate body rhythms and movements that, in turn, influence your mood. When you hear some upbeat music, the rhythm and melody tend to induce body movement (such as bobbing your head). These movements are associated with positive mood; your body tends to move more quickly and vigorously when you're happy than when you're depressed. The body movement induced by music, then, may create a more positive mood (Scherer, 2004)—just as you might expect from research reviewed earlier on mood and physical activities.

> Do you find it hard to resist moving your body when you hear music? If so, what is the effect on your mood?

⚡ WHAT DO YOU KNOW?...

10. Which of the following statements are true about factors that can change mood? Check all that apply.

___a. In one study, exercise was as powerful as antidepressants in increasing positive mood among adults suffering from chronic depression.

___b. In one study, yoga was as powerful as walking in reducing anxious arousal.

___c. Massage has been demonstrated to reduce anxious tension.

___d. Singing has been shown to be a more powerful way to increase positive mood than listening to music.

Mood, Thought, and Behavior

Preview Questions

› Can today's weather influence how satisfied we are with life in general?
› Are people more likely to help others when in a positive mood or negative mood?

Mood is inherently interesting. Variations in mood state intrigue psychologists and nonpsychologists alike. Yet, to the psychological scientist, mood is intriguing for a second reason, namely, because it systematically affects thinking and behavior. Let's first look at the influence of mood on thought.

MOOD AS INFORMATION. Consider the following questions:

1. How much do you like the college in which you are enrolled?

2. How good is your car?

3. How satisfied are you with your life in general?

We posed those questions in order to ask you a different one: How did you go about answering them?

In theory, you might have answered each question by contemplating a long list of facts and then systematically adding the facts together. To answer the life satisfaction question, you could have written down a long list of every person, place, and thing associated with your life; weighed the good with the bad; averaged all the pieces of information together; and computed a level of life satisfaction. But, in reality, that's probably not what you did.

When evaluating a target of judgment—a school, a car, a life—people rarely enumerate and compile long lists of facts. Instead, they rely on something else: their mood, specifically, the mood they are in when making the evaluation.

The **mood-as-information hypothesis** (Schwarz & Clore, 2007) proposes that when people evaluate a target of judgment, their moods directly inform their evaluations. In the psychological process of evaluation, mood acts *as if* it is a source of information. The idea behind the theory is that, when confronted with a question such as "How satisfied are you with your life?" people answer by consulting their feelings. If a person thinks about her life, is feeling good when thinking about it, and then formulates an evaluation of her life in general, she'll tend to say, "I'm very satisfied." Her feelings inform her evaluation.

The mood-as-information hypothesis thus has a fascinating implication: Irrelevant factors may affect people's evaluations. People's evaluations of a target—their college, their car, their life—may be influenced by extraneous factors that happen to affect their mood, but that otherwise have nothing to do with the object being evaluated. One such factor is the weather.

A study by the social psychologists Norbert Schwarz and Gerald Clore (1983) vividly illustrates mood-as-information processes. In a telephone interview, they asked people to rate their level of satisfaction with their life as a whole. Schwarz and Clore conducted interviews on both damp, rainy days and warm, sunny days. You might think that weather would have no effect on interview responses because people were rating their overall life, not the day's weather. But that's not what Schwarz and Clore thought; they predicted that weather would influence mood, and mood, in turn, would affect evaluations of life. As the researchers predicted, those interviewed on a sunny day evaluated their life more positively than those interviewed on a rainy day (Figure 10.12).

Interestingly, if the researchers first asked participants, "How's the weather?" their life evaluations on sunny and rainy days did not differ (Schwarz & Clore, 1983). The "how's the weather" question reminded people that something irrelevant, the weather that day, might bias their judgments. Once reminded, participants no longer used their mood as a source of information. There's a practical lesson here! When making an important life decision, stop and think—or your conclusions could be biased by trivial factors that affect your mood.

On a day like this, she may not like her city. Or her clothes. Or her life in general. Foul weather can put you in a bad mood that affects your judgment through mood-as-information processes.

Michael Blann / Getty Images

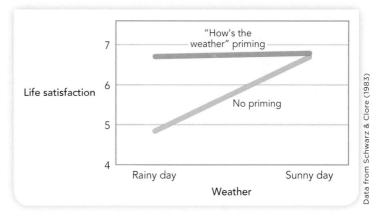

Data from Schwarz & Clore (1983)

figure **10.12**
Life satisfaction and weather If someone asked how satisfied you are with your life as a whole, your answer might be influenced by on two factors: (1) the weather, and (2) whether the person first *asked you about* the weather. Weather can affect your mood and your judgments, if you don't stop to think about this effect.

MOOD AND HELPING. Mood can also influence behavior. How you feel affects what you do. One type of social behavior that is strongly influenced by mood is helping others.

People often have opportunities to help. Salvation Army workers ask for donations. Community service organizations seek volunteers. Indigent and homeless citizens ask for assistance. Do you help them? Research suggests that you are much more likely to do so if you are in a good mood.

mood-as-information hypothesis
A proposal about the way in which feeling states influence thinking processes; in this hypothesis, moods inform thinking directly, as if they were sources of information.

Chris Fryer / MLIVE.COM / Landov

Keep smiling! Research shows that putting people in a good mood increases the chances that they will help you out.

Even simple, subtle influences on mood can affect willingness to help. Isen and Levin (1972) conducted a study in which they left a dime in the coin return slot of telephones in a phone booth. (This was well before the advent of cell phones, at a time when the value of a dime was equivalent to about 50 cents in today's money.) After participants found the dime and left the booth, a researcher nearby would drop a folder full of papers on the ground. The dependent measure of the study was whether participants helped pick up the papers. Finding a dime—an event that temporarily induced a positive mood—increased helping behavior. Most people who found a dime helped pick up the papers. Most people in a second experimental condition, in which there was no dime, did not help.

> Can any of your acts of generosity have been influenced by something as small as a dime?

🧠 WHAT DO YOU KNOW?...

11. An electronics company needs people's honest opinions about a phone it is developing. The company plans to ask a group of people to participate in a test trial using the phone, then fill out a questionnaire. For their trouble, people will receive a valuable gift. Should the company provide the people with the gift before or after they fill out the questionnaire? Consider the research by Norbert Schwarz and Gerald Clore (1983) on the mood-as-information hypothesis and explain your answer.

Emotion and the Brain

Now that you've learned about the psychology of emotion and mood, let's move down a level of analysis to the biology. What systems in the brain enable humans to have a mind filled not only with thoughts, but also feelings? This question has been addressed since the dawn of experimental psychology. We'll begin by looking back to the late nineteenth century.

Classic Conceptions of Body, Brain, and Emotion

Preview Questions

> Do we first have to experience bodily arousal in order to experience an emotion?
> Are all emotions produced via the same process, and according to a step-by-step sequence of events, as the James–Lange and Cannon–Bard theories had predicted?

James–Lange theory of emotion
A theory of how the brain and body generate emotional experience in which physiological arousal, in response to an event, is said to precede and cause a subsequent emotional response.

JAMES–LANGE THEORY OF EMOTION. In the mid-1880s, a coincidence occurred. Two psychologists working independently, William James and Carl Lange, developed similar, novel ideas about how the brain and body generate emotional experience. The most novel aspect of their ideas concerned the causal relation between emotion and physiological activities in the body.

Intuitively, it seems that emotions cause physiological arousal: You experience an emotion (e.g., fear), which causes your bodily arousal to increase. But James and Lange thought this conception was backwards. The **James–Lange theory of emotion** proposes that physiological activity causes emotional experience. When something happens—someone insults you; an onrushing car heads your way; your lottery number is chosen (Figure 10.13)—your brain receives information from sensory systems and generates a physiological response in your body. Signals are then sent from your body to your brain, informing the brain that bodily arousal has occurred. Only then, after the brain receives these signals, do you experience an emotion.

The James–Lange theory contends that if you were unaware of the changes in your body, you would not experience an emotion (James, 1884). You would have thoughts—you'd see that you had won the lottery—but they would be cold pieces of information rather than hot feelings.

Years later, two psychologists added a component to the James–Lange formulation. Stanley Schachter and Jerome Singer (1962) suggested that when people experience physiological arousal, they "label" it, that is, they categorize the experience they are having. Social factors influence the labels people use. Different people experiencing the same physiological arousal might use different labels and thus experience different emotions. Schachter and Singer conducted research (detailed in Research Toolkit, Chapter 12) showing that, when in the vicinity of an angry person, people tend to label their own physiological arousal as anger; but if people are with a happy person, they label that same arousal as happiness. Schachter and Singer's theory attracted much attention in the 1960s and 1970s, but by the 1980s research testing the theory had "yielded disappointing results" (Leventhal & Tomarken, 1986, p. 574) that called into question some of the theory's assumptions. Other theoretical approaches—such as the appraisal theories discussed earlier in this chapter—became more influential guides to emotion research.

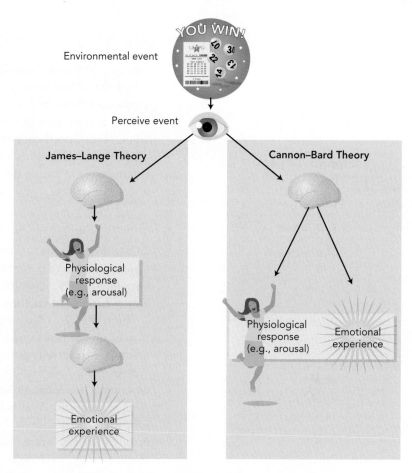

figure 10.13
Classic theories of emotion

CANNON–BARD THEORY OF EMOTION. In the 1920s, two scientists, Walter Cannon and Philip Bard, developed a major alternative to the James–Lange theory. It is known as—no surprise here—the *Cannon–Bard theory of emotion.*

According to the **Cannon–Bard theory of emotion,** information about emotionally arousing events travels from the sensory system to structures in the brain's limbic system (especially the thalamus; Cannon, 1927). Signals sent from the limbic system, in turn, accomplish two functions simultaneously: (1) They produce the experience of emotion, and (2) they generate the bodily changes (in physiological arousal, facial expression, and body posture) that are distinctive of emotion (see Figure 10.12). Unlike the James–Lange theory, then, in the Cannon–Bard theory bodily arousal does not precede, and is not the cause of, emotion.

Cannon and Bard rejected the James–Lange theory based on evidence unavailable to James and Lange back in the 1880s. By the 1920s, researchers had performed experimental surgeries with animals in which they cut the nervous system connections from the heart, lungs, stomach, and other organs to the brain. After the surgeries, the animals appeared just as emotional as they were previously (Cannon, 1927), a finding inconsistent with the expectations of the James–Lange theory.

Cannon–Bard theory of emotion
A theory of the generation of emotional states in which emotionally arousing events produce physiological and emotional responses simultaneously, rather than one leading to the other.

THINK ABOUT IT

Is one of these theories of emotion (James–Lange, Cannon–Bard) right and the other wrong? Or might emotions be generated in different ways on different occasions, with the implication that both theories are valid sometimes but not all the time? Compare your experiences when you (1) suddenly are frightened by a loud noise and (2) gradually figure out the implications of some bad news. Are emotions generated in the same way in these different situations?

CONTEMPORARY STATUS OF THE CLASSIC THEORIES. James, Lange, Cannon, and Bard's contributions were significant in their days. Those days, however, were long ago. Contemporary advances highlight two main limitations of both the James–Lange and Cannon–Bard approaches.

Both theories tried to identify the way in which emotion is generated. But there may be no *one way* in which emotion is generated. Some emotions may arise through one type of psychological process, whereas others arise through some other process. Contemporary researchers recognize that multiple processes contribute to emotional experience (LeDoux, 1994; Pessoa & Adolphs, 2010).

A second limitation is that both theories depict a step-by-step sequence of events. One event occurs in the brain, and then another, and then another. Contemporary research on the brain, however, shows that large numbers of brain events occur *simultaneously*. Networks of neurons provide continuous communication among multiple brain systems that are active simultaneously (Sporns, 2011). Developments in psychological science as a whole have therefore moved the study of emotion beyond the contributions of the James–Lange and Cannon–Bard theories.

WHAT DO YOU KNOW?...

12. True or False?
    a. One criticism of the James–Lange and Cannon–Bard theories of emotion is that they treat all emotions as if they arise through the same processes.
    b. Another criticism of the James–Lange and Cannon–Bard theories of emotion is that they are not sequential enough; rather, they assume that brain events leading to emotional experiences happen simultaneously.

The Limbic System and Emotion

Preview Question

> What subcortical brain structures are key to emotional life? How do we know?

One region of brain that is key to emotional life is the limbic system. The *limbic system* is a set of brain structures residing below the cortex and above the brain stem (see Chapter 3). Limbic system structures are involved in the processing of rewarding, punishing, and threatening stimuli whose presence generates emotional reactions.

THE AMYGDALA. A structure within the limbic system that is particularly important to emotional response is the *amygdala* (Gallagher & Chiba, 1996; Hamann, 2011;

Figure 10.14). The amygdala plays multiple roles in emotional experience and is particularly active in processing events that have the power to generate negative emotions such as fear.

One function of the amygdala is to detect stimuli that might be threatening to the organism. These stimuli often involve novelty; in general, familiar people and places are less threatening than novel ones. Brain-imaging studies show that the amygdala responds particularly strongly when people see images of other people who are novel, that is, who are strangers to them (Balderston, Schultz, & Helmstetter, 2011).

Research on people with damage to the amygdala provides further evidence of its role in processing emotional information. Such people can recognize the identity of others but have difficulty identifying emotions expressed in others' faces (Adolphs et al., 1994).

THE CASE OF SM. The amygdala plays a role not only in recognizing threatening stimuli, but also in generating the emotion of fear. Evidence of this comes from a remarkable case—that of SM.

SM is a woman who has experienced bilateral amygdala damage, that is, damage to the amygdala on both the left and right sides of her brain. To learn about her experience of fear, experimenters (Feinstein et al., 2011) exposed her to stimuli that would scare almost anybody: handling a snake and a tarantula in a pet store; going to a haunted house; watching a scary movie. Other people found these stimuli quite scary—but not SM. When exposed to these stimuli, she showed no fear at all! Instead, SM wanted to play with the snakes and tarantulas, even after a store employee said they were dangerous. She smiled and laughed her way through the haunted house, while others screamed with fear. The scary movie—film clips depicting torture, mutilation, and murder—elicited no fear in SM.

> What would your life be like without fear?

SM was not emotionless, however. When she saw the snakes and tarantulas, she showed interest. When she saw funny movies, she laughed. The deficit produced by her amygdala damage was highly specific: It eliminated only one emotion, fear. When researchers asked her to complete surveys of her emotions during daily life, she reported a full range of emotion—sadness, happiness, disgust, anger—except for fear (Feinstein et al., 2011).

Does SM's case mean that the amygdala, by itself, produces the emotion of fear? No, not at all. Consider this analogy. If the thermostat in your home is damaged, you can't control your home's temperature. But the thermostat, by itself, does not produce the hot or cool air that maintains a home's temperature. It's just one component in a large system of parts. Analogously, if the amygdala in your brain is damaged, your emotional life is altered. Yet the amygdala is just one component in a large system of brain structures involved in emotional experience.

Warner Bros. / The Kobal Collection

figure 10.14
Amygdala The amygdala, a structure in the limbic system, is important to the processing of emotionally arousing stimuli. Note that, like virtually all brain structures, there is an amygdala in both the left and right hemispheres of the brain.

Limbic system

Amygdala

It may be scary to you But not to a patient known as SM, whose amygdala damage makes her immune to fear. The amygdala is a brain structure that is active in processing events with the power to generate feelings of fear. So while this character from the 1973 horror film *The Exorcist* caused audience members at the time to scream, faint, and run out of the theatre during scenes of demonic possession, SM would not have felt any fear at all.

❤ WHAT DO YOU KNOW?...

13. The workings of the limbic system are better understood thanks to SM, a person with bilateral _____ damage. She did not find snakes and tarantulas _____, as most would; as a result, she didn't experience the emotion of _____.

The Cortex and Emotion

Preview Question

> How can we explain the psychologically complex phenomenon of emotional experience at the biological level of analysis?

If you think back to what you learned earlier in this chapter, you can figure out for yourself that emotion must involve brain structures beyond the amygdala. You learned that the psychology of emotion includes the following:

> *Thinking processes:* Cognitive appraisals shape emotional experience.

> *Motor movements:* Movements of facial muscles communicate emotions to others.

> *Consequences for motivation and decision making:* Emotions affect our behavior and decisions.

In addition, you saw that these psychological components of emotion are highly coordinated. Your thoughts, feelings, facial expressions, and motives are synchronized. If you think you were insulted, you immediately feel angry; anger is immediately displayed on your face; and you immediately are motivated to act against the person who insulted you.

EMOTION AND INTERCONNECTED BRAIN SYSTEMS. These psychological facts have biological implications. The biological systems of emotion must be capable of explaining the psychological phenomena that you learned about. This means that the biology of emotion must include the following:

1. *Brain structures involved in emotion-related thoughts, motor movements, motivation, and decision making.* It is known that many of the brain structures underlying thought, decision making, and behavior are not in the limbic system, but in the brain's highest region, the cortex (see Chapter 3). The cortex, then, must play a big role in emotion.

2. *Interconnections among these brain structures.* Brain structures in the limbic system and cortex must be highly interconnected. If they weren't, then there couldn't be such a high degree of synchronization among the various psychological components of emotion (thoughts, feeling, motivations, and facial expressions).

EVIDENCE FROM BRAIN-IMAGING METHODS. In recent years, psychologists have employed brain-imaging methods to discover the neural systems involved in emotional experience. Large numbers of studies have visually identified systems within the brain that are most active when people experience emotions. A team of researchers (Kober et al., 2008) has reviewed evidence from more than 150 such studies, in order to obtain an overall depiction of the brain structures involved.

Their results show that a complex network of brain structures contributes to emotion (Figure 10.15). Specifically, six interconnected groups of neural systems are involved. Two of them are in the limbic system, and the others are in the brain's cortex. The latter include regions of the cortex that play a role in paying attention to stimuli, processing visual information, controlling motor movement, and planning one's actions.

Furthermore, just as you'd expect from what you learned about the psychology of emotion, these brain systems of emotion were found to be highly interconnected. Activation in one region of the brain tended to co-occur with activation in another and another (Figure 10.15).

Research at a biological level of analysis, then, complements findings at a psychological level of analysis. Psychologically, emotions consist of a number of distinct

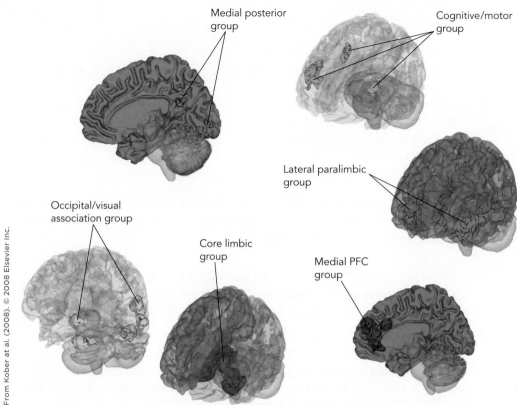

Medial posterior group

Cognitive/motor group

Lateral paralimbic group

Occipital/visual association group

Core limbic group

Medial PFC group

From Kober at al. (2008). © 2008 Elsevier Inc.

figure **10.15**
Brain systems in emotion Brain-imaging methods reveal that six different neural groups in the limbic system and the cortex of the brain contribute to emotional experience, and that the six groups are highly interconnected.

components. These include both high-level thinking processes through which people determine the meaning of events and low-level, "gut" feelings that add power to emotional experience. Biologically, emotions activate a number of distinct components in the brain systems. These include both low-level mechanisms in the brain's limbic system and high-level neural networks in the cortex (Pessoa & Adolphs, 2010).

WHAT DO YOU KNOW?...

14. Match the fact about emotional experience on the left with its biological component on the right.

1. Emotional experience is complex and includes lots of different kinds of activities.

2. Cognitive appraisals shape emotional experiences.

3. There is synchronization among thoughts, feelings, motivations, and facial expressions.

a. When people experience emotions, not one, but at least *six* neural systems are involved.

b. The brain systems that are activated during emotional processing are highly interconnected.

c. One of the areas of the brain that is active during emotional experience is its highest region, the cortex, an area associated with thinking.

Stress and Health

Some emotions are relaxing: the calm tranquility your experience lazing under a warm sun. Some are uplifting: the pride and sense of power you experience after winning a big game. But some emotions are stressful. Tragic news (the death of a loved one), physical threats (a mugging), personal challenges (an upcoming exam), and interpersonal crises (a relationship break-up) create feelings of intense stress.

In this final section of the chapter, we'll look at the nature of stress, how it can affect the body and your health, and how you can cope with the stresses of life.

Stress

Preview Questions

› How do psychologists classify environmental stressors? Are they always negative?
› What psychological features determine whether we experience a given environment as stressful?
› Through what biological process do our bodies enable us to respond adaptively to stress?
› What is the role of hormones in the stress response?

The word "stress" can be used in three different ways. It can refer to (1) environmental events, (2) subjective feelings, and (3) bodily reactions, specifically, the body's response to stressful events. Let's look at all three.

ENVIRONMENTAL STRESSORS. An environmental event is called a "stressor" if it is potentially damaging to an individual. Researchers distinguish among three types of environmental stressors (Lazarus & Lazarus, 1994):

1. *Harms* are damaging events that have already occurred. The recent death of a family member or close friend would be a stressful harm.

2. *Threats* are potentially damaging events that might occur in the future. If you're walking at night and see someone who looks dangerous walking toward you, the potential danger he represents is a threat.

3. *Challenges* are upcoming or ongoing activities that pose obstacles which, if overcome, can lead to personal growth. If you are working on a big exam, there not only is a threat of failing; there also is an opportunity to solve the exam's challenging problems and thereby prove your abilities to yourself.

In addition to the three types of stressors, stressors—of any type—also differ in duration (Segerstrom & Miller, 2004). *Acute stressors* last a brief amount of time. They would include, for example, the stress of slipping and falling on the ice, or suddenly being called on in class to answer a question for which you're unprepared. *Chronic stressors* are present through a prolonged period of a person's life. They include stressors such as chronic poverty, living in a war zone, or caring for a person with a severe mental disability.

These distinctions identify different *types* of stressors. What specific life events, though, tend to be most stressful? Psychologists have developed lists of stressful life events, ranked according to the degree to which they disrupt established patterns of life (Holmes & Rahe, 1967). As you can see (Table 10.2), they include not only negative events (e.g., personal injury, being fired from work) but also some positive ones (e.g., an addition to the family) that require life adjustments that may present major challenges.

What positive life events have you experienced that required life adjustments?

SUBJECTIVE STRESS. Stress must be understood not only from the outside—stressors in the environment—but also from the inside. People's inner thoughts can determine whether any given environmental event is stressful. This is especially true for events in the social world, which can be interpreted differently by different people. A job interview may be a "valuable opportunity" to one person but a "stressful evaluation" to another. One student looks forward to classroom discussions, which she sees as a chance to show off her intelligence, whereas another is stressed out because she sees only the possibility of saying something stupid. **Subjective stress** is the psychological

subjective stress The psychological impact of a potentially stressful event from the perspective of the individual experiencing it.

table **10.2**

Stressful Events			
Event	**Stress Scores**	**Event**	**Stress Scores**
Death of spouse	100	Change in work responsibilities	29
Divorce	73	Trouble with in-laws	29
Marital separation	65	Outstanding personal achievement	28
Jail term	63	Spouse begins or stops work	26
Death of close family member	63	Starting or finishing school	26
Personal injury or illness	53	Change in living conditions	25
Marriage	50	Revision of personal habits	24
Fired from work	47	Trouble with boss	23
Marital reconciliation	45	Change in work hours, conditions	20
Retirement	45	Change in residence	20
Change in family member's health	44	Change in schools	20
Pregnancy	40	Change in recreational habits	19
Sex difficulties	39	Change in church activities	19
Addition to family	39	Change in social activities	18
Business readjustment	39	Mortgage or loan under $10,000	17
Change in financial status	38	Change in sleeping habits	16
Death of close friend	37	Change in number of family gatherings	15
Change to a different line of work	36	Change in eating habits	15
Change in number of marital arguments	35	Vacation	13
Mortgage or loan over $10,000	31	Christmas season	12
Foreclosure of mortgage or loan	30	Minor violation of the law	11

Reprinted from *Journal of Psychosomatic Research*, 11:213–218, Holmes & Rahe, The social readjustment rating scale, © 1967, with permission from Elsevier

impact of a potentially stressful event from the perspective of the individual who is experiencing it.

People experience subjective stress when situational demands and personal resources are out of balance (Lazarus & Lazarus, 1994). If demands outweigh resources ("I can't figure out these calculus problems—and the exam is tomorrow!"), stress results. Stress also can arise if the balance tips in the other direction. When personal resources greatly outweigh situational demands—for example, you're a skilled musician stuck in a music class for beginners—people become bored, and the boredom itself can be

Have you experienced a lot of these events? Let's hope not! They are life events that cause stress because they disrupt established patterns of life. The stress scores indicate the typical degree of disruption (Holmes & Rahe, 1967).

stressful. Calm, stress-free moments arise when personal skills and environmental demands are in synch (Csikszentmihalyi, 1990).

Measures of subjective stress differ from tests designed to measure environmental stressors (see Table 10.2). Subjective stress is measured using test items such as the following (Horowitz, Wilner, & Alvarez, 1979):

> "I have difficulty falling asleep because of images or thoughts related to the event."

> "Things I saw or heard suddenly reminded me of it."

> "I stayed away from things or situations that might remind me of it."

These items tap personal responses to stressful circumstances. They enable psychologists to identify individual differences in subjective reactions to the same objective event.

PHYSIOLOGICAL STRESS REACTIONS. "Stress" also refers to physiological reactions. When you experience a stressor, your body reacts. It produces a **stress response,** a coordinated series of physiological changes that prepare you for "fight or flight," that is, to confront or flee the stressor (Rodrigues, LeDoux, & Sapolsky, 2009).

The physiological changes that comprise the stress response occur in multiple systems within the body. Your heart rate increases, which delivers more oxygen to muscles to fuel bodily movement. Your thinking changes; signals from body to brain cause your attention to focus in on the stressor. Your immune system alters its functioning; as we discuss in detail below, this change means that stress can affect your health.

In the mid-twentieth century, the biologist Hans Selye (1950) identified the **general adaptation syndrome (GAS),** a sequence of physiological reactions that occur in response to stressors. The GAS consists of three stages:

1. *Alarm reaction:* When a stressor first occurs, the body's "internal alarm" system goes off, preparing the organism for fight or flight.

2. *Resistance:* If a stressor continues to be present—that is, if it is a chronic stressor—our bodies adapt. Our immune systems respond to the environment's high demands by "working overtime" to protect the body.

3. *Exhaustion:* The resistance stage requires energy. If a chronic stressor persists long enough, we run out of bodily energy and experience exhaustion. Immune system functioning breaks down, bodily organs can become damaged, and we are at high risk of illness.

The biological mechanisms that enable the body to respond adaptively to stress involve *hormones,* chemical substances that travel throughout the body and influence the activity of bodily organs (Chapter 3). When a stressful event occurs, hormones make intelligent use of the body's overall energies (Sapolsky, 2004). Hormones increase the supply of blood sugar and oxygen, which gives you extra energy to either flee from or confront the stressor. They suppress physiological activities that don't help you cope with the stressor; for example, under stress, digestive processes and sexual drives are reduced. This makes sense in evolutionary terms. Over the course of evolution, if you were under threat from a predator, that was no time to sit around digesting food or having sex.

Which exact hormones and bodily organs are involved in stress reactions? The central system is the **hypothalamic–pituitary–adrenal (HPA) axis,** an interconnected set of structures and hormone pathways that regulates stress response (Figure 10.16). As the name suggests, the HPA includes three structures: (1) the hypothalamus (a small structure in the lower-central area of the brain), (2) the pituitary gland (located just below the hypothalamus), and (3) the adrenal glands (which sit on top of the kidneys). A sequence of activities occurs when the hypothalamus is activated by stress (Sternberg & Gold 1997):

1. The hypothalamus releases a hormone, *corticotropin-releasing hormone* (CRH), into a duct that leads to the pituitary gland.

2. CRH causes the pituitary gland to release *adrenocorticotropic hormone* (ACTH). ACTH is carried by the bloodstream to the adrenal glands.

---

stress response A coordinated series of physiological changes that prepare you for "fight or flight"; that is, to confront the stressor, or flee.

general adaptation syndrome (GAS) A sequence of physiological reactions in response to stressors: alarm, resistance, and exhaustion.

hypothalamic–pituitary–adrenal (HPA) axis An interconnected set of structures and hormone pathways regulating stress response.

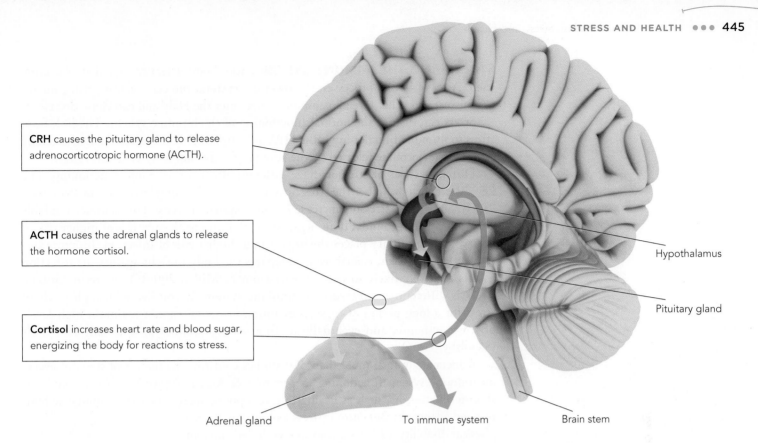

CRH causes the pituitary gland to release adrenocorticotropic hormone (ACTH).

ACTH causes the adrenal glands to release the hormone cortisol.

Cortisol increases heart rate and blood sugar, energizing the body for reactions to stress.

Hypothalamus

Pituitary gland

Adrenal gland

To immune system

Brain stem

figure **10.16**
Hypothalamic–pituitary–adrenal (HPA) axis

3. ACTH causes the adrenal glands to release another hormone, *cortisol,* into the bloodstream. Cortisol increases heart rate and blood sugar, thus energizing the body to react to stress.

The HPA axis also has a feedback mechanism. Some of the cortisol from the adrenal glands makes its way back to the hypothalamus and inhibits further hypothalamic release of CRH. This prevents the body as a whole from overreacting to the stressor (Sternberg & Gold, 1997).

WHAT DO YOU KNOW?...

15. When we perceive that situational demands are not in _____ with personal resources, we experience _____ stress. The first stage of the general _____ syndrome (GAS) is the _____ reaction, followed by _____, during which time our immune system works overtime to protect us. If the stressor continues, we experience the final stage of the GAS, _____. During a stress reaction, the _____–pituitary–adrenal (HPA) axis is active. The _____ releases corticotropin-releasing hormone to the pituitary gland, which then releases _____ (ACTH) hormone via the bloodstream to the adrenal glands, which in turn release _____ into the bloodstream, thereby energizing the body.

Health Effects of Stress

Preview Questions

› How does stress affect the functioning of our immune system? What are the implications for health?
› How can researchers test the effects of stress on immune system functioning in a way that controls for how hectic one's life is?
› How can stress make us old before our time?

How does stress influence health? A primary way is through the effects of stress on the immune system.

STRESS AND THE IMMUNE SYSTEM. Your body generally is good at protecting itself. A set of bodily processes, the **immune system,** protects against germs, microorganisms, and other foreign substances that enter the body and can cause disease.

Stress can disrupt the normal functioning of the immune system. The link from stress to immune functioning is the HPA axis. Immune system response is affected by cortisol, the hormone released by the adrenal glands (Sternberg & Gold, 1997).

Different types of stressors have different effects on immune functioning. The key difference is whether the stressor is a short-term or long-lasting event (Sapolsky, 2004). Short-term stressors increase immune system activity. This is understandable on evolutionary grounds. If an organism is fighting or fleeing, it is at higher risk of injury, and any injury places the organism at higher risk of infection. Immune system activation, then, is adaptive; it prepares the body to fight against the infection that is relatively likely to occur (Segerstrom & Miller, 2004). Long-term, chronic stress is different. It *suppresses* the immune system. If you live with high levels of stress for a long period of time, your immune system cannot maintain high levels of stress response, and eventually its functioning declines to unusually low levels (Sapolsky, 2004).

A meta-analysis of more than 300 studies confirms the impact of stressful events on immune system functioning (Segerstrom & Miller, 2004). When confronted by short-term stressors, such as having to give a public speech, people's immune systems respond adaptively. But chronic stressors—for instance, a physical disability, caring for someone with dementia, or being forced to move from one's home due to war—cause people's immune systems to work less well than normal.

> Have you experienced more illness during times of chronic stress?

STRESS AND HEALTH OUTCOMES. As you would expect, when the immune system is impaired, people experience poor health (Lovallo, 2005). Nurses who work for years on night shifts experience more heart disease (Kawachi et al., 1995). People who care for relatives with dementia are slower to heal from physical wounds

Poverty, stress, and health More than a billion people in the world live on less than $1 a day (World Health Organization, n.d.). Poverty impairs health not only because the poor have more exposure to environments that create illness and less access to health care, but also because poverty creates stress that impairs the immune system. These individuals live in Svay Reing, a province in the southeastern region of Cambodia.

Jerry Redfern / LightRocket via Getty Images

---

immune system A set of bodily processes that protects against germs, microorganisms, and other foreign substances that enter the body and can cause disease.

(Kiecolt-Glaser et al., 1995). Children, too, are affected by stress. Those who grow up in poverty experience more stress and, as adults, have more cardiovascular problems and do not live as long as people from wealthier backgrounds (Cohen et al., 2010). A range of *aversive childhood experiences* (*ACEs*), including exposure to physical abuse, mental abuse, domestic violence, or other criminal behavior, predict poorer health when the child reaches adulthood (Palusci, 2013).

Psychologists have linked stress to health through two types of research strategies. One is correlational; researchers determine whether levels of stress correlate with later health outcomes. For example, in the study of marital stress, correlational findings indicate that high levels of marital distress predict high numbers of physician visits, higher levels of self-reported health problems (symptoms of colds, flu, and gastrointestinal difficulties), and higher levels of health problems affected by poor immune system functioning, such as arthritis (Kiecolt-Glaser & Newton, 2001).

Correlational studies are informative but not entirely convincing. They leave open two possibilities. One is that stress directly impacts health. The other is that stress impacts health only indirectly; for example, highly stressed people may lead more hectic lifestyles that expose them to more people and thus more viruses. This exposure—not stress itself—may affect health. The second research strategy circumvents this problem.

In the second strategy, researchers experimentally manipulate people's exposure to viruses. Sheldon Cohen and colleagues randomly assigned participants to conditions in which they received nasal drops containing (1) a respiratory virus or (2) a simple mixture of salt and water (Cohen, Tyrrell, & Smith, 1993). Participants were quarantined in their apartments for two days before and seven days after receiving the drops. Each day, a physician examined each participant and recorded signs of illness. In addition, Cohen and colleagues measured stress. Participants indicated the number of stressful life events they were experiencing and whether they believed that these stressors exceeded their ability to cope. This sophisticated research strategy demonstrated that stress directly predicts health; among those exposed to the virus, people with more stressful lives were more likely to develop colds (Figure 10.17).

STRESS AND THE RATE OF AGING. When he served as vice president of the United States, an energetic, youthful Richard Nixon—who looked like a man in his

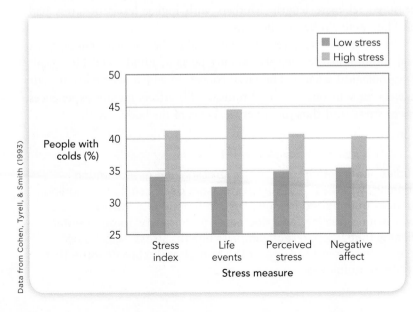

Data from Cohen, Tyrell, & Smith (1993)

People with colds (%)

Legend: ■ Low stress   ■ High stress

Stress measure: Stress index, Life events, Perceived stress, Negative affect

figure 10.17

Under stress? Feel a cold coming on? Maybe it's not a coincidence. Research findings indicate that people who experience high levels of stress are relatively more likely to develop colds. This is true no matter how the stress is measured. The chart illustrates the results for four different stress-measuring techniques—counting stressful life events, asking people their perceptions of life stress, measuring negative emotional experiences, or creating a stress index (bars on the left) that combines all three of the other measures.

Stress and aging The U.S. presidency is stressful for any office holder—but was particularly so for Richard M. Nixon, who resigned from office in the midst of the Watergate scandal. These images of a rapidly aging Nixon are consistent with scientific evidence showing that stress can speed the aging process. The two photos of Nixon were taken only 14 years apart (in 1960 and 1974).

early 40s—ran for the presidency. (Nixon lost to an even more youthful and energetic-looking John F. Kennedy.) When the Watergate scandal reached its crescendo later on, the President Nixon who resigned looked perhaps 30 years older, with greying hair, sagging skin, and a lined, worn face. But the two Nixons shown in the pair of photos differ in age not by three decades, but by only 14 years. What could have caused Nixon to age so much during that time period?

In part, it was the natural effects of aging (Olshansky, 2011). But the stress couldn't have helped. Life stress can accelerate the rate at which people age. Stress influences aging by affecting small bits of DNA called *telomeres* (Epel et al., 2004).

DNA, which is contained in chromosomes in the nuclei of cells, is the molecular material that contains the genetic instructions used to build organisms. A *telomere* is a small strand of DNA at the end of each chromosome. Telomeres maintain a cell's "youthfulness." When a cell loses too much of its telomere, it cannot replicate. Evidence suggests that, when this happens, body tissues age more rapidly (Sanders & Newman, 2013).

Research shows that stress can alter the body's internal chemistry in a way that causes telomeres to shorten (Epel et al., 2004). The researchers studied a group of mothers, some of whom experienced the stress of caring for a chronically ill child. They measured the level of stress experienced by each mother and, by analyzing blood samples, also measured telomere length. Mothers with higher levels of stress had shorter telomeres. They were old before their time.

Research on stress and telomeres reveals, once again, the intimate connections between body and mind, and the interplay among person-, mind-, and biological-level analyses in psychological science. The social context in which people live (in our example, as caregivers for someone who is chronically ill) affects mental experiences (increased feelings of stress) and thus the inner workings of the body.

⚡ WHAT DO YOU KNOW?...

16. Over 300 studies confirm that _____-term stressors increase immune system functioning, whereas _____-term stressors decrease its functioning. The consequences of impaired immune system functioning include _____ disease, slower wound healing, and decreases in longevity. Experimental research indicates that _____ directly impairs health. Stress ages us by shortening _____, the strand of DNA at the end of each chromosome that maintains a cell's youthfulness.

Coping with Stress

Preview Questions

> When coping with stressful events, is it more advantageous to try to change the problem or to focus on one's emotions?
> How and why do men and women's coping strategies differ?
> How is social support beneficial to physical and mental health?

How do you deal with stress? Some of the following strategies (from Internet discussions) might sound familiar:

> "When I am stressed, I cope by writing or sleeping."
> "I cope by simply walking out the door and sitting quietly in a nearby coffee shop, nursing a lo-cal drink until my anger and stress subside."
> "I cope by focusing on one task at a time . . . multitasking is just beyond me right now. So, I look at my day's to-do list, and prioritize things based on importance and the energy level required."
> "When I am stressed I cope by eating. If I've just come away from a stressful conversation or feel overwhelmed by everything I need to do, my stress reliever is to pause and have a little snack. Wow, if I am having a very stressful day or week, you can imagine how those extra unnecessary calories can add up!"
> "Well personally, I get extremely stressed with all the work I get. I'm in a couple of AP's right now and those stress me out incredibly. I cope by getting my work done early so I get sleep."
> "I cope by playing Electric Avenue on repeat and eating Grape Nerds."

You're probably thinking that some of these coping strategies are better than others. You might also have noticed that they are of two different types: *problem-focused* and *emotion-focused* coping strategies.

PROBLEM-FOCUSED AND EMOTION-FOCUSED COPING. In a classic book on stress and coping, Richard Lazarus and Susan Folkman (1984) identified two primary ways in which people cope with stressful events:

1. *Problem-focused coping* is an effort to change some aspects of the problem that is causing stress, so the problem is more manageable.
2. *Emotion-focused coping* is an effort to alter one's own feelings, which have been affected by a stressful problem, rather than altering the problem itself.

Look back to the examples of coping we presented above. You can tell which type of coping each exemplifies. "Prioritize things based on importance" is problem-focused; that person is making the source of stress, school activities, more manageable. "Playing Electric Avenue and eating Grape Nerds" is emotion-focused; it does not address one's problems, but it might put a person in a more relaxed mood.

Which way of coping is better? It depends; "coping processes are not inherently good or bad" (Folkman & Moskowitz, 2004, p. 753). Focusing on problems to be solved is often advantageous. Yet sometimes—such as when a problem is out of your control—it may be better to work on your emotional state. Problem-focused coping might be best when, for example, you have to cope with a heavy workload at the end of a busy semester. But emotion-focused coping may be the best strategy if you are dealing with the breakup of a relationship or the death of a loved one.

Research points to the advantages of coping *flexibly:* adjusting your coping style to the possibilities available in the situation at hand. One researcher (Cheng, 2001)

CONNECTING TO BRAIN SYSTEMS AND PSYCHOLOGICAL THERAPIES

(P)

PERSON

Chapter 15: Coping strategies are key elements of psychological therapies designed to enhance people's ability to handle stress and anxiety.

(M)

MIND

Here, we focus on mental strategies that are helpful in coping with stress.

(B)

BRAIN

Chapter 3: The brain's frontal lobes are the biological hardware that enables people to devise coping strategies and thereby regulate their emotional life.

PMB CONNECTIONS

measures flexibility by asking people how they have coped with a variety of different stressors that occur on different days. Some people, she finds, tend to cope in the same way from one situation to the next. Others are more flexible; they adjust coping strategies to different situations. Findings show that people who cope flexibly are less anxious when a highly stressful event, such as a major health problem, occurs (Cheng, 2003). Workers who are taught strategies for coping flexibly (e.g., using emotion-focused coping when problems seem uncontrollable) are less likely than others to become depressed when they experience stress at work (Cheng, Kogan, & Chio, 2012).

GENDER DIFFERENCES IN COPING. When it comes to coping with stress, men and women differ. To see the difference, we have to distinguish between two types of coping responses: *fight-or-flight* and *tend-and-befriend* (Taylor et al., 2000). (This distinction differs from the problem-focused/emotion-focused distinction, as you will see.)

Many members of the animal kingdom display a fight-or-flight response pattern (Cannon, 1932). A **fight-or-flight response** pattern is one in which an organism facing a threat does one of two things: (1) attack or (2) flee from the threat. If challenged by a predator, an animal might (1) fight or (2) run away. If challenged in an argument, you might (1) fight back verbally or (2) flee from confrontation by accepting the other person's point of view. Organisms usually opt for flight, rather than fight, when they see themselves as incapable of fighting back successfully. (Note that both fight and flight are problem-focused strategies; a problem is confronted or avoided.)

The psychologist Shelley Taylor and colleagues (Taylor et al., 2000) explain that women often cope in ways that

Consistent with research findings, both readers are men!

fight-or-flight response A behavioral pattern in which an organism facing a threat does one of two things: attack or flee.

are neither fight nor flight. Instead, women often **tend-and-befriend,** a strategy defined by two coping responses:

1. *Tending:* Taking action to reduce the distress and increase the safety of others, especially one's offspring

2. *Befriending:* Maintaining close personal connections with other people whose support might be helpful in coping with stress

Women are more likely than men to tend and to befriend. For example, compared with men, women have more same-sex friendships, more frequently seek support from their friends, and provide more emotional support to their friends (Taylor et al., 2000).

Why do men and women differ? Taylor suggests that biological evolution provides the answer. Across the course of evolution, females have been more heavily involved in parenting than males. During pregnancy, females carry the offspring. Afterward, they provide more biological support during nursing. For females, then, fight-or-flight often doesn't make sense. Both fighting and fleeing are hard at advanced stages of pregnancy. Both strategies leave offspring unprotected (while the mother fights or flees). By contrast, tending to the needs of offspring helps them survive during times of stress, and befriending others creates social networks that can help to support the mother. Women have therefore evolved a tendency to tend-and-befriend that is relatively lacking in men. Taylor and colleagues (Taylor et al., 2000) outline biochemical factors that contribute to the observed gender differences in coping behavior.

SOCIAL SUPPORT. Taylor's analysis of befriending raises a key point: When coping with stress, you don't have to go it alone. Friends and family can reduce the impact of stressful events by providing loving care and personal assistance, or **social support.** Research shows that people who receive more social support during times of stress tend to experience better physical and mental health (Cohen & Wills, 1985; Taylor & Stanton, 2007).

Psychologists have identified two ways in which social support is beneficial (Cohen & Wills, 1985). One is *stress buffering.* When stressful events occur, support from others can lower—or "buffer"—their impact. Suppose you experience a financial crisis. Friends and family might help with both problem-focused coping (by lending you money) and emotion-focused coping (by helping to reduce your anxiety). In this way, they buffer the impact of the crisis.

Social support's other benefit occurs even *before* you experience stress. Large networks of supportive friends and family increase people's overall psychological well-being. Increased well-being, in turn, lowers the chances that people will experience severe negative emotions when a setback occurs (Cohen & Wills, 1985).

Research documents the impact of social support in multiple areas of life. One is intimate relationships. Psychologists suggest that one key to the success of relationships is the social support that partners provide one another (Reis & Patrick, 1996). When partners make each other feel understood and emotionally supported, relationships thrive. In a study of remarkable scope, researchers studied couples over a 10-year period (Sullivan et al., 2010). In year 1, couples went to a laboratory and discussed marital problems they were facing. Researchers coded the degree to which partners provided positive emotional social support to one another during the discussions. At year 10, the researchers determined marital status (i.e., whether each couple was still married). Social support at year 1 significantly predicted marital status at year 10. Husbands and wives who were more socially supportive at year 1 were more likely to still be husbands and wives at year 10.

Another area where social support brings benefits is parenting. Parenting can be stressful for anyone, but is particularly so for parents of children with disabilities. In one research project (Ha, Greenberg, & Seltzer, 2011), African American parents

tend-and-befriend A coping strategy identified particularly in women in which the response to threat involves taking action to help others (tending) while maintaining a close support network (befriending).

social support Loving care and personal assistance from friends and family, particularly as provided during times of stress.

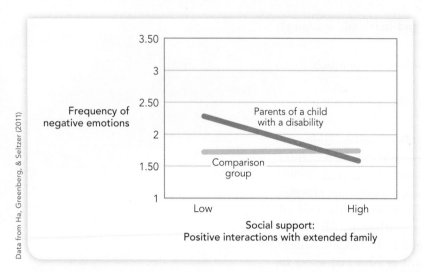

Data from Ha, Greenberg, & Seltzer (2011)

figure 10.18
Families buffer stress Parents whose child has a disability, but who benefit from high levels of social support from extended family members, experience levels of negative emotion that are no higher than parents of children with no disability (the "comparison group"). The study measured frequency of negative emotions such as sadness, nervousness, and feeling hopeless.

of children with disabilities such as autism (a disorder in which children fail to develop normal interactions with other people; see Chapter 14) and epilepsy (a nervous system disorder in which people experience seizures), plus a comparison group of parents whose children had no disabilities, were studied over a number of years. This group of parents was of particular interest because African American communities often contain extended families whose members provide one another with substantial social support.

A key dependent variable in this study was the emotional state of parents; the researchers measured negative emotion experienced by parents with, and without, children with disabilities. As you can see in Figure 10.18, social support buffered parents against negative emotions. Consider the parents of children with a disability. Among those with low social support, stressful negative emotions were frequent. But among those with high levels of social support, negative emotions were no more frequent than they were among other parents.

👀 WHAT DO YOU KNOW?...

17. True or False?
    a. The effectiveness of problem-focused and emotion-focused coping strategies depends on whether you have control over the stressor.
    b. Researchers advocate we cope flexibly, by adjusting our strategies to the type of problem.
    c. Men, more often than women, use the tend-and-befriend strategy, which involves reducing others' distress and maintaining a social support network.
    d. Research demonstrates that social support can contribute to physical and mental health by buffering the impact of a stressor.

↩️ Looking Back and Looking Ahead

In Chapter 1, you learned that psychology is diverse. Some psychologists study brains, and others study cultures. Some do basic research, and others apply psychological knowledge to practical problems. As you've seen in this chapter, the study of emotion is a microcosm of psychology as a whole, with emotion researchers tackling an extraordinarily wide range of problems, from basic questions about the causes of emotion to practical questions about reducing stress and improving health.

Although this ends our chapter, it's not the last you'll see of emotions. Developmental psychologists study growth in children's ability to control their emotional reactions. Personality theorists explore how emotions are one facet of the individual as a whole. And clinical psychologists seek therapies that empower people to gain control of their emotional lives.

Chapter Review

Now that you have completed this chapter, be sure to turn to Appendix B, where you will find a **Chapter Summary** that is useful for reviewing what you have learned about emotion, stress, and health.

Key Terms

appraisals (p. 423)

appraisal theories of emotion (p. 423)

Cannon–Bard theory of emotion (p. 437)

emotion (p. 409)

Facial Action Coding System (FACS) (p. 419)

facial feedback hypothesis (p. 417)

fight-or-flight response (p. 450)

general adaptation syndrome (GAS) (p. 444)

hypothalamic–pituitary–adrenal (HPA) axis (p. 444)

immune system (p. 446)

Iowa Gambling Task (p. 412)

James–Lange theory of emotion (p. 436)

mood (p. 410)

mood dimensions (p. 431)

mood-as-information hypothesis (p. 435)

moral judgments (p. 420)

social support (p. 451)

stress response (p. 444)

subjective stress (p. 442)

suppression (p. 427)

tend-and-befriend (p. 451)

Questions for Discussion

1. Review the section on the Facial Action Coding System (FACS).
   a. Without the FACS, how good do you think you are at detecting emotions based on facial expressions? What explains your skill? [Comprehend]
   b. Devise your own FACS to detect lying or some other behavior. [Apply]
   c. How will you validate the FACS you devised for lying? That is, how will you demonstrate whether you are correct? In determining your validation method, consider what biases you might have about the effectiveness of your emotion detection skills and how you can overcome them. [Synthesize]

2. Research using the Iowa Gambling Task demonstrates that "going with your gut" can lead you to make better decisions. However, in Chapter 1, you were cautioned against relying solely on intuition. Instead, you were encouraged to answer questions scientifically—that is, by collecting data or by relying on the reports of others who had published their findings. In what way is the intuition relied on during the Iowa Gambling Task scientific? In what way is it unscientific? [Analyze]

3. You learned that emotions may have evolved to motivate certain adaptive behaviors. For example, interest motivates us to spend more time on tasks and fear motivates us to avoid dangerous circumstances. Think of four emotions and discuss their evolutionary significance; that is, what problems did they likely evolve to solve? [Analyze]

4. According to appraisal theories of emotion, your appraisal of an experience can determine your emotional response to it. Does this suggest we can learn new emotional responses to past experiences through reappraisal? Explain. [Analyze]

5. You learned that people tend to overestimate the impact of life events on emotions, such that they think a positive event will be more satisfying than it eventually is and a negative event more devastating. Why do you suppose this is? Do you think we can learn how to correct for this bias and become more skilled at predicting our feelings? [Synthesize]

6. You learned that we experience subjective stress when situational demands and personal resources are out of balance, and that this goes both ways. That is, when demands exceed resources, we experience stress, but we also experience stress when resources (e.g., time) exceed demands (e.g., work). Describe an experience that fits each of these situations. Would others have perceived the situations in the same way? Why or why not? [Comprehend]

7. You learned that an effective method for changing emotions is to change anticipatory appraisals. Consider the type of anticipatory appraisals individuals make when they experience the subjective stress of expecting that situational demands and personal resources will be out of balance. Describe a time when you anticipated this imbalance. How could you have changed this anticipatory appraisal to make the event less stressful? [Comprehend]

Chapter Review

Self-Test

1. Which of the following conclusions was supported by Bechara and colleagues' study in which participants engaged in the Iowa Gambling Task?
   a. Emotions can impair decision making.
   b. Emotions can help us make good decisions.
   c. Emotions make it difficult to describe our thoughts.
   d. Emotions make it easier to describe our thoughts.

2. You are anxious about an upcoming exam, so you study extra hard for it. What does this illustrate about emotions?
   a. They have motivational power.
   b. They help us to communicate our thoughts.
   c. Their accompanying facial expressions are universal.
   d. They are difficult to measure.

3. Researchers presented Western Caucasian and East Asian participants with photos of individuals of varying facial expressions and asked them to identify the underlying emotion in each. What did the researchers find and what could they conclude?
   a. Both groups paid attention to the same facial structures when making their judgments. Culture plays a role in emotion detection.
   b. When making their judgments, Western Caucasians paid attention to the eyebrows and mouth, whereas East Asians paid attention to the direction of gaze. Culture does not play a role in emotion detection.
   c. Both groups paid attention to the same facial structures when making their judgments. Culture does not play a role in emotion detection.
   d. When making their judgments, Western Caucasians paid attention to the eyebrows and mouth, whereas East Asians paid attention to the direction of gaze. Culture plays a role in emotion detection.

4. Which of the following emotions contributes to moral judgment?
   a. Embarrassment
   b. Anxiety
   c. Disgust
   d. Fear

5. Joan receives an invitation to a party and is immediately filled with dread. Jemma gets the same invitation and is thrilled. According to appraisal theories of emotion, what explains their different emotional reactions?
   a. Joan is processing the information in a brain area that is different than Jemma's.
   b. Joan has assigned a different meaning to the event than has Jemma.

   c. Joan is experiencing bodily arousal, whereas Jemma is not.
   d. Joan is an introvert and Jemma is an extrovert.

6. Hindu women from northern India, a collectivistic culture, experience *lajja* when they feel they are acting according to their social obligations. Westerners do not experience this emotion. Which of the following theories can best account for cultural variations in emotion such as this?
   a. Cannon–Bard theory of emotion
   b. Schachter–Singer theory of emotion
   c. James–Lange theory of emotion
   d. Appraisal theories of emotion

7. The chapter describes a study by Gross (1998) in which participants watched a film of a leg being amputated under one of two experimental conditions. They were instructed to either appraise the film in a scientific manner or to suppress their emotions. A control group was given no instruction. What did the results of the study suggest?
   a. Suppression is an effective strategy for reducing arousal.
   b. Changing appraisals is an effective strategy for reducing arousal.
   c. Suppressing emotions is as effective as changing appraisals for reducing arousal.
   d. Some events are so horrible to watch that arousal cannot be reduced by any means.

8. If you're like most people, how would you respond to the question "How would you feel if you got a failing grade in this class?"
   a. I would overestimate its impact on my emotions and predict that I would be devastated.
   b. I would underestimate its impact on my emotions and predict that I wouldn't be bothered.
   c. I would not have much insight into my emotions; people typically "draw a blank" when asked to predict future emotions.
   d. I would immediately experience a "fight or flight" reaction.

9. Which of the following is true of the two-dimensional structure of mood?
   a. Theoretically, your mood can be located at only one place in the "mood map."
   b. Arousal and valence are opposites.
   c. Theoretically, you can simultaneously be calm and tense.
   d. These dimensions were identified to help explain why we have mixed emotions.

10. According to research on mood-as-information hypothesis, how will you respond to the question "How much do you like the town where you live?"
    a. If I'm in a good mood, I will probably say that I like it quite a bit.
    b. If I'm in a bad mood, I will probably say that I like it quite a bit.
    c. If I'm in a good mood, I'll be motivated to lie about how much I like it.
    d. If I'm in a bad mood, I'll be motivated to lie about how much I like it.

11. It is the middle of the night. You hear a loud banging noise, then your heart starts racing. You become very scared. In this scenario, your arousal preceded emotion and was the cause of it. Which of the following theories of emotion best accounts for this pattern?
    a. Cannon–Bard theory of emotion
    b. Schachter–Singer theory of emotion
    c. James–Lange theory of emotion
    d. Appraisal theories of emotion

12. A team of researchers evaluated over 150 brain-imaging studies to come to some conclusions about what brain structures are involved in emotion. What did they find?
    a. Complex emotional experience is produced entirely by the limbic system.
    b. Complex emotional experience is produced entirely by the cortex.
    c. Complex emotional experience is produced entirely by the thalamus.
    d. Complex emotional experience is produced by several interconnected structures within the limbic system and cortex.

13. We experience subjective stress when we judge that situational demands outweigh our resources, which means that two people can experience the same situation, yet experience different levels of stress. Which contemporary theory of emotion best accounts for this difference?
    a. Cannon–Bard theory of emotion
    b. Schachter–Singer theory of emotion
    c. James–Lange theory of emotion
    d. Appraisal theories of emotion

14. The body regulates the stress response via activity in the hypothalamic–pituitary–adrenal (HPA) axis. What is the final step in this process?
    a. ACTH is carried by the bloodstream to the adrenal glands.
    b. ACTH causes the adrenal glands to release cortisol into the bloodstream.
    c. The hypothalamus releases corticotropin-releasing hormone (CRH) into a duct that leads to the pituitary gland.
    d. The pituitary gland releases adrenocorticotropic hormone (ACTH).

15. Which of the following is true of successful coping?
    a. Emotion-focused strategies are typically the most advantageous.
    b. Adjusting coping strategies to meet situational demands is most advantageous.
    c. Problem-focused strategies are typically the most advantageous.
    d. The tend-and-befriend strategy is typically the most advantageous.

Answers

You can check your answers to the preceding Self-Test and the chapter's What Do You Know? questions in Appendix B.

Motivation

11

DO YOU EVER FEEL UNMOTIVATED? YOU MIGHT know that you should be getting more exercise—running, lifting weights, riding a bike—yet you struggle to get yourself off the couch. Some little excuse always gets in the way: It's raining; I'm tired; the second-to-last episode of my third-favorite TV show is on.

If this describes you, you're not alone. Many people have trouble motivating themselves. But not everybody. One day in 2002, a 24-year-old man in Ghana, Emmanuel Ofusu Yeboah, got off his couch, climbed on a bicycle, and motivated himself to bike *across his country*. "I am giving all my effort to this," Mr. Yeboah said. "I don't want to give up. I don't want to give up" (Associated Press, 2005).

His trip took months, but he finished it—and then made *another* trip, flying more than 7500 miles to San Diego, California, to compete in the biking portion of a triathlon.

Mr. Yeboah motivated himself into action despite obstacles that, to others, might have been excuses for inaction:

> Childhood presented the first obstacle to bike riding: His family couldn't afford a bike. The first time he was able to ride one was by taking some change his mother had given him for lunch and spending it on a bike rental instead.

> > In adulthood, Mr. Yeboah still couldn't afford a bike; his job as a shoe shiner gave him little spare income. The bike he rode across Ghana was donated by a charitable organization.

> > The same charitable organization also supported Mr. Yeboah's trip to San Diego. Yet the trip still wasn't easy: When he arrived, on his first trip outside of Ghana, he had with him only three dollars.

But these obstacles were the small ones. The big one? Mr. Yeboah could only pedal his bike with *one leg*! His right leg had been deformed from birth—so severely, in fact, that, in childhood, his mother had to carry him back and forth to school every day.

Mr. Yeboah's motivation was deeply rooted. He knew that, in Ghana, physically challenged people like himself were treated poorly; they were seen as incapable of contributing positively to society. "I want," he explained, "to show everyone that physically challenged people can do something" (Coffey, 2005).

Tim Mantoani, Challenged Athletes Foundation®

Gallery Stock

This he did. Mr. Yeboah's ability to overcome challenges made him a hero in his nation. Rather than basking in personal glory, though, he next directed his efforts to helping others. In Ghana, he established athletic training facilities that are open to all people, and he worked with government officials to improve the civil rights and personal opportunities of physically challenged individuals.

What were the sources of Mr. Yeboah's motivation? A deeply felt need to improve the welfare of others. Concrete goals and a determination to reach them. And this belief: "There's something always I believe myself," Yeboah said, "that I can do it, I can do it" (ABC News, 2005).

We explore these sources of motivation in the chapter ahead. ◉

LET'S BEGIN THIS chapter by assessing the field of psychology. From what you've learned so far, do you think psychology is succeeding? Providing scientific explanations of what you would want a science of psychology to explain? Or is it falling short?

One well-known criticism of the field is that psychologists often leave their subject "lost in thought." They devote so much time to inner mental life—memory, thinking, feeling, problem solving—that, if you didn't know better, you would think their subject matter, people, spent most of their time sitting around in quiet contemplation.

But you do know better. When you observe people, they usually are not just thinking and feeling, but *doing*. They are at work or play, studying, exercising, talking, driving, reading, or updating their Facebook pages. People are in action. They are motivated. **Motivation** refers to the psychological and biological processes that impel people, and other organisms, into action and sustain their efforts over time. This chapter introduces you to the psychology of motivation.

The Variety of Motives

Preview Question

> What did Maslow mean when saying that the needs that motivate human behavior form a hierarchy?

In the psychology of motivation, the first question to ask is a hard one: "What motivates behavior?" The difficulty is that there are so many potential answers. People are motivated to make money, to make peace; to rise in status, to rise to heaven; to feel good about themselves, to make others feel good—or bad—about themselves. How can we bring order to the diversity of motives?

One psychologist who provided order was Abraham Maslow. He organized the diversity of human motives according to five basic needs that form a hierarchy, known as **Maslow's hierarchy of needs** (Maslow, 1943, 1954; Figure 11.1). A need is a necessity of life that an organism is motivated to pursue. *Hierarchy* means that the needs are at different levels and you have to fulfill one level before you can move up to the next.

At the lowest level of Maslow's hierarchy are needs for *biological survival,* such as food, water, and sleep. If unmet, these needs become overwhelming. When your stomach grumbles or your eyelids droop, it's not time to make friends or money; it's time to eat or sleep.

Next are *safety* needs, that is, needs for protection against physical harm. These include harms that may be staring you in the face (e.g., a predator) and those you anticipate in the future (e.g., potentially losing a job and thus being unable to pay your rent).

The third need is evident from the 200 million tweets that Twitter users send every day or the more than $50 billion that Facebook Inc. is worth. People need to feel

Man lives by bread alone—when there is no bread.

—Maslow (1943)

motivation The psychological and biological processes that impel people, and other organisms, into action and sustain their efforts over time.

Maslow's hierarchy of needs A classification of human motives according to five basic needs, with lower-level needs requiring fulfillment before moving up to higher levels.

Self-Actualization → Fulfillment through engagement in challenging, innovative, creative projects

Ego/Esteem → Tackling important projects that bring prestige, status, and recognition from others

Social/Belonging → Being accepted by members of a group and identifying with groups that succeed

Safety/Security → Freedom from physical or economic threats to safety and security

Physiological → Basic bodily needs, such as the need for food, water, and sleep

figure 11.1

Maslow's hierarchy of needs Abraham Maslow theorized that five basic needs (those in the triangle) motivate human behavior. In his theory, they exist in a hierarchy. If needs at one level (e.g., safety/security) are unfulfilled, you can't be motivated to pursue a higher level (e.g., the social need for belonging).

connected to others. They have *social belonging* needs—to be in contact and establish relationships with members of their society and to belong to social groups.

Fourth, people need to be not only members of a group, but also *valued* members. People have an *esteem* need, according to Maslow; that is, a need to be well regarded by others.

Finally, at the highest level is a *self-actualization* need. **Self-actualization** is realizing one's inner potential. Even successful professionals might feel they are in the wrong profession; for example, a successful lawyer might have always felt that her true calling was to be a successful artist. If so, they will feel unfulfilled. People need to "be true to their own nature" (Maslow, 1970, p. 22). To learn about this need, Maslow studied people who fulfilled it: self-actualized persons. He found that—contrary to what the word "self" may suggest—they often were concerned with the welfare of others, taking strong stands on moral and ethical issues that promoted others' well-being.

How close are you to self-actualization? Are you realizing your inner potential?

Pixellover RM 9 / Alamy

Social networking Why do people spend so much time on social networks? The psychologist Abraham Maslow would say that it reflects a universal human need for social belonging.

Fotosearch / Getty Images

Self-actualization Maslow proposed that some people are motivated primarily by self-actualization—a desire to realize one's inner potential—and that the self-actualization need motivates ethical behavior that improves the welfare of others. Maslow cited, as an example, Eleanor Roosevelt, shown here in her role as chairperson of the United Nations Commission on Human Rights. An in-depth study of her personality (Piechowski & Tyska, 1982) found that she had many self-actualizing traits: a concern with personal growth rather than the attainment of honors and awards; a focus on large-scale problems of humanity rather than small personal concerns; and a high standard for moral and ethical behavior.

self-actualization A motivation to realize one's inner potential.

THINK ABOUT IT

Maslow's hierarchy of needs may accurately describe many people; individuals often need to satisfy basic biological needs before moving to higher motivational levels. But does it describe *all* people? What about South Asian *sādhus*, Hindu holy men and women who choose to live in poverty, outside of mainstream society, while seeking spiritual enlightenment? Are they pursuing high-level needs while leaving lower-level needs in the hierarchy unfulfilled?

Maslow formulated his theory decades ago. In the years since, researchers have recognized its limitations. Some note a lack of research support for the idea that the needs form a strict hierarchy (Wahba & Bridgewell, 1976). Others suggest that Maslow paid insufficient attention to the role of cultural factors in shaping needs and their pursuit (Smith & Feigenbaum, 2013). Nonetheless, Maslow valuably reminds us of the breadth of topics that must be included in a psychology of motivation. In the remainder of this chapter, we'll organize them as follows.

The first three sections explore *biological needs, achievement needs,* and *social needs.* We then turn to motivation and thinking processes, in a section on *cognition and motivation.* Next, you'll learn about motivation in groups, including schools and work settings. Finally, we'll move down a level of explanation: from motivational processes of the mind to their biological underpinnings in the brain.

🔥 WHAT DO YOU KNOW?...

1. The following statement is incorrect. Explain why: "Research indicates that the hierarchy of needs Maslow proposed we all possess is a strict hierarchy—that is, we all attempt to fulfill needs in the particular order he specified."

See Appendix B for answers to What Do You Know? questions.

Biological Needs and Motivation

All organisms must meet **biological needs.** They need, at minimum, to survive and to reproduce. You already are familiar with the relevant biological mechanisms. Organisms meet survival needs by transferring material between themselves and the environment, bringing in environmental nutrients (food, drink) and excreting bodily waste. Most complex species meet reproduction needs by transferring material *between* two organisms: a male and female engaging in sex, with sperm and egg uniting and developing into an embryo.

That is the biology. Here, we are interested in the psychology; we need to identify the psychological processes that *motivate* organisms to meet these biological needs. We'll do so starting with the need for food, the behavior of eating, and the psychological experience of hunger.

Hunger and Eating

Preview Question
› Does hunger alone motivate us to eat?
› What characterizes eating disorders? What causes them?

What motivates an organism to eat? Part of the answer is **hunger,** a feeling of food deprivation that motivates organisms to seek food. The psychological experience of hunger is created by biological systems in the body and brain. When the body needs nutrients, biochemicals circulating throughout the body signal a brain structure known as the *hypothalamus* (see Chapter 3). The hypothalamus, in turn, sends out biochemical signals that create the experience of hunger (Goldstone, 2006). When we have eaten enough, the hypothalamus sends signals that result in **satiety,** a feeling of having enough food, or being "full."

> How soon after you experience satiety do you typically stop eating?

---

biological needs Necessities required for an organism's survival (food, drink) and for reproduction.

hunger A feeling of food deprivation that motivates organisms to seek food.

satiety A feeling of having eaten enough food, or being "full."

It sounds simple: When the body needs nutrients, we experience hunger and eat; when we have enough nutrients, we experience satiety and stop. But, as often occurs with simple stories in psychological science, the story is *too* simple. The true story of eating and hunger is more complex, both psychologically and biologically (Berridge, 2004). One main complication is that there is not one, but two types of hunger (Lowe & Butryn, 2007): *homeostatic hunger* and *hedonic hunger.*

HOMEOSTASIS. *Homeostasis* is the maintenance of a stable state. **Homeostatic processes,** then, are processes that maintain stability. For example, a thermostat maintains stable room temperature by detecting current temperature and activating heating or air conditioning systems when that temperature deviates from a desired temperature.

Homeostatic hunger is a motivation to eat that is based on the body's need for energy (Lowe & Butryn, 2007). If you go for a long time without food, your body, as noted above, detects the lack of energy and produces feelings of hunger that motivate you to eat. The eating maintains *energy homeostasis,* that is, a stable supply of bodily energy (Woods et al., 2000). According to **set-point theories** of hunger and eating (see Pinel, Assanand, & Lehman, 2000), homeostatic processes control food consumption. People are motivated to eat when their energy supplies fall below their *set point,* the level that the body naturally tries to maintain. They stop eating when energy needs are met.

However, set-point theories are only part of the story; they do not fully explain when and why people eat (Pinel et al., 2000; Stroebe, Papies, & Aarts, 2008). If you think about it, you can probably figure out their limitation. Consider two examples:

1. Have you ever had a big meal in a restaurant—perhaps the double cheeseburger or the spaghetti and meatballs—and then ordered a dessert? And then eaten it? That behavior raises problems for a set-point analysis. Having finished the main course, you couldn't have been experiencing homeostatic hunger; the meal provided plenty of calories. Yet, contrary to what set-point theory would predict, you were motivated to eat dessert.

"How many salads do I have to eat before I can get dessert?"

© Donna Barstow 2011

Thomas Northcut / Getty Images

Homeostasis A thermostat is a part of a homeostatic system; the system seeks to maintain a stable temperature. Some motivational processes are homeostatic, such as *homeostatic hunger,* which motivates eating to maintain a stable supply of bodily energy.

DreamPictures / Getty Images

Dessert looks good! After dinner, your body doesn't need more calories. But you still might order dessert due to *hedonic hunger,* eating for the pleasure of eating.

homeostatic processes Processes that maintain a stable biological state in an organism.

homeostatic hunger Motivation to eat based on the body's need for energy.

set-point theories Theoretical explanations of hunger and eating which propose that homeostatic processes control food consumption, with people being motivated to eat (or not) when their energy supplies fall below (or above) their set point.

2. Have you ever been so busy—working the holiday rush in a store, finishing a paper due the next morning—that you forgot to eat? People commonly report being so busy that they didn't even notice any hunger pangs (Herman, Fitzgerald, & Polivy, 2003). Again, this violates the assumptions of set-point theory. When busy, people burn up more energy than usual, which should put them below their set point. Yet they still might forget to eat.

HEDONISM. There is a second motive to eat, and it's simple: Food tastes good. Even when people do not need more calories, they are motivated to eat because eating high-quality food is pleasurable. **Hedonic hunger** arises from the anticipated pleasure of eating good food (Lowe & Butryn, 2007). When it looks good, you'll order dessert—even if the last thing you need is more calories.

From an evolutionary perspective, hedonic hunger makes a lot of sense (Pinel et al., 2000). Consider the distant evolutionary past, when all humans hunted animals and foraged for edible foods. The food supply was unpredictable. Eating only when homeostatically hungry—that is, when nutrition was needed immediately—would

have been risky. At the moment nutrition was needed, there might not have been any food available, or an injury might have prevented hunting and gathering. It thus made sense for organisms to eat lots of food whenever it was available. Their bodies could store extra calories as fat, which could fuel the body if food supplies ran short later on. Organisms that were motivated to eat good-tasting food even when they did not need the calories were therefore more likely to survive and reproduce. We all inherit that motivational tendency today.

Evidence that factors beyond homeostasis motivate eating comes from a study of two patients with amnesia (Rozin et al., 1998). On each of a series of days, researchers offered them lunch, engaged them in conversation, offered them lunch again, engaged them in conversation again, and then offered them a third lunch. Being amnesic, they did not remember having already eaten when the subsequent lunches were offered. If eating were controlled by homeostatic signals, signals of satiety would have caused them to refuse the second and third lunches. But, instead, they ate again! On most days, the patients consumed most of the second lunch and much of the third (Rozin et al., 1998).

Although the hedonistic "eat tasty food whenever available" strategy might have been good in the distant past, today it has drawbacks. In contemporary industrialized societies, most people can readily access food. Wherever you are right now, you probably have eaten recently (i.e., within the past few hours) and are near a food source (refrigerator, supermarket, restaurant, vending machine). The evolved tendency to stock up on food, combined with a plentiful supply of tasty foods in the contemporary world's "food-rich environments" (Stroebe, Papies, & Aarts, 2008, p. 172), contributes to high rates of obesity in industrialized societies.

EATING DISORDERS. The two types of hunger—homeostatic and hedonic—are so motivating that many people find it difficult to control the urge to eat. A small subset of people, however, face challenges beyond the ordinary. These are people with **eating disorders:** disturbances in eating in which people lose the ability to control their intake of food and, as a result, experience serious health risks (National Institute of Mental Health, 2011).

hedonic hunger Hunger that arises from the anticipated pleasure of eating good food.

eating disorders Disturbances in eating in which people lose the ability to control their intake of food, resulting in serious health risks.

There are three types of eating disorders: *anorexia nervosa, bulimia nervosa,* and *binge eating disorder* (Heaner & Walsh, 2013; National Institute of Mental Health, 2011).

1. People with **anorexia nervosa** are so fearful of being fat that they starve themselves; they severely restrict their intake of food in order to attain thinness. The restrictions can be so severe that they create physical problems such as bone thinning and a loss of muscle mass. Despite being objectively thin, people with anorexia nervosa often see themselves as overweight and are dissatisfied with their bodies (Cash & Deagle, 1997).

2. People with **bulimia nervosa** exhibit a pattern of eating that fluctuates dramatically. They binge and then purge; that is, they eat uncontrollably large amounts of food (binging) and then try to avoid weight gain by getting rid of it (purging), often through self-induced vomiting. Bulimia's binge–purge cycle creates numerous medical problems, including dehydration, tooth decay (from repeated exposure to stomach acids), and disruptions of the body's internal chemistry (National Institute of Mental Health, 2011).

3. People with **binge eating disorder** repeatedly eat excessively large amounts of food, as is seen in bulimia nervosa. But, unlike people with bulimia, those with binge eating disorder do not purge. The binge eating pattern thus causes obesity.

When eating disorders strike, they usually begin in the teenage years or early adulthood. Surveys suggest that 0.5 to 1% of people experience anorexia or bulimia and that rates of binge eating disorder are about twice as high (Kessler et al., 2013; Preti et al., 2009). The disorders are much more common among women than men.

What causes eating disorders? In particular, why do some people take dramatic measures (e.g., starving themselves, purging) to reduce their intake of calories? There are a number of possible reasons. One is social. Society surrounds people—women, especially—with idealized images of thinness. Flip open a magazine, and you are sure to find ads that tell you, either explicitly or subtly, that thinness is preferred. The social pressure for thinness can become so great that it overpowers the motive to avoid hunger. The finding that eating disorders are more common in cultures that idealize thinness (Polivy & Herman, 2002) supports the idea that social and cultural factors are one important cause.

Another potential cause lies in the family environment. Parents who criticize their children's appearance and demand that they be thin may contribute to the development of eating disorders (Polivy & Herman, 2002). However, when eating disorders occur, parents are not necessarily to blame. Researchers emphasize that parenting is only one of a large number of factors that can contribute to eating disorders and that no one parenting style is strongly linked to their occurrence (Le Grange et al., 2010).

Finally, a psychological factor that can contribute to the development of eating disorders is perfectionism, that is, a general tendency to strive to fully meet high standards of excellence. The psychotherapist Hilde Bruch (1973) argued that many girls become obsessed with meeting other people's goals for them; they strive to be a "perfect child." Controlling one's eating can become a way of achieving this sense of perfection. Findings suggest that people who are more perfectionistic are more vulnerable to experiencing eating disorders (Bardone-Cone et al., 2007).

slimness keeps you in the swim

How many eyes on the ball! How many on pretty Miss Ryvita! No prizes for guessing the answer—a figure as slim and graceful as hers catches all eyes wherever it goes. Does yours do the same! No reason why not, for slimming is no problem at all, these days. Just three simple rules— trim down with amusing exercises, follow a diet, *and eat Ryvita from now on.* 1/1d for 22 crisp, crunchy pieces. Buy some today.

RYVITA makes you fit – keeps you slim

Jeff Morgan 09 / Alamy

"Slim" is the message For many years, media messages have promoted the idea that thinness is good. Such media messages may contribute to the occurrence of eating disorders.

○ ○
○
THINK ABOUT IT

Media images of thinness contribute to eating disorders. But do media influences fully explain why the disorders occur? Virtually everyone is exposed to images of thinness in ads, movies, and TV shows, yet only a small percentage of people experience eating disorders. There must therefore be other factors at play.

anorexia nervosa Eating disorder characterized by such a fear of being fat that people severely restrict their intake to the point of starvation.

bulimia nervosa Eating disorder characterized by a fluctuating pattern of binging and purging.

binge eating disorder A pattern of repeatedly eating excessively; binging without purging.

"This is who I am. And I am proud at any size."
That is what Lady Gaga told fans when launching the *Body Revolution 2013* page at her LittleMonsters Web site; it encourages people to be accepting of their bodies. Gaga, whose weight has fluctuated during her career, revealed that she has battled anorexia and bulimia since the age of 15.

🔥 WHAT DO YOU KNOW?...

2. Contrary to set-point theories of hunger, people don't always eat to maintain energy _____; rather, they often eat because they enjoy doing so, a phenomenon called _____ hunger. Of the three types of eating disorders described here, only _____ _____ is characterized by a restriction of food intake. The tendency to strive to meet high standards, known as _____, is a psychological factor that can contribute to eating disorders.

Sexual Desire

Preview Questions

› How does sexual motivation differ from the motivation to eat?
› What is the biological basis of sexual desire?

Sex, like hunger, is biologically basic. Humans and other animals desire, pursue, and enjoy sexual activity. The reason is obvious: In the evolutionary past, organisms who were motivated for sex out-reproduced those who were not. We thus inherit sexual motivation.

Although the motivations for both food and sex are biological basics, they differ in two main ways. First, unlike our need for food, we do not literally *need* sex. Without food, you die. Without sex, you could get by. Many celebrated historical figures have been celibate—sexually inactive for much or all of their lives. Science's greatest figure, Isaac Newton, was celibate, as was the Renaissance's greatest genius, Leonardo da Vinci, a homosexual who remained celibate to avoid detection (Abbott, 2000). Today, celibacy is a requirement for clergy in a number of the world's religions. A celibate life commonly has been prized; some cultures have made it a condition for holding a place of honor. Ancient Rome's Vestal Virgins were charged with keeping alight the central symbol of the Roman Empire: a perpetual fire that honored Vesta, goddess of home and family, and symbolized the empire's enduring strength. Keeping the fire burning wasn't difficult. But to get the job, one had to agree to remain celibate for 30 years (Zoch, 1998).

DIVERSITY IN SEXUAL DESIRE. A second way that sexual motivation differs from hunger is its diversity. Hunger motivates one type of behavior, the eating of food. But sexual motivation is diverse in four ways:

1. *Diversity of people toward whom sexual desires are directed.* Most adults are sexually attracted to members of the opposite sex; in one representative survey of young

adults, about 94% of men and 84% of women described themselves as "100% heterosexual" (Savin-Williams, Joyner, & Rieger, 2012). Those numbers, though large, are far from 100%; many people find members of their same sex to be sexually arousing. (Chapter 4 discusses biological and environmental factors that contribute to diversity in sexual orientation.)

An entirely different type of diversity is seen in cases of sexual deviance in which desires are directed toward nonhuman objects or nonconsenting individuals (Kafka, 2010). A particularly problematic form of sexual deviance is *pedophilia*, in which adult sexual motivations are directed toward children (Fagan et al., 2002).

2. *Diversity of stimuli that trigger sexual arousal.* The biological purpose of sex is reproduction, yet stimuli that have little or nothing to do with reproduction can trigger sexual arousal. Research on **fetishism,** sexual arousal in which stimuli that typically are not sexual in nature stir desires (Kafka, 2010), illustrates the point. A survey of Yahoo! discussion groups revealed 2938 groups whose publicly available information included the word "fetish" (Scorolli et al., 2007). Tens of thousands of group members were discussing their sexual attraction to stimuli such as body parts (e.g., feet, hair) and articles of clothing (stockings, shoes, boots, costumes).

3. *Diversity of activities motivated by sexual desires.* Sexual desires may motivate a diverse range of behaviors that are not inherently sexual. Sigmund Freud (1900) famously proposed that the human mind redirects sexual energy to nonsexual activities (also see Westen, 1999). According to Freud, when sexual activity is un-available or prohibited, the sexual energies build in pressure and must be released. A writer whose sexual energies are frustrated may redirect them into the writing of love poems. A painter or sculptor may use sexual energies to power the many hours of activity required to produce a great work of art.

4. *Diversity of reasons for having sex.* Why do people eat? To consume tasty foods. Why do people have sex? There's no shortage of reasons. Investigators who asked a large number of men and women why they have sex identified 237 reasons in the responses (Meston & Buss, 2007, 2009). In addition to obvious ones, such as the sensual pleasure of sexual activity, participants cited reasons such as relieving

Motives behind art? John the Baptist is said to have lived in the wilderness, where he survived by eating insects and wild honey. He traditionally is depicted as a gaunt individual surviving in a rugged environment, as in the image on the left. The Renaissance artist Leonardo da Vinci depicted him as on the right. Why? Sigmund Freud suggested that the motivation behind da Vinci's work was not primarily spiritual or artistic, but sexual. Da Vinci's homosexual sexual energies, Freud claimed, powered his art, resulting in a John the Baptist with soft features, flowing curly hair, and ambiguous sexuality.

fetishism Sexual arousal in which stimuli that typically are not sexual in nature stir desires.

boredom, punishing an unfaithful partner, attaining a job promotion, making someone jealous, improving a partner's emotional state, and (last but not least) expressing affection and love.

What accounts for the diversity of human sexuality? There are two "sides" to human sexual life (Tolman & Diamond, 2001). First is the biological side that we share with other species. Animals (including us) inherit biological mechanisms that impel sexual desire. Second, there is a social side. Unlike other animals, humans' sexual activities are suffused with social meaning: worries about your partner's enjoyment of the activity; concerns about your own attractiveness and performance; age-linked expectations for engaging in sex; social and moral prohibitions against doing so; media images that shape expectations and desires. Human sexual motivation, then, is much more than a simple expression of biological drives.

SEXUAL DESIRE AND HORMONES. Despite these social aspects of human sexuality, however, sexual motivation does have a core biological foundation: *hormones,* the chemical messengers that travel through the bloodstream and activate biological processes in the body (see Chapter 3). A hormone central to sexual life is **testosterone,** which is produced in the gonads—the testes of men and the ovaries of women.

Testosterone's role in sexual motivation is evident from studies that manipulate testosterone levels experimentally. This is done medically to treat *hypogonadism,* a condition in which the body produces too little testosterone. Among adult men, hypogonadism results in low levels of sexual motivation; additional symptoms include reduced facial hair growth and muscle mass. When testosterone is administered to people with hypogonadism, these symptoms reverse. In one study, patients received testosterone on a daily basis for six months. After 30 days, their sexual motivation increased. Men reported more frequent sexual daydreams, flirting, and sexual interactions (Wang et al., 2000). Similar results have been obtained among women reporting low levels of sexual desire. Compared with women in a placebo drug condition, those receiving daily doses of testosterone reported more sexual desire, as well as more arousal during sexual activities (Buster et al., 2005).

Just as you need gasoline to fuel a car, you need testosterone to fuel sexual motivation. Once you've got some gas in your car, though, varying levels of gas (a quarter tank, half a tank, etc.) do not make your engine more or less powerful. Similarly, once hormone levels are in a normal range, variations in testosterone are relatively unrelated to levels of sexual activity. Research with couples finds that although women's testosterone levels are correlated with their frequency of sexual experience, men's levels are unrelated to the couple's frequency and quality of sexual experiences. Sexual experiences reflect the quality of the couple's interpersonal relationship, not variations in hormone levels (Zitzmann & Nieschlag, 2001).

⚇ WHAT DO YOU KNOW?...

3. True or False?
   a. The diversity of human sexuality supports the idea that human sexual motivation is solely the product of biological drives.
   b. Research demonstrates that variations in men's testosterone levels are associated with variations in sexual activity.

Achievement Needs

Biological needs are compelling; they spur you into action. Other needs are compelling, too. Psychologists have long recognized that a wide variety of needs contribute to human motivation (Murray, 1938). Among these is the *need for achievement.*

testosterone Hormone that plays a role in motivating sexual desire in both men and women.

The Need to Achieve

Preview Question

> Is everyone equally motivated to achieve? How can we measure the need for achievement?

Have you ever put in extra practice to win a competition? Or "pulled an all-nighter" working on a school assignment because you wanted an A? If so, motivational psychologists would say you were displaying a **need for achievement:** a desire to succeed on challenging activities that require skilled, competent performance (Elliot & Sheldon, 1997; McClelland, 1985).

The human need for achievement is evident early in life. Consider young children. In principle, they could sit around passively, just staring into space. But in reality, they are active: knocking over cups, stacking blocks, and looking proud or frustrated as their efforts succeed or fail. Their need to develop skills and mastery over the environment—to achieve—drives them on (White, 1959). Later in life, this need powers the persistent efforts that so often are necessary for success.

The strength of the need for achievement varies from one person to the next. Some people are highly motivated to achieve, whereas others do not give achievement much thought. Researchers measure these individual differences indirectly (McClelland, 1985). In other words, rather than directly asking how motivated you are to achieve, they use tasks that subtly reveal people's personal motives.

How motivated to achieve are *you?*

In one commonly used indirect measure, the *Thematic Apperception Test* (*TAT*), people tell stories in response to ambiguous pictures (Figure 11.2). The pictures activate achievement needs in some people but not others, and story content reveals these individual differences. For instance, a TAT story filled with characters who strive for success would indicate that the storyteller has a high level of the achievement need. TAT measures of achievement motivation predict motivated behavior and professional success (McClelland, 1987); two meta-analyses confirm the positive correlation between TAT measures of motivation and performance outcomes, including professional career success (Collins, Hanges, & Locke, 2004; Spangler, 1992). Indirect measures of the need for achievement such as the TAT often reveal individual differences in motivation that are not detected when researchers simply ask people how motivated they are (McClelland, Koestner, & Weinberger, 1989).

Jose Luis Pelaez Inc. / Getty Images

She can do it! Even at a young age, children display a need to develop competence and achieve success.

Science Source

figure **11.2**

Measuring motives Motivation researchers assess the strength of motives by asking people to tell stories about pictures, such as the one shown here. If a story contains achievement-related themes (e.g., discussion of these characters' desires to prepare an excellent meal, or one character's goal of excelling in comparison to the other), it reveals that the storyteller has strong achievement needs.

need for achievement A desire to succeed on challenging activities requiring skilled, competent performance.

4. A friend tells you, "Story-based measures such as the Thematic Appercep-tion Test are an ineffective way to measure the need for achievement." What can you say to refute this? *Hint:* Do these measures predict any outcomes?

The Need to Avoid Failure

Preview Question

> What kind of person is most likely to seek out challenges?

The need to achieve is not the only motivational force that influences people's perfor-mance. The **need to avoid failure** is a desire to avoid situations in which you might fail due to a lack of competence. The two needs—to achieve success and to avoid failure—combine to influence behavior. Classic research shows how this works.

In this study (Atkinson & Litwin, 1960), researchers mea-sured both needs in a population of college students (Fig-ure 11.3). Two groups of students—(1) people high in the need to achieve and low in the need to avoid failure, and (2) people low in the need to achieve and high in the need to avoid failure—were asked to play a game in which they tried to toss a 10-inch-diameter ring over a wooden peg. They could decide where to stand when throwing the ring: very close, where there was little chance of missing; very far, where there was little chance of getting the ring over the peg; or at a middle distance (8 to 10 feet from the peg), where there was about a 50-50 chance of getting the ring over the peg.

Although the game and the instructions were the same for everyone, people approached the task differently. Those high in need for achievement and low in need to avoid failure looked for a challenge: They made most of their throws from the middle distance, where a particularly skillful toss could succeed. The other group—people low in need for achievement and high in the need to avoid failure—*avoided* challenge: They made most throws from either very close to the peg (where they couldn't miss) or very far away (where no one could be expected to succeed; a lack of success, from that distance, thus would not be seen as a personal failure).

The point of the study is not, of course, that achievement motives influence choices on games. People often choose among varying amounts of risk, such as when choosing a profession to pursue or deciding how to invest money. Achievement needs may affect behavior on a wide variety of activities in which success requires taking chances and exercising your highest level of skill (McClelland, 1985).

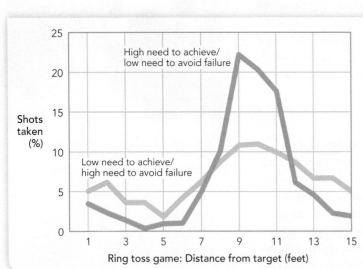

figure 11.3
Need for achievement People differ in achievement needs. Research shows that these differences affect their approach to challenges (Atkinson & Litwin, 1960). When playing a ring toss game and given the choice of how far away from the target to stand, people high in the need for achievement and low in the need to avoid failure looked for a challenge: They often stood moderately far from the target, a distance from which a skillful toss could succeed. People low in the need for achievement and high in the need to avoid failure, by contrast, *avoided* challenge. They often stood either very close to the target or so far away from it that no one would expect them to succeed.

5. a. People low in the need for achievement and high in the need to avoid failure chose either a close or a very far distance for the peg toss game. Why did both of these choices represent the avoidance of challenge?
   b. People high in the need to achieve and low in the need to avoid failure chose a middle distance for the peg toss game. Why did this represent a choice for challenge?

need to avoid failure A desire to avoid situations in which lack of competence might lead to failure.

Social Needs

Biological needs serve the body. Achievement needs fuel activity on challenging physical, intellectual, and professional tasks. But people live in a social world. Thus, they also are motivated by **social needs,** that is, desires that motivate us to interact with others and to achieve a meaningful role in society.

You often can feel your own social needs. You might be sitting at home, perfectly safe, snacks in the refrigerator, after a week of work. Your biological needs are met. Your work achievements are complete. Yet you want more. You want to hang out with your friends; to see a movie; to start a new relationship; to be involved in your community. These are your social needs.

Many psychologists have, over the years, tried to develop a comprehensive list of social needs (e.g., Murray, 1938). The job is difficult, especially because the needs that people experience may vary from culture to culture. Despite these difficulties, many contemporary psychologists (e.g., Fiske, 2009; Ryan & Deci, 2000) judge that five social needs are universally important to human motivation: needs for (1) belonging, (2) understanding, (3) mastery and control, (4) enhancing the self, and (5) trusting. (These needs overlap somewhat with the ones proposed by Maslow, discussed earlier. However, unlike Maslow, most contemporary psychologists do not think that the needs are arranged in a fixed hierarchy.)

Belonging

Preview Question

> Does everyone feel the need to belong?

"No man is an island." The poet John Donne's sentence is one of the most famous phrases in English literature, and for good reason. Donne captured an essential fact of human life: Psychologically, people need to live among others. Loneliness can be unbearable. A social **need for belonging** motivates people to spend time with other individuals and to become part of social groups.

Research suggests that this need is universal. People in all societies and cultures experience the need for belonging. To fulfill this need, people the world over form enduring social relationships and try to maintain the relationships they have established (Baumeister & Leary, 1995).

The need for belonging is so powerful that failing to fulfill it is painful—literally. When people become *dis*connected from others—for example, when a relationship breaks up—they often describe the experience using words that describe physical pain: The breakup "hurt," "broke my heart," "was emotionally scarring," and so forth. One reason for the choice of words is that the pain of the breakup is literal pain; that is, the bodily systems active during physical pain are the same ones that are active during "painful" social experiences (MacDonald & Leary, 2005). Brain research reveals this. Participants were exposed to either physical pain (a hot stimulus on their forearm) or social pain (looking at a picture of a former partner who had rejected them) while researchers obtained images of brain activation. The different types of painful experience activated the same brain regions (Kross et al., 2011). Rejection—a failure to fulfill the need to belong—thus is truly painful.

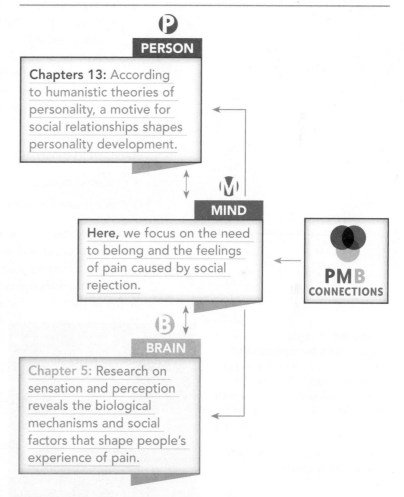

CONNECTING TO SENSATION AND PERCEPTION AND TO PERSONALITY DEVELOPMENT

P PERSON

Chapters 13: According to humanistic theories of personality, a motive for social relationships shapes personality development.

M MIND

Here, we focus on the need to belong and the feelings of pain caused by social rejection.

PMB CONNECTIONS

B BRAIN

Chapter 5: Research on sensation and perception reveals the biological mechanisms and social factors that shape people's experience of pain.

What have you done recently to maintain any of your social relationships?

social needs Desires that motivate people to interact with others and to achieve a meaningful role in society.

need for belonging A social need that motivates people to spend time with others and to become part of social groups.

Many argue that our contemporary need to belong is rooted in our evolutionary past. Tens of thousands of years ago, early humans faced harsh living conditions, such as ice ages that threatened the species' survival. To cope, people banded together into groups. Rather than living as isolated individuals or small families, they formed larger units that, through group efforts, were better able to battle the elements (Morris, 2010). A desire to belong to such groups was therefore an evolutionary advantage. People who felt a need to belong benefited from the advantages of group living. Individuals who were *not* motivated to live in social groups missed out on these benefits, and thus were less likely to survive. Thanks to evolution through natural selection, then, we contemporary humans inherit a need to belong (Hogan, 1983).

☙ WHAT DO YOU KNOW?...

6. For each of the "answers" below, provide the question. The first one is done for you.
   a. Answer: Poet John Donne's famous quotation about human social needs.
      Question: What is "No man is an island"?
   b. Answer: A social desire or motivation that in our evolutionary past would have better enabled us to battle the elements by engaging in group living.
   c. Answer: The brain regions activated during social pain—such as after a breakup—are also active during this experience.

Understanding

Preview Question

› Are we satisfied with a vague understanding of events?

A second social need is a **need for understanding,** that is, a motive to comprehend why events occur and to predict what the future might bring.

If you reflect on your own thoughts, you'll quickly recognize this need in yourself. What sorts of thoughts tend to run through your head? If you're like most people, many of them are efforts at understanding. Suppose a friend cancels plans to get together. You want to understand why. If your parents say they want to visit you next weekend, you want to understand why. We're like detectives: When things happen, we put together clues, think about other people's thoughts, and try to find out what causes the events of our lives.

The need for understanding is a social need in that we rely on others for knowledge. We gain information and figure out the meanings of events by interacting with other people in person and electronically (Kruglanski et al., 2006). In fact, one of the major topics explored in social psychology (see Chapter 12) is a form of thinking fueled by the need for understanding: *attributions,* or thoughts about the causes of people's social behavior.

People often seek a particular type of understanding. They want to achieve not merely a vague grasp of events, but *cognitive closure:* a firm, definitive understanding grounded in information that resolves ambiguities and eliminates confusions about events (Kruglanski & Webster, 1996). Although some people are more bothered by uncertainty than others, people generally prefer to reach closure on issues, that is, to resolve puzzles, get missing information, and gain a firm understanding of the world around them.

Why are people so fascinated by detectives? Their professional work is like our intuitive "work": Our need for understanding drives us to search for clues, look for motives, and figure out "who done it" and why. Pictured is Robert Downey Jr. as Sherlock Holmes, in the 2009 movie of the same title.

Warner Bros. / Photofest

need for understanding A social need to comprehend why events occur and to predict what the future might bring.

Control

Preview Question

> How do we benefit from having control over outcomes?

Who should decide what clothes you wear, how long your hair is, and who your friends are? Most people would say "*I should.*" You may not mind if others offer some opinions, but *you* want to be the final decision maker. People have a *need for control*.

The **need for control** is a desire to select one's life activities and to have the capacity to influence environmental events (Leotti, Iyengar, & Ochsner, 2010). Some suggest that two distinct needs are at play in the overall need for control: (1) a need for *autonomy,* that is, a need to direct and organize one's own activities so they are consistent with one's inner sense of self (Ryan & Deci, 2000); and (2) a need for *mastery,* that is, to be competent and able to influence events.

You may have felt your own need for autonomy in school. Did you ever have a teacher who issued a lot of commands, set a lot of deadlines, and thus gave students little choice in what to do, and how and when to do it? Teachers who reduce students' autonomy in this way may lower motivation. Students are found to be more interested in school material when they have more choices and options—more autonomy—in the classroom (Tsai et al., 2008).

The need for mastery is evident in many areas of life. One is coping with health problems. Studies of cancer patients, for example, reveal that after receiving their diagnosis, people differ in how they respond psychologically. Those who respond with strong feelings of mastery—feeling that they can overcome their illness by working closely with their physician—are better able to battle the disease (Taylor, 1983). For instance, in a study of patients whose cancer had reached an advanced stage, those who believed they still could influence their health outcomes reported less pain and less fatigue during treatment (Kurtz et al., 2008).

> Think about an upcoming exam. To what extent do you feel you have mastery over its outcome?

Conversely, a lack of control can reduce well-being. People who feel that they can't control life events are prone to *learned helplessness,* a psychological state in which they give up trying and become depressed (Seligman, 1975; see also Chapter 7, which discusses learned helplessness in greater detail).

"I will survive." Feelings of optimism and personal strength can benefit cancer patients as they battle their illness.

Cass Green / Getty Images

Enhancing the Self

Preview Question

> What kinds of behaviors are explained by the need to enhance the self?

A fourth social need is the **need to enhance the self,** that is, to grow as a person, to develop a life that is psychologically meaningful and potentially beneficial to others, and to realize your true potential. Personality theorists such as Carl Rogers

---

need for control A desire to select one's life activities and to be able to influence events.

need to enhance the self A social need to grow as a person, to live a meaningful life, and to realize your true potential.

Why spend a fortune making this window? Some motivation psychologists suggest that the construction of great cathedrals was motivated by needs for personal understanding and self-actualization. To Carl Jung, the cathedrals' circular windows symbolized people's motivation to attain a stable, "centered" understanding of self.

(see Chapter 13) and, as you saw earlier, the motivation theorist Abraham Maslow referred to this need as a motive for self-actualization.

The desire to enhance, or actualize, the self explains behavior that otherwise would be puzzling. Consider the effort that billions of people, throughout world history, have invested in religious practices. In medieval Europe, for example, most citizens lived in relative poverty, yet societies spent hundreds of millions of dollars (in contemporary currency) building each of Europe's great cathedrals (Scott, 2003). If people were driven solely by biological needs, this behavior would be inexplicable; you'd expect societies to expend money exclusively on food and shelter. The psychologist Carl Jung suggested, however, that people's desire to understand themselves and their place in the universe motivated these vast, costly efforts (Jung, 1964). In the contemporary world, people's personal goals in life frequently include aims that are directly or indirectly related to spiritualism (e.g., "live my life at all times for God," "approach life with mystery and awe"; Emmons, 2005, p. 736). Spiritual goals, Robert Emmons (2005) suggests, provide a sense of meaning in life, and thus contribute to an integrated, coherent sense of self.

Needs to enhance the self can be a source of motivation that benefits others. People can attain meaning in their own life by contributing to others' welfare—including others who will make up future generations (Erikson, 1963). Our opening story about the achievements of Emmanuel Ofusu Yeboah illustrates the motivational power of concern for others; Mr. Yeboah was motivated to improve the welfare of other Ghanaians who faced physical challenges. Although Mr. Yeboah's achievements are extraordinary, this source of motivation is relatively common. Psychologist Dan McAdams finds that, when people discuss their lives, their stories often contain a commitment to improving the lives of future generations (McAdams & de St. Aubin, 1992). Teachers helping their students grow, or environmentalists helping our planet do the same, attain a more meaningful sense of self by benefiting humanity's future.

🕊 WHAT DO YOU KNOW?...

9. You learned that engaging in religious practices and helping others are examples of self-actualization. What would make training for a marathon another example?

Trust

Preview Questions

> What are everyday examples of our uniquely human need for trust?
> What is the biological basis of trust?

A fifth social need is trust. Many psychologists argue that people have a basic need to trust in their fellow humans beings (Fiske, 2009; Kosfeld et al., 2005).

IN STRANGERS WE TRUST. At first, the idea that trust is a universal need might sound puzzling. When a car salesman says he has "a great deal" for you or a dating partner says he has a "good excuse" for showing up an hour late, you feel suspicion rather than trust. Nonetheless, much of everyday social life does rest on trust. If you go to a restaurant, you're served food before you pay: The owner trusts that you won't bolt out the door after downing his cuisine. If someone in a police uniform indicates where you should drive your car, you follow the instruction: You trust that it's a police officer, not someone who rented a uniform from a costume shop.

The economist Paul Seabright (2004) explains that the trust displayed by humans is unique in the animal kingdom. In other species, individuals exchange food only with others to whom they are genetically related. By contrast, humans exchange food and other value items with complete strangers. Grocery store workers hand you sacks of food; stores trust that your scribbled signature on a piece of paper will bring them money in exchange. You hand money over to bank tellers, trusting that they will keep it safe for you.

Human societies have advanced through social systems that rest on trust.

You give him your car, and you get a small piece of cardboard? Valet parking illustrates how social life rests on trust between strangers. Unlike other species, humans exchange food and other valued items with individuals to whom they are not genetically related, and whom they may not even know personally.

Juan Monino / Getty Images

> Who showed trust in you recently?

The need to convey a sense of trust may have contributed to the evolution of emotional reactions. Smiles and laughter indicate that people are not a threat; genuine expressions of positive emotion indicate that people are cooperative individuals who can be trusted. Smiles and laughter, then, may have evolved to promote human cooperation and trust (Owren & Bachorowski, 2003).

TRUST AND OXYTOCIN. Some research suggests that trust has a biochemical basis: oxytocin. **Oxytocin** is a hormone that is released into the body and the brain. One of its primary functions involves birth and the survival of children; oxytocin activates muscles necessary for childbirth and stimulates the release of milk for breastfeeding. In the brain, it may stimulate feelings of trust.

In research on oxytocin and trust (Kosfeld et al., 2005), participants played a game in which they were financial investors; they received money and, across a series of trials, chose how much to invest. To invest, they gave money to a second individual who had the power to decide, at a later point in time, how much money (the initial sum plus a portion of profit from investment) to return to the investor. The amount invested, then, revealed participants' level of trust in the other person. Before the game, researchers manipulated oxytocin levels. Participants received a nasal spray containing (a) oxytocin or (b) a placebo (i.e., no oxytocin).

Results indicated that oxytocin increased trust. Investors who received the oxytocin spray invested more money (i.e., displayed more trust) than those receiving the placebo spray (Kosfeld et al., 2005). The effects were substantial; more than twice as many people in the oxytocin condition made the maximum investment; they fully trusted the other individual.

The results suggest that oxytocin is like a "switch" that flips on a biological system that generates feelings of trust and good will. If true, the implications are significant; they suggest that people's behavior could be controlled—by investment professionals, sales persons, or others seeking their trust—merely by spraying some oxytocin. Recent results, however, have begun to provide a more nuanced understanding of the exact effects of oxytocin on motivation and behavior (see This Just In).

🐾 WHAT DO YOU KNOW?...

10. Humans' willingness to exchange food and other goods with those who are not _____ related indicates a universal need for trust. Experimental research indicates that the hormone _____ may stimulate feelings of trust.

oxytocin Hormone that activates muscles needed for childbirth and stimulates the release of breast milk; in the brain, it may stimulate feelings of trust.

Cover art Stephanie Gormory, Courtesy Pacific Standard Magazine, formerly Miller-McCune

Oxytocin and trust Some research suggests that oxytocin automatically produces feelings of trust. But recent findings complicate the picture.

THIS JUST IN

Oxytocin and Individual Differences

In the first decade of the twenty-first century, oxytocin went from obscurity to "stardom." Oxytocin-related Internet searches increased by 5000% from 2004 to 2011 (Bartz et al., 2011). Newspapers reported that oxytocin was a "love hormone" that could change your social life (Alleyne, 2010). The research on oxytocin and trust described in the main text triggered a wave of subsequent studies exploring its effect on emotion and motivation.

But when the results of this research came in, they weren't quite what people had expected. Nearly half the studies exploring oxytocin's effects on behaviors involving trust and helping showed *no* effect. More complex studies showed that oxytocin was influential in some settings but not others; for example, it increased trust toward people *unless* they appeared untrustworthy or were members of a threatening social group (Bartz et al., 2011). Why might oxytocin have variable effects on motivated behavior?

The key to answering this question is to rephrase it at a *person* level of analysis: Why do *people* react variably to oxytocin? This phrasing highlights a critical fact: People differ. They have different life experiences, skills, beliefs, and personal goals. They think differently about social situations and personal relationships. All these personal factors affect motivation. Thus, it is natural to expect that oxytocin (or any biochemical) might have different effects on different people in different situations.

One study shows that oxytocin's effects vary among people with varying levels of social skill (Bartz, Zaki, Bolger et al., 2010). Researchers first measured social skills, specifically, the skill of understanding other people's thoughts and feelings. Next, they showed participants a film in which an individual discussed emotional events. They then asked participants to estimate the person's feelings and measured the accuracy of the estimates. Before the film, the researchers gave half the participants a dose of oxytocin and gave the other half a placebo. Oxytocin did not have a uniform effect. Instead, it increased accuracy among people with very low social skills, but not among others.

Another study examined the effects of oxytocin on adults' recollections of their childhood interactions with their mothers. Rather than studying the average effects of oxytocin on people in general, the researchers explored an individual difference variable: people's levels of anxiety about close personal relationships. Oxytocin had different effects on different types of people. Among people low in anxiety about relationships, oxytocin created more positive recollections; people remembered their mother as a caring individual to whom they felt close. But among people high in anxiety, oxytocin created *less* positive recollections; they remembered their mothers as less caring and close (Bartz, Zaki, Ochsner et al., 2010).

Thus, in both studies there was no single effect of oxytocin; it was not a "love hormone" that filled everyone with fond memories and a deep understanding of others. Oxytocin's effects varied. The variability cautions us against presuming that any biochemical will affect all people in exactly the same way, all the time.

WHAT DO YOU KNOW?...

11. Which of the following statements correctly describe exceptions to the rule that oxytocin increases trust and other positive social outcomes? Check all that apply.

_____ a. It did not increase trust in people who seemed untrustworthy or were part of a threatening social group.

_____ b. It only increased the ability to understand others' thoughts and feelings among people who were low in social skills.

_____ c. It only increased the positivity of recollections about close personal relationships among people who were high in anxiety about those relationships.

TRY THIS!

Before you start reading the next section of this chapter, which is about motivation and thinking processes, or cognition, do something else first: Complete this chapter's Try This! activity. Motivate yourself to go to www.pmbpsychology.com and complete that activity for Chapter 11. ◉

Cognition and Motivation

The motivational forces we've covered so far—hunger, sexual desire, needs for mastery and autonomy—paint a portrait of human nature that is, in some respects, depressing. Motivation seems out of your control—an endless struggle to cope with biological and social needs that you never chose to have in the first place.

Things aren't quite so bad, though. The factors that affect motivation include thinking. People's thoughts about themselves and their activities can affect their motivation and success. This simple fact has major implications. Because thoughts are at least partly under your control, the influence of thinking on motivation gives you **personal agency:** the power to influence your own level of motivation, and thus your daily activities and the course of your life (Bandura, 2001).

Let's look at different types of thoughts that affect motivation and thereby power personal agency. We begin with *goals*.

Goals

Preview Questions

> What kinds of goals are most motivationally powerful?
> How important is feedback in motivation?
> What type of goals can impose organization on our lives?
> Can features of the environment activate goals that affect our behavior without our awareness?

"What do you want to do today?"

"I don't know, what do you want to do today?"

"I've got nothing planned; whatever you want to do."

These people aren't likely to be doing much today. They lack goals. In the psychology of motivation, a **goal** is a mental representation of the aim of an activity (Kruglanski et al., 2002). Goals are key to motivation (Locke & Latham, 1990).

CONCRETE, CHALLENGING GOALS. Not all goals are effective. People often have goals that they never seem to get started on. You might hear people say, "I know smoking is bad for me, and one day I'm gonna quit!" or "Someday I'm going to start knocking off some of this extra weight." And you might hear them say these same things month after month, year after year.

The problem with those goals is that they're so vague. When is "one day"? Exactly what does it mean to merely "start knocking off some" weight? If you want to motivate yourself, set goals that are *specific* and *challenging* (Locke & Latham, 1990):

> *Specificity:* Specific goals indicate exactly what you want to accomplish. For example, if you're trying to lose weight (Franz et al., 2007), don't aim for a vague goal such as "knocking off some weight." Set a specific one, such as "lose 5 pounds this month" or "count calories and reduce them to 2100 a day."

> We have an added layer on top of the bird's (and the ape's and the dolphin's) capacity to decide what to do next. . . . We can ask each other to do things, and we can ask ourselves to do things. . . . It is this kind of asking, which we can also direct to ourselves, that creates a special category of voluntary actions that sets us apart.
>
> —Daniel Dennett (2003, p. 251)

personal agency People's capacity to influence their motivation, behavior, and life outcomes by setting goals and developing skills.

goal A mental representation of the aim of an activity; more simply, goals are thoughts about future outcomes that people value.

The power of goal setting Goal setting is key to athletic success. Michael Johnson, the only athlete ever to win 200-meter-dash and 400-meter-dash gold medals in the same Olympics, attributes much of his success to the motivational effects of highly specific goals. "The importance of specificity can't be overstated. If I'd just set goals of running *well* in the 400 and the 200 . . . I might have settled for less" (Johnson, 1996, p. 13).

AP Photo / Doug Mills

What are your goals for today? Are they sufficiently challenging? Specific rather than vague?

› *Challenge:* If you want to motivate yourself, set goals that are challenging (while not being unrealistically difficult). People who set challenging goals (e.g., "I'm going to raise my GPA by 0.5 point this year") generally outperform those who set easier goals (e.g., "I'm going to raise my GPA by 0.1 point this year"; Locke & Latham, 1990).

PROXIMAL GOALS. Compare these two people, both preparing for a marathon in six months: (1) "I'm going to run 600 miles during the next six months"; (2) "I'm going to run 25 miles a week during the next six months." Both goals are specific. Both are challenging; in fact, they're equally challenging, since 25 miles a week equals 100 miles a month equals 600 miles in six months. Yet if you want to keep yourself motivated, Goal #2 is better than Goal #1.

Compared to Goal #1, Goal #2 is a **proximal goal,** one that specifies what you should do in the near ("proximal") future. Goal #1 is a **distal goal;** it specifies an achievement in the distant future. Distal goals can be discouraging. Before you get started, they seem so hard ("600 miles?!"). Once you do start, they still seem so far away ("I've been running for one week, and there's 575 miles to go?!"). Proximal goals seem more manageable, and once you get started, there are markers of progress ("I did it—25 miles in the first week!").

A study with schoolchildren having trouble learning arithmetic illustrates the power of proximal goals (Bandura & Schunk, 1981). One group of children was given a distal goal: completing a 42-page booklet of arithmetic problems in seven days. A second group received a proximal goal: completing six pages of arithmetic problems a day for seven days. (Yes, those are "the same," but because the children were just starting to learn arithmetic, the ones in the distal goals condition were unable to divide 42 by 7 to arrive at the strategy of completing 6 pages a day.) At the end of the program, children with proximal goals greatly outperformed others on an arithmetic test and were more interested in learning arithmetic (Bandura & Schunk, 1981).

Keep this result in mind when you have a long-term project. For example, at the start of a college semester, your list of required reading might look overwhelming: "My heavens, my psych textbook has over 750 pages." Don't just think of the distal goal (read the whole book in 16 weeks). Set proximal goals (e.g., read one chapter a week). The proximal goals don't seem as daunting. Achieving them builds your confidence (Stock & Cervone, 1990). And your greater confidence and motivation can boost your achievement.

FEEDBACK. Setting goals is a first step in getting yourself motivated. To see the second step, compare these two situations:

1. You've got a final exam in two weeks, and your first aim in getting ready for it is to read 50 pages of your textbook.

proximal goal A goal that specifies what should be done in the near ("proximal") future.

distal goal A goal that specifies an achievement in the distant future.

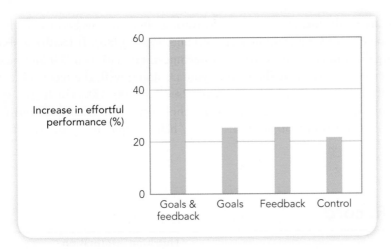

figure 11.4
Goals and feedback If you want to be motivated, it's good to know what you want to do (to have clear *goals*) and to know how well you're doing (to get feedback on your *progress*). The combination of goals and feedback enhances motivation, compared with either factor alone (Bandura & Cervone, 1983).

Maridav / Shuttstock

Motivational feedback One key to motivation is getting feedback: information about progress toward a goal. Feedback lets you know when you are falling short and encourages you when you are doing well. But where can you get accurate and honest feedback? Technology is candid! Electronic devices that monitor physiological states provide feedback that can motivate behavior.

2. You've got a paper due in two weeks, and your first aim in writing it is to come up with a good idea for a paper topic.

Now imagine that somebody asks, a few days later, how you are doing. For Situation #1, you can tell precisely; if you have read 20 pages, you know "I'm 40% of the way toward my goal." For Situation #2, you can't tell; if you have been thinking about the paper but do not have a good idea yet, you do not know if you'll need five more minutes or five more days of thinking to come up with one.

In Situation #1 you have *feedback:* information indicating your progress toward a goal. In Situation #2, you lack feedback; you cannot tell exactly how much progress you have made. Situations with feedback are motivating. Situations without feedback can be frustrating and demotivating. Research manipulating feedback, as well as goals, shows this.

In this study (Bandura & Cervone, 1983), participants performed a tiring task: riding an exercise bike. Some participants were given the goal of reaching a specific high level of performance, whereas others were encouraged merely to do their best. In addition, half the participants received feedback showing their exact level of performance, whereas others did not. The only situation that was highly motivating was the combination of goals with feedback (Figure 11.4). The lesson? If you want to motivate people (including yourself), make sure that (1) the goals are clear and (2) people get feedback on how they are doing as they work toward achieving the goals.

This lesson may remind you of our opening story about Emmanuel Yeboah. He not only was deeply committed to his goal. He also (1) possessed a goal that was clear (he aimed not to "ride his bike a lot" but, specifically, to ride from one end of Ghana to the other) and (2) received feedback on his progress (he knew where he was during the trip, and thus was aware of his progress and the miles remaining before he reached his goal).

CONNECTING TO BRAIN SYSTEMS AND DEVELOPMENT

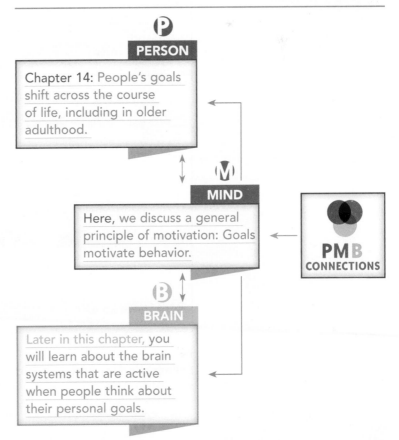

P
PERSON

Chapter 14: People's goals shift across the course of life, including in older adulthood.

M
MIND

Here, we discuss a general principle of motivation: Goals motivate behavior.

PMB
CONNECTIONS

B
BRAIN

Later in this chapter, you will learn about the brain systems that are active when people think about their personal goals.

Why are goals and feedback so motivating? It is mostly because of how they affect people's thinking (Bandura & Cervone, 1983, 1986). If feedback shows you are falling short of your goals, you may become angry with yourself and push yourself harder to succeed. If it shows that you are doing well, the feedback can boost your confidence, or *perceived self-efficacy* (see Chapter 13), which can spur you on to more success (Bandura, 1997). Psychologists have used goal-and-feedback principles in a variety of applications to help people motivate their behavior (Figure 11.5).

Daily Food Record

Date _____

Foods eaten	Nutrition information					
Breakfast	Calories	Fat	Protein	Carbs	Sugar	Sodium
Morning snack						
Lunch						
Afternoon snack						
Dinner						
Evening snack						
Totals for day	Calories	Fat	Protein	Carbs	Sugar	Sodium

figure **11.5**

Self-monitoring chart Trying to knock off a few pounds? A good first step is to get feedback on your eating: precise information about amounts and types of food consumed. Programs to help people control their diet often include food-intake diaries of the sort shown here. By tracking their daily food consumption, people receive motivating feedback on their progress toward their goal of weight loss.

PERSONAL PROJECTS. Some goals motivate behavior that involves one specific task. Consider these three goals:

1. Get myself to the gym tomorrow morning.
2. Bake a cake for Sue; it's her birthday.
3. Memorize all the formulas before tomorrow's chemistry exam.

Each goal can be fulfilled by performing one specific activity in the near future. Other goals, however, are broader in nature. Consider these three:

1. Get myself into shape before next summer.
2. Be a good friend.
3. Get into medical school.

This second list contains *personal projects,* which are goals with two defining qualities: Personal projects (1) incorporate a number of different actions with a common purpose that (2) extend over a significant period of time (Little, Salmela-Aro, & Phillips, 2007). To fulfill getting into shape before next summer, for instance, you need to (1) engage in a number of activities (running, dieting, working out in a gym) (2) over a period of weeks or months.

Personal projects help to organize life. Thanks to your personal projects, many of your daily activities are not disconnected behaviors, but meaningfully interconnected efforts to fulfill a long-term goal. The personal project to get into medical school, for example, might motivate activities as diverse as "memorize all the formulas before tomorrow's chemistry exam," "make friends with some juniors and seniors who know about medical school applications," and "move to a quieter dorm where I can study." People feel happier, and feel that their daily activities are more meaningful, when they are confident in completing projects of personal significance to them (McGregor & Little, 1998; Salmela-Aro, 2009).

Personal projects should sound familiar to you from this chapter's Try This! activity. The project assessments that you completed are essentially the same as those used in the psychology research you are reading about here.

People have more difficulty achieving their aims when different personal projects conflict with one another. Suppose that your goals include both "finding more time for studying" and "finding more time for exercise," or both "making myself appear smart to others" and "being honest with others." The incompatibility, or conflict, between the goals can create stress and interfere with their achievement (Emmons & King, 1988; Presseau et al. 2013).

Personal projects contribute to a human quality we mentioned earlier: *personal agency* (Bandura, 2001). People can motivate themselves and thereby influence their lives and personal development by setting, and remaining committed to, meaningful personal projects.

AP Photo / The Commercial Appeal, Mike Brown

TRY THIS!

Projects Participation in the work of the nonprofit organization Clean Memphis, which aims to "make Memphis the cleanest city in the country" (cleanmemphis.org), is an example of what motivation psychologists call a *personal project.* Personal projects consist of a set of actions that are organized for a common purpose and that extend over a significant period of time. In the Clean Memphis project, participants take part in a set of activities (street cleaning, environmental education, identifying violations of environmental laws) that contribute to the overall aim of a cleaner city.

THINK ABOUT IT

Goals are important to motivation, but might there be more to the study of cognition and motivation than just goal setting? What about those times when you have the goal of doing something but somehow "never get around to it"? (You'll read more about this later in the chapter.)

AUTOMATICALLY ACTIVATED GOALS. By setting goals, then, you can influence your behavior, "motivating yourself" into action. Goals thus give you more control over your behavior . . . sometimes.

Other times, goals give you *less* control. This happens when goals are activated automatically, that is, outside of your conscious awareness. Sometimes a subtle cue in the environment—a sign, a song, a snippet of overhead conversation—will activate a goal in your mind. Once the goal is activated, or cognitively *primed* (see Chapter 6), it may influence your behavior without you even knowing it.

In one study (Bargh et al., 2001, Study 1), the subtle cues that activated goals automatically came from the words in a word-search puzzle (a matrix of letters in which words are embedded). Participants worked on puzzles containing words that were either (1) achievement-related (succeed, strive, etc.) or (2) motivationally neutral (carpet, river, etc.). Afterward, they tried a second puzzle on which their performance was measured. Participants who read the achievement-related words performed at a higher level on the second puzzle. Though they didn't realize it, participants' achievement goals were activated by the puzzle words.

One everyday stimulus that can activate goals automatically is advertising logos. For example, after being shown the logo of Apple, a company known for its creativity, people performed at higher levels on a creativity task (Fitzsimons, Chartrand, & Fitzsimons, 2008). After being shown the logo of Disney, a company that people associate with honesty, participants answered a self-report personality test more honestly. If you asked people why they behaved so creatively or honestly, they couldn't tell you; automatically activated goals affect people's behavior without their even knowing it (Custer & Aarts, 2010).

> What goals are being potentially activated by the stimuli in your current environment?

🐾 WHAT DO YOU KNOW?...

12. True or False?
    a. The goal "Get better grades" is likely to be more motivating than "Form a study group and meet prior to each exam."
    b. The goal "Exercise for at least 6 hours (360 minutes) per month" is likely to be more motivating than "Exercise at least 90 minutes per week."
    c. A treadmill that tells you how fast you are moving and how many calories you are burning will be more motivating than one that provides you with no information about your progress.
    d. Personal projects organize our lives by specifying different actions we must engage in over extended periods of time to achieve our goals.
    e. Research demonstrates that stimuli as diverse as advertising logos can activate goals that influence performance.

Implementation Intentions

Preview Question

> How detailed should we be in our goal setting?

Goals enhance motivation. Sometimes, though, people set concrete goals yet fail to act. Your goal is to start working on a term paper, but a friend calls, you lose track of time, and never get around to it. Your goal is to pay a bill on time, but you start reading a book, forget about the bill, and remember only weeks later that you forgot to pay it. You know what you want to do, but it's hard to get yourself to do it.

The psychologist Peter Gollwitzer and his colleagues have devised a method to help you achieve the goals you set: *implementation intentions*. Goals indicate *what* you want to achieve, whereas **implementation intentions** specify exactly *when* and *where*

implementation intentions Plans that specify exactly when and where you will work on achieving a goal.

you will work on achieving those goals (Gollwitzer & Oettingen, 2013). The setting of implementation intentions, then, is another way in which thinking can contribute to motivation.

A study with college students on Christmas vacation shows how implementation intentions work. Prior to Christmas break, experimenters gave all participants in their study a goal: to write, and submit to the experimenters by the end of the day on December 26th, a report about how they spent Christmas Eve. They instructed half of these participants to form an implementation intention; specifically, these participants, before Christmas, wrote down when and where they would write the Christmas Eve report. The implementation intention helped students achieve their goal of writing the report on time. Three out of four participants with implementation intentions wrote the report, but two-thirds of the participants without implementation intentions failed to do so (Gollwitzer, 1999).

Many subsequent studies confirm that implementation intentions help people put their goals into action (Gollwitzer & Sheeran, 2006). For example, in a study of employees of a large company, researchers used implementation intentions to boost the number of employees receiving flu shots (Milkman et al., 2011). Some employees received a mailer listing times and locations at which free flu shots were available. Others received this same information plus an implementation intention: encouragement to write down an exact day and time at which they would get their shots (Figure 11.6). Implementation intentions worked; significantly more employees with implementation intentions got flu shots. In percentage terms, the effect was not large; flu-shot rates went up by 4.2%. Yet, even that increase represents a significant benefit to public health that was obtained at very little cost.

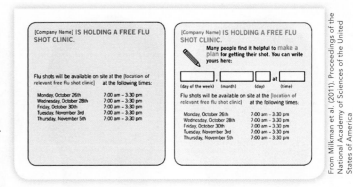

figure 11.6
Implementation intentions Compared with the mailer on the left, more employees of a large company got flu shots when they received the mailer on the right. The one on the right asks for an implementation intention: an exact time at which one will meet the goal of getting the flu shot.

> ### 👣 WHAT DO YOU KNOW?...
>
> 13. If you were to set an implementation intention for reading the remainder of this chapter, what two things would you need to specify?

Making the Distant Future Motivating

Preview Question

> Can implementation intentions motivate you to save for retirement?

Implementation intentions are good when you need to accomplish a goal (e.g., start a paper assignment; get a flu shot) in the near future. What about goals in the *distant* future, such as having enough money for a comfortable retirement or being a healthy, physically fit older adult? Implementation intentions are not much help with distant goals. You can't fill out a form indicating hundreds of specific occasions, over decades of time, when you will, for example, take steps to be more physically fit ("January 12, 2043, 8 A.M.: Jog 2 miles; January 13, 2043, 7 P.M.: Pass up dessert"). It's not practical.

Distant goals pose one of the greatest challenges to motivation. Even when they are important, short-term enticements may overwhelm them. Saving money for retirement and being a healthy older adult might be important distant goals for you. But if you see a nice outfit for sale or somebody offers you a couple cookies, it is difficult to pass them up. Today's temptations trump tomorrow's goals. Thoughts about the distant future tend to be more abstract than thoughts about the present (Trope & Liberman, 2003). Today's concrete, here-and-now temptations are so compelling that people often engage in behavior that they know is bad for them in the long run.

Here's the challenge: How can one make abstract, distant goals more motivating? Hal Hershfield and colleagues (2011) devised a clever strategy based on the following

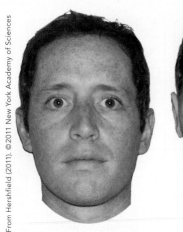
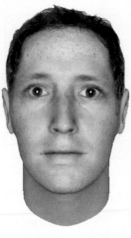
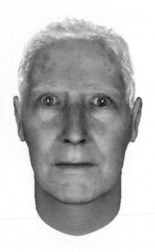

figure 11.7

The guy on the right looks like he'll need some retirement funds! Old age is so distant that goals such as saving for retirement usually are not very motivating. But they become more motivating if you can see yourself in the future. Researchers digitized regular photos (left, above) to create either present-day self (middle) or future-self (right) images. Participants who saw their future self hypothetically allocated more money to a retirement fund.

reasoning. Distant goals are not motivating because people do not relate strongly to their future self—the hard-to-picture-me-of-the-future who benefits from distant goals such as saving money for retirement. Hershfield and colleagues thus made the future self easier to envision. They did so with digitally altered photographs. Researchers took pictures of the participants, digitized them, and used computer software to alter the images to make them look older (Figure 11.7).

In different experimental conditions, participants looked at a digitized image of either (1) their present-day self or (2) their digitally altered future self. Afterward, when participants were asked what they would do if they received $1000, people who had viewed their future self said they would put more than twice as much of the money into a retirement account than did others (Hershfield et al., 2011). An image of the future self made the long-term goal more concrete and motivating.

⚑ WHAT DO YOU KNOW?...

14. The distal goal of maintaining your health into old age is difficult to work toward because there are so many temptations (e.g., fatty foods) in the present and because the future *you* is an abstract concept. Short of altering a digital photo of yourself as the researchers did in the text described above, what can you do to make the future you less abstract and the distal goal thus more motivating?

Motivational Orientations

Preview Questions

› Can your belief in your own capacity for growth influence motivation?
› Why does motivation decrease when we receive external rewards for activities we enjoy?
› When working toward a goal, should you focus on strategies that can help you achieve your goal or strategies that can help you avoid failure?
› How can you achieve a "flow" state?

Goals and implementation intentions, reviewed above, are thinking processes that can increase your motivation and performance on specific tasks. Psychologists also have identified **motivational orientations,** which are broad patterns of thoughts and feelings that can affect people's behavior across a wide variety of tasks. Let's begin our look at motivational orientations with the type of thoughts known as *mindsets*.

MINDSETS. The psychologist Carol Dweck has identified a motivation orientation she calls *mindsets*. A **mindset** is a belief about the nature of psychological attributes, such as intelligence. People's mindsets differ. Some people believe, for example, that their level of intelligence is fixed; they've either "got it" or not. Such people are said to have a *fixed mindset*. Others believe that intelligence can change; it grows over time, as new experiences convey new skills. Such people have a *growth mindset* (Dweck, 2006).

What kind of mindset do you possess: growth or fixed?

Mindsets shape people's interpretations of how they're doing. Suppose you try a new activity—such as a college class in a field unfamiliar to you—and at first you have

motivational orientations Broad patterns of thoughts and feelings that can affect people's behavior across a wide variety of tasks.

mindset A belief about the nature of psychological attributes, such as whether intelligence is fixed or can change.

some difficulty learning the material. If you have a growth mindset, you'll interpret the difficulty as an opportunity to learn; challenges and setbacks will be seen as opportunities to grow your skills. But if you have a fixed mindset, you'll tend to interpret setbacks as signs that you don't have enough intelligence. This will make you discouraged, reducing your motivation.

Dweck and colleagues have shown that people's mindsets can be changed. They enrolled a group of seventh-graders in an educational program designed to instill a growth mindset. Students were taught that their intelligence can grow and that the growth occurs because nerve cells in their brains form new connections when they work hard at their studying (which is true; see Chapter 3). A separate group of seventh-graders learned basic facts about the brain, but were not told that school experiences could cause their intelligence to grow. Afterward, the researchers asked teachers to report on children's levels of motivation, and they also recorded the grades children earned during the school year. Children who were taught a growth mindset became more motivated and earned higher grades (Blackwell, Trzesniewski, & Dweck, 2007).

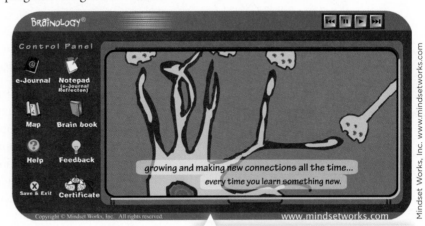

www.mindsetworks.com

Mindset Works, Inc. www.mindsetworks.com

Changing mindsets The software program Brainology tries to instill in children a *growth mindset* by teaching them how their brains form new connections when they learn.

INTRINSIC MOTIVATION. People often are motivated by factors and forces outside of themselves: a parent's rules, a teacher's grades, a company's salary. But sometimes people are motivated by factors *inside* themselves. **Intrinsic motivation** is the desire to engage in activities because they are personally interesting, challenging, and enjoyable (Ryan & Deci, 2000).

One aspect of life that highlights the power of intrinsic motivation is hobbies. If you take up a hobby—music, knitting, fishing, bird watching, stamp collecting, or whatever strikes your fancy—the activity might not serve any fundamental biological or achievement need. You might not do it with any specific goal in mind. You might not be trying to earn money or win a prize. It's just something you find interesting—an enjoyable, relaxing, intrinsically interesting break from the duties and demands of the rest of your day.

A unique feature of intrinsic motivation is that rewards from others can decrease, rather than increase, motivation. In classic research, researchers studied a group of children who were interested in drawing, in other words, who were intrinsically motivated to draw (Lepper, Greene, & Nisbett, 1973; see Chapter 7). The researchers gave some of these children a reward for drawing: a gold star. As a motivator, the gold star backfired in the long run; it reduced the children's intrinsic motivation. When they had some free time, children who had received the gold star were less motivated to engage in drawing.

In subsequent years, additional research examined the effects of external rewards on intrinsically motivated behavior. Results confirmed the original findings. A meta-analysis of 128 studies indicated that when people are intrinsically motivated to engage in an activity, and then receive an external reward for that activity (a prize or money), their intrinsic motivation goes down (Deci, Koestner, & Ryan, 1999).

Why do rewards lower intrinsic motivation? One reason is that they reduce people's sense of *autonomy,* that is, the sense that one is personally in charge of one's own behaviors, which are consistent with one's own personal values and interests (Ryan & Deci, 2000). If you choose an activity yourself (e.g., learning to play the guitar), the personal choice increases your feeling of autonomy, and the activity seems interesting. If somebody gives you a reward to engage in an activity (e.g., offers to pay you to learn

Hulton-Deutsch Collection / Corbis

Intrinsic motivation President Franklin D. Roosevelt collected stamps. Why? Hobbies such as stamp collecting are not externally motivated; FDR did not get money or prizes for stamp collecting. They are intrinsically motivated: driven by personal preferences and interests rather than external rewards.

intrinsic motivation The desire to engage in activities because they are personally interesting, challenging, and enjoyable.

Martha Campbell / Cartoonstock
www.CartoonStock.com

"My class can't wait to start multiplication. I made them sign a pledge never to use it for evil purposes."

the guitar), the external reward reduces your sense of personal autonomy, and you have less intrinsic motivation.

Theorists have viewed autonomy as a universal need (Ryan & Deci, 2000), in other words, one experienced in the same manner by people everywhere in the world. Although research conducted with people from Western cultures (North America, Western Europe) supports this view, research with people from other parts of the world suggests that cultures may differ (see Cultural Opportunities).

⊚ CULTURAL OPPORTUNITIES

Choice and Motivation

A basic principle of motivation research is that personal choice increases people's motivation. People don't like being told what to do; they like autonomy, that is, having a choice. When people don't have a choice—when someone makes them do something—they are less motivated.

Does this principle describe the psychological makeup of all people? In one effort to find out, Asian American children either chose an activity to perform or worked on one chosen by their mothers. Later, when given another opportunity to try the activity, Asian American children, contrary to the principle above, were less motivated if they had chosen the activity themselves than if their mothers had made the choice (Iyengar & Lepper, 1999).

Other research has yielded similar results. In a study by Savani, Markus, and Conner (2008, Study 5), people in the United States and India participated in research in exchange for a small gift: a new pen. Half the participants could choose one pen from a group of five. The other half were shown five pens and then the experimenter chose one for them. Among Americans, choice increased liking; people liked the pen they received more if they had chosen it themselves. Among Indians, choice had no effect; they liked the pen just as much if the experimenter had chosen it for them. Other findings show that people in American cultural contexts are more likely to think about their own actions in terms of personal choices than are people in Indian cultural contexts (Savani et al., 2010).

Why do the cultures differ? Differences in motivation reflect deep differences in cultural backgrounds (Tripathi, 2014). Indian culture is steeped in Hindu philosophy that highlights people's moral duty to fulfill obligations to others and act in a manner consistent with one's social role. American culture, by comparison, is grounded in Western European principles of individual rights, liberty, and the pursuit of personal happiness. People who grow up in the different cultures develop different views about personal choice, and thus different motivational tendencies.

⟲ WHAT DO YOU KNOW?•••

15. The following statement is incorrect. Explain why: "Personal choice, or autonomy, is universally desirable and motivating."

PROMOTION, PREVENTION, AND REGULATORY FIT. If you walk around a college library during final exam week, you will see a lot of people studying. If you ask them why they are studying, they might all say much the same thing: to do well on finals. But if you probe a little deeper, you will find differences. One person might respond, "I'm studying because it's important to reaching my long-term goal of being a doctor." Another might answer, "I'm studying because I don't want to disappoint my family; they're counting on me to be a doctor." These people have different motivational orientations known as *promotion* and *prevention* (Higgins, 1997):

› **Promotion focus:** In a promotion focus, the mind is focused on accomplishments that one personally hopes to attain. People think about accomplishments they can

promotion focus A mental approach to activities in which the mind is focused on accomplishments that one personally hopes to attain.

reach (or potentially miss out on) when engaged in a task. The mind is centered on outcomes that promote their personal growth.

> **Prevention focus:** In a prevention focus, the mind is focused on responsibilities and obligations. People think about obligations they may live up to (or fail to live up to) when doing the task. This is called a *prevention* focus because people's minds are centered on threats (in the example, failing to live up to obligations) they hope to prevent.

Note that motivational orientations can differ even among people taking part in exactly the same activity. The motivational orientation does not describe what people are doing. It describes *the way people think about* what they are doing.

How do motivational orientations relate to behavior? They do so through a principle known as *regulatory fit*. **Regulatory fit** is the match between a motivational orientation and a behavioral *strategy* (Higgins, 2005), that is, a behavior means for reaching a goal. Just as there are different motivational orientations, there are different behavioral strategies. Sometimes strategies and motivational orientations go together psychologically: They "fit" together, like pieces of a jigsaw puzzle (Figure 11.8). When this happens—when there's a fit—people are happier and more satisfied with what they're doing. Here's an example.

In one study, researchers experimentally manipulated prevention versus promotion focus through an essay task (Freitas & Higgins, 2002). Some participants wrote essays about their personal hopes and aspirations, which created a promotion focus in those participants. Others wrote about their duties and obligations in life. This created a prevention focus. Afterwards, everyone evaluated different strategies for earning a high GPA in college. Some strategies were accomplishments one could attain (e.g., *Complete schoolwork promptly*). Others were negative outcomes to avoid (e.g., *Stop procrastinating*). Which strategies did the students like more? It depended on their motivational orientation. When promotion-focused, students liked the accomplishment-based strategies. When prevention-focused, they liked the avoidance-based strategies. In short, they liked the strategies that "fit" their current motivational orientation.

FLOW STATES. A fourth motivational orientation has been given the name *flow* by the psychologist Mihaly Csikszentmihalyi (1990). (In case you were wondering what sound to make when seeing those letters, his last name is pronounced roughly *chick-SENT-me-hi*.) **Flow** is a psychological state in which people's attention is directed intently on an activity for a prolonged period of time. During flow states, people feel immersed in the activity. They are at one with the environment and the challenges it presents and are not distracted by thoughts about themselves, how they look, or their daily concerns. In flow states, people are motivated (they engage in sustained activity and often achieve high levels of performance), yet they are not focusing on motivational inducements such as pay or enhanced self-esteem. Rather, they are focusing on the activity itself.

Flow experiences are distinctive states of consciousness (Weber et al., 2009; see Chapter 9). In flow states, there is intense concentration. Events seem ordered, meaningful, and controllable. Activities may appear to unfold more slowly than normal. People experience a pleasurable, powerful sense of control during flow states.

> On what tasks have you experienced a flow state?

One group of people who you may hear describing flow states is athletes. Successful competitors may say they were "in the zone": an altered state of concentration in which the game seems easy. Its flow of activity, fast and frantic for most people, is slow and calm for the athlete "in the zone"—or, in Csikszentmihalyi's terms, in a flow state.

figure 11.8
Regulatory fit People feel better about their behavior when there is a *regulatory fit*—when their motivational orientation and behavioral strategy fit like pieces of a puzzle. A fit occurs either when someone with a promotion orientation works on strategies that bring achievement, or when someone with a prevention orientation works on strategies that avoid negative outcomes.

> My thoughts are very positive. . . . The moment starts to become the moment for me. Once you get in the moment you know you're there. Things start to move slowly. . . . I let the time tick. I felt like I had the court right where I wanted to.
>
> —Michael Jordan, describing his final seconds of play for the Chicago Bulls (as quoted by NBA Entertainment, 1999)

prevention focus A mental approach to activities in which the mind is focused on responsibilities and obligations.

regulatory fit The match between a motivational orientation and a behavioral strategy.

flow A psychological state in which your attention is directed intently on an activity for a long period of time, and you feel immersed in the activity.

CONNECTING TO CHILD DEVELOPMENT AND THE BRAIN

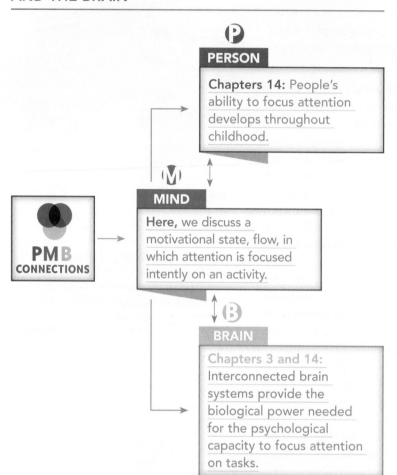

PERSON

Chapters 14: People's ability to focus attention develops throughout childhood.

MIND

Here, we discuss a motivational state, flow, in which attention is focused intently on an activity.

BRAIN

Chapters 3 and 14: Interconnected brain systems provide the biological power needed for the psychological capacity to focus attention on tasks.

PMB CONNECTIONS

There is nothing unique about athletics. A wide variety of activities can produce states of flow. The two key ingredients for creating flow states are the presence of (1) challenges that do not exceed people's skills, and (2) clear task goals and feedback (Csikszentmihalyi, 1990). Any activity with these ingredients can provide a sense of flow. People may have flow experiences while, for example, playing a musical instrument, working on a craft or hobby, playing chess, or painting. Even video games can produce flow experiences when they provide challenges that match players' skills (Hsu & Lu, 2004).

Researchers study flow experiences by measuring the quality of people's experiences. They do so at multiple times a day, while people engage in a variety of everyday activities (see Research Toolkit). This enables the researcher to determine whether certain types of activities are more likely to produce flow experiences. In one study (Csikszentmihalyi & LeFevre, 1989), a diverse group of more than 100 adults reported on their activities and experiences multiple times a day for a week. Specifically, they reported three key pieces of information: (a) whether their current activity was challenging and appropriate to their skills; (b) what they were doing (working, socializing, eating, etc.), and (c) whether they were experiencing psychological flow and its accompanying feelings of alertness, motivation, and happiness.

As predicted, participants reported more flow experiences when they were doing something challenging and had skills to meet the challenges. When there were no challenges, they were bored (Csikszentmihalyi & LeFevre, 1989). Surprisingly, however, high-flow activities were more likely to occur at work than during free time. Managers discussing workplace problems, clerical workers typing information, and blue-collar workers fixing equipment each reported flow experiences on the job. When at leisure, flow was less common. This is surprising; you might expect that in their free time, people would pick activities they enjoy. But nearly half of people's free time was spent watching TV—which provides few challenges and thus often induces boredom rather than flow. Also surprising were the results associated with a major activity for commuters: driving. People often complain about their commute. But driving presents challenges and skills; you navigate at high speeds through highway traffic. Driving produced the highest rates of flow experiences (Csikszentmihalyi & LeFevre, 1989).

Flow experiences occur when people undertake challenging activities that call upon their skills. These engrossing experiences can prove to be a means for self-expression, as in the work of painter Jackson Pollock.

Martha Holmes / Time Life Pictures / Getty Images

luckyraccoon / Shutterstock

He doesn't have flow Research shows that people experience periods of intense concentration, immersion in activities, and a powerful sense of control—or flow states—when they are engaged in challenging activities whose requirements do not exceed their skills. In this state, they feel alert, motivated, and happy. But in their free time, they often choose to engage in an activity that is not challenging, such as TV watching, and they become bored.

🌐 WHAT DO YOU KNOW?...

16. Match the motivational orientation on the left with the quotation that best characterizes it on the right.

1. Fixed mindset	a.	"I work hard at this because I'm hoping to achieve great things."
2. Growth mindset	b.	"I engage in this activity because I find it interesting. I don't need external rewards to do it."
3. Intrinsic motivation	c.	"You're born with all the intelligence you'll ever have and it can't be changed."
4. Promotion focus	d.	"When I am working on a complex problem I know I can solve, I am completely absorbed."
5. Prevention focus	e.	"I work hard at this because I'm hoping to avoid failure."
6. Flow	f.	"Intelligence is something that can grow with experience."

⊕ RESEARCH TOOLKIT

Experience Sampling Methods

Psychologists often study motivation in the lab. There, they can manipulate variables experimentally to determine their impact on motivation. However, psychologists aren't fundamentally interested in motivation in laboratories. They want to know about motivation in everyday life. They thus need a research tool to measure experiences of motivation—and lack of motivation—that occur when people encounter the activities that make up their day.

A problem is that there are so many activities. People do lots of different things, one after another, all day long, day after day. How could you measure all that?

In principle, researchers might videotape everything that people do over the course of a few days, assess motivation-related thoughts and feelings every few minutes, and obtain a complete motivational record. But this is infeasible. It's too difficult and intrusive for research participants, and it leaves the researcher with too much data—mountains of information that would take ages to analyze for each participant in a study.

What's the solution? *Hint:* You read about a similar problem back in Chapter 2. Its solution is relevant here. That problem occurred in survey research. Survey researchers are interested in populations that are so big (e.g., all voters) that it is infeasible to get information from all of them. The solution is to obtain a random sample: a subset of the population that resembles the population as a whole.

Motivation researchers use a similar strategy. Rather than trying to get information about every motivation-relevant experience a person has, they obtain a random sample of experiences, using the *experience sampling method* (Bolger, Davis, & Rafaeli, 2003; Csikszentmihalyi, Larson, & Prescott, 1977).

The **experience sampling method** is a research procedure in which participants carry an electronic device (e.g., a pager or a smartphone) throughout the course of a study (which might run for one or more weeks). The device signals the participant to respond at random intervals during the day. When signaled, participants report on motivational variables occurring at the time they are signaled. For example, in a study described in the main text (Csikszentmihalyi & LeFevre, 1989), when participants were beeped they reported (1) the activity in which they were engaged, (2) whether it was challenging, and (3) whether they were experiencing psychological *flow*.

Experience sampling methods solve three problems (two were noted above). (1) They tap motivation in everyday life, not the lab. (2) They yield a useful amount of information—enough to characterize a person's day, but not so much that the researcher is overwhelmed with data (participants usually are beeped only a few times a day). (3) The third advantage is accuracy. If participants were to report on their daily experiences only at the end of each day, they might forget some experiences or not remember exactly how they felt when the experience occurred. The experience sampling method, by contrast, asks people to report on their experiences "in the moment," when beeped. This reduces memory errors, increases accuracy, and thus yields portraits of life as it is lived.

Contemporary technological advances expand the range of data that can be sampled by researchers, as well as the ease with which those data can be collected. A major advance is wearable technology (Doherty, Lemieux, & Canally, 2014). Research participants may wear watches, wristbands, or "smart clothes" containing electronic sensors. These devices can monitor variables such as physiological state (e.g., heart rate) and participants' location (using GPS technology). By combining these measures with traditional self-report evidence, researchers obtain multilevel scientific evidence—data on social settings, personal experiences, and bodily states—as events unfold in everyday life.

AP Photo / Ben Margot

Wearable technology Watches, wristbands, and "smart clothes" containing electronic sensors enable researchers to collect a wide range of data while people live their everyday lives.

✪ WHAT DO YOU KNOW?...

17. Which of the following describe advantages of experience sampling methods? Check all that apply.

_____ a. They capture events in everyday life rather than in the laboratory.

_____ b. They provide a useful amount of information.

_____ c. They enable researchers to manipulate variables to determine their effect on motivation.

_____ d. They ask participants to report their behaviors as they happen, thus increasing the accuracy of their memories for them.

Motivation in Groups

Most of the motivation research we've covered so far in this chapter focuses on the individual. An individual person is struggling to control her diet, is being challenged on a laboratory task, or is being beeped in an experience sampling study. But much of motivation occurs in groups. Whether at work or at play, people are observed by others, compete with others, and team up with others. Let's look, then, at interaction with others.

experience sampling method
A research procedure in which participants carry an electronic device throughout the course of a study, signaling the participant to respond at random intervals throughout the day.

Social Facilitation

Preview Question

> Does the presence of others improve or worsen performance?

Back in the 1890s, psychologist Norman Triplett (1898) noticed something interesting about bicycle racers. When they rode as fast as possible on a track by themselves, they were slower than when they rode as fast as possible in a race with others. What he observed is a phenomenon known as *social facilitation,* a motivational phenomenon that occurs in groups. In **social facilitation,** the mere presence of other people improves people's performance on tasks on which they are skilled (Aiello & Douthitt, 2001). Social facilitation does not make a person skilled; if you don't know how to ride a bike, you won't suddenly be able to ride if other people are watching. However, it does enhance motivation. If you're a skilled bike rider and you're trying to pedal at maximum speed, the presence of others—whether competitors racing against you, or just an audience watching you—will speed you up.

Triplett (1898) conducted an experiment to test the effects of others' presence on motivation. Ironically, his own experiment did not provide strong evidence of social facilitation effects, a fact that only became clear when contemporary researchers analyzed his data with modern statistical methods that were lacking in his day (Stroebe, 2012). But the phenomenon is real; in many settings, social facilitation does boost motivation and performance.

Clear evidence of social facilitation effects came from a classic paper by the social psychologist Robert Zajonc (1965), whose review of social facilitation research accomplished three major goals. First, Zajonc showed that social facilitation occurs in not only humans, but also other organisms. Humans, rats, chickens—even insects—perform simple responses more quickly or strongly in the presence of other members of their species. Second, Zajonc provided an explanation, suggesting that the presence of others increases physiological arousal. Because all complex organisms experience varying states of arousal, social facilitation occurs across species. Third, Zajonc identified a circumstance in which social facilitation does *not* improve performance. It's one we noted above: When you are not good at a task—when you're just learning it and thus have not yet perfected the basic skills—the presence of an audience will not improve your performance. Social facilitation increases the strength of a *dominant* response, that is, the response that is an organism's most likely response in a given setting. If you're not skilled on a task, your dominant response might not help you to succeed, so an audience will not boost your performance.

On what tasks has the presence of others improved your performance? On what tasks has the presence of others decreased your performance?

Can you think of an exception to the social facilitation principle that the presence of others improves performance? This question might help: Have you ever worked on a group project for class and noticed that, while you were working hard on the project, somebody else in your group was playing video games? That person was displaying **social loafing,** a reduction in motivation on group tasks in which people work together. Groups often reduce the motivation of people who expect that, thanks to others' efforts, the group is likely to succeed, even if they goof off (Karau & Williams, 1993).

✌ WHAT DO YOU KNOW?...

18. Which of the following statements accurately describe Zajonc's findings from his work on social facilitation? Check all that apply.
    _____ a. It occurs in humans, rats, chickens, and insects.
    _____ b. It occurs because the presence of others increases physiological arousal.
    _____ c. It does not improve performance when you are not good at a task.
    _____ d. It reduces the strength of a dominant response.

social facilitation A phenomenon in which the mere presence of other people improves people's performance on tasks on which they are skilled.

social loafing A reduction in individual motivation on group tasks in which some people expect that the group is likely to succeed without their efforts.

Motivation in Schools

Preview Questions

> Do school grades measure intelligence or self-discipline?
> How can teachers increase students' motivation?

If you're like most people, a large percentage of your waking hours have been spent in a group setting in which you are supposed to be motivated to achieve: school. U.S. schoolchildren spend about 32.5 hours a week at school, plus more time doing homework (Juster, Ono, & Stafford, 2004).

MOTIVATION AND GRADES. How important is motivation to school achievement? You might think that grades are just a matter of smarts; maybe some kids have a lot of intelligence and get good grades, and motivation makes little difference. But consider the following study. At the beginning of an eighth-grade school year, researchers collected measures designed to predict children's grades at the end of the school year (Duckworth & Seligman, 2005). One was a standard measure of intelligence (see Chapter 9). Others involved motivation—not just trying hard when working on school, but *self-discipline,* that is, the skills and motivation needed to avoid distractions and start working in the first place. The self-discipline measures included a behavioral test, ratings by teachers, and students' own ratings of their abilities to control their emotions and follow rules. The researchers used both variables, intelligence and discipline, to predict grades.

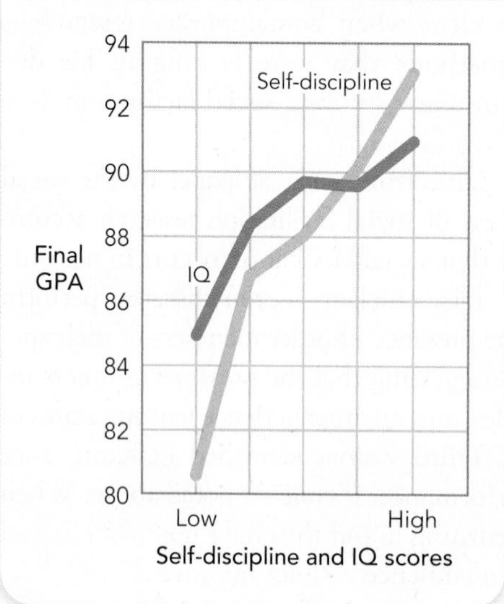

The results are shown in Figure 11.9. If intelligence predicted grades and self-discipline were unimportant, then the line relating intelligence to grades would be steep, and the line relating self-discipline to grades would be flat. But the self-discipline line not only isn't flat, it's steeper than the intelligence line! Self-discipline was a *more* important predictor of grades than was intelligence (Duckworth & Seligman, 2005).

This study's findings are consistent with other research. For example, in a study of high school students, study time was found to predict grades about as strongly as intelligence did (Keith, 1982).

figure 11.9
It's not just "smarts" Individual differences in a motivational variable, self-discipline, are even better predictors of school grades than is IQ (Duckworth & Seligman, 2005).

INCREASING STUDENT MOTIVATION. How can teachers increase students' motivation? Motivational processes you read about earlier in this chapter are relevant to the classroom (Covington, 2000). One important motivational process involves goals. Students who set a goal of learning and mastering material, rather than merely earning high grades, often achieve greater success (Ames, 1992; Nicholls, 1984). Goals are particularly important when students are struggling to learn material. Those aiming for high grades may worry that they aren't smart enough, whereas those whose goal is to learn will recognize that the struggles are a natural part of learning (Dweck, 1986). The *mindset* program described earlier in this chapter, in which students are taught about how the brain makes new connections when learning, is designed in part to alter students' goals (Dweck, 2006). Once students learn how the brain changes with experience, they may be less concerned about their current level of "smarts" and more focused on putting in the effort to learn material and develop a more powerful brain.

Others emphasize that goals are only part of the story of motivation in schools. Students—like anyone—try to fit in with others and to maintain a sense of personal worth (Covington, 2000). Many students may not associate academic success with their personal worth, or may even live in settings in which school success is undervalued, or even disparaged, in their peer group. For example, the anthropologist John Ogbu explained that Black inner-city students in the United States live in a setting that must be understood historically: Due to a history of racial barriers, previous generations of family members could not experience the same path from school success to professional success that whites could experience. As a result, they may be less personally invested in school success, which in turn could lower their achievement. In general, people who have become part of a country against their will (through slavery or colonization) are less likely to share the belief, often held by people in the more powerful majority group, that everyone can "make it" in society by succeeding in school and following the rules of society (Ogbu & Simons, 1998).

✪ WHAT DO YOU KNOW?...

19. Self-discipline may be more predictive of grades than is _____. To increase students' motivation, teachers can help them emphasize the goal of learning and _____ the material rather than getting high _____. This strategy, however, may be less useful to students who do not associate academic success with personal _____, or whose academic success won't predict professional success.

Motivation at Work

Preview Questions

› What payment plan should you adopt if you want to motivate your employees?
› What type of leadership style is most motivating?

After they're done with school, most people spend much of their time in another group setting: work. Employment commonly immerses workers in complex organizations in which people work as teams—either in person, at work sites, or in "virtual teams" in today's information-based workplace.

PAY. What motivates employees at work? At the risk of stating the obvious, a big part of the answer is pay. Yet there are some nonobvious facts about how pay motivates employees. Consider the question of what type of payment plan is best for motivating employees: pay based on (1) the amount of time an employee spends on a job, (2) the amount of work the employee produces, or (3) the success of the company as a whole? There is no single, correct answer in all cases. Different payment plans work best in different work settings (Helper, Kleiner, & Wang, 2010).

› In some jobs, any given employee individually produces a product (or stand-alone part of a product) that a company sells. In these jobs, the most motivating pay systems focus on the individual employee. Companies can maximize their productivity by paying individuals according to the amount of work each produces. Different individuals, who work at different rates, may earn different amounts.

› In other jobs, people work in coordinated teams that jointly strategize, solve problems, and produce a product. In these settings, the optimal payment plan focuses on the group. Companies can maximize productivity by paying everyone in the group roughly the same amount of money, and providing pay raises based on the success of the group as a whole. When people work in teams, group payment plans increase their motivation and satisfaction with their jobs.

GOALS. Success at work requires not only wanting to do well, but also knowing what to do. In job settings, employee motivation and performance are increased by the setting of goals. The goal-setting principles discussed earlier in this chapter have been applied extensively in work settings. Hundreds of studies show that goals that are specific—indicating exact levels of performance to be achieved—boost motivation and performance. Employees who are committed to specific job goals and who receive feedback on their progress toward those goals generally outperform those who have only vague goals, such as "do your best" on a job (Latham & Pinder, 2005).

LEADERSHIP STYLES. Another factor that can affect workplace motivation is *leadership style,* the typical behavior and overall approach to managing employees that is adopted by managers in charge of a work group. Early research on leadership styles contrasted (1) *democratic* styles, in which everyone (leader and subordinates) participates in setting organizational goals; (2) *autocratic* styles, in which the leader dictates what others do; and (3) *laissez-faire* styles, in which leaders are uninvolved in workers' decision making (Lewin & Lippitt, 1938; Lewin, Lippitt, & White, 1939). More recent research has identified other styles. In *transformational* leadership, the leader seeks to gain the trust of workers and to inspire them to reach goals. In *transactional* leadership, the leader simply appeals to workers' self-interest by providing rewards to them if they meet objectives (Eagly, Johannesen-Schmidt, & van Engen, 2003).

Although different styles may be effective in different types of groups, in general, transformational leadership has significant advantages. Inspiring transformational leadership predicts greater employee motivation and greater satisfaction with the leader (Judge & Piccolo, 2004). Interestingly, women in leadership roles are somewhat more likely to be transformational-style leaders than are men, who are more likely to engage in transactional leadership (Eagly et al., 2003).

> What leadership style do you find most appealing?

Transformational leadership Indra Nooyi sings karaoke with friends from work, plays rock guitar at company meetings, and is known as a caring individual who is concerned about the health of our planet (Useem, 2008). She also is the Chief Executive Officer (CEO) of Pepsico. Ms. Nooyi exemplifies a *transformational* leadership style, in which a leader motivates employees by gaining their trust and inspiring them.

❤ WHAT DO YOU KNOW?...

20. You manage a small company that employs potters to make handmade ceramic pieces, such as mugs, bowls, and plates. Every item the workers produce is a stand-alone product that you can sell. Choose one option from each pair below to maximize their productivity.

Option 1
a. Pay according to the amount of work produced, such that people may earn different amounts from each other.
b. Pay everyone about the same, and give raises when the group achieves certain goals.

Option 2
a. Remind them to "do their best."
b. Provide goals and feedback.

Option 3
a. Be a transactional leader, and appeal to their self-interest by providing rewards if they achieve their objectives.
b. Be a transformational leader, and gain their trust and inspire them to achieve their goals.

Motivation and the Brain

Let's conclude our coverage of motivation by moving down a level of analysis. We've just seen how mental contents—needs, goals, and related beliefs—can energize and direct behavior. Let's now examine brain systems that make it possible for us to experience motivational states. We'll consider three topics: (1) brain systems that are active during *approach* and *avoidance* motivation; (2) cases in which people are too motivated, namely, *addictions*; and (3) neural systems that enable people to set goals that guide their behavior.

Approach, Avoidance, and the Brain

Preview Question

> What are the biological bases of approach and avoidance motivation?

We've said throughout this chapter that motivational forces are diverse. Yet there is a simple distinction—between *approach* and *avoidance* motivation—that simplifies the diversity.

Approach motivation refers to a broad class of motives that concern the growth and enhancement of an organism (Harmon-Jones, 2011). Efforts to obtain food or attain a higher social status are both cases of approach motivation. **Avoidance motivation** is a drive to protect the self against threats and dangers. Staying away from physical threats (e.g., a dark alley that looks dangerous) and from social threats (e.g., a party where you might embarrass yourself socially) are both cases of avoidance motivation. A number of the specific motives and motivational orientations we encountered earlier in the chapter (e.g., needs to achieve and to avoid failure; or motivational orientations involving promotion or prevention) can be seen as relating to one of the two motivations, approach or avoidance.

The approach/avoidance distinction is psychological; it claims that approach and avoidance are psychologically distinct states. Are they also biologically distinct? In other words, are there distinct systems in the brain that correspond to these distinct types of motivation?

Much theory and research suggests that there are. A theoretical framework developed by British scientist Jeffrey Gray (reviewed in Smillie, Pickering, & Jackson, 2006) is useful for thinking about motivation and the brain. Gray conducted research on animals. In laboratory studies, they were exposed to stimuli that signaled the later occurrence of either rewards (which the animal would be inclined to approach) or punishments (which the animal would want to avoid). Gray then explored the brain systems when the two types of signals were presented. Based on this research, he distinguished between a *behavioral approach system* and a *behavioral inhibition system*. Both systems can be understood in terms of two types of biological mechanisms—the neurotransmitters that activate the systems, and the exact brain anatomy that is activated, as we'll see now.

BEHAVIORAL APPROACH SYSTEM. Stimuli that signal the future presence of rewards activate a *behavioral approach system*. The **behavioral approach system** is a neural system that arouses an organism, energizing it to seek out rewarding stimuli (e.g., food).

The neurotransmittiter *dopamine* is the biochemical key to this reward system. Although there is some disagreement on its precise functions, dopamine is known to be released when an organism encounters reward signals, and to activate brain regions needed for pursuing those rewards (Pickering & Corr, 2008).

Regarding the anatomy of this system—that is, the exact neural structures within the brain that are involved—the key mechanisms are in lower regions of the brain: the brain stem and limbic system. Dopamine travels along a bundle of nerve fibers, the *medial forebrain bundle,* to a set of neurons that is central to the pursuit of rewards, the *nucleus accumbens* (Wise, 1998; Figure 11.10). Many see this overall system of biochemistry and neural anatomy as a *reward system* in the brain (e.g., Makris et al., 2008), that is, a system dedicated to producing the pleasurable and motivating states that drive organisms to pursue rewarding stimuli.

approach motivation A broad class of motives that concern the growth and enhancement of an organism, from obtaining food to attaining a higher social status.

avoidance motivation A drive to protect oneself from threats and dangers, both physical and social.

behavioral approach system A neural system activated by stimuli that signal the future presence of rewards, energizing an organism to seek out rewarding stimuli.

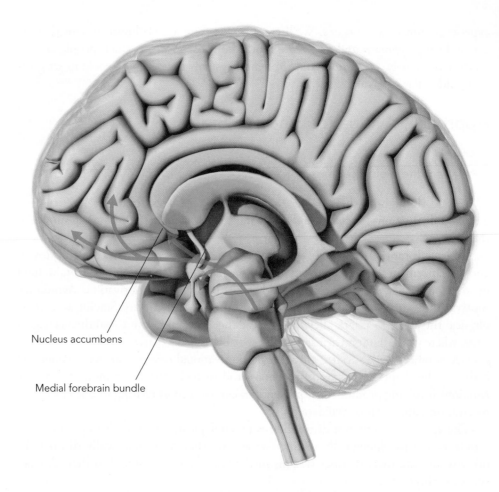

figure 11.10

Brain systems and motivation Two brain structures that are key to the brain's reward system are the medial forebrain bundle and the nucleus accumbens. Dopamine, the key biochemical component in the reward systems, travels from the medial forebrain bundle to the nucleus accumbens during the experience of rewarding stimuli.

Nucleus accumbens

Medial forebrain bundle

BEHAVIORAL INHIBITION SYSTEM. Signals of punishment activate a *behavioral inhibition system.* The **behavioral inhibition system** is a neural system within the brain that increases levels of arousal and feelings of anxiety. Activation of this system causes organisms to stop pursuing rewards and to attend, instead, to environmental threats. The behavioral inhibition system is activated by stimuli that signal punishment, by novel stimuli that could be threatening, and by stimuli that innately trigger fear.

Both the biochemistry and the anatomy of the behavioral inhibition system differ from those of the approach system. In terms of the biochemistry, the most important neurotransmitter is not dopamine but *serotonin* (Graeff, 2004). Anatomically, the key neural systems are located in the hippocampus and the amygdala (Barrós-Loscertales et al., 2006; Gray & McNaughton, 2000).

The biological differences between the systems are consistent with the psychological distinctions you learned earlier. Time and again, psychologists proposed that motives to attain positive outcomes and to avoid harms and threats were psychologically distinct. Brain research reveals that they are distinct biologically, too.

Brain research with humans provides further evidence of these distinctions, while also widening the scope of brain mechanisms involved. In addition to the lower-level brain regions that we share with animals, higher-level regions that are uniquely human are involved. These include biological matter in the front of the brain, that is, the *frontal cortex.* Findings indicate that different sides of the frontal cortex—the left and right hemispheres of the brain (see Chapter 3)—play different roles. The left side is more strongly involved in approach motivation, whereas the right side is more strongly involved in avoidance (Harmon-Jones, 2011).

behavioral inhibition system
A neural system activated by signals of punishment, increasing levels of arousal and feelings of anxiety.

Addiction and the Brain

Preview Question

> What is the biological basis of addiction?

Sometimes people are too motivated. They incessantly seek out substances or behaviors that are attractive, but ultimately harmful. These are people who suffer from *addictions*. **Addictions** are psychological disorders in which people use a drug or engage in an activity repeatedly and uncontrollably (Goldman, Oroszi, & Ducci, 2005).

Addictions are costly to individuals and to society as a whole. At a personal level, substance abuse can ruin friendships, romantic relationships, and family life. In economic terms, the cost of addictions is staggering: an estimated $600 billion a year in the United States in health-, crime-, and productivity-related costs (National Institute on Drug Abuse, 2012). Addictions also are costly to society's cultural life. The careers of numerous great musicians and artists have been cut short by drug abuse.

Why are so many people so prone to develop addictions? Addictive substances tap into a neural system found in everyone's brain: the *reward system* (behavioral approach system) described in the preceding section. A wide variety of addictive substances activate the brain circuitry that normally becomes active during rewarding, pleasurable experiences (Wise, 1998).

Addictive substances affect the reward system by increasing dopamine activity. Different substances increase dopamine in different ways. For example, nicotine increases the amount of dopamine released into the spaces between neurons (Stahl, 2002). Cocaine blocks a molecular process in which previously released dopamine is taken back into brain cells (Nestler, 2006; Figure 11.11). Either way, activity in the reward center of the brain increases.

Furthermore, addictive substances create two long-lasting changes in the brain that make it particularly difficult for people to break an addictive habit (Koob & Le Moal, 2005). First, they reduce the normal functioning of the brain's reward system. As a result, naturally occurring events become less rewarding and people lose motivation for everyday activities. Second, they increase the activity of brain systems that produce emotionally negative *withdrawal* states when a person's levels of an addictive substance are low.

Evidence indicates that the addictive *behaviors* have an effect on the brain that is similar to that of addictive *substances*. For instance, gambling—a behavior that becomes addictive for millions of people—has been shown to activate the same reward center that is activated by addictive drugs (Holden, 2001). When researchers study the brains of pathological gamblers and addictive drug users, they find similar patterns of response; regions of the brain involved in the processing of reward are particularly active in response to both drugs and monetary cues (Clark et al., 2013).

addictions Psychological disorders in which people use a drug or engage in an activity repeatedly and uncontrollably.

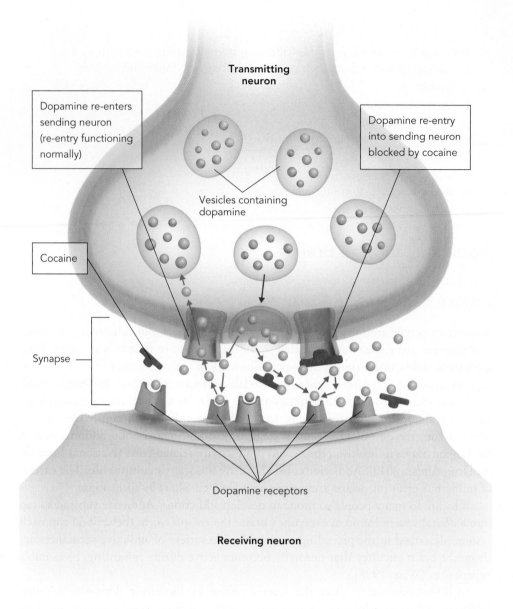

Transmitting neuron

Dopamine re-enters sending neuron (re-entry functioning normally)

Dopamine re-entry into sending neuron blocked by cocaine

Vesicles containing dopamine

Cocaine

Synapse

Dopamine receptors

Receiving neuron

figure 11.11

Cocaine and the brain Cocaine blocks a process within the brain in which dopamine is taken back into brain cells. This increases the amount of dopamine in the space between cells, which increases activity in the reward center of the brain.

🐾 WHAT DO YOU KNOW?...

22. Addictive substances activate the behavioral approach system, also known as the _____ system. Nicotine affects this system by _____ the amount of dopamine released into the space between neurons, whereas _____ blocks dopamine from being taken back up into the cell. Gambling has been shown to activate the same _____ center as addictive substances.

Goals and the Brain

Preview Question

> What brain regions are active during goal processing?

Goals shape motivation. This simple sentence captures a main theme of research on motivation and the mind. Research on motivation and the brain is beginning to shed light on the biological mechanisms that make it possible for people to formulate personal goals.

Psychologically, goals have two key features: (1) thoughts about the future and (2) thoughts that a person cares about. Goals, then, are not simple statements of fact (e.g., "Someday my hair will be gray"). They represent future states that one values (e.g., "Someday I will earn a college degree"). Because goals have more than one aspect psychologically, you might expect that more than one brain region will be involved in goal processing.

To study the neural basis of people's thoughts about goals, researchers (D'Argembeau et al., 2010) first asked participants to think of some future possibilities that were personal goals for them, and some other possible future events that they might experience but that were not personal goals. Later, they used a brain scanner to create images of regions of the brain that were highly active while participants were thinking about their personal goals, future activities that were not personal goals, and also some routine activities such as taking a shower.

Consistent with what one would expect from a psychological analysis of goals, two different brain regions—not just one region—were active during goal processing (D'Argembeau et al., 2010; Figure 11.12). One region, the *posterior cingulate cortex,* is known to be active when people contemplate future events. The other, the *ventral medial prefrontal cortex,* is involved in computing value, that is, the degree to which a piece of information is valuable to oneself. Input from these two neural systems—a future events system and a personal value system—combines to produce the representation of personal goals. Future research on goal setting and the brain is sure to provide more insight into the biological mechanisms that enable people to motivate themselves (Figure 11.13).

Thinking about personal goals

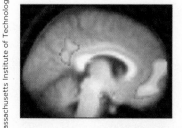

Thinking about future events that are not personal goals

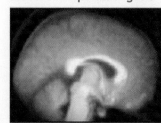

From D'Argembeau et al. (2010). © 2010 Massachusetts Institute of Technology

figure **11.12**
Goals and the brain Goals are thoughts about (1) future outcomes that (2) people value. It's no coincidence that thinking about goals activates two areas of the brain: (1) the posterior cingulate cortex (in the brain scan on the top, the highlighted area on the left; this area is active when people contemplate future possibilities) and (2) the ventral medial prefrontal cortex (in the brain scan on the top, the highlighted area on the right; this brain region is active in the computation of value, that is, whether a given piece of information is valuable to oneself). Their combined input enables people to think about goals that direct their behavior.

🔋 WHAT DO YOU KNOW?...

23. Brain-imaging research indicates that two areas of the brain are active when people think about goals: the posterior cingulate, an area known to be active when thinking about events in the _____, and the ventral medial prefrontal _____, an area known to be active when thinking about information that is important to the self.

↩↪ Looking Back and Looking Ahead

Early in this chapter, we noted a potential complaint about psychology. Psychologists devote so much time to studying inner mental life, some say, that they leave their subject matter, people, "lost in thought"—contemplative but inactive. Now that you have reached the end of the chapter, you see what the psychology of motivation has accomplished: It has "found" what otherwise might have been "lost." Today's psychological science of motivation squashes the complaint by providing a rich understanding of the diverse needs, goals, and social influences that motivate people into action—and sometimes leave them unmotivated even when they should act.

The power of motivation is seen in many other areas of psychology. Motivational forces influence people's perceptions of the world (Chapter 5). They power conscious and unconscious processes of personality (Chapter 13). Clinicians harness people's capacity to motivate themselves when formulating programs to benefit their clients (Chapter 14).

figure 11.13

PMB IN ACTION

DO ENVIRONMENTAL STIMULI CONTROL PEOPLE'S MOTIVATION?

(P) PERSON

No; people have a capacity for personal agency—an ability to motivate themselves to achieve their desires.

(M) MIND

Personal agency can be understood in terms of goals, mental representations of future achievement that direct and motivate behavior.

Project: → Win Olympic Medal

Task-Specific Goals: → Improve Race Start 10%   Sprint Drills 4x/week

Weight Training 3x/week

(B) BRAIN

At a brain level of analysis, goal-setting relies on neural systems that enable people to think about the future and to value future outcomes.

From D'Argembeau et al. (2010). © 2010 Massachusetts Institute of Technology

Popperfoto / Getty Images

Chapter Review

Now that you have completed this chapter, be sure to turn to Appendix B, where you will find a **Chapter Summary** that is useful for reviewing what you have learned about motivation.

Key Terms

addictions (p. 495)
anorexia nervosa (p. 463)
approach motivation (p. 493)
avoidance motivation (p. 493)
behavioral approach system (p. 493)
behavioral inhibition system (p. 494)
binge eating disorder (p. 463)
biological needs (p. 460)
bulimia nervosa (p. 463)
distal goal (p. 476)
eating disorders (p. 462)
experience sampling method (p. 488)
fetishism (p. 465)
flow (p. 485)
goal (p. 475)

hedonic hunger (p. 462)
homeostatic hunger (p. 461)
homeostatic processes (p. 461)
hunger (p. 460)
implementation intentions (p. 480)
intrinsic motivation (p. 483)
Maslow's hierarchy of needs (p. 458)
mindset (p. 482)
motivation (p. 458)
motivational orientations (p. 482)
need for achievement (p. 467)
need to avoid failure (p. 468)
need for belonging (p. 469)
need for control (p. 471)
need to enhance the self (p. 471)

need for understanding (p. 470)
oxytocin (p. 473)
personal agency (p. 475)
prevention focus (p. 485)
promotion focus (p. 484)
proximal goal (p. 476)
regulatory fit (p. 485)
satiety (p. 460)
self-actualization (p. 459)
set-point theories (p. 461)
social facilitation (p. 489)
social loafing (p. 489)
social needs (p. 469)
testosterone (p. 466)

Questions for Discussion

1. Hedonic hunger likely evolved to ensure that we would consume calories when they were available, thereby increasing our chances for survival when food was scarce. Food is highly available now, even in improbable places; stores like Home Depot make sure you can buy candy bars at their registers. Given the prevalence of stimuli that would trigger hedonic hunger, what are some strategies you can adopt for overcoming it and instead focusing on homeostatic hunger? [Apply]

2. What brain system is likely activated in the person planning to skydive for fun? What particular neurotransmitters and brain regions are activated by this system? Is the same system also activated in the individual who is addicted to video games? Explain. [Comprehend]

3. Of approach motivation and avoidance motivation, which does a better job explaining the following behaviors? Explain your answer. [Apply]
   a. A student picks a challenging yet interesting term paper topic.
   b. A child quits in the middle of a board game.
   c. A man goes to a party but does not talk to anyone.
   d. A runner maps out a longer-than-usual route.

4. You read about research by Bandura and Cervone (1983) which indicated that having a goal and getting feedback on how you're doing relative to that goal are highly motivating. If you're not doing well, your disappointment can spur you into action; if you are doing well, the positive feedback can boost your confidence. Identify a goal you're trying to achieve now. How might you solicit feedback on your progress so that you too can experience the motivational benefits of disappointment or a boost in confidence? [Apply]

5. You read about a study by Gollwitzer and Sheeran (2006) in which participants who had been asked to make implementation intentions about when and where to get a flu shot were more likely to achieve their goal of getting a flu shot. Why do you suppose implementation intentions are effective? What knowledge about the types of goals that are most motivating can you draw on to help you answer? [Analyze]

6. According to research on regulatory fit, people with a promotion focus tend to seek out different strategies to attain goals compared to people with a prevention focus. Consider a goal you would like to achieve. What would your promotion-focused strategies for its attainment look like? Your prevention-focused strategies? [Apply]

Chapter Review

7. Identify an upcoming due date, perhaps for a term paper or some other large-scale project. Specify a set of implementation intentions, if you haven't already. Now examine those intentions. Do they tend to be more promotion- or prevention-focused? [Apply]

8. You read about research by Duckworth and Seligman (2005) in which self-discipline was shown to be a better predictor of grades than is intelligence. What *is* self-discipline? What goal-setting principles from this chapter might help you achieve greater self-discipline? [Synthesize]

9. Given the information presented in the chapter on the factors that increase motivation, what recommendations can you make right now to your teacher for how he or she can help you achieve your potential? [Synthesize]

Self-Test

1. With which of Maslow's claims do contemporary researchers find fault?
   a. Humans are driven by a self-actualization need.
   b. The needs form a fixed hierarchy.
   c. Everyone has a need to belong.
   d. Safety needs are universal.

2. Which of the following behaviors is explained by set-point theory?
   a. After a day of judging science fair projects, Al realizes he missed lunch.
   b. Sunny didn't finish eating the large lunch her dad packed for her because she was full.
   c. After a big meal, Marty sees his roommates eating popcorn and helps himself to some.
   d. Aliza orders a second dessert in spite of her mother's glare.

3. What does research on the effects of testosterone on sexual desire reveal?
   a. The more testosterone one has, the greater the sexual desire.
   b. Among those with hypogonadism, testosterone increased sexual desire.
   c. The more testosterone one has, the greater the sexual desirability.
   d. Testosterone levels predict sexual desire in men only.

4. Callie was excellent at darts, so when she challenged her friend Erik to a game, she gave him the opportunity to pick how far away he stood from the dartboard. Consider the study by Atkinson and Litwin (1960) described in the text in which people high and low in the need to achieve and to avoid failure got to stand wherever they wanted relative to a target. If Erik was high in the need to achieve and low in the need to avoid failure, where would he choose to stand?
   a. Ridiculously close (no challenge at all)
   b. Very close (very little challenge)
   c. A middle distance so it's not clear whether he will miss (some challenge)
   d. Very far (too much challenge)

5. Imagine you wanted to motivate your younger brother to do a good job keeping his room tidy. One way to do so might be to increase his sense of autonomy. Which of the following could help you achieve that end?
   a. Give him step-by-step instructions for how to keep his room tidy.
   b. Provide him with a checklist of tasks that need to be completed.
   c. Describe your expectations and let him choose how he will meet them.
   d. Each time he gets successively closer to the goal, reinforce him.

6. According to research described in the text, which of the following statements is false?
   a. Experimental research indicates that oxytocin has been shown to universally increase trust and helping.
   b. Oxytocin decreases trust toward people who appear to be part of a nonthreatening social group.
   c. Among people low in social skills, oxytocin increases the ability to accurately infer the emotional state of others.
   d. Oxytocin causes people to recall more positive memories of their mothers, but only if they were anxious about their relationship with her.

7. Which of the following words is most synonymous with *personal agency*?
   a. "Motivation"
   b. "Belonging"
   c. "Hedonism"
   d. "Autonomy"

8. Considering the specificity, level of challenge, and proximity of the following goal statements, which would be most motivating?
   a. "I'd like to lose 12 pounds this week."
   b. "I'd like to lose 12 pounds in 3 months."
   c. "I'd like to lose 1 pound per week for 3 months."
   d. "I'd like to lose some weight in the next 3 months."

9. You've just failed a math exam. Considering Carol Dweck's research on mindsets, which of the following thoughts could keep you from becoming discouraged about your future math performance?
   a. "I tried my best, but I'm just not good at math and that's that."
   b. "It's clear to my teacher that I didn't inherit a gene for math skill."
   c. "I sure did blow it. I wonder what I can do to learn the material."
   d. "Well, at least I'm blessed with good reading and writing skills."

10. Which of the following is true of autonomy?
    a. It is defined as the need to be competent and able to influence events.
    b. It increases motivation among people of all cultures.
    c. It cannot be reduced by external rewards.
    d. In classroom contexts, it can increase interest in school material.

11. Sophia and Bella joined the local orchestra and had their first performance. During practice, they performed equally well, but on the day of the show, Bella made several mistakes, whereas Sophia played better than she ever had. Considering Zajonc's work on social facilitation, which of the following could best explain this difference?
    a. Sophia is well practiced in violin, whereas Bella is not.
    b. Sophia is taking advantage of an opportunity to engage in social loafing.
    c. Bella is well practiced in violin, whereas Sophia is not.
    d. Bella is taking advantage of an opportunity to engage in social loafing.

12. According to research described in the text, what do grades measure?
    a. Intelligence only
    b. Autonomy and intelligence
    c. Intelligence and self-discipline
    d. Self-discipline and autonomy

13. Which of the following motives and motivational orientations is categorized as an approach motivation?
    a. Need to avoid failure
    b. Prevention
    c. Need for punishment
    d. Promotion

14. What is the key function of the behavioral inhibition system?
    a. To motivate the organism to seek out novel stimuli
    b. To motivate the system to seek out rewards
    c. To motivate the system to attend to environmental threats
    d. To motivate the system to avoid rewards at all costs

15. Cocaine increases the activity of which of the following chemicals in the reward center of the brain?
    a. Serotonin
    b. Dopamine
    c. Testosterone
    d. Oxytocin

Answers

You can check your answers to the preceding Self-Test and the chapter's What Do You Know? questions in Appendix B.

How could human behavior be described? Surely only showing the actions of a variety of humans, as they are all mixed up together. Not what one man is doing now, but the whole hurly-burly.

– Ludwig Wittgenstein

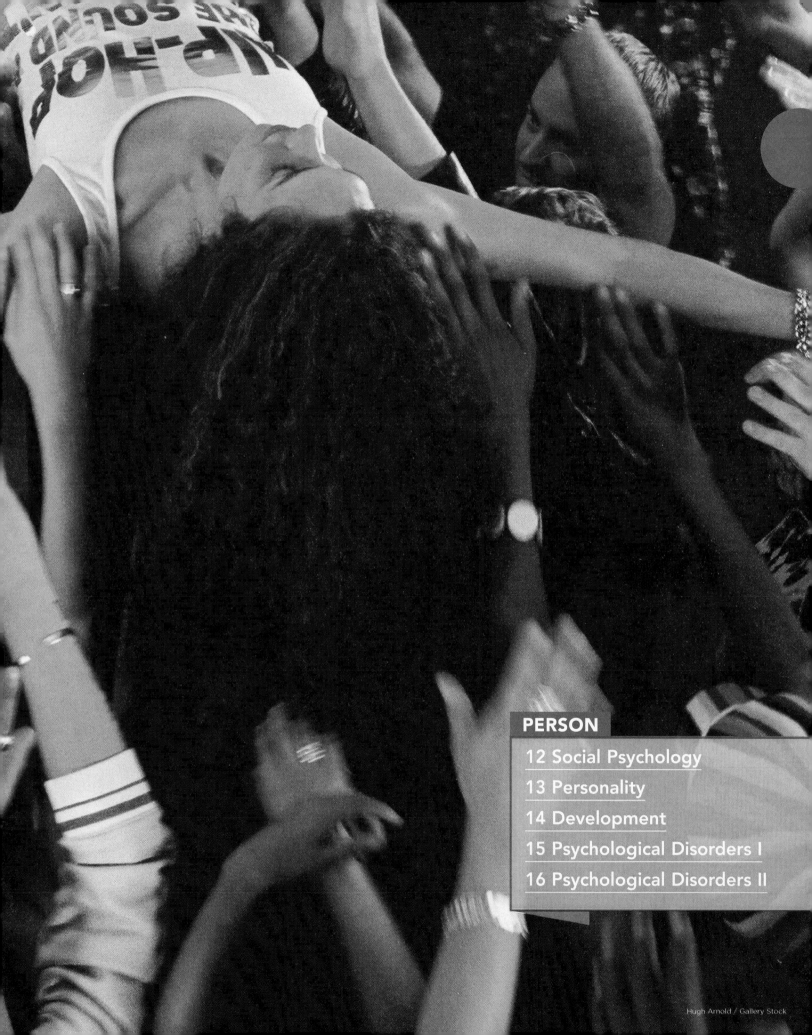

Social Psychology

12

HOW CAN WE UNDERSTAND THE PSYCHOLOGY OF HUMAN BEINGS? A natural first step is to look at what humans do. Here are some examples of human behavior:

› Nearly two-thirds of Americans help others by donating to charity. Total annual donations are about $300 billion—roughly $1000 per person.

› In Brooklyn, New York, a woman in a hospital emergency room waited nearly 24 hours for medical care. Hospital staff saw her waiting but provided no help—even as she fell to the floor, suffered convulsions for about an hour, and died.

› In Sweden, Norway, and Denmark, roughly 9 out of 10 citizens "never or rarely" attend religious services.

› In Allahabad, India, organizers held a religious festival at a place where legend says that divine nectar once fell to Earth while gods and demons wrestled over a water pitcher. More than 80 million people attended.

› A poll in the United States indicates that 40% of people think marriage is becoming obsolete.

› Chinese authorities recently arrested four men for digging up corpses and selling them to people desperate to arrange marriages: "ghost marriages" that would prevent the deceased from being lonely in the afterlife.

› Out of concern for the welfare of family at home, American travelers annually purchase more than 150,000 insurance policies that provide coverage should they die in a plane crash. The policies are popular, even though the risk of a fatal airline crash is infinitesimally small: 45 million to 1.

› During the holiday season, people in many parts of the world bring dead trees into their homes and place electric lights on them. The tradition is popular, even though the risk to the home and its inhabitants is significant; in the United States alone, enough trees catch fire to cause about $6 million in property damage annually.

So what are humans like? Hard to say, isn't it? In one situation, people seem caring. In another situation, they seem callous. In one culture, they are religious. In another, they are not. One social group values marriage, another finds it obsolete. In one role (traveler), people are cautious, and in another role (holiday decorator), tradition sweeps caution aside.

H&D Zielske / Gallery Stock

Getty Images, from left to right: Sbayram; Craftvision

Social and cultural diversity in human behavior The human brain and people's basic mental abilities are the same throughout the world. Yet human social behavior varies dramatically. For example, in Northern Europe (left), rates of attendance at religious events are low. In India, a religious festival in Allahabad, the Kumbh Mela (right), draws more than 80 million people.

Petr Svarc / Alamy

How could human behavior be described? Surely only by showing the actions of a variety of humans, as they are all mixed up together. Not what one man is doing now, but the whole hurly-burly.

—Wittgenstein (1967, p. 567)

social psychology Branch of psychology that studies people's thoughts, feelings, and actions as they contemplate, interact with, and are influenced by others in society.

social behavior Behavior that occurs in interaction with other people.

crowds Large gatherings of people who do not necessarily know one another.

groups Collections of people who know and communicate with each other, have distinctive roles (e.g., a group leader), and may work together toward a common goal.

close relationships One-on-one interactions in which a person is in frequent contact with, and feels a strong connection to, another person.

How, then, can we understand the psychology of human beings? We must study people *as well as* the situations, cultures, groups, and roles they inhabit. The perplexing diversity of human behavior can be comprehended only by studying the social world people inhabit and their beliefs about that world. This is the lesson of social psychology, as you will see in the chapter ahead. ◉

WHEN IS THE last time you spent a day alone—seeing no people, making no phone calls, exchanging no texts or emails, not even watching people on TV? Did you *ever* spend a day completely isolated from society?

David Pearson / Alamy

Social isolation is unnatural. The world of friends and neighbors, fellow students and coworkers, small groups and big crowds, social roles and responsibilities—the *social* world—is humanity's natural habitat. This chapter introduces you to **social psychology,** the branch of psychology that studies people's thoughts, feelings, and actions as they contemplate, interact with, and are influenced by others in society.

If you want to learn about psychology as a whole, social psychology is a great place to start. The social world contains most of "the drama" (Scheibe, 2000) of human life: people texting and shopping; gossiping and arguing; making friends and enemies; following rules and breaking them; falling in and out of love. It is where individuals become members of teams, clubs, schools, companies, religions, communities, and nations and develop a sense of who they are and what is meaningful in life. If psychologists in the rest of the field neglected social psychology, they wouldn't know what people are doing with their lives. And knowing this is the first step in building a science of person, mind, and brain.

We begin with social psychology's study of *social behavior* as it occurs in crowds, groups, and interpersonal relationships. We then turn to *social cognition*—people's thoughts about the individuals with whom they interact. The chapter's final two sections show how social cognition can be more deeply understood by studying (1) culture and (2) the brain.

Social Behavior

Much human behavior is **social behavior,** that is, behavior that occurs in interaction with other people. Let's look at social behavior in three types of settings, ranging from large to small:

1. **Crowds:** Large gatherings of people who do not necessarily know one another
2. **Groups:** Collections of people who know and communicate with each other, have distinctive roles (e.g., a group leader), and may work together toward a common goal
3. **Close relationships:** One-on-one interactions in which you are in frequent contact with, and feel a strong connection to, another person

Crowds

Preview Questions

> How does treating a crowd as a physical object help us understand behavior?
> How do we know that social norms—and not anonymity—shape crowd behavior?
> How does a crowd's actual response to disaster square with how the media portrays it?

Would you kill someone to get a good seat at a concert? Your answer surely is no. How many of your friends would kill somebody to get a good seat at a concert? Your answer is probably zero. Who would kill someone just to get a good seat?

In Cincinnati in 1979, tragedy struck at a concert. Eleven people were killed by concertgoers trying to get a good seat for a show by the British rock band The Who.

How could this have happened? Were there 11 Who fans crazy enough to kill somebody to get a good seat? Was there one crazed murderer who needed seats for himself and 10 friends?

There is no evidence that the concert attracted any crazed murderers. It attracted normal people like yourself who wouldn't choose to kill anybody; reports indicate that fans were "not riotous or violent" (The Who Concert Tragedy Task Force, 1980, p. 1). The culprit, then, was not any individual person. It was something bigger, with a force of its own: a crowd. The uncontrollable behavior of the crowd resulted in those 11 deaths.

Here is what happened. Seating at the concert was not reserved. Thousands of fans lined up ahead of time to get a good seat when the doors opened. There were few doors. As a result, a huge physical force, the crowd, propelled itself through a small physical space, the few doorways. "Rippling human waves of pressure knocked people down and rendered them helplessly trapped and fighting for breath" (http://www.crowdsafe.com/taskrpt/).

Unfortunately, this crowd disaster was not unique. About 2000 people a year die from being trapped in crowds (Hughes, 2003). Sometimes these tragedies are much larger in scope than the Who concert tragedy. In early 2006, roughly 1 million people were in Mecca, Saudi Arabia, for the Hajj, the annual Islamic pilgrimage. Crowding on a pedestrian bridge resulted in the death of 345 of these pilgrims, who were crushed, trampled, or suffocated (Murphy, 2006).

These tragedies teach us something important about people's social behavior in crowds. The behavior cannot be explained in terms of the desires of the individual people in the crowd. No individual Who fan wanted to kill anybody. No individual person on the Hajj wanted anyone else to be trampled to death. The tragedies resulted from the action of the crowd *as a whole.*

How, then, can we begin to understand the force of the crowd as a whole? One way is to treat the crowd as a physical object.

THE PHYSICAL CROWD. People take up space. A big crowd of people thus requires a lot of space. If too big a crowd is crammed into too small a space, people can be squeezed so tightly that they will literally be unable to breathe. One way to understand the behavior of crowds and to avert crowd tragedies is to study the physical nature of crowds in tight spaces. This is what the government of Saudi Arabia concluded after the deaths of the 345 religious pilgrims in 2006.

When people watched videos of that tragedy, they saw that the crowding problem occurred at a very precise spot on the pilgrims' path: a narrow "pinch point" (Murphy, 2006) on the overall route. Might the sheer physical force of the crowd at this particular point have caused the tragedy?

Have you ever been part of a crowd too big for a given space?

To find out, the Saudi government sought the advice of physicist Dirk Helbing (Helbing et al., 2014; Holden, 2007). In analyzing crowd flow through the physical layout of the Hajj route, Helbing developed an analogy: A human crowd is analogous to a fluid. Specifically, the flow of a crowd through walkways and bridges is like the flow of a liquid through trenches or pipes. Whether crowd flow is smooth or turbulent does not depend on the psychological characteristics of the individual people in the crowd. It depends on the rate of flow of the crowd as a whole and the space through which the crowd flows. If flow is too fast or the space is too small, flow—of a liquid or a human crowd—becomes turbulent.

The Who concert tragedy Clothing and shoes that remained after the crowd crush that killed 11 people before a performance of The Who in Cincinnati.

AP Photo / Brian Horton

Crowd flow The behavior of crowds in Mecca during the Hajj has been analyzed by treating the crowd as a physical object, a flowing liquid. The flow of a crowd often depends on physical characteristics (the size of the crowd and the layout of the space through which it moves) rather than psychological characteristics of individual crowd members.

Kazuyoshi Nomachi / HAGA / The Image Works

The crowd-as-fluid approach enabled Helbing not only to identify turbulent spots on the Hajj route (e.g., narrow passages that did not allow for a consistently smooth flow of people), but also to redesign the route to eliminate the turbulence. He reconfigured walkways, barriers, and plazas to create more elongated spaces that reduced "bottlenecks" in the system. The Saudi government then reconstructed the Hajj route according to his plan, and the changes worked: The next year's pilgrimage proceeded safely (Helbing, Johansson, & Al-Abideen, 2007) and there have been no Hajj crowding disasters since.

THE PSYCHOLOGY OF THE CROWD. Treating a crowd as a physical object—a giant flowing liquid—tells us only part of the story of crowds. Crowds aren't *only* physical. They are also psychological. There might be a unique "psychology of the crowd."

This possibility was addressed in one of the first works in the history of social psychology, by a nineteenth-century Frenchman, Gustave Le Bon (1896). Le Bon's interests were both psychological and political. In nineteenth-century Europe, political power shifted from royal dynasties to the public. Although most of us today would applaud this, Le Bon was concerned. He believed that individuals, once gathered into crowds, would become unruly and violent. "Isolated," Le Bon wrote, "[a person] may be a cultivated individual; in a crowd, he is a barbarian—that is, a creature acting by instinct" (Le Bon, 1896, p. 36).

About a half-century later, some American social psychologists proposed a similar theory (Festinger, Pepitone, & Newcomb, 1952). They suggested that people in a crowd lose their normal sense of self and act impulsively, failing to judge whether actions are right or wrong. *Anonymity* was thought to trigger impulsive, aggressive action. In a huge crowd, you're anonymous, and that anonymity might cause you to disregard rules of civilized behavior (Zimbardo, 1970).

If you are thinking like a psychological scientist, you are skeptical. Just because Le Bon and others said that anonymity causes crowd violence does not mean their conclusion is correct; you need to consider research findings. As it turns out, quantitative and qualitative research findings (Chapter 2) highlight factors *other than* anonymity. Let's look at the quantitative (numerical) data first.

Many researchers have measured levels of aggression displayed by participants in two types of experimental conditions. In one, participants are made anonymous (e.g., by dressing them in oversized coats with hoods). In the other, they are identifiable (they wear regular clothing and name tags). People in both conditions have the opportunity to act aggressively; for example, they may deliver electric shocks to people in another room (Zimbardo, 1970). A summary of 60 such experiments did *not* support the view that anonymity increases aggression (Postmes & Spears, 1998). Rather, results highlighted a different psychological factor: *social norms.*

A **social norm** is a socially shared belief about the type of behavior that is acceptable in any given setting. In almost any setting, some types of behavior are acceptable or "normative," whereas others are not. At a funeral, the norm is quiet, somber behavior. At a party, carefree, sociable behavior is normative. Norms often are not stated explicitly; instead, you learn them by observing others. In crowds, people learn social norms by observing others who are near them; they respond to "norms in the immediate social context" (Postmes & Spears, 1998, p. 254). If people near you in a crowd of political protesters are cursing loudly at government officials, you learn that it is acceptable to curse loudly in this setting, and you may do so, too. Crowds, then, affect behavior by defining local social norms.

> **THINK ABOUT IT**
>
> Have you ever been in a large crowd (e.g., at a concert or sporting event)? Once in the crowd, did you immediately lose your sense of self and act in an uncivilized manner? If not, what does that say about Le Bon's theory?

> What are the norms of the place where you are reading this book?

social norm A socially shared belief about the type of behavior that is acceptable in any given setting.

Qualitative data (information derived from interviews or written descriptions of behavior; Chapter 2) reveal a second cause of crowd violence, when it occurs. Some people in crowds *intend to* act violently. They do not lose their sense of self and ability to plan. Rather, they do plan—to be violent (McPhail, 1994). Consider an interview of a British soccer "hooligan" who took part in attacks on fans of a rival team. "I go to a [soccer] match for one reason only: the aggro [the opportunity to act aggressively]," he said. "It's an obsession, I can't give it up" (McPhail, 1994, p. 23). In an interview, one member of a Los Angeles gang said, "It's going to be hard to bring [the violence] to an end. A lot of us been doing this for years and don't want it to stop" (p. 24). Analysis of crowd behavior reveals that small groups of people who intend to act violently create much of the violence in a crowd (McPhail, 1994).

Think about how this finding conflicts with Le Bon's explanation of crowd violence. Le Bon claimed that crowds cause peaceful people to become impulsively violent. But qualitative evidence shows that people who are *not* peaceful strategically choose to engage in violence in crowds.

The puzzle of mob violence
In Athens, Greece, rioting erupted in 2008 after a police action that resulted in the death of a teenager. Why does violence occur in crowds? One possibility is that crowds cause peaceful people to become violent. However, another possibility is that some people enter into peaceful crowds with the intention of engaging in violence.

CROWD RESPONSE TO DISASTER. Crowds often gather for a purpose: to hear a concert, cheer for the home team, or support a politician. Yet sometimes, people don't intentionally gather at all. Instead, they are thrown together unexpectedly. People who previously had no shared purpose—who merely happened to be in the same place at the same time—suddenly can have a common purpose thrust upon them. This happens when disasters strike.

Many of us will never experience firsthand a disaster such as a plane crash, terrorist bombing, or natural catastrophe (earthquake, hurricane, etc.). Yet disasters are more common than you might think. An Internet service (http://hisz.rsoe.hu/alertmap/index.php?lang=eng) that details current disasters and emergencies worldwide lists, at the time of this writing, not just one or two disasters worldwide, but 15: 3 floods, 4 tropical storms or other cases of extreme weather, 5 disasters involving biological contaminants or the release of hazardous materials, 1 forest fire; 1 outbreak of an epidemic disease; and 1 explosion. How do people respond to such events?

One possibility is that they panic. Movies and TV programs sometimes show people responding to disasters by waving their hands in the air and screaming. Yet this is not what people usually do; evidence suggests that widespread panic is rare (Drury, 2004, p. 119). People usually follow instructions from authorities and help each other. Consider some examples:

> In 1977 a fire engulfed a crowded supper club in Southgate, Kentucky. Interviews indicated that people behaved calmly. Employees of the club instructed guests how to reach safety and the guests followed their instructions. No evidence of panic was found (Johnston & Johnson, 1989).

> During the 9/11 disaster, thousands of people who were in the World Trade Center when the planes struck poured into dark stairwells, their only route to safety. How did they act—panicked, clawing over one another for survival? Not at all. Interviews indicate that people treated each other "like old friends." They descended calmly, helping each other. One survivor reported a stranger saying to him, "You know, you look kind of tired, buddy, let me hold your jacket" (Ripley, 2008, p. 112).

> News reports from the 2013 Boston Marathon bombing indicate that, rather than fleeing the scene, large numbers of ordinary citizens remained there in order to help the injured. "The people on the street, the sidewalk volunteers, instead of running away, they stopped and . . . worked the people," a physician reported (Langfield & Briggs, 2013, April 16). The area quickly turned into a relatively calm, orderly medical-care site.

Volunteering in the face of disaster Rather than panicking when disaster strikes, people often respond calmly and helpfully. For example, numerous volunteers assisted New York City police and firefighters in the immediate aftermath of the 9/11 attacks.

Why do people so often respond to disasters by helping rather than panicking? A crowd thrown together by a disaster develops a sense of "shared identity" (Drury & Cocking, 2007, p. 4). The disaster reminds them of something they otherwise might forget: that they are part of the human family, their fate bound together with that of neighbors, coworkers, and even complete strangers. They recognize that they must pull together—and they usually do.

> Have you experienced unexpected kindness in an emergency?

🔥 WHAT DO YOU KNOW?...

1. Which of the following is true of crowds? Check all that apply.

_____ a. Treating the flow of a crowd as analogous to the flow of liquid has allowed for the redesign of public places to avoid crowding disasters.

_____ b. Research indicates that anonymity alone can account for increased aggression in crowds.

_____ c. In crowds, people may be prompted to act according to local norms; if the norms are to behave aggressively, crowd violence can occur.

_____ d. Crowd violence is often instigated by small groups who intend to act violently.

_____ e. During disasters, widespread panic is quite common.

See Appendix B for answers to What Do You Know? questions.

Groups and Social Influence

Preview Questions

› What is the minimum group size necessary for people to cave in to conformity?
› How can you get someone to comply with a request?
› What are the implications of Milgram's research on obedience to authority?

We now move from crowds to groups. This might not seem like much of a move, but it is. The psychological dynamics of crowds and groups differ.

Unlike crowds, the collections of people called *groups* generally know each other, communicate with one another, and share a common purpose. Group members often have well-defined responsibilities; one may be a leader, another an assistant to the leader, and still others may primarily follow the leader's command. Group members may have different goals, creating conflict within the group. Some may hold opinions that differ from those of others in the group and feel pressure to change their opinions. These psychological processes involving communication, conflict, and pressure among group members are **group dynamics.**

Social psychologists try to understand how group dynamics influence the behavior of individuals in the group. Research addresses three types of group influence: *conformity, compliance,* and *obedience.*

CONFORMITY. Conformity occurs when people alter their behavior to match the norms of a group (Cialdini & Goldstein, 2004). If you show up for your first day at work wearing jeans but notice everybody else is wearing a suit, deciding to dress in a suit the next day would be conforming to the group of employees at work.

Classic research by social psychologist Solomon Asch (1955) shows the power of conformity. Participants, upon arriving at Asch's laboratory, joined a small group of people taking part in an experiment that supposedly was about visual perception. Across a series of 18 trials, they were shown a "standard line" and three "comparison lines" and were asked to judge which comparison line was the same length as the standard (Figure 12.1).

> In what situations have you conformed to fit in? When have you refused to conform?

---

figure 12.1

Asch conformity experiment Stimulus material used in Asch's conformity experiment. Participants were asked which of the lines a, b, or c matched the length of the line on the left. This task may seem easy—until everyone else in the room answers "a" instead of "c."

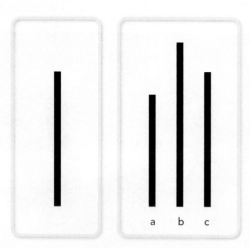

group dynamics Psychological processes involving communication, conflict, and pressure among group members.

conformity The altering of one's behavior so that it matches the norms of a group.

People expressed their judgments out loud; group members, one at a time, indicated which line they thought matched the standard line.

Had you participated in this experiment, you would have found the task easy. On the first trial, one line clearly matches the standard, whereas the other lines differ. The experimenter goes around the room and everyone gives the same answer. On the second trial, the same thing happens: The perceptual task is easy and everyone gives the same answer. But on the third trial, something strange happens. It looks to you, a participant, as if one line obviously matches the standard and the others do not. Yet the first person who responds gives an answer that seems wrong. You think the person just made a mistake. Then the *next* person gives the *same* wrong answer. One by one, *everybody* gives that same incorrect answer. Next it's your turn. What do you do? "Stick to your guns" and give the answer you believe is right, or conform to the group and give the answer everyone else did?

Participants faced this dilemma on 12 of 18 trials. Each time, all other participants gave the same answer, but it plainly was wrong. Did participants conform, that is, give answers that matched those of others in the group?

Before learning the results, you need to know a key piece of information. The other people—the group members who gave the wrong answer—were accomplices of the experimenter (or experimental "confederates"; see Research Toolkit, on the next page). Asch scripted their responses, instructing them to answer incorrectly on 12 of the 18 trials. The real research participant, of course, thought the others were real participants, too.

Asch found that conformity—the degree to which people conformed to the opinions of the group—depended on two factors that he manipulated experimentally: group size and unanimity.

> *Group size.* In different experimental conditions, Asch varied the number of confederates from 1 to 15. Conformity reached its maximum with only three confederates. When there were only one or two confederates, almost all of the real research participants stuck to their own beliefs. But once three or more people answered incorrectly, participants conformed to those incorrect views about one-third of the time; they gave the wrong answer even though the right answer was staring them in the face.

The first lesson about conformity, then, is that even small groups create powerful pressure to conform.

> *Unanimity.* In some studies, Asch eliminated unanimity. He instructed one confederate to give the right answer, while all the others answered incorrectly. With unanimity eliminated, conformity was greatly reduced. Even when only one other person in the group agreed with the participant, the participant was much less likely to conform.

The second lesson about conformity is that group pressures for conformity are greatest when the group is unanimous. When in a group—even a small one—in which no one else's opinions or behaviors match yours, you feel enormous pressure to conform.

The puzzled gent in the center is a participant in Asch's conformity study. The others are confederates whose responses were the same, but seemed to the participant to be wrong. In this situation, Asch found that people often conformed. When asked to speak, many participants gave the same clearly incorrect answer that was offered by others in the group.

Remarkably, conformity occurred in Asch's study even though group members (1) did not explicitly ask the participant to conform (they merely voiced their own answers) and (2) were not in a position of authority with respect to the participant (they seemed merely to be other people who signed up for the study). Group pressures may increase when people make explicit requests or are in positions of authority, as you'll see below.

⊕RESEARCH TOOLKIT

Confederates

Consider this classic social psychology study (Schachter & Singer, 1962). Pairs of people were invited to a lab room and were asked to complete a questionnaire that included the following items:

(1) With how many men (other than your father) has your mother had extramarital relationships?

    a. 4 and under

    b. 5–9

    c. 10 and over

(2) List the childhood diseases you have had and the age at which you had them in the blank spaces below.

    _____

    _____

(3) For which member of your immediate family is each of the following items most applicable? Please write the name of the family member in the blank space following the item.

Does not bathe or wash regularly. _____

Seems to need psychiatric care. _____

When seeing the items, one of the two people flew into a rage. "I get annoyed at this childhood disease question," he said angrily. "I can't remember what childhood diseases I had! . . . 'Does not bathe or wash regularly'—that's a real insult. . . . The hell with it!" he eventually said, "I don't have to tell them all this." The critical point here is that this happened *every time* the experiment was run: precisely the same rage, by the same person.

This person was a **confederate,** an accomplice of the experimenter who pretends to be a real research participant. Every time a real participant took part in the experiment, the confederate took part, too. His responses were the same every time because they were scripted by the experimenter as part of an "anger condition," that is, a condition in which the real participant interacted with someone who was angry. In another experimental condition, a "euphoria" condition, the confederate was consistently happy and upbeat. By assigning participants randomly to the anger or euphoria conditions, the experimenters could determine the effect of a social cue—another person's emotional reaction—on participants' emotional reactions.

In the history of social psychology, confederates have been used frequently. They enable researchers to overcome the conflict between two goals: (1) studying social interactions and (2) conducting research that is well controlled. Naturally occurring social interactions are out of the researcher's control; once two regular people interact, almost anything can happen. But if one of the two is a confederate who looks, acts, and speaks in the same manner each time a participant takes part in a given experimental condition, the researcher gains experimental control.

confederate In a research study, an accomplice of the experimenter who pretends to be a participant.

One might object to the use of confederates because of the deception; the participants are being tricked. Some argue that the costs to participants of deception outweigh the benefits to research (Oliansky, 1991). Yet ethics boards that review research (Chapter 2) often judge that the scientific gains outweigh the costs and grant psychologists permission to use confederates.

In summary, when the social psychologist's job is to create the seemingly impossible—social interactions with experimental control—their research tool is the confederate.

☙ WHAT DO YOU KNOW?...

2. Why is it difficult to maintain experimental control when studying social interactions? How do confederates solve this problem?

Conformity pressures also are influential when groups come together to make a joint decision. Pressure for conformity can produce **groupthink,** a decision-making phenomenon in which group members are so motivated to avoid disagreement, and to reach a shared decision, that they do not properly evaluate the quality of the decision they are reaching (Esser, 1998). Case study research launched social psychology's interest in groupthink. Irving Janis (1971) analyzed historical cases in which government officials made poor decisions, such as the Bay of Pigs decision in which the Kennedy administration invaded Cuba with a military force that was far too small for the task. Janis did not find that Kennedy administration officials were unintelligent. Rather, despite their high intelligence, groupthink produced a decision that was poor. Decision makers neglected critical information that conflicted with the most popular opinion in the group. As a result, their final decision was misguided and costly.

COMPLIANCE. Everyday life bombards us with requests: donate to our charity; learn about our candidate; complete our survey; try our new energy drink. Often you just say no. But sometimes, you find yourself saying yes. You donate, take some campaign materials, complete the survey, or try a free sample of the drink. If you do, your actions are cases of **compliance,** behavior in which individuals agree to an explicit request.

> When was the last time you complied with a request?

Social psychologists have identified techniques that increase compliance. One method is the *foot-in-the-door* technique.

The **foot-in-the-door technique** is a compliance strategy in which someone first makes a small request, in order later to convince people to comply with a larger request. The initial request is so small that almost everyone will agree to it; the small request gets your "foot in the door." Once you're "in," compliance with a big request is more likely. In one study (Freedman & Fraser, 1966/1971), the small request was an appeal to homeowners to sign a "safe driving" petition. The request was so simple that almost everyone agreed. A couple of weeks later, experimenters visited the homes of these people, plus a second group who had not been contacted about the petition. On the visit, the experimenters made a big request: to install a large "drive carefully" sign on their front lawn—a sign so big that workmen would have to dig a hole for a post to hold it. Who'd ever agree to that? People who had previously signed the "foot-in-the-door" petition would! A majority of them agreed to have the sign installed. Among people who had *not* signed the petition, more than four out of five people refused to have the sign installed. Subsequent research confirms that foot-in-the-door enhances compliance (Burger, 1999; Cialdini & Goldstein, 2004).

---

groupthink A decision-making phenomenon in which group members are so motivated to avoid disagreement, and to reach a shared decision, that they do not properly evaluate the quality of the decision they are reaching.

compliance Agreement to an explicit request.

foot-in-the-door technique A compliance strategy in which someone first makes a small request, in order to later convince people to comply with a larger request.

Before you sign a petition, think about the findings of social psychology research Foot-in-the-door research shows that the simple act of agreeing to sign a group's petition makes it much more likely that, in the future, you will comply with a larger request from the group.

Why is foot-in-the-door so effective? It can change the way people think about themselves. For example, after signing the petition, people may feel personally involved in the cause of safe driving. This sense of personal involvement increases later compliance (Freedman & Fraser, 1966/1971).

Another compliance strategy uses distraction. When asked to comply with a request, people often have two reactions in sequence: (1) positive feelings about the request, because it supports a good cause, and (2) negative thoughts about it, because it requires an expenditure of time or money. The **disrupt-then-reframe technique** (Davis & Knowles, 1999) increases compliance by distracting people, so they cannot formulate any negative thoughts. In one demonstration of the technique, researchers conducted door-to-door sales of $3 boxes of Christmas cards for a purportedly good cause; profits went to charity. In one experimental condition, researchers said, "They're $3. It's a bargain." In a second condition, they said, "They're 300 pennies . . . that's $3. It's a bargain." The unusual "pennies" phrasing distracts people. The distraction increased compliance: About one-third of the people purchased cards after hearing that they were $3, but *two*-thirds bought them after hearing that they cost 300 pennies.

Compliance research has significant real-world implications. Findings reveal that people can be affected by compliance techniques without being fully aware of what happened to them. Outside the lab, these techniques can become "weapons of influence" (Cialdini, 2009)—forces that cause people to comply unwittingly with requests from advertisers, political parties, and others who wish to change public opinion and behavior.

OBEDIENCE. Research on conformity and compliance shows that ordinary people who hold no position of power can influence our behavior. What about people who *are* in positions of power? Their influence is explored in social psychological research on **obedience,** which occurs when people adhere to the instructions and commands of an authority figure.

Historically, social psychologists were motivated to study obedience by events of the past century. The twentieth century witnessed extraordinarily horrific genocides, such as the deaths of 800,000 Tutsis in Rwanda (1994), 1.5 million Armenians in Turkey (1915–1918), 2 million Cambodians (1975–1979), and 6 million Jews in the Nazi Holocaust of World War II (1938–1945). It was, as one of the century's leading historians put it, an "age of extremes" (Hobsbawm, 1994).

No one person can individually kill hundreds of thousands of others. For a genocidal system to work, a large number of people must participate. How are we to understand the actions of the thousands of people who played some role in these twentieth-century genocides? Were they all crazed maniacs—Le Bon's "primitive beings"?

For the most part, no, these people weren't crazed maniacs. Many would have described themselves as ordinary employees who were merely following the orders of their superiors. Consider one of the twentieth century's most unforgettable images— "unforgettable" because it was so mundane. When Nazi officers who ran the genocidal system that put 6 million Jews to death were brought to trial after World War II, what did the world see? The officials often looked more like pencil-pushing middle managers running a bureaucracy than mass murderers running a massacre. Adolph Eichmann, who administered the transportation system that took Jews to Nazi death camps, didn't declare his hatred for Jews when he appeared in court. He told the world that he was just following orders: "[I] had no choice but to obey the orders of the Reich government" (Von Lang & Sibyll, 1983, p. 30).

The social psychologist Stanley Milgram observed these trials and posed a scientific question: Why are some orders from authority figures so powerful that people will

disrupt-then-reframe technique A compliance strategy in which targets of compliance efforts are distracted, so they cannot formulate negative thoughts about a compliance request.

obedience Adherence to the instructions and commands of an authority figure.

obey them even if it means harming or killing other human beings? He then devised experimental procedures to identify social determinants of obedience to authority. They proved to be the most compelling studies in the history of psychological science.

Before learning about the experimental procedures, first take note of Milgram's question. He did not ask about the type of person who obeys orders. He asked about the orders themselves and the situation in which those orders are issued. Once again, then, we see a social psychologist reasoning that some social factors are so powerful that they can affect anyone.

Milgram's experiment included three people: an experimenter, a research participant who was assigned the role of "teacher," and a confederate who played the role of "learner" and acted according to a fixed script. In the study, the learner attempted to memorize a series of words. Whenever he made a mistake, the teacher (the real research participant) was instructed to punish him by delivering an electric shock, using the machine pictured here. As the learner made more and more mistakes (according to the script), the experimenter ordered the research participant to deliver stronger and stronger shocks. The dependent variable was the harshest punishment—that is, the highest level of shock—the teacher would deliver before refusing to go on with the experiment. (The machine did not actually deliver electric shocks to the confederate, but research participants did not know this.)

Milgram added three features to the experiment that were so extreme that one would probably expect everyone to refuse to follow the experimenter's orders:

1. Punishments were severe. Shocks ranged from 15 to 450 volts, with the highest ones labeled "Danger: Severe Shock" and "X X X."

2. The learner, a middle-aged man, reported that he had a heart condition.

3. As the shocks were delivered, the learner yelled out in pain and protested against the experimenter. Although seated in an adjacent room, his protests could be heard through the wall: "Let me out of here. My heart is bothering me. . . . Let me out of here! You have no right to keep me here!" During these protests, the experimenter calmly ordered the participant to "please continue. The experiment requires that you continue." The learner's protests continued until the teacher reached the 315-volt mark, at which point the learner ominously fell silent.

Participants faced incredible stress. They had agreed to be in the experiment, and the authority figure running it was ordering them to go on. Yet a person was screaming in pain and demanding to be released from the study. Who would continue to deliver shocks to the learner in a circumstance like this?

It turns out that most people would. In Milgram's study, 26 of 40 participants—about two-thirds—obeyed the authority figure's orders and continued delivering shocks, despite the learner's protests, all the way up to 450 volts, the highest shock level!

Why? Did those participants not care about the learner? That's not it. They cared a lot and, as a result, were under severe strain. "Tension," Milgram reports, "reached extremes. . . . [S]ubjects were observed to sweat, tremble, stutter, bite their lips, groan, and dig their fingernails into their flesh" (1963/1971, p. 536). Yet the majority followed orders. Situational forces caused people—ordinary people who cared very much about the welfare of the learner—to deliver severe shocks.

Milgram's results have profound implications. They show that people will obey authorities even when ordered to harm others, and even when the authority figure is merely an experimental psychologist. Real authority figures—police, government officials, military officers—have greater power to induce obedience. No wonder, then, that governments were able to order the violent campaigns that marked twentieth-century history.

Both: Stanley Milgram

Milgram experiment In the Milgram experiment, a confederate playing the role of a "learner" (top) was strapped into an electrical apparatus that (purportedly) delivered electric shocks administered by the research participant, who was the "teacher." The bottom photo shows the shock generator used by participants in the experiment to (purportedly) deliver electric shocks to the learner. The participant was instructed to flick switches at the bottom of the box to deliver increasingly severe punishments when the learner made errors.

THINK ABOUT IT

Do you think Milgram should have been allowed to run his obedience to authority experiment? His participants were under tremendous stress; they thought they might have killed somebody! Does the knowledge gained from the experiment justify this cost to the participants?

"Maybe," the optimists among you may be thinking, "this sort of brutality can only happen when someone is issuing direct orders. Otherwise, people would treat each other with kindness and respect." Unfortunately, this sunny view of human nature is darkened by the social psychological research you'll read about next.

🌀 WHAT DO YOU KNOW?...

3. Match the concepts on the left with their description on the right.

1. Conformity		a.	A variable that increased the probability that people in Asch's study would conform
2. Unanimity		b.	An agreement to an explicit request
3. Groupthink		c.	Changing behavior to match group norms
4. Compliance		d.	A technique that uses distraction to increase compliance
5. Foot-in-the-door technique		e.	A technique in which a large request is preceded by a smaller request to increase compliance
6. Disrupt-then-reframe technique		f.	Adherence to instructions and commands of an authority figure
7. Obedience		g.	A decision-making process driven by the desire to maintain agreement that results in poor decisions

4. A friend says, "Adolph Eichmann was a monster. Why else would he have played such an integral role in the killing of so many innocent people?" How might Milgram hope you would respond?

Roles and Group Identity

Preview Questions

> Can wearing the uniform of a prison guard cause you to be abusive?
> What force is powerful enough to reduce group rivalry?
> When people don't intervene during an emergency, is it because they are callous and uncaring?

"All the world's a stage," Shakespeare wrote. Of all the metaphors to describe human social life—"It's a rat race," "It's a jungle out there"—none is more apt than Shakespeare's. The stage has actors, the actors have roles, and the roles shape the actors' behavior. When you're assigned a role in a play, you know what you are expected to do. If your role is that of a hero, you shouldn't look scared when the villains arrive. If you're the evil stepmother, it's a license for cruelty.

Everyday life resembles a play or movie (Scheibe, 2000). People have roles. A **role** is a set of behaviors that is expected of a person in a given situation. Here's a simple example. When your psychology class meets, one person has the role of course instructor. Everyone expects a certain type of behavior from the person in that role: showing up on time for class, organizing class plans, doing a lot of talking once class begins. Maybe outside of class your professor is chronically late, disorganized, and quiet. But in class, in the role of course instructor, he or she likely is punctual, organized, and talkative.

What roles will you play this week?

ROLES AND THE STANFORD PRISON EXPERIMENT. How can one study the impact of roles experimentally? In everyday life, people differ not only in their roles in society, but in their personalities, intelligence, physical appearance, and many other qualities—and these factors are jumbled together. Suppose a sports coach is

role A set of behaviors that is expected of a person in a given situation.

competitive and strong-willed. Did the role of coach create that behavior, or was it her natural personality? To study the causal impact of roles, you could create an "experimental society" in which people are assigned to roles randomly. Thanks to random assignment, if people with different roles behaved differently, you'd know the cause was the roles, not the people's personalities.

Stanford University psychologist Philip Zimbardo and his colleagues created such a society. It was a simulated prison. In the Stanford Prison Experiment (Haney, Banks, & Zimbardo, 1973; Zimbardo, 2007), 24 college students participated in what was planned as a two-week-long study of simulated prison life. Students were randomly assigned to the role of guard or prisoner. Guards wore khaki uniforms and sunglasses, carried nightsticks, and were assigned to 8-hour work shifts. Prisoners wore loose-fitting smocks (with no undergarments) with an ID number printed on the front and back, a nylon cap on their heads, and a chain around one of their ankles. They spent 24 hours a day in the simulated prison, in the basement of the Stanford University psychology department.

Zimbardo, the "Superintendent" of the prison, gave students little explicit information about their roles. He merely told the guards to maintain order and told the prisoners that, in the simulated jail, they were to be prisoners. Unlike the Milgram experiment, there were no specific orders about exactly how to act. In principle, prisoners and guards could have behaved however they liked; they could have spent the week just relaxing.

But that's not what they did. Instead, students assigned to the role of guard treated prisoners in a "negative, hostile, affrontive, and dehumanizing" manner (Haney et al., 1973, p. 80). They belittled the prisoners. "I got tired of seeing prisoners in their rags and smelling the strong odors of their bodies" (p. 88), a guard reported. They abused prisoners physically. "I went to cell 2 to mess up a bed which the prisoner had made," another guard reported, "and he grabbed me, screaming that he had just made it, and . . . I lashed out with my stick and hit him in the chin" (p. 88).

Students assigned to the role of prisoner behaved passively, seemingly accepting that the guards were in control. They experienced great stress from the guards' abuse, with five prisoners having to be released from the experiment due to depression, anxiety, or bouts of crying. Prisoners reported personality changes. "I began to feel," one said, "[that] I was losing my identity, that . . . the person who volunteered to get me into this prison [in other words, the person's pre-prison self] was distant from me. . . . I was [prisoner number] 416, I was really my number and 416 was going to have to decide what to do" (Haney et al., 1973, p. 87).

Eventually, the experiment spiraled out of control. Some prisoners staged a rebellion. Guards suppressed it forcefully. Afterward, guards treated prisoners even more harshly, compelling them to perform demeaning tasks, such as cleaning toilet bowls. Prisoners showed more and more signs of emotional disturbance. Finally, Zimbardo had to halt the experiment—after only 6 of the planned 14 days.

Why were the guards abusive and the prisoners passive? It can't be due to their personalities, since people were assigned to their roles randomly; with a different flip of a coin, the guards would have been the prisoners and vice versa. Their differences in behavior, then, were caused by their different social roles. Once assigned to their roles, guards and prisoners knew how to act. From stories, movies, news reports, TV shows, and so forth, they understood the expected behavior of a guard and a prisoner, and their actions fit those expectations.

Zimbardo (2007) argues that the Stanford Prison experiment's lessons extend to real-world events. For American citizens, one of the most shocking events of recent history was the abuse of prisoners by U.S. soldiers during the Iraq War. News reports and photographic evidence revealed that soldiers at the Abu Ghraib prison, near Baghdad, Iraq, had beaten prisoners, stripped them and made them assume humiliating poses,

Karen Ballard / Redux

Philip Zimbardo conducted the Stanford Prison experiment, whose results suggested that situational forces can cause ordinary people to commit evil acts.

Philip G. Zimbardo, Inc.

Stanford Prison experiment These "prisoners" in the Stanford Prison experiment were research participants randomly assigned to the role of prisoner rather than guard. Above, a group of prisoners is lined up against a wall by a participant assigned to the role of "guard."

and intimidated them with military work dogs (Hersh, 2004). Were the American soldiers inherently evil people? Zimbardo argues they were not. The source of evil was not the personality of the soldiers but the situation they were in, which caused people—even people who were not inherently evil—to mistreat prisoners. "The Pentagon blamed the whole thing on a 'few bad apples,'" Zimbardo noted, but "I knew from our experiment, if you put good apples into a bad situation, you'll get bad apples" (Dreifus, 2007, April 3).

The Stanford Prison experiment has limitations. As the researchers themselves were aware (Haney et al., 1973), it was not a carefully designed study with multiple experimental and control conditions (see Chapter 2). It was merely a demonstration of the power of social factors over the behavior of individuals assigned to different roles. Zimbardo's presence within the prison (as Superintendent) complicates interpretations of these factors. His behavior may have influenced participants in a manner that went beyond the effects of their assigned roles, per se (Griggs, 2014; Haslam & Reicher, 2003). Yet, even if so, the Stanford Prison experiment stands as a compelling demonstration of one of the major lessons of social psychology: the potential power of social forces over the behavior of ordinary people.

GROUP IDENTITY AND ROBBERS CAVE. Prisons are unusual—virtually the only place where one group has complete control over another. Do groups exert much influence in typical, everyday situations?

Anecdotal evidence suggests that they do. Whatever group you are a part of—a group of friends, a neighborhood, a church, an ethnic group, a city, a nation—if it is important to you, not only do you become part of the group, the group also becomes a part of you. Social psychologist Marilyn Brewer (1991, p. 467) explains that people develop *social identities*—an understanding of who they are in the social world—that is based significantly on their group membership. Once you identify with a group, your social identity influences your thoughts, feelings, and behavior.

Social identities are apparent in how people describe themselves. Self-descriptions commonly include not only a personal identity (e.g., physical characteristics, personality traits) but also a social identity; people say that they see themselves as members of groups (Hornsey, 2008).

Group identities can form rapidly. Even people who have been members of groups for only a few days may

> How do you describe yourself to others?

strongly identify with their group and see others as rivals. A classic study by Muzafer Sherif and collaborators (1954), conducted at Robbers Cave State Park in Oklahoma, illustrates this. Sherif divided 22 fifth-grade boys at a summer camp into two random, equally sized groups. The groups spent time apart during the camp's first week. In that week, boys quickly became attached to their group, even giving their group a nickname: the "Rattlers" and the "Eagles." When the boys were then brought together for sports competitions, they were heated rivals. They called each other names, burned each other's group flag, and planned raids of the others' campsite. They looked like lifelong enemies—even though the groups were formed randomly just a week earlier!

Sherif was able to eliminate the group rivalry as quickly as he created it. In the last week of camp, he presented challenges that could only be accomplished if the two groups worked together: He disrupted the camp water supply (which required the two groups to work together on repairs), told the boys that the camp couldn't afford to rent a movie (which prompted the Rattlers and Eagles to pitch in money together), and caused a truck to become stuck in mud (with the boys literally pulling together to get it out). Working together toward shared goals transformed the groups. Former enemies became friends; they sang songs together and laughed about

Group identity People from diverse backgrounds, who might even be complete strangers, can quickly identify with one another as members of a group, especially when they are competing against some other group.

Altrendo Images / Getty Images

their earlier rivalry. By the time camp ended, the Eagles and Rattlers wanted to leave camp together, on one bus, and cheered when staff said they could.

Sherif's results have fascinating implications. They suggest that group rivalries can be reduced by having rivals work together toward a shared goal. History shows that shared goals foster a sense of unity. For example, the 9/11 tragedy enhanced American's sense of national unity, as people realized that they needed to work cooperatively, as one big group, to achieve their aim of national security (Li & Brewer, 2004).

ROLE AMBIGUITY AND BYSTANDER INTERVENTION. The studies you've read about so far have something in common: Participants know their role. They are teachers or learners, prisoners or guards, Rattlers or Eagles. But sometimes we don't know what our role is. If a friend is drinking heavily at a party, what is your role—to be the voice of reason who tells him to stop drinking or the party buddy who encourages more fun? If two friends are arguing, what is your role—to act as the moderator who tries to resolve their differences or the passive onlooker who gets out of their way? And what, the social psychologist asks, determines the role you choose?

Research exploring this question was sparked by a tragedy in 1964. New York City resident Kitty Genovese was stabbed to death while returning home from work. Thirty-eight local residents heard her screams. Some looked out their apartment windows and witnessed the violence. But during the long and bloody attack, none intervened. It wasn't until the attack was long over that anyone even called the police.

Why did people just stand by instead of trying to help? Research on *bystander intervention* by John Darley and Bibb Latané (1968) suggests an answer. Darley and Latané invited participants to a discussion of issues in college life. The discussion took place through an intercom system; each participant could hear, but not see, the other participants, who were in nearby rooms. In reality, only one discussant was a real research participant; the others were confederates. During the discussion, the experimenters staged an emergency in which one of the confederates appeared to be having a seizure. "I'm-er-er-h-h-having a-a-a real problem," said a voice on the intercom, "gonna die-er-help-er-er-seizure-er-." The dependent variable was the time that elapsed before the real research participant took action to help the apparent seizure victim. The independent variable was group size. Based on the number of voices heard over the intercom, the real participant thought the group consisted of either two, three, or six people.

Group size strongly influenced helping behavior (Figure 12.2). In bigger groups, there was a *bystander effect:* People were slower to intervene, and in many cases never intervened at all, when a lot of other bystanders were around. Half the participants

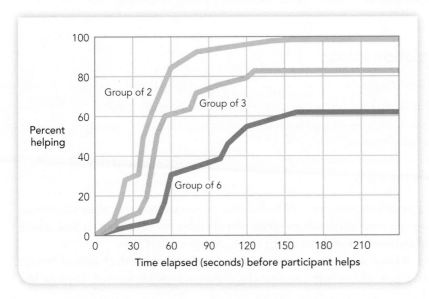

figure 12.2
Bystander intervention
The graph shows the speed with which people helped someone who apparently was having a seizure. Participants were assigned to groups of varying size (2, 3, or 6 persons, where the other members were confederates). Helping behavior varied in the different-sized groups. In larger groups—that is, when more bystanders were around—participants were slower to help (Darley & Latané, 1968).

assigned to six-person groups took nearly two minutes to respond. By comparison, in the two-person groups, when participants believed they were the only bystander who could help, almost everyone responded in less than a minute.

Why was group size so important? In emergencies, bystanders are aware of the people involved in the emergency and also the other bystanders in the vicinity. When there are no other bystanders, an individual knows that he or she is the only person who can provide help. But when lots of bystanders are around, one of them might provide assistance. The presence of other bystanders creates a **diffusion of responsibility:** lowered feelings of personal obligation to respond to someone in need, because others may respond. Larger groups diffuse responsibility and thereby lower people's tendency to intervene.

Darley and Latané's findings teach an important lesson. When hearing that city dwellers failed to respond to an emergency, one might conclude that city dwellers are callous and uncaring. But research indicates that the explanation is the situation, not the people. In big cities, there are likely to be more bystanders, more diffusion of responsibility, and thus less helping. No matter who you are, diffused responsibility causes you to be less likely to help.

WHAT DO YOU KNOW?...

5. True or False?
   a. In the Stanford Prison experiment, participants were not randomly assigned to the condition of guard or prisoner, so it is likely that their outrageous behavior was caused by the personalities of the people within each condition.
   b. Philip Zimbardo, in applying the lesson learned from the Stanford Prison experiment, has pointed out that the behavior of the U.S. soldiers at Abu Ghraib prison in Iraq was the result of a "few bad apples."
   c. In the Robbers Cave study, campers were not randomly assigned to their groups (which they later named the Rattlers and Eagles), so it is likely that their eventual rivalry was caused by the personalities of the people within each group.
   d. Ultimately, it was working toward shared goals that united the Rattlers and Eagles at Robbers Cave.
   e. In Darley and Latané's experiment on bystander intervention, the more participants there were available to help the person having a seizure, the faster any one person intervened to help.
   f. One reason the bystander effect occurs is that the greater the number of people present, the greater the diffusion of responsibility.

Close Relationships

Preview Questions

> What is the most sure-fire strategy to get someone to like you?
> To attract a mate, should you emphasize your psychological strengths or your physical attractiveness?
> Is romantic love anything more than sexual passion? How long does it last?
> How is love like a drug?

Crowds and groups can affect your behavior. But the encounters that most affect your life as a whole are *close relationships*—those that involve frequent contact and strong psychological connections with another person (Kelley et al., 1983).

Some close relationships occur naturally. From birth, we are in the hands of parents and other caregivers, with whom our first close relationships are formed. Later in life,

diffusion of responsibility Lowered feelings of personal obligation to respond to someone in need, because others might respond instead.

however, we have choices. We make friends with people we like, develop romantic relationships with people to whom we are attracted, and form committed relationships with people we love. Let's look at the social psychology of liking and friendships, attraction and romantic relationships, and love and commitment.

LIKING AND FRIENDSHIPS. Look at Figure 12.3, a diagram of an apartment building. Which people, from which of the 10 apartments, do you think are most likely to be friends?

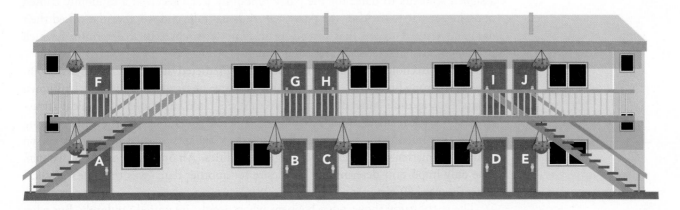

figure 12.3

Location, location, location Diagram of an apartment building similar to the one studied in research on liking and friendship by Festinger and colleagues (1950). Their results showed that, when it comes to the question of which residents would be friends with one another, a major determinant was location. People were most likely to develop friendships with their next-door neighbors.

The question might sound ridiculous. How can you predict who will be friends before you know more about the individual people—which ones like loud parties or quiet teas, Mozart or hip-hop, cats or dogs?

As it turns out, you can predict quite well. The big predictor, a team of social psychologists found, is physical distance (Festinger, Schachter, & Back, 1950). The people in the apartment complex shown in Figure 12.3 who tended to like each other and be friends were those who lived near each other; the building's most common friendship pattern, by far, was that people were friends with their next-door neighbors. Across different floors of the building, the placement of stairwells influenced friendship patterns. People who were closely connected by a stairwell (e.g., people in apartments 7 and 1) were more likely to be friends than others (e.g., people in apartments 7 and 3).

> Where do your favorite friends live?

A study of trainees at a police academy produced a similar result (Segal, 1974). The academy assigned seats in classrooms alphabetically, by last name. After their academy training, officers named their closest friends in the police force. Nearly half the time, they named people right next to them in the alphabet—the people who were closest to them physically in the classroom (Segal, 1974).

Why would physical distance have such a big effect? One explanation is *mere exposure*; people tend to like things more after they encounter them frequently (see the section on mere exposure and attitude change later in this chapter). We see the folks next door more frequently than the folks far away, and so we like them.

Proximity is not the only factor that affects liking, however. People also tend to like friends who support their opinions, help them to take part in activities they enjoy, and make them feel better about themselves (Finkel & Eastwick, in press). But one factor that reliably causes people to like each other is living next door.

ATTRACTION AND ROMANTIC RELATIONSHIPS. Some close relationships are just friendships. But others have that special spark: romance. What causes us to be romantically attracted to some people but not others?

To find out, social psychologists threw a party—that, in reality, was a psychology experiment (Walster et al., 1966). At the start of an academic year, they invited more than 700 university freshman to a dance party. Three aspects of the party made it a research study: Before the party, (1) students reported their psychological qualities (social attitudes, personality styles, intelligence) to researchers, and (2) the researchers assigned students to dates for the party randomly (each received a randomly chosen opposite-sex partner). After the party, (3) students indicated whether they liked their date and wanted to see that person again. The researchers then determined which psychological characteristics predicted romantic attraction.

Which psychological quality do you think predicted attraction? As it turns out, *none* were strong predictors. But something else was: physical attractiveness. Unknown to students, as each entered the party, researchers rated their level of physical attractiveness. Physical attractiveness strongly predicted romantic attraction; if a dating partner was rated as highly physically attractive, students wanted to see that person again—no matter what their psychological qualities. Among both men and women, "the only important determinant" of desire for another date "was the date's physical attractiveness" (Walster et al., 1966, p. 508).

The party study shows what happens when people are paired randomly. But what happens when people have a choice? How do they select others to date? Most can tell, intuitively, that things might not work out if they pursue the singularly most attractive and popular person in town. People therefore tend to "match," that is, to pursue dating partners whose level of physical attractiveness and popularity is similar to their own (Taylor et al., 2011). In the game of dating, people are strategic.

Without that wall in the middle, it wouldn't have been much of a game On ABC's *The Dating Game*, TV's first dating show, people selected a date from among three contestants. Key to the game was that they could not see the contestants. Instead, they posed questions (e.g., "If you were in charge of everything, what would you make the national pastime?") and made their selection based on the contestants' answers. It may have made for a good show, but it had little to do with real life. Social psychology research suggests that, if they had seen their dating prospects, most people would have simply chosen the most attractive contestant, no matter what answer was given.

LOVE AND COMMITMENT. Sometimes the spark of romance triggers the enduring flame of love. Social psychology cannot unravel all the mysteries of love, but it can answer some questions. One asks: What is it—what psychological ingredients have to be present for you to say that you are "in love"?

To find out, psychologists asked a large group of people to rate whether each of a large number of psychological experiences is a component of love (Aron & Westbay, 1996). Statistical analyses of their ratings identified three main components of love: (1) euphoric and sexually aroused feelings of *passion;* (2) honest and supportive *intimacy;* and (3) loyal, devoted *commitment* (Table 12.1). Love, then, is more than romantic attraction; it includes deep commitment within a relationship that is open and supportive.

Can all three components of love last a lifetime? You may worry that passion is a flame that inevitably flickers out, even if intimacy and commitment remain. If so, then scientific evidence can calm your worry. Research shows that, for some lucky couples, the flames of passion burn for a lifetime. Both qualitative and quantitative evidence support this conclusion (Acevedo & Aron, 2009). When married couples are interviewed, qualitative analyses reveal substantial subgroups of couples who say that they are intensely, romantically in love, even after decades of marriage. When feelings are measured quantitatively, many long-term-married couples are found to have levels of passion that match those of newlyweds.

These happy marriages have major benefits. People in romantically successful marriages are happier with their life as a whole, enjoy better mental health, and even experience better physical health (Acevedo & Aron, 2009).

That last result might sound mysterious: Why would love cause people to feel better physically? Research has begun to unravel that mystery. In one study, participants were asked to rate the amount of pain they experienced when exposed to a very hot physical stimulus (Younger et al., 2010). While this was happening, the participants looked at pictures showing either (1) their romantic partner or (2) an equally attractive acquaintance. When viewing their romantic partner, participants were in less pain. Brain images taken during the study showed why. Pictures of the romantic partner activated the brain's reward centers (i.e., neural systems involved in the processing of positive, rewarding stimuli). Activation of reward centers, in turn, directly reduces the experience of pain. Romantic love thus was like a pain-relieving drug; it activates biological mechanisms that reduce pain.

Lifelong love Research shows that, for some lucky couples, romantic passion still burns bright after decades of marriage.

table **12.1**

Components of Love		
Passion	**Intimacy**	**Commitment**
Gazing at the other	Openness	Devotion
Euphoria	Feel free to talk about anything	Commitment
Butterflies in stomach	Supportive	Put other first
Heart rate increases	Honesty	Need each other
Sexual passion	Understanding	Protectiveness
Sex appeal	Patience	Loyalty

The relationships that we call "love" have three features: passion, intimacy, and commitment (Aron & Westbay, 1996). The table lists the psychological experiences that people most strongly associate with each.

TRY THIS!

Before you start the next section of this chapter, on social thinking (or social cognition), it's time to do some thinking yourself. Go to www.pmbpsychology.com and try your hand at the Try This! activity for Chapter 12. Do it now, before we discuss it a little later in this chapter. ◉

CONNECTING TO THE SOCIAL PERCEPTION OF FACES AND EMOTIONAL STATES

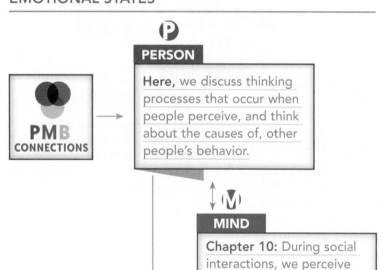

Ⓟ
PERSON

Here, we discuss thinking processes that occur when people perceive, and think about the causes of, other people's behavior.

Ⓜ
MIND

Chapter 10: During social interactions, we perceive others' emotional states by recognizing facial muscle movements that are associated with distinct emotions.

Ⓑ
BRAIN

Chapter 5: We recognize that other people are, in fact, *people* thanks to a brain region (the fusiform gyrus) that is key to facial perception.

PMB CONNECTIONS

Social Cognition

We spend a lot of our time doing things with other people. But we spend even more of our time *thinking about* other people. "Why did my brother sound so weird on the phone when he told me about his new girlfriend?" "Is my new friend from psych class a real friend, or does she just want somebody to help her with her homework?" "How embarrassing that I forgot my professor's name—I wonder what she thinks of me?" Thoughts like these can swirl through your head, hour after hour, day after day.

Social psychologists call these thoughts *social cognition*. **Social cognition** refers to people's beliefs, opinions, and feelings about the individuals and groups with whom they interact socially. Three main topics in the study of social cognition are *attributions, attitudes,* and *stereotypes.*

Attributions

Preview Question

› How good are we at figuring out the causes of others' behavior?

In everyday life, we often ask *why:* Why aren't my grades higher? Why are people saying no when I ask them out? Your answers to such questions are called *attributions.* An **attribution** is a belief about the causes of a social behavior.

Attributions are important in two ways. First, they affect motivation and emotion. For example, students who attribute school difficulties to a lack of ability rather than to a lack of effort become less motivated (Weiner, 1985). Teenagers who attribute personal problems to causes that cannot be changed, rather than to changeable ones, tend to become depressed (Hankin, Abramson, & Siler, 2001). Second, accurate attributions—correct diagnoses of the causes of events—are a first step in altering behavior you want to change. If you want to improve your grades or get people to start saying "yes" when you ask them out, you first want to figure out the cause of the current problems.

PERSONAL VERSUS SITUATIONAL CAUSES. When we try to figure out the causes of someone's behavior, two types of causes stand out: personal and situational. If a friend says, "I am struggling in calculus; I might not pass," the cause could be:

> *Personal:* Perhaps he lacks math ability, or has not exerted enough effort.

> *Situational:* Maybe the course (the situation he is in) is extremely difficult.

What determines whether we make personal or situational attributions? According to an attribution theory developed by Harold Kelley (1967; Kelley & Michela, 1980), the key factor is the degree to which potential causes *covary* with the behavior to be explained—that is, whether the potential causes co-occur with the behavior. Consider two cases:

1. Your friend struggles in *many* courses, and most other students in the calculus class find it easy. The behavior covaries with personal factors (qualities of your friend), so you make a personal attribution; for example, you conclude that your friend isn't very good at math.

2. Most people are struggling in calculus—even students who find other courses easy. Here, the behavior (struggling in courses) covaries with a situational factor (the calculus class), so you make a situational attribution; for example, you conclude that calculus is difficult.

THE FUNDAMENTAL ATTRIBUTION ERROR. Thus far, attributions seem simple, so you might expect people to be very good at attributional reasoning. But it turns out that people commonly commit an error—the *fundamental attribution error* (Ross, 1977). The **fundamental attribution error** is a pattern of thinking in which people underestimate the causal influence of situational factors on people's behavior and overestimate the causal influence of personal factors. Recall, as an example, the case of Kitty Genovese. If you first thought that the cause of people's failure to help was the callous personality of city dwellers, you committed the fundamental attribution error.

The fundamental attribution error is evident in a study in which participants made attributions about the causes—personal or situational—of the content of a political essay (Jones & Harris, 1967). They read an essay expressing either favorable or unfavorable opinions about the Cuban revolutionary leader Fidel Castro. In different experimental conditions, participants learned that the essay writer had either (1) a *choice* of what to write (pro- or anti-Castro) or (2) *no choice,* that is, the writer had to compose either a pro- or an anti-Castro essay. After reading the essay, participants judged the writer's true opinion of Castro; that is, they made an attribution about whether a personal factor (the writer's political opinion) determined the essay's content.

Imagine yourself in this experiment. In the *choice* condition, the task is easy: The writer chose the essay content, so it must match his true opinion of Castro. In the *no-choice* condition, it also seems easy; because the writer had no choice about the content, you have no idea of his true opinion. You might expect that, in the no-choice condition, participants' thoughts about the essay writer would be the same whether the essay was pro- or anti-Castro.

Now look at the results (Figure 12.4). In the *choice* conditions, when the essay said good (or bad) things about Castro, participants of course judged that the writer's true opinion about Castro was positive (or negative). The surprising result occurred in the *no-choice* conditions. Here, people committed the fundamental attribution error: They judged that the writer's personal opinion was the cause of the essay's content, even though a situational factor, the instruction given to the writer, was its true cause.

Do you think this worker likes Vitaminwater? Logically, you have no idea what he thinks of it; he is only driving the truck because that's his job. But research on the fundamental attribution error shows that people would still tend to conclude that the worker likes the product; they erroneously would attribute his behavior, driving the truck, to personal factors (his attitude toward the beverage) rather than to situational causes (driving the truck is his job).

Jochen Tack / ImageBroker / Newscom

social cognition People's beliefs, opinions, and feelings about the individuals and groups with whom they interact socially.

attributions Beliefs about the causes of social behaviors.

fundamental attribution error Pattern of thinking in which people underestimate the causal influence of situational factors on people's behavior and overestimate the causal influence of personal factors.

figure 12.4

Attributions When participants read an essay expressing favorable opinions of Fidel Castro (a pro-Castro essay), they judged that the writer truly had relatively favorable opinions of Castro. This occurred even in a *no-choice* condition in which participants knew that the writer had no choice over whether to write a pro- or an anti-Castro essay (Jones & Harris, 1967). Participants, then, attributed the writer's behavior to a personal characteristic—the writer's attitude—rather than to a situational feature—the fact that the writer had no choice about which type of essay to write.

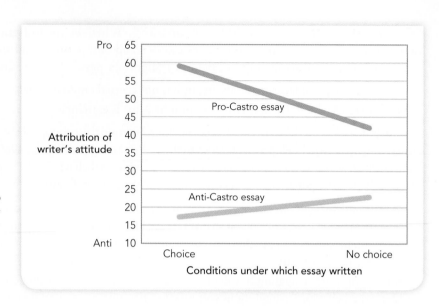

"**Sure, all the answers are in front of him,** but he just seems like some kind of super-genius" (actual comment in an online chat about *Jeopardy* host Alex Trebek). What do you think of quiz show hosts? Exceptionally smart? If you think so, you're committing the fundamental attribution error. Sure, he knows the answers, but there's a situational cause for that.

In another fundamental attribution error study, participants played a quiz game in which pairs of participants were randomly assigned to the role of questioner or answerer (Ross, Amabile, & Steinmetz, 1977). The questioner role was relatively easy: devising quiz questions on a topic of one's own choosing. The answerer role was difficult: trying to answer the questions devised by the questioner. After playing the game, both the questioner and answerer rated their own "general knowledge" and that of the other participant. A third person, who simply watched the quiz, also rated their general knowledge.

On logical grounds, there is no reason to think one participant was more knowledgeable, in general, than the other. Even if the answerer had trouble answering questions correctly, this doesn't mean the questioner was smarter. Participants were assigned to these roles randomly. If questioners had been answerers instead, maybe they wouldn't have looked so smart. Yet when people made their ratings after the quiz game, the winner was the fundamental attribution error: Contestants and observers of the game made personal attributions, judging that the questioner was more knowledgeable than the answerer.

> Can you think of a time when someone attributed your behavior to personal factors when it could have been explained by situational factors?

In summary, when considering the causes of others' behavior, people often overestimate the influence of stable personal qualities (e.g., attitudes, personality, intelligence) and underestimate the impact of situational forces (but see This Just In).

 **THIS JUST IN**

Attributions—Causes or Reasons?

In the social cognition research you just read about, researchers tried to determine whether people attribute behavior to personal or situational causes. Social psychologist Bertram Malle (2011) has raised a different question: When explaining behavior, do people always cite *causes*?

Consider the following examples:

Example 1: On a wintry day, someone slips on ice and falls. The person explains her behavior this way: "The ice caused me to slip and fall."

Example 2: In a comedy skit, a clown winds up to throw a pie at someone, but slips and falls, landing facedown on the pie. The clown explains her behavior this way: "When planning my comedy routine, I reasoned that it would be funnier to slip and fall on the pie than throw it."

The examples differ in two ways:

1. Whether the behavior was *accidental* or *intentional*. Falling on the ice was an accident. Falling on the pie was intentional.

2. Whether the explanation cited a *cause* of behavior or a *reason* for behavior. The slippery ice was a cause. But the desire to be funny was the reason for the clown's planned fall.

Causes differ from reasons. When mentioning a cause, the person could be wrong; maybe she slipped on a banana peel she didn't notice, not a piece of ice. But when explaining a personal reason for action, the speaker normally can't be wrong. The clown knows, absolutely for sure, that the reason she fell is because she planned it, thinking her fall would be funny.

People tend to explain *un*intentional behavior in terms of causes: factors that directly produce the behavior. However, they commonly explain intentional actions—planned, strategic behaviors—in terms of reasons (Malle, 2007; Figure 12.5). Reason-based explanations often are miniature "stories" that involve people in situations, with thoughts and actions that unfold over time (e.g., "My sister went to the other party instead because she wants to meet some guy who she hopes will be there").

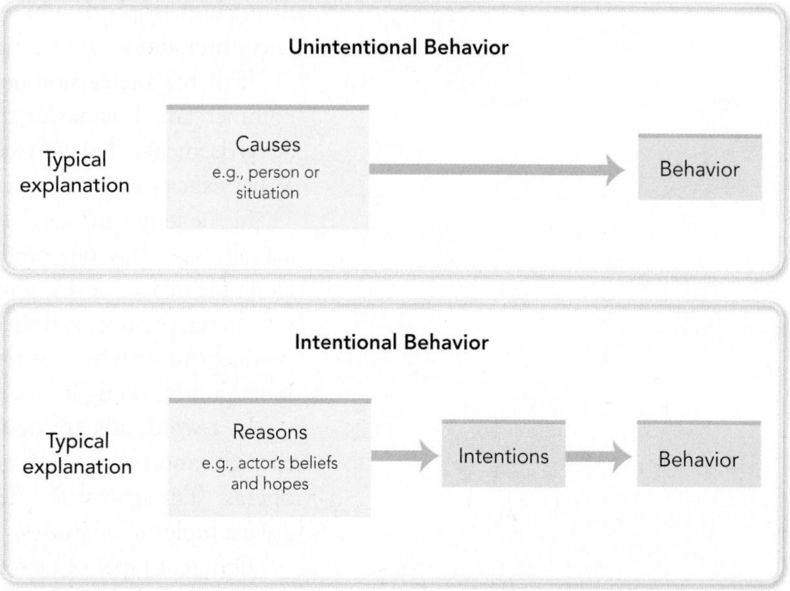

figure **12.5**
Intentional and unintentional behavior People typically give different types of explanations for unintentional versus intentional behavior. Unintentional behavior, such as slipping on ice and falling, is explained in terms of causes (e.g., "The ice caused the person to slip"). Intentional behavior, such as falling on purpose for comedic reasons, is explained in terms of a person's *reasons* for behavior (e.g., "The reason she fell is because she thought it would make the audience laugh").

🏵 WHAT DO YOU KNOW?...

7. For the two descriptions below, determine whether the given attribution is best characterized as a reason or a cause.
   a. When explaining why she missed the train, Mia said, "I guess I misread the schedule."
   b. When explaining why he apologized to the grocery store clerk, Ron said, "I accused her of giving me the wrong change, but it turns out, she was right. I had been a real jerk and I felt awful about it."

Attributions, as you have seen, involve thinking (about causes of behavior). In a second aspect of social cognition, thoughts combine with feelings to form social *attitudes*.

🏵 WHAT DO YOU KNOW?...

8. Up ahead, you notice an empty space in the crowded parking lot. As you get closer, you see that there isn't enough room to pull in because the car next to it is parked crookedly. You mutter to yourself, "What kind of a jerk would do that?" Have you made the fundamental attribution error? Explain.

9. In the quiz game study, the contestants and observers of the game rated the questioner as more knowledgeable than the answerer. Why was this interpreted as the fundamental attribution error?

Attitudes

Preview Questions

› Are strong arguments always more persuasive?
› When do our behaviors change our attitudes?
› When do our attitudes predict our behavior?

A quick question: If you're the average American, what feature of our society did you encounter about 40,000 times a year while growing up (Comstock & Paik, 1991)?

If there's a television nearby while you're reading this, you've got a big hint: It's TV commercials. Businesses spend billions of dollars a year on the tens of thousands of advertisements that you see on TV—plus the Internet, radio, billboards, and so on. What exactly are they trying to accomplish with these ads?

In the long run, they're trying to get you to buy their products. Yet, many ads don't actually say, "Buy our products!" They're more subtle. Advertisers present their product alongside images of sex, power, prestige, or sheer fun. They know that people tend to like sex, power, prestige, and sheer fun, and hope that some of this liking will "rub off" on their product. Advertisers thus try to shape your thoughts and feelings; they want you to think more positive thoughts about Coke than Pepsi (or iPhones than Samsung Galaxys, etc.).

In a word, ads are designed to change your *attitudes*. An **attitude** is a combined thought and feeling that is directed toward some person, object, or idea. "I don't like opera," "I'm against the death penalty," and "I think all the Kardashians are terrific" are examples of attitudes.

Different types of factors can cause attitude change. Let's look at three: (1) *persuasive messages* and their influence on thinking processes; (2) *cognitive dissonance* that occurs when people act in a manner inconsistent with their attitudes, and (3) *mere exposure,* that is, attitude change that occurs merely as a result of repeatedly being exposed to an object.

PERSUASIVE MESSAGES AND ATTITUDE CHANGE. Suppose a political ad tells you that a smiling, well-groomed candidate has "the best experience for the job." How—that is, through what psychological processes—might the ad affect your attitudes? A theory developed by Shelly Chaiken and her colleagues (Chaiken, Liberman, & Eagly, 1989) identifies two types of thinking processes (or "information processes") that come into play: *systematic* and *heuristic.*

1. **Systematic information processing** is careful, detailed, step-by-step thinking. If you scrutinize arguments ("Does this candidate really have 'the best experience'?") and carefully consider alternatives ("Sure, he's experienced at government, but maybe he doesn't know anything else"), you are thinking systematically.

2. **Heuristic information processing** is thinking that employs mental shortcuts or simple rules of thumb (also see Chapter 8). For example, if you rely on superficial appearances ("He looks like he knows what he's doing"), you are thinking heuristically.

How systematically are you thinking when you watch TV?

Any given persuasive message may have different effects, depending on whether people are thinking systematically or heuristically. This is evident from research that experimentally manipulated two factors: (1) *argument strength* (participants heard arguments that were either strong or weak), and (2) *information-processing style* (in one of two conditions, participants were distracted and given little time to think about the arguments, thereby forcing them to think heuristically rather than systematically). Stronger arguments produced more attitude change—but *only* when participants could think systematically (Mackie & Worth, 1989).

This finding explains why advertisers often do not even bother to present strong, carefully worded arguments in TV commercials. Much of the time, people are so distracted that they wouldn't pay enough attention for the arguments to make any difference.

Systematic and heuristic information processes are two psychological routes through which persuasive messages can change attitudes. Another way of changing attitudes is cognitive dissonance.

COGNITIVE DISSONANCE AND ATTITUDE CHANGE. **Cognitive dissonance** is a negative psychological state that occurs when people recognize that two (or more) of their ideas or actions do not fit together sensibly. Here's an example. Suppose you

---

attitude A combined thought and feeling directed toward some person, object, or idea.

systematic information processing Careful, detailed, step-by-step thinking.

heuristic information processing Thinking that employs mental shortcuts or simple rules of thumb.

cognitive dissonance A negative psychological state that occurs when people recognize that two (or more) of their ideas or actions do not fit together sensibly.

I should get myself one of those sale items, whatever they are While multitasking, our attitudes may be affected by media messages that would be ineffective if we were paying more attention to them. We rely on heuristic rather than systematic thinking processes when distracted, so our opinions may be affected even by arguments that are weak.

Bruce Sallan / BoomerTechtalk.com; Desktop image: Martin Poole / Getty Images

are an environmentalist, but to make some extra money, you take a part-time job for a company that is drilling for oil in a wildlife preserve. Taking the job conflicts with—in other words, is "dissonant" with—your environmentalist attitudes. When you recognize this, you may feel bad about the conflict. The bad feeling is known as cognitive dissonance.

Cognitive dissonance is psychologically uncomfortable. People thus are motivated to reduce it. One way to reduce dissonance is to change your attitudes. If you convince yourself that "maybe oil drilling in wildlife preserves isn't all that bad," your behavior (taking the job) and attitude ("isn't all that bad") are not as dissonant anymore. Cognitive dissonance theory predicts that when people engage in behavior that conflicts with their attitudes, the attitudes will change.

Researchers tested this theory by targeting people's attitudes about a boring task (Festinger & Carlsmith, 1959). In the first step of the experiment, participants spent an hour working on a task that was extraordinarily dull and monotonous (participants turned pegs in a pegboard). Their attitudes toward the task were negative because it was so boring. Afterwards, participants were told that the experiment was over—but in reality, it had barely begun. There were three more research steps:

1. Participants were asked to tell the *next* participant in the study that the experiment was very interesting. This behavior (saying it was interesting) conflicted with participants' attitudes (that the associated task was boring).

2. In different experimental conditions, participants were paid either $1 or $20 for telling the next participant that the boring study was interesting.

3. Later, participants were interviewed by someone who appeared to be unconnected with the experiment, who determined participants' true attitudes about the experiment and its boring task.

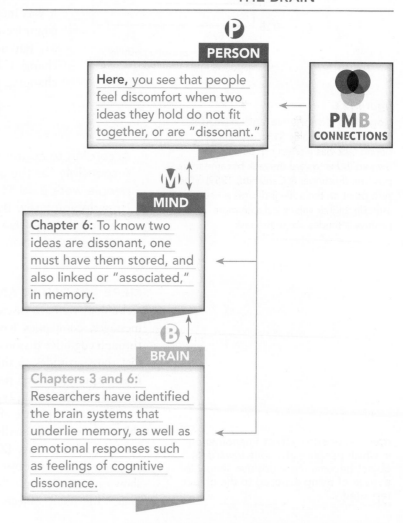

CONNECTING TO MEMORY AND THE BRAIN

PERSON

Here, you see that people feel discomfort when two ideas they hold do not fit together, or are "dissonant."

PMB CONNECTIONS

MIND

Chapter 6: To know two ideas are dissonant, one must have them stored, and also linked or "associated," in memory.

BRAIN

Chapters 3 and 6: Researchers have identified the brain systems that underlie memory, as well as emotional responses such as feelings of cognitive dissonance.

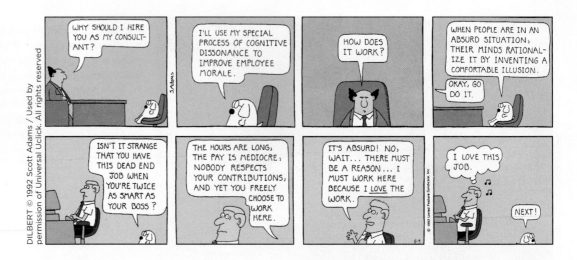

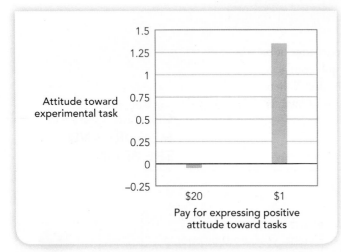

figure 12.6
Cognitive dissonance and attitudes
After being paid only $1 to say that a boring task was interesting, participants' own attitudes toward the task became more positive. (Festinger & Carlsmith, 1959). (The zero point on the scale indicates a neutral attitude; higher values indicate more positive attitudes about the task.)

After all this, who do you think would have more positive attitudes about the experiment? You might guess it was the people who were paid $20 rather than $1; people like getting money. But cognitive dissonance theory predicts the opposite result. When paid $20, people experience little cognitive dissonance because they know why they said that the boring task was interesting: to earn a lot of money. But when paid only $1, the low income does not justify the action of lying to a fellow student. In this condition, participants experienced dissonance between two conflicting ideas: (1) "the task was boring" and (2) "I said it was interesting (for a mere $1)." Just as the theory predicted, this cognitive dissonance produced attitude change (Figure 12.6). In the $1, but not the $20, condition, people's attitudes toward the task changed, becoming positive. People reduced cognitive dissonance by changing their attitudes.

THINK ABOUT IT

According to cognitive dissonance theory, feelings of dissonance were responsible for the attitude change that occurred in the study where people were paid $1 or $20 to say that a boring task was interesting. How do you know that this is true? The researchers did not measure feelings of cognitive dissonance. Maybe some other psychological process was responsible for the results.

MERE EXPOSURE AND ATTITUDE CHANGE. The first two attitude change techniques we have discussed take effort. To change your attitudes with persuasive messages, companies have to create advertisements. To change people's attitudes through cognitive dissonance, you have to get them to perform behaviors that contradict those attitudes. A third method of attitude change takes no effort at all. In the **mere exposure effect,** people's attitudes toward an object become more positive simply as a result of being exposed to the object repeatedly (Zajonc, 2001).

The mere exposure effect is surprising. You might expect people to be bored by things they see repeatedly, and to like them less. Yet mere exposure reliably makes attitudes more positive (Zajonc, 1980, 2001). In research demonstrating this, participants see pictures of objects. Some are displayed only once or twice, whereas others are shown repeatedly (e.g., 25 times). Participants then indicate how much they like each object. Inevitably, objects seen repeatedly are liked more.

mere exposure effect Phenomenon in which people's attitudes toward an object become more positive simply as a result of being exposed to the object repeatedly.

Mere exposure should seem familiar to you from this chapter's Try This! activity. There you saw exactly the sort of research procedures that provide scientific evidence of the influence of mere exposure on attitudes.

TRY THIS!

Three aspects of the mere exposure effect are particularly remarkable:

> It works for an extremely wide range of objects. Mere exposure increases the liking of even meaningless objects, such as geometric shapes or words from a foreign language people do not know (Zajonc, 1980).

> It works for both people and animals. Researchers played different sounds to baby chicks before they were hatched and then, after the chicks were born, determined which of the various sounds they preferred. The chicks liked the sounds they heard most often before they had hatched (reviewed in Zajonc, 2001).

> It works even when objects are shown so briefly that people can't recognize them. When researchers display pictures of objects for just a few thousandths of a second, the displays are so brief that, later on, people do not remember seeing the objects. Yet they like the ones that are shown more frequently (Bornstein & D'Agostino, 1992).

Mere exposure helps to explain phenomena that otherwise would be puzzling. Consider what happens when people are asked which of two photos they like more: a normal picture of themselves or a left–right reversed picture (created by "flipping" the normal image horizontally). A large majority prefer the reversed photo (Mita, Dermer, & Knight, 1977). Why? Mere exposure! People usually see themselves by looking in a mirror. Mirrors reverse images from left to right. (If you look in the mirror and touch your right ear, you appear to be seeing someone who is touching his or her left ear.) Because people have been exposed to a reversed image of themselves repeatedly, they like that image more.

FROM ATTITUDES TO BEHAVIOR. You've seen how attitudes can change. A second question is whether attitudes predict behavior.

How could people's attitudes not predict their behavior? If you have more positive attitudes toward Pepsi than Coke, you buy Pepsi. If you like candidate Williams more than Washington, you vote for Williams. But, reflecting on what you've learned in this chapter, you will realize that people's attitudes often do *not* predict their behavior. "Teachers" in the Milgram study did not express negative attitudes toward "learners," yet they administered seemingly lethal shocks to them. It is unlikely that bystanders in the Darley and Latané study had negative attitudes about the person having a seizure, yet many failed to help.

So when do attitudes predict behavior? Under three circumstances (Ajzen & Fishbein, 1977):

1. *When situational influences are weak.* Powerful situational forces—the orders in the Milgram study, for example— overwhelm personal attitudes. But when situational

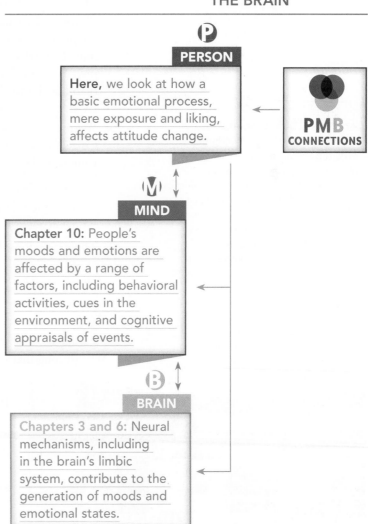

Eventually, you'll like it Thanks to mere exposure effects, people's attitudes toward unusual objects gradually become more positive.

Lonely Planet Images / Getty Images

CONNECTING TO EMOTION AND THE BRAIN

Ⓟ PERSON

Here, we look at how a basic emotional process, mere exposure and liking, affects attitude change.

PMB CONNECTIONS

Ⓜ MIND

Chapter 10: People's moods and emotions are affected by a range of factors, including behavioral activities, cues in the environment, and cognitive appraisals of events.

Ⓑ BRAIN

Chapters 3 and 6: Neural mechanisms, including in the brain's limbic system, contribute to the generation of moods and emotional states.

Mirror exposure On the left is a normal photo of President Obama. On the right is that same photo reversed from left to right. To you, the photo on the right might look odd. But to the president, it probably looks just fine—in fact, if he is like most people, he prefers it to the one on the left. Whenever Barack Obama looks into a mirror, he sees an image like the one on the right. Mere exposure effects would result in his liking it more.

Both: Pete Souza / Obama Transition Office via Getty Images

influences are weak, attitudes predict behavior. Consider a voting booth. No one can see who you are voting for; situational factors are essentially eliminated. Your voting behavior, then, directly expresses your political attitudes.

2. *When people pause to think about their attitudes and themselves.* You often go about daily activities without stopping to think, "What is my attitude about this activity?" You might, for instance, have positive attitudes about dental hygiene, but if you have a big exam tomorrow, you might not have time to think about dental hygiene and forget to brush your teeth. Attitudes predict behavior more strongly when people do stop to think about themselves and their attitudes. Social psychologists have demonstrated this through a simple experimental manipulation: the presence of a mirror. Mirrors draw people's attention to themselves, making it more likely that they will think about their personal attitudes. People's attitudes predict their behavior more strongly when they are in the presence of a mirror than not (Froming, Walker, & Lopyan, 1982; see Carver & Scheier, 1998).

> In what situations do you feel self-conscious? Do these situations make you more aware of your attitudes?

3. *When attitudes and behaviors are equally specific.* Consider the following two questions about your attitudes:

> How much do you like popular music in general?

> How much do you like the band that performed the song you most recently downloaded?

These questions differ in how *specific* they are. The first question asks about popular music in general, whereas the second asks about one specific band.

Now consider two questions about your behavior:

> How much money are you likely to spend on music (downloads and concert tickets) this year?

> How likely are you to buy downloads or concert tickets by the band who performed the last song that you downloaded?

Again, the first question is general, and the second one is specific.

Attitudes most strongly predict behavior when the attitude and the behavior being measured are equally specific (Ajzen & Fishbein, 1977). In our example, people's attitudes about music in general might predict their overall music purchasing, and their attitudes about a particular band might predict their purchasing behavior toward that band. But when attitudes and behavior are at different levels—for example, attitudes toward music in general, and behavior toward one particular band—the behavior and

Hill Street Studios / Getty Images

Attitudes, behavior, and the voting booth People's attitudes toward political candidates accurately predict voting behavior. Voting possesses all three of the characteristics that maximize the relation between attitudes and behavior: (1) Situational influences are weak (no one can see your vote or disrupt you while you are voting); (2) people pause to think about their attitudes and their choices (voters can take as long as they like, so they have plenty of time to think); (3) attitudes and behavior are equally specific (the candidates you like and dislike are listed on the ballot, for you to choose).

attitudes may be unrelated. Lots of factors other than your attitudes toward music in general will determine your behavior toward a particular band.

In summary, attitudes do predict behavior, but not always. They predict best when situational factors are weak, people think about their attitudes, and measures of attitudes and behavior are equally specific.

🕊 WHAT DO YOU KNOW?...

10. True or False?
    a. If you have crafted a strong argument for why your friends should vote for your candidate, the degree to which you can change their attitude will be greater if they are listening very carefully than if they are distracted.
    b. In the Festinger and Carlsmith cognitive dissonance study, the participants who had been paid $20 to lie about how enjoyable the task was experienced cognitive dissonance, which led to attitude change.
    c. According to the mere exposure effect, a person may come to really like his or her cell phone simply because he or she is repeatedly exposed to it.

11. For each of the scenarios described below, specify whether the attitude is likely to predict the behavior.
    a. Attitude: I like spicy food in general.
       Behavior: Choosing a particular restaurant that is known for its hot sauces, among all the possible choices of restaurants.
    b. Attitude: I think men and women should be paid equally.
       Behavior: Deciding whether a new female hire deserves the same pay as the new male hire, when your sounding board consists of your feminist coworkers who remind you of your ideals.
    c. Attitude: I think the union should authorize a strike.
       Behavior: Voting that the union should authorize a strike, when voting is done orally, and so far, everyone has voted "no" on the matter.

Stereotyping and Prejudice

Preview Questions

› Is it even possible to avoid stereotyping?
› How can being reminded of your own group's stereotype interfere with intellectual performance?
› How do psychologists measure attitudes that no one wants to admit having?
› What cognitive, emotional, motivational, and social factors cause prejudice?
› How can prejudice be reduced?

Not all beliefs are equally important to the life of society. Some, such as our views of sports teams, soft drinks, or celebrities, play only a minor role. Others affect the fabric of social life. One of these is *stereotypic* beliefs.

A **stereotype** is a simplified set of beliefs about the characteristics of members of a group. For instance, a person who believes that everyone of British ancestry is intelligent but aloof, or that all people of Italian ancestry are friendly and emotional, would be said to hold stereotypes about those groups.

Stereotyping has been a part of human life throughout history. One after another, different groups have been the target of negative stereotypes, with members of other groups seeing them as, say, cheap, lazy, aggressive, unintelligent, or unscrupulous. Sometimes stereotypes contain positive content, too; for example, in U.S. society there is a stereotype that Asian Americans are particularly skilled at mathematics (Cheryan & Bodenhausen, 2000). (Though it contains positive content, this stereotype can have social costs for Asian Americans; Wong & Halgin, 2006.)

stereotype A simplified set of beliefs about the characteristics of members of a group.

Votes for women The denial of votes to women is an instance of discrimination: unjust treatment of individuals based on their group membership. In the United States, women were not assured the right to vote until 1920.

Archive Photos / Getty Images

The presence of stereotypic beliefs in a society fosters **prejudice,** which is a negative attitude toward individuals based on their group membership. Disparaging thoughts and feelings about individuals in a group are the hallmark of prejudice.

Stereotyping and prejudice, in turn, contribute to **discrimination,** or the unjust treatment of people based on their membership in a particular group. The history of the United States, a nation founded on the notion that all people are created equal, is laced with examples of stereotyping, prejudice, and discrimination. For example, members of the group "women" could not vote until the year 1920. Members of the group "Black" could not be sure of exercising this basic right until the passage of the national Voting Rights Act in 1965.

SOCIAL-COGNITIVE PROCESSES IN STEREOTYPING AND PREJUDICE. Most people are aware of society's stereotypes—it's hard to miss them—but do not want to make prejudiced statements. Can they avoid it? Research suggests that it is nearly impossible to stop stereotypic thoughts from coming to mind, but it *is* possible to stop yourself from saying them in public. To understand this, one has to distinguish between two types of thinking: *automatic* and *controlled* (Devine, 1989; also see Chapter 6). Automatic thinking processes occur rapidly—so fast that you cannot control them. Controlled thinking processes require effort and can be influenced by the person doing the thinking (Kahneman, 2011).

In a study of automatic and controlled thinking (Devine, 1989), a researcher first identified two groups of participants: people (1) high and (2) low in racial prejudice toward African Americans. She then gave both groups two tasks:

1. *Automatic thinking:* The task measured the degree to which words stereotypically associated with African Americans automatically influence people's thoughts.

2. *Controlled thinking:* People wrote down thoughts that came to mind for them when they thought of African Americans; the task measures controlled thinking because people can control what they write, excluding certain thoughts that come to mind.

On the first task, the groups did not differ. The automatic thinking measure revealed that stereotypic thoughts can pop into anyone's mind. But on the second task, they *did* differ; low-prejudice people wrote down fewer negative thoughts about African Americans. The findings show that although the minds of people low in racial prejudice did contain society's negative stereotypes about African Americans, these individuals could exert the mental effort needed to prevent themselves from expressing those thoughts (Devine, 1989).

> When have you had to remind yourself to rethink a stereotype?

The lesson is that, if you live in a society with stereotypes, it is almost impossible not to learn them. However, you can counteract prejudice by reminding yourself, through controlled thinking processes, that stereotypes are simplistic, inaccurate portrayals of your fellow citizens.

STEREOTYPE THREAT. The research on stereotyping we just discussed focuses on people who *hold* stereotypes. But what about those who are the *targets* of stereotypes?

Research pioneered by Claude Steele (whom you met in the opening pages of this book) shows that stereotypes can harm people's intellectual performance. This occurs through **stereotype threat,** which is a negative emotional reaction people have when they realize that they might confirm a negative stereotype about their group (Steele, 1997). When threatened by a stereotype, people perform less well on tests of intellectual ability.

---

prejudice A negative attitude toward individuals based on their group membership, involving disparaging thoughts and feelings about individuals in a group.

discrimination Unjust treatment of people based on their group membership.

stereotype threat A negative emotional reaction that occurs when people recognize the possibility of their confirming a negative stereotype about their group.

Stereotype threat occurs when three factors coincide:

> An individual is trying to perform well on a task.
> The individual belongs to a group that, according to a social stereotype, is expected to perform poorly on this task.
> The individual is reminded of the stereotype.

When these occur together, people face a psychological threat: They might confirm the negative stereotype. Even if they know the stereotype to be false, they still may worry about performing in a way that confirms it. These worries can interfere with people's performance, causing them to achieve at levels below their true ability.

Steele tested this idea in a study of stereotype threat among Black college students taking an intellectually challenging test. White and Black students completed the test in two different experimental conditions. In one, they simply took the test. In the other, they first completed a demographic questionnaire asking them to indicate their racial background. This simple manipulation affected test scores. When participants indicated their race—which activated stereotype threat among Black students—Black students obtained lower test scores, and White students outperformed them to a large degree. When students did not indicate their race, the difference between Black and White students' scores was substantially reduced (Figure 12.7).

Racial and ethnic stereotypes are not the only ones that can create stereotype threat. Another is gender stereotypes. Women are subjected to a stereotype portraying them as inferior to men in math. Research shows how this stereotype can affect performance. In one experimental condition, male and female participants were told that, on a set of math problems they were to attempt, men's and women's test scores usually differed (information consistent with the stereotype). In this condition, men outperformed women. However, in another experimental condition, participants were told that men's and women's scores usually did *not* differ on the math problems they would be given—an instruction that reduced stereotype threat. Here, women and men performed equally well (Steele, 1997). Women therefore had the ability to perform as well as men, but did not do so when subjected to stereotypes.

A meta-analysis of more than 100 stereotype threat studies confirms Steele's original finding, that stereotype threat can impair intellectual performance (Nguyen & Ryan, 2008). When researchers study the flow of conscious thinking during task performance (see Chapter 9), they find that stereotype threat causes people's thoughts to "wander," that is, it causes people to become distracted and to begin thinking about topics other than the task at hand. These mental distractions impair performance (Mrazek et al., 2011).

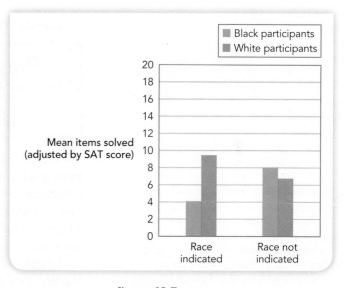

figure 12.7
Stereotype threat and intellectual performance In research by Claude Steele and colleagues (1997), Black and White participants took a test under experimental conditions in which they either did or did not indicate their racial background. Indicating race activated stereotype threat among Black students, lowering their test scores.

IMPLICIT MEASURES OF STEREOTYPES AND PREJUDICE. In the study of stereotypes and prejudice, a big scientific challenge involves measurement. Suppose one tried to measure racial stereotypes by asking people, "Do you think that [people of a given ethnic group] are inferior to your group?" You can see the problem: Even people who believe their group is superior may not want to *admit* that they think this. People might not answer honestly. What you need is some strategy to measure stereotypic beliefs that does not rely on explicit self-reports. Fortunately, psychologists have created one: *implicit measures*.

An *implicit measure* is one in which participants cannot tell what a psychologist is measuring. The test does not contain explicit statements that would give participants clues about its purpose, and when taking the test, participants do not directly report on their personal qualities. Nonetheless, the test measures people's beliefs. To see how implicit tests work, let's look in detail at one: the implicit association test, or IAT (Greenwald, McGhee, & Schwarz, 1998).

In an IAT that measures racial stereotypes, participants are shown two types of stimuli: (1) names that are typically European American (Heather) or African American (Ebony), and (2) words that are either emotionally positive ("happy") or negative ("evil"). When a name or word appears, participants must press, as quickly as possible, one of two keys on a computer keyboard. On some experimental trials, participants are asked to press the keys according to the following rule:

Press A if:	**Press B if:**
European American name	African American name
or	or
Positive Word	Negative Word

On other trials, they press the keys according to another rule:

Press A if:	**Press B if:**
European American name	African American name
or	or
Negative Word	Positive Word

When people's personal thoughts match the rules of the task, they perform the task more quickly. If, for example, people have mostly positive thoughts about European Americans and negative thoughts about African Americans, they would perform the task more quickly when a negative word is paired with an African American name than when a negative word is paired with a European American name. The measure of stereotyping compares the speed with which people perform the task under the two conditions.

Research shows that European Americans perform the task more quickly under the first condition than the second. Even among European Americans who disavow racial stereotypes when asked explicitly about race, the IAT reveals an implicit preference for European American names (Greenwald et al., 1998). In the years since the IAT's development, many studies have found that implicit measures reveal stereotypic beliefs and attitudes that are not identified by traditional questionnaires (Petty, Fazio, & Briñol, 2009). Implicit measures of attitudes open a window into the mind, revealing mental content that previously was hidden.

> What implicit beliefs would you be surprised to learn you held?

PREJUDICE: ORIGINS AND REDUCTION. How did prejudice originate? And, whatever its origins, how can it be reduced? Let's conclude our coverage of stereotyping and prejudice by addressing these questions.

When searching for origins of prejudice, there are two factors to consider: (1) psychological processes and (2) historical factors, specifically, the history of the people toward whom prejudice is directed.

Gordon Allport (1954) discussed three psychological processes that contribute to prejudice: generalization, hostility, and scapegoating:

1. *Generalization* occurs when people regard different things as essentially the same. When people think that all individuals in a group are basically the same—that is, when they generalize about a group—they are more likely to become prejudiced toward it.

2. *Hostility* is a negative emotion that people direct toward others who are seen as rivals or enemies. When people see themselves as competing with another group, they are prone to express hostility verbally, for example, by using ethnic or racial slurs.

Competition, hostility, and prejudice The nation of Italy is, relatively speaking, a racially tolerant country; surveys indicate that its citizens' views about racial and ethnic diversity are similar to those of many other European nations (Berggren & Nilsson, 2012). Yet it recently was the scene of a shocking act of hostile prejudice. During a soccer game, Black players from the team AC Milan were subjected to racial abuse by fans of the opposing team. AC Milan player Kevin Prince Boateng took a stand—he walked off the field in protest. His teammates joined him, and the game was stopped. The abuse occurred in exactly the type of situation that psychologist Gordon Allport identified as one that triggers prejudice: an interaction in which members of a different racial or ethnic group are rivals, in competition with one another.

Imago sportfotodienst / Newscom

3. **Scapegoating** occurs when people who are frustrated with their own circumstances blame members of another group for their plight (Glick, 2005). This blame may reflect people's motivation to maintain a positive view of themselves, which they can do by avoiding thoughts about their own faults and shifting blame onto others (Newman & Caldwell, 2005). Allport illustrated this with the example of a worker who "was unhappy in his job . . . had failed to become an engineer as he had once hoped . . . [and] railed against 'the Jews who run this place'" even though, in reality, "not a single Jew was connected with either the ownership or the management" (Allport, 1954, p. 349).

An analysis of general psychological processes, such as Allport's, is valuable yet limited. It implies that individual cases of prejudice can be understood as examples of the three psychological processes (hostility, generalization, and scapegoating). Yet some cases of prejudice may require not only a psychological analysis, but also a historical one. Consider the case of African Americans.

The psychologists Stanley Gaines and Edward Reed (1995) have argued that a full understanding of prejudice and the African American experience requires that one confront the unique history of this group. The African American experience involves not only generalization, hostility, and scapegoating, but also "the exploitation of a people [who were] stripped forcibly of home, property, and, to some extent, culture and family" (p. 99) in the slave trade.

Gaines and Reed draw on the insights of the great African American scholar W. E. B. Du Bois, who identified a unique aspect of African American psychological experience. Du Bois explained that African Americans experience a "divided social world" (Gaines & Reed, 1995, p. 99). On the one hand, they are Americans—citizens of the nation. On the other, they find it hard to identify with their nation because, historically, it treated African Americans as property. Even after slavery was abolished, mainstream society subjected African Americans to prejudice and discrimination. If you are African American, they explain, you are "both an American and not an American" (Gaines & Reed, 1995, p. 97)—a citizen, yet aware that your nation has treated your group shamefully. Others similarly explain that the African American experience includes a unique "tension between the individual's 'blackness' and the broader white society" (Sellers et al., 1998, p. 21).

Intergroup contact Research on intergroup contact shows that when members of different ethnic and racial groups work together, prejudice is reduced.

Whatever its roots, can prejudice be reduced? A large body of research (Paluck & Green, 2009) suggests that it can—through intergroup contact. In **intergroup contact** interventions, psychologists arrange for members of different groups to meet and spend time together. For instance, students from different racial and ethnic groups may spend time together in the same classroom, or employees from different groups may work together on the job. An analysis of results from more than 500 intergroup contact studies yields results that are encouraging for those hoping to reduce prejudice (Pettigrew & Tropp, 2006). Groups that spend more time together are found to express less prejudice toward one another. (This finding should remind you of Sherif's "Rattlers" and "Eagles" study, discussed earlier in this chapter.)

The cases of stereotyping and prejudice we have reviewed occurred in one region of the world, the United States. Let's now widen our world view by considering questions of culture.

scapegoating Blaming members of another group when frustrated with one's own circumstances.

intergroup contact A technique for reducing prejudice in which members of different groups meet and spend time together.

> ⚡ WHAT DO YOU KNOW?...

12. Thanks to _____ thinking processes, people are able to counteract prejudice. Reminding people that they belong to a group for which there is a stereotype may cause them to worry that they will _____ that stereotype. When doing the IAT, people who associate men with science and women with humanities would perform the task more quickly when a science word is paired with a _____ name than when a science word is paired with a _____ name. Allport identified three processes inherent in prejudice: generalization, hostility, and _____, but ignored prejudice that was rooted in the exploitation of African Americans in the _____ trade.

Culture

In your daily life, you take a lot of things for granted; certain behaviors are so common that you give them little thought. Consider these:

> When you meet somebody, she tells you her name and asks yours.

> If a child is given a toy, he sees it as his personal property and puts it in his toy chest.

> If you talk to a physician about a seriously ill relative, she may provide a medical prognosis, including an estimate of how much time the relative has left to live.

There's nothing surprising about these examples. It's normal to learn a person's name, to treat a gift as personal property, and to get a medical prognosis from a doctor. Pretty much everyone you know does these things and believes them to be appropriate.

In any large group of people, there inevitably are beliefs about people, social settings, and the world at large that all essentially share. People's shared beliefs, and the social practices that reflect those beliefs, constitute a group's **culture.**

Knowing the cultural beliefs and practices of your group is essential for navigating everyday life. Cultural knowledge enables you to figure out what things mean (Geertz, 1973). Without

> What cultural practices do you take for granted, if any?

this knowledge, everyday circumstances can be baffling. Tourists, for example, often lack this knowledge and experience *culture confusion* (Hottola, 2004). When traveling in a new part of the world, they notice that their native cultural knowledge does not fully apply to their current circumstances. Everyday encounters—such as forms of introduction to strangers, eye contact and how it is interpreted, conversational topics that are judged to be private, daily schedules and expectations regarding punctuality (Spradley & Phillips, 1972)—violate tourists' expectations, leaving them baffled.

Cultural Variability in Beliefs and Social Practices

Preview Question

> What are some examples of how culture shapes what we think and do?

Cultures vary; what is commonplace in one may be taboo in another. For example, you might think people always say their name and ask for yours when introduced. But they don't. On the Indonesian island of Bali, names traditionally have been "treated as though they are military secrets" (Geertz, 1973, p. 375). Balinese introduce themselves instead by referring to their place in their community (e.g., "I am the village chief") or family ("I am the mother of the village chief"). This social practice reflects the culture's great valuing of community and family ties (Geertz, 1973).

The other behaviors listed at the beginning of this section also vary culturally. In some cultures outside the United States, people view property as shared rather than personally owned. A child might see a toy, or an article of clothing, as family property rather than personal property (Trumbull, Rothstein-Fisch, & Greenfield, 2001).

Travel Etiquette Recommendations

In Asia, never touch any part of someone else's body with your foot.

In Fiji, an affectionate handshake can be very long, and may even last throughout an entire conversation.

In Nepal, it is considered bad manners to step over someone's outstretched legs, so avoid doing that.

In Italy, pushing and shoving in busy places is not considered rude, so don't be offended by it.

—Robert Reid (2011)

---

culture People's shared beliefs and the social practices that reflect those beliefs.

Regarding medical prognoses, in some Southeast Asian cultures, people do not want one. They believe that "only God knows when someone will die naturally." The implication is that "the only way a physician could know when someone will die is if that physician planned to kill the patient" (Galanti, 2000, p. 336).

Cultural Variability in Social Psychological Processes

Preview Question

> What assumption can social psychologists be faulted for making?

Now that you've read about cultural variability, think back for a moment to the material earlier in this chapter. The social psychology experiments discussed had something in common. Did you notice it? Almost all of them were carried out in the same culture, namely, that of the United States or Western Europe, or what is generally called "Western" culture. Would the research have yielded the same results in different cultures?

For many years, social psychologists rarely asked this question. They assumed that their research results would be the same anywhere in the world. More recently, however, the field of cultural psychology (Kitayama & Cohen, 2007; Shweder & Sullivan, 1993) has emerged, grown rapidly, and questioned this assumption. (The growth is evident in the Cultural Opportunities features that appear throughout this book.) **Cultural psychology** is a branch of psychology that studies how the social practices of cultures and the psychological qualities of individuals mutually influence one another. Let's revisit one of the topics explored earlier, attribution, and view it through the lens of cultural psychology.

Private road? If you live in the United States, the idea of a private road may seem commonplace to you. But in other parts of the world, it may seem alien. In some cultures, social practices highlight the interest of the community rather than the individual, and property more commonly is seen as shared rather than individually possessed.

Steve Shepard / Getty Images

◎ CULTURAL OPPORTUNITIES

Social Psychology

As you have seen, each chapter of *Psychology: The Science of Person, Mind, and Brain* explores the role of cultural factors in psychological experience. The study of culture is particularly prominent in social psychology. Today's social psychologists recognize that people's beliefs about social situations—and about themselves—are shaped by the culture in which they live (Markus & Hamedani, 2010).

The theory and research described throughout this section on culture show how social psychology has advanced by seizing upon the opportunity to study behavior and cognition in cultural contexts.

Culture and Attribution to Personal Versus Situational Causes

Preview Question

> Just how fundamental is the fundamental attribution error?

In 1984 psychologist Joan Miller ran a study that, in some respects, looked like a traditional attribution experiment. She asked participants to explain some everyday

cultural psychology Branch of psychology that studies how the social practices of cultures and the psychological qualities of individuals mutually influence one another.

TRUCK STOP / Alamy

Culture and the fundamental attribution error In the United States, people often commit the fundamental attribution error; they attribute behavior to personal characteristics and underestimate the influence of situational factors (e.g., one might wonder, "What was that crazy driver thinking to drive the bus on a muddy road?") Cross-cultural research shows that people in India are more likely to attribute behavior to social circumstances and thus are less likely to commit the attribution error (e.g., someone in India might think it was the driver's duty to try to navigate the bus along a route determined by others in a position of authority).

THINK ABOUT IT

What other psychological processes, beyond attributions, might vary across cultures? Might cultures differ in the degree to which they experience cognitive dissonance? Or are influenced by pressures for conformity?

cross-cultural study Research in which identical research procedures are carried out in different cultures.

individualistic In the study of cultural variations, a pattern of cultural beliefs and values that emphasizes individual rights to pursue happiness, speak freely, and "be yourself."

collectivistic In the study of cultural variations, a pattern of cultural beliefs and values that emphasizes individuals' ties to larger groups such as family, community, and nation.

actions. Based on fundamental attribution error research, you would expect her participants to overestimate the causal impact of people and underestimate the impact of situations. Miller, however, took an extra research step: conducting the study in both the United States and southern India. Hers was a **cross-cultural study,** that is, research in which identical research procedures are executed in different cultures.

Her work identified cultural differences in attribution. People in the United States primarily explained other people's behavior in terms of person qualities, for example, "That's just the type of person she is" (Miller, 1984, p. 967). Citizens of India, though, more frequently made attributions to social context; for example, "The man is unemployed" or "She did not have the [social] power" to act differently (Miller, 1984, p. 968). In India, then, the fundamental attribution error was not nearly as evident as in the United States.

Subsequent research confirmed this finding. When making attributions about the causes of events such as crime or sports performance, people in countries in the Middle East, South Asia, and East Asia are less likely than Americans to attribute behavior to personal dispositions; they more frequently cite situational factors (Oyserman, Coon, & Kemmelmeier, 2002).

Why do the cultures differ? One possibility is differing cultural beliefs and practices (Markus & Kitayama, 1991; Triandis, 1995). In the Western nations of North America and Western Europe, the dominant culture is **individualistic**—one that emphasizes individual rights to pursue happiness, speak freely, and "be yourself." Many Eastern (e.g., South and East Asian) nations have **collectivistic** cultures, which emphasize individuals' ties to larger groups (or "collectives"), such as family, community, and nation. Collectivistic cultural practices highlight the obligations of the individual to his or her society.

Different cultures foster different ways of thinking (Nisbett et al., 2001). People who develop in collectivistic cultures tend to think holistically. In *holistic thinking,* people pay attention to the overall setting—the physical and social environment—within which events occur. Individualistic cultures, by comparison, promote *analytic thinking,* in which people focus on the qualities of an individual person or object, in isolation from its context.

The holistic/analytic distinction explains the cultural variation in attribution discovered in the study by Miller. The holistic thinking of Eastern cultures draws people's attention to situational factors rather than to qualities of the person whose behavior is being explained. As a result, people consider situational factors when explaining behavior, thereby avoiding the fundamental attribution error.

Brain research provides additional evidence that cultures differ in analytic and holistic thinking (Lewis, Goto, & Kong, 2008). The research participants, Americans of either European or East Asian (primarily Chinese) ancestry, were shown a series of stimuli. Some were "target" stimuli on which participants focused most of their attention. Others were contextual stimuli, that is, visual information that was part of a background context. On some trials, the background context changed unexpectedly. EEG recordings measured the degree to which participants' brains responded to this change. Findings showed that the brains of East Asian Americans changed more; their brains responded more strongly to changes in background context (Figure 12.8). This means that different cultural practices (individualistic and collectivistic) can produce not only different thinking styles (analytic and holistic), but also different types of brain activity in members of the cultures.

Now that we have seen how the study of the brain can deepen one's understanding of culture and thought, let's focus our attention on social cognition and the brain.

figure 12.8

WHAT DO PEOPLE SAY IS THE CAUSE OF AN ACCIDENT?

PMB
IN ACTION

PERSON Ⓟ

Thoughts about causes vary across cultures. In the United States, people often attribute behavior to personal factors (e.g., "that crazy bus driver"). In India, citing contextual factors is common (e.g., "The driver may have been instructed, by someone in authority, to take this dangerous route").

MIND Ⓜ

The different attributions reflect different thinking styles. Analytic thinking (focusing on persons in isolation from their surrounding context) is relatively common in Western cultures. Holistic thinking (attending to contexts in which a person is embedded) is more common in Eastern cultures.

BRAIN Ⓑ

Neural Response, Unexpected Contextual Event

— East Asian Americans
— European Americans

EEG recordings indicate that, compared to European Americans, the brains of people from some Asian nations respond more strongly to unexpected changes in contextual information (Lewis et al., 2008); their brains, in other words, are attuned to context.

© AP / Corbis

15. The following statement is incorrect. Explain why: "People from collectivistic cultures such as India tend to process information analytically, which is why they attribute behaviors to social context, thereby avoiding the fundamental attribution error."

Social Cognition and the Brain

The history of social psychology illustrates a theme of the book. The field has incorporated three levels of analysis:

1. Social psychologists first conducted research at a *person* level of analysis. They examined the behavior of people in social settings (e.g., in crowds, groups, and social roles).

2. The study of social cognition introduced a *mind* level of analysis. Researchers identified thinking processes underlying people's attitudes and social behavior.

3. More recently, social psychologists have deepened their understanding by moving down to a *brain* level of analysis. In the rapidly growing field of **social neuroscience,** they explore biological systems in the brain that underlie social cognition and behavior (Cacioppo, Berntson, & Decety, 2012).

Researchers who study social cognition and the brain face two main challenges. One is figuring out how to study the brain. Technological advances help to meet this challenge. Researchers commonly use brain-imaging techniques, especially fMRI (see Chapters 2 and 3), to identify areas of the brain that are most active during social thinking.

The other challenge involves social cognition itself. Different types of social cognition may activate different regions of the brain. To relate psychological experience to biological mechanisms, then, researchers cannot just study the brain. They first must distinguish among different types of social thinking. The following distinction has proven valuable (Van Overwalle, 2009):

› *Thinking about others' ongoing psychological experiences:* When thinking about others, you sometimes focus on their ongoing psychological experiences, especially their current goals and feelings. You ask yourself, in essence, "What are they trying to do?" and "How do they feel about it?" If, for example, you observe someone telling jokes at a party, you might ask yourself what the person is trying to accomplish by telling jokes, and how he or she feels if nobody laughs.

› *Thinking about others' enduring personal characteristics:* Other times, you focus on the stable, enduring characteristics of other individuals; you try, in essence, to figure out what kind of person you are observing. For example, returning to our joke-teller at the party, you might ask yourself whether the individual is an extrovert (an enduring personality trait) or is intelligent (an enduring mental capability).

Brain research indicates that different parts of the brain are active during these two different types of thinking (Van Overwalle, 2009). So let's consider them one at a time.

Thinking About Others' Ongoing Experiences

Preview Question

› Why do we wince when we see other people in pain?

If you see someone being injured, you wince—even though you're not the one in pain. If you're watching a horse race and cheering on a horse and jockey, you lean forward in your chair and may yell encouragement to the horse—even though you're not the one riding it. It is as if your brain is creating, in you, a simulated version of the experiences of the person you are observing.

social neuroscience A field of study that explores biological systems in the brain that underlie social cognition and behavior.

Research indicates that this is exactly what your brain is doing. When you observe someone else, your brain simulates the other person's ongoing experiences (Gallese, Eagle, & Migone, 2007). It does this by automatically activating some of the same neural systems that are active in the other person's brain. The brain regions that simulate other people's activity are called a *mirror system* (Gallese et al., 2007; Rizzolatti et al., 2001; Van Overwalle, 2009) because they reflect the observed actions of others.

As also discussed in Chapter 7, the mirror system—or "mirror neurons"—was discovered in research with monkeys (Rizzolatti et al., 2001). When one monkey observed a second monkey grasping a piece of food, brain systems that control the motor movement of grasping were active in *both* monkeys. The observer's brain simulated ("mirrored") the observed action.

The mirror system helps organisms to not only imitate others, but also understand them. By simulating actions, the brain creates feelings in the observer that mimic those of the observed organism. This enables the observer to understand the ongoing experiences of the organism (monkey or person) being observed.

A meta-analysis of more than 200 fMRI studies (Van Overwalle, 2009) indicates that this mirroring function is executed, at least in part, in a region of the brain known as the *temporo-parietal junction* (TPJ). As the name suggests, the TPJ is at the junction of two lobes of the brain: the temporal and parietal lobes (Figure 12.9). Action in this region enables people to infer other people's goals and intentions for action—to judge, in essence, their *reasons* for action (as discussed earlier in the section on attribution).

Evidence of the TPJ's role comes from studies in which participants think about other people's behavior while the participants' brains are scanned. The TPJ is not particularly active when participants consider the background characteristics of

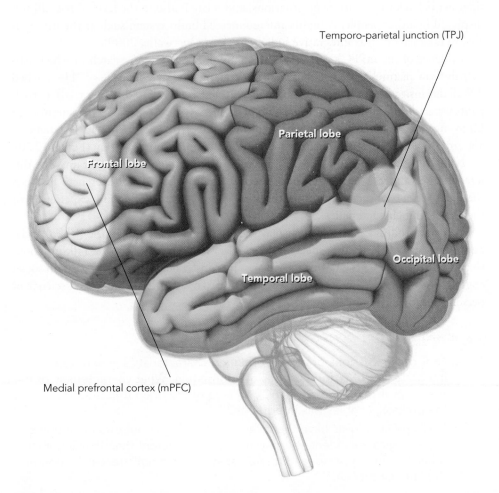

Temporo-parietal junction (TPJ)

Parietal lobe

Frontal lobe

Occipital lobe

Temporal lobe

Medial prefrontal cortex (mPFC)

figure **12.9**
Social cognition and the brain
Two brain regions that are key to social cognition: the temporo-parietal junction (TPJ) and the medial prefrontal cortex (mPFC).

others, such as where they grew up or what job they have. But it is highly active when participants contemplate other people's *behavior*. This is particularly true for unusual behavior (e.g., learning that a person has joined a cult) that prompts extra thinking about the other person's thoughts and feelings (Saxe & Wexler, 2005).

🐦 WHAT DO YOU KNOW?...

16. One reason we are able to understand what others are feeling is that we have a _____ system in the brain that simulates their experiences. Hundreds of fMRI studies indicate that this system's functioning occurs, at least in part, at the junction of two lobes in the brain: the _____ lobe and the _____ lobe.

Thinking About Others' Enduring Characteristics

Preview Question

> Is thinking about what people are experiencing different from thinking about what they are like?

When people think about enduring characteristics of others—long-lasting traits and abilities—a different region of brain is active. It is the *medial prefrontal cortex* (mPFC; Van Overwalle, 2009). The mPFC is located—again, as the name suggests—in a central region of the frontal lobes of the brain.

The mPFC is highly interconnected with other brain regions. This may explain its role in judgments about people's enduring traits. To make a trait judgment, you have to integrate different types of information. For instance, if you see someone acting in a friendly manner, you can't conclude that "she's a friendly person" until you first consider her behavior in a variety of situations, and relate it also to the level of friendliness displayed by other people. A highly interconnected brain system such as the mPFC is able to take part in this integrative judgment (Van Overwalle, 2009).

Evidence of the mPFC's role in social cognition comes from research in which participants saw pictures of people that were accompanied by statements (e.g., "He watched TV all day instead of looking for a job"; Mitchell et al., 2006). On different trials, participants were asked (1) to form an impression of the person's psychological characteristics or (2) to engage in a memory task in which they remembered the order in which statements appeared. The mPFC was particularly active during impression formation (Figure 12.10).

Note that the mPFC and the TPJ are very different regions of the brain. The differences in brain research correspond, then, to the psychological differences between these two aspects of social thinking: thinking about someone's ongoing experiences or their enduring characteristics.

Research findings such as this display the rapid advances made in the field of social neuroscience. Not long ago, social psychologists never expected to be talking about the TPJ or the mPFC; theirs was a science of persons. Then—thanks to work in social cognition—it also became a science of the mind. Today, it is an integrated science of person, mind, and brain.

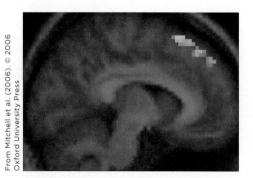

figure 12.10
Brain activity during social cognition Thinking about other people activates a distinctive area of the brain: the medial prefrontal cortex (mPFC). This brain image shows activation in the mPFC that occurred when research participants formed an impression of other people's personality characteristics.

🐦 WHAT DO YOU KNOW?...

17. a. To form impressions of others' enduring characteristics, you have to integrate lots of different types of information. What characteristic of the medial prefrontal cortex (mPFC), an area of the brain that is active during the process, enables this integration?

    b. Social psychologists have theorized that thinking about others' ongoing psychological experiences is psychologically different than thinking about others' enduring personality characteristics. Does brain research confirm this? Briefly explain.

⮂ Looking Back and Looking Ahead

At the start of this chapter, we said that to learn about psychology as a whole, social psychology is the place to start. By looking ahead to other topics in psychology, you can see why. Psychologists who study thinking processes must grapple with discoveries about social thinking, including the way thinking styles vary across cultures. Students of learning must explain how people learn skills, behaviors, and opinions when they interact with others. Research on emotion must include study of emotions that occur only in the social world: jealousy, envy, pride. Students of development must explain how both biological and psychological development occurs as people interact with the social world—the world we need in order to develop into fully human persons.

Chapter Review

Now that you have completed this chapter, be sure to turn to Appendix B, where you will find a **Chapter Summary** that is useful for reviewing what you have learned about social psychology.

Key Terms

attitude (p. 528)
attributions (p. 524)
close relationships (p. 506)
cognitive dissonance (p. 528)
collectivistic (p. 540)
compliance (p. 513)
confederate (p. 512)
conformity (p. 510)
cross-cultural study (p. 540)
crowds (p. 506)
cultural psychology (p. 539)
culture (p. 538)

diffusion of responsibility (p. 520)
discrimination (p. 534)
disrupt-then-reframe technique (p. 514)
foot-in-the-door technique (p. 513)
fundamental attribution error (p. 525)
group dynamics (p. 510)
groups (p. 506)
groupthink (p. 513)
heuristic information processing (p. 528)
individualistic (p. 540)
intergroup contact (p. 537)
mere exposure effect (p. 530)

obedience (p. 514)
prejudice (p. 534)
role (p. 516)
scapegoating (p. 537)
social behavior (p. 506)
social cognition (p. 524)
social neuroscience (p. 542)
social norm (p. 508)
social psychology (p. 506)
stereotype (p. 533)
stereotype threat (p. 534)
systematic information processing (p. 528)

Questions for Discussion

1. You're in charge of developing a strategy for keeping a screaming group of 11- and 12-year-olds calm during a concert. Discuss the merits of treating the crowd as a physical entity (as did Helbing) versus a psychological entity (as did social psychologists in their study of social norms). [Apply]

2. Conformity (as illustrated by Asch's study), compliance (as illustrated by the success of the foot-in-the-door technique), and obedience (as illustrated by Milgram's study) are three forms of social influence that may seem very similar. How do they differ from one another? [Analyze]

3. Milgram conducted his first obedience to authority study in the early 1960s. Zimbardo conducted his

Stanford Prison experiment in the early 1970s. Would a current-day Institutional Review Board determine that these studies are acceptable? To answer, consider the three principles that guide ethical research in psychology (discussed in more detail in Chapter 2): (1) Research participation must be voluntary; (2) participants must be informed; and (3) participants must be able to withdraw. Redesign the studies so as to minimize harm to the participants, then reflect on what knowledge would be lost or gained within these redesigns. [Synthesize, Analyze]

4. Your friend is angry because she sent an email to her chess club two weeks ago requesting that someone

Chapter Review

volunteer to host the next meeting, yet no one has responded. What recommendations will you give to her, in light of social psychological research on bystander intervention? [Apply]

5. Recall a memorable commercial and identify its central message. Did you evaluate the central message of the ad heuristically or systematically? If you processed the message heuristically, do you think you would have been more or less persuaded by it if you had processed the message systematically? Explain. [Apply]

6. We all have friends whose opinions on highly important topics differ from our own, but very few people know how to harness the power of social psychology to bend friends to their will. Capitalize on Festinger and Carlsmith's (1959) research on dissonance-induced attitude change to hatch a plan for getting a friend to change his or her mind on a topic on which you disagree. [Apply]

7. Design an experiment that might demonstrate how being reminded of the stereotype of one's group can enhance, rather than impair, performance in some domain. [Synthesize]

8. Identify an everyday behavior or custom in which you engage (e.g., tweeting) and describe it in such a way that individuals from other cultures might find the behavior odd (e.g., "Individuals in this culture sometimes interrupt their live social interactions to engage in computer-facilitated real-time social interactions, in which they describe how lonely they are"). How does this perspective-taking activity enhance our understanding of the role of culture in explaining human behavior? [Apply]

9. You read that intergroup contact interventions are an effective way to reduce prejudice. Why do you suppose these interventions work? Why is Sherif's Robbers Cave study an example of an intergroup contact intervention, whereas Zimbardo's Stanford Prison experiment is not? [Analyze]

Self-Test

1. In a crowd, which of the following variables is likely to increase aggression?
   a. Anonymity
   b. Shared identity
   c. Social norms
   d. Self-focus

2. How do people typically respond during disasters?
   a. By panicking
   b. By helping others
   c. By behaving aggressively
   d. By looting

3. If Asch's participants had been aware that the other "participants" were confederates, what might the results have been?
   a. The pressure to conform would have increased greatly.
   b. It would have taken fewer people to convince them to conform.
   c. The effect of unanimity on conformity would have been stronger.
   d. The pressure to conform would have decreased greatly.

4. What recommendation can you make to someone who would like to avoid groupthink?
   a. Increase pressure for the group to come to a consensus.
   b. Appoint a member to argue against dissenting opinions.
   c. Guide the group to identify and defend the most popular opinion.
   d. Appoint a member to introduce a dissenting opinion.

5. Jasmine attended a talk at an academic conference. When she entered the room, she was approached by a peer and asked to wear a special ribbon on her lapel that indicated she was a proud supporter of the organization that sponsored the talk. She was later asked to join the organization, which required paying $50. Which of the following techniques was used to increase the likelihood she would comply?
   a. Obedience to authority
   b. Increased systematic information processing
   c. Foot-in-the-door
   d. Disrupt-then-reframe

6. What did Milgram hope to demonstrate with his initial obedience experiments?
   a. Some situations are so powerful that they can override personal convictions.
   b. People will gladly harm others if they know there are no repercussions.
   c. Certain types of people are more likely to obey than others.
   d. Americans are incredibly gullible.

7. In what way was Milgram's obedience study similar to Zimbardo's Stanford Prison experiment?
   a. Participants in both studies were randomly assigned to conditions.
   b. They both demonstrated that powerful situational forces can override personality.
   c. Participants in both studies were preselected based on personality characteristics.
   d. They both demonstrated that people will willingly and happily harm others.

8. You are the teacher of a third-grade classroom whose boys and girls have developed quite a rivalry. Given what you know about Sherif's Robbers Cave study, what can you do to increase harmony among the boys and girls?
   a. Ask them to come up with a name for their "teams."
   b. Bring them together for fun competitions.
   c. Ask them to describe what makes their "team" great.
   d. Have them work toward a shared goal.

9. You're getting ready to move from one apartment to another and need to recruit some friends to help. Given what we know about the bystander effect, which of the following strategies will be most effective?
   a. Use social media to alert every one of your friends and/or followers at once that you need help.
   b. Contact your friends individually and explain to each why you thought of him or her in particular.
   c. Send an email to everyone in your address book stating that you need their help.
   d. Contact each of your friends separately. Tell each one that you're asking as many people as you can for help.

10. When taking cookies out of the oven, you burn your hand slightly. According to research described in the text, what can you do to reduce the pain?
    a. Think of your romantic partner.
    b. Remind yourself of your social identity.
    c. Process information holistically.
    d. Pretend you're a prison guard.

11. Most people in your social circle like you except for one person. What kind of attribution are you likely to make for his feelings about you?
    a. A personal attribution; there's something about *him* that is causing him to not like you.
    b. A situational attribution; there's something about *him* that is causing him to not like you.
    c. A personal attribution; there's something about *you* that is causing him to not like you.
    d. A situational attribution; there's something about *you* that is causing him to not like you.

12. You just got a speeding ticket. If you engage in the fundamental attribution error, how will you characterize the officer who wrote that ticket?
    a. "He wrote me a ticket because he's a jerk."
    b. "He wrote me a ticket because I was speeding."
    c. "He wrote me a ticket because I'm a jerk."
    d. "He wrote me a ticket because speeding is a dangerous moving violation."

13. In Festinger and Carlsmith's (1959) classic study on cognitive dissonance, which group of participants had the *least* amount of justification for their behavior and why? Those who were paid
    a. $20 to tell the next participant the study wasn't boring, because $20 is too little money to be paid to lie.
    b. $20 to tell the next participant the study wasn't boring, because $20 is too much money to be paid to lie.
    c. $1 to tell the next participant the study wasn't boring, because $1 is too little money to be paid to lie.
    d. $1 to tell the next participant the study wasn't boring, because $1 is too much money to be paid to lie.

14. Which of the following studies described in the text illustrated the effects of an intergroup contact intervention?
    a. Zimbardo's Stanford Prison experiment
    b. Milgram's obedience study
    c. Sherif's Robbers Cave study
    d. Asch's conformity experiment

15. What psychological experience is attributed to the functioning of the mirror system?
    a. We are able to infer the traits others possess simply by observing them.
    b. We are able to understand why people behave as they do by observing them.
    c. People experience less pain when they look at a picture of their romantic partner.
    d. People are likely to agree to a larger request if they've first agreed to a small one.

Answers

You can check your answers to the preceding Self-Test and the chapter's What Do You Know? questions in Appendix B.

Personality

> **MY PERSONALITY IS BEST DESCRIBED** as adventurous, wild, spontaneous, easygoing, flexible, open-minded, flirtatious, playful, friendly, kind, humorous, witty, intellectual, low maintenance, sensitive, nurturing."

> "My personality is best described as easygoing/flexible/open-minded, friendly/kind, humorous/witty, outgoing, self-confident."

> "My personality is constantly changing and evolving, either in a direction that I choose or in a direction I'm not choosing. There is no middle ground."

> "I've got an eclectic personality, so my personality is all over the place."

> "My personality is good. I have my blonde moments like all blondes do. I like the outdoors and love to just have a good time."

> "My personality is a little bit of everything I guess. I can be very shy, quiet, yet blunt and loud. Just depends on the situation. Different people describe me in very opposite ways."

> "I would say that my personality is like a flame that burns bright and that's hard to extinguish, easy for someone to warm to!"

Most people who read these personality descriptions ask themselves, "Would I like to meet these individuals?" The descriptions come from online dating services.

You might also be asking yourself this question: Are these statements accurate descriptions of the people's real personalities, or just things they said to make a good impression?

In this chapter on personality psychology, we'll pose simple, yet deeper questions: What are these people even talking about—what is this thing that can be wild and witty, shy and loud, changing and eclectic, and like a flame burning bright? What is personality? Whatever it is, where does it come from? Can it change? Can you measure it? ◉

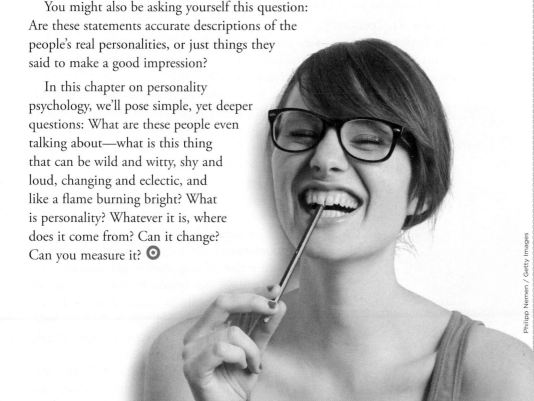

Michael Prince / Gallery Stock

Philipp Nemen / Getty Images

LET'S BEGIN WITH an exercise. Pause for a moment to reflect on your own personality characteristics and to answer this question: What is your personality like?

You've barely begun this chapter on personality yet, already, you can complete the exercise. Just like the people in the chapter opening, you can provide a description of your personality. You have an understanding of what "personality" means and you know what your personality is like. Everybody is, in a sense, a personality theorist.

This chapter introduces the work of people who are personality theorists for a living: psychologists who study personality. We will present personality psychology in three steps:

1. We first examine what *personality* means in psychology.
2. We then present four theories of personality: *psychodynamic, humanistic, trait,* and *social-cognitive* theories. You will learn the main theoretical ideas and see the measurement tools that psychologists use to investigate personality characteristics.
3. Finally, we move "down" a level of analysis to explore brain research that deepens our understanding of psychological characteristics studied in the personality theories.

What Is Personality?

Like most words, "personality" can mean different things. The statements below illustrate three uses of the word:

1. "I can't stand my psychology course. The professor has no personality."
2. "My personality is best described as adventurous, wild, spontaneous, easygoing, flexible, open-minded, flirtatious, playful, friendly, kind, humorous, witty, intellectual, low maintenance, sensitive, nurturing."
3. "Her personality is marked by a hidden, inner conflict between a motivation to succeed and fear of success. Her confident exterior is not her true self. It is a strategy that hides an inner turmoil of which she is only partly aware."

In Statement #1, "personality" essentially means "charisma." If your professor merely reads lecture notes in a quiet monotone, she lacks charisma; you say she has "no personality." If she darts about the lecture hall, mixing incisive scholarship with irreverent humor, you say she's got "a lot of personality."

Does Jack Black have "a lot of personality"? Yes, you might say that. But if you did, you would not be using the word "personality" in the same way that it is used in personality psychology. In the scientific field, "personality" does not mean "charisma"—as it does when we say that someone has "a lot" of personality. It refers to people's distinctive and relatively consistent patterns of feeling, thinking, and behaving, and the inner psychological qualities that contribute to those consistent patterns.

© Paul Schmulbach / Globe Photos / ZUMAPRESS.com

Before moving to Statements #2 and #3, note that, in psychological science, personality does *not* mean charisma. This chapter is not about "the psychology of charisma." The next two meanings of the word identify our topic.

In Statement #2, personality refers to a person's typical, observable behavior. If someone describes herself as adventurous, wild, spontaneous, and easygoing, she essentially is saying that, if you observe her long enough, you will see her behave in this way—not all the time (nobody is adventurous and wild 24 hours a day), but relatively frequently. Personality, then, can refer to how people typically think, feel, and behave.

Statement #3 differs from #1 and #2. It does not refer to observable behavior, but to inner mental life—in this case, a hidden mental conflict. If you were to observe this person casually, you might not see the conflict; her outer behavior might mask her inner turmoil. In this third instance, personality thus refers to the inner structure and workings of mental life: a person's characteristic thoughts, emotions, and desires.

Defining "Personality"

Preview Question

> What two scientific goals do personality psychologists try to accomplish?

Personality psychologists are interested in both observable behavior and inner mental life. Their definition of personality thus combines Statements #2 and #3: **Personality** refers to relatively consistent, observable patterns of feeling, thinking, and behaving and to the inner psychological systems that explain these patterns.

Because the definition of personality combines two features, psychologists who study personality pursue two scientific goals (Cervone, 1991):

> Describing people's typical behavior and individual differences in that behavior (do people differ from one another consistently in their tendency, for example, to be anxious or aggressive?)

> Explaining personality characteristics by identifying systems in the mind and brain that account for individuals' observable personal qualities (what beliefs, emotions, motivations, and brain systems lie "beneath the surface" and explain a person's anxious or aggressive behavior?)

We'll conclude this discussion of "what is personality" by noting two additional ideas. Because you already know, intuitively, what personality means, both ideas will be familiar to you. One is *distinctiveness;* personality is what makes you distinctive, that is, what sets you apart from others. When you described your personality in our opening exercise, you probably didn't say something like "I get angry when people intentionally insult me." *Everybody* gets angry when that happens; it isn't distinctive. Your personality qualities are what make you *unlike* everybody else. Personality psychologists recognize this and aim to describe scientifically the primary ways in which people differ.

What psychological qualities distinguish you from others?

The second idea is *consistency.* Personality refers to qualities that people have across time and place (Allport, 1937). If a friend appears anxious consistently—day after day, in different situations, with different people—you would say that "anxiety" is part of her personality. By contrast, if she appears anxious *in*consistently (e.g., only right before final exam week), you likely would not say this. A major task for personality psychologists is to explain patterns of consistency in people's experiences and behavior (Cervone, 2004).

© Thierry Orban / Sygma / Corbis

Persona The idea that public appearances may hide, or mask, inner personality characteristics is ancient. In Greek tragedy, actors wore a theatrical mask called (in Latin) a *persona*—the origin of the contemporary word "personality."

🐾 WHAT DO YOU KNOW?...

1. Personality psychologists pursue two scientific goals: (1) describing the major ways individuals _____ from one another and (2) explaining personality by identifying systems in the mind and _____ that explain behavior. Personality refers to qualities that make you _____ from others and that are _____ across time and place.

See Appendix B for answers to What Do You Know? questions.

personality The relatively consistent, observable patterns of feeling, thinking, and behaving that distinguish people from one another, and the inner psychological systems that explain these patterns.

Personality Theories

To explain personality qualities, psychologists formulate *personality theories*. A **personality theory** is a comprehensive scientific model of human nature and individual differences.

Let's begin by seeing what goes into a personality theory—its "basic ingredients." Then we'll present four theories of personality.

Personality Structures and Processes

Preview Question

> What aspects of personality are structures and processes meant to account for?

Personality theories contain two main parts: analyses of *personality structures* and *personality processes*.

> **Personality structures** are those elements of personality that remain consistent over significant periods of time. Many of your qualities—things you like, your typical emotional reactions, your long-term goals in life, personal values and moral standards—remain stable over months and years. These stable elements are personality structures.

> **Personality processes** are changes in mental life and behavior that occur from one moment to the next. If you think about your experiences, you can see personality processes in action. At any time recently, did your mood change from good to bad? Did you suddenly lose interest in an activity and stop pursuing it? Did you feel comfortable talking to some people and uncomfortable with others? Although the core of your personality—your personality structures—remained consistent from day to day, your experiences fluctuated across time and situations. Personality psychologists explain individuals' distinctive patterns of variation in mood, motivation, and behavior by developing theories of personality processes.

personality theory A comprehensive scientific model of human nature and individual differences.

personality structures Those elements of personality that remain consistent over significant periods of time.

personality processes Individuals' distinctive patterns of change in psychological experience and behavior that occur from one moment to the next.

Frederic J. Brown / AFP / Getty Images

Adam Pretty / Bongarts / Getty Images

Fluctuating personality processes Maria Sharapova's personality *structure* did not change from one time to another. But she did experience shifting personality *processes*, with her thoughts, feelings, and demeanor changing from one time to another.

In this chapter, you'll learn how each of a series of personality theories has addressed personality structures and personality processes. You'll also learn how each theory has handled a third major topic in the psychology of personality: assessment.

Personality Assessment

Preview Question

› What tool enables personality psychologists to study people scientifically?

Personality psychologists don't want to merely speculate about human nature. They want to study it scientifically. To do so, they need objective, reliable methods for learning about individuals. In other words, they need *personality assessments*.

A **personality assessment** is a structured procedure for learning about the distinctive psychological qualities of an individual. Each of the personality theories you'll learn about provides guidelines for assessing personality.

So let's now turn to the personality theories and their approach to personality structure, processes, and assessment.

Freud's Psychoanalytic Theory

If you could travel back to 1880s Vienna, you could meet a young man destined to become psychology's most famous figure: Sigmund Freud. In some ways, he would "look the part": intelligent, well-educated, insightful, ambitious. But if you were to ask him what he did for a living, his answer would surprise you. The young-adult Freud (he was born in 1856) was not a psychologist. He was a physician planning a career in biomedical research.

Science Source / Getty Images

Sigmund Freud The Austrian physician and psychologist, and creator of the psychoanalytic theory of personality, lived in Vienna until the last year of his life. In 1938 Freud, who was Jewish, moved from Vienna to London to escape the threat of growing Nazi power in Central Europe.

personality assessment A structured procedure for learning about an individual's distinctive psychological qualities.

Circumstances changed his plans. Freud fell in love, needed to make money to get married, and thus sought a career more lucrative than that of research. He became a practicing physician (Jones, 1953)—a career move that had huge consequences. Freud's work with patients launched his theory of personality, **psychoanalytic theory** (Freud, 1900, 1923)—also called a *psychodynamic* theory because it addresses the changing flow, or dynamics, of mental energy.

Freud's patients presented him with a puzzle. They reported bodily symptoms that had no obvious physical cause; a patient might report paralysis of a hand, yet have no injury or illness that could cause paralysis. Freud concluded that the cause was not physical, but psychological. Memories of traumatic events buried deep in patients' minds, he said, created physical symptoms.

Freud based this conclusion on his therapy experiences. With Freud's encouragement, patients in therapy would talk about their problems. Gradually, after great effort, many would recall highly traumatic events they had not remembered for years (e.g., experiences of childhood sexual abuse). Recalling the long-forgotten event was itself traumatic; patients relived painful events. But the pain brought gain as well. After uncovering the traumatic memories, the patients' symptoms improved: Physical problems lessened and psychological well-being increased. (Contemporary scientific evidence confirms that therapies inspired by Freud's approach significantly improve patients' well-being; Shedler, 2010.) From this progress, Freud concluded that the bottled-up memories had been causing the physical distress.

> How easy do you suppose it is to forget a traumatic event from the past?

Freud later modified his conclusion, however. He judged that many of his patients' long-buried thoughts were not accurate memories but rather "fantasies built on the basis of memories" (Freud, 1913, p. 393). The bottled-up ideas were a mix of reality and fantasy.

Freud's ideas raise extraordinarily difficult questions. How could memories and fantasies cause physical symptoms? Why are traumatic memories so hard to recall? When people don't recall such memories, where within the mind are they stored? Freud's personality theory contained his answers.

Structure: Conscious and Unconscious Personality Systems

Preview Questions

> According to Freud, what are the three main structures of the mind?
> According to Freud's "iceberg" metaphor, at what levels of consciousness does each structure of the mind reside?

Freud proposed that personality is not a single, unitary part of the mind. Rather, personality consists of different parts—three personality structures called the *id, ego,* and *superego.*

ID. The **id** is the personality system we are born with. It motivates people to satisfy basic bodily needs. The body needs food, and the id says, "Get it, now!" The body needs sex, and the id says, "Get it, now!" The id doesn't do anything except say, "Get it, now!" The id operates according to the *pleasure principle:* It seeks immediate pleasure and the avoidance of pain.

The id thus is impulsive. It doesn't care about what is "appropriate," "acceptable," and "moral." It doesn't even care what makes sense in the world of reality; a hungry infant will chew on both food and toys, even though the latter won't reduce its hunger.

EGO. The second personality structure, the **ego,** is a mental system that balances the demands of the id with opportunities and constraints in the world of reality.

---

psychoanalytic theory Freud's theory of personality, also called psychodynamic theory.

id In Freud's psychoanalytic theory, the personality structure that motivates people to satisfy basic bodily needs.

ego In Freud's psychoanalytic theory, the mental system that balances the demands of the id with the opportunities and constraints of the real world.

The ego operates according to the *reality principle:* It tries to delay the id's demands until there are circumstances in reality that enable the person to obtain pleasure while avoiding pain, including painful punishment that comes from breaking social rules.

Ride 'em, egoboy In psychoanalysis, the id is the most powerful personality system. Freud explained that the relation of the ego to the id is like the relation of a rider to a wild horse. The rider (the ego) has goals and strategies for the ride, but the powerful horse (the id) is the one who's really in charge.

To do this, the ego devises strategies. If a child wants a cookie, the ego's strategy might be to sneak into the cookie jar when no one is looking. If a guy wants a date, his ego's strategy is to tell the woman, "I'll be getting a great, high-paying job soon." If your romantic partner breaks up with you, your ego says, "I never really liked him that much." These strategies protect the person from harm: punishment from parents; rejection from a potential date; recognition of how much you really wanted a relationship to continue.

The ego, according to Freud, is weaker than the id. Its strategies are feeble compared with the id's impulsive desires. The ego is "like a man on horseback, who has to hold in check the superior strength of the horse" (Freud, 1923, p. 15).

SUPEREGO. Do you ever have sudden pangs of guilt? Almost everyone does. Freud believed they're generated by a third personality structure, the *superego*. The **superego** represents society's moral and ethical rules—rules indicating what types of behavior are bad and good. If the ego devises a strategy for dealing with the id's demands that violates these rules, the superego detects it and the person feels guilt. The superego thus helps to align behavior with social rules. In addition to rules dictating behavior one should avoid, the superego contains an *ego ideal:* an image of an idealized self that the ego should try to achieve.

> Is there someone in your life who is the embodiment of the superego? Of the id?

In psychoanalytic theory, the superego develops as children interact with their parents. Parental commands ("Don't hit") gradually become internalized as superego rules ("Hitting is bad").

LEVELS OF CONSCIOUSNESS. Personality structures operate, according to psychodynamic theory, at different levels of consciousness. *Consciousness* refers to people's awareness of mental contents and processes (Chapter 9). **Levels of consciousness** are variations in the degree to which people are aware of the contents of their mind.

Freud distinguished among three levels of consciousness. The **conscious** regions of mind contain the mental contents of which we are aware at a given moment. For instance, if you're paying attention to the words on this page, then ideas about Freud's theory of personality are in your conscious mind now. The **preconscious** contains ideas that you easily could bring to consciousness awareness if you wanted to. If, for example, someone asked for your phone number, you could think of it; before you were asked, the information was in your preconscious. Finally, the **unconscious** regions of mind contain ideas that you are not aware of and could not become aware of even if you wanted. Freud believed that a vast collection of painful memories is

superego In Freud's psychoanalytic theory, the personality structure that represents society's moral and ethical rules.

levels of consciousness Variations in the degree to which people are aware, and can become aware, of the contents of their minds.

conscious In Freud's analysis of levels of consciousness, the regions of mind containing the mental contents of which you are aware at any given moment.

preconscious In Freud's analysis of levels of consciousness, regions of mind containing ideas you can easily bring to awareness.

unconscious In Freud's analysis of levels of consciousness, regions of mind containing ideas you are not aware of and generally cannot become aware of even if you wanted to.

figure 13.1

Danger: There's a lot under the surface Freud suggested that the structure of personality was like an iceberg. The three Freudian levels of consciousness—conscious, preconscious, and unconscious—are like regions of an iceberg that, respectively, float above the surface of the water, are visible just below the surface, and lurk, invisibly, below the surface. Most of personality, including the entire id, resides below the surface in the unconscious region of the mind.

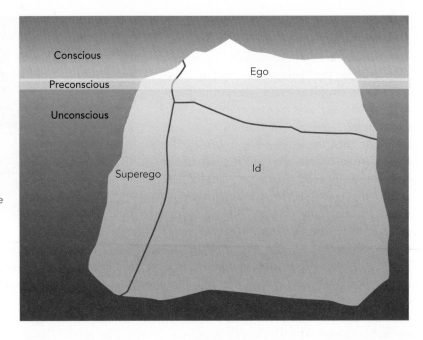

CONNECTING TO THE CONSCIOUS AND UNCONSCIOUS MIND AND BRAIN

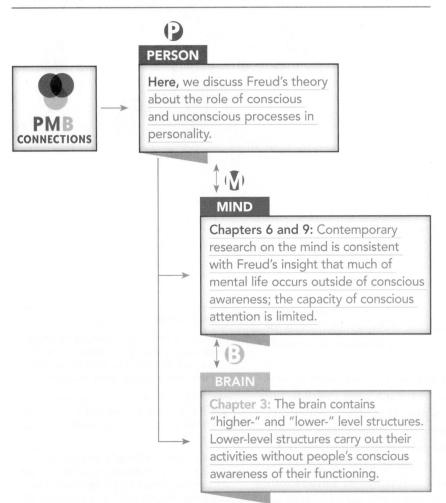

PMB CONNECTIONS

Ⓟ PERSON

Here, we discuss Freud's theory about the role of conscious and unconscious processes in personality.

Ⓜ MIND

Chapters 6 and 9: Contemporary research on the mind is consistent with Freud's insight that much of mental life occurs outside of conscious awareness; the capacity of conscious attention is limited.

Ⓑ BRAIN

Chapter 3: The brain contains "higher-" and "lower-" level structures. Lower-level structures carry out their activities without people's conscious awareness of their functioning.

stored unconsciously—especially the memories of traumatic events that he believed were the cause of his patients' unexplained physical symptoms. This material is so emotionally disturbing that the mind protects the person from even thinking about it by keeping it buried in the unconscious.

Metaphorically, Freud suggested that the mind is like an iceberg: A small tip (consciousness) floats above the surface; a thin layer (the preconscious) is visible just below the surface; and the vast bulk of material (the unconscious) lurks below, out of sight (Figure 13.1).

The id is entirely unconscious. People cannot consciously "look into" their mind and directly see its desires. Both the ego and the superego are partly unconscious. Sometimes we aren't aware of our ego strategies; you may really think that your ex is a terrible person, not recognizing that this conclusion is a strategy devised by the ego. Similarly, sometimes you may feel guilty without realizing how the superego has created this guilt. But sometimes, people are aware of the ego's and superego's contents. In general, Freud's key insight—one that shaped Western civilization's understanding of human nature—is that much of the mental activity that causes our experiences and actions is *unconscious:* outside of our awareness and control.

4. Match the personality structure on the left with the quote that exemplifies it on the right.

   1. Id   a. "I'm going to find a reasonable way to get that."
   2. Ego   b. "I really shouldn't have that."
   3. Superego   c. "I want it now."

5. Match the type of thought on the left with the structure of the mind that stores it on the right.

   1. The thoughts running through your mind right now   a. Unconscious
   2. What you had for dinner last night   b. Preconscious
   3. A traumatic memory from when you were a toddler   c. Conscious

Process: Anxiety and Defense

Preview Questions

› What are the two basic types of mental energies according to Freud's theory?
› According to Freud, how can experiences in childhood stages of development have lifelong effects?
› How, according to Freud, do individuals keep themselves from experiencing excessive anxiety or expressing socially unacceptable behavior?

The id, ego, and superego are stable personality structures. Their basic nature is consistent from one day of your life to the next. Let's now look at the personality processes of psychoanalytic theory, which explain changes in psychological experience.

PSYCHODYNAMICS. Psychoanalytic theory views the mind as an energy system. Just as the physical energy of burning fuel powers an automobile engine, mental energy powers the mind. In the physical sciences, the changing physical energies of objects in motion are called *dynamics*. In psychoanalysis, mental energies are called *psychodynamics*. **Psychodynamic processes** are changes in mental energy that occur as energy flows from one personality structure to another or is directed to desired objects.

Freud proposed two types of mental energies: life energies (or a *life instinct*) and death energies (a *death instinct*):

› *Life energies* motivate the preservation of life and reproduction. The life energies are primarily sexual; they motivate people to pursue sex and, more generally, to desire pleasurable, sensual activities.

› *Death energies* oppose the life energies. Freud believed that humans possess an instinctive awareness of their mortality and a mental energy that motivates them to attain a final resting place (i.e., to die).

The life and death energies can power a wide variety of behavior. The ego directs them to diverse activities that are related symbolically to survival and sex or to death (see Chapter 11; also see Chapter 9 for Freud's analysis of dreams and mental energy). Sexual energies power the efforts of an artist painting nudes or a musician composing sensual music. Death energies—once deflected away from the self—are destructive forces that power behaviors ranging from sarcasm and ridicule to violent acts of aggression.

THINK ABOUT IT

Freud could not measure mental energies. How strong then is the evidence behind his theory?

psychodynamic processes In Freud's theory, changes in mental energy that occur as energy flows from one personality structure to another, or is directed to desired objects.

Terror management theory predicts that ideas of death and of patriotism are closely linked. Death is so terrifying that, in order to cope with the terror, people affiliate with institutions that will live on after they have died, such as their nation.

Few contemporary psychologists endorse Freud's precise ideas about the death instinct. Yet research does confirm his general intuition about the power of death-related feelings. **Terror management theory** (Greenberg & Arndt, 2012; Solomon, Greenberg, & Pyszczynski, 2004) proposes that death is so terrifying that when people think about it, the mind plays a mental trick: It increases feelings of identification with institutions that will survive one's death. Some institutions—such as nations, religions, and cultures—are, in a sense, immortal. The theory predicts that thoughts of death heighten identification with these institutions, causing people temporarily to become more religious or patriotic, or to attend more closely to cultural norms.

In one test of the theory, researchers led participants to take a walk that either (1) passed through a cemetery or (2) did not pass through, or in sight of, a cemetery. All participants then overheard a conversation (in which the speaker was an experimental confederate; see Chapter 12) that exposed participants to a reminder of a cultural value, namely, helpfulness. Finally, participants encountered a stranger who needed help. People who had walked through the cemetery were more helpful (Gailliot et al., 2008); the reminder of death caused them to attend to the cultural norm of helpfulness. A meta-analysis of more than 200 experiments confirms that thinking about death increases adherence to cultural norms, as well as pride in one's nation, race, and cultural group (Burke, Martens, & Faucher, 2010).

PSYCHODYNAMIC DEVELOPMENT. In addition to identifying mental energies, Freud provided a theory of their development. He proposed that the id's sexual energies develop in a series of steps, or stages. A **psychosexual stage** is a period in child development during which the child focuses on obtaining sensual gratification through a particular part of the body. The specific part of the body changes from one stage to another.

Freud identified five psychosexual stages (Table 13.1). In the **oral stage** (age 0 to 18 months), children seek gratification through the mouth by eating, sucking, and chewing. In the **anal stage** (18 months to 3½ years), they experience gratification from the release of tension that comes from the control and elimination of feces. In the **phallic stage** (3½ to 6 years), the source of gratification shifts to the genitals. At the end of the phallic stage, children enter a **latency stage** during which sexual desires are repressed into the unconscious until puberty. The **genital stage,** which starts at puberty, signals the reawakening of sexual desire.

terror management theory A theory proposing that death is so terrifying that thinking about it increases feelings of identification with institutions (e.g., religions, nations) that will survive one's death.

psychosexual stage In Freud's theory of psychological development, a period during which the child focuses on obtaining sensual gratification through a particular part of the body.

oral stage In Freud's theory of psychological development, the developmental stage (ages 0 to 18 months) during which children seek gratification through the mouth.

anal stage In Freud's theory of psychological development, the developmental stage (18 months to 3½ years) during which children experience gratification from the release of tension resulting from the control and elimination of feces.

phallic stage In Freud's theory of psychological development, the developmental stage (3½ to 6 years) during which the source of gratification is the genitals.

latency stage In Freud's theory of psychological development, the developmental stage during which sexual desires are repressed into the unconscious until puberty.

genital stage In Freud's theory of psychological development, the developmental stage that starts at puberty, signaling the reawakening of sexual desire.

table **13.1**

Freud's Stages of Psychosexual Development		
Stage	**Age**	**Adult Characteristics Associated with a Fixation**
Oral	0 to 18 months	Demanding, impatient; behaviors such as smoking, chewing gum
Anal	18 months to 3½ years	Psychologically rigid; concerned about control and neatness
Phallic	3½ to 6 years	Male: competitive, "macho" Female: flirtatious
Latency	6 to 12 years	None
Genital	12 years through adulthood	If no fixations at an earlier stage, person can achieve emotionally mature sexual intimacy

Freud claimed that the emotional themes of the childhood psychosexual stages are repeated throughout life. The adult who frequently smokes and chews gum is repeating themes from the oral stage. Adult love and sexual attraction to a romantic partner repeat the child's first love and attraction, experienced toward the opposite-sex parent during the phallic stage. Themes repeat most strongly when the child experiences a developmental **fixation,** which is a disruption in development that occurs when an individual experiences either too little or too much gratification at a psychosexual stage. This occurs if parents overly indulge the child or provide inadequate physical and emotional support. Table 13.1 lists some adult psychological characteristics associated with fixations at each psychosexual stage of development.

At each psychosexual stage, the child encounters prohibitions. At the oral stage, parents tell children to stop chewing on nonfood items. At the anal stage, they tell children to control the elimination of feces and use the bathroom. Each developmental stage, then, features a *conflict:* Biological urges conflict with social rules. Conflict is particularly intense at the phallic stage. At this stage, children experience sexual attraction toward the opposite-sex parent, view the same-sex parent as a rival, and thus want to eliminate the same-sex parent in order to have the opposite-sex parent for themselves. Freud called this constellation of feelings the *Oedipus complex,* after the Greek tragedy *Oedipus Rex,* whose main character unknowingly kills his father and marries his mother.

What motivates muscle building? In Freudian theory, a fixation at the phallic stage of child development could motivate "manly" behaviors, such as bodybuilding, in adulthood.

© Jim McHugh / Sygma / Corbis

> **THINK ABOUT IT**
>
> How can Freud's theory be reconciled with principles of evolution? Wouldn't it have been bad, from an evolutionary perspective, to be motivated to eliminate (kill off) a parent?

Recall that children progress through the key psychosexual stages—oral, anal, phallic—early in life. Because Freud believed that developmental stages shape personality, he concluded that personality was largely "fixed"—stable and unchanging—by the time the child exited the phallic stage (usually by age 6).

> Freud believed that at the end of the first five years of life, an individual's personality is set for the rest of his or her life. Do you agree?

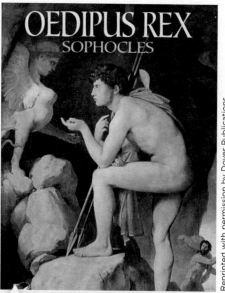

Reprinted with permission by Dover Publications

Oedipus complex Sigmund Freud believed all children experience an Oedipus complex—a constellation of psychological impulses central to the ancient Greek tragedy by Sophocles.

DEFENSE MECHANISMS. As you've just seen, the desires of the id conflict with the rules of society. The conflict, Freud explained, creates anxiety; people become anxious when they recognize that their desires conflict with moral rules. When this happens, *defense mechanisms* come to the rescue. A **defense mechanism** is a mental strategy devised by the ego to protect oneself against anxiety. Defense mechanisms reduce anxiety in two ways:

› *Block anxiety-provoking ideas:* The ego can protect against anxiety by blocking anxiety-provoking ideas from reaching consciousness. In the defense mechanism **repression,** for example, memories of highly traumatic experiences are kept in the unconscious and thereby are blocked from awareness.

› *Distort anxiety-provoking ideas:* The ego can distort ideas so that, if they do reach consciousness, they arrive in a socially acceptable form. In **sublimation,** for example, an animalistic instinct toward sex or aggression is redirected to the service of

fixation In Freud's theory of psychological development, a disruption in development occurring when an individual experiences either too little or too much gratification at a psychosexual stage.

defense mechanism A mental strategy that, in psychoanalytic theory, is devised by the ego to protect against anxiety.

repression A defense mechanism in which traumatic memories are kept in the unconscious, thereby blocked from awareness.

sublimation A defense mechanism in which an instinct toward sex or aggression is redirected to the service of a socially acceptable goal.

table **13.2**

Some Freudian Defense Mechanisms		
Defense Mechanism	**Definition**	**Example**
Denial	Failure to admit the existence or true nature of emotionally threatening information	After buying a house in an earthquake-prone area, a person denies the existence of valid scientific evidence showing that an earthquake is likely to strike.
Repression	Failure to remember anxiety-provoking information about one's past	An adult does not recall an emotionally disturbing event from childhood.
Rationalization	Formulating a logical reason or excuse that hides one's true motives or feelings	After being turned down for a date, you say you weren't really attracted to the person anyway.
Projection	Concluding that other people possess undesirable qualities that actually exist in oneself	A hostile, aggressive person starts a fight with someone but blames the other person for initiating it.
Reaction formation	Expressing thoughts and behaviors that are the opposite of one's true motives	You are extremely friendly and generous toward someone you actually dislike.
Sublimation	Expressing socially undesirable motives in a socially acceptable form	A person releases aggressive energy by taking a class in martial arts.
Displacement	Redirecting mental energy from a threatening target to an unrelated and less threatening target	An employee angry at his or her boss yells at family members, thus redirecting the anger to them.

Does the high-rise have psychological foundations? Freud would say that, whether the architect knew it or not, this towering building is a phallic symbol. Sexual energies stored in the id were the ultimate source of motivation behind the architect's work.

a socially acceptable goal. For instance, a medical student might direct aggressive impulses toward the practice of surgery, where cutting into a patient releases aggressive energy.

Which of your daily activities, if any, can be construed as sublimation?

Freud believed that all people use defense mechanisms (Cameron & Rychlak, 1985). Table 13.2 lists a number of defense mechanisms that people frequently employ.

> **✋ WHAT DO YOU KNOW?...**
>
> 6. True or False?
>   a. Freud suggested that a wide variety of behaviors are driven by two basic energies: a life energy and a death energy.
>   b. According to terror management theory, when people are reminded of their own imminent demise, they tend to increasingly adhere to cultural norms.
>   c. A fixation at any of the psychosexual stages of development only occurs when parents provide too little gratification at a given stage.
>   d. Gilbert, who is very consumed with his masculinity and with competition, is most likely fixated at the oral stage of psychosexual development.
>   e. The Oedipus complex is a constellation of feelings that arise during the anal stage of psychosexual development.
>   f. Defense mechanisms are strategies devised by the superego to satisfy the wishes of the ego within the constraints of the id.

fotoVoyager / Getty Images

Assessment: Uncovering the Unconscious

Preview Questions

> According to Freud, why is the free association method the best way to assess personality?

> What kinds of outcomes should projective tests be able to predict if they are valid? Do they?

Freud's psychoanalytic theory complicates the task of personality assessment. A simple assessment strategy—self-report (i.e., directly asking people about their personality characteristics; see Chapter 2)—cannot be used. To a psychoanalyst, self-report methods are inadequate for two reasons: (1) Much mental content is unconscious, so people can't recognize and discuss it; and (2) even when people do have insights into themselves, they may not *want* to talk about those insights because they reveal ideas that are socially unacceptable and anxiety provoking. Psychoanalytic psychologists thus need alternatives to self-report methods. They have developed two: the *free association method* and *projective tests.*

FREE ASSOCIATION METHOD. In the **free association method,** devised by Freud, psychologists encourage people to let their thoughts flow freely. They instruct people to say whatever comes to mind, even if it seems irrelevant or ridiculous. This procedure might sound odd, but Freud thought it was the best way to assess personality. He reasoned that the mind is like a machine. If a machine makes a sound (e.g., a banging in a car engine), something inside the machine must have caused it. The sound thus is a clue to the machine's inner workings. Similarly, if an idea pops into someone's mind, something inside the mind must have caused it. The flow of free associations thus provides clues to how the mind works.

Freud accepted a limitation of the free association method: It is slow. Patients may be in therapy for months before they associate to deeply significant material. (Freud's therapy method is detailed in Chapter 15.) Others sought quicker methods and thus devised *projective tests.*

PROJECTIVE TESTS. A **projective test** is a personality assessment tool in which test items are ambiguous and psychologists are interested in how test takers interpret the ambiguity. For example, test takers might tell a story about people depicted in a drawing whose feelings and actions are unclear. The idea behind the tests is that when people interpret ambiguous items, they inevitably will draw on information in their own personalities. Elements of personality are thus "projected" onto the test.

A famous projective test is the **Rorschach inkblot test** (or, simply, the "Rorschach"), developed in 1921 by Swiss psychiatrist Hermann Rorschach. The test items are symmetrical blobs of ink (Figure 13.2). Test takers say what the images look like to them, and explain their interpretations. Based on these responses, the psychologist usually tries to identify the test taker's style of thinking: Did the test taker focus on the image as a whole or just a small part of it? Did his or her interpretation rely only on the inkblot image itself, or did it include imaginative flights of fantasy that went beyond the image?

The Rorschach is personality psychology's most famous test. Unfortunately, it is more famous than accurate. Research shows that Rorschach test responses are poor predictors of important life outcomes, such as who might become depressed or who might perform well under high stress (Lilienfeld, Wood, & Garb, 2000). Even when Rorschach responses do predict outcomes accurately, similar predictions often can be made through much simpler procedures (e.g., directly asking people if they tend to become depressed or perform well under stress; Mischel, 1968).

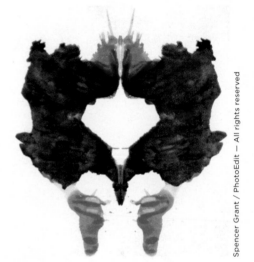

figure **13.2**
Rorschach Inkblot This item is from the Rorschach, a projective personality test. According to psychodynamic theory, test takers "project" some of their own personality onto the test item when interpreting what the image represents.

---

free association method A method of both personality assessment and therapy devised by Freud in which psychologists encourage people to let their thoughts flow freely and say whatever comes to mind.

projective test Personality assessment tool in which items are ambiguous and psychologists are interested in the way test takers interpret the ambiguity, "projecting" elements of their own personality onto the test.

Rorschach inkblot test A projective test in which the test items are symmetrical blobs of ink that test takers are asked to interpret.

> The problem of psychoanalysis is not the body of theory that Freud left behind, but the fact that it never became a medical *science*. It never tried to test its ideas.
>
> —Eric Kandel (quoted in Dreifus, 2012)

These negative results with the Rorschach reveal a limitation of the psychoanalytic approach. Freud and many of his followers neglected the principles of measurement and research design that make psychology scientific. One result of this neglect is their failure to develop efficient and accurate measures of personality.

🔧 WHAT DO YOU KNOW?...

7. The following statements are incorrect. Explain why.
   a. One of the reasons Freud so valued the free association method was that it was a relatively quick way to assess the contents of the unconscious.
   b. A necessary feature of projective tests is that their images must be unambiguous in their meaning.
   c. The value of the Rorschach is that it consistently predicts important outcomes such as depression.

The Neo-Freudians

Preview Question

> How did the ideas of the neo-Freudian personality theorists differ from those of Freud?

Freud's followers may have faltered when developing psychological tests. But they excelled at creating novel, insightful psychological theory. After Freud proposed his theory of personality, **neo-Freudian personality theories** developed—that is, new ("neo") theories inspired by Freud that attempted to overcome limitations in his work. Let's look at three neo-Freudian theories: those of Alfred Adler, Carl Jung, and Erik Erikson.

Adler (1927) felt that Freud underestimated the importance of social motives. People compare themselves to others in the social world—friends, classmates, coworkers—and are motivated to compensate for personal qualities that they feel are inferior to those of others. In particular, people are motivated to compensate for organ inferiorities: body organs that, due to disease or genetic defect, work less well than normal. Someone with impaired hearing, for example, may compensate by developing his or her musical skills. (Both Beethoven, the great classic composer, and Brian Wilson, songwriter for the Beach Boys, the American rock band with the all-time most Top 40 hits, had impaired hearing.) Adler judged that, to fully understand personality development, the motivation to compensate for inferiority—which Adler called an *inferiority complex*—must be added to the motives proposed by Freud.

Carl Jung (1939) judged that Freud underestimated the role of evolution. Specifically, Jung proposed that there are two different unconscious minds: (1) the one identified by Freud, which stores memories of events from one's own life, and (2) another, overlooked by Freud, which stores ideas inherited from humans' ancestral evolutionary past. Jung called this second unconscious mind the *collective unconscious*. The **collective unconscious** is a storehouse of mental images, symbols, and ideas that all humans inherit, in exactly the same form, thanks to their common evolutionary past. Throughout the history of our species, all humans experienced, for example, darkness (which is frightening), mothers (who are comforting), and wise older adults (who acquired wisdom during their long lives). Jung suggested that, as a result, concepts of darkness, mothers, and wise elders are stored in our collective unconscious. Without our even knowing it—because the ideas are unconscious!—these inherited mental symbols influence our thoughts and emotions.

neo-Freudian personality theories Theories of personality inspired by Freud that attempted to overcome limitations in his work.

collective unconscious Jung's concept of a storehouse of mental images, symbols, and ideas that all humans inherit thanks to evolution.

Look familiar? In his neo-Freudian theory of personality, Carl Jung suggested that humans possess a collective unconscious which contains images that are inherited and thus exist in the same manner in the minds of all humans. A prediction of Jung's theory is that some symbols would appear in stories and myths repeatedly— because all creators of these stories and myths have the same symbols in their collective unconscious. Shown are three examples of a "wise old man" symbol posited by Jung: Gandalf from *The Lord of the Rings* movies, Dumbledore from *Harry Potter*, and Obi Wan Kenobi from *Star Wars*.

Erik Erikson (1950) worked to overcome two limitations in Freud's theory of personality development:

1. Freud had focused only on development in early childhood. Erikson, by contrast, proposed a neo-Freudian theory of developmental processes in childhood, adolescence, and early, middle, and older adulthood.

2. Freud had focused on developmental processes that are internal to the person (sensual gratification focused on a part of the body). Erikson looked to the external world, proposing that development is a social process.

At each stage of development, people experience an emotional conflict, or "crisis," that involves interactions between oneself and the social world. Infants, for example, face a crisis involving trust in others, on whom they are entirely dependent for survival. Table 13.3 summarizes Erikson's theory.

table **13.3**

Erikson's Stages of Development		
Stage of Life	**Approximate Age**	**Predominant Psychological Crisis**
Infancy	0 to 1 year	Trust versus mistrust
Early childhood	1 to 3 years	Feeling of autonomy versus doubt in one's ability
Preschool	4 to 5 years	Initiative (doing things on one's own) versus guilt (about activities not valued by adults)
School age	6 to 12 years	Industriousness and competence versus inferiority
Adolescence	13 to 19 years	Clear sense of identity versus confusion
Early adulthood	20 to 25 years	Achieving intimacy versus superficial relationships and isolation
Middle adulthood	26 to 64 years	Fulfilling, generative work versus stagnation
Older adulthood	65+ years	Sense of order and meaning in life versus despair and regret

WHAT DO YOU KNOW?...

8. Adler believed Freud ignored the fact that when we compare ourselves to others, we are often motivated to compensate for feelings of _____. Jung suggested that we inherit the contents of our _____ unconscious from our common _____ past. Erikson highlighted the idea that development is also a _____ process that includes conflict between oneself and others at each stage.

Evaluation

Preview Question

> What disadvantages of Freud's theory call into question its usefulness?

Freud's theory of personality had immense impact. His insights revolutionized people's view of human nature; the idea that most memories and feelings are unknown to the individual, buried in the unconscious, was startling. Beyond psychology, scholars in other fields—history, art history, film and literary criticism—applied Freud's concepts. An artist's work, for example, could be interpreted as the symbolic expression of his or her unconscious desires.

Dalí's *The Persistence of Memory*
The Spanish painter Salvador Dalí, a student of Freud's writing, created art that depicted unreal, irrational images produced by the unconscious mind.

How valuable, though, are Freud's ideas as a scientific theory of personality? Freud, as you've seen, depicts personality as an energy system with three structures (id, ego, and superego) that regulate the flow of two types of energy (life/sex, death/aggression). In this model, much of mental life occurs outside of conscious awareness, and much of it is a struggle between biological urges and social rules. What are the advantages and disadvantages of this model?

An advantage is that it captures the complexity of personality. Mental life truly is a mix of conscious experiences and unconscious processes. People often do experience conflict within themselves and between personal desires and social rules. Freud's theory is complex enough to address these aspects of human experience. Some other theories of personality are not.

Yet the complexity brings costs. The major cost is that elements of Freud's theory are difficult—and sometimes impossible—to test. To test a theory, you generally need good measurement tools (see Chapter 2). Freud developed no tools for measuring personality precisely and thus provided no means for putting his theory to the test.

A final limitation is that, in some respect, psychoanalytic theory is not complex enough. Does the mind contain only three main personality structures (id, ego, and superego)? Most contemporary psychologists don't think so. As discussed elsewhere (especially Chapters 6 and 11), research suggests that the mind contains numerous mental systems that contribute to memory, thought, and motivation—more than Freud had imagined.

Such limitations motivated psychologists to develop alternative theories of psychoanalytic personality, as we'll see next.

WHAT DO YOU KNOW?...

9. On what bases can Freud's psychoanalytic theory be criticized? Check all that apply.
   ___a. It lacks the tools for precisely and objectively measuring the structures of personality.
   ___b. There are not enough structures specified to account for the full range of human behavior.
   ___c. It treats people as if they are more complex than they actually are.

TRY THIS!

Before you learn about the next theory of personality, take part in an activity that might lead you to learn something about yourself. Go to www.pmbpsychology.com and complete the Try This! activity for Chapter 13. It's a personality assessment that you will learn about in the next section of the chapter—so complete it now! ◉

Humanistic Theory

Preview Question

> What does humanistic theory emphasize, in contrast with psychoanalysis?

Who's your favorite person—the person you'd choose to spend your time with on a free afternoon, a long car trip, or the rest of your life? And how do you feel when you're with this person? Sure, your feelings vary as you gossip, joke, and talk seriously. Yet, if you're lucky and this person is a really good friend, you consistently feel like *yourself*. You don't hide your thoughts or try to make a good impression. You know your friend accepts you for who you are, which gives you the freedom to express your true self.

Freud said little about friendships and experiences of one's true self. *Humanistic theory* rectifies this oversight. **Humanistic theory** is an approach to personality that focuses on people's thoughts and feelings about themselves and the ways that interpersonal relationships shape those feelings. Humanistic psychologists emphasize people's conscious experiences (rather than Freud's emphasis on the unconscious), their search for meaning in life, and their capacity to make choices that can make their lives more meaningful.

In these regards, the humanistic viewpoint is the very opposite of Freud's. In Freudian theory, the most powerful personality system is the id, which is concerned with gratifying bodily needs. In humanistic theory, the major personality structure is the *self*, and the major personality process is the individual's quest to develop a meaningful self-concept. In Freudian theory, most significant personality processes are unconscious. In humanistic theory, conscious self-reflection is key to personality. Finally, Freud treated personality as a kind of machine: a set of parts put in motion by energy. Humanistic psychologists treat people as human beings who, unlike machines, have hopes, plans, dreams, and personal values and whose psychological makeup cannot easily be dissected into separate parts.

Many psychologists contributed to humanistic personality theory. But unique contributions were made by a psychologist from Illinois, Carl Rogers. Rogers first planned to be a minister. His religious training made him aware of people's struggle to attain a deep sense of personal meaning in their lives (Kirschenbaum, 1979). After studying scientific psychology and receiving training as a psychotherapist, Rogers developed a theory of personality centered on the self.

Just goofing around? Humanistic psychologists suggest that goofing around with a friend is more meaningful than it may appear. Relationships in which you can relax with someone who accepts you as you are help you grow psychologically.

How important have your personal relationships been to the development of your personality?

❂ WHAT DO YOU KNOW?...

10. In what ways does the humanistic viewpoint differ from Freud's psychoanalytic theory? Check all that apply.

___ a. Humanistic psychologists are more concerned with humans' quest to develop a meaningful self-concept.

___ b. Humanistic psychologists place more focus on humans' search for meaning in life.

___ c. Humanistic psychologists see people as machine-like.

___ d. Humanistic psychologists place more emphasis on unconscious processes.

___ e. Humanistic psychologists place less emphasis on the true self.

humanistic theory An approach to personality that focuses on people's thoughts and feelings about themselves and the ways that interpersonal relationships shape these feelings.

Structure: The Self Concept

Preview Questions

> What is "the self" and why did Rogers emphasize it in his theory of personality?
> What is the source of our emotions according to humanistic theory?

Carl Rogers (second from right) leading a discussion group. Rogers's humanistic theory provided personality psychology with an alternative to Freud's psychoanalysis.

Michael Rougier / Time & Life Pictures / Getty Images

Rogers was an exceptionally skilled therapist. By listening attentively to his clients, he not only helped them, but also learned from them. The critical lesson he learned was that the overarching question people ask themselves is, "Who am I—what is my true self?" The central personality structure in Rogers's theory is thus the *self*.

THE SELF. In Rogers's humanistic theory of personality, the **self** refers to people's conception of who they are. Rogers's idea is straightforward: Through our daily experiences, we learn about ourselves. We observe our strengths and weaknesses. We learn how we're similar to and different from other people. We learn what others think of us. When we consciously reflect on all this information, we try to organize it into a coherent portrait of who we really are. The result is the *self* (or *self-concept*), an organized set of self-perceptions of our personal qualities.

When conducting therapy, Rogers repeatedly heard his clients describe their experiences "through the lens" of the self. When an experience went poorly, they would say, "I was disappointed in myself." When surprised by their own actions, they'd say, "I wasn't acting like myself." These statements caused Rogers to center his theory on the self.

Therapy taught Rogers a second lesson: The self can change. People can alter and improve their self-concept. Just as you change your beliefs about other people when you discover something new about them, you may change your self-concept when you discover

> What would your life be like if you didn't have a sense of self? Could you experience disappointment? Satisfaction?

something new about yourself. Consider a client of Rogers's. She reported that "several parts of herself"—an interest in the arts and theatre; a playful, fun-loving style of behavior—had, in recent years, "been lost" (McMillan, 2004, p. 50). Once she rediscovered them, her sense of self changed; she developed a more positive self-concept, that is, a higher sense of *self-esteem*. In therapy, Rogers provided a supportive relationship in which people could engage in self-discovery and regain their true sense of self (Chapter 15).

ACTUAL AND IDEAL SELF. Rogers identified two aspects of the self: the *actual* and *ideal* self. The **actual self** is people's perceptions of how they are in the present. The **ideal self** is a set of self-perceptions about qualities that a person would like to possess; it is a future self that the individual hopes to attain.

The actual and ideal often do not match up. People would like to be a certain kind of person, but when they look in the mirror they see someone else. For instance, you might see yourself as fun-loving and irresponsible, but wish you were responsible and conscientious. If so, Rogers would say you're experiencing a discrepancy between your actual and ideal self.

Discrepancies between the actual and ideal self produce distress. People feel disappointment in their actual self, guilty about

> How would you describe your actual and ideal selves?

not being better, and worried about ever attaining their ideal. Rather than accepting themselves as they are, they imagine an ideal self—perhaps a thinner, smarter, or richer self—and then criticize themselves for not reaching this ideal. In Rogers's personality theory, then, the self—not the Freudian id—is the key source of emotion.

self In humanistic theories, such as that of Rogers, an organized set of self-perceptions of our personal qualities; people's conceptions of who they are.

actual self People's perceptions of psychological qualities they possess currently, in the present.

ideal self People's perceptions of psychological qualities that they optimally would possess in the future.

WHAT DO YOU KNOW?...

11. According to Rogers, the result of our tendency to consciously reflect on our experiences is an organized _____, which has the capacity to _____. The key source of emotion is a discrepancy between the _____ and _____ selves.

Process: The Growth of the Self

Preview Questions

> What is the fundamental human motive according to Rogers?
> How can our relationships with others foster or hinder self-actualization?

Rogers proposed an optimistic, positive view of personality processes. Rather than emphasizing sexual and aggressive drives, as Freud did, Rogers highlighted people's desire for *self-actualization*.

SELF-ACTUALIZATION. In humanistic personality theory, **self-actualization** is a motivation to enhance one's psychological state, that is, to achieve a personal meaning in life and attain a state of psychological maturity (Rogers, 1951). Self-actualization is a universal psychological drive. All people, in other words, are inherently motivated toward the attainment of psychological growth and maturity. (In the study of motivation, the humanistic theorist Abraham Maslow similarly proposed a motivating self-actualization need; see Chapter 11.)

Again, it was experiences in therapy that guided Rogers's theorizing. In case after case, he observed clients recovering from personal setbacks. They fought to improve their psychological lives, and they usually succeeded. Rogers attributed their success to their inner strength—their inherent capacity, and tendency, to overcome problems and attain personal growth. His clients, he concluded, were driven by a motive for self-actualization.

CONDITIONS OF WORTH. If we're all motivated toward self-actualization, as Rogers suggests, why aren't we always happy? Why do we experience so much psychological distress?

Rogers's answer is that people often experience *conditions of worth*. A **condition of worth** is a requirement for a person's behavior; specifically, it is a requirement that must be met if the person is to be fully valued, loved, and respected by others. Imagine, for example, a child who is interested in art, uninterested in sports, and whose parents are big sports fans. If the parents indicate, by their words or actions, that the child will be fully loved and respected only by excelling at sports rather than art, then they are imposing a condition of worth. The parents' behavior may cause the child to reject his interest in art, to pursue sports instead, and thus to lose touch with an aspect of his true self.

Contrast this situation with one in which the parents love and respect their child no matter what his interests may be. In this case, the child experiences **unconditional positive regard,** a consistent expression of respect and acceptance.

self-actualization A motivation to realize one's inner potential.

condition of worth In Rogers's theory of personality, a behavioral requirement imposed by others, such as parents, as a condition for being fully valued, loved, and respected.

unconditional positive regard A display of respect and acceptance toward others that is consistent and not dependent on their meeting behavioral requirements.

Acceptance First Lady Michelle Obama, addressing the Democratic National Convention, told listeners that her parents "poured everything they had into me. . . . It was the greatest gift a child could receive: never doubting for a single minute that you're loved, and cherished." Carl Rogers suggested that such unconditional acceptance enables people to realize their full potential.

Rogerian theory predicts that these different types of relationships have different effects on personality development. Unconditional positive regard enables people to explore the world confidently and to develop their true self. People know that they can try out new activities, take chances, and sometimes fail without losing the acceptance of others. By contrast, when relationships feature conditions of worth, people are forced to deny aspects of their true self in order to gain the acceptance of others. They become defensive and cautious, lose touch with their true self, and fail to grow toward self-actualization. Conditions of worth are therefore the ultimate source of distress.

> Who are the people in your life who love you unconditionally?

🎯 WHAT DO YOU KNOW?...

12. The following statements are incorrect. Explain why.
    a. Rogers claimed that there are individual differences in the drive to attain self-actualization.
    b. Imposing conditions of worth on a child frees the child to develop his or her true sense of self.

Assessment: Measuring Self-Perceptions

Preview Question

> How can we measure self-concept?

Unlike Freud, Rogers used the methods of psychological science to assess personality in an efficient, reliable manner. Because the central structure in Rogers's theory is the self, his main assessment goal was to assess self-concept.

ASSESSING SELF-CONCEPT. Rogers did not personally invent a method for assessing self-concept. Instead, he and his colleagues used an existing method, the *Q-sort* technique (Stephenson, 1953). The **Q-sort** is an assessment procedure in which people indicate whether each of a series of words and phrases describes them; they categorize or "sort" statements according to their self-descriptiveness.

When taking a Q-sort, one receives a large set of cards with printed statements such as "I am highly anxious" or "I do not easily express anger." Test takers sort cards along a continuum ranging from "most characteristic of me" to "least characteristic of me" (Figure 13.3). This enables psychologists to identify clusters of characteristics that are most and least descriptive of the individual test taker, from that individual's own perspective.

The Q-sort can be used to measure discrepancies between the two aspects of self identified by Rogers, the *actual* and *ideal* self. Psychologists ask participants to complete the Q-sort twice; participants sort the personality statements according to their conception of their (1) actual self and (2) ideal self. By comparing the two Q-sorts, psychologists can gauge the degree of discrepancy between these two aspects of self-concept.

The Q-sort method should seem familiar to you. It is the personality assessment method you completed in this chapter's Try This! activity. By comparing your own Q-sorts, you could see the relation between your actual and ideal self.

Q-sort measures have proven valuable in a number of areas of research, such as the study of psychological disorders (Fowler & Lilienfeld, 2007) and personality development (Block, 1961). One creative application of the method used Q-sorts to study the personalities of parents and their children (Zentner & Renaud, 2007). Parents and children ages 15 to 19 categorized Q-sort statements describing their actual personality and their ideal life goals (e.g., "having a high status career," "having children," "having fun," "working to promote the welfare of others"). A comparison of parents' ratings to their children's identified a gender difference: Girls' ideal self-concepts were more

TRY THIS!

Q-sort An assessment procedure in which people categorize words and phrases according to how well or poorly the descriptions fit them.

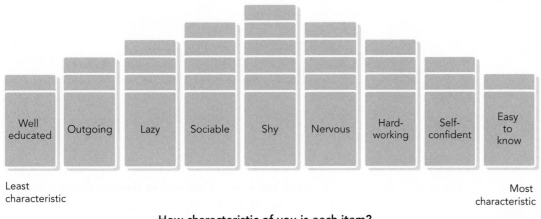

Least
characteristic

Most
characteristic

How characteristic of you is each item?

figure **13.3**
The Q-sort method In the Q-sort method, test takers create psychological self-portraits by categorizing statements that describe personal characteristics (e.g., well educated, outgoing, lazy) into categories ranging from "least" to "most" descriptive of their personality.

similar to their parents than were those of boys. Boys, in other words, were more likely to develop personal aspirations *unlike* those of their parents.

✔ WHAT DO YOU KNOW?...

13. True or False?
  a The Q-sort can be used to measure discrepancies between the ideal self and the actual self.
  b. Research using the Q-sort indicates that girls' ideal selves are more similar to their parents than are boys' ideal selves.

Evaluation

Preview Questions

> In what way does Rogers's theory improve upon Freud's?
> In what way is Rogers's theory limited as a theory of personality?

Rogers's humanistic theory was historically significant for personality psychology. It shifted the field's focus from the unconscious mind to conscious thoughts about the self, and from animalistic drives to the uniquely human tendency to actualize the self. Rogers developed a positive, uplifting psychology that drew attention to people's capacity to recover from setbacks and attain meaningful lives. The enduring importance of his thinking is evident from recent developments in psychology. Many psychologists today contribute to a *positive psychology* movement that focuses attention on human strengths, virtues, and conditions of life that enable people to develop optimally (Gable & Haidt, 2005; Keyes, Fredrickson, & Park, 2012). These are precisely the themes highlighted by Rogers. If he were still alive, he surely would be pleased to see twenty-first-century psychologists focusing on positive psychological growth.

The main limitation of Rogers's theory is that it is not sufficiently comprehensive. There are significant aspects of personality about which Rogers's theory says little. One is personality's "biological side"—individual differences in personality that may be inherited and evident early in life. As knowledge of human genetics grew in the second half of the twentieth century, researchers became increasingly interested in the biological foundations of personality. This interest triggered the development of a third approach to personality, trait theory.

CULTURAL OPPORTUNITIES

Self-Esteem

Personality theorists have global ambitions. They aim to develop theories that apply universally, to all cultures of the world. Have they succeeded?

In many ways, they have; numerous aspects of psychological life described in personality theories are universal (Brown, 1991). No matter where you go, people engage in both conscious and unconscious thinking (as psychoanalytic theory suggests), benefit from warm human relationships (as humanistic theory emphasizes), learn from psychological models (explored in social-cognitive theory, below), and differ from one another in part due to inherited biology (as trait theorists discovered). Yet cultures also differ in ways not anticipated by the personality theorists. One difference involves **self-esteem,** which is a person's overall sense of self-worth. Self-esteem scales ask people whether, for example, they are proud of themselves and believe they possess good qualities (Rosenberg, 1965).

In the United States, most people score well above the midpoint on self-esteem scales (Heine et al., 1999). The majority say, "I am satisfied with myself" and "I am a person of worth, at least on an equal plane with others." This is what you might expect from Rogers's humanistic theory of personality, which posits a universal motive to develop and enhance the self. But in other cultures, responses differ. When self-esteem scales are given to people in Japan, just as many people report having *low* self-esteem as high self-esteem (Heine et al., 1999).

Cultural factors explain this difference. In the United States, many social practices and institutions are designed to enhance self-esteem. Schools give students positive, esteem-enhancing feedback—so much so that we tend to believe, as humorist Garrison Keillor puts it, that "all the children are above average." In Japan, in contrast, "this discourse of the importance of self-esteem is rarely heard" (Heine et al., 1999, p. 779). Japanese culture emphasizes the need for individuals to get *along* with others rather than to get ahead of them. The Japanese strive to improve themselves in order to benefit their society (Kitayama et al., 1997).

Students' reactions to test results reveal this cultural difference. In Japan, university students who receive negative feedback tend to accept it as valid; bad test scores prompt them to question their abilities. In North America, students tend to question not themselves but the test; they often are as sure of their high abilities after receiving a bad test score as before (Heine, Kitayama, & Lehman, 2001).

To achieve their global ambitions, personality theorists need to attend to the diversity of the world's cultures.

You're the best! U.S. culture contains many social practices designed to build children's self-esteem. But in Japan, self-esteem–building practices are far less common. Japanese culture emphasizes the need to get *along* with others rather than to get ahead of them.

Randy Faris / Corbis

self-esteem A person's overall sense of self-worth.

Trait Theory

Preview Question

> What characterizes the measurement of personality in trait theory?

In personality psychology, a **trait** is a person's typical style of behavior and emotion. ("Trait" contrasts with the concept of psychological *state*—a person's current thoughts and feelings, which may vary from moment to moment.) **Trait theories** are theoretical approaches that try to identify, describe, and measure people's personality traits. A key word in that last sentence was "measure" (discussed in Chapter 2); reliable measurement is the foundation on which trait theory is built (Cattell, 1965).

Trait theorists recognize that good measurement benefits not only basic science, but also practical applications. Suppose you are hiring people to fill jobs at a company and want a sociable salesperson, an honest accountant, and a manager with a calm leadership style. There will be many applicants. Which would be best for each job? To find out, you need good measurement tools: efficient and reliable measures of the traits of interest. This is exactly what trait theory provides.

By way of background, trait theory has a long history. Early in the twentieth century, psychologists recognized that measurement principles used in the study of intelligence (see Chapter 8) could be applied to personality. By asking people a large number of questions and scoring their responses, personality could be measured. In the latter half of the twentieth century, research on genes and individual differences indicated that variations in personality trait scores were, to a significant degree, based on inherited biology (see Chapter 4). By the century's close, the combination of quantitative measures and genetic findings made trait psychology a major force in the science of personality.

Structure: Stable Individual Differences

Preview Question

> What scientific method do trait theorists use to reduce the thousands of traits in our language into the Big Five (or Six)?
> What does Eysenck's research suggest is the biological basis of the trait extraversion?

The major structure in personality trait theory is—no surprise here—the personality *trait*. As noted, a trait is a person's typical style of behavior and emotion. More specifically, personality traits have three defining qualities that refer to *consistent* ways in which people *differ* in their *average* tendencies:

1. *Consistency:* According to trait theory, personality traits express themselves consistently, across time and situations (Allport, 1937; Epstein, 1979). A person who is high in the trait *conscientiousness*, for example, would be expected to display conscientious behavior in a consistent manner (e.g., the person might be a reliable employee, a hardworking student, and a law-abiding citizen).

2. *Individual differences:* Personality traits refer to differences among people. Most trait psychologists try to identify a small number of traits that can be used to describe individual differences in any population of people.

3. *On average:* Traits refer to what people typically are like; in other words, what they are like on average. Suppose you are very friendly and pleasant with everyone except one particular person, whom you dislike. A trait measure of friendliness would average your behavior across all these relationships. Because you are friendly with most people, you would get a high score on friendliness. The score reflects your typical behavior.

trait In personality psychology, a person's typical style of behavior and emotion.

trait theories Theoretical approaches that try to identify, describe, and measure people's personality traits.

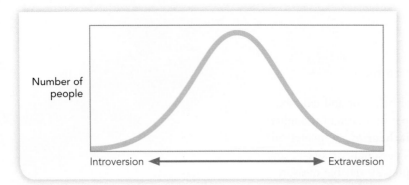

Number of people

Introversion ◄────────────► Extraversion

figure 13.4
Trait dimensions Trait theorists view personality traits as dimensions. For a trait dimension such as introversion–extraversion, most people are in the middle of the dimension; relatively few have extremely low or high levels of the trait.

In addition to these three defining qualities, the word "trait" has two extra meanings to most trait theorists. One is that it refers to a *dimension,* not a category. This means that there are gradual variations in levels of the trait. In this way, personality traits are like physical traits such as height. Although we sometimes talk about "tall people" and "short people," we know that these are not distinct categories of people; height varies along a dimension. Similarly, although we may talk about "agreeable people" and "disagreement," the trait of agreeableness varies dimensionally. For any given trait dimension, most people are near the middle of the dimension, and small numbers of people are at the very high or low ends (Figure 13.4).

Second, theorists see traits as *causes* of behavior (McCrae & Costa, 1995, 1996). Again, an analogy with height is useful. If someone buys shirts with extra-long sleeves and pants with extra-long legs, and he sometimes bumps his head on the top of doorways, the cause is his high standing on the physical dimension of height. Analogously, if someone helps people with errands, avoids getting into arguments, and cooperates cheerfully with team members on work projects, his behavior, according to trait theory, would be caused by his high standing on the personality dimension of *agreeableness*—an overall tendency to be pleasant, helpful, and accommodating (Graziano, Jensen-Campbell, & Finch, 1997; but see This Just In).

With the meaning of "trait" established, the next question to ask is what are the most important personality traits? There are two approaches to answering this question; we'll look at both in the sections ahead. The first is to examine words in everyday language (Ashton & Lee, 2007; Goldberg, 1981). The **lexical approach** to trait theory presumes that people will notice, and invent words for, all significant differences among people, and thus that words in the language contain clues about the most significant personality traits.

The other approach is to examine biology (Stelmack & Rammsayer, 2008). Neural or biochemical differences between people may produce variations in personality.

> If an extraterrestrial were to come to Earth and ask, "What are the most important ways in which individuals differ from one another?" what would your answer be?

PERSONALITY TRAITS IN THE LANGUAGE. Imagine opening a dictionary and listing all the words that describe personality traits. You start with "abrasive," move to "absent-minded" and "abstemious," and—if you can keep yourself awake long enough—eventually arrive, appropriately enough, at "zonked."

Incredibly, two personality psychologists once did just that: They listed every trait word in English—more than 4000 of them (Allport & Odbert, 1936).

The length of that list poses a problem: Measuring 4000 traits is impractical. It's too much work to develop 4000 tests, and even if you did develop them, who would ever take them all? Trait theorists need to identify a small set of traits that correspond to the most significant individual differences in personality. They do so by using *factor analysis.*

Factor analysis is a statistical technique that identifies patterns in a large set of correlations (*correlations* are described in Chapter 2). Suppose you measure numerous personality characteristics—for instance, reliable, emotional, insecure, generous, hardworking, nervous, punctual, self-conscious, ambitious, and creative—by asking many people to rate, on a 7-point scale, whether each characteristic describes them. For any two characteristics (e.g., insecure and nervous), the correlation between the two measures indicates how strongly the characteristics go together (i.e., whether people who say they are insecure also tend to say they are nervous).

lexical approach A perspective on the task of identifying personality traits which presumes that all significant individual differences among people will be represented by naturally occurring words in everyday language.

factor analysis A statistical technique that identifies patterns in large sets of correlations.

Now suppose you want to know how, in general, the traits correlated with one another. You suddenly are faced with a lot of numbers: If 10 traits were measured, there are 45 pairs of traits and thus 45 correlations. If 100 traits are measured, there are 4950 correlations—way too many to keep track of without a mathematical tool. Factor analysis is that tool. It enables psychologists to sort through the correlations to find groups of measures that are correlated strongly. Trait psychologists reason that each of these strongly correlated groups represents one trait. In our example, the group including reliable, hardworking, punctual, and ambitious would represent the trait of conscientiousness.

In the study of personality traits, factor analysis usually yields a simple result. Only five or six traits are needed to describe the main individual differences in personality. One group of five traits is found so commonly that it is called the "Big Five" (Goldberg, 1993; John, Naumann, & Soto, 2008). The **Big Five** personality traits are found consistently when people's descriptions of personality are analyzed with factor analysis. The same five traits are found when analyzing people's descriptions of their own personality and people's descriptions of others' personalities (e.g., close friends or one's spouse; McCrae & Costa, 1987). The Big Five traits—*extraversion, agreeableness, conscientiousness, neuroticism,* and *openness to experience*—are described in Table 13.4. (A hint for remembering them is that the first letters of the traits can be arranged to spell "ocean.")

The Big Five can be assessed easily. Table 13.5 contains a simple 10-item measure of the five personality factors (Gosling, Rentfrow, & Swann, 2003).

Some trait theorists think that the Big Five trait model is missing something—a sixth trait called honesty/humility (Ashton & Lee, 2007). People with high scores on this trait display sincerity and a lack of pretentiousness. Evidence of this sixth factor came from a multinational study. Native speakers of each

THINK ABOUT IT

Do you think that everyone has the same five traits? Or might you have some distinctive personality traits that make you unique, yet that are not represented within the Big Five approach?

table **13.4**

The Big Five Traits		
Big Five Trait	**Definition**	**Characteristics**
Extraversion	A tendency to approach the social and material world in an energetic manner	Sociable, active, assertive
Agreeableness	An orientation toward positive, prosocial feelings and behaviors when interacting with others	Altruistic, trusting, modest
Conscientiousness	A tendency to control inappropriate emotions and impulses and to follow social rules	Reliable, hardworking, organized
Neuroticism	A tendency to experience negative emotions	Anxious, nervous, sad
Openness to experience	An orientation toward a complex mental and behavioral life, and a diversity of experiences	Creative, artistic, liberal

Research from John, Naumann, & Soto (2008)

Big Five A set of personality traits that is found consistently when researchers analyze, via factor analysis, people's descriptions of personality.

table **13.5**

A Simple Big Five Measure						
Disagree strongly	Disagree moderately	Disagree a little	Neither agree nor disagree	Agree a little	Agree moderately	Agree strongly
1	2	3	4	5	6	7

I see myself as:

1. _____ Extraverted, enthusiastic
2. _____ Critical, quarrelsome
3. _____ Dependable, self-disciplined
4. _____ Anxious, easily upset
5. _____ Open to new experiences, complex
6. _____ Reserved, quiet
7. _____ Sympathetic, warm
8. _____ Disorganized, careless
9. _____ Calm, emotionally stable
10. _____ Conventional, uncreative

Reprinted from *Journal of Research in Personality*, 37:504–528, Gosling et al., A very brief measure of the Big-Five personality domains, © 2003, with permission from Elsevier

In this measure of the Big Five trait variables, two items tap each of the factors: Extraversion (1, 6*), Agreeableness (2*, 7); Conscientiousness (3, 8*), Emotional Stability (4*, 9), and Openness to Experiences: (5, 10*). The asterisk indicates that the item is scored in reverse; strongly agreeing with the item gives one a lower score on the trait.

of seven different languages—Dutch, French, German, Hungarian, Italian, Korean, and Polish—rated themselves on a list of about 400 personality trait adjectives, some of which had not been included in prior Big Five studies. In each language, factor analysis revealed that six, not five, factors were needed to describe individual differences, the sixth being honesty/humility (Ashton et al., 2004).

In sum, the lexical approach summarizes personality traits found in everyday language. The big question, though, is whether that is good enough. Ultimately, psychologists don't just want to know about the *language* of personality; they want to know the "flesh-and-bones" of personality: the biological structures underlying differences between people.

Library of Congress

Don Carl Steffen / Gamma-Rapho via Getty Images

On what trait did they differ? Both men were smart, ambitious, and hardworking. Neither was highly extraverted. Both may have been somewhat high on neuroticism. But they differed dramatically on the personality trait of honesty/humility. The humble Abe Lincoln was known as Honest Abe. Richard Nixon, known for saying that "I always do more than I say. I always produce more than I promise," resigned from office due to the dishonesty of the Watergate scandal.

🌀 THIS JUST IN

Traits as Networks

When researchers give people personality tests, groups of test items correlate with one another. For example, people who say that they are (1) self-conscious also tend to report that they tend to (2) worry, (3) feel anxious, and (4) experience frightening thoughts, which creates positive correlations among the items. Why do the items correlate?

The cause, according to trait theory, is the influence of traits. In our example, the trait of neuroticism is said to cause the items to correlate with one another (Figure 13.5).

Although trait psychologists believe this, there are other ways of thinking about it. A research team in the Netherlands recently developed an alternative conception: not traits as causes of behavior, but traits as descriptions of "networks" of thoughts and actions (Cramer et al., 2012). In this view, networks arise because the psychological qualities measured by test items *causally influence each other* (Figure 13.6). Consider the four qualities we just mentioned. Self-consciousness might cause one to worry; worrying can cause anxiety; anxiety could cause frightening thoughts to enter the mind; and the frightening thoughts could feed back into the network, causing one to become more anxious—which, in turn, might result in greater self-consciousness.

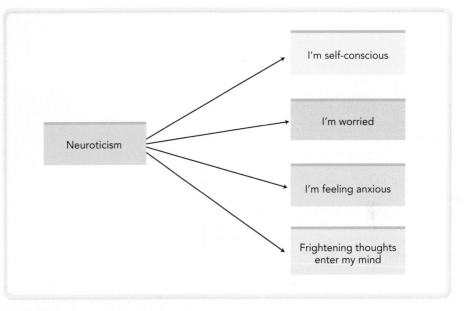

figure 13.5
Trait theory view

Researchers use a statistical technique called *network analysis* to depict the relations among individual test items. The technique is complex, but the idea behind it is simple. Instead of adding up test items to give people a single score, network analysis analyzes the items one by one. A network graph depicts the ways in which items are linked (i.e., correlated with one another). As you can see in Figure 13.7, when researchers analyze personality test items this way, they find overlapping clusters of items that roughly correspond to the Big Five traits (Cramer et al., 2012). The findings are consistent with the theoretical analysis in Figure 13.7—the network analysis.

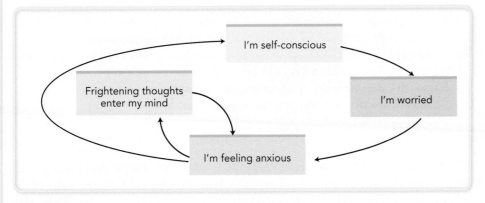

figure 13.6
Network analysis view

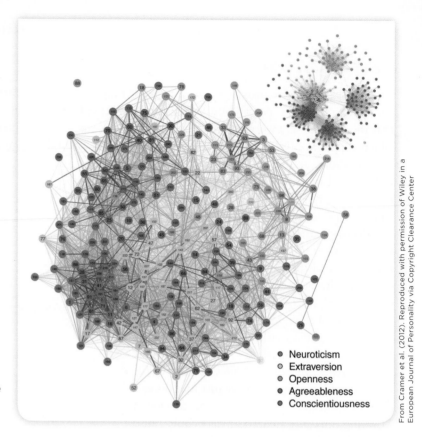

From Cramer et al. (2012). Reproduced with permission of Wiley in a European Journal of Personality via Copyright Clearance Center

figure 13.7

Is a trait a "thing"—a single structure in the mind or brain that causes consistent patterns of behavior? Maybe not. Trait terms might just be words that describe patterns of correlations among personality test items that are inherently interconnected. That is an implication of network analysis. In this network analysis of the correlations among items designed to measure the Big Five personality traits, items (indicated by numbers) that are closer in the network are more highly correlated. Traits (neuroticism, extraversion, etc.) do not cause the correlations to occur; they merely describe naturally occurring patterns in the data. The inset diagram in the upper right is what the network would look like if the five traits were independent.

Legend (in figure):
- Neuroticism
- Extraversion
- Openness
- Agreeableness
- Conscientiousness

Why is network analysis so important? There's a critical difference between Figures 13.6 and 13.7: In Figure 13.7, there is no single "neuroticism" variable. In the network analysis, neuroticism is not a real "thing"—that is, not a structure in the mind that causes consistent patterns of behavior. Neuroticism is merely a term that describes networks of thoughts, feelings, and actions that go together inevitably. The same holds true for the other Big Five traits as well; each is reconceptualized as a description of networks of experiences and actions, rather than as a psychological structure that causes behavior.

The picture reveals something interesting. Items measuring the Big Five traits do not fall into five separate clumps; they do not appear as five distinct traits. Rather, items representing the supposedly different traits are intertwined. Network analysis thus suggests that personality structure consists not of five separate, discrete traits, but of an interconnected system of thoughts, feelings, and actions.

🐦 WHAT DO YOU KNOW?...

17. True or False?
   a. In the network analysis view, your responses to items on a conscientiousness questionnaire are caused by the trait of conscientiousness.
   b. According to trait theory, your responses to items on a conscientiousness questionnaire are caused by the other items on the questionnaire.
   c. Research using network analysis indicates that items on personality questionnaires are often highly interconnected, just as our thoughts, feelings, and actions are.

Hans Eysenck, who identified extraversion and neuroticism as the two primary traits of personality.

PERSONALITY TRAITS IN THE NERVOUS SYSTEM. People differ biologically in many ways (height, weight, blood pressure, bone density, etc.). Might some of the biological differences produce individual differences in personality traits? Many trait psychologists have pursued this possibility (Stelmack & Rammsayer, 2008). One of the first was the British psychologist Hans Eysenck.

Eysenck (1970) searched for the biological basis of extraversion. He hypothesized that extraverts (high-energy people who like lots of activity and social interaction) and introverts (reserved individuals who are happy sitting quietly, reading a book) should differ in brain functioning. Specifically, Eysenck predicted they would differ in cortical arousal, that is, activation in the surface regions of the brain (the cortex; see Chapter 3). People with naturally low levels of arousal should compensate for this by pursuing arousing activities that raise their arousal level. People with high levels of cortical arousal should avoid simulating environments, which make them overly aroused. Arousal level therefore causes people to become extraverts (low arousal) or introverts (high arousal).

Some evidence supports Eysenck's idea. In electroencephalographic (EEG) research (see Chapter 2), investigators record the brain activity of introverts and extraverts while presenting simple stimuli, such as flashes of light or moderately loud noises. Just as Eysenck predicted, the brains of introverts react more strongly than those of extraverts to this physical stimulation (Stelmack & Rammsayer, 2008). Outside of the lab, in everyday life, the differences in brain reactivity may create differences in introverted versus extraverted behavior.

Eysenck also sought the biological basis of neuroticism, that is, the tendency to feel anxious and worried. Here, he predicted that individual differences in neuroticism would be linked to variations in the reactivity of the autonomic nervous system (ANS), which responds to environmental threats (see Chapter 3). People with high scores on neuroticism should have "jumpy" nervous systems. This prediction, however, has received less support (Stelmack & Rammsayer, 2008). Individual differences in self-reported neuroticism and ANS activity are related only weakly. Factors not anticipated by Eysenck, such as people's subjective interpretations of events, contribute to anxious, neurotic response styles (M. Eysenck, 2013). This weak result has motivated some trait psychologists to seek an alternative to Eysenck's theory.

One alternative was advanced by the British psychologist Jeffrey Gray and his colleagues (Corr, 2004; Gray & McNaughton, 2000; Pickering & Corr, 2008). Gray identified a problem in Eysenck's theory of neuroticism: It failed to distinguish between two fundamentally different emotions, namely, fear and anxiety. In Gray's theory of personality and motivation, different brain systems are said to underlie these different emotional responses.

Philip Game / Lonely Planet Images / Getty Images

Does it take an extravert to lead a social movement? The Indian spiritual and political leader Mohandas Gandhi led millions of Indian citizens in a struggle for human rights and political independence. Yet he was introverted. In his youth, he avoided contact with others. "My books and my lessons were my sole companions," Gandhi reported. "I literally ran back [home from school] because I could not bear to talk to anybody" (Easwaran, 1997, p. 13).

🌜 WHAT DO YOU KNOW?...

18. Trait refers to the major ways in which people _____ from each other in their average tendencies. They are _____ versus categorical and are said to be the _____ of behavior. The statistical tool of _____ _____ is used to identify the major individual differences in personality. Hans Eysenck hypothesized that differences between introverts and extraverts could be tied to differences in _____ arousal. His hypothesis that differences in neuroticism could be tied to differences in reactivity of the _____ nervous system has received little support.

Process: From Traits to Behavior

Preview Question

> How can Eysenck's work link structures to processes in trait theory?

Traits are the personality structures of trait theory. What about personality processes?

Trait theorists have devoted less attention to dynamically shifting personality processes than to stable personality structures (Hampson, 2012; McCrae & Costa, 1996). The lexical approach to personality traits, for example, analyzes personality structure exclusively.

Biological research, however, does shed light on personality processes. Consider again the work of Eysenck. His analysis of cortical arousal and extraversion identifies brain processes that come into play as people encounter situations featuring low and high levels of stimulation. Other researchers have extended Eysenck's analyses by showing how extraversion may be linked to bodily arousal, which, in turn, affects thinking processes (Humphreys & Revelle, 1984). Nonetheless, the analysis of personality processes is not the strong point of trait theories.

> ### 🌀 WHAT DO YOU KNOW?...
>
> 19. Research that links extraversion to bodily _____ is a promising way for trait theorists to link structure to _____.

Assessment: Measuring Individual Differences

Preview Question

> › How do trait theorists assess personality and what outcomes can be predicted by these assessments?

We've seen that analysis of personality processes is not a strength of trait theory. Personality assessment, however, is. Trait theorists have developed tests that reliably measure individual differences in personality traits.

COMPREHENSIVE SELF-REPORT QUESTIONNAIRES. The most common personality tests are self-report questionnaires in which people indicate their personal preferences and tendencies. Some of these tests aim for comprehensiveness; test creators seek to measure all the major personality traits, to provide a complete psychological portrait of the individual. Let's look at one such test in detail.

The NEO-Personality Inventory (NEO-PI-R; Costa & McCrae, 1992; McCrae & Costa, 2010) measures individual differences in each of the Big Five personality traits: neuroticism, extraversion, openness to experience, conscientiousness, and agreeableness. (Through a historical quirk, it gets its name, NEO, from only the first three of those traits. It exists in different forms, called the NEO-PI-R and NEO-PI-3.)

The NEO includes about 50 test items that measure each of the five traits. Why so many? No one question can measure a broad personality trait. But a large set of questions can. For example, conscientiousness (see Table 13.4) test items ask about keeping one's possessions in neat order, paying bills on time, working efficiently, finishing jobs, and so on. Adding together responses across the items provides an accurate measure of the trait.

As noted earlier, there are shorter tests (Gosling, Rentfrow, & Swann, 2003; Rammstedt & John, 2007). Brevity sacrifices accuracy, however. When psychologists want highly accurate measures of Big Five traits, they prefer to use longer tests, such as the NEO.

PREDICTING BEHAVIOR. Do these personality tests predict people's behavior? Often they do. Let's see two examples, the first of which involves personality and personal space.

Most people have one or two personal spaces, that is, areas they decorate themselves. In your bedroom, for instance, you might arrange the furniture and choose art for the walls. Personality predicts decoration preferences. Researchers sent participants to individuals' office spaces and bedrooms and asked them to judge the personality traits of the inhabitants. They made the judgments without ever meeting the occupants. Separately, the inhabitants of the rooms completed questionnaires measuring their personality traits. The ratings of conscientiousness, extraversion, and openness to experience

Zoonar RF / Thinkstock / Getty Images

David Hughes / Shutterstock

Guess what types of people live in these rooms? Trait theory research indicates that people can judge the personality of the inhabitants merely by viewing the rooms, without even meeting the inhabitants themselves.

that participants gave to occupants based on their rooms correlated significantly with the occupants' self-ratings on those traits (Gosling et al., 2002).

Personality traits also predict a more serious outcome: mortality. Researchers (Terracciano et al., 2008) measured personality traits in a large group of adults, and then followed their life course over decades. During this time, some research participants died. Remarkably, personality traits predicted length of life (Figure 13.8). People with more emotionally stable (low neuroticism) personalities, and those with higher levels of conscientiousness, lived longer (Terracciano et al., 2008).

Why would personality predict mortality? People with more emotional personalities may experience more life stress, which can impair health (Chapter 10). More conscientious people may maintain healthier lifestyles and have regular medical check-ups, which can prolong life.

THINK ABOUT IT

Conscientiousness predicts the neatness and organization of people's living spaces. Does this mean that the trait of conscientiousness causally affects people's behavior? Or might it be the opposite: Behavior affects self-reported conscientiousness? Self-report measures of conscientiousness ask people if they are "careless" and "disorganized." People might base answers to these questions on knowledge of their everyday behavior, such as the care of their living spaces.

✔ WHAT DO YOU KNOW?...

20. True or False?
   a. Briefer personality assessments tend to more accurately measure traits than do longer ones.
   b. Personality measures such as the NEO-PI-R are notoriously poor predictors of behavior.
   c. In one study, both conscientiousness and neuroticism predicted mortality.

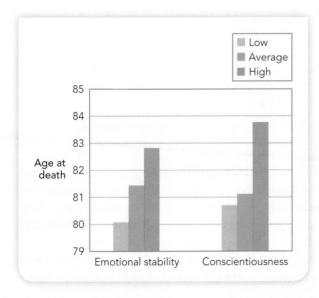

Legend:
- Low
- Average
- High

Age at death axis: 79, 80, 81, 82, 83, 84, 85

Categories: Emotional stability, Conscientiousness

figure **13.8**
Personality traits predict longevity
The graph shows longevity (age at death) among people with low, average, and high scores on the personality traits of emotional stability and conscientiousness. People with high scores on both emotional stability and conscientiousness lived longer (Terracciano et al., 2008).

Evaluation

Preview Question

> What are some strengths and weaknesses of trait theory?

Trait theories have three major strengths. They provide simple methods for assessing individual differences. They have spurred research into the connection between personality traits and biology. Their use of sophisticated statistical techniques brings scientific rigor that was sometimes lacking in prior theories of personality.

However, trait theories have limitations, too. One is that, like Rogers's humanistic theory, they are insufficiently comprehensive. As we've noted, trait theory says little about personality processes—the dynamic interactions among thoughts and feelings that were highlighted, for example, by Freud. Trait theory also says little about *in*consistencies in behavior. When asked to describe themselves, people often report behavior that is inconsistent; sometimes they act one way, sometimes another: "I am very shy, but I talk a lot once I get to know someone"; "I am organized for the most part, but I'm very rushed and messy at home"; "I have a very welcoming personality, but another aspect of my personality is my mean side" (Orom & Cervone, 2009). If you observe people's behavior, you see these inconsistencies; most individuals sometimes look like they're extraverts and other times look like they're introverts (Fleeson, 2001). Because trait variables refer to average levels of behavior, they don't explain such variations around the average. The psychologists who developed the fourth, and last, personality theory you'll learn about have tried to overcome these two limitations of the trait approach.

🌀 WHAT DO YOU KNOW?...

21. Which of the following statements about the strengths and weaknesses of trait theories are true? Check all that apply.
    ___ a. They provide simple methods for assessing individual differences in personality traits.
    ___ b. They have halted research into the connection between personality traits and biology.
    ___ c. Their use of sophisticated statistical techniques such as factor analysis brings scientific rigor that was sometimes lacking in psychoanalytic and humanistic theories.
    ___ d. They say little about dynamic interactions among thoughts and feelings—that is, personality processes.
    ___ e. They do a particularly good job of explaining variations around average levels of behavior.

Social-Cognitive Theory

Preview Question

> What did social-cognitive theory's two most prominent theorists—Bandura and Mischel—emphasize in their conceptualization of personality?

The fourth of our personality theories is **social-cognitive theory,** an approach to personality that emphasizes the social experiences through which people acquire knowledge, skills, and beliefs about themselves. According to social-cognitive theory, these cognitions—one's knowledge, skills, and beliefs—explain an individual's distinctive patterns of emotion and behavior.

Social-cognitive theory differs from the other three theories you've learned about in both substance and style. In substance, it attends more carefully to social context.

social-cognitive theory A theoretical approach to personality in which the core of personality consists of personal knowledge, beliefs, and skills acquired through social interaction.

Social-cognitive theorists examine the way personality develops and reveals itself as people interact with others in the social world (Shoda, Cervone, & Downey, 2007). In style, social-cognitive theory is integrative. Theorists have built a personality theory by drawing on research findings from throughout psychological science (Cervone & Mischel, 2002). The advantages of this style of theory building may seem obvious, yet it's not what the other personality theorists were doing. Psychodynamic, humanistic, and trait theories were relatively isolated from advances in psychology as a whole; Freud, for example, was famously *un*interested in experimental evidence in psychology.

Many psychologists have contributed to the social-cognitive approach (see Cervone & Shoda, 1999). Two, however, stand out: Albert Bandura and Walter Mischel.

Albert Bandura's social-cognitive theory of personality (1986, 1999, 2001) has two emphases. The first is personality's social foundations. Bandura recognizes that, were it not for our experiences in a social world, we would not have the personalities we do. Our social skills, personal beliefs, and life goals arise through interaction with the social world. The other emphasis is **personal agency,** which refers to people's capacity to influence their own life outcomes. By setting goals and developing new skills, people can guide the course of their own development.

Early in his career, Bandura worked with families of children who were highly aggressive (Bandura & Walters, 1959, 1963). Interviews with the children and their parents raised questions about how people learn to behave aggressively that Bandura then addressed in laboratory research. Throughout his long career, Bandura maintained this pattern, conducting basic laboratory research on personality processes while simultaneously addressing problems of great social significance.

Walter Mischel's social-cognitive approach views personality as a system. A *system* is anything made up of a large number of parts that influence one another. The view that personality is a system contrasts with, for example, the trait approach you learned about earlier. In trait theory, personality was viewed as a collection of structures (the traits) that were independent of one another; there was little analysis of how one trait influenced another. But in his social-cognitive systems approach, Mischel focuses on interactions among the parts of personality. Those parts include thoughts (or *cognitions*) as well as feelings (or *affects*); personality is thus a cognitive–affective system (Mischel, 2004, 2009; Mischel & Shoda, 1995). A person's distinctive pattern of interconnected thoughts and emotional reactions is the core of his or her personality structure. Regarding personality dynamics, Mischel emphasizes subjective meaning, that is, the processes through which people figure out, or assign meaning to, the events of their lives (Mischel, 1968; Orom & Cervone, 2009).

Mischel (1968, 2009) also is a critic of personality theories. He argues that trait theorists' decision to study what people are like "on average"—their average level of neuroticism or conscientiousness—is costly. It sacrifices too much information about personality. Much of what is interesting about personality is the way an individual *varies around* his or her average: conscientious at work but not at home; confident with some people but anxious with others. To Mischel, this variability in thought and

Albert Bandura

Albert Bandura, whose theory of personality explains the social foundations of people's beliefs, skills, and experiences.

Association for Psychological Science

Walter Mischel, whose research has shown how personality is revealed in the way that people adapt their behavior to varying social contexts.

It might be worth attending to the patterns of variability. . . . Although conspicuously absent in most personality psychology, such patterns are portrayed in virtually every character study in literature, revealing as they unfold the protagonists' underlying motivations and character structures, and making them come alive.

—Walter Mischel (2004, p. 6)

personal agency People's capacity to influence their motivation, behavior, and life outcomes by setting goals and developing skills.

Personality inconsistencies
According to social-cognitive theory, *inconsistencies* in behavior are revealing of personality. Consider the case of Eliot Spitzer: Leader of student government in college. Graduate of Harvard Law School. As a district attorney, he fought organized crime. As attorney general of the State of New York, he continued to battle white collar crime. He was elected governor of New York in a landslide and pledged to restore confidence in government (Gershman, 2006). Spitzer seemed to be a model citizen and leader, high on traits such as reliability, conscientiousness, and trustworthiness—until a prostitution scandal forced him to resign from office.

self-referent cognitions Thoughts people have about themselves as they interact with the world and reflect on their experiences.

action, which arises as people confront the diverse challenges and opportunities of life, is key to personality.

Bandura's and Mischel's contributions complement one another. In combination, they form the foundation of a social-cognitive approach to personality that is furthered by many contemporary personality psychologists (Cervone & Shoda, 1999).

⚡ WHAT DO YOU KNOW?...

22. Which of the following quotes are likely to have been uttered by a social-cognitive theorist such as Albert Bandura or Walter Mischel? Check all that apply.

____ a. "Experimental evidence is not useful for building theories of personality."

____ b. "Any theory of personality should emphasize the fact that people have the ability to influence their own life outcomes."

____ c. "Most theories of personality overemphasize the social foundations of our skills, beliefs, and goals."

____ d. "Personality can be viewed as a system whose interacting parts include cognitions and affects."

____ e. "Personality is adequately described by measuring average levels of behavior."

Structure: Socially Acquired Cognition

Preview Question

> What defines each of the three different types of personality structures within social-cognitive theory: self-referent cognition, skills, and affective systems?

Social-cognitive theory identifies three types of personality structures: (1) thoughts about the self, or *self-referent cognition;* (2) *skills;* and (3) *affective systems.* They are all personality structures in that they are enduring elements of the mind that contribute to people's distinctive and consistent styles of behavior.

SELF-REFERENT COGNITION. Much of our thinking concerns ourselves. When starting a new job, you think not only about the job, but also about yourself: "Will I be able to handle the work?" When choosing a major in college, you think not only about the courses to take, but also about yourself: "Does this major really help me accomplish my aims in life?" These thoughts about oneself are called **self-referent cognitions** (or, equivalently, *self-reflective thought*). Social-cognitive theory claims that self-referent cognitions directly affect emotion and behavior (Bandura, 1986). If you doubt that you can handle the job, you become anxious at work. The cause is not a "trait of anxiety," but rather your thoughts about yourself. If you think the major isn't for you, you may become unmotivated in classes. The cause is not a "trait of low motivation," but, again, your self-referent cognition.

Social-cognitive theorists distinguish among three types of self-referent cognition: beliefs, goals, and standards. *Beliefs* are ideas that we think are true. *Self-referent* beliefs, then, are ideas about yourself that you think are true. You may believe that you're attractive, smart, or clumsy. Or hardworking, independent, or shy. Beliefs are key to personality because they shape people's flow of thinking and of behavior. People who believe they're so shy that they will embarrass themselves at big social gatherings worry about parties and tend to avoid them. People who believe they're smart and resourceful feel confident in themselves and take on difficult challenges.

Bandura places particular emphasis on **self-efficacy beliefs,** which are judgments about one's own capabilities for performance. "I'm confident I can get an A in calculus"; "I just can't get myself to stop overeating"; and "When I have to speak in front of a group, I can't control my anxiety" are all self-efficacy beliefs. Self-efficacy beliefs critically benefit human achievement. People attempt difficult tasks and persist when the going gets rough if they have a strong belief in their self-efficacy—their ability to succeed (Bandura, 1997).

Goals are thoughts about what we hope to achieve in the future. Goals are important to personality due to their power to organize and direct people's actions over long periods of time (Little, Salmela-Aro, & Phillips, 2007; Pervin, 1989). Whether you're exercising to look better and be healthier in the future, studying to do well on upcoming exams, or working at two part-time jobs in order to pay tuition next semester, your goals (health, good grades, remaining in school) are guiding your current behavior (the exercising, studying, or working).

Standards are ideas about types of behavior that are acceptable or unacceptable. Our personal standards are the criteria we use to evaluate how we're doing. Statements such as "Ugh, that sentence I just wrote for the term paper was terrible" or "Uh oh, I look really fat" indicate that people are evaluating behavior according to internalized standards that prescribe types of behavior that are acceptable and unacceptable. The way people feel about themselves—proud, disappointed, elated, disgusted—is often determined by the standard they use to evaluate their achievements (Bandura, 1986). People with high, perfectionistic standards frequently are highly motivated (Bandura, 1978; Carver & Scheier, 1998), yet also prone to becoming depressed when they don't meet their own standards of excellence (Hewitt & Flett, 1991).

Standards, in social-cognitive theory, play a role similar to the superego in psychodynamic theory. In both cases, the personality structure represents criteria for evaluating whether behavior is socially acceptable. Yet the theories differ. Social-cognitive theory takes a more flexible view of personality than does psychoanalysis. In psychoanalysis, the superego is said to develop early in life, through interactions with parents, and to be fixed after that. Social-cognitive theory, by comparison, recognizes that personal standards may change throughout life. If, at any point in life, people's life circumstances change—they move to a new country, join a new religion, or experience some other major life change—their personal standards may change, too.

SKILLS. Sometimes the cause of behavior is not people's thoughts about themselves, but another aspect of personality: skills (or lack thereof). **Skills** are abilities that develop through experience. Although you might think of skills in connection with activities such as jobs or sports, they also are relevant to personality. Some social situations—such as diffusing an argument among friends or having a good time at a party where you don't know other people—require substantial interpersonal skills. Individual differences in behavior in those situations are caused by individual differences in the skills people possess (Wright & Mischel, 1987).

Differences in personality style, then, can reflect differences in skills. Some people develop a relatively high degree of social skill and knowledge about themselves. These

Vivienne Wagner; thevspotblog.com

LOVE EACH OTHER
BE IN THE MOMENT
BE THANKFUL
PICK UP AFTER YOURSELF
LAUGH OFTEN
DON'T PLAY BALL IN THE HOUSE
SAY YOUR PRAYERS
CHEW, SWALLOW, SPEAK
SLOW DOWN
KEEP YOUR PROMISES
NO WHINING
USE YOUR MANNERS
PAY IT FORWARD
ALWAYS TELL THE TRUTH
BE RESPECTFUL
SHARE AND TAKE TURNS
DO THE RIGHT THING

Do this. Don't do that. Society surrounds us with guidelines for behavior. If we learn and follow them, they become personal *standards*—internal guides for behavior that, according to social-cognitive theory, are enduring features of our personalities.

self-efficacy beliefs Judgments about one's own capabilities for performance.

skills Abilities that develop through experience, including interpersonal skills.

figure **13.9**
Social intelligence The diagrams represent the knowledge possessed by two hypothetical people who differ in *social intelligence* (Cantor & Kihlstrom, 1987). The person whose knowledge is diagrammed on top is socially intelligent when it comes to exam preparation; this individual possesses a rich collection of knowledge about how to prepare for a test and cope with stress. The less socially intelligent person, depicted on the bottom, has a much more limited set of knowledge and strategies. In social-cognitive theory, such differences in knowledge and skills are seen as a key source of individual differences in personality.

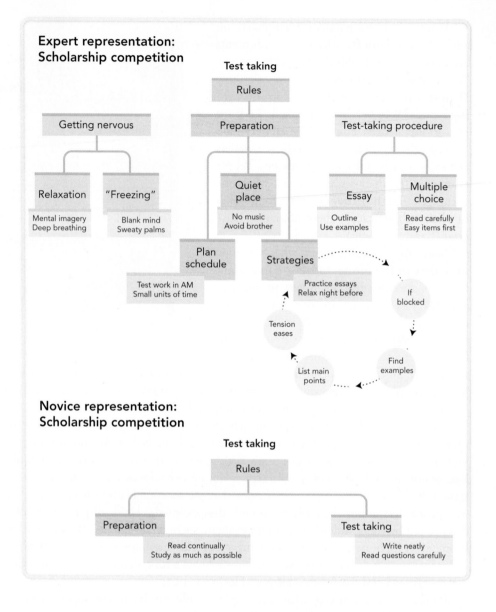

personality "experts" are said to have a high level of *social intelligence* (Cantor & Kihlstrom, 1987). Their knowledge is a valuable personal resource; it helps them adapt to unexpected challenges in situations they encounter (Figure 13.9).

AFFECTIVE SYSTEMS. People think, but they don't *only* think. People experience moods that linger from hour to hour and day to day, and emotions that can flare up and dissipate in minutes. A comprehensive theory of personality must address this "feeling" side of personality.

Social-cognitive theory does this by proposing that thinking or cognitive systems of personality interact with *affective systems*. The word "affect" refers to "feeling states," such as moods and emotions. **Affective systems** are psychological systems that generate moods and emotional states.

Social-cognitive theory suggests that cognition (thinking) and affect (feeling) are closely interrelated (Metcalfe & Mischel, 1999). Our thoughts influence our feelings, and our feelings, in turn, influence our thoughts. For example, perfectionistic standards for performance (a cognition) often cause people to become depressed (a prolonged negative mood). Perfectionistic people are more likely to develop depression than others (Enns, Cox, & Clara, 2002).

affective systems In social-cognitive theory, psychological systems that generate moods and emotional states.

Conversely, negative moods cause people to become perfectionistic. People who temporarily suffer from a negative mood are more likely to develop self-critical, perfectionistic standards for evaluating their own behavior (Cervone et al., 1994).

◊ WHAT DO YOU KNOW?...

23. Match the personality structure on the left with the quote that exemplifies it on the right.

    1. Self-efficacy belief
    2. Goal
    3. Standard

    a. "I'd like to do some volunteer work this summer."
    b. "Watching videos of kittens on the Internet is a poor use of my time."
    c. "I think I'd be really good at tutoring kids in math."

24. List a few examples of how thoughts can influence feelings and of how feelings can influence thoughts.

Process: Acquiring Skills and Self-Regulating Behavior

Preview Questions

› According to research by Bandura and others, through what process do individuals acquire skills?
› According to research by Mischel and colleagues, through what strategies can individuals control their emotions and impulses?

Beliefs, skills, and affective systems are stable personality structures; they comprise the structural aspects of social-cognitive theory. The theory addresses the process side of personality—changes in experience and behavior—by analyzing two topics: learning and self-regulation.

LEARNING. Where do people get their social skills? How did you first learn effective ways of participating in conversations, resolving conflicts with others, or making a good impression on people?

Social-cognitive theorists propose that the major way people learn life skills is through modeling. **Modeling** is the acquisition of skills by observing others who display those skills. If you learn to cook by watching a chef on TV, or learn to study more effectively by observing the study habits of academically successful friends, or learn to smoke by observing smokers light up (the behaviors learned can be both positive and negative), you are learning through modeling. People have the mental ability to remember others' behavior and to use this memory to guide their own actions in the future (Bandura, 1986). (Modeling is also called "observational learning" because a person can learn new information and skills by observing others.)

Other people's behavior thus serves as a kind of "instruction manual for life." Instead of just guessing how we should act, we can observe others and learn from them. When learning the culture of the workplace at a new job, you don't try out random styles of behavior—say, a formal suit one day, jeans and sandals the next—and learn only by trial and error. You observe the other employees and model their behavior.

A classic study by Bandura and colleagues shows that even brief exposure to a model can powerfully influence people's behavior (Bandura, Ross, & Ross, 1961; also see Chapter 7). Preschool children viewed a short film showing an adult punching and kicking an inflated clown doll, or Bobo doll. A second group of children, who constituted a control group, did not see the film. Later, children from both groups were sent one at a time into a playroom that contained a variety of toys, including a Bobo doll. Experimenters observed the children through a one-way mirror and recorded any acts of aggression toward the Bobo doll. As Bandura predicted, children who had seen the

modeling A form of learning in which knowledge and skills are acquired by observing others; also known as *observational learning*.

Courtesy of Albert Bandura

You can learn a lot from TV In Bandura's research on modeling, children quickly learned acts of aggression they observed on TV. The televised model of aggression is shown in the first row of pictures. The behavior of two children, after seeing the model, is shown in the second and third rows.

film behaved much more aggressively toward the Bobo doll than those who had not. They punched, kicked, and pummeled the Bobo doll with a hammer—just as they had seen in the film. They even devised novel acts of aggression toward the doll that went beyond what they had seen the model do.

As Bandura explained, this result contradicted the predictions of psychoanalytic theory. Psychoanalysis, as you learned, claims that aggressive energy is stored in the id. Viewing the film should have released some of this energy and reduced children's later aggression. But just the opposite happened. As social-cognitive theory predicted, children became more aggressive; they acted like the model.

THINK ABOUT IT

After they saw an adult hit a Bobo doll, children hit the doll, too. But Bobo dolls are made to be hit; given their design (bouncing right back up after being knocked down), hitting them is natural. Do you think that, as social-cognitive theory seems to suggest, the children would have modeled the adult's behavior no matter what she had hit (e.g., a potted plant; a piece of candy)? Are some behaviors more readily modeled than others?

CONNECTING TO LEARNING AND THE BRAIN

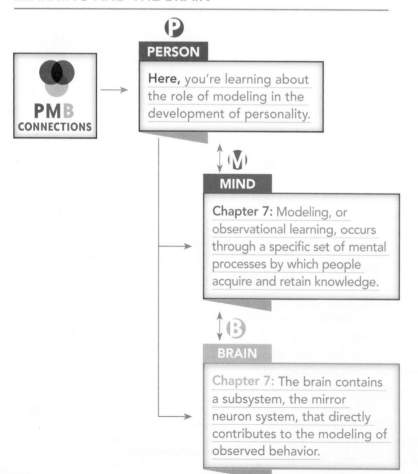

PMB CONNECTIONS

P PERSON

Here, you're learning about the role of modeling in the development of personality.

M MIND

Chapter 7: Modeling, or observational learning, occurs through a specific set of mental processes by which people acquire and retain knowledge.

B BRAIN

Chapter 7: The brain contains a subsystem, the mirror neuron system, that directly contributes to the modeling of observed behavior.

Subsequent research reveals that watching large amounts of violent television can have long-term effects. Children who watch large amounts of TV violence in childhood are more likely than others to develop into adults who behave aggressively (Huesmann et al., 2003). Violent video games similarly can increase aggressiveness (Bushman & Anderson, 2002). Although media violence, of course, is not the only factor that contributes to aggression in society, research shows that it does have a significant effect (Kirsh, 2012).

Modeling influences also can be positive. People who model socially valuable behaviors can have beneficial effects. Sometimes these effects are widespread. Consider a project in the East African nation of Tanzania, which suffers from high rates of HIV/AIDS infections (Mohammed, 2001; Vaughn et al., 2000). Social scientists working in collaboration with government officials designed a radio soap opera that educated listeners about HIV/AIDS. Some of the show's characters provided information about the causes of the disease. Other characters initially did not engage in safe-sex practices but, thanks to the positive influence of others, gradually adopted them. The show thus provided models of behaviors that promote health.

The government evaluated the program through an experiment of incredible scope. For two years, the show was broadcast in some regions of Tanzania but not others. Researchers conducted surveys to gauge its effects and found that the radio broadcast significantly improved the health behaviors of the nation's citizens. In areas where the show was broadcast, Tanzanian citizens reported more awareness of the risks of the disease and fewer HIV/AIDS risk factors (such as unprotected sex; Mohammed, 2001; Vaughn et al., 2000).

SELF-REGULATION. The second personality process of interest to social-cognitive theorists is self-regulation. **Self-regulation** refers to people's efforts to control their own behavior and emotions.

Sometimes people "give in to" impulses and emotions. You don't feel like doing your assigned reading, so you surf the Web instead. The triple-brownie delight looks good, so you order two. These are *not* cases of self-regulation. People self-regulate when they overcome impulses and emotions through their powers of thinking.

A major advance in scientific understanding of self-regulation was made by Walter Mischel, who studied a self-regulatory challenge known as *delay of gratification*. In delay of gratification, a person tries to put off (i.e., delay) an impulsive desire. For example, putting off a late-afternoon desire for a burger and waiting until dinner time to eat would be a case of delaying gratification. In Mischel's research, children in a nursery school were told that an adult who had been taking care of them had to leave for a while, but would come back. Before leaving, the adult left several marshmallows on the table in front of the children. If the children waited until the adult's return, they would get a reward: some marshmallows to eat. If they couldn't wait, they could ring a bell, and the adult would return—but the child would get only a small reward: one little marshmallow. Because children had an impulsive desire to eat the marshmallows, the length of time they waited was a measure of their ability to delay gratification.

The scientific question Mischel asked is: What can people do to delay gratification? In other words, what psychological processes enable people to control their behavior? He found that a major psychological process involves attention. What children pay attention to, while waiting, strongly affects their success at self-regulation. In a key study (Mischel & Baker, 1975), attention was manipulated experimentally:

> In one experimental condition, children were instructed to pay attention to how tasty marshmallows are: "When you look at marshmallows, think about how sweet they are when you eat them . . . how soft and sticky they are in your mouth" (Mischel & Baker, 1975, p. 257).

> In a second condition, children were *distracted from* the taste of the marshmallows; their attention was drawn to qualities other than taste: "When you look at marshmallows, think about how white and puffy they are. Clouds are white and puffy too—when you look at the marshmallows, think about clouds" (Mischel & Baker, 1975, p. 257).

Children whose attention was directed to qualities other than taste were much better at delaying gratification; they were able to wait 3 times longer than children who thought about how tasty marshmallows are. The findings show that the human ability to control thinking—to exert "executive control" over the flow of one's thoughts (Chapter 6)—enables people to control their impulsive desires.

Children differ in self-control abilities; some are better able to control their impulses than others. These differences predict outcomes later in life. Children with higher self-control skills tend, in adulthood, to experience better physical health and lower rates of substance abuse and are less likely to commit criminal offenses (Moffit et al., 2011; see Chapter 14).

PCI Media Impact

The nonprofit organization PCI Media Impact (formerly named Population Communications International) has put principles of social-cognitive theory into practice. They produce media broadcasts in which characters model beneficial behaviors, such as safe-sex practices. Here, broadcasters in Mexico work on the TV drama program *Mucho Corazon* (Much Heart), whose characters confront and cope with issues involving gender-based violence, financial literacy, and sustainable development. PCI Media Impact has produced approximately 100 TV and radio serial dramas that have reached over 1 billion people in 50 countries.

Jeff Greenberg / agefotostock

Want to avoid ordering a lot of fast food? If so, don't look at the picture or think about how good it would taste. Mischel's research on delay of gratification shows that forming mental images of things you want to avoid makes it harder to avoid them.

self-regulation People's efforts to control their own behavior and emotions.

25. True or False?
   a. According to social-cognitive theory, modeling is the major process by which we acquire new skills.
   b. Bandura's "Bobo doll" study illustrated how children are able to delay gratification.
   c. According to psychoanalytic theory, children who had seen an adult punch and kick the Bobo doll should have behaved less aggressively than they actually did.
   d. Evidence suggests that watching televised violence is linked to aggressive behavior.
   e. Self-regulation can be defined as the ability to overcome impulses and emotions by thinking.
   f. In Mischel's study, children who imagined the marshmallows as puffy clouds had the most trouble delaying gratification.
   g. Though there are individual differences in the ability to control impulses, they do not actually predict life outcomes.

Assessment: Evaluating Persons in Context

Preview Question

› What does it mean to assess cognition and behavior "in context"?

Social-cognitive theory, as you have seen, highlights (1) thinking processes and (2) the impact of thinking on behavior. When social-cognitive theorists assess personality, they have these same two targets in mind; they try to assess both thoughts and behavior. Before reading about how they do it, ask yourself this question: What are your thoughts and behaviors like? If you think about it, you will realize that the best answer to that question is, "It depends." You think about different things in different situations (at school, at work, with friends). Your behavior varies across varying social circumstances (with family, with one close friend, with a group of people you don't know well). Social *contexts*—the situations of your life—matter greatly.

Social-cognitive personality theorists recognize this. When assessing personality, they measure people's thoughts and actions as they occur within specific social contexts that are significant to people's lives (Cervone, Shadel, & Jencius, 2001; Shoda, Cervone, & Downey, 2007). (Note how this contrasts with trait theory, which assessed typical, average personality tendencies and thus paid much less attention to social context.) Let's look at some methods used to do this.

ASSESSING COGNITION IN CONTEXT. One method for assessing personality and thinking processes is self-report: asking people to report their beliefs about themselves and their actions. People usually give a lot of thought to themselves, their goals, and the personal standards they try to live up to. As a result they are, in some ways, "experts" about their own personality (Cantor & Kihlstrom, 1987). Social-cognitive theorists often draw on this expertise by asking people to report information about themselves.

Assessments of self-efficacy illustrate the strategy. Researchers ask people to report their confidence in performing specific types of behavior in specific settings (Bandura, 1997). For example, in a study of adolescents in school (Caprara et al., 2003), students were asked to report how confident they were in performing actions in specific contexts, such as "express[ing] your own opinions when other classmates disagree with you." These self-efficacy measures predicted behavior over a long period of time. Children who initially had higher self-efficacy beliefs regarding behavior at school were less shy

Perceived self-efficacy in the context of school Research on social-cognitive personality variables and school success shows that one determinant of success is perceived self-efficacy. Adolescents who are more confident in their abilities develop into more outgoing and assertive students.

at school two years later. Self-efficacy beliefs predicted behavior even after accounting for children's behavioral style at the start of the study (Caprara et al., 2003).

A second assessment strategy is *implicit* measures of personality, that is, measures that do *not* rely on people's explicit reports about themselves (see Research Toolkit). In social-cognitive psychology, the speed with which people respond to test questions is a commonly used implicit measure. People who, in their everyday lives, tend to dwell on a particular feature of their personality tend to respond more quickly when asked questions about that personality feature (Cervone et al., 2007; Markus, 1977).

⊕RESEARCH TOOLKIT

Implicit Measures of Personality

"Tell me about your personality."

This might seem easy. Everybody can tell you *something* about their personality. But is what they tell you accurate?

Two factors can create inaccuracy. People might not have an accurate conception of their personality. Alternatively, they might be motivated to create a good impression and thus describe their personality in a false manner. For example, people applying for a job that requires employees to act in an extraverted manner (e.g., sales or marketing) may describe themselves as extraverted—even if they're really not (Krahé, Becker, Zöllter, 2008).

To measure personality accurately, then, researchers need tools in addition to self-reports. One such tool is *implicit* measures of personality (Gawronski, LeBel, & Peters, 2007; also see Chapter 12 for a discussion of implicit measures).

The term "implicit measure" is most easily defined by first considering its opposite: *explicit measure*. An **explicit measure** of personality is one in which people directly state answers to questions, and the substance of their answers is interpreted as an index of their personality qualities. Interviews in which people discuss their personality, or questionnaires in which they describe themselves on rating scales, are explicit measures. An **implicit measure** of personality is one in which responses *other than* explicit self-reports provide information about personal qualities. For example, the length of time taken to answer a question may be revealing; people who take longer to answer a question may be hiding some aspect of their true self (Weinberger, Schwartz, & Davidson, 1979).

Let's see how implicit measures work in a specific case: measuring self-esteem, people's overall sense of self-worth.

In an explicit measure of self-esteem, participants simply make statements about themselves. Researchers might, for example, ask them to indicate whether "I have high self-esteem" (Robins, Hendin, & Trzesniewski, 2001, p. 153).

One popular implicit measure of self-esteem is the *implicit association test* (IAT, Greenwald & Farnham, 2000). In an IAT measure of self-esteem, people perform tasks that involve positive and negative ideas about the self. Their relative speed in making positive and negative responses on these tasks indicates their self-esteem level. In one task, people decide whether words fit the following rule: The word "is pleasant or describes me." In another, they decide whether each word "is *un*pleasant or describes me." Greater speed on the former task (pleasant or me) than the latter indicates a higher level of self-esteem. The speed reveals stronger mental associations between the concepts of "pleasant" and "self."

Intriguingly, implicit and explicit measures of self-esteem are not strongly related (Hofmann et al., 2005). Some people with low implicit self-esteem have high explicit self-esteem (and vice versa); they seem to doubt themselves, but don't express these

explicit measure An assessment of psychological qualities (e.g., personality characteristics) in which test items directly inquire about the psychological quality of interest, and people's responses are interpreted as a direct index of those qualities.

implicit measure An assessment of psychological qualities (e.g., personality characteristics) that does not rely on test takers' direct reports of their qualities; instead, measures such as length of time taken to answer a question provide information about psychological qualities.

doubts publicly. The implicit measure, then, provides unique information. It may reveal, for instance, that someone who speaks highly of herself publicly also has—at a hidden, implicit level—substantial self-doubts.

🦅 WHAT DO YOU KNOW?...

26. Researchers concerned about the accuracy of _____ measures may wish to instead rely on implicit measures of personality. On the IAT measure of self-esteem, high implicit self-esteem would be indicated if someone was faster to associate "describes me" with _____ words. Implicit and explicit measures are not strongly _____, indicating that the implicit measures do indeed provide unique information.

ASSESSING BEHAVIOR IN CONTEXT. The second target of assessment for social-cognitive theory, after thinking processes, is people's behavior. A particularly valuable method for assessing behavior was developed by Walter Mischel and colleagues. In the ***if . . . then . . . profile method,*** researchers chart variations in behavior that occur when people encounter different situations (Mischel & Shoda, 1995). The technique rests on the following idea. If you look at people's behavior, it varies. For example, you might be extraverted with close friends and introverted around strangers. Why average together these different behaviors in different situations (as is done in the trait approach)? Instead, assess the variability: "*If* you are with close friends, *then* you are extraverted," but "*If* you are with strangers, *then* you are introverted."

The *if . . . then . . .* profile method has been used to study children's aggressive behavior (Shoda, Mischel, & Wright, 1994). Psychologists recorded not only acts of aggression but also the particular situation a child was in when acting aggressively. They then plotted *if . . . then . . .* graphs showing how each person acted in different situations (Figure 13.10). Children who, on average, displayed similar levels of aggression differed from one another in the situations (the "ifs") that triggered their aggressiveness. For instance, some picked fights with other children but were not aggressive toward adults, whereas others were aggressive toward adults who reprimanded them but did not pick fights with other children. The profile method, then, reveals personality characteristics that would be missed if one only studied average levels of behavior.

🦅 WHAT DO YOU KNOW?...

27. Social-cognitive assessments are designed to find out what people are like in _____ versus what they are like on average. Research using the *if . . . then . . .* profile method revealed that children differed in the _____ that provoked aggression.

Evaluation

Preview Question

> What are the strengths and limitations of social-cognitive theory?

Social-cognitive theory has many strengths. It is supported by a firm base of research. That research base is diverse; it includes research conducted in the laboratory and in the real world, with adults and with children. By attending to social situations, social-cognitive theory helps to show how personality develops in interaction with the settings in which people live.

Like other theories, however, social-cognitive theory also has its limitations. It does not directly address some important phenomena. The theory says little about how unconscious motives, particularly those involving sex and aggression, can express

if . . . then . . . profile method A method for assessing behavior in which researchers chart variations in behavior that occur when people encounter different situations.

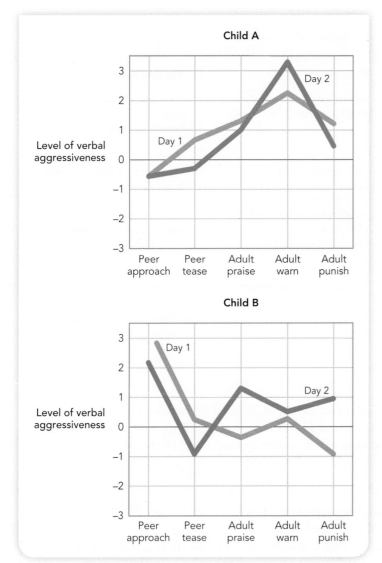

figure **13.10**
Personality in context Social-cognitive theorists explain that, to learn about personality, you should study people across a variety of social contexts. *If . . . then . . .* profile graphs show how personality reveals itself in the way that people's behavior varies from one context to another. The two graphs represent two children's levels of verbal aggression in each of five different social contexts involving interactions with peers and adults. The two lines in each graph represent the child's behavior as measured on two different days. On average—that is, if you averaged across the five contexts—the children score about the same. However, their reactions to specific social contexts are entirely different (Mischel & Shoda, 1995).

themselves in people's actions (a main concern of psychodynamic theory). It does not explicitly explain how the quality of interpersonal relationships can enhance personal growth (a main topic in humanistic theory). In addition, its assessment methods are valuable yet complex; they do not yield simple, quick assessment measures (of the sort provided by trait theory). But social-cognitive theory is still evolving. Expanding its scope is a challenge for its future.

🐦 WHAT DO YOU KNOW?...

28. Which of the following statements about the strengths and weaknesses of social-cognitive theory are true? Check all that apply.

___a. It is supported by both laboratory research and research in real-world settings.

___b. It is supported by research on adults, but unfortunately, not on children.

___c. It specifies how personality develops in interaction with other people.

___d. It does an excellent job specifying how unconscious motives drive behavior.

___e. Like humanistic theory, it excels at describing how relationships enhance personal growth.

table **13.6**

Personality Theory Structures, Processes, and Assessment Strategies			
Theory	**Structures**	**Processes**	**Assessment**
Psychodynamic theory	Conscious and unconscious mental systems: id, ego, and superego	Anxiety and defense mechanisms	Free association and projective tests (e.g., Rorschach test)
Humanistic theory	Self-concept: the actual and ideal self	Self-actualization, conditions of worth	Measures of self-concept (e.g., Q-sort technique)
Trait theory	Stable individual differences in average behavioral tendencies	Trait-based individual differences in reactions to stimuli	Comprehensive self-report questionnaires (e.g., NEO-PI-R)
Social-cognitive theory	Socially acquired cognition (self-referent cognition, skills) and affective systems	Acquiring skills, regulating emotion and behavior	Contextualized measures of cognition and behavior (e.g., self-efficacy measures, *if . . . then . . .* profiles)

We've reached the end of our survey of personality theories. Table 13.6 summarizes their structures, processes, and assessment strategies. With this information now in place, let's turn to the topic of personality dynamics and the brain.

Personality and the Brain

The history of personality psychology (Lombardo & Foschi, 2003) exemplifies the *person-first* theme of this textbook. Personality psychology began at a *person* level of analysis; theorists such as Freud, Rogers, and Bandura studied people in therapy and in everyday social contexts. Next, the field moved to a *mind* level. Researchers explored cognitive and emotional processes that might explain people's distinctive personality styles (e.g., Cantor & Kihlstrom, 1987; Cervone, 2004; Erdelyi, 1985).

In recent years, researchers have been able to move down a level, to the *brain*. Let's see how brain research has deepened psychology's understanding of two types of personality processes: (1) unconscious processes (as emphasized in psychodynamic theory) and (2) conscious, self-reflective processes (as emphasized in humanistic and social-cognitive theories).

Unconscious Personality Processes and the Brain

Preview Question

> Does research on the brain support the idea that thinking can occur unconsciously?

Freud's theory of the unconscious mind is psychological, not biological. Freud never identified parts of the brain associated with his psychodynamic structures and processes—but he wanted to. Freud began to formulate a biological theory of mind early in his career (Pribram & Gill, 1976), but abandoned the effort after concluding that scientific knowledge at the time was insufficient to support a biologically grounded theory of unconscious processes.

Times have changed, thanks to advances in biology. Today, psychologists recognize that biological evolution naturally gave rise to a mind that, to a large degree, acts unconsciously (Bargh & Morsella, 2008). During the course of evolution, quick, unconscious processes were often beneficial compared to slow, conscious ones; when chasing prey or avoiding predators, there's no time to sit around consciously deliberating on the best course of action. Organisms benefit from an unconscious mind that triggers actions rapidly.

This evolutionary reasoning suggests that brain researchers should be able to identify regions of the brain that trigger people's decisions even before they are consciously aware that they have decided. In one experiment with this goal, researchers studied a simple decision: when to press a button. Participants were asked to press one of two buttons whenever they "felt the urge to do so" (Soon et al., 2008, p. 543). To find out when people had the conscious experience of deciding to press a button, researchers flashed a series of letters on a computer screen and asked participants to remember which letter was on screen when they felt they were making their decision. (The researchers knew exactly when each letter appeared and thus could pinpoint the time at which participants had the conscious experience of making a decision.)

Throughout the task, fMRI was used to record participants' brain activity. The researchers identified two brain regions that predicted button pressing; in other words, when these regions became active, participants pressed a button soon afterward. Researchers then compared two time points: (1) when the brain regions became active, and (2) when people had the conscious experience of making the decision.

Of critical importance is that the brain activity occurred well *before* the conscious experience—often 7 to 10 seconds earlier (Figure 13.11). The implications are remarkable: The researchers could determine (from recordings of brain activity) when participants would press a button *before the participants themselves knew* (from their conscious experience) when they would do so. This and related findings (e.g., Libet et al., 1983) suggest that, outside of conscious awareness, brain systems "make a decision" and subsequently send information about the decision to the conscious part of the mind.

Another study provides a brain-level analysis of the phenomenon that launched Freud's psychodynamic theory of personality: the impact of mental content (memories, thoughts) on physical symptoms. Researchers (Voon et al., 2010) studied patients with *conversion disorder,* in which people experience physical symptoms—for example, odd muscular movements such as tremors and tics—that cannot be explained by any medical condition (also see Chapter 16). Their physical symptoms thus appear to have mental causes. What could connect the mental and the physical? Brain-imaging research indicated strong connections between the motor area (which controls muscular movement) and the amygdala (which is involved in emotional arousal). Just as Freud might have predicted, among people with conversion disorder, when the emotion region of the brain became active, the motor area of the brain became active, too. This emotion–motor connection in the brain was *not* seen in a second group of people who did not have conversion disorder.

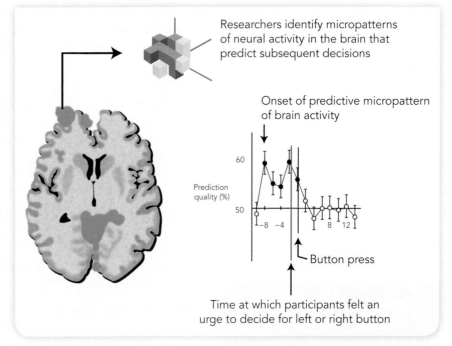

Researchers identify micropatterns of neural activity in the brain that predict subsequent decisions

Onset of predictive micropattern of brain activity

Prediction quality (%)

Button press

Time at which participants felt an urge to decide for left or right button

figure 13.11
Decision making and conscious awareness To determine when people had the *conscious experience* of making a decision, researchers recorded (1) when they were consciously aware of making the decision, and (2) brain activity that might predict decision making. Researchers identified a brain region that became active and predicted decision making 7 to 10 seconds *before* people were aware that they were making decisions. The results highlight the role of *nonconscious* processes in decision making.

THINK ABOUT IT

How do contemporary research findings on unconscious processes relate to Freud's theory? Is the unconscious studied in today's research the unconscious of Freud—one dominated by sexual and aggressive urges and repressed memories?

Connections in the brain thus may explain the connections between mind and body first analyzed by Freud. In patients with conversion disorder, emotional arousal may directly disrupt motor movements.

⚡ WHAT DO YOU KNOW?...

29. Brain _____ research indicates that different brain regions become active during conscious and _____ processing. It also indicates that among those with _____ disorder, there are strong connections between the emotion region, or the _____, and the motor area of the brain, which helps to explain why emotions can disrupt movements.

Conscious Self-Reflection and the Brain

Preview Question

> How have researchers studied the brain and people's ability to think about themselves, or self-reflect?

As you learned earlier, both humanistic and social-cognitive personality theorists analyzed the self, arguing that people's reflections upon themselves are a central personality process. They made these arguments on psychological, not biological, grounds. At the time the theories were formulated, researchers had little knowledge of the brain systems involved in self-reflection.

Again, times have changed. In the past decade, researchers have begun to identify the neural systems that enable people to reflect upon, and develop knowledge about, themselves (Lieberman, Jarcho, & Satpute, 2004).

One line of research has explored self-reflection and the brain through a two-step strategy (D'Argembeau et al., 2008). The steps exemplify the mind and brain levels of analysis we have discussed throughout:

> *Distinguish among mental processes:* The first step was to distinguish among different types of mental processes. Here, a key factor to consider is time. Sometimes people store information about, and reflect on, their current self—their present, here-and-now psychological characteristics. Other times people store and reflect on information about their past or future self—psychological characteristics they possessed earlier in life or might possess someday.

> *Identify neural system in the brain:* The second step was to identify brain systems that come into play during these different types of mental processes involving the self. The researchers used brain imaging to accomplish this, in the following research procedure.

Participants rated a series of adjectives (e.g., "modest," "shy"), judging, for each one, whether the word described them (D'Argembeau et al., 2008). In different experimental conditions, participants reflected on whether the words (1) described them now (their present self) or (2) described them as they were five years ago (their past self). They also rated whether adjectives described a close friend now and in the past; this combination of conditions enabled the researchers to identify regions of the brain that are most active specifically when people reflect upon themselves. Self-reflection, they found, was associated with *cortical midline structures,* that is, with activation in the middle of the upper regions of the brain; see Figure 13.12 (the cortex; Chapter 3). Central regions of the frontal cortex and rear, or posterior, cingulate cortex were more active when participants thought about themselves in the present than the past.

Twenty-first-century findings on personality and the brain deepen the understanding of human nature developed by twentieth-century psychologists. More generally, they show how contemporary psychology is integrative. Decades ago, research on

Self-reflection, the psychological activity of thinking about one's own characteristics, has long been the focus of art (as shown here in Picasso's *Girl Before a Mirror*). In twentieth-century personality theory, it was the focus of psychology, as personality theorists came to view self-reflection as a central personality process. In the twenty-first century, self-reflection is also targeted by neuroscientists, who search for brain regions that give people the power to reflect upon themselves.

Album / Oronoz / Album / SuperStock

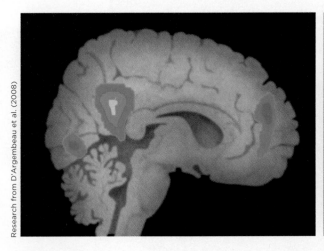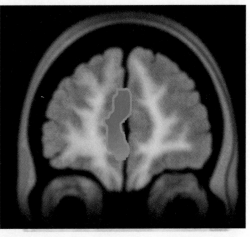

Research from D'Argembeau et al. (2008)

figure **13.12**

What your brain may have looked like when you did the exercise at the beginning of this chapter. Researchers took brain images while participants engaged in the same sort of task you performed at the start of this chapter: reflecting on your personality. Self-reflecting is associated with activity in structures in the middle of the brain, in the frontal lobes (colored region on the right side of image on the left; and image on the right) and the cingulate cortex (large green-and-blue-colored region in the brain image on the left).

self-concept, thinking processes, and the brain took part in disconnected sections of the field. Today, they are integrated. Findings from research with persons inform, and are enriched by, research on the brain (Figure 13.13).

🐸 WHAT DO YOU KNOW?...

30. Brain-imaging research indicates that different areas of the brain become active when people reflect on their past versus _____ selves. Such research is an example of how research on persons and on the brain _____ or unites the field of psychology.

⟳ Looking Back and Looking Ahead

In this chapter, you learned about the four main theories that have guided research in the psychology of personality. As you look back on them, you may ask yourself, "Why four? Couldn't psychology settle on just one?"

There may be benefits to four, rather than "just one." Theories are intellectual tools that help scientists explain events. Each of the theories you learned about provides a unique explanation; each, in other words, covers some aspects of personality that the other theories do not address thoroughly. In combination, then, the four theories give psychology a wide array of tools for explaining the life of individuals and the differences among them.

Psychologists in other fields have put these tools to work, as shown elsewhere in this book. Emotion researchers use the insights of personality psychology to understand why different people may have different emotional reactions in response to the same event (Chapter 10). Researchers studying nature, nurture, and genetics (Chapter 4) employ personality assessments when studying the interplay of inheritance and experience. Clinical psychologists draw on personality theories when formulating therapy strategies (Chapter 15). Motivation researchers draw on them to understand the forces that impel, and impede, human behavior (Chapter 11). "Psychology," as Hans Eysenck (1972) put it, "is about people." It's no surprise, then, that the branch of the field that focuses most explicitly on the individual person—the study of personality—has such wide-ranging implications for psychology as a whole.

figure **13.13**

PMB
IN ACTION

ARE THERE DIFFERENT COMPONENTS OF SELF-CONCEPT?

P **PERSON**

Personality theorists identify different components of self-concept that involve variations in time. Self-concept includes not only one's current, "actual" self, but also beliefs about one's development in the past and personal goals in the future.

M **MIND**

These aspects of personality and self-concept are possible only because of a distinctively human mental ability: mental time-travel. In the mind, information about the past and images of the future can be stored, retrieved, and contemplated.

Past   Present   Future
← *Mental Time Travel* →
Information Storage
and Retrieval

B **BRAIN**

Specific brain systems support the mental ability to contemplate not only the present, but also the past and future. Different neural systems are active when people think about themselves at different points in time.

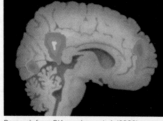

Research from D'Argembeau et al. (2008)

Rae Merrygold

Chapter Review

Now that you have completed this chapter, be sure to turn to Appendix B, where you will find a **Chapter Summary** that is useful for reviewing what you have learned about personality.

Key Terms

actual self (p. 566)
affective systems (p. 584)
anal stage (p. 558)
Big Five (p. 573)
collective unconscious (p. 562)
condition of worth (p. 567)
conscious (p. 555)
defense mechanism (p. 559)
ego (p. 554)
explicit measure (p. 589)
factor analysis (p. 572)
fixation (p. 559)
free association method (p. 561)
genital stage (p. 558)
humanistic theory (p. 565)
id (p. 554)
ideal self (p. 566)
if . . . then . . . profile method (p. 590)
implicit measure (p. 589)

latency stage (p. 558)
levels of consciousness (p. 555)
lexical approach (p. 572)
modeling (p. 585)
neo-Freudian personality theories (p. 562)
oral stage (p. 558)
personal agency (p. 581)
personality (p. 551)
personality assessment (p. 553)
personality processes (p. 552)
personality structures (p. 552)
personality theory (p. 552)
phallic stage (p. 558)
preconscious (p. 555)
projective test (p. 561)
psychoanalytic theory (p. 554)
psychodynamic processes (p. 557)
psychosexual stage (p. 558)

Q-sort (p. 568)
repression (p. 559)
Rorschach inkblot test (p. 561)
self (p. 566)
self-actualization (p. 567)
self-efficacy beliefs (p. 583)
self-esteem (p. 570)
self-referent cognitions (p. 582)
self-regulation (p. 587)
skills (p. 583)
social-cognitive theory (p. 580)
sublimation (p. 559)
superego (p. 555)
terror management theory (p. 558)
trait (p. 571)
trait theories (p. 571)
unconditional positive regard (p. 567)
unconscious (p. 555)

Questions for Discussion

1. If you could be described by only one of the assessment techniques explained in this chapter, which would you prefer and why? Which technique do you think would reveal the most about your own personality? [Analyze, Evaluate]

2. If you were to build your own theory of personality, what particular behaviors or aspects of personality would you most want to explain? What particular structures would be important for you to include and why? Are there structures you would exclude? If so, why? [Analyze, Evaluate]

3. Which of your own personality qualities is most puzzling to you? How would each of the theories discussed in this chapter explain it? Which seems to do the best job in explaining it? Pick a different quality (your most outstanding quality, perhaps) and address the same questions. Did the same theory do the best job this time around? What might this suggest about how to evaluate the various personality theories? [Apply, Analyze, Synthesize, Evaluate]

4. Which of your personality qualities do you think you could change if you really had to? Which of your qualities

do you regard as unchangeable? How do your intuitions about what can and cannot change in your personality match up to the ideas and research findings associated with each of the four personality theories discussed in this chapter? [Analyze]

5. Imagine that, instead of being raised by your actual parents, there was a mix-up at the hospital and you were raised by different parents. Do you think your current personality would be different? Why or why not? Relate your intuitions to the personality theories discussed in this chapter. [Analyze, Synthesize]

6. Einstein said, "The most important human endeavor is the striving for morality in our actions. . . . Only morality in our actions can give beauty and dignity to life." Do you believe that the personality theories discussed in this chapter stated enough about morality, that is, about what constitutes "right" and "wrong" behavior and what constitutes a morally and ethically good life? Should theorists have told us more about how we should live our lives? Or is that the sort of question a psychological scientist should avoid even trying to answer? [Evaluate]

Chapter Review

Self-Test

1. Though you would describe yourself as outgoing, there are situations in which your confidence decreases and you therefore appear very shy. This situational variability in your outward behavior highlights the need for personality psychologists to distinguish between _____ and _____, that is, between the stable traits and dynamic qualities of people.
   a. thought; expression
   b. actual self; ideal self
   c. id; superego
   d. structures; processes

2. In a flash of insight, you realize that the reason you're being so nice to your sister is that you feel guilty for having secretly wished her bad luck earlier. This insight was possible due to the fact that the _____ is/are partly available to consciousness.
   a. ego
   b. superego
   c. ego and superego
   d. id and ego

3. According to Freud, fixation is caused by either too much gratification or too little gratification at a given stage of development. This suggests that, theoretically, fixation
   a. should be common.
   b. should be rare.
   c. is impossible.
   d. is only possible at the oral stage.

4. Allie claims that Bruce has a big crush on her and she goes to great lengths to demonstrate how much she dislikes him. She is likely engaging in the defense mechanisms of _____ and _____ to protect herself from the possibility that she is sexually attracted to him.
   a. sublimation; projection
   b. projection; sublimation
   c. projection; reaction formation
   d. reaction formation; projection

5. Which of the following is *untrue* of projective tests?
   a. They consistently predict important outcomes.
   b. They are slow to administer, relative to other assessments.
   c. Their scoring is very subjective.
   d. They can consist of ambiguous images.

6. Discrepancies between the actual and ideal self cause distress, but theoretically they may also motivate us to
   a. become more like our ideal selves.
   b. seek out conditions of worth from others.
   c. become more like our actual selves.
   d. seek out opportunities to engage in defense.

7. Why would Freud *not* be interested in using the Q-sort to assess his structures of personality?
   a. The Q-sort was designed to measure the unconscious, which was of little interest to Freud.
   b. The Q-sort takes a long time to administer, and Freud favored quick and efficient assessment techniques.
   c. The Q-sort was designed to measure aspects of the self that people can consciously reflect upon, which was of little interest to Freud.
   d. The Q-sort is not a valid assessment technique, and Freud valued the validity of his measures above all else.

8. Research on cultural differences in self-esteem indicate that Americans report having higher self-esteem than do Japanese. As a consequence, when American students receive negative feedback on an exam, they question the validity of the test, whereas Japanese students question their understanding of the material. What is the implication?
   a. Japanese students will be motivated by the negative feedback to work harder, but American students won't.
   b. American students will be motivated by the negative feedback to work harder, but Japanese students won't.
   c. Both Japanese and American students will be motivated by the negative feedback to work harder.
   d. Japanese policy makers should consider putting programs in place that will increase their students' self-esteem.

9. According to the logic behind the use of factor analysis, if people who score high on the trait *altruistic* also score high on the traits *trusting* and *modest,* then
   a. their scores were caused by one trait: extraversion.
   b. their scores were caused by one trait: agreeableness.
   c. their scores were caused by two traits: extraversion and agreeableness.
   d. the meaning of their scores is inconclusive.

10. Recent research on the Big Five using the statistical technique network analysis indicates that
    a. the Big Five continue to fall into five separate "clumps," just as they do when factor analysis is used.
    b. when test items are correlated, it's because they cause each other, not because they are caused by one of the Big Five.
    c. when test items are correlated, it's because they are caused by one of the Big Five.
    d. the Big Five continue to be distinct, even when moving from factor analysis to network analysis.

11. Research on the differences in cortical arousal of introverts and extraverts suggests that
    a. shy people may avoid parties because they do not provide enough arousal.
    b. shy people may avoid parties because they provide too much arousal.
    c. shy people may seek out parties because they provide enough arousal.
    d. shy people would seek out parties if they were more arousing.

12. Unlike _____, who believed that personality development was largely fixed by age 6, _____ stressed the idea that individuals have personal agency, and can influence the course of their development throughout their lives.
    a. Bandura; Freud
    b. Bandura; Mischel
    c. Freud; Bandura
    d. Freud; Eysenck

13. The importance of self-referent cognitions can be summarized best by which of the following statements?
    a. People have personal agency and can direct their behavior toward positive life changes.
    b. People think about themselves, and these thoughts influence other thoughts, feelings, and behaviors.
    c. People vary in their behavior from situation to situation, and these changes are integral to personality.
    d. People learn much of their behavior not through trial and error, but by modeling others.

14. Implicit measures such as the implicit association test are based on the logic that
    a. when people interpret ambiguous stimuli, their responses will tell you something about their unconscious.
    b. when people fill out self-report measures, they provide information about their self-referent cognitions.
    c. when people take a long time to respond to a test item, they may be revealing something about themselves.
    d. when people are allowed to freely discuss whatever comes to mind, they will eventually reveal something about themselves.

15. Research using the *if . . . then . . .* procedure for assessing personality in context indicated that children differed from one another in the situations that provoked aggression. Which aspect of trait theory does this finding call into question?
    a. Trait theory's insistence that traits are biologically based
    b. Trait theory's insistence that traits are entirely shaped by the environment
    c. Trait theory's insistence that traits should be consistent from situation to situation
    d. Trait theory's insistence that traits should vary from situation to situation

Answers

You can check your answers to the preceding Self-Test and the chapter's What Do You Know? questions in Appendix B.

Development

Interviewer:	Do you see this stone? Why is it round?
Child Age 5:	*Because it wants to be round.*
Interviewer:	Have you seen the clouds moving?
Child Age 6½:	*Yes.*
Interviewer:	Can you make them move yourself?
Child Age 6½:	*Yes. By walking.*
Interviewer:	What happens when you walk?
Child Age 6½:	*It makes them move.*
Interviewer:	Do you see this stone? Do you think you could make a bigger stone with it?
Child Age 7:	*Oh, yes, you could take a big stone then you could break it and that would turn it into a bigger stone.*
Interviewer:	What is the moon like?
Child Age 12:	*Round.*
Interviewer:	Always?
Child Age 12:	*No.*
Interviewer:	What else does it look like?
Child Age 12:	*It's cut through the middle. In the evening it's round, and in the day it's cut in two.*
Interviewer:	Where is the other half?
Child Age 12:	*Gone away.*
Interviewer:	Where to?
Child Age 12:	*To another country where it's night.*

—All statements from Piaget (1929/1951)

THESE KIDS' IDEAS ARE WEIRD: NOT JUST factually wrong, but illogical. Objects don't "want" things or get bigger when broken.

Where do you think they got such ideas? No first-grade lesson plan includes "How walking controls clouds." They might have learned them from other kids—but then where did the *other* kids get the ideas?

Psychologists have another explanation. These ideas were not learned from teachers or other children. They were generated by the minds of the children themselves. The "weirdness" of the ideas is key to the nature of psychological development. ⊙

Getty Images, from top to bottom:
Stattmayer; Jasper James

Hugh Arnold / Gallery Stock

COMPARE YOURSELF TODAY to yourself as a child. You were different back then—maybe more impulsive and spontaneous, or less self-conscious and opinionated. Yet you probably were similar in some ways, too. If you're a fun-loving joker now, you might have been like that in grade school. If you're shy when meeting strangers today, you might have been shy around strangers years ago.

The ways people change, and remain the same, across the course of life are explored in **developmental psychology.** This chapter will introduce you to three main areas of study in developmental psychology: cognitive, social, and moral development.

1. **Cognitive development** is growth in intellectual capabilities, particularly during the early years of life. The interviews that opened this chapter, which were conducted by the Swiss cognitive-developmental psychologist Jean Piaget, illustrate the remarkable ways in which children's thinking differs from that of adults.

2. **Social development** is growth in people's ability to function effectively in the social world, both in childhood and across the life span. Developing abilities to control one's emotions, maintain relationships with others, establish a meaningful personal identity, and cope with the challenges of older adulthood are all aspects of social development.

3. **Moral development** is growth in reasoning about personal rights, responsibilities, and social obligations, especially regarding the welfare of other people. Questions about rules, laws, and circumstances in which it may be acceptable to challenge existing laws are the types of topics studied in moral development.

All three aspects of psychological development occur as people develop physically. The chapter thus also reviews aspects of physical development, including changes in brain structure that accompany growth in children's intellectual abilities; motor development (i.e., ability to move one's body skillfully) and the way it can be affected by the social environment; and the many biological changes that occur when adolescents reach puberty.

Let's begin with cognitive development.

Cognitive Development

You know a lot of things. Two and two is four. Alaska is the largest U.S. state. George Washington was the first president. You also know *how* you know these facts: People taught them to you, and you committed them to memory. Now consider some other things you know:

> If you take a ball of dough and flatten it out to make a pizza, you don't have more dough after flattening it out than when you started.

> If you paint white stripes on a black horse, you end up with a horse with white stripes, not a zebra.

> If you move someone's book from one location to another when that person isn't looking, he or she will first look for the book in its original location, not its actual location, and will be surprised when it is not there.

How did you learn these things? It's unlikely that a biology teacher ever taught you the one about horses and zebras, yet you know it is true. And *when* did you learn them? Were you born with such knowledge, or did you acquire it gradually during childhood? Questions like these are the focus of study in cognitive development.

---

developmental psychology The field of study that explores the ways people change, and remain the same, across the course of life.

cognitive development Growth in intellectual capabilities, particularly during the early years of life.

social development Growth in ability to function effectively in the social world, especially by controlling emotions, maintaining relationships, and establishing a personal identity.

moral development Growth in reasoning about personal rights, responsibilities, and social obligations regarding the welfare of others.

The Psychology of Jean Piaget

Preview Questions

> What were the key features of Piaget's research method?
> What cognitive tools enable us to solve logical reasoning problems we've never encountered before?
> How does our existing knowledge enable us to adapt to the environment? Through what process do we update that knowledge?
> What makes Piaget's approach a nature *and* nurture one?
> Which comes first: learning or development?
> What characterizes each of Piaget's stages of cognitive development?

Any review of cognitive development must begin with the monumental contributions of Jean Piaget, among the most influential figures in the history of psychology (Haggbloom et al., 2002). Piaget was trained as a biologist. But a job working with children aroused his interest in a psychological question: How do children's thinking abilities develop? To find out, he studied young children (including his own) from the 1920s until his death in 1980.

Piaget achieved scientific breakthroughs that were not appreciated immediately. However, English-language summaries of his findings, particularly that of John Flavell (1963, 1996), spread the word. By the 1980s, "almost everything people think and do" in cognitive development "had some connection with questions that Piaget raised" (Flavell & Markman, 1983, p. viii).

Bill Anderson / Photo Researchers / Getty Images

Jean Piaget, whose studies of children's abilities to solve problems laid foundations for the contemporary study of cognitive development.

PIAGET'S METHOD. Piaget devised a research method that was simple yet powerful. It had two key features (Flavell, 1963):

> *Ask children to solve problems that are novel:* Rather than asking children to recall facts they had already learned, Piaget asked them to solve problems they had never seen before. This enabled him to study the developing mind in action, as it tackles new challenges. For example, in a classic problem (discussed in detail below), Piaget poured water from a wide container into a tall, narrow one and asked children a novel question: During this process, did the total amount of water change or remain the same?

At what age do you suppose children are able to correctly solve this problem?

> *Ask children about their answers:* Rather than merely recording the correctness of children's answers, Piaget asked them to explain *why* they chose those answers. This simple step provided more insight into the developing mind.

SCHEMAS AND OPERATIONS. How can children solve problems they have never seen before? Piaget's answer is simple. Anything a person does—from picking up a toy to solving a math problem—requires that person to possess some mental structure that makes the action possible. Psychological abilities, Piaget reasoned, are like biological abilities. For example, because people digest food, they must possess a biological structure that enables digestion of that food. Analogously, if they solve a psychological problem, they must possess a mental structure that enables that type of problem to be solved.

Piaget called these mental structures *schemas.* A **schema,** in Piagetian theory, is a mental structure that makes organized, meaningful action possible. A schema for

schema A mental structure that makes organized, meaningful action possible.

CONNECTING TO PROBLEM SOLVING AND BRAIN NETWORKS

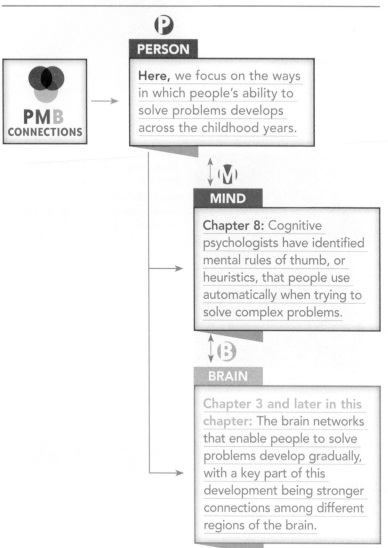

PMB CONNECTIONS

P

PERSON

Here, we focus on the ways in which people's ability to solve problems develops across the childhood years.

M

MIND

Chapter 8: Cognitive psychologists have identified mental rules of thumb, or heuristics, that people use automatically when trying to solve complex problems.

B

BRAIN

Chapter 3 and later in this chapter: The brain networks that enable people to solve problems develop gradually, with a key part of this development being stronger connections among different regions of the brain.

operation In Piagetian theory, a reversible action that modifies an object or set of objects, either physically or conceptually.

assimilation In Piagetian theory, a cognitive process in which one understands an object or event by incorporating it into a preexisting schema.

accommodation In Piagetian theory, a cognitive process in which a schema is modified as response to feedback from the environment.

grasping enables an infant to grab hold of a variety of toys. A schema for dogs enables a child to point to a picture of a dog in a book when asked to do so. A schema for proportions (i.e., relations between two amounts; Boulanger, 1976) enables an older child to figure out that a car that takes 15 minutes to travel 2 miles is faster than a car that takes 10 minutes to travel 1 mile. Once in possession of the schemas, children can grasp toys, identify dogs, and solve proportion problems that they have never come across before.

Schemas enable children to engage in **operations** (Piaget, 1964), which are actions that modify an object or set of objects. The modification can be physical (e.g., arranging objects from smallest to largest) or conceptual (e.g., placing words in alphabetical order). Operations are reversible; the logical system used in the operation can go in two directions (objects can be ordered from largest to smallest or placed in reverse alphabetical order). Operations, to Piaget, are "the essence of knowledge" (1964, p. 20). Knowledge therefore consists of not merely facts, but the ability to do things: to conduct operations using schemas.

ASSIMILATION AND ACCOMMODATION. People use their schemas to adapt to the environment. Piaget's theory highlights two processes of adaption: *assimilation* and *accommodation*.

In **assimilation,** external events are incorporated into an existing schema; children think about events and act on objects in ways that reflect the schemas they possess. If a child with a grasping schema used previously on toys grasps an adult's eyeglasses, she is assimilating eyeglasses to her grasping schema. If a child with a schema for chickens sees a Thanksgiving turkey and says, "Cluck, cluck, chicken," he is assimilating the turkey to his chicken schema.

Accommodation is the modification of schemas as a result of environmental feedback. In accommodation, schemas change. If, in the preceding example, adults explain that "no, it's a turkey, not a chicken," the child will eventually accommodate to the environment by dividing his original one schema into two: a chicken schema and a turkey schema. Experience, then, increases the number and precision of children's schemas.

Piaget's theory of schemas, assimilation, and accommodation addresses two questions of interest to all psychologists. The first is the *nature–nurture* question (see Chapters 1 and 4): Do psychological qualities originate in inherited biology (nature) or environmental experience (nurture)? Piaget's approach is neither a strict "nature" nor a strict "nurture" position. Rather, it uniquely mixes the two. The child learns by experience; in accommodation, "nurture" refines schemas. But children's mental powers (e.g., the ability to store and use schemas) have a biological origin, consistent with a "nature" perspective (Flavell, 1996).

The second question is the relation between learning and development. In some other psychological theories, "development" refers merely to changes in behavior that result from learning (see Chapter 7). Learning, in this view, drives development. But Piaget thought this was backward; he believed that development—specifically, the development of mental schemas—drives learning. Children spontaneously modify and elaborate their schemas as they interact with the world. The development of these knowledge structures, in turn, enables them to learn from parents and teachers.

STAGES OF DEVELOPMENT. Piaget claimed that cognitive development occurs in a fixed series of steps, or *stages*. A **developmental stage** is a period of time (months or years) during which one form of thinking is predominant. In a *stage theory* of development, the child is said to maintain one level of development for a given time period, and then to transition relatively rapidly to a new, higher level. Metaphorically, development is like a flight of stairs rather than a ramp: There are discrete steps, traversed in a fixed order.

Piaget proposed four stages of development: the (1) *sensorimotor,* (2) *preoperational,* (3) *concrete operational,* and (4) *formal operational* stages (Table 14.1).

In the **sensorimotor stage** (birth to 2 years), the child interacts with the world through his or her sensory systems (e.g., hearing, vision) and systems for motor movement (e.g., sucking, grasping). Children at this stage are preverbal; they cannot think in words. Although they cannot formulate a thought such as "I'd like to play with my new toy," they can see the new toy and play with it. Schemas involving sensation and motor movement enable purposeful action.

During the sensorimotor stage, children develop a concept you normally take for granted: *object permanence.* **Object permanence** is the understanding that objects continue to exist even when they can no longer be seen or otherwise perceived. Early in the sensorimotor stage, infants lack this capacity. If they are playing with a toy and an adult covers it with a piece of cloth, they will be baffled and won't look under the cloth for the toy. Later in the sensorimotor stage, they will. The child must develop a conception that the object still exists, despite being out of sight.

In the **preoperational stage** of development (ages 2 to 7), children can use mental symbols—words, numbers, images— to think. The capacity to use symbols is a major step "up"

Doug Goodman / Science Photo Library

I think that development explains learning, and this opinion is contrary to the widely held opinion that development is a sum of discrete learning experiences. . . . Development is the essential process and each element of learning occurs as a function of total development.

—Piaget (1964, p. 20)

Here one minute, gone forever the next In tests of object permanence, children are shown an object and then a barrier blocks it from view. Later in the sensorimotor period, the children will reach around and get the object. But early in the sensorimotor period, they appear baffled. They fail to search behind the barrier for the object because they do not yet understand that the object has a permanent existence.

Do you suppose the "peek-a-boo" game capitalizes on infants' ignorance of object permanence?

table **14.1**

Piagetian Stages		
Stage	**Age**	**Description**
Sensorimotor	Birth to 2 years	Child's interactions with the environment are based on sensory and motor systems; no logical operations occur.
Preoperational	2 to 7 years	Child can use mental symbols (words, numbers), yet still cannot perform logical operations.
Concrete operational	7 to 11 years	Child can perform logical operations on physical ("concrete") objects.
Formal operational	11 years to adulthood	Child can perform operations on physical and hypothetical objects; he or she can also engage in abstract reasoning.

developmental stage In Piaget's theory of child development, a period of months or years during which one form of given thinking is predominant.

sensorimotor stage In Piaget's theory of child development, the stage (birth to 2 years) in which a child interacts with the world through his or her sensory and motor systems.

object permanence The understanding that objects continue to exist even when they can no longer be seen or otherwise perceived.

preoperational stage In Piaget's theory of child development, the stage (ages 2 to 7) in which children can use mental symbols, such as words and numbers, to think, yet still cannot perform logical operations.

Spencer Grant / Photo Researchers, Inc.

figure 14.1

Conservation Piaget studied conservation, the ability to recognize that an object maintains some essential physical properties even when physically transformed. He asked children whether more or less water is present when liquid from a wide container is poured into a narrow container. Children do not understand that the amount of water is the same, or is conserved, until they reach the concrete operational stage of development.

Formal operations Solving algebraic equations with variables requires the cognitive skills of Piaget's formal operational stage of development, starting around age 11.

conservation In Piagetian psychology, the recognition that an object maintains some of its essential physical properties even when it is physically transformed.

concrete operational stage In Piaget's theory of child development, the stage (ages 7 to 11) in which children can perform reversible logical operations (e.g., basic arithmetic) limited to "concrete" objects that actually exist.

formal operational stage In Piaget's theory of child development, the stage (age 11 to adulthood) in which children can execute mental operations on both actual objects and hypothetical ones, using abstract rules.

in development. Yet at this stage, the child still cannot engage in *operations.* Recall that operations are reversible (e.g., items can be ordered from small to large or large to small). In the preoperational stage, children cannot make these logical reversals. This mental limitation is strikingly demonstrated by the phenomenon of *conservation.*

Conservation, in Piagetian psychology, is the recognition that an object maintains some essential physical properties even when it is physically transformed. In other words, those properties are conserved. Suppose you spread a ball of dough into a flat pizza. If you recognize that this spreading does not give you any more (or less) dough, then you have exhibited conservation; you know the dough's mass is conserved in spite of the transformation of its shape. Conservation requires a reversible mental operation. You must be able to see that going back and forth—from ball to flat pizza and back—does not alter physical mass.

Piaget discovered that, in the preoperational stage, children are *not* capable of conservation. They cannot perform the reversible mental operations needed to understand that physical properties are conserved. In a classic demonstration, Piaget poured water from a short, wide beaker into a tall, narrow one and asked children whether the amount of water was the same or different (Figure 14.1). "Different," they said! Children in the preoperational stage use a simple physical cue, the height of the water, to judge how much water there is; they thus believe more water is present when the liquid is poured into the narrow beaker.

In the **concrete operational stage** of development (ages 7 to 11), the child can perform reversible logical operations. Many of these operations have the same structure as basic arithmetic: adding and subtracting; judging that amounts are greater or lesser than one another; dividing groups into subgroups of items. If shown a group of six cats and two dogs and asked if there are more animals than there are cats, the child in the concrete operational stage can solve the problem; that child recognizes that cats are a subgroup of a larger group, animals. In earlier stages, however, children cannot perform this mental operation and are likely to say that there are more cats. Thanks to the ability to perform reversible operations, children in the concrete operational stage of development can begin to solve the conservation problems described earlier.

A mental limitation in the concrete operational stage is that children can execute operations only on objects, that is, things that actually exist in the child's experience. In the **formal operational stage** (age 11 through adulthood), they can execute operations on both actual objects and hypothetical ones. Questions about blue unicorns and flying dogs (e.g., if there are six blue unicorns and two flying dogs, are there more animals than dogs?) can be contemplated logically, even though the objects do not exist. The child thinks about hypothetical objects by applying abstract rules. For example, if asked to think of a number that has the following property—*the number, plus 20, is twice itself*—the formal operational child does not have to rely on trial-and-error guessing, as the concrete operational child would. A child in the formal operational stage of development can apply the rule that for any number x, if $x + y = 2x$, then $x = y$, so the number must be 20 (Ault, 1977).

SeanShot / Getty Images

THINK ABOUT IT

Piaget studied a relatively small number of children living in Europe in the mid-twentieth century. Is it possible that other children—living in other parts of the world, or at different historical times—developed differently than the children studied by Piaget?

Piaget recognized that children reach the stages at different ages; diverse experiences might accelerate or slow development. However, he claimed that the stages occur in a fixed order. You can't skip any. The ordering reflects the logical relation among stages. To engage in concrete operational thinking, you first have to be able to think using symbols (the achievement of preoperational thought). To engage in formal operational thinking, you first have to be able to think using operations (the achievement of concrete operational thought).

WHAT DO YOU KNOW?...

1. Bette had grasped conservation and therefore was able to judge that pouring the water from the wide pitcher to the tall pitcher did not increase the volume of the water.
   a. In this example, what is the *schema* and what is the *operation*?
   b. What makes her behavior an example of assimilation and not accommodation?

2. Willem loved dogs and regularly approached them without fear. One day, he approached a dog to pet it, but the dog snapped at him and barked ferociously. After that, Willem was more careful about approaching dogs. What makes Willem's experience an example of accommodation and not assimilation?

3. Match the Piagetian stage on the left with the characteristics on the right. There are one to three characteristics listed for each stage.

1. Sensorimotor	**a.** Reversible logical operations such as conservation are first possible.
2. Preoperational	**b.** Ability to think using words emerges.
3. Concrete operational	**c.** Child can execute operations on concrete and hypothetical objects.
4. Formal operational	**d.** Interaction with the world occurs, in large part, by sucking and grasping.
	e. Child can execute operations, but only on objects.
	f. Reversible logical operations such as dividing groups into subgroups are first possible.
	g. The child can think about hypothetical situations by applying abstract rules.
	h. Children cannot think in words; that is, they are preverbal.
	i. Object permanence develops.

See Appendix B for answers to What Do You Know? questions.

Domain-Linked Cognitive Development

Preview Question

> › In what domains of thinking are children actually smarter than Piaget had predicted?

Piaget's contributions are of unparalleled importance. Yet developmental psychology has moved beyond his contributions. Contemporary research suggests that Piaget overlooked a factor critical to children's cognitive development: *domains*.

In the study of cognition, a *domain* is an area of knowledge and mental ability (Hirschfeld & Gelman, 1994). For example, knowledge about plants (e.g., that they grow, need water, and are not manmade) and about household objects (e.g., that they do not grow or need watering and are not manmade) would be two separate domains. The ability to use language (see Chapter 8) or to appreciate and produce music (Justus & Hutsler, 2005) similarly may be distinct domains.

Piaget's theory was domain-general; that is, his theoretical principles were meant to generalize across domains. When Piaget said a child was, for example, in the concrete operational stage of development, he expected the child to exhibit concrete operational thinking, no matter what the topic of the child's thought.

Research challenges this expectation of Piagetian theory. In particular domains of thinking, children seem "smarter"—that is, engage in more complex thinking processes—than Piaget would expect (Bloom, 2004; Wellman & Gelman, 1992). Let's look at three of these domains: thinking about (1) objects, (2) living things, and (3) people's minds.

OBJECTS. Piaget found that, in infancy, children lack object permanence. They seem to have no understanding that there is such a thing as an object with a permanent, fixed existence. Recent research, however, reveals that they understand more than Piaget had thought. Much of this modern research uses a valuable research tool that was not employed by Piaget: looking-time studies (see Research Toolkit).

⊕ RESEARCH TOOLKIT

Looking-Time Methods

Imagine that you show people an empty box, place a ball in it, place another ball in it, and want to know how many balls they then expect are in the box. How would you find out? Just ask them. They will say they expect two. Similarly, if people see a toy car rolling along a floor and you want to find out what they expect will happen when it reaches a wall, you can ask them. They will say they expect it will hit the wall and stop. Their expectations reveal their knowledge. The people know that 1 plus 1 is 2 and that walls are solid.

But what if the people are infants? How could you find out what they know?

Infants can't state their expectations. But that doesn't mean they don't have any. Infants might have sophisticated expectations about events while lacking the ability to put those expectations into words. To learn about infants' knowledge, researchers thus need a measuring tool that does not require language.

One such tool is *looking-time* studies, which measure the amount of time infants look at events. The direction and duration of their gaze provide an indirect measure of the knowledge that infants possess. Two steps link knowledge to gaze:

1. Knowledge guides expectations. For example, because we know that walls are solid, we expect toy cars to stop rolling when they reach them.

2. Expectations influence gaze. People generally look longer at events that are unexpected; unexpected events "catch the eye" of observers.

Researchers infer that if babies look longer at one event than another, then, all other things being equal, the babies must have been surprised by that event. The event must, in other words, have violated their expectations.

Many studies have used looking-time measures to reveal infants' knowledge. For example, one researcher showed infants a rolling toy car. In one condition of the experiment, a block was placed near, but not in, the path of the car (Figure 14.2). In another condition, the block was placed directly in the car's path. In both instances, after infants saw the block, a small screen was placed in front of it, hiding just that section of the car path. The car then rolled along its normal path—even if the block had been placed in the way. Children displayed longer looking times in the condition in which the car seemed to have passed through the block (Baillargeon, 1986). This indicates that they expected the block would stop the car; they knew that the block still existed (despite being hidden by the screen) and that it was a solid object that would stop the car.

Whatever happened, she wasn't expecting it Babies can't tell you what they know and don't know. But you can figure it out. Researchers study the direction and duration of infants' gaze to determine whether they expected events or were surprised by them.

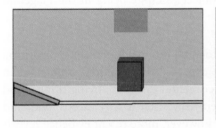
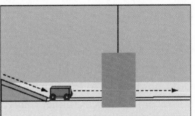
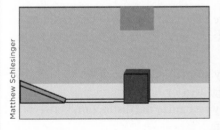
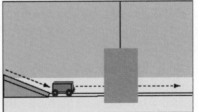

figure **14.2**
Looking-time methods These images depict events shown to infants in a looking-time study. Findings show that infants look longer at the display on the bottom, where the red block is on the "roadway." There, the car seems to pass through the block when the block is hidden behind a screen. From this fact, researchers infer that infants expected that the car would be stopped by the hidden block.

Other looking-time research shows that even 6- to 9-month-olds understand numerosity, that is, the number of objects in a scene (Berger, Tzur, & Posner, 2006). In this work, children saw (1) a puppet, (2) a screen that was placed in front of the puppet, and then (3) a second puppet being placed behind the screen. The screen was then removed, at which point, in different conditions, either one or two puppets appeared from behind the screen. Children looked longer when only one puppet appeared. This implies that children—even though they could not state their expectations in words—expected there to be more than one puppet. They knew that 1 plus 1 was not equal to 1.

In sum, infants know a lot more than they can say, and looking-time studies reveal some of their knowledge.

🕹 WHAT DO YOU KNOW?...

4. A child would spend more time looking at which of the following two events?
   a. An object is placed on a table behind a solid screen; then the screen tilts back and lands on the table without hitting the object.
   b. An object is placed on a table behind a solid screen; then the screen tilts back and lands on the table, hitting the object.

As the developmental psychologist Paul Bloom (2004) reviews, results of looking-time studies reveal that infants are surprised if any of the following events happen:

> They pull on one piece of an object and, instead of the whole object moving toward them, a piece comes off.

> An object moving from left to right passes behind one of two barriers (on the left) and then reappears from behind the other barrier (on the right) without being seen passing between the two barriers.

> An object is placed on a table behind a solid screen, and then the screen tilts back and lands on the table without hitting the object.

> One object moves toward another, on a path to hit it, but the second object moves before the first one hits it.

Their surprise indicates that they held expectations. The infants expected that objects were coherent wholes (not a collection of pieces that would break off); that they moved continuously (and thus couldn't jump from one barrier to another); and that they had a permanent existence, were solid, and could not move spontaneously. The infants could not put their knowledge into words. Nevertheless, their expectations reveal that they possessed knowledge of objects, despite being in the Piagetian sensorimotor period.

LIVING THINGS. A second domain about which young children display surprising amounts of knowledge is livings things. Piaget expected that children younger than school age would not be able to form the abstract mental category "living things" and thus would not recognize, for example, that their baby sister is alive, needs food, and sleeps, whereas their baby doll does not. Again, however, more recent evidence reveals that Piaget underestimated young children's knowledge. As Wellman and Gelman (1992) review:

> Three-year-olds distinguish between inanimate objects and animate livings things (i.e., animals, but not plants). They know that animals have feelings and that rocks, for example, do not.

> When 12-month-olds are shown a series of toy animals and then either another toy animal or a toy boat, they are surprised (as measured by how long they look) if the object presented was the boat. This means they recognize the distinction between the categories "animals" and "inanimate objects."

> Children's ability to distinguish inanimate objects from living things is not based merely on the superficial appearance of the items. If shown a realistic-looking mechanical animal, children do not think it needs to sleep or can have babies.

"Hey, Clanky, you're not fooling anybody." Research shows that even young children know the difference between a real living thing and a mechanical replica.

Steve bent Mirrorpix / Newscom

PEOPLE AND THEIR MINDS. Children also display more knowledge than Piaget expected when they think about the human mind. Even at a young age, children know that the people they encounter have minds, and that the plants and toys they encounter do not. Children possess a **theory of mind,** an understanding that other people have feelings and thoughts (Wellman, Cross, & Watson, 2001).

Evidence of theory of mind comes from a cleverly designed experimental task (Wimmer & Perner, 1983). Children of varying ages are shown a series of pictures: Someone places an object in one location and then leaves the vicinity (Figure 14.3). While the first person is away, a second person moves the object to a different location. Children are asked to indicate where the first person will look for the item when she returns. Yes, it's easy for you—but not for very young children. To know where the person will look, you have to have a theory of mind. You must understand that she has personal beliefs that guide her actions and that her beliefs are acquired from experience.

Ability to perform this task correctly develops during the preschool years (Wellman et al., 2001; Wimmer & Perner, 1983). At age 3, children cannot get it right; they think that, upon returning, the person will look for the object in its actual, new location. By age 6, more than half of children get the problem correct, and by age 8 to 9, the vast majority of children answer it correctly.

Other research shows that substantial elements of a theory of mind are in place even earlier (Wellman & Gelman, 1992). If asked why someone is looking in a particular location for an object, 4-year-olds will explain the action in terms of beliefs ("She thought it was there").

Many researchers suggest that theory of mind is central to a disorder of psychological development, autism. More formally known as *autism spectrum disorder,* **autism** refers to a range of symptoms whose central features include impaired communication and social interaction with other people (National Institute of Mental Health, 2011). Children with autism might, for instance, focus their attention on objects while failing to establish eye contact with other people. Children who lack a theory of mind, and thus fail to understand that others have feelings and thoughts, may be those who experience symptoms of autism (Baron-Cohen, Leslie, & Frith, 1985). Research shows that individuals with autism perform particularly poorly on tests of the ability to automatically make inferences about other people's beliefs (Schneider et al., 2013).

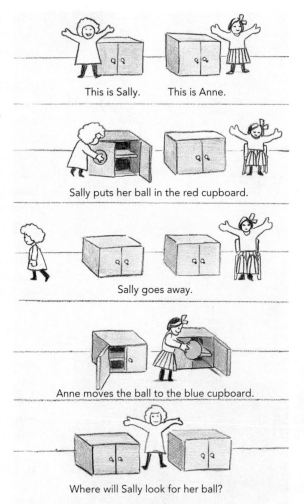

This is Sally.   This is Anne.

Sally puts her ball in the red cupboard.

Sally goes away.

Anne moves the ball to the blue cupboard.

Where will Sally look for her ball?

figure 14.3

Theory of mind By age 6, most children know that Sally will look in the red cupboard, even though the ball is in the blue cupboard (Baron-Cohen, Leslie, & Frith, 1985). This shows that they have a theory of mind: the idea that other people have beliefs that guide their actions.

🐾 WHAT DO YOU KNOW?...

5. True or False?
   a. Though infants lack object permanence, they do understand objects in other ways; for instance, they would show surprise if a ball jumped out of the way before being hit by another ball.
   b. Infants are particularly bad at distinguishing between living things and inanimate objects.
   c. By 3 years old, children understand that other people have beliefs that are acquired by experience.

Alternatives to Piagetian Theory

Preview Questions

› Are children born knowing things?
› How do children's social interactions influence their development?
› To aid development, is it a good idea to challenge children with problems that are above their current abilities?

theory of mind An intuitive understanding that other people have feelings and thoughts.

autism Autism spectrum disorder, a range of symptoms whose central features include impaired communication and social interaction with other people.

Novel research findings prompt psychologists to develop novel theories. Let's consider two attempts to move beyond Piagetian theory. The first proposes the existence of innate mental structures.

INNATE MENTAL STRUCTURES. As you've seen, children possess domain-linked knowledge—about objects, living things, and the mind—that is hard to explain from a Piagetian perspective. Piaget thought that ideas were learned by experience. But children develop complex beliefs at such an early age that it's hard to see how experience alone could account for their mental abilities. Parents, for example, rarely try to teach their children that other human beings have minds, yet kids somehow seem to know this.

Research on domain-linked knowledge prompts many contemporary developmental psychologists to conclude that Piaget underestimated the role of nature. They propose that children possess mental structures—elements of mind that enable them to interpret the world—that are products of biological inheritance. These inherited mental structures enable them to think accurately about objects, animate living things, and other people's minds.

One theory of innate mental structures has been developed by Harvard psychologist Susan Carey (2009, 2011). She proposes that children possess innate *input analyzers,* that is, biologically inherited mental mechanisms designed to detect and process specific types of information. The type of information corresponds to the domains of knowledge we have just reviewed. For example, an innate input analyzer that detects *agents* (entities that have goals and pursue them through their actions) contributes to children's ability to distinguish animate living things from objects as well as to their development of a theory of mind.

SOCIAL AND CULTURAL EXPERIENCE. A second alternative to Piagetian theory is grounded in the work of Lev Vygotsky, a Russian psychologist living in the first third of the twentieth century (Daniels, Cole, & Wertsch, 2007). Vygotsky believed that Piaget underestimated the importance of social and cultural experience and provided a theory of cognitive development that put sociocultural factors in their proper place.

In Piagetian theory, development primarily is an individual process. The lone child encounters the world, puzzles through various experiences, and thus advances in logical thinking. But Vygotsky notes that much development occurs through social interaction. Children acquire the cognitive tools of their culture—language, counting, reading, writing, mathematical symbols, diagrams, flowcharts, musical notation—by interacting with adults and older peers (Wertsch, 2007).

Once children have practice using cultural tools, they *internalize* them (Vygotsky, 1978). What first was a social activity becomes a feature of the child's inner mental life. Consider language. At first, it is a way to communicate with others. But once learned, it dominates inner thoughts; people "talk to themselves" in sentences and internal dialogues (Hermans, 1996). This inner speech serves important functions.

Are you ever aware of your own inner dialogue?

Children gain control over their behavior by listening to instructions (e.g., "Timmie, don't touch the stove") and internalizing them ("I must not touch the stove"; see Meichenbaum, 1977).

Unlike Piaget, Vygotsky (1978) thought that children, at any given time, should be characterized at *two* developmental levels: their current level of cognitive development and their *potential* level. Potential levels are mental achievements children cannot reach by themselves, but that they can reach through interacting with others who support them (e.g., with hints, examples, or leading questions). Vygotsky called the region between the two levels the **zone of proximal development.** This zone, then, contains problems the child cannot do independently, yet can do collaboratively

Baobao ou / Getty Images

Developing minds in a social world Analyses of development by Russian psychologist Lev Vygotsky highlighted the ways in which children develop cognitively by interacting with others.

zone of proximal development In Vygotsky's theory of cognitive development, the region between a child's current level of independent cognitive development and the level he or she can achieve only through interaction with others.

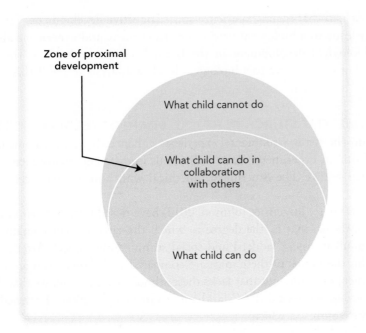

figure 14.4
Zone of proximal development In his theory of cognitive development, Vygotsky recognized that children most rapidly develop through challenges in their zone of proximal development, that is, problems that they can accomplish in collaboration with others.

(Figure 14.4). Vygotsky encouraged educators to challenge learners with problems in their zone of proximal development. Doing so, he said, would speed learning and psychological development.

Children often learn through zone-of-proximal-development interactions (Rogoff, 1990). When mothers explain classifications among animals (e.g., a house cat and a lion are both cats) while reading to children, the children's ability to categorize animals improves. When parents provide strategies for remembering words, children's memory improves. When children work together on logic problems and discuss their thoughts about the problem, they become more skillful problem solvers.

In summary, Vygotsky showed how the development of the mind is enhanced by the social experiences of the person. In so doing, he uncovered key connections between person and mind, and between social and cognitive development.

🦉 WHAT DO YOU KNOW?...

6. a. What feature of Piaget's theory does Susan Carey's concept of innate input analyzers challenge?
    b. What feature of Piaget's theory does Lev Vygotsky's concept of the zone of proximal development challenge?

Cognitive Development and the Brain

Preview Questions

> Does being raised in a more enriched environment increase brain size?
> Does the brain's development actually map onto Piaget's stages of cognitive development?
> How does the brain's connectivity change across the life span?

You have learned that social experience spurs cognitive development. This psychological fact leads to a biological prediction: Environmental experience also should spur the biological development in the brain because the brain is the organ of cognition. Let's now move to a biological level of analysis to see if this prediction holds true.

ENVIRONMENTAL ENRICHMENT AND BRAIN DEVELOPMENT. How could you find out whether environmental experience enhances brain development? Ideally, you would run an experiment: Raise individuals in different environments and then measure their brains. The experiment, unethical with humans, has been conducted with animals.

Researchers (e.g., Jurgens & Johnson, 2012) have raised mice in environments that vary in *enrichment,* that is, the degree to which the environment contains complex physical stimuli (tunnels, ladders) and social stimuli (other mice). After a period of development, the brains of these mice are compared with others who are raised in a low-enrichment environment that lacks these stimuli. Research shows that the brains of the two groups of mice differ (Markham & Greenough, 2004). Enriched environments produce brains in which:

› The cerebral cortex (the outer layer of the brain) is thicker.

› Individual brain cells form more connections with other cells.

› Brain cells are covered by more myelin, an insulating material that speeds nervous system communications.

› Blood vessels in the brain are more fully developed.

From Jurgens & Johnson (2012). Reprinted with permission from Elsevier

The enriched environment in which researchers raised mice (Jurgen & Johnson, 2012). The brains of mice raised in this setting differed significantly from those of mice raised in a less enriched environment.

These results demonstrate a key fact about the brain (also see Chapter 3). The exact structure of the brain, for any organism, is a product of both inheritance and experience. Just as physical exercise builds stronger muscles, the mental exercise that occurs in enriched environments builds a stronger brain.

THE DEVELOPMENT OF SUBSYSTEMS OF THE BRAIN. Another psychological fact suggests another prediction about brain development. Psychologically, as you learned, children experience a sequence of stages; at one stage they cannot perform tasks that, at a later stage, are easy for them. This suggests that the brain should develop through a sequence of stages, too.

It does. "In general, the sequence in which the cortex matures parallels cognitive milestones in human development" (Casey et al., 2005, p. 104). To understand the brain's maturation, you have to recall that the brain contains different parts that specialize in different tasks (e.g., understanding language, processing visual images, generating emotions, thinking about oneself). It turns out that these different parts develop in a fixed sequence. Consider three regions of the brain: (1) sensorimotor cortex (involved in basic perceptual processes and motor movement), (2) parietal and temporal cortices (whose many functions include language processing), and (3) prefrontal cortex (critical to sustaining attention on tasks and controlling emotional impulses). Brain research indicates that (Casey et al., 2005; Figure 14.5):

› The sensorimotor cortex matures first, with rapid development occurring in the first months of life.

› The parietal and temporal cortices develop later, with major biological development occurring between ages 8 months and 2 years.

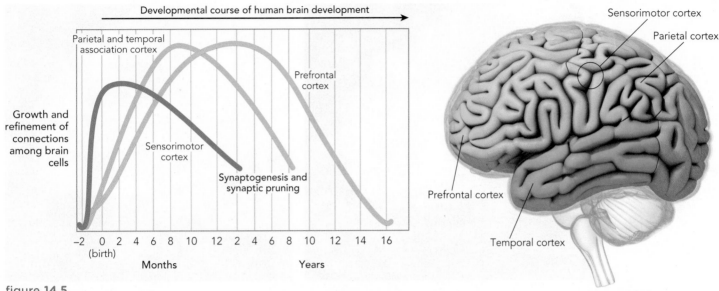

figure 14.5

Brain development Different regions of the brain develop at different points during childhood. The sensorimotor cortex develops rapidly in the first months of life, the parietal and temporal cortices display major development between ages 8 months and 2 years, and the prefrontal cortex does not begin to reach biological maturity until well into the teenage years.

> The prefrontal cortex evolves last, with this region of brain not reaching substantial maturity until well into the teenage years, and with final refinements of neural structure still occurring in a person's 20s (Johnson, Blum, & Giedd, 2009).

No wonder Piaget discovered a sensorimotor stage at which children can think, but not in words. At this Piagetian stage, children's sensorimotor cortex is developed, but language-processing regions of the brain are not. Contemporary brain research thus complements Piaget's earlier psychological research. Similarly, research on neural development shows, at a brain level of analysis, why children have more difficulty controlling emotions than adults do: Their prefrontal cortex, which is needed to control emotions, is less developed.

THE DEVELOPMENT OF BRAIN NETWORKS. The brain's specialized parts are interconnected. Nerve cells link distinct neural systems, creating information networks within the brain (Sporns, 2010). When people engage in complex mental activities, such as solving a problem, multiple interconnected regions of their brains are active (Gerlach et al., 2011).

A major feature of brain development is that, over time, these networks change (Fair et al., 2009). In childhood, most of the brain's connections are "local"; that is, they interconnect neurons within one region of the brain. Later in life, connections become "global"; different regions of the brain become more strongly interconnected (Khundrakpam et al., 2013).

Advances in brain imaging let us see these interconnections. Researchers obtained brain images in two groups of people: children aged 7 to 9 and adults aged 19 to 22 (Uddin et al., 2011). They focused on connections between two regions of the brain:

1. The brain's *central executive* system (shown in blue in Figure 14.6): The central executive system enables people to manipulate information in their minds, develop strategies, and make decisions in order to achieve their goals.

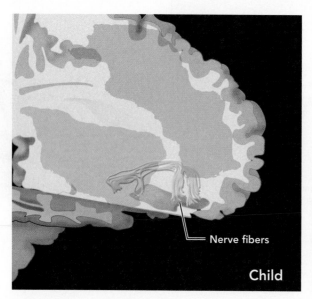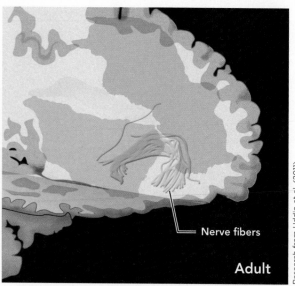

Research from Uddin et al. (2011)

figure 14.6

It's all about communication Compared to a child's brain, the different regions of an adult's brain are better able to communicate with each other, thanks to the development of cellular connections that link one brain region to another. Shown are two regions in the front of the brain that are involved in paying attention to information in the environment (lavender) and maintaining, in mind, information about personal goals (green). Also shown, in yellow, are nerve fibers that connect the two regions. The connections are stronger in adulthood than in childhood.

2. An *attentional* network (shown in red in the figure): specifically, a brain region used to pay attention to multiple external events and internal signals (hunger, pain, etc.) and to focus attention on those that are most important to well-being at any given time (Seeley et al., 2007).

As you can see in Figure 14.6, the two brain regions do not change significantly from childhood to adulthood. But the *interconnections between them* do (Uddin et al., 2011). The connections are stronger—thicker and more elaborate—in adulthood than in childhood.

What is the psychological implication of this biological finding? The brain connections enable people to gain greater control over their thoughts, emotions, and behavior (Menon & Uddin, 2010). Early in life, when the connections are weak, children may respond in a quick, reflexive manner to environmental events that grab their attention. For example, a child who is supposed to be doing homework might become distracted by a toy or by even slight feelings of hunger. Later in life, people are better at controlling what they pay attention to and concentrating on problems to be solved. This greater control is due, in part, to the stronger connections between the brain's central executive and attentional networks.

In sum, brain research deepens our understanding of cognitive development. As children age and interact with the world, their growing cognitive abilities are accompanied by growth in the biological systems of the brain (Figure 14.7).

Cognitive abilities are not the only aspects of life that change with development. People also develop emotions and motivation, the ability to control their emotions and behavior, and a sense of self—an understanding of who they are and their place in the world. These topics are studied in the field of social development, which we turn to next, beginning with the start of social life: infancy.

figure 14.7

HOW DO PEOPLE DEVELOP CONTROL OVER THEIR OWN BEHAVIOR?

PMB IN ACTION

PERSON Ⓟ

At a person level of analysis, self-control is an ability to work toward goals, avoid distractions, and suppress unwanted emotional reactions. It first develops in childhood. Individual differences in childhood self-control predict self-control abilities in later life.

MIND Ⓜ

Attention
Which Stimuli Are Important

Executive Control
What Are My Goals
What Can I Do To Reach Them

At a mind level of analysis, self-control ability reflects the workings of interconnected mental systems that are concerned with attention and executive control.

BRAIN Ⓑ

At a brain level of analysis, the abilities reflect interconnections (in red circle) between brain regions, which grow stronger across development.

Research from Uddin et al. (2011)

Gallery Stock

617

7. Which of the following findings are consistent with the prediction that environmental experiences should spur biological development in the brain? Check all that apply.

_____ a. Rats raised in enriched environments had brains that were more fully developed than those of rats raised in low-enrichment environments.

_____ b. The brain's cortices develop in a fixed sequence of stages that roughly correspond to Piaget's cognitive developmental stages.

_____ c. As children develop, their neural connections between brain regions become thicker and more elaborate.

Social Development: Biological and Social Foundations

The next time you have a chance, pay attention to some infants. You'll notice they differ. Some are active and energetic. Others frequently nap. Some are happy and easygoing. Others are cranky.

The differences are partly based in inherited biology. Genetic differences (also see Chapter 4) produce varying *temperament.*

Biological Foundations: Temperament

Preview Questions

› What is temperament, and why do psychologists study it?
› Is temperament the same in all contexts?

Temperament refers to variations in emotional and behavioral tendencies that are evident very early in life and are based, at least in part, in inherited biology (Zentner & Bates, 2008). Differences in emotional reactions—such as tendencies to be calm, angry, or shy—as well as differences in children's ability to *control* their emotions are aspects of temperament (Rothbart, 2012).

Temperament has intrigued scholars for ages (Strelau, 1998). In ancient Greece, the physician Hippocrates said that people possess four temperament styles, based on excesses of certain bodily fluids in an individual's system. Excess black bile, for example, was said to produce a sad, moody temperament; excess phlegm, he thought, created a calm, peaceful, *phlegmatic* style.

Although it was popular for more than 2000 years, Hippocrates's theory is wrong; the bodily fluids he proposed are not the source of temperament. Yet his work resembles contemporary ideas in a number of ways. Like Hippocrates, many scientists today search for a small number of temperament styles with biological origins.

Two pioneers in this search were Alexander Thomas and Stella Chess (1977). To study temperament, they interviewed parents. Parents reported their children's behavioral characteristics (e.g., "How much does your baby move around?"), regularity of daily experiences ("Could you tell . . . when during the day [your child] would be hungry, asleep, or awake?"), and adaptability ("How would you describe the way your child responded to changed circumstances?") (from Thomas & Chess, 1996). By analyzing these reports, Thomas and Chess identified three types of

temperament Biologically based emotional and behavioral tendencies on which individuals differ.

Jie Xu / Thinkstock/ Getty Images

Arthur Tilley / Getty Images

Maskot / Getty Images

Babies differ Even in the early months of life, infants differ psychologically. These differences, which stem primarily from variations in inherited biology, are what psychologists call temperament. The psychologists Thomas and Chess identified the three temperament styles represented here: *easy*, *difficult*, and *slow-to-warm-up*.

temperament, that is, three temperament categories into which individual children could be classified:

1. *Easy temperament:* Calm, cheerful adaption to new situations
2. *Difficult temperament:* Intense negative reactions to unexpected events and slow to adjust to changes in routine
3. *Slow-to-warm-up temperament:* Mild negative reactions to new events, but positive reactions develop if a situation is experienced repeatedly

Later psychologists followed Thomas and Chess's lead, but with a change in emphasis. Rather than focusing on temperament *types,* they searched for temperament *dimensions.* A **temperament dimension** is a biologically based psychological quality that all children possess to a greater or lesser degree.

Three important temperament dimensions are *emotionality, activity,* and *sociability* (Buss & Plomin, 1984; Table 14.2). Some children are more easily upset than others (emotionality), some are more energetic (activity), and some show a greater preference to spend time with other people (sociability). Many personality psychologists view these temperament dimensions as early-life precursors to adult personality traits (see Chapter 13.)

> What were your levels on each of these three temperament dimensions?

table **14.2**

Measuring Temperament Dimensions	
Emotionality	• Cries easily • Tends to be somewhat emotional • Reacts intensely when upset
Activity	• Is always on the go • When moving about, usually moves slowly* • Is off and running upon waking in the morning
Sociability	• Likes to be with people • Prefers playing with others rather than alone • Finds people more stimulating than anything else

Research from Buss & Plomin (1984); Spinath & Angleitner (1998)

One way to measure temperament is to ask parents to report on the qualities of their children. Three main dimensions of temperament identified with this measurement strategy are *emotionality*, *activity*, and *sociability*; the test items shown are designed to measure the dimensions. Note that the item marked with an asterisk is "reverse-worded," that is, a higher score on the item indicates a lower level of the associated dimension.

temperament dimension A biologically based psychological quality possessed by all children to a greater or lesser degree, such as emotionality, activity, or sociability.

THINK ABOUT IT

Temperament is biologically based. The biology of the brain consists of large numbers of neural systems and large numbers of neurotransmitters through which brain cells communicate. The biology of inheritance consists of thousands of genes. Does it seem right that the number of temperament dimensions is only three?

THE LONG-TERM SIGNIFICANCE OF EARLY-LIFE TEMPERAMENT. In principle, temperament styles might be temporary. Maybe most of the highly emotional 2-year-olds are calm and even-tempered when they reach age 3 to 4. It turns out, however, that temperament endures. When researchers study children at different points of time, they find that many children's temperament style is consistent across time. Here are two examples.

Researchers in Norway observed children at ages 18 months, 30 months, and 4 to 5 years (Janson & Mathiesen, 2008). At each age, they classified children into the Thomas and Chess temperament categories. Many children displayed consistent temperament across time. Almost half the children had the same temperament at 30 months as at 18 months, and almost half had the same temperament at 4 to 5 years of age as at 30 months.

Researchers in Finland measured temperament in a large group of teenagers (Hintsanen et al., 2009). Nine years later, they determined the employment status of these same individuals. Teenage temperament predicted adult employment. Teens whose temperament featured high levels of activity and low levels of negative emotion were more likely to be employed.

These are but two of many examples in which early-life temperament predicts later-life personality and life outcomes. Who you are, and the type of life you lead, are affected by temperament qualities you inherit. Further evidence of this comes from a temperament characteristic that is familiar to many of us: shyness.

Jose Luis Pelaez Inc / Getty Images

The happy businessperson
Research has linked temperament to life outcomes. People who are predisposed by temperament to be highly active and to experience positive emotions are less likely to be unemployed when they are adults.

SHYNESS. Many people say they are shy. In one survey, 40 percent said so when describing their present self, and 80 percent said they were shy at some point in their life (Zimbardo, 1977). High rates of shyness may be found in all cultures (Saunders & Chester, 2008).

Do you think that all people who claim they are shy are psychologically the same? Harvard University psychologist Jerome Kagan does not think so. His research findings suggest that a subgroup of people is distinctive; they inherit **inhibited temperament,** which is a tendency to experience high levels of distress and fear, especially in unfamiliar situations (the fearful reactions trigger shy, inhibited behavior) or in the presence of unfamiliar people. Furthermore, a second distinct subgroup inherits **uninhibited temperament,** a tendency to experience little fear and to act in a spontaneous and sociable manner. Before detailing his findings, let's examine his research methods. Kagan was wary of relying on parents' reports because parents' views of their own children could be inaccurate. They might, for example, see their child's behavior as wonderfully unique when it actually is commonplace (see Saudino, 1997; Spinath & Angleitner, 1998). Kagan thus brought children to his lab, where they could be directly observed by researchers.

inhibited temperament A tendency to experience high levels of distress and fear, especially in unfamiliar situations or in the presence of unfamiliar people.

uninhibited temperament A tendency to experience little fear and to act in a spontaneous and sociable manner.

In what situations do you feel shy?

Children first visited his lab at 4 months of age (Kagan & Snidman, 1991). Kagan videotaped them while they were exposed to novel events, such as a popping balloon. They returned at 9 and 14 months of age, when they again were exposed to novel stimuli (e.g., flashing lights, an unfamiliar loud toy, an unfamiliar adult). At age 7, they returned again and were observed while interacting with peers. Kagan hypothesized that two subgroups of children—those displaying either very inhibited or very uninhibited temperament at 4 months of age—would show consistent temperament styles across time.

Findings strongly supported his hypothesis. Children who had reacted fearfully at 4 months of age reacted fearfully again at 9 and 14 months. Most who were *un*inhibited at the earliest time periods remained uninhibited later. At age 7, the children who had been inhibited infants were shy when interacting with peers (Kagan, 1997).

These results show that temperament is often stable across long time periods. This, however, does not mean that temperament cannot change. Some experiences can alter temperament. One is childcare outside the home. Researchers compared inhibited children in either of two types of settings: (1) entirely in a home environment, or (2) multiple hours each week spent in childcare with teachers and other children. Childcare altered temperament. Socially inhibited children who spent 10 or more hours a week outside the home became less shy (Fox et al., 2001). Another factor is parenting. Mothers who avoid being overly protective of children tend to produce children who are better able, on their own, to develop strategies for dealing with fears and anxiety (Degnan et al., 2008).

Temperament is a biological foundation for social development. Another foundation is the family—in particular, the relation between children and parents.

CONNECTING TO EMOTIONS AND BRAIN STRUCTURES

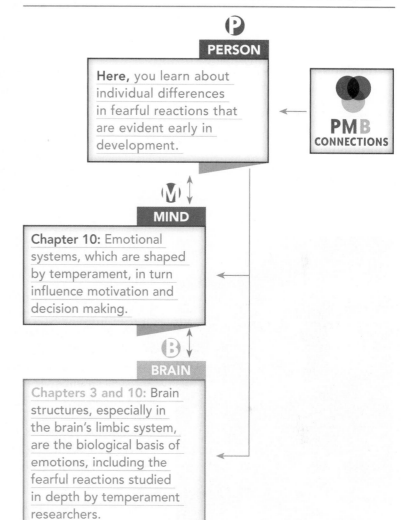

P PERSON

Here, you learn about individual differences in fearful reactions that are evident early in development.

PM B CONNECTIONS

M MIND

Chapter 10: Emotional systems, which are shaped by temperament, in turn influence motivation and decision making.

B BRAIN

Chapters 3 and 10: Brain structures, especially in the brain's limbic system, are the biological basis of emotions, including the fearful reactions studied in depth by temperament researchers.

skynesher / Getty Images

Temperament and social experience
Social experiences can affect temperament. Children with a shy temperament style who spend time in daycare can become less shy.

WHAT DO YOU KNOW?...

8. Which of the following are true of temperament? Check all that apply.

_____ a. Generally speaking, temperament consists of emotional reactions and the ability to control emotions.

_____ b. Early psychologists treated temperaments as consisting of dimensions, but contemporary psychologists prefer to treat them as distinct categories or types.

_____ c. Jerome Kagan found that subgroups of children who displayed inhibited and uninhibited temperaments showed consistent temperament across time.

_____ d. Research indicates that children who spent 10 or more weeks in childcare outside of the home became less shy.

_____ e. Research indicates that children whose parents are overprotective are better able to cope with anxiety.

Thomas D. McAvoy / Time & Life Pictures / Getty Images

Let's follow . . . um . . . that guy! Imprinting was discovered by Konrad Lorenz, who was awarded a Nobel Prize in 1973 for his breakthrough. Lorenz showed that young geese will form a lasting social bond with the first moving being they encounter after birth—even if it is Konrad Lorenz.

imprinting A phenomenon in some species in which newborns fix attention upon, and follow, the first moving object they encounter.

critical period For a given psychological process, a span of time early in life during which a psychological process must occur if it is ever to develop.

Social Foundations: Bonding Between Parent and Child

Preview Questions

› Why do goslings follow Mother Goose?

› Food or physical comfort: Why do babies bond with caregivers?

› According to attachment theory, how do early life experiences exert lifelong effects?

› How can putting children in a "strange situation" help us to understand attachment styles?

› Do negative childhood experiences scar us for life?

Across animal species, the development of offspring depends on the support of parents. Let's start our review of family foundations of development with a phenomenon that occurs in species other than ours: *imprinting*.

IMPRINTING. Look at the photo of baby geese. It shows them following . . . a man? Shouldn't they be following Mother Goose?

The geese have *imprinted* on the man. In **imprinting,** newborns fix attention upon, and follow, the first moving object they encounter (Sluckin, 2007). That object is usually the mother; imprinting therefore bonds mother and offspring. However, newborns of some species will imprint on almost anything that moves. Imprinting occurs only in species whose young are able to move about soon after birth (Hess, 1958); thus, it does not occur in humans.

Lorenz (1952/1997) explained that imprinting occurs only during a *critical period*. A **critical period** for a given psychological process is a span of time, usually early in life, during which the psychological process must occur if it is ever to occur (Hensch, 2004). A gosling, for example, will imprint on a moving object only if the object is encountered in the first few hours after birth. Once imprinted, the bond is permanent.

CONTACT AND COMFORT. In species that do not imprint, children still bond with parents. What drives parent–child bonding? You might guess it's the newborn's need for nourishment; offspring need food, so maybe evolution predisposes them to bond with food-providing parents. However, classic research by Harry Harlow identified a different factor: the need for physical contact and comfort.

Harlow studied infant macaque monkeys, whose early-life mother–child interactions (nursing, clinging to the mother) resemble those of humans. Monkeys were exposed to two artificial mothers: (1) a wire mother that provided nourishment through a bottle, and (2) a soft, terrycloth mother that was warm and cuddly but provided no food.

Which "mom" did infant monkeys prefer? Warm and cuddly mom. Throughout the first month of life, they spent much more time with this artificial mother than with the wire food-provider. When frightened, they turned to the terrycloth mom for support (Harlow, 1958). Harlow's experiments, then, showed that the need for warm-and-fuzzy physical comfort is the primary need that drives bonding with a parent.

Contact with a comforting mother is not only preferred; it is necessary. Infants need this contact for normal development. Monkeys who lack it display abnormal behavior as adults. Consider the fate of female rhesus monkeys that had no contact with a comforting mother during infancy. When, in adulthood, they became mothers themselves, they behaved abnormally, neglecting their own offspring (Hensch, 2004).

Harlow Primate Laboratory

Which one would you prefer to hang out with? Warm-and-fuzzy mom, or wire food-provider mom? As shown, infant monkeys usually prefer the warm-and-fuzzy option.

ATTACHMENT. Macaque monkeys are not the only primates for whom parental bonds are critical to social development. The same holds true for humans. We develop particularly slowly; a newborn monkey can move around independently within days of birth, but a human infant takes months to become mobile (Hayes, 1994). This enhances the importance, for human children, of parent–child *attachment*.

Attachment is a strong emotional bond between two people, especially a child and a caretaker, such as a parent. According to the **attachment theory** of British psychologist John Bowlby, bonds of attachment between parent and child have a lifelong impact on the child (1969, 1988).

How could early-life experiences have lifelong effects? Bowlby (1988) proposed that parent–child interactions shape children's beliefs. Once formed, beliefs endure and are applied to new relationships later in life. Suppose parents provide a child with reliable emotional support. Bowlby's attachment theory predicts that the child will develop the general belief that people will be supportive and, as an adult, will anticipate emotional support when entering into new relationships. Parental attachments thus create a foundation on which beliefs about future relationships are built.

Not all parent–child relationships are the same, however. Research identifies different *styles* of attachment. **Attachment styles** are characteristic ways in which the child and parent interact.

Different attachment styles have been identified through qualitative research (see Chapter 2). Mary Ainsworth (1967; Ainsworth et al., 1978) observed parent–child interactions in home environments and identified three styles of attachment: *secure, avoidant,* and *anxious-ambivalent* (Bretherton, 1992):

> **Secure attachment:** Securely attached infants have a positive relationship with their mother. The mother comforts the child when he or she is distressed, and the child complies with the mother's requests. If separated from the mother, the infant is happy to see her when reunited. Attachment security enables the child to explore the world, knowing that the mother's comfort is available if problems arise.

> **Avoidant attachment:** Avoidantly attached infants react in a relatively indifferent manner to the parent. If separated from the mother and then reunited, the infant may turn away from contact rather than try to be physically close. The child does not count on the parent as a source of security and comfort.

> **Anxious-ambivalent attachment.** In anxious-ambivalent attachment, the child experiences conflicting emotions: a desire for closeness with the mother combined with worry and anger toward the parent.

Which attachment style characterized you as a child?

attachment A strong emotional bond between two people, especially a child and a caretaker, such as a parent.

attachment theory Bowlby's theory of the ways in which bonds of attachment between parent and child have a lifelong impact on the child.

attachment styles Characteristic ways in which children and parents interact and relate to one another emotionally.

secure attachment The attachment style in which a child has a positive relationship with his or her mother, with a sense of security that enables the child to explore the world, confident of the mother's comfort.

avoidant attachment The attachment style in which a child reacts to a parent in a relatively indifferent manner; the child does not count on the parent as a source of security and comfort.

anxious-ambivalent attachment An attachment style in which an infant experiences conflicting emotions: a desire for closeness with the mother combined with worry and anger toward the parent.

Attachment In all the world's cultures, bonds of attachment between mother and child promote healthy child development.

If the mother is away and then returns, the child displays ambivalent reactions—desiring closeness, yet expressing anger and resentment.

Ainsworth and colleagues then developed a behavioral measure of attachment style called the **strange situation paradigm** (Ainsworth et al., 1978). In this procedure, the mother and child participate in a structured sequence of events in a laboratory. First, the mother and child spend a few minutes alone in a room. Then a stranger enters. Next, the mother leaves. Subsequently, the stranger leaves and the mother returns to the room. Psychologists observe the child's responses, especially when the parent returns. Secure infants are those who are easily comforted by the returning parent. Avoidant children look away and move away from the mother. Anxious-ambivalent children desire to be picked up by the mother yet also demand to be put down.

Numerous researchers have related behavioral measures of attachment styles to personality later in life. A meta-analysis of 60 studies finds that securely attached children are less likely to become shy, withdrawn, and depressed (Madigan et al., 2013). Others have employed behavioral measures in cross-cultural research. Findings indicate that secure attachment is the most common style in Asia, Europe, and North America, with more than half of children being securely attached (van IJzendoorn & Kroonenberg, 1988).

Psychologists also have related attachment styles to styles of behavior in adult romantic relationships (Fraley & Shaver, 2000). They find that some adults are secure in their romantic relationships, others find it hard to get close to romantic partners (i.e., they are avoidant), and still others want to get close yet are anxious about the possibility of being abandoned (they are anxious-ambivalent). Childhood attachment patterns may set a foundation for later-life relationships.

RESILIENCE AND THE CAPACITY FOR CHANGE. Attachment researchers thought that early-life experiences have lifelong consequences. Harlow and Bowlby suggested that poor attachment experiences in childhood can scar a person for life.

Other evidence, however, shows that many people bounce back from early-life hardships (Kagan, 1998). They display **resilience,** a capacity to retain or recover psychological functioning after negative experiences (Luthar, Cicchetti, & Becker, 2000; Masten & Gewirtz, 2006).

Striking evidence of resilience comes from a study of 200 children in Hawaii who experienced difficult conditions early in life, often due to parental alcoholism or mental illness (Werner, 1993; Werner & Smith, 1982). If the negative effects of such experiences are inevitable and permanent, one would expect all 200 children to display lifelong problems. But instead, many turned out fine. One-third "grew into competent, confident, and caring young adults" (Werner, 1993, p. 504). Temperament played a role in resilience; children with an active and easy temperament style were more likely to develop in a resilient, positive manner. So were children who experienced supportive relationships with adults other than their parents (e.g., grandparents, church and community leaders; Werner, 1993).

Further evidence of resilience comes from a study of more than 600 adolescents who, in childhood, experienced abuse (either physical or sexual) or neglect (parents not providing food, clothing, and shelter; DuMont, Widom, & Czaja, 2007). In adolescence, almost half (48%) were developing quite well: progressing in school; experiencing normal relationships; and showing no sign of substance abuse, criminal behavior, or psychiatric problems. Stable living conditions contributed to these positive outcomes. Children who lived consistently with the same parent or parents, or in the same foster-care placement, were much more likely than others to show positive social development despite early-life hardships.

strange situation paradigm A behavioral measure of attachment style in which researchers record a child's responses to a sequence of events in which the mother and child interact, are separated, and reunite.

resilience The capacity to retain or recover psychological functioning after negative experiences.

Ron Sachs / CNP / Corbis

AF archive / Alamy

Research on social development, then, delivers good news. Social environments can enable people to bounce back from early-life difficulties. Let's look more closely at these social settings now.

🐾 WHAT DO YOU KNOW?...

9. True or False?

   a. Imprinting does not occur in humans because human babies cannot move about when they are born.

   b. Harlow's research with macaque monkeys confirmed the belief that nourishment is ultimately what bonds parents and children.

   c. In his theory of attachment, Bowlby predicted that parent–child attachment would have lifelong effects by shaping children's beliefs about the support they could expect from others.

   d. The anxious-ambivalent attachment style is characterized by complete indifference toward the parent by the child.

   e. Although attachment styles have been shown to predict personality traits such as shyness later in life, they do not seem to predict behavior in adult romantic relationships.

   f. Research indicates that children who grew up in unsupportive environments, either due to parental alcoholism, mental illness, or abuse, often showed a great deal of resilience.

   g. Resilience against negative experiences can be explained, in part, by an active and easy temperament and by the stability of one's living conditions.

Social Settings for Development

Preview Questions

> What is a systems view of families? According to a systems view, what parenting style is best for social development?

> How do features of the family environment affect motor development?

> How do siblings influence development—both directly and indirectly?

> How do interactions with peers shape personality development?

> Can preschool help to combat the negative effects of poverty on personality development?

The world's children develop in widely varying environments. Some live in a high-tech world, sending texts while being shuttled from soccer games to music lessons. Others live in rural villages, work on farms, and receive little formal education. In some communities, most children are born into two-parent families. In others, two-parent households are relatively rare.

Despite this diversity, there are some constants. Most children grow up with one or both *parents;* many have *siblings;* virtually all interact with *peers;* and all inevitably develop within the *economic conditions* of their family, community, and nation. Let's examine these settings for social development.

PARENTS AND SOCIAL DEVELOPMENT. To understand the role of parents in children's development, it's important to recognize that families are "systems" (Parke, 2004; Sameroff, 1994; Thelen & Smith, 1994). A *system* is any collection of people or objects that influence one another. Families are like this. Not only do parents affect their children, but also children affect their parents, siblings influence one another's development, and the relationship between siblings affects parents (Parke, 2004).

Interactions in the family system make it hard to predict how any one variable will affect the family as a whole. Research on parenting styles illustrates this.

In one *longitudinal study*—a study in which the same individuals are observed at different periods of time—researchers first obtained two key measures when children were 1 to 2 years old: (1) *parenting style* (parents' level of warnings and punishments) and (2) *children's temperament* (whether a child was difficult or easy to manage). Later, when children were 7 to 10 years old, teachers and mothers reported their levels of aggressiveness (arguing, fighting) and delinquency (stealing, vandalism, substance abuse). How did parenting style affect these outcomes? It depended; in the complex system that is a family, parenting style did not have one consistent effect. Rather, the effects of parents' style varied depending on children's temperament (Figure 14.8). Among easy-to-manage children, a "laid back" parenting style was better. Among children with a difficult-to-manage temperament, a stricter parenting style was better (Bates et al., 1998).

This result teaches a general lesson about social development. The media often present "facile sound bites about parenting" (Collins et al., 2000, p. 228)—simple reports of what's best for children in general. But scientific evidence shows there is no single "best way" to parent. Parenting styles have different effects on different children.

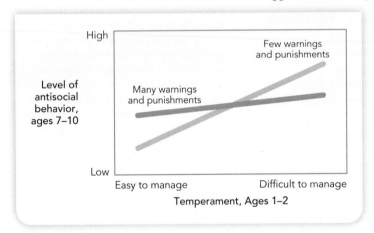

figure **14.8**
Temperament and parenting style
What parenting style is best if you want your child to be well behaved? It depends on your child. Parenting and temperament interact. A strict parenting style reduces antisocial behavior among children with difficult temperaments, but among children who are easy to manage, a parenting style that features few warnings and punishments is better (Bates et al., 1998).

PARENTS AND MOTOR DEVELOPMENT. In addition to social development, parenting can affect *physical* development. Children's physical skills are shaped not only by inherited biology, but also by experiences in the home (Kopp, 2011). An example of this is children's *motor development,* that is, growth in the ability to coordinate muscular movements in order to move one's body skillfully (Adolph, Karasik, & Tamis-LeMonda, 2010).

Motor development is marked by a series of "milestones"—significant changes that reflect a child's growing skill. For most children, motor development milestones occur in the sequence shown in Figure 14.9. Children achieve these milestones through practice. Observations of 12- to 19-month-olds, for example, reveal that during an average hour of free play, they take more than 2000 steps and fall about 17 times (Adolph et al., 2012). These experiences enable children to refine their motor skills.

The rate at which children develop motor skills is influenced by factors in the family environment. One is socioeconomic status. Children born into wealthier families tend to outperform children from poor households on tests of motor skill (Venetsanou &

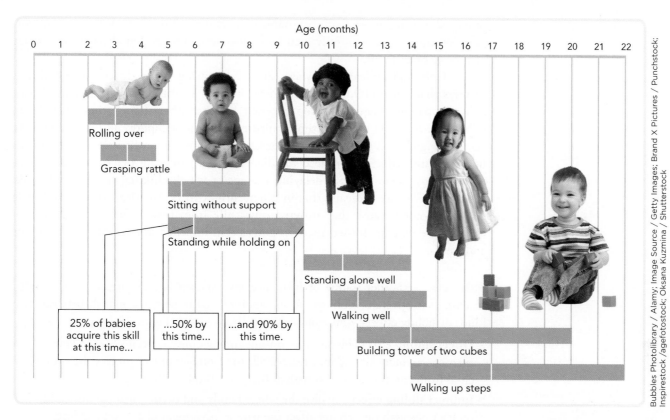

Age (months)

Rolling over

Grasping rattle

Sitting without support

Standing while holding on

Standing alone well

Walking well

Building tower of two cubes

Walking up steps

25% of babies acquire this skill at this time...

...50% by this time...

...and 90% by this time.

Bubbles Photolibrary / Alamy; Image Source / Getty Images; Brand X Pictures / Punchstock; Inspirestock /agefotostock; Oksana Kuzmina / Shutterstock

figure 14.9
Motor development milestones Most children progress through a series of achievements in motor development during the first 22 months of life.

Kambas, 2010). In wealthier households, children usually have more space to run around (e.g., a backyard) and more interactive toys, which may speed motor development.

A second factor is more surprising: parental choices about diapers. Researchers observed children's walking under each of three experimental diaper conditions: (1) no diapers (i.e., naked), (2) disposable diapers, or (3) cloth diapers (Cole, Lingeman, & Adolph, 2012). In each condition, children walked on a pressure-sensitive carpet that recorded their steps. Diapers impaired walking, as compared to the naked-walking condition (Figure 14.10). When wearing diapers, infants' walking was more wobbly and they fell more often (Cole et al., 2012). Cloth diapers

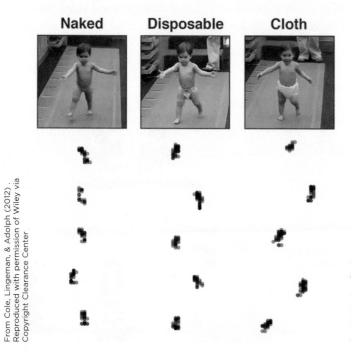

Naked   Disposable   Cloth

From Cole, Lingeman, & Adolph (2012). Reproduced with permission of Wiley via Copyright Clearance Center

figure 14.10
These diapers aren't made for walkin'
Children's level of motor coordination is affected not only by their biological development, but by how parents dress them. Diapers impair walking, in comparison to naked walking.

impaired walking more than disposable diapers did. Children's level of motor coordination thus reflects not only their biological development, but also parents' choice of how to dress them.

As Cole and colleagues review (2012), parenting styles differ across cultures in ways that affect children's motor development. In some Caribbean and African cultures, parents frequently prop up their infants rather than letting them lie in cribs. As a result, children in those cultures sit without support at a relatively early age (see Figure 14.9). In some areas of China, infants lie on fine sand that absorbs bodily waste, reducing the need for diapers. This parenting practice reduces freedom of movement, though, delaying the age at which children first sit and walk. Historical evidence indicates that in nineteenth-century America, children did little crawling—not because they differed physically from twenty-first-century infants, but because parents dressed them in gowns that impeded movement of their hands and knees.

SIBLINGS. Another source of influence on children's development is siblings. In studying the effects of siblings on one another, researchers distinguish between two kinds of sibling effects: *direct* and *indirect* (Brody, 2004; Figure 14.11).

> **Direct sibling effects** involve one-on-one interactions between siblings. For example, an older sibling may teach skills to a younger one or protect the younger child from emotional distress such as bullying (Brody, 2004).

> **Indirect sibling effects** involve the whole family and occur when parent–child interactions with one sibling affect the parents' treatment of a second sibling.

Three *indirect* sibling effects involve (1) parenting skill, (2) birth order, and (3) pecking order.

Parents' skills change from one child to the next. When raising their first child, parents are learning on-the-go. But thanks to their experiences with the firstborn, mom and dad are more skilled at parenting when the second child arrives; they tend to employ more effective parenting strategies that lower parent–child conflict (Whiteman, McHale, & Crouter, 2003).

Birth order effects are differences between the oldest child in the family and later-born children. On average, first- and second-born children differ in conformity, that is, the tendency to conform to, as opposed to rebel against, parental rules. Firstborn children are more likely to conform. Second-borns tend to rebel, particularly if the

figure 14.11
Sibling effects How do a child's siblings affect his or her social development? Direct effects involve one-on-one interactions between siblings. Indirect effects involve the family system. Interactions between one child and the parents affect the parents in ways that then affect the other sibling.

direct sibling effects Developmental influence involving one-on-one interactions between siblings.

indirect sibling effects Developmental influence in which parents' interactions with one sibling affect treatment of a second sibling.

Sibling effects on development

Direct effects

Sibling-to-sibling interactions

Indirect effects

Sibling–parent interactions affect parents; influence on parents then affects next sibling

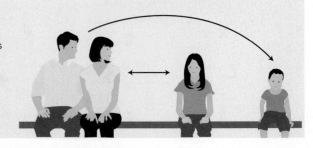

age difference between children is not large (Healey & Ellis, 2007; Sulloway, 1996). For example, among young adults in Belgium, second-born children were found to be less religious than their older siblings (Saroglou & Fiasse, 2003); they tended to rebel against the family's religious traditions. Birth order differences result from indirect sibling effects (Sulloway, 1996). Firstborn children have a family role available to them: maintain family traditions. Second-borns find that role already filled (by the firstborn); thus, they seek alternative lifestyles that establish their individuality.

> What is your role or niche in the family? Do the birth order effects hold true in your family's case?

Pecking order (Conley, 2004) refers to the relative status of children within a family. Many families face scarce resources and must therefore make difficult decisions about allocating family funds. Children judged to be brighter or more socially skilled may get more resources; they rise in the pecking order. Consistent with a pecking-order analysis, within-family differences in economic success in the United States are large: "In America, sibling differences represent about *three-quarters* of all the differences [i.e., the overall statistical differences] between individuals" (Conley, 2004, p. 6).

PEERS. Schoolchildren spend much of their time with *peers*, that is, boys and girls of their age group. Peers interact in classrooms, on playgrounds, and "virtually" in electronic communication.

Psychologist Judith Rich Harris (1995) explains that peer interactions shape children's development in two ways: They cause individuals to (1) fit in with, and (2) stand out from, others. The effects are called *group assimilation* and *within-group differentiation.*

> In *group assimilation,* a child's behavior becomes more similar to that of his or her peers. For example, through peer pressure, individuals may feel a need to develop interests, ways of speaking, and styles of dress that match others in the group. If they don't, they may be teased, mocked, and ultimately rejected by others.

> In *within-group differentiation,* group members draw distinctions among people in the group. They notice physical and psychological differences and may label them with nicknames ("Skinny," "Professor," "Four-Eyes").

> In what ways have you assimilated to your current peer group? In what ways are you differentiated from them?

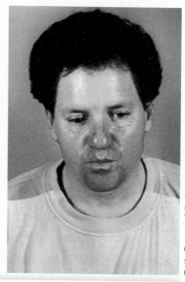

Both: Reuters / Corbis

Within-family differences in life outcomes Bill Clinton is shown, at age 46, receiving the oath of office as the 42nd President of the United States. His half-brother Roger Clinton, at age 44, is shown in a police booking, after being charged with drunk driving—an incident that occurred about a month after Roger was granted a presidential pardon erasing an earlier cocaine-related offense for which he had spent a year in jail. The Clinton family illustrates the large differences in developmental outcomes that can occur within families.

Kathrin Ziegler / Getty Images

They all seem to like big sunglasses Peer group interactions can create *group assimilation,* in which people's behavior becomes similar to that of their peers. As a result of assimilation, people's interests, behaviors, and appearances can become highly similar to one another.

As I came in . . . he whispered in a mysterious tone.

"Hush, please don't make noise, Anton is working!"

"Yes, dear, our Anton is working," Evgenia Yakovlevna the mother added, making a gesture indicating the door of his room. I went further. Maria Pavlovna, his sister, told me in a subdued voice, "Anton is working now."

In the next room, in a low voice, Nikolai Pavlovich told me, "Hello, my dear friend. You know, Anton is working now," he whispered, trying not to be loud. Everyone was afraid to break the silence.

—A visitor describing his arrival at the home of the Russian writer Anton Chekhov, who clearly was at the top of the pecking order (in Parks, 2012)

Peer interactions contribute to gender differences in behavior. In childhood and adolescence, girls' and boys' interactions with peers differ. For example, girls spend more time conversing with each other, revealing their private thoughts and feelings to close friends and seeking social support. Boys more frequently compete in games in large groups and engage in physical play. In conversation, boys are more likely to talk about their superiority to their peers (Rose & Rudolph, 2006). Where do these gender differences come from? In part, they are created by interactions with peers. Researchers measured the degree to which kindergartners played in mixed-sex groups or same-sex groups (Martin & Fabes, 2001). Over time, children who played in same-sex groups displayed more behavior that was typical of their gender. They appeared to learn behaviors that were typical for girls and for boys by interacting with other same-sex children.

Social experience and gender differences Compared to girls, boys spend more time in rough-and-tumble play. Social experiences contribute to these gender differences. When researchers studied children's behavior over a long period of time, they found that children who played in same-sex groups developed more behavior that was typical of their gender (Martin & Fabes, 2001). Through social interaction, they appeared to learn behaviors that were typical for girls and boys.

Laurence Mouton / Getty Images

Yellow Dog Productions / Getty Images

ECONOMIC STATUS. The world's families differ greatly in wealth. Many can easily provide children with adequate food, shelter, clothing, and education, whereas others struggle to obtain these necessities of life.

Economic status affects psychological development. Greater wealth provides children with opportunities to develop skills that bring success later in life. Poverty presents big disadvantages: fewer opportunities to experience music and the arts, to read and write at home, and to learn about the world beyond one's own neighborhood (Heckman, 2006). The lack of stimulation may slow development of personal motivation and skills.

Good news is that interventions can make up for a lack of intellectual stimulation at home. Evidence comes from a large-scale experimental study, the Perry Preschool Program (Schweinhart et al., 2005), which was launched in 1962 in Ypsilanti, Michigan.

More than 100 children aged 3 to 4 from economically disadvantaged African American families took part in the Perry Preschool Study. A subgroup of these children, chosen at random, experienced an enriched, high-quality educational program featuring an extra 2½ hours of preschool education per day and home visits from teachers, who consulted on each child's educational progress and overall development. To find out if this extra education had any effect, researchers tracked the children's development for an extraordinarily long time: until they reached age 40. Extra educational resources were found to have long-lasting effects (Figure 14.12). Children with enriched education were more likely to graduate from high school, less likely to ever be arrested, and earned more money as adults.

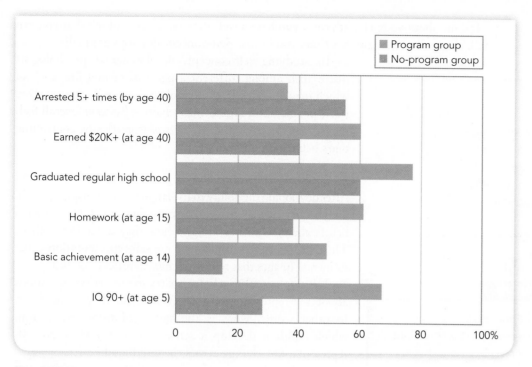

figure 14.12

The long-term benefits of early education The Perry Preschool Study, started in a low-SES neighborhood in 1962, shows that high-quality education early in life has long-lasting effects. In this study, the children in the program group received enriched education in preschool. As shown, they were more successful in adolescence and adulthood than those who did not receive such educational enrichment (Schweinhart et al., 2004).

🌐 WHAT DO YOU KNOW?...

10. a. Briefly describe the research finding that supports the claim that "parenting styles have different effects on different children."
    b. Briefly describe one research finding that supports the claim that "children's physical skills are shaped not only by inherited biology, but also by experiences in the home."
    c. What makes pecking order an example of an indirect effect of siblings?
    d. In which environment would you expect a girl to develop more typically feminine traits: one in which she grew up interacting primarily with same-sex groups or one in which she grew up interacting with mixed-sex groups? Briefly explain.
    e. A subgroup of children in the Perry Preschool Study experienced an enriched education that included things like 2½ extra hours of education per day. Name at least one of the long-lasting benefits of this enrichment.

The Development of Self-Concept

Preview Questions

› How do children acquire a sense of self? How do these self-representations change over time?
› How does self-esteem change across childhood?
› Why doesn't everybody have the same level of self-esteem?
› What skill do we need in order to exert self-control?
› Does the ability to delay gratification in childhood predict anything important?

CONNECTING TO CONSCIOUSNESS AND BRAIN SYSTEMS

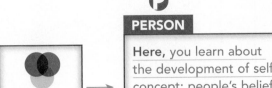

P

PERSON

Here, you learn about the development of self-concept: people's beliefs about their personal qualities.

M

MIND

Chapter 9: A wide variety of species have conscious feelings, but none have self-concept (in the human sense of the term) and few even have the human ability to recognize themselves.

B

BRAIN

Chapters 3 and 9: The capacity for consciousness, self-awareness, and self-concept rests on networks of interconnected brain systems.

"Tell me about yourself." It's easy; you have a well-developed sense of self that you can talk about. But once upon a time, you didn't. Self-concept develops gradually.

In studying self-concept, developmental psychologists distinguish among different aspects of mental life, each of which involves oneself. We'll look at three: *self-representations* (facts people know about themselves), *self-esteem* (overall feelings about oneself), and *self-control* (specifically, controlling one's behavior and emotions).

FACTS ABOUT THE SELF: SELF-REPRESENTATIONS. After developing the ability to use language (see Chapter 8), children begin to use language to describe themselves. They develop beliefs about who they are and how they differ from others. These beliefs, stored in memory, are **self-representations**, that is, mental images that represent characteristics of oneself.

Developmental psychologists try to answer two questions about self-representations: (1) Where do they come from; in other words, what is the source of information from which children develop a sense of self? (2) How do self-representations change across the childhood years?

Schoolchildren take classes on reading and writing, not on "the self." So where do they get their sense of self? A major source of information is the opinions and actions of others. Other people are like mirrors (Cooley, 1902): They reflect back to you information about yourself. Input from other people—not only others' statements but also their behavioral reactions to individuals (Leary et al., 1995)—teaches people about their skills, distinctive personality characteristics, and level of popularity.

The way in which self-representations change can be seen with some examples. They come from, respectively, a preschooler, a first-grader, and a fourth-grader:

"I'm 3 years old and I live in a big house with my mother and father and my brother, Jason, and my sister, Lisa. I have blue eyes and a kitty that is orange. . . . I like pizza and I have a nice teacher at preschool. I can count up to 100, want to hear me?"

"I have a lot of friends, in my neighborhood, at school, and at my church. I'm good at schoolwork, I know my words, and letters, and my numbers. . . . I can throw a ball real far, I'm going to be on some kind of team when I'm older. I can do lots of stuff real good. . . . My parents are real proud of me when I do good at things. It makes me really happy and excited when they watch me!"

"I'm in fourth grade this year, and I'm pretty popular, at least with the girls. That's because I'm nice to people and helpful and can keep secrets. Mostly I am nice to my friends, although if I get in a bad mood I sometimes say something that can be a little mean. I try to control my temper, but when I don't, I'm ashamed of myself. . . . Even though I'm not doing well in [math and science] . . . I still like myself as a person . . . how I look and how popular I am are more important."

—from Harter (1999, pp. 37, 41, 48)

self-representations Beliefs about the characteristics of oneself and the ways in which one differs from other people.

As you can see, self-representations change as children get older. They become richer and more complex (Harter, 1999). In the preschool years, children think of themselves in terms of simple, concrete attributes that may appear unrelated (e.g.,

"I live in a big house"; "I like pizza"). When they reach ages 5 to 7, children connect self-representations to one another. For example, the first-grader quoted above connects ideas causally; parents are proud *because* the child is good at things, and being on a team is likely *because of* the ability to throw a ball. By the fourth grade, self-representations consist of not only concrete actions and preferences, but also abstract traits. The fourth-grader quoted above knows not only that she has friends (a concrete fact), but also that she is "popular," a more abstract description of the self.

FEELINGS ABOUT THE SELF: SELF-ESTEEM. Now let's turn from facts (self-representations) to feelings about the self and children's development of *self-esteem*. **Self-esteem** refers to people's overall sense of self-worth—their feelings about how valuable and worthy they are. Psychologists distinguish between two aspects of self-esteem. **Global self-esteem** is a person's overall feelings of self-worth. **Differentiated self-esteem** refers to the varying feelings people may have about themselves when thinking about different aspects of their lives.

Self-esteem changes across the childhood years (Robins & Trzesniewski, 2005). Children's self-esteem tends to be high around ages 9 to 10 and to drop in early adolescence (around ages 12 to 13). Changes at school may contribute to this drop; middle school students face more academic competition and receive less personalized attention from teachers than in grade school (Harter & Whitesell, 2003). The adolescent decline in self-esteem is slightly larger for girls than boys. A combination of biology and culture may underlie the gender difference. Girls naturally gain weight during puberty but encounter a culture that idealizes thinness (Kling et al., 1999).

Self-esteem also becomes more differentiated as children age (Harter, 1999). Around ages 4 to 7, there are two distinct aspects to children's self-esteem: *competence* (children's evaluations of their behavioral effectiveness) and *social adequacy* (evaluations of social behavior and personal appearance). At ages 8 to 12, there are five: Children differentiate among competence at school, competence in athletics, physical appearance, self-control, and being liked by peers (Harter, 1999).

In what areas of your life is your self-esteem the highest? Lowest?

Individuals differ in self-esteem. Many factors contribute to these differences. One factor is inherited temperament. Children who inherit a tendency to experience negative emotions tend to develop low self-esteem (Neiss et al., 2009).

Another influence is parenting style. A classic study (Coopersmith, 1967) identified two aspects of parenting that predict self-esteem: (1) acceptance and (2) style of discipline. Parents who are consistently accepting of their children—who display interest in and affection toward them—produce children with higher self-esteem. A discipline style that features clear-cut rules, and their enforcement in a manner that is respectful of children, also boosts self-esteem.

Some factors have surprisingly little influence on self-esteem. One is social prestige; on average, children whose parents are wealthy and have prestigious jobs do not have higher self-esteem than others (Coopersmith, 1967). Another is adoption. Children who are adopted face unique challenges (e.g., living in foster care prior to adoption), yet their self-esteem is as high as children living with their biological families (Juffer & van IJzendoorn, 2007). Divorce is another factor with little influence. It disrupts family life, but does not substantially lower children's self-esteem and overall psychological adjustment. Its negative effects on children's sense of well-being are "small in magnitude and not universal" (Lansford, 2009, p. 140).

MASTERY OVER BEHAVIOR: SELF-CONTROL. If you want to, you usually can stifle inappropriate laughter, stop yourself from eating two desserts, and study for an exam when you'd rather be hanging out with friends. You can exert **self-control,**

Didier Robcis / Getty Images

Self-concept develops Research on child development suggests that the content of what this girl writes about herself in her diary will change systematically over time. Preschool children think of themselves in terms of simple, concrete attributes (e.g., "I like pizza"). By the time they reach fourth grade, their thoughts include more abstract social qualities (e.g., "I am popular").

self-esteem A person's overall sense of self-worth.

global self-esteem A person's overall sense of self-worth.

differentiated self-esteem The varying feelings people may have about themselves when thinking about different aspects of their lives.

self-control The ability to act in a manner consistent with long-term goals and values, even when one feels an impulse to act differently.

CONNECTING TO MENTAL SYSTEMS AND BRAIN MECHANISMS IN SELF-CONTROL

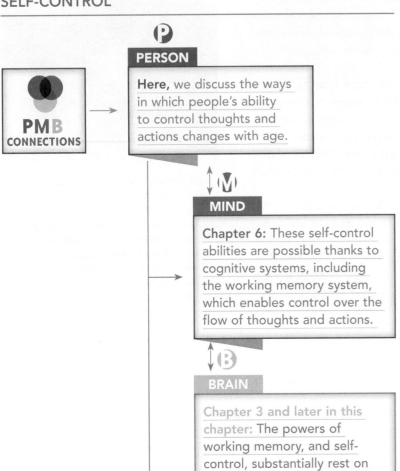

P

PERSON

Here, we discuss the ways in which people's ability to control thoughts and actions changes with age.

M

MIND

Chapter 6: These self-control abilities are possible thanks to cognitive systems, including the working memory system, which enables control over the flow of thoughts and actions.

B

BRAIN

Chapter 3 and later in this chapter: The powers of working memory, and self-control, substantially rest on the functioning of the brain's prefrontal cortex, which is highly interconnected with other brain regions that contribute to motor movement and emotional experience.

which is the ability to act in a manner consistent with long-term goals and values, even if you feel an emotional impulse to act differently. You may feel like laughing out loud or overeating, but you know that, in the long run, it's better to keep your mouth shut.

As an infant, however, you were unable to stifle your laughter, control your eating, or work toward long-term goals; you hadn't yet developed self-control. Those abilities develop rapidly during the first few years of life (Eisenberg, 2012). In one study, children of three different ages—18, 24, and 30 months—performed impulse-control tasks; for instance, they were asked to avoid playing with a telephone placed next to them. On average, 18-month-olds started playing with the phone in only 10 seconds. But 24- and 30-month-olds were much better at self-control; they refrained from playing with it for 70 and 113 seconds, respectively.

Children's ability to control their emotions and behavior rests, to a large degree, on a mental ability known as *cognitive control*. **Cognitive control** is the ability to suppress emotions and impulsive behaviors that are undesired or inappropriate (Casey et al., 2011). By concentrating attention on a task at hand, people can avoid distractions and maintain control over their impulses. This ability changes with age; older children are better able to focus their attention on tasks than are younger ones (Rothbart, Posner, & Kieras, 2006). When asked to pay attention to one aspect of images on a computer screen (the type of animal that an image depicted) while ignoring another aspect (the location of the image on the screen), 3-year-olds significantly outperformed 2½-year-olds who, in turn, outperformed 2-year-olds (Rothbart et al., 2003).

> How easily are you able to control your attention right now in spite of distractions in your environment?

Self-control abilities are remarkably consistent over time. Children with high (or low) self-control ability in childhood tend to have high (or low) self-control ability later in life. Striking evidence of this comes from *delay of gratification* research by Walter Mischel and colleagues. Delay of gratification is the ability to refrain from consuming a desired reward in order to get a better reward later (also see Chapter 13). If you stop yourself from eating a piece of cake in order to remain thin, you are delaying gratification. Mischel studied delay of gratification in children by asking them to delay eating a small food treat in order to obtain a bigger treat in the near future. The amount of time they could delay was the measure of individual differences in self-control ability. Ten years later, the researchers contacted the participants (high schoolers by then) and their families and asked the parents to describe their adolescents' personalities. Amazingly, ability to delay gratification in childhood predicted adolescent personality (Shoda, Mischel, & Peake, 1990). Children who were better at controlling their behavior in childhood were more capable of coping with everyday problems, pursuing personal goals, and avoiding distractions in high school. Delay ability even predicted SAT scores; better childhood self-control predicted higher test scores.

cognitive control The mental ability to suppress one's emotions and impulsive behaviors that are undesired or inappropriate.

TRY THIS!

Before moving to the next section of this chapter (on social development in adolescence and adulthood), go to www.pmbpsychology.com for the Chapter 14 Try This! activity. While doing it, ask yourself: How might the research activity relate to the topic of social development in adolescence and adulthood? ◉

Social Development Across the Life Span

Thus far in this chapter, we have focused most of our attention on childhood. Let's now look at social development across the span of life, starting with adolescence.

Adolescence

Preview Questions

› How do biology and social environment interact to influence behavior during puberty?
› What are four ways in which adolescents cope with the challenge of establishing a personal identity?

Adolescence is the period between childhood and adulthood. Societies differ in beliefs about its exact time span (Arnett & Taber, 1994). However, adolescence generally is thought to begin around ages 12 to 13 and to run throughout the teenage years.

Adolescence features numerous changes: physical, emotional, social, intellectual. Think back to your own experience. In adolescence, you suddenly did not look like a child anymore. Your peer groups changed when you entered middle and high school. Adults expected you to be more self-reliant. You developed romantic interests.

Adolescence poses two big psychological challenges. One stems from the biological changes of puberty. Another is the psychological challenge of establishing a personal identity.

PUBERTY. Puberty is the time when a child reaches sexual maturity. Girls and boys experience physical changes that transform them into women and men who are biologically capable of reproduction (Figure 14.13).

adolescence The period between childhood and adulthood; roughly the teenage years.

puberty The time when a child reaches sexual maturity and is biologically capable of reproduction.

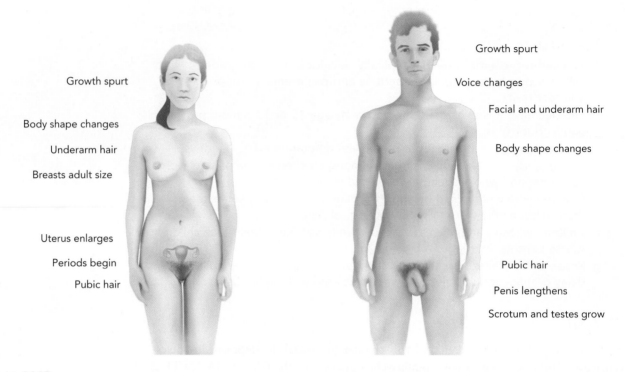

figure 14.13
Physical changes at puberty Girls and boys experience a range of physical changes at puberty, the period of life during which a child reaches sexual maturity. The biological changes of puberty begin, on average, at age 11 among girls and age 12 among boys. However, many individuals begin to experience puberty earlier, or later, than those average ages.

Behavioral changes accompany the biological ones. Compared with children, adolescents are more likely to have conflicts with parents (Laursen, Coy, & Collins, 1998; Paikoff & Brooks-Gunn, 1991); to engage in antisocial behavior (fighting, damaging property, using illegal drugs; Moffitt, 1993); and to experience bad moods and "swings" in mood (from good to bad and back) during the day (Larson & Ham, 1993).

How do the biological and behavioral changes relate to one another? There are two theoretical possibilities (Figure 14.14):

1. *Biological model.* A biological model says that changes in biology cause changes in behavior. Because all normally developing adolescents experience physical changes, this model suggests that changes in behavior during adolescence are inevitable; all adolescents should, for example, show increased antisocial behavior during the adolescent years, according to the biological model.

figure 14.14
Models of biological and social development
Different conceptual models guide research on biology and social development. In a biological model, biological factors directly produce behavioral effects. In a biopsychosocial model, the effects of biology interact with the environment. Biological factors may shape social experiences that, in turn, shape social behavior.

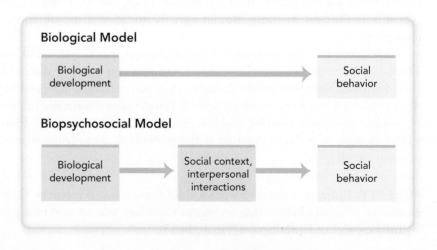

2. *Biopsychosocial model.* A **biopsychosocial model** says that the impact of biology on behavior depends on adolescents' social experiences. Social behavior, then, reflects an interaction between the biologically changing person and the social environment, which reacts to those changes. Behavioral changes, according to this model, are not inevitable.

How can you tell which model is correct? It's not easy; it requires longitudinal research that measures both biological changes and social environments. One example of such work is research on antisocial behavior among girls who reached puberty at different ages, by Swedish psychologist David Magnusson (1992).

If the biological model (Figure 14.14) were correct, then among all girls, those who reach puberty at a relatively young age should differ behaviorally from others. Biology should drive behavior. This, however, is not what Magnusson found. Rather, biological changes affected behavior only among some girls, and the effects depended on the social environment. A key social factor was peer groups. Some (but not all) early-maturing girls hung out with other early-maturing girls who, in turn, tended to hang out with older boys. The girls who hung out with older boys were more likely to engage in antisocial behavior such as drinking, drug use, and cheating at school (Magnusson, 1992). Similarly, other research shows that a main reason why girls and boys who experience early puberty are more likely to develop drinking problems is social: They are more likely to hang out with peers who drink (Biehl, Natsuaki, & Ge, 2007).

Results therefore support a biopsychosocial model. Biological changes can create social changes that, in turn, affect the development of behavior.

IDENTITY. Suppose you were asked to describe yourself: your personal history, social roles, and goals in life. Your answer would indicate your *identity*. In the study of social development, **identity** is people's overall understanding of themselves, their role in society, their strengths and weaknesses, their history, and their future potential.

Questions about identity strongly arise in adolescence (Erikson, 1959; see Chapter 13). Many adolescents begin to ask: What is my true personality? What are my strengths and limitations? What will I do in my future? In essence: Who am I?

People differ in whether and how they think about identity, and in how long they take to decide on a life path. Some find an answer quickly and commit themselves to a role in life. Others experience prolonged doubt and confusion. Still others give identity questions little thought at all. The psychologist James Marcia (1980) summarizes these differences by suggesting four different **identity statuses,** that is, different approaches to coping with the challenge of establishing a personal identity. (Marcia's efforts capitalize on earlier analyses of personal development by Erik Erikson; see Chapter 13.)

> **Identity achievement:** People who have deeply contemplated life options, chosen a career path, and are firmly committed to it thanks to deep personal values have the status *identity achievement.* For example, someone who has decided to be a doctor because she values the alleviation of people's physical suffering has reached *identity achievement* status.

> **Foreclosure:** People who know their role in life and prospective future occupation, but who feel these were imposed on them by others, have the identity status *foreclosure.* The term means that others, by imposing their values and expectations, have foreclosed one's opportunity to explore novel life paths. Foreclosure can reduce people's commitment to their activities.

> **Identity diffusion:** People who feel directionless, with no firm sense of where they're headed in life, have the status *identity diffusion.* These individuals generally have not given deep thought to their personal values or goals; they just know that they *don't* know exactly where they're headed in life.

biopsychosocial model A way of explaining developmental events (e.g., behavioral changes at puberty) in which the impact of biology on behavior is said to depend on social experiences.

identity People's overall understanding of themselves, their role in society, their strengths and weaknesses, their history, and their future potential.

identity statuses In Marcia's theory, four different approaches to coping with the challenge of establishing a personal identity.

identity achievement According to Marcia, the identity status achieved by people who have deeply contemplated life options and are committed to a career path based on their values.

foreclosure According to Marcia, the identity status of people who know their role in life and prospective future occupation, but feel these were imposed on them by others.

identity diffusion According to Marcia, the identity status of people who feel directionless, with no firm sense of where they're headed in life.

> **Moratorium:** Some people contemplate many life options but are unable to commit to any one set of goals. These people have an identity status called *moratorium.* The word refers to a suspension of activity. When people can't commit to a life path, their lives are, in a sense, "suspended" until they can settle on a path to pursue. Moratorium status can cause people to experience anxiety about themselves and their future.

Which identity status describes you?

People with different identity statuses differ in their behavior—particularly in **prosocial behavior,** which is actions that directly benefit others (e.g., comforting those in distress). Researchers find that people with identity achievement status are the most likely to act prosocially, whereas people with identity diffusion status are the least likely to do so (Padilla-Walker et al., 2008). People who have achieved a clear personal identity appear better able to look beyond themselves and consider their responsibility for the welfare of others.

🌎 WHAT DO YOU KNOW?...

12. In Magnusson's research, what was the social experience that led early-maturing girls to engage in antisocial behaviors? How does this illustrate a biopsychosocial model of behavior change?

13. Match the identity status on the left with the statement that illustrates it on the right.

1. Achievement	a. "My parents always valued education, so I figured I might as well become a teacher to make them happy."
2. Foreclosure	b. "I had so many ideas for what to do as a career, but I got overwhelmed and am now just working a part-time retail job until I can figure things out."
3. Diffusion	c. "It became clear to me that the best way for me to help people out of poverty was to use my talents to become a teacher."
4. Moratorium	d. "I have so many interests, but no idea which one I should pursue. I hardly even know who I am or what I'm good at."

⊚ CULTURAL OPPORTUNITIES

Ethnic and Racial Identity

We live in a "globalized" world. You can access a worldwide web of information. Many people work for multinational corporations. Movies and TV shows have an international reach; *The Simpsons,* for example, is so popular in China that the government once banned it from prime-time TV to boost the ratings of Chinese shows (McDonald, 2006).

How does globalization affect **ethnic identity,** people's personal identification with the ethnic group to which they belong? You might expect globalization would reduce it. Criss-crossing information from around the globe might create a single "world culture" in which people did not care about their own ethnicity. But in many places, the opposite seems to occur: Ethnic identity is celebrated and strengthened. New York City, for example, is home to an annual West Indian American Day parade, a Caribbean American festival, a Brazil Independence Day festival, a Latinos Unidos

---

moratorium According to Marcia, the identity status of people who contemplate many life options but are unable to commit to any one set of goals.

prosocial behavior Actions that directly benefit others, such as comforting those in distress.

ethnic identity People's personal identification with the ethnic group to which they belong.

parade, a Muslim Day parade, an African American Day Parade, the Italian American Feast of San Gennaro, the German American Steuben Day parade, and an International Cultures parade—and that's just in September (http://www.carnaval.com/newyork/parades/fall/)! These events seem to represent "a form of opposition or resistance to the global . . . a defense against the overruling process of globalization" (Hermans & Kempen, 1998, p. 1114).

A study of African American, Asian American, European American, and Latino American high school students in Southern California (Phinney, 1989) showed that students of this age differ in ethnic identity. The differences corresponded to three stages of identity noted above: *diffusion, moratorium,* or *achieved.*

> *Diffusion:* Some students had given little thought to their ethnic identity. "Why do I need to know who was the first black woman to do this or that?" one student said. "I'm just not too interested" (Phinney, 1989, p. 44).

> *Moratorium:* Others gave a lot of thought to their ethnicity, yet still were puzzling over their relation to their ethnic group. "There are a lot of non-Japanese people around me and it gets pretty confusing to try and decide who I am," said an Asian American male (Phinney, 1989, p. 44).

> *Identity achieved:* A third set of students had a firm sense of ethnic identity. They understood their group and their relation to it. "I have been born Filipino and am born to be Filipino. . . . I don't consider myself only Filipino, but also American" (Phinney, 1989, p. 44).

By contrast, European American students (the majority group in this study) "did not show evidence of these stages. . . . [E]thnicity was not an identity issue to which they could relate" (Phinney, 1989, p. 41, 44). European Americans primarily said they were "American"; their ethnic ancestry generally was not important to their personal identity. Ethnicity is more likely to be a part of your identity if your ethnic group is in the minority.

A theory developed by Robert Sellers and colleagues (Sellers et al., 1998; Figure 14.15) explains how the identities of group members differ from one another. These researchers focused on African American racial identity and identified four dimensions of variation:

1. *Salience:* Whether individuals judge that their race is relevant to them in a given situation
2. *Centrality:* Whether race is self-defining for a person
3. *Regard:* Positive or negative feelings about the racial group
4. *Ideology:* A person's beliefs about how members of the group should act

Racial identity, then, cannot be reduced to a single quality that is common to all members of a group.

In sum, ethnic and racial identity is complex. One can't be sure of an individual's identity beliefs just from knowing the individual's ethnic group. But one thing we can be sure of is that, despite globalization, ethnic identity is here to stay.

Ethnic identity Although we live in a "globalized" world, many ethnic groups maintain a strong, distinctive ethnic identity—as seen here at a National Puerto Rican Day Parade in New York.

© Richard Drew / AP / Corbis

Racial identity

Racial salience | Racial centrality | Racial regard | Racial ideology

figure **14.15**
Sellers's model of racial identity In the model of racial identity developed by Robert Sellers and colleagues (1998), there are four dimensions of racial identity. People vary in the degree to which race is *salient* and *central* to them, in how they *regard* their racial group, and in their *ideological* beliefs about how group members should act.

[Sellers, R. M., Smith, M. A., Shelton, J. N., Rowley, S. A., & Chavous, T. M. (1998). Multidimensional model of racial identity: A reconceptualization of African American racial identity. *Personality and Social Psychology Review, 2,* 18–39, © 1998 by Society for Personality and Social Psychology, Inc. Reprinted by permission of SAGE Publications.]

🌀 WHAT DO YOU KNOW?...

14. High school students' ethnic identity corresponded to Marcia's identity stages. Which stage is exemplified by the following statement? "I speak Chinese at home and English at school. I feel like I'm stuck between two worlds. Sometimes I don't know who I am."

Emerging Adulthood

Preview Question

> Are 18-year-olds really full-fledged adults?

Decades ago, most Americans entered into the work and family life of adulthood soon after adolescence. In the 1950s and 1960s, the average age of first marriage was under 23 for men and 21 for women (Information Please Database®, 2009). But times have changed. Today, the average age of first marriage is more than five years later for both men and women.

This change creates, for many people in their early 20s, a relatively novel developmental period. The psychologist Jeffrey Arnett (2000) calls it *emerging adulthood*. **Emerging adulthood** is a period of life in the very late teen years and early 20s (roughly ages 18 to 25). It is experienced by people who, on the one hand, have the rights and psychological independence of adulthood but, on the other, do not yet have the obligations and responsibilities of family life (Arnett, 2000). Surveys show that people experience this period of life as unique. When asked whether they feel like adults, most people do not say yes or no. They say, "Yes and no" (Figure 14.16).

Emerging adulthood is a time of exploration. People may try one job, quit, then try another; move from one city to another; and explore new relationships before settling down into marriage. The relationships of emerging adulthood often are in flux. Research shows that, among emerging adults who experience a relationship break-up, about half get back together with their ex-mate (Halpern-Meekin et al., 2013). This finding suggests that traditional relationship categories ("going out," "broken up") may not describe emerging adulthood relationships, which "go through periods of being undefined or . . . fluid" (Halpern-Meekin et al., 2013, p. 183).

Today's emerging adults allocate time to activities that did not exist in the past: an average of 3½ hours a day on the Internet and 45 minutes a day texting or making phone calls (Coyne, Padilla-Walker, & Howard, 2013). Major developmental tasks, such as establishing a social identity, are now accomplished electronically.

> ### THINK ABOUT IT
>
> When you hear the phrase "stages of human development," it might sound as if a fixed set of stages has characterized the development of all people, in all times and places, throughout human history. Is that true? Researchers studying emerging adulthood see this stage as a recent development in human history. Might other stages also be relatively new? *Hint*: The entire concept of adolescence as a life stage that exists prior to adulthood did not develop until about 120 years ago (Kett, 2003).

figure 14.16

Are you an "adult"? When asked if they felt they had "reached adulthood," most Americans aged 18 to 25 did not answer either "no" or "yes." They endorsed an ambiguous answer instead: "In some respects, yes; in some respects, no" (indicated by the "Yes and no" data in the graph). Their answers suggest that they are not yet in adulthood, but in a distinct developmental stage, emerging adulthood (Arnett, 2000).

emerging adulthood The period of life in the late teens and early 20s (roughly 18 to 25) experienced by people who have the rights and psychological independence of adulthood but do not yet have the obligations and responsibilities of family life.

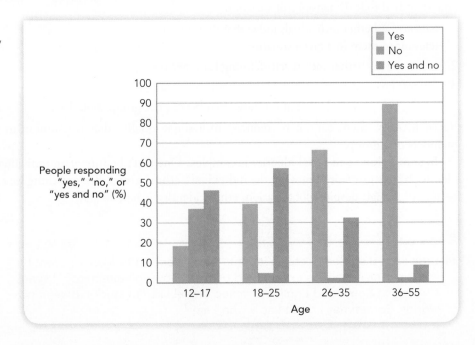

⚘ WHAT DO YOU KNOW?...

15. Individuals in emerging adulthood have the psychological independence and _____ of adults but not the responsibilities of _____ life.

Midlife Development

Preview Questions

> Is a midlife crisis inevitable?
> What are some common themes of individuals' life stories?

Some years from now, you'll be done with school. You might have a job and a family and be settled into "the afternoon of life," the *midlife* years. Or maybe you're already there.

Biologically, midlife is not sharply defined. Culture shapes people's thoughts about this life period. In fact, the entire concept of "middle age" is a cultural construction (Shweder, 1998); nothing about human biology delineates an exact middle-age period. Nonetheless, many cultures recognize a middle age that starts around age 35 and continues to 60. Midlife adults share numerous concerns that are particularly relevant to this time period: advancing professionally, establishing and maintaining a family, preparing for retirement, and coping with the illness and death of older relatives (Lachman, 2001).

MIDLIFE CRISIS? Fill in the blank: *midlife* _____. Many people would say "crisis." A stereotype is that midlifers become overwhelmed with their loss of youth, experience a crisis, and do surprising things: quit their job, join a new religion, buy a flashy sports car.

Research findings challenge this stereotype. Most midlife adults do *not* experience a sudden crisis and drastically change their lifestyle (Wethington, Kessler, & Pixley, 2004). Midlifers do "take stock" of their lives—assessing past accomplishments and future challenges. But this rarely triggers a crisis (Wethington, 2000). Even when it does, the crises often center on problems that could occur at any age, such as job loss or the death of a family member.

Similarly, some midlife events have less psychological impact than you might guess. Consider, for example, *menopause,* the end of female reproductive fertility, which generally occurs around age 50. Is menopause a psychologically negative event because it signals advancing age? Interviews with women suggest not; their "attitudes toward menopause ranged from neutral to positive" (Sommer et al., 1999, p. 871). So many women live such busy lives that menopause isn't a major event. For example, among African American women, who had the most positive attitudes toward this life transition, "menopause seemed a minor stressor," especially compared with others, such as "the consequences of racism they had experienced throughout their lives" (Sommer et al., 1999, p. 872).

LIFE STORIES AT MIDLIFE. By early adulthood, people usually have developed a **life story**—a narrative understanding of the major events and themes of their lives (Habermas & Bluck, 2000). Midlife stories often reflect on accomplishments, after decades of time devoted to work and family.

Everyone's life story is unique, yet life stories have common themes. Two are generativity and redemption:

> *Generativity* is a concern for future generations (Erikson, 1963). Some adults see themselves as contributing to the welfare of future generations, whereas others' stories lament their failure to contribute anything of lasting value.

"A spoiler is standard on all sports cars. It helps protect your hair transplant."

Mike Baldwin / Cartoonstock.com

life story A narrative understanding of the major events and themes of one's life.

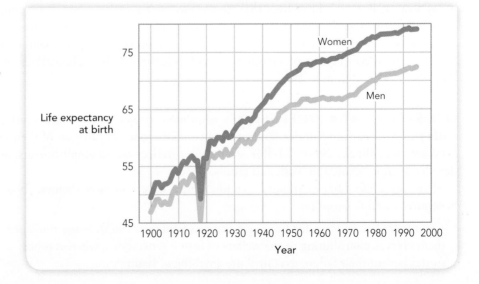

He could spend his free time
at the beach, but actor Sean
Penn instead is working with a relief
organization to help citizens of Haiti
recover from an earthquake. His work
is exceptional, yet it reflects a motive
common to human development: the
desire to help others and to improve
the well-being of the next generation
of society.

Ramon Espinosa / AP / Corbis

> *Redemption* is a theme in which life is transformed when a personal crisis is over-come (McAdams, 2006). With the crisis behind them, people are poised to contrib-ute to the world.

Researchers have studied these themes by asking people to tell stories highlighting "turning points" in their life and to describe what they personally are striving for (McAdams et al., 2001). Adults whose life stories included themes of generativity and redemption were more well-adjusted—they were less depressed, more satisfied with life, and saw life as comprehensible and manageable.

Midlife, then, is not a time of inevitable crisis. Midlifers assess their lives and expe-rience greater psychological well-being if they feel they have coped with life challenges and are contributing to the next generation.

🌐 WHAT DO YOU KNOW?...

16. True or False?
   a. Consistent with the stereotype, most individuals eventually do experience a midlife crisis.
   b. Consistent with the stereotype, most women perceive menopause to be an overwhelmingly negative major life event.
   c. People whose life stories include themes of generativity and redemption tend to be more well adjusted.

Older Adulthood

Do you think much about old age—life when you're 65, or 75, or 85? If you're like most people reading this book, older adulthood is so far away that you don't give it much thought.

For many years, developmental psychologists didn't give it much thought, either; they primarily studied life's early years. But more recently, researchers have forged the field of **lifespan developmental psychology,** which explores human development from the start of life to old age (Baltes, Staudinger, & Lindenberger, 1999). They did so, in part, in response to changes in the human population.

The human life span has lengthened considerably (see Figure 14.17 for U.S. data). In wealthy nations with modern medical care, people born today can expect to live twice as long as those born only a few generations ago. This increases the population of older adults.

figure **14.17**
Life expectancy in the United States People are living a lot longer than they used to. Except for a decline around 1918 (as a result of a flu pandemic, as well as casualties of World War I), life expectancy for women and men in the United States generally increased throughout the twentieth century (Wilmoth, 2000).

lifespan developmental psychology
The field of study that explores human psychological development from the start of life through old age.

Lifespan developmental psychology explores a segment of life that did not exist in the evolutionary past. For example, 40,000 years ago, typical humans lived only into their late 20s or early 30s (Wilmoth, 2000). Evolution thus could not shape psychological mechanisms for solving problems uniquely encountered by 70- and 80-year-olds (Baltes et al., 1999). This makes older adulthood unique with respect to psychology's nature–nurture questions (see Chapters 1 and 4). Nature does not provide psychological mechanisms that evolved to solve the unique problems of older adulthood. Yet, as you'll see, older adults are quite good at solving them.

Well-Being in Older Adulthood

Preview Question

> Do most people experience declines in well-being in older adulthood?

If you're young now, old age might sound depressing; you'll be slower, weaker, and grayer. Yet most older adults are not depressed about their age; their psychological well-being commonly is as high as that of younger persons (Baltes & Graf, 1996; Brandtstädter & Wentura, 1995). This is true despite the many significant challenges that older adults face (e.g., managing chronic health problems; Christensen et al., 2009). A 4-year-long study of adults ranging in age from their late 50s to early 80s found that the older participants reported physical declines but a level of personal contentment that matched younger persons (Rothermund & Brandtstädter, 2003). Older adults knew they were declining physically, but didn't seem to mind!

German psychologist Paul Baltes, whose research and theories provided critical foundations for the contemporary psychological study of lifespan development.

Max Planck Institute for Human Development, Berlin.

> **☙ WHAT DO YOU KNOW?...**

17. True or False?

Because of the significant challenges they face, older adults tend to be more depressed about their age than younger adults.

Goals, Strategies, and the SOC Model

Preview Question

> How do selection, optimization, and compensation contribute to successful psychological adjustment in older adulthood?

How do so many older adults maintain a sense of well-being? They prioritize. They determine what's important to them, devote time to that, and avoid wasting time on irrelevant tasks. This prioritization is described in the **selection, optimization, and compensation (SOC) model** of successful aging devised by Baltes and colleagues (Baltes, 1997; Freund, 2008; Freund & Baltes, 2002). They identify three psychological processes that promote positive personal development: selection, optimization and compensation.

1. **Selection** is the process of setting personal goals for a given period of your life. Older adults often narrow down their goals, focusing on fewer tasks than when they were younger. They "concentrate all . . . [their] energy on a few things" and "always focus on the one most important goal at a given time" (Freund & Baltes, 2002, pp. 661–662).

2. **Optimization** is the process of devising plans to achieve goals that have been set. People who optimize say they "keep working on what I have planned until I succeed" and that "when I choose a goal, I am also willing to invest effort in it" (Freund & Baltes, 2002, pp. 661–662).

3. **Compensation** is the identification of alternative strategies to achieve goals, if at first you don't succeed. Everyone experiences setbacks. But older adults, in particular, need compensation to adjust to setbacks caused by physical declines.

selection, optimization, and compensation (SOC) model A model of successful aging that identifies three psychological processes that promote positive personal development: selection, optimization, and compensation.

selection In the selection, optimization, and compensation (SOC) model of successful aging, the process of setting personal goals for a given period of your life.

optimization In the selection, optimization, and compensation (SOC) model of successful aging, the process of devising plans to achieve goals you set.

compensation In the selection, optimization, and compensation (SOC) model of successful aging, the identification of alternative strategies to achieve goals, if at first you don't succeed.

Strategies for successful aging
Pianist Arthur Rubinstein did not retire from stage performances until the age of 89. How did he keep playing for so long? He selected a small number of pieces to play, practiced them frequently to optimize his skill, and compensated for a loss in muscular speed by playing slow passages more slowly than he had in his youth (thus making the fast passages seem faster). These are the three strategies of Baltes's selection, optimization, and compensation model of successful adult aging.

A person taking medication on a regular schedule, for example, may compensate for memory declines by buying a calendar pill box.

These strategies are simple, yet successful. Older adults who are better at selection, optimization, and compensation experience more positive emotions, a higher sense of personal well-being, and a greater sense of purpose in life (Freund, 2008; Freund & Baltes, 2002).

The SOC model does not specify which goals an older adult should pursue, however. Its message is that in older adulthood, *whatever* you choose to do, you should avoid doing too many things at once; stick to goals once they are set; anticipate setbacks; and plan ways to compensate for them.

🐱 WHAT DO YOU KNOW?...

18. Match the process on the left with the statement that illustrates it on the right.

1. Selection	a. "Instead of giving just a few hours to many volunteer organizations, I'm going to give more time to the one that is most important to me."
2. Optimization	b. "I'm going to set a realistic goal of walking for 20 minutes a day, 4 days a week, to make it more likely that I'll exercise."
3. Compensation	c. "I'm going to set an alarm to remind me to do my physical therapy exercises so that I no longer forget to do them."

Motives and Socioemotional Selectivity Theory

Preview Question

❯ How does knowing you're at the end of your life affect how you want to spend your time?

Blissful grandparenthood
Research indicates that older adults show a strong preference for spending time on emotionally significant activities, such as playing with grandchildren.

No one knows what the future will bring. But if you're in your teens or early 20s, you do know that there's likely to be a lot of it; you can expect more than a half-century of future ahead of you. Older adults, however, know that more of life is behind them than ahead of them.

Socioemotional selectivity theory, developed by Laura Carstensen (1995, 2006), explains how perceptions of the amount of time remaining in life affect motivation. Young adults, knowing they have decades of life ahead, are motivated to pursue activities with long-term payoff: acquiring information and skills (which has long-term professional benefit) and engaging in activities that develop a firm sense of self and personal identity (which is a foundation for personal development later in life). Older adults, knowing they have fewer years remaining, are less attracted to activities with only long-term benefit. They prefer activities that are emotionally meaningful (e.g., spending time with family and close friends). Motives thus shift across the life course (Figure 14.18).

socioemotional selectivity theory
A lifespan developmental theory of motivational processes that explains how perceptions of the amount of time remaining in life affect motivation.

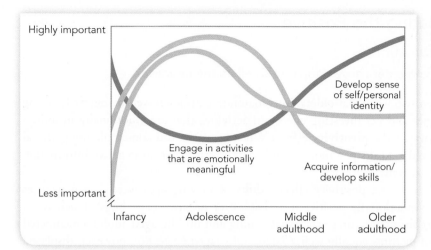

figure **14.18**
Socioemotional selectivity theory Carstensen's socioemotional selectivity theory predicts that the salience of social motives—that is, the relative importance of the motives to individuals—will change across the life span, due to people's awareness of the amount of time left in their life (Carstensen, 1995). The curves show shifts in three social motives: seeking information, developing self-concept, and regulating emotion in order to maintain an emotionally positive day-to-day life. In older adulthood, people are most motivated to experience social interactions—with family or longtime friends—that are emotionally meaningful to them.

Research confirms the theory's predictions. When choosing to spend free time with (1) a family member, (2) an author of a book recently read, or (3) an acquaintance with common interests, older adults, unlike younger adults, more frequently chose #1 (Fung, Carstensen, & Lutz, 1999). When shown advertisements, older adults preferred ones with emotion-based, rather than information-based, messages (Fung & Carstensen, 2003; Figure 14.19). These findings are consistent with socioemotional selectivity theory's prediction that older adults are more attracted to activities that are emotionally meaningful.

These research methods should sound familiar to you—they are the same ones you encountered in this chapter's Try This! activity. Your responses to the Try This! items may have differed from those of someone a few decades older than yourself— or from your own responses if you answer these same questions a few decades from now.

TRY THIS!

☻ WHAT DO YOU KNOW?...

19. According to socioemotional selectivity theory, what activities will be most motivating for older adults?

Bringing you closer to the people you love

Reach out and explore the world

Both: Lost Horizon Images / Getty Images

figure **14.19**
Advertising, age Researchers showed younger and older adults pairs of advertisements that highlighted a single product's benefits in two ways: its benefit to acquiring information about the unknown, or its benefit to maintaining a positive emotional life (Fung & Carstensen, 2003). Consistent with the prediction of socioemotional selectivity theory, older adults preferred advertisements such as the one on the left, which emphasizes an emotional appeal, to the one on the right, which highlights the knowledge gained from new experiences.

Accentuating the Positive

Preview Question

› Does getting older cause people to dwell on the negative?

You have seen two ways that older adults maintain emotional well-being: by (1) using SOC strategies and (2) investing energy in activities that are emotionally meaningful. A third way is the **positivity effect:** When recalling and contemplating personal experiences, older adults pay more attention to positive than to negative information (Mather & Carstensen, 2005).

In research on the positivity effect, adults of varying ages were shown pictures of two types: emotionally positive (e.g., babies) or negative (e.g., bugs). Later, when their memory for the pictures was tested, young and middle-aged adults remembered both kinds of pictures equally well. Older adults (aged 65 to 80), however, displayed a positivity effect: They had much better memory for the positive pictures (Charles, Mather, & Carstensen, 2003).

The positivity effect is also evident in neural activity. When people view emotionally positive and negative pictures, younger adults' brains respond equally to both picture types, but older adults' brains respond more strongly to positive than negative images (Mather et al., 2004).

Has evolution equipped humans with strategies, such as the positivity effect, that enhance well-being in older adulthood? That may sound plausible, but it is extremely unlikely. As noted earlier, principles of evolution seem incapable of explaining the present-day tendencies of older adults (Baltes, 1997). Rather, the explanation must involve older adults' strategies for making the most of the time that is left to them.

"Something's just not right—our air is clean, our water is pure, we all get plenty of exercise, everything we eat is organic and free-range, and yet nobody lives past thirty."

Alex Gregory The New Yorker Collection / The Cartoon Bank

😈 WHAT DO YOU KNOW?...

20. Two photos are presented to a group of young, middle-aged, and older adults: one depicting flowers and one depicting an overflowing garbage can. Which photo will older adults be more likely to remember? How will their memory for the photos compare to those of the young and middle-aged adults?

Moral Development

Is it OK to slingshot rocks at people and buildings if it's for a good cause? Why or why not? Psychologists ask research participants such questions in order to learn about their moral reasoning, that is, the way they think about problems having to do with personal responsibilities, rights, and obligations. The photo shows a protester in Egypt during the Arab Spring uprisings of 2011.

msheshtawy / Demotix / Corbis

Internet reports tell of a Chinese man whose girlfriend needed treatments for cancer that the couple could not afford. Desperate, the man stole money to pay for the treatment. He was caught and jailed for 4 years—but was allowed to leave jail to attend a wedding ceremony with his new wife, who now was terminally ill (stubear, 2010, November 18).

Was it wrong for the man to steal money to save the woman's life? Why or why not?

We ask this question not to determine the right answer but to note that there is no "right answer"—at least not in the same sense that there is a right answer to "What is 2 + 2?" or "Does the amount of water change when you pour it from a wide container into a narrow one?" The question about stealing money is not a factual question, but a moral question. The *moral domain*

positivity effect A phenomenon in which older adults pay more attention to positive information when recalling and contemplating personal experiences.

is a domain of reasoning that concerns personal rights, responsibilities, and obligations, especially with regard to the welfare of others. We'll conclude this chapter by examining *moral development,* that is, the development of thinking about the moral domain.

Moral Stages

Preview Question

> How do we develop our morality?

Psychologist Lawrence Kohlberg established key foundations for the study of moral development. Inspired by Piaget, Kohlberg suggested that moral development occurs in stages. A **moral stage** is a period of development during which a person's moral reasoning is consistently organized around a single way of thinking (Kohlberg & Hersh, 1977).

To identify moral stages, Kohlberg interviewed boys living in the Chicago area at 4-year intervals from childhood through young adulthood (Garz, 2009). He asked them questions such as the one above about stealing, and charted shifts in their moral thinking across time. Analysis of their responses led Kohlberg to propose three levels of moral thinking, each with two stages:

1. *Preconventional level:* Children's thinking is organized around ideas about rewards and punishments. In the first stage, "good" behavior consists of actions that avoid punishment. In the second stage, children recognize that actions that bring personal rewards also are good.

2. *Conventional level:* Children evaluate actions in terms of social conventions and norms. In the first stage of the conventional level, children assess whether behavior is consistent with being a "good girl" or "good boy." This is an advance over the preconventional level, in that the child recognizes that a behavior might be wrong even if it is not punished. At the second stage, children have a "law and order" orientation. They think about their duty to uphold rules established by authorities.

3. *Postconventional level:* Individuals can transcend the rules of authority figures and base their reasoning in abstract principles. At the first stage of the post-conventional level, people think about individual rights. They recognize that if laws laid down by authorities violate those rights, the laws should be changed to protect the individual. At the second postconventional stage, the most advanced level of moral reasoning in Kohlberg's system, people evaluate actions according to universal ethical principles such as justice and respect for the dignity of the individual.

According to Kohlberg, social experiences affect people's rate of progress through these stages and whether they ever reach the highest stage. Kohlberg called for moral education to increase the complexity of students' moral reasoning (Kohlberg & Hersh, 1977).

Kohlberg's work, although enormously influential, has been criticized, however. One criticism involves *domains* of reasoning. Kohlberg (like Piaget) assumed children would reason in a similar manner across different domains. But, evidence reveals domain specificity. For example, when thinking about the personal domain (i.e., actions that involve only oneself, such as hair style or food preferences), children employ principles involving personal choices and rights to privacy that are distinct to that domain (Nucci & Turiel, 2009).

A second criticism, which we will consider in detail after This Just In, involves gender.

Postconventional thinking The African National Congress rallies supporters for its Campaign of Defiance Against Unjust Laws. The campaign illustrates moral thinking at a postconventional level. In the 1950s, thousands began protesting against laws that oppressed Black South Africans. The protestors moved beyond the "law and order" orientation of conventional thinking to a higher level of moral reasoning that centered on universal principles of human rights. The campaign strengthened the African National Congress, which became South Africa's governing political party after the elimination of South Africa's apartheid system in the early 1990s (www.anc.org.za).

Photo by Jurgen Schadeberg / Hulton Archive / Getty Images

moral stage According to Kohlberg, a period of development during which a person's moral reasoning is consistently organized around a single way of thinking.

WHAT DO YOU KNOW?...

21. Match the level of moral thinking on the left with the statement that illustrates it on the right.

1. Preconventional	a. "I helped my mom with my little brother because my dad told me that's what a good sister does."
2. Conventional	b. "I volunteered for the animal shelter because I believe all creatures deserve to be treated with dignity."
3. Postconventional	c. "I stopped pulling the cat's tail because I didn't want to get punished."

THIS JUST IN

Moral Babies

Do babies think of behavior as being "right" or "wrong," "good" or "bad"? Kohlberg did not think so. As you learned, he said people did not achieve that type of thinking until the conventional level of moral development, which might not be reached until adolescence.

Research suggests, however, that babies are more moral than Kohlberg thought. Remarkable findings come from research in which babies 9 months of age and younger watched a puppet show (Hamlin & Wynn, 2011; Figure 14.20). In the show, one puppet tried to open a plastic box. Two other puppets either (1) helped the first to open the box or (2) jumped up and landed on the box's lid, slamming it closed. The researchers then showed the babies both puppets—the helpful one and the "mean" one that slammed the lid closed—to see which they preferred. The one they reached for was presumed to be the puppet they preferred. There were three possible findings:

Both: Kiley Hamlin

figure **14.20**

Good dog, bad dog In research by Hamlin and Wynn (2011), infants watched a puppet show in which a dog either helped another animal open a box (left photo) or interfered with an animal's attempt to open a box by jumping up and landing on the box's lid, slamming it closed (right photo). After seeing the show, children liked the helpful dog more than the other dog. This means that the infants could tell the difference between good and bad social behavior—and preferred the good.

1. *No preference.* The infants might have had no understanding of the moral content of the puppet show (i.e., the fact that one puppet's actions were "good" and the other's "bad"), and thus have shown no preference for one or the other puppet.

2. *Prefer the "mean" puppet.* The mean puppet was active and powerful; it jumped up in the air and slammed the lid. Babies might be attracted to action and power.

3. *Prefer the "good" puppet.* If babies understand good and bad behavior, they would prefer the helpful puppet, that is, the one whose actions were morally good.

Results confirmed possibility #3: Babies preferred the "good" puppet. Nearly 75% of them reached out to touch the puppet that, in the show, had been helpful. This means that babies are aware of good and bad behavior—and prefer the good (Hamlin & Wynn, 2011; also see Hamlin, Wynn, & Bloom, 2007). More recent research provides further evidence that babies less than 1 year old evaluate whether social actors are helping or hindering another individual (Hamlin et al., 2013). In sum, results suggest that, even in infancy, the way people treat others is "fundamental to perceiving the social world" (Hamlin & Wynn, 2011, p. 30).

✿ WHAT DO YOU KNOW?•••

22. The following statement is incorrect. Explain why: "In one study, infants preferred puppets that were mean yet powerful over puppets that were helpful, suggesting that they are attracted to action and power."

Gender and Moral Thinking

Preview Question

> How does women's moral reasoning differ from men's?

You may have noticed something unusual about Kohlberg's research, reviewed earlier: All the participants were male. The psychologist and feminist scholar Carol Gilligan (1977) noticed this and something more: None of the questions Kohlberg posed to participants dealt specifically with concerns unique to women's lives. Furthermore, the style of moral thinking Kohlberg deemed most advanced—reasoning according to universal principles—may be preferred by men more than women. Kohlberg's work, Gilligan concluded, was gender-biased; its procedures favored one gender (male) over the other.

Gilligan (1977) suggested that women's moral reasoning differs from men's. Women, she proposed, focus on personal relationships rather than abstract principles. They value obligations to others and try to solve problems without hurting others physically or psychologically.

In research, Gilligan posed moral questions pertinent to women's lives (e.g., questions about pregnancy and a prospective abortion). She found that women progress through moral stages distinct from the ones identified by Kohlberg in research with men. The highest stage for women, Gilligan found, involved reasoning according to a principle of nonviolence; rather than adhering to abstract principles of justice, women adhered to the concrete human principle of not harming others (Gilligan, 1977).

Gilligan's critique of Kohlberg's research was powerful. But research conducted after she formulated her approach indicates that gender differences in moral reasoning are smaller than she expected. A meta-analysis of research on moral reasoning revealed that women do pay more attention to the care of others and men attend more to universal principles of justice. Yet the gender differences were small—so small that the findings did not support Gilligan's claim that women's and men's moral thinking differs fundamentally (Jaffee & Hyde, 2000).

This result, in which men and women were more similar than many anticipated, is not unusual. In many aspects of cognitive and social development, gender differences are smaller than people expect (Hyde, 2005). The relative lack of differences is important. Scientific findings do not support social stereotypes about stark differences between men's and women's tendencies and potentials. Instead, they are consistent with the idea that society should give all people, of both genders, equal opportunities for personal and professional success.

✿ WHAT DO YOU KNOW?...

23. Carol Gilligan argued that because all of Kohlberg's research participants were _____ , his procedures were biased in their favor. In her research, she found that women's highest moral stage was characterized by a principle of _____ and obligation to others, rather than adherence to abstract values of _____ . A later meta-analysis supported this sex difference, but indicated that it was much _____ than Gilligan would have predicted.

⟳ Looking Back and Looking Ahead

Developmental psychology is home to many of psychological science's greatest discoveries: remarkable changes in children's thought identified by Piaget; thinking capacities of infants that even Piaget had underestimated; the human aptitude for resilience in the face of hardship and setbacks; the ability of older adults to maintain psychological well-being despite the challenges of aging. In recent years, these findings, uncovered in research conducted at *person* and *mind* levels of analysis, have been complemented by brain research that deepens our understanding of the developing individual.

These discoveries answer questions that often go unresolved in other branches of the field. Adults possess complex concepts and problem-solving abilities (Chapter 8 on thinking, language, and intelligence)—but where did those concepts and abilities come from? Adults differ from one another in emotional styles and beliefs about the self (Chapter 13 on personality)—but how did those differences develop? Adults possess complexly interconnected neural networks in their brains (Chapter 3 on the brain and the nervous system)—but how did those connections form? Lessons from developmental psychology complement material in other chapters of this book by answering questions you might not even have thought about when reading them.

Chapter Review

Now that you have completed this chapter, be sure to turn to Appendix B, where you will find a **Chapter Summary** that is useful for reviewing what you have learned about development.

Key Terms

accommodation (p. 604)
adolescence (p. 635)
anxious-ambivalent attachment (p. 623)
assimilation (p. 604)
attachment (p. 623)
attachment styles (p. 623)
attachment theory (p. 623)
autism (p. 611)
avoidant attachment (p. 623)
biopsychosocial model (p. 637)
cognitive control (p. 634)
cognitive development (p. 602)
compensation (p. 643)
concrete operational stage (p. 606)
conservation (p. 606)
critical period (p. 622)
developmental psychology (p. 602)
developmental stage (p. 605)
differentiated self-esteem (p. 633)
direct sibling effects (p. 628)
emerging adulthood (p. 640)

ethnic identity (p. 638)
foreclosure (p. 637)
formal operational stage (p. 606)
global self-esteem (p. 633)
identity (p. 637)
identity achievement (p. 637)
identity diffusion (p. 637)
identity statuses (p. 637)
imprinting (p. 622)
indirect sibling effects (p. 628)
inhibited temperament (p. 620)
life story (p. 641)
lifespan developmental psychology (p. 642)
moral development (p. 602)
moral stage (p. 647)
moratorium (p. 638)
object permanence (p. 605)
operation (p. 604)
optimization (p. 643)
positivity effect (p. 646)

preoperational stage (p. 605)
prosocial behavior (p. 638)
puberty (p. 635)
resilience (p. 624)
schema (p. 603)
secure attachment (p. 623)
selection (p. 643)
selection, optimization, and compensation (SOC) model (p. 643)
self-control (p. 633)
self-esteem (p. 633)
self-representations (p. 632)
sensorimotor stage (p. 605)
social development (p. 602)
socioemotional selectivity theory (p. 644)
strange situation paradigm (p. 624)
temperament (p. 618)
temperament dimension (p. 619)
theory of mind (p. 611)
uninhibited temperament (p. 620)
zone of proximal development (p. 612)

Questions for Discussion

1. Characterize the schema of a child at the preoperational stage of development who cannot yet solve the conservation problem. What kind of experience might cause him or her to need to accommodate this schema? [Analyze]

2. Identify a novel situation you recently encountered—perhaps you met a new acquaintance or started a new job. How did you respond to this novelty? According to research by Jerome Kagan, your temperament might help explain your behavior. Ask a parent or caregiver whether he or she would characterize you as having had an inhibited or uninhibited temperament as a child, then reflect on whether this provides insight into your current personality. [Apply]

3. Which attachment style best characterizes you? Are you securely attached? Avoidant? Anxious-ambivalent? Reflect on how your attachment style manifests itself in your friendships and, if applicable, your romantic relationships. [Apply]

4. Parenting magazines are filled with advice on how to raise children. Think back to the text's discussion of the *systems* view of families and of research demonstrating the interactive effect of parenting styles and child temperaments on antisocial behavior. Write a letter to the editor of one of these magazines, outlining your recommendations. [Synthesize]

5. Where are you in Dalton Conley's *pecking order*? How can his theory of how the allocation of family funds affects personality development help you understand your experiences growing up? [Apply]

6. The text describes research on mice that were raised in environments that varied in their enrichment and research on students in the Perry Preschool Study who were provided enriched educational experiences. Review the results of these studies and discuss how they complement each other. How might they illustrate the way in which research at the brain level complements research at the mind level? [Analyze, Synthesize]

Chapter Review

7. James Marcia identifies four different identity statuses to describe how people cope with the challenge of establishing a personal identity. To which of these statuses do you belong? Where would you like to be and what issues will you need to consider to get there? [Apply]

8. Review the section on midlife development and on life stories. What will your *life story* look like? Will it include themes of *generativity* and *redemption*? [Comprehend]

9. Think about how your grandparents or other older relatives approach life. Do you see evidence that they are engaging in *selection*, *optimization*, and *compensation*? How can socioemotional selectivity theory explain how their priorities differ from yours? [Analyze]

10. You learned that at the first stage of the postconventional level of Kohlberg's moral development, people recognize that if laws violate human rights, they should be changed. What are some examples of laws that you believe should be changed because they violate human rights? [Comprehend]

Self-Test

1. Five-year-old Brandi's *sharing* schema led her to walk up and down the aisle of the train, offering sticks of gum to strangers. Her mother dragged her back to her seat and angrily explained that there are some circumstances under which it is not okay to share. In this example, the environmental feedback from her mother led to
   a. assimilation.
   b. accommodation.
   c. object permanence.
   d. conservation.

2. The "concrete" in the concrete operational stage of development refers to
   a. actual objects.
   b. animate objects.
   c. inanimate objects.
   d. hypothetical objects.

3. Which of the following behaviors violates what Piaget would have predicted?
   a. A child in the preoperational stage watches someone pour water from a low, squat pitcher into a tall, thin pitcher and claims that the second pitcher holds more water.
   b. A child in the concrete operational stage can solve basic computational problems (e.g., 3 + 4 = 7) but has trouble with algebra because it involves abstract concepts.
   c. A child in the sensorimotor stage of development seems surprised when the string attached to the pull-toy he wants falls off with the slightest tug.
   d. A child early in the sensorimotor stage appears to believe that a doll no longer exists when a blanket is thrown over it.

4. Which of the following does not accurately compare Piaget's and Vygotsky's theories of development?
   a. According to Vygotsky, Piaget's theory ignored social and cultural factors that influence development.
   b. Unlike Piaget, Vygotsky thought that children should be characterized according to both their current and potential levels of development.

   c. Piaget and Vygotsky both believed that children possess innate input analyzers, biologically inherited mental mechanisms that help them think.
   d. Piaget's theory characterizes development as something that happens as an individual process, whereas Vygotsky characterizes it as a socially embedded process.

5. Alfred and Brian are identical twins who were raised separately. Alfred was raised in an enriched environment that gave him access to the arts, music, sports, and other activities. Brian's environment was much less enriched. He lived in an impoverished area and didn't have access to the kinds of activities Alfred did. How has this difference in environments likely affected their brains?
   a. Alfred's cerebral cortex is thinner.
   b. Alfred's brain cells are more highly connected with each other.
   c. Alfred's brain cells are covered by less myelin.
   d. Alfred's and Brian's brains do not differ from each other.

6. Given what is known about each of Piaget's stages of development and of brain development, what area of the brain would be expected to develop first?
   a. Parietal cortex
   b. Prefrontal cortex
   c. Temporal cortex
   d. Sensorimotor cortex

7. Which of the following is true of temperament?
   a. It is inherited, shows remarkable stability across time, and cannot change.
   b. It is inherited, and though it tends to be stable across time, it can change.
   c. It is not inherited, but once acquired, it tends to be stable across time.
   d. It is not inherited, and once acquired, it tends to change quite a bit across time.

8. Parental attachment shapes our expectations for future relationships. What do individuals with an avoidant attachment style tend to expect from others?
   a. That they cannot be relied on as a source of security and comfort.
   b. That they can be relied on to provide security, but not comfort.
   c. That they can be relied on to provide too much security and comfort.
   d. That they can be relied on as a source of security and comfort.

9. Siblings affect our development directly and indirectly. Which of the following is an example of an indirect effect of a sibling on development?
   a. An older brother explains to his sister how to figure out who can be trusted.
   b. A pitcher's speed increases as a result of doing pitching drills with his brother.
   c. A smart sibling is sent to private school while her sister attends public school.
   d. A sibling takes her brother's advice to sing a happy song whenever she feels blue.

10. What did the results of the experiment conducted at Perry Preschool demonstrate regarding the protective effects of preschool interventions on development among those low in socioeconomic status?
   a. This experiment is still in progress, so we do not yet know the effects of such interventions.
   b. Enriched high-quality education programs can have long-lasting effects, including higher graduation rates.
   c. The effects of enriched high-quality education programs are too short-lived to justify the costs.
   d. The effects of enriched high-quality education programs are too small to justify the costs.

11. Which of the following factors has been shown to have little to no influence on self-esteem?
   a. Adoption
   b. Temperament
   c. Acceptance by parents
   d. Parental discipline style

12. Which of the following is a feature of Magnusson's findings on the effect of early biological maturation on antisocial behavior that supports a biopsychosocial model?
   a. The effect of early maturation was the same for all girls.
   b. There was no effect of early maturation on antisocial behavior.
   c. The effect of girls' early maturation on antisocial behavior depended on how puberty was measured.
   d. The effect of girls' early maturation depended on whether they hung out with older peers.

13. "I just started college last semester and right away, I started getting pressured by my mom to declare a major. She wants me to major in business, but I want to major in psychology because, after thinking about it a lot, I really believe I can make a difference in people's lives after studying it. The whole ordeal has me so mixed up and anxious that right now, I've kind of given up and I'm just taking my required classes 'til I can figure things out." Which of Marcia's identity statuses is exemplified by this student's lament?
   a. Identity achievement
   b. Foreclosure
   c. Identity diffusion
   d. Moratorium

14. According to socioemotional selectivity theory, which of the following options will be most attractive to an older adult?
   a. Working out with a personal trainer who specializes in older populations
   b. Having lunch with a professor with a PhD in mathematics
   c. Attending a talk by a renowned physicist
   d. Spending the day with grandchildren

15. Rafael was enraged to find that his sister hadn't been punished for sneaking cookies into bed with her. At what moral stage is he according to Kohlberg?
   a. Preconventional level
   b. Periconventional level
   c. Conventional level
   d. Postconventional level

Answers

You can check your answers to the preceding Self-Test and the chapter's What Do You Know? questions in Appendix B.

Psychological Disorders I: Anxiety and Mood Disorders

15

HICH OF THE FOLLOWING PEOPLE SOUND TO YOU as if they have a mental disorder? Which, in other words, show signs of mental illness?

> A girl, aged 14, is continually anxious. "Each and every day [of my life] is filled with tension. Expectation and hope generate tension, as does fear—for example, [of] a noise inside or outside the house." In addition to the constant anxiety, the girl's behavior toward her father is odd for a teenager: "I crawl into Father's bed every night for comfort."

> In public, in front of a group of people, a man starts babbling. His word-like sounds are incomprehensible not only to the crowd, but also to himself. "Aish nay gum nay tayo . . . aish nay gum . . . aish nay . . . anna gayna . . . ayna ganna keena . . . kayna geen anna gaymanna naymanna." He continues like this for a few minutes, then starts crying.

> A political activist aims to improve the welfare of patients hospitalized for the treatment of severe mental illness. She investigates conditions at the hospitals and finds that many patients have been mistreated. Some have been abused sexually. Hospitalized children who misbehave have been punished with electric shocks. She writes a newspaper article alerting the public to these unethical practices.

You'll learn more about these three people in the chapter ahead, which introduces the study of psychological disorders. As you'll see, psychologists studying disorders face numerous challenges. One is to develop effective treatments for people who experience the disorders. Another is to figure out exactly who has a mental disorder in the first place. ◉

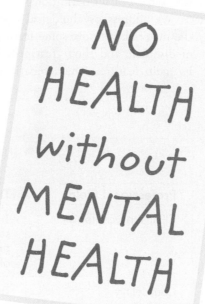

Image Source / Getty Images

Amani Willett / Gallery Stock
This woman does not have a mental disorder.

WHAT DO PSYCHOLOGISTS do for a living? As you saw in Chapter 1, we're "all over the map." Some study the brain's neural networks. Others study people's social networks. Some try to understand genes. Others try to comprehend cultures. Some work with adult humans and others with newborn animals. It may seem that no central goal motivates the majority of psychologists.

That perception, however, is not accurate. Consider these numbers from the United States Bureau of Labor Statistics. Of the approximately 190,000 people in the United States employed as psychologists, more than 60% work in clinical or counseling psychology—fields where the primary goal is to reduce psychological distress. Tens of thousands more work as school psychologists, where job duties include helping students overcome behavioral and emotional problems.

Thus, there is a central goal that motivates the work of most psychologists: reducing psychological distress, thereby improving mental health. Psychologists try to benefit mental health by treating **psychological disorders,** which are prolonged experiences of psychological distress or poor psychological functioning that interfere with a person's everyday life. Psychological disorders are often called *mental disorders;* we'll use the terms interchangeably. They also have been called *mental illnesses* (a controversial term, as we discuss later). The study of psychological disorders is called *psychopathology.* Because the disordered psychological experiences are atypical or "abnormal," the branch of psychology that studies and treats them is often called *abnormal psychology.* A variety of professionals treat psychological disorders, including **clinical psychologists, counseling psychologists, psychiatrists,** and social workers (see Table 15.1 for definitions).

We address psychological disorders in this chapter and the next. To preview the material, we note some features of our coverage. A key feature is that coverage of disorders and their treatment is integrated. For any given disorder, we present its main features (characteristic experiences of individuals with the disorder and

psychological disorders Prolonged experiences of psychological distress or poor psychological functioning that interfere with a person's everyday life; mental disorders.

clinical psychologists Professionals trained not only in principles of psychological science, but also in the application of those principles to the diagnosis of, and provision of therapy for, psychological disorders.

counseling psychologists Professionals whose training and professional activities are similar to those of clinical psychologists, but with particular emphasis on the provision of advice regarding not only mental health, but also personal and vocational development.

psychiatrists Physicians trained in the diagnosis and treatment of mental disorders, with particular emphasis on the biological basis of disorders and the use of drugs to combat them.

table **15.1**

Some of the Professionals Who Treat Psychological Disorders	
Professional Field	**Training and Emphasis**
Clinical psychologist	Trained not only in principles of psychological science, but also in the application of those principles to the diagnosis of, and provision of therapy for, psychological disorders
Counseling psychologist	Training and professional activities similar to those of clinical psychology, but with particular emphasis on the provision of advice (regarding not only mental health, but also personal and vocational development)
Psychiatrist	Physician trained in the diagnosis and treatment of mental disorders, with particular emphasis on the biological basis of disorders and the use of drugs to combat them
Social worker	Trained in the provision of counseling and therapy, with particular emphasis on environmental factors (social and community contexts) that impact individual well-being

diagnostic categories for classifying those experiences) and then review therapies designed to treat that disorder. You thus will see how contemporary psychologists devise therapies designed to alleviate specific types of psychological distress (Nathan & Gorman, 2007).

This integration of disorders and their treatment occurs consistently throughout Chapters 15 and 16. Here, in Chapter 15, we focus our attention on two classes of psychological disorder that are particularly prevalent: those involving (1) anxiety and (2) depression. In Chapter 16, we explore the nature of, and treatment for, disorders that are somewhat less common yet that affect the brain, the mind, and people's lives in a particularly profound and enduring manner: schizophrenia, personality disorders, and dissociative disorders.

Before learning about individual disorders and their treatment, however, you need to know (1) what "counts" as a disorder (i.e., psychologists' methods for determining whether people have a psychological disorder) and (2) the overall options available for treating disorders (i.e., the available strategies for meeting the challenge of reducing psychological distress). We therefore begin with an overview of psychological disorders and therapies.

Psychological Disorders

Mental disorders have been part of the human experience for as long as there have been humans. In the ancient world, people believed disorders were caused by evil spirits. Treatments reflected this belief. In ancient Egypt, for example, people with mental disorders were taken to temples, where animal sacrifices were performed to appease the gods (Kellogg, 1897). Many cultures have used magical amulets (jewelry thought to have mystical power) to drive away evil spirits (Coury, 1967; Millon, Grossman, & Meagher, 2004). A surgical procedure called trephination, in which a hole is cut in the skull (presumably to let evil spirits escape), was used to treat mental disorders as early as 3500 years ago (Mashour, Walker, & Martuza, 2005).

Modern science, of course, rejects the idea that supernatural forces cause mental disorders. A leading candidate to replace this perspective is a natural-science viewpoint, the "medical model" of psychological disorders.

The Medical Model of Psychological Disorders

Preview Questions

> Do we diagnose and treat psychological disorders in the same way as we do physical illness?
> What are the advantages and disadvantages of focusing on the internal causes of psychological illness?

The **medical model of psychological disorders** is a framework for thinking about causes of, and treatments for, disorders. Although different people use the term "medical model" in slightly different ways (Shah & Mountain, 2007), the general assumption is that psychological disorders are similar to physical illnesses. To understand the medical model of psychological disorders, then, let's first consider how professionals think about physical illnesses.

When diagnosing and treating physical illnesses, physicians distinguish symptoms from their underlying causes. If you experience fatigue, fever, or a sore throat, these are symptoms. Your doctor tries to diagnose their underlying biological cause (e.g., a bacterial infection). Once a diagnosis is determined, treatment targets the cause, not just the symptoms (e.g., your doctor gives you an antibiotic to fight the infection, not an energy drink to fight the fatigue).

The Extraction of the Stone of Madness, 1475-1480 (oil on panel), Bosch, Hieronymus (c.1450-1516) / Prado, Madrid, Spain / Mondadori Portfolio / Electa / Remo Bardazzi / The Bridgeman Art Library

The psychological disorder must be in there somewhere Numerous cultures have, in the past, tried to relieve psychological disorders through trephination, a surgical procedure in which a hole is cut in the skull. The scene is from the painting *The Extraction of the Stone of Madness,* by the Dutch artist Hieronymus Bosch.

medical model of psychological disorders Framework for thinking about the causes of, and treatments for, psychological disorders in a way that mimics thinking about physical illnesses.

In the medical model of psychological disorders, psychological experiences (e.g., prolonged, intense feelings of anxiety or depression) are seen as symptoms. A psychologist or psychiatrist who adopts the medical model looks for the symptoms' underlying cause (Elkins, 2009). The cause might be conceptualized at a psychological level of analysis (e.g., a troubling memory or belief) or at a biological level (e.g., abnormal brain functioning). Therapists then treat the underlying cause; for example, they might prescribe a medication designed to alter brain functioning in a way that alleviates a person's depression.

Many mental health professionals embrace the medical model of psychological disorders (Elkins, 2009; also see Nesse & Stein, 2012; Shah & Mountain, 2007). However, many others question it. The medical model has both advantages and disadvantages.

Belgian cage In the past, people with mental disorders were treated in ways that today seem inhumane. Shown is the "Belgian cage," which was used to confine mental patients until the practice was outlawed by the government of Belgium in 1850 (Letchworth, 1889).

ADVANTAGES OF THE MEDICAL MODEL. One big advantage is that the medical model has promoted the ethical treatment of people suffering from severe mental illness. This advantage is stark if you compare current society to earlier history, before the medical model was formulated.

In Europe hundreds of years ago, mental disorders were seen as a personal moral failing—a sign that the devil was at work in a person's soul. People with disorders thus were seen as "demonic" and were punished (Laffey, 2003).

The medical model opened the door to more humane care. Once psychological disorders were viewed as illnesses rather than evils, society pursued treatment rather than punishment.

A second advantage is that the medical model ushered in the modern era of drug therapies. Once it was recognized that mental disturbances could have biological causes, research sought drugs to alter the problematic biology. As you will see in this chapter and the next, drug therapies have greatly benefited individuals suffering from some types of psychological disorder.

DISADVANTAGES OF THE MEDICAL MODEL. So what are the medical model's drawbacks? One was first identified in the 1960s by psychiatrist Thomas Szasz (1960, 2011) and sociologist Erving Goffman (1961; see Mac Suibhne, 2011): The medical model can detrimentally affect psychologists' and psychiatrists' views of their patients. The effect is based on the term, or "label," the medical model uses to describe people who suffer from psychological distress.

In the medical model, people experiencing psychological distress are said to be mentally "ill." The label "ill" (or "illness") can change the way therapists—and society at large—think of these individuals. People labeled as "ill" may be thought of as less mentally competent than others (because illnesses generally weaken people, lowering their capabilities). In particular, people labeled as mentally ill may be seen as incompetent to make decisions about their own care. If so, procedures may be performed on them "for their own good," whether they want the procedures or not. This is a substantial drawback. It may cause patients to be viewed as "object[s]" (Goffman, 1961, p. 344) rather than as capable, intelligent human beings with the ability, and right, to make decisions about their own care. In its efforts to help people, the medical model might inadvertently dehumanize them instead.

When have you been assigned a label that influenced others' treatment of you?

A second potential drawback of the medical model concerns the search for the causes of mental disorders. The medical model directs professionals' attention to causes "inside the head" of the patient: inner illnesses that explain observed symptoms. The drawback is that looking "inside" may distract attention from important causes "outside" in the environment. Life stress, interpersonal relationships, and other social and environmental factors may be the root causes of many people's distress and thus the appropriate targets of interventions to improve mental health.

These drawbacks motivate alternatives to the medical model. Rather than searching for a specific mental illness inside the person, some therapists try to understand the person as a whole and the social world in which he or she lives (Barker, 2004). They avoid calling people "mentally ill" or "patients" because those terms make people sound sickly and incompetent. Instead, they refer to distressed individuals as their *clients* (Rogers, 1951) or, simply, as *persons* (Tudor & Worrall, 2006). Humanistic therapy, discussed below, is one prominent approach that rejects the medical model.

🌐 WHAT DO YOU KNOW?...

1. The following statement is incorrect. Explain why: "An advantage of the medical model of psychological disorders is that it encourages an examination of both internal and external causes of symptoms."

See Appendix B for answers to What Do You Know? questions.

What "Counts" as a Psychological Disorder?

Practicing psychologists face the question you encountered in this chapter's opening: Who is, and is not, suffering from a psychological disorder? Many people feel sad or anxious. Many display behavior that's "quirky." Are they all suffering from a mental disorder?

In principle, the definition of "psychological disorders"—prolonged experiences of unusual psychological distress or poor psychological functioning—might seem to answer this question. But the definition leaves some significant questions unanswered: How prolonged? How unusual? What level of distress? Who judges that functioning is "poor"? Essentially, what "counts" as a psychological disorder?

That question has no simple answer. There are no sharp boundaries of "normality" and "abnormality" (McNally, 2011). Even highly unusual behavior may not signal a psychological disorder. To see this, let's return to the three cases in the chapter opening: the anxious girl, babbling man, and political activist working to improve the welfare of hospitalized patients.

Psychological Disorder or Normal Reaction to the Environment?

Preview Question

> What caution must we exercise when evaluating unusual behavior?

What did you think of the people described in the opening of this chapter? The girl seemed weird: constantly anxious and jumping into her father's bed every night. The man seemed weirder: babbling incoherently and breaking into tears. The woman, though, seemed quite normal: working diligently to benefit people in need. Now let's learn more about them.

The anxious teenager is Anne Frank, a Jewish girl living in Amsterdam when it was occupied by Nazi Germany during World War II. The Frank family needed to hide from the Nazis; if found, they would be arrested and likely killed. (Ultimately, this is exactly what happened; Anne Frank died in a Nazi concentration camp.) The Franks went into seclusion, hiding for years in a secret apartment hidden behind an office. Throughout this period, the family lived under constant threat of detection. No wonder she was so anxious! As her remarkable diary (Frank, 1952) shows, Anne Frank was not psychologically disordered. Her extreme anxiety was a perfectly normal reaction to an extremely disordered environment. The problem lay not in Anne Frank, but in the war-torn world in which she lived.

John Elk / Getty Images

Is this "normal" behavior? Behavior that is indicative of a psychological disorder in some social and cultural contexts is perfectly normal, and thus not indicative of a disorder, in others. For example, in many contexts, intentionally injuring oneself physically is a sign of a psychological disorder. However, in the context shown here, it is not. Some adherents of Islam willingly harm themselves on the holy day of Ashura, as a way of commemorating an event in the early history of the religion. In general, claims that a given behavior reveals a disorder must be made carefully, with attention paid to the social, cultural, and historical context in which the behavior occurs.

> We have for too long been taught that the sight of a man speaking to himself is a sign of eccentricity or madness.
>
> —Teju Cole (2011, p. 5)

© Vova Pomortzeff / Demotix / Corbis

Is it "crazy" to disagree with the government? In 1968 the poet Natalya Gorbanevskaya protested actions of her country's government (an invasion of Czechoslovakia by the armed forces of the Soviet Union) and published a newsletter to promote human rights. In response, a Soviet court judged her to be mentally unstable. She was confined to a mental hospital for three years. As another Soviet writer put it, "If one does not think along the prescribed lines, they say, 'You are not normal'" (G. v. D., 1970).

The babbling man is a Pentecostal Christian (Higley, 2007). Pentecostals believe in the power of speaking in tongues, an ability that they trace back to a New Testament event in which the Holy Spirit gave the Disciples of Christ the power to speak in multiple languages (Macchia, 2006). To Pentecostals, the man's speaking is perfectly normal—not crazy babbling, but a meaningful gift from God. His crying was normal, too: an expected emotional reaction to a profoundly moving religious event.

In both cases, Anne Frank and the Pentecostal, social context is critical. The behavior seems "weird." You might think the person is "crazy." But when you understand the context in which the person lives, you recognize that the behavior was a normal response to a situation with which you were unfamiliar.

> What is a behavior that you engaged in today that, out of context, might appear unusual?

What about the third case from the chapter opening, that of the political activist? She seemed normal. Yet, soon after her newspaper article appeared, government officials "forcibly detained [her] in a psychiatric clinic" (Gee, 2007). The government ran the hospitals she investigated, reportedly felt threatened by her article, and responded to the threat by labeling her "mentally ill." Her case is not unique. Soon after, Russian government officials labeled a political protestor a "confused and paranoid lunatic" and, similarly, confined him to a mental hospital (Holdsworth, 2008). Doctors claimed that when he was hauled away to the insane asylum, he seemed "stressed . . . suspicious of others, argumentative and confused."

"It's hardly surprising I seemed like that," the man later noted, "given the circumstances" (Holdsworth, 2008).

Such cases raise a critical question: *Who judges* that a person is mental ill? People in society differ enormously in power, that is, their degree of influence over social events and others' lives. Typically, people with greater power judge the mental health or illness of people with less power (Foucault, 1965). Government officials can call protesters "mentally ill" and, in some countries, send them to asylums. Protestors can't do the same to government officials.

Social and historical factors also affect judgments about mental illness. Behavior that seems normal in one time period can seem abnormal in another. For instance, modern professionals do *not* view any sexual orientation as disordered—yet a half-century ago, they did. In the 1950s and 1960s, psychiatrists classified homosexuality as a mental illness. Millions of people, merely as a result of their sexual orientation, were said to have a mental disorder. It was not until the early 1970s that psychiatrists changed their stance, voting to drop homosexuality from the list of mental illnesses (McNally, 2011).

As these examples make clear, claims that a person is mentally ill must be made cautiously. Sometimes unusual behavior reflects unusual life circumstances. Behavior that appears abnormal in one social or historical setting may seem completely normal in another.

🌐 WHAT DO YOU KNOW?...

2. A careful consideration of whether to classify someone as having a mental illness must take into account the _____ in which the unusual behavior occurs.

Classifying Disorders

Preview Questions

> What is the major tool mental health professionals use to diagnose and classify psychological problems?

> What are some criticisms of the major tool mental health professionals use to diagnose and classify psychological problems?

Despite these cautions, there is no question that millions of people the world over suffer from serious psychological disorders. A first step in helping them is to diagnose their disorders, that is, to classify them as being of a certain type. Just as physicians diagnose and classify physical problems as a first step in formulating medical treatment, mental health professionals diagnose and classify psychological problems as a first step in formulating therapy.

THE DIAGNOSTIC AND STATISTICAL MANUAL (DSM). The tool that psychologists use to classify disorders is a book: the ***Diagnostic and Statistical Manual of Mental Disorders,*** or **DSM.** The DSM comprehensively lists and organizes the mental disorders identified by health care professionals. Each listing specifies behavioral and emotional responses a person must experience to be classified as having the given disorder. Here's an example.

Imagine you're a clinical psychologist whose client says that she's extraordinarily anxious in social settings and that the anxiety is disrupting her life. If you open your copy of the DSM, you'll find a relevant diagnostic category: *Social Anxiety Disorder.* Furthermore, you'll find specific criteria for determining whether your client's condition qualifies as a case of this disorder. The DSM criteria for Social Anxiety Disorder include the following (American Psychiatric Association, 2013):

> High levels of fear about social situations that involve scrutiny by others, including fear of seeming anxious and being humiliated.

> These situations induce such fear consistently.

> The person avoids the situations or finds them extremely difficult to endure.

> The person has experienced these feelings typically for six months or more, and they cause significant distress or interfere with daily functioning.

> The fear is extreme in comparison to the actual danger posed in the situation.

You would then talk to the client; assess the frequency, severity, and duration of her anxiety; and use that information to determine whether she qualifies as having the disorder. The DSM includes guidelines of this sort for each of an enormous variety of disorders, including all the disorders mentioned in this chapter and the next.

DSM-5 The recently revised *Diagnostic and Statistical Manual of Mental Disorders*, the DSM, is the most widely used system for identifying and classifying psychological disorders.

Macmillan Education Archive

Diagnostic and Statistical Manual of Mental Disorders (DSM) Reference book that comprehensively lists and classifies mental disorders, specifying diagnostic criteria.

When diagnosing clients using the DSM, therapists recognize that any given client could have more than one disorder; psychological disorders often are *comorbid*. **Comorbidity** refers to the presence of symptoms of two or more disorders in any one individual (Kessler et al., 1994). Comorbidity can occur for a number of reasons. A biological factor (e.g., a genetic predisposition) could contribute to more than one disorder. One disorder may trigger another; for example, a person may become depressed about her persistent social anxiety. Alternatively, comorbidity can occur simply because disorders overlap; that is, some psychological experiences are, according to the DSM, symptoms of more than one disorder (Cramer et al., 2010).

THE DSM: NOBODY'S PERFECT. The DSM is the most influential book in the field of mental health. Its diagnostic categories provide therapists, researchers, drug companies, insurance companies, and government agencies with a common language for identifying and communicating about mental disorders. Many countries outside the United States use a different diagnostic system, the *International Classification of Disorders*, or *ICD*; however, the ICD's content has been shaped significantly by the categorization system of the DSM (APA Monitor, 2009), thus extending the DSM's influence. Given the widespread use of the DSM's diagnostic categories, it is important to examine them critically. Three points stand out:

1. *The DSM's diagnostic categories change.* The DSM has evolved across five editions (the first in 1952 and the fifth, **DSM-5,** in 2013; Blashfield et al., 2014). In this evolution, its content has changed substantially. Newer editions list more disorders than do earlier editions, while also discarding some diagnostic categories that had been used previously.

   How could the classifications of mental disorders change so much? Did science discover new disorders and find that some old ones no longer exist?
   The DSM's categories are only partly grounded in scientific research. They also rest on professional opinion; health care professionals meet and debate the book's contents. Professional opinions change, reflecting both scientific findings and shifting social trends (as we saw with homosexuality). The categories thus change from one DSM edition to the next. Ideally, the manual's categories would be grounded more thoroughly in scientific findings.

2. *DSM categories are descriptions, not causes.* When diagnosing physical disorders, physicians distinguish between (a) symptoms and (b) their causes. If you tell your doctor that you have chest pain, that is a symptom. When your doctor diagnoses the problem, she does not say that you have "chest pain disorder"; that diagnosis merely would describe the problem you have. Instead, she looks for causes. She seeks a diagnosis (e.g., a digestive system disorder, a muscular injury, a heart attack) that will explain why your symptom occurred. The DSM diagnostic categories, however, are not like this. DSM categories merely describe symptoms; the DSM classifies disorders according to "surface similarity of signs and symptoms, not in terms of their causes" (McNally, 2011, p. 176). Although a physician does not diagnose a person experiencing chest pains as having "chest pain disorder," the DSM *does* diagnose a person experiencing prolonged depressed feelings as having "depressive disorder."

3. *The DSM may cause mental illness to be overdiagnosed.* What percentage of people do you think have mental illness? Intuitively, you probably would expect this number to be small; although people have their "quirks," most people you know don't literally seem mentally ill. Yet, when DSM criteria are employed, the percentage of people with a disorder is remarkably large. In one survey of thousands of college students, almost *half* (46%) qualified as having had a mental disorder in the preceding year (Blanco et al., 2008). A similar survey in Europe yielded the startling

comorbidity The presence of symptoms of two or more disorders in any one individual.

DSM-5 The current edition of the DSM manual, published in 2013 with substantial changes in content.

Monarchy / Regency / The Kobal Collection

Yonhap News / YNA / Newscom

Psychological diversity in DSM categories DSM categories classify people according to the symptoms, not the causes, of psychological disorder. As a result, people with different psychological backgrounds can receive the same DSM diagnosis. Based on biographical information, both U.S. film star Kim Basinger (shown here in the 1997 film *L.A. Confidential*) and South Korean hip-hop musician Daniel Lee (also known as Tablo, in the group Epik High) appear to meet DSM criteria for the same disorder: social anxiety disorder. Yet their backgrounds differ. Ms. Basinger has been socially anxious since childhood; she appeared to teachers to be having a nervous breakdown whenever asked to read aloud in class (Cuncic, 2010). Mr. Lee, by contrast, developed social anxiety only later in life, due to a prolonged and public traumatic event. After graduating from Stanford University and returning to his home country, Mr. Lee was wrongly accused of falsifying his academic records. Newspaper articles and Internet sites attacked him for purported dishonesty. He eventually proved that he earned his degrees, but the attacks traumatized him, making him afraid to appear in public. "I'm damaged," he says. "And I don't know if I'll ever be better" (Davis, 2011).

news headline, "38% of Europeans Are Mentally Ill" (Associated Press, 2011). The percentages are so large that some ask whether the DSM is overdiagnosing mental illness by labeling some everyday, normal human experiences as disorders.

A particular concern is that, when diagnosed using the DSM, some people who are experiencing normal sadness are labeled as "mentally disordered" (Horwitz & Wakefield, 2007, p. 6). Throughout human history, people have experienced sadness in response to bad events (e.g., the death of a loved one; the breakup of a relationship). If people's sadness lasts long enough, they might qualify as having a mental illness, despite experiencing an emotion that is a normal part of human nature (Horwitz & Wakefield, 2007).

Feminist scholars raise another concern. Historically, the professionals who have formulated the DSM and used it to diagnose patients have been men. Some male clinicians may misunderstand women's experiences. Others may hold gender biases that cause them to treat women negatively. These factors could cause male clinicians to mistakenly judge psychologically normal women as mentally ill (Chesler, 1997). Research shows that clinicians' views of mental health can be gender-biased. When clinicians described (1) a normal male, (2) a normal female, or (3) a "healthy, mature, socially competent adult" (Broverman et al., 1970, p. 2), their descriptions of a healthy adult resembled their

STAN, I'M WORRIED ABOUT HOW CONTENTED YOU SEEM —I THINK YOU NEED THERAPY

CHRIS MADDEN

Chris Madden

descriptions of a normal male and differed from their descriptions of a normal female. Clinicians' beliefs about psychological normality, then, were biased against women.

Finally, cultural and social group differences might cause disorders to be overdiagnosed. Consider cultural differences in reactions to tragedy. In some cultures, such as in urban societies in Cairo, Egypt (Rosenblatt, 1993), grief reactions are extremely prolonged. Just within the United States, grief after the loss of a loved one is, on average, more prolonged among African American college students than European American students (Laurie & Neimeyer, 2008). A mental health professional unaware of these cultural differences might classify as "abnormal" grief reactions that are typical, and perfectly normal, among individuals of the given culture.

Despite its limitations, the DSM is the "gold standard"—the book that holds the greatest authority when professionals classify the different types of mental disorders that require therapy. Now that you've learned about this diagnostic tool, let's look at those therapies.

> ⚡ **WHAT DO YOU KNOW?...**
>
> 3. Though the DSM is the gold standard, it can be criticized on several grounds. For which of the following reasons can the DSM be criticized? Check all that apply.
> _____ a. Its categories are too grounded in scientific research and not enough on professional opinion.
> _____ b. Its categories are descriptions of symptoms of disorders, not underlying causes.
> _____ c. It was formulated by clinicians whose beliefs about psychological health may be biased against women.
> _____ d. Its use could lead to the overdiagnosis of mental illness among certain cultural and social groups.

Therapy

Every year, about 24 million Americans receive therapy for psychological disorders. They spend, in total, more than $16 billion for these services (Olfson & Markus, 2010). And those figures are just for *outpatient* mental health services, that is, therapies delivered to people who do not require an overnight hospital stay. Many others experience severe mental disorders that require hospitalization; for example, more than a third of a million people in the United States are hospitalized for schizophrenia, a disease whose total cost to the U.S. economy runs in the tens of billions of dollars ("Schizophrenia Facts and Statistics," 1996–2010).

These numbers raise two questions: (1) What are the therapies for which tens of millions of people are spending tens of billions of dollars? (2) Do they work? We'll address these questions in the rest of the chapter.

Therapy Strategies

Preview Question

> › Why are there so many different types of therapy?

The therapies on which people spend time and money are, in a word, diverse. Two factors fuel diversity. One is the diversity of disorders and people who suffer from them (Nathan & Gorman, 2007). Clinicians develop different therapies for different psychological problems. Furthermore, they adapt standard methods to individual clients; one prominent therapist (Irvin Yalom, interviewed in Howes, 2009) even suggests that "you have to develop a separate new therapy for every single patient. So for some patients the goal will be this and for some the goal will be that."

The second factor is that different clinicians embrace different *therapy strategies,* that is, different approaches to reducing psychological distress and improving mental health. There are two main types of strategies, *psychological therapies* and *drug therapies:*

1. **Psychological therapies** (also called **psychotherapies**) are interactions between a therapist and one or more clients in which therapists speak with, and may create novel behavioral experiences for, the clients. These psychological interactions between therapist and client are designed to improve clients' well-being. In psychological therapies, clinicians try to improve clients' emotional state, increase the quality of their thinking, and enhance their behavioral skills.

2. **Biological therapies** are interventions that directly alter the biochemistry or anatomy of the nervous system. The most common biological therapies are **drug therapies,** in which patients receive pharmaceuticals (i.e., chemical substances designed for medical treatment) that alter the biochemistry of the brain. These alterations are designed to improve clients' emotional state and thinking abilities.

Let's first explore the psychological therapies.

© Wavebreak Media Ltd. / Corbis

Psychotherapy In psychotherapy, mental health professionals interact with clients in personal encounters designed to improve the client's psychological well-being.

> ### 😈 WHAT DO YOU KNOW?...
>
> 4. The main goals of _____ therapies are to improve clients' emotional state, increase the quality of their thinking, and enhance their behavioral skills. The goal of drug therapies is to alter the biochemistry of the _____.

Psychological Therapies

Preview Questions

> › What are some of the most prominent types of psychotherapy and what is it like to experience each of them?
> › Which psychological therapy is most popular?

Professionals who provide psychological therapies are called **psychotherapists.** What exactly do psychotherapists do?

It depends. Psychologists hold different beliefs about the best psychological techniques for improving mental health; thus, there are different types of psychological therapy. Five types are particularly prominent: *psychoanalysis, behavior therapy, cognitive therapy, humanistic therapy,* and the family of *group therapies.* (The approaches to psychotherapy are very closely related to the various personality theories; see Chapter 13.)

PSYCHOANALYSIS. Psychoanalysis is a psychotherapy strategy developed late in the nineteenth century by Sigmund Freud, a physician in Vienna, Austria (Freud, 1900; Freud & Breuer, 1895). It is an example of **insight therapy,** in which therapists help clients identify and understand—or "gain insight into"—the root causes of their psychological symptoms. Insight into one's own mental life is thought to improve psychological well-being (Cameron & Rychlak, 1985). Freud developed a unique method for gaining insight: the *free association method.*

The **free association method** is a therapy technique in which patients are encouraged to say anything that comes to mind when they contemplate their psychological problems; they "free associate" to the problems. Freud instructed his patients not to hold anything back. They were to voice any thought that came to mind, even if it seemed trivial (Bellak, 1961). Freud did not interfere with the free associations. He merely took notes on the client's thoughts and analyzed their content. The idea was that, eventually, the free associations would lead to deeply significant psychological content, such as memories of traumatic events in the past.

psychological therapies (psychotherapies) Interactions between a therapist and client(s) in which the therapist speaks with the client, with a goal of improving emotional state, thinking, and behavioral skills.

biological therapies In the treatment of psychological disorders, interventions that directly alter the biochemistry or anatomy of the nervous system.

drug therapies In the treatment of psychological disorders, treatment with pharmaceuticals that alter the biochemistry of the brain to improve emotional state and thinking abilities.

psychotherapists Professionals who provide psychological therapies.

psychoanalysis The psychotherapy strategy originally developed by Sigmund Freud; a type of insight therapy.

insight therapy A type of psychotherapy in which therapists help clients identify and understand the root causes of their psychological symptoms.

free association method A method of both personality assessment and therapy devised by Freud in which psychologists encourage people to let their thoughts flow freely and say whatever comes to mind.

Next? Freud in his office, apparently waiting for his next patient. When conducting psychoanalytic therapy, Freud would sit in this chair and his patient would lie down on the sofa to his left.

Why not just ask clients directly to talk about this significant psychological content? Freud's answer is that they are unable to do so. Troubling memories are stored in the *unconscious,* a region of mind whose contents are hidden and unusually inaccessible. In Freud's theory, the mind is like a library with different levels, and the unconscious is like a large basement level that is locked. The unconscious contains a lot of material, but you can't access it without a key. The free association method is the key that lets people into the unconscious mind.

Freud explains that some life experiences are so emotionally disturbing that people don't want to think about them. To stop doing so, people *repress* them; that is, they transfer memories of the events from their conscious mind (the part of mind of which you are aware) into the unconscious. Once deposited there, the unconscious thoughts do not just go away. Rather, their emotional energy endures. This energy can break out of the unconscious and cause emotional and physical distress. People experience distress but don't know why; they lack insight into its unconscious causes.

Through the free association method, people gain this insight. As therapy proceeds, they uncover topics of deeper and deeper emotional significance, eventually encountering the underlying cause of their emotional disturbance. This process can be slow. Patients may be in psychoanalysis for years, overcoming their resistance to thinking about emotionally disturbing past events only gradually (Sandell et al., 2000). But once they gain insight into this material, aided by interpretations provided by the therapist, their mental health is expected to improve. Their conscious mind should gain strength, the unconscious should lose strength, and the person should become relatively free of debilitating psychological distress (Cameron & Rychlak, 1985). A large-scale meta-analysis of the effectiveness of psychoanalytic therapy provides scientific evidence that the approach has long-term benefits for the majority of clients (de Maat et al., 2009; also see Shedler, 2010).

Freud's approach exemplifies the medical model of psychological disorders (Elkins, 2009; Macklin, 1973). The patients' problems of living—their disturbances in thinking, emotion, and behavior—are interpreted as symptoms. In the free association, Freud searches for their underlying causes in the unconscious. Therapy ultimately targets the purported causes: the unconscious content.

Another key psychoanalytic process is **transference,** which occurs when a patient unintentionally responds to a therapist as if the therapist were a significant figure (e.g., a parent) from the patient's past. Emotions originally experienced with the significant figure are "transferred" to the therapist. Transference is significant in that, once past emotions are re-experienced in therapy, they can be analyzed. Through this analysis, the patient can gain insight into how past emotional experiences are causing current distress (Cameron & Rychlak, 1985).

During and after Freud's lifetime, a large number of other therapists developed therapy methods that were inspired by, but were not identical to, Freud's approach. The resulting set of therapy approaches—Freud's psychoanalytic therapy and the related methods—are referred to as *psychodynamic therapies.* The

⬭ **THINK ABOUT IT**

Freud kept notes on his patients' progress and, based on those records, concluded that psychoanalytic therapy works. Is that good scientific evidence? How could you test the effectiveness of psychoanalytic therapy scientifically?

transference A psychoanalytic process in which a patient unintentionally responds emotionally to a therapist as if the therapist were a significant figure from the patient's past, such as a parent.

Have you ever met someone who reminded you of a significant person in your life? Did you treat this person in ways that were similar to the way you treat the significant person? This experience is similar to transference.

term *psychodynamic* refers to a flow of mental energies within the mind (Chapter 13). Psychodynamic therapists share a concern with identifying, in therapy, aspects of mental life that may be unknown to the client, yet that contribute to emotional distress. They attend to the ways in which past life events affect clients' present-day experiences, and they encourage clients to discuss not only problems of everyday life, but also thoughts that arise in fantasy, dreams, and daydreams (Shedler, 2010).

BEHAVIOR THERAPY. Behavior therapy is a strategy in which therapists aim to directly alter clients' patterns of behavior. By learning more adaptive ways of behaving, clients' psychological lives improve (O'Donohue & Krasner, 1995).

Behavior therapy differs considerably from psychoanalysis. Psychoanalysts analyze the client's past. Behavior therapists focus, instead, on the present and the future. They try to identify behavioral problems the client is experiencing now, and to teach new behaviors that will be effective in meeting upcoming challenges. This practical, problem-focused approach can sometimes produce behavior change quite rapidly (O'Donohue, Fisher, & Hayes, 2003).

Behavior therapists change clients' behavior by altering their environment. They know that, in general, environmental experiences shape behavior (Skinner, 1953). Strategically changing clients' environments therefore may change their behavior and improve their well-being. Here's an example. If a client is depressed, the behavior therapist might direct the client into new environments that can lift the depression mood—such as settings in which they dress attractively, engage in meaningful conversations, have a good meal, and spend time with other people who are not depressed (Lewinsohn & Graf, 1973). No matter what the past causes of clients' depression might have been, these new environments can alleviate depressed mood.

Behavior therapy is grounded in research on learning (Chapter 7). Historically, learning researchers first identified environmental factors that modify emotion and behavior in laboratory studies. Behavior therapists then put the research findings into practice, via three steps of reasoning: (1) Clients experience distress because environments they experienced in the past did not teach them behaviors that are useful in their present circumstances; (2) it's never too late to learn, thus clients can learn useful new behaviors in therapy; and (3) factors shown, in basic research on learning, to modify emotion and behavior could be used to teach clients the new behaviors (Bandura, 1969; Schachtman & Reilly, 2011).

To see how the behavior therapy strategy can be put into practice, consider an application in which therapists worked with couples experiencing high levels of marital distress (Christensen et al., 2004). For the couples, being in therapy was like taking a class—on "how to be a good marital partner." Therapists taught them behaviors that are good for relationships. For instance:

> *Behavioral exchange:* The couples were taught to generate lists of positive things that they could do for their partners.

> *Communication training:* Therapists taught couples new ways of speaking, with a key behavior being first-person statements (e.g., "I feel bad when you make a mess around the house") instead of second-person statements that make people defensive (e.g., "You are a slob.")

> *Listening skills:* Couples learned how to summarize and paraphrase statements their partner made during conversations. Paraphrasing makes people know they are being understood, which benefits conversations and, more generally, relationships.

Couples therapy One of many settings in which behavior therapists may work is therapy for couples. Therapists may try to build couples' listening and communication skills and help clients behave in a more positive manner toward their relationship partners.

behavior therapy A therapy strategy grounded in research on learning, in which therapists aim to directly alter clients' patterns of behavior by teaching more adaptive ways of behaving.

CONNECTING TO LEARNING AND TO BIOLOGICAL MECHANISMS

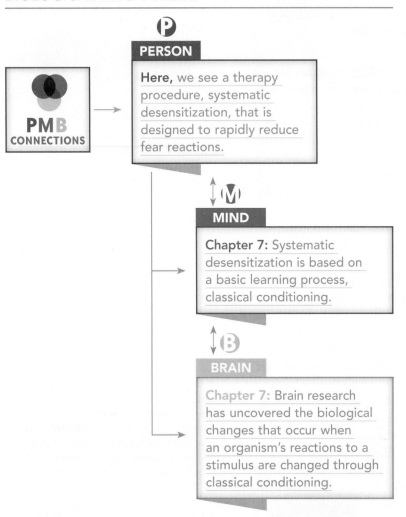

PMB CONNECTIONS

Ⓟ
PERSON

Here, we see a therapy procedure, systematic desensitization, that is designed to rapidly reduce fear reactions.

Ⓜ
MIND

Chapter 7: Systematic desensitization is based on a basic learning process, classical conditioning.

Ⓑ
BRAIN

Chapter 7: Brain research has uncovered the biological changes that occur when an organism's reactions to a stimulus are changed through classical conditioning.

---

token economy A behavior therapy technique in which therapists reward desirable behavior with tokens that serve as reinforcers, making the behavior more likely to reoccur.

exposure therapy A behavior therapy technique in which therapists combat the emotions of fear and anxiety by bringing clients into direct contact with an object or situation that arouses their fear, while ensuring that no harm occurs.

extinguishing (of emotion) In exposure therapy, the reduction in emotional response that occurs when an anticipated emotionally arousing consequence does not occur.

systematic desensitization An exposure therapy that reduces fear by exposing clients to feared objects in a slow, gradual manner.

To determine whether therapy worked, therapists measured marital satisfaction both before and after therapy. Behavior therapy significantly improved couples' satisfaction with their marriages (Christensen et al., 2004).

An effective behavior therapy technique is the **token economy,** in which therapists reward desirable behavior by administering reinforcers that make those behaviors more likely to occur (see Chapter 7). The reinforcers are tokens—for example, a plastic chip—that people later can exchange for something valuable (e.g., food). Token economies are designed to increase the frequency with which people perform desirable behaviors. In one study (Maley, Feldman, & Ruskin, 1973), conducted with female patients in a mental hospital, psychologists gave women tokens when they engaged in desirable behaviors such as personal grooming or communicating appropriately with hospital staff. The tokens later could be exchanged for snacks and cigarettes. Compared to patients who did not experience the token economy, token-economy patients displayed better communication, less confusion and strange behavior, and more positive mood. Tokens, then, reduced abnormal behavior.

Token economies illustrate a fundamental principle of behavior therapy, namely, that behavior is controlled by its consequences. People do things that bring rewards. They avoid performing behaviors that bring punishments. Following this simple yet powerful principle enables behavior therapists to reduce people's maladaptive behavior.

In addition to modifying behavior, some behavior therapy techniques directly target emotional reactions. Behavior therapists combat the emotions of fear and anxiety with **exposure therapy,** in which clients are brought into direct contact with an object or situation that arouses their fear (McNally, 2007). A client who is obsessively anxious about germs, for example, may be exposed to materials that are dirty. Someone afraid of heights may be brought to a high floor of a tall building. Therapists ensure that no harm occurs to the client during exposure. The client, then, simultaneously experiences (1) the feared object and (2) an absence of harm. This two-part experience modifies the client's emotional reactions (Foa & Kozak, 1986). The emotion lessens or *extinguishes;* the **extinguishing** of an emotion is the reduction in emotional response that occurs when an anticipated emotionally arousing consequence does not occur.

The behavior therapist Joseph Wolpe (1958) pioneered an exposure therapy called *systematic desensitization.* **Systematic desensitization** reduces fear by exposing clients to feared objects in a slow, gradual manner. The exposure can occur through real-life experience or by having clients imagine themselves in a feared situation. In either case, clients first confront a circumstance that is only moderately challenging for them (e.g., someone afraid of heights might be asked to imagine standing only a few feet off the ground). They then confront increasing levels of challenge (e.g., the person imagines looking out from the second, third, and fourth floors of a building). The goal is for clients to remain calm, so that they associate the objects with calmness rather than fear.

> Did any of your grade school teachers create a token economy in the classroom?

Virtual systematic desensitization Systematic desensitization reduces clients' fears by exposing them to feared objects in a gradual, step-by-step manner. Thanks to modern technology, this can be accomplished through virtual reality, which immerses clients in a computer-generated environment. In the photo, a client with spider phobia (an excessive fear of spiders) confronts her fear in a virtual environment (Hoffman et al., 2003), which gives people the virtual experience of interacting with a spider.

This reduces their fear response. Exposure therapies have proven highly effective in reducing anxiety (McNally, 2007) across a number of different anxiety disorders, as we discuss later in this chapter.

COGNITIVE THERAPY. In **cognitive therapy,** therapists try to improve mental health by changing the way in which clients think. They try, in other words, to change clients' cognitions.

Cognitive therapy is grounded in a simple yet important idea: Thinking processes are at the heart of psychological distress. Certain types of thoughts—negative interpretations of statements people make about you, pessimistic expectations about your own abilities, blaming yourself for circumstances that may be beyond your control—can make you depressed or anxious.

These negative thoughts are self-defeating; that is, they interfere with people's ability to successfully improve their lives. A person whose thoughts about the future are pessimistic may give up on life plans that actually could succeed. Someone who sets unrealistically high goals may make herself tense and doom herself to disappointment. People with low opinions about their value as a person makes themselves depressed. The causes of the bad outcomes—giving up, tension, disappointment, depression—are the cognitions: the pessimistic beliefs, unrealistic goals, and low opinions of oneself.

Cognitive therapists argue that many of these negative beliefs are *irrational*. **Irrational beliefs** are demanding, dogmatic thoughts that cause people to experience negative emotions (Ellis & Dryden, 1997). The beliefs are called "irrational" because they distort reality illogically. In so doing, they bring about psychological distress; people irrationally make themselves feel bad through their own beliefs.

The irrational thoughts targeted in cognitive therapy may be familiar to you. Do you ever think that you can't be happy unless you have more friends? Or more money? Or that you *must* become more successful in school or *must* make someone else happy for you to be happy yourself? Such beliefs are common yet, to the cognitive therapist, irrational because they can doom you to unhappiness. The cognitive therapist thus combats them. For instance, when a client said he was unhappy because his wife's pushy parents did not respect him, his cognitive therapist explained that his unhappiness was caused not by the in-laws, but by the client's own irrational beliefs (Barry, 2009)—in particular, the belief that he must have his in-laws' respect to be happy. The therapist challenged the belief: "Why do you need your [in-laws'] approval . . . where did you learn that you have a duty to obey [their] wishes?"

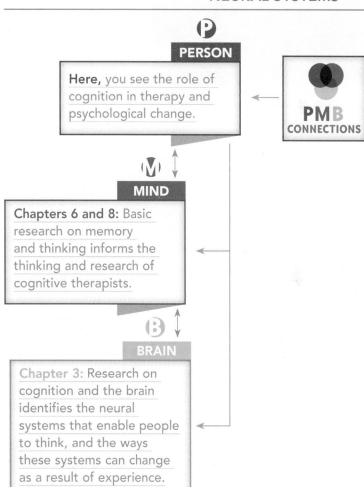

CONNECTING TO COGNITIVE PROCESSES AND TO NEURAL SYSTEMS

PERSON
Here, you see the role of cognition in therapy and psychological change.

PMB CONNECTIONS

MIND
Chapters 6 and 8: Basic research on memory and thinking informs the thinking and research of cognitive therapists.

BRAIN
Chapter 3: Research on cognition and the brain identifies the neural systems that enable people to think, and the ways these systems can change as a result of experience.

cognitive therapy A psychological therapy in which therapists try to improve mental health by changing the way in which clients think, reducing negative, self-defeating thoughts.

irrational beliefs Demanding, dogmatic thoughts that distort reality illogically and cause people to experience negative emotions.

Clem Murray / MCT / Newscom

Aaron Beck, who pioneered cognitive therapy for depression.

One proven method for changing negative, irrational cognitions is **Beck's cognitive therapy,** developed by the physician Aaron T. Beck (1979). Beck explains that the thoughts which create distress often are **automatic thoughts,** that is, thoughts that spring to mind rapidly and unintentionally. People don't intend to think thoughts that create distress. They just pop into mind. When contemplating the future, the depressed person automatically thinks, "Things will go badly." When considering an upcoming social event, the socially anxious person automatically thinks, "I'm going to look like an idiot."

Cognitive therapists try to change automatic thoughts through conversations with clients that aim to achieve a number of therapeutic goals:

> *Increasing awareness:* Clients may be unaware of how negative their thoughts are. The cognitive therapist's first goal, then, is to increase awareness, that is, to help clients see how their own negative thinking contributes to their emotional distress.

> *Challenging negative thoughts:* Therapists then challenge the negative thoughts they have identified. They question the logic and evidence behind the thoughts.

> *Suggesting positive thoughts:* Therapists not only attack negative thoughts. They also encourage clients to replace them with more positive, adaptive ways of thinking.

Let's see how cognitive therapy works in a case involving a suicidal patient (P). The therapist (T) tries to prevent a suicide attempt by changing the patient's thoughts—specifically, by replacing thoughts about reasons for dying with thoughts about reasons for living (Williams & Wells, 1989, pp. 212–213).

T: Are there any other reasons for dying?

P: I just feel I'm wasting everyone's time. No one can help me. I've been like this since I was a child.

T: Some reasons for dying are that you would escape from your despair, the children would not have to put up with you, that John would realize how bad you've been feeling, that you wouldn't be wasting people's time any more. Is there anything else?

P: [Pause] No, I don't think so.

T: Can you think of any disadvantages that there may be to trying to kill yourself?

P: Disadvantages?

T: Yes.

P: [Long pause] I think I might fail—end up with brain damage or worse and be more of a burden.

T: Any other disadvantage?

P: Sometimes, when things are going a bit better, I realize how upset the children would be. Michael and Marion climbed into bed last Saturday morning and gave me a big kiss. They'd tried making some toast. The marmalade got everywhere. [Smiles, then tearful.]

T: Anything else?

P: Well, I don't know what's on the other side—of death, I mean. I don't have any religious beliefs, but I sort of think, well, it scares me. It might not be peaceful.

T: So sometimes you see there may be disadvantages to dying, or to attempting to die: that you could end up worse off—physically damaged in some way; that the children would miss you; that the other side might not be peaceful.

As you can see, the cognitive therapist tried to change the client's way of thinking. The therapist did so subtly—not by proclaiming, "You must live!" but by leading the client into a personal exploration of reasons why suicide might not be a good idea.

In some ways, cognitive therapy resembles behavior therapy. Both endeavor to teach clients new skills. Both focus on challenges in the here-and-now environment rather than emphasizing causes of distress that lie deep in a person's past, as in psychoanalysis. Because of these similarities, cognitive therapy often is called *cognitive-behavioral therapy.* Yet the approaches do differ. Unlike behavior therapy, cognitive

Beck's cognitive therapy A therapy method for changing negative, irrational thoughts by increasing clients' awareness of their automatic thoughts, challenging those thoughts, and suggesting positive alternative ones.

automatic thoughts Thoughts that spring to mind rapidly and unintentionally.

therapy focuses on personal beliefs and skills that involve thinking. Rather than trying to change the client's environment, the cognitive therapist changes how clients *think about* their environments and personal experiences. New thoughts, in turn, lead to new, more adaptive behavior.

HUMANISTIC THERAPY. **Humanistic therapy** is a strategy in which therapists provide clients with supportive interpersonal relationships. In humanistic therapy, the quality of the relationship between the therapist and the client is key. Therapist and theorist Carl Rogers explains the approach: "If I can provide a certain type of relationship, the other person will discover within himself the capacity to use that relationship for growth and change, and personal development will occur" (Rogers, 1961, p. 33).

Humanistic therapists believe that a good client–therapist relationship is fundamentally similar to relationships that may occur outside of therapy. Do you have a particularly strong, supportive relationship with someone whose wisdom and insight you value and who listens carefully when you talk about yourself? Maybe it's a relative, a coach, or a minister or other religious figure? If so, you may sense that the relationship benefits you psychologically. You can converse seriously, exploring questions about your life, your future, and yourself. This, in turn, helps you to understand, as well as be more accepting of, yourself, and thus to grow psychologically—to achieve greater maturity. This is the sort of relationship humanists try to establish in therapy.

Of course, for many people the answer to the question above is no; they *lack* a strong, supportive relationship with someone who listens closely to them. This absence can harm psychological development. Humanistic therapists tell us that just as a seed needs water to grow, a person needs personal relationships to grow. By providing such relationships in therapy to people who may lack them outside of therapy, the humanistic psychologist provides the support that clients need to achieve psychological growth.

To develop strong personal relationships with their clients, humanistic therapists follow three basic guidelines—what Rogers (1961) calls three "conditions" needed for therapeutic success. They are *genuineness, acceptance,* and *understanding.*

1. *Genuineness:* In therapy, humanistic therapists express their true, genuine feelings to their clients. They do not maintain a cold, detached, "scientific" personal style of the sort you might find when talking to a physician. Rather, the humanistic therapist is an open and honest person who is willing to express his or her genuine feelings as they arise during the therapy encounter.

2. *Acceptance:* Humanistic therapists are accepting of their clients. They never reject a client's thoughts and actions as being foolish or inappropriate. The client is always respected as a person of dignity and worth. This acceptance establishes a psychologically safe setting in which clients can freely explore their personal experiences. The humanistic therapist's term for this acceptance is **unconditional positive regard,** which is the expression of positive feelings toward the client no matter what the client does and says; the positive feelings, in other words, are expressed unconditionally.

3. *Empathic understanding:* Humanistic therapists strive to display **empathic understanding,** which is an understanding of the clients' psychological life *from the perspective of the client.* The humanistic therapist does not try to diagnose an inner mental illness that is unknown to the client. Instead, the therapist strives to understand what clients know about, and feel about, themselves. Furthermore, they ensure that clients know they are being understood. They do this through active listening, that is, listening in which one conveys to speakers that they are being understood from their own point of view (Rogers & Farson, 1987).

   A key active-listening technique is **reflection,** in which therapists recurringly summarize statements made by the client; they "reflect" the content of

humanistic therapy A psychological therapy in which therapists provide clients with supportive interpersonal relationships; the quality of the relationship between therapist and client is key to the client's growth and change.

unconditional positive regard A display of respect and acceptance toward others that is consistent and not dependent on their meeting behavioral requirements.

empathic understanding In humanistic therapy, the therapist's understanding of the client's psychological life from the perspective of the client.

reflection In psychotherapy, an active-listening technique in which the therapist recurringly summarizes statements made by the client, "reflecting" the content back to the client.

The Conversation (oil on canvas), Kroll, Leon (1884–1974) / National Academy Museum, New York, USA / Bridgeman Images

Humanistic therapy as an interpersonal encounter Carl Rogers's humanistic therapy emphasizes a type of human encounter that can occur both inside and outside therapy: deep, meaningful, supportive conversation.

clients' statements back to them. For example, a client might say, "I've been feeling really bad that I haven't done better at college; my parents had been hoping I'd do well; they never got a chance to go to college themselves and they're counting on me, and I'm blowing it." The therapist could reply, "You've got a deep sense of guilt about not meeting your parent's expectations." By encapsulating the meaning and emotional tone of the statement, the therapist shows the client that she is being understood empathically.

> Do you ever "reflect" statements made by your friends in everyday conversation?

Humanistic therapists believe that these three therapeutic conditions are not only necessary for therapy to succeed, but also are sufficient. Humanistic therapists do not try to modify their clients' thoughts, as cognitive therapists do. They instead try to develop a relationship in which they can understand their clients' thoughts. Once this relationship is achieved, the client naturally "will discover *within himself* the capacity" to grow (Rogers, 1961, p. 35). The agent of psychological change, in the humanistic view, is not the therapist. It is the client.

GROUP THERAPY. Therapy does not always consist of one-on-one encounters between a therapist and client. Therapy also can be conducted in groups. **Group therapy** is any type of psychological therapy in which a therapist meets together with two or more clients.

One benefit of group therapy is efficiency. Mental health services can be delivered to more people, in any given amount of time, when therapy is conducted in groups. Efficiency, however, is not group therapy's main advantage. As Yalom (1970) explained in a classic text, group therapy introduces a number of psychological processes that may benefit clients, including the following:

> *"Misery loves company"*: In group therapy, clients see that they are not alone. They encounter others who share similar psychological difficulties. This makes clients aware that their life circumstances are not as unusual or "strange" as they may have thought.

Group therapy Many psychologists conduct therapy in groups. Interpersonal interactions within the therapy group can provide insight into interpersonal problems that occur in clients' lives outside of therapy.

David Harry Stewart / Getty Images

group therapy Any type of psychological therapy in which a therapist meets with two or more clients together.

> *Helping others:* Clients in group therapy may help others by providing advice or emotional support. The experience of helping others can prove beneficial to the person providing the help.

> *Building social skills:* In group therapy, people often receive feedback from others on their behavior. As a result, they may learn about personal behaviors that leave a bad impression on others, such as failing to establish eye contact or talking obsessively about oneself. By correcting these tendencies, people can increase their social skills and thus develop more positive relationships.

> *Therapy group as a microcosm of everyday life:* After a number of group therapy sessions, people's behavior in the group may resemble their behavior in everyday life. In particular, individuals may exhibit, in the group, the same negative behavior that interferes with their everyday relationships. Someone who is domineering toward relatives may become domineering toward group members. People concerned about social rejection in everyday life may become concerned about rejection from group members. When this happens, the therapist and group members can provide feedback that enables people to become aware of negative aspects of their behavior. This awareness is a first step in bringing about change.

Group therapists foster these beneficial group dynamics through a number of steps (Yalom, 1970). First, they form and maintain the group, ensuring that members show up and participate in discussions. Second, they establish and maintain norms for group behavior—a particular challenge because these norms differ from those of ordinary life; in group therapy, people comment about others in an open, emotional manner that would be inappropriate elsewhere. Finally, therapists draw group members' attention to what Yalom calls the "here and now": thoughts and emotions as they are occurring during the course of the therapy session. The group scrutinizes its own experiences. Members thus gain insight into their interpersonal behavior.

Table 15.2 summarizes the five different therapy strategies we have discussed.

table **15.2**

Therapy Strategies			
Therapy	**Main Therapeutic Goal**	**Key Therapy Processes/ Techniques**	**Key Figure**
Psychoanalysis	Gain insight into unconscious causes of psychological distress	• Insight • Transference	Sigmund Freud
Behavior therapy	Use environmental experiences to teach new behavioral and emotional responses	• Reward desirable behaviors • Extinguish anxious emotions	Joseph Wolpe
Cognitive therapy	Identify and modify clients' irrational, self-defeating thinking	• Challenge negative thoughts • Teach positive thinking	Aaron Beck
Humanistic therapy	Provide an interpersonal relationship that enables psychological growth	• Unconditional positive regard • Reflection	Carl Rogers
Group therapy	Use group dynamics to instill hope and increase self-understanding	• Establish open, honest group discussion • Explore "here-and-now" group experiences	Irvin Yalom

TRY THIS!

Could you tell the difference between the different approaches to psychotherapy if you saw them put into practice? Find out with this chapter's Try This! activity. Go to www.pmbpsychology.com, where you will see videos of therapists who illustrate different forms of therapy. ◉

ECLECTIC, INTEGRATIVE PSYCHOLOGICAL THERAPIES. After learning about these different forms of therapy, you might be wondering which is most popular. It turns out, rather than "picking one," a popular strategy is to combine the virtues of different approaches to fit the needs of the individual client. **Integrative psychotherapy** is an effort to combine systematically the methods of different schools of therapy (Thoma & Cecero, 2009). The resulting combination is described as **eclectic therapy,** an approach that creatively draws upon any therapeutic method available (Jensen, Bergin, & Greaves, 1990). (The notions of "integrative" and "eclectic" therapy overlap; some therapists describe their approach as "eclectic-integrative"; Garfield, 1995.)

In surveys, more than two-thirds of practicing therapists in the United States describe their orientation as eclectic (Jensen et al., 1990). Therapists trained in one approach commonly explore therapy methods developed in others (Thoma & Cecero, 2009).

❤ WHAT DO YOU KNOW?...

5. Match the therapy type on the left to its key feature on the right.

1. Psychoanalysis	a. Based on the belief that a strong supportive relationship is key to psychological growth
2. Behavior therapy	b. Its benefits to clients include the opportunity to provide help to others in a similar situation and to build social skills.
3. Cognitive therapy	c. Its goal is to change behavior by changing the clients' environment, often by introducing reinforcers.
4. Humanistic therapy	d. Rooted in the belief that clients' traumatic memories are buried in the unconscious and that the only way to access them is the free association method
5. Group therapies	e. The psychotherapist uses conversation as a tool to challenge irrational beliefs such as "In order to be happy, I must have a lot of friends."
6. Eclectic therapy	f. A very popular approach that creatively draws on many therapeutic methods

---

Drugs and Other Biological Therapies

Preview Questions

› How did physicians figure out that psychological disorders could be treated with drugs?
› How do drugs affect mental health?
› What are some alternatives to drug therapies?

Psychological disorders are just that: psychological. Their defining features are troubling alterations in psychological experience: thought, emotion, and behavior. Yet if you want to treat these disorders, one option is to shift from a psychological to a biological level of analysis.

eclectic therapy (integrative psychotherapy) Therapy that draws upon any therapeutic method available, with the therapist combining the methods of different therapy schools in designing an optimal approach for therapy in general or an individual client.

Psychological disorder can result from a malfunctioning brain. If so, then altering brain function might relieve psychological distress. Biological therapies for psychological disorders, as noted earlier, are therapy approaches that alter the anatomy or physiology of the brain in an effort to improve mental health. By far the most popular of the biological therapies are drug therapies.

THE HISTORY OF DRUG THERAPIES. The discovery that drugs could alleviate mental illness was accidental. In the 1940s, a physician in France was searching for a drug that would help surgical patients during their postoperative recovery. The drug he tried, *thorazine,* worked; postoperative patients were calm and relaxed. Psychiatrists guessed that this drug might benefit others—not only people who were anxious about surgery, but also those whose emotions stemmed from a mental disorder.

Their guess proved correct. The drug originally designed for surgical patients calmed people suffering a state of severe excitation known as mania (discussed later in the chapter). It had additional beneficial effects as well. After taking the drug, patients whose thinking was confused and who were worried that others were out to get them began to think more clearly.

These unexpected findings triggered a burst of scientific research in the 1950s that ushered in a new era in the treatment of severe mental illness (Valenstein, 1998). The medical community quickly embraced the finding that psychotic disorders (Chapter 16) could be treated with drugs.

Other accidental findings followed. Physicians noticed that when patients received a drug designed to treat tuberculosis, their mood changed; the drug made them happy. This drug quickly was put to use in the treatment of depression (Valenstein, 1998).

Not all drug therapies were developed accidentally, however. A treatment for depression was based on a theory about brain functioning (Carlsson, 1999). The theory was that the neurotransmitter *serotonin* is related to mood; specifically, greater serotonin activity in the brain should make mood more positive. Scientists designed **selective serotonin reuptake inhibitors,** or **SSRIs,** to alleviate depression by increasing serotonin activity. They do so by interfering with a biochemical process known as *reabsorption*. In reabsorption, some of the serotonin that one neuron could use to communicate with a second neuron is absorbed back into the first neuron. SSRIs block reabsorption (Figure 15.1). The amount of serotonin available for neuron-to-neuron communication thus increases. Some of the most popular antidepressants, such as Prozac and Zoloft, are selective serotonin reuptake inhibitors.

Drug therapies have revolutionized the treatment of mental illness. The biggest change occurred in the treatment of psychotic disorders. Until the mid-twentieth century, patients with severe mental disorders generally were unable to care for themselves. They commonly lived in mental hospitals under conditions that, today, seem inhumane: herded into overcrowded psychiatric wards where they received few if any beneficial treatments (Frank & Glied, 2006). Antipsychotic drugs improved their plight. The drugs increased patients' thinking abilities, enabling them to leave hospital care; the mental hospital population plummeted (Manderscheid, Atay, & Crider, 2009; Figure 15.2). Patients who previously would have been isolated in psychiatric wards lived productively in the community. As a result, "the lives of most people with mental illness are better today than they were fifty years ago" (Frank & Glied, 2006, p. 2).

WHY DRUGS HAVE PSYCHOLOGICAL EFFECTS. You learned in Chapter 2 (also see Chapter 3) that brain cells communicate chemically. Chemical substances known as neurotransmitters travel from one brain cell, or neuron, to another. These chemical transmissions determine the level of activity of the cells of the brain.

These basic facts about brain functioning are key to understanding why drugs affect mental health. Drugs are chemical substances. Most chemical substances you ingest

selective serotonin reuptake inhibitors (SSRIs) Pharmaceuticals designed to alleviate depression by increasing serotonin activity through interference with the biochemical process known as reabsorption or reuptake.

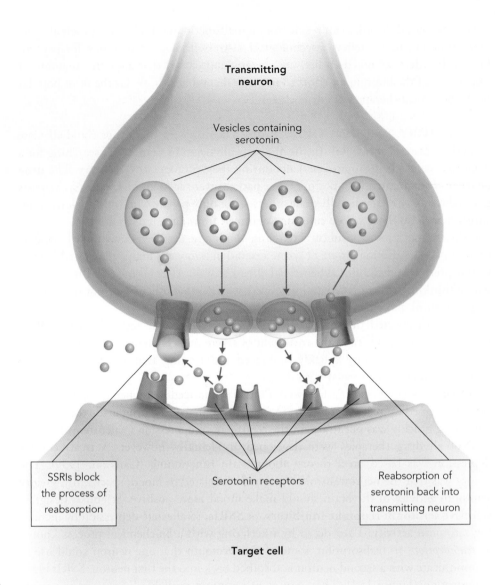

figure 15.1

SSRIs increase serotonin activity by interfering with reabsorption, the process through which serotonin that one neuron could use to communicate with a second neuron is absorbed back into the first neuron. By blocking reabsorption, SSRIs increase the amount of serotonin available for neuron-to-neuron communication.

figure 15.2

Antipsychotic drugs and mental hospital admissions The figure displays the number of admissions and the number of patients in residence in mental hospitals in the United States. As you can see, the numbers came down considerably in the 1950s and 1960s, thanks to the discovery of antipsychotic drugs (Manderscheid, Atay, & Crider, 2009).

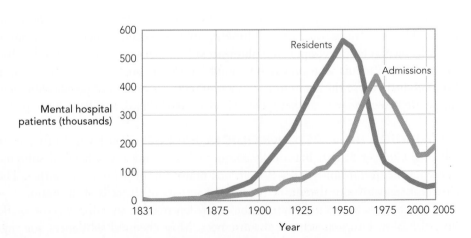

have little or no effect on brain functioning because of the body's built-in protection system: the **blood–brain barrier,** which is a set of biological mechanisms in the body's circulatory system that stops substances in the bloodstream from entering into brain tissue. The molecules of some chemical substances, however, are small enough that they permeate the blood–brain barrier and make their way into the brain (Julien, 2005). Some of these small chemical substances affect the functioning of brain cells and therefore alter thinking. They are known as **psychoactive substances,** chemical substances that affect psychological processes of perception, thinking, or emotion (World Health Organization, 2004). (We'll discuss specific psychoactive drugs later in this chapter and in Chapter 16, when we explore specific mental disorders and their treatment.)

One way in which drugs have psychological effects, then, is that they directly alter chemical activity in the brain. A second way that drugs can affect mental health is through *placebo effects.* A **placebo effect,** in drug therapies, is any medical benefit that is *not* caused by biologically active properties of the drug. Researchers demonstrate placebo effects by giving some patients pills that have no medicinal qualities— fake, "placebo" pills. Patients are not told whether they are receiving real medicine or a placebo. Although the placebo has no biological effects, many patients improve anyway. Among depressed persons, 30% show reduced depressive symptoms after taking a placebo (Rutherford, Wager, & Roose, 2010).

How would you feel if you learned that an improvement in your own health was due to a placebo effect?

What is the cause of placebo effects? The main source appears to be people's beliefs. People who get a medication (or, in the case of a placebo, a pill that *they think* is a medication) believe that, as a result, they will improve. This expectation of improvement becomes a "self-fulfilling prophecy"; the expectation of improvement creates an actual improvement (Kirsch, 2010; Rutherford et al., 2010).

Placebo effects raise challenges for researchers who want to show that a real drug uniquely benefits mental health. They must demonstrate not only that people who receive the drug improve; they also need to show that people on the drug improve more than those who get a fake drug—a placebo. Sometimes this is surprisingly difficult to demonstrate (see This Just In later in the chapter).

OTHER BIOLOGICAL THERAPIES. The psychological effects of drug therapies can be slow. Even the manufacturers of antidepressant drugs recognize that patients may not experience benefits until after taking them consistently for four weeks or more ("Highlights of Prescribing Information," 2014). If a patient is severely depressed and suicidal, or if a range of medications has not helped, some therapists then employ *electroconvulsive therapy.*

In **electroconvulsive therapy (ECT),** physicians deliver electrical currents to the brain. The electricity creates a brief brain *seizure,* that is, a period of abnormal electrical activity in the brain, during which a person loses consciousness. Studies indicate that electroconvulsive therapy benefits severely depressed individuals, reducing depressive symptoms in the majority of such patients (Rudorfer, Henry, & Sackeim, 2003). Why does it work? Good question; the mechanisms through which ECT reduces severe depression are not well understood. However, recent evidence indicates that the therapy may disrupt connections in the brain that contribute to depression. Specifically,

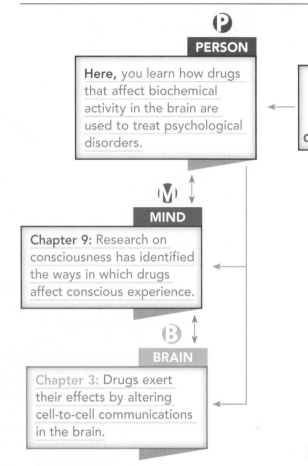

CONNECTING TO CONSCIOUSNESS AND TO CELLULAR COMMUNICATIONS

PERSON

Here, you learn how drugs that affect biochemical activity in the brain are used to treat psychological disorders.

PMB CONNECTIONS

MIND

Chapter 9: Research on consciousness has identified the ways in which drugs affect conscious experience.

BRAIN

Chapter 3: Drugs exert their effects by altering cell-to-cell communications in the brain.

blood–brain barrier A set of biological mechanisms in the circulatory system that prevents most substances in the bloodstream from entering brain tissue.

psychoactive substances Chemical substances small enough to cross the blood–brain barrier that affect psychological processes of perception, thinking, or emotion.

placebo effect In drug therapies, any medical benefit not caused by biologically active properties of the drug, but by the patient's expectation that the drug will help him.

electroconvulsive therapy (ECT) A biological therapy for severe depression in which electrical currents are delivered to the brain.

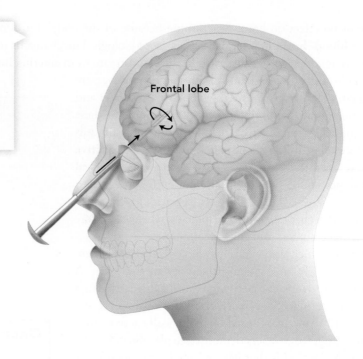

Lobotomy In the mid-twentieth century, surgeons performed lobotomies in an effort to eliminate severe mental illness. The procedure—which, fortunately, has gone out of fashion—was crude. In one form of lobotomy, the surgeon would sever connections among brain regions with an ice pick (Lerner, 2005).

Frontal lobe

the brains of people with severe depression often feature atypically strong connections among those parts of the brain involved in thinking and in emotion. ECT can disrupt these connections, which reduces depressive symptoms (Perrin et al., 2012).

Another alternative to drug therapies that has been tried is surgery. In principle, surgeons could treat mental disorders by intervening directly in the brain. They could remove a malfunctioning brain system or sever its connections to other regions of the brain, thereby cutting off its influence. In **lobotomy**, a surgeon damages brain tissue in the frontal regions of the brain, specifically, the brain's frontal cortex.

The origins and popularity of lobotomy lie in the past. Physicians in the first half of the twentieth century believed that a malfunctioning frontal cortex was the root of severe mental illness. They thus reasoned that damaging the cortex and its connections to the rest of the brain would alleviate mental illness (Lerner, 2005). This idea affected medical practice; by mid-century, about 20,000 lobotomies had been performed in the United States (Govan, 2011). Today, the procedure is rare. Contemporary health professionals view lobotomy as a crude and inhumane process. Drug therapies are, by far, the preferred alternative for alleviating psychoses.

🧠 WHAT DO YOU KNOW?...

6. For each of the "answers" below, provide the question. The first one is done for you.
   a. Answer: Though many drug therapies were developed accidentally, the use of this class of drugs was based on the theory that the neurotransmitter serotonin was related to mood.
      Question: What are selective serotonin reuptake inhibitors (SSRIs)?
   b. Answer: These are drugs that can cross the blood–brain barrier to affect perception, thinking, or emotion.
   c. Answer: People's belief in the effectiveness of a drug they are taking alleviates their symptoms, even in the absence of the drug's actual effectiveness.
   d. Answer: A type of therapy in which the therapist delivers electrical currents to the brain.
   e. Answer: A procedure in which a surgeon damages tissue in the brain's frontal cortex.

lobotomy An outmoded surgical procedure for treating mental disorders in which a surgeon would damage brain tissue in the frontal cortex.

Evaluating the Interventions: Empirically Supported Therapies

Preview Question

> What's wrong with using case studies as evidence for a therapy's effectiveness?

People who suffer from psychological problems have one big question: Which therapies work best? They want therapies that will improve their mental health, and quickly.

In the early days of clinical psychology, it was hard to tell which therapies worked best. Actually, it was hard to tell if they worked at all. Evidence of therapy effectiveness was meager and of poor quality. The predominant evidence was case studies; therapists reported on the effectiveness of their favored therapy method with individual patients. Case study evidence has two big limitations (see Chapter 2):

1. *Potential bias:* Because therapists prefer their own therapy method, they may be biased when interpreting and reporting on its effectiveness (Kendall, 1998).

2. *Lack of a control group:* When an individual patient improves during therapy, there is no way of knowing whether that person would have improved in a similar manner even without therapy; some mental health problems dissipate naturally over time.

To identify cause and effect—that is, to determine whether therapy was the true cause of a change in symptoms—one must compare people receiving therapy to other people, in a control group, who receive no therapy.

Today, this superior evidence is readily available. Clinical psychologists conduct research to identify **empirically supported therapies** (Kendall, 1998), that is, therapies whose effectiveness is established in carefully controlled experimental research. To qualify as an empirically supported therapy, a therapy method must be shown to be superior to no-therapy control groups, placebo medications, or other treatments known to be effective (Chambless & Ollendick, 2001).

Many types of therapy have, in fact, received empirical support—in other words, many really do work. Key evidence comes from studies with controls groups that eliminate the possibility of experimenter bias (see Research Toolkit). In the remainder of this chapter and in Chapter 16, we'll review therapies after presenting the characteristic experiences associated with a given psychological disorder. When, in this review, we say that a given type of therapy has been shown to benefit people suffering from the disorder, we mean that it is empirically supported—shown, in experimental research with control conditions, to work.

🐾 WHAT DO YOU KNOW?...

7. A theory is _____ supported when it has been demonstrated to be more effective than a no-therapy control group, a placebo, or some other effective therapy.

⊕ RESEARCH TOOLKIT

The Double-Blind Clinical Outcome Study

Scientists are people, too. When conducting a study, they usually hope it will work. They hope, for example, that a therapy they have devised will prove superior to a no-therapy control group, or that a promising new drug will prove superior to a placebo.

These hopes raise the possibility of bias. Scientists may make observations, and interpret results, in a way that is favorable to their own theory.

empirically supported therapies Treatments whose effectiveness is established in carefully controlled experimental research.

The virtues of randomness Double-blind clinical outcome studies rely on a principle you learned about in Chapter 2: the random assignment of research participants to experimental conditions. In a double-blind clinical study, neither the participant nor the therapist interacting with the participants is aware of the condition to which the participant has been assigned.

Lyon Fred / Getty Images

Such bias can occur in any science. But in psychology, the possibility for bias is doubled because the object of study—people—have hopes, expectations, and potential biases, too. In therapy studies, the research participants are not neutral observers. They want their therapy to succeed. If, at the end of therapy, participants are asked to report on their mental health, they may be biased to say that they have improved.

How can researchers overcome these biases and obtain results that are not "colored" by their hopes and those of their participants? The best strategy is the *double-blind clinical outcome study.*

A **double-blind clinical outcome study** is an experiment in which neither the research participants nor the researcher who interacts with them knows the condition of the experiment to which the participant has been assigned. Suppose there are two conditions in an experiment: (1) a drug condition (participants receive an actual drug that is designed to reduce mental illness) and (2) a placebo condition (participants receive an inert substance that looks like a real drug). Because both researchers and participants are ignorant of the condition to which participants are assigned, their expectations cannot bias the results—cannot, in other words, contribute to differences between the drug condition and the placebo condition.

You might be wondering, "Well, if nobody knows who's in which condition, how can they tell if the experiment worked?" The answer is that in a double-blind study, there are *two* researchers. One assigns people to conditions (e.g., real drug versus placebo) and keeps a codebook indicating the condition to which each participant has been assigned. A second, who does not see the codebook, runs the study. At the end of the study, the code is "broken," everyone finds out which participant was in which condition, and analyses are conducted to see if the outcome for the two conditions differed. Voilà, bias is eliminated!

👤 WHAT DO YOU KNOW?...

8. Why is it that in a double-blind clinical outcome study, neither the researcher's nor the participant's expectations can bias the results?

Depressive Disorders

Everybody feels depressed sometimes. A bad exam grade, a bad haircut, rejection by a college, or rejection by somebody you asked out on a date can ruin your mood for hours or days. Yet these temporary changes in mood are *not* what psychologists mean by "depression." To a psychologist, the term refers to a condition that is more severe. **Depression** is a psychological disorder that includes feelings of sadness, hopelessness, and fatigue; a loss of interest in activities; and changes in typical patterns of eating and sleep. In depression, these symptoms last for weeks (National Institute of Mental Health [NIMH], 2011).

The term "depression" does not refer to a single disorder. Rather, there is a family of *depressive disorders,* that is, distinct psychological conditions that each include depressive symptoms. Let's explore two prominent depressive disorders: *Major Depressive Disorder* and *Bipolar Disorder* (previously called *Manic-Depressive Disorder*). As we review them, and also when we review anxiety disorders later in this chapter, we will cover two main topics: (1) the given disorder's defining features and its prevalence (i.e., the number of people in a population who have the disorder), and (2) therapies that effectively treat the disorder.

double-blind clinical outcome study A research procedure to evaluate the effectiveness of therapy in which neither the research participants nor the researcher interacting with them knows the condition of the experiment to which the participant has been assigned.

depression A family of psychological disorders that include feelings of sadness and hopelessness, fatigue, loss of interest in activities, changes in eating and sleeping patterns, and that continues for weeks.

Major Depressive Disorder

Preview Questions

> What defines major depressive disorder and how prevalent is it?
> What therapies effectively treat major depressive disorder?

"It hit me what a complete mess I had made of my life. That hit me quite hard. We were as skint [poor] as you can be without being homeless and at that point I was definitely clinically depressed. That was characterized by a numbness, a coldness and an inability to believe you will feel happy again. All the color drained out of life" (ABC News, 2009).

The woman quoted above was suffering from *major depression.* But it didn't ruin her life. She managed to cope quite successfully, in part—by writing a novel, and then another novel, and another. They constituted the *Harry Potter* series. J. K. Rowling's epic novels (and their associated movies) originated in her need to overcome a psychological disorder, major depression.

DEFINING FEATURES AND PREVALENCE. **Major depressive disorder** is defined by a set of symptoms; a person is diagnosed with major depressive disorder only if these symptoms last two weeks or longer. They include the following:

> Consistent depressed mood
> Loss of interest in most daily activities
> Change in body weight
> Change in sleep patterns
> Fatigue
> Feelings of worthlessness, hopelessness, or helplessness
> Difficulty concentrating
> Thoughts of suicide

No one symptom is necessary in order to be diagnosed with the disorder. Individuals with major depression are people who exhibit a majority of the symptoms for at least a two-week period.

Major depression is a relatively prevalent disorder. A survey of U.S. adults indicated that 6.7% of the population suffered from major depressive disorder at some point during the previous year (Kessler et al., 2005). That's about 15 million people experiencing a disorder that brings despair and lethargy that can utterly disrupt one's life. Furthermore, the *lifetime prevalence* of the disorder—that is, the percentage of people who experience the disorder at least once in their life—is even higher, about 15% (Kessler et al., 1997).

Different groups have varying chances of becoming depressed. Major depression is more frequent among people living in poverty than among those above the poverty line (Riolo et al., 2005). Ethnic groups also differ. In one large-scale study of Americans of European, African, and Mexican ancestry, European Americans were the most likely to experience severe major depression. African Americans and Mexican Americans had higher rates of *dysthymic disorder,* a prolonged period of low mood whose symptoms are not as severe as those of major depression (Riolo et al., 2005). Finally, in the population at large, women are more likely to experience depression at some point in their lifetime than are men (Kessler et al., 1997).

TREATMENT. A number of the treatment strategies discussed earlier in this chapter have been used successfully to treat major depression. Let's now look at

Ron Bull / Getty Images

Depression in fact and fiction J. K. Rowling's *Harry Potter* series includes, among its cast of characters, Dementors, creatures that create despair and depression among those they encounter. The fictional creations reflect Rowling's own experience battling major depression.

Every day, though, sometimes more than once a day, sometimes all day, a coppery taste in my mouth, which I termed intense insipidity, heralded a session of helpless, bottomless misery in which I would lie curled in a foetal position on the sofa with tears leaking from my eyes, my brain boiling with the confusion of stuff not worth calling thought or imagery: it was more like shredded mental kelp marinated in pure pain. During and after such attacks, I would be prostrate with inertia, as if all my energy had gone into a black hole.

—Les Murray, *Killing the Black Dog*

major depressive disorder A disorder in which individuals experience some (but not necessarily all) of the following symptoms: depressed mood lasting at least two weeks, loss of interest in daily activities, changes in weight and sleep, fatigue, feelings of worthlessness and hopelessness, difficulty concentrating, and thoughts of suicide.

four options: behavior therapy, cognitive therapy, interpersonal therapy (which draws from psychodynamic and humanistic therapies), and drug therapy.

Behavioral therapists emphasize that the environment affects people's psychological life. Some environmental events make almost anyone feel bad, whereas others make virtually everyone feel good. People become depressed, according to the behavioral approach, when they do not experience enough pleasant activities (Lewinsohn & Graf, 1973). If you sit around by yourself doing nothing at all, day after day—and thereby experience no pleasant events—you'll eventually feel depressed.

What, then, should you do to alleviate depression? The behavioral strategy involves two steps. First, therapists instruct clients to keep track of both their daily activities and their mood during these activities; this enables clients to see how environmental events trigger good and bad moods. Second, therapists devise strategies that enable clients to avoid events that trigger depression and to engage in more activities that improve mood. One team of behavior therapists applied this approach when working with a depressed single mother. They found that the woman had eliminated virtually all positive social events from her life in order to cope with the demands of parenting. Therapists showed her how to increase her social contacts while also handling depressing household chores more efficiently so that she would have time for a social life. After a few weeks, her mood substantially improved (Lewinsohn, Sullivan, & Grosscup, 1980).

In what environments do you experience good moods?

A second approach is cognitive therapy. Aaron Beck (1987) identified a "cognitive triad"—three interconnected types of thoughts—that contribute to depression. People who are depressed tend to have excessively negatively thoughts about (1) themselves, (2) the world, and (3) the future. If a relationship breaks up and you think (1) "I'm unattractive," (2) "The dating scene is a cruel meat market," and (3) "I'll never be in a relationship again," you are exhibiting the cognitive triad of negative beliefs. In therapy, cognitive therapists challenge these thoughts and help clients replace them with ones that are more accurate and adaptive.

Good news for people suffering from depression is that cognitive therapy works. Meta-analyses that summarize the effectiveness of therapy have long shown that cognitive therapy significantly reduces symptoms of depression (Dobson, 1989). As we've seen, cognitive therapy is not the only effective therapy strategy, and there is some question about whether cognitive therapy is superior to all alternative approaches to psychotherapy (Cuijpers et al., 2008). Nonetheless, there is no question that cognitive therapy substantially reduces depressive symptoms.

Another effective approach is *interpersonal therapy*. In **interpersonal therapy,** therapists try to identify, and change, interpersonal problems that contribute to a client's current depression. A key aim is to reduce the client's social isolation by expanding his or her network of relationships (Klerman et al., 1984). Interpersonal therapy is inspired by two of the broad therapy strategies you learned about earlier: the psychodynamic approach, which, in developments made after Freud's lifetime, began to emphasize the importance of analyzing client's interpersonal relationships (Sullivan, 1953); and the humanistic approach, whose central tenet is that strong interpersonal relationships are the foundation of healthy psychological growth. In practice, interpersonal therapy is similar to cognitive therapy for depression, with both approaches targeting irrational thoughts about interpersonal relationships (Ablon & Jones, 2002).

A fourth strategy to combat depression is drug therapy. Antidepressants are among the most widely prescribed of all prescription drugs in the United States. Nearly 1 in 10 women, and about half as many men, take antidepressants (Barber, 2008; Breggin & Breggin, 2010).

Paul Bradbury / Gallery Stock

Friends can lift your mood
To treat depression, behavior therapists may instruct clients to engage in more positive social activities, such as hanging out with friends. Social activities can improve mood.

interpersonal therapy A therapy approach in which therapists try to identify and change interpersonal problems contributing to clients' psychological distress, especially by reducing clients' social isolation.

⏰ THIS JUST IN

Do Antidepressants Work Better Than Placebos?

Americans spend and spend on antidepressant drugs. Prozac, one popular antidepressant, attained annual sales of $800 million just a few years after its 1988 release (Stipp, 2005). Today, Americans shell out $10 *billion* a year on antidepressant medicines—the second-most prescribed class of drugs in the United States (Hensley, 2011). If people are spending $10 billion, the drugs must be working great, right?

The exact answer depends on how "working" is defined. People who take antidepressants do improve compared with people who receive no treatment (no medication, no psychotherapy) for their depression. In this sense, then, antidepressants work. But as the psychologist Irving Kirsch (2010) emphasizes, this does not mean that the active ingredients in antidepressant drugs effectively reduce depression. The problem is that substances with *no active ingredients whatsoever*—that is, placebo substances—also reduce depression.

Placebo effects are fundamentally psychological, not biochemical (Kirsch, 2010). When people take prescribed substances, they expect them to work; the prescriptions give people hope. Hope combats the feelings of hopelessness that accompany depression. As a result, depressed people who take medication improve. This improvement occurs whether the drugs are real pharmaceuticals or placebos; both instill hope and reduce depression. Placebos can even induce changes in brain activity that resemble changes found in people taking real medication (Benedetti et al., 2005; Figure 15.3).

The key question, then, is whether antidepressant drugs work better than placebos. Kirsch (2010) reviewed all existing research studies on this question, and found the difference between drug effects and placebo effects to be remarkably small. Specifically, 82% of the effects of drugs were due to placebo effects. In other words, there was a unique effect of drugs, but it was only about 20% larger than the effect obtained from placebos. Even this 20%, Kirsch argues, is small. On a 52-point measurement scale used to measure people's level of depression, the advantage of drugs over placebos was only 1.8 points—a difference that is statistically significant but, in practice, not that big (Kirsch, 2010). For many people, the effect is even smaller. The drug–placebo difference is larger for people who are very severely depressed and smaller for the many people who are only moderately depressed.

Others reach similar conclusions. One research team reviewed therapy outcomes among more than 700 individuals with mild, severe, or very severe levels of depression. Among people whose depression levels were very severe, antidepressant drugs were of substantial benefit. But for the remaining two-thirds of the population, with depression in the mild-to-severe range, the "benefit of antidepressant medication [was] . . . minimal to nonexistent" (Fournier et al., 2010, p. 47). Another meta-analysis, involving more than 4,000 patients, reached similarly pessimistic conclusions (Pigott et al., 2010).

A final bit of evidence "just in" compares the effects of antidepressant medication to a simple intervention: exercise. Reviews of research findings indicate that, for mild to moderate levels of depression, a program of intense physical exercise is as effective as antidepressant medications in alleviating depression (Carek et al., 2011; Cooney et al., 2013).

Courtesy of Adbusters Media Foundation, adbusters.org

How much better is it than plain water? Research findings raise questions about the effectiveness of antidepressant medications, such as Prozac, in treating mild and moderate depression.

THINK ABOUT IT

When a therapy works, ask *why*. What are its *active ingredients*—the components that actually caused it to succeed? Did a drug work because of its chemical substances or merely because taking a drug caused people to believe they would improve? Did people benefit from a psychotherapy strategy because of specific components of that strategy or merely because they had a warm, socially skilled individual (therapist) who was paying attention to them?

Like most people, I used to think that antidepressants worked.

—Irving Kirsch (2010, p. 1)

🧠 WHAT DO YOU KNOW?...

9. True or False?
   a. Kirsch's extensive review of research led him to conclude that most of the effectiveness of antidepressants is due to placebo effects.
   b. Among the studies demonstrating that antidepressants work, the size of the effect was large.

figure 15.3

PMB IN ACTION

DO FAKE (PLACEBO) DRUGS HAVE PSYCHOLOGICAL EFFECTS?

(P) PERSON

Yes, placebo drugs affect people's psychological experiences. For example, many people with depression experience an improvement in symptoms after taking placebo medication.

(M) MIND

At a mind level of analysis, placebos work by altering beliefs. The belief that a medication will work triggers improvement, even if the medication is a fake.

(B) BRAIN

People who believe placebos will work and then improve psychologically display changes in brain activity similar to those seen in people who take real medication and expect it to work.

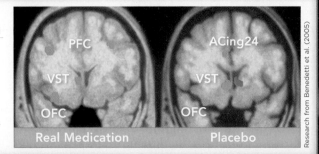

PFC · VST · OFC — Real Medication
ACing24 · VST · OFC — Placebo

Research from Benedetti et al. (2005)

Because both drug therapies and psychotherapy are available to treat depression, a significant question for people experiencing the disorder is how the different therapy strategies compare. Much research has investigated this question. Findings commonly indicate either that cognitive therapy is superior to drugs in relieving major depression or that the two approaches are about equally effective (Butler et al., 2006; Cox et al., 2012). Drug therapy rarely is found to be superior. In light of recent findings comparing antidepressant drugs to placebo medications (see This Just In), this result is not surprising. Antidepressant medications have proven to be less effective than the pharmaceutical industry, and depression sufferers, had hoped.

✋ WHAT DO YOU KNOW?...

10. The following statement is incorrect. Explain why: "To be diagnosed with major depressive disorder, an individual has to exhibit all depressive symptoms (consistent depressed mood; loss of interest in most daily activities; change in body weight; change in sleep patterns; fatigue; feelings of worthlessness, hopelessness, or helplessness; difficulty concentrating; and thoughts of suicide) for at least two weeks."

11. Aaron Beck observed that individuals with major depression displayed a cognitive triad of negative thoughts about themselves, the world, and the _____. Research indicates that cognitive therapy is superior to, or at least equal to _____ therapies in relieving the symptoms of major depression.

◎ CULTURAL OPPORTUNITIES

Diagnosing Disorders

People in all cultures experience psychological disorders. But do they experience the *same* disorders?

In the United States, a particularly common disorder is major depression. As you learned in the main text, its central features are prolonged low mood and feelings of personal worthlessness and hopelessness.

You might expect that diagnoses of major depression would be common everywhere in the world. They aren't. Research conducted in Hunan, a large province of South-Central China, shows that diagnoses of major depression there are rare (Kleinman & Kleinman, 1985). Far more common are diagnoses of "neurasthenia." This diagnostic category differs from depression in that its main features are not thoughts and emotions of the mind, but physical conditions of the body: fatigue, insomnia, and headache.

The difference in diagnostic categories used in the United States and China has two possible causes. People in the different countries may experience fundamentally different disorders. Alternatively, they may experience similar disorders but think and talk about them differently. Cultural differences may affect how people conceptualize their personal distress. Some evidence supports the latter view.

Researchers (Kleinman & Kleinman, 1985) carefully analyzed the psychological conditions of 100 Hunanese patients diagnosed with neurasthenia. The vast majority of them, they found, showed signs of major depression as it is diagnosed in the United States. In other words, even though they were diagnosed in China with neurasthenia, not depression, in the United States, major depression would have been the diagnosis.

What accounts for this discrepancy? It appeared that when the Chinese patients talked to their Chinese physicians, their conversations did not focus on the patient's thoughts and emotional life. Rather, as in other non-Western cultures (Tsai & Chentsova-Dutton, 2002), Chinese patients and physicians

Mental health is a worldwide issue When diagnosing and treating psychological disorders, mental health professionals must pay attention to cultural factors that can influence how people experience, and discuss, psychological distress. Shown is a government-run mental health facility in the Indian state of Jammu and Kashmir, whose population experiences high rates of anxiety and stress disorders due to ongoing, and often violent, political conflicts in the region.

Robert Nickelsberg / Getty Images

discussed bodily states more than thoughts and feelings. This tendency reflects long-held cultural beliefs (Kleinman & Kleinman, 1985). In China, unlike the United States, prolonged sadness can bring shame upon oneself and one's family. People thus are reluctant to talk about such emotion. Furthermore, traditional Chinese medicine suggests that the expression of negative emotion is a cause of illness, which further adds to people's reluctance to discuss their depressed mood.

Thus, cultural factors shape the way health professionals discuss and diagnose the conditions of their patients.

✪ WHAT DO YOU KNOW?...

12. In Hunan, major _____ is less likely to be diagnosed than in the United States, largely because of what the Hunanese _____ about when describing their symptoms. They tend to focus on _____ symptoms and not emotional ones because, in their culture, sadness is shameful.

Bipolar Disorder

Preview Questions

› What defines bipolar disorder and how prevalent is it?
› What therapies effectively treat bipolar disorder?

"I have two moods. One is . . . rollicking . . . the wild ride of a mood. [The other] stands on the shore and sobs . . . Sometimes the tide is in, sometimes it's out."

The writer suffers from **bipolar disorder,** also known as **manic-depressive disorder.** Bipolar disorder is a depressive disorder characterized by extreme variations in mood. People's mood "swings" from severe depression to **mania,** which is a period of abnormally high energy, arousal, and positive mood.

Intense positive mood might sound like fun. But to people with bipolar disorder, both depression and mania bring difficulties (Gruber, 2011). In manic states, people sometimes engage in reckless behavior they later regret. It's "a world of bad judgment calls," the writer above continues. During the manic periods, "[I display] every kind of bad judgment because it all seems like a good idea at the time. A great idea. . . . So if it's talking, if it's shopping, if it's—the weirdest one for me is sex. That's only happened twice. But then it's wow, who are you?"

Like J. K. Rowling, this writer also overcame her depressive disorder and achieved great professional success. She is Carrie Fisher—*Star Wars*'s Princess Leia, one of the great heroines of film history. "I outlasted my problems," says Fisher. "I am mentally ill. I can say that. I am not ashamed of that. I survived that, I'm still surviving it, but bring it on. Better me than you" (Prime Time, 2000).

In her memoir entitled *Wishful Drinking*, Carrie Fisher reacts to learning that her image graced the title page of an abnormal psychology textbook chapter on bipolar disorder: "Obviously my family is so proud. Keep in mind, though, I'm a PEZ dispenser *and* I'm in the *Abnormal Psychology* textbook. Who says you can't have it all?" (Fisher, 2008, p. 114)

Lucasfilm / 20th Century Fox / The Kobal Collection

Battling bipolar disorder
As Princess Leia in *Star Wars*, Carrie Fisher battled Darth Vader and Jabba the Hutt. Off screen, Carrie Fisher is one of millions of Americans who have battled bipolar disorder.

bipolar disorder (manic-depressive disorder) A depressive disorder characterized by extreme variations in mood, from severe depression to mania.

mania A period of abnormally high energy, arousal, and often positive mood that can be accompanied by reckless behavior.

DEFINING FEATURES AND PREVALENCE. To be categorized according to the DSM as a person with bipolar disorder, an individual must display two types of symptoms:

› *Depression:* One or more episodes of depression, that is, periods of at least two weeks during which a person experiences depressed mood, loss of interest in activities, fatigue, and feelings of worthlessness.

› *Mania:* A period of at least four days in a row marked by abnormally high energy, racing thoughts, extreme talkativeness, high levels of self-esteem, or involvement in fun activities that are costly or risky (e.g., the person decides, on a whim, to check into the most expensive hotel in town). Manic periods may also include episodes of extreme irritability.

These mood swings, from depression to mania and back, distinguish bipolar disorder from major depression. Note that a person with bipolar disorder generally will experience substantial periods of normal mood state; the deviations from this state are what characterize the disorder.

About 1% of adults suffer from bipolar disorder (NIMH, 2007). In terms of overall numbers of people, then, bipolar disorder is quite prevalent; in the United States alone, 1% of adults translates into about 2 million people. Bipolar disorder is a long-term illness for which there is no surefire cure. The personal and social costs of the disorder are huge and include high risks of suicide; estimates of suicide rates among persons diagnosed with the disorder range from 8 to 20% (Nakic, Krystal, & Bhagwagar, 2010). Because it is prevalent, severe, and chronic, the World Health Organization ranks it as the sixth most severe of *all medical disorders* in terms of years of life lost to disability and death (Nakic et al., 2010).

TREATMENT. The primary form of treatment for bipolar disorder is drug therapy. The reasoning behind drug therapy is that bipolar disorder's mood swings may stem from abnormal variations in brain functioning. The brain's neurotransmitter systems generally are seen as the biological culprits (Nakic et al., 2010). **Mood stabilizers,** which are drugs designed to influence neurotransmitters in the brain in a manner that calms and steadies the patient's swinging mood states, thus are a major form of treatment (Stahl, 2002).

Three types of drugs are most commonly used as mood stabilizers (Stahl, 2002):

1. *Lithium:* The drug **lithium,** a chemical compound that centrally includes the physical element lithium, is the classic drug of choice for treating bipolar disorder. Findings support its effectiveness. Lithium reduces bipolar symptoms, even in long-term use among patients who take the drug for years (Tondo, Baldessarini, & Floris, 2001).

2. *Anticonvulsants:* As we've seen, sometimes drugs used to treat one disorder turn out to benefit another. **Anticonvulsants,** which are drugs used to treat epileptic seizures, also reduce bipolar symptoms (Bowden, 2009).

3. *Antipsychotics:* As you'll learn in the next chapter, a variety of drugs are used to treat psychotic disorders such as schizophrenia. Some of the more recently developed antipsychotic drugs also have been found to reduce bipolar symptoms (Perlis et al., 2006).

The best evidence that these drugs work comes from meta-analyses of studies that compared the experiences of people receiving a mood stabilizer to those of people receiving a placebo drug. One such meta-analysis has documented the effectiveness of lithium, which was particularly effective in reducing manic episodes (Geddes et al., 2004). Another indicates that some antipsychotics can reduce bipolar symptoms particularly rapidly (Cruz et al., 2010).

Major depression and bipolar disorder are not the only depressive disorders. In **postpartum depression,** which affects 10 to 15% of women who give birth (Pearlstein et al., 2009), women experience symptoms akin to those of major depression beginning within a few weeks of childbirth (NIHM, 2011). In **seasonal affective disorder,** individuals tend to experience depressed mood during late autumn and winter, periods when there is less sunlight (Rosenthal, 2009). Light therapy can help sufferers. Exposure to bright light for about half an hour a day relieves symptoms, an effect that may be due to the influence of intense light on neurotransmitters in the brain (Virk et al., 2009).

© B. Boissonnet / Bsip / Bsip / Corbis

Want to brighten your mood? Exposure to bright light can help relieve symptoms of *seasonal affective disorder*, in which individuals experience depressed mood during late autumn and winter.

mood stabilizers Drugs designed to reduce symptoms of bipolar disorder by affecting neurotransmitters in a way that calms and steadies a patient's mood swings.

lithium A mood-stabilizing drug that centrally includes the physical element lithium; the classic drug of choice for treatment of bipolar disorder.

anticonvulsants Drugs typically used to treat epileptic seizures but that also are used to reduce bipolar symptoms.

postpartum depression A depressive disorder in which some women experience symptoms akin to major depression beginning within weeks of childbirth.

seasonal affective disorder A depressive disorder in which individuals experience depressed mood during late summer and winter, periods when there is less sunlight.

13. Which of the following statements are true of bipolar disorder? Check all that apply.

———a. It is marked by swings between depression, lasting at least two weeks, and mania, lasting at least four days in a row.

———b. Its manic symptoms include a decrease in self-esteem and an aversion to making decisions that are costly or risky.

———c. Only about .01% of adults suffer from it, making it one of the least prevalent medical disorders.

———d. It is typically treated with mood-stabilizing drugs, including lithium, anticonvulsants, and antipsychotics.

Anxiety Disorders

How do you feel at the start of a job interview? Anxious. At the start of a big date? Anxious. When beginning a final exam? Anxious. Everyone sometimes experiences **anxiety,** an agitated emotional state that includes feelings of apprehension about impending danger or misfortune.

Although everyone experiences it, some people's experiences of anxiety are extreme—far more severe and frequent than is normal. These people suffer from **anxiety disorders,** long-lasting psychological states involving strong and persistent feelings of anxiety that interfere with everyday life (NIMH, 2009).

Anxiety is a unique emotion. It differs from fear (Sylvers, Lilienfeld, & LaPrairie, 2011). People are fearful when danger is staring them in the face: a mugger in an alley; a fast-moving car headed right at them. Anxiety, however, arises when threats are vague and hard to identify. Nothing may go wrong in the interview, on the date, or during the exam, yet you're still anxious. People often feel anxiety without knowing exactly what is making them anxious.

Just as there are different depressive disorders, there also are different types of disorders in which anxiety is a central symptom. We'll look at five: *Generalized Anxiety Disorder, Panic Disorder, Social Anxiety Disorder, Posttraumatic Stress Disorder,* and *Obsessive-Compulsive Disorder.*

Generalized Anxiety Disorder

Preview Questions

> What defines generalized anxiety disorder and how prevalent is it?
> What therapies effectively treat generalized anxiety disorder?

> I've put up with this constant severe anxiety thrashing my body for 4 years now. I'm now 17 starting my senior year and I can't function in school. My anxiety has been at a level which basically takes over my day, almost every day, and it has for the past 4 years. I wake up with the fight or flight response, walk downstairs with it, eat breakfast with it, struggle being around my family with it, and go to school barely managing to get through the classes. I have missed days of school and ditched classes a number of times because I got to the point I just couldn't force myself to do it every day. I honestly don't know how I even went through this for the past 4 years, completely out of control.
>
> Am I alone? I don't know. I feel even worse after I wrote this. Like the seriousness of it all hit me, and the question, "Am I one of the very few with this severe of anxiety?"
>
> —(losthobbit, 2011)

anxiety An agitated emotional state that includes feelings of apprehension about impending danger or misfortune.

anxiety disorders Long-lasting psychological states involving strong and persistent feelings of anxiety that interfere with everyday life.

The writer, a contributor to an online chat room, is not alone. She is one of millions of Americans suffering from generalized anxiety disorder (Newman et al., 2013).

DEFINING FEATURES AND PREVALENCE. **Generalized anxiety disorder** is a psychological disorder in which people experience high and persistent levels of tension, agitation, apprehension, and worry, even in the absence of a current event that provokes the feelings of anxiety (NIMH, 2009). DSM criteria for the disorder include the following (Andrews et al., 2010):

> Worry about two or more aspects of life (e.g., relationships, health, finances, family affairs, or work).

> The worry and anxiety occur on the majority of days.

> The symptoms persist for at least three months.

In addition to the emotional reactions (anxiety) and thoughts (worry), people suffering from generalized anxiety disorder often display distinctive behaviors. They tend to avoid situations that provoke worry, to procrastinate when they need to take action or make decisions, and to spend excessive time preparing for activities. The disorder thus can disrupt many aspects of people's lives.

Another common feature of generalized anxiety disorder is a perceived lack of control. People not only worry excessively, they also believe that stopping their worrying is beyond their capabilities (Andrews et al., 2010).

Generalized anxiety disorder affects nearly 7 million adults in the United States, which makes it the most prevalent of the anxiety disorders (Wittchen & Hoyer, 2001). It occurs about twice as often among women as among men.

TREATMENT. Both drugs and psychological therapies are used to treat generalized anxiety disorder (Portman, 2009). Drug therapies employ **anti-anxiety drugs,** pharmaceuticals designed to alter brain functioning in a manner that reduces feelings of anxiety. Anti-anxiety drugs work by affecting neurotransmitters in the brain (Chapter 3). For example, one popular class of drug, benzodiazepines, increases the effectiveness of a neurotransmitter that, in turn, *decreases* the level of electrical activity of brain cells. Benzodiazepines thus lead to a reduction in brain activity, including within regions of the brain that produce emotional response. As a result, they reduce anxiety. The anti-anxiety medications Valium and Xanax are benzodiazepines.

Drug therapies do not cure generalized anxiety disorders, however. They merely dampen the symptoms. To fully combat the disorder, then, therapists commonly combine drugs with psychological therapy strategies.

Two strategies you saw earlier in this chapter—behavior therapy and cognitive therapy—are used frequently to treat generalized anxiety disorder (Huppert & Sanderson, 2009). Behavior therapy targets anxious emotions; therapists aim to reduce clients' tension and anxious arousal by providing them with new behavioral experiences. Cognitive therapy targets the tendency to worry; therapists restructure clients' anxious cognitions. In practice, psychologists often combine the approaches into one cognitive-behavioral treatment package.

Despite these effects, psychotherapy for generalized anxiety disorder is less effective than one would hope. Therapy outcome studies do show that clients in psychotherapy improve, on average, compared with those in control groups. Nonetheless, many individual clients who receive therapy still do not improve substantially (Borkovec & Costello, 1993). Even the most effective cognitive therapies benefit only about half of the clients who receive them (Huppert & Sanderson, 2009).

Van D Bucher / Getty Images

Valium, an anti-anxiety drug, works by affecting a neurotransmitter that decreases levels of electrical activity in the brain.

generalized anxiety disorder A psychological disorder in which people experience high and persistent levels of tension, agitation, apprehension, and worry, even in the absence of a current event that provokes the feelings.

anti-anxiety drugs Pharmaceuticals designed to alter brain functioning by affecting neurotransmitters in a manner that reduces feelings of anxiety.

Panic Disorder

Preview Questions

› What defines panic disorder and how prevalent is it?

› What therapies effectively treat panic disorder?

In generalized anxiety disorder, worry and anxiety are persistently present. The next anxiety disorder we will consider is different: **Panic disorder** is a psychological disorder in which people experience sudden bouts of intense terror and extreme physiological arousal (NIMH, 2009).

DEFINING FEATURES AND PREVALENCE. The key defining feature of panic disorder is the occurrence of panic attacks. A **panic attack** is an episode of extreme fear, including high levels of physical arousal, that occurs suddenly and without apparent cause. During panic attacks, sufferers do not merely feel "worried"; they feel as if they are losing control of their body, having a heart attack, dying, or going insane. A 24-year-old woman describes her symptoms: "lightheadedness . . . my chest was tightening . . . I felt like I could not breathe. My heart was racing and I had shortness of breath . . . totally terrifying" (Stevenson, 2014).

The DSM specifies criteria for the disorder. They include the following:

› The panic attacks are recurrent.

› For one month or more, the person worries about the attack and its consequences.

› The panic attacks are not side effects of a medication or other drug.

The prevalence of panic disorder is similar to that of generalized anxiety disorder. It affects about 6 million Americans and is twice as common among women as among men.

TREATMENT. A variety of psychotherapy strategies can benefit people suffering from panic disorder. One is psychoanalysis. In one study, participants diagnosed with panic disorder were assigned randomly to one of two types of therapy: (1) relaxation training, in which they were taught to relax various muscle groups, or (2) psychoanalytic therapy, in which therapists explored the personal meaning of participants' panic symptoms. One patient, for example, was highly critical of herself during panic attacks, and psychoanalytic therapy indicated that negative experiences with her mother were at the root of the self-criticism and panic. Psychoanalytic therapy reduced panic symptoms more than did relaxation training (Milrod et al., 2007).

Cognitive-behavioral therapy is another approach to alleviating panic disorder. Cognitive-behavioral therapists try to alter clients' thoughts about panic (e.g., the thought that a high heart rate will lead to a heart attack or death). They also teach

Kyle Gustafson / For The Washington Post via Getty Images

Jeff Tweedy, lead singer for the band Wilco, suffers from panic disorder. "One of the things that happens a lot with panic disorder is that you'll have an actual panic attack and for weeks or months after that you'll have a fear of a panic attack that can heighten your anxiety and heighten your stress levels to the point where you end up having another panic attack" (Tweedy, 2008).

panic disorder A psychological disorder in which people experience the sudden bouts of intense terror and extreme physiological arousal known as panic attacks.

panic attack An episode of extreme fear, including high levels of physical arousal, that occurs suddenly and without apparent cause.

strategies for lowering the arousal itself (e.g., strategies to slow one's breathing; Barlow & Craske, 2007).

Yet another strategy for combating panic disorder is a behavioral approach discussed earlier, namely, *exposure therapy*. Therapists place clients into contact with the object or situation that triggers their panic, while ensuring that no harm will come to clients in the situation. Gradually, clients' fear dissipates as they experience prolonged, harmless encounters with the situation that had triggered panic. A review of therapy outcome studies documents that exposure therapy effectively reduces panic symptoms (Sánchez-Meca et al., 2010).

Finally, drug therapies are also an option for treating panic disorder. SSRIs, used to treat depression, as you learned earlier, have been shown to also be effective in reducing panic disorder symptoms (Batelaan, Van Balkom, & Stein, 2012). In practice, mental health professionals often combine drug therapies with a psychotherapy such as cognitive-behavioral therapy. An advantage of this combination is that the psychotherapy provides clients with psychological skills that endure after they stop taking the medication (Batelaan et al., 2012).

> **What strategies do you use to lower arousal?**

✪ WHAT DO YOU KNOW?...

15. Which of the following statements are true of panic disorder? Check all that apply.

_____ a. It is marked by panic attacks: recurrent sudden bouts of intense terror and extreme physiological arousal.

_____ b. To be diagnosed, an individual must worry about such attacks and their consequences for one month or more.

_____ c. A person can be diagnosed with panic disorder even if the panic attack was a side effect of a medication or other drug.

_____ d. It has been successfully treated with psychoanalysis, cognitive-behavioral therapy, and exposure therapy sessions in which the individual is put in situations that have triggered the attacks in the past.

Social Anxiety Disorder

Preview Questions

> What defines social anxiety disorder and how prevalent is it?
> What therapies effectively treat social anxiety disorder?

In the two anxiety disorders we just reviewed, generalized anxiety disorder and panic disorder, anxiety and worry can occur in virtually any type of situation. The next disorder is different. **Social anxiety disorder** is defined by extreme levels of anxiety and self-consciousness specifically in situations involving other people.

People who suffer from social anxiety disorder are intensely worried about embarrassing themselves in front of others who, they believe, are observing and evaluating them (NIMH, 2009). Everyone sometimes has worries about social embarrassment. But in social anxiety disorder, people experience "overwhelming terror" in response to even the "simple process of interacting with people" (Turk, Heimberg, & Magee, 2008, p. 123). These reactions can substantially lower socially anxious people's overall quality of life, with fear of embarrassment interfering with the ability to take part in routine activities. For example,

Laura Neal / Getty Images

What if all the world were a public speech? Some situations, such as giving a public speech, are anxiety provoking for most individuals, who worry about embarrassing themselves in front of others. People who suffer from social anxiety disorder have such worries in a wide range of situations, including everyday circumstances that provoke little or no anxiety in most other people.

social anxiety disorder A disorder characterized by extreme levels of anxiety and self-consciousness specifically in situations involving other people.

a mother with social anxiety disorder reports that "I feel anxious when I attend parents' meetings in my children's classes. . . . I am afraid that I will blush. . . . [I] go completely blank and cannot think of anything to say" (Jensen, Hougaard, & Fishman, 2013, p. 288).

DEFINING FEATURES AND PREVALENCE. According to DSM criteria, individuals have social anxiety disorder only if their anxiety is persistent and extreme. Criteria include the following:

> Persistent fear of social situations and anticipation of humiliation and embarrassment in such situations.

> A recognition by the individual that the anxiety is excessive.

> The anxiety interferes with the person's normal professional or social activities.

> These symptoms last at least six months.

Social anxiety disorder is very prevalent. Surveys indicate that 12.1% of U.S. citizens experience social anxiety disorder at some point in their adult lives (Turk et al., 2008). This percentage is so high that, to some, it raises a possibility discussed earlier in this chapter, namely, that the disorder is *over*diagnosed. Some express concern that normal, everyday shyness may inappropriately be diagnosed as a psychological disorder (Swinson, 2005). Despite this concern, however, millions of individuals unquestionably do experience extreme levels of social anxiety that erode the quality of their life. Let's consider therapies available for them.

TREATMENT. A variety of therapy strategies have been used to combat social anxiety disorder, and the good news is that many are effective. Meta-analyses indicate that therapies significantly benefit people with the disorder (Acarturk et al., 2009; Gould et al., 1997).

Different therapy strategies can each be effective in treating social anxiety disorder. As with other anxiety disorders, anti-anxiety drugs reduce the symptoms of social anxiety (Turk et al., 2008). Cognitive and behavioral therapies also are effective for individuals. In addition, people with social anxiety disorder benefit from group therapy; in fact, group therapy has unique advantages.

One advantage of group therapy involves social skills. People with social anxiety disorder may lack some skills; for instance, they might not be good at starting a conversation or establishing eye contact with others. Furthermore, even when their skills are adequate, they may underestimate themselves and judge that they are socially inept (Heimberg, 2002). Group therapy gives clients an opportunity to learn new social skills that they can test out in the group. In one study, clients received instruction on topics to discuss in social conversation, appropriate ways of speaking in those conversations (e.g., maintaining sufficient voice volume), and nonverbal behavior to perform when conversing (e.g., establishing eye contact, displaying appropriate facial expressions). They also received "homework assignments" to practice those skills. Compared with others, clients receiving social skills training in a group setting showed a substantial reduction in social anxiety disorder symptoms (Herbert et al., 2005).

Overcoming social anxiety disorder
After Ricky Williams won the Heisman Trophy, awarded annually to America's best college football player, one might have expected that Williams's future would be filled with nothing but success. But he experienced social anxiety disorder; he had trouble interacting with fans, media, and even friends and family. Fortunately for Mr. Williams, an accurate diagnosis and therapy helped. "After I was diagnosed with social anxiety disorder, I felt immense relief because it meant that there was a name for my suffering. I wasn't crazy or weird, like I thought for so many years," said Williams. "Soon [after therapy began] I was able to start acting like the real Ricky Williams" (Anderson, n.d.).

© ZUMA Press, Inc. / Alamy

16. Which of the following statements are true of social anxiety disorder? Check all that apply.

_____ a. Individuals diagnosed with it avoid social situations because they expect to be embarrassed and humiliated by others, even though they know this fear is excessive.

_____ b. In order to be diagnosed, individuals must experience symptoms for at least six months.

_____ c. About 12% of U.S. citizens are diagnosed with it, raising the issue of whether it is overdiagnosed.

_____ d. It is treated with anti-anxiety drugs, cognitive and behavioral therapies, and group therapy, which is especially effective because clients can learn and test out social skills.

Phobias

Preview Questions

> What defines phobias and how prevalent are they?
> What therapies effectively treat phobias?

In a panic attack, as you learned, people experience extreme fear but do not know why. In another type of disorder, people know why; they can readily tell you what causes them to become afraid. Their excessive fear reactions are called *phobias*.

DEFINING FEATURES AND PREVALENCE. **Phobias** are strong, persistent fears caused by situations that pose little or no actual threat. There are different types of phobic disorder. **Specific phobias** are fears directed toward particular objects or situations (LeBeau et al., 2010). People who are afraid of flying, heights, snakes, spiders, or closed-in spaces suffer from specific phobias. Sometimes people develop phobias toward objects you might never expect; Chapter 7 of this book begins with some cases in which people are phobic of buttons.

Agoraphobia is a fear of being in diverse social situations outside one's home. Someone with agoraphobia might avoid stores, theatres, public transportation, or any setting in which crowds are present (Wittchen et al., 2010). (The word *agora* is Greek for "gathering place" and refers to the location in a town where people meet socially; "agoraphobia" thus is a fear of people in such social gathering places.)

Specific phobias are common. Nearly 20 million adult Americans (8 to 9% of adults) experience some form of specific phobia (NIMH, 2009). Agoraphobia is much rarer, afflicting about one-half of 1% of adults (Grant et al., 2006; McCabe et al., 2006).

TREATMENT. When it comes to treating phobias, it is worth remembering the old adage "You have to get back on the horse that threw you." A particularly effective way for people to overcome phobias is by directly confronting their fears, rather than merely talking about them.

A key strategy for confronting fears is thus exposure therapy. Exposure therapy treats phobias effectively (Choy, Fyer, & Lipsitz, 2007), especially when it increases clients' beliefs in their personal ability to cope with the feared stimulus (Bandura, 1986).

A closely related strategy is *mastery therapy* (Williams & Zane, 1997). In mastery therapy, therapists accompany clients to situations that they fear and perform activities with them. Therapists treating agoraphobia, for example, might join clients shopping at a mall or riding on a bus (Gloster et al., 2011). Therapists gradually reduce the amount of help they give to clients, so clients can learn to master their fears on their own.

phobias Strong, persistent fears caused by situations that pose little or no actual threat.

specific phobias Fears directed toward particular objects or situations, such as fear of flying, heights, spiders, or closed-in spaces.

agoraphobia Fear of being in diverse social situations outside one's home, such as in stores, public transportation, or among crowds.

Treating phobia A particularly effective way of overcoming phobias (such as height phobia) is to have people directly confront their fears. Therapists may encourage clients to expose themselves to anxiety-provoking situations in a safe manner.

In therapy, these behavioral experiences are commonly combined with cognitive strategies designed to boost clients' confidence in their ability to overcome their fears.

The cognitive-behavioral strategy for treating phobias is a success story, benefiting people with specific phobias and agoraphobia (Butler et al., 2006). Treatments for specific phobias are particularly powerful; they often eradicate phobic reactions in the large majority of clients (Bandura, Adams, & Beyer, 1977). If you know someone with phobia, psychology can help.

Research finds that therapies change phobic behavior by affecting not only the mind (e.g., people's beliefs about feared stimuli and their ability to cope with them), but also the brain (Paquette et al., 2003). People with spider phobias participated in a cognitive-behavioral therapy that combined exposure to spiders with cognitive strategies for changing fearful beliefs. The therapy worked; it reduced the phobic reactions of all participants. Before and after therapy, researchers scanned participants' brains to identify regions that were highly active when they viewed films depicting spiders. Therapy changed brain activity. Before therapy, spider films activated regions of the frontal cortex that normally are active when people worry excessively about harmful events. After therapy, the films did not activate these same brain regions. As the researchers summarize, "Change the mind and you change the brain" (Paquette et al., 2003, p. 401). Cognitive-behavioral therapy changed people's beliefs; they no longer viewed spiders as threats. As a result, brain activity in regions that are active when people worry about threats was reduced.

We'll conclude this chapter with two disorders that involve anxiety, yet have enough distinctive features that DSM-5 classifies them as separate disorders: (1) *Obsessive-Compulsive Disorder* (*OCD*) and (2) trauma-related disorders, especially *Posttraumatic Stress Disorder* (*PTSD*).

WHAT DO YOU KNOW?...

17. When it comes to successfully treating phobias, why are treatments that force clients to "get back on the horse that threw them" more effective than those that simply let them talk about their fears?

Obsessive-Compulsive Disorder

Preview Questions

> What defines obsessive-compulsive disorder and how prevalent is it?
> What therapies effectively treat obsessive-compulsive disorder?

"Feeding the dog took two hours as I checked and re-checked I'd given him the right food and the right amount." The British homemaker Hayley Martin suffered from *obsessive-compulsive disorder.* As its name suggests, **obsessive-compulsive disorder (OCD)** is defined by the presence of two symptoms: obsessions and compulsions (Abramowitz, Taylor, & McKay, 2009).

1. *Obsessions* are recurring, intrusive thoughts about potential danger or harm.
2. *Compulsions* are repetitive actions taken to prevent the dangers and harms imagined in the obsessions. People with OCD engage, over and over, in actions such as checking the locks of a door, washing their hands, or arranging household items in a strict order.

Dog feeding unfortunately was the least of Hayley Martin's problems. Obsessive thoughts dominated her family relationships: "The fear I had, that someone I love would be hurt or die as a result of me not checking everything is safe, was all-consuming. It was taking four hours to check and re-check that the gas was off." OCD affected her relations with friends: "If I phoned someone I was terrified I'd offended them and had to call them back to make sure I hadn't." It also affected her health; she eventually had a heart attack from the stress of OCD ("Checking House Was Safe," 2010).

DEFINING FEATURES AND PREVALENCE. In the DSM, the defining features of obsessive-compulsive disorder include the following:

> Recurring thoughts that the individual attempts to suppress

> Repetitive behaviors performed in response to those thoughts

> The obsessive thoughts and compulsive behaviors take up more than an hour a day of the person's time and interfere with his or her social or professional life

The compulsive behavior of OCD is irrational—and people with OCD know it. They know that the gas is turned off, the water isn't running, the door is locked, and their hands are clean. Yet this cold, factual knowledge is not enough. They still experience anxiety about potential harm and compulsively engage in behavior that the anxiety triggers.

As with other psychological disorders, the symptoms of OCD may sound familiar to you. Most of us, from time to time, worry excessively about everyday harms and engage in some extra "checking" behavior. However, OCD is more severe, and more rare, than this. The extreme anxiety and compulsiveness of obsessive-compulsive disorder strike about 1% of the adult population (Franklin & Foa, 2011).

TREATMENT. A number of therapeutic strategies benefit people with OCD. One is *exposure and response prevention* (Franklin & Foa, 2011). In **exposure and response prevention** therapy, therapists cause clients to come into contact with the stimuli that trigger their obsessions. They then prevent the clients from engaging in their usual compulsive behavior. Suppose, for example, that the therapist is working with a client who compulsively washes her hands to avoid germs. The therapist might lead the client to touch an object that is not perfectly clean, and then prevent her from washing her hands. At first, this is anxiety provoking for the client. After repeated exposure, however, the anxiety tends to dissipate as the client sees that no harm results when the typical compulsive behaviors are not performed.

In addition, both cognitive therapy and drug therapy can treat OCD successfully. Cognitive therapists combat clients' irrational beliefs, such as the belief that harm will befall people if the client does not compulsively check and recheck situations. In drug therapies, drugs used to treat depression also have been found to benefit OCD patients. However, a drawback is that they have these benefits only while patients continue to take the drugs (Franklin & Foa, 2011). By comparison, cognitive-behavioral therapy instills skills that remain with clients long after therapy concludes. This advantage leads many therapists to promote "skills, not pills"—that is, to endorse cognitive and behavioral approaches rather than drugs.

Photofusion / UIG via Getty Images

People with obsessive-compulsive disorder engage in repetitive behaviors, such as repeated hand washing.

obsessive-compulsive disorder (OCD) A mental disorder involving both recurring, intrusive thoughts about potential danger or harm (obsessions) and repetitive actions (compulsions) taken to prevent the imagined dangers and harms.

exposure and response prevention A type of therapy for obsessive-compulsive disorder in which therapists cause clients to come into contact with the stimuli that trigger their obsessions while preventing them from engaging in their usual compulsive behavior.

Trauma and Posttraumatic Stress Disorder

Preview Questions

> What defines posttraumatic stress disorder and how prevalent is it?

> What therapies effectively treat posttraumatic stress disorder?

I haven't really slept for twenty years. I lie down but I don't sleep. I'm always watching the door, the window, then back to the door. . . . It's like that until the sun begins to come up, then I can sleep for an hour or two. . . . Once a guy was burned real bad when some hydraulic fluid caught fire. . . . I got through Vietnam without a scratch (but) the smell of burning flesh f***ed me up real bad afterward. . . . I didn't notice it at the time the guy caught fire, but for the next few weeks I kept having flashbacks. . . . I don't deserve my wife. What kind of life it is for her married to me? . . . I once threw her out of bed. . . . I thought there was an NVA potato-masher [a North Vietnamese Army hand grenade] come in on us.

—Shay (1994, pp. xiv–xv)

This Vietnam veteran experienced an emotional trauma and is paying the price. He is not alone. Among many people, traumas trigger *trauma-related disorders,* those in which people experience any of a wide range of disturbances in emotional life (anxiety, depression, anger, loss of interest in social life) following a stressful traumatic event (American Psychiatric Association, 2013).

Psychologists have studied the psychological effects of trauma throughout the field's history. In the late 1800s, cases in which patients reported traumatic sexual abuse were the foundation for Freud's theory of personality (Chapter 13). In the 1970s, the study of trauma advanced when psychologists studied soldiers returning from the Vietnam War (Boscarino & Figley, 2012). They identified, in many veterans, a syndrome known as *posttraumatic stress disorder.*

DEFINING FEATURES AND PREVALENCE. **Posttraumatic stress disorder,** or **PTSD,** develops when people encounter extremely high levels of stress (e.g., military combat experience or a sexual assault; Nemeroff et al., 2006). Months or even years after the stressful event, people with PTSD experience *flashbacks,* which are vivid memories of past traumas. A crime victim may frequently re-experience the sights and sounds of the crime. A war veteran may uncontrollably relive the images and feelings of battle. The flashbacks can trigger intense anxiety that interferes with everyday life—as you read in the case of the Vietnam veteran quoted earlier. Symptoms of PTSD also include alterations in emotions, including anxiety when encountering

posttraumatic stress disorder (PTSD) A mental disorder characterized by flashbacks to previously encountered highly stressful experiences, such as military combat or sexual assault.

anything that reminds one of the traumatic event, persistent negative emotions (anger, guilt, horror), and high levels of arousal that cause people to easily startle.

Many people experience PTSD symptoms; at any given time, its prevalence among adults in the United States is 3.5% (American Psychiatric Association, 2013). Rates are considerably higher if one examines populations in which all individuals have experienced a trauma. For instance, more than 12% of rescue and recovery volunteers who assisted at the World Trade Center after the 9/11 attacks experienced PTSD (Perrin et al., 2007).

TREATMENT. Fortunately, therapy can help people cope with the disorder (Foa, Keane, & Friedman, 2000). One popular therapy strategy is a cognitive-behavioral approach in which clients learn how to cope with their traumatic memories effectively. For example, in a therapy for female combat veterans (Schnurr et al., 2007), women were encouraged to think about the traumatic events they had experienced rather than avoiding such thoughts. As they maintained their mental focus on the events, their emotional distress gradually reduced. They thus learned that they were able to think about past traumas without losing control of their thoughts and emotions. A meta-analysis of therapy effectiveness shows that when therapy alters people's beliefs about the traumatic event and its consequences, PTSD symptoms are reduced (Bisson et al., 2007).

Modern technology can enhance the effectiveness of PTSD therapy. Rather than relying on clients' ability to form mental images of traumatic events, therapists use virtual reality technologies to present images of trauma (e.g., military combat scenes; Rizzo et al., 2013). Virtual reality immerses clients in vivid computer-generated environments (see photo). They thus can develop skills for coping with their emotions while experiencing lifelike representations of traumatic events.

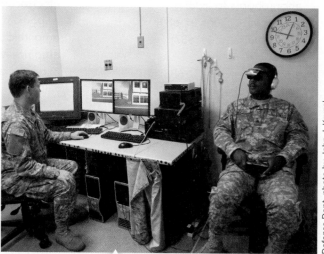

Virtual reality therapy and PTSD
A major challenge to military personnel is PTSD experienced after traumatic combat experiences. Virtual reality technology can help veterans learn how to manage the emotions that combat flashbacks can create.

✔ WHAT DO YOU KNOW?...

19. Experiencing an extremely traumatic stressful event, such as a sexual assault, may cause an individual to develop _____ _____ _____, or PTSD. Individuals with PTSD may experience _____, vivid memories of the events that interfere with everyday life. Cognitive-behavioral therapies help people cope with the negative thoughts and _____ that accompany stress-inducing memories, rather than avoiding them.

↺ Looking Back and Looking Ahead

This chapter has been a long journey. We started with the question of how to define psychological disorders, traversed through strategies for diagnosing and treating them, and then took a detailed tour of disorders involving depression, anxiety, obsessions and compulsions, and trauma.

Our trip is not over. In the next chapter, we'll visit a different realm of disorders— those in which people's normal ability to perceive the world of reality is lost.

Chapter Review

Now that you have completed this chapter, be sure to turn to Appendix B, where you will find a **Chapter Summary** that is useful for reviewing what you have learned about psychological disorders.

Key Terms

agoraphobia (p. 693)
anti-anxiety drugs (p. 689)
anticonvulsants (p. 687)
anxiety (p. 688)
anxiety disorders (p. 688)
automatic thoughts (p. 670)
Beck's cognitive therapy (p. 670)
behavior therapy (p. 667)
biological therapies (p. 665)
bipolar disorder (manic-depressive disorder) (p. 686)
blood–brain barrier (p. 677)
clinical psychologists (p. 656)
cognitive therapy (p. 669)
comorbidity (p. 662)
counseling psychologists (p. 656)
depression (p. 680)
Diagnostic and Statistical Manual of Mental Disorders (DSM) (p. 661)
double-blind clinical outcome study (p. 680)
drug therapies (p. 665)
DSM-5 (p. 662)
eclectic therapy (integrative psychotherapy) (p. 674)

electroconvulsive therapy (ECT) (p. 677)
empathic understanding (p. 671)
empirically supported therapies (p. 679)
exposure and response prevention (p. 695)
exposure therapy (p. 668)
extinguishing (of emotion) (p. 668)
free association method (p. 665)
generalized anxiety disorder (p. 689)
group therapy (p. 672)
humanistic therapy (p. 671)
insight therapy (p. 665)
interpersonal therapy (p. 682)
irrational beliefs (p. 669)
lithium (p. 687)
lobotomy (p. 678)
major depressive disorder (p. 681)
mania (p. 686)
medical model of psychological disorders (p. 657)
mood stabilizers (p. 687)
obsessive-compulsive disorder (OCD) (p. 695)

panic attack (p. 690)
panic disorder (p. 690)
phobias (p. 693)
placebo effect (p. 677)
postpartum depression (p. 687)
posttraumatic stress disorder (PTSD) (p. 696)
psychiatrists (p. 656)
psychoactive substances (p. 677)
psychoanalysis (p. 665)
psychological disorders (p. 656)
psychological therapies (psychotherapies) (p. 665)
psychotherapists (p. 665)
reflection (p. 671)
seasonal affective disorder (p. 687)
selective serotonin reuptake inhibitors (SSRIs) (p. 675)
social anxiety disorder (p. 691)
specific phobias (p. 693)
systematic desensitization (p. 668)
token economy (p. 668)
transference (p. 666)
unconditional positive regard (p. 671)

Questions for Discussion

1. In the medical model, the individual experiencing psychological distress is labeled as "ill." This label can be considered a hypothesis—that is, the therapist may or may not be correct in the label applied. Once this hypothesis is in place, though, how might confirmation bias (the tendency to seek out information that is consistent with, and thus confirms, one's beliefs) influence what behaviors the therapist notices and remembers? Should therapists avoid labeling? [Analyze, Evaluate]

2. Once a therapist labels a client as having a psychological disorder, how might that labeling become a self-fulfilling prophecy? For example, are there ways the therapist might act toward a client diagnosed with major depression that might elicit responses that resemble symptoms? [Analyze]

3. You read about several criticisms of the DSM, including the idea that its use can lead to overdiagnosis of

disorders. For instance, in Cairo, Egypt, it is normal for grief to last a very long time following the loss of a family member. This prolonged grief might be diagnosed as a disorder following the DSM criteria. How should cultural differences like these be handled? Does the DSM need to change in response, or is it up to the clinician to take these factors into account? [Evaluate]

4. In the text, an individual with OCD was quoted as saying, "The fear I had, that someone I love would be hurt or die as a result of me not checking everything is safe, was all-consuming. It was taking four hours to check and re-check that the gas was off." How does this quote illustrate a principle emphasized by behavior therapists, namely, that behavior is controlled by its consequences? What behavior was being reinforced and what was the reinforcer? How might the control of behavior by its consequence help us understand how OCD symptoms may maintain themselves over time? [Analyze]

5. You learned that in cognitive therapies, the therapist's goal is to get the client to change his or her automatic thoughts. Identify an automatic thought you may have had in response to a failed exam. If it was a thought that ultimately helped you do better in the future, what about it was so motivating? If it was one that led to future failure, what was it about the thought that was so demotivating? How could you change it? [Analyze]

6. Humanistic theorists claim that in therapy, three conditions are necessary *and sufficient* for fostering psychological change: genuineness, acceptance, and empathic understanding. That is, if a therapist can provide these three conditions in therapy, the individual *will* experience positive growth. Do you agree? Are there other conditions you see as necessary for helping individuals achieve their goals in therapy? [Evaluate]

7. Jhin's friends have noticed that he never shows up for kickball games anymore, even though it used to be the highlight of his Wednesdays. When he does show up to class, he often seems kind of confused, so his teachers rarely call on him anymore. All he seems to want to do is sleep all day. He rarely eats and appears to be very tired. When his best friend expressed concern for him, he replied, "What does it matter whether I'm happy or not?" Do you have enough information to diagnose Jhin with a mental disorder? If not, what other information would you like? [Analyze]

8. Consider why exposure therapy is useful. (*Hint:* Do clients experience the negative consequences they expect, following exposure to an anxiety-arousing stimulus?) When group therapy is used to treat social anxiety disorder, is it a form of exposure therapy? Explain. [Analyze]

Self-Test

1. Dr. Reed met with his client for a couple of weeks before determining that the cause of her symptoms, including a marked disinterest in activities and a deep sadness, was depression. Dr. Reed's approach, characterized by a search for the inner causes of outward symptoms, is commonly referred to as
   a. the medical model.
   b. the diagnostic model.
   c. the mental illness model.
   d. the disorder model.

2. Homosexuality was included as a disorder in the first edition of the *Diagnostic and Statistical Manual of Mental Disorders* (DSM) but doesn't appear in the current edition. What does this suggest about the process through which disorders are included and excluded in the DSM?
   a. The process is free of clinician bias.
   b. The process is always firmly grounded in scientific research.
   c. The process includes consideration of social trends.
   d. The process does not make room for public opinion.

3. Shayna wanted to get over her fear of dogs, so she employed the help of a therapist who asked her to imagine different situations that included dogs. In these situations, she got successively closer to interacting with a dog. Throughout this process, her therapist helped her to remain calm. Eventually, Shayna learned that that she could pet a dog without any negative consequences. What therapeutic technique did her therapist use?
   a. Beck's cognitive therapy
   b. Systematic desensitization
   c. Free association
   d. Group therapy

4. Throughout the course of several sessions, Sasha hypothesized that much of her client's psychological distress stemmed from his belief that he couldn't trust anyone. Sasha asked her client questions to make him aware of the belief, but also to challenge it. What type of therapy was Sasha most likely using?
   a. Cognitive therapy
   b. Psychoanalysis
   c. Humanistic therapy
   d. Eclectic therapy

Chapter Review

5. Which of the following is true of the approach called cognitive-behavioral therapy?
   a. Contrary to its name, it is not at all focused on teaching new behaviors.
   b. Like psychoanalysis, it is very focused on traumatic events from the past.
   c. It is employed when it would be useful to target clients' emotions and thinking.
   d. Its primary goal is to provide for clients interpersonal relationships than enable them to discover, within themselves, the capacity for psychological growth.

6. Which of the following is true of how therapists choose their therapeutic strategies?
   a. Therapists in the United States are required to draw on at least two theoretical orientations.
   b. Most therapists in the United States describe their theoretical orientation as eclectic.
   c. Therapists in the United States are required to stick to one theoretical orientation.
   d. Most therapists in the United States prefer to stick with one theoretical orientation.

7. Under which of the following circumstances could individuals experience a placebo effect?
   a. When they didn't know they were taking a drug
   b. When they believed the drug they took will make them feel better
   c. When they believed that drugs are of little use in treating disorders
   d. When they were told the drug they took would not make them feel better

8. What proportion of individuals in the United States will experience major depressive disorder in their lifetime?
   a. 1%
   b. 5%
   c. 10%
   d. 15%

9. For which of the following disorders is someone most likely to be prescribed mood stabilizers such as lithium, anticonvulsants, or antipsychotics?
   a. Obsessive-compulsive disorder
   b. Bipolar disorder
   c. Generalized anxiety disorder
   d. Panic disorder

10. To what does the "mastery" in mastery therapy (used to treat phobias) refer?
    a. Clients give mastery to the therapist to cure them.
    b. Clients gain mastery to control fear on their own.
    c. Clients give mastery to a higher power to help them.
    d. Clients gain a master's degree in fear management.

11. DeWan's sister suffers from generalized anxiety disorder and he does his best to be compassionate. However, one day he found himself blurting, "If you would just stop worrying about everything, you'd get better!" Considering the symptoms of the disorder, which of the following is most problematic about his outburst (besides its insensitivity)?
    a. His sister may feel she lacks the ability to control her worrying.
    b. His sister may enjoy worrying.
    c. His sister may not feel she is ready to stop worrying.
    d. The worrying itself may be adaptive.

12. Why is exposure therapy an effective approach for treating panic disorder?
    a. Many people believe that it works, so its effectiveness is largely due to placebo effects.
    b. Many find exposure therapy exhilarating and are therefore distracted by the positive arousal it creates.
    c. Clients learn there are no harmful consequences to being placed in situations that had in the past triggered panic attacks.
    d. Clients are encouraged to identify past traumas that may have triggered panic attacks and to make meaning of them.

13. Why is group therapy an effective approach for treating social anxiety disorder?
    a. Its sessions are dominated by the therapist, who is a master of social interaction.
    b. Its group membership changes every week, so clients don't have to worry about meeting others again.
    c. Its sessions are highly scripted and clients enjoy their comfort and familiarity.
    d. It provides an opportunity for clients to practice social skills and to have mastery experiences in social settings.

14. Why is exposure and response prevention therapy an effective approach for treating obsessive-compulsive disorder?
    a. Clients eventually learn there are no harmful consequences to not engaging in their compulsions.
    b. Clients are given "tokens" for refraining from engaging in their compulsions, which they use to purchase other valued items.
    c. Clients are led to understand that their compulsions are largely the result of past unresolved traumas.
    d. Clients learn to replace old compulsive behaviors with those that are more socially acceptable.

15. Bertram was the sole survivor of a head-on collision that killed his family three years ago. He is often visited by vivid and horrific memories of the accident and feels extremely guilty that he survived. He is easily startled. What disorder is characterized by these particular symptoms?

a. Panic disorder
b. Social anxiety disorder
c. Major depressive disorder
d. Posttraumatic stress disorder

Answers

You can check your answers to the preceding Self-Test and the chapter's What Do You Know? questions in Appendix B.

Psychological Disorders II: Schizophrenia, Personality Disorders, and Dissociative Disorders

16

The 17-year-old girl attacked herself. She burned her wrists and slashed her arms and legs. To protect her from herself, authorities moved her to what they thought was a safe location: a secluded room containing only a bed and chair. She couldn't hurt herself here, they thought. But they were wrong. The girl banged her head repeatedly against the wall and floor. She wanted to die.

She survived her ordeal. Looking back on it, she later said that her "whole experience of these episodes was that someone else was doing it; it was like 'I know this is coming, I'm out of control, somebody help me; where are you, God?'" (Carey, 2011).

THIS CLINICAL CASE IS DESCRIBED FOR US BY DR. MARSHA LINEHAN, Professor of Psychology at the University of Washington. Dr. Linehan, an internationally known clinical psychologist, created a form of psychotherapy that you will learn about in this chapter.

Consider now a second case. This one also is described by a prominent scholar: Dr. Elyn Saks, Professor of Law, Psychology, and Psychiatry at the University of Southern California and winner of an academic prize so prestigious it's nicknamed the "genius award."

One night, when studying with friends at a library, a student blurted out, "Have you ever killed anyone?" When her friends asked what she was talking about, she said, "Heaven, and hell. Who's what, who's who." She then coaxed her friends out onto the library roof, where she waved her arms above her head while shouting, "Come to the Florida lemon tree! Come to the Florida sunshine bush! Where they make lemons. Where there are demons" (Saks, 2007). Her friends were scared. Teachers who saw her behavior knew something was deeply wrong. Within a day, authorities had taken her to a mental hospital.

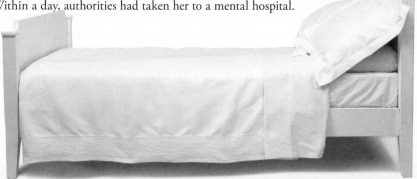

Erin Mulvehill

Getty Images, left to right: Dorling Kindersley; C Squared Studios

In both cases, the young women suffered from severe psychological disorders. Their normal personalities were profoundly disturbed. Their thoughts were detached from the world of reality. In this chapter, you'll learn about these disorders, their causes, and the therapies available to treat them.

But first, take a guess about the following. Where do you think these two troubled girls are today? Confined to a mental hospital? On the streets, homeless?

The cases turned out better than you might expect. Drs. Linehan and Saks were describing themselves. They battled their disorders and, today, help others to do the same. Their lives testify to both the burden of mental illness and the possibility of overcoming it. ◉

WHAT ARE SOME things you believe—basic beliefs about the world and yourself? You surely believe that you are a human being, composed of the same biological matter as other humans. You probably believe that government officials are no more interested in you than in hundreds of millions of other citizens. Whatever your religious beliefs, you probably believe that your relationship to the spiritual world does not differ fundamentally from that of billions of other people.

But now consider the following beliefs expressed by individuals in a public discussion forum on the Internet:

› "God wants me to start a new religion."
› "I have a spirit guide who speaks to me, and I'll swear I have seen him out on the street."
› "Mel Gibson and I used to be married."
› "I believed everyone was a robot but they didn't know they were. But I knew."
› "License plates have special messages for me, and the CIA is transmitting data to me through the TV and other media."
› "I am one of the Virgin Mary's guards when she comes to Earth. I have been told this is a delusion, but I have dreams of this. I can't tell if they are real or not. I am proud to be so high up as to be one of her guards. It is something that makes me feel good about myself."
› "My delusion was that my family had been murdered and replaced with androids who stole my blood while I slept and replaced it with a poison of some sort. Now, I'm still convinced that I'm going to die someday due to these said androids. But I no longer believe my family is dead."

The writers expressing these beliefs have a mental illness known as *schizophrenia*. In this chapter, we'll examine schizophrenia in depth. We'll then look at other forms of mental disorder, including the persistent styles of behavior known as *personality disorders* and the disruptions to normal conscious experience that are the *dissociative disorders.*

In covering these disorders, we will maintain a strategy employed in Chapter 15. After reviewing a given disorder, we review therapies developed to treat that particular disorder. In today's clinical psychological science, researchers rarely ask whether therapy approaches work "in general." Instead, "the overwhelming majority of randomized clinical trials in psychotherapy"—that is, studies evaluating the effectiveness of therapy—"compare the efficacy of specific treatments for specific disorders" (Norcross & Wampold, 2011, p. 127). Our linking of disorders and therapies thus reflects the state of psychological science. Just as you did in Chapter 15, in this chapter you will see how contemporary psychologists devise and evaluate therapies that target specific disorders of the mind and brain.

Psychotic Disorders and Schizophrenia

Preview Questions

› What does it mean to suffer from a psychotic disorder?
› How prevalent is schizophrenia?

The previous chapter focused on depressive and anxiety disorders. Those disorders can disrupt people's lives, yet they generally leave two psychological qualities intact. One is that people are in touch with reality. For example, a socially anxious person's level of worry about social relationships may be excessive, but the relationships really do exist. Another quality is that thinking is organized logically. A depressed person may say, "I just feel I'm wasting everyone's time. No one can help me" (see Chapter 15), but is unlikely to say, "I have a sort of silver bullet which held me by my leg, that one cannot jump in, where one wants, and that ends beautifully like the stars" (McKenna & Oh, 2005, p. 2)—a disorganized jumble of ideas.

In *psychotic disorders,* people lose these basic mental abilities. **Psychotic disorders** are psychological disorders whose core symptoms are that people's thoughts and actions are disorganized and their thinking loses touch with reality; people see and worry about things that do not exist (Heckers et al., 2013).

A particularly severe psychotic disorder, which we will focus on first, is *schizophrenia.* The *Diagnostic and Statistical Manual of Mental Disorders* (DSM, discussed in Chapter 15) defines **schizophrenia** as a disorder in which people exhibit multiple psychotic symptoms (detailed below) for a period of at least one month. Schizophrenia is prevalent globally. A meta-analysis of nearly 200 studies from 46 different nations indicated that schizophrenia occurs in 4.6 out of 1000 people (i.e., about 1 out of every 200; Saha et al., 2005). Rates do not vary across countries or between genders (Eranti et al., 2013); wherever you go, between 4 and 7 people out of 1000 experience the disease. Schizophrenia is costly not only to sufferers and their families, but also to society as a whole. In a wide range of industrialized countries, between 1.5 and 3% of nations' *overall healthcare budgets* are expended on schizophrenia treatment and care (Knapp, Mangalore, & Simon, 2004).

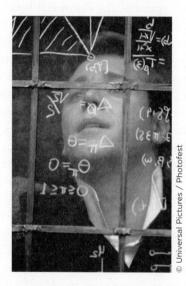

Professional success despite schizophrenia John Nash achieved breakthroughs in mathematics that earned him a Nobel Prize in 1994, despite first suffering from symptoms of schizophrenia in 1959. On the left is Russell Crowe, who portrayed Nash in the Oscar-winning film *A Beautiful Mind.* On the right is the real-life Nash.

Let's first learn about schizophrenia at a *person level* of analysis. We'll examine symptoms that haunt the lives of people with schizophrenia, as well as the illness's typical development across the course of people's lives. Next, we'll move "down" to mind and brain levels of analysis to show how schizophrenia affects information processing in the mind and physiological functioning in the brain. The study of mind and brain, as you'll see, helps to explain the symptoms experienced by people with schizophrenia. Finally, you'll learn how mental health professionals treat this mental illness.

People with Schizophrenia

Preview Questions

> What are the positive and negative symptoms of schizophrenia?
> What cognitive impairments do people with schizophrenia experience?

People with schizophrenia face exceptional challenges. Schizophrenia symptoms severely disrupt their experience of the world and their sense of self (Estroff, 1989). The symptoms are of three types (National Institute of Mental Health, 2009):

1. **Positive symptoms:** Mental events that are experienced by people with schizophrenia but rarely by others (e.g., hallucinations). The word "positive" here

psychotic disorders Psychological disorders in which thoughts and actions are disorganized and thinking loses touch with reality; people see and worry about things that do not exist.

schizophrenia Psychological disorder in which people exhibit multiple psychotic symptoms.

positive symptoms (of schizophrenia) Undesirable mental events experienced by people with schizophrenia but rarely by others.

indicates the presence, rather than absence, of a symptom; a positive symptom adds something unwanted to one's life.

2. **Negative symptoms:** The absence, among people with schizophrenia, of desirable psychological experiences common among most people (e.g., the experience of enjoying social events). The word "negative" indicates an absence of a desirable quality; negative symptoms subtract something desirable from one's life.

3. **Cognitive impairments:** Reduced ability to perform everyday thinking tasks (e.g., an inability to concentrate on information).

Let's examine these in detail, beginning with positive symptoms.

POSITIVE SYMPTOMS. One positive symptom of schizophrenia is **delusional beliefs,** which are personal convictions that contradict known facts about the world but that a person clings to even when faced with conflicting evidence (Heckers et al., 2013). You read some delusional beliefs in the quotes above. The idea that one's family has been replaced by androids or that one is receiving messages from the CIA through the TV is typical of the delusional beliefs experienced by people with schizophrenia (Elgie et al., 2005). Such beliefs are so bizarre that you can't help but wonder how anyone could take them seriously. Yet, to people with schizophrenia, they are vivid, compelling, and convincing. Some common delusional beliefs are somatic delusions (e.g., believing that one has been injured, is ill, or has been poisoned) and delusions of grandeur (believing one has special abilities or powers; Tateyama et al., 1998).

A second positive symptom of schizophrenia is *hallucination.* **Hallucinations** are experiences—sights, sounds, smells, tastes, or feelings (touch)—of people or things that are not really there. A person with schizophrenia may, for instance, hallucinate an evil demon. He may have the experience of seeing and hearing the demon, standing right there in front of him, issuing orders. The majority of people with schizophrenia experience hallucinations, which often recur across decades of life (Goghari et al., 2013).

Some people with schizophrenia experience delusions and hallucinations, yet otherwise retain their normal thinking abilities. For example, when they express strange beliefs (e.g., "The demon is telling me what to do"), they do so in sentences that are organized logically. But others with the disease suffer a third positive symptom of schizophrenia: *disorganized thinking.* In **disorganized thinking,** people cannot structure their thoughts and spoken words in a manner consistent with standard rules of language use. Their thoughts are garbled and unintelligible.

Sometimes disorganized thinking is evident in sentence-to-sentence connections within a conversation. In normal dialogue, ideas flow logically from one sentence to the next. In conversation marked by disorganized thinking, however, ideas jump illogically. Consider this interview with a patient with schizophrenia, who begins by discussing his fear of other people:

"I'm so scared I could tell you that picture's got a headache."

"Can you tell me more about that?" the interviewer asks.

"When a sperm and an egg go together to make a baby, only one sperm goes up the egg and when they touch there are two contact points touched before the other two then it's carried up in the air. When they fuse it's like nuclear fusion except it's human fusion. There's a mass loss of the proton. When heat abstraction goes up in the electron, spins around, comes back down into the proton to form the mind. And the mind could be reduced to one atom."

—Neuroslicer (2007, April 18)

It's not merely that the content of the person's beliefs is bizarre (e.g., "picture's got a headache"). In addition, the sentence-to-sentence flow of thoughts does not follow

Is he looking at somebody? If you had schizophrenia, you might think that Uncle Sam is an actual person and is looking and speaking directly to you. People with the disorder sometimes believe that media images are addressing them personally.

© K. J. Historical / Corbis

negative symptoms (of schizophrenia) The absence, among people with schizophrenia, of desirable psychological experiences common among most others (e.g., enjoying social events).

cognitive impairments (in schizophrenia) Among people with schizophrenia, reduced ability to perform everyday thinking tasks such as concentrating, remembering, and planning social interactions.

delusional beliefs Personal convictions that contradict known facts about the world but that a person clings to even when faced with conflicting evidence.

hallucinations Experiences (sights, sounds, smells, tastes, or touches) of people or things that are not really there.

disorganized thinking A positive symptom of schizophrenia in which thoughts and speech are not properly structured, and speech is thus unintelligible.

normal rules of conversation. The interviewer asks about the picture. In response, the patient discusses human conception.

Disorganized thinking can also occur at the level of sentences and individual words. Patients' sentences may be schizophrenic *word salads:* seemingly random jumbles of words that are meaningless to listeners. When talking to someone with schizophrenia, you may hear sentences such as, "Tramway flogging into my question, are you why is it thirty letters down under peanut butter, what is it" (an example frequently cited online).

A final positive symptom of schizophrenia is disorders of *motor movement* (Arango & Carpenter, 2011). Patients may display odd mannerisms, such as a strange grimace on their face. Others engage in repeated movements, such as spinning a lock of hair over and over again. Still others exhibit *catatonia,* which is a lack of motor movement. Some people with schizophrenia display little movement throughout the day and thus appear withdrawn from the outside world. "No movement from me," one writes. "It's as if I was an old oak tree, the blank stare, the silent face" (www.schizophrenia. com posting).

NEGATIVE SYMPTOMS. The negative symptoms of schizophrenia consist of emotional and behavioral deficits (Kirkpatrick et al., 1989). People with schizophrenia lack emotional experiences enjoyed by others and fail to engage in valuable social behaviors. These deficits in emotion and behavior reduce schizophrenic individuals' overall sense of well-being (Blanchard et al., 2011); in fact, their quality of life is reduced even more by the negative symptoms of schizophrenia than the positive ones (Rabinowitz et al., 2012).

One negative symptom is **flat affect** (pronounced AFF-ect), an absence of normal emotional expression (Kring & Moran, 2008). Rather than the typical "ups" and "downs" of emotion—a smile, a frown, a look of interest, a look of annoyance—people with schizophrenia may display no emotions at all; they may appear lethargic and emotionless. When asked by researchers, people with schizophrenia do report *experiencing* emotions—yet, at the same time, they may show little or no sign of emotion on their faces (Kring et al., 1993). Not all persons with schizophrenia display flat affect. However, those who do display it report lower quality of life and, in the long run, are less likely to see their schizophrenic symptoms improve (Gur et al., 2006).

Another negative symptom is a lack of interest in social activities. Normally, people find some daily activities interesting. You might look forward to lunch, or meeting friends, or shopping, or playing video games—or maybe even learning about psychology! However, many people with schizophrenia experience little pleasure in any everyday activity. As a result, they are not motivated to plan or engage in them (Kirkpatrick et al., 1989). This lack of interest can extend to behaviors that seem like necessities of life, such as hygiene and overall personal care.

People with schizophrenia often are well aware of this neglect: "Lately I've noticed that my personal hygiene has been (expletive)," one person writes. "I only shower once every two weeks, I don't shave my face, I just don't care how I look anymore" (www.schizophrenia.com posting). They also may possess insight into why they lack motivation for personal care: "When we discover that our futures are impacted by an incurable disease, we give up on it."

COGNITIVE IMPAIRMENTS. On top of the positive and negative symptoms of schizophrenia, individuals with the disease also experience *cognitive impairments,* which, as noted previously, are reduced abilities to execute mental skills that are simple for most people (Kuperberg & Heckers, 2000). We'll look at three, which involve

Alex Telfe / Gallery Stock

A negative symptom of schizophrenia: Flat affect Rather than experiencing the typical "ups" and "downs" of emotion, people with schizophrenia may display flat affect: little emotion at all. Flat affect is a negative symptom of schizophrenia because it involves an absence of a typical and desirable human quality: variations in emotional state.

flat affect An absence of normal emotional expression; a negative symptom of schizophrenia.

concentration, memory, and *social cognition*—that is, thinking about other people and social interactions (see Chapter 12).

1. *Concentration:* Many people with schizophrenia have difficulty concentrating their attention on tasks (Hilti et al., 2010). This includes everyday tasks such as attending to what a person is saying. They often are painfully aware of this problem. "Do you [i.e., like me] have trouble understanding/reading what people say to you?" one patient asks. "My head is currently scrambled, noisy, can't concentrate and scared people will talk to me because I can't understand much" (www.schizophrenia.com posting). "I have TERRIBLE problems with this," another writes. "[I] forget what I was saying or what the conversation is about midway through it. It is a horrible, awful symptom of the disease" (www.schizophrenia.com posting).

2. *Remembering:* People with schizophrenia do not lose all of their memory ability; rather, the illness impairs their ability to remember certain *types* of material. One is visual information; people with schizophrenia perform relatively poorly when trying to recall images or the spatial location of objects (Palmer et al., 2010). Another is *episodic memory* (see Chapter 6), or memory for personal experiences. Their episodic memory for emotional experiences is particularly poor (Herbener, 2008). These memory deficits degrade quality of life—in particular, because it makes it difficult to plan new activities (Herbener, 2008). People often make plans by asking themselves, "What would I like to do today?" and consulting memories of experiences that were enjoyed in the past. People with schizophrenia who cannot easily remember past activities thus have trouble making plans. As a result, they engage in fewer professional and social activities, which further reduces their quality of life.

> How well do you know your way around a keyboard? This largely depends on your ability to recall spatial location.

3. *Social cognition:* People with schizophrenia experience a number of social-cognitive problems. They err when thinking about the reasons behind other people's behavior. For example, if someone fails to return a phone call of theirs quickly, they may think, wrongly, that the other person is expressing hostility toward them (Green et al., 2005). They also have lower social-cognitive skills, with less ability to initiate conversation and maintain eye contact. The skill deficits make it difficult for them to succeed in the workplace, where many jobs require skillful social behavior (Dickinson, Bellack, & Gold, 2007). Finally, individuals with schizophrenia may display inappropriate social emotions (Cole & Hall, 2008). They have trouble controlling their emotions and matching emotional expressions to their present circumstances. "The other day in group [therapy]," one patient relates, "the counselor asked us . . . have we bursted out laughing at inappropriate times? I told him I had and while I was telling him the story I was laughing. It was sad because it had to do with my principal dying while I was in high school" (www.schizophrenia.com posting).

Table 16.1 summarizes the range of symptoms—positive, negative, and cognitive impairments—experienced in schizophrenia. Not all patients experience all symptoms; people with schizophrenia can exhibit different patterns of symptomatology.

TRY THIS!

Now that you have read about the experiences of people with schizophrenia, it's time for you to also see and hear about them. Go to www.pmbpsychology.com now for this chapter's Try This! activity. ◉

table **16.1**

Symptoms of Schizophrenia		
Positive Symptoms	**Negative Symptoms**	**Cognitive Impairment**
Delusional beliefs	Flat affect	Difficulty concentrating
Hallucinations	Lack of pleasure and interest in activities	Difficulty remembering, especially personal experiences and emotions
Disorganized thinking		Impaired social cognition

🌏 WHAT DO YOU KNOW?...

1. Classify the following statements as illustrating either positive or negative symptoms of schizophrenia.
   a. "I just can't seem to motivate myself to start a new project."
   b. "If you come in from the rain, use a laser pointer to run the bookstore."
   c. "I know you're supposed to talk to people at parties, but I just don't care to."
   d. "I can't believe you don't see the yellow rabbit standing over there."
2. Jean, a person with schizophrenia, noticed that a man sitting across from her in the train station was smiling at her. Though the other person meant to convey friendliness, Jean thought he was mocking her. Of the three types of cognitive impairments described in this section (concentration, memory, and social cognition), which does Jean's misinterpretation best exemplify? Briefly explain.

See Appendix B for answers to What Do You Know? questions.

Schizophrenia and Information Processing

Preview Questions

> Why are the thoughts of people with schizophrenia so disorganized?
> Why are people with schizophrenia so poor at making decisions?

Why do people with schizophrenia experience this broad range of symptoms? Some answers come from research on how the illness affects information-processing systems of the mind and the biological machinery of the brain. One key information-processing system is working memory.

WORKING MEMORY. Working memory (see Chapter 6) is the mental system you use to store information in mind for brief periods (e.g., a phone number you keep in mind until you have time to write it down), to manipulate stored information (e.g., adding up a set of digits), and, importantly, to control your own mental activities. Working memory contains a "central executive" that people use to focus attention on tasks. When you concentrate on solving a problem while avoiding distractions from nearby sounds and sights, you're employing the central executive component of your working memory system.

In schizophrenia, working memory is impaired (Barch, 2005). Individuals with schizophrenia perform less well than others on laboratory tasks that assess working memory ability (Barch, 2005). This working memory impairment helps

CONNECTING TO THINKING, EMOTION, AND THE BRAIN

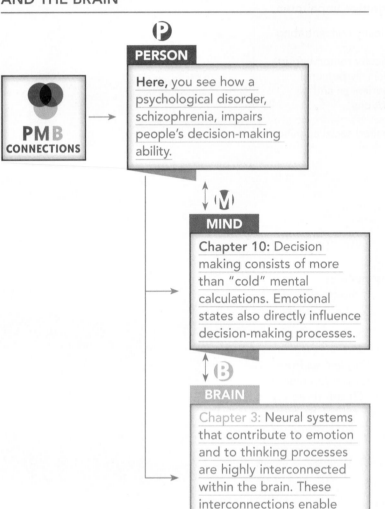

PMB CONNECTIONS

Ⓟ PERSON

Here, you see how a psychological disorder, schizophrenia, impairs people's decision-making ability.

Ⓜ MIND

Chapter 10: Decision making consists of more than "cold" mental calculations. Emotional states also directly influence decision-making processes.

Ⓑ BRAIN

Chapter 3: Neural systems that contribute to emotion and to thinking processes are highly interconnected within the brain. These interconnections enable emotional processes to influence thinking.

to explain symptoms experienced by people with schizophrenia, discussed earlier, such as disorganized thinking (where words and sentences are not connected logically). Working memory is the "executive" mental system that enables people to organize their thoughts. Breakdowns in this component of the mind thus contribute to a positive symptom of schizophrenia, disorganized thought.

An additional information-processing problem in schizophrenia is information-processing speed. Individuals with schizophrenia do not process information as quickly as others. They take longer to complete various timed laboratory tasks (Mesholam-Gately et al., 2009).

EMOTION AND DECISION MAKING. In addition to affecting working memory, schizophrenia impairs mental systems that are needed for decision making. These systems involve both thinking and emotion. When people who are not affected by schizophrenia make decisions, their emotions often improve the quality of their decision making (see Chapter 10). Specifically, negative emotions experienced after bad decisions help people avoid making those same poor decisions in the future. Key evidence of this comes from research where people played a gambling task in which participants' emotional reactions and decisions were recorded. Negative emotions after bad gambling decisions helped people improve the decisions they made on future gambles (Bechara et al., 1994).

What happens when people with schizophrenia play this gambling game? Unlike most others, they show little improvement across trials of the task (Shurman, Horan, & Nuechterlein, 2005). Even after big gambling losses, schizophrenic patients do not have the emotion-induced changes in decision making that nonpatients exhibit. As a result, they perform poorly on the task.

ⓦ WHAT DO YOU KNOW?...

3. Answer the following questions about impairment in schizophrenia.
   a. How does an impairment in working memory lead to the disorganized thinking seen in many people with schizophrenia?
   b. How does impairment in the functioning of emotions lead to the decision-making impairments observed in many people with schizophrenia?

Schizophrenia and the Brain

Preview Questions

› How can the delusional thinking displayed by people with schizophrenia be explained at the mind and brain levels of analysis?

› How are the brains of people with schizophrenia different from those without the disorder?

We've now seen what life is like for people with schizophrenia. They experience delusions and flat affect, and they have difficulty focusing on tasks and planning daily events. We've also seen how schizophrenia affects information-processing systems of the mind. It impairs the central executive system of working memory, as well as the thinking and emotional systems involved in decision making.

Let's now move to a biological level of analysis. How does schizophrenia affect the brain and how do these biological effects explain the psychological ones?

As discussed in Chapters 2 and 3, the brain contains both neurons (the cells of the brain) and neurotransmitters (the chemical substances through which neurons communicate). We'll look at both, starting with the role of a specific neurotransmitter, dopamine, in schizophrenia.

DOPAMINE. The brain contains a variety of neurotransmitters. When searching for biochemical bases of schizophrenia, then, two questions arise: Which neurotransmitter is most central to schizophrenia? And why do high or low levels of that neurotransmitter cause schizophrenic symptoms?

Most researchers agree that the answer to the first question is dopamine. Dopamine is a neurotransmitter found in multiple regions of the brain (Figure 16.1). Thanks to its widespread presence, it can affect multiple aspects of mental life.

More than half a century ago, researchers discovered that dopamine and schizophrenia were linked. The discovery originated with an unexpected finding: Some drugs originally designed to treat other medical problems were found to reduce symptoms of schizophrenia (Valenstein, 1998). The drugs, it turned out, were those that blocked the neuron-to-neuron transmission of dopamine. This finding fueled

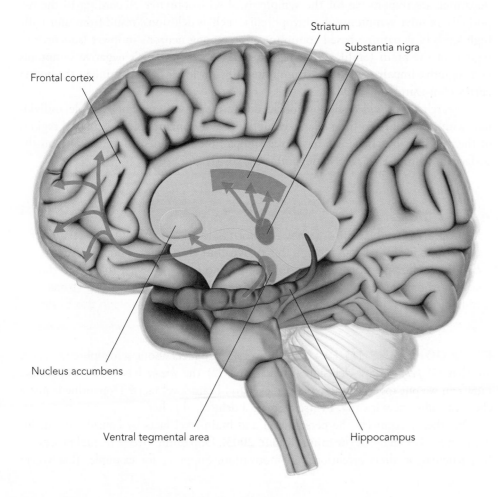

figure 16.1

Dopamine pathways The neurotransmitter dopamine affects activity in the brain, thereby affecting psychological experience and behavior. Its effects are widespread, thanks to dopamine pathways, which are routes within the brain that transfer dopamine from one brain region to another. The pathways take dopamine to a set of lower-level brain regions that control motor movement and the experience of pleasure in activities; these include the nucleus accumbens, ventral tegmental area, striatum, substantia nigra, and hippocampus. Pathways also lead to the frontal cortex, which is involved in self-reflection and the planning of goal-directed behavior. According to the dopamine hypothesis of schizophrenia, abnormal levels of dopamine are responsible for schizophrenia symptoms.

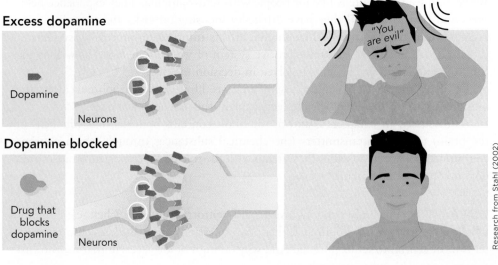

figure **16.2**

Dopamine hypothesis of schizophrenia According to the dopamine hypothesis of schizophrenia, excessively high levels of dopamine in the brain cause the positive symptoms of schizophrenia, such as hearing the voice of an evil demon (top panel). The theory receives support from the finding that drugs that block dopamine relieve the symptoms (bottom panel).

the **dopamine hypothesis of schizophrenia,** which states that abnormal levels of dopamine are responsible for the symptoms of schizophrenia. According to the hypothesis, positive symptoms of schizophrenia, such as delusions, result from unusually high levels of dopamine-based communication among neurons in lower (subcortical) regions of the brain (Stahl, 2002; Figure 16.2). Schizophrenia's negative symptoms and cognitive impairments result from unusually low levels of dopamine in the brain's cortex (Abi-Dargham, 2004).

Research has provided support for the dopamine hypothesis. For example, individuals with schizophrenia have relatively high levels of dopamine in subcortical regions of their brains; they may also have excess dopamine receptors, the molecules on the surface of neurons that receive dopamine signals (Kapur, 2003).

> At a clinical level the doctor–patient interaction proceeds mainly at a "mind" or "behavioral" level of description . . . [while] theorizing and therapeutics proceed largely at a "brain" level. . . . So, when the patient asks, "Doctor, how does my chemical imbalance lead to my delusions?" the doctor has no simple framework within which to cast an answer.
>
> —Kapur (2003, p. 13)

dopamine hypothesis of schizophrenia A hypothesis stating that abnormal levels of dopamine are responsible for the symptoms of schizophrenia.

THINK ABOUT IT

If people with schizophrenia have abnormal levels of the neurotransmitter dopamine in their brains, does this prove that dopamine caused them to develop schizophrenia? You should be saying no by now! It might be that some other factor caused schizophrenia to develop and that the stress of living with schizophrenia affected neurotransmitter levels in the brain.

FROM DOPAMINE TO DELUSIONS. Two key facts about schizophrenia, then, are that (1) *people* have delusional beliefs and (2) the *brain* has excess dopamine. How can we put together these person-level and brain-level facts? Dopamine is just a chemical substance; it can't, by itself, create a delusional belief.

One theory connects the person-level and brain-level facts by considering an in-between level of analysis: the mind (Kapur, 2003). Dopamine affects mental processes. In particular, it alters attention and motivation. Suppose, for example, that you're hungry and are driving past road signs. You hardly notice most of them—but one that says "EAT" grabs your attention. You concentrate on it and are motivated to find the restaurant ahead. Dopamine contributes to this attention grabbing. It converts the EAT sign from "cold" information to a "hot," motivating, attention-grabbing stimulus (Berridge & Robinson, 2003).

What does this have to do with schizophrenia? In schizophrenia, excess dopamine causes even trivial stimuli—a picture on the wall, a TV commercial—to grab people's attention. Objects and events that once seemed irrelevant now seem deeply significant. This is confusing to people with schizophrenia, who struggle to understand the profound change in their everyday experience ("Why does this TV commercial feel so important?"). To make sense of their experiences, they invent explanations. Because the experiences are weird, the explanations are, too ("The TV commercial must be a message directly to me!"). The strange, delusional beliefs seen in schizophrenia, then, are created by people trying to understand the alterations in mental life caused by excess dopamine (Kapur, 2003).

BRAIN STRUCTURES AND SCHIZOPHRENIA. Let's now turn from neurotransmitters to brain structures, to examine activity in the various parts of the brain, each of which contains millions of neurons (Chapter 3).

Which brain structures does schizophrenia affect? You name it—"Almost every cortical and subcortical brain structure has been found to be abnormal in schizophrenia" (Antonova et al., 2004, p. 118). Schizophrenia affects not only individual brain regions, but also the brain as a whole. Brain volume—that is, the overall amount of cellular material in the brain—is reduced among people with the disorder.

One brain area is enlarged, rather than reduced, in people with schizophrenia: the brain's ventricles (Palmer, Dawes, & Heaton, 2009). The **ventricles** are spaces in the brain filled with a fluid that supports the brain's functioning. These spaces do not contain neurons. Larger ventricles mean that a smaller percentage of the brain's overall volume contains the neurons that power thinking.

Although schizophrenia affects the whole brain, some brain regions are likely to be more central to the disease than others. How could you find them? The search has benefited from a strategy you see often in this book: using research on the mind to guide research on the brain. Earlier, you saw that one aspect of mind that schizophrenia strongly impairs is working memory. This mind-level finding suggests a strategy for brain research: Compare the brain activity of people with and without schizophrenia while they perform a task that places great demands on the working memory system. When researchers do this (Glahn et al., 2005; Figure 16.3), they find that brain activity in people with schizophrenia differs in two ways:

1. It is lower in the *dorsolateral prefrontal cortex,* a brain structure known to be key to working memory (Curtis & D'Esposito, 2003).

2. It is higher in the anterior cingulate, a brain region known to be active when people detect errors in their performance. The lower task performance caused by reduced activity in the prefrontal cortex (point #1) heightens people's sensitivity to errors they are making (Glahn et al., 2005).

Once again, one can connect these brain-level findings to person-level symptoms of schizophrenia. You'll recall that people with schizophrenia have difficulty concentrating on tasks and planning daily events. Schizophrenia and planning events are connected through a three-step process involving the brain, the mind, and the person's ability to plan (Figure 16.4): (1) Schizophrenia impairs neural communication in the

ventricles Spaces in the brain filled with a fluid that supports brain functioning but without neurons; enlarged in people with schizophrenia.

figure **16.3**

Brain activity and schizophrenia The image shows areas in which brain activity in people with and without schizophrenia differed while performing a task that placed demands on the working memory system. The yellow-orange areas are those in which people with schizophrenia had less brain activity than others. The purple-pinkish areas are ones in which they showed greater activity. Differences between groups of people, then, were complex. People with schizophrenia did not have less brain activity across all regions of the brain but did have less activity in regions of the brain known to be involved in memory performance.

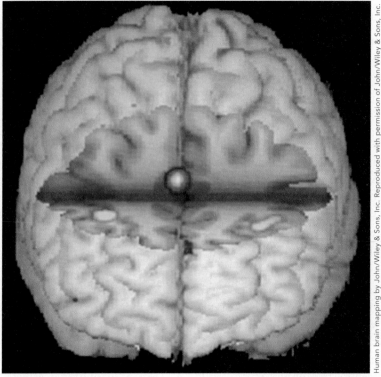

frontal cortex; (2) impaired communication in the frontal cortex reduces working memory; and (3) impaired working memory makes it difficult for people to perform tasks that require concentration, such as planning daily events.

WHAT DO YOU KNOW?...

4. Which of the following statements about dopamine and delusions are true? Check all that apply.

_____ a. According to the dopamine hypothesis, positive symptoms are the result of too little dopamine-based communication in subcortical regions of the brain, and negative symptoms are the result of too much of this activity in the brain's cortex.

_____ b. Excess dopamine can cause lots of stimuli to grab attention, even when those stimuli are not important.

_____ c. People with schizophrenia may experience delusions because they try to invent explanations for the overwhelming amount of stimuli that grabs their attention.

_____ d. In individuals with schizophrenia, brain volume is larger and ventricles are reduced in size.

_____ e. When people with schizophrenia perform an activity that tasks working memory capacity, they experience higher activity in the dorsolateral prefrontal cortex, an area known to be active during tasks that require working memory capacity, than people without schizophrenia.

_____ f. When people with schizophrenia perform an activity that tasks working memory capacity, they experience lower activity in the anterior cingulate, an area known to be active when people detect their own errors.

figure **16.4**

PMB
IN ACTION

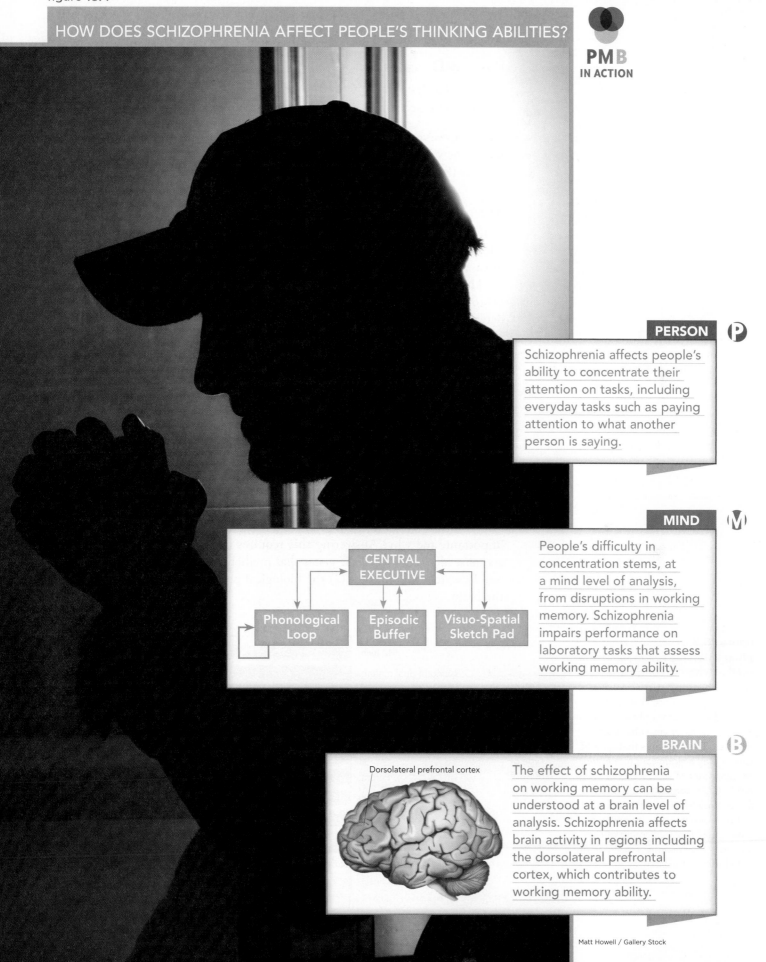

PERSON P

Schizophrenia affects people's ability to concentrate their attention on tasks, including everyday tasks such as paying attention to what another person is saying.

MIND M

CENTRAL EXECUTIVE

Phonological Loop

Episodic Buffer

Visuo-Spatial Sketch Pad

People's difficulty in concentration stems, at a mind level of analysis, from disruptions in working memory. Schizophrenia impairs performance on laboratory tasks that assess working memory ability.

BRAIN B

Dorsolateral prefrontal cortex

The effect of schizophrenia on working memory can be understood at a brain level of analysis. Schizophrenia affects brain activity in regions including the dorsolateral prefrontal cortex, which contributes to working memory ability.

Matt Howell / Gallery Stock

The Development of Schizophrenia

Preview Questions

> Do genes alone determine whether someone will develop schizophrenia?
> When does schizophrenia first develop?

Now that we've seen how schizophrenia affects people, the mind, and the brain, let's look at how it develops. One factor to consider in the development of the disease is genetics (Riley, 2011).

GENES AND THE ENVIRONMENT. When asking about genes and the development of schizophrenia, two scientific questions require answers: (1) Do genes have an effect? (2) If so, why? Which genes are important, and how do they contribute to the disease's development?

The first question can be answered through *twin studies,* which compare identical to fraternal twins (see Chapter 4). In a twin study of schizophrenia, researchers determined whether twin pairs differ in *concordance,* that is, whether the two individuals in a twin pair have the same outcome (i.e., schizophrenia or not). Figure 16.5 shows the results. As you can see, identical, or monozygotic (MZ), twins—who share 100% of their genes—are far more concordant for schizophrenia than are any other pairs of relatives. Fraternal, or dizygotic (DZ), twins are far less similar. They share the same prenatal environment and grow up together in the same household, as is the case for MZ twins. But (like any pair of siblings), on average, they share only 50% of their genes and, as a result, are less concordant for schizophrenia than are MZ twins.

This finding establishes that genetic factors have an effect; specifically, they are a *diathesis* for schizophrenia (Fowles, 1992). For any medical or psychological disorder, a diathesis is any factor that predisposes a person to experience the disorder.

With that established, one can turn to the second question: Which genes are important, and why? Answering this requires more than twin studies. Researchers must identify (1) specific genes that predict the development of schizophrenia (see Research Toolkit) and (2) the biological processes through which they affect the brain.

figure **16.5**
What relatives are most similar when it comes to schizophrenia? Identical twins. They are much more likely to be concordant for schizophrenia than fraternal twins or any other pair of relatives. This indicates that genetic factors play a significant role in the development of schizophrenia (Riley, 2011). ("Concordant" means that the two relatives have the same status; if one has schizophrenia, the other does, too. "Offspring of Dual Matings" are children whose parents both have schizophrenia.)

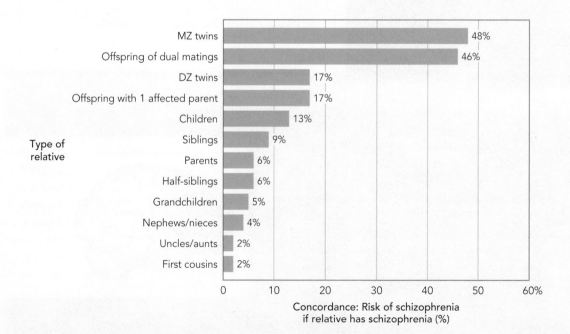

Finding genes that make people susceptible to developing schizophrenia is very difficult (Duan, Sanders, & Gejman, 2010). The number of potential genes (more than 1000) is large (Xu et al., 2013). Furthermore, studies require the participation of large numbers of people with schizophrenia—a challenge, since 99% of the population does not have the disease. In general, "progress in the identification of susceptibility genes has been slow" (Xu et al., 2013, p. 1). For example, a large-scale study in China involving thousands of participants was able to identify general regions of the genome that differ in people with and without the illness, but it could not pinpoint specific genes or explain how they contribute to the disease (Cyranoski, 2011).

⚇ RESEARCH TOOLKIT

Genome-Wide Association Studies

If you want to find a location, a helpful tool is a map. This is true whether the desired location is the nearest entrance to the interstate or a place along the genome where people who have a psychological disorder differ from other people. The genetic map exists; biologists have mapped the human genome—the full set of molecular information required to build a human organism (Chapter 4). With this map, they can search for specific individual genes that contribute to specific mental illnesses. The research method they use in this search is the *genome-wide association study.* In **genome-wide association studies,** scientists analyze thousands of small variations in the human genome in order to identify places along the genome where people with and without a disease differ.

It sounds complex, but the principle behind the method is simple (Figure 16.6). In a study of genes and schizophrenia, researchers would obtain genetic material (DNA) from people with and without the disorder and then would search for differences in that material.

figure 16.6
Genome-wide association study

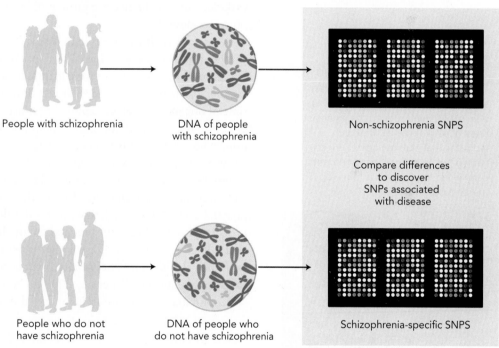

People with schizophrenia

DNA of people with schizophrenia

Non-schizophrenia SNPS

Compare differences to discover SNPs associated with disease

People who do not have schizophrenia

DNA of people who do not have schizophrenia

Schizophrenia-specific SNPS

What the researchers are looking for, specifically, is variations in *nucleotides,* which are the molecules that make up strands of DNA. The variations are called *polymorphisms,* which means "more than one form." Because polymorphisms occur at the level of single, individual nucleotides, researchers look for **single-nucleotide polymorphisms,** or **SNPs** (pronounced "snips"). SNPs are locations along the genome at which one molecule—that is, one nucleotide—differs from one individual to the next. In genome-wide association studies, researchers may scan 100,000 or more SNPs to identify tiny molecular variations that might have big biological effects (Gibbs & Singleton, 2006).

Have researchers identified the SNPs that contribute strongly to schizophrenia? Not yet. The search has been frustrating. Genome-wide association studies have produced "false starts" (Chi, 2009, p. 713). One study would produce an interesting result, but the next would find something different. The cause of schizophrenia "remains elusive" (Zhang et al., 2014, p. 26).

genome-wide association study A method in which researchers study the relation between a psychological characteristic (e.g., a psychological disorder) and hundreds or thousands of genetic variations simultaneously, in order to identify places along the human genome that are associated with the presence versus absence of the characteristic.

single-nucleotide polymorphisms (SNPs) Locations along the genome at which one molecule (i.e., one nucleotide) differs from one individual to another.

The difficulties reflect the sheer numbers involved. In traditional psychological research (see Chapter 2), one or two variables might be studied. But in a genome-wide association study, there are more than 100,000 potential variables—all the nucleotides that might vary from one person to another. To grapple with this complexity, scientists need a lot of research participants, statistical skills, and patience.

🔥 WHAT DO YOU KNOW?...

5. If you were conducting a _____-_____ association study for schizophrenia, you would compare genetic material of people with and without the disease to see how they differed. In particular, you would examine _____-_____ _____ (SNPs) to identify differences in molecules.

Some recent progress has come from a change in strategy. Rather than studying the presence or absence of the disease as a whole, researchers have related genetic material to specific *symptoms of* schizophrenia. A meta-analysis (Xu et al., 2013) has identified five points along the genome at which variations in genetic material were strongly associated with the disease's negative symptoms (the impaired emotional reactions and social behavior discussed earlier). Initial evidence suggests that the genetic variations may influence the growth of brain cells and the speed with which the brain processes information.

Whatever their precise role in schizophrenia, genes alone will never tell the whole story of how this mental illness develops. You can see this for yourself if you look back at Figure 16.6. How similar were identical twins? Their concordance for schizophrenia was not 100% or 99% or 98%. It was only 48%. This means that more than half the time, if one member of an identical twin pair has schizophrenia, the other twin—who of course is genetically identical—does *not*. Genes by themselves, then, do not determine who develops this mental illness.

What other factors are important? It's hard to say; science does not fully understand the causes of schizophrenia. However, some research points to the prenatal environment. A vast amount of brain development occurs before a child's birth, and prenatal events may interfere with this development in a way that, later in life, results in schizophrenia. Harmful prenatal factors include bodily infections and exposure to lead (Opler & Susser, 2005). Another is poor nutrition. Research conducted in China examined the life outcomes of children conceived in the years 1959 to 1961, a time of catastrophic famine (Xu et al., 2009). These children were twice as likely to develop schizophrenia as were children conceived in other, non-famine historical periods.

SCHIZOPHRENIA ACROSS THE LIFE COURSE. It is rare for anyone to develop schizophrenia in early childhood. It is very rare for individuals to develop schizophrenia in their 40s or later in life if they have not had it previously. Among people who have the mental illness, schizophrenia usually first develops between the ages of 16 and 30 (Mueser & McGurk, 2004). Biological changes occurring during puberty may explain why the disease does not develop until the teenage years (Galdos, van Os, & Murray, 1993).

Bad news for sufferers is that schizophrenia persists. The disease generally lasts throughout a person's lifetime (Mueser & McGurk, 2004), although the severity of positive symptoms of schizophrenia often decreases in older adulthood (Schultz et al., 1997). The vast majority of people who experience an initial episode of schizophrenia will relapse (i.e., will have another such period) subsequently; studies report relapse rates of 95% (Emsley et al., 2013). Treatments for schizophrenia, which we'll learn about next, help people manage the symptoms, but do not eradicate the disease.

Famine, child development, and schizophrenia Among the terrible effects of famine is that it can increase rates of schizophrenia. Research indicates that children born during a famine are, due to a lack of nutrients early in life, more likely to develop the disorder.

Per-Anders Pettersson / Liaison / Getty Images

> **WHAT DO YOU KNOW?...**

6. Answer the following questions about schizophrenia.
   a. If schizophrenia was entirely caused by genes, how would the bar for MZ twins in Figure 16.5 change?
   b. Cite at least one factor, other than genes, that may cause schizophrenia.
   c. At what age does schizophrenia develop and how long-lasting is it?

Therapy for Schizophrenia

Preview Questions

> What drugs are used to treat schizophrenia? What are the side effects? Do they work?

> What psychotherapies are used to treat schizophrenia?

Schizophrenia exerts a huge cost on individuals and society at large. Treating the disorder is thus one of the greatest challenges for psychological science. Let's see how it's done.

DRUG THERAPY. You've learned enough about schizophrenia that, when it comes to the question of how to treat it, you can take an educated guess. Excess dopamine-based signals in the brain produce symptoms of schizophrenia. What's the treatment? Drugs that reduce these dopamine-based signals.

To treat schizophrenia, psychiatrists prescribe **antipsychotic drugs,** which are medications that alter the action of neurotransmitters in the brain in a manner that reduces psychotic symptoms. The drugs generally target the neurotransmitter dopamine.

Two types of antipsychotic drugs are available: *typical* and *atypical* antipsychotics. Their names indicate the historical time of their development. **Typical antipsychotics** are those developed first, in the 1950s. **Atypical antipsychotics** were developed in the 1990s, by which time use of the previously developed drugs was "typical." One commonly used typical antipsychotic is *chlorpromazine* (which has the trade name *thorazine*). A common atypical antipsychotic is the drug *clozapine.*

Both typical and atypical antipsychotics lower dopamine-based communication among neurons. How? They do not lower the brain's overall amount of dopamine. Instead, they block dopamine receptor sites. With the sites already filled, dopamine molecules thus cannot land there and deliver their signals. This reduction of dopamine-based neural activity alleviates the positive symptoms—the delusions and hallucinations—of schizophrenia (Stahl, 2002; see Figure 16.2).

Although typical and atypical antipsychotics both affect dopamine in this manner, in other ways they differ. Atypical antipsychotics affect not only dopamine signaling, but also signaling by a second neurotransmitter, serotonin. Serotonin contributes to emotional feelings that occur when people pursue activities that they find rewarding (Kranz, Kasper, & Lanzenberger, 2010). By influencing serotonin, atypical antipsychotic drugs thus may benefit not just positive symptoms of schizophrenia, but negative symptoms such as flat affect and lack of motivation, too (Stahl, 2002). A second difference is that the typical antipsychotics have a side effect that is not usually produced by the atypical drugs (Geddes et al., 2000), namely, uncontrollable, "shaking" muscular movements.

Unfortunately for patients with schizophrenia, both types of antipsychotic medication can produce a side effect known as *tardive dyskinesia.* **Tardive dyskinesia** consists of repetitive, involuntary movements of facial muscles. These movements result in odd

antipsychotic drugs Medications designed to alter neurotransmitter activity in the brain in a manner that reduces psychotic symptoms.

typical antipsychotics One of two major types of antipsychotic drugs, specifically, the first such drugs developed, in the 1950s.

atypical antipsychotics One of two major types of antipsychotic drugs, specifically, the second class of such drugs to be developed, in the 1990s. Atypical antipsychotics may relieve a wider range of symptoms while having fewer side effects than typical antipsychotics.

tardive dyskinesia Repetitive, uncontrollable muscular movements, typically of the face, such as odd grimacing and lip smacking; a side effect of antipsychotic medication.

symptoms such as repeated grimacing and lip smacking. For some patients, tardive dyskinesia is irreversible; it continues even after they stop taking the antipsychotic medication that triggered it (Muench & Hamer, 2010). Tardive dyskinesia rates are lower with atypical than typical antipsychotics (Kane, 2004).

EFFECTIVENESS OF ANTIPSYCHOTIC DRUGS. The good news is that antipsychotic drugs work for many patients, substantially reducing their positive symptoms of schizophrenia. As a result, people who otherwise might be hospitalized can live in their regular community. One study finds that, among patients treated for schizophrenia, 40% experience significant periods of recovery, that is, periods during which they are free from schizophrenic symptoms and can hold a job and take part in social activities (Harrow et al., 2005). The scholar you read about in this chapter's opening, Dr. Elyn Saks, is an example. She lives with schizophrenia yet leads an exceptionally productive professional life, in part thanks to antipsychotic drugs (Saks, 2007).

There are, however, two pieces of bad news. First, antipsychotic drugs do not always work. Reviews indicate that at least half the patients taking the drugs do not experience substantial long-term reductions in schizophrenic symptoms (Hegarty et al., 1994). Second, the drugs have side effects that include not only tardive dyskinesia, as just noted, but also sluggishness, sexual dysfunction, and weight gain (Muench & Hamer, 2010). The side effects cause many patients to stop taking the medications—which results in their losing out on the drugs' potential benefits. In one large study (Lieberman et al., 2005), the *majority* of schizophrenic patients—between two-thirds and four-fifths, depending on the drug—stopped taking their medication after either experiencing side effects or concluding that the drug didn't work. A major challenge is to develop antipsychotic drugs that are both effective and tolerable for more patients.

PSYCHOTHERAPY. Drugs can reduce the delusions and hallucinations of schizophrenia, but these symptoms are only part of the story. Schizophrenia affects the person as a whole. People with schizophrenia question themselves—their capabilities, their identity, their purpose in life. "It's hard for us," one person with schizophrenia writes, "because we lose everything that we thought we were. Our identity is taken from us in a sense" (www.schizophrenia.com posting). Psychotherapy (i.e., psychological therapy) can help people cope with the distress that schizophrenia brings (Lysaker et al., 2010).

A key question about psychotherapies for schizophrenia is which ones work. Which therapies, in other words, are empirically supported? (Also see Chapter 15.) One approach with empirical support is cognitive therapy. Cognitive therapists engage in a dialogue with patients about their delusional beliefs (Beck & Rector, 2002). They encourage patients to question the accuracy of the beliefs—to think of them as ideas they have about the world, rather than as statements of fact. (For example, they might encourage a patient to think, "It seems to me that the TV is sending a message directly to me, but that might not be true.") Patients learn how to question the evidence behind their beliefs and to cope with distress that the beliefs create. Evidence indicates that cognitive therapy can reduce both positive and negative symptoms of schizophrenia (Dickerson et al., 2002).

Some therapists employ cognitive strategies while also emphasizing the usefulness of humanistic approaches. The humanistic approach to therapy for schizophrenia focuses on the person as a whole: the individual who must cope not only with symptoms of schizophrenia, but also with the changes in lifestyle and self-concept that schizophrenia brings. In the humanistic approach, the quality of the personal relationship between therapist and client is seen as integral to therapy. The job of the therapist is not merely to teach clients but to collaborate with them (Chadwick, 2006); therapist and client work together to reduce the distress of mental illness.

Courtesy of USC Gould School of Law

Elyn Saks, Professor of Law, Psychology, and Psychiatry and the Behavioral Sciences at the Gould School of Law at the University of Southern California, has made significant scholarly contributions to the understanding of mental illness. In her personal life, she also copes with a severe mental illness, schizophrenia.

🔥 WHAT DO YOU KNOW?...

7. Which of the following statements about treatments for schizophrenia are true? Check all that apply.

_____ a. Both typical and atypical antipsychotic drugs reduce dopamine signals by blocking receptor sites.

_____ b. Both typical and atypical antipsychotic drugs alleviate positive symptoms, and atypical psychotics can additionally alleviate negative symptoms, by affecting serotonin signaling.

_____ c. Most people with schizophrenia who take antipsychotics experience significant periods of recovery, enabling them to live relatively normal lives.

_____ d. Side effects of antipsychotics include tardive dyskinesia, sluggishness, weight gain, and sexual dysfunction.

_____ e. The side effects of antipsychotics are mild enough that few people stop taking the drugs.

_____ f. Cognitive therapists help people with schizophrenia to challenge their delusional beliefs and to cope with the stress those beliefs create.

_____ g. Humanistic therapists help people with schizophrenia cope with changes in their self-concept.

Other Psychotic Disorders

Preview Question

> Is schizophrenia the only psychotic disorder?

We have examined schizophrenia in depth for two reasons. One, as noted earlier, is that its personal cost to individuals and its economic cost to society—estimated at more than $60 billion in the United States in any given year (Wu et al., 2005)—are so large that the disease demands attention. Second, its symptoms are so diverse and severe that, in schizophrenia, one sees the range of psychotic symptoms that people with psychotic disorders may experience.

Schizophrenia, however, is not the only psychotic disorder. There are other psychological disorders in which people experience psychotic symptoms, but not with the severity and duration seen in schizophrenia. Two of them are *brief psychotic disorder* and *delusional disorder*.

In **brief psychotic disorder,** people experience the same types of symptoms as in schizophrenia (delusions, hallucinations, etc.). However, they experience them—as you can guess from the disorder's name—for only a brief period of time. DSM-5 classifies people as having brief psychotic disorder if they exhibit these symptoms for at least one day but less than one month.

In **delusional disorder,** people experience only one psychotic symptom, delusions, which may persist indefinitely. People with the disorder may believe, without evidence, that they are being spied upon, that someone is trying to poison them, or that they have made some profoundly important discovery that society has not recognized. Some beliefs held by people with delusional disorder may be wildly implausible (DSM-5 gives the example of the belief that a stranger has removed one's internal organs and replaced them with somebody else's).

Brief psychotic disorder and delusional disorder illustrate that psychoses exist on a continuum. There is, in other words, a dimension—ranging from low to high severity—along which psychoses vary. Schizophrenia is at the high end of the severity dimension; brief psychotic disorder and delusional disorder are lower in severity. At the very low end are the experiences of people who occasionally exhibit one of

brief psychotic disorder A disorder in which people experience symptoms typical of schizophrenia, but for only a brief period of time.

delusional disorder A psychological disorder in which people hold convictions that contradict known facts (e.g., that someone is trying to harm them).

IMAGINE IF YOU GOT BLAMED FOR HAVING CANCER.

END THE STIGMA & DISCRIMINATION OF MENTAL ILLNESS ® bring change 2 mind.org

Battling misconceptions of psychological disorders Organizations such as bringchange2mind.org work to fight social stigmas that are associated with psychotic disorders by correcting misconceptions of mental illness.

the symptoms of psychosis, yet do not have any psychological disorder at all. Such people are not all that rare. Surveys indicate that about 10% of people experience a hallucination (e.g., hearing voices) at least once in their life, and that much larger numbers of people hold beliefs that qualify as delusional. For example, a belief in ghosts was expressed by 25% of survey respondents in Great Britain (a nation where, unlike some parts of the world, the existence of ghosts is not a culturally accepted belief; Johns & van Os, 2001). In a large-scale survey conducted in 52 countries, an average prevalence rate of about 5% was found for the belief that one's thoughts were sometimes controlled by another person or other outside force (Nuevo et al., 2010).

These survey findings can help reduce the social stigma associated with psychotic disorders. *Social stigma* refers to widespread negative beliefs about a group. Societies around the world stigmatize people with psychotic disorders (Lee, 2002). The stigma portrays them as "lunatic, "crazy" individuals who differ fundamentally from "normal" members of society. In surveys of people with schizophrenia, 4 in 5 individuals report overhearing hurtful, offensive comments about mental illness from other people or the media, and the majority indicate that people sometimes try to avoid them (Wahl, 1999). These experiences can create stress, lower self-esteem, and thus make it even harder for individuals to cope with the disorder. "People attempting to recover from mental illnesses . . . often feel that they suffer as much from being labeled mentally ill as they do from mental illnesses itself" (Link & Phelan, 2009, p. 571).

> ## 🌀 WHAT DO YOU KNOW?...
>
> 8. The following statement is incorrect. Explain why: "Two pieces of information suggest that psychotic disorders are best conceptualized as distinct categories, rather than dimensions: (1) 10% of people have experienced delusions such as hallucinations, and (2) brief psychotic disorder and delusional disorder share symptoms with schizophrenia, but in lesser form."

Personality Disorders

Preview Question

> › What's the difference between having a personality disorder and just being quirky?

The disorders you've learned about previously, in this chapter and in Chapter 15, disrupt people's typical styles of behavior. Rather than being their usual selves, people become intensely anxious, or gloomily depressed, or begin hearing voices. Now we'll consider a different type of disorder—one in which the disorder *is* the person's typical style of behavior.

Personality disorders are chronic styles of thinking, behavior, and emotion that severely lower the quality of people's personal relationships. These personal styles create conflict with others and, in the long run, harm the person with the disorder. People with personality disorders may not realize that the problems they experience in relationships are caused by their own behavior; as a result, they tend to blame others for interpersonal conflict.

People with personality disorders are particularly likely to experience difficulties when under stress. Stress can occur in different situations of a person's life: work, relations with parents, social relationships, dealing with financial problems, and so forth.

personality disorders Psychological disorders that feature chronic styles of thinking, behavior, and emotion that severely lower the quality of people's relationships, creating conflict with others.

In general, it is good to be "flexible" when dealing with stress; that is, to develop different strategies for coping with different types of stress (Cheng & Cheung, 2005). However, people with personality disorders are relatively *in*flexible; their personal style is consistent across different situations. As a result, they do not cope with stress as effectively as most other people (Bijttebier & Vertommen, 1999).

Why do psychologists say that some personality styles are "disorders" rather than merely saying that a person is "unusual" or "quirky" or "difficult"? The term *disorder* implies that the personality style is directly harmful to mental health. Psychologist Theodore Millon (2004) explains that people with personality disorders contribute to their own psychological distress in a number of ways:

> *Inflexible interactions with a given person.* If you're in a relationship and find that certain behaviors of yours bother the other person, you might change how you act in order to improve the relationship. But people with personality disorders tend to maintain the same style of behavior, which creates ever-increasing interpersonal stress.

> *Inability to adapt to different people and roles.* You probably act differently toward different people: family, friends, teachers, or a boss at work. You might politely follow an order from a job supervisor, but not a friend. People with personality disorders are less able to adapt to different people and roles. They often seek to control situations, rather than adapt to them.

> As a result of this inflexibility, people with personality disorders do not grow psychologically, gaining in maturity, as others do. Instead, time and again, their inflexible behavior creates the same type of interpersonal conflict with others.

When the DSM is used to diagnose people, personality disorders are found to be remarkably prevalent. A large survey in the United States, involving a representative sample of more than 9000 adults, found that roughly 1 out of every 11 adults exhibits a diagnosable personality disorder (Lenzenweger et al., 2007).

😟 WHAT DO YOU KNOW?...

9. In what ways do people with personality disorders contribute to their own distress? Check all that apply.

_____ a. They refuse to believe that their visual hallucinations are not grounded in reality, even if acknowledging this would improve interactions.

_____ b. They inflexibly maintain the same style of interaction with a particular person, even if changing it would improve the relationship.

_____ c. They do not change their behavior to suit the type of people with whom they are interacting, preferring instead to control situations.

Types of Personality Disorder

Preview Question

> What characterizes the six main types of personality disorder: antisocial, avoidant, borderline, obsessive-compulsive, narcissistic, and schizotypal personality disorder?

Identifying and distinguishing among personality disorders is a tricky task. DSM-5 contains two different classifications of the disorders; one maintains older classifications, and the other is a new, simpler model. We will rely here on the newer model, which recognizes six types of personality disorder: (1) antisocial, (2) avoidant, (3) borderline, (4) obsessive-compulsive, (5) narcissistic, and (6) schizotypal personality disorder. Each, as you will see, is a distinctive pattern of personality processes—an interconnected system of thoughts, feelings, and interpersonal behaviors (Shedler et al., 2010).

"The only sensible way to live in this world is without rules." So said the Joker, a fictional character who illustrates antisocial personality disorder, played here by Heath Ledger in *The Dark Knight*.

ANTISOCIAL PERSONALITY DISORDER. **Antisocial personality disorder** is defined by a set of negative personality traits. People with antisocial personalities are manipulative (using others to achieve their own goals), callous (not caring about harm to others), hostile (often angry and vengeful), and are risk takers (engaging calmly in dangerous behaviors). They lack empathy; that is, they are unconcerned about the feelings, rights, and safety of others. If a person displays these traits consistently, and they harm the individual's interpersonal relationships, then the person meets DSM criteria for antisocial personality disorder.

The center point of antisocial personality disorder, at a deeper psychological level, is what Sigmund Freud called a weak superego (Meloy, 2007) and what contemporary psychological scientists refer to as moral reasoning (Raine & Yang, 2006). Most people adhere to moral rules that prevent them from harming others and motivate them to perform behaviors that are good for society. In antisocial personality disorder, these rules seem to be absent; people lack an inner "voice of conscience." Even after harming another person, an individual with antisocial personality disorder experiences no guilt or remorse. Such people can be dangerous to themselves, to society at large, and to the therapists who try to help them. One therapist reports an antisocial personality disorder client saying, after numerous therapy sessions, "You know a lot about me, Doc, and sometimes when people know too much they get killed" (Meloy, 2007, p. 779).

People who fit the diagnostic category *antisocial personality disorder* are not all the same. The category is broad and, within it, researchers have identified distinct subgroups of people with somewhat different personalities (Poythress et al., 2010). One subgroup has a high level of a trait called *psychopathy* (Hare & Neumann, 2008). **Psychopathy** is a personality style defined not only by the hostility toward others and lack of guilt that characterize antisocial personality disorder in general, but also by a tendency to lie to others and manipulate them. Psychopaths are "social predators who charm [and] manipulate . . . leaving a broad trail of broken hearts, shattered expectations, and empty wallets" (Hare, 1999, p. xi). Many of the serial killers who have plagued recent world history displayed psychopathic characteristics (LaBrode, 2007). Psychopathy is less prevalent among women than men (Cale & Lilienfeld, 2002). By contrast, a different subgroup shows signs of antisocial personality disorder (a callous lack of empathy) but *not* psychopathy (manipulativeness and lying; Poythress et al., 2010).

Can you think of any fictional characters who could be characterized as psychopaths?

AVOIDANT PERSONALITY DISORDER. Consider the case of "Ms. K," a 24-year-old pursuing a degree in nursing (Gilbert & Gordon, 2013; following quotes pp. 115–116). Ms. K entered psychotherapy to address "a lifetime of significant interpersonal passivity." She reported "low positive mood throughout her adolescence and

antisocial personality disorder
A psychological disorder defined by a set of negative personality traits such as being manipulative, callous, hostile; taking risks; and lacking empathy.

psychopathy A personality style defined by hostility toward others, lack of guilt, and a tendency toward dishonesty and manipulation of others.

young adult life," and chronic feelings of inadequacy that caused her to be unable to express opinions to professional associates or to friends. A tendency to avoid other people "had been present her entire life," her therapist reported, "and affected all areas of functioning."

Ms. K's is a case of **avoidant personality disorder,** which is characterized by feelings of social inadequacy and low self-esteem, as well as preoccupation with the possibility of being evaluated negatively by others (Sanislow, Bartolini, & Zoloth, 2012). These feelings and thoughts contribute to a style of behavior that is shy, withdrawn, and inhibited. People's insecurity about themselves causes them to miss out on social contact with others.

Research suggests that, among people with avoidant personality disorder, feelings of insecurity are particularly acute in a certain type of situation: when others might be criticizing them. In one study (Bowles et al., 2013), participants were asked to imagine themselves working busily on particular projects and receiving feedback from others. In one experimental condition, the feedback was fully supportive ("I'm really impressed"). In another, it was ambiguous with a suggestion of criticism ("Don't spread yourself too thin"). More so than other individuals, people with avoidant personality disorder felt badly about themselves after being exposed to the ambiguous feedback.

BORDERLINE PERSONALITY DISORDER. You encountered borderline personality disorder at the outset of this chapter, in our opening vignette. The 17-year-old girl who attacked herself—and who, as an adult, became the eminent clinical psychologist Marsha Linehan—was a sufferer.

Borderline personality disorder is the most commonly diagnosed personality disorder, with a prevalence rate of 2 to 3% of the adult population (Gunderson & Links, 2008). Borderline personality disorder is difficult to describe precisely; professionals are not in complete agreement on its defining characteristics. However, it has the following main features:

> *Unstable sense of self.* People's self-image varies. Sometimes they seem self-confident, and other times they seem to have poor self-esteem. Rather than maintaining a stable set of personal goals and plans, their goals vary in a seemingly erratic manner.

> *Emotional instability.* Variations in self-image are accompanied by variations in emotion. People with borderline personality disorder experience a range of negative emotions; sometimes they feel depressed and worthless, yet they also experience outbursts of anger.

> *Unstable interpersonal relationships.* People with borderline personality disorder experience extreme difficulties maintaining relationships. They tend to view friends and romantic partners in an extreme black-and-white manner, sometimes seeing their partner as being a wonderful, ideal person, but other times experiencing intense disappointment in, and anger toward, that same person. Their relationships with others often lack empathy. Rather than understanding the emotional life of another person, people with borderline personality disorder use the relationships to bolster their own self-image and calm their own emotional troubles.

> *Sense of abandonment.* People with borderline personality disorder have recurring worries that other people will reject or abandon them.

This combination of symptoms is exceptionally stressful. Borderline individuals report feeling lonely, worthless, and overwhelmed by the stresses of life (Zanarini at al., 1998). They experience a spectrum of negative emotions and have difficulty controlling those emotions. Borderline individuals dwell on, or go over and over,

Damon Winter / The New York Times / Redux

Marsha Linehan, who developed dialectical behavior therapy as a treatment for borderline personality disorder.

avoidant personality disorder
A psychological disorder characterized by feelings of social inadequacy, low self-esteem, and preoccupation with potential negative evaluations by others, leading to behavior that is shy, withdrawn, and inhibited.

borderline personality disorder
A psychological disorder involving an unstable sense of self, emotional instability, unstable interpersonal relationships, and a sense of abandonment.

their emotions. As a result, feelings of anger, anxiety, and despair can last for weeks and disrupt their lives (Conklin, Bradley, & Westen, 2006).

People with borderline personality disorder sometimes take desperate steps to escape this stress. One step is self-harm—that is, deliberately harming oneself physically. Some individuals cut themselves or burn themselves with lit cigarettes. Why would anyone engage in self-destructive behavior? Borderline individuals often report that self-harm temporarily relieves their anxieties (Linehan, 1993). Although the behavior is harmful in the long run, its short-term effect is to reduce tension and distract people from the daily worries that commonly overwhelm them (Brown, Comtois, & Linehan, 2002).

Another tragic step taken by many borderline patients is suicide. Suicide is a risk associated with many mental health problems; different forms of distress and despair can drive people to the ultimate, final escape from life's problems (Nordentoft, Mortensen, & Pedersen, 2011). Borderline patients, however, are particularly at risk. The majority of borderline patients attempt suicide, and 10% of individuals with borderline personality disorder die from their attempts (Soloff et al., 2005). Research sheds light on the reasons behind this act. Interviewers spoke with women who had tried unsuccessfully to take their own lives. They indicated that a primary reason for suicide was to make other people better off (Brown et al., 2002). Individuals with borderline personality disorder perceived themselves as a burden on others and tried to take their own lives to relieve others of this burden.

NARCISSISTIC PERSONALITY DISORDER. **Narcissistic personality disorder** is a personality pattern in which individuals are excessively self-centered. They pay little attention to the thoughts and feelings of others, focusing instead on themselves and how to enhance their own self-image. According to the DSM, this personality pattern qualifies as a disorder when it occurs repeatedly across time and place and lowers the quality of the interpersonal relationships that an individual is able to form.

Narcissistic individuals possess personality characteristics that are contradictory (Morf & Rhodewalt, 2001). On the one hand, they hold views of themselves that seem extraordinarily positive. Narcissists crave attention and, when they get it, talk about

Narcissistic personality disorder derives its name from Greek mythology (Hamilton, 1942). In the ancient myth, Narcissus was an exceedingly handsome lad and a paragon of self-centeredness. When he saw his reflection in water (as depicted here in *Echo and Narcisssus*, by John William Waterhouse, 1903), he was so entranced by his own image that he stared endlessly at himself, wasted away, and died.

Echo and Narcissus, 1903 (oil on canvas), Waterhouse, John William (1849–1917) / © Walker Art Gallery, National Museums Liverpool / Bridgeman Images

narcissistic personality disorder
A psychological disorder characterized by self-centeredness, concern with enhancing one's self-image, and disregard for the thoughts and feelings of others.

how great they are. On the other hand, their opinion of themselves seems "fragile." If you know a narcissist, you might get the impression that, down deep, the person isn't confident in all the great things he's saying about himself. This uncertainty, in fact, is why he craves attention. Narcissists need to find other people to support their grandiose, yet fragile, views of self. The political dictator who surrounds himself with "yes men" illustrates these personality dynamics.

OBSESSIVE COMPULSIVE PERSONALITY DISORDER. As you may recall, Chapter 15 discusses *obsessive-compulsive disorder* (OCD), in which people experience obsessions (recurring thoughts about danger and harm) and engage in compulsions (repetitive actions taken to prevent the dangers and harms). People with OCD repeatedly check locks, arrange household items in a strict order, or engage in other such compulsive behavior.

More than a century ago, the French psychologist Pierre Janet observed this OCD—and something in addition. He noticed some personality characteristics that seemed to predict the onset of OCD symptoms. Individuals who were highly perfectionistic, he judged, were more likely to develop obsessions and compulsions later in life (Mancebo et al., 2005).

The observations of Janet, and many subsequent psychologists and psychiatrists, led to the recognition of **obsessive-compulsive personality disorder (OCPD).** People with OCPD are, as Janet observed, highly perfectionistic. They also seek order and control over activities, stick rigidly to rules for behavior, and pay extraordinary attention to small details (Mancebo et al., 2005). OCPD individuals are so highly devoted to work that they commonly are, in practice, less devoted to family and friends (Van Noppen, 2010). Unlike individuals with OCD, who generally are aware of their psychological problems, people with OCPD often see their dysfunctional behavior as perfectly normal.

Research reveals a strong relation between the personality disorder, OCPD, and the anxiety disorder, obsessive-compulsive disorder. The populations of people with OCPD and OCD overlap significantly, and individuals with perfectionistic OCPD tendencies are relatively less likely to benefit from therapy for obsessive-compulsive symptoms (Garyfallos et al., 2010; Pinto et al., 2011).

SCHIZOTYPAL PERSONALITY DISORDER. **Schizotypal personality disorder** is characterized by two predominant features. One is its distinctive patterns of thinking (Chemerinski et al., 2013). In this disorder, individuals have odd beliefs that diverge from those of most members of society; individuals may, for example, believe in "paranormal" phenomena, such as the ability of thoughts alone to control physical objects. They also may exhibit odd mannerisms, styles of dressing and speaking that differ from most other people, and suspiciousness of other people. People with schizotypal personality disorder are, in short, individuals whom you might call "eccentric."

The second distinctive feature is that people with schizotypal personality disorder have few close friends (e.g., Bergman et al., 1996). Their odd personal style, combined with their suspicions of others, appear to undermine their capacity to form close personal relationships with people outside of their immediate families. Many people with the disorder lead lives that are socially isolated from others.

The odd beliefs that characterize this personality disorder are related to schizophrenia; the name itself, "schizotypal," suggests that the disease is a type of schizophrenia. However, research on brain mechanisms in the two disorders suggests that they are distinct (Haznedar et al., 2004).

Table 16.2 summarizes the characteristics of the six disorders we have reviewed.

Imagno / Getty Images

Van Gogh Dutch painter Vincent Van Gogh exhibited personal eccentricities and, in adulthood, was often socially isolated from others. Some therefore suggest that he experienced schizotypal personality disorder (www.schizophrenia.com). If so, his extraordinary work demonstrates that schizotypy can co-exist with creative genius. Indeed, research suggests that individuals with schizotypal personality disorder may have a greater capacity for creative thinking than most other individuals (Folley & Park, 2005).

obsessive-compulsive personality disorder (OCPD) A psychological disorder characterized by perfectionism, a seeking of order and control, rigid adherence to rules for behavior, and attention to small details.

schizotypal personality disorder A psychological disorder characterized by (1) odd beliefs, eccentricity in manner or dress, and suspiciousness; and (2) few close friends, that is, social isolation resulting from these beliefs and behaviors.

table **16.2**

Six Types of Personality Disorder	
Personality Disorder	**Defining Characteristics**
Antisocial personality disorder	Lack of empathy; disregard for others' feelings, rights, and safety; manipulative, callous, and often hostile personality traits.
Avoidant personality disorder	Feelings of inadequacy and low self-esteem; preoccupation with the prospect of negative evaluation by others; behavior is withdrawn, shy, and inhibited.
Borderline personality disorder	Unstable sense of self, unstable relationships, and unstable emotional life; feelings of abandonment and concern about being rejected by others.
Narcissistic personality disorder	Excessively self-centered; opinions of self are highly positive yet also "fragile"; people crave the attention of others who support their grandiose sense of self.
Obsessive-compulsive personality disorder	Perfectionism, a desire for order and control over activities, and rigid adherence to rules; devotion to work may impair personal relationships.
Schizotypal personality disorder	Odd, eccentric patterns of thinking or behavior, combined with social isolation resulting from an inability to form close personal relationships with people outside of immediate family.

✿ WHAT DO YOU KNOW?...

10. People with _____ personality disorder are often, among other things, manipulative and callous and engage in risky behaviors. Serial killers tend to be particularly high in the trait of _____, characterized by the tendency to lie and to manipulate. People with _____ personality disorder seem very confident yet need others to support their grandiose views of themselves. Though a precise definition of _____ personality disorder has not been attained, most can agree it is characterized by instability in self-concept, interpersonal relations, and emotions, as well as a fear of abandonment.

Causes of Personality Disorder: Nature, Nurture, and the Brain

Preview Questions

> How do nature and nurture contribute to the development of antisocial behavior?
> What does the psychopathic brain look like?
> How are the brains of people with borderline personality disorder different from those without the disorder?

Nature and nurture both contribute to the development of personality disorders. Genes and environmental experience play significant roles and interact with one other. Research on antisocial personality disorder illustrates this general point.

GENE–ENVIRONMENTAL INTERACTION AND ANTISOCIAL PERSONALITY DISORDER. A meta-analysis of twin studies—in other words, a statistical summary of numerous past twin studies—reveals the substantial impact of both genetic and environmental factors on antisocial behavior. Genes were found to account for 41% of overall individual differences in antisocial conduct. Environmental factors thus explained the majority of the differences between people: 59% (Rhee & Waldman, 2002).

This twin-study finding establishes that both nature and nurture—genes and the environment—play important roles. But it does not tell us what those roles are. To determine this, researchers examine how genes and environmental experiences affect the workings of the brain. A landmark study of antisocial behavior (Caspi et al., 2002) shows how genes and the environment interact in affecting brain functioning and antisocial conduct.

In this study, researchers (Caspi et al., 2002) focused on two factors, one environmental and one genetic:

> *Childhood maltreatment:* The environmental factor was maltreatment during childhood. Maltreatment, which included harsh physical punishment and sexual abuse, was identified by interviewing parents and by speaking with their children years later, when they reached adulthood.

> *A gene that affects neurotransmitter levels:* The genetic factor was person-to-person variation in a gene that affects neurotransmitter activity in the brain. Specifically, the gene influences the body's production of a biochemical that alters the chemical structure of neurotransmitters. Once altered, signaling activity in the brain is reduced.

These two factors have opposing effects within the brain. Childhood maltreatment is a highly stressful event that causes neurotransmitter activity to increase. The gene causes neurotransmitter activity to decrease; in particular, it enables the brain to return to a normal activity level after a stressful event occurs. Research findings show that these two factors combine in their influence on antisocial behavior. Among children who did not experience maltreatment, genetic variations did not make much difference. No matter what their genetic makeup, children who do not experience maltreatment are unlikely to develop antisocial personalities (Figure 16.7). However, among children who *do* experience maltreatment, genes make a big difference. Some of these children are quite likely to become antisocial adults, whereas others, who have a different genetic makeup, are not. Children who experience maltreatment, but who also possess genes that produce a biochemical that quickly restores their normal level of activity after stress, are "resilient" in the face of maltreatment (see Chapter 14); they are less likely to become antisocial adults.

ANTISOCIAL AND PSYCHOPATHIC DISORDERS AND THE BRAIN. In addition to neurotransmitters, researchers studying the biology of antisocial personality disorder and psychopathy also investigate neurons, the brain's cells. They compare people with different personality styles and search for neural differences.

A challenge is figuring out where in the brain to search. Psychological findings provide a clue. As you learned, the main psychological component of antisocial behavior is deficits in empathy and moral reasoning. Psychopathic individuals also display a lack of guilt feelings. Brain regions

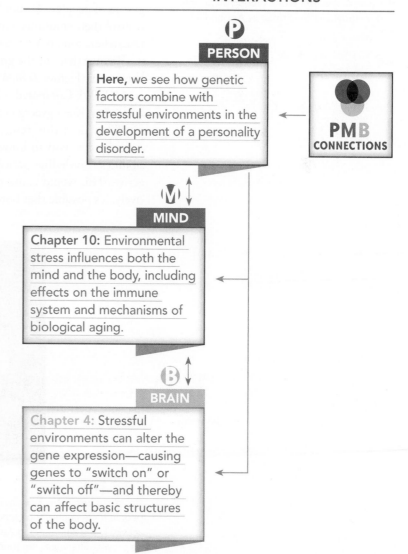

CONNECTING TO STRESS AND COPING AND GENE–ENVIRONMENT INTERACTIONS

PERSON

Here, we see how genetic factors combine with stressful environments in the development of a personality disorder.

PMB CONNECTIONS

MIND

Chapter 10: Environmental stress influences both the mind and the body, including effects on the immune system and mechanisms of biological aging.

BRAIN

Chapter 4: Stressful environments can alter the gene expression—causing genes to "switch on" or "switch off"—and thereby can affect basic structures of the body.

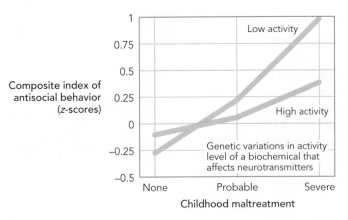

Research from Koenigsberg et al. (2009)

figure 16.7

Gene–environment interaction and antisocial behavior Genes and the environment interact in the development of antisocial behavior. Children who possess a genetic predisposition to the disorder and also experience severe maltreatment are most likely to display antisocial behavior later in life (Caspi et al., 2002). (The z-scores indicate how far people's scores are from the overall average score, among all people in the study; see the Statistics Appendix.)

that already are known to be involved in these thoughts and feelings, then, are the place to look when conducting brain research.

In one study (Gregory et al., 2012), researchers examined a population of men who had been convicted of violent crimes (e.g., murder). Within this population, they identified one subgroup with antisocial personality disorder and psychopathic personality qualities, and a second with antisocial personality disorder but *without* psychopathic qualities. Brain scans revealed differences between the groups. The psychopathic group had lower brain volume in parts of the brain that are active when people (1) evaluate others' ongoing social behavior and emotions (a region in the brain's frontal cortex) and (2) relate ongoing behavior to personal memories and stored knowledge of social rules (a region in the temporal lobe). These brain regions are needed to understand when, and why, one's own behavior violates social rules, and thus to experience emotions such as embarrassment and guilt (Gregory et al., 2012). The brain-level findings thus complement mind-level analyses of psychopathic persons.

BORDERLINE PERSONALITY DISORDER AND THE BRAIN. Brain research sheds light on the biological underpinnings of other personality disorders, including borderline personality disorder. Researchers (Koenigsberg et al., 2009) asked two groups of people—(1) borderline patients and (2) individuals without the disorder—to control their emotions while viewing a series of pictures with emotional content. The researchers took brain images while participants performed this task.

Brain activity in the groups differed. Variations were seen within the anterior cingulate cortex (Figure 16.8), a region known to be involved in emotional control (Ochsner et al., 2004). Compared with other people, in borderline patients, this brain region was less active (Koenigsberg et al., 2009).

What does this result say about borderline personality disorder and the brain? Actually, it's hard to know precisely without additional research. There are two possibilities. Borderline patients may inherit a brain structure that is less developed and active. This would cause them to have less ability to control their emotions. Alternatively, it's possible that borderline patients less frequently try to control their emotions.

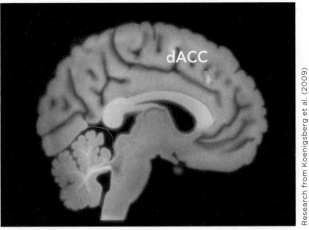

figure 16.8

Brain research on borderline personality disorder Brain research shows that, when people try to control their emotions, individuals with borderline personality disorder have less activity in the anterior cingulate cortex, a brain region known to be involved in emotional control. As shown, differences are found, specifically, in the dACC, the dorsal anterior cingulate cortex.

This could cause them to have less neural development in regions of the brain involved in emotional control (Giuliani, Drabant, & Gross, 2011). Behavioral activities (such as controlling emotions) can change the brain (see Chapter 3).

🐾 WHAT DO YOU KNOW?...

11. True or False?
   a. A meta-analysis of twin studies indicated that 59% of the differences in antisocial conduct were attributable to the influence of genes.
   b. Research by Caspi and colleagues indicated that the effect of genes on antisocial behavior was apparent only among those who had been mistreated as children.
   c. Research indicates that among men who have antisocial personality disorder with psychopathic personality qualities, brain volume is lower in regions integral to feelings of embarrassment and guilt: one region associated with evaluating others' emotions and another relating behavior to knowledge of social rules.
   d. In one study, the anterior cingulate, an area associated with emotional control, was less active among those with borderline personality disorder.
   e. Finding that the anterior cingulate is less active among those with borderline personality disorder enables one to conclude that these individuals were born with a deficit in this brain structure.

Therapy for Personality Disorders

Preview Question

> How do therapists treat personality disorders?

When it comes to formulating therapy, personality disorders pose unique challenges. The disorders consist of emotional and behavioral patterns that are highly ingrained. There is no quick-and-easy way to alter fundamental personality styles that have been exhibited for years.

Despite the challenge, the need for therapy is compelling. In antisocial personality disorder, sufferers may inflict harm on others. In borderline personality disorder, people often inflict harm on themselves. Therapists need to act quickly to minimize the harm that these disorders can bring.

PSYCHOANALYTIC THERAPY AND COGNITIVE THERAPY. For many years, the primary psychotherapy for personality disorders was psychoanalysis (Waldinger, 1987). Psychoanalytic therapists focused on clients' unconscious defense mechanisms (mental strategies to protect against anxiety; see Chapter 13) and their interpersonal relationship with the therapist. They judged that transference—a process in which a patient unconsciously responds to the therapist as a significant figure from earlier in his or her life (see Chapter 15)—is central to therapeutic insight and improvement.

More recently, many therapists have employed cognitive therapy for personality disorders (Beck, Freeman, & Davis, 2004). In comparison to psychoanalysis, cognitive therapy places greater emphasis on conscious processes. Therapists believe clients are consciously aware of personal beliefs that contribute to their chronic psychological distress, and they try to modify these cognitions in therapy.

In addition, like psychoanalysts, cognitive therapists attend closely to the interpersonal relationship they have with their clients. In therapy for personality disorders, therapists must become familiar with a client's life as a whole and must build a therapeutic relationship strong enough that the client will come to accept the therapist's suggestions for significant personal change (Beck et al., 2004).

Andrey Prokhorov / Getty Images

Dialectical behavior therapy for borderline personality disorder incorporates principles of Eastern philosophy, including the idea that, to gain understanding, one should acknowledge opposing points of view and then search for a viewpoint that reconciles them. In Eastern philosophy, this perspective is commonly represented with a yin and yang symbol (Xinyan, 2013).

DIALECTICAL BEHAVIOR THERAPY. Psychoanalysis and cognitive therapy were not originally designed to treat personality disorders. Instead, they have been adapted to the need of the personality disorder client. We'll now consider a therapy designed specifically to benefit clients with a personality disorder, specifically, borderline personality disorder.

Dialectical behavior therapy is a treatment for borderline personality disorder developed by the psychologist Marsha Linehan (1993). Her therapy combines principles of behavior therapy with principles of Eastern and Western philosophy.

A primary philosophical principle is *dialectic*. Dialectic is a form of argument—that is, a way of resolving disagreements—that has been known for thousands of years. In dialectical argument, one identifies opposing points of view and then searches for a single viewpoint that reconciles them. Rather than "sticking to your guns," you think flexibly and remain open to changing your opinions. Linehan and colleagues explain (Lynch et al., 2007) how dialectic works when patients harm themselves. Rather than merely arguing that self-harm is bad, therapists recognize two opposing facts: Self-injury is (1) harmful in the long run (it creates scars and risks severe bodily damage), but (2) has short-term benefits (it temporarily relieves emotional turmoil, as borderline patients report; Kemperman, Russ, & Shearin, 1997). The therapist acknowledges the validity of both points and then reconciles them by searching for a new way to remove emotional distress that avoids the long-term harm of self-injury (Lynch et al., 2007). Dialectical thinking counteracts the tendency among borderline patients to engage in black-and-white thinking.

A second philosophical principle is *acceptance*. The term is used as in Zen Buddhism, where it refers to recognizing, and accepting, that some aspects of the world are unchangeable. This principle shifts the therapist's focus. Rather than constantly striving for therapeutic change, the dialectical behavior therapist teaches clients to accept themselves, and their circumstances, as they are.

Linehan grafts these philosophical principles onto standard cognitive and behavior therapy practices. As in behavior therapy (see Chapter 15), the dialectical therapist strives to increase clients' skills in problem solving and to reduce their anxiety. This is accomplished through both individual psychotherapy and group settings in which clients can develop and test their interpersonal skills (Linehan, 1993).

Good news for people with borderline personality disorder is that dialectical behavior therapy works. Numerous research studies comparing dialectical therapy to other treatments document that dialectic behavior therapy uniquely improves the emotional lives and behavioral experiences of borderline patients (Lynch et al., 2007). Critically, dialectical therapy also substantially reduces their risk of suicide (Linehan et al., 2006).

🔥 WHAT DO YOU KNOW?●●●

12. In _____ therapy for personality disorders, therapists help patients become conscious of the beliefs that contribute to their distress. Dialectical behavior therapy is used to treat _____ personality disorder. Dialectic refers to a type of _____, one in which the validity of two opposing viewpoints is acknowledged. The therapist searches for a third viewpoint that can _____ the differences between the two. The Zen Buddhist principle of _____ that some things cannot be changed is a major feature of dialectical behavior therapy.

---

dialectical behavior therapy
A therapy for borderline personality disorder whose core element is a dialectic approach that attempts to identify and reconcile opposing points of view on psychological problems, in an effort to reduce emotional distress.

Dissociative and Conversion Disorders

Let's hear once again from some people on an Internet discussion forum.

> "Earlier this week, my therapist and I were talking and he determined that maybe the reason why Megan got constantly depressed is because she wanted attention.

I gave her some and she made weird requests throughout the day. When I got to bed, she asked for a plushie to sleep with. I got her one from our closet (she has like thirty from an amusement park)."

> "[They're] all so different. I think it depends on their age. . . . For example, I know that Skip has had lengthy discussions about how much he wants to race (someone) to see who can run faster. He's a young child, so this is important to him."

> "Kyle and Hera are married. Axel is something of a family friend to them. Mark and Kyle have been friends for years. Hera seems to know everyone in the system, and most people respect her and obey pretty much everything she says."

These reports seem so different from those written by people with schizophrenia, which you read earlier in this chapter. These people don't report that God is speaking directly to them, that everyone else is a robot, or other such delusional beliefs. You might wonder what these stories about Megan, Skip, Kyle, and the others are even doing in a chapter on psychological disorders.

Here's a hint: Megan doesn't exist. Neither does Skip. The same goes for Kyle, Hera, and their friends. They don't exist anywhere except within the minds of the writers (from http://www.psychforums.com/dissociative-identity). All these characters are *alters*—alternative personalities—invented by people with *dissociative identity disorder*.

In this section of the chapter, we'll learn about the *dissociative disorders* and will then complete our coverage of psychological disorders by reviewing a puzzling syndrome known as *conversion disorder*.

Dissociative Disorders

Preview Questions

> Do people with dissociative identity disorder truly have multiple independent personalities?
> What causes dissociative identity disorder?
> What defines depersonalization/derealization disorder?
> Can people completely lose their memory for who they are?

Dissociative disorders are a category of psychological disorders in which people experience profound alterations in their sense of personal identity, their conscious experiences of events, or their memory of their own past. Clinicians have identified a range of dissociative disorders; they include *dissociative identity disorder, depersonalization/ derealization disorder,* and *dissociative amnesia and fugue.*

DISSOCIATIVE IDENTITY DISORDER. In **dissociative identity disorder,** people experience more than one self; that is, more than one personality seems to inhabit their mind. (The disorder was formerly known as *multiple personality disorder.*) According to the DSM, people qualify as having the disorder when they experience two or more personalities that are distinct. The different personalities are experienced as possessing different behavioral styles, emotional experiences, and personal goals. An additional factor in diagnosis involves memory. People with dissociative identity disorder experience memory disruptions; when in one personality state, they report being unable to remember what they were doing when in another.

The disorder became well known in American society more than half a century ago thanks to a movie. The film *The Three Faces of Eve* (1957) told the story of Eve White, a modest

Have you seen dramatic depictions of dissociative identity disorder on TV or film?

dissociative disorders Category of psychological disorders characterized by alterations in one's sense of personal identity, conscious experiences of events, or memory of one's own past.

dissociative identity disorder A psychological disorder in which people experience more than one self; that is, more than one personality seems to inhabit their mind.

The Three Faces of Eve, a 1957 movie starring Joanne Woodward as Eve, brought multiple personality disorder (now known as dissociative identity disorder) to the attention of the general public.

woman with a wild alternative personality, as well as a third personality that was able to discuss the other two.

There can be no doubt that dissociative identity disorder severely disrupts people's lives. Yet substantial questions about the disorder are unresolved (Gillig, 2009). One concerns the alternative personalities. Are they really separate psychological beings, each with its own, independent mental life? Or are they just ways of talking about normal variations in emotion and behavior (Merckelbach, Devilly, & Rassin, 2002)? Everyone is in a good mood sometimes and a bad mood other times. Everyone is fun-loving and outgoing in some settings, and quiet and shy in others. These variations do not indicate that everyone has multiple personalities, but merely that people's experiences and behaviors naturally vary from one situation to another. It can be difficult, then, to discern whether people with dissociative identity disorder truly have multiple personalities or simply observe variations in their own behavior, try to understand themselves, and, in so doing, create stories in which they describe themselves in terms of different characters.

A second question is the cause of dissociative identity disorder. Many clinicians have suggested that its causes lie in childhood (Gillig, 2009). Children who experience mistreatment, including sexual abuse, may cope with the trauma by convincing themselves that it happened "to somebody else"—an alternative personality. This was the explanation given in the famous case of Sybil (Schreiber, 1973), a woman whose multiple personalities reportedly were caused by physical abuse suffered at the hands of her mother (but see This Just In). Others, while recognizing the reality of the disorder, question whether evidence truly supports trauma-based explanations. They suggest, instead, that the disorder may develop through social processes in which people adopt different social roles that call for different types of behavior and gradually come to think of these roles as "selves" or "personalities" (Lilienfeld et al., 1999).

◐ THIS JUST IN

Sybil

Dissociative disorder burst into the public awareness in the 1970s, thanks to psychology's most famous case study of the past half-century. The case of Sybil (a pseudonym, to protect her identity) was bizarre and gripping. Sybil displayed multiple personalities—16 of them! There emerged from her mind a toddler, a grandmother, a couple of promiscuous girls, a couple of boys, and more, each with distinctive names, voices, and characteristics.

Sybil's therapist, a well-known psychoanalyst named Connie Wilbur, worked with Sybil to uncover the origins of her multiple personalities. Together, they searched Sybil's mind for buried memories of childhood trauma—and found them. While in therapy with Dr. Wilbur, Sybil recalled horrific instances of child abuse perpetrated by her parents, while she was being raised in a small rural town in the Midwest.

Dr. Wilbur and Sybil made her case public. They collaborated with a professional writer, Flora Rheta Schreiber, on *Sybil: The True Story of a Woman Possessed by Sixteen Separate Personalities* (Schreiber, 1973), a book detailing the childhood horrors that presumably gave birth to Sybil's multiple personalities.

It sold like hotcakes. Although many professional books on mental health sell only a few thousand copies, Schreiber's sold 6 million! *Sybil* the book was then turned into *Sybil* the TV miniseries, which was seen by 40 million Americans.

The case of Sybil affected society, including the mental health professions. *Sybil* made therapists and patients more aware of dissociative disorder. As a result, far more cases of the disorder were diagnosed after its publication than before. The case contributed to the inclusion of the disorder in the DSM. Wilbur and Schreiber appeared to have done a great service to mental health by uncovering facts about multiple personality . . . until the following news came in.

Much of the content of Wilbur's and Schreiber's report was a hoax. That was the conclusion reached by author Debbie Nathan, whose painstaking journalistic research has punched huge holes in the Sybil story. When she traveled to Sybil's hometown and spoke with people who had known her family well, none reported any sign of child abuse. When she read correspondence between Sybil and Dr. Wilbur, she found a confession; Sybil had informed her analyst that she was "none of the things I pretended to be. . . . I do not have any multiple personalities. . . . I have been essentially lying. . . . I was trying to show you I felt I needed help." Sybil had become emotionally dependent on her doctor, made up stories she thought her doctor wanted to hear, and explained to Wilbur that she had been afraid that if she told the truth, "you would be angry . . . [and] would not let me come to talk with you anymore" (Nathan, 2011, p. 106).

Sybil Sally Field (with glasses) played Sybil in a 1976 TV movie based on the book *Sybil: The True Story of a Woman Possessed by Sixteen Separate Personalities*. Joanne Woodward, who starred in *The Three Faces of Eve*, played her therapist.

NBC / Photofest

Incredibly, despite the confession, Wilbur remained certain that her original diagnosis of Sybil was correct! She stuck to her diagnosis of multiple personality disorder and worked to convince Schreiber that Sybil's symptoms were real and that their causes were childhood abuse. Nathan's journalistic detective work suggests that this book involved blatant deception, including the creation of a fake diary that told of Sybil's mental distress in the years before she knew Wilbur.

Sybil truly was mentally distressed. But the bizarre details—the 16 personalities, the stories of childhood abuse—apparently were fictions. Ultimately, what the famed case primarily illustrates is how patients may try to please their therapists, how therapists may be overconfident in their diagnoses, and how everybody is prone to bending the truth when trying to sell a lot of books.

✅ WHAT DO YOU KNOW?...

13. What motivated Sybil to lie to her therapist about her childhood trauma and to create 16 different alters?

There is no single, standard therapy strategy for treating dissociative identity disorder. Some therapists employ cognitive therapy designed to teach clients ways of coping with stress that are more adaptive than switching personalities (Gillig, 2009). Others use hypnosis (see Chapter 9) in an effort to help clients remain calm while focusing their attention on traumatic memories or feelings that may underlie their disorder (Kluft, 2012).

DEPERSONALIZATION/DEREALIZATION DISORDER. A second dissociative disorder is *depersonalization/derealization disorder,* which is defined by a change in people's conscious experiences. In **depersonalization/derealization disorder,** people do not feel fully involved in their own experiences. They go through their day with strange detachment, as if they are merely observing the day's events rather than taking part in them (Sierra, 2009). According to DSM-5 criteria, a person is classified as having depersonalization/derealization disorder (previously known as depersonalization disorder) based on the persistent presence of either (or both) of these two key symptoms:

> *Depersonalization:* Feeling as if one is merely observing, in a detached manner, one's ongoing thoughts and actions

depersonalization/derealization disorder A psychological disorder in which people feel detachment from their own experiences; key symptoms are depersonalization (a sense of merely observing with detachment) and derealization (feeling as if objects and others are unreal or foggy).

> *Derealization:* Feeling as if objects and other people are unreal; the world appears dreamlike or "foggy"

Adam Duritz, lead singer of the band *Counting Crows,* describes—from personal experience with depersonalization/derealization disorder—what it's like to have this particular dissociative disorder. It "makes the world seem like it's not real, as if things aren't taking place. It's hard to explain, but you feel untethered. . . . Because nothing seems real, it's hard to connect with the world or the people in it because they're not there. You're not there . . . you feel like you don't exist" (Duritz, 2008).

Not all cases of depersonalization are alike; there is a range of severity (Sierra, 2009). For some people, feelings of detachment occur only rarely and do not substantially disrupt their lives. For others, depersonalization/derealization experiences are nearly continual, and personal well-being is severely impaired.

DISSOCIATIVE AMNESIA AND FUGUE. The third dissociative disorder we'll review disrupts memory. In **dissociative amnesia,** people are unable to remember significant personal information—facts and experiences that normally would be highly memorable. Some people with dissociative amnesia forget specific personal experiences that were highly stressful or traumatic. Others' memory loss is more widespread; they may forget major aspects of their own life history.

On rare occasions, individuals with dissociative amnesia experience **dissociative fugue,** which is a complete loss of memory for one's own personal identity. Fugue states, when they occur, commonly prompt unexpected travel (the word *fugue,* in Italian, means "escape" or "take flight"). People move to a new location and may establish a new identity. When they recover memory of their original, true identity, they may have no memory of the fugue period. Cases of dissociative fugue are rare but have been documented, including among well-known people.

Case study evidence shows what it's like to experience dissociative amnesia and fugue. Consider these two cases:

> A 27-year-old businessman reported that, one morning, "When I woke up, I wondered what room I was in and where I was. I found my ID card in my wallet, which showed that I was a company businessman, but I was not otherwise aware of that fact" (Kikuchi et al., 2010, p. 603).

> "When a colleague was talking to [a 52-year-old man] on the telephone, they both became aware of his retrograde amnesia. He could recall nothing about the company, his job, and events over the last few decades. He said afterward that he had thought, 'Who am I talking to? What is that company?'" (Kikuchi et al., 2010, p. 605).

These two cases are particularly interesting in that they were reported by neuroscientists who used brain-imaging techniques to identify the biological bases of the men's psychological problems. The men were found to have lower than normal activity in the hippocampus, a brain region known to be involved in the formation of new memories (Kikuchi et al., 2010).

Adam Duritz, lead singer of the band *Counting Crows,* suffers from depersonalization/derealization disorder.

dissociative amnesia A psychological disorder in which people are unable to remember significant personal information that typically would be highly memorable.

dissociative fugue A psychological disorder featuring complete loss of memory of one's own personal identity.

💢 WHAT DO YOU KNOW?...

14. Match the disorder on the left with three facts about it on the right:

    1. Dissociative identity disorder

    2. Depersonalization/ derealization disorder

    a. May involve the feeling that things are dreamlike or unreal.

    b. May have its origin in childhood trauma or could simply be an extreme manifestation of the different social roles a person adopts.

3. Dissociative amnesia

c. In rare cases, individuals experience fugue states that prompt unexpected travel

d. Characterized by a feeling of detachment from one's own experiences

e. Characterized by loss of memory for significant personal information

f. Was once known as multiple personality disorder

g. People question whether individuals with this disorder truly experience separate personalities

h. Characterized by the feeling that objects and other people are not real

i. Associated with decreased functioning of the hippocampus

Popperfoto / Getty Images

Agatha Christie, author of *Murder on the Orient Express* and other mystery novels, became the world's best-selling fiction writer. She also provided the world with a nonfiction mystery: One winter's night she disappeared without telling anyone—including her 7-year-old daughter—of her plans or whereabouts. Days later, people took notice of an outgoing, intellectual woman calling herself "Mrs. Theresa Neale" who had checked into a hotel about 250 miles from Christie's home. Mrs. Neale turned out to be Christie. Some suggest that the author suffered from a dissociative fugue in which she forgot her own identity, took up a new one, and began traveling. She later regained her identity and said she'd experienced a "nervous breakdown" (Elliot, 2009).

◎ CULTURAL OPPORTUNITIES

Latah

Boo!

If you sneak up on people and yell, "Boo," they will startle. The response is usually brief: a sudden wide-eyed facial expression, a quick bodily reaction, and a temporary increase in breathing and heart rate. Then psychological life returns to normal.

In the Southeast Asian nation of Malaysia, however, some people display a response to startle, called *latah* (Simons, 1996), that might strike you as *ab*normal. A nineteenth-century British traveler named O'Brien was the first Westerner to describe it.

O'Brien observed that startling stimuli—a loud noise, a snake in the woods—initially produced the same reactions in Malaysians as in people from the West: surprise, jumping back, and often an "involuntary exclamation . . . characterized by . . . obscenity." But some Malaysians would then enter a trance state in which they lost voluntary control of their behavior. Their actions appeared to be controlled by other people and environmental events rather than by themselves. "Without encouragement," O'Brien wrote, people would "involuntarily imitate the words, sounds or gestures of those around them . . . [they would] completely abandon themselves to my will and powers of direction" (in Tanner & Chamberland, 2001, p. 528). Latah is this "mindless" imitation of others and obedience to their commands.

Evidence suggests that, here in the twenty-first century, latah still exists. Researchers (Tanner & Chamberland, 2001) interviewed 15 Malaysian women known, in their communities, to experience latah. They found that, when startled, the women repeated sounds, imitated gestures, and obeyed commands in a manner that appeared largely out of their control.

Latah can be understood, in part, in terms of biology. Throughout the world, some people experience larger startle reactions than others due to differences in the brain systems that produce the startle response (Dreissen et al., 2012). Within Malaysia, it's likely such people are the individuals prone to experiencing latah. But culture is also critical. Latah is a culturally linked psychological syndrome; in other words, people only experience it if they grow up in cultures where it is an established and socially accepted pattern of response (Tseng, 2006).

What do you think of latah? It resembles dissociative disorders, in that conscious experience is altered and people's normal personal identity escapes them. But is this a mental disorder?

This is the sort of question mental health professionals face when working with people from a culture unfamiliar to them. If people's behavior seems strange, is it safe to conclude that they have a psychological disorder? In general, no. The behavior might be a normal reaction within the culture in which it originated. As one psychiatrist explained, "From a diagnostic point of view, it is necessary to be careful in labeling 'peculiar behavior' as a 'disorder' simply because it is unfamiliar. A good example is provided by . . . latah. (Many) behavioral scientists favor the view that latah is a social behavior and not a 'disorder' . . . even though some psychiatrists have considered it a psychopathological condition" (Tseng, 2006, p. 559).

✦ WHAT DO YOU KNOW?...

15. In Malaysia, many individuals experience latah, a trance state following a _____ response during which they imitate and obey those around them. Latah resembles _____ disorders, but prior to concluding that it is a disorder, we should consider the context or _____ in which it occurs.

Dissociative Disorders and the Law

Preview Question

› Are people with dissociative identity disorder responsible for crimes committed by their alternative personalities?

Dissociative identity disorder raises not only psychological questions, but also moral and legal concerns.

Sometimes we condemn behavior as immoral. We do this when the behavior violates a moral rule. What about behavior that violates a rule, but is performed by an *alter*—an alternative personality that seizes control of the actions of someone suffering from dissociative identity disorder? One sufferer writes, "One of my alters (a 17-year-old sexual deviant) went and had sex with someone a few times over multiple years. . . . Logically I understand that my body went and had sex with someone that was not my husband. . . . Logically he understands that the person that had the affair was not his wife. . . . But emotionally we're a bit of a mess" (http://www.psychforums.com/dissociative-identity/topic24140.html).

A similar question arises in legal settings (Farrell, 2011). Suppose a crime is committed, but the criminal, a person with dissociative identity disorder, reports the following: "I would never do that. I don't even remember any of the criminal behavior. The crime wasn't done by me. It was done by my alter." Does this individual, who suffers from a severe mental illness, have the same legal responsibility as someone without a mental illness who planned and intentionally committed a crime?

Legal scholars have addressed this issue. Elyn Saks (featured in this chapter's opening vignette) explains that a standard legal principle is the following: People are found innocent of acts if they "did not have the capacity . . . *not* to act" (Saks, 1991, p. 431; emphasis added). In other words, people with no control over their behavior cannot be found guilty. Imagine someone who is sleepwalking. If the person sleepwalks into a store and walks out without paying, she can't be found guilty of shoplifting. Because she was asleep, she had no control over her behavior—she was not able "not to act." Lawyers defending a person with dissociative identity disorder may argue, similarly, that their client had no control over the actions of an alter.

The psychologist John Kihlstrom (2005) notes a different legal circumstance. Suppose a person insists on his innocence in a criminal case, but one day an alter confesses to the crime. Should the legal system convict the person based on the confession of his alter?

People charged with crimes have the legal option of pleading *not guilty by reason of insanity*. In the insanity defense, people admit to committing the crime—to being the physical agent who caused the crime to occur—but claim that, due to mental illness, their physical behavior was out of their control. For example, people might claim that

Hillside Strangler Kenneth Bianchi was one of two men charged in the Hillside Strangler case, involving a series of kidnappings and murders in Southern California in the late 1970s. His defense? Multiple personality disorder. Bianchi claimed that the crimes had not been committed by him, but by an alter—one of his alternative personalities. The legal strategy failed; Bianchi received a sentence of life imprisonment.

© Bettmann / Corbis

they suffer from dissociative identity disorder and that, at the time of the crime, their behavior was controlled not by themselves, but by an alter.

How successful is this defense? Not very. The claim of insanity due to dissociative disorder rarely has produced not-guilty verdicts (Farrell, 2011). Sometimes courts are not convinced that the defendant really is mentally ill. Other times they accept the claim of mental illness, but judge that it is not an excuse; for instance, a court may decide that whatever the defendant's personality at the time of a crime, that personality had the responsibility to tell right from wrong. Either way, the insanity defense fails (Fouche & Klesty, 2011).

♥ WHAT DO YOU KNOW?...

16. The following statement is incorrect. Explain why: "The insanity defense works in the case of dissociative disorder because most courts are easily convinced the defendant is mentally ill and because they typically agree that this type of mental illness is a reasonable excuse."

Conversion Disorder

Preview Question

> What could cause an individual to experience paralysis in the absence of a medical condition?

The last psychological disorder we will review, *conversion disorder*, is among the first to be studied systematically. Freud saw patients with the disorder in the late nineteenth century and based much of his psychoanalytic theory of personality on ideas about how conversion disorder develops and how it can be cured.

PHYSICAL SYMPTOMS AND EMOTIONAL DISTRESS.
Conversion disorder is a psychological disorder in which people experience physical symptoms that cannot be explained by any medical condition. A person might report paralysis of a hand or arm, or difficulty seeing or hearing, without there being any detectable biological cause. Most editions of the DSM, including DSM-5, have suggested that the physical symptoms may have an emotional basis, with psychological stress or trauma triggering the disorder. Treatment of the disorder is particularly difficult because patients commonly believe they are afflicted by a malady that is physical, not psychological, and thus may resist psychological therapy (Krull & Schifferdecker, 1990).

Freud explained such cases through his theory of the unconscious. The unconscious mind, according to the founder of psychoanalysis, holds repressed ideas that the physical symptoms symbolically represent. A repressed traumatic memory that involved the use of one's hand, for example, might cause a hand paralysis.

Today, most psychologists do not endorse Freud's explanation of the disorder. In fact, some question the entire existence of conversion disorder. They say patients might be faking their symptoms to get attention from others, or might be overly sensitive to minor physical symptoms with ordinary medical causes. Recent brain-imaging evidence, however, may quiet the skeptics.

CONVERSION DISORDER AND BRAIN RESEARCH. Researchers (Voon et al., 2010) studied patients with motor conversion disorder, in which the symptoms are motor movement disorders (e.g., muscular shaking) with no medical explanation. They compared

Jean Charcot, a nineteenth-century French physician, is shown demonstrating to colleagues a case of conversion disorder (called hysteria in Charcot's time): a female patient exhibiting a physical symptom, fainting, in the absence of any biomedical condition that could explain the symptom. Early in his career, Sigmund Freud studied under Charcot and was greatly influenced by his theories on the psychological causes of physical symptoms.

Erich Lessing / Art Resource, NY

conversion disorder A psychological disorder characterized by physical symptoms (e.g., partial paralysis, difficulty seeing or hearing) that cannot be explained by a medical condition.

them with a control group of psychologically healthy individuals lacking any sign of conversion disorder. The researchers took brain images while participants responded to a series of pictures displaying either fearful or happy human faces. Afterward, they conducted analyses to determine not only which brain regions were active during the task, but also how different regions of the brain interacted with each other during task performance.

The results provided remarkable brain-level insight into conversion disorder. Compared with psychologically healthy participants, in the brains of people with conversion disorder there was more communication between two regions of the brain: (1) the amygdala, which is involved in the detection of emotionally relevant stimuli (see Chapter 10), and (2) the motor cortex, which controls the planning and execution of muscular movements (Voon et al., 2010). These links between emotion and motor-movement centers of the brain may be a biological basis for the unusual physical symptoms experienced by emotionally distressed people with conversion disorder.

OTHER PSYCHOLOGICAL SOMATIC DISORDERS. In DSM-5, conversion disorder is part of a broader category of disorders in which psychological factors substantially affect the experience of one's body and potential physical illness. This broader category also includes somatic symptom disorder and illness anxiety disorder.

In *somatic symptom disorder,* people are excessively distressed about a physical symptom. Unlike conversion disorder, the cause of the physical symptom may be known; it may have a clear medical basis. The psychological problem is the person's degree of reaction to the symptom. For example, a heart attack victim who has a medical prognosis predicting full recovery, but who obsessively worries about having another heart attack and substantially restricts work and social activities to avoid one, would be exhibiting somatic symptom disorder.

In *illness anxiety disorder,* a person is excessively distressed about his or her physical well-being even in the complete absence of physical symptoms. The disorder is present when people are highly anxious about their health and frequently check themselves for signs of illness, despite being physically fit.

🐾 WHAT DO YOU KNOW?...

17. The following statement is incorrect. Explain why, briefly citing brain research: "All people diagnosed with conversion disorder are faking their symptoms."

18. In somatic symptom disorder and illness anxiety disorder, individuals are excessively stressed about physical symptoms; however, it is only in _____ _____ disorder that the individual has an actual physical symptom to worry about.

⟳ Looking Back and Looking Ahead

At first sight, the psychological disorders discussed in this chapter are profoundly puzzling. How could people think the TV is talking to them, speak in random jumbles of words, injure themselves, or callously harm others? But now that you have finished this chapter, the disorders should look different. You have seen that disorders, rather than being mysterious oddities, often result from breakdowns in simple, understandable psychological abilities that you normally take for granted—such as the ability to figure out what is real and what is not, to order information in memory in a logical manner, and to control emotional states and their influence on thinking and behavior.

Now that you have seen this, you can also see the connection between psychological disorders and the rest of psychology: the study of thinking, memory, emotion, and their biological underpinnings. Basic research in these other areas of psychology not only teaches lessons about the mind and brain. It can also provide understanding of—and, in the long run, benefit to—people who are experiencing psychological disorders.

Chapter Review

Now that you have completed this chapter, be sure to turn to Appendix B, where you will find a **Chapter Summary** that is useful for reviewing what you have learned about psychological disorders.

Key Terms

antipsychotic drugs (p. 719)

antisocial personality disorder (p. 724)

atypical antipsychotics (p. 719)

avoidant personality disorder (p. 725)

borderline personality disorder (p. 725)

brief psychotic disorder (p. 721)

cognitive impairments (p. 706)

conversion disorder (p. 739)

delusional beliefs (p. 706)

delusional disorder (p. 721)

depersonalization/derealization disorder (p. 735)

dialectical behavior therapy (p. 732)

disorganized thinking (p. 706)

dissociative amnesia (p. 736)

dissociative disorders (p. 733)

dissociative fugue (p. 736)

dissociative identity disorder (p. 733)

dopamine hypothesis of schizophrenia (p. 712)

flat affect (p. 707)

genome-wide association studies (p. 717)

hallucinations (p. 706)

narcissistic personality disorder (p. 726)

negative symptoms (p. 706)

obsessive-compulsive personality disorder (OCPD) (p. 727)

personality disorders (p. 722)

positive symptoms (p. 705)

psychopathy (p. 724)

psychotic disorders (p. 705)

schizophrenia (p. 705)

schizotypal personality disorder (p. 727)

single-nucleotide polymorphisms (SNPs) (p. 717)

tardive dyskinesia (p. 719)

typical antipsychotics (p. 719)

ventricles (p. 713)

Questions for Discussion

1. You read that among people with schizophrenia, an excess of dopamine causes trivial stimuli to grab their attention and that their attempts to explain why these stimuli are so distracting lead to delusional beliefs. Can the same process explain the bizarreness of dreams among people who do *not* have schizophrenia? Some suggest (see Chapter 9) that dreams are the result of attempts by higher-level brain structures to interpret random neural signals from lower-level structures. How do the processes compare? Explain. [Analyze]

2. You learned that people with schizophrenia experience deficits in episodic memory, particularly for emotional experiences, and that these deficits make planning for the future difficult because people who suffer from this disorder cannot consult past experiences to decide what to do in the future. You also learned that people with schizophrenia experience deficits in social-cognitive skills, such as the ability to initiate conversation and to maintain eye contact. What are other examples of social-cognitive skills and how could deficits in these areas affect quality of life? [Comprehend, Apply]

3. Dissociative identity disorder is depicted in television dramas (e.g., *Law & Order*) and in movies (e.g., *Me, Myself & Irene*) at a rate that is disproportionate to its actual prevalence. Why do you think it is so popular in plot lines? [Analyze]

4. You learned that the insanity defense rarely results in not-guilty verdicts in the cases of people with dissociative identity disorder. One reason is that courts are rarely convinced that the individual is mentally ill. A similar level of disbelief existed about individuals with conversion disorder, but brain-level research indicates that they are not faking their symptoms. Design a brain-imaging study that would address the question of whether people with dissociative identity disorder are faking their symptoms. What groups of people will you compare? What brain differences will you examine? [Analyze]

5. People with personality disorders were described in the text as being inflexible in their approach to situations, with the result that they do not cope effectively with stress. In a stressful situation, what does it look like to be flexible? Provide an example of a situation in which inflexibility would lead to ineffective coping and, ultimately, stress. [Comprehend]

6. You learned that in cognitive therapy, the goal is to make clients aware of the beliefs that create chronic psychological distress and to then try to modify those cognitions through techniques such as questioning. How successful is this technique likely to be in treating people with antisocial personality disorder who are high in psychopathy? Explain. [Synthesize]

7. What could explain why dialectical behavior therapy is effective in treating borderline personality disorder in particular? [Analyze]

Chapter Review

8. Review the case of Sybil, described in This Just In. In spite of Sybil's confession that she did not have multiple personalities, her therapist, Connie Wilbur, continued to assert that she did suffer from dissociative identity disorder and that childhood abuse was the cause. What would have compelled Wilbur to come to this conclusion, despite all the evidence to the contrary? Was she just trying to market and sell her book or do additional explanations exist? [Analyze]

Self-Test

1. Michaela's description of why aliens are monitoring her thoughts makes sense if you suspend your disbelief in aliens. Which of the following statements is true of her schizophrenic symptoms?
   a. She has a negative symptom, delusional thinking, but does not suffer from disorganized thinking, a positive symptom.
   b. She has a positive symptom, delusional thinking, but does not suffer from disorganized thinking, a positive symptom.
   c. She has a negative symptom, delusional thinking, and suffers from disorganized thinking, a negative symptom.
   d. She has a positive symptom, delusional thinking, and suffers from disorganized thinking, a negative symptom.

2. What qualifies flat affect as a negative symptom of schizophrenia?
   a. It is an absence of a psychological experience (affect) that others devalue.
   b. It is an absence of a psychological experience (affect) that is valued by others.
   c. It is the presence of a psychological experience (affect) that others devalue.
   d. It is the presence of a psychological experience (affect) that is valued by others.

3. Ronnie, a person with schizophrenia, is playing a game of Monopoly with her family. In this game, players can invest in real estate. Earlier in the game, she made the risky decision to spend nearly all of her savings on hotels in a "neighborhood" she owned. Her investment nearly left her bankrupt. On her next turn, she had an opportunity to make another risky investment and she did, which completely bankrupted her. Which of the following is the best explanation for her behavior?
   a. People with schizophrenia tend to engage in very risky behavior, especially when it comes to money.
   b. People with schizophrenia have deficits in social cognition that make it difficult to infer others' intentions.
   c. People with schizophrenia have a difficult time visualizing the spatial location of objects.
   d. People with schizophrenia, when faced with bad outcomes, tend to be poor decision makers.

4. What is the relation between the enlarged brain ventricles of people with schizophrenia and their overall brain volume?
   a. The larger the ventricles, the more neurons, and the greater the overall brain volume.
   b. The larger the ventricles, the fewer the neurons, and the lower the overall brain volume.
   c. The smaller the ventricles, the more neurons, and the lower the overall brain volume.
   d. There is no relation between ventricle size and brain volume.

5. Which of the following statements is true of the role of genes and environment in the development of schizophrenia?
   a. Twin studies indicate that genes contribute to the development of schizophrenia, and genome-wide association studies have identified the particular genes.
   b. Twin studies indicate that the concordance rate for MZ twins is 100%, suggesting that genes are the only factor influencing the development of schizophrenia.
   c. Twin studies indicate that genes contribute to the development of schizophrenia, but because the concordance rate for MZ twins is only 48%, the environment must play a role.
   d. Twin studies indicate that the concordance rate for MZ twins is 0%, suggesting that genes play no role in influencing the development of schizophrenia.

6. Which of the following statements is true of the effects of antipsychotic drugs in the treatment of schizophrenia?
   a. The majority of patients discontinue taking the drugs because of side effects such as tardive dyskinesia.
   b. At least half the patients who take the drugs do not experience long-term alleviation of their symptoms.
   c. A small minority of patients discontinue taking the drugs because of side effects such as tardive dyskinesia.
   d. Both (a) and (b) are correct.

7. The text notes that the differences in severity between schizophrenia and other psychotic disorders, such as brief psychotic disorder, suggest that these disorders exist on a continuum. Keeping in mind what defines a psychotic disorder, which of the following symptoms would be at the lowest end of severity?
   a. A belief in ghosts
   b. Word salad
   c. Narcissism
   d. Anger

8. Toni is puzzled by the behavior of a new guy she has been dating, Marcus. She used to think of him as having a dynamic personality, but has started to become frustrated by his instability. In her words, "Some days, he thinks I'm the most wonderful person in the world, and other days, he thinks I'm a soul-crushing tyrant. Most days, he expresses panic that I will leave him. I can hardly keep up with his moods, and frankly, sometimes his self-esteem is so low, I'm afraid he's going to hurt himself." From what disorder does Marcus likely suffer?
   a. Narcissistic personality disorder
   b. Antisocial personality disorder
   c. Borderline personality disorder
   d. Schizoid personality disorder

9. One subgroup of individuals with antisocial personality disorder is particularly manipulative and deceitful. What trait do members of this subgroup possess?
   a. Psychopathy
   b. Schizotypy
   c. Narcissism
   d. Dyskinesia

10. Caspi and colleagues conducted a study to investigate the role of genes and the environment in shaping antisocial behavior. What did they find?
    a. There was a gene that caused antisocial behavior, even in the absence of childhood maltreatment.
    b. Childhood maltreatment alone was enough to cause someone to develop antisocial behavior.
    c. Variations in genes and in childhood maltreatment combined to predict antisocial behavior.
    d. Strangely, neither genes nor childhood maltreatment caused antisocial behavior to develop.

11. Which of the following psychological therapies is characterized by a technique in which the therapist teaches patients with borderline personality disorder how to avoid black-and-white thinking by acknowledging the validity of their thoughts, even when those thoughts are potentially harmful in the long term?
    a. Dialectic behavioral therapy
    b. Psychoanalysis
    c. Cognitive therapy
    d. Drug therapy

12. Some have argued that dissociative identity disorder has its origin in childhood trauma, such as sexual abuse. What is the rationale for this particular explanation?
    a. The child copes with the trauma by feeding a therapist stories to gain attention.
    b. The child copes with the trauma by inventing an alternative personality who suffered the abuse.
    c. The child copes with the trauma by distracting him- or herself with imaginary friends.
    d. The child copes with the trauma by imitating and obeying those around him or her.

13. Ajit woke up disoriented in a hotel he had no memory of checking into. When he called the front desk, he learned that he had booked the room a week ago under a name he didn't recognize. He had no memory of the events during the past week. Ajit is most likely experiencing which of the following disorders?
    a. Dissociative identity disorder
    b. Depersonalization/derealization disorder
    c. Delusional disorder
    d. Dissociative amnesia with fugue

14. By law, who is responsible for a crime committed by people with dissociative identity disorder?
    a. People diagnosed with the disorder because they have absolute control over their alters.
    b. People diagnosed with the disorder, if it is established they actually were in control of their behavior.
    c. People diagnosed with the disorder because the disorder is a hoax.
    d. People who treat those diagnosed with the disorder because therapists control their patients' thinking.

15. Some have suggested that conversion disorder may have its basis in emotional problems. Did the brain research described in the text support this proposition?
    a. Yes. Among people with conversion disorder, there was less communication between areas of the brain associated with emotion and movement.
    b. Yes. Among people with conversion disorder, there was higher than normal activity in the brain area associated with emotion.
    c. No. Among people with conversion disorder, there was actually heightened communication between areas of the brain associated with emotion and movement.
    d. No. The brains of people with conversion disorder looked no different than those of controls.

Answers

You can check your answers to the preceding Self-Test and the chapter's What Do You Know? questions in Appendix B.

Appendix A
Statistics
by Tracy L. Caldwell

What Does Statistics Have to Do with Psychology?

The answer to this question has to do with something you may recall from Chapter 2—namely, that psychology is a science. To make sense of human nature, psychologists do not rely on intuition; they go into the natural world to gather data and test hypotheses. But they do not make their observations haphazardly; rather, they *operationally define* their variables so that others can verify their findings. Let's start with an example to illustrate the need for the scientific approach, and then we'll spell out the role of statistics within this framework.

Imagine you are a developmental psychologist who wants to find out whether adolescent boys and girls differ in their self-esteem. You approach teens at a nearby high school and ask them, "So, how's your self-esteem?" and write down their answers. At the end of the day, you have two columns of data: one for boys and one for girls. Within these two columns, you might find responses like "great" and "okay" and "just fine, thank you." How far would you get in finding out whether there are differences in self-esteem between boys and girls?

Careful readers will have already picked up on the idea that you could have gathered much more useful information by assigning *numbers* to the variable of self-esteem. This would enable you to succinctly summarize the data by calculating averages for boys and girls. In doing so, you would be using *statistics* to describe self-esteem.

Statistics refers simultaneously to three things. First, statistics is a field of study; statisticians are mathematicians who focus on analyzing large sets of numbers to extract meaning from them. Second, a statistic is a number that describes some aspect of a larger set of numbers. For instance, the statistic that describes the average of a sample of numbers is the *mean,* whereas the statistic that tells us the middlemost score in a set of scores is the *median* (as in "median family income"). Third, statistics is a mathematical tool for helping scientists describe and make inferences about data. The purpose of this appendix is to introduce you to some of the statistical methods researchers use to describe data and draw inferences based on them. The first section will focus on **descriptive statistics,** or mathematical techniques geared toward helping scientists summarize their data. Then you will be introduced to **inferential statistics,** or mathematical techniques that enable scientists to make inferences about populations based on data collected from samples.

Descriptive Statistics: Summarizing Data

Have you ever had to describe a live music performance to a friend who missed the show? If so, you know that you had to answer questions about the band's performance, such as, "Did they play a long set? Did the singer talk to the crowd at all?" Perhaps you've also had to answer the question, "What were people in the crowd like?"

How would you answer this last question? "Well, they were . . . tall. They all faced the stage. They seemed to enjoy clapping." Of course, this is not the kind of information your friend is looking for. She is probably interested in knowing *who* the crowd was—that is,

descriptive statistics
Mathematical techniques geared toward summarizing data.

inferential statistics
Mathematical techniques that enable scientists to make inferences about populations based on data collected from samples.

did it include people you know? Did the audience just stand around or did they dance? Were they young or old? How should you go about answering *these* questions?

Let's imagine you decide to answer her question in terms of how old the crowd was. Without even realizing it, you may quickly try to compute some descriptive statistics. In other words, you might try to summarize what the crowd was like by using numbers to describe its characteristics. You come up with an average age—say, 30—but then qualify that estimate by indicating that people seemed as young as 21 and as old as 40. In your assessment, the *average* age tells your friend the typical age of the crowd and the *range* of ages around that mean helps her understand just *how* typical that age is.

In providing these statistics, you are relying on memory and intuition. But to answer this question scientifically, you need to be more precise. You need to adopt the systematic methods psychologists and other scientific researchers use to summarize the characteristics of groups of people. Some of these methods are described below.

Tabular Summaries: Frequency Distributions

Preview Question

> What tabular methods do researchers use to organize and summarize data?

Imagine that in anticipation of your friend's request for information, you had decided to systematically collect data about the age of all the people at the show by asking a sample of 30 individuals to state their age as they walked through the door (let's just assume they told the truth).

Here are your data: 28, 32, 30, 30, 32, 30, 30, 28, 35, 29, 29, 30, 32, 30, 31, 25, 29, 32, 29, 29, 27, 27, 31, 34, 28, 30, 31, 33, 31, and 26.

How can you make sense of these data so that you can easily describe them to your friend? The first thing you might do is organize them into a **frequency distribution table.** Instead of listing every single age, you might order them from lowest to highest in one column. Then in a column to the right of that, note how often that score occurs, as shown in Table A-1.

Presenting these data in a table should help summarize the crowd's age. You might begin by scanning the frequency column for the age that best describes the center of the distribution; here, the most frequently occurring age is 30. You might then proceed by determining just *how* descriptive the age 30 is of the rest of the crowd by comparing its frequency to the frequencies of the other ages. Notice that only two people were younger than 27 and that only three people were older than 32. Later, you'll read about some handy statistics you can use to depict the most typical score and for determining just *how* typical that score is. But first, let's look at some graphical methods for depicting a distribution of scores in a sample. Throughout the chapter, you will see the term **distribution** used to refer to a set of scores that can be described by the frequency of each score.

table **A-1**

Frequency Distribution Table	
Age	**Frequency**
25	1
26	1
27	2
28	3
29	5
30	7
31	4
32	4
33	1
34	1
35	1

frequency distribution table A table that lists all the scores in a distribution in numeric order, as well as the frequency of each score.

distribution A set of scores that can be described by the frequency of each score.

histogram A frequency distribution graph in which bars are used to represent the frequency of each score.

🤔 WHAT DO YOU KNOW?...

1. According to Table A-1, how many individuals in this crowd were 32 years old?

See Appendix B for answers to What Do You Know? questions.

Pictures of Data: Histograms and Polygons

Preview Question

> What graphical methods do researchers use to organize and summarize data?

Often the easiest way to depict how scores are distributed is to draw a frequency distribution graph. For instance, you might create what's called a **histogram,** a frequency

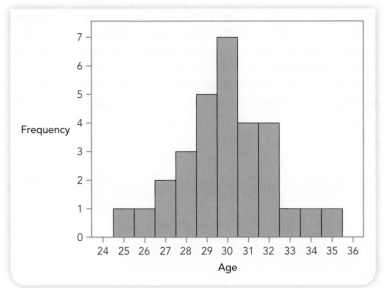

figure **A-1**
Histogram for age data A histogram is a frequency distribution graph in which each bar represents the frequency of scores at a given interval.

distribution graph in which each bar represents the frequency of scores at a particular interval. Figure A-1 is a histogram depicting our crowd age data.

Age is depicted on the horizontal or **x-axis,** and the frequency of each of these ages is depicted on the vertical or **y-axis.** You can find the frequency of any given age by locating the top of its bar on the y-axis. Try this yourself by determining how many individuals were 29. By describing the data with a histogram, you can immediately see how scores are distributed. Our histogram shows that most of the concert attendees were between the ages of 27 and 32; that the most frequently occurring age was 30; and that none of the concert attendees were younger than 25 or older than 35. You can also tell by "eyeballing" the data that, because the ages taper off as they get farther away from 30, 30 is a fairly typical or representative age. By the way, did you find that five people were 29?

Some researchers prefer **frequency polygons** to histograms. Frequency polygons provide the same information as histograms, but with dots and lines rather than with bars. As you can see in Figure A-2, frequency polygons provide the same information.

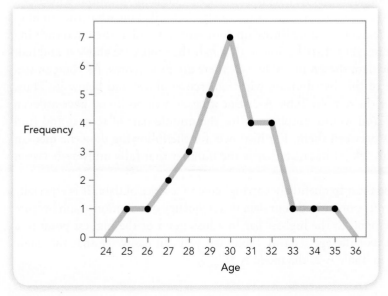

figure **A-2**
Frequency polygon for age data Frequency polygons provide the same information as histograms, but with dots and lines rather than bars.

x-axis In any graph, the horizontal axis.

y-axis In any graph, the vertical axis.

frequency polygon A frequency distribution graph that uses dots connected by lines to represent frequency.

One of the benefits of depicting data in a frequency distribution graph is that you can get a better sense of the shape of the distribution, which is information you will need to find the most representative score. Many psychological variables are distributed symmetrically in the population; if you cut a symmetrical distribution in half, half its scores are above the midpoint and half the scores are below, and you will see that the halves are mirror images. How symmetrical are the age data? Not perfectly symmetrical, but they are close.

⚘ WHAT DO YOU KNOW?...

2. According to the frequency histogram (Figure A-1) or polygon (Figure A-2), how many individuals in this crowd were older than 32?

Central Tendency: Mean, Median, and Mode

Preview Question

> What statistical measures do researchers use to find the most representative score of a distribution?

Creating tables and graphs to describe data is useful but time-consuming. Earlier, you read that you can describe distributions of ages by figuring out what the most "typical" or "representative" score is. In fact, there are three different ways to find the most representative score; you can find the *mean, median,* or *mode*. These are all **measures of central tendency:** statistics that describe the most representative score in a distribution.

The **mean** is the average score, which is calculated by adding up all the scores in the distribution and dividing the sum by the number of scores in the distribution. More succinctly, the formula is

$$\mu = \frac{\Sigma X}{N}$$

where

$$\mu = \text{mean}$$
$$X = \text{each of our scores}$$
$$\Sigma X = \text{"summation } X\text{"}$$

ΣX is shorthand for the "sum all the values of X." For example, for the data in Table A-2, $\Sigma X = 27$. The advantage of the mean is that it takes into account every score in a distribution and so is very representative as a measure of central tendency.

The **median** is a measure of central tendency that tells you what the middle-most score is. You "calculate" it by lining up your scores in order, then determining which score separates your distribution so that half the scores are above it and half are below it. In the data shown in Table A-2, there are nine scores. As you can see, 3 is in the middle of the distribution, with four scores above and below it. Thus, 3 is the median for the data in Table A-2. But what do you do if you have an even number of scores? You would simply look for the middle pair of scores, and find the value that falls between them. For instance, for the following data the median is 24: 1, 13, 22, 26, 29, 33 because that is the number that falls midway between 22 and 26.

The **mode** is the most frequently occurring score in a series of data. It is especially easy to spot when you've organized your data in a frequency distribution graph because it will always correspond to the highest bar in a histogram or the highest point in a frequency polygon. For the age data in Table A-1, you can easily see that the mode is 30. For the data in Table A-2, the mode is 3.

table **A-2**

Summation X
X
1
2
2
3
3
3
4
4
5
$\Sigma X = 27$
$N = 9$
$\mu = 3$

measures of central tendency
Statistics that describe the most representative score in a distribution, including mean, median, and mode.

mean The average score in a distribution.

median The middlemost score in a distribution.

mode The most frequently occurring score in a distribution.

3. Here are data describing the number of doctor visits this year for six people: 3, 2, 2, 1, 2, 2. Find the mean, median, and mode.

Shapes of Distributions: Normal, Skewed, and Symmetrical

Preview Question

› When is it appropriate to use the mean, median, or mode as a measure of central tendency?

So far, you have learned that (1) the goal of descriptive statistics is to summarize data and that (2) you can summarize data by creating tables or graphs. You have also seen that it is faster to describe data by using three measures of central tendency: the mean, median, and mode. But why do you need *three* measures of central tendency? To answer this question, you will need a little background.

Take another look at Table A-2. Note that the mean, median, and mode were exactly the same. Why? The answer has to do with the way the scores were distributed. Notice how symmetrically the nine scores are distributed in the frequency distribution graph for these data in Figure A-3. Each half of the distribution is a mirror image of the other. Notice also that the majority of the scores are clustered around the midpoint of the distribution and that they become less frequent as you move away from this point. When a distribution has these two qualities—that is, when symmetrical and **unimodal** (only having one mode)—it is said to be a **normal distribution.** In a normal distribution, the mean, mode, and median are equal; they are all equally good at telling us what the most representative score is.

It is not always the case that the mean, median, and mode are equally good indicators of the most representative score. Take a look at Figure A-4, which depicts two distributions of exam scores. Both distributions are **skewed:** They are asymmetrical; most students got either extremely high or extremely low scores. The scores in distribution (a) are **positively skewed,** which means that the majority of scores is low. The scores in distribution (b) are **negatively skewed,** which means that the majority of scores is high. A simple way to remember the distinction between positively and negatively skewed distributions is that in a negatively skewed distribution, the tail is

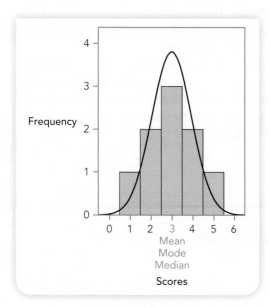

figure A-3

A normal distribution When a distribution is symmetrical and unimodal (has one mode), it is said to be a *normal distribution.* In a normal distribution, the mean, mode, and median are equal to each other.

unimodal Term describing a distribution having only one mode.

normal distribution A distribution that is symmetrical and unimodal; the mean, mode, and median are equal.

skewed distribution An asymmetrical distribution in which the mean is no longer in the middle because it is "pulled" by extreme scores.

positively skewed Description of a distribution in which the majority of scores is low, but there is one or more extreme high score in the "tail."

negatively skewed Description of a distribution in which the majority of scores is high, but there is one or more extreme low score in the "tail."

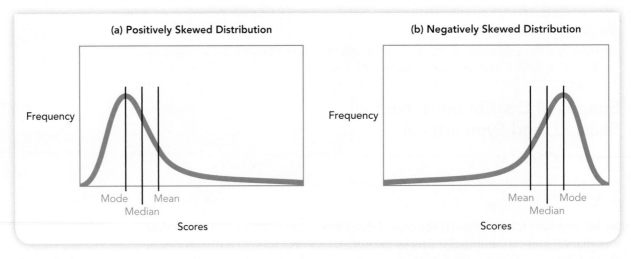

figure **A-4**
Measures of central tendency in skewed distributions These two distributions of scores are asymmetrical, or *skewed*. Distribution (a) is positively skewed; its tail extends toward the higher, more "positive" values of the distribution. Distribution (b) is negatively skewed; its tail extends toward the lower, more "negative" values of the distribution. In a skewed distribution, the mean is no longer a useful measure of central tendency because it is influenced by extreme scores. In a skewed distribution, the mode or median is the most appropriate measure of central tendency.

"pulled" by the "negative" or lower scores, and in a positively skewed distribution, the tail is "pulled" by the "positive" or higher scores.

In any skewed distribution, the three measures of central tendency are no longer equal to each other. Which one will do the best job representing a skewed distribution, then? In normal distributions, the mean is desirable because it takes into account *all* scores in the distribution. In a skewed distribution, however, it can be strongly affected by extreme scores. To illustrate, consider the following data, representing scores on a recent exam:

80, 80, 90, 90, 90, 100, 100

The mean of this dataset is equal to 90, a very representative score. What if we add an extreme score—say, a 30? The dataset is then

30, 80, 80, 90, 90, 90, 100, 100

The mean would now be 82.5, which is not very representative. Our mean was "pulled" by the extreme score.

If you were to rely on the mean to describe this distribution, you would be led to believe that the class did not perform nearly as well on this exam as they actually did, because the mean was influenced by one very extreme score.

In the case of skewed distributions, you should use the median. The median is not influenced by extreme scores; it simply tells us the midpoint of the distribution. You might also describe the distribution using the mode because it simply describes the most frequently occurring score. In this case, the median and mode are better descriptors of this distribution of scores than is the mean.

☾ WHAT DO YOU KNOW?•••

4. What are the median and mode of our skewed distribution of scores?

Variability: Range and Standard Deviation

Preview Question

> What statistical measures do researchers use to describe the variability of a distribution?

Now that you can answer the question of *which* score is most representative of a distribution, let's turn to a new question: *How representative is a given score?* Take a look at the two distributions in Figure A-5. For which distribution is the mean more representative? Intuitively, you know that the answer has to be Distribution A, because the scores are packed in closer to the mean than they are in Distribution B. Statisticians have a slightly more elaborate way of describing this state of affairs; they note that the scores in Distribution A have less *variability* than those in Distribution B. A distribution's **variability** describes how far the scores spread out above and below the mean. Two popular measures of variability are the range and standard deviation.

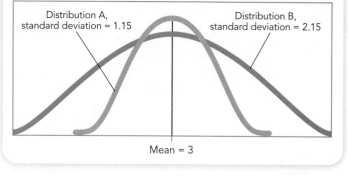

figure A-5
Variability and representativeness
The mean is more representative of Distribution A than it is of B because the scores in Distribution B are more spread out, or *variable*.

The **range** is the difference between the highest and lowest score in a distribution; you find it by subtracting the lowest score from the highest score. For example, the range for the age data in Table A-1 is $35 - 25 = 10$.

An advantage of the range is its simplicity; however, this simplicity comes at the cost of information—specifically, information about how much the individual scores differ from each other. To illustrate, take a look at the two sets of scores below. Both have a range of 9.

3 3 3 3 3 3 3 3 3 3 3 3 3 3 12

1 1 2 2 3 3 4 4 5 6 7 8 9 9 10

How comfortable are you with the idea that these two datasets are functionally the same in their variability? If you said "not very," it was probably because you recognized that in the first set most of the scores are 3s; that is, there's hardly any variability. However, in the second set, most of the scores differ from each other. Clearly, you need an index of variability that takes into account how different the scores are from one another. The *standard deviation* accomplishes this.

The standard deviation is a measure of variability that tells you how far, on average, any score is from the mean (see Chapter 2). The mean serves as an anchor because in a normal distribution, it is the most representative score. The standard deviation tells you just *how* representative the mean is by measuring how much, on average, you can expect *any* score to differ from it. Note that "standard" and "average" mean the same thing in this context. The advantage of the standard deviation over the range is that it gives a sense of just how accurately the mean represents the distribution of scores.

Examining the method for calculating it will help you understand why the standard deviation is an index of the representativeness of scores. Look at the data in column 1 of Table A-3. The sum of scores (ΣX) and the mean (μ) have already been calculated. Because you're interested in finding out how much, on average, the scores deviate from the mean (remember, that's what the standard deviation tells us!), the next step is to determine how much each score deviates from the mean. You find this distance or deviation by subtracting the mean from every score. The results are shown in column 2.

The summation sign in the next operation, $\Sigma(X - \mu)$, at the bottom of column 2, tells you to sum the deviations you just calculated. Before you find that sum, though, take a moment to look over the deviation scores. You can see that the smallest *absolute* distance between the scores and the mean is 0 and that the largest absolute distance is 2. At the outset, you know that the standard (average) deviation won't be greater than 2.

As you can see at the bottom of column 2, when we sum our deviation scores we find that $\Sigma(X - \mu) = 0$. This is because the distances above the mean, which is the center of our distribution, equal the distances below our mean in the distribution. Does this suggest that the standard deviation is 0 and that there is no variability

variability The degree to which the scores in a distribution spread out above and below the mean.

range A simple measure of the variability of a distribution; the difference between the highest and lowest scores.

table **A-3**

Calculating the Squared Deviations from the Mean		
X	**X − μ**	**(X − μ)²**
5	5 − 3 = 2	2² = 4
4	4 − 3 = 1	1² = 1
4	4 − 3 = 1	1² = 1
3	3 − 3 = 0	0² = 0
3	3 − 3 = 0	0² = 0
3	3 − 3 = 0	0² = 0
2	2 − 3 = −1	1² = 1
2	2 − 3 = −1	1² = 1
1	1 − 3 = −2	2² = 4
ΣX = 27	Σ(X − μ) = 0	Σ(X − μ)² = 12
N = 9	N = 9	N = 9
μ = 3	Σ(X − μ)/N = 0	Σ(X − μ)²/N = 1.33

around the mean? Of course not; you know this isn't true because the scores do, in fact, differ from each other. You can remedy this situation by squaring each of the deviation scores, as shown in Column 3. The scores are squared for a reason you may remember from high school math: The product of two negative numbers is always positive. This step brings us closer to finding the standard deviation. You'll see that the sum of these squared deviations is 12. Now divide these squared deviations by N, the number of scores, to get a value called the *variance:*

$$12/9 = 1.33$$

Because you got this value by squaring the deviations, you'll need to take the square root to get it back into its original units: $\sqrt{1.33} = 1.15$. The standard deviation (symbolized by the Greek lowercase sigma, σ) is 1.15, which means that, on average, the scores deviate from the mean by 1.15 points. Earlier in our computations, you predicted that the average deviation would fall somewhere between 0 and 2. This is correct! For the record, the formula for the standard deviation is

$$\sigma = \sqrt{\frac{\sum(X - \mu)}{N}}$$

So, what does it mean to have a standard deviation of 1.15? Earlier you read that the standard deviation is a measure of how accurately the mean represents a given distribution. To illustrate this idea, take a look back at Figure A-5, which depicts two distributions, both with a mean of 3. Compare the shape of Distribution A, which has a standard deviation of 1.15, with that of B, whose standard deviation is 2.15. For which of these distributions is the mean the more representative score? You know the answer is A because the scores are more closely situated around the mean. The smaller the standard deviation, the more accurately the mean represents the distribution.

An interesting characteristic of normal distributions is that almost all scores tend to fall within 3 standard deviations of the mean. Thus, if the mean of a distribution was 5 and its standard deviation was 1, you could figure out that most (about 99%) of its scores will fall between 2 and 8, as long as the distribution is normal. In fact, the **empirical rule** tells you approximately how the scores will be distributed as you get

empirical rule A rule stating that in a normal distribution, roughly 68% of scores will fall within 1 standard deviation of the mean; 95% will fall within 2 standard deviations; and 99% will fall within 3 standard deviations.

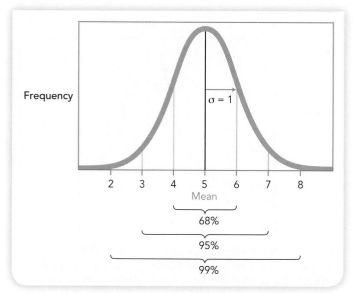

figure **A-6**

Empirical rule According to the empirical rule, roughly 68% of scores in a normal distribution tend to fall within 1 standard deviation of the mean; roughly 95% tend to fall within 2 standard deviations of the mean; and roughly 99% tend to fall within 3 standard deviations of the mean. In a normal distribution in which the mean is 5 and the standard deviation is 1, 68% of scores will fall between 4 and 6; 95% of scores will fall between 3 and 7; and 99% of scores will fall between 2 and 8.

farther away from the mean. As Figure A-6 illustrates, the empirical rule states that roughly 68% of scores in a normal distribution will fall within 1 standard deviation of the mean; 95% will fall within 2 standard deviations; and 99% will fall within 3 standard deviations. This characteristic of normal distributions makes the standard deviation even more useful because it enables you to estimate how scores will be distributed around the mean.

WHAT DO YOU KNOW?...

5. Without doing any calculations, figure out the standard deviation for this distribution: 1, 1, 1, 1, 1.

6. A distribution of scores has a mean of 5. Its highest score is 7 and its lowest score is 3. Why can't the standard deviation be greater than 2?

7. A distribution of scores is normal and has a mean of 5 and a standard deviation of 1. According to the empirical rule, what proportion of scores will fall between 4 and 6, 3 and 7, and 2 and 8?

Using the Mean and Standard Deviation to Make Comparisons: z-scores

Preview Question

› How do statistics enable researchers to compare scores from different distributions?

As far as measures of variability go, the standard deviation is useful because it tells you how far scores are from the mean, on average, and thus provides an index of how representative the mean is. Why should you care about the variability of distributions? A little context might help. Imagine you're a student who took a test worth 100 points and you would like to know how well you did relative to your peers. Will the mean alone be informative? Sure: If the mean were 75 and you got an 85, you would be 10 points above the mean, which is certainly a nice place to be. The standard deviation additionally tells you just *how* far above the mean you are. To illustrate, take a look at Figure A-7, which depicts two distributions of scores, both of which have a mean of 75.

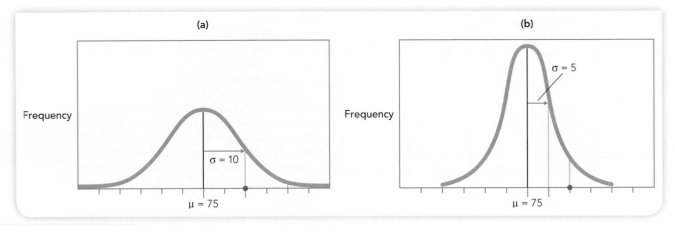

figure **A-7**
The standard deviation and distance from the mean Here are two distributions of exam scores, each with the same mean of 75, but one with a standard deviation of 10 (a) and one with a standard deviation of 5 (b). If you had gotten an 85 on an exam (red dot on graphs) in which the mean was 75, you would probably prefer that the standard deviation were 5 (b) rather than 10 (a), because then you would have outperformed more of your classmates. You would be 2 standard deviations above the mean rather than 1.

In distribution (a), the standard deviation is 10, while in distribution (b), the standard deviation is 5. Take a look at where your score of 85 is relative to the mean in both distributions. For which distribution should you be happier with your performance? You should be happier with your performance in distribution (b), because your score would be farther above the mean, signifying that you had outperformed almost all your classmates because your score is 2 standard deviations above the mean.

Simply put, the mean acts as an anchor against which you can compare scores and the standard deviation tells you how far the scores are from that anchor. Here are some more examples. If you got an 80 on an exam for which the mean was 70 and the standard deviation was 10, how far would you be from the mean? One standard deviation. If you got a 90, how far would you be from the mean? Two standard deviations. If you got an 84.30, how far would you be from the mean? Maybe it's time to introduce a formula that will enable you to very quickly calculate how far, in standard deviation units, a given score is from the mean. The formula below enables you to calculate what's called a **z-score,** a statistic that tells you how far a given score is from the mean, in standard units. Saying that your exam score is 2 standard deviations from the mean is synonymous with saying that you have a z-score of 2 on the exam.

$$z = \frac{X - \mu}{\sigma} = \frac{90 - 70}{10} = 2.00$$

The beauty of the z-score is that it provides two valuable pieces of information: (1) how far a given score is from the mean in standard units, and (2) whether that score is above or below the mean. A positive z-score indicates that a score is above the mean, whereas a negative z-score indicates that a score is below the mean. For example, if instead of getting a 90 on the above exam, you had received a 60, your z-score of −1.00 would very quickly tell you that you are 1 standard deviation below the mean.

Perhaps an even greater beauty of z-scores is that they enable you to compare scores from two different distributions—figuratively speaking, they enable you to "compare apples to oranges." For instance, imagine you were bragging to your French cousin that you bought a pair of Nikes for a price that was considerably lower than the average. Imagine further that your cousin had coincidentally bought the same pair, also considerably below the average, and believed that he had gotten the better deal. Calculating your and his z-scores will enable you to determine who is right. If you had

z-score A statistic that tells you how far a given score is from the mean of a distribution, in standard units.

paid $85 in a market in which the average price is $110 and the standard deviation was $10, then your z-score would be

$$z = \frac{X - \mu}{\sigma} = \frac{85 - 110}{10} = -2.50$$

If he had paid 64 euros in a market in which the average price is 78 euros and the standard deviation was 7 euros, his z-score would be

$$z = \frac{X - \mu}{\sigma} = \frac{64 - 78}{7} = -2.00$$

Given that your price is 2.50 standard deviations below the mean, whereas your cousin's is only 2 standard deviations below, we can conclude that you, in fact, got the better deal.

✔ WHAT DO YOU KNOW?...

8. You like to tease your aunt, who is older than you, about how much faster than her you ran a recent 5K race. You ran it at a rate of 9 minutes per mile, whereas she ran it in 10 minutes per mile. In your age group, the mean rate was a 10-minute mile with a standard deviation of 1; in her age group, the mean rate was an 11-minute mile with a standard deviation of 1.
   a. What are your respective z-scores?
   b. Given these z-scores, are you justified in teasing her?

Correlations

Preview Question

> How do researchers determine whether variables are correlated?

Sometimes researchers are interested in the extent to which two variables are related; in other words, they are interested in whether a *correlation* exists between them. Variables are said to be correlated if a change in the value of one of them is accompanied by a change in the value of another. For instance, as children age, there is a corresponding increase in their height. As people eat more junk food, there is typically a corresponding increase in weight (and decrease in energy and other health-related variables). How can you determine whether there is a correlation between two variables? Take a look at Table A-4a, which lists people's scores on two variables: number of hours spent studying per week and GPA.

It is difficult to get a sense of the relation between the two variables based on a quick glance at the data alone, so you might construct a *scatterplot:* a graph that plots the values for two variables (see Figure A-8).

The number of hours spent studying is depicted on the *x*-axis of the scatterplot, and individuals' GPAs are depicted on the *y*-axis. The scatterplot enables us to see the point at which each of these scores intersect. For instance, you can see that Candace, who spent 8 hours per week studying, has a GPA of 3.8, whereas her classmate Denise, who spent only 2 hours per week studying, has a GPA of 2.0.

So what does this scatterplot tell you about the relation between these variables? Take a look at the pattern of the data: It doesn't seem random, does it? It seems to cluster around a line. In fact, when two variables are correlated, they are said to have a *linear relationship*— as the value of one changes, the other does, too, at approximately the same rate.

Researchers distinguish between correlations that are positive and negative. When there is a *positive correlation* between two variables, an increase in one of the variables corresponds to an increase in the other—that is, as one goes up, so does the other. According to the GPA data, hours spent studying and GPA are positively correlated. Other variables that are likely to be positively correlated include hours spent chewing gum and amount of jaw pain, the amount of caffeine consumed and jitteriness, and outside temperature and ice cream sales.

table **A-4a**

	Calculating the Sum of the Cross-Products	
Person	**Hours Studied (X)**	**GPA (Y)**
Candace	8	3.8
Denise	2	2
Joaquin	2	2.3
Jon	7	3.4
Milford	5	2.4
Rachel	5	2.5
Shawna	1	1.7
Leroi	9	3.7
Jeanine	6	3.2
Marisol	10	4
Lee	2	1.5
Rashid	9	3.9
Sunny	3	2.6
Flora	6	3
Kris	4	2.9
Denis	11	3.9

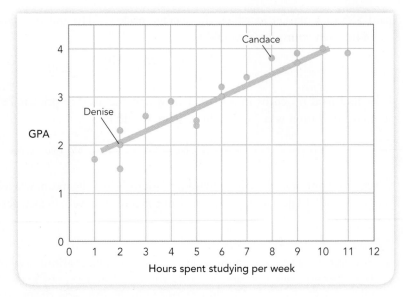

figure **A-8**
Scatterplot This graph plots the intersection of each individual's scores for two variables. The fact that these scores do not deviate much from a straight line suggests that there is a linear relationship between these two variables. That is, as a score on one variable changes by 1 unit, so does the score for the other variable.

When there is a *negative correlation* between two variables, an increase in one of the variables corresponds to a decrease in the other—as one goes up, the other goes down. For instance, as the number of textbooks you buy for class increases, there is a corresponding decrease in your money. Other variables that are likely to be negatively correlated include self-esteem and depression, test anxiety and exam scores, and calories consumed and weight loss. Figure A-9 includes scatterplots depicting positive and negative correlations.

In a correlation between two variables, one variable can be designated the *predictor variable* and the other as the *criterion variable.* The **predictor variable** is used to predict the value of the **criterion variable.** In the caffeine and jitteriness example, caffeine was the predictor variable and jitteriness was the criterion variable.

Instead of continuously constructing scatterplots to detect relationships between variables, researchers calculate a *correlation coefficient:* a figure that indicates the strength and direction of the relationship between variables. The formula for the correlation coefficient (also known as *r*) is as follows:

$$r = \frac{\sum z_x z_y}{N}$$

where

$$z_x = z\text{-scores of our predictor variable}$$
$$\text{and}$$
$$z_y = z\text{-scores of our criterion variable}$$

Take a moment to reflect on why it would be necessary to convert raw scores into *z*-scores to calculate the correlation between any two variables. Here's a hint: In the preceding example, you were interested in the relation between hours spent studying and GPA—in other words, you were interested in the relation between time and academic achievement. Are these variables measured on the same scale? They are not, and to compare scores from two different distributions, you must standardize them by converting them into *z*-scores. In Table A-4b, this was done for the predictor, number of hours each person studied (*X*), in the column headed by z_x, and for the criterion, GPA (*Y*), in the column headed by z_y.

predictor variable In a correlation between two variables, the variable that is used to predict the value of the other (criterion) variable.

criterion variable In a correlation between two variables, the variable whose value is predicted by the other (predictor) variable.

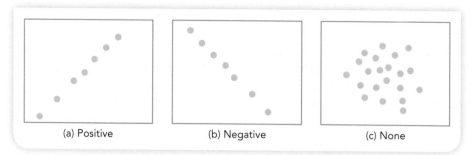

figure **A-9**
Correlations (a) In a perfect positive correlation, the data form a line that originates at the lower left corner and reaches to the upper right corner. (b) In a perfect negative correlation, the data form a line that originates at the upper left corner and reaches to the lower right corner. (c) When variables are unrelated, hardly any pattern is discernible in the data.

Once you've standardized your scores, you need to find the *cross-product* of each person's scores—that is, you need to multiply each person's z_x score by her z_y score, as was done in the last column of Table A-4b. You then sum these cross-products, as directed by the numerator of the correlation coefficient formula. The sum of the cross-products for our example is 14.16. We divide this value by N to find the average cross-product. The correlation coefficient is the average cross-product of the two variables you're studying. In this example, $r = .89$. But what does this mean?

table **A-4b**

Calculating the Sum of the Cross-Products					
Person	Hours Studied (X)	GPA (Y)	z_x	z_y	$z_x z_y$
Candace	8	3.8	0.75	1.07	0.80
Denise	2	2	−1.15	−1.13	1.30
Joaquin	2	2.3	−1.15	−0.76	0.88
Jon	7	3.4	0.44	0.58	0.25
Milford	5	2.4	−0.20	−0.64	0.13
Rachel	5	2.5	−0.20	−0.52	0.10
Shawna	1	1.7	−1.46	−1.50	2.19
Leroi	9	3.7	1.07	0.95	1.01
Jeanine	6	3.2	0.12	0.34	0.04
Marisol	10	4	1.38	1.31	1.82
Lee	2	1.5	−1.15	−1.74	2.00
Rashid	9	3.9	1.07	1.19	1.27
Sunny	3	2.6	−0.83	−0.40	0.33
Flora	6	3	0.12	0.09	0.01
Kris	4	2.9	−0.51	−0.03	0.02
Denis	11	3.9	1.70	1.19	2.02
				$\Sigma z_x z_y =$	14.16

It would help to know how to interpret a correlation coefficient. A correlation coefficient has two parts: sign and magnitude. Sign, sometimes known as direction, indicates whether the correlation is positive or negative (above, we talked about the difference between a positive relation [time studying and GPA] and a negative relation [number of textbooks bought and amount of money]). Magnitude is an indication of the strength of the relationship; it can range from 0 to 1.00. A correlation coefficient of 1.00 would indicate that two variables are perfectly positively correlated; you would expect, for instance, that the temperature at which a pot roast is cooked is nearly perfectly correlated with the time it takes to reach a safe eating temperature.

The scatterplot in Figure A-9a depicts what the data would look like in this case: a perfect diagonal line originating at the lower left corner and reaching to the upper right corner. Likewise, a correlation coefficient of −1.0 would indicate that two variables are perfectly negatively correlated; you would expect, for instance, that the number of days one spends in solitary confinement is nearly perfectly correlated with how many conversations one has with another person. The scatterplot in Figure A-9b depicts what the data would look like in this case: a perfect diagonal line originating at the upper left corner and reaching to the lower right corner.

The scatterplot in Figure A-9c depicts how the scores would be situated if the correlation coefficient were 0. For example, you might expect that the daily temperature in San Francisco is uncorrelated with how many times its citizens talk about koala bears. Notice how there is little discernible pattern to the data; it is hard to anticipate how often koala bears will come up in conversation given changes in daily temperature. Can you think of other pairs of variables whose correlation coefficient would be 0?

Rarely will you find that two variables are perfectly correlated because there are usually several factors that determine an individual's score on some outcome. For instance, the correlation coefficient for the relationship between how many hours one spends studying for an exam and one's exam score is very high (.89, in our example)— but it's not perfect because many other factors, including *how* one studies, could also predict one's exam score.

⚙ WHAT DO YOU KNOW?...

9. Match the correlations on the left with the most plausible correlation coefficient on the right.

1. Highest educational degree received and salary at first job	a. −.90
2. Number of times the letter T appears in one's name and GPA	b. .67
3. In one hour, time spent checking email and amount of time remaining to study for exam	c. .04

Inferential Statistics

Preview Question

› What is the value of the experimental method for testing cause–effect relations?

Let's introduce inferential statistics in the context of an important empirical question: Does driving while talking on a cell phone affect one's driving? Many legislators seem to think so: As of this writing, the use of handheld cellular telephones while driving has been banned in 14 states plus Washington, D.C., Puerto Rico, Guam, and the U.S. Virgin Islands. Many other states have left it to local jurisdictions to ban their use, including Massachusetts, Michigan, Ohio, and Pennsylvania. Note, however, that no state currently bans all drivers from using *hands-free* cell phones while driving. Presumably, the rationale behind this decision is that cell phones are harmful because they reduce the number of hands on the wheel from two to one. The loss of that hand is what causes individuals to drive carelessly; therefore, hands-free technology should restore the driver to conditions similar to those they experience when they're simply talking to their passengers. Makes sense, right? Being a critical thinker, you are probably thinking, "Yes, but even the most commonsense beliefs should be regarded with skepticism. Show me the scientific evidence!" Likewise, if you've ever had the displeasure of driving behind people using even hands-free devices, you may have noticed that they still don't seem as attentive as those who are simply talking to passengers.

Hunton and Rose (2005) investigated our opening question experimentally. They tested the hypothesis that driving performance would grow increasingly worse across three conditions: (1) during no conversation, (2) during a conversation with a passenger, and (3) during a hands-free cell phone conversation (for the purposes of this discussion, focus your attention on the last two conditions). Participants engaged in a realistic simulated driving task while they either spoke with a passenger seated to their right or with an individual on a cell phone using a hands-free device. Table A-5 includes data that could have been generated by this study.

The descriptive statistics indicate that the means between these two experimental conditions are different; those who used a hands-free device to talk committed more errors than those who simply spoke to a passenger. Note that we have new symbols for the number of people in each condition (n), for the mean (M), and for the standard deviation (s). These symbols indicate that we are working with samples rather than populations.

Based on the means, can you now conclude that hands-free devices cause declines in performance? Well, that depends on whether you can rule out two different classes of alternative explanations: one concerned with experimental design and one concerned with chance. Let's first briefly review the explanation that has to do with experimental design, then move on to chance.

Recall from Chapter 2 that in order to comfortably make the claim that a manipulation *caused* changes in a dependent variable, you have to hold all other factors constant—factors having to do with preexisting differences between groups (e.g., personality traits, skills, motivation) and factors having to do with the research environment or procedure (e.g., the time of day the study is run, the setting in which it is held). Ideally, the only factor that should differ between conditions is the manipulation of the independent variable.

So, did this study (Hunton & Rose, 2005) pass this test? First, take a moment to think about what possible individual differences could have influenced participants' performance during the driving simulations. If you reasoned that differences in individuals' driving skills could be a factor, then you are on the same page as the researchers. How might they have controlled for these differences? People's driving skills were controlled by—you guessed it—random assignment. Professional and amateur drivers had an equal chance of being assigned to either condition; thus, any differences in performance on the driving task couldn't be attributed to preexisting differences between groups.

Of course, the researchers also had to be very careful to rule out alternative explanations having to do with the research procedure, so they held a number of environmental variables constant. For instance, participants in *both* conditions were told that the purpose of the study was to test the quality of the simulation software and that they would be observed by a representative of the manufacturer. The "representative," who was actually a confederate of the researchers, was instructed to ask participants the *same* set of questions, in the *same* order, and at the *same* pace. This way, if the groups did differ, no one could argue that it was due to differences in the way they experienced the experimental procedure.

table **A-5**

Number of Errors Committed in Passenger Versus Cell-Phone Conditions	
Passenger Condition	**Cell-Phone Condition**
3	5
3	5
5	7
5	7
5	7
5	7
7	9
7	9
7	9
7	9
7	9
7	9
9	11
9	11
9	11
9	11
11	13
11	13
$\Sigma X = 126$	$\Sigma X = 162$
N (or n) = 18	N (or n) = 18
μ (or M) = 7	μ (or M) = 9
σ (or s) = 2.38	σ (or s) = 2.38

In summary, the researchers (Hunton & Rose, 2005) ruled out several alternative explanations for any differences they observed in the number of errors by randomly assigning participants to conditions and by treating both groups in exactly the same way, except for the manipulation. Are you justified in concluding that hands-free cell phone use leads to more crashes and less careful driving? In a word, no. You haven't ruled out the possibility that our findings were simply due to chance. *Inferential statistics* will enable you to do this. As noted earlier, inferential statistics are mathematical techniques that enable researchers to draw conclusions about populations based on data collected from samples.

✪ WHAT DO YOU KNOW?...

10. A researcher wanted to test the hypothesis that when someone hears a description of a person, the traits presented first in a list will be more influential in forming an impression than those presented last. She asked participants to listen to her as she read a list of traits describing an individual, then to rate how much they like her. Half the participants were randomly assigned to a condition in which positive words were presented first, and half to a condition in which positive words were presented last.
    a. How could the researcher ensure that any preexisting differences between groups would not influence the results of the study?
    b. The researcher made sure that the traits in the list were identical across the two conditions. What feature of the way the list was presented would have been important to hold constant?

Were the Observed Differences Due to Chance?

Preview Question

> › How do researchers determine whether the differences they observe in an experiment are due to the effect of their manipulation or due to chance?

Imagine for the moment that someone wants to convince you he has a magic coin. You know that if the coin were *not* magic, and he were to flip it a bazillion times, there is a 50-50 chance that it would come up heads (or tails). Now you don't have all the time in the world to sit there and watch this guy flip his coin, but imagine you're willing to wait as he flips it 10 times. Further imagine that he comes up with 7 heads and 3 tails. Should you accept his claim that he is in possession of a magic coin? Probably not. Over trials lasting just a few coin flips, you know that there will be variations in the proportions of heads versus tails—variations that have more to do with chance and less with magic.

Here is your challenge, then: You want to test the hypothesis that this is a magic coin. You know that the most thorough and convincing test of this hypothesis would involve flipping the coin an infinite number of times, but by definition you cannot do that. Researchers face a similar problem when they want to test their hypotheses. For example, imagine a researcher wanted to test the hypothesis that the majority of the people in New Haven, Connecticut, prefer organically grown produce to conventionally grown produce. She knows that the most convincing test of this hypothesis would involve asking the *entire population* of New Havenites their preference, but she has neither the time nor the funding to do so. What would you recommend she do? If you carefully read Chapter 2, you recognize that this situation calls for representative sampling. You might recommend that she randomly select a sample of New Havenites, ask them "Do you prefer organically grown produce to conventionally grown produce?" then tabulate her results.

Imagine she finds that 56% of those sampled said they prefer organically grown produce. Can she reasonably conclude that her hypothesis is correct? Alert readers will point out that this depends entirely on how successful she was in selecting a representative sample. Even if the majority of people in New Haven prefer convention-ally grown produce, she could, by chance alone, have randomly selected a sample that included a majority of people who prefer organic. How can she find out whether her results are attributable to chance? She might begin by asking, "If I repeatedly sampled the population of New Havenites, how often would I find results that *dis*confirmed my hypothesis?" As explained below, this is the question that essentially drives infer-ential statistics.

THE NULL VERSUS ALTERNATIVE HYPOTHESIS. The researcher above was interested in testing the hypothesis that most of the people of New Haven preferred organically grown produce. For the sake of introducing hypothesis testing, though, it may help to go back to the study that asked whether driving while talking with a hands-free cell phone is less safe than driving while talking with a passenger. Before you can answer this question, though, you'll need to formally state some hypotheses about two populations: drivers who speak to passengers and those who talk on cell phones. Though it seems strange to think of these groups as discrete populations, we assume that the sample of people who participated in each of your study's conditions was selected from them. Whenever scientists test hypotheses, they assume they are working with samples drawn from populations. In fact, inferential statistics is so-called because you use samples to make *inferences* about populations.

You will start by hypothesizing that in the populations from which you drew your samples, there are *no differences* in safety between those who talk to passengers and those who talk on cell phones. Why? Odd as it may sound, when researchers want to test a hypothesis, they begin by assuming it's not true. In doing so, they test what is called the **null hypothesis**—which states that no relationship exists between the variables they are observing and that any relationship they do observe is attributable to chance. The null hypothesis for this particular study is that in the population of drivers who talk to passengers, people commit the same number of errors, on average, as in the population of drivers who talk on cell phones.

The hypothesis you are truly interested in, of course, is that there *is* a difference in the mean number of errors committed between the population of people who talk on a hands-free phone compared with the population of people who talk to a passenger. Researchers call this the **alternative hypothesis** (also known as the *research hypothesis*)—a hypothesis that states a relationship will exist between the observed variables. Let us now discuss how we will evaluate which of our hypotheses is more likely.

THE DISTRIBUTION OF SAMPLE MEANS AND SAMPLING ERROR. Earlier, you learned that when you sample from a population, you're not always going to draw samples whose means perfectly represent the population's mean. By chance alone, you could draw samples whose means differ from the mean of the population. The difference between the mean of the population and the means of the samples drawn from it is called **sampling error.**

To illustrate sampling error, imagine that you have a (very small) population consist-ing of four people whose scores are: 4, 6, 8, and 10, with a mean of 7. If you were to re-peatedly draw samples of two people from this population, then replace them, how often would you obtain samples whose means were also 7? You can find out by listing all the possible combinations of samples of $n = 2$ people. Table A-6 lists all the possible samples of $n = 2$ you could draw from this population, as well as the means of those samples.

Each of those means is plotted on the frequency distribution graph depicted in Figure A-10. What do you notice about the shape of this distribution? It's that

null hypothesis A hypothesis stating that any relationship observed between variables will be due to chance.

alternative hypothesis A hypothesis stating that a relationship will exist between observed variables (also known as the *research hypothesis*).

sampling error Chance differences between sample statistics and population statistics (called *parameters*); for example, the difference between the mean of a population and the mean of a sample drawn from it.

table A-6

All Possible Samples of $n = 2$ from a Population in Which $N = 4$, and the Scores Are 4, 6, 8, and 10			
Sample Number	First Score	Second Score	Sample Means
1	4	4	4
2	4	6	5
3	4	8	6
4	4	10	7
5	6	4	5
6	6	6	6
7	6	8	7
8	6	10	8
9	8	4	6
10	8	6	7
11	8	8	8
12	8	10	9
13	10	4	7
14	10	6	8
15	10	8	9
16	10	10	10

figure A-10

Sampling error By repeatedly drawing and replacing samples of $n = 2$ people from the population in which $N = 4$ and $\mu = 7$, you created a distribution of sample means whose mean was also 7. Notice that you drew samples with means as low as 4 and as high as 10. This suggests that when you randomly sample from the population, you won't always get a sample whose mean perfectly represents the population mean. Researchers refer to these chance differences between samples and populations as *sampling error.*

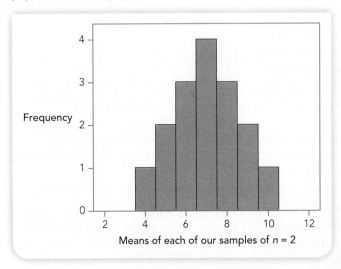

standard normal distribution again! Most of your scores are clustering around a mean of 7—exactly what you'd expect, given that your samples come from a population with this mean. However, sometimes by chance alone you would draw samples whose means were not 7. Sometimes you might draw samples whose means are hardly representative of the population mean of 7—some as extreme as 4 and 10. When you randomly select people from this (or any) population, you won't always get a sample whose mean perfectly represents the population mean. Again, these chance differences between the sample and population means constitute *sampling error.* Luckily, there is a far more efficient method by which you can determine how much sampling error exists. You simply calculate a statistic called the **standard error.** The standard error quantifies sampling error or chance and is used to help determine whether you can reject the null hypothesis. We will return to this point shortly.

What you just constructed by plotting the sample means for all possible combinations of samples is a **distribution of sample means,** which is a hypothetical distribution of all possible sample means of a given sample size from a specified population. Do researchers really plot the means for all possible combinations of samples? No, they don't. As you've probably figured out by now, the distribution of sample means is hypothetical; no one would painstakingly list all possible combinations of samples of a given size just to find out the probabilities of randomly selecting various sample means. Statisticians have created computer simulations that calculate and plot these sample mean differences in frequency distribution graphs so that we don't have to.

Psychologists use the distribution of sample means, also called a *sampling distribution,* to help them draw inferences about the probability of their particular data if the null hypothesis is true. In particular, they ask, "If the null hypothesis were true, how likely is it that we would observe the particular outcome of our study?"

Let's return to the data presented in Table A-5, that is, the full group of 18 drivers in each condition studied. The mean number of errors committed by your sample of participants who spoke to a passenger was 7 and for your sample of participants who spoke to someone via hands-free cell phone, 9. Though your sample means differ by 2 errors, you have to entertain the possibility that you happen to have selected exceptional samples—that is, two samples whose difference does not represent the actual difference between the populations. We will now calculate a test statistic to tell us how unlikely it would be to observe this difference, if the null hypothesis is true.

SIGNIFICANCE TESTING AND *t*-TESTS. When you are interested in testing whether two groups' means are different beyond chance, you will be evaluating differences between two samples in a statistical procedure called a **t-test.** The particular *t*-test you will learn about is often referred to as the independent-samples *t*-test.

You will use the data in Table A-5 to calculate something called the **t-statistic,** a statistic used in the *t*-test that is the ratio of the hypothesized difference against chance differences:

$$t = \frac{(M_1 - M_2) - (\mu_1 - \mu_2)}{s_{M1 - M2}}$$

Take a look at the numerator of the *t*-statistic formula, in particular, the term "$\mu_1 - \mu_2$," which refers to the hypothesized difference between the experimental groups in the *population.* Because you're testing the null hypothesis, you hypothesize this value to be 0; in other words, under the null you expect that there will be *no* difference between the two groups in the population from which you're sampling. The term "$(M_1 - M_2)$" refers to the difference between our sample means. The denominator contains the standard error, which as mentioned previously is a value that quantifies sampling error or chance. The standard error for this example is .79, a value that takes into account the variability of your samples and sample size. Conceptually, it can be represented as

$$\text{standard error} = \frac{\text{standard deviation of the samples}}{\text{square root of sample sizes}}$$

It was calculated following a procedure you can learn about when you take a class in statistics for the behavioral sciences. Plugging in the values to the *t*-statistic formula, you will find

$$t = \frac{(7 - 9) - (0)}{.79} = -2.53$$

The fact that you have divided the mean difference by a standard score (the standard error) enables you to make use of the empirical rule to determine the probability of our data under the null hypothesis. Earlier, you learned that according to the empirical rule, about 68%, 95%, and 99% of scores tend to fall within 1, 2, and 3 standard deviations of the mean, respectively. The same rule applies even when the distribution is of sample means instead of scores and even when using the standard error instead of standard deviation. If 95% of scores tend to fall within 2 standard errors of the mean of the sampling distribution, then

standard error A statistic that quantifies sampling error or chance differences between the sample and the population.

distribution of sample means A hypothetical distribution of all possible sample means of a given sample size from a specified population.

t-test The statistical procedure for evaluating whether differences observed between two sample means represent true population mean differences or chance.

t-statistic A statistic used in the *t*-test that is the ratio of the hypothesized difference against chance differences.

5% of scores tend to fall outside of this region. These are values we would be less likely to observe if the null hypothesis were true. A *t*-statistic of ±2 would correspond to a mean difference that was highly improbable; the probability of observing it would be about 5%.

Our actual *t*-statistic, −2.53, was even more improbable; in fact, the actual probability of observing it happens to be about .02, which means that if the null hypothesis were true, you would have a 2% chance of obtaining a mean difference as extreme as this one. Consequently, you will happily reject the null hypothesis and conclude that driving while speaking on a hands-free cell phone results in more errors than driving while speaking to a passenger.

To reiterate, if the null hypothesis were true, the difference in errors you observed between your samples would have been so unlikely that you would be comfortable rejecting the null hypothesis. Researchers refer to this procedure as **null hypothesis significance testing**—the process through which statistics are used to calculate the probability that a research result could have occurred by chance alone. Your data were extremely unlikely under the null hypothesis, so you would conclude that your results were *statistically significant,* in other words, *very unlikely to have occurred by chance alone.*

How improbable should your observed difference have been for you to decide to reject the null hypothesis? This is up to the researcher; however, convention dictates that you set a probability level, or ***p*-level,** of .05, meaning the probability that you got these results by chance is 5%. The probability that our observed difference was due to chance, 2%, was lower than our 5% cutoff.

TYPE I ERRORS. Does having rejected the null hypothesis mean you can state with certainty that you *proved* the alternative hypothesis is true? In a word, no. When a researcher decides to set his or her *p*-level at .05, he or she is essentially saying, "My findings are unlikely to be due to chance. However, it is still possible that I selected samples whose mean differences were this extreme by chance alone and the probability of this is 5%." In other words, whenever you reject the null hypothesis, you risk doing so incorrectly. You risk making what is called a **type I error**—*rejecting the null hypothesis when it is, in fact, true.* What is the probability of making a type I error? It is the probability level (the *p*-level) you set at the outset (more professionally referred to as the "alpha level"). Though your mean differences were unlikely to have been obtained by chance, the probability is not nil, so you can never feel comfortable saying that you *proved* the hypothesis to be correct (which is why researchers often prefer to say that they have "demonstrated" a relationship between variables).

VARIABILITY, SAMPLE SIZE, AND CHANCE. How does the amount of variability within a sample affect your ability to reject the null hypothesis? This can be answered in the context of the cell-phone experiment. You invited people into your lab and randomly assigned them to one of two groups. For the sake of this example, imagine that you manipulated your variable perfectly—you held all aspects of your experiment constant by randomly assigning people to groups and by treating everyone across each of the two groups in exactly the same way, except for your manipulation.

There's *still* one aspect of the experiment over which you have no control: pre-existing individual differences. As we've discussed, people walked into your lab with their own unique learning histories, interests, moods, and importantly, driving skills. So even though you treated the groups in exactly the same way (except for the manipulation), and even though you randomly assigned them to conditions, you know at the outset that your manipulation isn't going to make everyone *within* each of the groups get the same exact score. People differ. Figures A-11a and b depict pairs of hypothetical frequency distributions for groups whose means differ. The difference between Panel A and Panel B lies in how much variability exists within each of our passenger versus cell phone user groups. This will have implications for the conclusions that can be drawn about the effect of the manipulation and, by extension, about the null and alternative hypotheses.

null hypothesis significance testing A statistical procedure that calculates the probability that a research result could have occurred by chance alone.

p-level The probability that results are due to chance, under the null hypothesis.

type I error In statistics, rejecting the null hypothesis when it is, in fact, true.

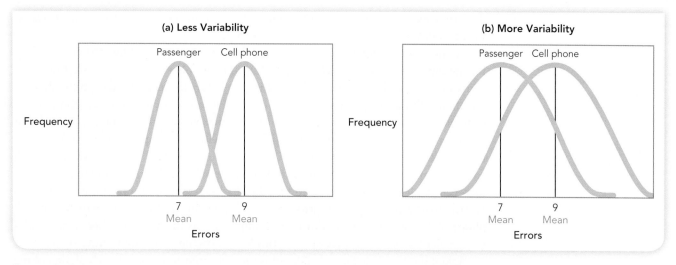

figure A-11

Two pairs of distributions that differ in variability Notice how little variability exists within each of the groups in (a); the manipulation seemed to have the effect of making everyone in each of the groups look very similar. Note also that, because there is little variability within the groups, there is very little overlap between these two distributions of scores. The frequency distributions in (b) represent what would happen if the two samples still differed, on average, but had a lot more variability within them. This increase in variability increases the amount of overlap between the two distributions of scores. If they do differ, on average, chance is probably playing a role.

Figure A-11a shows two frequency distributions: one for the passenger group and one for the hands-free cell phone group. Notice how little variability there is within each of these groups: The scores are tightly distributed around the means, such that the means represent the groups fairly well; the manipulation seems to have the effect of making everyone in each of the groups look basically the same. Note also that because little variability exists within the groups, there is very little overlap between these two distributions of scores; the people in the passenger group are so distinct from those in the hands-free cell phone group that you would feel fairly comfortable asserting that it was due to your manipulation and not chance.

Now take a look at Figure A-11b. These frequency distributions represent what would happen if the two samples still differed, on average, but had a lot more variability within them. Note how this increase in variability increases the amount of overlap between the two distributions of scores—it's hard to even distinguish between them! If they do differ, on average, it's difficult to make the case that it's because of anything an experimenter did to them, since the effect of the manipulation was so inconsistent across people within each of the groups. Chance is probably playing a role here. If your samples' data had been distributed like this, you would probably not be able to reject the null hypothesis.

Statisticians had exactly the above idea in mind when creating the formula for t. Here is the t-statistic formula again:

$$t = \frac{(M_1 - M_2) - (\mu_1 - \mu_2)}{s_{M1 - M2}}$$

As noted, the term in the denominator, the standard error ($s_{M1 - M2}$), is calculated by dividing the standard deviation of the samples by the square root of n:

$$\text{standard error} = \frac{\text{standard deviation of the samples}}{\text{square root of sample sizes}}$$

What's important here is that the standard deviation is an index of how much variability exists within the samples. If there is a lot of variability, the standard deviation, and by extension the standard error, will increase. Keep this in mind as you take another look at the t-statistic formula. What would happen to the value of t if the standard deviation were to increase? As the standard deviation increases, t would decrease, as would your ability to confidently reject the null hypothesis.

So, how does sample size affect your ability to reject the null hypothesis? Read on for the intuitive answer and then the technical one. Whose data would you find more convincing for making the case that talking on hands-free cell phones is more dangerous than talking to a passenger while driving: Professor Small Sample's, who found a difference between his samples, with only one person in each condition; or Professor Large Sample's, who found the same difference, with 100 people in each group? If you remember the discussion of sample size, you should *not* have chosen Professor Small Sample's data because you reasoned that two people hardly represent the population of drivers. For all you know, he could have by chance assigned auto racing driver Danica Patrick to the passenger condition and a visually impaired centenarian to the cell phone condition. But if Professor Large Sample detects the difference between samples using lots of people, you may start to think, "Maybe he's onto something there. . . ."

Again, the t-statistic formula takes this very idea into account in its calculation of the standard error. Take another look at the formula for the standard error; you'll see that, as sample size increases, the standard error decreases. So if you're planning a study and want to lower the probability that chance is playing a role in your results, recruit lots of people!

✿ WHAT DO YOU KNOW?...

11. Match the concept on the left with its corresponding description on the right. The context is the study in which participants interacted with someone on a hands-free phone or talked to a passenger, and the dependent variable is the number of errors committed during a driving simulation.

1. Null hypothesis	a. Participants in the cell-phone condition will commit more errors than those in the passenger condition.
2. Alternative hypothesis	b. The statistic that would quantify our sampling error.
3. Sampling error	c. Incorrectly rejecting the (null) hypothesis that there are no differences in errors between our cell-phone and passenger conditions.
4. Statistically significant	d. The difference in errors between the drivers using cell phones and the drivers with passengers was unlikely to have been due to chance.
5. Null hypothesis significance testing	e. Participants in the cell-phone condition will commit the same number of errors as those in the passenger condition.
6. Standard error	f. The difference between the mean of the sample of cell-phone drivers and the mean of the population of cell-phone drivers; also, our operational definition of chance.
7. t-test	g. The statistical test we would use to test our hypothesis if we were using two samples to represent our two populations (drivers using cell phones and drivers with passengers).
8. Type I error	h. The process by which we determine whether the differences in errors we observe between our drivers using cell phones and drivers of passengers is due to chance.

12. For the pair of variables below, specify whether the correlation is positive or negative:
   a. Variability within samples and ability to reject the null hypothesis
   b. Sample size and ability to reject the null hypothesis

How Large Are the Observed Differences?

Preview Question

> How do researchers determine just how meaningful their results are?

In your cell phone study, you ruled out chance as an explanation for the differences in errors between the cell phone and passenger groups. Should you now lobby your legislators to ban all cell phone use? Before you risk being ostracized by your community for taking away the joy of talking to loved ones while stuck in traffic, you need to consider whether the differences you observed were more than just statistically significant. You should consider whether the effect you observed was sizable. **Effect size** is a measure of how big the effect is; however, it's more than that. It tells us how big the effect is when you control for the amount of variability that existed within your sample(s).

What the significance test told you was the probability that your differences are due to chance; it told you nothing about whether your findings were "significant" in the way you're probably accustomed to using the term—that is, it didn't tell you if your findings were important, newsworthy, or even noteworthy. Nor did it tell you how *consistent* the effect was across people. As an example, take a look at the fictional data depicted in Table A-7.

If you were to only pay attention to the mean differences between your groups, you might be quite impressed with the data: There is, on average, a difference of *four* errors between the two conditions. When you take a closer look, though, you can see that the effect of your manipulation wasn't consistent from person to person—in fact, the effect was so inconsistent that the majority of participants were unfazed by it! Even if you had found, by doing a *t*-test, that your mean difference "beat chance" (it doesn't—can you figure out why?), you'd have a hard time selling the idea that we should demand a ban on the use of cell phones while driving. The size of the effect is just too inconsistent from person to person—that is, there's too much variability in the data.

"But you just told us that the standard error takes this variability into account!" you must be thinking. Yes, of course, you're right: When calculating the standard error, you divide the variability within your groups (quantified by the standard deviation) by the square root of your sample size. Here's where things get interesting. Because there is an inverse relationship between sample size and standard error, if an effect is inconsistent from person to person (as it is above), your findings can still be

table **A-7**

Inconsistencies in the Effect of the Manipulation on Errors	
Passenger	**Hands-free cell phone**
10	10
10	10
10	10
10	10
0	20
M = 8	M = 12
s = 4.72	s = 4.72

Danica Patrick? → 0

20 ← Visually-impaired centenarian?

effect size A measure indicating how big an effect is (e.g., how great the difference between two means) that takes into account the consistency of the effect and that ignores sample size.

statistically significant. Check it out. Earlier, you found that there was a 2-point mean difference between your two groups. In calculating the *t*-statistic, you also learned that you were able to reject the null hypothesis, owing to the fact that your standard error was outweighed by the mean difference, by a factor of 2.53:

$$t = \frac{(7 - 9) - (0)}{.79} = -2.53$$

Recall that the standard error, your operational definition of chance, is calculated by dividing the standard deviation of our samples by the square root of your sample size.

$$\text{standard error of the mean} = \frac{\text{standard deviation of the samples}}{\text{square root of sample sizes}}$$

Immediately you can see that even if there were a lot of variability within your cell phone and passenger conditions, a sufficiently large sample size could enable you to reject the null hypothesis; however, if there had been a lot variability in your data, it would've been hard to make the case that the effect of your manipulation had been fully consistent across people. In short, the size of your sample can work to reduce standard error enough so that you can reject the null, even if the effect doesn't hold for most individuals.

So if sample size poses problems for the inferences we make about our data, what would you suggest we do? If you're thinking, "Why not come up with a formula for effect size that takes into account the size of the effect and the consistency of the effect and that ignores sample size?" then you're right on. Psychologists rely on a number of formulas for determining effect size. The formula to focus on here is *Cohen's d*:

$$d = \frac{\text{mean difference}}{\text{standard deviation}}$$

Cohen's *d* is a measure of effect size that expresses the difference between sample means in standard deviation units. Cohen's *d* offers a benchmark against which you can evaluate the size of your differences. These criteria, set forth by Cohen (1992), are presented in Table A-8.

In the cell-phone study, the absolute mean difference between our groups was 2 and the standard deviation, which was calculated for you, was 3.35, and so *d* would be

$$\frac{2}{3.35} = 0.60$$

In this example, your *d* indicates you have a medium effect, because .60 is closest to the cutoff of .50. What you have just learned is that participants in your cell-phone group committed, on average, 0.60 of a standard deviation more errors than your passenger drivers.

Is it time to call the legislators? Well, notice first that the above table provides standardized guidelines, but not standardized recommendations (e.g., "Medium effect: Start panicking"). The decision concerning how to act, armed with your data, will depend on various considerations. For instance, your dependent variable happened to be errors, but what if the numbers referred not to errors but to highway fatalities? In this circumstance, you might wish to call your legislators right away (but not while driving). Statistics do not do our thinking for us—they are instead tools that enable us to make informed decisions on our own. Finally, remember that these data, while based in reality, are not the actual data from the study. You are encouraged to read the actual study!

table **A-8**

Effect Sizes: Cohen's *d*	
d	Size of effect
.2	Small
.5	Medium
.8	Large

Cohen's *d* A measure of effect size that expresses the difference between sample means in standard deviation units.

WHAT DO YOU KNOW?...

13. What is one advantage of relying on effect size to determine the meaning of your findings?

Chapter Review

Now that you have completed this statistics appendix, be sure to turn to Appendix B, where you will find a **Chapter Summary** that is useful for reviewing what you have learned about statistics.

Key Terms

alternative hypothesis (p. A-17)
Cohen's *d* (p. A-24)
criterion variable (p. A-12)
descriptive statistics (p. A-1)
distribution (p. A-2)
distribution of sample means (p. A-18)
effect size (p. A-23)
empirical rule (p. A-8)
frequency distribution table (p. A-2)
frequency polygon (p. A-3)
histogram (p. A-2)
inferential statistics (p. A-1)

mean (p. A-4)
measures of central tendency (p. A-4)
median (p. A-4)
mode (p. A-4)
negatively skewed (p. A-5)
normal distribution (p. A-5)
null hypothesis (p. A-17)
null hypothesis significance
  testing (p. A-20)
p-level (p. A-20)
positively skewed (p. A-5)
predictor variable (p. A-12)

range (p. A-7)
sampling error (p. A-17)
skewed distribution (p. A-5)
standard error (p. A-18)
t-statistic (p. A-19)
t-test (p. A-19)
type I error (p. A-20)
unimodal (p. A-5)
variability (p. A-7)
x-axis (p. A-3)
y-axis (p. A-3)
z-score (p. A-10)

The following terms from Chapter 2 are important here also: *correlation, correlation coefficient, negative correlation, positive correlation, scatterplot, standard deviation, statistically significant,* and *statistics*.

Questions for Discussion

1. If you were to measure your friends' love of classical music on a 5-point scale with 1 = no love at all and 5 = lots of love, how do you suppose the scores would be distributed? Would they be normally distributed, with most people answering at the midpoint, or would they be skewed? If skewed, would they be positively or negatively skewed? What would be the most appropriate measure of central tendency? How much variability would be in these scores— that is, would the standard deviation be high or low? [Apply]

2. A brother and sister, fraternal twins, are arguing about who is taller, relatively speaking. The brother is 72 inches and the sister is 67 inches. In a 2004 report, the Centers for Disease Control (CDC) published data on the average heights of males and females (Ogden et al., 2004), indicating that 19-year-old males are, on average, 69.6 inches with a standard deviation of 4.97 and that 19-year-old women are, on average, 64.2 inches with a standard deviation of 4.56. Treat these data as if they come from the entire population of 19-year-olds and figure out who, in fact, is relatively taller. *Hint:* Calculate *z*-scores for both groups and ask yourself, "Who is farther away from the mean?" [Apply]

3. What are some examples of variables that are positively correlated? Negatively correlated? How about variables that have zero correlation? [Comprehend]

4. In the nineteenth episode of Season 20 of the popular Fox television program *The Simpsons*, Lisa laments that Springfield Elementary is fully 2 standard deviations below the mean on school performance. Explain to someone who has no exposure to the concept of *z*-scores what she means. *Hint:* Look at Figure A-7 for a refresher. [Apply]

5. Imagine you learned of a study in which researchers randomly assigned individuals to memorize a list of words while either listening to music or not. Results indicated that there was a statistically significant difference in the number of items they were later able to recall, with those in the no music condition outperforming those in the music condition. What effect size (small, medium, or large) would be large enough for you to take these results to heart and perhaps change the conditions under which you study? What if the dependent variable had instead been grades? [Apply, Analyze]

Appendix B
Chapter Summaries and Answers to Chapter Questions

CHAPTER 1
Chapter Summary

What is psychology?

Psychology is the scientific study of persons, the mind, and the brain.

What are some examples of the diversity characterizing the field of psychology?

The field of psychology is exceptionally diverse. Some psychologists work as researchers, investigating topics such as Internet communication among people or cell communication in the brain. Others have exceptional interpersonal skills and use them to help people in therapy.

What's so bad about intuition?

When people have strong intuitions, they are tempted to think that they don't need other additional information. Moreover, different people have different intuitions about the same question.

What's a good alternative to intuition?

An alternative that psychologists rely on is the scientific method, which refers to a broad array of evidence-based procedures. The scientific method enables one to approach problems with open-minded skepticism, a concept introduced in the Research Toolkit feature.

What makes a question "scientific"?

Scientific questions are those for which one collects evidence through scientific methods that could convincingly demonstrate the correct answer. Normative questions, questions of faith, and questions of logic are not scientific because they are not answered by gathering evidence.

What characterizes the "levels-of-analysis" approach to explaining psychological phenomena?

One may study a psychological phenomenon at any of three distinct yet complementary levels: person, mind, and brain. The person level of analysis addresses the individual as a whole and the social settings in which he or she lives. The mind level of analysis addresses thinking processes, emotions, and other mental events. The brain level of analysis refers to the anatomy and functioning of the brain.

How can sex differences in math performance be explained at the person, mind, and brain levels?

At the person level, research indicates that women are affected by stereotypes that lower their performance. At the mind level, research indicates that these stereotypes create anxiety that reduces memory and lowers math performance. At the brain level, research indicates that these stereotypes influence activity in a part of the brain known to be involved in producing emotions, which are detrimental to performance on a math test.

In what ways were Aristotle and the Buddha similar to and different from modern psychologists?

Aristotle asked scientific questions about psychology and developed a scheme for classifying mental capacities. The Buddha wanted to understand the causes of emotions and then developed a "therapy" to reduce emotional suffering: meditation. Modern psychologists address these and other concerns but evaluate their ideas using the scientific method.

How did the philosophers Locke and Kant believe that humans acquire knowledge?

Locke believed the mind is a "blank slate," shaped entirely by experience, whereas Kant believed some knowledge, such as the understanding that we exist in three-dimensional space, is innate.

Why are Wundt and James considered the founders of scientific psychology?

Wundt wrote *Principles of Physiological Psychology*, which included information about biological aspects of psychology and of the mind. In 1875 he established one of the first experimental psychological laboratories. James also established a laboratory but is better known for his textbook *The Principles of Psychology*, which defines the field's breadth.

What characterizes six of the most prominent schools of thought in psychology?

Structuralists were interested in how the simple components of the mind came together to create complex perceptual experiences. The functionalists focused on the mental activity of the mind, especially as it interacted with the body and with the environment. Psychoanalysts were interested in how the mind's hidden conflicts influenced ongoing behavior. Behaviorists concentrated on how the environment shapes observable behavior, by studying simple systems such as rats. Humanistic psychologists shifted the focus back to people—in particular, the study of the human experience of the whole person. The cognitive revolution ushered in a focus on the mind as an information-processing system—that is, as a device that can acquire, store, and manipulate symbols to transform information.

Answers to What Do You Know?

1. Lynne Owens Mock creates new scientific knowledge when she conducts research evaluating the efficacy of programs such as those designed to develop the leadership skills of girls 10 to 18 years old. She applies existing knowledge to help others when she runs support groups for grandparents raising children.

2. intuition/hunches; scientific

3. Scientists record how they make their observations so that other scientists can verify them.

4. faith; normative/should; scientific; evidence/data

5. skepticism

6. analysis; person

7. mind; memory; brain; emotions

8. Aristotle: 1 and 3

9. Buddha: 4 and 5

10. His thinking is in line with Kant's belief that certain ideas, such as those related to space, are innate.

11. experimental; scientific

12. One opportunity afforded by an increase in global scope is that psychologists can test whether their results might differ in another culture. Another is they can study the impact of culture on the individual.

13. 1d, 2b, 3a, 4e, 5f, 6c

Answers to Self-Test

1. c	6. c	11. a
2. d	7. d	12. d
3. b	8. a	13. d
4. a	9. b	14. c
5. d	10. c	15. c

CHAPTER 2
Chapter Summary

What are some flaws that can reduce the value of a study in psychology?

(1) People might not honestly answer a researcher's questions; (2) the research process might alter people's opinions instead of merely measuring them; (3) people might respond differently at different times; (4) people not included in a study might respond in a manner that differs from those who are included; (5) the psychologist's phrasing of questions may affect a research participant's answers; (6) some responses by a participant may be ambiguous; and (7) the researcher's record of participants' responses may be inaccurate.

Who is capable of thinking critically about problems in psychological research?

You are. You have the ability to detect flaws and apply the critical thinking skills you use in everyday life to fix them.

What are the three goals of scientific research?

In psychology, or any science, a researcher usually has one of three goals: description, prediction, and causal explanation.

What is the survey method?

In the survey method, psychologists learn about a large group of people by studying a subgroup of them. Researchers typically measure psychological qualities using this method, by asking questions, either in interviews or in survey items.

How do samples differ from populations? Why do researchers collect data from samples rather than from whole populations?

The overall group in whose opinions a researcher is interested is called the study's population. The subgroup of the population to whom a survey is administered is called the study's sample. Researchers don't administer their surveys to all the people in the population because it is too big.

Why does random sampling increase the representativeness of a sample?

Random sampling minimizes the possibility that the sample differs from the population as a whole.

What is a correlational study?

A correlational study is a research design whose aim is to determine the relation between two measured variables.

What scientific goal does a correlational study help psychologists to achieve?

Psychologists achieve the scientific goal of prediction through the use of correlational designs. The results of a correlational study indicate the degree to which one variable predicts another.

What is a scatterplot and how is it interpreted?

A scatterplot is a graph depicting the relation between two variables. The dots in the scatterplot indicate whether the two variables go together, that is, whether higher levels of one variable are associated with higher (or lower) levels of the other variable.

What is a positive correlation? A negative correlation?

A positive correlation is one in which a higher amount of one variable co-occurs with higher amounts of the other variable, whereas a negative correlation is one in which a *lower* amount of one variable co-occurs with higher amounts of the other variable.

What is a correlation coefficient? What are examples of strong and weak positive and negative correlation coefficients?

A correlation coefficient is a number that represents the strength of a correlation between any two variables. If the correlation is close to +1.0, then there is a very strong positive correlation. If it is close to −1.0, then there is a very strong negative correlation. If the correlation coefficient is close to 0, there is little or no correlation.

What is the major limitation of correlational designs?

The major limitation is that researchers cannot tell whether the relation between two variables is causal, coincidental, or based on a third variable that affects both.

What scientific goal is achieved through experimental designs?

Experimental designs enable psychologists to achieve the goal of causal explanation. By manipulating one variable and seeing whether the manipulation affects a second variable, the psychologist can determine whether the first variable is a cause of the second one.

How does an independent variable differ from a dependent variable?

In an experimental design, the independent variable is the manipulated variable, whereas the measured variable, or outcome, is the dependent variable.

What is a hypothesis?

In psychology, a hypothesis is a prediction about the result of a study.

What is a control group?

A control group is an experimental condition that does not receive the experimental treatment.

What are the two defining characteristics of an experiment?

An experiment is a form of research in which there is (1) more than one experimental condition and (2) the random assignment of research participants to experimental conditions.

How does random assignment enable researchers to establish a causal effect between independent and dependent variables?

Random assignment eliminates the effects of preexisting individual differences by evenly distributing them across conditions so the only thing that theoretically differs between the conditions is the independent variable(s).

What is measurement? What are three examples of measurement in psychology?

Measurement is any procedure in which numbers are assigned to objects or events. Three examples are: (1) counting the number of correct answers on a test; (2) creating numerical scales to represent a continuum of opinions; and (3) measuring the time it takes to solve a problem.

What is an operational definition?

An operational definition is the specification of a procedure that can be used to measure a variable.

In the measurement of variables, what are reliability and validity?

A measure possesses reliability if it consistently measures a psychological property. It possesses validity if it measures what it is supposed to measure—that is, if it is accurate.

What are some potential advantages and disadvantages of quantitative methods?

Numbers can describe events precisely; quantitative data yield concise summaries of research, and numbers are easier to compare to one another than are words and sentences. One potential disadvantage is that people might have thoughts and feelings not included in the measurement scale.

What does it mean to say that a study's outcomes are statistically significant?

The outcomes of research are called statistically significant if they vary from what would be expected by chance.

What are qualitative research methods? What are three examples of qualitative research strategies?

In qualitative research, researchers observe people's statements and actions and describe their observations without using numberings. Three qualitative research strategies include clinical case studies, observational studies, and community-participation studies.

What are three advantages of qualitative data? What are some reasons most psychologists prefer quantitative to qualitative data?

Three advantages of qualitative data are that they are well suited to understanding (1) personal meaning and (2) the storylike quality of lives, and that they enable psychologists to (3) obtain evidence that is naturalistic. However, qualitative data do not provide the comparison, conciseness, and precision that quantitative data do, which is why so many psychologists prefer quantitative data.

What are three forms of psychological evidence that researchers obtain to study people's thoughts, feelings, and behaviors?

(1) Self-report methods are a form of evidence in which participants provide information about themselves. (2) Observer-report methods ask people to report on someone else whom they know well. (3) Direct observation of behavior is a method of gathering evidence in which the researcher views the actions of research participants firsthand.

What are two limitations of self-reports as a source of evidence about people's behavior?

In self-report studies, people may be (1) *unwilling* or even (2) *unable* to accurately report some information about themselves.

What are two main targets for research in studies of psychology and biology, and how do scientists learn about them?

Two main targets for research are psychologically relevant activity in the brain and the body. Two ways of studying the electrical activity in the brain are (1) electroencephalography (EEG), in which electrodes placed on the scalp record electrical activity, and (2) functional magnetic resonance imaging (fMRI), in which the brain's blood flow is recorded while a person performs a mental task. Psychophysiological evidence provides information about the body. Psychophysiologists use tools such as skin conductance response to record levels of bodily arousal.

What is a scientific theory?

A scientific theory is a systematic, data-based explanation for a phenomenon or set of phenomena.

What is the relation between theory and evidence?

There is a back-and-forth, "two-way street" relation between theory and evidence. After scientists formulate a theory, scientific evidence is collected to determine whether the theory's hypotheses can be confirmed. But before scientists formulate a theory, scientific evidence provides information about the world that guides theory development.

How are decisions about the ethics of a research proposal made?

In the United States, every major institution in which research is conducted has an Institutional Review Board (IRB), which assesses the ethics of proposed research by weighing the study's benefits (the scientific knowledge gained) against its costs (the inconvenience and potential risk to participants).

What three principles guide ethical research in psychology?

First, research participation must be voluntary; participants cannot be made to feel coerced in any way. Second, potential participants must be informed—that is, they must be given all the information they would need to make a decision about whether or not to participate, in an informed consent form. Third, they have the right to withdraw at any time without penalty. In addition, researchers must provide participants with a debriefing: an explanation of the research at the conclusion of the study.

Answers to What Do You Know?

1. F

2. This statement is incorrect because nearly *anyone* is capable of thinking critically about problems in psychological research.

3. 1b, 2c, 3a

4. Back translation is designed to avoid errors in translation.

5. population; sample; random; representative

6. (a) positive, (b) negative

7. b

8. One possible third variable would be quality of education, especially quality of education about good nutrition. Other answers are possible.

9. This statement is incorrect because random assignment increases the chances that any observed differences between experimental and control conditions are due to *manipulation*, rather than preexisting differences. This is why it is so useful.

10. 1f, 2d, 3b, 4e, 5a, 6c

11. data; mining; causation

12. (a) What is an operational definition? (b) What is validity? (c) What is the standard deviation?

13. All but *d* and *e* should be checked.

14. One benefit of methods like the Stroop Task is that they do not rely on human memory, which can be unreliable. Another benefit is that responses cannot be influenced by people's tendency to want to make a good impression on others.

15. electroencephalography; functional magnetic resonance imaging (fMRI); psychoactive; skin conductance response

16. F

17 (a) theory to evidence; (b) evidence to theory

18. Tuskegee Study; costs/harm

19. (a) T, (b) F

Answers to Self-Test

1. d	6. c	11. a
2. b	7. c	12. d
3. b	8. b	13. c
4. b	9. a	14. a
5. d	10. c	15. b

CHAPTER 3
Chapter Summary

What analogies have been used to describe the brain through the ages?

The ancient Romans described the brain as being like a pump that propels fluids. In the eighteenth century, scientists suggested that the brain and the body are like a machine. In the nineteenth century, psychologists and physicians such as Freud proposed that the brain is an energy system. Over the past half-century, psychologists have suggested that the brain is like a computer.

What valuable points are highlighted by using a brain-as-tool analogy?

First, you can use a tool for tasks that didn't exist in the evolutionary past (e.g., reading). Second, when you use a tool to perform a job, it is you—not the tool—who is responsible for completing the job.

How have researchers demonstrated that the brain is like muscle?

Like a muscle, the brain grows with experience. Researchers found that among people who learned to juggle, there was growth in an area of the brain related to processing visual information, whereas no changes occurred in the brains of nonjugglers.

What can brain damage tell us about the structure and function of the brain?

Brain damage helps to identify which structures are associated with which functions. When the brain is damaged, some thinking abilities remain completely intact, whereas others are lost.

How does Aristotle's model of the brain compare to more recent conceptualizations of the brain?

In Aristotle's model, the vegetative mind is responsible for growth and reproduction; the animal mind is responsible for feelings of pleasure and pain; and the rational mind enables people to engage in logical thought. In MacLean's triune brain, a model proposed in the twentieth century, the reptilian brain, similar to the vegetative mind, executes simple functions like regulating body temperature and breathing; the paleomammalian brain, similar to the animal brain, produces emotions; and the neomammalian brain, similar to the rational mind, enables us to put experiences into words.

What did MacLean mean when he said that we have "three brains in one"?

MacLean, in his triune brain model, suggested that our contemporary human brains have three main parts that evolved at different points in history and that each performs unique functions. Each is, in a sense, a brain.

What are the structures of the lowest level of the brain and their functions?

The brain stem is made up of the medulla, the pons, and the midbrain. The medulla plays a major role in homeostasis. The pons contains structures that control your rate of breathing and also conveys signals among other brain regions. One region of the midbrain protects the organism by generating defensive reactions to threatening events. The reticular formation is a system that influences arousal. The cerebellum is involved in motor movement.

What are the structures of the middle level of the brain and their functions?

The limbic system includes the hypothalamus, the hippocampus, and the amygdala. The hypothalamus plays a critical role in the regulation of bodily states and behaviors such as eating, drinking, and sexual response. The hippocampus is a structure that you need for remembering and for spatial memory. The amygdala contributes to the processing of information about danger in risky situations.

Other structures in the limbic system include the fornix, the olfactory bulbs, and the cingulate gyrus. The fornix connects the hippocampus and the hypothalamus and helps them to work as a system. The olfactory bulbs are required for a sense of smell. The cingulate gyrus contributes to people's ability to stop themselves from doing one thing and to switch to something else.

What are the structures of the highest level of the brain and their functions?

The cerebral cortex consists of four lobes: occipital, parietal, temporal, and frontal. The occipital lobe, commonly called the visual cortex, is heavily involved in the processing of visual information and also becomes active when you engage in mental imagery. The parietal lobes contain brain matter needed for somatosensory processing. The sensory cortex of the parietal lobe receives sensory information from all parts of the body, which are, in essence, "mapped" onto the cortex. The temporal lobe is crucial to hearing and to memory. The auditory cortex of the temporal lobe is active whenever you listen to sounds, detecting their pitch, volume, and timing in relation to one another.

The frontal lobes enable humans to think about themselves; to set goals and stick to them; to control their emotions; and to recognize themselves as social beings who are evaluated by others. The frontal lobes also contain the motor cortex, which sends out signals that move the body's muscles. The association areas of the cerebral cortex receive sensory information and connect it to stored knowledge of the world. The prefrontal cortex contributes to the ability to concentrate on facts, focus attention, and manipulate information in the mind; and to the ability to align behavior with social rules and conventions.

What is the relation between the left and right sides of the brain?

Information from the left side of the body reaches the right cerebral hemisphere, and information from the body's right side reaches the left cerebral hemisphere. Similarly, commands sent out from the brain to the body switch sides. The hemispheres are connected through the corpus callosum, a structure containing more than 200 million cells that transmit signals from one side of the brain to the other.

As discussed in Cultural Opportunities: Arithmetic and the Brain, there are cultural variations in which parts of the left cerebral hemisphere are active during tasks such as arithmetic. Among native English speakers, an addition task activated the visual–spatial region and Broca's area; among Chinese speakers, Broca's area was almost entirely *in*active during arithmetic.

For what functions are the left and right sides of the brain specialized?

The left hemisphere specializes in analytic tasks, including arithmetic and the ability to produce and understand spoken language. The right hemisphere is specialized for spatial thinking, the ability to create images in your mind.

If the left and right sides of the brain were cut off from each other, would you have two brains? How do we know?

If the corpus callosum were severed, your left and right hemispheres would function as if they were two separate brains. Sperry and his colleagues placed patients in front of a projection screen, asked them to concentrate on a dot in the middle of the screen, and then briefly flashed words, simultaneously, on the screen's left and right sides. When split brain patients were asked what word or words they saw, they inevitably named only the word on the right, though they were aware the other word had been shown and could even identify it by reaching for the correct object, as long as they did so with their left hand.

How does the architecture of our brains enable us to process large amounts of information simultaneously?

Even though different parts of the brain are specialized, the brain is organized into networks that enable communication between different regions. Many of these transmissions run through a brain structure known as the thalamus, which serves as a "relay station" for connections among brain regions.

What distinguishes nerve cells from other cells of the body?

Two features distinguish neurons from other cells: (1) their shape, which is unique due to the presence of dendrites and axons, and (2) their ability to communicate with one another, due to specialized structures found at synapses.

How do neurons communicate electrochemically?

Neurons produce action potentials, electrochemical events in which an electrical current travels down the length of the axon, from the soma to the axon terminals. When at rest, the neuron's interior mostly contains substances that are charged negatively. On the outside of the cell are positively charged sodium ions. During an action potential, the sodium ions briefly enter the neuron through channels in the neuron's cell wall. This flow of charged particles generates an electric impulse. The electrical impulse moves down the length of the axon and is sped along by the myelin sheath, a fatty substance that surrounds the axon and acts as an electrical insulator.

How do neurons send signals from the axon terminal of one neuron to the dendrites of another?

A sending neuron stores neurotransmitters in small sacs known as synaptic vesicles, which move within the neuron, down the length of the axon. They reach the end of the axon and "dock" with the outer edge of the axon terminal, where they are able to release their neurotransmitters into the synapse. Some of these neurotransmitters reach receptors on dendrites of the receiving neuron. When a neurotransmitter from the sending neuron binds to the receptor of a receiving neuron, one bit of communication between neurons is complete.

As discussed in This Just In, neural communication can also occur outside of the synapse.

What determines whether a neuron will fire?

Neurotransmitters determine whether a receiving neuron will fire. Some neurotransmitters bind to receptors that increase the likelihood the neuron will fire, whereas others bind to receptors that decrease this likelihood. The receiving neuron integrates these inputs to determine whether to fire.

How do neurons stay in place?

Glial cells hold neurons in place, as well as support the biological functioning of neurons, supplying them with nutrients and disposing of the brain's biological waste matter.

What are the structures of the central nervous system and their functions?

The central nervous system consists of the brain and the spinal cord. The spinal cord participates in communications between the brain and body. In one direction, information from the environment is directed into the spinal cord and then passed on to the brain via sensory neurons. After outgoing messages from the brain reach the spinal cord, motor neurons send out signals to the body's muscles.

What are the structures of the peripheral nervous system and their functions?

The peripheral nervous system consists of the somatic nervous system and the autonomic nervous system. The somatic nervous system provides the brain-to-periphery communications that enable you to control your bodily movement. The autonomic nervous system provides the communications that control bodily functions generally *not* under your control. The autonomic nervous system is further divided into the sympathetic nervous system, which prepares you for action by activating the biological systems required for "fight" or "flight" responses, and the parasympathetic nervous system, which maintains normal functioning of the body when you are not under threat or stress.

What is the endocrine system and how does it differ from the nervous system?

The endocrine system is a collection of glands that produce and secrete hormones, which carry messages from the brain to organs via the bloodstream. The nervous system is fast and specific, whereas the endocrine system is slow with lingering effects. The nervous system communicates electrically, whereas the endocrine system's communications are entirely chemical.

What are the major endocrine glands and their functions?

The pineal gland produces a hormone called melatonin that influences patterns of sleeping and wakefulness. The pituitary gland releases hormones that influence biological activity in several other glands, including those that respond to stress, contribute to reproduction, and regulate the body's use of energy. It is also the point of contact between the nervous systems and endocrine system via the hypothalamus. The thyroid gland releases hormones that regulate the body's metabolic rate. The thymus produces hormones that influence the development and functioning of the immune system. The adrenal glands produce hormones that respond to stress, as well as sex hormones, which are produced also by the gonads. The pancreas releases hormones that include insulin, which regulates the level of sugar in the bloodstream. The gonads are the organs that produce reproductive cells; the ovaries in women produce ova (eggs) and the testes in men produce sperm. The gonads also produce hormones. The ovaries produce estrogens and progesterone; the testes produce testosterone.

How does estrogen affect memory and behavior?

The research of Pauline Maki and colleagues indicated that memory varied across the menstrual cycle; when estrogen levels were high, memory was superior. Martie Haselton and colleagues' research indicated that during high-fertility periods, women tended to wear more fashionable clothes that showed more skin—presumably to make themselves more sexually attractive.

Answers to What Do You Know?

1. analogies/metaphors

2. The statement is incorrect because the brain-as-tool analogy reminds us that it is the *person using the tool* (in this case, the brain) who performs the tasks.

3. Plasticity refers to how the brain changes physically as a result of experiences. In this way, it is like a muscle that increases in strength when used.

4. If parts of the brain were not specialized, Phineas Gage may have lost his ability to think or his thinking may have been impaired.

5. functional; blood

6. 1e, 2f, 3i, 4h, 5b, 6c, 7a, 8k, 9g, 10j, 11d

7. (b) What is the right hemisphere?

   (c) What is the corpus callosum?

   (d) What is the right hemisphere?

   (e) What is the field of vision on the right?

8. (a) The brain's networks enable these functions.

   (b) It is the thalamus that acts as a relay station.

9. The statement is incorrect because it was only among the native English speakers that Broca's area became active when they solved an arithmetic problem, illustrating that culture does, in fact, play a role in brain development.

10. 1c, 2g, 3i, 4h, 5d, 6a, 7b, 8f, 9e

11. synapse

12. (a) What are sensory neurons?

    (b) What are motor neurons?

    (c) What are reflexes?

13. somatic; sympathetic; parasympathetic

14. Whereas the nervous system is fast and specific and communicates electrically, the endocrine system is slow and less specific and communicates chemically via hormones, which travel through the bloodstream.

15. 1b, 2d, 3g, 4f, 5a, 6e, 7c

16. fashionably/sexily/attractively

Answers to Self-Test

1. c	6. b	11. d
2. b	7. a	12. a
3. c	8. d	13. a
4. c	9. d	14. d
5. b	10. c	15. d

CHAPTER 4
Chapter Summary

What explains intelligence? Nature? Nurture? Both?

Both. In a twin study conducted in 2003, the degree to which genes affected intelligence differed at the different socioeconomic status (SES) levels. Among participants in high-SES families, genetics explained most of the variations in intelligence, but among poor families, genetics explained hardly anything at all. The influence of genes depended upon the environment.

What can lactose intolerance tell us about whether biology or culture came first?

Cultural differences created variations in "lactose tolerance" genes. If milk was a major food source in a given culture, then, and only then, did most people develop the ability to digest lactose, because those who had the ability to digest lactose were more likely to survive to reproduce.

The Cultural Opportunities feature describes examples of how biology can shape culture (e.g., higher levels of pathogens are associated with greater collectivism) and how culture can shape biology (e.g., the cultural practice of marrying within one's group is associated with decreased genetic diversity).

What does it mean to say that nature is dependent on nurture?

Nature and nurture work together to produce the psychological characteristics that make us human. For example, according to research on genes, intelligence, and poverty, in some environments most of the differences between people are accounted for by genes. In other settings, environmental factors account for most of the differences.

How can identical and fraternal twins' data be used to tell us about the influence of genes?

In the twin method, researchers compare the psychological similarity of monozygotic (identical; MZ) twins and dizygotic (fraternal; DZ) twins. If MZ twins resemble one another more closely than do DZ twins, the cause of the greater resemblance must be genetic because the only difference between the two types of twins, presumably, is their genetic similarity (although recent research, described in This Just In, indicates that not all identical twins are genetically identical!).

What do twin studies tell us about the heritability of personality, psychological disorders, and intelligence?

Twin studies commonly find that identical twins are more similar, psychologically, than are fraternal twins and that heritability depends on the quality being measured. Schizophrenia, for instance, is highly heritable, whereas social and political attitudes are lower in heritability.

What false conclusions should we avoid making when interpreting the results of twin studies?

First, do not assume that the heritability of psychological characteristics indicates those traits cannot change. Second, 50% heritability for a trait does not mean that half of each individual's trait is inherited. Third, high heritability within a group does not mean that differences between that group and some other group must be due to genetics.

What is the relation between chromosomes, DNA, genes, and the genome?

Genetic information is contained in chromosomes; a critical molecule found in the chromosome is deoxyribonucleic acid, or DNA, which contains the instructions for building an organism. These instructions are encoded in sequences of molecules that contain instructions for building *protein* molecules. A gene is a stretch of DNA that provides the full information needed to produce a protein. The genome is the entire set of genes for an organism.

How do we get from DNA to protein building?

In the process known as gene expression, a molecule in the cell reads the information in DNA and creates another molecule called ribonucleic acid, or RNA. The RNA, which contains the information needed for protein building, moves to a mechanism in the cell that contains the biochemical machinery needed to build those proteins. Once there, cellular machinery reads the information encoded in RNA, gathers the molecules needed to build a protein, and assembles them into a protein.

How do our experiences affect gene expression? In other words, how does nurture influence nature?

Environmental experiences "switch on" genes, causing them to become active in the production of proteins. For example, in one study, researchers found that people with one type of genetic makeup rarely contemplated suicide, no matter how many stressful events they experienced. However, among people genetically predisposed to experience depression, those who suffered a large number of stressful life events were far more likely than others to consider suicide.

How do characteristics—psychological and otherwise—evolve?

Nature selects them. In any naturally occurring environment, some features possessed by an organism are more adaptive than others, thereby helping organisms to survive and reproduce in that environment. Across generations, these features become more frequent because the reproducing organisms pass them down to their offspring.

According to evolutionary psychologists, how did the mind evolve to produce our contemporary mental abilities, desires, and preferences?

Some evolutionary psychologists propose that the human mind acquired mental modules: elements of the mind and nervous system that perform a specific task in response to a specific type of environmental input. According to this concept, elements of mind that evolved in the evolutionary past shape our present preferences (e.g., a male's preference for women with wide hips is a preference that evolved because it increased the odds of successfully reproducing).

What are three limitations of evolutionary explanations of the modern mind?

First, subsequent research findings failed to confirm some original findings. Second, much human mental activity cannot be explained by mental modules alone. Third, genes do not, by themselves, determine the nature of an organism; rather, organisms develop through dynamic interactions between nature and nurture.

Can evolutionary theory explain homosexuality?

Some scholars have suggested that homosexuality itself may not have evolved. Instead, what evolved is a particular gene that has different effects for men and women. In men, the gene increases the likelihood of homosexuality, whereas in women, it increases the likelihood of childbirth.

What does research suggest concerning the genetic basis of homosexuality?

Twin studies indicate that genetics explains slightly more than one-third of the overall variability in sexual orientation, whereas shared environmental factors have no effect at all. Prenatal factors may influence sexual orientation. Men who have larger numbers of older brothers are more likely to be homosexual, possibly because the mother's immune system recognizes a male child as biologically "foreign" (because she is female) and produces antibodies that affect fetal brain development in a way that increases the likelihood of homosexuality.

How do genes shape brain development?

Genetic information causes neurons to connect from one general region of the brain to another; however, these region-to-region connections are not precise enough for the brain to function properly. The brain requires experience to form the exact neuron-to-neuron connections.

How does environmental experience shape brain development?

Environmental experience influences the connections among brain cells. When environmental stimulation causes a group of neurons to fire at the same time, the interconnections among those neurons grow stronger. Connections among neurons that don't fire together grow weaker, and through neural pruning, these unneeded connections are eliminated. Environmental experience also affects neural connections by influencing gene expression.

Answers to What Do You Know?

1. (b) Nature and nurture are interdependent.
2. In cultures where people raised and milked dairy cows and encouraged the drinking of milk, possessing the gene that enabled lactose digestion would have been an evolutionary advantage because it would increase the odds of survival and it would enable one to pass along those same genes. Genes therefore depend on culture.
3. nature/genes; environment

4. We must conclude that genes are the likely cause.

5. All but *a* should be checked.

6. Items *a* and *c* should be checked.

7. DNA; genes; alleles; gene

8. alleles

9. In epigenetics, researchers study how the environment affects the expression of genes. Environmental experiences, such as stress, can determine whether or not a given gene is expressed. An epigenetics researcher would argue that neither nature nor nurture is more important to the process of gene expression; rather, nature is dependent on nurture.

10. gene

11. Sweating evolved to keep us cool in warm environments. Having the ability to sweat does not mean we will; it is a combination of the ability to sweat and a warm environment that causes us to sweat.

12. (a) T, (b) T, (c) F

13. The increase in pathogens could cause societies to adopt practices that would shield them from germs, such as fostering conformity and marrying within one's local group. Biology therefore shaped these collectivist cultural practices.

14. (a) T, (b) F, (c) T, (d) T

15. Genes can't entirely explain which neurons connect with which other neurons because there just isn't enough information in the genetic code to account for the trillions of neural interconnections.

16. wire; pruning; gene

Answers to Self-Test

1. c	6. d	11. b
2. b	7. d	12. b
3. a	8. a	13. c
4. b	9. a	14. d
5. b	10. a	15. a

CHAPTER 5
Chapter Summary

What is the difference between sensation and perception?

As biological mechanisms, sensation occurs when cells at the periphery of the body detect physical stimuli, and perception occurs when systems in the brain process these signals and produce conscious awareness of sensory inputs.

How are physical events translated into psychological events?

In transduction, physical stimuli reaching the body activate receptor cells in the body's nervous system; these cells then send nerve impulses toward the brain. Processing of the signals in the brain itself gives rise to perceptual and sensory experience.

How are we able to perceive depth even with one eye closed?

We rely on monocular cues such as converging vertical lines, variations in visual texture, occlusion, shading, clarity, and environmental context.

What are the advantages of having two eyes?

Binocularity's advantages include a "spare" eye, a wider visual field, and more accurate depth perception. The superior depth perception occurs thanks to two binocular cues to depth: stereopsis and convergence.

How does the visual system enable us to perceive motion?

Your visual system delivers information about the movement of an object in the environment (with respect to you, who are not moving), such that you can detect immediately not only that an object is moving, however slightly, but also where it's going and how fast. It also delivers information about your own movement through an environment (which is not moving).

How do past experiences and current context influence perception of shape?

There are several examples of this. One is that in the context of the numbers 12 and 14, a vertical line next to a curved letter "m" shape on its side looks like the number 13. In the context of letters, that same shape looks like a B. Another example concerns cultural contexts. As seen in this chapter's Cultural Opportunities, Japanese students, raised in a culture that values holistic thinking, were better at reproducing the relative (versus absolute) length of a line. North American students, raised in a culture that values analytic thinking, showed the opposite pattern of perception.

What does it take for us to notice whether someone dimmed the lights?

A just noticeable difference's (JND's) value depends on how much light is already in the environment. If a lot of light is present, then a larger change in illumination is needed for us to notice the change in brightness.

How does our attention to the overall environment enable us to experience color?

The psychological experience of color is determined not only by the wavelength of light, but also by our ability to mentally compute how changes in illumination in the environment will affect perception; this ability is responsible for color constancy.

Do colors have opposites?

Yes. For example, you can imagine a reddish brown but not a reddish green because red and green are opposites, as are yellow and blue. Opponent processes in perception create visual experiences that consist of these opposing color pairs. Biological mechanisms involved in perceiving one color weaken over time, which causes mechanisms that perceive the opposite color to dominate your perceptual experience.

Through what biological process are we able to convert light energy into information that is sent to the brain?

The cornea focuses light, which passes through the pupil, whose size is controlled by the iris. The lens further focuses incoming light, which is projected onto the retina, which contains two types of photoreceptors: rods and cones. The retina picks up most of its visual information during visual fixations, which occur between saccades.

How is visual information processed once it reaches the brain?

Rods and cones send information via ganglion cells, which form the optic nerve. These visual signals cross at the optic chiasm. After crossing, signals reach the lateral geniculate nucleus, which perform "computations" on these signals.

Given the complexity of visual information, how are we able to perceive objects accurately?

Visual properties such as the shape, brightness, texture, and color of objects influence one another, due to complex information processing in the cortex that integrates information about these perceptual features. This integration produces more accurate perception of objects.

What are the qualities of sound?

They are loudness, pitch, timbre, and location.

How do we know where a sound is coming from?

We use cues based on timing (how long it takes a sound to reach your right or left ear) and differences in pressure created by sound waves on our right and left ears. These cues can make right/left localization easy but can make front/back localization difficult. Up/down localization is made possible by the asymmetrical shape of the ear.

What psychological processes enable you to not only hear sounds, but also recognize them?

Auditory recognition—that is, recognizing sounds—requires you to maintain a sound in short-term memory, to activate knowledge of sounds stored in long-term memory, and to compare the two (the incoming sound and the sound stored in memory).

Through what biological process are we able to convert sound waves into meaningful information?

The outer ear captures sound waves and directs them down the auditory canal. In the middle ear, motion of the eardrum causes motion in ossicles, which, in turn, creates activity in the inner ear. Transduction occurs in the cochlea, which contains auditory hair cells whose movement triggers neural impulses that travel via the auditory nerve to the brain's auditory cortex, in the temporal lobe. Signals from the left ear reach the right side of the brain and vice versa. The auditory cortex is organized systematically according to pitch; similar sound wave frequencies are processed in neighboring areas. In addition, specialized regions of the auditory cortex process information about the location of sounds, the source of sounds, and vocalizations by members of one's own species.

What are some types of stimuli we can smell?

We can smell food, pheromones (though not as well as other species), and disease.

Through what biological process are we able to convert airborne chemical signals into information that is sent to the brain?

Signals from the receptor cells (activated by odorants, pheromones, and disease-related molecules in the air) are sent to the olfactory bulbs, which send information to the olfactory cortex, where the processing of the signals that allow you to recognize smells is completed.

Why are some people more sensitive to odors than others?

Researchers have been able to link genetic variations that produce variations in the number and diversity of receptors to individual differences in olfaction.

Besides salty and sweet, what are the other types of tastes we can detect? What the heck is umami?

Humans perceive five distinct taste qualities: sweet, salty, bitter, sour, and umami. Umami is a recently discovered quality; it corresponds to the taste sensation we usually call "savory."

Why don't all salty foods taste the same?

Even when two foods share a quality, such as saltiness, there are four other dimensions that can influence their taste. Hedonics refers to how much you like the taste. Localization is perception of where within the mouth a taste is experienced. Onset/aftertaste describes whether a taste will linger or vanish. Intensity describes the strength of the gustatory experience. Two foods might both be salty, but one could have a much greater intensity of saltiness than the other and perhaps a longer aftertaste, too.

What is the difference between flavor and taste?

When you eat, some of the perceptual information you gather comes from taste and some of it comes from smell. The combination of two perceptual systems—gustation and olfaction—contributes to its flavor.

What is a supertaster?

Supertasters are people whose have greater sensitivity to tastes than others.

Through what biological process are we able to convert gustatory information from our mouths to our brains?

When taste receptors, bundled together in taste buds, are stimulated by food chemicals, they release neurotransmitters that begin the process of transmitting gustatory information to the brain. Signals from taste receptors travel along neural pathways to the brain stem and then to the gustatory cortex, which is highly connected to other regions of the brain. This means that taste perception is affected by other sensory inputs and the overall state of the body. As we saw in This Just In, five distinct regions of the cortex process each of the five types of gustatory signals: sweet, salty, bitter, sour and umami.

On what parts of the body is touch perceived most accurately?

The greatest acuity is found at the fingers. The lowest is found at the shoulder, back, and areas of the leg.

How do hand and finger movements deliver information about texture, temperature, and hardness?

When you move your fingertips back and forth across the surface of an object, you acquire information about texture. To get temperature information, you hold your fingers still on an object's surface. Pressing against the surface of an object tells you how hard it is.

How do we detect mass?

We detect mass by holding objects and moving them around. Size influences judgments of weight; when given two objects of the same weight but different size, people judge the larger object to be lighter.

Through what biological process are we able to convert haptic information from our skin to our brains?

Cutaneous receptors convert physical stimulation into nervous-system impulses, which send impulses that travel to your spinal cord and then to your brain.

What is our sixth sense?

Our sixth sense is the kinesthetic system, the perceptual system that delivers information about the orientation of your body and its various parts.

What explains pain?

Nociceptors send electrical signals to the brain when activated by harmful stimuli, such as a cut or burn. Nociceptors send fast signals, which produce sudden, sharp pain, as well as slow signals, which produce prolonged, lingering, dull pain. According to the gate control theory of pain, the spinal cord contains a biological mechanism that acts like a gate. When it's closed, pain signals can't get past the spinal cord to the brain, so people don't feel pain even though their nociceptors have fired.

Why are we so good at recognizing faces?

Across the course of evolution, the ability to recognize others would have been critical to survival, reproduction, and the survival of offspring. Natural selection thus would have favored the evolution of this ability.

Does motivation—one's goals and desires—influence perception?

Yes. One example of research providing initial evidence on this question came from a study in which children estimated the size of either of two objects: (1) coins or (2) cardboard disks of the same size as coins. The children judged that the coins—a desired object—were larger than the disks, especially if the children were poor.

Do people hear only what they want to hear?

People can, in fact, selectively attend to some auditory information while simultaneously tuning out other information, although some unattended information can still grab attention.

Do people see only what they want to see?

People can, in fact, selectively attend to some visual information and simultaneously miss unexpected information.

Our perceptions—including what we see—are guided at least in part by current motives.

Answers to What Do You Know?

1. sensation; perception

2. receptor

3. When using analytic thinking, we analyze objects in terms of their distinct parts, thereby enabling us to easily reproduce them. When using holistic processing, we view objects in relation to their overall context, which fosters estimates of relative length. People of Asian cultures tend to engage in holistic processing, whereas those in North America tend to engage in analytic processing.

4. 1d, 2a, 3b, 4f, 5c, 6e

5. shape; just noticeable difference; color constancy; red

6. retinas; duration/length

7. 1g, 2d, 3h, 4f, 5e, 6c, 7b, 8a

8. (b) What is frequency? (c) What is timbre? (d) What is front/back localization? (e) What is up/down localization?

9. eardrum; ossicles; cochlea; hair; auditory; nerve; neighboring/nearby

10. (a) T, (b) F, (c) T

11. receptor; olfactory bulbs; olfactory; limbic; duration; genetic

12. The fifth type of taste is umami. It is triggered by proteins in foods, so its detection enables us to identify (and ingest) this vital nutrient. The experience of flavor combines the gustatory and olfaction systems.

13. receptors; gustatory; parietal

14. It means there is a direct spatial correspondence between activity in the different types of taste receptors and activity in different areas of the gustatory cortex.

15. (a) F, (b) T

16. cutaneous; breadth; speed

17. kinesthetic

18. Stimulating nocioreceptors does not guarantee pain according to the theory because people can use high-level thinking processes to close the gate, so to speak.

19. selection

20. needs/motives

21. The finding was that, even though people only attended to information in one ear, they could still notice personally relevant information, such as their names, presented in the unattended ear.

22. (a) T, (b) T

Answers to Self-Test

1. d	6. d	11. a
2. d	7. c	12. b
3. a	8. a	13. d
4. d	9. c	14. d
5. b	10. b	15. c

CHAPTER 6
Chapter Summary

What are some examples of everyday experiences that rely on the ability to remember?

Examples include experiences involving attitudes, personal goals, and perceptions of the type of person you are. Improvements in psychological well-being that result when people think about these experiences in a new way would not occur if they were unable to remember their attitudes, goals, and past experiences.

What is memory, and what do the cases of AJ and HM teach us about the varieties of remembering?

Memory is the capacity to retain knowledge. AJ and HM had exceptionally good (AJ) and poor (HM) abilities to retain some types of knowledge, but relatively ordinary abilities to retain other types of knowledge. This variability shows that there is more than one type of remembering.

What is sensory memory and what are two types of sensory memory?

Sensory memory is an ability to retain information that is based on the functioning of sensory systems. Two types of sensory memory are iconic memory, which is sensory memory of visual images, and echoic memory, which is sensory memory for sound.

What are short-term memory and encoding? What is the capacity of short-term memory?

Short-term memory is a system that enables people to keep a limited amount of information actively in mind for brief periods of time. Encoding is the process through which information is transferred from sensory memory to short-term memory. Contemporary evidence suggests that the capacity of short-term memory is four pieces of information.

Why do we forget information soon after it reaches short-term memory? What strategies can we use to reduce forgetting?

Two factors that cause people to forget information after it reaches short-term memory are decay, which is the fading of information from memory, and interference, which is a failure to retain information in short-term memory that occurs when material learned earlier or later prevents its retention. Both rehearsal and deep processing are strategies for reducing forgetting.

How does working memory differ from short-term memory? What are its three components?

Working memory expands the original concept of short-term memory by recognizing that there are three components, each of which keeps information in mind for brief periods of time: the phonological loop, visuospatial sketchpad, and central executive.

What is long-term memory? How long does it last? How much can it hold? What are different types of long-term memory?

Long-term memory is a mental system that stores knowledge for extended periods of time and whose capacity is essentially unlimited. The different types of long-term memory are semantic memory, which is memory for factual information; procedural memory, which is memory of how to do things; and episodic memory, which is memory for events.

One type of episodic memory is autobiographical memory. As described in Cultural Opportunities, American children, who are from an individualist culture, had more specific autobiographical memories than did Chinese children, who are from a collectivist culture.

Once information enters long term-memory, does it automatically become unforgettable?

No, in fact, it can take hours or days for information in long-term memory to consolidate, that is, to change from a fragile state in which information can be lost, to a more fixed state in which the memory is available relatively permanently.

What two factors enable us to retrieve information from long-term memory?

They are retrieval cues, which are bits of information related to memories you are trying to recall, and context, that is, contextual cues from the situation or environment you were in when you originally encountered the information you are trying to remember.

What is a network?

A network is any collection of interconnected elements, such as interconnected bits of information in memory.

In a semantic network model of memory, what determines how closely any two concepts in the mind are related?

In a semantic network model, the meaning of concepts determines how closely they are related. Concepts with similar meaning are related more closely.

Are people generally aware of when ideas in their minds have been primed?

No, people are not always aware of when ideas have been primed, which means that information can influence our thoughts and feelings without our even knowing it.

What are the basic elements in a parallel distributed processing model of mind?

The basic elements are simple units of knowledge that do nothing other than turn on or off. Concepts are represented in a PDP system by patterns of activation in large numbers of these units.

How does an embodied cognition approach to memory differ from semantic network and PDP models?

In semantic network and PDP models, perceptual systems play no role in remembering; they are active only when people first experience an event. In the embodied cognition model, perceptual and motor systems are what enable people to think about and remember events. Embodied cognition can help us understand physical metaphors, whereas semantic network and PDP models cannot.

How do errors of memory show that human memory processes differ substantially from memory storage in an electronic device, such as a computer's memory system?

Electronic devices record information passively, whereas human memory processes involve active thinking; unlike electronic devices, people combine different pieces of information creatively. When they do so, they sometimes exhibit errors of memory.

What is chunking and how does it increase the amount of information a person can store in short-term memory?

Chunking is a strategy for increasing the amount of information you can retain in short-term memory by combining different pieces of information into one "chunk." If each chunk contains a few pieces of information, then the overall amount of information in short-term memory increases.

What are mnemonics and how do they improve memory?

Mnemonics are strategies for organizing information in long-term memory. The organization makes it easier to find information in memory when it's needed, thereby improving memory.

What part of the brain is active when we concentrate on and manipulate information?

Contemporary evidence indicates that the frontal lobes are key to this working memory activity.

What brain systems are critical for the formation of more permanent memories? How can they be enhanced?

The hippocampus, a neural system within the temporal lobes, is critical for memory consolidation—that is, for the formation of permanent memories. Consolidation occurs during long-term potentiation, when cell-to-cell communications become more efficient due to changes in the biochemical processes through which brain cells influence one another's firing. The amygdala also takes part in this process, especially for the consolidation of information acquired during shallow processing. Research indicates that aerobic exercise can enhance memory by increasing the size of the hippocampus.

What brain system is critical for our ability to make cognitive maps?

The hippocampus is particularly critical for this ability, which is one of many spatial memory skills.

Does the way information is stored in the brain resemble the way a book is stored in a library?

No. A book is stored in a library in a single spot. By contrast, our memories for experiences are stored across multiple parts of the brain.

Answers to What Do You Know?

1. An ability to remember personal events coupled with an inability to engage in rote memorization suggests that there are different types of memory.

2. mind; brain

3. Participants did not know which tone would sound and therefore did not know which row they would have to report. Thus, they had to have stored *all* of the rows in iconic memory before hearing the tone in order to be correct, which they were.

4. F

5. (a) T, (b) F, (c) T, (d) F, (e) F, (f) T

6. store; semantic; procedural; explicit; happy

7. T

8. Any concepts that are semantically related to relocating may be primed, such as packing, boxes, a moving truck, and the like.

9. In the semantic network model, concepts are the simplest elements, whereas in the parallel distributed processing (PDP) model, units of knowledge are the simplest elements. These knowledge units resemble, in their processing, the simplest units of the brain, the neurons.

10. embodied; cold

11. Human memory processes are far more active than those of electronic devices. As Loftus's (1997) study illustrates, when people are asked to recall events that never happened, like getting lost in a shopping mall, their imaginations can lead them to experience false memories. Her research on biases in eyewitness memory illustrates that our experiences after an event can alter our memory for it (e.g., being asked how fast cars were traveling before they hit versus smashed into each other can affect estimates of speed).

12. The recollections of children from the United States were more specific than those of children from China, indicating that culture does, in fact, shape our memories.

13. 1b, 2c, 3a

14. lobes

15. temporal; potentiation; spatial; amygdala

16. According to parallel distributed processing models of memory, activity in the temporal cortex works to coordinate these different memories so you experience a coherent whole.

Answers to Self-Test

1. d	6. c	11. c
2. a	7. b	12. a
3. a	8. a	13. d
4. d	9. b	14. c
5. c	10. b	15. d

CHAPTER 7
Chapter Summary

What is an example of classical conditioning in everyday life?

In classical conditioning, we learn that one stimulus predicts another. For example, if you were in a relationship that broke up during a trip to an amusement park, you might avoid amusement parks because, for you, they "predict" a breakup.

In classical conditioning, what is the association that an animal learns?

In classical conditioning, animals learn an association between an unconditioned stimulus (US), which elicits reactions prior to any learning experiences, and a conditioned stimulus (CS), which originally is neutral but subsequently elicits a reaction, after being associated with the unconditioned stimulus.

What types of organisms learn through classical conditioning?

A wide range of organisms, from very simple (such as fruit flies) to very complex (such as humans), learn through classical conditioning.

Why did a research participant known as Little Albert become afraid of a small white rat during the course of a psychology experiment, when the rat itself did nothing to make Albert afraid?

Albert's fear developed through classical conditioning. Through classical conditioning, he learned to associate something that at first was not fear-provoking, the rat, with something that was fear-provoking, a loud noise. Once this association was formed, the rat elicited fear in Albert.

If you want to teach an animal to associate a conditioned stimulus with an unconditioned stimulus, about how long should you wait, after the conditioned stimulus, before presenting the unconditioned stimulus?

You should wait only a very brief amount of time—less than a second. If you wait longer, the animal will be slower to learn the CS–US connection.

In classical conditioning, if you slightly alter the conditioned stimulus that an animal previously has learned to associate with an unconditioned stimulus, what happens?

If you slightly alter the stimulus, organisms still respond, but not quite as strongly as they had responded to the original stimulus. This process is known as generalization.

In classical conditioning, what is extinction?

Extinction is a gradual lessening of a conditioned response when a CS is presented repeatedly without any presentations of the US.

What happens when a stimulus that normally produces a response in an organism is presented over and over again?

The organism habituates to the stimulus, that is, it responds to a lesser and lesser degree to the stimulus.

How does research on compensatory responses explain some cases of drug overdose?

Drug users sometimes suffer fatal overdoses from a drug when they use the drug in a setting in which they previously have not taken it. In the new situation, their bodies do not produce compensatory responses, the biological reactions that are the opposite of the effects of a stimulus and that counteract the drug effect. The absence of compensatory responses results in the overdose.

What is blocking and how did the discovery of blocking alter psychologists' understanding of the psychological processes involved in classical conditioning?

Blocking is a phenomenon in which animals fail to learn an association between a conditioned stimulus and an unconditioned stimulus that are repeatedly paired; specifically, they fail to learn the association when they already are able to predict the occurrence of the US, even before being exposed to the CS. It tells us that animals do not learn only about simple pairings of stimuli. Rather, they acquire information about the environment as a whole.

What happens when animals learn that they cannot control unpleasant outcomes they wish to avoid?

When animals learn that their own behavior cannot control unpleasant outcomes, they experience learned helplessness, a reduction in motivation that causes the animal to not even try to avoid outcomes that harm it.

How does conditioned taste aversion (the Garcia effect) provide information about the role of evolution and biology in classical conditioning?

The Garcia effect, which is the rapid learning of a connection between the taste of food and illness, shows that not all associations are learned in the same manner. Stimulus–response connections that were important to a species across the course of evolution are learned particularly rapidly.

Through what research strategy have scientists succeeded in identifying the biological bases of classical conditioning?

A valuable research strategy for identifying the biological bases of classical conditioning has been to study a simple organism that has relatively few neurons. Eric Kandel has pursued this strategy in studies of classical conditioning in *Aplysia*, a sea slug that has only about 20,000 neurons.

What happens at the level of the nervous system when an animal experiences habituation?

Neurons reduce the amount of neurotransmitters that they send. For example, when an *Aplysia* is touched by an object, it reflexively retracts its gill. When a stimulus strikes the *Aplysia* repeatedly, the neuron that detects this stimulus gradually sends lesser amounts of neurotransmitters to the neuron that controls motor movement. When this latter neuron receives fewer neurotransmitters, it is less likely to fire and to thus cause the gill to retract.

What is an example of operant conditioning in everyday life?

Consequences alter behavior. For example, when a parent "gives in" to a child's demands, the child is more likely to argue in the future because "giving in" is a positive consequence that raises the likelihood of the child repeating the behavior.

What are the two main differences between classical conditioning and operant conditioning?

Unlike classical conditioning, in which a stimulus triggers a subsequent response, in operant conditioning, a behavior is followed by a stimulus, known as a response consequence. In classical conditioning, behaviors are internal physiological reactions; in operant conditioning, they are actions that affect the external world.

What was the main research result in Thorndike's studies of how animals learn to escape from puzzle boxes?

Thorndike discovered that the time cats needed to escape from the box decreased across trials. Initially, it would take them a couple of minutes to escape, but eventually they could do so in just a matter of seconds. Thus, they learned from their trial-and-error experiences.

What is the law of effect?

The law of effect is a principle of learning which states that when an organism performs a behavior that leads to a satisfying outcome in a given situation, it will be more likely to perform that behavior when it encounters the same situation in the future.

In Skinner's analysis of operant conditioning, what is a reinforcer?

A reinforcer is any stimulus that occurs after a response and raises the future probability of that response.

What is the difference between positive and negative reinforcement?

In positive reinforcement, the occurrence of a stimulus increases the likelihood that the given type of behavior occurs. In negative reinforcement, the removal of an unpleasant stimulus increases the likelihood of a given type of behavior.

How does reinforcement differ from punishment?

Punishment is a stimulus that decreases the likelihood of a behavior. It differs from reinforcement (positive or negative), in that reinforcement *increases* the probability of the behavior.

What is a schedule of reinforcement?

A schedule of reinforcement is a timetable that indicates when reinforcers occur, in relation to the occurrence of behavior.

How do different reinforcement schedules affect behavior?

Different schedules of reinforcement produce different rates of behavior. For example, ratio schedules produce higher response rates than interval schedules.

What is a discriminative stimulus?

A discriminative stimulus is a stimulus that provides information about the relation between a behavior and a reinforcer. Specifically, a discriminative stimulus signals whether a behavior is or is not likely to be reinforced.

How does research on discriminative stimuli explain people's tendency to act differently in different situations?

Many everyday situations contain discriminative stimuli that indicate the type of behavior likely to be reinforced in that situation. Because these stimuli vary from one situation to another, and people respond to them, individuals' behavior varies from one situation to the next.

How can organisms learn complex behaviors through operant conditioning?

In operant conditioning, organisms learn complex behaviors through shaping, a step-by-step learning process in which, at first, psychologists reinforce behaviors that merely approximate a desired, final behavior.

What does it mean to say there are "biological constraints" on learning?

This means that it is difficult for organisms to learn some behaviors, in some situations, due to their inherited biology. The ability to learn the behavior, then, is "constrained" by their biological predispositions.

Do research findings in the study of biological constraints on learning confirm, or call into question, the principles of learning developed by Skinner?

Research findings in the study of biological constraints on learning indicate that some combinations of behavior and reinforcement fail to work; that is, the likelihood of behavior in organisms does not increase. Skinnerian principles presumed that all combinations of behavior and reinforcers would work the same way, and thus these principles are violated by such findings.

Why might rewards sometimes lower people's tendency to engage in an activity?

Rewards can lower people's tendency to engage in an activity when the activity initially is performed because it is interesting, but then the provision of rewards changes people's understanding of their own behavior, causing them to see it as something done not out of personal interest, but to gain external rewards.

How do psychologists know that the brain contains a "reward center"?

They know this thanks to research in which electrical stimulation of an area of the limbic system was used as a response consequence. Rats repeatedly pressed a lever in order to gain stimulation of this area. This brain region, then, was a reward center whose stimulation reinforced behavior. Subsequent research indicates that rewards influence behavior through their effect on the dopamine system.

How do the results of Bandura's Bobo doll experiment contradict the expectations of operant conditioning analyses of learning?

The results of the Bobo doll experiment contradict the expectations of an operant conditioning analysis in that children in the study learn a relatively complex behavior in the absence of reinforcement, which Skinnerians had seen as necessary to learning. Also, they learn without any gradual, step-by-step learning trials of the sort observed in Skinnerian analyses of shaping.

What psychological processes are involved in observational learning, that is, what processes are required for a person to learn to perform a behavior displayed by a psychological model?

The four subprocesses are attention (paying attention to the model's behavior), retention (retaining memory for the model's actions), production (using a mental representation of the model's behavior to guide your own behavior), and motivation (being motivated to perform the modeled behavior).

Can spanking increase aggression in children?

Research indicates that, in the long run, spanking is associated with an increase in children's aggressiveness. Evidence of this comes from a long-term study relating spanking at 3 years of age to level of aggressiveness at age 5.

Does research on the effects of spanking support theoretical predictions made by operant conditioning or observational learning analyses?

Spanking, a punishment for unruly behavior, fails to reduce that behavior, as you might expect from an operant conditioning analysis. Instead, the spanking seems to serve as a model of aggressive behavior and is associated with increases in aggressiveness in children, as you might expect from an observational learning analysis.

What is one way in which modern computer technology can enhance the power of modeling?

One way that this technology can enhance the power of modeling is through the use of *virtual representations of the self* (VRSs), in which people see an image of themselves performing a desired behavior. This technology enables learners to see a psychological model that is of great personal relevance to them.

What neural system directly contributes to organisms' tendency to imitate the behavior of others?

The brains of complex organisms—people and nonhuman animals—contain mirror neurons, which are neurons in the brain's motor cortex that fire not only when you engage in a certain type of action, but also when you observe someone else engage in that same action.

Answers to What Do You Know?

1. response or reaction
2. US = surprise; UR = startle; CS = tune; CR = startle
3. unconditioned; aversive noise; cookie jar; conditioned
4. 1c, 2a, 3b
5. US = nutrients from pork roll; UR = hunger reduction/increase in energy; CS = appearance/flavor of pork roll; CR = hunger reduction/increase in energy
6. (a) T, (b) F, (c) T
7. The neuron is sending lesser amounts of neurotransmitters to the neuron that controls motor movement.
8. F
9. (a) operant, (b) classical
10. This statement is incorrect because Thorndike's work with cats in puzzle boxes led him to conclude that cats can, in fact, learn through their experiences. This work led him to formulate the law of effect, which states that the likelihood of a behavior increases when followed by positive consequences.
11. 1bg, 2ae, 3dh, 4cf
12. replicate
13. A well-intentioned person might say things like "That must really hurt!" or "Are you okay?" which could unintentionally reinforce pain behavior and cause more pain.
14. ratio; variable; variable; punished; reinforced
15. (a) This statement is incorrect because it is, in fact, easier to teach a pigeon to peck than to flap its wings; this indicates that our evolutionary history *constrains* our ability to learn through operant conditioning.

    (b) This statement is incorrect because, contrary to what Skinner would have predicted, rewards can actually decrease the likelihood of a behavior, when people are intrinsically motivated to do something.
16. biologically/physiologically; dopamine
17. Skinner would have predicted that because the children had not been reinforced for engaging in the behaviors enacted by the model, they would be unlikely to engage in those same behaviors.

18. Though individuals may acquire the knowledge and therefore the potential to engage in aggression, they may not be sufficiently motivated to actually perform it.

19. If operant conditioning were more powerful than observational learning, spanking should decrease unruly and aggressive behavior.

20. Spanking is associated with increases in aggressiveness in children. In one study, spanking children at age 3 resulted in greater aggression at age 5, suggesting that parents had inadvertently modeled aggressive behavior.

21. virtual representations of self

22. mirror

Answers to Self-Test

1. a	6. d	11. b
2. c	7. b	12. c
3. a	8. a	13. a
4. d	9. d	14. d
5. b	10. a	15. b

CHAPTER 8
Chapter Summary

What categories are most natural to use?

The categories most natural to use are those that are basic-level: moderately abstract categories that provide a good combination of being informative and efficient.

What is the structure of categories?

Classical categories possess a set of features that determine, unambiguously, whether individual items belong to the category, whereas the boundaries of fuzzy categories are ambiguous. A family resemblance category is one in which category members share a large number of features, but no single feature is absolutely necessary for membership in the category. Within categories, prototype refers to the most central member of a category. Categories vary in abstraction. One category is more abstract than a second if the second category is contained within the first. Ad hoc categories are groupings of items that go together because they relate to a goal that people have in a specific situation.

Do dogs use language?

No, though they do communicate, often with scent. Language differs from general communication in two ways: (1) There is an arbitrary relation between words and things and (2) language's rules are generative.

How is language organized?

Language is organized by levels. At the highest level is conversation, followed by sentences, phrases, and words. Words are made up of parts called morphemes that themselves convey meaning. At the lowest level of analysis, language consists of sounds.

What do the rules of syntax do?

Rules of syntax specify whether a series of phrases form a sentence that is grammatically correct and how a core sentence can be transformed. A transformational grammar is the full set of rules that indicates how components of a sentence can be shifted around to create other sentences that are grammatically correct.

How do children acquire language?

B. F. Skinner proposed that children learn language through environmental rewards. Noam Chomsky proposed that all humans possess a mechanism in the brain that is dedicated to processing the syntax of language, that is, a universal grammar (although, as we saw in This Just In on universal grammar, more recent research indicates that grammar may not be as universal as Chomsky believed). Statistical language learning proposes that children acquire language by learning patterns of sounds and words that are statistically more common than others.

What did early discoveries in the study of language and the brain say about brain regions involved in producing and understanding language?

This evidence suggested that the brain contained two distinct regions dedicated entirely to, and independently responsible for, the use of language. One, Broca's area, produced grammatical language, and the other, Wernicke's area, was responsible for the understanding of spoken language.

How has contemporary brain imaging evidence altered scientists' earlier beliefs about language and the brain?

Contemporary brain imaging evidence reveals that multiple areas of the brain, beyond merely Broca's area and Wernicke's area, contribute to language use. Furthermore, Broca's area and Wernicke's area take part in psychological functions other than just language.

Why don't animals have language?

To answer this question, Herbert Terrace tried to teach a chimp, Nim Chimpsky, to use sign language to communicate. Terrace found that Nim never combined sequences of signs in a novel manner to express ideas—a behavior that defines language use.

Does language shape reality?

According to the Sapir–Whorf hypothesis, yes. The Sapir–Whorf hypothesis states that language shapes our thinking, implying that individuals who speak different languages could have fundamentally different views of reality.

What does research on the Sapir–Whorf hypothesis tell us about the effect of language on thinking?

One prediction from the Sapir–Whorf hypothesis is that if language affects thought, people who speak languages with different numbers of color terms should think differently about colors. However, a study by Berlin and Kay (1969) demonstrated that people who spoke different languages thought similarly about colors. This and other evidence contradict the Sapir–Whorf hypothesis and reminds us that people's thoughts about color are embodied cognitions determined, in part, by the workings of the visual system.

How do we know that thought influences language?

Psychologists have used as evidence the difficulty we experience when trying to express ideas in words that we already communicated by gesturing. Moreover, as we saw in Cultural Opportunities, there are cultural variations in patterns of thinking that are reflected in language. Individuals from Australia use more adjectives and fewer state verbs than do individuals from South Korea.

What psychological processes get in the way of good logical reasoning?

People's ability to reason logically is impaired by confirmation bias, the tendency to seek out information that is consistent with initial conclusions and to disregard information that might contradict them. Confirmation bias is dangerous because it may cause us to overlook important information.

Do people always have difficulty with logical reasoning?

No. Leda Cosmides's research demonstrates that people can reason accurately about problems involving the possibility of cheating when goods are exchanged, even if they do poorly on other reasoning tasks.

How do people judge the likelihood of uncertain events?

People judge the likelihood of uncertain events by using judgmental heuristics, which are simple cognitive procedures for making estimates that otherwise might be made through formal calculations. In the availability heuristic, people base their judgments on the ease with which information comes to mind. In the representativeness heuristic, people base judgments about the likelihood that an individual belongs to a given category on the degree to which the person or object resembles the category. In the anchoring-and-adjustment heuristic, people estimate an amount by formulating an initial guess (the "anchor") and adjusting it to reach a final judgment. These heuristics can be helpful but they can also lead us to make judgmental errors.

How logically do we make decisions?

Though the standard model of decision making suggests that we make decisions by considering the subjective value and net worth of outcomes, framing effects and mental accounting suggest that people are not always this logical. In a framing effect, people's decisions are influenced by the way that alternative choices are described, not by the subjective value of choices. In mental accounting, people divide their assets and expenditures into distinct cognitive categories and, in doing so, ignore net costs.

How do people solve problems?

We know the answer to this question thanks, in part, to think-aloud protocol analysis (see Research Toolkit). Because people can't envision a problem's entire problem space, they rely on problem-solving heuristics, such as means–ends analysis. In means–ends analysis, instead of imagining every possible step that could lead to a desired outcome, people simply try to reduce the distance between where they are now and where they want to end up.

How do computers solve problems?

Researchers studying problem solving have written computer programs that solve problems using means–ends analysis. When they compare the computer's performance to human performance, results are similar, which suggests that both computers and humans use a means–ends problem-solving strategy.

What determines how quickly we can rotate images in our head?

According to research by Shepard and colleagues, the time it takes people to rotate images correlates almost perfectly with the number of actual degrees the images must be mentally rotated.

What does research on mental distance suggest about how we use mental imagery?

Kosslyn and colleagues' research indicates that people take longer to answer a question about a mental image if they have to cover more distance across the image in their minds to do so.

What is—and isn't—intelligence?

Intelligence is the ability to acquire knowledge, to solve problems, and to use acquired knowledge to create new, valued products. It does not refer to personality traits, physical abilities, or specific skills.

How has intelligence been measured?

In the early 1900s, French psychologist Alfred Binet constructed a test including items important to school achievement: logical reasoning, vocabulary use, and factual knowledge. He found that individual differences in test performance predicted individual differences in classroom achievement, a finding that holds true today. A German psychologist, William Stern, supplemented Binet's efforts with a scoring system that included children's mental age in a formula for intelligence quotient, or IQ: IQ = (mental age/chronological age) × 100. When intelligence tests are given to adults, the tests are scored so that the mean score in a population is 100 and the standard deviation 15; about two-thirds of people, then, get IQ scores between 85 and 115.

Is there a "general" intelligence?

People's scores on tests measuring different mental abilities tend to correlate positively. These positive correlations can be explained by proposing that there exists general intelligence, an overall mental ability that affects performance on different types of tests.

What cognitive processes contribute to individual differences in general intelligence?

Individual differences in fluid intelligence, which refers to mental abilities that are useful in the performance of almost any challenging task that a person may attempt, can be explained by individual differences in working memory capacity, which refers to the ability to focus attention and avoid distraction.

Is inherited biology the only determinant of intelligence?

Four findings suggest that biological factors alone cannot explain people's level of intelligence. The first is the Flynn effect, which refers to the rise in a population's average IQ over time. This change has occurred over decades—too fast to be accounted for by genetic changes. The second is the finding that education increases intelligence. The third is that individual differences in intelligence can change over time. The fourth is that the effect of genes on intelligence depends on the population being studied.

Are there multiple types of intelligence?

According to Howard Gardner's multiple intelligences theory, people possess a number of different mental abilities, each of which is a distinct form of intelligence. He cites as evidence the existence of child prodigies. Another source of evidence is savant syndrome, characterized by mental impairment in most areas of life but exceptional performance in one domain. A third type of evidence consists of cases in which people develop exceptional intellectual abilities late in life, in the midst of declining overall mental capacity.

Do people with big brains tend to be smarter?

Yes, but the correlation is only of modest size, which means that many people with smaller brains can have relatively higher levels of intelligence, and vice versa.

How are brain connections related to intelligence?

Intelligent behavior requires the use of multiple regions of the brain. People who have relatively strong neural connections among these brain regions can process information more efficiently, and thus tend to get higher IQ scores.

Answers to What Do You Know?

1. furniture, chair, stool
2. chair
3. 1b, 2a, 3c
4. Answers will vary. Examples of prototypical sculptures include Rodin's *The Thinker* and Michelangelo's *David*.
5. sounds; generativity
6. 1c, 2d, 3a, 4b
7. universal
8. instinct; grammar; common; culture
9. (a) Easterner, (b) Westerner
10. (a) F, (b) F, (c) F, (d) T
11. Chimps cannot be said to use language because they do not take into account the knowledge and goals of the recipient of their communication and because they cannot combine components of language into an indefinite variety of sentences.
12. T
13. visual; Sapir–Whorf
14. a
15. All but *b* should be checked.
16. 1c, 2a, 3b
17. Most people will choose Protocol 2 because they tend to prefer a risky option over certain loss when the choice is framed in terms of avoiding loss (in this case, death).
18. Most people will answer yes for Choice #2 because, in Choice #1, the individual may have already mentally accounted for the $40 expenditure.
19. problem; means–ends
20. F
21. Only *a* should be checked.
22. T
23. It will take longer to report the color of the clown's shoes because there is a greater mental distance to cover.

24. Items *a, b,* and *e* should be checked.

25. If you were 10 and you scored the same as the average 10-year-old on an intelligence test, your mental age would be 10 and your IQ would be 100.

26. If you scored high on the WAIS Verbal Comprehension, Perceptual Reasoning, and Working Memory abilities, you can predict that you would score similarly on the WAIS Processing Speed ability because these scores tend to be positively correlated.

27. The ability to figure out how many events are in a decathlon by thinking about the similarity between the words "decathlon" and "decade" (choice *b*) is an example of fluid intelligence because the ability to compare word roots to determine their meaning is a skill you can apply broadly.

28. If an individual scores high on tests of fluid intelligence, you can predict that the capacity of his or her working memory will be relatively large.

29. F

30. All the research findings are consistent with the claim that intelligence cannot only be biologically determined.

31. prodigies; general; triarchic; knowledge-acquisition; executive; performance

32. volume/size; connected

Answers to Self-Test

1. a	6. c	11. a
2. b	7. a	12. c
3. d	8. c	13. a
4. d	9. b	14. d
5. b	10. b	15. c

CHAPTER 9
Chapter Summary

What could have made consciousness an "unmentionable topic" by the 1980s?

Behaviorists argued that because consciousness could not be directly measured, it could not be studied scientifically and therefore should be dropped from scientific investigation. In the 1960s, psychologists' interests were guided by the metaphor that human thinking processes are similar to a computer's information processing. Though computers can be said to think, they cannot be said to have feelings, so this metaphor left little room for studies of consciousness.

What does it mean to say that consciousness is "subjective"?

This means that it only exists, and can only be assessed, from the viewpoint of the individual who is having the conscious experience.

What psychological quality must something have in order to say that it has "consciousness"?

Consciousness involves feelings. Only beings with subjective feelings can be said to have consciousness.

On what basis did the French philosopher Rene Descartes declare that consciousness is a basic fact of life?

In searching for facts he could identify as true, Descartes concluded that the *only* thing he could not doubt was that he existed and that he had conscious experience. The act of doubting his existence further proved he existed because *someone* had to be doing the doubting.

When, during development, do humans first experience consciousness?

Consciousness begins before birth: In one study conducted with both 27- and 35-week-old fetuses (Shahidullah & Hepper, 1994), researchers found that all the fetuses were aware of a sound presented outside their mother's abdomen.

Do animals have consciousness? How do we know?

Yes. When animals perform tasks, they are distractible in much the same way that people are. Biological evidence indicates that the brain systems necessary for human consciousness exist in mammals other than humans.

Do animals have self-consciousness? How do we know?

Mirror self-recognition tests suggest that few animals show any sign of self-consciousness. Great apes and dolphins pass this test, but dogs and cats do not.

Why don't robots have consciousness?

Robots are programmed to process information according to logical rules. Consciousness involves not only logical thought, but also emotions, sensations, and other feelings.

Is the mind separate from the body?

According to dualism, the mind and body are said to be two separate entities. The physical body projects images of the world into one location in the brain, where the nonphysical mind views it.

What are some limitations of dualism?

One limitation is the mind–body problem. If the mind were a nonphysical entity, it would be impossible for it to influence the body. Another limitation is the homunculus problem. To say there is a structure in the brain that consciously experiences sights and sounds is to suggest that the brain contains a small conscious person-in-the-head, or homunculus, which raises the question: "How is it that the homunculus is conscious?"

How can one explain consciousness without proposing that the images of the outer world are reproduced within the brain?

In Daniel Dennett's theory of consciousness, the brain does not reproduce stimuli. It merely detects features of stimuli and makes guesses about what type of object is out there. In this theory, different parts of the brain detect different features. There is no "theatre" in the mind in which the world is reproduced.

What is the evolutionary advantage of consciousness?

Consciousness enables organisms to take different types of information into account, and combine these facts when deciding how to act.

How evolutionarily old is consciousness?

Consciousness has been around for about 300 million years.

What subsystems of the brain are necessary for an organism to have conscious experience? How do we know?

Thalamo-cortical circuits integrate activity in multiple brain regions and thus serve as a basis for consciousness. Research by Alkire et al. (2008) indicates that anesthetics induce unconsciousness by reducing activity in the thalamus, implying that the thalamo-cortical circuits are key to consciousness.

What characterizes REM and non-REM sleep?

During REM sleep, heart rate, blood pressure, and breathing rate vary, just as they do during waking periods, and men and women experience genital arousal. During non-REM sleep, heart rate and blood pressure are lower than when you are awake and are very consistent, as is your breathing rate. Body temperature drops during non-REM sleep. Brain activity during REM sleep resembles brain activity during waking periods far more than brain activity during non-REM sleep. People dream during both REM and non-REM sleep, but during REM sleep, dreams are more frequent and more vivid.

Why, during REM sleep, do our eyes move rapidly but our muscles stay relatively still?

Our eyes may be "scanning" the dream imagery or they themselves may contribute to the production of the dream images. Our bodies remain still because the brain changes the release of neurotransmitters that, during waking periods, activate cells that control motor movement.

What characterizes sleep stages?

During the first 90 minutes of sleep, you experience a series of three non-REM sleep stages during which heart and breathing rates progressively decrease, and brain waves look less like those that occur when you are awake. After about 90 minutes, instead of remaining in deep sleep, you emerge from it and experience your first period of REM sleep, after which you head back down again, through the non-REM stages. As this cycle repeats itself during the night, the REM periods become longer and you do not descend all the way down to the deepest stage of non-REM sleep.

How have sleep labs been used to study the timing of the body's internal clock?

Sleep labs can create an environment where external cues to length of day, such as patterns of light and dark, are altered from a 24-hour cycle. Research participants are monitored to see if shifts in the external environment change their biological rhythms. In one study, two groups spent a month living in a lab. One was placed on a 28-hour-day schedule, and the other on a 20-hour-day schedule. Results indicated that both groups had a 24-hour circadian rhythm.

Why do we sleep?

The low metabolic rate of non-REM sleep gives the body time to repair damage, though recent research indicates that sleep may only be necessary for repairing the brain, not the body as a whole. The mental activity of REM sleep may help the brain to establish neural connections required for processing stimuli when awake. Food needs may influence sleeping patterns.

In what ways does sleep deprivation impair performance?

Sleep deprivation can make individuals feel more anxious and depressed, and exhibit higher levels of paranoid thought. It can reduce the ability to concentrate, remember information, and solve problems, and it can also impair performance on activities that require sustained concentration and quick reactions, such as driving.

What characterizes sleep disorders?

Narcolepsy is a disorder in which people experience sudden, extreme feelings of sleepiness during the day that are sometimes accompanied by "microsleeps." In sleep apnea, people suffer from brief pauses in breathing which awaken them. Insomnia is a prolonged difficulty in falling asleep or staying asleep when you have an opportunity to sleep.

How bizarre is the content of our dreams?

Not very. People dream about conversations and work activities in school or a work environment; interactions with either romantic partners or family members, generally in indoor settings; sports activities; flying, fighting, or war (men's dreams); or shopping or colors (women's dreams); and motion, such as running or driving fast, combined with violence, threats, and fear.

Why do people dream?

According to Freud, dreams fulfill wishes, thereby releasing sexual and aggressive energies that would otherwise disrupt our sleep. According to the activation-synthesis theory, dreams are the brain's way of making sense of random brain signals. An evolutionary perspective is that dreams are mental simulations that serve as a kind of rehearsal for real-life threats.

What is meditation designed to do and what are its two main techniques?

Meditative methods are designed to increase people's ability to concentrate. In one technique, people concentrate their attention on a particular object or event while meditating. In a second method, people may try to clear their mind of all thoughts.

How do we know that meditation improves mental abilities?

In one study (Slagter et al., 2007), people who received meditation training showed greater increases in the ability to focus and sustain their attention on a task than did the control group.

Is everyone hypnotizable?

People differ considerably in their susceptibility to hypnosis.

How is a hypnotic state induced?

Participants are encouraged to focus their attention on an object while relaxing. The hypnotist provides suggestions to promote deep relaxation. If the person's eyes close, the hypnotist instructs the participant to focus on the words of the hypnotist, and then leads the person into a hypnotic state from which, the hypnotist suggests, the participant will not emerge until told to do so.

How do we know hypnosis works?

In one study (Hilgard et al., 1975), a hypnotist made two suggestions to participants: (1) They would not consciously experience any pain when one of their hands was placed in ice cold water but (2) a "hidden part" of them would be aware of the pain. The participants were then asked to put a hand in extremely cold water. Indeed, individuals did not consciously experience the pain of the ice water, though the "hidden part" did.

What are the effects of hallucinogens, opioids, stimulants, and depressants and how do they work?

Hallucinogens cause people to hallucinate and to lose contact with reality. The drug affects the actions of the neurotransmitter serotonin.

Opiate drugs such as morphine contain opioids, chemical substances that reduce pain by lessening the transmission of pain signals from the body to the brain. Opiates reduce pain but can also produce powerful feelings of euphoria and ecstasy, making them highly addictive.

Stimulants such as caffeine are psychoactive drugs that increase nervous system activity and thus enhance alertness and energy. Stimulants also can enhance people's sense of psychological well-being and self-esteem and can lower their inhibitions. Amphetamines are powerful stimulants that increase alertness and produce euphoric feelings by affecting multiple neurotransmitters, including dopamine.

Depressants are psychoactive drugs that reduce arousal in the central nervous system. In so doing, they can lower conscious experiences of excitability and anxiety. Depressants achieve these effects, in part, by increasing the effects of inhibitory neurotransmitters, that is, neurotransmitters that reduce activity in the brain. Benzodiazepines are depressants that activate the brain's reward center and thus produce pleasurable feelings.

Answers to What Do You Know?

1. (a) T, (b) F
2. phantom; subjective
3. Your bathroom scale cannot be said to have consciousness because even though it detects and responds to your weight, it does not *feel* the weight.
4. consciousness; born
5. Distractibility is evidence for consciousness because there would otherwise be nothing for the animal to be "distracted from."
6. The ability to recognize the self is a precursor to the ability to think about oneself.
7. feelings/emotions
8. (b) Who is Descartes? (c) What is the pineal gland?
9. a

10. b

11. (a) Dennett, (b) Descartes, (c) Dennett

12. Items *b* and *c* should be checked.

13. (a) T, (b) T, (c) F

14. This statement is incorrect because modern research suggests that it is the integrated workings of several brain structures that produce consciousness; key among them are the thalamus and cortex.

15. (a) F, (b) F

16. Items *a, e, f,* and *h* describe REM sleep; items *b, c, d,* and *g* describe non-REM sleep.

17. sleep; circadian

18. Items *a* and *c* should be checked.

19. attention; 20%; narcolepsy; sleep apnea; insomnia

20. bizarre; higher

21. 1b, 2c, 3a

22. Items *b* and *d* should be checked.

23. All but *c* should be checked.

24. induction; hypnotized; suggestible; implicit; brain

25. LSD, morphine, stimulant, dopamine; hallucinogen; alcohol; inhibitory; excitatory

Answers to Self-Test

1. b	6. b	11. c
2. c	7. a	12. d
3. d	8. a	13. c
4. a	9. d	14. b
5. b	10. a	15. b

CHAPTER 10
Chapter Summary

What are the four key components of an emotion?

An emotion is a psychological state that combines (1) feelings, (2) thoughts, and (3) bodily arousal and that often has (4) a distinctive accompanying facial expression. In the Research Toolkit, you learned that the Facial Action Coding System (FACS) is a system for detecting emotions from facial expressions that avoids reliance on self-reports.

How do moods differ from emotions?

Moods last longer than emotions; moods are not necessarily accompanied by a specific pattern of thinking; and moods are not strongly linked to facial expressions.

What are four psychological activities that we can accomplish with the help of emotions?

Emotions can aid in our decision making; they have motivational power; they communicate information; and they support moral judgments.

How does our thinking affect our emotions?

Emotions result from the meaning that people give to events, not from the events themselves. If thinking varies from person to person, so too will emotions. This idea was well illustrated in research presented in Cultural Opportunities, where you learned that Hindu women in northern India, who are part of a culture that values social obligation, feel the emotion *lajja* when they sense that they are behaving consistently with those values. People from cultures that don't emphasize those values do not experience lajja.

What kinds of thoughts influence emotional experience?

According to appraisal theories of emotion, a small number of appraisals can generate a wide variety of emotional experiences. They include appraisals of: motivational significance (is the event relevant to my concerns and goals?), motivational congruence (does it facilitate my goals or hinder them?), accountability (who is to blame or who deserves credit for an event?), future expectancy (can things change?), problem-focused coping potential (can I myself bring about change that solves a problem?), and emotion-focused coping potential (can I adjust, psychologically, to the event?).

What can we do to control our emotions? What shouldn't we do?

Because appraisals shape emotion, people can control emotions by altering their anticipatory appraisals, the thoughts they have prior to the occurrence of an event. For example, when children are taught to think of a marshmallow as a ball they can play with rather than a food, they are able to refrain from eating it. Altering anticipatory appraisals is more effective than emotion suppression, which can ironically increase arousal.

How well can we predict the degree of our happiness if we win a lot of money?

Not very well. People tend to overestimate the impact of life events on emotions. They anticipate that bad events will be emotionally worse and good events more emotionally uplifting than they actually turn out to be. In This Just In, you further learned that when predicting our happiness, we shouldn't overestimate the effect of genes. As it turns out, social factors, such as setting goals for altruistic behavior, can increase happiness.

What does it mean to say that we can describe any mood with two simple structures: valence and arousal?

Arousal refers to the level of activation of the body and brain during the mood state. Valence refers to the positivity or negativity of the mood. By combining these two dimensions, psychologists can describe the full variation in mood in terms of a two-dimensional structure that functions like a map. No matter what your mood at any given time, it can be located somewhere in the "mood map."

What activities have been demonstrated to improve mood?

One activity is exercise, including yoga, which can increase positive emotions and decrease negative arousal (stress). The same is true of massage therapy. Other activities include listening to music and singing.

Can today's weather influence how satisfied we are with life in general?

Yes. The mood-as-information hypothesis proposes that people evaluate life satisfaction by consulting their feelings. One implication is that irrelevant factors, such as the weather, may affect people's evaluations. This was supported by an experiment whose results indicated that people who were interviewed on a sunny day evaluated their life more positively than did people interviewed on a rainy day.

Are people more likely to help others when in a positive mood or a negative mood?

Research suggests that people are much more likely to help if they are in a positive mood. Even subtle influences on mood can affect willingness to help, such as finding a small amount of money.

Do we first have to experience bodily arousal in order to experience an emotion?

According to the James–Lange theory of emotion, yes. When an event occurs, your brain receives information from sensory systems and generates a bodily response, arousal. The body then alerts the brain of this arousal, and you experience an emotion. The Cannon–Bard theory of emotion, on the other hand, suggests that bodily arousal does not precede, and is not the cause of, emotion. Instead, information about emotionally arousing events travels from the sensory system to structures in the brain's limbic system, which simultaneously produces the experience of emotion and generates the bodily changes that are distinctive of emotion.

Are all emotions produced via the same process, and according to a step-by-step sequence of events, as the James–Lange and Cannon–Bard theories had predicted?

No. Contemporary researchers recognize that multiple processes contribute to emotional experience. Moreover, contemporary research on the brain shows that large numbers of brain events occur simultaneously.

What subcortical brain structures are key to emotional life? How do we know?

The limbic system, a set of brain structures that resides below the cortex and above the brain stem, is key to emotional life. A structure within the limbic system that is particularly important to emotional response is the amygdala, which is especially active in processing fear-inducing events. Evidence of this comes from the remarkable case of SM, a woman who experienced bilateral amygdala damage and, consequently, showed no fear.

How can we explain the psychologically complex phenomenon of emotional experience at the biological level of analysis?

A biological analysis of emotion must include the brain structure that underlies the psychological components of emotion (thoughts, feeling, motivations, and facial expressions): the cortex. It must also include the interconnections between the cortex and limbic system, to account for the synchronization of the psychological components. Evidence from studies using brain-imaging methods confirms that six interconnected groups of neural systems contribute to the complex phenomenon of emotional experience: two in the limbic system and four in the cortex.

How do psychologists classify environmental stressors? Are they always negative?

Researchers distinguish among three types of stressors: harms (damaging events that have already occurred), threats (potentially damaging events that might occur in the future), and challenges (upcoming or ongoing activities that pose difficulties and that are damaging if you cannot handle them). Acute stressors last a brief amount of time, whereas chronic stressors are present through a prolonged period of a person's life. Stressors are often negative events, but they can also include positive events that require life adjustments, which can be challenging.

What psychological features determine whether we experience a given environment as stressful?

People experience subjective stress when situational demands and personal resources are out of balance; if demands outweigh resources, stress results. Likewise, when personal resources greatly outweigh situational demands, people become bored, and the boredom itself can be stressful.

Through what biological process do our bodies enable us to respond adaptively to stress?

When you experience a stressor, your body produces a stress response, a coordinated series of physiological changes that prepare you to confront or flee the stressor. Your heart rate increases to deliver more oxygen to muscles; your thinking changes to focus your attention on the stressor; and your immune system alters its functioning.

Selye's general adaptation syndrome (GAS) is a sequence of physiological reactions that occur in response to stressors. The first stage is alarm reaction; when a stressor first occurs, the body produces the stress response described above. The second is resistance; if a stressor continues to be present, the immune system responds by "working overtime." If a chronic stressor persists long enough, we may experience the third stage, exhaustion, when we run out of energy and are at high risk of illness.

What is the role of hormones in the stress response?

The central system involved in stress reactions is the hypothalamic–pituitary–adrenal (HPA) axis. A sequence of hormone-releasing activities occurs when the hypothalamus is activated by stress. First, the hypothalamus releases corticotropin-releasing hormone (CRH) into a duct that leads to the pituitary gland. CRH causes the pituitary gland to release adrenocorticotropic hormone (ACTH), which is carried by the bloodstream to the adrenal glands. Finally, ATCH causes the adrenal glands to release cortisol into the bloodstream, which increases heart rate and blood sugar, thus energizing the body to react to stress.

How does stress affect the functioning of our immune system? What are the implications for health?

Short-term stressors increase immune system activity, whereas long-term or chronic stress suppresses the immune system. When immune system functioning is impaired, people experience poor health.

How can researchers test the effects of stress on immune system functioning in a way that controls for how hectic one's life is?

They can take an experimental approach, as Sheldon Cohen and colleagues did. They randomly assigned participants to receive nasal drops that contained either a respiratory virus or a mixture of salt and water. They then quarantined participants in their apartments to control for virus exposure. Each day, a physician examined each participant and the researchers measured their subjective stress. Results indicated that, among those receiving the respiratory virus, people who reported more subjective stress were more likely to develop colds.

How can stress make us old before our time?

Stress influences aging by affecting telomeres, small strands of DNA at the end of each chromosome that maintain a cell's "youthfulness." When a cell loses too much of its telomere, it cannot replicate.

When coping with stressful events, is it more advantageous to try to change the problem or to focus on one's emotions?

It depends. Focusing on problems to be solved can be advantageous unless, for instance, the problem is out of your control. Then it may be better to work on your emotional state. Research indicates that coping flexibly is advantageous.

How and why do men and women's coping strategies differ?

When faced with a stressor, people may engage in a fight-or-flight coping strategy or a tend-and-befriend strategy. Women use the tend-and-befriend strategy more than men do, perhaps because they have been more heavily involved in parenting than males. Fighting and fleeing isn't very compatible with protecting offspring and isn't always possible during advanced stages of pregnancy. Tending to the needs of offspring helps them survive during times of stress, and befriending others creates social networks that can help to support the mother.

How is social support beneficial to physical and mental health?

Even before a stressor occurs, social support aids in health by increasing our sense of well-being. Once a stressor, such as the difficulty associated with parenting, is present, social support from others can "buffer" its impact on emotions. Positive emotional social support between partners helps maintain marriages.

Answers to What Do You Know?

1. You would need to ask, "Did I experience bodily arousal?"

2. (a) mood, (b) mood, (c) emotion, (d) emotion

3. The text describes three problems with relying on self-report of emotions, all of which are relevant to measuring happiness: (1) People may try to create a positive impression by over- or underreporting happiness levels; (2) people may inaccurately report happiness levels because they change so often; and (3) asking people to report their levels of happiness may itself influence their happiness.

4. 1b, 2a, 3d, 4c

5. Answers will vary. Here is an example.
   Motivational significance: Failing an exam is certainly relevant to my goal to do well in school.
   Motivational congruence: This failure hinders my goal to do well in school.
   Accountability: The exam was difficult, but I could have studied harder, so I share the blame.
   Future expectancy: Things can change for the better.
   Problem-focused coping potential: Next time, I can study more often.

6. (a) This statement is incorrect because *lajja* cannot be said to be universal. It is not experienced by individuals in individualistic cultures such as in the United States.
(b) This statement is incorrect because appraisal theories of emotion are particularly well suited to explaining cultural differences in emotional experience. These theories suggest that emotions are shaped by people's beliefs—beliefs that are shaped, in part, by culture.

7. appraisals; suppression; over

8. All but *b* and *d* should be checked.

9. Sluggish: negative, low arousal; peppy: positive, high arousal; depressed: negative, low arousal; energetic: positive, high arousal

10. All but *b* should be checked.

11. If the company wants honest feedback, it would be better off giving the gift after people fill out the questionnaire. That way, the positive mood elicited by the gift cannot influence their judgments.

12. (a) T, (b) F

13. amygdala; scary; fear

14. 1a, 2c, 3b

15. balance; subjective; adaptation; alarm; resistance; exhaustion; hypothalamic; hypothalamus; adrenocorticotropic; cortisol

16. short; long; heart; stress; telomeres

17. (a) T, (b) F, (c) F, (d) T

Answers to Self-Test

1. b	6. d	11. c
2. a	7. b	12. d
3. d	8. a	13. d
4. c	9. a	14. b
5. b	10. a	15. b

CHAPTER 11
Chapter Summary

What did Maslow mean when saying that the needs that motivate human behavior form a hierarchy?

Maslow meant that needs exist at different levels and a person has to fulfill lower-level needs (e.g., biological survival needs like eating) in order to progressively move up to the highest level, self-actualization.

Does hunger alone motivate us to eat?

No. Set-point theories of hunger and eating propose that we eat to maintain an energy homeostasis, but they can't explain why we eat when we are not hungry. Hedonic hunger arises when delicious-looking food whets our appetite. This hunger was likely naturally selected, because it caused us to eat when food was available, thereby protecting us for times when food was unavailable.

What characterizes eating disorders? What causes them?

Anorexia nervosa is characterized by a fear of being fat, which results in individuals starving themselves, often so severely that they experience bone thinning and loss of muscle mass. Bulimia nervosa is characterized by a fluctuating pattern of binging and purging, often through self-induced vomiting. It can result in dehydration and tooth decay, among other problems. Binge eating disorder is characterized by binging without purging and can cause obesity. Eating disorders can be caused by factors that include social pressures for thinness, parental criticism, and perfectionism.

How does sexual motivation differ from the motivation to eat?

First, a person can live without sex but cannot live without food. Second, the diversity of behaviors associated with sexual motivation exceeds that associated with hunger; there is a diversity of people to whom sexual desires are directed and a diversity of stimuli that trigger sexual arousal. Moreover, sexual desires motivate diverse activities, including a range of behaviors that are not inherently sexual. Finally, there is a greater diversity of reasons for having sex.

What is the biological basis of sexual desire?

Experimental research indicates that testosterone plays a role in motivating sexual desire.

Is everyone equally motivated to achieve? How can we measure the need for achievement?

People differ in the strength of their need to achieve. Researchers assess these individual differences through indirect measures, such as asking participants to tell stories in response to pictures. People who tell stories about characters striving to achieve and who are concerned about success are people high in the need for achievement.

What kind of person is most likely to seek out challenges?

Research indicates that participants who are high in need for achievement and low in need to avoid failure tend to seek out greater challenges, relative to those who are low in need for achievement and high in the need to avoid failure, who tend to be more cautious.

Does everyone feel the need to belong?

Yes. Research suggests that the need to belong is universal. Many argue that this need is rooted in our evolutionary past. People who felt a need to belong benefited from the safety advantages of group living.

Are we satisfied with a vague understanding of events?

No. In pursuit of our need for understanding, we want to achieve not merely a vague grasp of events, but cognitive closure, a firm understanding that resolves ambiguities and eliminates confusion.

How do we benefit from having control over outcomes?

The need for control encompasses a need for autonomy and a need for mastery. Students whose teachers give them more autonomy over their classroom experiences show greater interest in school material. Cancer patients who respond to their diagnosis with feelings of mastery are better able to battle the disease. They report less pain and fatigue during treatment.

What kinds of behaviors are explained by the need to enhance the self?

The need to enhance the self can help us understand why we pursue goals related to spiritualism. For example, in medieval Europe, most citizens lived in relative poverty but societies spent hundreds of millions of dollars building great cathedrals. In the contemporary world, many people expend great time and effort on spiritual aims. These expenditures can't be explained by suggesting that we are only motivated by biological needs.

What are everyday examples of our uniquely human need for trust?

Much of everyday social life rests on trust. A grocery store gives you food in exchange for your signature on a piece of paper. You give money to bank tellers, trusting they will deposit it.

What is the biological basis of trust?

Experimental research suggests that the biochemical basis of trust is oxytocin, a hormone released into the body and the brain whose primary function is to aid the birth and survival of children. However, as you saw in This Just In, the effect of oxytocin can further depend on individual difference variables, such as one's level of social skills and the degree to which one is anxious about relationships.

What kinds of goals are most motivationally powerful?

The most motivationally powerful goals are specific and challenging, yet within the confines of your potential abilities. In addition, the proximity of goals is important. Proximal goals are those that specify what you should do in the short-term future and seem more manageable than distal goals, which specify what you should do in the distant future and can be overwhelming.

How important is feedback in motivation?

Experimental research indicates that having specific goals and specific feedback can be highly motivating because they provide people with the opportunity to become angry with themselves when they fall short and to feel proud when they succeed.

What type of goals can impose organization on our lives?

Personal projects are goals that (1) incorporate a number of different actions with a common purpose that (2) extend over a significant period of time. An example is getting into graduate school. One must engage in several diverse activities toward that goal, over a period of time. Personal projects lend organization to life by giving meaning to what might otherwise seem to be a series of disconnected behaviors.

Can features of the environment activate goals that affect our behavior without our awareness?

Yes. For example, in one study, participants who had been exposed to achievement-related words via a word-search puzzle later worked harder on a subsequent task than those who had been exposed to neutral words.

How detailed should we be in our goal setting?

Very detailed, according to research on implementation intentions. In one study, most participants who specified when and where they would write a report actually wrote the report, whereas two-thirds of the participants with no implementation intentions failed to do so.

Can implementation intentions motivate you to save for retirement?

Not easily. It's difficult to focus on the *when* and *where* of behavior for goals that are distal and abstract. In one study, however, researchers were able to increase participants' willingness to save for their retirement by digitizing photographs of participants to make them look older. The participants who viewed their "older selves" were led to see their future selves as less abstract and put more hypothetical money into a retirement plan than did other participants.

Can your belief in your own capacity for growth influence motivation?

Yes. Unlike people with a fixed mindset, who believe intelligence is fixed, those with a growth mindset see intelligence as something that can be changed; they consequently tend to interpret difficult tasks as opportunities to learn, seeing challenges and setbacks as opportunities to grow their skills. Those with a fixed mindset tend to interpret setbacks as signs that they don't have enough intelligence. Consequently, they experience discouragement and reduced motivation.

Why does motivation decrease when we receive external rewards for activities we enjoy?

When people are intrinsically motivated to engage in an activity, and then receive an external reward for doing so, their intrinsic motivation goes down because those rewards reduce their sense of autonomy. However, as you saw in Cultural Opportunities, this general finding may not replicate across all cultures. In one Asian American sample and two Indian samples, autonomy actually decreased motivation.

When working toward a goal, should you focus on strategies that can help you achieve your goal or strategies that can help you avoid failure?

That depends on whether you are promotion- or prevention-focused. If you are promotion-focused, a better regulatory fit for you would be to select accomplishment strategies, such as completing your work on time. If you are prevention-focused, a better regulatory fit for you would be to select avoidance strategies, such as to stop procrastinating.

How can you achieve a "flow" state?

The two key ingredients for creating flow states are the presence of (1) activities that are challenging yet do not exceed people's skills, and (2) clear task goals and feedback. Any activity with these ingredients can provide a sense of flow. Our knowledge of flow states has benefited greatly from research that employs experience sampling methods, as you saw in Research Toolkit.

Does the presence of others improve or worsen performance?

It can do both. The presence of others increases the strength of a dominant response, which is the response that is most likely in a given setting. On tasks in which you have less skill, this response is the wrong response, and so the presence of others will decrease performance. On tasks for which you're highly skilled, the presence of others should enhance performance.

Do school grades measure intelligence or self-discipline?

Research indicates that self-discipline is often a more important predictor of grades than is intelligence.

How can teachers increase students' motivation?

They can do so by helping students set a goal of learning and mastering material, rather than merely earning high grades. They can also adopt a mindset program, in which they teach students that the brain changes with experience. Research indicates that doing so decreases students' concern with "smarts" and encourages them to put more effort into learning material. However, if students do not associate academic success with their personal worth or if they live in settings in which school success is not valued in their peer group, they may be less personally invested in school success.

What payment plan should you adopt if you want to motivate your employees?

In settings in which employees work individually, companies can maximize productivity by paying individuals according to the amount of work each individual has produced. In settings in which people work in coordinated teams, companies can maximize productivity by paying everyone in the group roughly the same amount of money, and providing pay raises based on the success of the group as a whole.

What type of leadership style is most motivating?

Transformational leadership predicts greater employee motivation and greater satisfaction with the leader, relative to transactional leadership, in which the leader simply appeals to workers' self-interest by providing rewards to them if they meet objectives.

What are the biological bases of approach and avoidance motivation?

Signals of reward activate the behavioral approach system, energizing the organism to seek out those stimuli. The neurotransmitter dopamine is the biochemical key to this system and the exact neural structures within the brain are the brain stem and limbic system. Dopamine travels along a bundle of nerve fibers, the medial forebrain bundle, to a set of neurons that is central to the pursuit of rewards, the nucleus accumbens. Signals of punishment activate the behavioral inhibition system, prompting the organism to attend to environmental threats. The most important neurotransmitter is serotonin, and the key neural systems are in the hippocampus and the amygdala.

What is the biological basis of addiction?

Addictive substances affect the brain's reward system by increasing dopamine activity. Addiction can reduce the normal functioning of the brain's reward system so that naturally occurring events become less rewarding and people lose motivation for everyday activities. Addiction can also increase the activity of brain systems that produce emotionally negative withdrawal states when a person's levels of an addictive substance are low.

What brain regions are active during goal processing?

One brain-imaging study indicated that two different brain regions were active during goal processing: the posterior cingulate cortex, which is known to be active when people think about future events, and the ventral medial prefrontal cortex, which is involved in computing the degree to which a piece of information is valuable to oneself. Activation in these two areas of the brain is consistent with a psychological analysis of goal processing.

Answers to What Do You Know?

1. The statement is incorrect because there are notable exceptions. The *sādhus* of South Asia, for example, are Hindus who prioritize spiritual enlightenment over biological survival and safety needs.

2. homeostasis; hedonic; anorexia nervosa; perfectionism

3. (a) F, (b) F

4. You can tell your friend that people's responses to these measures have been shown to predict their future levels of professional success.

5. (a) It is not very challenging to get the ring on the peg from very close distance. From a far distance, the challenge is so great that it ironically ceases to be challenging, because no one expects the ring-tosser to succeed.
(b) The middle distance is considered challenging because it is not too easy but also not so difficult as to be impossible to succeed.

6. (b) What is the need for belonging?
(c) What is physical pain?

7. social; closure

8. In autonomy, you control your own behavior so it is consistent with your sense of self. In mastery, you have the ability to control your outcomes.

9. Training for a marathon would be an example of self-actualization because self-actualization is part of the need to enhance the self, which not only encompasses the need to engage in activities that are psychologically meaningful and potentially beneficial to others, but also those that realize your true potential.

10. genetically; oxytocin

11. Only *a* and *b* should be checked.

12. (a) F, (b) F, (c) T, (d) T, (e) T

13. You would need to specify when and where you would read it.

14. Answers will vary. One possibility would be to look at your parents or others who are similar to you and older than you, to get an idea of what you may be like in the future.

15. This statement is incorrect because research contradicts it. Asian American children were less motivated on tasks that they themselves chose. Moreover, among Indians, choice of pen had no effect, but among Americans, choice of pen increased its liking.

16. 1c, 2f, 3b, 4a, 5e, 6d

17. All but *c* should be checked.

18. All but *d* should be checked.

19. intelligence; mastery; grades; worth/regard/esteem

20. 1a, 2b, 3b

21. (a) ii, (b) i, (c) ii, (d) ii, (e) ii, (f) i, (g) i, (h) i

22. reward; increasing; cocaine; reward/brain

23. future; cortex

Answers to Self-Test

1. b	6. d	11. a
2. b	7. d	12. c
3. b	8. c	13. d
4. c	9. c	14. c
5. c	10. d	15. b

CHAPTER 12
Chapter Summary

How does treating a crowd as a physical object help us understand behavior?

In the case of the overcrowding of a pedestrian bridge in Mecca that led to the deaths of 345 religious pilgrims, treating the crowd as fluid helped researchers to identify a nonpsychological factor that could explain the tragedy: a narrowing of the bridge.

How do we know that social norms—and not anonymity—shape crowd behavior?

A summary of 60 experiments on aggression in crowds did not support the view that anonymity causes aggression. The results instead suggested that crowds cause people to tune into social norms to guide their behavior. Another factor in crowd violence, as revealed in qualitative data, is that a few people in the crowd who intend to act violently are often responsible for a large percentage of the damage that a crowd causes.

How does a crowd's actual response to disaster square with how the media portrays it?

Contrary to what movies and TV might have us believe, widespread panic during disaster is rare. People often react relatively calmly and adhere to social norms. Many even pitch in to help, owing to the sense of shared identity that develops.

What is the minimum group size necessary for people to cave in to conformity?

Solomon Asch found that individuals were more likely to conform to the opinions of others when the group contained as few as three other people, especially when all the other group members were unanimous in their opinions. The other group members consisted of confederates, described in the Research Toolkit of this chapter.

How can you get someone to comply with a request?

One example is the foot-in-the-door technique, a compliance strategy in which people first make a small request, as a means of later convincing people to comply with a larger request. Another strategy is the disrupt-then-reframe technique, which enhances compliance by disrupting an individual's ability to think of the costs of complying.

What are the implications of Milgram's research on obedience to authority?

Milgram's research showed that people will obey authorities even when ordered to harm others and even when the person giving the orders doesn't have a lot of authority. This implies that people of greater authority might be able to induce widespread obedience to orders. Numerous instances of genocide bear this out.

Can wearing the uniform of a prison guard cause you to be abusive?

According to the Stanford Prison experiment, yes. In that study, ordinary people were assigned randomly to the role of prisoner or guard. Even though they had never been in prison themselves, all had a sense of what is expected of prisoners and guards. In the case of guards, this caused them to act accordingly, by being abusive.

What force is powerful enough to reduce group rivalry?

As seen in Sherif's Robber's Cave study, group rivalry was eliminated when opposing groups were presented with challenges that could only be accomplished if the groups worked together.

When people don't intervene during an emergency, is it because they are callous and uncaring?

Not typically. As seen in research by Darley and Latané on the bystander effect, group size strongly influences the degree to which people intervene during an emergency. People respond less quickly when lots of people are around because there is a diffusion of responsibility—a sense that someone else is responsible for intervening.

What is the most sure-fire strategy to get someone to like you?

Become their next-door neighbor. Research indicates that physical proximity is a great predictor of friendship.

To attract a mate, should you emphasize your psychological strengths or your physical attractiveness?

You should definitely emphasize your physical attractiveness. Experimental research indicates that physical attractiveness strongly predicts romantic attraction, whereas psychological strengths are less predictive. In the "real world," however, people tend to strategically look for mates who match them in attractiveness.

Is romantic love anything more than sexual passion? How long does it last?

In one study, participants rated three components of love as being central: passion, intimacy, and commitment. All three components can last a lifetime—even passion, according to both qualitative and quantitative research.

How is love like a drug?

Results of a brain-imaging experiment indicated that, when people were exposed to a hot (painful) stimulus, simply viewing a picture of one's romantic partner at the same time reduced pain by stimulating reward centers in the brain.

How good are we at figuring out the causes of others' behavior?

Research indicates that people often make the fundamental attribution error—that is, they mistakenly see an individual's personal traits and attitudes as causes of behavior when, in reality, situational factors caused people to act as they did. As discussed in This Just In, people explain unintentional behavior in terms of causes and intentional behavior in terms of reasons.

Are strong arguments always more persuasive?

No. Research indicates that stronger arguments have a greater effect when participants are thinking systematically but are no more effective than weak arguments when people are thinking heuristically.

When do our behaviors change our attitudes?

According to cognitive dissonance theory, when people engage in behavior that is discrepant from their attitudes, they experience discomfort that motivates them to change their attitudes to align with their behavior.

When do our attitudes predict our behavior?

Attitudes predict behavior more strongly when situational influences are weak, when people pause to think about their attitudes and themselves, and when attitudes and behavior are equally specific.

Is it even possible to avoid stereotyping?

Stereotypic thoughts come to mind automatically; however, thanks to controlled thinking processes, one can counteract them.

How can being reminded of your own group's stereotype interfere with intellectual performance?

Knowledge of one's own group stereotype can interfere with intellectual performance through stereotype threat processes, in which people worry that they might confirm a negative stereotype about their group. This worry can distract people from the task they are performing and thus interfere with their performance.

How do psychologists measure attitudes that no one wants to admit having?

Psychologists measure such attitudes using implicit measures like the implicit association test (IAT). In the IAT, the speed with which participants respond to information related to different groups of people provides a measure of participants' attitudes toward those groups, without participants' knowledge that they are providing such information.

What cognitive, emotional, motivational, and social factors cause prejudice?

These include generalization (treating different members of a group as being essentially the same), hostility (negative emotions toward members of a group), and scapegoating (blaming members of another group for the failures of oneself or one's own group). A fourth factor is social, involving exploitation by a group in power.

How can prejudice be reduced?

The most promising technique for reducing prejudice is intergroup contact, that is, arranging circumstances in which members of different groups meet and spend a significant amount of time together.

What are some examples of how culture shapes what we think and do?

Many behaviors vary culturally. In some cultures outside the United States, people view property as shared rather than personally owned. In some Southeast Asians cultures, people honor the belief that "only God knows when someone will die naturally" by not asking for prognoses.

What assumption can social psychologists be faulted for making?

Social psychologists can be faulted for assuming their research results generalize to all cultures.

Just how fundamental is the fundamental attribution error?

Not very. Research indicates, for instance, that citizens of the Middle East, South Asia, and East Asia are more likely to make situational rather than personal attributions for behavior. These differences are explained by the holistic processing that is common among individuals in collectivistic cultures.

As described in This Just In, the question of whether people attribute behavior to situational or personal causes is based on the assumption that the behavior was unintentional. Intentional behaviors are better explained according to personal *reasons*.

Why do we wince when we see other people in pain?

When we see others in pain, our brain creates a version of their experiences. It does so by activating neurons in the brain's mirror system, a neural system that simulates the activities and experiences of other people.

Is thinking about what people are experiencing different from thinking about what they are like?

Yes. When people think about what others are experiencing, the mirror system, located in the temporo-parietal junction (TPJ), is activated. When people think about what people are like, the medial prefrontal cortex (mPFC) is active. The mPFC is highly interconnected with other brain regions, a quality that is necessary for the task of integrating different types of information to form an impression of someone.

Answers to What Do You Know?

1. Items *a, c,* and *d* should be checked.

2. Experimental control during social interactions is difficult because social interactions can vary quite a bit. Confederates solve this problem by behaving in the same exact manner within an experimental condition.

3. 1c, 2a, 3g, 4b, 5e, 6d, 7f

4. Milgram might agree that Eichmann's behavior was monstrous but would advise that you tell your friend to consider that a very powerful social factor was at play: our strong tendency to obey authority figures.

5. (a) F, (b) F, (c) F, (d) T, (e) F, (f) T

6. 1c, 2b, 3a

7. (a) This attribution is best characterized as a cause because Mia is citing a cause for a behavior that was unintentional. (b) This attribution is best characterized as a reason because Ron describes a planned strategic behavior he engaged in, and his explanation was story-like.

8. Yes, you have made the fundamental attribution error because you made a personal attribution, and failed to take into account the situational causes of the crooked parking. Perhaps the person who parked next to that car had pulled in crookedly.

9. This was interpreted as the fundamental attribution error because there was no reason to believe that either the questioner or answerer was more knowledgeable; they were randomly assigned to those conditions. People failed to take this situational information into account when they made their ratings.

10. (a) T, (b) F, (c) T

11. (a) No; the attitude and behavior are not equally specific. (b) Yes; attention is drawn to the self and to one's attitudes. (c) No; situational influences are not weak.

12. controlled; confirm; man's/male/masculine; woman's/female/feminine; scapegoating; slave

13. community

14. Cultural

15. This statement is incorrect because people from collectivistic cultures tend to process information holistically.

16. mirror; temporal; parietal

17. (a) The medial prefrontal cortex (mPFC) is highly interconnected with other brain areas, thus enabling it to integrate lots of information. (b) Yes, brain research confirms that different areas of the brain are active during these two tasks. Mirror neurons in the temporo-parietal junction (TPJ) are active when thinking about others' ongoing experiences, whereas the medial prefrontal cortex (mPFC) is active when thinking about others' enduring characteristics.

Answers to Self-Test

1. c	6. a	11. a
2. b	7. b	12. a
3. d	8. d	13. c
4. d	9. b	14. c
5. c	10. a	15. b

CHAPTER 13
Chapter Summary

What two scientific goals do personality psychologists try to accomplish?

One goal is to characterize individual differences in people's typical patterns of observable behavior. The other is to understand the inner workings of the mind. Personality psychologists' scientific understanding of the mind can help explain the individual differences in personality that they observe.

What aspects of personality are structures and processes meant to account for?

Personality structures are meant to account for people's enduring, consistent personality qualities. Personality processes explain variations in a person's thoughts and emotions that occur across relatively brief periods of time.

What tool enables personality psychologists to study people scientifically?

Psychologists rely on personality assessment, which refers to a structured procedure for learning about the distinctive psychological qualities of an individual.

According to Freud, what are the three main structures of the mind?

Freud proposed that the mind contains three structures that are inherently in conflict: the id, ego, and superego. The id seeks immediate release of mental energy; the superego tries to adhere to social norms, and the ego attempts to devise realistic strategies to cope with the demands of the superego and id.

According to Freud's "iceberg" metaphor, at what levels of consciousness does each structure of the mind reside?

In Freud's iceberg model, the id is entirely unconscious, whereas the ego and superego are partly conscious.

What are the two basic types of mental energies according to Freud's theory?

One is life energies, which motivate people to preserve their own lives and to reproduce. The other is energies associated with death, often expressed as aggression.

According to Freud, how can experiences in childhood stages of development have lifelong effects?

Freud believed that early life experiences create fixations specific to the childhood stage of development at which the experiences occur. Later in life, people relive the emotions, motivations, and conflicts of that developmental stage.

How, according to Freud, do individuals keep themselves from experiencing excessive anxiety or expressing socially unacceptable behavior?

People use defense mechanisms, which are mental strategies that protect against anxiety by blocking unacceptable ideas and impulses, or by distorting them so that the socially unacceptable desire ends up being expressed in a socially acceptable manner.

According to Freud, why is the free association method the best way to assess personality?

According to Freud, if something pops into mind during free association, it must have been due to the action of an inner mental structure that caused it to come to mind, so if a person just let his or her mind "run free," the ideas that come to mind will reveal its inner workings.

What kinds of outcomes should projective tests be able to predict if they are valid? Do they?

A projective test such as the Rorschach inkblot test should predict important life outcomes, such as who develops a psychological disorder, or who performs well under stress on the job. Research, however, reveals that Rorschach test scores commonly fail to accurately predict real-life psychological outcomes.

How did the ideas of the neo-Freudian personality theorists differ from those of Freud?

Alfred Adler (1927) believed that Freud underestimated the importance of social motives—in particular, the motivation to compensate for inferiority. Carl Jung (1939) judged that Freud underestimated the role that evolution played in shaping the mind—in particular, the collective unconscious. Erik Erikson (1950) expanded Freud's theory of development to the years beyond early childhood. He also sought to incorporate the conflicts or crises that people experience in their interactions with others throughout the life span.

What disadvantages of Freud's theory call into question its usefulness?

The theory cannot be easily tested. Likewise, the energy model of mind and its three mental structures may not explain the full range of variability in human social behavior.

What does humanistic theory emphasize, in contrast to psychoanalysis?

Humanistic theory, unlike psychoanalysis, emphasizes people's desire for freedom and their capacity to reflect on their lives, as well as individuals' personal, subjective, conscious experiences of themselves.

What is "the self" and why did Rogers emphasize it in his theory of personality?

The self, in Rogers's theory, is an organized set of self-perceptions of how we really are. It is the central personality structure through which people make sense of their daily experiences.

What is the source of our emotions according to humanistic theory?

People possess an ideal self—that is, the conception of how they ideally would like to be—and they become distressed when their actual experiences fall short of this ideal.

What is the fundamental human motive according to Rogers?

The fundamental human motive is self-actualization, a motivation to enhance one's psychological state, to achieve personal meaning in life, and to attain a state of psychological maturity.

How can our relationships with others foster or hinder self-actualization?

Relationships in which you experience unconditional positive regard allow you to freely explore and develop your true self-concept. Relationships in which people establish conditions of worth can force you to deny aspects of your true self, which hinders self-actualization.

How can we measure self-concept?

Self-concept can be measured through procedures such as the Q-sort, a personality assessment method in which people are asked to describe multiple aspects of their views of themselves. As you learned in Research Toolkit, aspects of the self-concept can also be gauged using implicit measures, such as the IAT.

In what way does Rogers's theory improve upon Freud's?

Rogers, unlike Freud, revealed the importance of conscious thinking processes and interpersonal relationships to personality and also showed the changes in personality that can occur in therapy. Rogers highlighted positive aspects of human nature that were largely overlooked by Freud.

In what way is Rogers's theory limited as a theory of personality?

A limitation of Rogers's theory is that it says little about the biological side of personality.

What characterizes the measurement of personality in trait theory?

Trait theory is known for the efficiency and reliability of its measures of personality.

What scientific method do trait theorists use to reduce thousands of traits in our language into the Big Five (or Six)?

Trait psychologists rely on factor analysis, a statistical tool that searches for patterns in large sets of correlations, such as correlations among measures of different personality traits. Factor analysis enables psychologists to determine whether some of the characteristics go together so frequently that they should be considered different aspects of one basic trait.

What does Eysenck's research suggest is the biological basis of the trait extraversion?

Eysenck's research suggests that individual differences in cortical activity in response to environmental stimulation are the basis of individual differences in extraversion. Extraverts have relatively low levels of cortical response and thus seek out more stimulation from the environment. Introverts have high levels of response and are prone to becoming overstimulated in some environments.

How can Eysenck's work link structures to processes in trait theory?

Eysenck's analysis of cortical arousal and extraversion identifies brain processes that come into play as people encounter situations featuring low and high levels of stimulation. Extraverts need lower levels of stimulation to experience cortical arousal.

How do trait theorists assess personality and what outcomes can be predicted by these assessments?

Trait theorists assess personality by using questionnaires in which people report their typical preferences and personal tendencies. Individual differences in questionnaire responses have been shown to predict real-life outcomes, including everyday behaviors (such as the style of one's personal spaces) and long-term life outcomes (such as longevity).

What are some strengths and weaknesses of trait theory?

Trait theory provides a simple method for assessing individual differences and spurs research into the connection between psychology and biology. However, it fails to address in detail the psychological processes through which traits express themselves in behavior, and it does not fully explain fluctuations in a person's behavior from one situation to another. Furthermore, as described in This Just In, the technique of network analysis suggests that trait theory's central assumption—that people's responses to items on trait questionnaires are caused by their traits—may not be supportable. Network analysis indicates that their responses to items are caused by their responses to other items.

What did social-cognitive theory's two most prominent theorists—Bandura and Mischel—emphasize in their conceptualization of personality?

Both Bandura and Mischel emphasize that personality consists of interconnected beliefs and skills that people develop as they interact with the social world. The theory and research of both underscore the fact that your personal development is not determined merely by inherited qualities outside of your personal control. Rather, you have a capacity for self-control. In addition, both theorists highlight the importance of social context.

What defines each of the three different types of personality structures within social-cognitive theory: self-referent cognition, skills, and affective systems?

Self-referent cognition refers to the thoughts people have about themselves as they interact with the world and reflect on their experiences. Skills are abilities that are developed through experience and that enable people to act in an effective manner. Affective systems are the moods and emotions that influence and are influenced by a person's style of thinking.

According to research by Bandura, through what process do individuals acquire skills?

People acquire skills through modeling, that is, the observation of others who display those skills. Bandura's research on the modeling of aggression showed that children quickly learn aggressive behavior patterns that are displayed in the media. In general, people can learn both negative and positive behaviors through modeling.

According to research by Mischel and colleagues, through what strategies can individuals control their emotions and impulses?

People can control their emotions and impulses by distracting themselves, in particular, by directing their attention away from some enticing object that they are trying to avoid.

What does it mean to assess cognition and behavior "in context"?

To assess cognition and behavior "in context" is to measure not only people's thoughts and actions, but also the situation they were in when thinking and acting.

What are the strengths and limitations of social-cognitive theory?

The strengths of social-cognitive theory include its extensive and diverse research base, which involves both basic and applied research methods. Other strengths are its comprehensiveness and its focus on the relationship between social contexts and personality. A limitation of social-cognitive theory is that it says little about exactly how unconscious motives are expressed in people's actions, emotions, and psychological distress.

Does research on the brain support the idea that thinking can occur unconsciously?

Yes. Research shows, for example, that activity in one region of the brain can predict the decision a person makes a few seconds before the person is even aware of having made it.

How have researchers studied the brain and people's ability to think about themselves, or self-reflect?

In brain-imaging research, people have been asked to reflect on their own characteristics, as well as those of others. Findings show that there are distinctive areas of the brain, known as cortical midline structures, that are particularly active when people think about themselves.

Answers to What Do You Know?

1. differ; brain; distinct/different; consistent
2. structures; processes
3. scientifically
4. 1c, 2a, 3b
5. 1c, 2b, 3a
6. (a) T, (b) T, (c) F, (d) F, (e) F, (f) F
7. (a) This statement is incorrect because the free association method is a time-consuming method for assessing the contents of the unconscious.
   (b) This statement is incorrect because a necessary feature of projective tests is that their images must be highly ambiguous in their meaning, so there is room for people to project their personalities onto them.
   (c) This statement is incorrect because the Rorschach does not consistently predict important outcomes.
8. inferiority; collective; evolutionary; social
9. Choices *a* and *b* should be checked.
10. Choices *a* and *b* should be checked.
11. self-concept; change; actual; ideal
12. (a) This statement is incorrect because Rogers claimed that the drive to attain self-actualization was universal.
    (b) This statement is incorrect because the child is only free to develop his or her true sense of self if he or she receives unconditional positive regard. Conditions of worth cause the child to deny aspects of the self.
13. (a) T, (b) T

14. F
15. U.S. culture emphasizes getting ahead rather than getting along; this emphasis explains why its citizens are more concerned with positive self-regard.
16. (a) F, (b) F
17. (a) F, (b) F, (c) T
18. differ; dimensional; cause; factor analysis; cortical; autonomic
19. arousal; process
20. (a) F, (b) F, (c) T
21. Choices *a, c,* and *d* should be checked.
22. Choices *b* and *d* should be checked.
23. 1c, 2a, 3b
24. Answers will vary. If you feel highly capable of performing a challenging task, you might feel less anxious. Likewise, anxiety may influence your estimate of how capable you are to perform a task.
25. (a) T, (b) F, (c) T, (d) T, (e) T, (f) F, (g) F
26. explicit; pleasant; related
27. context/situations; situations
28. Choices *a* and *c* should be checked.
29. imaging; unconscious; conversion; amygdala
30. present; integrates

Answers to Self-Test

1. d	6. a	11. b
2. c	7. c	12. c
3. a	8. a	13. b
4. c	9. b	14. c
5. a	10. b	15. c

CHAPTER 14
Chapter Summary

What were the key features of Piaget's research method?

First, he presented children with novel problems whose solution required reasoning. In a classic problem, Piaget poured water from a wide container into a tall, narrow container and asked children whether, during this process, the total amount of water remained the same. To solve it correctly, children had to apply a general principle about physical objects. The second feature is that Piaget did not merely record the correctness of children's answers. To learn more about their thinking, he also asked them why they chose the answer they did.

What cognitive tools enable us to solve logical reasoning problems we've never encountered before?

We have schemas that enable us to engage in operations. Schemas are mental structures that make organized, meaningful action possible. A schema for grasping, for example, enables an infant to grab hold of a variety of toys. Operations are actions that modify an object or set of objects. The modification could be physical (e.g., ordering a set of objects from smallest to largest) or conceptual (e.g., placing a series of words in alphabetical order). Operations are reversible; that is, the logical system used in the operation can go in two directions (e.g., one can order objects from largest to smallest or place them in reverse alphabetical order).

How does our existing knowledge enable us to adapt to the environment? Through what process do we update that knowledge?

We use schemas to adapt to the environment. We understand external events by incorporating their features into existing schemas. A child with a schema for chickens may look at a picture of a Thanksgiving turkey and say, "Cluck, cluck, chicken," for example. To update his or her chicken schema, the child would engage in a process called accommodation, whereby feedback from the environment ("No, this is not a chicken") would cause him or her to modify the schema, perhaps by dividing it into two: a chicken schema and a turkey schema. Through experience, then, schemas grow in number and become sharper in focus.

What makes Piaget's approach a nature *and* nurture one?

The child learns by experience, as a traditional "nurture" perspective would suggest. But the child does so using mental powers that have a biological origin, as a "nature" perspective would explain.

Which comes first: learning or development?

Many learning theorists believe learning drives development. Environmental experiences modify children's responses and provide them with information; these changes constitute learning; and through this learning, children develop. To Piaget, development drives learning. Children spontaneously modify and elaborate their schemas as they interact with the world. The development of these knowledge structures, in turn, enables children to learn from parents and teachers.

What characterizes each of Piaget's stages of cognitive development?

In the sensorimotor stage (birth to 2 years), children interact with the world through their sensory and motor systems only. They develop object permanence. In the preoperational stage of development (ages 2 to 7), children can use mental symbols to think about the world, but they cannot engage in operations. In particular, they do not have the capacity to make logical reversals, a mental limitation demonstrated by the phenomenon of conservation, the recognition that an object maintains some of its essential physical properties even when it is transformed.

In the concrete operational stage of development (ages 7 to 11), children are capable of performing reversible logical operations (e.g., if shown a group of 6 cats and 2 dogs and asked whether there are more animals than dogs, the child can solve the problem). This stage is limited in that children can execute operations only on things that actually exist in the child's experience. In the formal operational stage (ages 11 to adulthood), children can execute mental operations on actual objects as well as hypothetical ones that do not exist. They think about hypothetical objects by applying abstract rules, such as those found in algebra.

In what domains of thinking are children actually smarter than Piaget had predicted?

First, Piaget found that, in infancy, children lack object permanence, but research using the looking-time method described in Research Toolkit indicates that this is inaccurate. Second, research indicates that contrary to Piaget's beliefs, 3-year-olds can distinguish between inanimate objects and animate living things. Finally, children also display more knowledge than Piaget expected when thinking about the human mind. Even at a very young age, children know that the people they encounter have minds, and that the plants and toys they encounter do not. They also possess a theory of mind, an understanding that other people have feelings and thoughts.

Are children born knowing things?

Children develop complex beliefs at such an early age that it's hard to see how experience alone could account for their mental abilities. Harvard psychologist Susan Carey proposes that children possess innate input analyzers, that is, biologically inherited mental mechanisms designed to detect and process specific types of information, including information about objects, living things, and people's minds.

How do children's social interactions influence their development?

Vygotsky explains that by interacting with adults and older peers, children acquire the cognitive tools of their culture: language, counting systems, reading and writing; arithmetic and algebraic symbols, diagrams and flowcharts; musical notation. Once children have practice using these cultural tools, they internalize them. What first was a social activity becomes a feature of the child's inner mental life.

To aid development, is it a good idea to challenge children with problems that are above their current abilities?

Vygotsky believed that by challenging learners with problems that were a small degree above their current abilities, in a space called the zone of proximal development, teachers could speed their learning and psychological development. Research supports this belief.

Does being raised in a more enriched environment increase brain size?

Yes. In one study, the brains of mice raised in an enriched environment differed markedly from those raised in a low-enrichment environment. Their cerebral cortexes were thicker, their individual brain cells formed more connections with other cells, their brain cells were covered by more myelin, and their blood vessels in the brain were more fully developed.

Does the brain's development actually map onto Piaget's stages of cognitive development?

Yes. Brain research indicates that, in concert with development of motor movement, the sensorimotor cortex matures first, with rapid development occurring in the first months of life. In concert with development of language processing, the parietal and temporal cortices develop later, with major biological development occurring between ages 8 months and 2 years. In concert with the development of the ability to sustain attention and control emotional impulses, the prefrontal cortex does not reach substantial maturity until well into the teenage years, and it continues to develop through a person's 20s.

How does the brain's connectivity change across the life span?

In childhood, most of the brain's connections are "local"; that is, they interconnect neurons within one region of the brain. Later in life, connections become "global"; different regions of the brain become more strongly interconnected. For example, in one study, researchers found that the interconnections between the brain regions associated with the central executive system and the attentional network became stronger. This increase in connectivity enables people to gain greater control over their thoughts, emotions, and behavior.

What is temperament, and why do psychologists study it?

Temperament is a child's biologically based emotional and behavioral tendencies. Psychologists study temperament due to their intrinsic interest in understanding individual differences in childhood, because temperament qualities endure into later years of life and are important for understanding adolescent and adult development, and because temperament predicts socially significant behaviors.

Is temperament the same in all contexts?

Research reveals that a child's temperament is evident in some social contexts but not others. Children with inhibited temperament, for example, appear shy specifically in contexts that contain novel stimuli.

Why do goslings follow Mother Goose?

They are imprinting—that is, they are fixing their attention upon, and following, the first moving object they encounter, who is typically their mother. Imprinting bonds them permanently.

Food or physical comfort: Why do babies bond with caregivers?

Harlow's research indicated that macaque babies preferred "terrycloth mothers" over "wire mothers," even when the terrycloth mothers provided no nourishment, suggesting that the need for physical comfort was what drives caregiver–offspring bonding. Other research shows that human and animal babies that lack comforting attachment relationships in childhood tend to develop abnormal behavior patterns in adulthood.

According to attachment theory, how do early life experiences exert lifelong effects?

Parent–child interactions shape children's beliefs about what the child can expect from others, and these beliefs are applied to new relationships later in life. Attachments thus create a foundation on which beliefs about future relationships are built.

How can putting children in a "strange situation" help us to understand attachment styles?

The strange situation paradigm is a structured sequence of events in which mother and child interact, and researchers observe their interactions. The child's responses when separated from and then reunited with the mother indicate the child's attachment style. Secure infants are those who are easily comforted by the parent when she returns. Avoidant children look away and move away from the mother. Anxious-ambivalent children exhibit a desire to be picked up by the mother, yet also demand to be put down.

Do negative childhood experiences scar us for life?

Not typically. Research indicates that many people are resilient, that is, they have the capacity to retain or recover psychological functioning after negative experiences. For instance, in a study of more than 600 adolescents who had experienced childhood abuse or neglect, almost half were developing quite well. Stable living conditions contributed to these positive outcomes—that is, their social environments enabled them to bounce back from early-life difficulties.

What is a systems view of families? According to a systems view, what parenting style is best for social development?

A systems view of families is a theoretical viewpoint arguing that all members of the family influence one another. A systems view recognizes that there is no one style of parenting that is best for everyone; the effects of a parenting style on children depend on other factors in the family, such as the temperament of the child.

How do features of the family environment affect motor development?

The rate at which children develop motor skills is influenced by several aspects of the family environment, including socioeconomic status, whether parents choose to use diapers, and whether parents prop children up in a crib or let them lie down. On tests of motor skill, children born into wealthier families are more likely to outperform children from poor households because they tend to have more space to run around and more interactive toys, which may speed motor development. Research indicates that diapers interfere with walking, especially cloth ones. In some Caribbean and African cultures, children learn quickly how to sit without support because parents frequently prop up their infants rather than let them lie in cribs.

How do siblings influence development— both directly and indirectly?

In direct sibling effects, one-on-one interactions between siblings shape behavior and emotional life. For example, one sibling can teach another how to cope with bullies. In indirect effects, a sibling influences the parents who, in turn, interact with and affect another sibling. For instance, older siblings interact with parents, who then become more skilled at parenting younger siblings. Two other indirect effects include birth order and pecking order.

How do interactions with peers shape personality development?

Peer interactions have two types of effects: assimilation and within-group differentiation. Hanging out with peers causes us to become more similar to them—to assimilate. Simultaneously, group members identify and label differences within the group to highlight individuals' uniqueness.

Can preschool help to combat the negative effects of poverty on personality development?

People who live in poverty have fewer opportunities to experience stimuli, such as music and the arts, that aid in the development of personal motivation and skills. The Perry Preschool Study demonstrated that providing children with an enriched high-quality educational program featuring longer hours of preschool education per day and home visits from teachers had long-term effects. Children with enriched education were more likely to graduate from high school, less likely to ever be arrested, and earned more money as adults.

How do children acquire a sense of self? How do these self-representations change over time?

A major source of the child's self-concept, or self-representations, is others. Input from adults and other children teaches children about their skills, distinctive personality characteristics, and level of popularity. As children develop, self-representations grow more abstract. They become more complex and connected (e.g., the child is popular *because* she can keep a secret) and refer not only to concrete actions and preferences, but also to generalized personal traits.

How does self-esteem change across childhood?

Self-esteem tends to be high around ages 9 to 10. Levels of self-esteem then drop in early adolescence (around ages 12 to 13), with the drop being sharper for girls than boys.

Why doesn't everybody have the same level of self-esteem?

For starters, not everybody inherits the same temperament. People who inherit a tendency to experience negative emotions are more likely to develop low self-esteem. Not everybody experiences the same parenting, either. Children whose parents displayed interest in and affection toward them tend to experience higher self-esteem.

What skill do we need in order to exert self-control?

Self-control, the ability to act in a manner consistent with long-term goals and values, largely depends on cognitive control, the ability to suppress undesired or inappropriate emotions and impulsive behaviors. We do this by concentrating attention on a task at hand, and avoiding distractions. Luckily, this ability increases with age.

Does the ability to delay gratification in childhood predict anything important?

Yes. Walter Mischel's research shows that self-control abilities are highly stable over time and that they predict important life outcomes, such as SAT scores.

How do biology and social environment interact to influence behavior during puberty?

According to the biopsychosocial model, the effects of biological changes on behavior depend on the social environment. For example, Magnusson's research indicated that girls who reached puberty earlier than others tended to engage in more antisocial behaviors (e.g., drinking and cheating in school) because they were hanging out with older peers who also engaged in those behaviors.

What are four ways in which adolescents cope with the challenge of establishing a personal identity?

Marcia outlines four approaches to coping, or identity statuses: personally choosing and being committed to a status (identity achievement); having a status thrust upon you by others (foreclosure); feeling directionless (identity diffusion); and struggling with questions of identity without firmly committing to a life path (moratorium).

A study you read about in Cultural Opportunities indicated that among African Americans, Asian Americans, and Latino students, individual differences in ethnic identity mapped onto three of Marcia's statuses: diffusion, moratorium, and achieved.

Are 18-year-olds really full-fledged adults?

Sort of. People are getting married at a later age than they used to, prompting psychologists to identify a novel developmental period they call emerging adulthood, which refers to a period of life in the very late teen years and early 20s when people are technically adults but do not yet have the obligations and responsibilities of family life. When people this age are asked whether they feel like adults, most say, "Yes and no." This stage of life is a time of exploration.

Is a midlife crisis inevitable?

No. Research shows that this stereotype about midlife is wrong. Midlifers do "take stock" of their lives, but doing so rarely triggers a crisis. When it does, the crisis often centers on problems that could occur at any age.

What are some common themes of individuals' life stories?

Two key themes are generativity, or a concern with contributing to the welfare of the next generation, and redemption, in which people describe how they have overcome suffering or crisis.

Do most people experience declines in well-being in older adulthood?

In general, no. Older adults' level of well-being commonly is as high as that of younger persons.

How do selection, optimization, and compensation contribute to successful psychological adjustment in older adulthood?

These three strategies, which are identified in the selection, optimization, and compensation (SOC) model of Baltes and his colleagues, help older adults experience high levels of personal achievement on a limited set of daily activities, and maintain a strong sense of well-being. Selection is the process of setting personal goals for a given period of your life. Optimization is the process of devising plans to achieve goals that are set. Compensation is the identification of alternative strategies to achieve goals, if at first you don't succeed.

How does knowing you're at the end of your life affect how you want to spend your time?

Research supports socioemotional selectivity theory's prediction that when people recognize that there is little time left in their life, they are more motivated to pursue activities that are emotionally meaningful to them, such as spending time with family and longtime friends.

Does getting older cause people to dwell on the negative?

Just the opposite! Older adults display the positivity effect, which is the tendency to pay more attention to positive than to negative information. Older adults tend to have greater memory for emotionally positive information, suggesting that they attend more closely to such information when it is presented.

How do we develop our morality?

Kohlberg suggested that morality develops in distinct levels and stages. He identified three levels of moral thinking, each with two stages. At the preconventional level, children's thinking is organized around ideas about rewards and punishments. "Good" behavior consists of actions that avoid punishment (Stage 1) and, later, that bring them personal rewards (Stage 2). At the conventional level, children evaluate actions in terms of social conventions and norms. They assess whether behavior is consistent with being a "good girl" or "good boy" (Stage 1) and then think about their duty to uphold social rules (Stage 2). At the postconventional level, individuals can transcend the rules of authority figures and base moral reasoning on abstract principles. People recognize that if laws from authorities violate individual rights, the laws should be changed (Stage 1) and evaluate actions according to universal ethical principles such as justice and respect for the dignity of the individual (Stage 2).

How does women's moral reasoning differ from men's?

Gilligan found that women progress through moral stages that differ from those identified by Kohlberg in research with men. The highest stage for women, Gilligan found, involved reasoning according to a principle of nonviolence. Rather than adhering to abstract principles of justice, women followed the concrete human principle of not harming others. Research conducted after Gilligan formulated her approach, however, indicates that gender differences in moral reasoning are smaller than she expected.

Answers to What Do You Know?

1. (a) The schema is conservation, and the operation is the judgment that the volume of the water did not change when moved from one pitcher to another.
(b) This is an example of assimilation because her conservation schema enables her to correctly judge that the volume of the water does not change; she does not have to modify her existing schema, as is the case in accommodation.

2. This is an example of accommodation because Willem had to modify his existing schema for dogs based on environmental feedback; his existing schema did not enable him to easily assimilate this particular experience, as is the case in assimilation.

3. 1dhi, 2b, 3aef, 4gc

4. Event *a*

5. (a) T, (b) F, (c) F

6. (a) Susan Carey challenged Piaget's claim that children learn entirely through experience when she theorized that children possess innate input analyzers, mental mechanisms that detect and process specific types of information.
(b) Lev Vygotsky challenged Piaget's claim that children learn alone when he theorized that there exists a zone of proximal development, a gap between a child's current and potential level of development consisting of problems the child cannot do alone but can complete in collaboration with others.

7. All choices should be checked.

8. Choices *a, c,* and *d* should be checked.

9. (a) T, (b) F, (c) T, (d) F, (e) F, (f) T, (g) T

10. (a) Aggressiveness and delinquency were lowest among children whose temperament matched parenting style; easy-to-manage children benefited more from parenting that was laid back; and difficult-to-manage children benefited more from parenting that was strict.
(b) Five findings were cited in the text: (1) Children who grew up in wealthy households outperformed those of poor households in tests of motor skills, because they had more room in which to move and more interactive toys; (2) diapers (especially cloth ones) impair walking; (3) in some Caribbean and African cultures, parents' practice of propping up their children rather than laying them down in a crib causes the children to be able to sit up very early in life; (4) in some areas of China, parents sit their children on sand, which absorbs bodily waste, but also reduces freedom of movement, thereby delaying development; (5) in nineteenth-century America, children moved less than those of the twenty-first century because they wore gowns that impeded their movement.
(c) Pecking order is an indirect effect because it is the parents' decision to allocate resources to one sibling that affects the share another sibling will receive; the siblings thus do not directly influence one another.
(d) She would be more typically feminine if she had grown up interacting in same-sex groups because it is in that context where she would have learned behaviors appropriate for her gender.
(e) By age 40, children who received the enriched education earned more money, were more likely to graduate from high school, and were less likely to be arrested.

11. (a) T, (b) T, (c) F, (d) T, (e) F, (f) F, (g) T

12. In Magnusson's research, early-maturing girls hung out with other early-maturing girls and older boys who engaged in antisocial behaviors, which prompted them to do the same. This illustrates the biopsychosocial model because the effect of the biological change (early maturity) depended on a change in a social experience (their peer group).

13. 1c, 2a, 3d, 4b

14. This quote best exemplifies someone in the moratorium stage of development.

15. rights; family

16. (a) F, (b) F, (c) T

17. F

18. 1a, 2b, 3c

19. According to socioemotional selectivity theory, activities that are emotionally meaningful will be most motivating for older adults.

20. The older adults will be more likely to remember the photo of the flowers and the young and middle-aged adults will be equally likely to remember both photos.

21. 1c, 2a, 3b

22. The infants were actually attracted to the helpful puppet, suggesting that they understand bad and good behavior, and prefer the good.

23. males/men; nonviolence; justice; smaller

Answers to Self-Test

1. b	6. d	11. a
2. a	7. b	12. d
3. c	8. a	13. d
4. c	9. c	14. d
5. b	10. b	15. c

CHAPTER 15
Chapter Summary

Do we diagnose and treat psychological disorders in the same way as we do physical illness?

Diagnosis of psychological disorders follows a medical model, similar to the diagnosis of physical illness. Psychological experiences (e.g., feelings of anxiety or depression) are seen as symptoms that arise from a psychological or biological cause. Therapists try to alter the brain and/or psychological functioning of the individual to treat that cause and to alleviate symptoms.

What are the advantages and disadvantages of focusing on the internal causes of psychological illness?

One advantage is that it has stopped people from treating mental illness as a moral failing, thereby promoting the ethical treatment of people suffering from mental illness. A second advantage is that the search for biological causes of mental illness led to research on therapeutic drugs. A disadvantage is that once individuals are labeled as mentally ill, they may be perceived as mentally incompetent. A second disadvantage is that the medical model's process of diagnosis may lead professionals to search "inside the head" of the patient for causes that are "outside" in the environment.

What caution must we exercise when evaluating unusual behavior?

Sometimes unusual behavior reflects unusual life circumstances. Behavior that appears abnormal in one social or historical setting may seem completely normal in another.

What is the major tool mental health professionals use to diagnose and classify psychological problems?

Psychologists use the Diagnostic and Statistical Manual of Mental Disorders (DSM) to classify disorders. The DSM specifies criteria that a person must exhibit in order to be classified as having a given disorder.

What are some criticisms of the diagnostic tool mental health professionals use to diagnose and classify psychological problems?

First, though the DSM's categories are in part grounded in scientific research, they also rest on professional opinion, which can be unreliable. Second, the DSM classifies disorders according to symptoms, not causes. Finally, gender and other biases in the DSM may cause some mental illnesses to be overdiagnosed.

Why are there so many different types of therapy?

One reason is that there are a lot of different types of disorders and people who suffer from them. Another is that different clinicians embrace different therapy strategies.

What are some of the most prominent types of psychotherapy and what is it like to experience each of them?

Five types are particularly prominent: psychoanalysis, behavior therapy, cognitive therapy, humanistic therapy, and the family of group therapies. If you were to experience psychoanalysis, your therapist would use the free association method to reveal unconscious memories that are a source of distress. In this context, you may experience transference, whereby you unintentionally respond to the therapist as if he or she were a significant figure (e.g., a parent) from the past. This experience would enable you to analyze any emotions you may be re-experiencing.

A behavior therapist would alter your environment to teach you new ways of behaving, perhaps by providing reinforcers for desirable behaviors. In a token economy, for instance, you might be given tokens for desirable behaviors that you could later exchange for something valuable. If you had a fear you wanted to extinguish, you might experience exposure therapy, in which the therapist would reduce your fear by bringing you into direct contact with the feared object or situation, or systematic desensitization, in which this exposure would happen more gradually.

A cognitive therapist using Beck's cognitive therapy would target your negative irrational cognitions that come to mind automatically, to increase your awareness of them, challenge them, and suggest positive thoughts to replace them. A humanistic therapist would help you achieve positive growth by building a good relationship with you. Three conditions necessary for this growth are genuineness, acceptance (via unconditional positive regard), and empathic understanding. In group therapy, your therapist would form and maintain the group, establish norms for behaviors within the group, and encourage you to focus on your thoughts and feelings in the "here and now" to help you gain insight into your interpersonal behavior.

Which psychological therapy is most popular?

Most therapists try to integrate the best methods of different approaches to fit the needs of each individual patient. Some therapists describe their work as eclectic therapy.

How did physicians figure out that psychological disorders could be treated with drugs?

The discovery was accidental. In the 1940s, a physician in France was searching for a drug that would help surgical patients during their postoperative recovery. The drug he tried calmed his postoperative patients. Psychiatrists used this drug to calm people suffering from mania, and the sufferers' thinking became clearer.

Antidepressants such as Prozac and Zoloft were not discovered accidentally, but were developed based on the theory that targeting serotonin, a neurotransmitter associated with mood, could alleviate depressive symptoms. As revealed in This Just In, antidepressants are not as effective as originally theorized.

How do drugs affect mental health?

Once drugs permeate the blood–brain barrier, they affect the functioning of brain cells and therefore affect thinking and emotion. A second way that drugs can affect mental health is through placebo effects, which occur because people believe that taking medication will cause them to improve; that expectation can cause actual improvement, a self-fulfilling prophecy.

What are some alternatives to drug therapies?

One is electroconvulsive therapy, in which a physician delivers electrical currents to the brain. Another is the lobotomy, now rare, in which a surgeon damages tissue in the brain's frontal cortex.

What's wrong with using case studies as evidence for a therapy's effectiveness?

Case studies rely on the subjective observations of therapists, who may be biased in favor of their own therapy method. Case studies also lack a control group, so there is no way of knowing whether the client would have improved even without therapy. As you saw in Research Toolkit, the most carefully controlled method for empirically testing the efficacy of a therapy is the double-blind clinical outcome study.

What defines major depressive disorder and how prevalent is it?

A person is diagnosed with major depressive disorder only if a majority of the following symptoms last two weeks or longer: consistent depressed mood; loss of interest in most daily activities; change in body weight; change in sleep patterns; fatigue; feelings of worthlessness, hopelessness, or helplessness; difficulty concentrating; and thoughts of suicide. A survey of U.S. adults indicated that 6.7% of the population suffered from major depressive disorder at some point during the previous year. The lifetime prevalence of the disorder is about 15%, although the prevalence varies with different groups in American society. As you learned in Cultural Opportunities, prevalence rates differ across cultures. In Hunan, China, major depression is rarely diagnosed, largely because the Hunanese seldom talk about their emotional lives.

What therapies effectively treat major depressive disorder?

One approach is that of behavioral therapists, who emphasize that the environment affects people's psychological life. A second approach is cognitive therapy, where the therapist challenges negative beliefs in an effort to replace the depressive thoughts with more positive ones. A third approach is interpersonal therapy, in which therapists try to alleviate depression by identifying interpersonal problems that contribute to the client's current depression, and to reduce the client's social isolation by expanding his or her network of relationships. A fourth strategy is drug therapy.

What defines bipolar disorder and how prevalent is it?

To be diagnosed with bipolar disorder, an individual must display depression for at least two weeks and mania for at least four days in a row. Manic symptoms include abnormally high energy, racing thoughts, extreme talkativeness, high levels of self-esteem, and involvement in fun activities that are costly or risky. About 1% of adults suffer from bipolar disorder.

What therapies effectively treat bipolar disorder?

Bipolar disorder is treated with mood stabilizers including lithium, anticonvulsants, and antipsychotics.

What defines generalized anxiety disorder and how prevalent is it?

To be diagnosed with generalized anxiety disorder, an individual must worry about two or more aspects of life on the majority of days, and symptoms must persist for at least three months. Generalized anxiety disorder affects nearly 7 million adults in the United States and is about twice as common among women as men.

What therapies effectively treat generalized anxiety disorder?

Generalized anxiety disorder is treated with anti-anxiety drugs, typically benzodiazepines, in conjunction with cognitive therapy and behavior therapy.

What defines panic disorder and how prevalent is it?

The key defining feature of panic disorder is panic attacks: episodes of extreme fear, including high levels of physical arousal, that occur suddenly and without apparent cause. During panic attacks, sufferers feel as if they are losing control of their body, having a heart attack, dying, or going insane. To be diagnosed with the disorder, the person must worry about the attack and its consequences for at least one month and the panic attacks must not be side effects of a medication or other drug. Panic disorder affects about 6 million Americans and is twice as common among women as men.

What therapies effectively treat panic disorder?

Panic disorder is treated with psychoanalytic therapy, cognitive-behavioral therapy, exposure therapy, and drug therapies.

What defines social anxiety disorder and how prevalent is it?

Social anxiety disorder is marked by a persistent fear of social situations and the expectation that the individual will experience humiliation and embarrassment in them. Symptoms must last at least six months and sufferers must recognize that the anxiety is excessive. Surveys indicate that 12.1% of U.S. citizens experience social anxiety disorder at some point in their adult lives. Some have suggested the disorder is overdiagnosed.

What therapies effectively treat social anxiety disorder?

Social anxiety disorder is treated with anti-anxiety drugs in conjunction with cognitive and behavioral therapies. People with social anxiety disorder also benefit from group therapy, which has the unique advantage of building social skills.

What defines phobias and how prevalent are they?

Phobias are strong, persistent fears caused by situations that pose little or no actual threat; specific phobias are fears directed toward particular objects or situations. Nearly 8 to 9% of American adults experience some form of specific phobia.

What therapies effectively treat phobias?

A form of exposure therapy called mastery therapy is often effective. In it, therapists accompany clients to situations that they fear and perform activities with them, gradually reducing the amount of help they give, so clients can master their own fears. This approach is commonly combined with cognitive strategies designed to boost clients' confidence in their ability to overcome their fears.

What defines obsessive-compulsive disorder and how prevalent is it?

To be diagnosed with obsessive-compulsive disorder, the individual must have recurring thoughts about potential harm that they try to suppress and must engage in repetitive behaviors in response to those thoughts. These obsessive thoughts and compulsive behaviors must take up more than an hour a day of the person's time and interfere with his or her social or professional life.

What therapies effectively treat obsessive-compulsive disorder?

Exposure and response prevention therapy has been effective. In it, therapists expose clients to the stimuli that trigger their obsessions and prevent them from engaging in their compulsions. This is anxiety provoking at first, but after repeated exposure, clients notice that no harm has befallen them and their anxiety dissipates. Cognitive therapies and drug therapies have also been effective.

What defines posttraumatic stress disorder and how prevalent is it?

Posttraumatic stress disorder (PTSD) develops when people encounter extremely high levels of stress, such as during military combat experience. Individuals with PTSD experience flashbacks that can trigger intense anxiety that interferes with everyday life. Other symptoms are emotional, including anxiety when exposed to stimuli that trigger memories of the trauma, persistent negative emotions, and high levels of arousal. Its prevalence among adults in the United States is 3.5%.

What therapies effectively treat posttraumatic stress disorder?

Cognitive-behavioral therapy has been effective in helping clients learn to cope with their traumatic memories. Therapists have also used virtual reality technologies to present lifelike images of trauma to clients. The clients are then able to develop skills for coping with their emotions in a nonthreatening environment.

Answers to What Do You Know?

1. This statement is incorrect because the medical model focuses on the internal causes of symptoms and, in doing so, ignores possible environmental causes, such as life stresses.

2. context

3. All but *a* should be checked.

4. cognitive; brain

5. 1d, 2c, 3e, 4a, 5b, 6f

6. (b) What are psychoactive substances?
   (c) What is the placebo effect?
   (d) What is electroconvulsive therapy?
   (e) What is a lobotomy?

7. empirically

8. In a double-blind study, both the researcher and the participant are unaware of the condition to which the participant is assigned.

9. (a) T, (b) F

10. This statement is incorrect because an individual only has to experience a majority of these symptoms for two weeks in order to be diagnosed with major depressive disorder.

11. future; drug

12. depression; talk; physical

13. Only *a* and *d* should be checked.

14. All but *d* should be checked.

15. All but *c* should be checked.

16. All items should be checked.

17. Treatments that force clients to directly confront their fears (rather than simply talk about them) can increase the clients' belief in their ability to master their fears on their own.

18. All but *b* should be checked.

19. posttraumatic stress disorder; flashbacks; emotions

Answers to Self-Test

1. a	6. b	11. a
2. c	7. b	12. c
3. b	8. d	13. d
4. a	9. b	14. a
5. c	10. b	15. d

CHAPTER 16
Chapter Summary

What does it mean to suffer from a psychotic disorder?

Psychotic disorders are psychological disorders whose core symptoms are that people's thoughts and actions are disorganized and their thinking loses touch with reality; people see and worry about things that do not exist.

How prevalent is schizophrenia?

In a meta-analysis of nearly 200 studies from 46 different nations, schizophrenia was identified in about 1 out of every 200 people. Rates do not vary across countries or between genders.

What are the positive and negative symptoms of schizophrenia?

Positive symptoms consist of the presence of undesirable mental events experienced by people with schizophrenia but not by others. Two examples are delusional beliefs and hallucinations. Negative symptoms consist of the absence of desirable behaviors that most others engage in. Two examples are a lack of interest in social activities and flat affect.

What cognitive impairments do people with schizophrenia experience?

People with schizophrenia have difficulty with concentration and memory (especially memory for visual information and episodic memory) and display inaccurate social cognition.

Why are the thoughts of people with schizophrenia so disorganized?

In schizophrenia, impairments in working memory contribute to disorganized thought. In addition, individuals with schizophrenia do not process information as quickly as others.

Why are people with schizophrenia so poor at making decisions?

People with schizophrenia do not exhibit the emotion-induced changes in decision making that people ordinarily exhibit. They do not adjust their decision making on the basis of poor past results. Therefore, they perform poorly on decision-making tasks.

How can the delusional thinking displayed by people with schizophrenia be explained at the mind and brain levels of analysis?

People with schizophrenia have relatively high levels of dopamine in their brains and an excess of dopamine receptors. In schizophrenia, excess dopamine causes even trivial stimuli to grab people's attention and to seem important. People with schizophrenia try to make sense of this seemingly important yet disparate array of information by inventing explanations. Because this information is strange, their explanations are often delusional.

How are the brains of people with schizophrenia different from those without the disorder?

Brain volume is reduced among people with schizophrenia, in part, due to an enlargement of the ventricles, which are spaces in the brain that contain no neurons and are instead filled with a fluid that supports the brain's functioning. Activity in the dorsolateral prefrontal cortex, an area that supports working memory, is lower in people with schizophrenia. Activity in the anterior cingulate, an area known to be active when people detect their own errors, is higher in people with schizophrenia.

Do genes alone determine whether someone will develop schizophrenia?

No. Twin studies indicate that genes are only a diathesis for schizophrenia—that is, a factor that predisposes its development. As you read in Research Toolkit, it will be a long time before genome-wide association studies can pinpoint which genes, in particular, are important. Recent research points to the importance of harmful prenatal factors in the development of schizophrenia, including bodily infections and exposure to lead. Poor nutrition may also play a role.

When does schizophrenia first develop?

Among people who have the mental illness, schizophrenia usually first develops between the ages of 16 and 30.

What drugs are used to treat schizophrenia? What are the side effects? Do they work?

One commonly prescribed typical (traditional) antipsychotic drug is chlorpromazine (trade name thorazine). A common atypical (newer) antipsychotic drug is clozapine. Both work by blocking dopamine receptor sites, which alleviates positive symptoms. Atypical antipsychotics also affect serotonin signaling, which can alleviate negative symptoms. Both types of antipsychotic drugs can produce a side effect known as tardive dyskinesia, which consists of repetitive, uncontrollable muscular movements, typically in the face (e.g., grimacing).

Antipsychotic drugs can substantially reduce the positive symptoms of schizophrenia. Nonetheless, at least half the patients who take the drugs do not experience substantial long-term reductions in schizophrenic symptoms. Moreover, a great many patients stop taking the drugs to avoid their side effects.

What psychotherapies are used to treat schizophrenia?

Cognitive therapy has been empirically demonstrated to effectively reduce the positive and negative symptoms of schizophrenia. Cognitive therapists try to get patients to question the accuracy of their delusional beliefs—to think of them as ideas they have about the world, rather than as statements of fact. Other therapists draw on the humanistic approach by focusing on the person as a whole, a person who copes with not only symptoms, but also the changes in lifestyle and self-concept that the disorder brings.

Is schizophrenia the only psychotic disorder?

No. One other is brief psychotic disorder, in which people experience some of the same symptoms of schizophrenia, including delusions and hallucinations, but for only a brief period. Another is delusional disorder, in which people experience delusions that may persist indefinitely.

What's the difference between having a personality disorder and just being quirky?

Personality disorders are consistent styles of thinking, behavior, and emotion that severely lower the quality of people's personal relationships. These styles go beyond quirkiness by harming mental health. Three qualities are shared by personality disorders: inflexible interactions with a given person, an inability to flexibly adapt to different people and roles, and a resulting inability to mature psychologically.

What characterizes the six main types of personality disorder: antisocial, avoidant, borderline, obsessive-compulsive, narcissistic, and schizotypal personality disorder?

People with antisocial personality disorder are manipulative, callous, hostile, and are risk takers. Some individuals with antisocial personality disorder are high in psychopathy, which means that they are particularly dishonest and manipulative.

In avoidant personality disorder, people feel inadequate, have low self-esteem, and are preoccupied with possible negative evaluation by others. Their behavior is withdrawn, shy, and inhibited.

The main features of borderline personality disorder include instability of self-concept, emotions, and interpersonal relationships, as well as an intense fear of abandonment. Borderline individuals report feeling lonely, worthless, and overwhelmed by the stresses of life. They sometimes take desperate steps to escape their stress, including self-harm, and are at high risk for suicide.

Individuals with narcissistic personality disorder hold extraordinarily positive views of themselves, yet their opinions of themselves seem "fragile." This uncertainty causes them to crave the attention of other people, to support their grandiose but fragile views of self.

Obsessive-compulsive personality disorder is characterized by perfectionism, a desire for order and control over activities, and a rigid adherence to rules for behavior. People's devotion to work activities may impair their personal relationships.

In schizotypal personality disorder, odd, eccentric patterns of thinking or behavior are combined with social isolation that results from an inability to form close personal relationships with people outside of the immediate family.

How do nature and nurture contribute to the development of antisocial behavior?

According to Caspi and colleagues, nature and nurture interact in the development of antisocial behavior. In their research, among children who did not experience maltreatment, genes did not contribute to the development of antisocial behavior. However, among children who did experience maltreatment, genes greatly contributed to the development of antisocial behavior.

What does the psychopathic brain look like?

When brain scans of men with antisocial personality disorder who have psychopathic qualities are compared to those with the disorder who do not have psychopathic qualities, it is clear that there is lower volume in the frontal cortex, an area that enables us to evaluate others' behavior and emotions. Lower volume also exists in the temporal lobe, an area that is active when we consider the rules for a given context and monitor whether we are following them. Without this activity, one cannot experience embarrassment or guilt.

How are the brains of people with borderline personality disorder different from those without the disorder?

Brain activity in the anterior cingulate cortex of borderline patients is less developed relative to those without the disorder. This region is known to be involved in emotional control.

How do therapists treat personality disorders?

Some use cognitive therapy and try to modify patients' personal beliefs that contribute to psychological distress. They also try to build a therapeutic relationship strong enough that clients will come to accept their suggestions for significant personal change.

Dialectical behavior therapy is a therapy for borderline personality disorder. The therapist teaches patients to avoid black-and-white thinking by acknowledging that their thoughts, even if potentially harmful, are valid. The therapist also focuses on clients' acceptance of themselves and their circumstances, just as they are.

Do people with dissociative identity disorder truly have multiple independent personalities?

It can be difficult to ascertain whether people with dissociative identity disorder truly have multiple personalities, or whether they simply observe variations in their own behavior and create stories about different characters to understand themselves.

What causes dissociative identity disorder?

Dissociative identity disorder may develop when individuals who experience trauma try to convince themselves it happened to someone else. It may also develop when people adopt different social roles that call for different types of behavior and gradually come to see those differences as different "personalities." In This Just In, you learned that the most famous case of dissociative identity disorder, Sybil, was a hoax.

An interesting cultural variation on dissociative disorders, latah, was highlighted in Cultural Opportunities. There, you learned that following a startle response, people in Malaysia can enter a trance state in which they imitate and obey others.

What defines depersonalization/ derealization disorder?

In depersonalization/derealization disorder, people experience the events of their day with strange detachment, as if they are merely observing the events rather than taking part in them.

They also experience derealization, the feeling that objects and events in their lives are unreal.

Can people completely lose their memory for who they are?

Yes. In dissociative amnesia, people are unable to remember significant personal information that normally would be highly memorable. Individuals with this disorder may experience fugue states in which they completely lose memory of their own personal identity.

Are people with dissociative identity disorder responsible for crimes committed by their alternative personalities?

Legal scholars who have addressed this issue explain that people with no control over their behavior cannot be found guilty. If the alter confesses to a crime, the person has the legal option of pleading not guilty by reason of insanity. This defense is typically not very successful in the case of dissociative identity disorder.

What could cause an individual to experience paralysis in the absence of a medical condition?

In conversion disorder, people experience physical symptoms that cannot be explained by any medical condition. Recent brain-imaging evidence supports an explanation that these physical symptoms have an emotional basis.

Answers to What Do You Know?

1. Choices *a* and *c* are examples of negative symptoms of schizophrenia; choices *b* and *d* are examples of positive symptoms.

2. Jean's misinterpretation best exemplifies an impairment in social cognition because she is incorrect in her thinking about the reason behind the man's smile.

3. (a) Working memory ability includes the ability to store information in one's mind for brief periods, to manipulate that information, and to control one's thinking. Impairments in any of these abilities would make it difficult to think in an organized manner.
(b) Emotions enable us to learn from our mistakes to make better decisions; an impairment in emotional functioning can thus disrupt this process and impair decision making.

4. Choices *b* and *c* should be checked.

5. genome-wide; single-nucleotide polymorphisms

6. (a) If genes alone caused schizophrenia, the bar for MZ twins would be at or near 100%.
(b) The text cites two other factors: prenatal events, including bodily infections or exposure to lead, and poor nutrition.
(c) Schizophrenia develops between ages 16 and 30 and persists throughout one's lifetime.

7. All but *c* and *e* should be checked.

8. This statement is incorrect because those facts point to the conclusion that psychotic disorders are best conceptualized as dimensions that exist along a continuum.

9. Choices *b* and *c* should be checked.

10. antisocial; psychopathy; narcissistic; borderline

11. (a) F, (b) T, (c) T, (d) T, (e) F

12. cognitive; borderline; argument; reconcile; acceptance

13. Sybil lied because she had become emotionally dependent on her therapist and wanted to please her in order to continue their relationship.

14. 1bfg, 2adh, 3cei

15. startle; dissociative; culture

16. This statement is incorrect because the insanity defense rarely works in the case of dissociative disorder. It is also incorrect because juries rarely believe the defendant is mentally ill, and even when they do, such jurors do not agree that this diagnosis provides a reasonable excuse.

17. This statement is incorrect according to brain research indicating that, among people diagnosed with conversion disorder, there is greater communication between the amygdala (which is active during the detection of emotional stimuli) and the motor cortex. Research at the brain level, then, confirms the reality of a psychological experience.

18. somatic symptom

Answers to Self-Test

1. b	6. d	11. a
2. b	7. a	12. b
3. d	8. c	13. d
4. b	9. a	14. b
5. c	10. c	15. a

APPENDIX A: Statistics
Summary

What tabular methods do researchers use to organize and summarize data?

One such method is a tool known as a frequency distribution table, which lists all of the scores, as well as the frequency of those scores. Frequency distribution tables enable researchers to see which scores occur most often.

What graphical methods do researchers use to organize and summarize data?

Researchers create histograms and frequency polygons to graphically depict the frequencies of scores. For both types of graphs, the scores are depicted on the horizontal or *x*-axis, and the frequency of each of these scores is depicted on the vertical or *y*-axis. A histogram is a frequency distribution graph in which bars are used to represent the frequency of scores. Frequency polygons provide the same information as a histogram, but with dots and lines rather than with bars.

What statistical measures do researchers use to find the most representative score of a distribution?

Researchers use the mean, median, and mode—three measures of central tendency—to describe the most representative score of a distribution. The mean is the average score; the median is the middlemost score; and the mode is the most frequently occurring score.

When is it appropriate to use the mean, median, or mode as a measure of central tendency?

The appropriateness depends on the shape of the distribution. In a normal distribution, the mean, mode, and median equal each other and are equally good indicators of the most representative score. For distributions that are negatively or positively skewed, the median or mode is preferable to the mean.

What statistical measures do researchers use to describe the variability of a distribution?

Researchers use the range and the standard deviation. The range is found by subtracting the lowest score from the highest score. The standard deviation is the average distance of the scores from the mean. It is found by subtracting the mean from each of the scores, squaring those deviations, and finding the average of those deviations. The standard deviation is often a more accurate measure of the variability of a distribution.

How do statistics enable researchers to compare scores from different distributions?

Researchers make scores comparable to each other by standardizing them. One statistic they use to standardize scores is the *z*-score, which is calculated by finding the distance of any raw score from the mean of its distribution and dividing it by the standard deviation of that distribution. *Z*-scores enable researchers to compare scores from different distributions according to how far above or below the mean of their respective distributions they are.

How do researchers determine whether variables are correlated?

Researchers use a graphical tool called the scatterplot and a statistical tool known as the correlation coefficient. A scatterplot is a graph that depicts the relation between two variables by plotting the point at which people's scores on two variables intersect. If the scores appear to gather along an imaginary diagonal line, the variables are probably correlated. A correlation coefficient is a statistic that more accurately indicates the strength and direction of the correlation between variables. The strength of the relationship between two variables is indicated by the magnitude of the correlation coefficient (how far away it is from 0). The direction of the relationship is indicated by whether the coefficient is positive or negative. When two variables are positively correlated, an increase in one of the variables corresponds to an increase in the other and the coefficient will be positive. When variables are negatively correlated, an increase in one of the variables corresponds to a decrease in the other and the coefficient will be negative.

What is the value of the experimental method for testing cause–effect relations?

The experimental method uses random assignment, which enables researchers to hold constant or control for any pre-existing differences between groups. It also enables the researcher to control for other differences so that the only factor that will differ between conditions is the manipulation of the independent variable. When differences are observed between conditions, we are confident that they were due to the manipulation.

How do researchers determine whether the differences they observe in an experiment are due to the effect of their manipulation or due to chance?

Researchers use inferential statistics to calculate the probability that the differences they observed were due to chance. Researchers begin with the *null hypothesis*—a hypothesis that states that any relationship observed between variables is due to chance—though they are actually interested in the alternative hypothesis, which states that there will be a relationship between observed variables. In explaining relationships between variables, researchers hope to rule out sampling error—chance differences between samples and populations. Psychologists use the distribution of (all possible) sample means to help them draw inferences about the probability of their particular data, if in fact the null hypothesis is true. In doing so, they are engaging in null hypothesis significance testing—a statistical procedure that reports the probability that a research result could have occurred by chance alone. If data are extremely unlikely

under the null hypothesis, psychologists conclude that their findings were statistically significant.

How do researchers determine just how meaningful their results are?

Statistical significance tells you that your observed differences were not due to chance, but it doesn't indicate how big the effect was, so researchers calculate effect size—a measure of the size of the effect that takes into account the consistency of the effect and that ignores sample size. Though there are criteria for deciding whether the effect size is small, medium, or large, it is ultimately up to the researcher to determine the meaningfulness of the findings.

Answers to What Do You Know?

1. 4
2. 3
3. The mean, median, and mode of this distribution are all 2.
4. The median and mode are both 90.
5. The standard deviation would be 0 because the scores do not vary around the mean of 1.
6. The standard deviation cannot be greater than 2 because the absolute distance between the most extreme scores and the mean is not greater than 2.
7. According to the empirical rule, 68% of scores will fall between 4 and 6; 95% of scores will fall between 3 and 7; and 99% of scores will fall between 2 and 8.
8. (a) Your respective z-scores are 1.
   (b) Given that your z-scores are the same, you are not justified in teasing her, because you run at the same rate, relative to your age groups.
9. 1b, 2c, 3a
10. (a) She randomly assigned participants to conditions.
    (b) It would have been important for her to hold constant the rate at which she read the traits. Other answers are possible.
11. 1e, 2a, 3f, 4d, 5h, 6b, 7g, 8c
12. (a) negative, (b) positive
13. One advantage is that effect size takes into account the consistency of the effect. Another is that there are benchmarks for determining whether the effect is small, medium, or large.

Glossary

2D:4D ratio A relation between two finger lengths (the second and fourth digit of the hand) that is related to variations in sexual orientation. (p. 150)

accommodation In Piagetian theory, a cognitive process in which a schema is modified as response to feedback from the environment. (p. 604)

acquisition In the psychology of learning, attaining the ability to perform a new response; "acquiring" a response. (p. 266)

action potentials Nerve impulses (or spikes); electrochemical events in which an electrical current travels down the length of an axon. (p. 107)

activation-synthesis theory A theory about the processes through which dreams are generated, claiming that dreams are the brain's attempt to make sense of random brain signals. (p. 389)

actual self People's perceptions of psychological qualities they possess currently, in the present. (p. 566)

ad hoc categories Categories whose structure is defined according to the relevance of items to a goal; items in the category are useful for some common purpose. (p. 312)

addictions Psychological disorders in which people use a drug or engage in an activity repeatedly and uncontrollably. (p. 495)

adolescence The period between childhood and adulthood; roughly the teenage years. (p. 635)

adrenal glands Endocrine glands that produce hormones that respond to stress, as well as sex hormones. (p. 115)

affective systems In social-cognitive theory, psychological systems that generate moods and emotional states. (p. 584)

agoraphobia Fear of being in diverse social situations outside one's home, such as in stores, public transportation, or among crowds. (p. 693)

alcohol A depressant chemical compound found in beer, wine, and spirits that induces feelings of relaxation and a lessening of inhibitions. (p. 401)

alleles Variations in specific genes that produce different versions of a characteristic, such as eye color or blood type. (p. 134)

alternative hypothesis A hypothesis stating that a relationship will exist between observed variables; also known as the *research hypothesis*. (p. A-17)

Ames room An apparatus for studying the perception of size; the room is not cubic, contrary to the visual system's assumption, and this creates perceptual illusion involving size. (p. 165)

amphetamines Stimulants that strongly increase alertness and produce euphoric feelings. (p. 400)

amygdala A limbic system structure that contributes to the processing of threatening stimuli. (p. 92)

anal stage In Freud's theory of psychological development, the developmental stage (18 months to 3½ years) during which children experience gratification from the release of tension resulting from the control and elimination of feces. (p. 558)

anchoring-and-adjustment heuristic A psychological process in which people formulate estimates by starting with an initial guess (an "anchor") and adjusting it to reach a final judgment. (p. 333)

anorexia nervosa Eating disorder characterized by such a fear of being fat that people severely restrict their intake to the point of starvation. (p. 463)

anti-anxiety drugs Pharmaceuticals designed to alter brain functioning by affecting neurotransmitters in a manner that reduces feelings of anxiety. (p. 689)

anticonvulsants Drugs typically used to treat epileptic seizures but that also are used to reduce bipolar symptoms. (p. 687)

antipsychotic drugs Medications designed to alter neurotransmitter activity in the brain in a manner that reduces psychotic symptoms. (p. 719)

antisocial personality disorder A psychological disorder defined by a set of negative personality traits such as being manipulative, callous, hostile; taking risks; and lacking empathy. (p. 724)

anxiety An agitated emotional state that includes feelings of apprehension about impending danger or misfortune. (p. 688)

anxiety disorders Long-lasting psychological states involving strong and persistent feelings of anxiety that interfere with everyday life. (p. 688)

anxious-ambivalent attachment An attachment style in which an infant experiences conflicting emotions: a desire for closeness with the mother combined with worry and anger toward the parent. (p. 623)

aphasia An impairment of language abilities that occurs while other mental abilities remain intact. (p. 321)

appraisal theories of emotion Theories claiming that emotions arise from a psychological process in which people continuously monitor the relation between themselves and the world around them, with these appraisals determining the emotion they experience. (p. 423)

appraisals Evaluations of the personal significance of ongoing and upcoming events. (p. 423)

approach motivation A broad class of motives that concern the growth and enhancement of an organism, from obtaining food to attaining a higher social status. (p. 493)

assimilation In Piagetian theory, a cognitive process in which one understands an object or event by incorporating it into a preexisting schema. (p. 604)

association areas Areas of the cerebral cortex that receive sensory information from other regions of the brain and connect it to memories and stored knowledge, enabling psychologically meaningful experiences. (p. 97)

attachment A strong emotional bond between two people, especially a child and a caretaker, such as a parent. (p. 623)

attachment styles Characteristic ways in which children and parents interact and relate to one another emotionally. (p. 623)

attachment theory Bowlby's theory of the ways in which bonds of attachment between parent and child have a lifelong impact on the child. (p. 623)

attention The process of bringing an idea or an external stimulus into conscious awareness. (p. 204)

attentional effort Focusing attention on a stimulus in the environment; concentration. (p. 219)

attention-deficit hyperactivity disorder (ADHD) A condition marked by high distractibility, low ability to concentrate, and impulsive behavior such as fast and frequent moving and talking. (p. 400)

attitude A combined thought and feeling directed toward some person, object, or idea. (p. 528)

attributions Beliefs about the causes of social behaviors. (p. 524)

atypical antipsychotics One of two major types of antipsychotic drugs, specifically, the second class of such drugs to be developed, in the 1990s. Atypical antipsychotics may relieve a wider range of symptoms while having fewer side effects than typical antipsychotics. (p. 719)

auditory cortex A region of the temporal lobes that contributes to the processing of sounds and also is key to remembering facts and experiences. (p. 96)

auditory nerve A bundle of nerve cells that carries auditory information from the inner ear to the brain. (p. 189)

auditory system The perceptual system detecting environmental information that consists of sound waves. (p. 160)

autism Autism spectrum disorder, a range of symptoms whose central features include impaired communication and social interaction with other people. (p. 611)

autobiographical memory Your memory of facts and experiences from your own life. (p. 244)

automatic thoughts Thoughts that spring to mind rapidly and unintentionally. (p. 670)

autonomic nervous system Functionally, the part of the peripheral nervous system that provides the communications controlling bodily functions that generally are not under your control, such as breathing. (p. 112)

availability heuristic A psychological process in which people base judgments on the ease with which information comes to mind. (p. 332)

avoidance motivation A drive to protect oneself from threats and dangers, both physical and social. (p. 493)

avoidant attachment The attachment style in which a child reacts to a parent in a relatively indifferent manner; the child does not count on the parent as a source of security and comfort. (p. 623)

avoidant personality disorder A psychological disorder characterized by feelings of social inadequacy, low self-esteem, and preoccupation with potential negative evaluations by others, leading to behavior that is shy, withdrawn, and inhibited. (p. 725)

axon The thin and long projection from a neuron that sends outgoing signals to other neurons. (p. 107)

back translation A method to assure the accuracy of translation by having the research materials translated twice (by different individuals)—first into the second language, and then from the second language back into the first. (p. 41)

basic-level categories Categories that are informative and efficient, and that thus are used most commonly to categorize items. (p. 309)

Beck's cognitive therapy A therapy method for changing negative, irrational thoughts by increasing clients' awareness of their automatic thoughts, challenging those thoughts, and suggesting positive alternative ones. (p. 670)

behavior genetics Field of study that investigates the degree to which psychological variations are inherited. (p. 127)

behavior therapy A therapy strategy grounded in research on learning, in which therapists aim to directly alter clients' patterns of behavior by teaching more adaptive ways of behaving. (p. 667)

behavioral approach system A neural system activated by stimuli that signal the future presence of rewards, energizing an organism to seek out rewarding stimuli. (p. 493)

behavioral inhibition system A neural system activated by signals of punishment, increasing levels of arousal and feelings of anxiety. (p. 494)

behaviorism A school of thought focusing solely on the prediction and control of behavior, by studying how the environment shapes observable actions. (p. 28)

benzodiazepines Psychoactive drugs prescribed for anxiety that reduce feelings of anxiety while also inducing muscular relaxation and sleepiness; may also produce pleasurable feelings. (p. 400)

Big Five A set of personality traits that is found consistently when researchers analyze, via factor analysis, people's descriptions of personality. (p. 573)

binge eating disorder A pattern of repeatedly eating excessively; binging without purging. (p. 463)

binocular cues Depth cues that require two eyes. (p. 163)

biological constraint An evolved predisposition that makes it difficult or impossible for a given species to learn a certain type of behavior when reinforced with a certain type of reward. (p. 293)

biological needs Necessities required for an organism's survival (food, drink) and for reproduction. (p. 460)

biological therapies In the treatment of psychological disorders, interventions that directly alter the biochemistry or anatomy of the nervous system. (p. 665)

biopsychosocial model A way of explaining developmental events (e.g., behavioral changes at puberty) in which the impact of biology on behavior is said to depend on social experiences. (p. 637)

bipolar disorder (manic-depressive disorder) A depressive disorder characterized by extreme variations in mood, from severe depression to mania. (p. 686)

blind spot The location in the visual field at which nothing is seen because light from that location projects to an area of the retina in which there are no photoreceptors; this is the retinal area where the optic nerve exits the eye. (p. 179)

blocking A failure to learn an association between a conditioned stimulus and an unconditioned stimulus that occurs if other environmental stimuli already predict occurrences of the unconditioned stimulus. (p. 273)

blood–brain barrier A set of biological mechanisms in the circulatory system that prevents most substances in the bloodstream from entering brain tissue. (p. 677)

borderline personality disorder A psychological disorder involving an unstable sense of self, emotional instability, unstable interpersonal relationships, and a sense of abandonment. (p. 725)

brain stem The lowest region of the brain; its structures regulate bodily activities critical to survival. (p. 88)

brief psychotic disorder A disorder in which people experience symptoms typical of schizophrenia, but for only a brief period of time. (p. 721)

Broca's area A region of the frontal lobe in the left hemisphere of the brain needed to produce speech. (p. 321)

bulimia nervosa Eating disorder characterized by a fluctuating pattern of binging and purging. (p. 463)

caffeine A chemical compound found in coffee, tea, energy drinks, sodas, and chocolate that increases alertness. (p. 400)

Cannon–Bard theory of emotion A theory of the generation of emotional states in which emotionally arousing events produce physiological and emotional responses simultaneously, rather than one leading to the other. (p. 437)

case study A detailed analysis of one particular person or group of people; the person or group is the "case." (p. 62)

categorize To classify an item as a type of thing, that is, a member of a group. (p. 308)

category level A relation between categories; one category is of a lower level than another when all members of the former category are contained within the latter, higher-level category. (p. 309)

category structure The rules that determine category membership. (p. 310)

central nervous system The part of the nervous system found in the center of the body; its two main parts are the brain and the spinal cord. (p. 111)

cerebellum A brain structure located behind the brain stem that regulates motor movement and also contributes to emotion and thinking. (p. 89)

cerebral cortex A layer of cells on the brain's outer surface that is key to the human capacity for complex conceptual thought. (p. 94)

cerebral hemispheres The two sides of the brain; the left hemisphere specializes in analytical tasks including math and language, while the right hemisphere is specialized for spatial thinking, the ability to create and think about images. (p. 99)

child prodigies Children exhibiting exceptional mastery of a skill at a very early age. (p. 352)

chromosomes Biological structures within the nucleus of cells that contain genetic information (DNA). (p. 134)

chunking A strategy for increasing the amount of information retained in short-term memory in which distinct pieces of information are grouped into "chunks." (p. 246)

circadian rhythm The approximately 24-hour cycle of changes in internal bodily processes. (p. 382)

clarity The degree of distinctness, as opposed to fuzziness, of a visual image; a monocular depth cue. (p. 164)

classical categories Categories whose boundaries are unambiguous due to clear-cut rules for determining category membership. (p. 310)

classical conditioning A form of learning that occurs when an organism encounters a stimulus that repeatedly signals the occurrence of a second stimulus. (p. 260)

clinical case study In psychology, an analysis of someone receiving psychological therapy; generally a written summary of a case. (p. 62)

clinical psychologists Professionals trained not only in principles of psychological science, but also in the application of those principles to the diagnosis of, and provision of therapy for, psychological disorders. (p. 656)

close relationships One-on-one interactions in which a person is in frequent contact with, and feels a strong connection to, another person. (p. 506)

cocaine A powerful stimulant that increases alertness and produces euphoric feelings, and thus is highly addictive. (p. 400)

coevolution Processes through which biology and culture interact in the course of human evolution. (p. 124)

cognitive control The mental ability to suppress one's emotions and impulsive behaviors that are undesired or inappropriate. (p. 634)

cognitive development Growth in intellectual capabilities, particularly during the early years of life. (p. 602)

cognitive dissonance A negative psychological state that occurs when people recognize that two (or more) of their ideas or actions do not fit together sensibly. (p. 528)

cognitive impairments (in schizophrenia) Among people with schizophrenia, reduced ability to perform everyday thinking tasks such as concentrating, remembering, and planning social interactions. (p. 706)

cognitive revolution A school of thought focusing on the mind as an information-processing system; in so doing, it introduced novel forms of theory and research into psychological science. (p. 30)

cognitive therapy A psychological therapy in which therapists try to improve mental health by changing the way in which clients think, reducing negative, self-defeating thoughts. (p. 669)

Cohen's *d* A measure of effect size that expresses the difference between sample means in standard deviation units. (p. A-24)

collective unconscious Jung's concept of a storehouse of mental images, symbols, and ideas that all humans inherit thanks to evolution. (p. 562)

collectivistic In the study of cultural variations, a pattern of cultural beliefs and values that emphasizes individuals' ties to larger groups such as family, community, and nation. (p. 540)

color blindness An insensitivity to one or more of the colors red, green, or blue. (p. 176)

color constancy The tendency for a given object to be perceived as having the same color, despite changes in illumination. (p. 173)

community-participation study A type of research in which researchers collaborate with community residents to determine a study's goals and research procedures. (p. 62)

comorbidity The presence of symptoms of two or more disorders in any one individual. (p. 662)

compensation In the selection, optimization, and compensation (SOC) model of successful aging, the identification of alternative strategies to achieve goals, if at first you don't succeed. (p. 643)

compensatory response A biological reaction to a conditioned stimulus that is the opposite of the effects of the stimulus and therefore partially counteracts its effects. (p. 271)

compliance Agreement to an explicit request. (p. 513)

concrete operational stage In Piaget's theory of child development, the stage (ages 7 to 11) in which children can perform reversible logical operations (e.g., basic arithmetic) limited to "concrete" objects that actually exist. (p. 606)

condition of worth In Rogers's theory of personality, a behavioral requirement imposed by others, such as parents, as a condition for being fully valued, loved, and respected. (p. 567)

conditioned response (CR) A response to a conditioned stimulus that occurs as a result of learning through classical conditioning. (p. 262)

conditioned stimulus (CS) An event that elicits a response from an organism only after the organism learns to associate it with another stimulus that already evokes a response. (p. 262)

conditioned taste aversion (Garcia effect) The rapid learning of a connection between the taste of a food and illness that occurs after consuming that food. (p. 275)

cones Photoreceptors that are concentrated near the center of the retina and that provide visual detail and color. (p. 176)

confederate In a research study, an accomplice of the experimenter who pretends to be a participant. (p. 512)

confirmation bias The tendency to seek out information that is consistent with one's initial conclusions, and to disregard information that might contradict those conclusions. (p. 328)

conformity The altering of one's behavior so that it matches the norms of a group. (p. 510)

confound A factor other than the independent variable that might create differences between experimental conditions. (p. 49)

connectome The complete network of neural connections in the brain and overall nervous system of an organism. (p. 104)

conscious In Freud's analysis of levels of consciousness, the regions of mind containing the mental contents of which you are aware at any given moment. (p. 555)

consciousness Awareness and personal experience of oneself and one's surroundings. (p. 362)

consent procedure A process in which researchers describe a study's procedures and determine whether participants agree to take part. (p. 73)

conservation In Piagetian psychology, the recognition that an object maintains some of its essential physical properties even when it is physically transformed. (p. 606)

consolidation A transformation of information in long-term memory from a fragile state, in which information can be lost, to a more fixed state in which it is available relatively permanently. (p. 230)

control group An experimental condition that does not receive the experimental treatment. (p. 48)

convergence A binocular depth cue based on the effort eye muscles must exert to look at objects very close to the face. (p. 167)

converging vertical lines A monocular depth cue consisting of vertically oriented lines that get closer to one another, creating the perception of depth. (p. 163)

conversion disorder A psychological disorder characterized by physical symptoms (e.g., partial paralysis, difficulty seeing or hearing) that cannot be explained by a medical condition. (p. 739)

cornea The transparent material at the very front of the eye; its curvature begins the process of focusing light. (p. 175)

corpus callosum A brain structure that connects the two hemispheres of the brain, enabling them to work in synchrony. (p. 99)

correlation coefficient (correlation) A numerical value that represents the strength of a correlation between any two variables. (p. 44; see also pp. A-11, A-12)

correlational study A research design whose aim is to determine the relation between two or more measured variables. (p. 43)

counseling psychologists Professionals whose training and professional activities are similar to those of clinical psychologists, but with particular emphasis on the provision of advice regarding not only mental health, but also personal and vocational development. (p. 656)

cranial nerves Those parts of the peripheral nervous system found in the head; nerves that extend from the bottom of the brain to structures in the head such as eyes, nose, and tongue. (p. 112)

criterion variable In a correlation between two variables, the variable whose value is predicted by the other (predictor) variable. (p. A-12)

critical period For a given psychological process, a span of time early in life during which a psychological process must occur if it is ever to develop. (p. 622)

critical thinking Thinking skills that include the ability to think logically, to question assumptions, to evaluate evidence, and, generally, to be open-minded yet skeptical. (p. 12)

cross-cultural study Research in which identical research procedures are carried out in different cultures. (p. 540)

crowds Large gatherings of people who do not necessarily know one another. (p. 506)

cues to depth Sources of information that enable us to judge the distance between ourselves and the objects we perceive. (p. 163)

cultural psychology Branch of psychology that studies how the social practices of cultures and the psychological qualities of individuals mutually influence one another. (p. 539)

culture People's shared beliefs and the social practices that reflect those beliefs. (p. 538)

cutaneous receptors Receptor cells under the skin that convert physical stimulation into nervous-system impulses. (p. 200)

data Any type of information obtained in a scientific study. (p. 51)

decay The fading of information from short-term memory. (p. 221)

decision making The process of making a choice, that is, selecting among alternatives. (p. 334)

defense mechanism A mental strategy that, in psychoanalytic theory, is devised by the ego to protect against anxiety. (p. 559)

delusional beliefs Personal convictions that contradict known facts about the world but that a person clings to even when faced with conflicting evidence. (p. 706)

delusional disorder A psychological disorder in which people hold convictions that contradict known facts (e.g., that someone is trying to harm them). (p. 721)

dendrites Projections that branch out from the main body of a neuron, receiving incoming signals from other neurons. (p. 107)

deoxyribonucleic acid (DNA) The molecule found in chromosomes that encodes the instructions for building an organism. (p. 134)

dependent variable In an experimental design, the variable that is potentially influenced by the manipulation of the independent variable. (p. 47)

depersonalization/derealization disorder A psychological disorder in which people feel detachment from their own experiences; key symptoms are depersonalization (a sense of merely observing with detachment) and derealization (feeling as if objects and others are unreal or foggy). (p. 735)

depressants Psychoactive drugs that reduce arousal in the central nervous system, lowering conscious experiences of excitability and anxiety. (p. 400)

depression A family of psychological disorders that includes feelings of sadness and hopelessness, fatigue, loss of interest in activities, changes in eating and sleeping patterns, and that continues for weeks. (p. 680)

depth of processing The degree to which people think about meaningful rather than superficial aspects of presented information. (p. 224)

depth perception The perception of distance. (p. 163)

descriptive statistics Mathematical techniques geared toward summarizing data. (p. A-1)

developmental psychology The field of study that explores the ways people change, and remain the same, across the course of life. (p. 602)

developmental stage In Piaget's theory of child development, a period of months or years during which one form of given thinking is predominant. (p. 605)

Diagnostic and Statistical Manual of Mental Disorders (DSM) Reference book that comprehensively lists and classifies mental disorders, specifying diagnostic criteria. (p. 661)

dialectical behavior therapy A therapy for borderline personality disorder whose core element is a dialectic approach that attempts to identify and reconcile opposing points of view on psychological problems, in an effort to reduce emotional distress. (p. 732)

differentiated self-esteem The varying feelings people may have about themselves when thinking about different aspects of their lives. (p. 633)

diffusion of responsibility Lowered feelings of personal obligation to respond to someone in need, because others might respond instead. (p. 520)

direct observation A research method in which researchers view the actions of research participants firsthand and record the behaviors they observe, often by counting specific behaviors. (p. 66)

direct sibling effects Developmental influence involving one-on-one interactions between siblings. (p. 628)

discrimination (1) In the study of learning, a process in which organisms distinguish between stimuli, responding to one stimulus but not another. (p. 268); (2) In social psychology, unjust treatment of people based on their group membership. (p. 534)

discriminative stimulus Any stimulus that provides information about the type of consequences that are likely to follow a given type of behavior in particular situations. (p. 290)

disorganized thinking A positive symptom of schizophrenia in which thoughts and speech are not properly structured, and speech is thus unintelligible. (p. 706)

disrupt-then-reframe technique A compliance strategy in which targets of compliance efforts are distracted, so they cannot formulate negative thoughts about a compliance request. (p. 514)

dissociative amnesia A psychological disorder in which people are unable to remember significant personal information that typically would be highly memorable. (p. 736)

dissociative disorders Category of psychological disorders characterized by alterations in one's sense of personal identity, conscious experiences of events, or memory of one's own past. (p. 733)

dissociative fugue A psychological disorder featuring complete loss of memory of one's own personal identity. (p. 736)

dissociative identity disorder A psychological disorder in which people experience more than one self; that is, more than one personality seems to inhabit their mind. (p. 733)

distal causes In an evolutionary analysis, factors in the distant past that caused a biological mechanism to evolve. (p. 141)

distal goal A goal that specifies an achievement in the distant future. (p. 476)

distribution A set of scores that can be described by the frequency of each score. (p. A-2)

distribution of sample means A hypothetical distribution of all possible sample means of a given sample size from a specified population. (p. A-18)

dizygotic (DZ) twins Siblings produced during the same pregnancy who are conceived from two separately fertilized cells; fraternal twins. (p. 122)

dopamine hypothesis of schizophrenia A hypothesis stating that abnormal levels of dopamine are responsible for the symptoms of schizophrenia. (p. 712)

double-blind clinical outcome study A research procedure to evaluate the effectiveness of therapy in which neither the research participants nor the researcher interacting with them knows the condition of the experiment to which the participant has been assigned. (p. 680)

drug addiction Compulsive, habitual, uncontrollable use of a harmful chemical substance. (p. 397)

drug therapies In the treatment of psychological disorders, treatment with pharmaceuticals that alter the biochemistry of the brain to improve emotional state and thinking abilities. (p. 665)

DSM-5 The current edition of the DSM manual, published in 2013 with substantial changes in content. (p. 662)

dualism The proposition that the mind and body are two separate entities, with consciousness being a property of the nonphysical mind. (p. 368)

ear A biological mechanism for hearing with three overall parts: an outer ear, middle ear, and inner ear. (p. 187)

eardrum A thin membrane within the ear that vibrates when struck by sound waves. (p. 187)

eating disorders Disturbances in eating in which people lose the ability to control their intake of food, resulting in serious health risks. (p. 462)

echoic memory Sensory memory for sound. (p. 218)

eclectic therapy (integrative psychotherapy) Therapy that draws upon any therapeutic method available, with the therapist combining the methods of different therapy schools in designing an optimal approach for therapy in general or an individual client. (p. 674)

ecstasy A recreational drug that can reduce anxiety and create feelings of intimacy and euphoria while raising body temperature; both a stimulant and a hallucinogen. (p. 400)

EEG *See* electroencephalography

effect size A measure indicating how big an effect is (e.g., how great the difference between two means) that takes into account the consistency of the effect and that ignores sample size. (p. A-23)

ego In Freud's psychoanalytic theory, the mental system that balances the demands of the id with the opportunities and constraints of the real world. (p. 554)

electroconvulsive therapy (ECT) A biological therapy for severe depression in which electrical currents are delivered to the brain. (p. 677)

electroencephalography (EEG) A technique for recording and visually depicting electrical activity within the brain in which electrodes on the scalp record neural activity in underlying brain regions. The record of electrical activity through this method is called an *electroencephalogram*. (pp. 67, 381)

embodied cognition A conceptual model of knowledge representation in which parts of the mind previously thought to participate only in relatively simple mental activities, such as perceiving an event, also contribute to complex thought and memory. (p. 237)

emerging adulthood The period of life in the late teens and early 20s (roughly 18 to 25) experienced by people who have the rights and psychological independence of adulthood but do not yet have the obligations and responsibilities of family life. (p. 640)

emotion A psychological state that combines feelings, thoughts, and bodily arousal and that often has a distinctive accompanying facial expression. (p. 409)

empathic understanding In humanistic therapy, the therapist's understanding of the client's psychological life from the perspective of the client. (p. 671)

empirical rule A rule stating that in a normal distribution, roughly 68% of scores will fall within 1 standard deviation of the mean; 95% will fall within 2 standard deviations; and 99% will fall within 3 standard deviations. (p. A-8)

empirically supported therapies Treatments whose effectiveness is established in carefully controlled experimental research. (p. 679)

encoding The process through which information is transferred from sensory memory to short-term memory and, in the transfer, converted from physical stimulation to conceptual information (i.e., ideas). (p. 219)

endocrine system A collection of glands that produce and secrete hormones, which carry messages from the brain to organs via the bloodstream. (p. 113)

epigenetics The study of how environmental experience "switches on" genes, making them active in the production of proteins. (p. 136)

episodic memory Memory for events you have experienced. (p. 229)

ethnic identity People's personal identification with the ethnic group to which they belong. (p. 638)

evolution The biological process through which species develop and change across generations. (p. 140)

evolutionary psychology Field of study that explores the evolutionary foundations of contemporary human mental abilities, preferences, and desires. (p. 142)

evolved mechanisms Biological systems that developed over the course of evolution, thanks to their success in solving a specific problem faced repeatedly by members of a given species. (p. 141)

experience sampling method A research procedure in which participants carry an electronic device throughout the course of a study, signaling the participant to respond at random intervals throughout the day. (p. 488)

experiment A research design in which a variable is manipulated, with a goal of identifying the causes of events. (p. 47)

experimental conditions The different settings in a research design, which contain different levels of the independent variable. (p. 48)

experimental design The researcher's plan for manipulating one or more variables in an experiment. (p. 47)

explicit measure An assessment of psychological qualities (e.g., personality characteristics) in which test items directly inquire about the psychological quality of interest, and people's responses are interpreted as a direct index of those qualities. (p. 589)

explicit memory Conscious recall of previously encountered information or experience. (p. 229)

exposure and response prevention A type of therapy for obsessive-compulsive disorder in which therapists cause clients to come into contact with the stimuli that trigger their obsessions while preventing them from engaging in their usual compulsive behavior. (p. 695)

exposure therapy A behavior therapy technique in which therapists combat the emotions of fear and anxiety by bringing clients into direct contact with an object or situation that arouses their fear, while ensuring that no harm occurs. (p. 668)

extinction In the study of learning, a gradual lessening of a response that occurs when a stimulus is presented repeatedly without any presentations of an unconditioned stimulus (in classical conditioning) or reinforcer (in operant conditioning). (p. 269)

extinguishing (of emotion) In exposure therapy, the reduction in emotional response that occurs when an anticipated emotionally arousing consequence does not occur. (p. 668)

eyewitness memory Memory for events that are personally observed (rather than being learned of second-hand, through conversation or reading). (p. 241)

Facial Action Coding System (FACS) A method for measuring emotions that capitalizes on the link between emotional experience and facial expression; in this system, researchers code muscular movements occurring in specific parts of the face. (p. 419)

facial feedback hypothesis The prediction that biological feedback from facial muscles directly influences emotional experience. (p. 417)

factor analysis A statistical technique that identifies patterns in large sets of correlations. (p. 572)

false memory The experience of "remembering" an event that, in reality, never occurred. (p. 239)

family resemblance A category structure in which category members share many features but no single feature is absolutely necessary for membership. (p. 311)

fetishism Sexual arousal in which stimuli that typically are not sexual in nature stir desires. (p. 465)

fight-or-flight response A behavioral pattern in which an organism facing a threat does one of two things: attack or flee. (p. 450)

figure-ground perception The visual system's tendency to divide a scene into objects, or "figures," that are the focus of attention and the background context. (p. 172)

fixation In Freud's theory of psychological development, a disruption in development occurring when an individual experiences either too little or too much gratification at a psychosexual stage. (p. 559)

fixed schedule of reinforcement In operant conditioning research, a timetable for reinforcement that is consistent across trials. (p. 287)

flashbulb memory Vivid memory of unexpected, highly emotional, and significant events. (p. 242)

flat affect An absence of normal emotional expression; a negative symptom of schizophrenia. (p. 707)

flow A psychological state in which your attention is directed intently on an activity for a long period of time, and you feel immersed in the activity. (p. 485)

Flynn effect Name given to the relatively rapid rise in intelligence test scores that is evident across generations. (p. 347)

foot-in-the-door technique A compliance strategy in which someone first makes a small request, in order to later convince people to comply with a larger request. (p. 513)

foreclosure According to Marcia, the identity status of people who know their role in life and prospective future occupation, but feel these were imposed on them by others. (p. 637)

formal operational stage In Piaget's theory of child development, the stage (age 11 to adulthood) in which children can execute mental operations on both actual objects and hypothetical ones, using abstract rules. (p. 606)

fovea A region near the center of the retina that features a dense concentration of cones. (p. 176)

framing effect A phenomenon in decision making in which people's decisions are affected by the way in which outcomes are described, or "framed." (p. 335)

free association method A method of both personality assessment and therapy devised by Freud in which psychologists encourage people to let their thoughts flow freely and say whatever comes to mind. (pp. 561, 665)

frequency The physical property of sound waves that produces variations in pitch, based on the number of vibrations that occur during any fixed period of time. (p. 184)

frequency distribution table A table that lists all the scores in a distribution in numeric order, as well as the frequency of each score. (p. A-2)

frequency polygon A frequency distribution graph that uses dots connected by lines to represent frequency. (p. A-3)

frontal lobes A part of the cerebral cortex that is particularly large in humans and enables distinctive human mental abilities such as self-reflection (i.e., thinking about oneself). (p. 96)

functional magnetic resonance imaging (fMRI) A brain-scanning method that depicts activity in specific regions of the brain as people engage in psychological activities. (p. 67)

functionalism A school of thought focusing on the mental activity of the mind rather than on its structure, as it interacts with the body and adapts to the environment. (p. 27)

fundamental attribution error Pattern of thinking in which people underestimate the causal influence of situational factors on people's behavior and overestimate the causal influence of personal factors. (p. 525)

fuzzy categories Categories whose boundaries are ambiguous. (p. 310)

ganglion cells Cells that form the optic nerve and pass visual information from the retina to the brain. (p. 179)

Garcia effect *See* conditioned taste aversion

gate control theory of pain The theory that the spinal cord contains a biological mechanism that acts like a gate; when closed, pain signals do not reach the brain, resulting in no experience of pain even though there is pain receptor activity. (p. 202)

gene Any section of DNA that provides the full information needed to produce a protein. (p. 134)

gene expression A biological process in which information in DNA becomes active in the process of producing protein molecules. (p. 135)

general adaptation syndrome (GAS) A sequence of physiological reactions in response to stressors: alarm, resistance, and exhaustion. (p. 444)

general intelligence (g) A measure of overall mental ability based on total performance across a number of different types of intellectual tests. (p. 344)

generalization A learning process in which responses are elicited by stimuli that vary slightly from the stimuli encountered during acquisition of a response. (p. 267)

generalized anxiety disorder A psychological disorder in which people experience high and persistent levels of tension, agitation, apprehension, and worry, even in the absence of a current event that provokes the feelings. (p. 689)

generative A characteristic of language referring to the fact that linguistic rules enable speakers to produce (or "generate") an infinite number of sentences. (p. 314)

genital stage In Freud's theory of psychological development, the developmental stage that starts at puberty, signaling the reawakening of sexual desire. (p. 558)

genome The entire set of genes possessed by an organism. (p. 134)

genome-wide association study A method in which researchers study the relation between a psychological characteristic (e.g., a psychological disorder) and hundreds or thousands of genetic variations simultaneously, in order to identify places along the human genome that are associated with the presence versus absence of the characteristic. (p. 717)

glial cells Cells that hold neurons in place and also support their biological functioning, supplying nutrients to neurons and disposing of the brain's biological waste matter. (p. 110)

global self-esteem A person's overall sense of self-worth. (p. 633)

goal A mental representation of the aim of an activity; more simply, goals are thoughts about future outcomes that people value. (p. 475)

gonads The organs that produce reproductive cells—ovaries in women produce ova and testes in men produce sperm. (p. 115)

group dynamics Psychological processes involving communication, conflict, and pressure among group members. (p. 510)

group therapy Any type of psychological therapy in which a therapist meets with two or more clients together. (p. 672)

groups Collections of people who know and communicate with each other, have distinctive roles (e.g., a group leader), and may work together toward a common goal. (p. 506)

groupthink A decision-making phenomenon in which group members are so motivated to avoid disagreement, and to reach a shared decision, that they do not properly evaluate the quality of the decision they are reaching. (p. 513)

gustatory cortex The brain region in the parietal lobe that completes the processing of perceptual signals of taste. (p. 196)

gustatory system The perceptual system that is sensitive to chemical substances and provides the sense of taste. (p. 160)

habituation A lessening in response that occurs when a stimulus that normally evokes a reaction in an organism is presented (p. 270)

hair cells Auditory receptor cells in the inner ear that are responsible for transduction of sound waves. (p. 188)

hallucinations Experiences (sights, sounds, smells, tastes, or touches) of people or things that are not really there. (p. 706)

hallucinogens Substances that profoundly alter consciousness, causing people to experience phenomena such as hallucinations and a loss of contact with reality. (p. 398)

haptic system The perceptual system through which people acquire information about objects by touching them. (p. 160)

hedonic hunger Hunger that arises from the anticipated pleasure of eating good food. (p. 462)

heritability The degree to which genetic factors explain individual differences in a characteristic. (p. 129)

heuristic A rule of thumb, that is, a simple way of accomplishing something that otherwise would be done through a more complex procedure. (p. 331)

heuristic information processing Thinking that employs mental shortcuts or simple rules of thumb. (p. 528)

hippocampus A limbic system structure needed for forming permanent memories and central to spatial memory (the recall of geographic layouts). (p. 91)

histogram A frequency distribution graph in which bars are used to represent the frequency of each score. (p. A-2)

homeostatic hunger Motivation to eat based on the body's need for energy. (p. 461)

homeostatic processes Processes that maintain a stable biological state in an organism. (p. 461)

homunculus problem A problem in scientific explanation that arises if an organism's capacity for consciousness is explained by proposing that a structure in its mind or brain is conscious. The problem is the failure to explain how consciousness arises in the mind or brain structure. (p. 370)

hormones Chemicals that the endocrine system uses for communication; they travel through the bloodstream and carry messages to the body's organs. (p. 114)

Human Genome Project An international effort to map the entire sequence of molecular material in the human genetic code; initiated in 1990, the project was completed in 2003. (p. 138)

humanistic psychology An intellectual movement which argues that everyday personal experiences—thoughts, feelings, hopes, fears, sense of self—should be psychologists' main target of study. (p. 28)

humanistic theory An approach to personality that focuses on people's thoughts and feelings about themselves and the ways that interpersonal relationships shape these feelings. (p. 565)

humanistic therapy A psychological therapy in which therapists provide clients with supportive interpersonal relationships; the quality of the relationship between therapist and client is key to the client's growth and change. (p. 671)

hunger A feeling of food deprivation that motivates organisms to seek food. (p. 460)

hypnosis An altered state of consciousness characterized by the subject's unusual responsiveness to suggestions made by the hypnotist. (p. 394)

hypnotic induction The process of inducing a state of hypnosis in a subject, usually through procedures combining relaxation and focused attention. (p. 394)

hypothalamic–pituitary–adrenal (HPA) axis An interconnected set of structures and hormone pathways regulating stress response. (p. 444)

hypothalamus A limbic system structure key to the regulation of bodily states and behaviors such as eating, drinking, and sexual response. (p. 90)

hypothesis A prediction about the result of a study. (p. 48)

iconic memory Sensory memory of visual images. (p. 217)

id In Freud's psychoanalytic theory, the personality structure that motivates people to satisfy basic bodily needs. (p. 554)

ideal self People's perceptions of psychological qualities that they optimally would possess in the future. (p. 566)

identity People's overall understanding of themselves, their role in society, their strengths and weaknesses, their history, and their future potential. (p. 637)

identity achievement According to Marcia, the identity status achieved by people who have deeply contemplated life options and are committed to a career path based on their values. (p. 637)

identity diffusion According to Marcia, the identity status of people who feel directionless, with no firm sense of where they're headed in life. (p. 637)

identity statuses In Marcia's theory, four different approaches to coping with the challenge of establishing a personal identity. (p. 637)

if . . . then . . . profile method A method for assessing behavior in which researchers chart variations in behavior that occur when people encounter different situations. (p. 590)

immune system A set of bodily processes that protects against germs, microorganisms, and other foreign substances that enter the body and can cause disease. (p. 446)

implementation intentions Plans that specify exactly when and where you will work on achieving a goal. (p. 480)

implicit measure An assessment of psychological qualities (e.g., personality characteristics) that does not rely on test takers' direct reports of their qualities; instead, measures such as length of time taken to answer a question provide information about psychological qualities. (p. 589)

implicit memory Task performance that is affected by previous information or experience, even if the prior material is not explicitly remembered. (p. 229)

imprinting A phenomenon in some species in which newborns fix attention upon, and follow, the first moving object they encounter. (p. 622)

independent variable In an experimental design, any variable that the experimenter manipulates in order to see its effect on another variable. (p. 47)

indirect sibling effects Developmental influence in which parents' interactions with one sibling affect treatment of a second sibling. (p. 628)

individualistic In the study of cultural variations, a pattern of cultural beliefs and values that emphasizes individual rights to pursue happiness, speak freely, and "be yourself." (p. 540)

inferential statistics Mathematical techniques that enable scientists to make inferences about populations based on data collected from samples. (p. A-1)

information-processing system A device that can acquire, store, and manipulate symbols to transform information. (p. 30)

inhibited temperament A tendency to experience high levels of distress and fear, especially in unfamiliar situations or in the presence of unfamiliar people. (p. 620)

insight therapy A type of psychotherapy in which therapists help clients identify and understand the root causes of their psychological symptoms. (p. 665)

insomnia A sleep disorder involving prolonged difficulty in falling asleep or staying asleep. (p. 386)

instinct A behavioral tendency possessed by an animal due to its biological inheritance. (p. 317)

Institutional Review Board (IRB) A group of professionals who assess the ethics of a proposed research study. (p. 72)

integrative psychotherapy *See* eclectic therapy

intelligence The ability to acquire knowledge, to solve problems, and to use acquired knowledge to create new, valued products. (p. 342)

interference Failure to retain information in short-term memory that occurs when material learned earlier or later prevents its retention. (p. 222)

intergroup contact A technique for reducing prejudice in which members of different groups meet and spend time together. (p. 537)

interpersonal therapy A therapy approach in which therapists try to identify and change interpersonal problems contributing to clients' psychological distress, especially by reducing clients' social isolation. (p. 682)

interval schedule of reinforcement In operant conditioning research, a timetable for reinforcement in which the reinforcer is delivered subsequent to the first response an organism makes after a specific period of time elapses. (p. 287)

intrinsic motivation The desire to engage in activities because they are personally interesting, challenging, and enjoyable. (p. 483)

Iowa Gambling Task A method for studying, via a card game with monetary payoffs, the influence of emotions on decision making. (p. 412)

IQ (intelligence quotient) A measure of overall intelligence that takes into account a person's age. (p. 343)

iris The colorful eye structure that surrounds the pupil and responds to low and high light levels by dilating or constricting the pupil. (p. 175)

irrational beliefs Demanding, dogmatic thoughts that distort reality illogically and cause people to experience negative emotions. (p. 669)

James–Lange theory of emotion A theory of how the brain and body generate emotional experience in which physiological arousal, in response to an event, is said to precede and cause a subsequent emotional response. (p. 436)

just noticeable difference (JND) The minimal variation in a physical stimulus such as light or sound that a person can detect. (p. 172)

kinesthetic system The perceptual system that detects information about the location of body parts. (p. 160)

knowledge representation The format in which knowledge in long-term memory is retained, and in which elements of that knowledge are interconnected. (p. 232)

language A communication system in which sounds have meaning and rules govern the way in which linguistic units (e.g., words) can be combined. (p. 313)

latency stage In Freud's theory of psychological development, the developmental stage during which sexual desires are repressed into the unconscious until puberty. (p. 558)

lateral geniculate nucleus Cells that receive visual signals and perform "computations" on them before transmitting the same signals to the visual cortex. (p. 180)

law of effect A principle of learning which states that when an organism performs a behavior that leads to a satisfying outcome in a given situation, it will be more likely to perform that behavior when it again encounters the same situation. (p. 282)

learned helplessness A severe reduction in motivation that occurs when animals learn that their own behavior cannot control unpleasant outcomes. (p. 273)

learning Any relatively long-lasting change in behavioral abilities or emotional reactions that results from experience. (p. 260)

lens An adjustable, transparent mechanism in the eye that focuses incoming light. (p. 175)

levels of analysis Different ways of describing and explaining any given object or event. Psychological phenomena can be studied at three levels—person, mind, and brain. (p. 14)

levels of consciousness Variations in the degree to which people are aware, and can become aware, of the contents of their minds. (p. 555)

lexical approach A perspective on the task of identifying personality traits which presumes that all significant individual differences among people will be represented by naturally occurring words in everyday language. (p. 572)

life story A narrative understanding of the major events and themes of one's life. (p. 641)

lifespan developmental psychology The field of study that explores human psychological development from the start of life through old age. (p. 642)

limbic system A set of brain structures just above the brain stem, including the hypothalamus, hippocampus, and amygdala, that give mammals the capacity to experience emotional reactions. (p. 90)

lithium A mood-stabilizing drug that centrally includes the physical element lithium; the classic drug of choice for treatment of bipolar disorder. (p. 687)

lobotomy An outmoded surgical procedure for treating mental disorders in which a surgeon would damage brain tissue in the frontal cortex. (p. 678)

long-term memory The mental system that stores knowledge for extended periods of time. (p. 227)

long-term potentiation An enduring increase in the efficiency of communication between brain cells. (p. 249)

loudness The subjective experience of the intensity, or strength, of an auditory experience. (p. 183)

LSD (lysergic acid diethylamide) A synthetic chemical that affects the firing of neurons in the brain, thereby inducing widespread biological, and thus psychological, effects. (p. 398)

major depressive disorder A disorder in which individuals experience some (but not necessarily all) of the following symptoms: depressed mood lasting at least two weeks, loss of interest in daily activities, changes in weight and sleep, fatigue, feelings of worthlessness and hopelessness, difficulty concentrating, and thoughts of suicide. (p. 681)

mania A period of abnormally high energy, arousal, and often positive mood that can be accompanied by reckless behavior. (p. 686)

marijuana A drug that produces a wide range of effects that commonly include both euphoria and a relaxed, tranquil state. (p. 401)

Maslow's hierarchy of needs A classification of human motives according to five basic needs, with lower-level needs requiring fulfillment before moving up to higher levels. (p. 458)

mean The average score in a distribution (or set of numbers). (pp. 58, A-4)

means–ends analysis A strategy for solving complex problems in which, at each step toward a solution, people aim to reduce the distance between their current state of progress and the final problem-solving goal they want to achieve. (p. 337)

measurement Any procedure in which numbers are assigned to objects or events. (p. 52)

measures of central tendency Statistics that describe the most representative score in a distribution, including mean, median, and mode. (p. A-4)

median The middlemost score in a distribution. (p. A-4)

medical model of psychological disorders Framework for thinking about the causes of, and treatments for, psychological disorders in a way that mimics thinking about physical illnesses. (p. 657)

meditation Any practice in which people focus their attention for an extended period of time, as a method for increasing their ability to concentrate. (p. 391)

medulla A structure in the brain stem that contributes to homeostasis by regulating rates of physiological activity and that serves as the communications pathway from the brain to the rest of the body. (p. 89)

memory The capacity to retain knowledge. (p. 215)

mental accounting A thinking process in which people divide their assets and expenditures into distinct cognitive categories, rather than thinking about their overall costs and net assets. (p. 336)

mental age A measure of a child's intelligence based on both the child's test responses and the responses of other children who have taken the same test. The child's mental age is equivalent to the average age of other children who perform as well as that child. (p. 344)

mental imagery Thinking that involves pictures and spatial relationships rather than words, numbers, and logical rules. (p. 339)

mental module A proposed subsystem of the mind and nervous system that performs a specific task in response to a specific type of environmental input. (p. 142)

mental rotation The psychological process of turning an image in one's mind, much as a person might turn a physical object in the world. (p. 340)

mental time travel The ability to project yourself backward or forward in time in your mind. (p. 366)

mere exposure effect Phenomenon in which people's attitudes toward an object become more positive simply as a result of being exposed to the object repeatedly. (p. 530)

meta-analysis A statistical technique for combining results from multiple studies in order to identify overall patterns in the studies as a whole. (p. 59)

midbrain A structure of the brain stem that contributes to survival in several ways, such as by generating defensive reactions to threatening events. (p. 89)

mind–body problem A conceptual problem that arises within dualistic theories (see dualism), namely, that there is no way to explain how a nonphysical mind can influence the physical body without violating laws of science. (p. 370)

mindset A belief about the nature of psychological attributes, such as whether intelligence is fixed or can change. (p. 482)

mirror neurons Neurons in the motor cortex that fire not only when an organism engages in an action, but also when it observes another organism engaging in that same action. (p. 301)

mirror self-recognition test A method for evaluating an animal's capacity to recognize itself in which researchers determine whether the animal looking at itself in a mirror behaves in a manner indicating its recognition of a mark made on its body. (p. 366)

mnemonics Strategies for enhancing memory, in particular by organizing information in a manner that aids recall. (p. 246)

mode The most frequently occurring score in a distribution. (p. A-4)

modeling A form of learning in which knowledge and skills are acquired by observing others; also known as *observational learning*. (pp. 297, 585)

molecular genetic methods Biological techniques for studying specific genes and variations in those genes; researchers relate this genetic information to variations in behavior. (p. 137)

monocular cues Depth cues that are available even when we use only one eye. (p. 163)

monozygotic (MZ) twins Siblings who, at conception, develop from a single fertilized cell that splits; identical twins. (p. 122)

mood A prolonged, consistent feeling state, either positive or negative. (p. 410)

mood dimensions Universal variations in feeling states; variations that can describe the mood of any and all people. (p. 431)

mood stabilizers Drugs designed to reduce symptoms of bipolar disorder by affecting neurotransmitters in a way that calms and steadies a patient's mood swings. (p. 687)

mood-as-information hypothesis A proposal about the way in which feeling states influence thinking processes; in this hypothesis, moods inform thinking directly, as if they were sources of information. (p. 435)

moral development Growth in reasoning about personal rights, responsibilities, and social obligations regarding the welfare of others. (p. 602)

moral judgments Decisions that involve fundamental questions of right and wrong. (p. 420)

moral stage According to Kohlberg, a period of development during which a person's moral reasoning is consistently organized around a single way of thinking. (p. 647)

moratorium According to Marcia, the identity status of people who contemplate many life options but are unable to commit to any one set of goals. (p. 638)

morpheme The smallest unit of a language that itself conveys meaning; words contain one or more morphemes. (p. 315)

motivation The psychological and biological processes that impel people, and other organisms, into action and sustain their efforts over time. (p. 458)

motivational orientations Broad patterns of thoughts and feelings that can affect people's behavior across a wide variety of tasks. (p. 482)

motor cortex A region of the cerebral cortex that sends out signals controlling the body's muscular movements. (p. 97)

motor neurons Nerve cells that send out signals from the spinal cord to the body's muscles, enabling the brain to control bodily movement. (p. 112)

multiple intelligences theory A theory proposed by Gardner claiming that people possess a number of different mental abilities, each of which is a distinct form of intelligence. (p. 351)

myelin sheath A fatty substance that surrounds axons and acts as an electrical insulator. (p. 108)

narcissistic personality disorder A psychological disorder characterized by self-centeredness, concern with enhancing one's self-image, and disregard for the thoughts and feelings of others. (p. 726)

narcolepsy A sleep disorder in which people experience sudden, extreme feelings of sleepiness during the day, even if they've had adequate sleep; sometimes accompanied by "microsleeps." (p. 385)

natural selection The process whereby features of a population of organisms change, across generations, depending on the degree to which those features are adaptive (i.e., help organisms to survive and reproduce in a given environment). (p. 141)

nature In psychology, a biological origin of psychological characteristics. Characteristics that come from nature are those that are inherited. (p. 23)

need for achievement A desire to succeed on challenging activities requiring skilled, competent performance. (p. 467)

need to avoid failure A desire to avoid situations in which lack of competence might lead to failure. (p. 468)

need for belonging A social need that motivates people to spend time with others and to become part of social groups. (p. 469)

need for control A desire to select one's life activities and to be able to influence events. (p. 471)

need to enhance the self A social need to grow as a person, to live a meaningful life, and to realize your true potential. (p. 471)

need for understanding A social need to comprehend why events occur and to predict what the future might bring. (p. 470)

negative correlation A correlation in which higher levels of one variable co-occur with lower levels of the other variable. (p. 44; see also p. A-12)

negative reinforcement A stimulus whose removal following a behavior raises the future likelihood of that behavior. (p. 283)

negative symptoms (of schizophrenia) The absence, among people with schizophrenia, of desirable psychological experiences common among most others (e.g., enjoying social events). (p. 706)

negatively skewed Description of a distribution in which the majority of scores is high, but there is one or more extreme low score in the "tail." (p. A-5)

neo-Freudian personality theories Theories of personality inspired by Freud that attempted to overcome limitations in his work. (p. 562)

nervous system The complete collection of neurons that transmits signals among the parts of the body. (p. 111)

neural pruning Elimination of connections among neurons that occurs when the connections are not needed for an organism's functioning. (p. 152)

neurons Brain cells, also called nerve cells, distinguished by their unique shape and ability to communicate with one another. (p. 106)

neurotransmitters Chemical substances that travel across synapses between neurons; the primary way that neurons communicate. (p. 108)

nicotine A stimulant found in tobacco products that increases alertness while enhancing feelings of pleasure and emotional well-being. (p. 400)

nociceptors Specialized pain receptors that are activated by harmful stimuli such as a cut or burn. (p. 202)

non-REM sleep Sleep stage in which brain activity differs from that of waking states, and breathing rate, heart rate, blood pressure, and body temperature are relatively low. (p. 378)

normal distribution A distribution that is symmetrical and unimodal; the mean, mode, and median are equal. (p. A-5)

null hypothesis A hypothesis stating that any relationship observed between variables will be due to chance. (p. A-17)

null hypothesis significance testing A statistical procedure that calculates the probability that a research result could have occurred by chance alone. (p. A-20)

nurture The development of abilities through experiences in the world. Abilities that come from nurture are those that are learned rather than inherited. (p. 23)

obedience Adherence to the instructions and commands of an authority figure. (p. 514)

object permanence The understanding that objects continue to exist even when they can no longer be seen or otherwise perceived. (p. 605)

observational learning A form of learning in which knowledge and skills are acquired by observing others; also known as *modeling*. (p. 297)

observational study A type of research in which researchers observe people's behavior from a distance without interacting with them. (p. 62)

observer report A research method in which researchers learn about various characteristics of a given individual by obtaining reports from other people who know that person. (p. 64)

obsessive-compulsive disorder (OCD) A mental disorder involving both recurring, intrusive thoughts about potential danger or harm (obsessions) and repetitive actions (compulsions) taken to prevent the imagined dangers and harms. (p. 695)

obsessive-compulsive personality disorder (OCPD) A psychological disorder characterized by perfectionism, a seeking of order and control, rigid adherence to rules for behavior, and attention to small details. (p. 727)

occipital lobe The region of the cerebral cortex heavily involved in the processing of visual information and mental imagery; commonly called the visual cortex. (p. 95)

occlusion A monocular depth cue in which one object in the field of vision partly blocks another from view. (p. 164)

odorant Anything that smells; odorants include a variety of substances such as foods, pheromones, and chemical signals of cell damage and disease. (p. 190)

olfactory bulbs Collections of cells near the front of the brain that receive signals from olfactory receptor cells and begin the process of identifying odors. (p. 192)

olfactory cortex A neural system that completes the biological processing needed to recognize smells. (p. 192)

olfactory system The perceptual system that detects airborne chemical substances and provides the sense of smell. (p. 160)

operant conditioning A form of learning in which the future likelihood of performing a type of behavior is modified by consequences that follow performance of the behavior. (p. 279)

operation In Piagetian theory, a reversible action that modifies an object or set of objects, either physically or conceptually. (p. 604)

operational definition The specification of a procedure that can be used to measure a variable. (p. 52)

opioids Chemical substances whose primary psychoactive effect is the reduction of pain; can also induce feelings of euphoria and ecstasy. (p. 399)

optic chiasm The location in the brain where visual signals carried by the optic nerves cross, sending information from the left eye to the right side of the brain, and vice versa. (p. 179)

optic nerve The biological pathway along which information leaves the eye and moves toward the brain, formed by the long fibers of ganglion cells. (p. 179)

optical flow The continuous change in visual images that occurs when organisms move through the environment. (p. 170)

optimization In the selection, optimization, and compensation (SOC) model of successful aging, the process of devising plans to achieve goals you set. (p. 643)

oral stage In Freud's theory of psychological development, the developmental stage (ages 0 to 18 months) during which children seek gratification through the mouth. (p. 558)

ovaries The reproductive cells in women that produce ova (eggs). (p. 115)

oxytocin Hormone that activates muscles needed for childbirth and stimulates the release of breast milk; in the brain, it may stimulate feelings of trust. (p. 473)

pancreas The organ that releases hormones including insulin, which regulates the level of sugar in the bloodstream. (p. 115)

panic attack An episode of extreme fear, including high levels of physical arousal, that occurs suddenly and without apparent cause. (p. 690)

panic disorder A psychological disorder in which people experience the sudden bouts of intense terror and extreme physiological arousal known as panic attacks. (p. 690)

parallel distributed processing (PDP) A conceptual model of knowledge representation in which long-term memory consists of simple processing units that turn on and off; concepts are represented by patterns of activation in large numbers of units. (p. 235)

parasympathetic nervous system A component of the autonomic nervous system that maintains normal functioning of the body when one is not under threat or stress by activating digestion and waste elimination and restoring baseline heart rate and blood pressure. (p. 113)

parietal lobes The region of the cerebral cortex that processes somatosensory information (i.e., relating the body to the environment). (p. 95)

perception The biological process occurring when systems in the brain process sensory signals and produce awareness of sensory inputs. (p. 161)

perceptual systems Interconnected parts of the body that deliver sensory and perceptual information; humans have six perceptual systems. (p. 160)

peripheral nervous system That part of the nervous system found in the periphery of the body, outside of the central nervous system; it consists of the somatic nervous system and the autonomic nervous system. (p. 112)

personal agency People's capacity to influence their motivation, behavior, and life outcomes by setting goals and developing skills. (pp. 475, 581)

personality The relatively consistent, observable patterns of feeling, thinking, and behaving that distinguish people from one another, and the inner psychological systems that explain these patterns. (p. 551)

personality assessment A structured procedure for learning about an individual's distinctive psychological qualities. (p. 553)

personality disorders Psychological disorders that feature chronic styles of thinking, behavior, and emotion that severely lower the quality of people's relationships, creating conflict with others. (p. 722)

personality processes Individuals' distinctive patterns of change in psychological experience and behavior that occur from one moment to the next. (p. 552)

personality structures Those elements of personality that remain consistent over significant periods of time. (p. 552)

personality theory A comprehensive scientific model of human nature and individual differences. (p. 552)

phallic stage In Freud's theory of psychological development, the developmental stage (3½ to 6 years) during which the source of gratification is the genitals. (p. 558)

phantom limb syndrome The subjective conscious feeling that an amputated limb is still attached to one's body. (p. 363)

pheromones Chemical signals produced and secreted by one organism and detected by another organism of the same species, triggering a distinctive reaction. (p. 190)

phi phenomenon An illusory perception of visual motion that occurs when stationary objects flash in an alternating sequence and are perceived as a single object moving back and forth. (p. 169)

phobias Strong, persistent fears caused by situations that pose little or no actual threat. (p. 693)

photoreceptors Receptor cells in the eye that are sensitive to stimulation by light. (p. 162)

pineal gland An endocrine gland that produces a hormone called melatonin that influences patterns of sleeping and wakefulness. (p. 114)

pitch The sound experience that we usually describe with the words "low" or "high" (such as a musical note or voice). (p. 184)

pituitary gland The "master gland" of the endocrine system; it releases hormones that influence biological activity in several other glands, including those that regulate stress response, reproduction, and metabolic rate. (p. 115)

placebo effect In drug therapies, any medical benefit not caused by biologically active properties of the drug, but by the patient's expectation that the drug will help him. (p. 677)

plasticity The brain's capacity to change physically as a result of experience. (p. 84)

p-level The probability that results are due to chance, under the null hypothesis. (p. A-20)

pons A structure of the brain stem that carries out biological functions, including the control of breathing rate and generation of REM sleep. (p. 89)

population The overall, large group of people of interest to a researcher conducting a study. (p. 42)

positive correlation A correlation (statistical relation between two variables) in which higher levels of one variable co-occur with higher levels of the other variable. (p. 44; see also p. A-11)

positive psychology An intellectual movement that emphasizes positive individual traits such as love, courage, and forgiveness rather than human frailties. (p. 29)

positive reinforcement A stimulus whose occurrence following a behavior raises the future likelihood of that behavior. (p. 283)

positive symptoms (of schizophrenia) Undesirable mental events experienced by people with schizophrenia but rarely by others. (p. 705)

positively skewed Description of a distribution in which the majority of scores is low, but there is one or more extreme high score in the "tail." (p. A-5)

positivity effect A phenomenon in which older adults pay more attention to positive information when recalling and contemplating personal experiences. (p. 646)

postpartum depression A depressive disorder in which some women experience symptoms akin to major depression beginning within weeks of childbirth. (p. 687)

posttraumatic stress disorder (PTSD) A mental disorder characterized by flashbacks to previously encountered highly stressful experiences, such as military combat or sexual assault. (p. 696)

preconscious In Freud's analysis of levels of consciousness, regions of mind containing ideas you can easily bring to awareness. (p. 555)

predictor variable In a correlation between two variables, the value that is used to predict the value of the other (criterion) variable. (p. A-12)

prefrontal cortex The area of the brain immediately behind the forehead; a complex area that contributes to the ability to concentrate on facts, focus attention, manipulate information, and align behavior with social rules. (p. 97)

prejudice A negative attitude toward individuals based on their group membership, involving disparaging thoughts and feelings about individuals in a group. (p. 534)

prenatal environment The biological environment experienced before a person is born. (p. 149)

preoperational stage In Piaget's theory of child development, the stage (ages 2 to 7) in which children can use mental symbols, such as words and numbers, to think, yet still cannot perform logical operations. (p. 605)

preparedness The ease with which associations between a stimulus and a response can be learned; as a result of a species' experiences over the course of evolution, some stimulus–response connections are "prepared," that is, are easy to learn. (p. 275)

pressure In the study of auditory perception, a cue to the location of a sound source that is based on the difference in pressure on left and right ears produced by a sound wave coming from one side. (p. 186)

prevention focus A mental approach to activities in which the mind is focused on responsibilities and obligations. (p. 485)

priming The presentation of information (a "prime") that activates a concept stored in memory. (p. 234)

proactive interference A short-term memory impairment that occurs when material learned earlier impairs memory for material learned later. (p. 222)

problem solving A thinking process in which people try to reach a solution by working through a series of steps. (p. 336)

problem space The full set of steps it is possible to take when solving a problem. (p. 337)

procedural memory Memory for how to perform behaviors. (p. 229)

projective test Personality assessment tool in which items are ambiguous and psychologists are interested in the way test takers interpret the ambiguity, "projecting" elements of their own personality onto the test. (p. 561)

promotion focus A mental approach to activities in which the mind is focused on accomplishments that one personally hopes to attain. (p. 484)

prosocial behavior Actions that directly benefit others, such as comforting those in distress. (p. 638)

prototype The most typical, central member of a category. (p. 311)

prototype structure A category structure in which category membership is defined according to the resemblance of items to a central, most typical member (the prototype). (p. 311)

proximal causes In an evolutionary analysis, events and mechanisms in the present environment that determine an organism's responses. (p. 141)

proximal goal A goal that specifies what should be done in the near ("proximal") future. (p. 476)

psychiatrists Physicians trained in the diagnosis and treatment of mental disorders, with particular emphasis on the biological basis of disorders and the use of drugs to combat them. (p. 656)

psychoactive drug Any chemical substance that affects the nervous system in a manner that alters conscious experience. (p. 397)

psychoactive substances Chemical substances small enough to cross the blood–brain barrier that affect psychological processes of perception, thinking, or emotion. (p. 677)

psychoanalysis The psychotherapy strategy originally developed by Sigmund Freud; a type of insight therapy. (p. 665)

psychoanalytic theory Freud's theory of personality, also called psychodynamic theory. (p. 554)

psychodynamic processes In Freud's theory, changes in mental energy that occur as energy flows from one personality structure to another, or is directed to desired objects. (p. 557)

psychological disorders Prolonged experiences of psychological distress or poor psychological functioning that interfere with a person's everyday life; mental disorders. (p. 656)

psychological therapies (psychotherapies) Interactions between a therapist and client(s) in which the therapist speaks with the client, with a goal of improving emotional state, thinking, and behavioral skills. (p. 665)

psychology The scientific study of persons, the mind, and the brain. (p. 4)

psychopathy A personality style defined by hostility toward others, lack of guilt, and a tendency toward dishonesty and manipulation of others. (p. 724)

psychophysics A branch of psychology that studies relations between physical stimuli and psychological reactions. (p. 172)

psychophysiology A field of study that provides scientific information about the relation between physiological reactions and psychological experiences. (p. 68)

psychosexual stage In Freud's theory of psychological development, a period during which the child focuses on obtaining sensual gratification through a particular part of the body. (p. 558)

psychotherapists Professionals who provide psychological therapies. (p. 665)

psychotic disorders Psychological disorders in which thoughts and actions are disorganized and thinking loses touch with reality; people see and worry about things that do not exist. (p. 705)

puberty The time when a child reaches sexual maturity and is biologically capable of reproduction. (p. 635)

punishment In operant conditioning, a stimulus that lowers the future likelihood of a given behavior. (p. 284)

pupil The opening in the eye through which light passes. (p. 175)

Q-sort An assessment procedure in which people categorize words and phrases according to how well or poorly the descriptions fit them. (p. 568)

qualitative data Sources of scientific information that are not converted into numbers, but reported in words. (p. 51)

qualitative research methods Any of a wide range of methods in which researchers observe, record, and summarize behavior using words rather than numbers. (p. 51)

quantitative data Numerical data, that is, data in which scientific observations are recorded using numbers. (p. 51)

quantitative research methods Scientific methods in which participants' responses are described in terms of numbers. (p. 51)

questionnaire A set of questions or statements to which participants respond by choosing response options that best characterize their own thoughts. (p. 64)

random assignment A process in which participants are allocated to conditions of an experiment on an entirely chance basis. (p. 49)

random sample A sample in which each individual's inclusion, or not, is determined by a chance process. (p. 42)

range A simple measure of the variability of a distribution; the difference between the highest and lowest scores. (p. A-7)

ratio schedule of reinforcement In operant conditioning research, a timetable for reinforcement in which a reinforcer is administered only after an organism performs a certain number of responses. (p. 287)

reasoning The process of drawing conclusions that are based on facts, beliefs, and experiences, combining them to reach conclusions that go beyond the information originally perceived. (p. 328)

receptor cells Nervous system cells that are sensitive to specific types of physical stimulation from the environment and send signals to the brain when stimulated. (p. 162)

receptors Sites on the dendrites of receiving neurons to which neurotransmitters can attach; chemically, molecules to which specific types of neurotransmitters can bind. (p. 109)

reflection In psychotherapy, an active-listening technique in which the therapist recurringly summarizes statements made by the client, "reflecting" the content back to the client. (p. 671)

reflexes Automatic, involuntary responses to external stimulation. (p. 112)

regulatory fit The match between a motivational orientation and a behavioral strategy. (p. 485)

rehearsal The strategy of repeating information to retain it in short-term memory. (p. 223)

reinforcer In operant conditioning, any stimulus that occurs after a response and raises the future probability of that response. (p. 283)

reliability An attribute of a measure; specifically, a measure possesses "reliability" if it produces results that are consistent from one measurement occasion to another. (p. 54)

REM (rapid eye movement) sleep A sleep stage during which there is rapid eye movement, frequent dreams, and brain activity resembling that of waking periods. (p. 378)

representative sample A sample in which the qualities of the individuals included match those of the overall population. (p. 42)

representativeness heuristic A psychological process in which people judge whether a person or thing belongs to a given category by evaluating the degree to which the person or object resembles the category. (p. 332)

repression A defense mechanism in which traumatic memories are kept in the unconscious, thereby blocked from awareness. (p. 559)

research design Plans for the execution of scientific research projects. (p. 38)

resilience The capacity to retain or recover psychological functioning after negative experiences. (p. 624)

reticular formation A network of cells in the brain stem that influences bodily arousal. (p. 89)

retina The rear wall of the eye containing nerve cells that respond to light and send signals to the brain. (p. 175)

retrieval The access of information that has been stored in long-term memory. (p. 230)

retroactive interference A short-term memory impairment that occurs when material learned later impairs memory for material learned earlier. (p. 222)

rods Photoreceptors that enable vision in low illumination. (p. 177)

role A set of behaviors that is expected of a person in a given situation. (p. 516)

Rorschach inkblot test A projective test in which the test items are symmetrical blobs of ink that test takers are asked to interpret. (p. 561)

saccades Rapid movements of the eyes from one position to another. (p. 177)

sample The select subgroup of people contacted by a researcher, who uses information from the sample to draw conclusions about the population as a whole. (p. 42)

sampling error Chance differences between sample statistics and population statistics (called *parameters*); for example, the difference between the mean of a population and the mean of a sample drawn from it. (p. A-17)

Sapir–Whorf hypothesis A conception of the relation between language and thought which claims that language shapes thinking; this hypothesis implies that people who speak different languages think differently about the world around them. (p. 324)

satiety A feeling of having eaten enough food, or being "full." (p. 460)

savant syndrome A syndrome characterized by mental impairment in most areas of life but exceptional performance in one domain. (p. 353)

scapegoating Blaming members of another group when frustrated with one's own circumstances. (p. 537)

scatterplot A graph that displays the relation between two variables. Data points representing the measurements of the two variables "scatter" about the visual display. (p. 44; see also p. A-11)

schedule of reinforcement In operant conditioning research, a timetable that indicates when reinforcements occur, in relation to the occurrence of behavior. (p. 287)

schema A mental structure that makes organized, meaningful action possible. (p. 603)

schizophrenia Psychological disorder in which people exhibit multiple psychotic symptoms. (p. 705)

schizotypal personality disorder A psychological disorder characterized by (1) odd beliefs, eccentricity in manner or dress, and suspiciousness; and (2) few close friends, that is, social isolation resulting from these beliefs and behaviors. (p. 727)

scientific methods A broad array of procedures through which scientists obtain information about the world. Scientific methods involve three key steps: collect evidence, record observations systematically, and record how observations were made. (p. 9)

scientific questions Questions that can be answered by gathering evidence through scientific methods. (p. 10)

scientific theory In science, a systematic, data-based explanation for a phenomenon or set of phenomena. (p. 70)

seasonal affective disorder A depressive disorder in which individuals experience depressed mood during late summer and winter, periods when there is less sunlight. (p. 687)

secure attachment The attachment style in which a child has a positive relationship with his or her mother, with a sense of security that enables the child to explore the world, confident of the mother's comfort. (p. 623)

selection In the selection, optimization, and compensation (SOC) model of successful aging, the process of setting personal goals for a given period of your life. (p. 643)

selection, optimization, and compensation (SOC) model A model of successful aging that identifies three psychological processes that promote positive personal development: selection, optimization, and compensation. (p. 643)

selective attention The capacity to choose the flow of information that enters conscious awareness. (p. 204)

selective serotonin reuptake inhibitors (SSRIs) Pharmaceuticals designed to alleviate depression by increasing serotonin activity through interference with the biochemical process known as reabsorption or reuptake. (p. 675)

self In humanistic theories, such as that of Rogers, an organized set of self-perceptions of our personal qualities; people's conceptions of who they are. (p. 566)

self-actualization A motivation to realize one's inner potential. (pp. 459, 567)

self-consciousness The process of thinking about oneself, that is, thinking about one's own experiences and how one appears to others. (p. 366)

self-control The ability to act in a manner consistent with long-term goals and values, even when one feels an impulse to act differently. (p. 633)

self-efficacy beliefs Judgments about one's own capabilities for performance. (p. 583)

self-esteem A person's overall sense of self-worth. (pp. 570, 633)

self-referent cognitions Thoughts people have about themselves as they interact with the world and reflect on their experiences. (p. 582)

self-regulation People's efforts to control their own behavior and emotions. (p. 587)

self-report Research techniques in which researchers ask participants to provide information about themselves. (p. 64)

self-representations Beliefs about the characteristics of oneself and the ways in which one differs from other people. (p. 632)

semantic memory Memory for factual information. (p. 228)

semantic network model A conceptual model of knowledge representation in which long-term memory consists of a large set of individual concepts connected to one another. (p. 232)

sensation The biological process occurring when cells at the periphery of the body detect physical stimuli. (p. 161)

sensorimotor stage In Piaget's theory of child development, the stage (birth to 2 years) in which a child interacts with the world through his or her sensory and motor systems. (p. 605)

sensory cortex A region of the parietal cortex that receives sensory information from all parts of the body. (p. 96)

sensory memory Memory that is based on the workings of sensory systems. (p. 217)

sensory neurons Nerve cells that respond to external stimuli and send messages about the environment to the spinal cord. (p. 111)

serial position effect The tendency to display superior recall for items positioned at the beginning or end of a list rather than in the middle. (p. 223)

set-point theories Theoretical explanations of hunger and eating which propose that homeostatic processes control food consumption, with people being motivated to eat (or not) when their energy supplies fall below (or above) their set point. (p. 461)

sexual orientation A person's primary form of sexual and romantic attachment, whether to the opposite sex (heterosexual), the same sex (homosexual), or both (bisexual). (p. 147)

shading A monocular depth cue based on the presence within a visual image of a relatively dark area that appears to have been created by blocking a source of light. (p. 164)

shaping In operant conditioning, the learning of complex behavior through a step-by-step process in which behaviors that successively approximate a desired, final behavior are reinforced. (p. 291)

short-term memory A memory system that enables people to keep a limited amount of information actively in mind for brief periods of time. (p. 219)

sign language A language in which bodily movements, especially of the hands and fingers, are used to convey information. (p. 323)

single-nucleotide polymorphisms (SNPs) Locations along the genome at which one molecule (i.e., one nucleotide) differs from one individual to another. (p. 717)

skewed distribution An asymmetrical distribution in which the mean is no longer in the middle because it is "pulled" by extreme scores. (p. A-5)

skills Abilities that develop through experience, including interpersonal skills. (p. 583)

skin conductance response (SCR) A measure of electrical resistance at the skin that uses the activity of sweat glands to provide a physiological measure of anxiety. (p. 68)

Skinner box The primary laboratory apparatus in the study of operant conditioning; it includes a device for animals to act upon (e.g., a lever to press) and a mechanism for delivering reinforcers. (p. 286)

sleep apnea A disorder in which people suffer from brief pauses in breathing while they are asleep, causing them to wake up. (p. 386)

sleep deprivation Going without adequate sleep, which not only makes you tired but also impairs normal conscious experiences. (p. 384)

sleep disorder Any medical condition that disrupts normal patterns of sleep. (p. 385)

sleep laboratory A scientific facility for studying sleep; research participants spend nights sleeping while their biological rhythms and brain activity are monitored. (p. 382)

sleep stages The sequence of changes in REM and non-REM sleep that everyone experiences in the same order. (p. 380)

social anxiety disorder A disorder characterized by extreme levels of anxiety and self-consciousness specifically in situations involving other people. (p. 691)

social behavior Behavior that occurs in interaction with other people. (p. 506)

social cognition People's beliefs, opinions, and feelings about the individuals and groups with whom they interact socially. (p. 524)

social development Growth in ability to function effectively in the social world, especially by controlling emotions, maintaining relationships, and establishing a personal identity. (p. 602)

social facilitation A phenomenon in which the mere presence of other people improves people's performance on tasks on which they are skilled. (p. 489)

social loafing A reduction in individual motivation on group tasks in which some people expect that the group is likely to succeed without their efforts. (p. 489)

social needs Desires that motivate people to interact with others and to achieve a meaningful role in society. (p. 469)

social neuroscience A field of study that explores biological systems in the brain that underlie social cognition and behavior. (p. 542)

social norm A socially shared belief about the type of behavior that is acceptable in any given setting. (p. 508)

social psychology Branch of psychology that studies people's thoughts, feelings, and actions as they contemplate, interact with, and are influenced by others in society. (p. 506)

social support Loving care and personal assistance from friends and family, particularly as provided during times of stress. (p. 451)

social-cognitive theory A theoretical approach to personality in which the core of personality consists of personal knowledge, beliefs, and skills acquired through social interaction. (p. 580)

socioemotional selectivity theory A lifespan developmental theory of motivational processes that explains how perceptions of the amount of time remaining in life affect motivation. (p. 644)

somatic nervous system Functionally, the part of the peripheral nervous system that provides the brain-to-periphery communications that allow(s) you to control your bodily movement. (p. 112)

sound waves Variations in pressure that reach the ears and are converted by the auditory system into signals. (p. 182)

spatial memory The ability to recall the layout of one's physical environment. (p. 250)

specific phobias Fears directed toward particular objects or situations, such as fear of flying, heights, spiders, or closed-in spaces. (p. 693)

spinal cord A bundle of neurons and glial cells that extends from the brain stem down to the bottom of the spine; it participates in two-way communications between the brain and the body. (p. 111)

spinal nerves Those parts of the peripheral nervous system that extend from the spinal cord to the body's neck, torso, and limbs. (p. 112)

split brain A surgical procedure in which the corpus callosum is cut. The resulting disruption of information transmission between cerebral hemispheres alters conscious experience. (p. 101)

spontaneous recovery The reappearance of an extinguished conditioned response after a period of delay following extinction. (p. 269)

standard deviation A statistic that describes the degree to which numbers vary, or deviate, from the mean. (p. 58; see also p. A-7)

standard error A statistic that quantifies sampling error or chance differences between the sample and the population. (p. A-18)

statistical language learning A theory of language acquisition proposing that people acquire language by learning patterns of sounds and words that they hear frequently, that is, that are statistically common. (p. 318)

statistically significant An experimental result is said to be statistically significant if observed outcomes vary from what would be expected by chance. (p. 58; see also p. A-20)

statistics Mathematical procedures for summarizing sets of numbers. (p. 58; see also p. A-1)

stereopsis The perception of three-dimensional space produced by the fact that images reaching your two eyes vary slightly because your eyes are a few inches apart; a binocular depth cue. (p. 166)

stereotype A simplified set of beliefs about the characteristics of members of a group. (p. 533)

stereotype threat A negative emotional reaction that occurs when people recognize the possibility of their confirming a negative stereotype about their group. (p. 534)

stimulants Psychoactive drugs that increase nervous system activity and thus enhance alertness and energy. (p. 400)

strange situation paradigm A behavioral measure of attachment style in which researchers record a child's responses to a sequence of events in which the mother and child interact, are separated, and reunite. (p. 624)

stress response A coordinated series of physiological changes that prepare you for "fight or flight"; that is, to confront the stressor, or flee. (p. 444)

structuralism A school of thought focusing on the mind's basic components, or structures, and how they come together to create complex mental experiences. (p. 27)

subjective stress The psychological impact of a potentially stressful event from the perspective of the individual experiencing it. (p. 442)

subjective value The degree of personal worth that an individual places on an outcome. (p. 334)

sublimation A defense mechanism in which an instinct toward sex or aggression is redirected to the service of a socially acceptable goal. (p. 559)

superego In Freud's psychoanalytic theory, the personality structure that represents society's moral and ethical rules. (p. 555)

supertasters People who have greater sensitivity to tastes than others. (p. 195)

suppression Any conscious, intentional effort to prevent oneself from showing any visible sign of emotional arousal (or other such psychological states). (p. 427)

survey method A research design in which researchers obtain descriptive information about a large group of people by studying a select subgroup of them. (p. 40)

sympathetic nervous system A component of the autonomic nervous system that prepares organisms or action by activating biological systems required for "fight or flight" responses. (p. 112)

synapse The small gap that separates any two neurons; chemical signals between neurons must bridge this microscopic gap. (p. 108)

synaptic vesicles Small sacs that store and transport neurotransmitters within neurons and release neurotransmitters into synapses. (p. 108)

syntax The set of rules determining whether a series of phrases form a sentence that is grammatically correct. (p. 315)

systematic desensitization An exposure therapy that reduces fear by exposing clients to feared objects in a slow, gradual manner. (p. 668)

systematic information processing Careful, detailed, step-by-step thinking. (p. 528)

tardive dyskinesia Repetitive, uncontrollable muscular movements, typically of the face, such as odd grimacing and lip smacking; a side effect of antipsychotic medication. (p. 719)

taste buds Bundles of taste receptors, found primarily on the tongue but also on the roof of the mouth and throat. (p. 196)

taste receptors Cells that are stimulated by chemical substances in food, whose activation begins the process of transmitting gustatory information to the brain. (p. 196)

temperament Biologically based emotional and behavioral tendencies on which individuals differ. (p. 618)

temperament dimension A biologically based psychological quality possessed by all children to a greater or lesser degree, such as emotionality, activity, or sociability. (p. 619)

temporal lobe The region of the cerebral cortex crucial to psychological functions, including hearing and memory. (p. 96)

tend-and-befriend A coping strategy identified particularly in women in which the response to threat involves taking action to help others (tending) while maintaining a close support network (befriending). (p. 451)

terror management theory A theory proposing that death is so terrifying that thinking about it increases feelings of identification with institutions (e.g., religions, nations) that will survive one's death. (p. 558)

testes The reproductive cells in men that produce sperm. (p. 115)

testosterone Hormone that plays a role in motivating sexual desire in both men and women. (p. 466)

texture A monocular depth cue based on markings on the surface of objects in a visual scene. (p. 164)

thalamus A structure near the center of the brain that serves as a "relay station" for rapid connections among brain regions. (p. 103)

theory of mind An intuitive understanding that other people have feelings and thoughts. (p. 611)

think-aloud protocol analysis A research method in which participants verbalize their thoughts while solving a problem, which enables experimenters to record and analyze the problem-solving strategies used. (p. 338)

three-stage memory model A conceptual depiction of the memory system in which information is said to be stored in any of three storage systems: sensory memory, short-term memory, or long-term memory. (p. 217)

thymus An endocrine gland that produces hormones influencing the development and functioning of the immune system. (p. 115)

thyroid gland An endocrine gland that releases hormones regulating the body's metabolic rate. (p. 115)

timbre The distinctive "signature" of a sound, based on variations in the complexity of sound waves. (p. 185)

timing In the study of auditory perception, a cue to the location of a sound source that is based on the difference in time it takes a sound coming from your side to reach each ear. (p. 186)

token economy A behavior therapy technique in which therapists reward desirable behavior with tokens that serve as reinforcers, making the behavior more likely to reoccur. (p. 668)

trait In personality psychology, a person's typical style of behavior and emotion. (p. 571)

trait theories Theoretical approaches that try to identify, describe, and measure people's personality traits. (p. 571)

transduction A biological process in which physical stimuli activate cells in the nervous system, which then send nerve impulses to the brain, where processing gives rise to perceptual and sensory experience. (p. 162)

transference A psychoanalytic process in which a patient unintentionally responds emotionally to a therapist as if the therapist were a significant figure from the patient's past, such as a parent. (p. 666)

transformational grammar The set of rules governing how components of a sentence can be shifted to create other sentences that are grammatically correct. (p. 316)

triarchic theory of intelligence A theory of intelligence proposed by Sternberg, which says that intelligent behavior requires three distinct mental components: knowledge acquisition, executive planning, and performance. (p. 354)

triune brain Conceptual model of brain structure distinguishing among three main parts of the human brain that evolved at different points and perform distinct functions. (p. 87)

***t*-statistic** A statistic used in the *t*-test that is the ratio of the hypothesized difference against chance differences. (p. A-19)

***t*-test** The statistical procedure for evaluating whether differences observed between two sample means represent true population mean differences or chance. (p. A-19)

twin method A procedure for determining the degree to which genes account for individual differences by comparing degrees of similarity among MZ and DZ twins. (p. 128)

two-point procedure A method to measure haptic system acuity that assesses the smallest distance at the skin at which people can perceive two separate stimuli rather than one. (p. 198)

type I error In statistics, rejecting the null hypothesis when it is, in fact, true. (p. A-20)

typical antipsychotics One of two major types of antipsychotic drugs, specifically, the first such drugs developed, in the 1950s. (p. 719)

umami A taste sensation that is "savory," triggered by high protein levels in food. (p. 194)

unconditional positive regard A display of respect and acceptance toward others that is consistent and not dependent on their meeting behavioral requirements. (pp. 567, 671)

unconditioned response (UR) A reaction to an unconditioned stimulus that occurs automatically, prior to any learning. (p. 262)

unconditioned stimulus (US) A stimulus that elicits a reaction in an organism prior to any learning. (p. 262)

unconscious In Freud's analysis of levels of consciousness, regions of mind containing ideas you are not aware of and generally cannot become aware of even if you wanted to. (p. 555)

unimodal Term describing a distribution having only one mode. (p. A-5)

uninhibited temperament A tendency to experience little fear and to act in a spontaneous and sociable manner. (p. 620)

universal grammar A set of linguistic rules that, according to Chomsky, are possessed by all humans and that enable people to understand and produce sentences. (p. 317)

validity An attribute of a measure; specifically, a measure possesses "validity" if it measures what it is supposed to measure. (p. 54)

variability The degree to which the scores in a distribution spread out above and below the mean. (p. A-7)

variable Any property that fluctuates, such as from person to person or from time to time. (p. 43)

variable schedule of reinforcement In operant conditioning research, a timetable for reinforcement that is inconsistent across trials; the delivery of reinforcers changes unpredictably. (p. 287)

ventricles Spaces in the brain filled with a fluid that supports brain functioning but without neurons; enlarged in people with schizophrenia. (p. 713)

visual cortex A region in the rear of the brain devoted to processing visual information. (p. 180)

visual fixations Periods when a person's gaze is held in one location, when most visual information is picked up. (p. 177)

visual system The perceptual system detecting environmental information that reaches the body in the form of light. (p. 160)

Wechsler Adult Intelligence Scale (WAIS) A popular test of intelligence that assesses verbal comprehension, perceptual reasoning, working memory, and mental processing speed. (p. 344)

Wernicke's area A region in the temporal lobe of the left hemisphere of the brain needed to understand language and to produce meaningful sentences. (p. 321)

wish-fulfillment theory Freud's proposal that dreams help us stay asleep by depicting the fulfillment of unconscious wishes, thereby releasing pent-up mental energy. (p. 388)

working memory A set of interrelated systems that both store and manipulate information; its three components are the phonological loop, visuospatial sketchpad, and central executive. (p. 225)

***x*-axis** In any graph, the horizontal axis. (p. A-3)

***y*-axis** In any graph, the vertical axis. (p. A-3)

zone of proximal development In Vygotsky's theory of cognitive development, the region between a child's current level of independent cognitive development and the level he or she can achieve only through interaction with others. (p. 612)

***z*-score** A statistic that tells you how far a given score is from the mean of a distribution, in standard units. (p. A-10)

References

Abbott, E. (2000). *A history of celibacy: From Athena to Elizabeth I, Leonardo da Vinci, Florence Nightingale, Gandhi, & Cher.* New York, NY: Scribner.

ABC News. (2005, August 6). One-legged cyclist transforms African nation. Retrieved from http://abcnews.go.com/WNT/International/story?id=1005135

ABC News (Producer). (2009, July 16). J. K. Rowling: A year in the life, part 2: Author says period of depression inspired "Dementors" in "Harry Potter." Retrieved from http://abcnews.go.com/video/playerIndex?id=8105333

Abi-Dargham, A. (2004). Do we still believe in the dopamine hypothesis? New data bring new evidence. *The International Journal of Neuropsychopharmacology, 7*(1), S1–S5. doi:10.1017/S1461145704004110

Ablon, J. S., & Jones, E. E. (2002). Validity of controlled clinical trials of psychotherapy: Findings from the NIMH Treatment of Depression Collaborative Research Program. *American Journal of Psychiatry, 159,* 775–783. doi:10.1176/appi.ajp.159.5.775

Abramowitz, J. S., Taylor, S., & McKay, D. (2009). Obsessive-compulsive disorder. *The Lancet, 374,* 491–499. doi:10.1016/S0140-6736(09)60240-3

Acarturk, C., Cuijpers, P., van Straten, A., & de Graaf, R. (2009). Psychological treatment of social anxiety disorder: A meta-analysis. *Psychological Medicine, 39,* 241–254. doi:10.1017/S0033291708003590

Acevedo, B. P., & Aron, A. (2009). Does a long-term relationship kill romantic love? *Review of General Psychology, 13,* 59–65. doi:10.1037/a0014226

Adler, A. (1927). *Understanding human nature.* New York, NY: Garden City Publishing.

Adolph, K. E., Cole, W. G., Komati, M., Garciaguirre, J. S., Badaly, D., Lingeman, J. M., ... & Sotsky, R. B. (2012). How do you learn to walk? Thousands of steps and dozens of falls per day. *Psychological Science, 23,* 1387–1394. doi:10.1177/0956797612446346

Adolph, K. E., Karasik, L. B., & Tamis-LeMonda, C. S. (2010). Using social information to guide action: Infants' locomotion over slippery slopes. *Neural Networks, 23,* 1033–1042. doi:10.1016/j.neunet.2010.08.012

Adolphs, R., Tranel, D., Damasio, H., & Damasio, A. (1994). Impaired recognition of emotion in facial expressions following bilateral damage to the human amygdala. *Nature, 372,* 669–672. doi:10.1038/372669a0

Aghajanian, G. K., & Marek, G. J. (1999). Serotonin and hallucinogens. *Neuropsychopharmacology, 21,* 16S–23S. doi:10.1016/S0893-133X(98)00135-3

Agosta, L. (2010). Empathy in the context of philosophy. New York, NY: Palgrave Macmillan. doi:10.1057/9780230275249

Aiello, J. R., & Douthitt, E. A. (2001). Social facilitation from Triplett to electronic performance monitoring. *Group Dynamics: Theory, Research, and Practice, 5,* 163–180. doi:10.1037/1089-2699.5.3.163

Ainsworth, M. D. S. (1967). *Infancy in Uganda: Infant care and the growth of love.* Oxford, England: Johns Hopkins Press.

Ainsworth, M. D. S., Bleher, M. C., Waters, E., & Wall, S. (1978). *Patterns of attachment: A psychological study of the strange situation.* Hillsdale, NJ: Erlbaum.

Ajzen, I., & Fishbein, M. (1977). Attitude–behavior relations: A theoretical analysis and review of empirical research. *Psychological Bulletin, 84,* 888–918. doi:10.1037/0033-2909.84.5.888

Alkire, M. T., Haier, R. J., & Fallon, J. H. (2000). Toward a unified theory of narcosis: Brain imaging evidence for a thalamocortical switch as the neurophysiologic basis of anesthetic-induced unconsciousness. *Consciousness and Cognition, 9,* 370–386. doi:10.1006/ccog.1999.0423

Alkire, M. T., Hudetz, A. G., & Tononi, G. (2008). Consciousness and anesthesia. *Science, 322,* 876–380. doi:10.1126/science.1149213

Alleyne, R. (2010, September 23). Oxytocin—the love hormone—could cure shyness: A nasal spray could cure shyness, a new study suggests. *The Telegraph.* Retrieved from http://www.telegraph.co.uk/health/healthnews/8020464/Oxytocin-the-love-hormone-could-cure-shyness.html

Allison, K. R., & Rootman, I. (1996). Scientific rigor and community participation in health promotion research: Are they compatible? *Health Promotion International, 11,* 333–340. doi:10.1093/heapro/11.4.333

Allport, G. W. (1937). *Personality: A psychological interpretation.* New York, NY: Holt, Rinehart & Winston.

Allport, G. W. (1954). *The nature of prejudice.* Reading, MA: Addison-Wesley.

Allport, G. W. (1965). *Letters from Jenny.* New York: Harcourt, Brace.

Allport, G. W., & Odbert, H. S. (1936). Trait-names: A psycholexical study. *Psychological Monographs, 47,* i–171. doi:10.1037/h0093360

Ameri, A. (1999). The effects of cannabinoids on the brain. *Progress in Neurobiology, 58,* 315–348. doi:10.1016/S0301-0082(98)00087-2

American Psychiatric Association. (2013). *Diagnostic and statistical manual of mental disorders* (5th ed.). Arlington, VA: American Psychiatric Publishing.

American Sleep Apnea Association. (2013). *Enhancing the lives of those with sleep apnea.* Retrieved from http://www.sleepapnea.org

Ames, C. (1992). Classrooms: Goals, structures, and student motivation. *Journal of Educational Psychology, 84,* 261–271. doi:10.1037/0022-0663.84.3.261

Andersen, R. A., Snyder, L. H., Bradley, D. C., & Xing, J. (1997). Multimodal representation of space in the posterior parietal cortex and its use in planning movements. *Annual Review of Neuroscience, 20,* 303–330. doi:10.1146/annurev.neuro.20.1.303

Anderson, A. K., Christoff, K., Stappen, I., Panitz, D., Ghahremani, D. G., Glover, G., ... & Sobel, N. (2003). Dissociated neural representations of intensity and valence in human olfaction. *Nature Neuroscience, 6,* 196–202. doi:10.1038/nn1001

Anderson, J. R., Bothell, D., Byrne, M. D., Douglass, S., Lebiere, C., & Qin, Y. (2004). An integrated theory of the mind. *Psychological Review, 111*(4), 1036–1060.

Anderson, L. (n.d.). Ricky Williams: A story of social anxiety disorder. Retrieved from http://www.adaa.org/living-with-anxiety/personal-stories/ricky-williams-story-social-anxiety-disorder

Anderson, M. L. (2003). Embodied cognition: A field guide. *Artificial Intelligence, 149,* 91–130. doi:10.1016/S0004-3702(03)00054-7

Anderson, M., Ochsner, K., & Kuhl, B. (2004). Neural systems underlying the suppression of unwanted memories. *Science, 303,* 232–235. doi:10.1126/science.1089504

Anderson, S. R., & Lightfoot, D. W. (1999). The human language faculty as an organ. *Annual Review of Physiology, 62,* 697–722. doi:10.1146/annurev.physiol.62.1.697

Andreassi, J. L. (2007). *Human behavior and psychophysiological response* (4th ed.). Mahwah, NJ: Erlbaum.

Andrews, G., Hobbs, M. J., Borkovec, T. D., Beesdo, K., Craske, M. G., Heimberg, R. G., . . . & Stanley, M. A. (2010). Generalized worry disorder: A review of DSM-IV generalized anxiety disorder and options for DSM-V. *Depression and Anxiety, 27,* 134–147. doi:10.1002/da.20658

Angell, J. R. (1906). *Psychology: An introductory study of the structure and function of human conscious* (3rd ed., revised). New York, NY: Henry Holt and Company. doi:10.1037/10999-000

Antonova, E., Sharma, T., Morris, R., & Kumari, V. (2004). The relationship between brain structure and neurocognition in schizophrenia: A selective review. *Schizophrenia Research, 70,* 117–145. doi:10.1016/j.schres.2003.12.002

Anzai, Y., & Simon, H. A. (1979). The theory of learning by doing. *Psychological Review, 86,* 124–140. doi:10.1037/0033-295X.86.2.124

APA Monitor. (2009). ICD vs. DSM. *Monitor on Psychology, 40,* 63. Retrieved from http://www.apa.org/monitor/2009/10/icd-dsm.aspx

Apkarian, A. V., Bushnell, M. C., Treede, R.-D., & Zubieta, J.-K. (2005). Human brain mechanisms of pain perception and regulation in health and disease. *European Journal of Pain, 9,* 463–484. doi:10.1016/j.ejpain.2004.11.001

Appleton, K. M., Gentry, R. C., & Shepherd, R. (2006). Evidence of a role for conditioning in the development of liking for flavours in humans in everyday life. *Physiology & Behavior, 87,* 478–486. doi:10.1016/j.physbeh.2005.11.017

Aquino, K., Freeman, D., Reed, A., II, Lim, V. K. G., & Felps, W. (2009). Testing a social-cognitive model of moral behavior: The interactive influence of situations and moral identity centrality. *Journal of Personality and Social Psychology, 97,* 123–141. doi:10.1037/a0015406

Arango, C., & Carpenter, W. T. (2011). The schizophrenia construct: Symptomatic presentation. In D. R. Weinberger, & P. J. Harrison (Eds.), *Schizophrenia* (3rd ed., pp. 9–23). Oxford, UK: Wiley-Blackwell. doi:10.1002/9781444327298.ch2

Araque, A., & Navarrete, M. (2010). Glial cells in neuronal network function. *Philosophical Transactions of the Royal Society of London. Series B, Biological Sciences, 365,* 2375–2381. doi:10.1098/rstb.2009.0313

Ariely, D., Loewenstein, G., & Prelec, D. (2004). Arbitrarily coherent preferences. In I. Brocas & J. D. Carrillo (Eds.), *The psychology of economic decisions* (Vol. 2, pp. 131–161). Oxford, UK: Oxford University Press.

Aristotle. (1963 ce/350 bce). *Aristotle's Categories and de Interpretatione.* J. L. Ackrill & L. Judson, Eds. (J. L. Ackrill, Trans.). Oxford, UK: Oxford University Press.

Aristotle. *On the soul.* (J. A. Smith, Trans., 2010) Retrieved from http://ebooks.adelaide.edu.au/a/aristotle/a8so/

Armony, J., & Vuilleumier, P. (Eds.). (2013). *The Cambridge handbook of human affective neuroscience.* New York, NY: Cambridge University Press. doi:10.1017/CBO9780511843716

Arnett, J. J. (2000). Emerging adulthood: A theory of development from the late teens through the twenties. *American Psychologist, 55,* 469–480. doi:10.1037/0003-066X.55.5.469

Arnett, J. J., & Taber, S. (1994). Adolescence terminable and interminable: When does adolescence end? *Journal of Youth and Adolescence, 23,* 517–537. doi:10.1007/BF01537734

Aron, A., & Westbay, L. (1996). Dimensions of the prototype of love. *Journal of Personality and Social Psychology, 70,* 535–551. doi:10.1037/0022-3514.70.3.535

Art Tatum. (n.d.). *New World Encyclopedia.* http://www.newworldencyclopedia.org/entry/Art_Tatum.

Arya, P. U. (1978). *Superconscious Meditation.* Honesdale, PA: Himalayan Institute Press.

Asch, S. (1955). Opinions and social pressure. *Scientific American, 193,* 31–35. doi:10.1038/scientificamerican1155-31

Ashcraft, M. H., & Kirk, E. P. (2001). The relationships among working memory, math anxiety, and performance. *Journal of Experimental Psychology: General, 130,* 224–237. doi:10.1037//0096-3445.130.2.224

Ashton, M. C., & Lee, K. (2007). Empirical, theoretical, and practical advantages of the HEXACO model of personality structure. *Personality and Social Psychology Review, 11,* 150–166. doi:10.1177/1088868306294907

Ashton, M. C., Lee, K., Perugini, M., Szarota, P., de Vries, R. E., Di Blas, L., . . . & De Raad, B. (2004). A six-factor structure of personality-descriptive adjectives: Solutions from psycholexical studies in seven languages. *Journal of Personality and Social Psychology, 86,* 356–366. doi:10.1037/0022-3514.86.2.356

Aspinwall, L. G., & Staudinger, U. M. (Eds.). (2002). *A psychology of human strengths: Fundamental questions and future directions for a positive psychology.* Washington, DC: American Psychological Association.

Associated Press. (2005, July 16). Emmanuel Yeboah preps for Fitness Triathlon. Retrieved from http://www.ghanaweb.com/GhanaHomePage/NewsArchive/artikel.php?ID=85911

Associated Press. (2011, September 6). 38% of Europeans are mentally ill, study says. *CBS News.* Retrieved from http://www.cbsnews.com/stories/2011/09/06/health/main20102020.shtml

Association of Genetic Technologists. (2008, April 25). *Genetics in the Laboratory* [PowerPoint file]. Lenexa, KS. Retrieved from www.agt-info.org

Atkins, P. (2003). *Galileo's finger: The ten great ideas of science.* New York: Oxford University Press.

Atkinson, A. P., Dittrich, W. H., Gemmell, A. J., & Young, A. W. (2004). Emotion perception from dynamic and static body expressions in point-light and full-light displays. *Perception, 33,* 717–746. doi:10.1068/p5096

Atkinson, J. W., & Litwin, G. H. (1960). Achievement motive and test anxiety conceived as motive to approach success and motive to avoid failure. *The Journal of Abnormal and Social Psychology, 60,* 52–63. doi:10.1037/h0041119

Atkinson, R. C., & Shiffrin, R. M. (1968). Human memory: A proposed system and its control processes. In K. W. Spence and J. T. Spence (Eds.), *The psychology of learning and motivation: Advances in research and theory* (Vol. II, pp. 89–195). New York, NY: Academic Press.

Aubrey, A. (2011, October 19). IQ isn't set in stone, suggests study that finds big jumps, dips in teens. *NPR.* Retrieved from http://m.npr.org/news/Health/141511314

Ault, R. L. (1977). *Children's cognitive development: Piaget's theory and the process approach.* New York, NY: Oxford University Press.

Austin, J. H. (2013). Review of *The Heart of William James. Perspectives on Psychological Science, 8,* 314–315. doi:10.1177/1745691613483473

Austin, J. L. (1962). *How to do things with words.* Oxford, UK: Oxford University Press.

Auvray, M., & Spence, C. (2008). The multisensory perception of flavor. *Consciousness and Cognition, 17,* 1016–1031. doi:10.1016/j.concog.2007.06.005

Azevedo, F. A. C., Carvalho, L. R. B., Grinberg, L. T., Farfel, J. M., Ferretti, R. E. L., Leite, R. E. P., . . . & Herculano-Houzel, S. (2009). Equal numbers of neuronal and nonneuronal cells make the human brain an isometrically scaled-up primate brain. *The Journal of Comparative Neurology, 513,* 532–541. doi:10.1002/cne.21974

Baars, B. J. (2005). Subjective experience is probably not limited to humans: The evidence from neurobiology and behavior. *Consciousness and Cognition, 14,* 7–21. doi:10.1016/j.concog.2004.11.002

Babyak, M., Blumenthal, J. A., Herman, S., Khatri, P., Doraiswamy, M., Moore, K., . . . & Krishnan, K. R. (2000). Exercise treatment for major depression: Maintenance of therapeutic benefit at 10 months. *Psychosomatic Medicine, 62,* 633–638. doi:10.1097/00006842-20000 9000-00006

Baccus, J. R., Baldwin, M. W., & Packer, D. J. (2004). Increasing implicit self-esteem through classical conditioning. *Psychological Science, 15,* 498–502. doi:10.1111/j.0956-7976.2004.00708.x

Baddeley, A. (2003). Working memory: Looking back and looking forward. *Nature Reviews Neuroscience, 4,* 829–839. doi:10.1038/nrn1201

Baddeley, A., & Hitch, G. (1974). Working memory. In G. H. Bower (Ed.), *The Psychology of Learning & Motivation* (Vol. 8, pp. 47–89). New York, NY: Academic Press.

Baer, R. (2003). Mindfulness training as a clinical intervention: A conceptual and empirical review. *Clinical Psychology: Science and Practice, 10,* 125–143. doi:10.1093/clipsy.bpg015

Bailey, N., & Zuk, M. (2009). Same-sex sexual behavior and evolution. *Trends in Ecology & Evolution, 24,* 439–446. doi:10.1016/j.tree.2009.03.014

Baillargeon, R. (1986). Representing the existence and the location of hidden objects: Object permanence in 6- and 8-month-old infants. *Cognition, 23,* 21–41. doi:10.1016/0010-0277(86)90052-1

Balderston, N. L., Schultz, D. H., & Helmstetter, F. J. (2011). The human amygdala plays a stimulus specific role in the detection of novelty. *NeuroImage, 55,* 1889–1898. doi:10.1016/j.neuroimage.2011.01.034

Baldo, J. V, & Dronkers, N. F. (2007). Neural correlates of arithmetic and language comprehension: A common substrate? *Neuropsychologia, 45,* 229–235. doi:10.1016/j.neuropsychologia.2006.07.014

Baltes, E. B., & Graf, E. (1996). Psychological aspects of aging: Facts and frontiers. In D. Magnusson (Ed.), *The Lifespan Development of Individuals: Behavioural, Neurobiological and Psychosocial Perspectives* (pp. 427–460). Cambridge, England: Cambridge University Press.

Baltes, P. B. (1997). On the incomplete architecture of human ontogeny: Selection, optimization, and compensation as foundation of developmental theory. *American Psychologist, 52,* 366–380. doi:10.1037/0003-066X.52.4.366

Baltes, P. B., Staudinger, U. M., & Lindenberger, U. (1999). Lifespan psychology: Theory and application to intellectual functioning. *Annual Review of Psychology, 50,* 471–507. doi:10.1146/annurev.psych.50.1.471

Bandura, A. (1965). Vicarious processes: A case of no-trial learning. In L. Berkowitz (Ed.), *Advances in Experimental Social Psychology* (Vol. 2, pp. 3–57). New York, NY: Academic Press.

Bandura, A. (1969). *Principles of behavior modification.* Oxford, England: Holt, Rinehart, & Winston.

Bandura, A. (1978). The self system in reciprocal determinism. *American Psychologist, 33,* 344–358. doi:10.1037/0003-066X.33.4.344

Bandura, A. (1986) *Social foundations of thought and action: A social-cognitive theory.* Englewood Cliffs, NJ: Prentice-Hall.

Bandura, A. (1997). *Self-efficacy: The exercise of control.* New York, NY: Freeman.

Bandura, A. (1999). Social-cognitive theory of personality. In D. Cervone & Y. Shoda (Eds.), *The Coherence of Personality: Social-Cognitive Bases of Consistency, Variability, and Organization* (pp. 185–241). New York, NY: Guilford Press.

Bandura, A. (2001). Social cognitive theory: An agentic perspective. *Annual Review of Psychology, 52,* 1–26. doi:10.1146/annurev.psych.52.1.1

Bandura, A., & Cervone, D. (1983). Self-evaluative and self-efficacy mechanisms governing the motivational effects of goal systems. *Journal of Personality and Social Psychology, 45,* 1017–1028. doi:10.1037/0022-3514.45.5.1017

Bandura, A., & Cervone, D. (1986). Differential engagement of self-reactive influences in cognitive motivation. *Organizational Behavior and Human Decision Processes, 38,* 92–113. doi:10.1016/0749-5978(86)90028-2

Bandura, A., & Schunk, D. (1981). Cultivating competence, self-efficacy, and intrinsic interest through proximal self-motivation. *Journal of Personality and Social Psychology, 41,* 586–598. doi:10.1037/0022-3514.41.3.586

Bandura, A., & Walters, R. H. (1959). *Adolescent aggression.* New York, NY: Ronald.

Bandura, A., & Walters, R. H. (1963). *Social learning and personality development.* New York, NY: Holt, Rinehart, & Winston.

Bandura, A., Adams, N. E., & Beyer, J. (1977). Cognitive processes mediating behavioral change. *Journal of Personality and Social Psychology, 35,* 125–139. doi:10.1037/0022-3514.35.3.125

Bandura, A., Ross, D., & Ross, S. (1961). Transmission of aggression through imitation of aggressive models. *Journal of Abnormal and Social Psychology, 63,* 575–582. doi:10.1037/h0045925

Bangert, M., Peschel, T., Schlaug, G., Rotte, M., Drescher, D., Hinrichs, H., et al. (2006). Shared networks for auditory and motor processing in professional pianists: Evidence from fMRI conjunction. *NeuroImage, 30,* 917–926.

Banyard, V. L. (1995). "Taking another route": Daily survival narratives from mothers who are homeless. *American Journal of Community Psychology, 23,* 871–891. doi:10.1007/BF02507019

Barber, C. (2008). *Comfortably numb: How psychiatry is medicating a nation.* New York, NY: Pantheon Books.

Barch, D. M. (2005). The cognitive neuroscience of schizophrenia. *Annual Review of Clinical Psychology, 1,* 321–353. doi:10.1146/annurev.clinpsy.1.102803.143959

Bardone-Cone, A. M., Wonderlich, S. A., Frost, R. O., Bulik, C. M., Mitchell, J. E., Uppala, S., & Simonich, H. (2007). Perfectionism and eating disorders: Current status and future directions. *Clinical Psychology Review, 27,* 384–405. doi:10.1016/j.cpr.2006.12.005

Barger, B., Nabi, R. L., & Yu Hong, L. (2010). Standard back-translation procedures may not capture proper emotion concepts: A case study of Chinese disgust terms. *Emotion, 10,* 703–711. doi:10.1037/a0021453

Bargh, J. A., Gollwitzer, P. M., Lee-Chai, A., Barndollar, K., & Trötschel, R. (2001). The automated will: Nonconscious activation and pursuit of behavioral goals. *Journal of Personality and Social Psychology, 81,* 1014–1027. doi:10.1037/0022-3514.81.6.1014

Bargh, J. A., & Morsella, E. (2008). The unconscious mind. *Perspectives on Psychological Science, 3,* 73–79. doi:10.1111/j.1745-6916.2008.00064.x

Barker, P. J. (2004). *Assessment in psychiatric and mental health nursing: In search of the whole person* (2nd ed.). Cheltenham, UK: Nelson Thornes.

Barlow, D. H., & Craske, M. G. (2007). *Mastery of your anxiety and panic: Workbook.* Treatments that work. New York, NY: Oxford University Press.

Barnes, J., Bartlett, J. W., van de Pol, L. A., Loy, C. T., Scahill, R. I., Frost, C., . . . & Fox, N. C. (2009). A meta-analysis of hippocampal atrophy rates in Alzheimer's disease. *Neurobiology of Aging, 30,* 1711–1723. doi:10.1016/j.neurobiolaging.2008.01.010

Baron-Cohen, S., Leslie, A. M., & Frith, U. (1985). Does the autistic child have a "theory of mind"? *Cognition, 21,* 37–46. doi:10.1016/0010-0277(85)90022-8

Barrera, M. E., & Maurer, D. (1981). The perception of facial expressions by the three-month-old. *Child Development, 52,* 203–206. doi:10.2307/1129231

Barrett, L., Ochsner, K., & Gross, J. (2007). On the automaticity of emotion. In J. A. Bargh (Ed.), *Social Psychology and the Unconscious: The Automaticity of Higher Mental Processes* (pp. 173–217). Frontiers of social psychology. New York, NY: Psychology Press.

Barrett, L. F., Lindquist, K. A., & Gendron, M. (2007). Language as context for the perception of emotion. *Trends in Cognitive Science, 11,* 327–332. doi:10.1016/j.tics.2007.06.003

Barrós-Loscertales, A., Meseguer, V., Sanjuán, A., Belloch, V., Parcet, M. A., Torrubia, R., & Avila, C. (2006). Striatum gray matter reduction in males with an overactive behavioral activation system. *European Journal of Neuroscience, 24,* 2071–2074. doi:10.1111/j.1460-9568.2006.05084.x

Barry, J. (2009, September 7). A case using rational emotive behavior therapy. *Counselling connection.* Retrieved from http://www.counselling connection.com/index.php/2009/09/07/a-case-using-rational-emotive-behaviour-therapy/

Barsalou, L. W. (1999) Perceptual symbol systems. *Behavioral and Brain Sciences, 22,* 577–660.

Barsalou, L. W. (2010). Ad hoc categories. In P. Hogan (Ed.), *The Cambridge Encyclopaedia of the Language Sciences* (pp. 86–87). Cambridge, England: Cambridge University Press.

Barsalou, L. W., Simmons, W. K., Barbey, A. K., & Wilson, C. D. (2003). Grounding conceptual knowledge in modality-specific systems. *Trends in Cognitive Sciences, 7,* 84–91. doi:10.1016/S1364-6613(02)00029-3

Bartoshuk, L. M. (2000). Comparing sensory experiences across individuals: Recent psychophysical advances illuminate genetic variation in taste perception. *Chemical Senses, 25,* 447–460. doi:10.1093/chemse/25.4.447

Bartz, J. A., Zaki, J., Bolger, N., Hollander, E., Ludwig, N. N., Kolevzon, A., & Ochsner, K. N. (2010). Oxytocin selectively improves empathic accuracy. *Psychological Science, 21,* 1426–1428. doi:10.1177/0956797610383439

Bartz, J. A., Zaki, J., Bolger, N., & Ochsner, K. N. (2011). Social effects of oxytocin in humans: Context and person matter. *Trends in Cognitive Sciences, 15,* 301–309. doi:10.1016/j.tics.2011.05.002

Bartz, J. A., Zaki, J., Ochsner, K. N., Bolger, N., Kolevzon, A., Ludwig, N., & Lydon, J. E. (2010). Effects of oxytocin on recollections of maternal care and closeness. *Proceedings of the National Academy of Sciences of the United States of America, 107,* 21371–21375. doi:10.1073/pnas.1012669107

Batelaan, N. M., Van Balkom, A. J., & Stein, D. J. (2012). Evidence-based pharmacotherapy of panic disorder: An update. *The International Journal of Neuropsychopharmacology, 15,* 403–415. doi:10.1017/S1461145711000800

Bates, J. E., Pettit, G. S., Dodge, K. A., & Ridge, B. (1998). Interaction of temperamental resistance to control and restrictive parenting in the development of externalizing behavior. *Developmental Psychology, 34,* 982–995. doi:10.1037/0012-1649.34.5.982

Baumeister, R. F., & Leary, M. R. (1995). The need to belong: Desire for interpersonal attachments as a fundamental human motivation. *Psychological Bulletin, 117,* 497–529. doi:10.1037/0033-2909.117.3.497

Baumeister, R. F., Stillwell, A. M., & Heatherton, T. F. (1994). Guilt: An interpersonal approach. *Psychological Bulletin, 115,* 243–267. doi:10.1037/0033-2909.115.2.243

Bayard, S., & Lassonde, M. (2001). Cognitive, sensory and motor adjustment to hemispherectomy. In I. Jambaque, M. Lassonde, & O. Dulac (Eds.), *Neuropsychology of childhood epilepsy* (pp. 229–244). Hingham, MA: Kluwer Academic Publishers. doi:10.1007/0-306-47612-6_25

Bean, B. P. (2007). The action potential in mammalian central neurons. *Nature Reviews Neuroscience, 8,* 451–465. doi:10.1038/nrn2148

Beauregard, M., & O'Leary, D. (2008). Believing can make it so: The neuroscience of the placebo effect. *Advances in Mind–Body Medicine, 23,* 14–18.

Bechara, A., Damasio, A. R., Damasio, H., & Anderson, S. W. (1994). Insensitivity to future consequences following damage to human prefrontal cortex. *Cognition, 50,* 7–15. doi:10.1016/0010-0277(94)90018-3

Bechara, A., Damasio, H., Tranel, D., & Damasio, A. R. (1997). Deciding advantageously before knowing the advantageous strategy. *Science, 275,* 1293–1295. doi:10.1126/science.275.5304.1293

Bechara, A., Damasio, H., Tranel, D., & Damasio, A. R. (2005). The Iowa Gambling Task and the somatic marker hypothesis: Some questions and answers. *Trends in Cognitive Sciences, 9,* 159–162. doi:10.1016/j.tics.2005.02.002

Beck, A. T. (1979). *Cognitive therapy and the emotional disorders.* New York, NY: Meridian.

Beck, A. T. (1987). Cognitive models of depression. *Journal of Cognitive Psychotherapy: An International Quarterly, 1,* 5–37.

Beck, A. T., Freeman, A., & Davis, D. D. (2004). *Cognitive therapy of personality disorders* (2nd ed.). New York, NY: Guilford Press.

Beck, A. T., & Rector, N. A. (2002). Delusions: A cognitive perspective. *Journal of Cognitive Psychotherapy, 16,* 455–468. doi:10.1891/jcop.16.4.455.52522

Beck, A. T, Rush, A. J., Shaw, B. E, & Emery, G. (1979). *Cognitive therapy of depression.* New York: Guilford Press.

Beck, A. T., Steer, R. A., & Brown, G. K. (1996). *Manual for the Beck Depression Inventory-II.* San Antonio, TX: Psychological Corporation.

Becklen, R., & Cervone, D. (1983). Selective looking and the noticing of unexpected events. *Memory & Cognition, 11,* 601–608. doi:10.3758/BF03198284

Beilock, S. L., Lyons, I. M., Mattarella-Micke, A., Nusbaum, H. C., & Small, S. L. (2008). Sports experience changes the neural processing of action language. *Proceedings of the National Academy of Sciences of the United States of America, 105,* 13269–13273. doi:10.1073/pnas.0803424105

Bellak, L. (1961). Free association: Conceptual and clinical aspects. *The International Journal of Psychoanalysis, 42,* 9–20.

Belliveau, J., Kennedy, D., McKinstry, R., Buchbinder, B., Weisskoff, R., Cohen, M., . . . & Rosen, B. (1991). Functional mapping of the human visual cortex by magnetic resonance imaging. *Science, 254,* 716–719. doi:10.1126/science.1948051

Bem, D. J. (1987). Writing the empirical journal article. In M. P. Zanna & J. M. Darley (Eds.), *The compleat academic: A practical guide for the beginning social scientist* (pp. 171–201). New York, NY: Random House.

Bem, D. J. (2011). Feeling the future: Experimental evidence for anomalous retroactive influences on cognition and affect. *Journal of Personality and Social Psychology, 100,* 407–425. doi:10.1037/a0021524

Benedetti, F., Mayberg, H. S., Wager, T. D., Stohler, C. S., & Zubieta, J.-K. (2005). Neurobiological mechanisms of the placebo effect. *The Journal of Neuroscience, 25,* 10390–10402. doi:10.1523/jneurosci.3458-05.2005

Benjamin, L. T. Jr., & Baker, D. B. (2012). The internationalization of psychology: A history. In D. B. Baker (Ed.), *The Oxford Handbook of the History of Psychology: Global Perspectives* (pp. 1–17). New York: Oxford University Press. doi:10.1093/oxfordhb/9780195366556.013.0001

Bennet, M. R., & Hacker, P. M. S. (2003). Reductionism. In *Philosophical Foundations of neuroscience* (pp. 355–377). Malden, MA: Blackwell.

Berger, A., Tzur, G., & Posner, M. I. (2006). Infant brains detect arithmetic errors. *Proceedings of the National Academy of Sciences of the United States of America, 103,* 12649–12653. doi:10.1073/pnas.0605350103

Berggren, Niclas, & Nilsson, Therese. (2012). Does economic freedom foster tolerance? *Kyklos, 66,* 177–207.

Bergman, A. J., Harvey, P. D., Mitropoulou, V., Aronson, A., Marder, D., Silverman, J., . . . & Siever, L. J. (1996). The factor structure of schizotypal symptoms in a clinical population. *Schizophrenia Bulletin, 22,* 501–509. doi:10.1093/schbul/22.3.501

Berlin, B., & Kay, P. (1969). *Basic color terms: Their universality and evolution.* Berkeley, CA: University of California.

Berman, S. M., Kuczenski, R., McCracken, J. T., & London, E. D. (2009). Potential adverse effects of amphetamine treatment on brain and behavior: A review. *Molecular Psychiatry, 14,* 123–142. doi:10.1038/mp.2008.90

Bermudez-Rattoni, F. (2010). Is memory consolidation a multiple-circuit system? *Proceedings of the National Academy of Sciences, 107,* 8051–8052. doi:10.1073/pnas.1003434107

Berridge, K. C. (2004). Motivation concepts in behavioral neuroscience. *Physiology & Behavior, 81,* 179–209. doi:10.1016/j.physbeh.2004.02.004

Berridge, K. C., & Robinson, T. E. (2003). Parsing reward. *Trends in Neurosciences, 26,* 507–513. doi:10.1016/S0166-2236(03)00233-9

Berry, J. W. (2013). Global psychology. *South African Journal of Psychology, 43,* 391–401. doi:10.1177/0081246313504517

Bhattacharyya, N., Baugh, R. F., Orvidas, L., Barrs, D., Bronston, L. J., Cass, S., . . . & Haidari, J. (2008). Clinical practice guideline: Benign paroxysmal positional vertigo. *Otolaryngology-Head and Neck Surgery, 139,* S47–S81. doi:10.1016/j.otohns.2008.08.022

Biehl, M. C., Natsuaki, M. N., & Ge, X. (2007). The influence of pubertal timing on alcohol use and heavy drinking trajectories. *Journal of Youth and Adolescence, 36,* 153–167. doi:10.1007/s10964-006-9120-z

Bigelow, J., & Poremba, A. (2014). Achilles' ear? Inferior human short-term and recognition memory in the auditory modality. *PLoS One, 9,* e89914. doi:10.1371/journal.pone.0089914

Bijttebier, P., & Vertommen, H. (1999). Coping strategies in relation to personality disorders. *Personality and Individual Differences, 26,* 847–856. doi:10.1016/S0191-8869(98)00187-1

Bingham, G. P., & Pagano, C. C. (1998). The necessity of a perception–action approach to definite distance perception: Monocular distance perception to guide reaching. *Journal of Experimental Psychology: Human Perception and Performance, 24,* 145–168. doi:10.1037/0096-1523.24.1.145

Biological Sciences Curriculum Study. (2003). *Sleep, Sleep Disorders, and Biological Rhythms* (NIH Publication No. 04-4989). Retrieved from http://science.education.nih.gov/supplements/nih3/sleep/guide/info-sleep.htm

Bisson, J. I., Ehlers, A., Matthews, R., Pilling, S., Richards, D., & Turner, S. (2007). Psychological treatments for chronic post-traumatic stress disorder: Systematic review and meta-analysis. *The British Journal of Psychiatry, 190,* 97–104. doi:10.1192/bjp.bp.106.021402

Bitterman, M. E. (2006). Classical conditioning since Pavlov. *Review of General Psychology, 10,* 365–376. doi:10.1037/1089-2680.10.4.365

Blackwell, L. S., Trzesniewski, K. H., & Dweck, C. S. (2007). Implicit theories of intelligence predict achievement across an adolescent transition: A longitudinal study and an intervention. *Child Development, 78,* 246–263. doi:10.1111/j.1467-8624.2007.00995.x

Blanchard, J. J., Kring, A. M., Horan, W. P., & Gur, R. (2011). Toward the next generation of negative symptom assessments: The Collaboration to Advance Negative Symptom Assessment in Schizophrenia. *Schizophrenia Bulletin, 37,* 291–299. doi:10.1093/schbul/sbq104

Blanco, C., Okuda, M., Wright, C., Hasin, D. S., Grant, B. F., Liu, S. M., & Olfson, M. (2008). Mental health of college students and their non–college-attending peers: Results from the National Epidemiologic Study on Alcohol and Related Conditions. *Archives of General Psychiatry, 65,* 1429–1437. doi:10.1001/archpsyc.65.12.1429

Blashfield, R. K., Keeley, J. W., Flanagan, E. H., & Miles, S. R. (2014). The cycle of classification: DSM-I through DSM-5. *Annual Review of Clinical Psychology, 10,* 25–51. doi:10.1146/annurev-clinpsy-032813-153639

Bliss, T. V., & Collingridge, G. L. (1993). A synaptic model of memory: Long-term potentiation in the hippocampus. *Nature, 361,* 31–39. doi:10.1038/361031a0

Block, J. (1961). *The Q-sort method in personality assessment and psychiatric research.* Springfield, IL: Charles C Thomas. doi:10.1037/13141-000

Blood, A. J., & Zatorre, R. J. (2001). Intensely pleasurable responses to music correlate with activity in brain regions implicated in reward and emotion. *Proceedings of the National Academy of Sciences of the United States of America, 98,* 11818–11823. doi:10.1073/pnas.191355898

Bloom, G., & Sherman, P. W. (2005). Dairying barriers affect the distribution of lactose malabsorption. *Evolution and Human Behavior, 26,* 301.e1–301.e33. doi:10.1016/j.evolhumbehav.2004.10.002

Bloom, P. (2004). *Decartes' baby: How the science of child development explains what makes us human.* New York, NY: Basic Books.

Bloom, P., & Keil, F. C. (2001). Thinking through language. *Mind and Language, 16,* 351–367. doi:10.1111/1468-0017.00175

Blumenthal, A. L. (2001). A Wundt primer: The operating characteristics of consciousness. In W. Rieber & D. K. Robinson (Eds.), *Wilhelm Wundt in history: The making of a scientific psychology* (pp. 121–144). New York: Kluwer Academic/Plenum Publishers.

Blumenthal, J. A., Babyak, M. A., Moore, K. A., Craighead, W. E., Herman, S., Khatri, P., . . . & Krishnan, K. R. (1999). Effects of exercise training on older patients with major depression. *Archives of Internal Medicine, 159,* 2349–2356. doi:10.1001/archinte.159.19.2349

Bodhi, B. (Ed.). (1993). *A comprehensive manual of Abhidhamma (The Abhidhammattha Sangaha of Acariya Anuruddha).* Kandy, Sri Lanka: Buddhist Publication Society.

Bogaert, A. F. (2006). Biological versus nonbiological older brothers and men's sexual orientation. *Proceedings of the National Academy of Sciences of the United States of America, 103,* 10771–4. doi:10.1073/pnas.0511152103

Bohannon, J. (2010). A taste for controversy. *Science, 328,* 1471–1473. doi:10.1126/science.328.5985.1471

Bolger, N., Davis, A., & Rafaeli, E. (2003). Diary methods: Capturing life as it is lived. *Annual Review of Psychology, 54,* 579–616. doi:10.1146/annurev.psych.54.101601.145030

Bolton, R. (1978). Aristotle's definition of the soul: "De Anima" II, 1–3. *Phronesis, 23,* 258–278. doi:10.1163/156852878X00154

Bond, R. M., Fariss, C. J., Jones, J. J., Kramer, A. D. I., Marlow, C., Settle, J. E., & Fowler, J. H. (2012). A 61-million-person experiment in social influence and political mobilization. *Nature, 489,* 295–298. doi:10.1038/nature11421

Bookheimer, S. (2002). Functional MRI of language: New approaches to understanding the cortical organization of semantic processing. *Annual Review of Neuroscience, 25,* 151–188. doi:10.1146/annurev.neuro.25.112701.142946

Boring, E. G. (1929). *A history of experimental psychology.* New York, NY: The Century Company.

Boring, E. G. (1950). *A history of experimental psychology* (2nd ed.) New York: Appleton-Century-Crofts, 1950.

Borjon, J. I.., & Ghanzanfar, A. A. (2013). Neural tuning of human face processing. *Proceedings of the National Academy of Sciences, 110,* 16702–16703. doi:10.1073/pnas.1315621110

Borkovec, T. D., & Costello, E. (1993). Efficacy of applied relaxation and cognitive-behavioral therapy in the treatment of generalized anxiety disorder. *Journal of Consulting and Clinical Psychology, 61*, 611–619. doi:10.1037/0022-006X.61.4.611

Bornstein, R. F., & D'Agostino, P. R. (1992). Stimulus recognition and the mere exposure effect. *Journal of Personality and Social Psychology, 63*, 545–552. doi:10.1037/0022-3514.63.4.545

Borsboom, D., & Dolan, C. V. (2006). Why g is not an adaptation: A comment on Kanazawa (2004). *Psychological Review, 113*, 433–437. doi:10.1037/0033-295X.113.2.433

Borsboom, D., Mellenbergh, G. J., & van Heerden, J. (2004). The concept of validity. *Psychological Review, 111*, 1061–1071. doi:10.1037/0033-295X.111.4.1061

Boscarino, J. A., & Figley, C. R. (2012). Understanding the neurobiology of fear conditioning and emergence of PTSD psychobiology: Commentary on Blanchard et al. *The Journal of Nervous and Mental Disease, 200*, 740–744. doi:10.1097/NMD.0b013e318266b5ea

Boston Post. (1848, September 13). *Horrible Accident.* Retrieved from http://www.genling.nw.ru/Staff/Psycholinguistics/Computer.pdf

Bouchard, T., Lykken, D., & McGue, M. (1990). Sources of human psychological differences: The Minnesota study of twins reared apart. *Science, 250*, 223–228. doi:10.1126/science.2218526

Boulanger, F. D. (1976). The effects of training in the proportional reasoning associated with the concept of speed. *Journal of Research in Science Teaching, 13*, 145–154. doi:10.1002/tea.3660130207

Bowden, C. L. (2009). Anticonvulsants in bipolar disorders: Current research and practice and future directions. *Bipolar Disorders, 11*(s2), 20–33. doi:10.1111/j.1399-5618.2009.00708.x

Bower, G. H. (1970). Analysis of a mnemonic device: Modern psychology uncovers the powerful components of an ancient system for improving memory. *American Scientist, 58*, 496–510.

Bower, G. H. (1981). Mood and memory. *American Psychologist, 36*, 129–148. doi:10.1037/0003-066X.36.2.129

Bower, G. H., & Hilgard, E. R. (1981). *Theories of learning.* Englewood Cliffs, NJ: Prentice-Hall.

Bowlby, J. (1969). *Attachment and loss: Vol. 1. Attachment.* New York, NY: Basic Books.

Bowlby, J. (1988). *A secure base.* New York, NY: Basic Books.

Bowles, D. P., Armitage, C. J., Drabble, J., & Meyer, B. (2013). Self-esteem and other-esteem in college students with borderline and avoidant personality disorder features: An experimental vignette study. *Personality and Mental Health, 7*, 307–319. doi:10.1002/pmh.1230

Boyer, P. (2001). *Religion explained: The evolutionary origins of religious thought.* New York: Basic Books.

Bozarth, M. A. (1994). Pleasure systems in the brain. In D.M. Warburton (Ed.), *Pleasure: The politics and the reality* (pp. 5–14). New York, NY: John Wiley & Sons.

Brady, J. V, Porter, R. W., Conrad, D. G., & Mason, J. W. (1958). Avoidance behavior and the development of gastroduodenal ulcers. *Journal of the Experimental Analysis of Behavior, 1*, 69–72. doi:10.1901/jeab.1958.1-69

Brandão, M. L., Borelli, K. G., Nobre, M. J., Santos, J. M., Albrechet-Souza, L., Oliveira, A. R., & Martinez, R. C. (2005). Gabaergic regulation of the neural organization of fear in the midbrain tectum. *Neuroscience and Biobehavioral Reviews, 29*, 1299–1311. doi:10.1016/j.neubiorev.2005.04.013

Brandtstädter, J., & Wentura, D. (1995). Adjustment to shifting possibility frontiers in later life: Complementary adaptive modes. In R. A. Dixon, & L. Bäckman (Eds.), *Compensating for Psychological Deficits and Declines: Managing losses and promoting gains* (pp. 83–106). Mahwah, NJ: Lawrence Erlbaum Associates.

Braudel, F. (1992). *The structures of everyday life.* Civilization and capitalism, 15th–18th century (Vol. I, S. Reynold, Trans.). Berkeley and Los Angeles, CA: University of California Press. (Original work published 1979)

Brefczynski-Lewis, J. A., Lutz, A., Schaefer, H. S., Levinson, D. B., & Davidson, R. J. (2007). Neural correlates of attentional expertise in long-term meditation practitioners. *Proceedings of the National Academy of Sciences of the United States of America, 104*, 11483–11488. doi:10.1073/pnas.0606552104

Breggin, P. R., & Breggin, G. R. (2010). *Talking back to Prozac: What doctors aren't telling you about Prozac and the newer antidepressants.* New York, NY: E-Reads.

Breland, K., & Breland, M. (1961). The misbehavior of organisms. *American Psychologist, 16*, 681–684. doi:10.1037/h0040090

Brembs, B., Lorenzetti, F. D., Reyes, F. D., Baxter, D. A., & Byrne, J. H. (2002). Operant reward learning in *Aplysia*: Neuronal correlates and mechanisms. *Science, 296*, 1706–1709. doi:10.1126/science.1069434

Breslin, P., & Spector, A. (2008). Mammalian taste perception. *Current Biology, 18*, R148–R155. doi:10.1016/j.cub.2007.12.017

Bretherton, I. (1992). The origins of attachment theory: John Bowlby and Mary Ainsworth. *Developmental Psychology, 28*, 759–775. doi:10.1037/0012-1649.28.5.759

Breuer, J., & Freud, S. (1895). *Studies on hysteria.* In *Standard Edition* (Vol. 2). London: Hogarth Press. (Translation 1955.)

Brewer, M. B. (1991). The social self: On being the same and different at the same time. *Personality and Social Psychology Bulletin, 17*, 475–482. doi:10.1177/0146167291175001

Bringmann, W. G., & Ungerer, G. A. (1980). The foundation of the Institute for Experimental Psychology at Leipzig University. *Psychological Research, 42*, 5–18.

Brislin, R. W. (1970). Back-translation for cross-cultural research. *Journal of Cross-Cultural Psychology, 1*, 185–216. doi:10.1177/135910457000100301

Brody, G. H. (2004). Siblings' direct and indirect contributions to child development. *Current Directions in Psychological Science, 13*, 124–126. doi:10.1111/j.0963-7214.2004.00289.x

Brody, N. (1992). *Intelligence* (2nd ed.). San Diego, CA: Academic Press.

Brooks, S. N., & Kushida, C. A. (2002). Recent advances in the understanding and treatment of narcolepsy. *Primary Psychiatry, 9*, 30–36.

Broverman, I. K., Broverman, D. M., Clarkson, F. E., Rosenkrantz, P. S., & Vogel, S. R. (1970). Sex-role stereotypes and clinical judgments of mental health. *Journal of Consulting and Clinical Psychology, 34*, 1–7. doi:10.1037/h0028797

Brown, D. E. (1991). *Human universals.* Philadelphia, PA: Temple University Press.

Brown, J. (1958). Some tests of the decay theory of immediate memory. *Quarterly Journal of Experimental Psychology, 10*, 12–21. doi:10.1080/17470215808416249

Brown, M. Z., Comtois, K. A., & Linehan, M. M. (2002). Reasons for suicide attempts and nonsuicidal self-injury in women with borderline personality disorder. *Journal of Abnormal Psychology, 111*, 198–202. doi:10.1037/0021-843X.111.1.198

Brown, R. (1958). *Words and things.* New York, NY: Free Press.

Brown, R. (1973). *A first language: The early stages.* Cambridge, MA: Harvard University Press. doi:10.4159/harvard.9780674732469

Bruch, H. (1973). *Eating disorders: Obesity, anorexia nervosa, and the person within.* New York, NY: Basic Books.

Bruder, C., Piotrowski, A., Gijsbers, A. A., Andersson, R., Erickson, S., de Ståhl, T. D., . . . & Poplawski, A. (2008). Phenotypically concordant and discordant monozygotic twins display different DNA copy-number-variation profiles. *The American Journal of Human Genetics, 82*, 763–771. doi:10.1016/j.ajhg.2007.12.011

Bruner, J. S. (1957). On perceptual readiness. *Psychological Review, 64,* 123–152. doi:10.1037/h0043805

Bruner, J. S., & Goodman, C. C. (1947). Value and need as organizing factors in perception. *Journal of Abnormal Psychology, 42,* 33–44. doi:10.1037/h0058484

Buller, D. J. (2005). *Adapting minds: Evolutionary psychology and the persistent quest for human nature.* Cambridge, MA: MIT Press.

Bullmore, E., & Sporns, O. (2009). Complex brain networks: Graph theoretical analysis of structural and functional systems. *Nature Reviews Neuroscience, 10,* 186–198. doi:10.1038/nrn2575

Burch, C. (2000). *Top hundred words.* Retrieved from http://www.cs.cmu.edu/~cburch/words/top.html

Burger, J. M. (1999). The foot-in-the-door compliance procedure: A multiple-process analysis and review. *Personality and Social Psychology Review, 3,* 303–325. doi:10.1207/s15327957pspr0304_2

Burke, B. L., Martens, A., & Faucher, E. H. (2010). Two decades of terror management theory: A meta-analysis of mortality salience research. *Personality and Social Psychology Review, 14,* 155–195. doi:10.1177/1088868309352321

Bushman, B. J., & Anderson, C. A. (2002). Violent video games and hostile expectations: A test of the general aggression model. *Personality & Social Psychology Bulletin, 28,* 1679–1686. doi:10.1177/014616702237649

Buss, A. H., & Plomin, R. (1984). *Temperament: Early developing personality traits.* Hillsdale, NJ: Lawrence Erlbaum Associates.

Buss, D. (1989). Sex differences in human mate preferences: Evolutionary hypotheses tested in 37 cultures. *Behavioral and Brain Sciences, 12,* 1–49. doi:10.1017/S0140525X00023992

Buss, D. (1991). Evolutionary personality psychology. *Annual Review of Psychology, 42,* 459–491. doi:10.1146/annurev.ps.42.020191.002331

Buss, D. (1995). Evolutionary psychology: A new paradigm for psychological science. *Psychological Inquiry, 6,* 1–30. doi:10.1207/s15327965pli0601_1

Buss, D. M. (2009). How can evolutionary psychology successfully explain personality and individual differences? Perspectives *in Psychological Science, 4,* 359–366. doi:10.1111/j.1745-6924.2009.01138.x

Buster, J. E., Kingsberg, S. A., Aguirre, O., Brown, C., Breaux, J. G., Buch, A., . . . Casson, P. (2005). Testosterone patch for low sexual desire in surgically menopausal women: A randomized trial. *Obstetrics and Gynecology, 105,* 944–952. doi:10.1097/01.AOG.0000158103.27672.0d

Butler, A. C., Chapman, J. E., Forman, E. M., & Beck, A. T. (2006). The empirical status of cognitive-behavioral therapy: A review of meta-analyses. *Clinical Psychology Review, 26,* 17–31. doi:10.1016/j.cpr.2005.07.003

Butler, E. A., Young, V. J., & Randall, A. K. (2010). Suppressing to please, eating to cope: The effect of overweight women's emotion suppression on romantic relationships and eating. *Journal of Social and Clinical Psychology, 29,* 599–623. doi:10.1521/jscp.2010.29.6.599

Cabanac, A., & Cabanac, M. (2000). Heart rate response to gentle handling of frog and lizard. *Behavioural Processes, 52,* 89–95. doi:10.1016/S0376-6357(00)00108-X

Cabanac, M., Cabanac, A. J., & Parent, A. (2009). The emergence of consciousness in phylogeny. *Behavioural Brain Research, 198,* 267–272. doi:10.1016/j.bbr.2008.11.028

Cacioppo, J. T., Berntson, G. G., & Decety, J. (2012). A history of social neuroscience. In A. W. Kruglanski & W. Stroebe (Eds.), *Handbook of the History of Social Psychology* (pp. 123–136). New York, NY: Psychology Press.

Cacioppo, J. T., Berntson, G. G., Lorig, T. S., Norris, C. J., Rickett, E., & Nusbaum, H. (2003). Just because you're imaging the brain doesn't mean you can stop using your head: A primer and set of first principles. *Journal of Personality and Social Psychology, 85,* 650–661. doi:10.1037/0022-3514.85.4.650

Cain, W. (1979). To know with the nose: Keys to odor identification. *Science, 203,* 467–470. doi:10.1126/science.760202

Cain, W. S., & Gent, J. F. (1991). Olfactory sensitivity: Reliability, generality, and association with aging. *Journal of Experimental Psychology: Human Perception and Performance, 17,* 382–391. doi:10.1037/0096-1523.17.2.382

Cale, E. M., & Lilienfeld, S. O. (2002). Sex differences in psychopathy and antisocial personality disorder: A review and integration. *Clinical Psychology Review, 22,* 1179–1207. doi:10.1016/S0272-7358(01)00125-8

Cameron, N., & Rychlak, J. F. (1985). *Personality development and psychopathology: A dynamic approach* (2nd ed.). Boston, MA: Houghton, Mifflin and Company.

Camperio-Ciani, A., Corna, F., & Capiluppi, C. (2004) Evidence for maternally inherited factors favouring male homosexuality and promoting female fecundity. *Philosophical Transactions of the Royal Society of London. Series B, Biological Sciences, 271,* 2217–2221. doi:10.1098/rspb.2004.2872

Cannon, W. B. (1927). The James–Lange theory of emotions: A critical examination and an alternative theory. *The American Journal of Psychology, 39,* 106–124. doi:10.2307/1415404

Cannon, W. B. (1932). *The wisdom of the body.* New York, NY: Norton.

Canter, D. V. (2011). Resolving the offender "profiling equations" and the emergence of an investigative psychology. *Current Directions in Psychological Science, 20,* 5–10. doi:10.1177/0963721410396825

Cantor, N., & Kihlstrom, J. F. (1987). *Personality and social intelligence.* Englewood Cliffs, NJ: Prentice Hall.

Capellini, I., Barton, R. A., McNamara, P., Preston, B. T., & Nunn, C. L. (2008). Phylogenetic analysis of the ecology and evolution of mammalian sleep. *Evolution, 62,* 1764–1776. doi:10.1111/j.1558-5646.2008.00392.x

Capellini, I., Nunn, C. L., McNamara, P., Preston, B. T., & Barton, R. A. (2008). Energetic constraints, not predation, influence the evolution of sleep patterning in mammals. *Functional Ecology, 22,* 847–853. doi:10.1111/j.1365-2435.2008.01449.x

Caporael, L. R. (2001). Evolutionary psychology: Toward a unifying theory and a hybrid science. *Annual Review of Psychology, 52,* 607–628. doi:10.1146/annurev.psych.52.1.607

Caprara, G. V., Steca, P., Cervone, D., & Artistico, D. (2003). The contribution of self-efficacy beliefs to dispositional shyness: On social-cognitive systems and the development of personality dispositions. *Journal of Personality, 71,* 943–970. doi:10.1111/1467-6494.7106003

Carek, P. J., Laibstain, S. E., & Carek, S. M. (2011). Exercise for the treatment of depression and anxiety. *The International Journal of Psychiatry in Medicine, 41,* 15–28. doi:10.2190/PM.41.1.c

Carey, B. (2011, June 23). Expert on mental illness reveals her own fight. *The New York Times.* Retrieved from http://www.nytimes.com/2011/06/23/health/23lives.html

Carey, S. (2009). *The origin of concepts.* Oxford series in cognitive development. Oxford, England: Oxford University Press. doi:10.1093/acprof:oso/9780195367638.001.0001

Carey, S. (2011). Précis of the origin of concepts. *Behavioral and Brain Sciences, 34,* 113–124. doi:10.1017/S0140525X10000919

Carlsson, A. (1999). The discovery of the SSRIs: A milestone in neuropsychopharmacology and rational drug design. In S. C. Stanford (Ed.), *Selective Serotonin Reuptake Inhibitors (SSRIs): Past, Present and Future* (pp. 1–7). Austin, TX: R. G. Landes Co.

Carstensen, L. L. (1995). Evidence for a life-span theory of socioemotional selectivity. *Current Directions in Psychological Science, 4,* 151–156. doi:10.1111/1467-8721.ep11512261

Carstensen, L. L. (2006). The influence of a sense of time on human development. *Science, 312,* 1913–1915. doi:10.1126/science.1127488

Carter, C. S., Braver, T. S., Barch, D. M., Botvinick, M. M., Noll, D., & Cohen, J. D. (1998). Anterior cingulate cortex, error detection, and the online monitoring of performance. *Science, 280,* 747–749. doi:10.1126/science.280.5364.747

Carver, C. S., & Scheier, M. F. (1998). *On the self-regulation of behavior.* New York, NY: Cambridge University Press. doi:10.1017/CBO9781139174794

Casey, B. J., Somerville, L. H., Gotlib, I. H., Ayduk, O., Franklin, N. T., Askren, M. K., . . . & Shoda, Y. (2011). Behavioral and neural correlates of delay of gratification 40 years later. *Proceedings of the National Academy of Sciences of the United States of America, 108,* 14998–15003. doi:10.1073/pnas.1108561108

Casey, B. J., Tottenham, N., Liston, C., & Durston, S. (2005). Imaging the developing brain: What have we learned about cognitive development? *Trends in Cognitive Sciences, 9,* 104–110. doi:10.1016/j.tics.2005.01.011

Cash, T. F., & Deagle, E. A. (1997). The nature and extent of body-image disturbances in anorexia nervosa and bulimia nervosa: A meta-analysis. *International Journal of Eating Disorders, 22,* 107–126. doi:10.1002/(SICI)1098-108X(199709)22:2

Caspi, A., McClay, J., Moffitt, T. E., Mill, J., Martin, J., Craig, I. W., . . . & Poulton, R. (2002). Role of genotype in the cycle of violence in maltreated children. *Science, 297,* 851–854. doi:10.1126/science.1072290

Caspi, A., Sugden, K., Moffitt, T. E., Taylor, A., Craig, I. W., Harrington, H., . . . & Poulton, R. (2003). Influence of life stress on depression: Moderation by a polymorphism in the 5-HTT gene. *Science, 301,* 386–389. doi:10.1126/science.1083968

Casselman, A. (2008, April 3). Identical twin's genes are not identical. *Scientific American.* Retrieved from http://www.scientificamerican.com/article/identical-twins-genes-are-not-identical/

Cattell, R. B. (1965). *The scientific analysis of personality.* Baltimore, MD: Penguin.

Cattell, R. B. (Ed.). (1987). *Intelligence: Its structure, growth, and action.* Advances in Psychology. Amsterdam, Netherlands: Elsevier Science Publishers, B. V.

Ceci, S. J. (1991). How much does schooling influence general intelligence and its cognitive components? A reassessment of the evidence. *Developmental Psychology, 27,* 703–722. doi:10.1037//0012-1649.27.5.703

Ceci, S. J., Williams, W. M., & Barnett, S. M. (2009). Women's underrepresentation in science: Sociocultural and biological considerations. *Psychological Bulletin, 135,* 218–261. doi:10.1037/a0014412

Celizic, M. for TODAY, NBC News. (2010, March 25). *Meet the girl with half a brain: 9-year-old had radical surgery to fight seizures; today she's back in school.* Retrieved from http://today.msnbc.msn.com/id/36032653/

Cervone, D. (1991). The two disciplines of personality psychology. *Psychological Science, 6,* 371–377. doi:10.1111/j.1467-9280.1991.tb00169.x

Cervone, D. (2004). The architecture of personality. *Psychological Review, 111,* 183–204. doi:10.1037/0033-295X.111.1.183

Cervone, D. (2012). Diverse perspectives. *Program, 24th Annual Convention of the Association for Psychological Science,* Chicago, IL.

Cervone, D., Kopp, D. A., Schaumann, L., & Scott, W. D. (1994). Mood, self-efficacy, and performance standards: Lower moods induce higher standards for performance. *Journal of Personality and Social Psychology, 67,* 499–512. doi:10.1037/0022-3514.67.3.499

Cervone, D., & Mischel, W. (Eds.). (2002). *Advances in personality science.* New York, NY: Guilford.

Cervone, D., Orom, H., Artistico, D., Shadel, W. G., & Kassel, J. (2007). Using a knowledge-and-appraisal model of personality architecture to understand consistency and variability in smokers' self-efficacy appraisals in high-risk situations. *Psychology of Addictive Behaviors, 21,* 44–54. doi:10.1037/0893-164X.21.1.44

Cervone, D., Shadel, W. G., & Jencius, S. (2001). Social-cognitive theory of personality assessment. *Personality and Social Psychology Review, 5,* 33–51. doi:10.1207/S15327957PSPR0501_3

Cervone, D., & Shoda, Y. (Eds.). (1999). *The coherence of personality: Social-cognitive bases of consistency, variability, and organization.* New York, NY: Guilford.

Chadwick, P. D. J. (2006). *Person-based cognitive therapy for distressing psychosis.* Chichester, England: John Wiley & Sons. doi:10.1002/9780470713075

Chaiken, S., Liberman, A., & Eagly, A. H. (1989). Heuristic and systematic information processing within and beyond the persuasion context. In J. S. Uleman & J. A. Bargh (Eds.), *Unintended Thought* (pp. 212–252). New York, NY: Guilford Press.

Chalmers, D. J. (1996). *The conscious mind: In search of a fundamental theory.* Oxford, UK: Oxford University Press.

Chalmers, D. J. (2010). *The character of consciousness.* Oxford, UK: Oxford University Press. doi:10.1093/acprof:oso/9780195311105.001.0001

Chambless, D. L., & Ollendick, T. H. (2001). Empirically supported psychological interventions: Controversies and evidence. *Annual Review of Psychology, 52,* 685–716. doi:10.1146/annurev.psych.52.1.685

Champagne, F. A., & Curley, J. P. (2009). Epigenetic mechanisms mediating the long-term effects of maternal care on development. *Neuroscience and Biobehavioral Reviews, 33,* 593–600. doi:10.1016/j.neubiorev.2007.10.009

Chance, P. (1999). Thorndike's puzzle boxes and the origins of the experimental analysis of behavior. *Journal of the Experimental Analysis of Behavior, 72,* 433–440. doi:10.1901/jeab.1999.72-433

Chandrashekar, J., Hoon, M. A., Ryba, N. J. P., & Zuker, C. S. (2006). The receptors and cells for mammalian taste. *Nature, 444,* 288–294. doi:10.1038/nature05401

Charles, S. T., Mather, M., & Carstensen, L. L. (2003). Aging and emotional memory: The forgettable nature of negative images for older adults. *Journal of Experimental Psychology: General, 132,* 310–324. doi:10.1037/0096-3445.132.2.310

Chater, N., & Christiansen, M. H. (2010). Language acquisition meets language evolution. *Cognitive Science, 34,* 1131–1157. doi:10.1111/j.1551-6709.2009.01049.x

Checking house was safe 200 times a day gave me a heart attack. (2010, March 9). *The Sun.* Retrieved from http://www.thesun.co.uk/sol/homepage/woman/real_life/2884211/The-nightmare-of-living-with-obsessive-compulsive-disorder.html

Chemerinski, E., Triebwasser, J., Roussos, P., & Siever, L. J. (2013). Schizotypal personality disorder. *Journal of Personality Disorders, 27,* 652–679. doi:10.1521/pedi_2012_26_053

Chen, X., Gabitto, M., Peng, Y., Ryba, N. J. P., & Zuker, C. S. (2011). A gustotopic map of taste qualities in the mammalian brain. *Science, 333,* 1262–1266. doi:10.1126/science.1204076

Cheng, C. (2001). Assessing coping flexibility in real-life and laboratory settings: A multimethod approach. *Journal of Personality and Social Psychology, 80,* 814–833. doi:10.1037/0022-3514.80.5.814

Cheng, C. (2003). Cognitive and motivational processes underlying coping flexibility: A dual-process model. *Journal of Personality and Social Psychology, 84,* 425–438. doi:10.1037/0022-3514.84.2.425

Cheng, C., & Cheung, M. W. (2005). Cognitive processes underlying coping flexibility: Differentiation and integration. *Journal of Personality, 73,* 859–886. doi:10.1111/j.1467-6494.2005.00331.x

Cheng, C., Kogan, A., & Chio, J. H. M. (2012). The effectiveness of a new, coping flexibility intervention as compared with a cognitive–behavioural intervention in managing work stress. *Work & Stress, 26,* 272–288. doi:10.1080/02678373.2012.710369

Cheryan, S., & Bodenhausen, G. V. (2000). When positive stereotypes threaten intellectual performance: The psychological hazards of "model minority" status. *Psychological Science, 11,* 399–402. doi:10.1111/1467-9280.00277

Chesler, P. (1997). *Women and madness* (25th Anniversary Edition). New York, NY: Four Walls Eight Windows.

Chi, K. R. (2009). Hit or miss? Genome-wide association studies have identified hundreds of genetic clues to disease. Kelly Rae Chi looks at three to see just how on-target the approach seems to be. *Nature, 461,* 712–714. doi:10.1038/461712a

Chiao, J. Y., & Blizinsky, K. D. (2010). Culture–gene coevolution of individualism–collectivism and the serotonin transporter gene. *Philosophical Transactions of the Royal Society of London. Series B, Biological Sciences, 277,* 529–537. doi:10.1098/rspb.2009.1650

Chittka, L. (1996). Does bee color vision predate the evolution of flower color? *Naturwissenschaften, 83,* 136–138. doi:10.1007/BF01142181

Chochon, F., Cohen, L., van de Moortele, P. F., & Dehaene, S. (1999). Differential contributions of the left and right inferior parietal lobules to number processing. *Journal of Cognitive Neuroscience, 11,* 617–630. doi:10.1162/089892999563689

Chodron, T. (1990). *Open heart, clear mind.* Ithaca, NY: Snow Lion Publications.

Chomsky, N. (1959). A review of B. F. Skinner's "Verbal Behavior." *Language, 35,* 26–58. doi:10.2307/411334

Chomsky, N. (1965). *Aspects of the theory of syntax.* Cambridge, MA: MIT Press.

Chomsky, N. (1980). *Rules and representations.* New York, NY: Columbia University Press.

Choy, Y., Fyer, A. J., & Lipsitz, J. D. (2007). Treatment of specific phobia in adults. *Clinical Psychology Review, 27,* 266–286. doi:10.1016/j.cpr.2006.10.002

Christensen, A., Sevier, M., Simpson, L., & Gattis, K. (2004). Acceptance, mindfulness, and change in couple therapy. In S. C. Hayes, V. M. Follette, & M. M. Linehan (Eds.), *Mindfulness and Acceptance: Expanding the Cognitive-Behavioral Tradition* (pp. 288–309). New York, NY: Guilford Press.

Christensen, K., Doblhammer, G., Rau, R., & Vaupel, J. W. (2009). Ageing populations: The challenges ahead. *The Lancet, 374,* 1196–1208. doi:10.1016/S0140-6736(09)61460-4

Cialdini, R. B. (2009). *Influence: Science and practice* (5th ed.). Boston, MA: Pearson Education.

Cialdini, R. B., & Goldstein, N. J. (2004). Social influence: Compliance and conformity. *Annual Review of Psychology, 55,* 591–621. doi:10.1146/annurev.psych.55.090902.142015

Clark, L., Averbeck, B., Payer, D., Sescousse, G., Winstanley, C. A., & Xue, G. (2013). Pathological choice: The neuroscience of gambling and gambling addiction. *The Journal of Neuroscience, 33,* 17617–17623. doi:10.1523/JNEUROSCI.3231-13.2013

Clift, S. M., & Hancox, G. (2001). The perceived benefits of singing: Findings from preliminary surveys of a university college choral society. *The Journal of the Royal Society for the Promotion of Health, 121,* 248–256. doi:10.1177/146642400112100409

Coffey, Wayne. (2005, March 13). Ghana: From rags to riches, *New York Daily News.* http://www.nydailynews.com/archives/sports/ghana-rags-to-riches-abandoned-child-disabled-cyclist-rises-poor-streets-west-africa-change-world-article-1.595793

Cohen, D., & Eisdorfer, C. (2001). *The loss of self: A family resource for the care of Alzheimer's disease and related disorders (Revised and updated ed.).* London, England: W. W. Norton and Company.

Cohen, J. (1992). A power primer. *Psychological Bulletin, 112,* 155–159.

Cohen, S., Janicki-Deverts, D., Chen, E., & Matthews, K. A. (2010). Childhood socioeconomic status and adult health. *Annals of the New York Academy of Sciences, 1186,* 37–55. doi:10.1111/j.1749-6632.2009.05334.x

Cohen, S., Tyrrell, D., & Smith, A. (1993). Negative life events, perceived stress, negative affect, and susceptibility to the common cold. *Journal of Personality and Social Psychology, 64,* 131–140. doi:10.1037/0022-3514.64.1.131

Cohen, S., & Wills, T. A. (1985). Stress, social support, and the buffering hypothesis. *Psychological Bulletin, 98,* 310–357. doi:10.1037/0033-2909.98.2.310

Cohn, J., Ambadar, Z., & Ekman, P. (2007). Observer-based measurement of facial expression with the Facial Action Coding System. In J. A. Coan & J. J. B. Allen (Eds.), *The Handbook of Emotion Elicitation and Assessment* (pp. 203–221). Series in affective science. New York, NY: Oxford University Press.

Cole, N. S. (1997). *The ETS gender study: How females and males perform in educational settings.* Princeton, NJ: Education Testing Service.

Cole, P. M., & Hall, S. E. (2008). Emotion dysregulation as a risk factor for psychopathology. In T. P. Beauchaine, & S. P. Hinshaw (Eds.), *Child and Adolescent Psychopathology* (pp. 265–298). Hoboken, NJ: John Wiley & Sons.

Cole, S. W. (2009). Social regulation of human gene expression. *Current Directions in Psychological Science, 18,* 132–137. doi:10.1111/j.1467-8721.2009.01623.x

Cole, S. W., Hawkley, L. C., Arevalo, J. M., Sung, C. Y., Rose, R. M., & Cacioppo, J. T. (2007). Social regulation of gene expression in human leukocytes. *Genome Biology, 8,* R189. doi:10.1186/gb-2007-8-9-r189

Cole, T. (2011). *Open city.* New York, NY: Random House.

Cole, W. G., Lingeman, J. M., & Adolph, K. E. (2012). Go naked: Diapers affect infant walking. *Developmental Science, 15,* 783–790. doi:10.1111/j.1467-7687.2012.01169.x

Coleman, P. D. (1963). An analysis of cues to auditory depth perception in free space. *Psychological Bulletin, 60,* 302–315. doi:10.1037/h0045716

Collins, A. M., & Loftus, E. F. (1975). A spreading-activation theory of semantic processing. *Psychological Review, 82,* 407–428. doi:10.1037//0033-295X.82.6.407

Collins, C. J., Hanges, P. J., & Locke, E. A. (2004). The relationship of achievement motivation to entrepreneurial behavior: A meta-analysis. *Human Performance, 17,* 95–117. doi:10.1207/S15327043HUP1701_5

Collins, W. A., Maccoby, E. E., Steinberg, L., Hetherington, E. M., & Bornstein, M. H. (2000). Contemporary research on parenting: The case for nature and nurture. *American Psychologist, 55,* 218–232. doi:10.1037/0003-066X.55.2.218

Colom, R., Rebollo, I., Palacios, A., Juan-Espinosa, M., & Kyllonen, P. (2004). Working memory is (almost) perfectly predicted by g. *Intelligence, 32,* 277–296. doi:10.1016/j.intell.2003.12.002

Comstock, G., & Paik, H. (1991). Television and the American child. San Diego, CA: Academic Press.

Conklin, C. Z., Bradley, R., & Westen, D. (2006). Affect regulation in borderline personality disorder. *The Journal of Nervous and Mental Disease, 194,* 69–77. doi:10.1097/01.nmd.0000198138.41709.4f

Conley, D. (2004). *The pecking order: Which siblings succeed and why.* New York, NY: Pantheon.

Cooley, C. H. (1902). *Human nature and the social order.* New York, NY: Scribner's.

Cooney, G. M., Dwan, K., Greig, C. A., Lawlor, D. A., Rimer, J., Waugh, F. R., . . . & Mead, G. E. (2013). Exercise for depression (Review). *Cochrane Database of Systematic Reviews, 12,* CD004366. doi:10.1002/14651858.CD004366.pub6

Cooper, H., Hedges, L. V., & Valentine, J. C. (Eds.). (2009). *Handbook of research synthesis and meta-analysis.* New York, NY: Russell Sage Foundation.

Coopersmith, S. (1967). *The antecedents of self-esteem.* San Francisco, CA: W. H. Freeman.

Copeland, W. E., Angold, A., Shanahan, L., & Costello, E. J. (2014). Longitudinal patterns of anxiety from childhood to adulthood: The great smoky mountains study. *Journal of the American Academy of Child and Adolescent Psychiatry, 53,* 21–33.

Coren, S. (1998, March). Sleep deprivation, psychosis and mental efficiency. *Psychiatric Times, 15*(3).

Corkin, S. (2002). What's new with the amnesic patient H. M.? *Nature Reviews Neuroscience, 3,* 153–60. doi:10.1038/nrn726

Corkin, S., Amaral, D. G., González, R. G., Johnson, K. A., & Hyman, B. T. (1997). H. M.'s medial temporal lobe lesion: Findings from magnetic resonance imaging. *The Journal of Neuroscience, 17,* 3964–3979.

Corr, P. (2004). Reinforcement sensitivity theory and personality. *Neuroscience and Biobehavioural Reviews, 28,* 317–332. doi:10.1016/j.neubiorev.2004.01.005

Cosmides, L. (1989). The logic of social exchange: Has natural selection shaped how humans reason? Studies with the Wason selection task. *Cognition, 31,* 187–276. doi:10.1016/0010-0277(89)90023-1

Cosmides, L., & Tooby, J. (1997). Evolutionary psychology: A primer. Retrieved from http://www.psych.ucsb.edu/research/cep/primer.html

Cosmides, L., & Tooby, J. (2013). Evolutionary psychology: New perspectives on cognition and motivation. *Annual Review of Psychology, 64,* 201–229. doi:10.1146/annurev.psych.121208.131628

Costa, P. T., Jr., & McCrae, R. R. (1992). *NEO-PI-R: Professional manual.* Odessa, FL: Psychological Assessment Resources.

Costandi, M. (2008, August 27). *Wilder Penfield, neural cartographer.* Retrieved from http://neurophilosophy.wordpress.com/2008/08/27/wilder_penfield_neural_cartographer/

Coury, C. (1967). The basic principles of medicine in the primitive mind. *Medical History, 11,* 111–127. doi:10.1017/S0025727300011972

Covington, M. V. (2000). Goal theory, motivation, and school achievement: An integrative review. *Annual Review of Psychology, 51,* 171–200. doi:10.1146/annurev.psych.51.1.171

Cowan, N. (2001). The magical number 4 in short-term memory: A reconsideration of mental storage capacity. *Behavioral and Brain Sciences, 24,* 87–114. doi:10.1017/S0140525X01003922

Cowan, N., Morey, C. C., & Chen, Z. (2007). The legend of the magical number seven. In S. Della Sala (Ed.), *Tall Tales about the Mind & Brain: Separating Fact from Fiction* (pp. 45–59). Oxford, U.K.: Oxford University Press. doi:10.1093/acprof:oso/9780198568773.003.0005

Cox, G. R., Callahan, P., Churchill, R., Hunot, V., Merry, S. N., Parker, A. G., & Hetrick, S. E. (2012). Psychological therapies versus antidepressant medication, alone and in combination for depression in children and adolescents (Review). *Cochrane Database of Systematic Reviews 2012, 11,* CD008324. doi:10.1002/14651858.CD008324.pub2

Coyne, S. M., Padilla-Walker, L. M., & Howard, E. (2013). Emerging in a digital world: A decade review of media use, effects, and gratifications in emerging adulthood. *Emerging Adulthood, 1,* 125–137. doi:10.1177/2167696813479782

Craik, F. I., & Tulving, E. (1975). Depth of processing and the retention of words in episodic memory. *Journal of Experimental Psychology: General, 104,* 268–294. doi:10.1037/0096-3445.104.3.268

Craik, F. I., & Watkins, M. J. (1973). The role of rehearsal in short-term memory. *Journal of Verbal Learning and Verbal Behavior, 12,* 599–607. doi:10.1016/S0022-5371(73)80039-8

Cramer, A. O., Sluis, S., Noordhof, A., Wichers, M., Geschwind, N., Aggen, S. H., . . . & Borsboom, D. (2012). Dimensions of normal personality as networks in search of equilibrium: You can't like parties if you don't like people. *European Journal of Personality, 26,* 414–431. doi:10.1002/per.1866

Cramer, A. O., Waldorp, L. J., van der Maas, H. L., & Borsboom, D. (2010). Comorbidity: A network perspective. *Behavioral and Brain Sciences, 33,* 137–150. doi:10.1017/S0140525X09991567

Crews, F. C. (1998). *Unauthorized Freud: Doubters confront a legend.* New York, NY: Viking.

Crick, A. (2009, November 4). Shot and awe. *The Sun.* Available from http://www.thesun.co.uk/sol/homepage/news/campaigns/our_boys/2711716/Shot-and-awe.html

Cruz, N., Sanchez-Moreno, J., Torres, F., Goikolea, J. M., Valentí, M., & Vieta, E. (2010). Efficacy of modern antipsychotics in placebo-controlled trials in bipolar depression: A meta-analysis. *The International Journal of Neuropsychopharmacology, 13,* 5–14. doi:10.1017/S1461145709990344

Csikszentmihalyi, M. (1990). *Flow: The psychology of optimal experience.* New York, NY: Harper Row.

Csikszentmihalyi, M., Larson, R., & Prescott, S. (1977). The ecology of adolescent activity and experience. *Journal of Youth and Adolescence, 6,* 281–294. doi:10.1007/BF02138940

Csikszentmihalyi, M., & LeFevre, J. (1989). Optimal experience in work and leisure. *Journal of Personality and Social Psychology, 56,* 815–822. doi:10.1037/0022-3514.56.5.815

Cuijpers, P., van Straten, A., Andersson, G., & van Oppen, P. (2008). Psychotherapy for depression in adults: A meta-analysis of comparative outcome studies. *Journal of Consulting and Clinical Psychology, 76,* 909–922. doi:10.1037/a0013075

Cuncic, A. (2010, January 28). What is Kim Basinger's experience with social anxiety? *About.com.* Retrieved from http://socialanxietydisorder.about.com/od/celebrieswithsad/p/kimbasinger.htm

Curcio, C. A., Sloan, K. R., Kalina, R. E., & Hendrickson, A. E. (1990). Human photoreceptor topography. *Journal of Comparative Neurology, 292,* 497–523. doi:10.1002/cne.902920402

Curtis, C. E., & D'Esposito, M. (2003). Persistent activity in the prefrontal cortex during working memory. *Trends in Cognitive Sciences, 7,* 415–423. doi:10.1016/S1364-6613(03)00197-9

Custer, R., & Aarts, H. (2010). The unconscious will: How the pursuit of goals operates outside of conscious awareness. *Science, 329,* 47–50. doi:10.1126/science.1188595

Cutrell, E., & Guan, Z. (2007, April). What are you looking for?: An eye-tracking study of information usage in web search. In *Proceedings of the SIGCHI Conference on Human Factors in Computing Systems* (pp. 407–416). New York, NY: ACM. doi:10.1145/1240624.1240690

Cutting, J. E. (2012). Gunnar Johansson, events, and biological motion. In K. Johnson & M. Shiffrar (Eds.), *Visual Perception of the Human Body in Motion.* New York, NY: Oxford University Press.

Cyranoski, D. (2011, October 31). More clues in the genetics of schizophrenia: Chinese researchers add three chromosomal regions to a slow-growing list of genetic links. *Nature News.* doi:10.1038/news.2011.620

Czeisler, C. A., Duffy, J., Shanahan, T., Brown, E., Mitchell, J., Rimmer, D., . . . & Kronauer, R. (1999). Stability, precision, and near-24-hour period of the human circadian pacemaker. *Science, 284,* 2177–2181. doi:10.1126/science.284.5423.2177

Czeisler, C. A., & Fryer, B. (2006). Sleep deficit: The performance killer. *Harvard Business Review, 94,* 53–59.

D'Argembeau, A., Feyers, D., Majerus, S., Collette, F., Van der Linden, M., Maquet, P., & Salmon, E. (2008). Self-reflection across time: Cortical midline structures differentiate between present and past selves. *Social Cognitive and Affective Neuroscience, 3,* 244–252. doi:10.1093/scan/nsn020

D'Argembeau, A., Stawarczyk, D., Majerus, S., Collette, F., Van der Linden, M., Feyers, D., . . . & Salmon, E. (2010). The neural basis of personal goal processing when envisioning future events. *Journal of Cognitive Neuroscience, 22,* 1701–1713. doi:10.1162/jocn.2009.21314

Dalai Lama, & Cutler, H. C. (1998). *The art of happiness.* New York, NY: Riverhead Books.

Damasio, A. R. (1994). *Descartes' error: Emotion, reason, and the human brain.* New York, NY: Grosset/Putnam.

Damasio, H., Grabowski, T., Frank, R., Galaburda, A. M., & Damasio, A. R. (1994). The return of Phineas Gage: Clues about the brain from the skull of a famous patient. *Science, 264,* 1102–1105. doi:10.1126/science.8178168

Damisch, L., Stoberock, B., & Mussweiler, T. (2010). Keep your fingers crossed! How superstition improves performance. *Psychological Science, 21,* 1014–1020. doi:10.1177/0956797610372631

Daniels, H., Cole, M., & Wertsch, J. V. (Eds.). (2007). *The Cambridge companion to Vygotsky.* New York, NY: Cambridge University Press. doi:10.1017/CCOL0521831040

Danziger, K. (2008). *Marking the mind: A history of memory.* Cambridge, UK: Cambridge University Press. doi:10.1017/CBO9780511810626

Darley, J., & Latané, B. (1968). Bystander intervention in emergencies: Diffusion of responsibility. *Journal of Personality and Social Psychology, 8,* 377–383. doi:10.1037/h0025589

Darwin, C. (1872). *The expression of emotions in man and animals.* New York, NY: Philosophical Library. doi:10.1037/10001-000

Daugman, J. (2001). Brain metaphor and brain theory. In W. Bechtel, P. Mandik, J. Mundale, & R. S. Stufflebeam (Eds.), *Philosophy and the neurosciences: A reader* (pp. 23–36). Oxford, England: Blackwell Publishers.

Daum, I., Ackermann, H., Schugens, M. M., Reimold, C., Dichgans, J., & Birbaumer, N. (1993). The cerebellum and cognitive functions in humans. *Behavioral Neuroscience, 107,* 411–419. doi:10.1037/0735-7044.107.3.411

Davis, B. P., & Knowles, E. S. (1999). A disrupt-then-reframe technique of social influence. *Journal of Personality and Social Psychology, 76,* 192–199. doi:10.1037/0022-3514.76.2.192

Davis, J. (2011, July/August). The persecution of Daniel Lee. *Stanford Magazine.* Retrieved from http://alumni.stanford.edu/get/page/magazine/article/?article_id=40913

Dawood, K., Bailey, J. M., & Martin, N. G. (2009). Genetic and environmental influences on sexual orientation. In Y.-K. Kim (Ed.), *Handbook of Behavior Genetics* (pp. 269–279). New York, NY: Springer New York. doi:10.1007/978-0-387-76727-7_19

de Araujo, I. E., & Simon, S. A. (2009). The gustatory cortex and multisensory integration. *International Journal of Obesity, 33,* S34–S43. doi:10.1038/ijo.2009.70

De Beaumont, L., Tremblay, S., Poirier, J., Lassonde, M., & Théoret, H. (2012). Altered bidirectional plasticity and reduced implicit motor learning in concussed athletes. *Cerebral Cortex, 22,* 112–121. doi:10.1093/cercor/bhr096

de Maat, S., de Jonghe, F., Schoevers, R., & Dekker, J. (2009). The effectiveness of long-term psychoanalytic therapy: A systematic review of empirical studies. *Harvard Review of Psychiatry, 17,* 1–23. doi:10.1080/10673220902742476

De Martino, B., Camerer, C. F., & Adolphs, R. (2010). Amygdala damage eliminates monetary loss aversion. *Proceedings of the National Academy of Sciences of the United States of America, 107,* 3788–3792. doi:10.1073/pnas.0910230107

Deary, I. J. (2001). *Intelligence: A very short introduction.* Oxford, UK: Oxford University Press. doi:10.1093/actrade/9780192893215.001.0001

Deary, I. J., Penke, L., & Johnson, W. (2010). The neuroscience of human intelligence differences. *Nature Reviews Neuroscience, 11,* 201–211. doi:10.1038/nrn2793

Deary, I. J., Strand, S., Smith, P., & Fernandes, C. (2007). Intelligence and educational achievement. *Intelligence, 35,* 13–21. doi:10.1016/j.intell.2006.02.001

Deater-Deckard, K., Pike, A., Petrill, S. A., Cutting, A. L., Hughes, C., & O'Connor, T. G. (2001). Fast-Track Report: Nonshared environmental processes in social-emotional development: An observational study of identical twin differences in the preschool period. *Developmental Science, 4,* F1–F6. doi:10.1111/1467-7687.00157

Deci, E. L., Koestner, R., & Ryan, R. M. (1999). A meta-analytic review of experiments examining the effects of extrinsic rewards on intrinsic motivation. *Psychological Bulletin, 125,* 627–668. doi:10.1037/0033-2909.125.6.627

Degnan, K. A., Henderson, H. A., Fox, N. A., & Rubin, K. H. (2008). Predicting social wariness in middle childhood: The moderating roles of childcare history, maternal personality and maternal behavior. *Social Development, 17,* 471–487. doi:10.1111/j.1467-9507.2007.00437.x

Dehaene, S. (2004). Evolution of human cortical circuits for reading and arithmetic: The "neuronal recycling" hypothesis. In S. Dehaene, J. R. Duhamel, M. Hauser & G. Rizzolatti (Eds.), *From Monkey Brain to Human Brain* (pp. 133–157). Cambridge, MA: MIT Press.

Dehaene, S., & Naccache, L. (2001). Towards a cognitive neuroscience of consciousness: Basic evidence and a workspace framework. *Cognition, 79,* 1–37. doi:10.1016/S0010-0277(00)00123-2

DeKay, W. T., & Buss, D. M. (1992). Human nature, individual differences, and the importance of context: Perspectives from evolutionary psychology. *Current Directions in Psychological Science, 1,* 184–189. doi:10.1111/1467-8721.ep10770389

Dement, W. C. (1978). *Some must watch while some must sleep: Exploring the world of sleep.* New York, NY: Norton.

Dennett, D. C. (1991). *Consciousness explained.* Boston, MA: Little Brown.

Dennett, D. C. (1995). *Darwin's dangerous idea: Evolution and the meanings of life.* New York, NY: Simon & Schuster.

Dennett, D. C. (2003). *Freedom evolves.* New York, NY: Viking.

Dennett, D., & Kinsbourne, M. (1992). Time and the observer: The where and when of consciousness in the brain. *Behavioral and Brain Sciences, 15,* 183–247. doi:10.1017/S0140525X00068229

Denzin, N. K. & Lincoln, Y. S. (Eds.). (2011). *The Sage handbook of qualitative research* (4th ed.). Thousand Oaks, CA: Sage.

Department of Homeland Security. (2008, February 25). *Privacy impact assessment for the experimental testing of Project Hostile Intent technology* (DHS Publication No. DHS/S&T/PIA-005). Retrieved from http://www.dhs.gov/xlibrary/assets/privacy/privacy_pia_st_phi.pdf

Department of Homeland Security. (2011, December 21). *Privacy impact assessment update for the Future Attribute Screening Technology (FAST)/passive methods for precision behavioral screening* (DHS Publication No. DHS/S&T/PIA-012(a)). Retrieved from http://www.dhs.gov/xlibrary/assets/privacy/privacy_pia_st_fast-a.pdf

Devilbiss, D. M., & Berridge, C. W. (2008). Cognition-enhancing doses of methylphenidate preferentially increase prefrontal cortex neuronal responsiveness. *Biological Psychiatry, 64,* 626–635. doi:10.1016/j.biopsych.2008.04.037

Devine, P. G. (1989). Stereotypes and prejudice: Their automatic and controlled components. *Journal of Personality and Social Psychology, 56,* 5–18. doi:10.1037//0022-3514.56.1.5

Dickerson, F. B., Sommerville, J., Origoni, A. E., Ringel, N. B., & Parente, F. (2002). Experiences of stigma among outpatients with schizophrenia. *Schizophrenia Bulletin, 28,* 143–155. doi:10.1093/oxfordjournals.schbul.a006917

Dickinson, D., Bellack, A. S., & Gold, J. M. (2007). Social/communication skills, cognition, and vocational functioning in schizophrenia. *Schizophrenia Bulletin, 33,* 1213–1220. doi:10.1093/schbul/sbl067

Diener, E., Tay, L., & Oishi, S. (2013). Rising income and the subjective well-being of nations. *Journal of Personality and Social Psychology, 104,* 267–276. doi:10.1037/a0030487

Dobson, K. S. (1989). A meta-analysis of the efficacy of cognitive therapy for depression. *Journal of Consulting and Clinical Psychology, 57,* 414–419. doi:10.1037/0022-006X.57.3.414

Doherty, S. T., Lemieux, C. J., & Canally, C. (2014). Tracking human activity and well-being in natural environments using wearable sensors and experience sampling. *Social Science & Medicine, 106,* 83–92. doi:10.1016/j.socscimed.2014.01.048

Domhoff, G. W. (2005). Refocusing the neurocognitive approach to dreams: A critique of the Hobson versus Solms debate. *Dreaming, 15,* 3–20. doi:10.1037/1053-0797.15.1.3

Domjan, M., & Galef, B. G. (1983). Biological constraints on instrumental and classical conditioning: Retrospect and prospect. *Animal Learning & Behavior, 11,* 151–161. doi:10.3758/BF03199643

Downing, P. E. (2000). Interactions between visual working memory and selective attention. *Psychological Science, 11,* 467–473. doi:10.1111/1467-9280.00290

Doyle, A. C. (2007). *The Treasury of Sherlock Holmes.* Radford, VA: Wilder Publications.

Draganski, B., Gaser, C., Busch, V., Schuierer, G., Bogdahn, U., & May, A. (2004). Changes in grey matter induced by training. *Nature, 427,* 311–312. doi:10.1038/427311a

Dreifus, C. (2007, April 3). Finding hope in knowing the universal capacity for evil: A conversation with Philip G. Zimbardo. *The New York Times.* Retrieved from http://www.nytimes.com/2007/04/03/science/03conv.html

Dreifus, C. (2012, March 5). A quest to understand how memory works: A conversation with Eric R. Kandel. *The New York Times.* Retrieved from http://www.nytimes.com/2012/03/06/science/a-quest-to-understand-how-memory-works.html

Dreissen, Y. E., Bakker, M. J., Koelman, J. H., & Tijssen, M. A. (2012). Exaggerated startle reactions. *Clinical Neurophysiology, 123,* 34–44. doi:10.1016/j.clinph.2011.09.022

Dreyfus, G., & Thompson, E. (2007). Asian perspectives: Indian theories of mind. In P. D. Zelazo, M. Moscovitch, and E. Thompson (Eds.), *The Cambridge Handbook of Consciousness* (pp. 89–114). New York, NY: Cambridge University Press. doi:10.1017/CBO9780511816789.006

Dronkers, N. F., Plaisant, O., Iba-Zizen, M. T., & Cabanis, E. A. (2007). Paul Broca's historic cases: High resolution MR imaging of the brains of Leborgne and Lelong. *Brain, 130,* 1432–1441. doi:10.1093/brain/awm042

Drury, J. (2004). No need to panic. *The Psychologist, 3,* 118–119.

Drury, J., & Cocking, C. (2007). *The mass psychology of disasters and emergency evacuations: A research report and implications for practice.* Unpublished manuscript. University of Sussex, Brighton. Retrieved from http://www.sussex.ac.uk/affiliates/panic/Disasters%20and%20emergency%20evacuations%20%282007%29.pdf

Duan, J., Sanders, A. R., & Gejman, P. V. (2010). Genome-wide approaches to schizophrenia. *Brain Research Bulletin, 83,* 93–102. doi:10.1016/j.brainresbull.2010.04.009

Duckworth, A. L., & Seligman, M. E. P. (2005). Self-discipline outdoes IQ in predicting academic performance of adolescents. *Psychological Science, 16,* 939–944. doi:10.1111/j.1467-9280.2005.01641.x

Dudai, Y. (1988). Neurogenetic dissection of learning and short-term memory in *Drosophila. Annual Review of Neuroscience, 11,* 537–563. doi:10.1146/annurev.ne.11.030188.002541

Duffy, E. (1934). Emotion: An example of the need for reorientation in psychology. *Psychological Review, 41,* 184–198. doi:10.1037/h0074603

DuMont, K. A., Widom, C. S., & Czaja, S. J. (2007). Predictors of resilience in abused and neglected children grown-up: The role of individual and neighborhood characteristics. *Child Abuse & Neglect, 31,* 255–274. doi:10.1016/j.chiabu.2005.11.015

Durham, W. H. (1991). *Co-evolution: Genes, culture and human diversity.* Stanford, CA: Stanford University Press.

Duritz, A. (2008, April 17). The lonely disease: Counting Crows front man Adam Duritz reveals how he battled a debilitating mental disorder to record the best music of his career—and reclaim his life. *Men's Health.* Retrieved from http://www.menshealth.com/health/mental-illness

Dutton, D. G., & Aron, A. P. (1974). Some evidence for heightened sexual attraction under conditions of high anxiety. *Journal of Personality and Social Psychology, 30,* 510–517. doi:10.1037/h0037031

Dweck, C. S. (1986). Motivational processes affecting learning. *American Psychologist, 41,* 1040–1048. doi:10.1037/0003-066X.41.10.1040

Dweck, C. S. (2006). *Mindset: The new psychology of success.* New York, NY: Random House.

Dzierzewski, J. M., O'Brien, E. M., Kay, D., & McCrae, C. S. (2010). Tackling sleeplessness: Psychological treatment options for insomnia in older adults. *Nature and Science of Sleep, 2,* 47–61. doi:10.2147/NSS.S7064

Eagly, A., & Wood, W. (1999). The origins of sex differences in human behavior: Evolved dispositions versus social roles. *American Psychologist, 54,* 408–423. doi:10.1037/0003-066X.54.6.408

Eagly, A. H., Johannesen-Schmidt, M. C., & van Engen, M. L. (2003). Transformational, transactional, and laissez-faire leadership styles: A meta-analysis comparing women and men. *Psychological Bulletin, 129,* 569–591. doi:10.1037/0033-2909.129.4.569

Easwaran, E. (1997). *Gandhi the man: The story of his transformation.* Berkeley, CA: The Blue Mountain Center of Meditation.

Eaves, L., Heath, A., Martin, N., Maes, H., Neale, M., Kendler, K., . . . & Corey, L. (1999). Comparing the biological and cultural inheritance of personality and social attitudes in the Virginia 30 000 study of twins and their relatives. *Twin Research, 2,* 62–80.

Echeverría, J., & Niemeyer, H. M. (2013). Nicotine in the hair of mummies from San Pedro de Atacama (Northern Chile). *Journal of Archaeological Science, 40,* 3561–3568. doi:10.1016/j.jas.2013.04.030

Ecker, B., Ticic, R., & Hulley, L. (2012). *Unlocking the emotional brain: Eliminating symptoms at their roots using memory reconsolidation.* New York, NY: Routledge.

Edelman, G. M. (2003). Naturalizing consciousness: A theoretical framework. *Proceedings of the National Academy of Sciences of the United States of America, 100,* 5520–5524. doi:10.1073/pnas.0931349100

Edelman, G. M., & Tononi, G. (2000). *A universe of consciousness: How matter becomes imagination.* New York, NY: Basic Books.

Education: Ginny and Gracie go to school. (1979, December 10). *Time.* Retrieved from http://www.time.com/time/magazine/article/0,9171,912582,00.html.

Ehrlich, P. R. (2000). *Human natures: Genes, cultures, and the human prospect.* New York, NY: Penguin Books.

Eisenberg N. (2012). Temperamental effortful control (self-regulation) (Revised ed.). In R. E. Tremblay, M. Boivin, & R. DeV. Peters (Eds.), M. K. Rothbart (Topic Ed.), *Encyclopedia on Early Childhood Development* [online]. Montreal, Quebec: Centre of Excellence for Early Childhood Development and Strategic Knowledge Cluster on Early Child Development. Retrieved from http://www.child-encyclopedia.com/documents/EisenbergANGxp2-Temperament.pdf

Ekman, P. (1993). Facial expression and emotion. *American Psychologist, 48,* 376–379. doi:10.1037/0003-066X.48.4.384

Ekman, P. (2003). Darwin, deception, and facial expression. In P. Ekman, J. J. Campos, R. J. Davidson, & F. B. M. de Waal (Eds.), *Emotions Inside Out: 130 Years after Darwin's: The Expression of the Emotions in Man and Animals* (pp. 205–221). New York, NY: New York Academy of Sciences.

Ekman, P., & Friesen, W. (1971). Constants across cultures in the face and emotion. *Journal of Personality and Social Psychology, 17,* 124–129. doi:10.1037/h0030377

Ekman, P., O'Sullivan, M., & Frank, M. G. (1999). A few can catch a liar. *Psychological Science, 10,* 263–266. doi:10.1111/1467-9280.00147

Elgie, R., Amerongen, A. P. V., Byrne, P., D'Arienzo, S., Hickey, C., Lambert, M., . . . & Sappia, S. (2005, May). *Discover the road ahead: Support and guidance for everyone affected by schizophrenia* [Booklet]. Leopardstown, Ireland: Bristol-Myers Squibb and Otsuka Pharmaceuticals Europe Ltd.

Eliot, L. (1999). *What's going on in there? How the brain and mind develop in the first five years of life.* New York, NY: Bantam.

Elkins D. N. (2009). *Humanistic psychology: A clinical manifesto: A critique of clinical psychology and the need for progressive alternatives.* Colorado Springs, CO: University of the Rockies Press.

Elliot, A. J., & Sheldon, K. M. (1997). Avoidance achievement motivation: A personal goals analysis. *Journal of Personality and Social Psychology, 73,* 171–185. doi:10.1037/0022-3514.73.1.171

Elliot, S. M. (2009, August 20). The lady vanishes part I: Agatha Christie. *Swallowing the Camel.* Retrieved from http://swallowingthecamel.blogspot.com/2009/08/lady-vanishes-part-i-agatha-christie_20.html

Ellis, A., & Dryden, W. (1997). *The practice of rational emotive behavior therapy.* New York, NY: Springer Publishing.

Ellsworth, P. C., & Scherer, K. R. (2003). Appraisal processes in emotion. In R. J. Davidson, K. R. Scherer, & H. H. Goldsmith (Eds.), *Handbook of Affective Sciences* (pp. 572–595). New York, NY: Oxford University Press. doi:10.1037/1528-3542.3.1.81

Elman, J. L. (1991). Distributed representations, simple recurrent networks, and grammatical structure. *Machine Learning, 7,* 195–225. doi:10.1007/BF00114844

Elman, J. L., Bates, E. A., Johnson, M. H., Karmiloff-Smith, A., Parisi, D., & Plunkett, K. (1996). *Rethinking innateness: A connectionist perspective on development.* Cambridge, MA: MIT Press.

Emmons, R. A. (2005). Striving for the sacred: Personal goals, life meaning, and religion. *Journal of Social Issues, 61,* 731–745. doi:10.1111/j.1540-4560.2005.00429.x

Emmons, R. A., & King, L. A. (1988). Conflict among personal strivings: Immediate and long-term implications for psychological and physical well-being. *Journal of Personality and Social Psychology, 54,* 1040–1048. doi:10.1037/0022-3514.54.6.1040

Emsley, R., Chiliza, B., Asmal, L., & Harvey, B. H. (2013). The nature of relapse in schizophrenia. *BMC Psychiatry, 13,* 50–57. doi:10.1186/1471-244X-13-50

Engle, R. (2002). Working memory capacity as executive attention. *Current Directions in Psychological Science, 11,* 19–23. doi:10.1111/1467-8721.00160

Engle, R. W., Tuholski, S. W., Laughlin, J. E., & Conway, A. R. A. (1999). Working memory, short-term memory, and general fluid intelligence: A latent-variable approach? *Journal of Experimental Psychology: General, 128,* 309–331. doi:10.1037/0096-3445.128.3.309

Enns, M. W., Cox, B. J., & Clara, I. (2002). Adaptive and maladaptive perfectionism: Developmental origins and association with depression proneness. *Personality and Individual Differences, 33,* 921–935. doi:10.1016/S0191-8869(01)00202-1

Epel, E. S., Blackburn, E. H., Lin, J., Dhabhar, F. S., Adler, N. E., Morrow, J. D., & Cawthon, R. M. (2004). Accelerated telomere shortening in response to life stress. *Proceedings of the National Academy of Sciences of the United States of America, 101,* 17312–17315. doi:10.1073/pnas.0407162101

Epstein, S. (1979). The stability of behavior: I. On predicting most of the people much of the time. *Journal of Personality and Social Psychology, 37,* 1097–1126. doi:10.1037/0022-3514.37.7.1097

Eranti, S. V., Maccabe, J. H., Bundy, H., & Murray, R. M. (2013). Gender difference in age at onset of schizophrenia: A meta-analysis. *Psychological Medicine, 43,* 155–167. doi:10.1017/S003329171200089X

Erdelyi, M. H. (1985). *Psychoanalysis: Freud's cognitive psychology.* New York, NY: W. H. Freeman.

Erickson, K. I., Voss, M. W., Prakash, R. S., Basak, C., Szabo, A., Chaddock, L., . . . & Kramer, A. F. (2011). Exercise training increases size of hippocampus and improves memory. *Proceedings of the National Academy of Sciences, 108,* 3017–3022. doi:10.1073/pnas.1015950108

Ericsson, K. A., & Simon, H. (1984). *Protocol analysis: Verbal reports as data.* Cambridge, MA: MIT Press.

Erikson, E. (1950). *Childhood and society.* New York, NY: Norton.

Erikson, E. H. (1959). Identity and the life cycle: Selected papers. *Psychological Issues, 1,* 1–171.

Erikson, E. H. (1963). *Childhood and society* (2nd ed.). New York, NY: W. W. Norton.

Ermer, E., Guerin, S. A., Cosmides, L., Tooby, J., & Miller, M. B. (2006). Theory of mind broad and narrow: Reasoning about social exchange engages ToM areas, precautionary reasoning does not. *Social Neuroscience, 1,* 196–219. doi:10.1080/17470910600989771

Esser, J. K. (1998). Alive and well after 25 years: A review of groupthink research. *Organizational Behavior and Human Decision Processes, 73,* 116–141. doi:10.1006/obhd.1998.2758

Estroff, S. E. (1989). Self, identity, and subjective experiences of schizophrenia. *Schizophrenia Bulletin, 15,* 189–196. doi:10.1093/schbul/15.2.189

Evans, N., & Levinson, S. C. (2009). The myth of language universals: Language diversity and its importance for cognitive science. *The Behavioral and Brain Sciences, 32,* 429–448; discussion 448–494. doi:10.1017/S0140525X0999094X

Everett, G. E., Olmi, D. J., Edwards, R. P., Tingstrom, D. H., Sterling-Turner, H. E., & Christ, T. J. (2007). An empirical investigation of time-out with and without escape extinction to treat escape-maintained noncompliance. *Behavior Modification, 31,* 412–434. doi:10.1177/0145445506297725

Everitt, B. J., Belin, D., Economidou, D., Pelloux, Y., Dalley, J. W., & Robbins, T. W. (2008). Neural mechanisms underlying the vulnerability to develop compulsive drug-seeking habits and addiction. *Philosophical Transactions of the Royal Society of London. Series B, Biological Sciences, 363,* 3125–3135. doi:10.1098/rstb.2008.0089

Eysenck, H. J. (1970). *The structure of personality* (3rd edition). London, England: Methuen.

Eysenck, H. J. (1972). *Psychology is about people.* New York, NY: Library Press.

Eysenck, M. W. (2013). Social anxiety and performance. In D. Cervone, M. Fajkowska, M. W. Eysenck, & T. Maruszewski, T. (Eds.), *Personality Dynamics: Meaning Construction, the Scial World, and the Embodied Mind* (pp. 125–140). Warsaw Lectures in Personality and Social Psychology. Clinton Corners, NY: Eliot Werner Publications.

Fagan, P. J., Wise, T. N., Schmidt, C. W., & Berlin, F. S. (2002). Pedophilia. *Journal of the American Medical Association, 288,* 2458–2465. doi:10.1001/jama.288.19.2458

Fair, D. A., Cohen, A. L., Power, J. D., Dosenbach, N. U., Church, J. A., Miezin, F. M., . . . & Petersen, S. E. (2009). Functional brain networks develop from a "local to distributed" organization. *PLoS Computational Biology, 5*, e1000381. doi:10.1371/journal.pcbi.1000381

Fancher, R. E. (1979). *Pioneers of psychology.* New York: Norton.

Fantegrossi, W. E., Murnane, K. S., & Reissig, C. J. (2008). The behavioral pharmacology of hallucinogens. *Biochemical Pharmacology, 75*, 17–33. doi:10.1016/j.bcp.2007.07.018

Farah, M. J. (1984). The neurological basis of mental imagery: A componential analysis. *Cognition, 18*, 245–272. doi:10.1016/0010-0277(84)90026-X

Farrell, H. M. (2011). Dissociative identity disorder: Medicolegal challenges. *Journal of the American Academy of Psychiatry and the Law Online, 39*, 402–406.

Fedorenko, E., & Kanwisher, N. (2009). Neuroimaging of language: Why hasn't a clearer picture emerged? *Language and Linguistics Compass, 3*, 839–865. doi:10.1111/j.1749-818X.2009.00143.x

Feero, W. G., Guttmacher, A. E., & Collins, F. S. (2010). Genomic medicine—An updated primer. *New England Journal of Medicine, 362*, 2001–2011. doi:10.1056/NEJMra0907175

Feinstein, J. S., Adolphs, R., Damasio, A., & Tranel, D. (2011). The human amygdala and the induction and experience of fear. *Current Biology, 21*, 34–38. doi:10.1016/j.cub.2010.11.042

Feng, S., D'Mello, S., & Graesser, A. C. (2013). Mind wandering while reading easy and difficult texts. *Psychonomic Bulletin & Review, 20*, 586–592. doi:10.3758/s13423-012-0367-y

Ferster, C. B., & Skinner, B. F. (1957). *Schedules of reinforcement.* New York, NY: Appleton-Century-Crofts. doi:10.1037/10627-000

Festinger, L., & Carlsmith, J. M. (1959). Cognitive consequences of forced compliance. *The Journal of Abnormal and Social Psychology, 58*, 203–210. doi:10.1037/h0041593

Festinger, L., Pepitone, A., & Newcomb, T. (1952). Some consequences of de-individuation in a group. *The Journal of Abnormal and Social Psychology, 47*, 382–389. doi:10.1037/h0057906

Festinger, L., Schachter, S., & Back, K. W. (1950). *Social pressures in informal groups: A study of human factors in housing* (No. 3). Stanford, CA: Stanford University Press.

Fields, R. D. (Ed.). (2008). *Beyond the synapse: Cell–cell signaling in synaptic plasticity.* Cambridge, UK: Cambridge University Press.

Fields, R. D., & Ni, Y. (2010). Nonsynaptic communication through ATP release from volume-activated anion channels in axons. *Science Signaling, 3*, ra73. doi:10.1126/scisignal.2001128

Fincher, C. L., Thornhill, R., Murray, D. R., & Schaller, M. (2008). Pathogen prevalence predicts human cross-cultural variability in individualism/collectivism. *Philosophical Transactions of the Royal Society of London. Series B, Biological Sciences, 275*, 1279–1285. doi:10.1098/rspb.2008.0094

Finkel, E. J., & Eastwick, P. W. (in press). Interpersonal attraction: In search of a theoretical rosetta stone. In J. A. Simpson & J. F. Dovidio (Eds.), *Handbook of Personality and Social Psychology: Interpersonal Relations and Group Processes.* Washington, DC: American Psychological Association.

Firestein, S. (2001). How the olfactory system makes sense of scents. *Nature, 413*, 211–218. doi:10.1038/35093026

Fisher, C. (2008). *Wishful drinking.* New York, NY: Simon and Schuster.

Fiske, S. T. (2009). *Social beings: Core motives in social psychology* (2nd ed.). Hoboken, NJ: John Wiley & Sons.

Fitch, W. T., Hauser, M. D., & Chomsky, N. (2005). The evolution of the language faculty: Clarifications and implications. *Cognition, 97*, 179–210; discussion 211–225. doi:10.1016/j.cognition.2005.02.005

Fitzgerald, M. (2010). The lost domain of pain. *Brain, 133*, 1850–1854. doi:10.1093/brain/awq019

Fitzpatrick, S. M., Kaye, Q., Feathers, J., Pavia, J. A., & Marsaglia, K. M. (2009). Evidence for inter-island transport of heirlooms: Luminescence dating and petrographic analysis of ceramic inhaling bowls from Carriacou, West Indies. *Journal of Archaeological Science, 36*, 596–606. doi:10.1016/j.jas.2008.08.007

Fitzsimons, G. M., Chartrand, T. L., & Fitzsimons, G. J. (2008). Automatic effects of brand exposure on motivated behavior: How Apple makes you "think different." *Journal of Consumer Research, 35*, 21–35. doi:10.1086/527269

Flanagan, J. R., & Beltzner, M. A. (2000). Independence of perceptual and sensorimotor predictions in the size–weight illusion. *Nature Neuroscience, 3*, 737–741. doi:10.1038/76701

Flavell, J. H. (1963). *The developmental psychology of Jean Piaget.* The university series in psychology. Princeton, NJ: D Van Nostrand. doi:10.1037/11449-000

Flavell, J. H. (1996). Piaget's legacy. *Psychological Science, 7*, 200–203. doi:10.1111/j.1467-9280.1996.tb00359.x

Flavell, J. H., & Markman, E. M. (Eds.). (1983). *Handbook of child psychology: Cognitive development* (Vol. 3). New York, NY: Wiley.

Fleeson, W. (2001). Toward a structure- and process-integrated view of personality: Traits as density distributions of states. *Journal of Personality and Social Psychology, 80*, 1011–1027. doi:10.1037/0022-3514.80.6.1011

Floderus-Myrhed, B., Pedersen, N., & Rasmuson, I. (1980). Assessment of heritability for personality, based on a short-form of the Eysenck Personality Inventory: A study of 12,898 twin pairs. *Behavior Genetics, 10*, 153–162. doi:10.1007/BF01066265

Flynn, J. R. (1987). Massive IQ gains in 14 nations: What IQ tests really measure. *Psychological Bulletin, 101*, 171–191. doi:10.1037/0033-2909.101.2.171

Flynn, J. R. (1999). Searching for justice: The discovery of IQ gains over time. *American Psychologist, 54*, 5–20. doi:10.1037/0003-066X.54.1.5

Foa, E. B., Keane, T. M., & Friedman, M. J. (2000). Guidelines for treatment of PTSD. *Journal of Traumatic Stress, 13*, 539–588. doi:10.1023/A:1007802031411

Foa, E. B., & Kozak, M. J. (1986). Emotional processing of fear: Exposure to corrective information. *Psychological Bulletin, 99*, 20–35. doi:10.1037/0033-2909.99.1.20

Fodor, J. (1983). *The modularity of mind: An essay on faculty psychology.* Cambridge, MA: MIT Press.

Fodor J, & Piatelli-Palmerini M. (2010). *What Darwin got wrong.* New York, NY: Farrar, Straus and Giroux.

Foley, W. A. (1997). *Anthropological linguistics.* Oxford, UK: Blackwell Publishing Ltd.

Folkman, S., & Moskowitz, J. T. (2004). Coping: Pitfalls and promise. *Annual Review of Psychology, 55*, 27.1–27.30. doi:10.1146/annurev.psych.55.090902.141456

Folley, B. S., & Park, S. (2005). Verbal creativity and schizotypal personality in relation to prefrontal hemispheric laterality: A behavioral and near-infrared optical imaging study. *Schizophrenia Research, 80*, 271–282. doi:10.1016/j.schres.2005.06.016

Food and Drug Administration. (2007). *Medicines in my home: Caffeine and your body.* Retrieved from http://www.fda.gov/downloads/UCM200805.pdf

Foucault, M. (1965). *Madness and civilization* (R. Howard, Trans.). New York, NY: Pantheon.

Fouche, G., & Klesty, V. (2011, November 29). Norwegian mass killer ruled insane, likely to avoid. Reuters. Retrieved from http://www.reuters.com/article/2011/11/29/us-norway-killer-idUSTRE7AS0PY20111129

Fournier, J. C., DeRubeis, R. J., Hollon, S. D., Dimidjian, S, Amsterdam, J. D., Shelton, R. C., & Fawcett, J. (2010). Antidepressant drug effects and depression severity: A patient-level meta-analysis. *Journal of the American Medical Association, 303*(1): 47–53. doi:10.1001/jama.2009.1943.

Fowler, K. A., & Lilienfeld, S. O. (2007). The psychopathy Q-sort: Construct validity evidence in a nonclinical sample. *Assessment, 14,* 75–79. doi:10.1177/1073191106290792

Fowles, D. C. (1992). Schizophrenia: Diathesis-stress revisited. *Annual Review of Psychology, 43,* 303–336. doi:10.1146/annurev.ps.43.020192.001511

Fox, J., & Bailenson, J. N. (2009). Virtual self-modeling: The effects of vicarious reinforcement and identification on exercise behaviors. *Media Psychology, 12,* 1–25. doi:10.1080/15213260802669474

Fox, K. C. R., Nijeboer, S., Solomonova, E., Domhoff, G. W., & Christoff, K. (2013). Dreaming as mind wandering: Evidence from functional neuroimaging and first-person content reports. *Frontiers in Human Neuroscience, 7,* 412. doi:10.3389/fnhum.2013.00412

Fox, M. C., Ericsson, K. A., & Best, R. (2011). Do procedures for verbal reporting of thinking have to be reactive? A meta-analysis and recommendations for best reporting methods. *Psychological Bulletin, 137,* 316–344. doi:10.1037/a0021663

Fox, N. A., Henderson, H. A., Rubin, K. H., Calkins, S. D., & Schmidt, L. A. (2001). Continuity and discontinuity of behavioral inhibition and exuberance: Psychophysiological and behavioral influences across the first four years of life. *Child Development, 72,* 1–21. doi:10.1111/1467-8624.00262

Fraley, R. C., & Shaver, P. R. (2000). Adult romantic attachment: Theoretical developments, emerging controversies, and unanswered questions. *Review of General Psychology, 4,* 132–154. doi:10.1037/1089-2680.4.2.132

Frank, A. (1952). *Anne Frank: The diary of a young girl.* New York, NY: Doubleday & Co.

Frank, M. G. (2011). The ontogeny and function(s) of REM sleep. In B. N. Mallick, S. R. Pandi-Perumal, R. W. McCarley, & A. R. Morrison (Eds.), *Rapid Eye Movement Sleep: Regulation and Function.* Cambridge, UK: Cambridge University Press. doi:10.1017/CBO9780511921179.008

Frank, M. G., & Ekman, P. (1997). The ability to detect deceit generalizes across different types of high-stake lies. *Journal of Personality and Social Psychology, 72,* 1429–1439. doi:10.1037/0022-3514.72.6.1429

Frank, R. G., & Glied, S. A. (2006). *Better but not well: Mental health policy in the United States since 1950.* Baltimore, MA: Johns Hopkins University Press.

Franklin, M. E., & Foa, E. B. (2011). Treatment of obsessive-compulsive disorder. *Annual Review of Clinical Psychology, 7,* 299–243. doi:10.1146/annurev-clinpsy-032210-104533

Franz, M. J., VanWormer, J. J., Crain, A. L., Boucher, J. L., Histon, T., Caplan, W., . . . & Pronk, N. P. (2007). Weight-loss outcomes: A systematic review and meta-analysis of weight-loss clinical trials with a minimum 1-year follow-up. *Journal of the American Dietetic Association, 107,* 1755–1767. doi:10.1016/j.jada.2007.07.017

Freedman, J. L., & Fraser, S. L. (1971). Compliance without pressure: The foot-in-the-door technique. In J. L. Freedman, J. M. Carlsmith, & D. Sears (Eds.), *Readings in Social Psychology* (pp. 542–552). Englewood Cliffs, NJ: Prentice-Hall. (Reprinted from *Journal of Personality and Social Psychology, 4* (1966), 195–202. doi:10.1037/h0023552)

Freitas, A. L., & Higgins, E. T. (2002). Enjoying goal-directed action: The role of regulatory fit. *Psychological Science, 13,* 1–6. doi:10.1111/1467-9280.00401

Freud, S. (1900). *The interpretation of dreams.* In *Standard edition,* Vols. 4 & 5. London: Hogarth Press. (Translation 1953.)

Freud, S. (1913). *The interpretation of dreams* (3rd ed., A. A. Brill, Trans.). New York, NY: Macmillan.doi:10.1037/10561-000

Freud, S. (1923). *The ego and the id.* In *Standard edition,* Vol. 19 (pp. 1–59). London, England: Hogarth Press. (Translation 1961.)

Freud, S. (1930). *Civilization and its discontents.* New York, NY: Norton. (Translation 1961, J. Strachey.)

Freud, S., & Breuer, J. (1895). *Studies on hysteria.* In *Standard edition,* Vol. 2. London, England: Hogarth Press. (Translation 1955.)

Freund, A. M. (2008). Successful aging as management of resources: The role of selection, optimization, and compensation. *Research in Human Development, 5,* 94–106. doi:10.1080/15427600802034827

Freund, A. M., & Baltes, P. B. (2002). Life-management strategies of selection, optimization and compensation: Measurement by self-report and construct validity. *Journal of Personality and Social Psychology, 82,* 642–662. doi:10.1037/0022-3514.82.4.642

Fridlund, A. J., Beck, H. P., Goldie, W. D., & Irons, G. (2012). Little Albert: A neurologically impaired child. *History of Psychology, 15,* 302–327. doi:http://dx.doi.org/10.1037/a0026720

Froming, W. J., Walker, G. R., & Lopyan, K. J. (1982). Public and private self-awareness: When personal attitudes conflict with societal expectations. *Journal of Experimental Social Psychology, 18,* 476–487. doi:10.1016/0022-1031(82)90067-1

Fung, H. H., & Carstensen, L. L. (2003). Sending memorable messages to the old: Age differences in preferences and memory for advertisements. *Journal of Personality and Social Psychology, 85,* 163–178. doi:10.1037/0022-3514.85.1.163

Fung, H. H., Carstensen, L. L., & Lutz, A. M. (1999). Influence of time on social preferences: Implications for life-span development. *Psychology and Aging, 14,* 595–604. doi:10.1037/0882-7974.14.4.595

G. v. D. (1970, July 9). Soviet civil rights activist condemned to insane asylum. *Radio Free Europe Research.* Retrieved from http://osaarchivum.org/files/holdings/300/8/3/text/66-2-238.shtml

Gabbiani, F., & Midtgaard, J. (2001). Neural information processing. In *Encyclopedia of Life Sciences.* Nature Publishing Group. doi:10.1038/npg.els.0000149

Gable, S. L., & Haidt, J. (2005). What (and why) is positive psychology? *Review of General Psychology, 9,* 103–110. doi:10.1037/1089-2680.9.2.103

Gailliot, M. T., Stillman, T., Schmeichel, B. J., Plant, E. A., & Maner, J. K. (2008). Mortality salience increases adherence to cultural norms. *Personality and Social Psychology Bulletin, 34,* 993–1003. doi:10.1177/0146167208316791

Gaines, S. O., & Reed, E. S. (1995). Prejudice: From Allport to DuBois. *American Psychologist, 50,* 96–103. doi:10.1037/0003-066X.50.2.96

Galak, J., LeBoeuf, R. A., Nelson, L. D., & Simmons, J. P. (2012). Correcting the past: Failures to replicate Psi. *Journal of Personality and Social Psychology, 103,* 933–948. doi:10.1037/a0029709

Galanti, G. A. (2000). An introduction to cultural differences. *Western Journal of Medicine, 172,* 335–336. doi:10.1136/ewjm.172.5.335

Galdos, P. M., van Os, J. J., & Murray, R. M. (1993). Puberty and the onset of psychosis. *Schizophrenia Research, 10,* 7–14. doi:10.1016/0920-9964(93)90071-P

Gallagher, M., & Chiba, A. A. (1996). The amygdala and emotion. *Current Opinion in Neurobiology, 6,* 221–227. doi:10.1016/S0959-4388(96)80076-6

Gallese, V., Eagle, M. N., & Migone, P. (2007). Intentional attunement: Mirror neurons and the neural underpinnings of interpersonal relations. *Journal of the American Psychoanalytic Association, 55,* 131–175. doi:10.1177/00030651070550010601

Gallistel, C. R., Fairhurst, S., & Balsam, P. (2004). The learning curve: Implications of a quantitative analysis. *Proceedings of the National Academy of Sciences of the United States of America, 101,* 13124–13131. doi:10.1073/pnas.0404965101

Galton, F. (1883). *Inquiries into human faculty and its development.* London, UK: Macmillan and Company.

Garcia, J., & Koelling, R. A. (1966). Relation of cue to consequence in avoidance learning. *Psychonomic Science, 4,* 123–124. doi:10.3758/BF03342209

Gardner, H. (1985). *Frames of mind: The theory of multiple intelligences.* New York, NY: Basic Books.

Gardner, H. (1993). *Frames of mind: The theory of multiple intelligences* (10th Anniversary ed.). New York, NY: Basic Books.

Gardner, H. (1999). *Intelligence reframed: Multiple intelligences for the 21st century.* New York, NY: Basic Books.

Gardner, R. A., & Gardner, B. T. (1969). Teaching sign language to a chimpanzee. *Science, 165,* 664–672. doi:10.1126/science.165.3894.664

Garfield, S. L. (1995). *Psychotherapy: An eclectic-integrative approach,* 2nd edition. New York, NY: Wiley

Garyfallos, G., Katsigiannopoulos, K., Adamopoulou, A., Papazisis, G., Karastergiou, A., & Bozikas, V. P. (2010). Comorbidity of obsessive–compulsive disorder with obsessive–compulsive personality disorder: Does it imply a specific subtype of obsessive–compulsive disorder? *Psychiatry Research, 177,* 156–160. doi:10.1016/j.psychres.2010.01.006

Garz, D. (2009). *Lawrence Kohlberg—An Introduction.* Opladen & Farmington Hills, MI: Barbara Budrich Publishers.

Gasper, K., & Clore, G. L. (2000). Do you have to pay attention to your feelings to be influenced by them? *Personality and Social Psychology Bulletin, 26,* 698–711. doi:10.1177/0146167200268005

Gately, I. (2008). *Drink: A cultural history of alcohol.* New York, NY: Gotham Books.

Gatzounis, R., Schrooten, M. G., Crombez, G., & Vlaeyen, J. W. (2012). Operant learning theory in pain and chronic pain rehabilitation. *Current Pain and Headache Reports, 16,* 117–126. doi:10.1007/s11916-012-0247-1

Gawin, F. W., & Ellinwood, E. H., Jr. (1988). Cocaine and other stimulants: Actions, abuse and treatment. *New England Journal of Medicine, 318,* 1173–1182. doi:10.1056/NEJM198805053181806

Gawronski, B., LeBel, E. P., & Peters, K. R. (2007). What do implicit measures tell us? Scrutinizing the validity of three common assumptions. *Perspectives on Psychological Science, 2,* 181–193. doi:10.1111/j.1745-6916.2007.00036.x

Gazit, I., & Terkel, J. (2003). Domination of olfaction over vision in explosives detection by dogs. *Applied Animal Behaviour Science, 82,* 65–73. doi:10.1016/S0168-1591(03)00051-0

Gazzaniga, M. S., & Miller, M. B. (2009). The left hemisphere does not miss the right hemisphere. In S. Laureys & G. Tononi (Eds.), *The Neurology of Consciousness: Cognitive Neuroscience and Neuropathology* (pp. 261–270). London, England: Academic Press. doi:10.1016/B978-0-12-374168-4.00020-4

Geddes, J. R., Burgess, S., Hawton, K., Jamison, K., & Goodwin, G. M. (2004). Long-term lithium therapy for bipolar disorder: Systematic review and meta-analysis of randomized controlled trials. *American Journal of Psychiatry, 161,* 217–222. doi:10.1176/appi.ajp.161.2.217

Geddes, J., Freemantle, N., Harrison, P., & Bebbington, P. (2000). Atypical antipsychotics in the treatment of schizophrenia: Systematic overview and meta-regression analysis. *BMJ, 321,* 1371–1376. doi:10.1136/bmj.321.7273.1371

Gee, A. (2007, July 30). Russian dissident "forcibly detained in mental hospital." *London Independent.* Retrieved from http://infowars.net/articles/july2007/300707dissident.htm

Geertz, C. (1973). The impact of the concept of culture on the concept of man. In C. Geertz, *The Interpretation of Cultures: Selected Essays by Clifford Geertz* (pp. 33–54). New York, NY: Basic Books.

Gelfand, M. J., Chiu, C., & Hong, Y. (2013). *Advances in culture and psychology* (Vol. 3). New York: Oxford University Press.

Gerdin, I. (1981). The Balinese sidikara: Ancestors, kinship, and rank. *Bijdragen tot de Taal-, Land- en Volkenkunde (Journal of the Humanities and Social Sciences of Southeast Asia), 137,* 17–34.

Gerlach, K. D., Spreng, R. N., Gilmore, A. W., & Schacter, D. L. (2011). Solving future problems: Default network and executive activity associated with goal-directed mental simulations. *Neuroimage, 55,* 1816–1824. doi:10.1016/j.neuroimage.2011.01.030

Gershman, J. (2006, November 8). Spitzer, in a historic landslide, vows "a new brand." *The New York Sun.* Retrieved from http://www.nysun.com/new-york/spitzer-in-a-historic-landslide-vows-a-new-brand/43126/.

Geschwind, N. (1970). The organization of language and the brain. *Science, 170,* 940–944. doi:10.1126/science.170.3961.940

Gibbs, J. R., & Singleton, A. (2006). Application of genome-wide single nucleotide polymorphism typing: Simple association and beyond. *PLoS Genetics, 2,* e150. doi:10.1371/journal.pgen.0020150

Gibson, J. J. (1962). Observations on active touch. *Psychological Review, 69,* 477–491. doi:10.1037/h0046962

Gibson, J. J. (1966). *The senses considered as perceptual systems.* Oxford, England: Houghton Mifflin.

Gibson, J. J. (1968). What gives rise to the perception of motion? *Psychological Review, 75,* 335–346. doi:10.1037/h0025893

Gilbert, S. E., & Gordon, K. C. (2013). Interpersonal psychotherapy informed treatment for avoidant personality disorder with subsequent depression. *Clinical Case Studies, 12,* 111–127. doi:10.1177/1534650112468611

Gillath, O., Mikulincer, M., Birnbaum, G. E., & Shaver, P. R. (2008). When sex primes love: Subliminal sexual priming motivates relationship goal pursuit. *Personality and Social Psychology Bulletin, 34,* 1057–1069. doi:10.1177/0146167208318141

Gillespie, P., & Müller, U. (2009). Mechanotransduction by hair cells: Models, molecules, and mechanisms. *Cell, 139,* 33–44. doi:10.1016/j.cell.2009.09.010

Gillig, P. M. (2009). Dissociative identity disorder: A controversial diagnosis. *Psychiatry (Edmont), 6,* 24–29.

Gilligan, C. (1977). In a different voice: Women's conceptions of self and of morality. *Harvard Educational Review, 47,* 481–517.

Giovino, G., Mirza, S., Samet, J., Gupta, P., Jarvis, M., Bhala, N., . . . & Group, G. C. (2012). Tobacco use in 3 billion individuals from 16 countries: An analysis of nationally representative cross-sectional household surveys. *Lancet, 380,* 668–679. doi:10.1016/S0140-6736(12)61085-X

Giuliani, N. R., Drabant, E. M., & Gross, J. J. (2011). Anterior cingulate cortex volume and emotion regulation: Is bigger better? *Biological Psychology, 86,* 379–382. doi:10.1016/j.biopsycho.2010.11.010

Gjerdingen, R. O., & Perrott, David. (2008). Scanning the dial: The rapid recognition of music genres. *Journal of New Music Research, 37,* 93–100.

Glahn, D. C., Ragland, J. D., Abramoff, A., Barrett, J., Laird, A. R., Bearden, C. E., & Velligan, D. I. (2005). Beyond hypofrontality: A quantitative meta-analysis of functional neuroimaging studies of working memory in schizophrenia. *Human Brain Mapping, 25,* 60–69. doi:10.1002/hbm.20138

Glenberg, A. M. (2010). Embodiment as a unifying perspective for psychology. *Wiley Interdisciplinary Reviews: Cognitive Science, 1,* 586–596.

Glick, P. (2005). Choice of scapegoats. In J. F. Dovidio, P. Glick, & L. Rudman (Eds.), *Reflecting on the Nature of Prejudice* (pp. 244–261). Malden, MA: Blackwell Press. doi:10.1002/9780470773963.ch15

Gloster, A. T., Wittchen, H. U., Einsle, F., Lang, T., Helbig-Lang, S., Fydrich, T., . . . & Arolt, V. (2011). Psychological treatment for panic disorder with agoraphobia: A randomized controlled trial to examine the role of therapist-guided exposure in situ in CBT. *Journal of Consulting and Clinical Psychology, 79,* 406–420. doi:10.1037/a0023584

Gluck, M. A., Mercado, E., & Myers, C. E. (2008). *Learning and memory: From brain to behavior.* New York, NY: Worth.

Godden, D. R., & Baddeley, A. D. (1975). Context-dependent memory in two natural environments: On land and underwater. *British Journal of Psychology, 66,* 325–331. doi:10.1111/j.2044-8295.1975.tb01468.x

Goffman, E. (1959). *The presentation of self in everyday life.* New York, NY: Doubleday Anchor Books.

Goffman, E. (1961). *Asylums: Essays on the social situation of mental patients and other inmates.* Garden City, NY: Anchor Books.

Goghari, V. M., Harrow, M., Grossman, L. S., & Rosen, C. (2013). A 20-year multi-follow-up of hallucinations in schizophrenia, other psychotic, and mood disorders. *Psychological Medicine, 43,* 1151–1160. doi:10.1017/S0033291712002206

Gold, J. M., Tadin, D., Cook, S. C., & Blake, R. (2008). The efficiency of biological motion perception. *Perception & Psychophysics, 70,* 88–95. doi:10.3758/PP

Goldberg, L. R. (1981). Language and individual differences: The search for universals in personality lexicons. In L. Wheeler (Ed.), *Review of Personality and Social Psychology* (pp. 141–165). Beverly Hills, CA: Sage.

Goldberg, L. R. (1993). The structure of phenotypic personality traits. *American Psychologist, 48,* 26–34. doi:10.1037/0003-066X.48.1.26

Goldberg, T., Egan, M., Gscheidle, T., Coppola, R., Weickert, T., Kolachana, B., . . . & Weinberger, D. (2003). Executive subprocesses in working memory: Relationship to catechol-O-methyltransferase Val158Met genotype and schizophrenia. *Archives of General Psychiatry, 60,* 889–896. doi:10.1001/archpsyc.60.9.889

Goldhaber, D. (2012). *The nature–nurture debates: Bridging the gap.* New York, NY: Cambridge University Press.

Goldman, D., Oroszi, G., & Ducci, F. (2005). The genetics of addictions: Uncovering the genes. *Nature Reviews Genetics, 6,* 521–532. doi:10.1038/nrg1635

Goldsmith, H. H. (1983). Genetic influences on personality from infancy to adulthood. *Child Development, 54,* 331–355. doi:10.2307/1129695

Goldstone, A. P. (2006). The hypothalamus, hormones, and hunger: Alterations in human obesity and illness. *Progress in Brain Research, 153,* 57–73. doi:10.1016/S0079-6123(06)53003-1

Goleman, D. (1988). *The meditative mind: The varieties of meditative experience.* New York, NY: Tarcher/Putnam.

Gollwitzer, P. M. (1999). Implementation intentions: Strong effects of simple plans. *American Psychologist, 54,* 493–503. doi:10.1037/0003-066X.54.7.493

Gollwitzer, P. M., & Oettingen, G. (2013). Implementation intentions. In M. Gellman & J. R. Turner (Eds.), *Encyclopedia of Behavioral Medicine* (Part 9, pp. 1043–1048). New York, NY: Springer-Verlag.

Gollwitzer, P., & Sheeran, P. (2006). Implementation intentions and goal achievement: A meta-analysis of effects and processes. *Advances in Experimental Social Psychology, 38,* 69–119. doi:10.1016/S0065-2601(06)38002-1

González-Maeso, J., Weisstaub, N. V, Zhou, M., Chan, P., Ivic, L., Ang, R., . . . & Gingrich, J. A. (2007). Hallucinogens recruit specific cortical 5-HT(2A) receptor-mediated signaling pathways to affect behavior. *Neuron, 53,* 439–452. doi:10.1016/j.neuron.2007.01.008

Gosling, S. D., Ko, S. J., Mannarelli, T., & Morris, M. E. (2002). A room with a cue: Judgments of personality based on offices and bedrooms. *Journal of Personality and Social Psychology, 82,* 379–398. doi:10.1037/0022-3514.82.3.379

Gosling, S. D., Rentfrow, P. J., & Swann, W. B., Jr. (2003). A very brief measure of the Big Five Personality Domains. *Journal of Research in Personality, 37,* 504–528. doi:10.1016/S0092-6566(03)00046-1

Gottlieb, G. (1998). Normally occurring environmental and behavioral influences on gene activity: From central dogma to probabilistic epigenesis. *Psychological Review, 105,* 792–802. doi:10.1037/0033-295X.105.4.792-802

Gould, R. A., Buckminster, S., Pollack, M. H., & Otto, M. W. (1997). Cognitive-behavioral and pharmacological treatment for social phobia: A meta-analysis. *Clinical Psychology: Science and Practice, 4,* 291–306. doi:10.1111/j.1468-2850.1997.tb00123.x

Gould, S. J. (1981). *The mismeasure of man.* New York, NY: W. W. Norton & Co.

Govan, F. (2011, August 3). Lobotomy: A history of the controversial procedure. *The Telegraph.* Retrieved from http://www.telegraph.co.uk/news/worldnews/southamerica/argentina/8679929/Lobotomy-A-history-of-the-controversial-procedure.html

Graefe, A., Armstrong, J. S., Jones, R. J., & Cuzán, A. G. (2014). Accuracy of combined forecasts for the 2012 presidential election: The PollyVote. *PS: Political Science & Politics, 47,* 427–431. doi:10.1017/S1049096514000341

Graeff, F. G. (2004). Serotonin, the periaqueductal gray and panic. *Neuroscience & Biobehavioral Reviews, 28,* 239–259. doi:10.1016/j.neubiorev.2003.12.004

Grant, B. F., Hasin, D. S., Stinson, F. S., Dawson, D. A., Goldstein, R. B., Smith, S., . . . & Saha, T. D. (2006). The epidemiology of DSM-IV panic disorder and agoraphobia in the United States: Results from the National Epidemiologic Survey on Alcohol and Related Conditions. *Journal of Clinical Psychiatry, 67,* 363–374. doi:10.4088/JCP.v67n0305

Gray, J. A., & McNaughton, N. (2000). *The neuropsychology of anxiety: An enquiry into the function of the Septo-Hippocampal System* (2nd ed.). Oxford, UK: Oxford University Press.

Graziano, M. (2010). Ethologically relevant movements mapped on the motor cortex. In M. L. Platt & A. A. Ghazanfar (Eds.), *Primate neuroethology* (pp. 454–470). New York, NY: Oxford University Press.

Graziano, M., Taylor, C., Moore, T., & Cooke, D. (2002). The cortical control of movement revisited. *Neuron, 36,* 349–362. doi:10.1016/S0896-6273(02)01003-6

Graziano, W. G., Jensen-Campbell, L. A., & Finch, J. F. (1997). The self as a mediator between personality and adjustment. *Journal of Personality and Social Psychology, 73,* 392–404. doi:10.1037/0022-3514.73.2.392

Grbich, C. (2009). *Qualitative research in health: An introduction.* London, England: Sage.

Green, M. F., Olivier, B., Crawley, J. N., Penn, D. L., & Silverstein, S. (2005). Social cognition in schizophrenia: Recommendations from the Measurement and Treatment Research to Improve Cognition in Schizophrenia New Approaches Conference. *Schizophrenia Bulletin, 31,* 882–887. doi:10.1093/schbul/sbi049

Greenberg, D. L., & Verfaellie, M. (2010). Interdependence of episodic and semantic memory: Evidence from neuropsychology. *Journal of the International Neuropsychological Society, 16,* 748–753. doi:10.1017/S1355617710000676

Greenberg, J., & Arndt, J. (2012). Terror management theory. In P. A. M. Van Lange, A. W. Kruglanski, & E. T. Higgins (Eds.), *Handbook of Theories of Social Psychology* (Vol. 1, pp. 398–415). London, England: Sage Press. doi:10.4135/9781446249215.n20

Greene, J. D., Sommerville, R. B., Nystrom, L. E., Darley, J. M., & Cohen, J. D. (2001). An fMRI investigation of emotional engagement in moral judgment. *Science, 293,* 2105–2108. doi:10.1126/science.1062872

Greenwald, A. G., & Farnham, S. D. (2000). Using the implicit association test to measure self-esteem and self-concept. *Journal of Personality and Social Psychology, 79,* 1022–1038. doi:10.1037/0022-3514.79.6.1022

Greenwald, A. G., McGhee, D. E., & Schwartz, J. L. K. (1998). Measuring individual differences in implicit cognition: The implicit association test. *Journal of Personality and Social Psychology, 74,* 1464–1480. doi:10.1037/0022-3514.74.6.1464

Gregory, S., Simmons, A., Kumari, V., Howard, M., Hodgins, S., & Blackwood, N. (2012). The antisocial brain: Psychopathy matters: A structural MRI investigation of antisocial male violent offenders. *Archives of General Psychiatry, 69,* 962–972. doi:10.1001/archgenpsychiatry.2012.222

Greven, C., Harlaar, N., Kovas, Y., Chamorro-Premuzie, T., & Plomin, R. (2009). More than just IQ: School achievement is predicted by self-perceived abilities—but for genetic rather than environmental reasons. *Psychological Science, 20,* 753–762. doi:10.1111/j.1467-9280.2009.02366.x

Grice, H. P. (1975). Logic and conversation. In P. Cole and J. L. Morgan (Eds.), *Syntax and Semantics Volume 3: Speech Acts* (pp. 41–58). New York, NY: Academic Press.

Griggs, R. A. (2014). Coverage of the Stanford Prison Experiment in Introductory Psychology Textbooks. *Teaching of Psychology, 41,* 195–203. doi:10.1177/0098628314537968

Grimbos, T., Dawood, K., Burriss, R. P., Zucker, K. J., & Puts, D. A. (2010). Sexual orientation and the second to fourth finger length ratio: A meta-analysis in men and women. *Behavioral Neuroscience, 124,* 278–287. doi:10.1037/a0018764

Gross, J. J. (1998). Antecedent- and response-focused emotion regulation: Divergent consequences for experience, expression, and physiology. *Journal of Personality and Social Psychology, 74,* 224–237. doi:10.1037/0022-3514.74.1.224

Groves, R. M., Fowler, F. J., Couper, M. P., Lepkowski, J. M., Singer, E., & Tourangeau, R. (2009). *Survey methodology* (2nd ed.). Hoboken, NJ: Wiley.

Gruber, J. (2011). Can feeling too good be bad? Positive emotion persistence (PEP) in bipolar disorder. *Current Directions in Psychological Science, 20,* 217–221. doi:10.1177/0963721411414632

Guenther, H. V., and Kawamura, L. (1975). *Mind in Buddhist Psychology: Necklace of Clear Understanding by Yeshe Gyaltsen.* Tibetan translation series. Berkeley, CA: Dharma.

Guillot, A., Collet, C., Nguyen, V. A., Malouin, F., Richards, C., & Doyon, J. (2009). Brain activity during visual versus kinesthetic imagery: An fMRI study. *Human Brain Mapping, 30,* 2157–2172. doi:10.1002/hbm.20658

Gunderson, J. G., & Links, P. (2008). *Borderline personality disorder: A clinical guide* (2nd ed.). Washington, DC: American Psychiatric Press, Inc.

Gupta, V., Saluja, S., Ahuja, G. K., & Walia, L. (2010). Reticular formation—A network system of brain. *Journal of Anaesthesiology Clinical Pharmacology, 26,* 143–148.

Gur, R. E., Kohler, C. G., Ragland, J. D., Siegel, S. J., Lesko, K., Bilker, W. B., & Gur, R. C. (2006). Flat affect in schizophrenia: Relation to emotion processing and neurocognitive measures. *Schizophrenia Bulletin, 32,* 279–287. doi:10.1093/schbul/sbj041

Gygi, B., Kidd, G. R., & Watson, C. S. (2004). Spectral–temporal factors in the identification of environmental sounds. *The Journal of the Acoustical Society of America, 115,* 1252–1265. doi:10.1121/1.1635840

Ha, J. H., Greenberg, J. S., & Seltzer, M. M. (2011). Parenting a child with a disability: The role of social support for African American parents. *Families in Society: The Journal of Contemporary Social Services, 92,* 405–411. doi:10.1606/1044-3894.4150

Haber, S. N., & Knutson, B. (2010). The reward circuit: Linking primate anatomy and human imaging. *Neuropsychopharmacology, 35,* 4–26. doi:10.1038/npp.2009.129

Habermas, T., & Bluck, S. (2000). Getting a life: The emergence of the life story in adolescence. *Psychological Bulletin, 126,* 748–769. doi:10.1037/0033-2909.126.5.748

Hacker, P. M. S. (2004). The conceptual framework for the investigation of emotions. *International Review of Psychiatry, 16,* 199–208. doi:10.1080/09540260400003883

Hacker, P. M. S. (2010). *Human nature: The categorical framework.* Chichester, UK: Wiley-Blackwell.

Haggbloom, S. J., Warnick, R., Warnick, J. E., Jones, V. K., Yarbrough, G. L., Russell, T. M., . . . & Monte, E. (2002). The 100 most eminent psychologists of the 20th century. *Review of General Psychology, 6,* 139–152. doi:10.1037//1089-2680.6.2.139

Haidt, J. (2001). The emotional dog and its rational tail: A social intuitionist approach to moral judgment. *Psychological Review, 108,* 814–834. doi:10.1037/0033-295X.108.4.814

Halpern-Meekin, S., Manning, W. D., Giordano, P. C., & Longmore, M. A. (2013). Relationship churning, physical violence, and verbal abuse in young adult relationships. *Journal of Marriage and Family, 75,* 2–12. doi:10.1111/j.1741-3737.2012.01029.x

Halpin, T., & Booth, J. (2009, May 27). Feral girl in Siberian city of Chita was brought up by cats and dogs. *Times.* Retrieved from http://www.thetimes.co.uk/tto/news/world/europe/article2600036.ece

Hamann, S. (2011). Affective neuroscience: Amygdala's role in experiencing fear. *Current Biology, 21,* R75–R77. doi:10.1016/j.cub.2010.12.007

Hamilton, J. for NPR Science News. (2010, October 5). *Twitchy nerves (literally) may explain epilepsy, pain.* Retrieved from http://www.npr.org/templates/story/story.php?storyId=130244715

Hamlin, J. K., & Wynn, K. (2011). Young infants prefer prosocial to antisocial others. *Cognitive Development, 26,* 30–39. doi:10.1016/j.cogdev.2010.09.001

Hamlin, J. K., Ullman, T., Tenenbaum, J., Goodman, N., & Baker, C. (2013). The mentalistic basis of core social cognition: Experiments in preverbal infants and a computational model. *Developmental Science, 16,* 209–226. doi:10.1111/desc.12017

Hamlin, J. K., Wynn, K., & Bloom, P. (2007). Social evaluation by preverbal infants. *Nature, 450,* 557–559. doi:10.1038/nature06288

Hammarlund, M., Palfreyman, M. T., Watanabe, S., Olsen, S., & Jorgensen, E. M. (2007). Open syntaxin docks synaptic vesicles. *PLoS Biology, 5,* e198. doi:10.1371/journal.pbio.0050198

Hampden-Turner, C. (1981). *Maps of the mind: Charts and concepts of the mind and its labyrinths.* New York, NY: Macmillan.

Hampson, S. E. (2012). Personality processes: Mechanisms by which personality traits "get outside the skin." *Annual Review of Psychology, 63,* 315–339. doi:10.1146/annurev-psych-120710-100419

Han, J., Kamber, M., & Pei, J. (2012). Data mining: Concepts and techniques (2nd ed.). Waltham, MA: Elsevier.

Haney, C., Banks, W. C., & Zimbardo, P. G. (1973). Interpersonal dynamics in a simulated prison. *International Journal of Criminology and Penology, 1,* 69–97.

Hankin, B. L., Abramson, L. Y., & Siler, M. (2001). A prospective test of the hopelessness theory of depression in adolescence. *Cognitive Therapy and Research, 25,* 607–632. doi:10.1023/A:1005561616506

Hanson, N. R. (1961). *Patterns of discovery: An inquiry into the conceptual foundations of science.* Cambridge, UK: Cambridge University Press.

Hare, R. D. (1999). *Without conscience: The disturbing world of the psychopaths among us.* New York, NY: Guilford Press.

Hare, R. D., & Neumann, C. S. (2008). Psychopathy as a clinical and empirical construct. *Annual Review of Clinical Psychology, 4,* 217–246. doi:10.1146/annurev.clinpsy.3.022806.091452

Harlow, H. F. (1958). The nature of love. *American Psychologist, 13,* 673–685. doi:10.1037/h0047884

Harmon-Jones, E. (2011). Neural bases of approach and avoidance. In M. D. Alicke, & C. Sedikides (Eds.), *The Handbook of Self-Enhancement and Self-Protection* (pp. 23–48). New York, NY: Guilford Press.

Harper, R. S. (1950). The first psychological laboratory. *Isis, 41,* 158–161. doi:10.1086/349141

Harré, R. (2000). Acts of living. *Science, 289,* 1303–1304. doi:10.1126/science.289.5483.1303

Harré, R. (2002). *Cognitive science: A philosophical introduction.* London, U. K.: Sage Publications.

Harré, R. (2012). The brain can be thought of as a tool. *Integrative Psychological and Behavioral Science, 46,* 387–394. doi:10.1007/s12124-012-9195-x

Harré, R., & van Langenhove, L. (1999). *Positioning theory.* Oxford, UK: Blackwell Publishers.

Harris, J. R. (1995). Where is the child's environment? A group socialization theory of development. *Psychological Review, 102,* 458–489. doi:10.1037/0033-295X.102.3.458

Harrow, M., Grossman, L. S., Jobe, T. H., & Herbener, E. S. (2005). Do patients with schizophrenia ever show periods of recovery? A 15-year multi-follow-up study. *Schizophrenia Bulletin, 31,* 723–734. doi:10.1093/schbul/sbi026

Harter, S. (1999). *The construction of the self: A developmental perspective.* New York, NY: Guilford Press.

Harter, S., & Whitesell, N. R. (2003). Beyond the debate: Why some adolescents report stable self-worth over time and situation, whereas others report changes in self-worth. *Journal of Personality, 71,* 1027–1058. doi:10.1111/1467-6494.7106006

Haselton, M. G., Mortezaie, M., Pillsworth, E. G., Bleske-Rechek, A., & Frederick, D. A. (2007). Ovulatory shifts in human female ornamentation: Near ovulation, women dress to impress. *Hormones and Behavior, 51,* 40–45. doi:10.1016/j.yhbeh.2006.07.007

Hasin-Brumshtein, Y., Lancet, D., & Olender, T. (2009). Human olfaction: From genomic variation to phenotypic diversity. *Trends in Genetics, 25,* 178–184. doi:10.1016/j.tig.2009.02.002

Haslam, S. A., & Reicher, S. (2003). Beyond Stanford: Questioning a role-based explanation of tyranny. *Dialogue, 18,* 22–25.

Hatemi, P. K., Funk, C. L., Medland, S. E., Maes, H. M., Silberg, J. L., Martin, N. G., & Eaves, L. J. (2009). Genetic and environmental transmission of political attitudes over a lifetime. *The Journal of Politics, 71,* 1141. doi:10.1017/S0022381609090938

Hauser, M. D. (2006). *Moral minds: How nature designed our universal sense of right and wrong.* New York, NY: Ecco.

Hauser, M. D., Chomsky, N., & Fitch, W. T. (2002). The faculty of language: What is it, who has it, and how did it evolve? *Science, 298,* 1569–1579. doi:10.1126/science.298.5598.1569

Havas, D. A., Glenberg, A. M., Gutowski, K. A., Lucarelli, M. J., & Davidson, R. J. (2010). Cosmetic use of botulinum toxin-A affects processing of emotional language. *Psychological Science, 21,* 895–900. doi:10.1177/0956797610374742

Hayes, A. (1994). *Normal and impaired motor development: Theory into practice.* London, England: Chapman & Hall Publishers.

Haznedar, M. M., Buchsbaum, M. S., Hazlett, E. A., Shihabuddin, L., New, A., & Siever, L. J. (2004). Cingulate gyrus volume and metabolism in the schizophrenia spectrum. *Schizophrenia Research, 71,* 249–262. doi:10.1016/j.schres.2004.02.025

Headey, B., Muffels, R., & Wagner, G. G. (2010). Long-running German panel survey shows that personal and economic choices, not just genes, matter for happiness. *Proceedings of the National Academy of Sciences of the United States of America, 107,* 17922–17926. doi:10.1073/pnas.1008612107

Healey, M. D., & Ellis, B. J. (2007). Birth order, conscientiousness, and openness to experience: Tests of the family-niche model of personality using a within-family methodology. *Evolution and Human Behavior, 28,* 55–59. doi:10.1016/j.evolhumbehav.2006.05.003

Heaner, M. K., & Walsh, B. T. (2013). A history of the identification of the characteristic eating disturbances of bulimia nervosa, binge eating disorder and anorexia nervosa. *Appetite, 65,* 185–188. doi:10.1016/j.appet.2013.01.005

Heckers, S., Barch, D. M., Bustillo, J., Gaebel, W., Gur, R., Malaspina, D.,... & Carpenter, W. (2013). Structure of the psychotic disorders classification in DSM-5. *Schizophrenia Research, 150,* 11–14. doi:10.1016/j.schres.2013.04.039

Heckman, J. J. (2006). Skill formation and the economics of investing in disadvantaged children. *Science, 312,* 1900–1902. doi:10.1126/science.1128898

Hegarty, J. D., Baldessarini, R. J., Tohen, M., Waternaux, C., & Oepen, G. (1994). One hundred years of schizophrenia: A meta-analysis of the outcome literature. *American Journal of Psychiatry, 151,* 1409–1416.

Heimberg, R. G. (2002). Cognitive-behavioral therapy for social anxiety disorder: Current status and future directions. *Biological Psychiatry, 51,* 101–108. doi:10.1016/S0006-3223(01)01183-0

Heine, S. J., Kitayama, S., Lehman, D. R. (2001). Cultural differences in self-evaluation: Japanese readily accept negative self-relevant information. *Cross-Cultural Psychology, 32,* 434–443. doi:10.1177/0022022101032004004

Heine, S. J., Lehman, D. R., Markus, H. R., & Kitayama, S. (1999). Is there a universal need for positive self-regard? *Psychological Review, 106,* 766–794. doi:10.1037/0033-295X.106.4.766

Helbing, D., Brockmann, D., Chadefaux, T., Donnay, K., Blanke, U., Woolley-Meza, O.,... & Perc, M. (2014). Saving human lives: What complexity science and information systems can contribute. *Journal of Statistical Physics, 156,* 1–47. doi:10.1007/s10955-014-1024-9

Helbing, D., Johansson, A., & Al-Abideen, H. Z. (2007). Dynamics of crowd disasters: An empirical study. *Physical Review E, 75,* 046109. doi:10.1103/PhysRevE.75.046109

Helm, B. W. (2009). Emotions as evaluative feelings. *Emotion Review, 1,* 248–255. doi:10.1177/1754073909103593

Helper, S., Kleiner, M. M., & Wang, Y. (2010, November). *Analyzing compensation methods in manufacturing: Piece rates, time rates, or gain-sharing?* (NBER Working Paper No. 16540). Cambridge, MA: National Bureau of Economic Research.

Hennenlotter, A., Dresel, C., Castrop, F., Ceballos-Baumann, A. O., Wohlschläger, A. M., & Haslinger, B. (2009). The link between facial feedback and neural activity within central circuitries of emotion—New insights from Botulinum toxin–induced denervation of frown muscles. *Cerebral Cortex, 19,* 537–542. doi:10.1093/cercor/bhn104

Hensch, T. K. (2004). Critical period regulation. *Annual Review of Neuroscience, 27,* 549–579. doi:10.1146/annurev.neuro.27.070203.144327

Hensley, S. (2011). Look around: 1 in 10 Americans takes antidepressants. *Health News from NPR.* Retrieved from http://www.npr.org/blogs/health/2011/10/20/141544135/look-around-1-in-10-americans-take-antidepressants

Herbener, E. S. (2008). Emotional memory in schizophrenia. *Schizophrenia Bulletin, 34,* 875–887. doi:10.1093/schbul/sbn081

Herbert, J. D., Gaudiano, B. A., Rheingold, A. A., Myers, V. H., Dalrymple, K., & Nolan, E. M. (2005). Social skills training augments the effectiveness of cognitive behavioral group therapy for social anxiety disorder. *Behavior Therapy, 36,* 125–138. doi:10.1016/S0005-7894(05)80061-9

Herman, C. P., Fitzgerald, N. E., & Polivy, J. (2003). The influence of social norms on hunger ratings and eating. *Appetite, 41,* 15–20. doi:10.1016/S0195-6663(03)00027-8

Hermans, H. J. (1996). Voicing the self: From information processing to dialogical interchange. *Psychological Bulletin, 119,* 31–50. doi:10.1037/0033-2909.119.1.31

Hermans, H. J., & Kempen, H. J. (1998). Moving cultures: The perilous problems of cultural dichotomies in a globalizing society. *American Psychologist, 53,* 1111–1120. doi:10.1037/0003-066X.53.10.1111

Herring, A. H., Attard, S. M., Gordon-Larsen, P., Joyner, W. H., and Halpern, C. T. (2013). Like a Virgin (Mother): Analysis of data from a longitudinal, U.S. population representative sample survey. *British Medical Journal, 347*:f7102.

Herrnstein, R. J., & Murray, C. (1994). *The bell curve: Intelligence and class structure in American life.* New York, NY: Free Press.

Hersh, S. M. (2004, May 10). Torture at Abu Ghraib: American soldiers brutalized Iraqis. How far up does the responsibility go? *The New Yorker.* Retrieved from http://www.newyorker.com/archive/2004/05/10/040510fa_fact

Hershberger, S. L., & Segal, N. L. (2004). The cognitive, behavioral, and personality profiles of a male monozygotic triplet set discordant for sexual orientation. *Archives of Sexual Behavior, 33,* 497–514. doi:10.1023/B:ASEB.0000037430.17032.7d

Hershfield, H. E. (2011). Future self-continuity: How conceptions of the future self transform intertemporal choice. *Annals of the New York Academy of Sciences, 1235,* 30–43.

Hershfield, H. E., Goldstein, D. G., Sharpe, W. F., Fox, J., Yeykelis, L., Carstensen, L. L., & Bailenson, J. N. (2011). Increasing saving behavior through age-progressed renderings of the future self. *Journal of Marketing Research, 48,* S23–S37. doi:10.1509/jmkr.48.SPL.S23

Hess, E. (2008). *Nim Chimpsky: The chimp who would be human.* New York, NY: Bantam.

Hess, E. H. (1958). Imprinting in animals. *Scientific American, 198,* 81–90. doi:10.1038/scientificamerican0358-81

Hewitt, P. L., & Flett, G. L. (1991). Dimensions of perfectionism in unipolar depression. *Journal of Abnormal Psychology, 100,* 98–101. doi:10.1037/0021-843X.100.1.98

Heyes, C. (2003). Four routes of cognitive evolution. *Psychological Review, 110,* 713–727. doi:10.1037/0033-295X.110.4.713

Heyes, C. (2012). New thinking: The evolution of human cognition. *Philosophical Transactions of the Royal Society of London. Series B, Biological Sciences, 367,* 2091–2096. doi:10.1098/rstb.2012.0111

Higbee, K. L. (1996). *Your memory: How it works & how to improve it* (2nd ed.). New York, NY: Marlowe & Company.

Higgins, E. T. (1987). Self-discrepancy: A theory relating self and affect. *Psychological Review, 94,* 319–340. doi:10.1037/0033-295X.94.3.319

Higgins, E. T. (1997). Beyond pleasure and pain. *American Psychologist, 52,* 1280–1300. doi:10.1037/0003-066X.52.12.1280

Higgins, E. T. (2005). Value from regulatory fit. *Current Directions in Psychological Science, 14,* 209–213. doi:10.1111/j.0963-7214.2005.00366.x

Highlights of prescribing information. (2014, March 13). Indianapolis, IN: Eli Lilly and Co. Retrieved from http://pi.lilly.com/us/prozac.pdf

Higley, S. L. (2007). *Hildegard of Bingen's Unknown language: An edition, translation, and discussion.* New York, NY: Palgrave Macmillan. doi:10.1057/9780230610057

Hilgard, E. R., Morgan, A. H., & Macdonald, H. (1975). Pain and dissociation in the cold pressor test: A study of hypnotic analgesia with "hidden reports" through automatic key pressing and automatic talking. *Journal of Abnormal Psychology, 84,* 280–289. doi:10.1037/h0076654

Hilti, C. C., Delko, T., Orosz, A. T., Thomann, K., Ludewig, S., Geyer, M. A., . . . & Cattapan-Ludewig, K. (2010). Sustained attention and planning deficits but intact attentional set-shifting in neuroleptic-naïve first-episode schizophrenia patients. *Neuropsychobiology, 61,* 79–86. doi:10.1159/000265133

Hines, M. (2010). Sex-related variation in human behavior and the brain. *Trends in Cognitive Sciences, 14,* 448–456. doi:10.1016/j.tics.2010.07.005

Hintsanen, M., Lipsanen, J., Pulkki-Råback, L., Kivimäki, M., Hintsa, T., & Keltikangas-Järvinen, L. (2009). EAS temperaments as predictors of unemployment in young adults: A 9-year follow-up of the Cardiovascular Risk in Young Finns Study. *Journal of Research in Personality, 43,* 618–623. doi:10.1016/j.jrp.2009.03.013

Hiraishi, K., Sasaki, S., Shikishima, C., & Ando, J. (2012). The second to fourth digit ratio (2D:4D) in a Japanese twin sample: Heritability, prenatal hormone transfer, and association with sexual orientation. *Archives of Sexual Behavior, 41,* 711–724. doi:10.1007/s10508-011-9889-z

Hirschfeld, L. A., & Gelman, S. A. (Eds.). (1994). *Mapping the mind: Domain specificity in cognition and culture.* Cambridge, UK: Cambridge University Press. doi:10.1017/CBO9780511752902

Hirstein, W., & Ramachandran, V. (1997). Capgras syndrome: A novel probe for understanding the neural representation of the identity and familiarity of persons. *Proceedings of the Royal Society of London. Series B, Biological Sciences, 264,* 437–444. doi:10.1098/rspb.1997.0062

Hishikawa, Y., & Shimizu, T. (1995). Physiology of REM sleep, cataplexy, and sleep paralysis. A*dvances in Neurology, 67,* 245–271.

Hobsbawm, E. J. (1994). *Age of extremes: The short twentieth century, 1914–1991.* London, England: Michael Joseph.

Hobson, J., & McCarley, R. (1977). The brain as a dream state generator: An activation-synthesis hypothesis of the dream process. *American Journal of Psychiatry, 134,* 1335–1348.

Hobson, J. A. (1988). *The dreaming brain: How the brain creates both the sense and the nonsense of dreams.* New York: Basic Books.

Hodgkin, A. L., & Katz, B. (1949). The effect of sodium ions on the electrical activity of giant axon of the squid. *Journal of Physiology, 108,* 37–77.

Hoffman, A. (1979). *LSD, My problem child: Reflections on sacred drugs, mysticism, and science.* New York, NY: McGraw-Hill.

Hoffman, H. G., Garcia-Palacios, A., Carlin, A., Furness, T. A., III, & Botella-Arbona, C. (2003). Interfaces that heal: Coupling real and virtual objects to treat spider phobia. *International Journal of Human-Computer Interaction, 16,* 283–300. doi:10.1207/S15327590IJHC1602_08

Hoffmann, H., Janssen, E., & Turner, S. L. (2004). Classical conditioning of sexual arousal in women and men: Effects of varying awareness and biological relevance of the conditioned stimulus. *Archives of Sexual Behavior, 33,* 43–53. doi:10.1023/B:ASEB.0000007461.59019.d3

Hofmann, S. G., Moscovitch, D. A., Litz, B. T., Kim, H.-J., Davis, L. L., & Pizzagalli, D. A. (2005). The worried mind: Autonomic and prefrontal activation during worrying. *Emotion, 5,* 464–475. doi:10.1037/1528-3542.5.4.464

Hofmann, W., Gschwendner, T., Friese, M., Wiers, R. W., & Schmitt, M. (2008). Working memory capacity and self-regulatory behavior: Toward an individual-differences perspective on behavior determination by automatic versus controlled processes. *Journal of Personality and Social Psychology, 95,* 962–977. doi:10.1037/a0012705

Hogan, R. (1983). A socioanalytic theory of personality. In M. Page (Ed.), *Nebraska Symposium on Motivation* (pp. 58–89). Lincoln, NE: University of Nebraska Press.

Holden, C. (2001). 'Behavioral' addictions: Do they exist? *Science, 294,* 980–982. doi:10.1126/science.294.5544.980

Holden, C. (2007). Modeling Mecca's crowds. *Science, 316,* 347. doi:10.1126/science.316.5823.347d

Holden, J. E., Jeong, Y., & Forrest, J. M. (2005). The endogenous opioid system and clinical pain management. *AACN Advanced Critical Care, 16,* 291–301.

Holdsworth, N. (2008, February 10). Student sectioned for anti-Putin activities. *The Telegraph*. Retrieved from http://www.telegraph.co.uk/news/worldnews/1578228/Student-sectioned-for-anti-Putin-activities.html

Holmes, T., & Rahe, R. (1967). The social readjustment rating scale. *Journal of Psychosomatic Research, 11*, 213–218. doi:10.1016/0022-3999(67)90010-4

Hong, C. C. H., Harris, J. C., Pearlson, G. D., Kim, J. S., Calhoun, V. D., Fallon, J. H., . . . & Pekar, J. J. (2009). fMRI evidence for multisensory recruitment associated with rapid eye movements during sleep. *Human Brain Mapping, 30*, 1705–1722. doi:10.1002/hbm.20635

Hong, C. C. H., Potkin, S. G., Antrobus, J. S., Dow, B. M., Callaghan, G. M., & Gillin, J. C. (1997). REM sleep eye movement counts correlate with visual imagery in dreaming: A pilot study. *Psychophysiology, 34*, 377–381. doi:10.1111/j.1469-8986.1997.tb02408.x

Hornsey, M. J. (2008). Social identity theory and self-categorization theory: A historical review. *Social and Personality Psychology Compass, 2*, 204–222. doi:10.1111/j.1751-9004.2007.00066.x

Horowitz, M., Wilner, N., & Alvarez, W. (1979). Impact of event scale: A measure of subjective stress. *Psychosomatic Medicine, 41*, 209–218. doi:10.1097/00006842-197905000-00004

Horwitz, A. V., & Wakefield, J. C. (2007). *The loss of sadness: How psychiatry transformed normal sorrow into depressive disorder.* New York, NY: Oxford University Press.

Hottola, P. (2004). Culture confusion: Intercultural adaptation in tourism. *Annals of Tourism Research, 31*, 447–466. doi:10.1016/j.annals.2004.01.003

Houston, M. B., Bettencourt, L. A., & Wenger, S. (1998). The relationship between waiting in a service queue and evaluations of service quality: A field theory perspective. *Psychology & Marketing, 15*, 735–753. doi:10.1002/(SICI)1520-6793(199812)15:8<735::AID-MAR2>3.0.CO;2-9

Howes, R. (2009, March 25). Seven questions for Irvin Yalom. *Psychology Today*. Retrieved from http://www.psychologytoday.com/blog/in-therapy/200903/seven-questions-irvin-yalom

Hsu, C. L., & Lu, H. P. (2004). Why do people play on-line games? An extended TAM with social influences and flow experience. *Information & Management, 41*, 853–868. doi:10.1016/j.im.2003.08.014

Hubel, D. H. (1963). The visual cortex of the brain. *Scientific American, 209*, 54–63. doi:10.1038/scientificamerican1163-54

Hubel, D. H., & Wiesel, T. N. (1968). Receptive fields and functional architecture of monkey striate cortex. *Journal of Physiology, 195*, 215–243.

Huesmann, L. R., Moise-Titus, J., Podolski, C., & Eron, L. D. (2003). Longitudinal relations between children's exposure to TV violence and their aggressive and violent behavior in young adulthood: 1977–1992. *Developmental Psychology, 39*, 201–221. doi:10.1037/0012-1649.39.2.201

Huff, N. C., Hernandez, J. A., Blanding, N. Q., & LaBar, K. S. (2009). Delayed extinction attenuates conditioned fear renewal and spontaneous recovery in humans. *Behavioral Neuroscience, 123*, 834–843. doi:10.1037/a0016511

Hughes, R. (2003). The flow of human crowds. *Annual Review of Fluid Mechanics, 35*, 169–182. doi:10.1146/annurev.fluid.35.101101.161136

Huk, A. C. (2008). Visual neuroscience: Retinotopy meets perceptotopy? *Current Biology, 18*, R1005–R1007. doi:10.1016/j.cub.2008.09.015

Humphreys, M. S., & Revelle, W. (1984). Personality, motivation, and performance: A theory of the relationship between individual differences and information processing. *Psychological Review, 91*, 153–184. doi:10.1037/0033-295X.91.2.153

Hunt, R. H., & Thomas, K. M. (2008). Magnetic resonance imaging methods in developmental science: A primer. *Development and Psychopathology, 20*, 1029–1051. doi:10.1017/S0954579408000497

Hunton, J., & Rose, J. M. (2005). Cellular telephones and driving performance: The effects of attentional demands on motor vehicle crash risk. *Risk Analysis, 25*, 855–866.

Huppert, J. D., & Sanderson, W. C. (2009). Psychotherapy for generalized anxiety disorder. In D. J. Stein, E. Hollander, & B. O. Rothbaum (Eds.), *Textbook of Anxiety Disorders* (2nd ed., pp. 141–155). Arlington, VA: American Psychiatric Publishing.

Hurtz, G. M., & Donovan, J. J. (2000). Personality and job performance: The Big Five revisited. *Journal of Applied Psychology, 85*, 869–879. doi: 10.1037//0021-9010.85.6.869

Hurvich, L., & Jameson, D. (1957). An opponent-process theory of color vision. *Psychological Review, 64*, 384–404. doi:10.1037/h0041403

Hyde, J. S. (2005). The gender similarities hypothesis. *American Psychologist, 60*, 581–592. doi:10.1037/0003-066X.60.6.581

Iacoboni, M., Woods, R. P., Brass, M., Bekkering, H., Mazziotta, J. C., & Rizzolatti, G. (1999). Cortical mechanisms of human imitation. *Science, 286*, 2526–2528. doi:10.1126/science.286.5449.2526

Iemmola, F., & Camperio-Ciani, A. (2009). New evidence of genetic factors influencing sexual orientation in men: Female fecundity increase in the maternal line. *Archives of Sexual Behavior, 38*, 393–399. doi:10.1007/s10508-008-9381-6

Iggo, A., & Andres, K. H. (1982). Morphology of cutaneous receptors. *Annual Review of Neuroscience, 5*, 1–31. doi:10.1146/annurev.ne.05.030182.000245

Information Please® Database. (2009). Median age at first marriage, 1890–2010. *United States statistics*. Pearson Education. Retrieved from http://www.infoplease.com/ipa/A0005061.html

Innocence Project. (2012, July 19). DNA evidence exonerates Oklahoma man who served 16 years for a burglary and robbery he didn't commit: Innocence Project urges state lawmakers to stop lagging behind the rest of the nation and enact DNA testing law. *Innocence Project*. Retrieved from http://www.innocenceproject.org/Content/3720PRINT.php

Intelligent Children More Likely to Become Vegetarian. (2006, December 15). *ScienceDaily*. Retrieved November 7, 2013, from http://www.sciencedaily.com/releases/2006/12/061215090916.htm

Isen, A. M., & Levin, P. F. (1972). Effect of feeling good on helping: Cookies and kindness. *Journal of Personality and Social Psychology, 21*, 384–388. doi:10.1037/h0032317

Ito, M. (2002). Historical review of the significance of the cerebellum and the role of Purkinje cells in motor learning. *Annals of the New York Academy of Sciences, 978*, 273–288. doi:10.1111/j.1749-6632.2002.tb07574.x

Ivry, R. B., & Keele, S. W. (1989). Timing functions of the cerebellum. *Journal of Cognitive Neuroscience, 1*, 136-152. doi:10.1162/jocn.1989.1.2.136

Iyengar, S. S., & Lepper, M. R. (1999). Rethinking the value of choice: A cultural perspective on intrinsic motivation. *Journal of Personality and Social Psychology, 76*, 349–366. doi:10.1037/0022-3514.76.3.349

Izhikevich, E. M., & Edelman, G. M. (2008). Large-scale model of mammalian thalamocortical systems. *Proceedings of the National Academy of Sciences, 105*, 3593–3598. doi:10.1073/pnas.0712231105

Jack, R. E., Caldara, R., & Schyns, P. G. (2012). Internal representations reveal cultural diversity in expectations of facial expressions of emotion. *Journal of Experimental Psychology: General, 141*, 19–25. doi:10.1037/a0023463

Jaffee, S., & Hyde, J. S. (2000). Gender differences in moral orientation: A meta-analysis. *Psychological Bulletin, 126*, 703–726. doi:10.1037/0033-2909.126.5.703

James, W. (1884). What is an emotion? *Mind, 9,* 188–205. doi:10.1093/mind/os-IX.34.188

James, W. (1890). *Principles of psychology.* New York, NY: Henry Holt. doi:10.1037/11059-000

Janis, I. L. (1971, November). Groupthink. *Psychology Today, 5*(6), 43–46, 74–76.

Janson, H., & Mathiesen, K. S. (2008). Temperament profiles from infancy to middle childhood: Development and associations with behavior problems. *Developmental Psychology, 44,* 1314–1328. doi:10.1037/a0012713

Javaheri, S., Parker, T. J., Liming, J. D., Corbett, W. S., Nishiyama, H., Wexler, L., & Roselle, G. (1998). Sleep apnea in 81 ambulatory male patients with stable heart failure types and their prevalences, consequences, and presentations. *Circulation, 97,* 2154–2159. doi:10.1161/01.CIR.97.21.2154

Jensen, A. R. (1969). How much can we boost IQ and scholastic achievement? *Harvard Educational Review, 39,* 1–123.

Jensen, J. P., Bergin, A. E., & Greaves, D. W. (1990). The meaning of eclecticism: New survey and analysis of components. *Professional Psychology: Research and Practice, 21,* 124–130. doi:10.1037/0735-7028.21.2.124

Jensen, V. L., Hougaard, E., & Fishman, D. B. (2013). Sara, a social phobia client with sudden change after exposure exercises in intensive cognitive-behavior group therapy: A case-based analysis of mechanisms of change. *Pragmatic Case Studies in Psychotherapy, 9,* 275–336. Retrieved from http://pcsp.libraries.rutgers.edu/index.php/pcsp/article/view/1825/3250

Jesteadt, W., Green, D. M., & Wier, C. C. (1978). The Rawdon–Smith illusion. *Perception & Psychophysics, 23,* 244–250. doi:10.3758/BF03204133

John, O. P., Naumann, L. P., & Soto, C. J. (2008). Paradigm shift to the integrative Big Five trait taxonomy: History, measurement, and conceptual issues. In O. P. John, R. W. Robins, & L. A. Pervin (Eds.), *Handbook of Personality: Theory and Research* (pp. 114–158). New York, NY: Guilford.

Johns, L. C., & van Os, J. (2001). The continuity of psychotic experiences in the general population. *Clinical Psychology Review, 21,* 1125–1141. doi:10.1016/S0272-7358(01)00103-9

Johnson, C. Y. (2009, September 18). Spotting a terrorist: Next-generation system for detecting suspects in public settings holds promise, sparks privacy concerns. *Boston Globe.* Retrieved from http://www.boston.com/business/technology/articles/2009/09/18/spotting_a_terrorist/

Johnson, M. (1996). *Slaying the dragon: How to turn your small steps to great feats.* New York, NY: HarperCollins.

Johnson, S. B., Blum, R. W., & Giedd, J. N. (2009). Adolescent maturity and the brain: The promise and pitfalls of neuroscience research in adolescent health policy. *Journal of Adolescent Health, 45*(3), 216–221. doi:10.1016/j.jadohealth.2009.05.016

Johnson, W., Turkheimer, E., Gottesman, I., & Bouchard, T. (2009). Beyond heritability: Twin studies in behavioral research. *Current Directions in Psychological Science, 18,* 217–220. doi:10.1111/j.1467-8721.2009.01639.x

Johnson-Laird, P. N. (1990). The development of reasoning ability. In G. Butterworth & P. Bryant (Eds.), *Causes of development: Interdisciplinary perspectives* (pp. 85–110). New York, NY: Harvester Wheatsheaf.

Johnson-Laird, P. N. (1999). Deductive reasoning. *Annual Review of Psychology, 50,* 109–135. doi:10.1146/annurev.psych.50.1.109

Johnston, D. M., & Johnson, N. R. (1989). Role extension in disaster: Employee behavior at the Beverly Hills Supper Club fire. *Sociological Focus, 22,* 39–51.

Jones, E. (1953). *The life and work of Sigmund Freud.* Oxford, England: Basic Books.

Jones, E. E., & Harris, V. A. (1967). The attribution of attitudes. *Journal of Experimental Social Psychology, 3,* 1–24. doi:10.1016/0022-1031(67)90034-0

Jonides, J., Lewis, R. L., Nee, D. E., Lustig, C. A., Berman, M. G., & Moore, K. S. (2008). The mind and brain of short-term memory. *Annual Review of Psychology, 59,* 193–224. doi:10.1146/annurev.psych.59.103006.093615

Josse, G., & Tzourio-Mazoyer, N. (2004). Hemispheric specialization for language. *Brain Research Reviews, 44,* 1–12. doi:10.1016/j.brainresrev.2003.10.001

Jouvet, M., & Delorme, F. (1965). Locus coeruleus et sommeil paradoxal. *Comptes Rendus des Séances de la Société de Biologie et de ses Filiales, 159,* 895–899.

Joye, Y. (2007). Architectural lessons from environmental psychology: The case of biophilic architecture. *Review of General Psychology, 11,* 305–328. doi:10.1037/1089-2680.11.4.305

Judge, T. A., & Piccolo, R. F. (2004). Transformational and transactional leadership: A meta-analytic test of their relative validity. *Journal of Applied Psychology, 89,* 755–768. doi:10.1037/0021-9010.89.5.755

Juffer, F., & van IJzendoorn, M. H. (2007). Adoptees do not lack self-esteem: A meta-analysis of studies on self-esteem of transracial, international, and domestic adoptees. *Psychological Bulletin, 133,* 1067–1083. doi:10.1037/0033-2909.133.6.1067

Julien, R. M. (2005). *A primer of drug action: A comprehensive guide to the actions, uses, and side effects of psychoactive drugs* (10th edition). New York, NY: Worth Publishers.

Jung, C. G. (1939). *The integration of the personality.* New York, NY: Farrar & Rinehart.

Jung, C. G. (Ed.). (1964). *Man and his symbols.* London, UK: Aldus Books.

Jurgens, H. A., & Johnson, R. W. (2012). Environmental enrichment attenuates hippocampal neuroinflammation and improves cognitive function during influenza infection. *Brain, Behavior, and Immunity, 26,* 1006–1016. doi:10.1016/j.bbi.2012.05.015

Juster, F. T., Ono, H., & Stafford, F. P. (2004). *Changing times of American youth: 1981–2003.* Ann Arbor, MI: Institute for Social Research, University of Michigan. Retrieved from http://www.nwf.org/~/media/PDFs/Eco-schools/teen_time_report.pdf

Justus, T., & Hutsler, J. J. (2005). Fundamental issues in the evolutionary psychology of music: Assessing innateness and domain specificity. *Music Perception, 23,* 1–27. doi:10.1525/mp.2005.23.1.1

Kaare, B., & Woodburn, J. (1999). The Hadza of Tanzania. In R. B. Lee and R. H Daly (Eds.), *The Cambridge encyclopedia of hunters and gatherers* (pp. 200–204). Cambridge, U.K.: Cambridge University Press.

Kafka, M. P. (2010). The DSM diagnostic criteria for paraphilia not otherwise specified. *Archives of Sexual Behavior, 39,* 373–376. doi:10.1007/s10508-009-9552-0

Kagan, J. (1988). The meanings of personality predicates. *The American Psychologist, 43,* 614–620. doi:10.1037/0003-066X.43.8.614

Kagan, J. (1997). Temperament and the reactions to unfamiliarity. *Child Development, 68,* 139–143. doi:10.1111/j.1467-8624.1997.tb01931.x

Kagan, J. (1998). *Three seductive ideas.* Cambridge, MA: Harvard University Press.

Kagan, J. (2002). *Surprise, uncertainty, and mental structures.* Cambridge, MA: Harvard University Press.

Kagan, J., & Snidman, N. (1991). Infant predictors of inhibited and uninhibited profiles. *Psychological Science, 2,* 40–44. doi:10.1111/j.1467-9280.1991.tb00094.x

Kagan, J., & Snidman, N. (1991). Temperamental factors in human development. *American Psychologist, 46,* 856–862. doi:10.1037/0003-066X.46.8.856

Kahn-Greene, E. T., Killgore, D. B., Kamimori, G. H., Balkin, T. J., & Killgore, W. D. S. (2007). The effects of sleep deprivation on symptoms of psychopathology in healthy adults. *Sleep Medicine, 8,* 215–221. doi:10.1016/j.sleep.2006.08.007

Kahneman, D. (1973). *Attention and effort.* Englewood Cliffs, NJ: Prentice-Hall.

Kahneman, D. (2011). *Thinking fast and slow.* New York, NY: Farrar, Straus and Giroux.

Kahneman, D., & Miller, D. T. (1986). Norm theory: Comparing reality to its alternatives. *Psychological Review, 93,* 136–153. doi:10.1037/0033-295X.93.2.136

Kahneman, D., & Tversky, A. (1979). Prospect theory: An analysis of decision under risk. *Econometrica, 47,* 263–292. doi:10.2307/1914185

Kahneman, D., & Tversky, A. (1982). The psychology of preferences. *Scientific American, 246,* 160–173. doi:10.1038/scientificamerican 0182-160

Kahneman, D., & Tversky, A. (1984). Choices, values, and frames. *American Psychologist, 39,* 341–350. doi:10.1037/0003-066X.39.4.341

Kahneman, D., Krueger, A. B., Schkade, D., Schwarz, N., & Stone, A. A. (2006). Would you be happier if you were richer? A focusing illusion. *Science, 312,* 1908–1910. doi:10.1126/science.1129688

Kamin, L. J. (1968). "Attention-like" processes in classical conditioning. In M.R. Jones (Ed.), *Miami symposium on the prediction of behaviour: Aversive stimulation* (pp. 9–33). Coral Gables, FL: University of Miami Press.

Kamphuisen, H. A., Kemp, B., Kramer, C. G., Duijvestijn, J., Ras, L., & Steens, J. (1992). Long-term sleep deprivation as a game: The wear and tear of wakefulness. *Clinical Neurology and Neurosurgery, 94,* S96–S99. doi:10.1016/0303-8467(92)90036-3

Kanamori, T., Kanai, M. I., Dairyo, Y., Yasunaga, K., Morikawa, R. K., & Emoto, K. (2013). Compartmentalized calcium transients trigger dendrite pruning in Drosophila sensory neurons. *Science, 340,* 1475–1478. doi:10.1126/science.1234879

Kandel, E. R. (1991). Cellular mechanisms of learning and the biological basis of individuality. In E. R. Kandel, J. H. Schwartz, & T. M. Jessell (Eds.), *Principles of Neural Science* (3rd ed., pp. 1009–1031). Norwalk, CT: Appleton & Lange.

Kandel, E. R. (2006). Essay: The new science of mind. *Scientific American Mind, 17,* 62–69. doi:10.1038/scientificamericanmind0406-62

Kandel, E. R. for CHARLIE ROSE, PBS. (2013, March 7). *Brain Series 2 Episode 13: Public Policy Implications of the New Science of Mind with Eric Kandel, Alan Alda, Daniel Kahneman, Michael Shadlen, and Walter Mischel.* Retrieved from http://www.charlierose.com/watch/60190667

Kandel, E. R., Schwartz, J. H., & Jessell, T. M. (Eds.). (2000). *Principles of neural science* (Vol. 4). New York, NY: McGraw-Hill.

Kane, J. M. (2004). Tardive dyskinesia rates with atypical antipsychotics in adults: Prevalence and incidence. *The Journal of Clinical Psychiatry, 65*(9), 16–20.

Kanizsa, G. (1976). Subjective contours. *Scientific American, 234,* 48–52. doi:10.1038/scientificamerican0476-48

Kanwisher, N. (2000). Domain specificity in face perception. *Nature Neuroscience, 3,* 759–763. doi:10.1038/77664

Kapur, R., & Smith, M. D. (2009). Treatment of cardiovascular collapse from caffeine overdose with lidocaine, phenylephrine, and hemodialysis. *The American Journal of Emergency Medicine, 27,* 253. e3–253.e6. doi:10.1016/j.ajem.2008.06.028

Kapur, S. (2003). Psychosis as a state of aberrant salience: A framework linking biology, phenomenology, and pharmacology in schizophrenia. *American Journal of Psychiatry, 160,* 13–23. doi:10.1176/appi.ajp.160.1.13

Karau, S. J., & Williams, K. D. (1993). Social loafing: A meta-analytic review and theoretical integration. *Journal of Personality and Social Psychology, 65,* 681–706. doi:10.1037/0022-3514.65.4.681

Karg, K., Burmeister, M., Shedden, K., & Sen, S. (2011). The serotonin transporter promoter variant (5-HTTLPR), stress, and depression meta-analysis revisited: Evidence of genetic moderation. *Archives of General Psychiatry, 68,* 444–454. doi:10.1001/archgen psychiatry.2010.189

Karmiloff-Smith, A. (2009). Nativism versus neuroconstructivism: Rethinking the study of developmental disorders. *Developmental Psychology, 45,* 56–63. doi:10.1037/a0014506

Kashima, Y., Kashima, E. S., Kim, U., & Gelfand, M. (2006). Describing the social world: How is a person, a group, and a relationship described in the East and the West? *Journal of Experimental Social Psychology, 42,* 388–396. doi:10.1016/j.jesp.2005.05.004

Kawachi, I., Colditz, G. A., Stampfer, M. J., Willett, W. C., Manson, J. E., Speizer, F. E., & Hennekens, C. H. (1995). Prospective study of shift work and risk of coronary heart disease in women. *Circulation, 92,* 3178–3182. doi:10.1161/01.CIR.92.11.3178

Kay, P., Berlin, B., Maffi, L., & Merrifield, W. (1997). Color naming across languages. In C. L. Hardin & L. Maffi (Eds.), *Color categories in thought and language* (pp. 21–56). Cambridge, England: Cambridge University Press. doi:10.1017/CBO9780511519819.002

Keith, T. Z. (1982). Time spent on homework and high school grades: A large-sample path analysis. *Journal of Educational Psychology, 74,* 248–253. doi:10.1037/0022-0663.74.2.248

Kelley, H. H. (1967). Attribution theory in social psychology. In D. Levine (Ed.), *Nebraska Symposium on Motivation, 1967.* Lincoln, NE: University of Nebraska Press.

Kelley, H. H., & Michela, J. L. (1980). Attribution theory and research. *Annual Review of Psychology, 31,* 457–501. doi:10.1146/annurev. ps.31.020180.002325

Kelley, H. H., Berscheid, E., Christensen, A., Harvey, J. H., Huston, T. L., Levinger, G., . . . & Peterson, D. R. (Eds.). (1983). *Close relationships.* New York, NY: Freeman.

Kellogg, T. H. (1897). *A text-book on mental diseases.* New York, NY: William Wood & Company.

Kelly, G. A. (1955). *The psychology of personal constructs.* New York, NY: Norton.

Kelly, J. G. (2004). The legacy of consultee-centered consultation for collaborative research. In N. M. Lambert, I. Hylander, & S. Sandoval (Eds.), *Consultee-centered consultation* (pp. 233–244). Mahwah, NJ: Lawrence Erlbaum.

Keltner, D. (1995). Signs of appeasement: Evidence for the distinct displays of embarrassment, amusement, and shame. *Journal of Personality and Social Psychology, 68,* 441–454. doi:10.1037//0022-3514.68.3.441

Kemperman, I., Russ, M. J., & Shearin, E. (1997). Self-injurious behavior and mood regulation in borderline patients. *Journal of Personality Disorders, 11,* 146–157. doi:10.1521/pedi.1997.11.2.146

Kendall, P. C. (1998). Empirically supported psychological therapies. *Journal of Consulting and Clinical Psychology, 66,* 3–6. doi:10.1037/ 0022-006X.66.1.3

Keppel, G., & Underwood, B. J. (1962). Proactive inhibition in short-term retention of single items. *Journal of Verbal Learning and Verbal Behavior, 1,* 153–161. doi:10.1016/S0022-5371(62)80023-1

Kessler, R. C., Berglund, P. A., Chiu, W. T., Deitz, A. C., Hudson, J. I., Shahly, V., . . . & Xavier, M. (2013). The prevalence and correlates of binge eating disorder in the World Health Organization World Mental Health Surveys. *Biological Psychiatry, 73,* 904–914. doi:10.1016/j.biopsych.2012.11.020

Kessler, R. C., Chiu, W. T., Demler, O., & Walters, E. E. (2005). Prevalence, severity, and comorbidity of 12-month DSM-IV disorders in the National Comorbidity Survey Replication. *Archives of General Psychiatry, 62,* 617–627. doi:10.1001/archpsyc.62.6.617

Kessler, R. C., McGonagle, K. A., Zhao, S., Nelson, C. B., Hughes, M., Eshleman, S., . . . & Kendler, K. S. (1994). Lifetime and 12-month prevalence of DSM-III-R psychiatric disorders in the United States: Results from the National Comorbidity Survey. *Archives of General Psychiatry, 51*, 8–19. doi:10.1001/archpsyc.1994.03950010008002

Kessler, R. C., Zhao, S., Blazer, D. G., & Swartz, M. (1997). Prevalence, correlates, and course of minor depression and major depression in the National Comorbidity Survey. *Journal of Affective Disorders, 45*, 19–30. doi:10.1016/S0165-0327(97)00056-6

Kett, J. F. (2003). Reflections on the history of adolescence in America. *The History of the Family, 8*, 355–373. doi:10.1016/S1081-602X(03)00042-3

Keyes, C. L. M., Fredrickson, B. L., & Park, N. (2012). Positive psychology and the quality of life. In K. Land, A. Michelos, & M. Sirgy (Eds.), *Handbook of Social Indicators and Quality of Life Research* (pp. 99–112). Dordrecht, Netherlands: Springer Netherlands. doi:10.1007/978-94-007-2421-1_5

Khundrakpam, B. S., Reid, A., Brauer, J., Carbonell, F., Lewis, J., Ameis, S., . . . & Fadale, D. (2013). Developmental changes in organization of structural brain networks. *Cerebral Cortex, 23*, 2072–2085. doi:10.1093/cercor/bhs187

Kiecolt-Glaser, J. K., Marucha, P. T., Malarkey, W. B., Mercado, A. M., & Glaser, R. (1995). Slowing of wound healing by psychological stress. *Lancet, 346*, 1194–1196. doi:10.1016/S0140-6736(95)92899-5

Kiecolt-Glaser, J. K., & Newton, T. L. (2001). Marriage and health: His and hers. *Psychological Bulletin, 127*, 472–503. doi:10.1037/0033-2909.127.4.472

Kihlstrom, J. F. (2005). Dissociative disorders. *Annual Review of Clinical Psychology, 1*, 227–253. doi:10.1146/annurev.clinpsy.1.102803.143925

Kihlstrom, J. F. (2006). Does neuroscience constrain social-psychological theory? *Dialogue, 21*, 16–17.

Kihlstrom, J. F. (2007). Consciousness in hypnosis. In P. D. Zelazo, M. Moscovitch, & E. Thompson (Eds.), *Cambridge Handbook of Consciousness* (pp. 445–479). Cambridge, UK: Cambridge University Press. doi:10.1017/CBO9780511816789.018

Kikuchi, H., Fujii, T., Abe, N., Suzuki, M., Takagi, M., Mugikura, S., . . . & Mori, E. (2010). Memory repression: Brain mechanisms underlying dissociative amnesia. *Journal of Cognitive Neuroscience, 22*, 602–613. doi:10.1162/jocn.2009.21212

Kim, Y.-K. (Ed.). (2009). *Handbook of behavior genetics*. New York, NY: Springer. doi:10.1007/978-0-387-76727-7

King, B. M. (2006). The rise, fall, and resurrection of the ventromedial hypothalamus in the regulation of feeding behavior and body weight. *Physiology and Behavior, 87*, 221–244. doi:10.1016/j.physbeh.2005.10.007

Kinney, H. C., Korein, J., Panigrahy, A., Dikkes, P., & Goode, R. (1994). Neuropathological findings in the brain of Karen Ann Quinlan—The role of the thalamus in the persistent vegetative state. *New England Journal of Medicine, 330*, 1469–1475. doi:10.1056/NEJM199405263302101

Kinsey, A. C., Pomeroy, W. B. and Martin, C. E. (1948). *Sexual behavior in the human male*. Philadelphia, PA: W. B. Saunders.

Kintsch, W. (1994). Text comprehension, memory, and learning. *American Psychologist, 49*, 294–303.

Kirk, R. (2009). Zombies. In E. N. Zalta (Ed.), *The Stanford Encyclopedia of Philosophy* (Summer 2009 Ed.). Retrieved from http://plato.stanford.edu/archives/sum2009/entries/zombies/

Kirkpatrick, B., Buchanan, R. W., McKenny, P. D., Alphs, L. D., & Carpenter Jr, W. T. (1989). The Schedule for the Deficit Syndrome: An instrument for research in schizophrenia. *Psychiatry Research, 30*, 119–123. doi:10.1016/0165-1781(89)90153-4

Kirsch, I. (2010). *The emperor's new drugs: Exploding the antidepressant myth*. New York, NY: Basic Books.

Kirschenbaum, H. (1979). *On becoming Carl Rogers*. New York, NY: Delacorte.

Kirsh, S. J. (2012). *Children, adolescents, and media violence: A critical look at the research* (2nd ed.). Thousand Oaks, CA: Sage.

Kitayama, S., & Cohen, D. (Eds.). (2007). *Handbook of cultural psychology*. New York, NY: Guilford Press.

Kitayama, S., Duffy, S., Kawamura, T., & Larsen, J. T. (2003). Perceiving an object and its context in different cultures: A cultural look at new look. *Psychological Science, 14*, 201–206. doi:10.1111/1467-9280.02432

Kitayama, S., & Markus, H. R. (1999). Yin and Yang of the Japanese self: The cultural psychology of personality coherence. In D. Cervone & Y. Shoda (Eds.), *The coherence of personality: Social-cognitive bases of consistency, variability, and organization* (pp. 242–302). New York, NY: Guilford Press.

Kitayama, S., Markus, H. R., Matsumoto, H., & Norasakkunit, V. (1997). Individual and collective processes of self-esteem management: Self-enhancement in the United States and self-depreciation in Japan. *Journal of Personality and Social Psychology, 72*, 1245–1267. doi:10.1037/0022-3514.72.6.1245

Klein, D., Zatorre, R. J., Milner, B., & Zhao, V. (2001). A cross-linguistic PET study of tone perception in Mandarin Chinese and English speakers. *Neuroimage, 13*, 646–653. doi:10.1006/nimg.2000.0738

Kleinman, A., & Kleinman, J. (1985). Somatization: The interconnections in Chinese society among culture, depressive experiences, and the meanings of pain. In A. Kleinman, & B. Good (Eds.), *Culture and Depression: Studies in the Anthropology and Cross-Cultural Psychiatry of Affect and Disorder* (pp. 429–490). Berkeley, CA: University of California Press.

Klerman, G. L., Weissman, M. M., Rounsaville, B. J., & Chevron, E. S. (1984). *Interpersonal psychotherapy of depression*. New York, NY: Basic Books.

Kling, K. C., Hyde, J. S., Showers, C. J., & Buswell, B. N. (1999). Gender differences in self-esteem: A meta-analysis. *Psychological Bulletin, 125*, 470–500. doi:10.1037/0033-2909.125.4.470

Kluft, R. P. (2012). Hypnosis in the treatment of dissociative identity disorder and allied states: An overview and case study. *South African Journal of Psychology, 42*, 146–155. doi:10.1177/008124631204200202

Knapp, M., Mangalore, R., & Simon, J. (2004). The global costs of schizophrenia. *Schizophrenia Bulletin, 30*, 279–293. doi:10.1093/oxfordjournals.schbul.a007078

Knight, S. (2009, April 10). Is high IQ a burden as much as a blessing? *Financial Times*. Retrieved from http://www.ft.com/intl/cms/s/0/4add9230-23d5-11de-996a-00144feabdc0.html#axzz34rPxUZjo

Knudsen, N., Laurberg, P., Rasmussen, L. B., Bülow, I., Perrild, H., Ovesen, L., & Jørgensen, T. (2005). Small differences in thyroid function may be important for body mass index and the occurrence of obesity in the population. *Journal of Clinical Endocrinology & Metabolism, 90*, 4019–4024. doi:10.1210/jc.2004-2225

Kobayakawa, T., Wakita, M., Saito, S., Gotow, N., Sakai, N., & Ogawa, H. (2005). Location of the primary gustatory area in humans and its properties, studied by magnetoencephalography. *Chemical Senses, 30*(suppl 1), i226–i227. doi:10.1093/chemse/bjh196

Kober, H., Barrett, L., Joseph, J., Bliss-Moreau, E., Lindquist, K., & Wager, T. D. (2008). Functional grouping and cortical–subcortical interactions in emotion: A meta-analysis of neuroimaging studies. *Neuroimage, 42*, 998–1031. doi:10.1016/j.neuroimage.2008.03.059

Koch, C., & Crick, F. (2001). The zombie within. *Nature, 411*, 893–893. doi:10.1038/35082161

Koch, S., Holland, R. W., Hengstler, M., & van Knippenberg, A. (2009). Body locomotion as regulatory process stepping backward enhances cognitive control. *Psychological Science, 20*, 549–550. doi:10.1111/j.1467-9280.2009.02342.x

Koelsch, S., Fritz, T., von Cramon, D. Y., Müller, K., & Friederici, A. D. (2006). Investigating emotion with music: An fMRI study. *Human Brain Mapping, 27*, 239–250. doi:10.1002/hbm.20180

Koenigsberg, H. W., Siever, L. J., Lee, H., Pizzarello, S., New, A. S., Goodman, M., . . . & Prohovnik, I. (2009). Neural correlates of emotion processing in borderline personality disorder. *Psychiatry Research: Neuroimaging, 172*, 192–199. doi:10.1016/j.pscychresns.2008.07.010

Kohlberg, L. (1969). Stage and sequence: The cognitive-developmental approach to socialization. In D. A. Goslin (Ed.), *Handbook of Socialization Theory and Research* (pp. 347–480). Chicago, IL: Rand McNally.

Kohlberg, L., & Hersh, R. H. (1977). Moral development: A review of the theory. *Theory Into Practice, 16*, 53–59. doi:10.1080/00405847709542675

Kolb, B., & Whishaw, I. Q. (1990). *Fundamentals of human neuropsychology* (3rd ed.). New York, NY: Freeman.

Koob, G. F., & Le Moal, M. (2005). Plasticity of reward neurocircuitry and the 'dark side' of drug addiction. *Nature Neuroscience, 8*, 1442–1444. doi:10.1038/nn1105-1442

Kopp, C. B. (2011). Development in the early years: Socialization, motor development, and consciousness. *Annual Review of Psychology, 62*, 165–187. doi:10.1146/annurev.psych.121208.131625

Kosfeld, M., Heinrichs, M., Zak, P. J., Fischbacher, U., & Fehr, E. (2005). Oxytocin increases trust in humans. *Nature, 435*, 673–676. doi:10.1038/nature03701

Kosslyn, S. M. (1973). Scanning visual images: Some structural implications. *Perception and Psychophysics, 14*(1), 90–94.

Kosslyn, S. M. (1980). *Image and mind*. Cambridge, MA: Harvard University Press.

Kosslyn, S. M., Thompson, W. L., Kim, I. J., Rauch, S. L., & Alpert, N. M. (1996). Individual differences in cerebral blood flow in area 17 predict the time to evaluate visualized letters. *Journal of Cognitive Neuroscience, 8*, 78–82.

Kouider, S., Stahlhut, C., Gelskov, S. V., Barbosa, L. S., Dutat, M., De Gardelle, V., . . . & Dehaene-Lambertz, G. (2013). A neural marker of perceptual consciousness in infants. *Science, 340*, 376–380. doi:10.1126/science.1232509

Kozol, J. (1991). *Savage inequalities: Children in America's schools*. New York, NY: Crown Publishers, Inc.

Krahé, B., Becker, J., & Zöllter, J. (2008). Contextual cues as a source of response bias in personality questionnaires: The case of the NEO-FFI. *European Journal of Personality, 22*, 655–673. doi:10.1002/per.695

Kranz, G. S., Kasper, S., & Lanzenberger, R. (2010). Reward and the serotonergic system. *Neuroscience, 166*, 1023–1035. doi:10.1016/j.neuroscience.2010.01.036

Krathwohl, D. R. (2002). A revision of Bloom's taxonomy: An overview. *Theory into Practice, 41*, 212–218.

Krendl, A., Richeson, J., Kelley, W., & Heatherton, T. F. (2008). The negative consequences of threat: A functional magnetic resonance imaging investigation of the neural mechanisms underlying women's underperformance in math. *Psychological Science, 19*, 168–175. doi:10.1111/j.1467-9280.2008.02063

Kreutz, G., Bongard, S., Rohrmann, S., Hodapp, V., & Grebe, D. (2004). Effects of choir singing or listening on secretory immunoglobulin A, cortisol, and emotional state. *Journal of Behavioral Medicine, 27*, 623–635. doi:10.1007/s10865-004-0006-9

Kring, A. M., Kerr, S. L., Smith, D. A., & Neale, J. M. (1993). Flat affect in schizophrenia does not reflect diminished subjective experience of emotion. *Journal of Abnormal Psychology, 102*, 507–517. doi:10.1037/0021-843X.102.4.507

Kring, A. M., & Moran, E. K. (2008). Emotional response deficits in schizophrenia: Insights from affective science. *Schizophrenia Bulletin, 34*, 819–834. doi:10.1093/schbul/sbn071

Kross, E., Berman, M. G., Mischel, W., Smith, E. E., & Wager, T. D. (2011). Social rejection shares somatosensory representations with physical pain. *Proceedings of the National Academy of Sciences of the United States of America, 108*, 6270–6275. doi:10.1073/pnas.1102693108

Kruglanski, A. W., Pierro, A., Mannetti, L., & De Grada, E. (2006). Groups as epistemic providers: Need for closure and the unfolding of group-centrism. *Psychological Review, 113*, 84–100. doi:10.1037/0033-295X.113.1.84

Kruglanski, A. W., Shah, J. Y., Fishbach, A., Friedman, R., Chun, W. Y., & Sleeth-Keppler, D. (2002). A theory of goal systems. In M. P. Zanna (Ed.), *Advances in Experimental Social Psychology* (pp. 331–378). New York, NY: Academic Press.

Kruglanski, A. W., & Webster, D. M. (1996). Motivated closing of the mind: "Seizing" and "freezing." *Psychological Review, 103*, 263–283. doi:10.1037/0033-295X.103.2.263

Krull, F., & Schifferdecker, M. (1990). Inpatient treatment of conversion disorder: A clinical investigation of outcome. *Psychotherapy and Psychosomatics, 53*, 161–165. doi:10.1159/000288360

Krumhansl, C. L. (1997). An exploratory study of musical emotions and psychophysiology. *Canadian Journal of Experimental Psychology/ Revue Canadienne de Psychologie Expérimentale, 51*, 336–353. doi:10.1037/1196-1961.51.4.336

Krumhansl, C. L. (2002). Music: A link between cognition and emotion. *Current Directions in Psychological Science, 11*, 45–50. doi:10.1111/1467-8721.00165

Kuffler, S. W., & Nicholls, J. G. (1976). *From neuron to brain: A cellular approach to the function of the nervous system*. Sunderland, MA: Sinauer Associates.

Kuhbandner, C., Spitzer, B., & Pekrun, R. (2011). Read-out of emotional information from iconic memory: The longevity of threatening stimuli. *Psychological Science, 22*, 695–700. doi:10.1177/0956797611406445

Kuhl, P. K. (2000). A new view of language acquisition. *Proceedings of the National Academy of Sciences, 97*, 11850–11857.

Kunz, M., Rainville, P., & Lautenbacher, S. (2011). Operant conditioning of facial displays of pain. *Psychosomatic Medicine, 73*, 422–431. doi:10.1097/PSY.0b013e318218db3e

Kuperberg, G., & Heckers, S. (2000). Schizophrenia and cognitive function. *Current Opinion in Neurobiology, 10*, 205–210. doi:10.1016/S0959-4388(00)00068-4

Kuppens, P., Van Mechelen, I., & Rijmen, F. (2008). Toward disentangling sources of individual differences in appraisal and anger. *Journal of Personality, 76*, 969–1000. doi:10.1111/j.1467-6494.2008.00511.x

Kurtz, M. E., Kurtz, J. C., Given, C. W., & Given, B. A. (2008). Patient optimism and mastery—Do they play a role in cancer patients' management of pain and fatigue? *Journal of Pain and Symptom Management, 36*, 1–10. doi:10.1016/j.jpainsymman.2007.08.010

La Mettrie, J. O. (1748). *L'homme machine*. Leyden: Elie Luzac.

Labar, K. (2007). Beyond fear: Emotional memory mechanisms in the human brain. *Current Directions in Psychological Science, 16*, 173–177. doi:10.1111/j.1467-8721.2007.00498

LaBrode, R. T. (2007). Etiology of the psychopathic serial killer: An analysis of antisocial personality disorder, psychopathy, and serial killer personality and crime scene characteristics. *Brief Treatment and Crisis Intervention, 7*, 151–160. doi:10.1093/brief-treatment/mhm004

Lachman, M. E. (Ed.). (2001). *Handbook of midlife development*. New York, NY: Wiley.

Laffey, P. (2003). Psychiatric therapy in Georgian Britain. *Psychological Medicine, 33*, 1285–1297. doi:10.1017/S0033291703008109

Lakoff, G. (1987). *Women, fire, and dangerous things: What categories reveal about the mind.* Chicago, IL: The University of Chicago Press. doi:10.7208/chicago/9780226471013.001.0001

Lakoff, G. (2012). Explaining embodied cognition results. *Topics in Cognitive Science, 4,* 773–785. doi:10.1111/j.1756-8765.2012.01222.x

Lakoff, G., & Johnson, M. (1999). *Philosophy in the flesh: The embodied mind and its challenge to western thought.* New York, NY: Basic Books.

Laland, K., Odling-Smee, J., & Myles, S. (2010). How culture shaped the human genome: Bringing genetics and the human sciences together. *Nature Reviews Genetics, 11,* 137–148. doi:10.1038/nrg2734

Landolfi, E. (2012). Exercise addiction. *Sports Medicine, 43,* 111–119. doi:10.1007/s40279-012-0013-x

Langfield, A., & Briggs, B. (2013, April 16). Amid the chaos and carnage in Boston, heroes emerge. *NBC News.* Retrieved from http://usnews.nbcnews.com/_news/2013/04/16/17780108-amid-the-chaos-and-carnage-in-boston-heroes-emerge?lite

Långström, N., Rahman, Q., Carlström, E., & Lichtenstein, P. (2010). Genetic and environmental effects on same-sex sexual behavior: A population study of twins in Sweden. *Archives of Sexual Behavior, 39,* 75–80. doi:10.1007/s10508-008-9386-1

Lansford, J. E. (2009). Parental divorce and children's adjustment. *Perspectives on Psychological Science, 4,* 140–152. doi:10.1111/j.1745-6924.2009.01114.x

Larson, R., & Ham, M. (1993). Stress and "storm and stress" in early adolescence: The relationship of negative events with dysphoric affect. *Developmental Psychology, 29,* 130–140. doi:10.1037/0012-1649.29.1.130

Latham, G. P., & Pinder, C. C. (2005). Work motivation theory and research at the dawn of the twenty-first century. *Annual Review of Psychology, 56,* 485–516. doi:10.1146/annurev.psych.55.090902.142105

Lattin, D. (2010). *The Harvard psychedelic club: How Timothy Leary, Ram Dass, Huston Smith, and Andrew Weil killed the fifties and ushered in a new age for America.* New York, NY: Harper Collins.

Laurie, A., & Neimeyer, R. A. (2008). African Americans in bereavement: Grief as a function of ethnicity. *OMEGA—Journal of Death and Dying, 57,* 173–193. doi:10.2190/OM.57.2.d

Laursen, B., Coy, K. C., & Collins, W. A. (1998). Reconsidering changes in parent–child conflict across adolescence: A meta-analysis. *Child Development, 69,* 817–832. doi:10.1111/j.1467-8624.1998.tb06245.x

Lazarus, R. S. (1991). *Emotion and adaptation.* New York, NY: Oxford University Press.

Lazarus, R. S., & Alfert, E. (1964). Short-circuiting of threat by experimentally altering cognitive appraisal. *Journal of Abnormal and Social Psychology, 69,* 195–205. doi:10.1037/h0044635

Lazarus, R. S., & Folkman, S. (1984). *Stress, appraisal, and coping.* New York, NY: Springer.

Lazarus, R. S., & Lazarus, B. N. (1994). *Passion and reason: Making sense of our emotions.* New York, NY: Oxford University Press.

Lazear, E. (1986). Salaries and piece rates. *Journal of Business, 59,* 405–431. doi:10.2307/2352711

Le Bihan, D., Mangin, J., Poupon, C., Clark, C. A., Pappata, S., Molko, N., & Chabriat, H. (2001). Diffusion tensor imaging: Concepts and applications. *Journal of Magnetic Resonance Imaging, 13,* 534–546. doi:10.1002/jmri.1076

Le Bon, G. (1896). *The crowd: A study of the popular mind.* London, England: Ernest Benn.

Le Grange, D., Lock, J., Loeb, K., & Nicholls, D. (2010). Academy for eating disorders position paper: The role of the family in eating disorders. *International Journal of Eating Disorders, 43,* 1–5. doi:10.1002/eat.20751

Leaper, C., & Ayres, M. M. (2007). A meta-analytic review of gender variations in adults' language use: Talkativeness, affiliative speech, and assertive speech. *Personality and Social Psychology Review, 11,* 328–363. doi:10.1177/1088868307302221

Leary, M. R., Tambor, E. S., Terdal, S. K., & Downs, D. L. (1995). Self-esteem as an interpersonal monitor: The sociometer hypothesis. *Journal of Personality and Social Psychology, 68(3),* 518–530. doi:10.1037/0022-3514.68.3.518

LeBeau, R. T., Glenn, D., Liao, B., Wittchen, H. U., Beesdo-Baum, K., Ollendick, T., & Craske, M. G. (2010). Specific phobia: A review of DSM-IV specific phobia and preliminary recommendations for DSM-V. *Depression and Anxiety, 27,* 148–167. doi:10.1002/da.20655

Lederman, S., & Klatzky, R. (2009). Haptic perception: A tutorial. *Attention, Perception, & Psychophysics, 71,* 1439–1459. doi:10.3758/APP

LeDoux, J. E. (1994). Emotion, memory and the brain. *Scientific American, 270,* 50–57. doi:10.1038/scientificamerican0694-50

Lee, J. L. C. (2009). Reconsolidation: maintaining memory relevance. *Trends in Neuroscience, 32,* 413–420. doi:10.1016/j.tins.2009.05.002

Lee, K. M., & Kang, S. Y. (2002). Arithmetic operation and working memory: Differential suppression in dual tasks. *Cognition, 83,* B63–B68. doi:10.1016/S0010-0277(02)00010-0

Lee, S. (2002). The stigma of schizophrenia: A transcultural problem. *Current Opinion in Psychiatry, 15,* 37–41. doi:10.1097/00001504-200201000-00007

Lefcourt, H. M. (1973). The function of the illusions of control and freedom. *American Psychologist, 28,* 417–425. doi:10.1037/h0034639

Lemmer, B. (2007). The sleep–wake cycle and sleeping pills. *Physiology & Behavior, 90,* 285–293. doi:10.1016/j.physbeh.2006.09.006

Lenzenweger, M. F., Lane, M. C., Loranger, A. W., & Kessler, R. C. (2007). DSM-IV personality disorders in the National Comorbidity Survey Replication. *Biological Psychiatry, 62,* 553–564. doi:10.1016/j.biopsych.2006.09.019

Leotti, L. A., Iyengar, S. S., & Ochsner, K. N. (2010). Born to choose: The origins and value of the need for control. *Trends in Cognitive Sciences, 14,* 457–463. doi:10.1016/j.tics.2010.08.001

Lepper, M. R., Greene, D., & Nisbett, R. E. (1973). Undermining children's intrinsic interest with extrinsic reward: A test of the "overjustification" hypothesis. *Journal of Personality and Social Psychology, 28,* 129–137. doi:10.1037/h0035519

Lerner, B. H. (2005). Last-ditch medical therapy: Revisiting lobotomy. *New England Journal of Medicine, 353,* 119–121. doi:10.1056/NEJMp048349

Letchworth, W. P. (1889). *The insane in foreign countries.* New York, NY: G. P. Putnam's Sons.

Leventhal, H., & Tomarken, A. (1986). Emotion: Today's problems. *Annual Review of Psychology, 37,* 565–610. doi:10.1146/annurev.ps.37.020186.003025

Levinson, S. C. (1996). Frames of reference and Molyneaux's question: Cross-linguistic evidence. In P. Bloom, M. Peterson, L. Nadel, & M. Garrett (Eds.), *Language and space* (pp. 109–169). Cambridge, MA: MIT Press.

Levy, R., & Goldman-Rakic, P. S. (2000). Segregation of working memory functions within the dorsolateral prefrontal cortex. *Experimental Brain Research, 133,* 23–32. doi:10.1007/s002210000397

Lewin, K., & Lippitt, R. (1938). An experimental approach to the study of autocracy and democracy: A preliminary note. *Sociometry, 1,* 292–300. doi:10.2307/2785585

Lewin, K., Lippitt, R., & White, R. K. (1939). Patterns of aggressive behavior in experimentally created "social climates." *The Journal of Social Psychology, 10,* 269–299. doi:10.1080/00224545.1939.9713366

Lewinsohn, P. M., & Graf, M. (1973). Pleasant activities and depression. *Journal of Consulting and Clinical Psychology, 41,* 261–268. doi:10.1037/h0035142

Lewinsohn, P. M., Sullivan, J. M., & Grosscup, S. J. (1980). Changing reinforcing events: An approach to the treatment of depression. *Psychotherapy: Theory, Research & Practice, 17,* 322–334. doi:10.1037/h0085929

Lewis, M., Haviland-Jones, J. M., & Barrett, L. F. (Eds.). (2008). *Handbook of emotions.* New York, NY: Guilford Press.

Lewis, R. S., Goto, S. G., & Kong, L. L. (2008). Culture and context: East Asian American and European American differences in P3 event-related potentials and self-construal. *Personality and Social Psychology Bulletin, 34,* 623–634. doi:10.1177/0146167207313731

Lewontin, R. C. (2000). *The triple helix: Gene, organism, and environment.* Cambridge, MA: Harvard University Press.

Lewy, A. J., Wehr, T. A., Goodwin, F. K., Newsome, D. A., & Markey, S. P. (1980). Light suppresses melatonin secretion in humans. *Science, 210,* 1267–1269. doi:10.1126/science.7434030

Li, Q., & Brewer, M. B. (2004). What does it mean to be an American? Patriotism, nationalism, and American identity after 9/11. *Political Psychology, 25,* 727–739. doi:10.1111/j.1467-9221.2004.00395.x

Li, X., Staszewski, L., Xu, H., Durick, K., Zoller, M., & Adler, E. (2002). Human receptors for sweet and umami taste. *Proceedings of the National Academy of Sciences, 99,* 4692-4696. doi:10.1073/pnas.072090199

Li, Y., Liu, Y., Li, J., Qin, W., Li, K., Yu, C., & Jiang, T. (2009). Brain anatomical network and intelligence. *PLoS Computational Biology, 5,* e1000395. doi:10.1371/journal.pcbi.1000395

Libet, B., Gleason, C. A., Wright, E. W., & Pearl, D. K. (1983). Time of conscious intention to act in relation to onset of cerebral activity (readiness potential): The unconscious initiation of a freely voluntary act. *Brain, 106,* 623–642. doi:10.1093/brain/106.3.623

Lickliter, R., & Honeycutt, H. (2003). Developmental dynamics: Towards a biologically plausible evolutionary psychology. *Psychological Bulletin, 129,* 819–835. doi:10.1037/0033-2909.129.6.819

Lickliter, R., & Honeycutt, H. (2013). A developmental evolutionary framework for psychology. *Review of General Psychology, 17,* 184–189. doi:10.1037/a0032932

Lieberman, J. A., Stroup, T. S., McEvoy, J. P., Swartz, M. S., Rosenheck, R. A., Perkins, D. O., . . . & Hsiao, J. K. (2005). Effectiveness of antipsychotic drugs in patients with chronic schizophrenia. *New England Journal of Medicine, 353,* 1209–1223. doi:10.1056/NEJMoa051688

Lieberman, M. D., Jarcho, J. M., & Satpute, A. B. (2004). Evidence-based and intuition-based self-knowledge: An fMRI study. *Journal of Personality and Social Psychology, 87,* 421–435. doi:10.1037/0022-3514.87.4.421

Lilienfeld, S. O., Kirsch, I., Sarbin, T. R., Lynn, S. J., Chaves, J. F., Ganaway, G. K., & Powell, R. A. (1999). Dissociative identity disorder and the sociocognitive model: Recalling the lessons of the past. *Psychological Bulletin, 125,* 507–523. doi:10.1037/0033-2909.125.5.507

Lilienfeld, S. O., Wood, J. M., & Garb, H. N. (2000). The scientific status of projective techniques. *Psychological Science in the Public Interest, 1,* 27–66. doi:10.1111/1529-1006.002

Linehan, M. M. (1993). *Cognitive-behavioral treatment of borderline personality disorder.* New York, NY: Guilford Press.

Linehan, M. M., Comtois, K. A., Murray, A. M., Brown, M. Z., Gallop, R. J., Heard, H. L., . . . & Lindenboim, N. (2006). Two-year randomized controlled trial and follow-up of dialectical behavior therapy vs. therapy by experts for suicidal behaviors and borderline personality disorder. *Archives of General Psychiatry, 63,* 757–766. doi:10.1001/archpsyc.63.7.757

Link, B. G., & Phelan, J. C. (2009). Labeling and stigma. In T. L. Scheid, & T. N. Brown (Eds.), *A Handbook for the Study of Mental Health: Social Contexts, Theories, and Systems* (2nd ed., pp. 571–588). New York, NY: Cambridge University Press. doi:10.1017/CBO9780511984945.034

Lissek, S., Biggs, A. L., Rabin, S. J., Cornwell, B. R., Alvarez, R. P., Pine, D. S., & Grillon, C. (2008). Generalization of conditioned fear-potentiated startle in humans: Experimental validation and clinical relevance. *Behaviour Research and Therapy, 46,* 678–687. doi:10.1016/j.brat.2008.02.005

Little, B. R., Salmela-Aro, K., & Phillips, S. D. (Eds.). (2007). *Personal project pursuit: Goals, action and human flourishing.* Mahwah, NJ: Lawrence Erlbaum Associates.

Little, D. R., Lewandowsky, S., & Heit, E. (2006). Ad hoc category restructuring. *Memory & Cognition, 34,* 1398–1413. doi:10.3758/BF03195905

Littner, M., Johnson, S. F., McCall, W. V., Anderson, W. M., Davila, D., Hartse, K., . . . & Woodson, B. T. (2001). Practice parameters for the treatment of narcolepsy: An update for 2000. *Sleep, 24,* 451–466.

Lo, J. C., Groeger, J. A., Santhi, N., Arbon, E. L., Lazar, A. S., Hasan, S., . . . & Dijk, D. J. (2012). Effects of partial and acute total sleep deprivation on performance across cognitive domains, individuals and circadian phase. *PLoS one, 7,* e45987. doi:10.1371/journal.pone.0045987

Locke, E. A., & Latham, G. P. (1990). *A theory of goal setting & task performance.* Englewood Cliffs, NJ: Prentice-Hall, Inc.

Loftus, E. F. (1975). Leading questions and the eyewitness report. *Cognitive Psychology, 7,* 560–572. doi:10.1016/0010-0285(75)90023-7

Loftus, E. F. (1997). Creating false memories. *Scientific American, 277,* 70–75. doi:10.1038/scientificamerican0997-70

Loftus, E. F. (2003). Make-believe memories. *American Psychologist, 58,* 867–873. doi:10.1037/0003-066X.58.11.867

Lohr, C., Thyssen, A., & Hirnet, D. (2011). Extrasynaptic neuron-glia communication: The how and why. *Communicative and Integrative Biology, 4,* 109–111. doi:10.4161/cib.4.1.14184

Lombardo, G. P., & Foschi, R. (2003). The concept of personality in 19th-century French and 20th-century American psychology. *History of Psychology, 6,* 123–142. doi:10.1037/1093-4510.6.2.123

Lopes da Silva, F. (1991). Neural mechanisms underlying brain waves: From neural membranes to networks. *Electroencephalography and Clinical Neurophysiology, 79,* 81–93. doi:10.1016/0013-4694(91)90044-5

Lorenz, K. Z. (1997). *King Solomon's ring: New light on animals' ways* (M. K. Wilson, Trans.). New York, NY: Penguin Group. (Original work published 1952)

Lorenzetti, F. D., Mozzachiodi, R., Baxter, D. A., & Byrne, J. H. (2006). Classical and operant conditioning differentially modify the intrinsic properties of an identified neuron. *Nature Neuroscience, 9,* 17–19. doi:10.1038/nn1593

losthobbit. (2011, August 25). Cant take it anymore. Feel like running away. but you cant runaway from anxiety. Anxiety forums and chat rooms. Retrieved from http://www.anxietyzone.com/index.php/topic,45308.0.html

Lovallo, W. R. (2005). *Stress and health: Biological and psychological interactions* (2nd ed.). Thousand Oaks, CA: SAGE.

Low, L. K., & Cheng, H.-J. (2006). Axon pruning: An essential step underlying the developmental plasticity of neuronal connections. *Philosophical Transactions of the Royal Society of London. Series B, Biological Sciences, 361,* 1531–1544. doi:10.1098/rstb.2006.1883

Lowe, M. R., & Butryn, M. L. (2007). Hedonic hunger: A new dimension of appetite? *Physiology & Behavior, 91,* 432–439. doi:10.1016/j.physbeh.2007.04.006

Luthar, S. S., Cicchetti, D., & Becker, B. (2000). The construct of resilience: A critical evaluation and guidelines for future work. *Child Development, 71,* 543–562. doi:10.1111/1467-8624.00164

Lutz, A., Slagter, H. A., Dunne, J. D., & Davidson, R. J. (2008). Attention regulation and monitoring in meditation. *Trends in Cognitive Sciences, 12,* 163–169. doi:10.1016/j.tics.2008.01.005

Lykken, D., & Tellegen, A. (1996). Happiness is a stochastic phenomenon. *Psychological Science, 7,* 186–189. doi:10.1111/j.1467-9280.1996.tb00355.x

Lynch, T. R., Cheavens, J. S., Cukrowicz, K. C., Thorp, S. R., Bronner, L., & Beyer, J. (2007). Treatment of older adults with co-morbid personality disorder and depression: A dialectical behavior therapy approach. *International Journal of Geriatric Psychiatry, 22,* 131–143. doi:10.1002/gps.1703

Lysaker, P. H., Glynn, S. M., Wilkniss, S. M., & Silverstein, S. M. (2010). Psychotherapy and recovery from schizophrenia: A review of potential applications and need for future study. *Psychological Services, 7,* 75–91. doi:10.1037/a0019115

Mac Suibhne, S. (2011). Erving Goffman's *Asylums* 50 years on. *The British Journal of Psychiatry, 198,* 1–2. doi:10.1192/bjp.bp.109.077172

MacCarthy-Leventhal, E. M. (1959). Post-radiation mouth blindness. *The Lancet, 274,* 1138–1139. doi:10.1016/S0140-6736(59)90117-5

Macchia, F. D. (2006). *Baptized in the spirit: A global Pentecostal theology.* Grand Rapids, MI: Zondervan.

MacDonald, G., & Leary, M. R. (2005). Why does social exclusion hurt? The relationship between social and physical pain. *Psychological Bulletin, 131,* 202–223. doi:10.1037/0033-2909.131.2.202

Mackie, D. M., & Worth, L. T. (1989). Processing deficits and the mediation of positive affect in persuasion. *Journal of Personality and Social Psychology, 57,* 27–40. doi:10.1037/0022-3514.57.1.27

Macklin, R. (1973). The medical model in psychoanalysis and psychotherapy. *Comprehensive Psychiatry, 14,* 49–69. doi:10.1016/0010-440X(73)90055-2

MacLean, P. D. (1990). *The triune brain in evolution: Role in paleocerebral functions.* New York, NY: Plenum.

MacLeod, C., & MacDonald, P. (2000). Interdimensional interference in the Stroop effect: Uncovering the cognitive and neural anatomy of attention. *Trends in Cognitive Sciences, 4,* 383–391. doi:10.1016/S1364-6613(00)01530-8

Macmillan, M. (2000). *An odd kind of fame: Stories of Phineas Gage.* Cambridge, MA: MIT Press.

MacVean, M. (2012, September 6). Popular kids more likely to smoke, research says. *Los Angeles Times.* Retrieved from http://articles.latimes.com/2012/sep/06/news/la-heb-popular-smoking-20120906

Maday, S., & Holzbaur, E. (2012). Autophagosome assembly and cargo capture in the distal axon. *Autophagy, 8,* 858–860. doi:10.4161/auto.20055

Maddox, W. T., Glass, B. D., Wolosin, S. M., Savarie, Z. R., Bowen, C., Matthews, M. D., & Schnyer, D. M. (2009). The effects of sleep deprivation on information-integration categorization performance. *Sleep, 32,* 1439–1448.

Madigan, S., Atkinson, L., Laurin, K., & Benoit, D. (2013). Attachment and internalizing behavior in early childhood: A meta-analysis. *Developmental Psychology, 49,* 672–689. doi:10.1037/a0028793

Magnusson, D. (1992). Individual development: A longitudinal perspective. *European Journal of Personality, 6,* 119–138. doi:10.1002/per.2410060205

Maier, S. F., & Seligman, M. E. (1976). Learned helplessness: Theory and evidence. *Journal of Experimental Psychology: General, 105,* 3–46. doi:10.1037//0096-3445.105.1.3

Maiti, S., Kumar, K. H. B. G., Castellani, C. A., O'Reilly, R., & Singh, S. M. (2011). Ontogenetic *de novo* copy number variations (CNVs) as a source of genetic individuality: Studies on two families with MZD twins for schizophrenia. *PloS ONE, 6,* e17125. doi:10.1371/journal.pone.0017125

Maki, P. M., Rich, J. B., & Rosenbaum, R. S. (2002). Implicit memory varies across the menstrual cycle: Estrogen effects in young women. *Neuropsychologia, 40,* 518–529. doi:10.1016/S0028-3932(01)00126-9

Makris, N., Oscar-Berman, M., Jaffin, S. K., Hodge, S. M., Kennedy, D. N., Caviness, V. S., . . . & Harris, G. J. (2008). Decreased volume of the brain reward system in alcoholism. *Biological Psychiatry, 64,* 192–202. doi:10.1016/j.biopsych.2008.01.018

Maley, R. F., Feldman, G. L., & Ruskin, R. S. (1973). Evaluation of patient improvement in a token economy treatment program. *Journal of Abnormal Psychology, 82,* 141–144. doi:10.1037/h0034975

Malle, B. F. (2007). Attributions as behavior explanations: Toward a new theory. In D. Chadee & J. Hunter (Eds.), *Current Themes and Perspectives in Social Psychology* (pp. 3–26). St. Augustine, Trinidad: SOCS, The University of the West Indies.

Malle, B. F. (2011). Time to give up the dogmas of attribution: An alternative theory of behavior explanation. In J. M. Olson & M. P. Zanna (Eds.), *Advances in Experimental Social Psychology* (Vol. 44, pp. 297–311). San Diego, CA: Academic Press.

Mancebo, M. C., Eisen, J. L., Grant, J. E., & Rasmussen, S. A. (2005). Obsessive compulsive personality disorder and obsessive compulsive disorder: Clinical characteristics, diagnostic difficulties, and treatment. *Annals of Clinical Psychiatry, 17,* 197–204. doi:10.3109/10401230500295305

Manderscheid, R., Atay, J., & Crider, R. (2009). Changing trends in state psychiatric hospital use from 2002 to 2005. *Psychiatric Services, 60,* 29–34. doi:10.1176/appi.ps.60.1.29

Mandik, P. (2001). Mental representation and the subjectivity of consciousness. *Philosophical Psychology, 14,* 179–202. doi:10.1080/09515080120051553

Maner, J. K., DeWall, C. N., & Gailliot, M. T. (2008). Selective attention to signs of success: Social dominance and early stage interpersonal perception. *Personality and Social Psychology Bulletin, 34,* 488–501. doi:10.1177/0146167207311910

Mani, A., Mullainathan, S., Shafir, E., & Zhao, J. (2013). Poverty impedes cognitive function. *Science, 341,* 976–980. doi:10.1126/science.1238041

Manna, A., Raffone, A., Perrucci, M. G., Nardo, D., Ferretti, A., Tartaro, A., . . . & Romani, G. L. (2010). Neural correlates of focused attention and cognitive monitoring in meditation. *Brain Research Bulletin, 82,* 46–56. doi:10.1016/j.brainresbull.2010.03.001

Marcel, A. (1983). Conscious and unconscious perception: Experiments on visual masking and word recognition. *Cognitive Psychology, 15,* 197–237. doi:10.1016/0010-0285(83)90009-9

Marchani, E. E., Watkins, W. S., Bulayeva, K., Harpending, H. C., & Jorde, L. B. (2008). Culture creates genetic structure in the Caucasus: Autosomal, mitochondrial, and Y-chromosomal variation in Daghestan. *BMC Genetics, 9,* 47–59. doi:10.1186/1471-2156-9-47

Marcia, J. E. (1980). Identity in adolescence. In J. Adelson (Ed.), *Handbook of Adolescent Psychology* (pp. 159–187). New York: Wiley

Marek, G. R. (1975). *Toscanini—A biography.* New York, NY: Atheneum.

Markham, J. A., & Greenough, W. T. (2004). Experience-driven brain plasticity: Beyond the synapse. *Neuron Glia Biology, 1,* 351–363. doi:10.1017/S1740925X05000219

Markman, A. B., & Gentner, D. (2001). Thinking. *Annual Review of Psychology, 52,* 223–247. doi:10.1146/annurev.psych.52.1.223

Markus, H. (1977). Self-schemata and processing information about the self. *Journal of Personality and Social Psychology, 35,* 63–78. doi:10.1037/0022-3514.35.2.63

Markus, H. R., & Hamedani, M. G. (2010). Sociocultural psychology: The dynamic interdependence among self systems and social systems. In S. Kitayama & D. Cohen (Eds.), *Handbook of Cultural Psychology* (pp. 3–39). New York, NY: US: Guilford Press.

Markus, H. R., & Kitayama, S. (1991). Culture and the self: Implications for cognition, emotion, and motivation. *Psychological Review, 98,* 224–253. doi:10.1037//0033-295X.98.2.224

Martin, C. L., & Fabes, R. A. (2001). The stability and consequences of young children's same-sex peer interactions. *Developmental Psychology, 37,* 431–446. doi:10.1037/0012-1649.37.3.431

Martin, K. M., & Aggleton, J. P. (1993). Contextual effects on the ability of divers to use decompression tables. *Applied Cognitive Psychology, 7,* 311–316. doi:10.1002/acp.2350070405

Martin, R. C. (2003). Language processing: Functional organization and neuroanatomical basis. *Annual Review of Psychology, 54,* 55–89. doi:10.1146/annurev.psych.54.101601.145201

Mashour, G. A., Walker, E. E., & Martuza, R. L. (2005). Psychosurgery: Past, present, and future. *Brain Research Reviews, 48,* 409–419. doi:10.1016/j.brainresrev.2004.09.002

Maslow, A. H. (1943). A theory of human motivation. *Psychological Review, 50,* 370–396. doi:10.1037/h0054346

Maslow, A. H. (1954). *Motivation and personality.* New York, NY: Harper.

Maslow, A. H. (1970). *Motivation and personality* (2nd ed.). New York, NY: Harper & Row.

Masten, A. S., & Gewirtz, A. H. (2006). Resilience in development: The importance of early childhood. In R. E. Tremblay, R. G. Barr, & R. DeV. Peters (Eds.), *Encyclopedia on Early Childhood Development* [online]. Montreal, Quebec: Centre of Excellence for Early Childhood Development. Retrieved from http://www.child-encyclopedia.com/pages/PDF/Resilience_EN.pdf

Masterpasqua, F. (2009). Psychology and epigenetics. *Review of General Psychology, 13,* 194–201. doi:10.1037/a0016301

Mather, M., Cacioppo, J. T., & Kanwisher, N. (2013). How fMRI can inform cognitive theories. *Perspectives on Psychological Science, 8,* 108–113. doi:10.1177/1745691612469037

Mather, M., Canli, T., English, T., Whitfield, S., Wais, P., Ochsner, K., . . . & Carstensen, L. L. (2004). Amygdala responses to emotionally valenced stimuli in older and younger adults. *Psychological Science, 15,* 259–263. doi:10.1111/j.0956-7976.2004.00662.x

Mather, M., & Carstensen, L. L. (2005). Aging and motivated cognition: The positivity effect in attention and memory. *Trends in Cognitive Sciences, 9,* 496–502. doi:10.1016/j.tics.2005.08.005

Matthews, P. (1982). Where does Sherrington's "muscular sense" originate? Muscles, joints, corollary discharges? *Annual Review of Neuroscience, 5,* 189–218. doi:10.1146/annurev.ne.05.030182.001201

Maurer, D., Le Grand, R., & Mondloch, C. J. (2002). The many faces of configural processing. *Trends in Cognitive Science, 6,* 255–260.

Mauss, I. B., & Robinson, M. D. (2009). Measures of emotion: A review. *Cognition and Emotion, 23,* 209–237. doi:10.1080/02699930802204677

McAdams, D. P. (2001). The psychology of life stories. *Review of General Psychology, 5,* 100–122. doi:10.1037/1089-2680.5.2.100

McAdams, D. P. (2006). The redemptive self: Generativity and the stories Americans live by. *Research in Human Development, 3,* 81–100. doi:10.1080/15427609.2006.9683363

McAdams, D. P. (2006). *The redemptive self: Stories Americans live by.* New York: Oxford University Press. doi:10.1093/acprof:oso/9780195176933.001.0001

McAdams, D. P., & de St. Aubin, E. (1992). A theory of generativity and its assessment through self-report, behavioral acts, and narrative themes in autobiography. *Journal of Personality and Social Psychology, 62,* 1003–1015. doi:10.1037/0022-3514.62.6.1003

McAdams, D. P., Reynolds, J., Lewis, M., Patten, A. H., & Bowman, P. J. (2001). When bad things turn good and good things turn bad: Sequences of redemption and contamination in life narrative and their relation to psychosocial adaptation in midlife adults and in students. *Personality and Social Psychology Bulletin, 27,* 474–485. doi:10.1177/0146167201274008

McAllister, T. W. (2011). Neurobiological consequences of traumatic brain injury. *Dialogues in Clinical Neuroscience, 13,* 287–300.

McCabe, L., Cairney, J., Veldhuizen, S., Herrmann, N., & Streiner, D. L. (2006). Prevalence and correlates of agoraphobia in older adults. *The American Journal of Geriatric Psychiatry, 14,* 515–522. doi:10.1097/01.JGP.0000203177.54242.14

McCauley, R. N. (1986). Intertheoretic relations and the future of psychology. *Philosophy of Science, 53,* 179–199.

McClelland, D. C. (1985). How motives, skills, and values determine what people do. *American Psychologist, 40,* 812–825. doi:10.1037//0003-066X.40.7.812

McClelland, D. C. (1987). *Human motivation.* Cambridge, UK: Cambridge University Press.

McClelland, D. C., Koestner, R., & Weinberger, J. (1989). How do self-attributed and implicit motives differ? *Psychological Review, 96,* 690–702. doi:10.1037//0033-295X.96.4.690

McClelland, J. L., & Rogers, T. T. (2003). The parallel distributed processing approach to semantic cognition. *Nature Reviews Neuroscience, 4,* 310–322. doi:10.1038/nrn1076

McCorduck, P. (2004). *Machines who think* (2nd ed.). Natick, MA: A. K. Peters, Ltd.

McCrae, R. R., & Costa, P. T., Jr. (1987). Validation of the five-factor model of personality across instruments and observers. *Journal of Personality and Social Psychology, 52,* 81–90. doi:10.1037/0022-3514.52.1.81

McCrae, R. R., & Costa, P. T., Jr. (1995). Trait explanations in personality psychology. *European Journal of Personality, 9,* 231–252. doi:10.1002/per.2410090402

McCrae, R. R., & Costa, P. T., Jr. (1996). Toward a new generation of personality theories: Theoretical contexts for the five-factor model. In J. S. Wiggins (Ed.), *The Five-Factor Model of Personality. Theoretical Perspectives* (pp. 51–87). New York, NY: Guilford.

McCrae, R. R., & Costa, P. T., Jr. (2010). *NEO inventories for the NEO Personality Inventory-3 (NEO PI-3), NEO Five-Factor Inventory-3 (NEO-FFI-3) and NEO Personality Inventory-revised (NEO PI-R): Professional Manual.* Lutz, FL: Psychological Assessment Resources.

McDaniel, M. (2005). Big-brained people are smarter: A meta-analysis of the relationship between in vivo brain volume and intelligence. *Intelligence, 33,* 337–346. doi:10.1016/j.intell.2004.11.005

McDonald, J. (2006, August 13). China bans 'Simpsons' from prime-time TV. *The Associated Press.* Retrieved from http://www.washingtonpost.com/wp-dyn/content/article/2006/08/13/AR2006081300242.html

McEwen, B. S., Eiland, L., Hunter, R. G., & Miller, M. M. (2012). Stress and anxiety: Structural plasticity and epigenetic regulation as a consequence of stress. *Neuropharmacology, 62,* 3–12. doi:10.1016/j.neuropharm.2011.07.014

McGaugh, J. L. (2000). Memory—A century of consolidation. *Science, 287,* 248–251. doi:10.1126/science.287.5451.248

McGinn, C. (1999). *The mysterious flame: Conscious minds in a material world.* New York, NY: Basic Books.

McGregor, I., & Little, B. R. (1998). Personal projects, happiness, and meaning: On doing well and being yourself. *Journal of Personality and Social Psychology, 74,* 494–512. doi:10.1037/0022-3514.74.2.494

McIntosh, D. N. (1996). Facial feedback hypotheses: Evidence, implications, and directions. *Motivation and Emotion, 20,* 121–147. doi:10.1007/BF02253868

McIntyre, C. K., McGaugh, J. L., & Williams, C. L. (2012). Interacting brain systems modulate memory consolidation. *Neuroscience & Biobehavioral Reviews, 36,* 1750–1762. doi:10.1016/j.neubiorev.2011.11.001

McKenna, P. J., & Oh, T. M. (2005). *Schizophrenic speech: Making sense of bathroots and ponds that fall in doorways.* Cambridge, UK: Cambridge University Press.

McKone, E., Crookes, K., & Kanwisher, N. (2009). The cognitive and neural development of face recognition in humans. In M. S. Gazzaniga (Ed.), *The cognitive neurosciences IV* (4th ed., pp. 467–482). Cambridge, MA: MIT Press, Bradford Books.

McLachlan, N., & Wilson, S. (2010). The central role of recognition in auditory perception: A neurobiological model. *Psychological Review, 117,* 175–196. doi:10.1037/a0018063

McMillan, M. (2004). *The person-centered approach to therapeutic change.* London, England: Sage.

McMullen, T. (2001). Getting rid of the homunculus: A direct realist approach. In J. R. Morss, N. Stephenson, & H. van Rappard (Eds.), *Theoretical issues in psychology* (pp. 159–167). New York, NY: Springer. doi:10.1007/978-1-4757-6817-6_14

McNally, R. J. (2007). Mechanisms of exposure therapy: How neuroscience can improve psychological treatments for anxiety disorders. *Clinical Psychology Review, 27,* 750–759. doi:10.1016/j.cpr.2007.01.003

McNally, R. J. (2011). *What is mental illness?* Cambridge, MA: Harvard University Press.

McNeill, D. (2005). *Gesture and thought.* Chicago, IL: University of Chicago Press. doi:10.7208/chicago/9780226514642.001.0001

McNulty, J. K., & Fincham, F. D. (2012). Beyond positive psychology? Toward a contextual view of psychological processes and well-being. *The American Psychologist, 67,* 101–110. doi:10.1037/a0024572

McPhail, C. (1994). Presidential address: The dark side of purpose: Individual and collective violence in riots. *The Sociological Quarterly, 35,* 1–32. doi:10.1111/j.1533-8525.1994.tb00396.x

Meichenbaum, D. (1977). *Cognitive-behavior modification: An integrative approach.* New York, NY: Plenum Press. doi:10.1007/978-1-4757-9739-8

Meier, M. H., Caspi, A., Ambler, A., Harrington, H., Houts, R., Keefe, R. S., . . . & Moffitt, T. E. (2012). Persistent cannabis users show neuropsychological decline from childhood to midlife. *Proceedings of the National Academy of Sciences, 109,* E2657–E2664. doi:10.1073/pnas.1206820109

Meloy, J. R. (2007). Antisocial personality disorder. In G. O. Gabbard (Ed.), *Treatments of Psychiatric Disorders* (4th ed., pp. 775–789). Washington, DC: American Psychiatric Press.

Melzack, R., & Wall, P. D. (1965). Pain mechanisms: A new theory. *Science, 150,* 971–979. doi:10.1126/science.150.3699.971

Menand, L. (2001). *The metaphysical club.* New York, NY: Farrar, Straus & Giroux.

Menon, R. S. (2012). Mental chronometry. *NeuroImage, 62,* 1068–1071. doi:10.1016/j.neuroimage.2012.01.011

Menon, V., Levitin, D., Smith, B., Lembke, A., Krasnow, B., Glazer, D., . . . & McAdams, S. (2002). Neural correlates of timbre change in harmonic sounds. *NeuroImage, 17,* 1742–1754. doi:10.1006/nimg.2002.1295

Menon, V., & Uddin, L. Q. (2010). Saliency, switching, attention and control: A network model of insula function. *Brain Structure and Function, 214,* 655–667. doi:10.1007/s00429-010-0262-0

Merckelbach, H., Devilly, G. J., & Rassin, E. (2002). Alters in dissociative identity disorder: Metaphors or genuine entities? *Clinical Psychology Review, 22,* 481–497. doi:10.1016/S0272-7358(01)00115-5

Merker, B. (2005). The liabilities of mobility: A selection pressure for the transition to consciousness in animal evolution. *Consciousness and Cognition, 14,* 89–114. doi:10.1016/S1053-8100(03)00002-3

Mesholam-Gately, R. I., Giuliano, A. J., Goff, K. P., Faraone, S. V., & Seidman, L. J. (2009). Neurocognition in first-episode schizophrenia: A meta-analytic review. *Neuropsychology, 23,* 315–336. doi:10.1037/a0014708

Meston, C. M., & Buss, D. M. (2007). Why humans have sex. *Archives of Sexual Behavior, 36,* 477–507. doi:10.1007/s10508-007-9175-2

Meston, C. M., & Buss, D. M. (2009). *Why women have sex.* New York, NY: Holt.

Meston, C. M., & Frolich, P. F. (2003). Love at first fright: Partner salience moderates roller-coaster induced excitation transfer. *Archives of Sexual Behavior, 32,* 537–544. doi:10.1023/A:1026037527455

Metcalfe, J., & Mischel, W. (1999). A hot/cool-system analysis of delay of gratification: Dynamics of willpower. *Psychological Review, 106,* 3–19. doi:10.1037/0033-295X.106.1.3

Meyerowitz, B. E., & Chaiken, S. (1987). The effect of message framing on breast self-examination attitudes, intentions, and behavior. *Journal of Personality and Social Psychology, 52,* 500–510. doi:10.1037/0022-3514.52.3.500

Michalsen, A., Grossman, P., Acil, A., Langhorst, J., Ludtke, R., Esch, T., . . . Dobos, G. J. (2005). Rapid stress reduction and anxiolysis among distressed women as a consequence of a three-month intensive yoga program. *Medical Science Monitor, 11,* CR555–CR561. Retrieved from http://www.yoga-vidya.de/fileadmin/yv/Yogatherapie/Artikel/StressreduktionYoga.pdf

Michalski, D. Kohout, J., Wicherski, M., & Hart, B. (2011). *2009 Doctorate Employment Survey.* APA Center for Workforce Studies.

Middlebrooks, J., & Green, D. (1991). Sound localization by human listeners. *Annual Review of Psychology, 42,* 135–159. doi:10.1146/annurev.ps.42.020191.001031

Milgram, S. (1971). Behavioral study of obedience. In J. L. Freedman, J. M. Carlsmith, & D. Sears (Eds.), *Readings in Social Psychology* (pp. 529–541). Englewood Cliffs, NJ: Prentice-Hall. (Reprinted from *Journal of Abnormal and Social Psychology, 67* (1963), 371–378. doi:10.1037/h0040525)

Milivojevic, B., Hamm, J. P., & Corballis, M. C. (2009a). Functional neuroanatomy of mental rotation. *Journal of Cognitive Neuroscience, 21,* 945–959. doi:10.1162/jocn.2009.21085

Milivojevic, B., Hamm, J. P., & Corballis, M. C. (2009b). Hemispheric dominance for mental rotation: It is a matter of time. *NeuroReport, 20,* 1507–1512. doi: 10.1097/WNR.0b013e32832ea6fd

Milkman, K. L., Beshears, J., Choi, J. J., Laibson, D., & Madrian, B. C. (2011). Using implementation intentions prompts to enhance influenza vaccination rates. *Proceedings of the National Academy of Sciences of the United States of America, 108,* 10415–10420. doi:10.1073/pnas.1103170108

Miller, B. L., Cummings, J., Mishkin, F., Boone, K., Prince, F., Ponton, M., & Cotman, C. (1998). Emergence of artistic talent in frontotemporal dementia. *Neurology, 51,* 978–982. doi:10.1212/WNL.51.4.978

Miller, G. A. (1956). The magical number seven, plus or minus two: Some limits on our capacity for processing information. *Psychological Review, 63,* 81–97. doi:10.1037/h0043158

Miller, G. A. (2003). The cognitive revolution: A historical perspective. *Trends in Cognitive Sciences, 7,* 141–144. doi:10.1016/S1364-6613(03)00029-9

Miller, J. G. (1984). Culture and development of everyday social explanation. *Journal of Personality and Social Psychology, 46,* 961–978. doi:10.1037/0022-3514.46.5.961

Miller, M. B., Van Horn, J. D., Wolford, G. L., Handy, T. C., Valsangkar-Smyth, M., Inati, S., . . . & Gazzaniga, M. S. (2002). Extensive individual differences in brain activations associated with episodic retrieval are reliable over time. *Journal of Cognitive Neuroscience, 14,* 1200–1214. doi:10.1162/089892902760807203

Miller, N. E. (1985). The value of behavioral research on animals. *American Psychologist, 40,* 423–440. doi:10.1037/0003-066X.40.4.423

Millon, T., Grossman, S. D., & Meagher, S. E. (2004). *Masters of the mind: Exploring the story of mental illness from ancient times to the new millennium.* Hoboken, NJ: John Wiley & Sons.

Millon, T., Millon, C. M., Meagher, S., Grossman, S., & Ramnath, R. (2004). *Personality disorders in modern life* (2nd ed.). Hoboken, NJ: John Wiley & Sons.

Milrod, B., Leon, A., Busch, F., Rudden, M., Schwalberg, M., Clarkin, J., . . . & Shear, M. (2007). A randomized controlled clinical trial of psychoanalytic psychotherapy for panic disorder. *American Journal of Psychiatry, 164,* 265–272. doi:10.1176/appi.ajp.164.2.265

Mischel, W. (1968). *Personality and assessment.* New York, NY: Wiley.

Mischel, W. (1974). Processes in delay of gratification. In L. Berkowitz (Ed.), *Advances in Experimental Social Psychology* (Vol.7, pp. 249–292). San Diego, CA: Academic Press.

Mischel, W. (2004). Toward an integrative science of the person. *Annual Review of Psychology, 55,* 1–22. doi:10.1146/annurev. psych.55.042902.130709

Mischel, W. (2009). From *Personality and Assessment* (1968) to Personality Science, 2009. *Journal of Research in Personality, 43,* 282–290. doi:10.1016/j.jrp.2008.12.037

Mischel, W. (2009). Becoming a cumulative science. *Observer, 22,* 18.

Mischel, W., & Baker, N. (1975). Cognitive transformations of reward objects through instructions. *Journal of Personality and Social Psychology, 31,* 254–261. doi:10.1037/h0076272

Mischel, W., & Peake, P. K. (1982). Beyond deja vu in the search for cross-situational consistency. *Psychological Review, 89,* 730–755. doi:10.1037/0033-295X.89.6.730

Mischel, W., & Shoda, Y. (1995). A cognitive-affective system theory of personality: Reconceptualizing the invariances in personality and the role of situations. *Psychological Review, 102,* 246–286. doi:10.1037/0033-295X.102.2.246

Mita, T. H., Dermer, M., & Knight, J. (1977). Reversed facial images and the mere-exposure hypothesis. *Journal of Personality and Social Psychology, 35,* 597–601. doi:10.1037/0022-3514.35.8.597

Mitchell, J. P., Cloutier, J., Banaji, M. R., & Macrae, C. N. (2006). Medial prefrontal dissociations during processing of trait diagnostic and nondiagnostic person information. *Social Cognitive and Affective Neuroscience, 1,* 49–55. doi:10.1093/scan/nsl007

Mithen, S. J. (1996). *The prehistory of the mind: A search for the origins of art, religion, and science.* London, England: Thames and Hudson.

Mobini, S., Chambers, L. C., & Yeomans, M. R. (2007). Effects of hunger state on flavour pleasantness conditioning at home: Flavour–nutrient learning vs. flavour–flavour learning. *Appetite, 48,* 20–28. doi:10.1016/j.appet.2006.05.017

Moffitt, T. E. (1993). Adolescence-limited and life-course-persistent antisocial behavior: A developmental taxonomy. *Psychological Review, 100,* 674–701. doi:10.1037/0033-295X.100.4.674

Moffitt, T. E., Arseneault, L., Belsky, D., Dickson, N., Hancox, R. J., Harrington, H., . . . & Caspi, A. (2011). A gradient of childhood self-control predicts health, wealth, and public safety. *Proceedings of the National Academy of Sciences of the United States of America, 108,* 2693–2698. doi:10.1073/pnas.1010076108

Mohammed, S. (2001). Personal communication networks and the effects of an entertainment-education radio soap opera in Tanzania. *Journal of Health Communication, 6,* 137–154. doi:10.1080/10810730117219

Monti, M. M., Vanhaudenhuyse, A., Coleman, M. R., Boly, M., Pickard, J. D., Tshibanda, L., . . . & Laureys, S. (2010). Willful modulation of brain activity in disorders of consciousness. *New England Journal of Medicine, 362,* 579–589. doi:10.1056/NEJMoa0905370

Moore, J. K., & Linthicum, F. H. (2004). Auditory System. In G. Paxinos & J. K. Mai (Eds.), *The Human Nervous System* (2nd ed., pp. 1241–1279). Amsterdam, Netherlands: Elsevier Academic Press.

Moors, A. (2007). Can cognitive methods be used to study the unique aspect of emotion: An appraisal theorist's answer. *Cognition and Emotion, 21,* 1238–1269. doi:10.1080/02699930701438061

Moors, A., & De Houwer, J. (2001). Automatic appraisal of motivational valence: Motivational affective priming and Simon effects. *Cognition & Emotion, 15,* 749–766. doi:10.1080/02699930143000293

Moos, R. H., & Moos, B. S. (2003). Long-term influence of duration and intensity of treatment on previously untreated individuals with alcohol use disorders. *Addiction, 98,* 325–337. doi:10.1046/j.1360-0443.2003.00327.x

Morf, C. C., & Rhodewalt, F. (2001). Unraveling the paradoxes of narcissism: A dynamic self-regulatory processing model. *Psychological Inquiry, 12,* 177–196. doi:10.1207/S15327965PLI1204_1

Morris, I. (2010). *Why the West rules—for now: The patterns of history, and what they reveal about the future.* New York, NY: Farrar, Straus and Giroux.

Moruzzi, G., & Magoun, H. W. (1949). Brain stem reticular formation and activation of the EEG. *Electroencephalography and Clinical Neurophysiology, 1,* 455–473. doi:10.1016/0013-4694(49)90219-9

Moskowitz, H. R., Dravnieks, A., & Klarman, L. A. (1976). Odor intensity and pleasantness for a diverse set of odorants. *Perception & Psychophysics, 19,* 122–128. doi:10.3758/BF03204218

Moyer, C. A., Rounds, J., & Hannum, J. W. (2004). A meta-analysis of massage therapy research. *Psychological Bulletin, 130,* 3–18. doi:10.1037/0033-2909.130.1.3

Mrazek, M. D., Chin, J. M., Schmader, T., Hartson, K. A., Smallwood, J., & Schooler, J. W. (2011). Threatened to distraction: Mind-wandering as a consequence of stereotype threat. *Journal of Experimental Social Psychology, 47,* 1243–1248. doi:10.1016/j.jesp.2011.05.011

Muench, J., & Hamer, A. M. (2010). Adverse effects of antipsychotic medications. *American Family Physician, 81,* 617–622.

Mueser, K. T., & McGurk, S. R. (2004). Schizophrenia. *The Lancet, 363,* 2063–2072. doi:10.1016/S0140-6736(04)16458-1

Mund, M., & Mitte, K. (2012). The costs of repression: A meta-analysis on the relation between repressive coping and somatic diseases. *Health Psychology, 31,* 640–649. doi:10.1037/a0026257

Munzenmaier C., & Rubin, N. (2013). *Bloom's taxonomy: What's old is new again.* Santa Rosa, CA: The eLearning Guild. http://onlineteachered.mit.edu/edc-pakistan/files/best-practices/session-2/Pre-Session-Munzenmaier-Rubin-2013.pdf

Munger, S. D. (2009). Olfaction: Noses within noses. *Nature, 459,* 521–522. doi:10.1038/459521a

Muraven, M., & Baumeister, R. F. (2000). Self-regulation and depletion of limited resources: Does self-control resemble a muscle? *Psychological Bulletin, 126,* 247–259. doi:10.1037/0033-2909.126.2.247

Murphy, Z. (2006, January 12). Tragedy despite huge investment. *BBC News.* Retrieved from http://news.bbc.co.uk/2/hi/middle_east/4607420.stm

Murray, H. A. (1938). *Explorations in personality.* Oxford, England: Oxford University Press.

Murray, L. (2009). *Killing the black dog.* Collingwood, Australia: Black Inc.

Myers, L. B. (2010). The importance of the repressive coping style: Findings from 30 years of research. *Anxiety, Stress & Coping, 23,* 3–17. doi:10.1080/10615800903366945

Nadel, L. (1991). The hippocampus and space revisited. *Hippocampus, 1,* 221–229. doi:10.1002/hipo.450010302

Nadel, L., & Moscovitch, M. (1997). Memory consolidation, retrograde amnesia and the hippocampal complex. *Current Opinion in Neurobiology, 7,* 217–227. doi:10.1016/S0959-4388(97)80010-4

Nakic, M., Krystal, J. H., & Bhagwagar, Z. (2010). Neurotransmitter systems in bipolar disorder. In L. N. Yatham, & M. Maj (Eds.), *Bipolar Disorder* (pp. 210–227). Chichester, UK: John Wiley & Sons. doi:10.1002/9780470661277.ch16

Nakielny, S., Fischer, U., Michael, W. M., & Dreyfuss, G. (1997). RNA transport. *Annual Review of Neuroscience, 20,* 269–301. doi:10.1146/annurev.neuro.20.1.269

Nantais, K. M., & Schellenberg, E. G. (1999). The Mozart effect: An artifact of preference. *Psychological Science, 10,* 370–373.

Nathan, D. (2011). *Sybil exposed: The extraordinary story behind the famous multiple personality case.* New York, NY: Free Press.

Nathan, P. E., & Gorman, J. M. (Eds.). (2007). *A guide to treatments that work* (3rd ed.). New York, NY: Oxford University Press.

National Academy of Sciences. (2008). *Science, Evolution, and Creationism.* Washington, D.C.: National Academies Press.

National Commission for the Protection of Human Subjects of Biomedical and Behavioral Research. (1979). *Belmont report: Ethical principles and guidelines for the protection of human subjects of research.* Bethesda, Md.: Author.

National Heart, Lung, and Blood Institute. (n.d.). *National Institutes of Health: National Center on Sleep Disorders Research.* Retrieved from http://www.nhlbi.nih.gov/about/ncsdr/

National Human Genome Research Institute, National Institutes of Health (NIH). (2003, April 14). *International consortium completes Human Genome Project: All goals achieved; new vision for genome research unveiled.* Retrieved from http://www.genome.gov/11006929

National Institute of General Medical Sciences, National Institutes of Health (NIH). (2006). *The new genetics* (NIH Publication No. 10-662) [Booklet]. Retrieved from http://publications.nigms.nih.gov/thenewgenetics/

National Institute of Mental Health (NIMH). (2009). *Schizophrenia* (NIH Publication No. 09-3517) [Booklet]. Retrieved from http://www.nimh.nih.gov/health/publications/schizophrenia/schizophrenia-booket-2009.pdf

National Institute of Mental Health [NIMH]. (2007, May 8). *Genetic roots of bipolar disorder revealed by first genome-wide study of illness* (Press Release). Retrieved from http://www.nimh.nih.gov/news/science-news/2007/genetic-roots-of-bipolar-disorder-revealed-by-first-genome-wide-study-of-illness.shtml

National Institute of Mental Health. (2009). *Anxiety disorders* (NIH Publication No. 09-3879). Bethesda, MD: National Institute of Mental Health. Retrieved from http://www.nimh.nih.gov/health/publications/anxiety-disorders/nimhanxiety.pdf

National Institute of Mental Health. (2009). *Schizophrenia* (NIH Publication No. 09-3517). Bethesda, MA: National Institute of Mental Health. Retrieved from http://www.nimh.nih.gov/health/publications/schizophrenia/schizophrenia-booket-2009.pdf

National Institute of Mental Health. (2011). *A parent's guide to autism spectrum disorder* (NIH Publication No. 11-5511). Bethesda, MD: National Institute of Mental Health. Retrieved from http://www.nimh.nih.gov/health/publications/a-parents-guide-to-autism-spectrum-disorder/parent-guide-to-autism.pdf

National Institute of Mental Health. (2011). *Depression* (NIH Publication No. 11-3561). Bethesda, MD: National Institute of Mental Health. Retrieved from http://www.nimh.nih.gov/health/publications/depression/depression-booklet.pdf

National Institute of Mental Health. (2011). *Eating disorders* (Revised, NIH Publication No. 11-4901). Retrieved from http://www.nimh.nih.gov/health/publications/eating-disorders/eating-disorders.pdf

National Institute on Drug Abuse. (2010). *Drugs, brains, and behavior: The science of addiction* (NIH Publication No. 10-5605). Retrieved from http://www.drugabuse.gov/sites/default/files/sciofaddiction.pdf

National Institute on Drug Abuse. (2011). *Facts on CNS depressants.* Retrieved from http://teens.drugabuse.gov/sites/default/files/peerx/pdf/PEERx_Toolkit_Depressants.pdf

National Institute on Drug Abuse. (2012). Costs of substance abuse. In *Trends & Statistics* (Updated December 2012). Retrieved from http://www.drugabuse.gov/related-topics/trends-statistics

National Institute on Drug Abuse. (2014). *Drug facts: Marijuana.* Retrieved from http://www.drugabuse.gov/publications/drugfacts/marijuana

National Institutes of Health, U.S. Department of Health and Human Services. (2009, July 15). *NIH launches the Human Connectome Project to unravel the brain's connections.* Retrieved from http://www.nih.gov/news/health/jul2009/ninds-15.htm

National Institutes of Health. (2012). *Attention Deficit Hyperactivity Disorder (ADHD)* (NIH Publication No. 12-3572). Retrieved from http://www.nimh.nih.gov/health/publications/attention-deficit-hyperactivity-disorder/adhd_booklet_cl508.pdf

National Institutes of Health. (updated 2011) *Your guide to healthy sleep* (NIH Publication No. 11-5271). Retrieved from http://www.nhlbi.nih.gov/health/public/sleep/healthy_sleep.pdf

NBA Entertainment. (1999). ESPN Internet Ventures and Starwave Corporation, http://web.archive.org/web/20000818063945/; http://www.nba.com/finals98/00738002.html

Neath, I. (1998). *Human memory: An introduction to research, data, and theory.* Belmont, CA: Thomson Brooks/Cole Publishing Co.

Neiss, M. B., Stevenson, J., Legrand, L. N., Iacono, W. G., & Sedikides, C. (2009). Self-esteem, negative emotionality, and depression as a common temperamental core: A study of mid-adolescent twin girls. *Journal of Personality, 77,* 327–346. doi:10.1111/j.1467-6494.2008.00549.x

Neisser, U. (1976). *Cognition and reality: Principles and implications of cognitive psychology.* San Francisco, CA: W. H. Freeman.

Neisser, U. (1997). Rising Scores on Intelligence Tests Test scores are certainly going up all over the world, but whether intelligence itself has risen remains controversial. *American Scientist, 85,* 440–447.

Neisser, U., & Becklen, R. (1975). Selective looking: Attending to visually specified events. *Cognitive Psychology, 7,* 480–494. doi:10.1016/0010-0285(75)90019-5

Nelson, K., & Fivush, R. (2004). The emergence of autobiographical memory: A social cultural developmental theory. *Psychological Review, 111,* 486–511. doi:10.1037/0033-295X.111.2.486

Nemeroff, C. B., Bremner, J. D., Foa, E. B., Mayberg, H. S., North, C. S., & Stein, M. B. (2006). Posttraumatic stress disorder: a state-of-the-science review. *Journal of Psychiatric Research, 40,* 1–21. doi:10.1016/j.jpsychires.2005.07.005

Nesse, R. M., & Ellsworth, P. C. (2009). Evolution, emotions, and emotional disorders. *American Psychologist, 64,* 129–139. doi:10.1037/a0013503

Nesse, R. M., & Stein, D. J. (2012). Towards a genuinely medical model for psychiatric nosology. *BMC Medicine, 10,* 5. doi:10.1186/1741-7015-10-5

Nestler, E. J. (2006). The addicted brain: Cocaine use alters genes. *Paradigm, 11,* 12–22.

Neubauer, D. N. (2004). Chronic insomnia: Current issues. *Clinical Cornerstone, 6,* S17–S22. doi:10.1016/S1098-3597(04)80044-9

Neuroslicer. (2007, April 18). *Schizophrenia: Gerald, Part 1* [Video file]. Retrieved from https://www.youtube.com/watch?v=gGnl8dqEoPQ

Newell, A., & Simon, H. A. (1961). Computer simulation of human thinking. *Science, 134,* 2011–2017. doi:10.1126/science.134.3495.2011

Newell, A., & Simon, H. A. (1972). *Human problem solving.* Englewood Cliffs, NJ: Prentice-Hall.

Newman, J. D., & Harris, J. C. (2009). The scientific contributions of Paul D. MacLean (1913–2007). *The Journal of Nervous and Mental Disease, 197,* 3–5. doi:10.1097/NMD.0b013e31818ec5d9

Newman, L. S. & Caldwell, T. L. (2005). Allport's "living inkblots": The role of defensive projection in stereotyping and prejudice. In J. F. Dovidio, P. Glick, & L. A. Rudman (Eds.), *On the Nature of Prejudice: 50 Years After Allport* (pp. 377–392). Malden, MA: Blackwell Publishing. doi:10.1002/9780470773963.ch23

Newman, M. G., Llera, S. J., Erickson, T. M., Przeworski, A., & Castonguay, L. G. (2013). Worry and generalized anxiety disorder: A review and theoretical synthesis of evidence on nature, etiology, mechanisms, and treatment. *Annual Review of Clinical Psychology, 9,* 275–297. doi:10.1146/annurev-clinpsy-050212-185544

Nguyen, H. H. D., & Ryan, A. M. (2008). Does stereotype threat affect test performance of minorities and women? A meta-analysis of experimental evidence. *Journal of Applied Psychology, 93,* 1314–1334. doi:10.1037/a0012702

Nicholls, J. G. (1984). Achievement motivation: Conceptions of ability, subjective experience, task choice, and performance. *Psychological Review, 91,* 328–346. doi:10.1037/0033-295X.91.3.328

Nichols, D. E. (2004). Hallucinogens. *Pharmacology & Therapeutics, 101,* 131–181. doi:10.1016/j.pharmthera.2003.11.002

Nickerson, R. S. (1998). Confirmation bias: A ubiquitous phenomenon in many guises. *Review of General Psychology, 2,* 175–220. doi:10.1037/1089-2680.2.2.175

Nicolas, S., & Levine, Z. (2012). Beyond intelligence testing: Remembering Alfred Binet after a century. *European Psychologist, 17,* 320–325.

NIDCD. (2013). *Noise-induced hearing loss.* NIH Pub 13-4233. Bethesda, MD: National Institute on Deafness and Other Communication Disorders. Available from www.nidcd.nih.gov/health/hearing/noise.asp

Nisbett, R. E. (2009). *Intelligence and how to get it: Why schools and cultures count.* New York, NY: W. W. Norton & Company.

Nisbett, R. E., Peng, K., Choi, I., & Norenzayan, A. (2001). Culture and systems of thought: Holistic versus analytic cognition. *Psychological Review, 108,* 291–310. doi:10.1037/0033-295X.108.2.291

Nolan, J., for the Associated Press. (1994, March 1). Suit against Cardinal is dropped: The plaintiff, a Philadelphia man, was no longer sure the Chicago prelate had abused him. *The Inquirer.* Retrieved from http://articles.philly.com/1994-03-01/news/25848095_1_cardinal-bernardin-steven-cook-chicago-prelate

Norcross, J. C., & Wampold, B. E. (2011). What works for whom: Tailoring psychotherapy to the person. *Journal of Clinical Psychology, 67,* 127–132. doi:10.1002/jclp.20764

Nordentoft, M., Mortensen, P. B., & Pedersen, C. B. (2011). Absolute risk of suicide after first hospital contact in mental disorder. *Archives of General Psychiatry, 68,* 1058–1064. doi:10.1001/archgenpsychiatry.2011.113

Nowak, A., & Vallacher, R. R. (1998). *Dynamical social psychology.* New York, NY: Guilford Press.

Nozick, R. (1981). *Philosophical explanations.* Cambridge, MA: Belknap Press of Harvard University Press.

Nucci, L., & Turiel, E. (2009). Capturing the complexity of moral development and education. *Mind, Brain, and Education, 3,* 151–159. doi:10.1111/j.1751-228X.2009.01065.x

Nuevo, R., Chatterji, S., Verdes, E., Naidoo, N., Arango, C., & Ayuso-Mateos, J. L. (2010). The continuum of psychotic symptoms in the general population: A cross-national study. *Schizophrenia Bulletin, 38,* 475–485. doi:10.1093/schbul/sbq099

O'Donohue, W., Fisher, J. E., & Hayes, S. C. (Eds.). (2003). *Cognitive behavior therapy: Applying empirically supported techniques in your practice.* New York, NY: Wiley.

O'Donohue, W., & Krasner, L. (Eds.). (1995). *Theories of behavior therapy: Exploring behavior change.* Washington, DC: American Psychological Association.

O'Reilly, J. X., Jbabdi, S., & Behrens, T. E. (2012). How can a Bayesian approach inform neuroscience? *European Journal of Neuroscience, 35,* 1169–1179. doi:10.1111/j.1460-9568.2012.08010.x

Ochsner, K. N., Ray, R. D., Cooper, J. C., Robertson, E. R., Chopra, S., Gabrieli, J. D., & Gross, J. J. (2004). For better or for worse: Neural systems supporting the cognitive down-and up-regulation of negative emotion. *Neuroimage, 23,* 483–499. doi:10.1016/j.neuroimage.2004.06.030

Ogbu, J. U., & Simons, H. D. (1998). Voluntary and involuntary minorities: A cultural-ecological theory of school performance with some implications for education. *Anthropology & Education Quarterly, 29,* 155–188. doi:10.1525/aeq.1998.29.2.155

Ogden, C. L., Fryar, C. D., Carroll, M. D., & Flegal, K. M. (2004). Mean body weight, height, and body mass index, United States 1960–2002. *Advance data from vital and health statistics; no 347.* Hyattsville, Maryland: National Center for Health Statistics.

Ohayon, M. M., & Zulley, J. (2001). Correlates of global sleep dissatisfaction in the German population. *Sleep, 24,* 780–787.

Öhman, A., & Mineka, S. (2001). Fears, phobias, and preparedness: Toward an evolved module of fear and fear learning. *Psychological Review, 108,* 483–522. doi:10.1037/0033-295X.108.3.483

Olds, J. (1958). Self-stimulation of the brain. *Science, 127,* 315–324. doi:10.1126/science.127.3294.315

Olds, J., & Milner, P. (1954). Positive reinforcement produced by electrical stimulation of septal area and other regions of rat brain. *Journal of Comparative and Physiological Psychology, 47,* 419–427. doi:10.1037/h0058775

Olejniczak, P. (2006). Neurophysiologic basis of EEG. *Journal of Clinical Neurophysiology, 23,* 186–189. doi:10.1097/01.wnp.0000220079.61973.6c

Olfson, M., & Marcus, S. C. (2010). National trends in outpatient psychotherapy. *American Journal of Psychiatry, 167,* 1456–1463. doi:10.1176/appi.ajp.2010.10040570

Oliansky, A. (1991). A confederate's perspective on deception. *Ethics & Behavior, 1,* 253–258. doi:10.1207/s15327019eb0104_3

Olshansky, S. J. (2011). Aging of US presidents. *Journal of the American Medical Association, 306,* 2328–2329. doi:10.1001/jama.2011.1786

Oltmanns, T. F., & Turkheimer, E. (2009). Person perception and personality pathology. *Current Directions in Psychological Science, 18,* 32–36. doi:10.1111/j.1467-8721.2009.01601.x

Omotoso, S. (1978). Storytelling: A cherished cultural tradition in Nigeria. *Language Arts, 55,* 724–727.

Opler, M. G., & Susser, E. S. (2005). Fetal environment and schizophrenia. *Environmental Health Perspectives, 113,* 1239–1242. doi:10.1289/ehp.7572

Ornstein, R., & Thompson, R. (1984). *The amazing brain.* Boston, MA: Houghton Mifflin.

Orom, H., & Cervone, D. (2009). Personality dynamics, meaning, and idiosyncrasy: Identifying cross-situational coherence by assessing personality architecture. *Journal of Research in Personality, 43,* 228–240. doi:10.1016/j.jrp.2009.01.015

Ostrov, J. M., & Keating, C. F. (2004). Gender differences in preschool aggression during free play and structured interactions: An observational study. *Social Development, 13,* 255–275. doi:10.1111/j.1467-9507.2004.000266.x

Overmier, J. B. & Murison, R. (2000). Anxiety and helplessness in the face of stress predisposes, precipitates, and sustains gastric ulceration. *Behavioural Brain Research, 110,* 161–174. doi:10.1016/S0166-4328(99)00193-X

Owen, A. M., Coleman, M. R., Boly, M., Davis, M. H., Laureys, S., & Pickard, J. D. (2006). Detecting awareness in the vegetative state. *Science, 313,* 1402. doi:10.1126/science.1130197

Owren, M. J., & Bachorowski, J.-A. (2003). Reconsidering the evolution of nonlinguistic communication: The case of laughter. *Journal of Nonverbal Behavior, 27,* 183–200. doi:10.1023/A:1025394015198

Oxley, D. R., Smith, K. B., Alford, J. R., Hibbing, M. V, Miller, J. L., Scalora, M., . . . & Hibbing, J. R. (2008). Political attitudes vary with physiological traits. *Science, 321,* 1667–1670. doi:10.1126/science.1157627

Oyserman, D., Coon, H. M., & Kemmelmeier, M. (2002). Rethinking individualism and collectivism: Evaluation of theoretical assumptions and meta-analyses. *Psychological Bulletin, 128,* 3–72. doi:10.1037//0033-2909.128.1.3

Padilla-Walker, L. M., Barry, C. M., Carroll, J. S., Madsen, S. D., & Nelson, L. J. (2008). Looking on the bright side: The role of identity status and gender on positive orientations during emerging adulthood. *Journal of Adolescence, 31,* 451–467. doi:10.1016/j.adolescence.2007.09.001

Pai, A., & You, L. (2009). Optimal tuning of bacterial sensing potential. *Molecular Systems Biology, 5,* 286. doi:10.1038/msb.2009.43

Paikoff, R. L., & Brooks-Gunn, J. (1991). Do parent-child relationships change during puberty? *Psychological Bulletin, 110,* 47–66. doi:10.1037/0033-2909.110.1.47

Palmer, B. W., Dawes, S. E., & Heaton, R. K. (2009). What do we know about neuropsychological aspects of schizophrenia? *Neuropsychology Review, 19,* 365–384. doi:10.1007/s11065-009-9109-y

Palmer, B. W., Savla, G. N., Fellows, I. E., Twamley, E. W., Jeste, D. V., & Lacro, J. P. (2010). Do people with schizophrenia have differential impairment in episodic memory and/or working memory relative to other cognitive abilities? *Schizophrenia Research, 116,* 259–265. doi:10.1016/j.schres.2009.11.002

Paluck, E. L., & Green, D. P. (2009). Prejudice reduction: What works? A review and assessment of research and practice. *Annual Review of Psychology, 60,* 339–367. doi:10.1146/annurev.psych.60.110707.163607

Palusci, V. J. (2013). Adverse childhood experiences and lifelong health. *JAMA Pediatrics, 167,* 95–96. doi:10.1001/jamapediatrics.2013.427

Panagopoulos, C. (2009). Polls and elections: Preelection poll accuracy in the 2008 General Elections. *Presidential Studies Quarterly, 39,* 896–907. doi:10.1111/j.1741-5705.2009.03713.x

Panayiotopoulos, C. P. (1999). *Benign childhood partial seizures and related epileptic syndromes.* London, England: John Libbey & Company.

Pandya, D. N., & Seltzer, B. (1982). Intrinsic connections and architectonics of posterior parietal cortex in the rhesus monkey. *Journal of Comparative Neurology, 204,* 196–210. doi:10.1002/cne.902040208

Paquette, V., Lévesque, J., Mensour, B., Leroux, J.-M., Beaudoin, G., Bourgouin, P., & Beauregard, M. (2003). "Change the mind and you change the brain": Effects of cognitive-behavioral therapy on the neural correlates of spider phobia. *NeuroImage, 18,* 401–409. doi:10.1016/S1053-8119(02)00030-7

Parish, S. M. (1991). The sacred mind: Newar cultural representations of mental life and the productions of moral consciousness. *Ethos, 19,* 313–351. doi:10.1525/eth.1991.19.3.02a00030

Parisi, D., & Petrosino, G. (2010). Robots that have emotions. *Adaptive Behavior, 18,* 453–469. doi:10.1177/1059712310388528

Parke, R. D. (2004). Development in the family. *Annual Review of Psychology, 55,* 365–399. doi:10.1146/annurev.psych.55.090902.141528

Parker, E. S., Cahill, L., & McGaugh, J. L. (2006). A case of unusual autobiographical remembering. *Neurocase, 12,* 35–49. doi:10.1080/13554790500473680

Parks, T. (2012, April 5). Chekhov: Behind the charm. *The New York review of books.* Retrieved from http://www.nybooks.com/articles/archives/2012/apr/05/chekhov-behind-charm/

Paulhus, D. L., & Reid, D. B. (1991). Enhancement and denial in socially desirable responding. *Journal of Personality and Social Psychology, 60,* 307–317. doi:10.1037/0022-3514.60.2.307

Pavlov, I. P. (1928). *Lectures on conditioned reflexes.* New York, NY: International Publishers.

Pearlstein, T., Howard, M., Salisbury, A., & Zlotnick, C. (2009). Postpartum depression. *American Journal of Obstetrics and Gynecology, 200,* 357–364. doi:10.1016/j.ajog.2008.11.033

Pedersen, N. L., Plomin, R., McClearn, G. E., & Friberg, L. (1988). Neuroticism, extraversion, and related traits in adult twins reared apart and reared together. *Journal of Personality and Social Psychology, 55,* 950–957. doi:10.1037/0022-3514.55.6.950

Penfield, W., & Boldrey, E. (1937). Somatic motor and sensory representation in the cerebral cortex of man as studied by electrical stimulation. *Brain, 60,* 389–443. doi:10.1093/brain/60.4.389

Penn, A. A., & Shatz, C. J. (1999). Brain waves and brain wiring: The role of endogenous and sensory-driven neural activity in development. *Pediatric Research, 45,* 447–458. doi:10.1203/00006450-199904010-00001

Pennisi, E. (2005). Why do humans have so few genes? *Science, 309,* 80. doi:10.1126/science.309.5731.80

Pentland, A. (2013). The Data-Driven Society. *Scientific American, 309,* 78–83. doi:10.1038/scientificamerican1013-78

Pepperberg, I. (1991). A communicative approach to animal cognition: A study of conceptual abilities of an African grey parrot. In C. A. Ristau (Ed.), *Cognitive ethology: The minds of other animals: Essays in honor of Donald R. Griffin* (pp. 153–186). Hillsdale, NJ: Lawrence Erlbaum Associates, Inc.

Perkel, J. M. (2013). This is your brain: Mapping the connectome. *Science, 339,* 350–352. doi:10.1126/science.339.6117.350

Perlis, R. H., Welge, J. A., Vornik, L. A., Hirschfeld, R. M., & Keck Jr, P. E. (2006). Atypical antipsychotics in the treatment of mania: A meta-analysis of randomized, placebo-controlled trials. *Journal of Clinical Psychiatry, 67,* 509–516. doi:10.4088/JCP.v67n0401

Perrin, J. S., Merz, S., Bennett, D. M., Currie, J., Steele, D. J., Reid, I. C., & Schwarzbauer, C. (2012). Electroconvulsive therapy reduces frontal cortical connectivity in severe depressive disorder. *Proceedings of the National Academy of Sciences of the United States of America, 109,* 5464–5468. doi:10.1073/pnas.1117206109

Perrin, M., DiGrande, L., Wheeler, K., Thorpe, L., Farfel, M., & Brackbill, R. (2007). Differences in PTSD prevalence and associated risk factors among World Trade Center disaster rescue and recovery workers. *American Journal of Psychiatry, 164,* 1385–1394. doi:10.1176/appi.ajp.2007.06101645

Pervin, L. A. (Ed.). (1989). *Goal concepts in personality and social psychology.* Hillsdale, NJ: Lawrence Erlbaum Associates, Inc.

Pessoa, L., & Adolphs, R. (2010). Emotion processing and the amygdala: From a 'low road' to 'many roads' of evaluating biological significance. *Nature Reviews Neuroscience, 11,* 773–783.

Peterson, L., & Peterson, M. J. (1959). Short-term retention of individual verbal items. *Journal of Experimental Psychology, 58,* 193–198. doi:10.1037/h0049234

Petrides, M., Alivisatos, B., Meyer, E., & Evans, A. C. (1993). Functional activation of the human frontal cortex during the performance of verbal working memory tasks. *Proceedings of the National Academy of Sciences, 90,* 878–882. doi:10.1073/pnas.90.3.878

Pettigrew, T. F., & Tropp, L. R. (2006). A meta-analytic test of intergroup contact theory. *Journal of Personality and Social Psychology, 90,* 751–783. doi:10.1037/0022-3514.90.5.751

Petty, R. E., Fazio, R. H., & Briñol, P. (Eds.). (2009). *Attitudes: Insights from the new implicit measures.* New York, NY: Psychology Press.

Phinney, J. S. (1989). Stages of ethnic identity development in minority group adolescents. *The Journal of Early Adolescence, 9,* 34–49. doi:10.1177/0272431689091004

Piaget, J. (1964), Part I: Cognitive development in children: Piaget development and learning. *Journal of Research in Science Teaching, 2,* 176-186. doi: 10.1002/tea.3660020306

Pickering, A. D., & Corr, P. J. (2008). J. A. Gray's reinforcement sensitivity theory (RST) of personality. In G. J. Boyle, G. Matthews, & D. H. Saklofske (Eds.), *The SAGE Handbook of Personality Theory and Assessment* (Vol 1, pp. 239–256). Thousand Oaks, CA: SAGE Publications. doi:10.4135/9781849200462.n11

Pickering, A. D., & Corr, P. J. (2008). The neuroscience of personality. In G. Boyle, G. Matthews, & D. H. Saklofske (Eds.), *Handbook of Personality Testing and Theory* (pp. 239–256). London, England: Sage.

Piechowski, M. M., & Tyska, C. (1982). Self-actualization profile of Eleanor Roosevelt, a presumed nontranscender. *Genetic Psychology Monographs, 105,* 95–153.

Pietiläinen, K. H., Kaprio, J., Rissanen, A., Winter, T., Rimpelä, A., Viken, R. J., & Rose, R. J. (1999). Distribution and heritability of BMI in Finnish adolescents aged 16y and 17y: A study of 4884 twins and 2509 singletons. *International Journal of Obesity and Related Metabolic Disorders: Journal of the International Association for the Study of Obesity, 23,* 107–115. doi:10.1038/sj.ijo.0800767

Pigott, H. E., Leventhal, A. M., Alter, G. S., & Boren, J. J. (2010). Efficacy and effectiveness of antidepressants: Current status of research. *Psychotherapy and Psychosomatics, 79,* 267–279. doi:10.1159/000318293

Pilley, J. W., & Reid A. K. (2011). Border collie comprehends object names as verbal referents. *Behavioural Processes, 86,* 184–195.

Pillsbury, W. B. (1911). *The essentials of psychology.* New York, NY: Macmillian.

Pinel, J. P. J., Assanand, S., & Lehman, D. R. (2000). Hunger, eating, and ill health. *American Psychologist, 55,* 1105–1116. doi:10.1037//0003-066X.55.10.1105

Pinker, S. (1994). The language instinct: How the mind creates language. New York, NY: Harper Collins. doi:10.1016/j.cub.2004.10.009

Pinker, S. (1997). *How the mind works.* New York, NY: Norton.

Pinker, S. (1999). *Words and rules: The ingredients of language.* New York, NY: Basic Books.

Pinker, S. (2002). *The blank slate: The modern denial of human nature.* New York, NY: Viking.

Pinker, S., & Jackendoff, R. (2005). The faculty of language: What's special about it? *Cognition, 95,* 201–236. doi:10.1016/j.cognition.2004.08.004

Pinto, A., Liebowitz, M. R., Foa, E. B., & Simpson, H. B. (2011). Obsessive compulsive personality disorder as a predictor of exposure and ritual prevention outcome for obsessive compulsive disorder. *Behaviour Research and Therapy, 49,* 453–458. doi:10.1016/j.brat.2011.04.004

Plack, C. J., & Carlyon, R. P. (1995). Differences in frequency modulation detection and fundamental frequency discrimination between complex tones consisting of resolved and unresolved harmonics. *The Journal of the Acoustical Society of America, 98,* 1355–1364. doi:10.1121/1.413471

Plomin, R., & Daniels, D. (1987). Why are children in the same family so different from one another? *Behavioral and Brain Sciences, 10,* 1–16. doi:10.1017/S0140525X00055941

Pogue-Geile, M., & Yokley, J. (2010). Current research on the genetic contributors to schizophrenia. *Current Directions in Psychological Science, 19,* 214–219. doi:10.1177/0963721410378490

Pokorny, J., Lutze, M., Cao, D., & Zele, A. J. (2006). The color of night: Surface color perception under dim illuminations. *Visual Neuroscience, 23,* 525–530. doi:10.1017/S0952523806233492

Polikovsky, S. S., Kameda, Y., & Ohta, Y. (2010). *Facial micro-expressions recognition using high speed camera and 3D-gradient descriptor.* Paper presented at the 3rd International Conference on Imaging for Crime Detection and Prevention (ICDP-09), London, UK. Retrieved from http://kameda-lab.org/research/publication/2009/20091203_ICDP/200912_ICDP_senya_revised.pdf

Polivy, J., & Herman, C. P. (2002). Causes of eating disorders. *Annual Review of Psychology, 53,* 187–213. doi:10.1146/annurev.psych.53.100901.135103

Polkinghorne, D. E. (2005). Language and meaning: Data collection in qualitative research. *Journal of Counseling Psychology, 52,* 137–145. doi:10.1037/0022-0167.52.2.137

Poo, C., & Isaacson, J. (2009). Odor representations in olfactory cortex: "Sparse" coding, global inhibition, and oscillations. *Neuron, 62,* 850–861. doi:10.1016/j.neuron.2009.05.022.Odor

Portman, M. (2009). *Generalized anxiety disorder across the lifespan: An integrative approach.* New York, NY: Springer. doi:10.1007/978-0-387-89243-6

Posner, M. I. (1978). *Chronometric explorations of mind.* Hillsdale, N.J: Lawrence Erlbaum Associates

Posner, M. I., & Rothbart, M. K. (2007). Research on attention networks as a model for the integration of psychological science. *Annual Review of Psychology, 58,* 1–23. doi:10.1146/annurev.psych.58.110405.085516

Posner, M. I., & Rothbart, M. K. (2011). Brain states and hypnosis research. *Consciousness and Cognition, 20,* 325–327. doi:10.1016/j.concog.2009.11.008

Postmes, T., & Spears, R. (1998). Deindividuation and antinormative behavior: A meta-analysis. *Psychological Bulletin, 123,* 238–259. doi:10.1037//0033-2909.123.3.238

Potter, J., & Hepburn, A. (2005). Qualitative interviews in psychology: Problems and possibilities. *Qualitative Research in Psychology, 2,* 281–307. doi:10.1191/1478088705qp045oa

Powell, R. A., Digdon, N., Harris, B., & Smithson, C. (2014). Correcting the record on Watson, Raynor, and Little Albert: Albert Barger as "psychology's lost boy." *American Psychologist, 69,* 600–611.

Poythress, N. G., Edens, J. F., Skeem, J. L., Lilienfeld, S. O., Douglas, K. S., Frick, P. J., . . . & Wang, T. (2010). Identifying subtypes among offenders with antisocial personality disorder: A cluster-analytic study. *Journal of Abnormal Psychology, 119,* 389–400. doi:10.1037/a0018611

Presseau, J., Tait, R. I., Johnston, D. W., Francis, J. J., & Sniehotta, F. F. (2013). Goal conflict and goal facilitation as predictors of daily accelerometer-assessed physical activity. *Health Psychology, 32,* 1179–1187. doi:10.1037/a0029430

Preti, A., Girolamo, G. D., Vilagut, G., Alonso, J., Graaf, R. D., Bruffaerts, R., . . . & Morosini, P. (2009). The epidemiology of eating disorders in six European countries: Results of the ESEMeD-WMH project. *Journal of Psychiatric Research, 43,* 1125–1132. doi:10.1016/j.jpsychires.2009.04.003

Pribram, K. H., & Gill, M. M. (1976). *Freud's 'Project' reassessed: Preface to contemporary cognitive theory and neuropsychology.* New York, NY: Basic Books.

Prime Time: Carrie Fisher interview. (2000, December 21). Retrieved from http://abcnews.go.com/Primetime/story?id=132315

Prinz, J. J. (2012). *The conscious brain: How attention engenders experience.* Oxford, U. K.: Oxford University Press. doi:10.1093/acprof:oso/9780195314595.001.0001

Punch, K. F. (2003). *Survey research: The basics.* Thousand Oaks, CA: Sage.

Quevedo, K., Smith, T., Donzella, B., Schunk, E., & Gunnar, M. (2010). The startle response: Developmental effects and a paradigm for children and adults. *Developmental Psychobiology, 52,* 78–89. doi:10.1002/dev.20415

Quinn, D. M., & Spencer, S. J. (2001). The interference of stereotype threat with women's generation of mathematical problem-solving strategies. *Journal of Social Issues, 57*, 55–71. doi:10.1111/0022-4537.00201

Rabagliati, A. (1881). Critical digests and notices of books. *Brain, 4*, 100–110. doi:10.1093/brain/4.1.100

Rabinowitz, J., Levine, S. Z., Garibaldi, G., Bugarski-Kirola, D., Berardo, C. G., & Kapur, S. (2012). Negative symptoms have greater impact on functioning than positive symptoms in schizophrenia: Analysis of CATIE data. *Schizophrenia Research, 137*, 147–150. doi:10.1016/j.schres.2012.01.015

Rachlin, H. (1976). *Behavior and learning.* San Francisco, CA: Freeman.

Raine, A., & Yang, Y. (2006). Neural foundations to moral reasoning and antisocial behavior. *Social Cognitive and Affective Neuroscience, 1*, 203–213. doi:10.1093/scan/nsl033

Rama. (1998). *Meditation and its practice* (Revised). Honesdale, PA: Himalayan Institute Press.

Ramachandran, V. W., & Hirstein, W. (1998). The perception of phantom limbs: The D. O. Hebb lecture. *Brain, 121*, 1603–1630. doi:10.1093/brain/121.9.1603

Rammstedt, B., & John, O. P. (2007). Measuring personality in one minute or less: A 10-item short version of the Big Five Inventory in English and German. *Journal of Research in Personality, 41*, 203–212. doi:10.1016/j.jrp.2006.02.001

Ramsden, S., Richardson, F. M., Josse, G., Thomas, M. S., Ellis, C., Shakeshaft, C., . . . & Price, C. J. (2011). Verbal and non-verbal intelligence changes in the teenage brain. *Nature, 479*, 113–116. doi:10.1038/nature10514

Randolph-Seng, B., & Nielsen, M. E. (2007). Honesty: One effect of primed religious representations. *The International Journal for the Psychology of Religion, 17*, 303–315. doi:10.1080/10508610701572812

Raney, G. E., Campbell, S. J., & Bovee, J. C. (2014). Using eye movements to evaluate the cognitive processes involved in text comprehension. *Journal of Visualized Experiments, 83*, e50780. doi:10.3791/50780

Rankin, C. H. (2002). A bite to remember. *Science, 296*, 1624–1625. doi:10.1126/science.1072683

Rasch, R., & Plomp, R. (1999). The perception of musical tones. In D. Deutsch (Ed.), *The psychology of music* (2nd ed., pp. 89–112). San Diego, CA: Academic Press. doi:10.1016/B978-012213564-4/50005-6

Rauschecker, J. P., & Tian, B. (2000). Mechanisms and streams for processing of "what" and "where" in auditory cortex. *Proceedings of the National Academy of Sciences of the United States of America, 97*, 11800–11806. doi:10.1073/pnas.97.22.11800

Raz, A., Fan, J., & Posner, M. I. (2005). Hypnotic suggestion reduces conflict in the human brain. *Proceedings of the National Academy of Sciences, 102*, 9978–9983. doi:10.1073/pnas.0503064102

Raz, A., & Shapiro, T. (2002). Hypnosis and neuroscience: A cross talk between clinical and cognitive research. *Archives of General Psychiatry, 59*, 85–90. doi:10.1001/archpsyc.59.1.85

Rebuschat, J., & Williams, J. N. (Eds.). (2012). *Statistical learning and language acquisition.* Berlin, Germany: Mouton de Gruyter.

Ree, M. J., & Earles, J. A. (1992). Intelligence is the best predictor of job performance. *Current Directions in Psychological Science, 1*, 86–89. doi:10.1111/1467-8721.ep10768746

Reep, R. L., Finlay, B. L., & Darlington, R. B. (2007). The limbic system in Mammalian brain evolution. *Brain, Behavior and Evolution, 70*, 57–70. doi:10.1159/000101491

Regier, T., Kay, P., & Cook, R. S. (2005). Focal colors are universal after all. *Proceedings of the National Academy of Sciences of the United States of America, 102*, 8386–8391. doi:10.1073/pnas.0503281102

Reid, R. (2011, May 6). Travel etiquette 101: Body language. *BBC Travel Tips.* Retrieved from http://www.bbc.com/travel/feature/20110405-travel-etiquette-101-body-language

Reinhardt-Rutland, A. H. (1998). Increasing-loudness aftereffect following decreasing-intensity adaptation: Spectral dependence in interotic and monotic testing. *Perception, 27*, 473–482. doi:10.1068/p270473

Reis, H. T., & Patrick, B. C. (1996). Attachment and intimacy: Component processes. In E. T. Higgins & A. W. Kruglanski (Eds.), *Social Psychology: Handbook of Basic Principles* (pp. 523–563). New York, NY: Guilford Press.

Reiss, D., & Marino, L. (2001). Mirror self-recognition in the bottlenose dolphin: A case of cognitive convergence. *Proceedings of the National Academy of Sciences of the United States of America, 98*, 5937–5942. doi:10.1073/pnas.101086398

Repovš, G., & Baddeley, A. (2006). The multi-component model of working memory: Explorations in experimental cognitive psychology. *Neuroscience, 139*, 5–21. doi:10.1016/j.neuroscience.2005.12.061

Rescorla, R. A. (1988). Pavlovian conditioning: It's not what you think it is. *American Psychologist, 43*, 151–160. doi:10.1037/0003-066X.43.3.151

Rescorla, R. A. (2004). Spontaneous recovery. *Learning & Memory, 11*, 501–509. doi:10.1101/lm.77504

Rescorla, R., & Wagner, A. (1972). A theory of Pavlovian conditioning: Variations in the effectiveness of reinforcement and nonreinforcement. In A. H. Black & W. F. Prokasy (Eds.), *Classical conditioning II: Current research and theory* (pp. 64–99). New York, NY: Appleton-Century-Crofts.

Revonsuo, A. (2000). The reinterpretation of dreams: An evolutionary hypothesis of the function of dreaming. *Behavioral and Brain Sciences, 23*, 877–901. doi:10.1017/S0140525X00004015

Rhee, S. H., & Waldman, I. D. (2002). Genetic and environmental influences on antisocial behavior: A meta-analysis of twin and adoption studies. *Psychological Bulletin, 128*, 490–529. doi:10.1037/0033-2909.128.3.490

Ribeiro, J. A., & Sebastião, A. M. (2010). Caffeine and adenosine. *Journal of Alzheimers Disease, 20*, S3–15. doi:10.3233/JAD-2010-1379

Richardson, J. T. E. (2003). Howard Andrew Knox and the origins of performance testing on Ellis Island, 1912–1916. *History of Psychology, 6*, 143–170.

Richardson, R., Williams, C., & Riccio, D. C. (1984). Stimulus generalization of conditioned taste aversion in rats. *Behavioral and Neural Biology, 41*, 41–53. doi:10.1016/S0163-1047(84)90706-4

Ridley, M. (2003). *Nature via nurture: Genes, experience, & what makes us human.* New York, NY: Harper Collins.

Rieke, F., & Baylor, D. A. (1998). Origin of reproducibility in the responses of retinal rods to single photons. *Biophysical Journal, 75*, 1836–1857. doi:S0006-3495(98)77625-8

Rieke, F., Warland, D., De Ruyter van Steveninck, R., & Bialek, W. (1997). *Spikes: Exploring the neural code.* Cambridge, MA: The MIT Press.

Riley, B. (2011). Genetic studies of schizophrenia. In J. D. Clelland (Ed.), *Genomics, Proteomics, and the Nervous System* (pp. 333–380). Advances in neurobiology 2. New York, NY: Springer.

Riolo, S. A., Nguyen, T. A., Greden, J. F., & King, C. A. (2005). Prevalence of depression by race/ethnicity: Findings from the National Health and Nutrition Examination Survey III. *American Journal of Public Health, 95*, 998–1000. doi:10.2105/AJPH.2004.047225

Ripley, A. (2008). *The unthinkable: Who survives when disaster strikes—and why.* New York, NY: Crown Publishing.

Ritchey, M., LaBar, K. S., & Cabeza, R. (2011). Level of processing modulates the neural correlates of emotional memory formation. *Journal of Cognitive Neuroscience, 23*, 757–771. doi:10.1162/jocn.2010.21487

Ritchie, S., Wiseman, R., & French, C. (2012). Failing the future: Three unsuccessful attempts to replicate Bem's "Retroactive facilitation of recall" effect. *PLoS ONE, 7*, e33423. doi:10.1371/journal.pone.0033423

Ritschel, T., & Eisemann, E. (2012). A computational model of afterimages. *Computer Graphics Forum, 31,* 529–534. doi:10.1111/j.1467-8659.2012.03053.x

Rivière, S., Challet, L., Fluegge, D., Spehr, M., & Rodriguez, I. (2009). Formyl peptide receptor-like proteins are a novel family of vomeronasal chemosensors. *Nature, 459,* 574–577. doi:10.1038/nature08029

Rizzo, A., John, B., Newman, B., Williams, J., Hartholt, A., Lethin, C., & Buckwalter, J. G. (2013). Virtual reality as a tool for delivering PTSD exposure therapy and stress resilience training. *Military Behavioral Health, 1,* 52–58. doi:10.1080/21635781.2012.721064

Rizzolatti, G., Fogassi, L., & Gallese, V. (2001). Neurophysiological mechanisms underlying the understanding and imitation of action. *Nature Reviews Neuroscience, 2,* 661–670. doi:10.1038/35090060

Roberts, N. A., Levenson, R. W., & Gross, J. J. (2008). Cardiovascular costs of emotion suppression cross ethnic lines. *International Journal of Psychophysiology, 70,* 82–87. doi:10.1016/j.ijpsycho.2008.06.003

Robie, C., Brown, D. J., & Beaty, J. C. (2007). Do people fake on personality inventories? A verbal protocol analysis. *Journal of Business and Psychology, 21,* 489–509. doi:10.1007/s10869-007-9038-9

Robins, R. W., Hendin, H. M., & Trzesniewski, K. H. (2001). Measuring global self-esteem: Construct validation of a single-item measure and the Rosenberg Self-Esteem Scale. *Personality and Social Psychology Bulletin, 27,* 151–161. doi:10.1177/0146167201272002

Robins, R. W., & Trzesniewski, K. H. (2005). Self-esteem development across the lifespan. *Current Directions in Psychological Science, 14,* 158–162. doi:10.1111/j.0963-7214.2005.00353.x

Robinson, D. K. (2002). Reaction-time experiments in Wundt's institute and beyond. In R. Rieber & D. Robinson (Eds.), *Wilhelm Wundt in history: The making of a scientific psychology* (pp. 161–204). New York, NY: Kluwer.

Röder, B., Ley, P., Shenoy, B.H., Kekunnaya, R., & Bottari, D. (2013). Sensitive periods for the functional specialization of the neural system for human face processing. *Proceedings of the National Academy of Sciences, 110,* 16760–16765. doi:10.1073/pnas.1309963110

Rodrigues, S. M., LeDoux, J. E., & Sapolsky, R. M. (2009). The influence of stress hormones on fear circuitry. *Annual Review of Neuroscience, 32,* 289–313. doi:10.1146/annurev.neuro.051508.135620

Roediger, H. L. (1980). Memory metaphors in cognitive psychology. *Memory & Cognition, 8,* 231–246. doi:10.3758/BF03197611

Roediger, H. L., & McDermott, K. B. (1995). Creating false memories: Remembering words not presented in lists. *Journal of Experimental Psychology: Learning, Memory, and Cognition, 21,* 803–814. doi:10.1037/0278-7393.21.4.803

Rogers, C. R. (1951). *Client-centered therapy: Its current practice, implications, and theory.* Boston, MA: Houghton Mifflin Harcourt.

Rogers, C. R. (1961). *On becoming a person: A therapist's view of psychotherapy.* Boston, MA: Houghton Mifflin.

Rogers, C. R., & Farson, R. E. (1987). Active listening. In R. G. Newman, M. A. Danzinger, & M. Cohen (Eds.), *Communication in Business Today.* Washington, DC: Heath and Co.

Rogers, G., Elston, J., Garside, R., Roome, C., Taylor, R., Younger, P., . . . & Somerville, M. (2009). The harmful health effects of recreational ecstasy: A systematic review of observational evidence. *Health Technology Assessment, 13,* xii–338. doi:10.3310/hta13060

Rogers, T. T., & McClelland, J. L. (2004). *Semantic cognition: A parallel distributed processing approach.* Cambridge, MA: MIT Press.

Rogoff, B. (1990). *Apprenticeship in thinking: Cognitive development in social context.* New York, NY: Oxford University Press.

Romberg, A. R., & Saffran, J. R. (2010). Statistical learning and language acquisition. *Wiley Interdisciplinary Reviews: Cognitive Science, 1,* 906–914.

Romero-Corral, A., Caples, S. M., Lopez-Jimenez, F., & Somers, V. K. (2010). Interactions between obesity and obstructive sleep apnea: Implications for treatment. *CHEST Journal, 137,* 711–719. doi:10.1378/chest.09-0360

Rorden, C., & Karnath, H.-O. (2004). Using human brain lesions to infer function: A relic from a past era in the fMRI age? *Nature Reviews Neuroscience, 5,* 813–819. doi:10.1038/nrn1521

Rosch, E. (1978). Principles of categorization. In E. Rosch, & B. Lloyd (Eds.), *Cognition and categorization.* Hillsdale, NJ: Erlbaum.

Rose, A. J., & Rudolph, K. D. (2006). A review of sex differences in peer relationship processes: Potential trade-offs for the emotional and behavioral development of girls and boys. *Psychological Bulletin, 132,* 98–131. doi:10.1037/0033-2909.132.1.98

Rose, J. D. (2002). The neurobehavioral nature of fishes and the question of awareness and pain. *Reviews in Fisheries Science, 10,* 1–38. doi:10.1080/20026491051668

Rosenberg, M. (1965). *Society and the adolescent self-image.* Princeton, NJ: Princeton University Press.

Rosenblatt, P. C. (1993). Grief: The social context of private feelings. In M. S. Stroebe, W. Stroebe, & R. O. Hansson (Eds.), *Handbook of Bereavement* (pp. 102–111). New York, NY: Cambridge University Press. doi:10.1017/CBO9780511664076.008

Rosenthal, N. (2009). Issues for DSM-V: Seasonal affective disorder and seasonality. *American Journal of Psychiatry, 166,* 852–853. doi:10.1176/appi.ajp.2009.09020188

Ross, L. (1977). The intuitive psychologist and his shortcomings: Distortions in the attribution process. In L. Berkowitz (Ed.), *Advances in Experimental Social Psychology* (Vol. 10). New York, NY: Academic Press.

Ross, L. D., Amabile, T. M., & Steinmetz, J. L. (1977). Social roles, social control, and biases in social-perception processes. *Journal of Personality and Social Psychology, 35,* 485–494. doi:10.1037/0022-3514.35.7.485

Rothbart, M. K. (2012). Advances in temperament: History, concepts, and measures. In M. Zentner, & R. L Shiner (Eds.), *Handbook of Temperament* (pp. 3–20). New York, NY: Guilford Press.

Rothbart, M. K., Ellis, L. K., Rueda, R. M., & Posner, M. I. (2003). Developing mechanisms of temperamental effortful control. *Journal of Personality, 71,* 1113–1144. doi:10.1111/1467-6494.7106009

Rothbart, M. K., Posner, M. I., & Kieras, J. (2006). Temperament, attention, and the development of self-regulation. In K. McCartney, & D. Phillips (Eds.), *Blackwell Handbook of Early Childhood Development* (pp. 338–357). Blackwell handbooks of developmental psychology. Malden, MA: Blackwell Publishing. doi:10.1002/9780470757703.ch17

Rothermund, K., & Brandstädter, J. (2003). Coping with deficits and losses in later life: From compensatory action to accommodation. *Psychology and Aging, 18,* 896–905. doi:10.1037/0882-7974.18.4.896

Rozin, P., Dow, S., Moscovitch, M., & Rajaram, S. (1998). What causes humans to begin and end a meal? A role for memory for what has been eaten, as evidenced by a study of multiple meal eating in amnesic patients. *Psychological Science, 9,* 392–396. doi:10.1111/1467-9280.00073

Rubin, D. C. (1995). *Memory in oral traditions: The cognitive psychology of counting-out rhymes, ballads, and epics.* New York, NY: Oxford University Press.

Rudgley, R. (1995). The archaic use of hallucinogens in Europe: An archaeology of altered states. *Addiction, 90,* 163–164. doi:10.1111/j.1360-0443.1995.tb01023.x

Rudorfer, M. V., Henry, M. E., & Sackeim, H. A. (2003). Electroconvulsive therapy. In A. Tasman, J. Kay, J. A. Lieberman (Eds.), *Psychiatry* (2nd ed., pp. 1865–1901). Chichester, England: John Wiley & Sons.

Rumelhart, D. E., McClelland, J. L., & PDP Research Group. (1986). *Parallel distributed processing: Explorations in the microstructure of cognition* (Vols. 1 and 2). Cambridge, MA: MIT Press.

Russell, E. (2011). *Evolutionary history: Uniting history and biology to understand life on earth.* New York, NY: Cambridge University Press. doi:10.1017/CBO9780511974267

Russell, J. A. (2003). Core affect and the psychological construction of emotion. *Psychological Review, 110,* 145–172. doi:10.1037/0033-295X.110.1.145

Ruthazer, E. S., & Aizenman, C. D. (2010). Learning to see: Patterned visual activity and the development of visual function. *Trends in Neurosciences, 33,* 183–192. doi:10.1016/j.tins.2010.01.003

Rutherford, B. R., Wager, T. D., & Roose, S. P. (2010). Expectancy and the treatment of depression: A review of experimental methodology and effects on patient outcome. *Current Psychiatry Reviews, 6,* 1–10. doi:10.2174/157340010790596571

Ryan, R. M., & Deci, E. L. (2000). Self-determination theory and the facilitation of intrinsic motivation, social development, and well-being. *American Psychologist, 55,* 68–78. doi:10.1037/0003-066X.55.1.68

Saavedra, L. M., & Silverman, W. K. (2002). Case study: Disgust and a specific phobia of buttons. *Journal of the American Academy of Child & Adolescent Psychiatry, 41,* 1376–1379. doi:10.1097/00004583-200211000-00020

Sacks, O. (2013, February 21). Speak, memory. *The New York Review of Books.* Retrieved from http://www.nybooks.com/articles/archives/2013/feb/21/speak-memory

Saffran, J. R. (2003). Statistical language learning: Mechanisms and constraints. *Current Directions in Psychological Science, 12,* 110–114. doi:10.1111/1467-8721.01243

Saha, S., Chant, D., Welham, J., & McGrath, J. (2005). A systematic review of the prevalence of schizophrenia. *PLoS Medicine, 2,* e141. doi:10.1371/journal.pmed.0020141

Saks, E. R. (1991). Multiple personality disorder and criminal responsibility. *UC Davis Law Review, 25,* 383–461.

Saks, E. R. (2007). *The center cannot hold: My journey through madness.* New York, NY: Hyperion.

Salmela-Aro, K. (2009). Personal goals and well-being during critical life transitions: The four C's—Channelling, choice, co-agency and compensation. *Advances in Life Course Research, 14,* 63–73. doi:10.1016/j.alcr.2009.03.003

Salmon, W. C. (1989). Four decades of scientific explanation. In P. Kitcher & W. C. Salmon (Eds.), *Minnesota studies in the philosophy of science, Vol. XIII. Scientific Explanation* (pp. 3–219). Minneapolis: University of Minnesota Press.

Sameroff, A. (1994). Developmental systems and family functioning. In R. D. Parke, & S. G. Kellam (Eds.), *Exploring Family Relationships with Other Social Contexts* (pp. 199–214). Hillsdale, NJ: Lawrence Erlbaum Associates.

Sánchez-Meca, J., Rosa-Alcázar, A. I., Marín-Martínez, F., & Gómez-Conesa, A. (2010). Psychological treatment of panic disorder with or without agoraphobia: A meta-analysis. *Clinical Psychology Review, 30,* 37–50. doi:10.1016/j.cpr.2009.08.011

Sandell, R., Blomberg, J., Lazar, A., Carlsson, J., Broberg, J., & Schubert, J. (2000). Varieties of long-term outcome among patients in psychoanalysis and long-term psychotherapy: A review of findings in the Stockholm Outcome of Psychoanalysis and Psychotherapy Project (STOPP). *The International Journal of Psychoanalysis, 81,* 921–942. doi:10.1516/0020757001600291

Sanders, J. L., & Newman, A. B. (2013). Telomere length in epidemiology: A biomarker of aging, age-related disease, both, or neither? *Epidemiologic Reviews, 35,* 112–131. doi:10.1093/epirev/mxs008

Saneyoshi, A., Niimi, R., Suetsugu, T., Kaminaga, T., & Yokosawa, K. (2011). Iconic memory and parietofrontal network: fMRI study using temporal integration. *Neuroreport, 22,* 515–519. doi:10.1097/WNR.0b013e328348aa0c

Sanislow, C. A., Bartolini, E. E., & Zoloth, E. C. (2012). Avoidant personality disorder. In V. S. Ramachandran (Ed.), *Encyclopedia of Human Behavior* (2nd ed., pp. 257–266). San Diego, CA: Academic Press. doi:10.1016/B978-0-12-375000-6.00049-5

Sansone, C., & Thoman, D. B. (2005). Interest as the missing motivator in self-regulation. *European Psychologist, 10,* 175–186. doi:10.1027/1016-9040.10.3.175

Sapolsky, R. M. (2004). Mothering style and methylation. *Nature Neuroscience, 7,* 791–792. doi:10.1038/nn0804-791

Sarbin, T. R. (1950). Contributions to role-taking theory: I. Hypnotic behavior. *Psychological Review, 57,* 255–270. doi:10.1037/h0062218

Saroglou, V., & Fiasse, L. (2003). Birth order, personality, and religion: A study among young adults from a three-sibling family. *Personality and Individual Differences, 35,* 19–29. doi:10.1016/S0191-8869(02)00137-X

Sarter, M., Gehring, W. J., & Kozak, R. (2006). More attention must be paid: The neurobiology of attentional effort. *Brain Research Reviews, 51,* 145–160. doi:10.1016/j.brainresrev.2005.11.002

Saudino, K. J. (1997). Moving beyond the heritability question: New directions in behavioral genetic studies of personality. *Current Directions in Psychological Science, 6,* 86–90. doi:10.1111/1467-8721.ep11512809

Saunders, P. L., & Chester, A. (2008). Shyness and the internet: Social problem or panacea? *Computers in Human Behavior, 24,* 2649–2658. doi:10.1016/j.chb.2008.03.005

Sauter, D. A., Eisner, F., Ekman, P., & Scott, S. K. (2010). Cross-cultural recognition of basic emotions through nonverbal emotional vocalizations. *Proceedings of the National Academy of Sciences of the United States of America, 107,* 2408–2412. doi:10.1073/pnas.0908239106

Savani, K., Markus, H. R., & Conner, A. L. (2008). Let your preference be your guide? Preferences and choices are more tightly linked for North Americans than for Indians. *Journal of Personality and Social Psychology, 95,* 861–876. doi:10.1037/a0011618

Savani, K., Markus, H. R., Naidu, N. V. R., Kumar, S., & Berlia, V. (2010). What counts as a choice? U.S. Americans are more likely than Indians to construe actions as choices. *Psychological Science, 21,* 391–398. doi:10.1177/0956797609359908

Savastano, H. I., & Miller, R. R. (1998). Time as content in Pavlovian conditioning. *Behavioural Processes, 44,* 147–162. doi:10.1016/S0376-6357(98)00046-1

Savin-Williams, R. C., Joyner, K., & Rieger, G. (2012). Prevalence and stability of self-reported sexual orientation identity during young adulthood. *Archives of Sexual Behavior, 41,* 103–110. doi:10.1007/s10508-012-9913-y

Saxe, R., & Wexler, A. (2005). Making sense of another mind: The role of the right temporo-parietal junction. *Neuropsychologia, 43,* 1391–1399. doi:10.1016/j.neuropsychologia.2005.02.013

Schachter, S., & Singer, J. (1962). Cognitive, social, and physiological determinants of emotional state. *Psychological Review, 69,* 379–399. doi:10.1037/h0046234

Schachtman, T. R., & Reilly, S. (2011). *Associate learning and conditioning theory: Human and non-human applications.* New York, NY: Oxford University Press. doi:10.1093/acprof:oso/9780199735969.001.0001

Schacter, D. L. (1987). Implicit expressions of memory in organic amnesia: Learning of new facts and associations. *Human Neurobiology, 6,* 107–118.

Schacter, D. L. (1996). *Searching for memory: The brain, the mind, and the past.* New York, NY: Basic Books.

Schaffhausen, J. (2011, April 26). The day his world stood still: The strange story of "H. M." *Brain Connection.* Retrieved from http://brainconnection.positscience.com/the-day-his-world-stood-still/

Schaller, M., Park, J. H., & Kenrick, D. T. (2007). Human evolution and social cognition. In R. I. M. Dunbar & L. Barrett (Eds.), *Oxford Handbook of Evolutionary Psychology* (pp. 491–504). Oxford, U. K.: Oxford University Press.

Scheef, L., Jankowski, J., Daamen, M., Weyer, G., Klingenberg, M., Renner, J., . . . & Boecker, H. (2012). An fMRI study on the acute effects of exercise on pain processing in trained athletes. *Pain, 153,* 1702–1714. doi:10.1016/j.pain.2012.05.008

Scheibe, K. E. (2000). *The drama of everyday life.* Cambridge, MA: Harvard University Press.

Scheibe, K. E. (2000). *The Drama of Everyday Life.* Harvard University Press, Boston, MA.

Schein, E., & Bernstein, P. (2007). *Identical strangers: a memoir of twins separated and reunited.* New York: Random House

Scherer, K. R. (2004). Which emotions can be induced by music? What are the underlying mechanisms? And how can we measure them? *Journal of New Music Research, 33,* 239–251. doi:10.1080/0929821042000317822

Scherer, K. R., Schorr, A., & Johnstone, T. (Eds.). (2001). *Appraisal processes in emotion: Theory, methods, research.* Series in affective science. New York, NY: Oxford University Press.

Schifano F., & Corkery, J. (2008). Cocaine/crack cocaine consumption, treatment demand, seizures, related offences, prices, average purity levels and deaths in the UK (1990–2004). *Journal of Psychopharmacology, 22,* 71–79. doi:10.1177/0269881107079170

Schiffman, S., & Pasternak, M. (1979). Decreased discrimination of food odors in the elderly. *Journal of Gerontology, 34,* 73–79. doi:10.1093/geronj/34.1.73

Schiller, D., Monfils, M. H., Raio, C. M., Johnson, D. C., LeDoux, J. E., & Phelps, E. A. (2010). Preventing the return of fear in humans using reconsolidation update mechanisms. *Nature, 463,* 49–53. doi:10.1038/nature08637

Schiller, F. (1979). *Paul Broca, founder of French anthropology, explorer of the brain.* Berkeley, CA: University of California Press.

Schiller, F. (1992). *Paul Broca: Explorer of the brain.* Oxford, England: Oxford University Press.

Schizophrenia facts and statistics. (1996–2010). *The internet mental health initiative.* Retrieved from http://www.schizophrenia.com/szfacts.htm

Schizophrenia Psychiatric Genome-Wide Association Study (GWAS) Consortium. (2011). Genome-wide association study identifies five new schizophrenia loci. *Nature Genetics, 43,* 969–976. doi:10.1038/ng.940

Schlesinger, M., & Casey, P. (2003). Where infants look when impossible things happen: Simulating and testing a gaze-direction model. *Connection Science, 15,* 271–280. doi:10.1080/09540090310001655093

Schmitz, T. W., & Johnson, S. C. (2007). Relevance to self: A brief review and framework of neural systems underlying appraisal. *Neuroscience and Biobehavioral Reviews, 31,* 585–596. doi:10.1016/j.neubiorev.2006.12.003

Schneider, D., Slaughter, V. P., Bayliss, A. P., & Dux, P. E. (2013). A temporally sustained implicit theory of mind deficit in autism spectrum disorders. *Cognition, 129,* 410–417. doi:10.1016/j.cognition.2013.08.004

Schnieder, S. (2007). Daniel Dennett on the nature of consciousness. In M. Velmans & S. Schneider (Eds.), *The Blackwell companion to consciousness* (pp. 313–324). Malden, MA: Blackwell. doi:10.1002/9780470751466.ch25

Schnurr, P. P., Friedman, M. J., Engel, C. C., Foa, E. B., Shea, M. T., Chow, B. K., . . . & Bernardy, N. (2007). Cognitive behavioral therapy for posttraumatic stress disorder in women: A randomized controlled trial. *Journal of the American Medical Association, 297,* 820–830. doi:10.1001/jama.297.8.820

Schreiber, F. R. (1973). *Sybil: The true story of a woman possessed by 16 different personalities.* Chicago, IL: Henry Regnery.

Schultz, S. K., Miller, D. D., Oliver, S. E., Arndt, S., Flaum, M., & Andreasen, N. C. (1997). The life course of schizophrenia: Age and symptom dimensions. *Schizophrenia Research, 23,* 15–23. doi:10.1016/S0920-9964(96)00087-4

Schultz, W. (2006). Behavioral theories and the neurophysiology of reward. *Annual Review of Psychology, 57,* 87–115. doi:10.1146/annurev.psych.56.091103.070229

Schwartz, N., Schohl, A., & Ruthazer, E. S. (2011). Activity-dependent transcription of BDNF enhances visual acuity during development. *Neuron, 70,* 455–467. doi:10.1016/j.neuron.2011.02.055

Schwartz, S. (2004). What dreaming can reveal about cognitive and brain functions during sleep: A lexico-statistical analysis of dream reports. *Psychologica Belgica, 44,* 5–42.

Schwarz, N., & Clore, G. (1983). Mood, misattribution, and judgments of well-being: Informative and directive functions of affective states. *Journal of Personality and Social Psychology, 45,* 513–523. doi:10.1037/0022-3514.45.3.513

Schwarz, N., & Clore, G. L. (2007). Feelings and phenomenal experiences. In A. Kruglanski & E. T. Higgins (Eds.), *Social Psychology: Handbook of Basic Principles* (2nd ed., pp. 385–407). New York, NY: Guilford.

Schwarz, S., Hassebrauck, M., & Dörfler, R. (2010). Let us talk about sex: Prototype and personal templates. *Personal Relationships, 17,* 533–555. doi:10.1111/j.1475-6811.2010.01289.x

Schweinhart, L. J., Montie, J., Xiang, Z., Barnett, W. S., Belfield, C. R., & Nores, M. (2005). *Lifetime effects: The HighScope Perry Preschool Study through age 40* (Monographs of the HighScope Educational Research Foundation, 14). Ypsilanti, MI: HighScope Press. Retrieved from http://www.highscope.org/Content.asp?ContentId=219

Scorolli, C., Ghirlanda, S., Enquist, M., Zattoni, S., & Jannini, E. A. (2007). Relative prevalence of different fetishes. *International Journal of Impotence Research, 19,* 432–437. doi:10.1038/sj.ijir.3901547

Scott, R. A. (2003). *The gothic enterprise: A guide to understanding the medieval cathedral.* Berkeley, CA: University of California Press.

Scoville, W. B., & Milner, B. (1957). Loss of recent memory after bilateral hippocampal lesions. *Journal of Neurology, Neurosurgery, and Psychiatry, 20,* 11–21. doi:10.1136/jnnp.20.1.11

Seabright, P. (2004). *The company of strangers: A natural history of economic life.* Princeton, NJ: Princeton University Press.

Searle, J. R. (1980). Minds, brains, and programs. *Behavioral and Brain Sciences, 3,* 417–424. doi:10.1017/S0140525X00005756

Searle, J. R. (1998). How to study consciousness scientifically. *Philosophical Transactions of the Royal Society of London. Series B, Biological Sciences, 353,* 1935–1942. doi:10.1098/rstb.1998.0346

Seeley, W. W., Menon, V., Schatzberg, A. F., Keller, J., Glover, G. H., Kenna, H., . . . & Greicius, M. D. (2007). Dissociable intrinsic connectivity networks for salience processing and executive control. *The Journal of Neuroscience, 27,* 2349–2356. doi:10.1523/JNEUROSCI.5587-06.2007

Segal, M. W. (1974). Alphabet and attraction: An unobtrusive measure of the effect of propinquity in a field setting. *Journal of Personality and Social Psychology, 30,* 654–657. doi:10.1037/h0037446

Segerstrom, S. C., & Miller, G. E. (2004). Psychological stress and the human immune system: A meta-analytic study of 30 years of inquiry. *Psychological Bulletin, 130,* 601–630. doi:10.1037/0033-2909.130.4.601

Segev, E., & Baram-Tsabari, A. (2012). Seeking science information online: Data mining Google to better understand the roles of the media and the education system. *Public Understanding of Science, 21,* 813–829. doi:10.1177/0963662510387560

Sekuler, R., Watamaniuk, S. N. J., & Blake, R. (2002). Visual motion perception. In H. Pashler (Series Ed.) & S. Yantis (Vol. Ed.), *Stevens' Handbook of Experimental Psychology: Vol. 1. Sensation and perception* (3rd ed., pp. 121–176). New York, NY: Wiley.

Sela, L., & Sobel, N. (2010). Human olfaction: A constant state of change-blindness. *Experimental Brain Research, 205,* 13–29. doi:10.1007/s00221-010-2348-6

Seligman, M. E. (1970). On the generality of the laws of learning. *Psychological Review, 77,* 406-418. doi:10.1037/h0029790

Seligman, M. E. P. (1975). *Helplessness: On depression, development, and death.* San Francisco, CA: W. H. Freeman.

Seligman, M. E., & Csikszentmihalyi, M. (2000). Positive psychology: An introduction. *American Psychologist, 55,* 5–14. doi:10.1037//0003-066X.55.1.5

Seligson, J. L., Huebner, E. S. & Valois, R. F. (2003). Preliminary validation of the Brief Multidimensional Students' Life Satisfaction Scale (BMSLSS). *Social Indicators Research, 61,* 121–145. doi:10.1023/A:1021326822957

Sellers, R. M., Smith, M. A., Shelton, J. N., Rowley, S. A., & Chavous, T. M. (1998). Multidimensional model of racial identity: A reconceptualization of African American racial identity. *Personality and Social Psychology Review, 2,* 18–39. doi:10.1207/s15327957pspr0201_2

Selye, H. (1950). *The physiology and pathology of exposure to stress.* Montreal: Acta.

Semendeferi, K., Lu, A., Schenker, N., & Damasio, H. (2002). Humans and great apes share a large frontal cortex. *Nature Neuroscience, 5,* 272–276. doi:10.1038/nn814

Sen, A. (2012). Socioeconomic status and mental health: What is the causal relationship? *Acta Psychiatrica Scandinavica, 125,* 187–188. doi:10.1111/j.1600-0447.2011.01829.x

Shah, P., & Mountain, D. (2007). The medical model is dead—Long live the medical model. *The British Journal of Psychiatry, 191,* 375–377. doi:10.1192/bjp.bp.107.037242

Shahidullah, S., & Hepper, P. G. (1994). Frequency discrimination by the fetus. *Early Human Development, 36,* 13–26. doi:10.1016/0378-3782(94)90029-9

Shamay-Tsoory, S. G., Harari, H., Aharon-Peretz, J., & Levkovitz, Y. (2010). The role of the orbitofrontal cortex in affective theory of mind deficits in criminal offenders with psychopathic tendencies. *Cortex, 46,* 668–677. doi:10.1016/j.cortex.2009.04.008

Shapley, R., & Hawken, M. J. (2011). Color in the cortex: Single- and double-opponent cells. *Vision Research, 51,* 701–717. doi:10.1016/j.visres.2011.02.012

Sharpe, L. T., Stockman, A., Jägle, H., & Nathans, J. (1999). Opsin genes, cone photopigments, color vision, and color blindness. In K. R. Gegenfurtner & L. T. Sharpe (Eds.), *Color Vision: From Genes to Perception* (pp. 3–51). Cambridge, UK: Cambridge University Press.

Shatz, C. J. (1992) The developing brain. *Scientific American, 267,* 60–67. doi:10.1038/scientificamerican0992-60

Shavers, V. L., Lynch, C. F., & Burmeister, L. F. (2000). Knowledge of the Tuskegee study and its impact on the willingness to participate in medical research studies. *Journal of the National Medical Association, 92,* 563–572.

Shay, J. (1994). *Achilles in Vietnam: Combat trauma and the undoing of character.* New York, NY: Scribner.

Shea, N. (2012). New thinking, innateness and inherited representation. *Philosophical Transactions of the Royal Society B: Biological Sciences, 367,* 2234–2244. doi:10.1098/rstb.2012.0125

Shedler, J. (2010). The efficacy of psychodynamic psychotherapy. *American Psychologist, 65,* 98–109. doi:10.1037/a0018378

Shedler, J., Beck, A., Fonagy, P., Gabbard, G. O., Gunderson, J., Kernberg, O., . . . & Westen, D. (2010). Personality disorders in DSM-5. *American Journal of Psychiatry, 167,* 1026–1028. doi:10.1176/appi.ajp.2010.10050746

Shepard, R. N. (1964). Attention and the metric structure of the stimulus space. *Journal of Mathematical Psychology, 1,* 54–87. doi:10.1016/0022-2496(64)90017-3

Shepard, R., & Metzler, J. (1971). Mental rotation of three-dimensional objects. *Science, 171,* 701–703. doi:10.1126/science.171.3972.701

Sherif, M. H., Harvey, O. J., White, B. J., Hood, W. R., & Sherif, C. (1954). *Experimental study of positive and negative intergroup attitudes between experimentally produced groups: Robbers Cave experiment.* Norman, OK: University of Oklahoma.

Sherman, G. D., Lee, J. J., Cuddy, A. J., Renshon, J., Oveis, C., Gross, J. J., & Lerner, J. S. (2012). Leadership is associated with lower levels of stress. *Proceedings of the National Academy of Sciences, 109,* 17903–17907. doi:10.1073/pnas.1207042109

Shevell, S. K., & Kingdom, F. A. A. (2008). Color in complex scenes. *Annual Review of Psychology, 59,* 143–166. doi:10.1146/annurev.psych.59.103006.093619

Shikata, H., McMahon, D. B., & Breslin, P. A. (2000). Psychophysics of taste lateralization on anterior tongue. *Perception & Psychophysics, 62,* 684–694. doi:10.3758/BF03206915

Shinbrot, T., & Young, W. (2008). Why decussate? Topological constraints on 3D wiring. *Anatomical Record, 291,* 1278–1292. doi:10.1002/ar.20731

Shiner, R. L., & Masten, A. S. (2012). Childhood personality traits as a harbinger of competence and resilience in adulthood. *Development and Psychopathology, 24,* 507–528. doi:10.1017/S0954579412000120

Shoda, Y., Cervone, D., & Downey, G. (Eds.). (2007). *Persons in context: Building a science of the individual.* New York, NY: Guilford Press.

Shoda, Y., Mischel, W., & Peake, P. K. (1990). Predicting adolescent cognitive and self-regulatory competencies from preschool delay of gratification: Identifying diagnostic conditions. *Developmental Psychology, 26,* 978–986. doi:10.1037/0012-1649.26.6.978

Shoda, Y., Mischel, W., & Wright, J. C. (1994). Intraindividual stability in the organization and patterning of behavior: Incorporating psychological situations into the idiographic analysis of personality. *Journal of Personality and Social Psychology, 67,* 674–687. doi:10.1037/0022-3514.67.4.674

Shurman, B., Horan, W. P., & Nuechterlein, K. H. (2005). Schizophrenia patients demonstrate a distinctive pattern of decision-making impairment on the Iowa Gambling Task. *Schizophrenia Research, 72,* 215–224. doi:10.1016/j.schres.2004.03.020

Shweder, R. A. (1993). The cultural psychology of the emotions. In M. Lewis & J. Haviland (Eds.), *The Handbook of Emotions* (pp. 417–431). New York: Guilford Press.

Shweder, R. A. (2003). Toward a deep cultural psychology of shame. *Social Research: An International Quarterly, 70,* 1109–1129.

Shweder, R. A. (Ed.). (1998). *Welcome to middle age! (And other cultural fictions).* Chicago, IL: University of Chicago Press.

Shweder, R. A., & Sullivan, M. A. (1993). Cultural psychology: Who needs it? *Annual Review of Psychology, 44,* 497–523. doi:10.1146/annurev.ps.44.020193.002433

Siegel, J. M. (2003). Why we sleep: The reasons that we sleep are gradually becoming less enigmatic. *Scientific American, 289,* 92–97. doi:10.1038/scientificamerican1103-92

Siegel, J. M. (2005). REM sleep. In M. H. Kryger, T. Roth & W. C. Dement (Eds.), *Principles and practice of sleep medicine.* Philadelphia, PA: W. B. Saunders Company.

Siegel, P., Han, E., Cohen, D., & Anderson, J. (2013). A dissociation between detection and identification of phobic stimuli: Unconscious perception? *Cognition & Emotion, 27,* 1153–1167. doi:10.1080/0269 9931.2013.774264

Siegel, S. (2001). Pavlovian conditioning and drug overdose: When tolerance fails. *Addiction Research & Theory, 9,* 503–513. doi:10.3109/16066350109141767

Siegel, S. (2005). Drug tolerance, drug addiction, and drug anticipation. *Current Directions in Psychological Science, 14,* 296–300. doi:10.1111/j.0963-7214.2005.00384.x

Siegel, S., & Ellsworth, D. W. (1986). Pavlovian conditioning and death from apparent overdose of medically prescribed morphine: A case report. *Bulletin of the Psychonomic Society, 24,* 278–280. doi:10.3758/BF03330140

Siegel, S., & Ramos, B. (2002). Applying laboratory research: Drug anticipation and the treatment of drug addiction. *Experimental and Clinical Psychopharmacology, 10,* 162–183. doi:10.1037/1064-1297.10.3.162

Sierra, M. (2009). *Depersonalization: A new look at a neglected syndrome.* Cambridge, UK: Cambridge University Press. doi:10.1017/CBO97805 11730023

Sigmon, S. C., Herning, R. I., Better, W., Cadet, J. L., & Griffiths, R. R. (2009). Caffeine withdrawal, acute effects, tolerance, and absence of net beneficial effects of chronic administration: Cerebral blood flow velocity, quantitative EEG, and subjective effects. *Psychopharmacology, 204,* 573–585. doi:10.1007/s00213-009-1489-4

Silber, M. H., Ancoli-Israel, S., Bonnet, M. H., Chokroverty, S., Grigg-Damberger, M. M., Hirshkowitz, M., . . . & Iber, C. (2007). The visual scoring of sleep in adults. *Journal of Clinical Sleep Medicine, 3,* 121–131.

Silventoinen, K., Magnusson, P. K. E., Tynelius, P., Kaprio, J., & Rasmussen, F. (2008). Heritability of body size and muscle strength in young adulthood: A study of one million Swedish men. *Genetic Epidemiology, 32,* 341–349. doi:10.1002/gepi.20308

Silvia, P. J. (2008). Interest—The curious emotion. *Current Directions in Psychological Science, 17,* 57–60. doi:10.1111/j.1467-8721.2008.00548.x

Simmons, R. (2014). *Success through stillness: Meditation made simple.* New York: Gotham Books.

Simon, H. (1990). Invariants of human behavior. *Annual Reviews of Psychology, 41,* 1–19. doi:10.1146/annurev.ps.41.020190.000245

Simon, H. A. (1969). *The sciences of the artificial.* Cambridge, MA: MIT Press.

Simon, H. A. (1979). *Models of thought.* New Haven, CT: Yale University Press. doi:10.5840/thought197954224

Simon, H. A. (1983). *Reason in human affairs.* Stanford, CA: Stanford University Press.

Simon, H. A. (1992). What is an "explanation" of behavior? *Psychological Science, 3,* 150–161. doi:10.1111/j.1467-9280.1992.tb00017.x

Simon, H. A. (1996). *The sciences of the artificial* (3rd ed.). Cambridge, MA: MIT Press.

Simons, D. J., & Chabris, C. F. (1999). Gorillas in our midst: Sustained inattentional blindness for dynamic events. *Perception, 28,* 1059–1074. doi:10.1068/p2952

Simons, R. C. (1996). *Boo! Culture, experience, and the startle reflex.* New York, NY: Oxford University Press.

Singh, D. (1993). Adaptive significance of female physical attractiveness: Role of waist-to-hip ratio. *Journal of Personality and Social Psychology, 65,* 293–307. doi:10.1037/0022-3514.65.2.293

Siok, W. T., Kay, P., Wang, W. S., Chan, A. H., Chen, L., Luke, K. K., & Tan, L. H. (2009). Language regions of brain are operative in color perception. *Proceedings of the National Academy of Sciences, 106,* 8140–8145. doi:10.1073/pnas.0903627106

Skinner, B. F. (1938). *The behavior of organisms: An experimental analysis.* Oxford, England: Appleton-Century.

Skinner, B. F. (1948). "Superstition" in the pigeon. *Journal of Experimental Psychology, 38,* 168–172. doi:10.1037/h0055873

Skinner, B. F. (1953). *Science and human behavior.* New York, NY: Simon & Schuster.

Skinner, B. F. (1956). A case history in scientific method. *American Psychologist, 11,* 221–233. doi:10.1037/h0047662

Skinner, B. F. (1957). *Verbal behavior.* Acton, MA: Copley Publishing Group. doi:10.1037/11256-000

Skinner, B. F. (1974). *About behaviorism.* New York, NY: Alfred A. Knopf, Inc.

Skitka, L. J. (2010). The psychology of moral conviction. *Social and Personality Psychology Compass, 4,* 267–281. doi:10.1111/j.1751-9004.2010.00254.x

Slagter, H. A, Lutz, A., Greischar, L. L., Francis, A. D., Nieuwenhuis, S., Davis, J. M., & Davidson, R. J. (2007). Mental training affects distribution of limited brain resources. *PLoS Biology, 5,* e138. doi:10.1371/journal.pbio.0050138

Slavich, G. M., & Cole, S. W. (2013). The emerging field of human social genomics. *Clinical Psychological Science, 1,* 331–348. doi:10.1177/2167702613478594

Sluckin, W. (2007). *Imprinting and early learning* (2nd ed.). Piscataway, NJ: Aldine Transaction.

Smillie, L. D., Pickering, A. D., & Jackson, C. J. (2006). The new reinforcement sensitivity theory: Implications for personality measurement. *Personality and Social Psychology Review, 10,* 320–335. doi:10.1207/s15327957pspr1004_3

Smith, C. A., & Lazarus, R. S. (1990). Emotion and adaptation. In L. A. Pervin (Ed.), *Handbook of Personality: Theory and Research* (pp. 609–637). New York, NY: Guilford Press.

Smith, D. V., & Margolskee, R. F. (2001). Making sense of taste. *Scientific American, 284,* 32–39. doi:10.1038/scientificamerican0301-32

Smith, K. D., Smith, S. T., & Christopher, J. C. (2007). What defines the good person? Cross-cultural comparisons of experts' models with lay prototypes. *Journal of Cross-Cultural Psychology, 38,* 333–360. doi:10.1177/0022022107300279

Smith, K., Alford, J. R., Hatemi, P. K., Eaves, L. J., Funk, C., & Hibbing, J. R. (2012). Biology, ideology, and epistemology: How do we know political attitudes are inherited and why should we care? *American Journal of Political Science, 56,* 17–33. doi:10.1111/j.1540-5907.2011.00560.x

Smith, M. B. (1990). Humanistic psychology. *Journal of Humanistic Psychology, 30,* 6–21. doi:10.1177/002216789003000402

Smith, R. A., & Feigenbaum, K. D. (2013). Maslow's intellectual betrayal of Ruth Benedict? *Journal of Humanistic Psychology, 53,* 307–321. doi:10.1177/0022167812469832

Solms, M. (2000). Dreaming and REM sleep are controlled by different brain mechanisms. *Behavioral and Brain Sciences, 23,* 843–850. doi:10.1017/S0140525X00003988

Soloff, P. H., Fabio, A., Kelly, T. M., Malone, K. M., & Mann, J. J. (2005). High-lethality status in patients with borderline personality disorder. *Journal of Personality Disorders, 19,* 386–399. doi:10.1521/pedi.2005.19.4.386

Solomon, R. (1993). The philosophy of emotions. In M. Lewis, & J. M. Haviland (Eds.), *Handbook of Emotions* (pp. 3–15). New York, NY: Guilford Press.

Solomon, S., Greenberg, J., & Pyszczynski, T. (2004). The cultural animal: Twenty years of terror management theory and research. In J. Greenberg, S. L. Koole, & T. Psyzczynski (Eds.), *Handbook of Experimental Existential Psychology* (pp. 13–34). New York, NY: Guilford.

Sommer, B., Avis, N., Meyer, P., Ory, M., Madden, T., Kagawa-Singer, M., . . . & Adler, S. (1999). Attitudes toward menopause and aging across ethnic/racial groups. *Psychosomatic Medicine, 61,* 868–875. doi:10.1097/00006842-199911000-00023

Sonoda, H., Kohnoe, S., Yamazato, T., Satoh, Y., Morizono, G., Shikata, K., . . . & Maehara, Y. (2011). Colorectal cancer screening with odour material by canine scent detection. *Gut, 60,* 814–819. doi:10.1136/gut.2010.218305

Soon, C. S., Brass, M., Heinze, H. J., & Haynes, J. D. (2008). Unconscious determinants of free decisions in the human brain. *Nature Neuroscience, 11,* 543–545. doi:10.1038/nn.2112

Sorjonen, K., Hemmingsson, T., Lundin, A., Falkstedt, D., & Melin, B. (2012). Intelligence, socioeconomic background, emotional capacity, and level of education as predictors of attained socioeconomic position in a cohort of Swedish men. *Intelligence, 40,* 269–277. doi:10.1016/j.intell.2012.02.009

Spangler, W. D. (1992). Validity of questionnaire and TAT measures of need for achievement: Two meta-analyses. *Psychological Bulletin, 112,* 140–154. doi:10.1037/0033-2909.112.1.140

Spanos, N. P., & Hewitt, E. C. (1980). The hidden observer in hypnotic analgesia: Discovery or experimental creation? *Journal of Personality and Social Psychology, 39,* 1201–1204. doi:10.1037/h0077730

Spearman, C. (1904). "General intelligence," objectively determined and measured. *The American Journal of Psychology, 15,* 201–292. doi:10.2307/1412107

Sperling, G. (1960). The information available in brief visual presentations. *Psychological Monographs: General and Applied, 74,* 1–29. doi:10.1037/h0093759

Sperry, R. (1982). Some effects of disconnecting the cerebral hemispheres. *Science, 217,* 1223–1226. doi:10.1126/science.7112125

Sperry, R. W. (1961). Cerebral organization and behavior. *Science, 133,* 1749–1757. doi:10.1126/science.133.3466.1749

Sperry, R. W., Gazzaniga, M. S., & Bogen, J. E. (1969). Interhemispheric relationships: The neocortical commissures; syndromes of hemisphere disconnection. In *Handbook of Clinical Neurology* (Vol. 4, pp. 273–290). Amsterdam: North Holland Publishing Company.

Spinath, F. M., & Angleitner, A. (1998). Contrast effects in Buss and Plomin's EAS questionnaire: A behavioral-genetic study on early developing personality traits assessed through parental ratings. *Personality and Individual Differences, 25,* 947–963. doi:10.1016/S0191-8869(98)00097-X

Sporns, O. (2010). *Networks of the brain.* Cambridge, MA: MIT Press.

Sporns, O. (2011). *Networks of the brain.* Cambridge, MA: MIT Press.

Sporns, O. (2012). *Discovering the human connectome.* Cambridge, MA: MIT Press.

Sporns, O., Tononi, G., Kötter, R. (2005). The human connectome: A structural description of the human brain. *PLoS Computational Biology, 1,* e42. doi:10.1371/journal.pcbi.0010042

Spradley, J. P., & Phillips, M. (1972). Culture and stress: A quantitative analysis. *American Anthropologist, 74,* 518–529. doi:10.1525/aa.1972.74.3.02a00190

Sprouse-Blum, A. S., Smith, G., Sugai, D., & Parsa, F. D. (2010). Understanding endorphins and their importance in pain management. *Hawaii Medical Journal, 69,* 70–71.

Squire, L. R. (1992). Memory and the hippocampus: A synthesis from findings with rats, monkeys, and humans. *Psychological Review, 99,* 195–231. doi:10.1037/0033-295X.99.2.195

Squire, L. R. (2009). Memory and brain systems: 1969–2009. *The Journal of Neuroscience, 29,* 12711–12716. doi:10.1523/JNEUROSCI.3575-09.2009

Squire, L. R., & Wixted, J. T. (2011). The cognitive neuroscience of human memory since H. M. *Annual Review of Neuroscience, 34,* 259–288. doi:10.1146/annurev-neuro-061010-113720

Stahl, S. M. (2002). *Essential psychopharmacology of antipsychotics and mood stabilizers.* Cambridge, UK: Cambridge University Press.

Stahl, S. M. (2002). *Essential psychopharmacology: Neuroscientific basis and practical applications* (2nd ed.). New York, NY: Cambridge University Press.

Stahl, S. M. (2002). *Essential psychopharmacology: Neuroscientific basis and practical applications* (2nd ed.). New York, NY: Cambridge University Press.

Steckel, R. H. (1995). "Percentiles of Modern Height Standards for Use in Historical Research," NBER Historical Working Papers 0075, National Bureau of Economic Research, Inc.

Steele, C. (1997). A threat in the air: How stereotypes shape intellectual identity and performance. *American Psychologist, 52,* 613–629. doi:10.1037/0003-066X.52.6.613

Steele, C. (2010). *Whistling Vivaldi: How stereotypes affect us and what we can do.* New York: Norton.

Steele, C. M., & Josephs, R. A. (1990). Alcohol myopia: Its prized and dangerous effects. *American Psychologist, 45,* 921–933. doi:10.1037/0003-066X.45.8.921

Stelmack, R. M., & Rammsayer, T. H. (2008). Psychophysiological and biochemical correlates of personality. In G. J. Boyle, G. Matthews, & D. H. Saklofske (Eds.), *The SAGE Handbook of Personality Theory and Assessment* (Vol 1, pp. 33–55). Thousand Oaks, CA: SAGE Publications. doi:10.4135/9781849200462.n2

Stephenson, W. (1953). *The study of behavior.* Chicago, IL: University of Chicago Press.

Stern, D. G. (1991). Models of memory: Wittgenstein and cognitive science. *Philosophical Psychology, 4,* 203–218. doi:10.1080/09515089108573027

Stern, K., & McClintock, M. K. (1998). Regulation of ovulation by human pheromones. *Nature, 392,* 177–179. doi:10.1038/32408

Sternberg, E. M., & Gold, P. W. (1997). The mind–body interaction in disease. *Scientific American, 7,* 8–15.

Sternberg, R. J. (1985). Implicit theories of intelligence, creativity, and wisdom. *Journal of Personality and Social Psychology, 49,* 607. doi:10.1037/0022-3514.49.3.607

Stevens, S. S. (1948). Sensation and psychological measurement. In E. G. Boring, H. S. Langfeld, & H. P. Weld (Eds.), *Foundations of psychology* (pp. 250–268). New York, NY: Wiley. doi:10.1037/11332-011

Stevens, S. S. (1955). The measurement of loudness. *Journal of the Acoustical Society of America, 27,* 815–829. doi:10.1121/1.1908048

Stevenson, J. (2014, July 14). How after 14 years of hell that stemmed from severe panic and anxiety attacks, I literally gained my life and self-confidence back and permanently put an end to my panic attacks within days. *My anxiety solution.* Retrieved from http://www.myanxietysolution.com/

Stipp, D. (2005, November 28). Trouble in Prozac nation. *Fortune, 152,* 154–156.

Stock, J., & Cervone, D. (1990). Proximal goal-setting and self-regulatory processes. *Cognitive Therapy and Research, 14,* 483–498. doi:10.1007/BF01172969

Stoerig, P. (2007). Hunting the ghost: Toward a neuroscience of consciousness. In P. D. Zelazo, M. Moscovitch, & E. Thompson (Eds.), *Cambridge Handbook of Consciousness.* New York, NY: Cambridge University Press. doi:10.1017/CBO9780511816789.026

Stoet, G., & Geary, D. C. (2012). Can stereotype threat explain the gender gap in mathematics performance and achievement? *Review of General Psychology, 16,* 93–102. doi:10.1037/a0026617

Stratton, G. M. (1917). The mnemonic feat of the "Shass Pollak." *Psychological Review, 24,* 244–247. doi:10.1037/h0070091

Streeter, C. C., Whitfield, T. H., Owen, L., Rein, T., Karri, S. K., Yakhkind, A., . . . & Jensen, J. E. (2010). Effects of yoga versus walking on mood, anxiety, and brain GABA levels: A randomized controlled MRS study. *Journal of Alternative and Complementary Medicine, 16,* 1145–1152. doi:10.1089/acm.2010.0007

Strelau, J. (1998). *Temperament: A psychological perspective.* Perspectives on individual differences. New York, NY: Springer Science+Business.

Strick, P. L., Dum, R. P., & Fiez, J. A. (2009). Cerebellum and nonmotor function. *Annual Review of Neuroscience, 32,* 413–434. doi:10.1146/annurev.neuro.31.060407.125606

Stroebe, W. (2012). The truth about Triplett (1898), but nobody seems to care. *Perspectives on Psychological Science, 7,* 54–57. doi:10.1177/1745691611427306

Stroebe, W., Papies, E. K., & Aarts, H. (2008). From homeostatic to hedonic theories of eating: Self-regulatory failure in food-rich environments. *Applied Psychology, 57,* 172–193. doi:10.1111/j.1464-0597.2008.00360.x

Stroop, J. R. (1935). Studies of interference in serial verbal reactions. *Journal of Experimental Psychology, 28,* 643–662. doi:10.1037/h0054651

stubear. (2010, November 18). *Man steals for dying girlfriend, marries her while in prison.* Retrieved from http://www.chinasmack.com/2010/pictures/man-steals-for-dying-girlfriend-marries-her-while-in-prison.html

Sturm, R., Duffy, D., Zhao, Z., Leite, F., Stark, M., Hayward, N., . . . & Montgomery, G. (2008). A single SNP in an evolutionary conserved region within intron 86 of the HERC2 gene determines human blue-brown eye color. *The American Journal of Human Genetics, 82,* 424–431. doi:10.1016/j.ajhg.2007.11.005.

Stuss, D. T. (2011). Traumatic brain injury: Relation to executive dysfunction and the frontal lobes. *Current Opinion in Neurology, 24,* 584–589. doi:10.1097/WCO.0b013e32834c7eb9

Substance Abuse and Mental Health Services Administration. (2010). *Results from the 2009 National Survey on Drug Use and Health: Volume I. Summary of National Findings* (Office of Applied Studies, NSDUH Series H-38A, HHS Publication No. SMA 10-4586Findings). Rockville, MD: Substance Abuse and Mental Health Services Administration. Retrieved from http://www.samhsa.gov/data/2k9/2k9Resultsweb/web/2k9results.pdf

Suddendorf, T., & Butler, D. L. (2013). The nature of visual self-recognition. *Trends in Cognitive Sciences, 17,* 121–127. doi:10.1016/j.tics.2013.01.004

Suddendorf, T., & Corballis, M. C. (2007). The evolution of foresight: What is mental time travel, and is it unique to humans? *The Behavioral and Brain Sciences, 30,* 299–313; discussion 313–351. doi:10.1017/S0140525X07001975

Sullivan, H. S. (1953). *The interpersonal therapy of psychiatry.* New York, NY: W. W. Norton & Co.

Sullivan, K. T., Pasch, L. A., Johnson, M. D., & Bradbury, T. N. (2010). Social support, problem solving, and the longitudinal course of newlywed marriage. *Journal of Personality and Social Psychology, 98,* 631–644. doi:10.1037/a0017578

Sulloway, F. J. (1996). *Born to rebel: Birth order, family dynamics and creative lies.* New York, NY: Pantheon.

Swinson, R. P. (2005). Social anxiety disorder. *The Canadian Journal of Psychiatry / La Revue Canadienne de Psychiatrie, 50,* 305–307.

Sylvers, P., Lilienfeld, S. O., & LaPrairie, J. L. (2011). Differences between trait fear and trait anxiety: Implications for psychopathology. *Clinical Psychology Review, 31,* 122–137. doi:10.1016/j.cpr.2010.08.004

Szasz, T. (2011). The myth of mental illness: 50 years later. *The Psychiatrist, 35,* 179–182. doi:10.1192/pb.bp.110.031310

Szasz, T. S. (1960). The myth of mental illness. *American Psychologist, 15,* 113–118. doi:10.1037/h0046535

Takahashi, Y. K., Nagayama, S., & Mori, K. (2004). Detection and masking of spoiled food smells by odor maps in the olfactory bulb. *Journal of Neuroscience, 24,* 8690–8694. doi:10.1523/JNEUROSCI.2510-04.2004

Talarico, J. M., & Rubin, D. C. (2003). Confidence, not consistency, characterizes flashbulb memories. *Psychological Science, 14,* 455–461. doi:10.1111/1467-9280.02453

Tan, K. R., Rudolph, U., & Lüscher, C. (2011). Hooked on benzodiazepines: GABA$_A$ receptor subtypes and addiction. *Trends in Neurosciences, 34,* 188–197. doi:10.1016/j.tins.2011.01.004

Tang, Y., Zhang, W., Chen, K., Feng, S., Ji, Y., Shen, J., . . . & Liu, Y. (2006). Arithmetic processing in the brain shaped by cultures. *Proceedings of the National Academy of Sciences of the United States of America, 103,* 10775–10780. doi:10.1073/pnas.0604416103

Tang, Y.-Y., & Posner, M. I. (2009). Attention training and attention state training. *Trends in Cognitive Sciences, 13,* 222–227. doi:10.1016/j.tics.2009.01.009

Tanner, C. M., & Chamberland, J. (2001). Latah in Jakarta, Indonesia. *Movement Disorders, 16,* 526–529. doi:10.1002/mds.1088

Tanner, J. M. (1978). *Foetus into man: Physical growth from conception to maturity.* Cambridge, MA: Harvard University Press.

Tassinary, L., & Hansen, K. (1998). A critical test of the waist-to-hip-ratio hypothesis of female physical attractiveness. *Psychological Science, 9,* 150–155. doi:10.1111/1467-9280.00029

Tateyama, M., Asai, M., Hashimoto, M., Bartels, M., & Kasper, S. (1998). Transcultural study of schizophrenic delusions. *Psychopathology, 31,* 59–68. doi:10.1159/000029025

Taylor, C. A., Manganello, J. A., Lee, S. J., & Rice, J. C. (2010). Mothers' spanking of 3-year-old children and subsequent risk of children's aggressive behavior. *Pediatrics, 125,* e1057–e1065. doi:10.1542/peds.2009-2678

Taylor, L. S., Fiore, A. T., Mendelsohn, G. A., & Cheshire, C. (2011). "Out of my league": A real-world test of the matching hypothesis. *Personality and Social Psychology Bulletin, 37,* 942–954. doi:10.1177/0146167211409947

Taylor, S. (1983). Adjustment to threatening events: A theory of cognitive adaptation. *American Psychologist, 38,* 1161–1173. doi:10.1037/0003-066X.38.11.1161

Taylor, S. E., Klein, L. C., Lewis, B. P., Gruenewald, T. L., Gurung, R. A., & Updegraff, J. A. (2000). Biobehavioral responses to stress in females: Tend-and-befriend, not fight-or-flight. *Psychological Review, 107,* 411–429. doi:10.1037/0033-295X.107.3.411

Taylor, S. E., & Stanton, A. L. (2007). Coping resources, coping processes, and mental health. *Annual Review of Clinical Psychology, 3,* 377–401. doi:10.1146/annurev.clinpsy.3.022806.091520

Terracciano, A., Löckenhoff, C. E., Zonderman, A. B., Ferrucci, L., & Costa, P. T. (2008). Personality predictors of longevity: Activity, emotional stability, and conscientiousness. *Psychosomatic Medicine, 70,* 621–627. doi:10.1017/S0033291709992029

Terzis, V., Moridis, C. N., and Economides, A. A. (2011). Measuring instant emotions based on facial expressions during computer-based assessment. *Personal and Ubiquitous Computing, 17,* 43–52. doi:10.1007/s00779-011-0477-y

Thayer, R. E. (1996). *The origin of everyday moods: Managing energy, tension, and stress.* New York, NY: Oxford University Press.

Thayer, R. E. (2003). *Calm energy: How people regulate mood with food and exercise.* New York, NY: Oxford University Press.

Thelen, E., & Smith, L. B. (1994). *A dynamic systems approach to the development of cognition and action*. Cambridge, MA: MIT Press.

Thiel, C. M., Studte, S., Hildebrandt, H., Huster, R., & Weerda, R. (2014). When a loved one feels unfamiliar: A case study on the neural basis of Capgras delusion. *Cortex, 52,* 75–85. doi:10.1016/j.cortex.2013.11.011

Thoma, N. C., & Cecero, J. J. (2009). Is integrative use of techniques in psychotherapy the exception or the rule? Results of a national survey of doctoral-level practitioners. *Psychotherapy: Theory, Research, Practice, Training, 46,* 405–417. doi:10.1037/a0017900

Thomas, A., & Chess, S. (1977). *Temperament and development*. Oxford, England: Brunner/Mazel.

Thomas, A., & Chess, S. (1996). *Temperament: Theory and practice*. New York, NY: Brunner/Mazel.

Thompson, E. M., & Morgan, E. M. (2008). "Mostly straight" young women: Variations in sexual behavior and identity development. *Developmental Psychology, 44,* 15–21. doi:10.1037/0012-1649.44.1.15

Thompson, R. F. (2000). *The brain: A neuroscience primer* (3rd ed.). New York, NY: Worth.

Tiest, W. M. B., & Kappers, A. M. (2009). Cues for haptic perception of compliance. *Haptics, IEEE Transactions on Haptics, 2,* 189–199. doi:10.1109/TOH.2009.16

Titchener, E. B. (1898). A psychological laboratory. *Mind, 7,* 311–331. doi:10.1093/mind/VII.27.311

Toga, A. W., & Thompson, P. M. (2003). Mapping brain asymmetry. *Nature Reviews Neuroscience, 4,* 37–48. doi:10.1038/nrn1009

Tolman, D. L., & Diamond, L. M. (2001). Desegregating sexuality research: Cultural and biological perspectives on gender and desire. *Annual Review of Sex Research, 12,* 33–74.

Tolman, E. C. (1948). Cognitive maps in rats and men. *Psychological Review, 55,* 189–208. doi:10.1037/h0061626

Tomkins, S. S. (1962). *Affect. Imagery. Consciousness* (Vol. I: The positive affects). New York, NY: Springer Publishing Co.

Tomkins, S. S. (1963). *Affect. Imagery. Consciousness* (Vol. II. The negative affects). New York, NY: Springer Publishing Co.

Tondo, L., Baldessarini, R. J., & Floris, G. (2001). Long-term clinical effectiveness of lithium maintenance treatment in types I and II bipolar disorders. *The British Journal of Psychiatry, 178,* s184–s190. doi:10.1192/bjp.178.41.s184

Tooby, J., & Cosmides, L. (2005). Conceptual foundations of evolutionary psychology. In D. M. Buss (Ed.), *The Handbook of Evolutionary Psychology* (pp. 5–67). Hoboken, NJ: Wiley.

Tootell, R. B. H., Silverman, M. S., Switkes, E., & De Valois, R. L. (1982). Deoxyglucose analysis of retinotopic organization in primate striate cortex. *Science, 218,* 902–904. doi:10.1126/science.7134981

Treffert, D. A. (2009). The savant syndrome: an extraordinary condition. A synopsis: Past, present, future. *Philosophical Transactions of the Royal Society B: Biological Sciences, 364,* 1351–1357. doi:10.1098/rstb.2008.0326

Treisman, A. (1969). Strategies and models of selective attention. *Psychological Review, 76,* 282–299.

Treisman, A. M., & Gelade, G. (1980). A feature-integration theory of attention. *Cognitive Psychology, 12,* 97–136. doi:10.1016/0010-0285(80)90005-5

Triandis, H. C. (1995). *Individualism and collectivism*. Boulder, CO: Westview Press.

Triesman, A. (1964). Selective attention in man. *British Medical Bulletin, 20,* 12–16.

Tripathi, R. (2014). The science and art of learning about cultures: Descriptions, explanations, and reflections–In conversation with Sri Sri Ravi Shankar. *IIMB Management Review, 26,* 122–129. doi:10.1016/j.iimb.2014.03.012

Triplett, N. (1898). The dynamogenic factors in pacemaking and competition. *American Journal of Psychology, 9,* 507–533. doi:10.2307/1412188

Trope, Y., & Liberman, N. (2003). Temporal construal. *Psychological Review, 110,* 403–421. doi:10.1037/0033-295X.110.3.403

Trumbull, E., Rothstein-Fisch, C., & Greenfield, P. M. (2001, Spring). Ours and mine. *Journal of Staff Development, 22,* 10–14.

Trzesniewski, K. H., Donnellan, M. B., & Robins, R. W. (2003). Stability of self-esteem across the lifespan. *Journal of Personality and Social Psychology, 84,* 205–220. doi:10.1037/0022-3514.84.1.205

Tsai, J. L., & Chentsova-Dutton, Y. (2002). Understanding depression across cultures. In I. H. Gotlib, & C. L. Hammen (Eds.), *Handbook of Depression* (pp. 467–491). New York, NY: Guilford Press.

Tsai, Y.-M., Kunter, M., Lüdtke, O., Trautwein, U., & Ryan, R. M. (2008). What makes lessons interesting? The role of situational and individual factors in three school subjects. *Journal of Educational Psychology, 100,* 460–472. doi:10.1037/0022-0663.100.2.460

Tseng, W. S. (2006). From peculiar psychiatric disorders through culture-bound syndromes to culture-related specific syndromes. *Transcultural Psychiatry, 43,* 554–576. doi:10.1177/1363461506070781

Tudor, K., & Worrall, M. (2006). *Person-centred therapy: A clinical philosophy*. Hove, UK: Routledge.

Tulving, E. (1972). Episodic and semantic memory. In E. Tulving & W. Donaldson (Eds.), *Organization of memory*. New York, NY: Academic Press.

Turk, C. L., Heimberg, R. G., & Magee, L. (2008). Social anxiety disorder. In D. H. Barlow (Ed.), *Clinical Handbook of Psychological Disorders: A Step-by-Step Treatment Manual* (4th ed., pp.123–163). New York, NY: Guilford Publications.

Turkheimer, E., Haley, A., Waldron, M., D'Onofrio, B., & Gottesman, I. (2003). Socioeconomic status modifies heritability of IQ in young children. *Psychological Science, 14,* 623–628. doi:10.1046/j.0956-7976.2003.psci_1475.x

Turvey, M. T., & Carello, C. (2011). Obtaining information by dynamic (effortful) touching. *Philosophical Transactions of the Royal Society of London. Series B, Biological Sciences, 366,* 3123–3132. doi:10.1098/rstb.2011.0159

Tversky, A., & Kahneman, D. (1974). Judgment under uncertainty: Heuristics and biases. *Science, 185,* 1124–1131. doi:10.1126/science.185.4157.1124

Tversky, A., & Kahneman, D. (1983). Extensional versus intuitive reasoning: The conjunction fallacy in probability judgment. *Psychological Review, 90,* 293–315. doi:10.1037/0033-295X.90.4.293

Tweedy, J. (2008, March 5). Shaking it off. *The New York Times*. Retrieved from http://migraine.blogs.nytimes.com/2008/03/05/shaking-it-off/

Uchino, B. N., Cacioppo, J. T., & Kiecolt-Glaser, J. K. (1996). The relationship between social support and physiological processes: A review with emphasis on underlying mechanisms and implications for health. *Psychological Bulletin, 119,* 488–531. doi:10.1037/0033-2909.119.3.488

Uddin, L. Q., Supekar, K. S., Ryali, S., & Menon, V. (2011). Dynamic reconfiguration of structural and functional connectivity across core neurocognitive brain networks with development. *The Journal of Neuroscience, 31,* 18578–18589. doi:10.1523/JNEUROSCI.4465-11.2011

United Nations Development Programme. (2012). Gender equality index 2012. Retrieved from https://data.undp.org/dataset/Table-4-Gender-Inequality-Index/pq34-nwq7, January 27, 2014.

United Nations Office on Drugs and Crime. (2009). *UNODC-WHO joint programme on drug dependence and care* [Booklet]. Retrieved from http://www.unodc.org/documents/drug-treatment/UNODC-WHO-brochure.pdf

Urban, P. P., & Caplan, L. R. (Eds.). (2011). *Brainstem disorders.* Berlin: Springer-Verlag. doi:10.1007/978-3-642-04203-4

Useem, M. (2008, Nov. 19). America's best leaders: Indra Nooyi, PepsiCo CEO: The karaoke-singing chief executive is taking Pepsi in an unlikely direction—toward healthful foods. *U.S. News and World Report.* Retrieved from http://www.usnews.com/news/best-leaders/articles/2008/11/19/americas-best-leaders-indra-nooyi-pepsico-ceo

Valenstein, E. S. (1998). *Blaming the brain: The truth about drugs and mental health.* New York, NY: Free Press.

Valenzuela, C. F. (1997). Alcohol and neurotransmitter interactions. *Alcohol Health and Research World, 21,* 144–148.

Valli, K., Strandholm, T., Sillanmäki, L., & Revonsuo, A. (2008). Dreams are more negative than real life: Implications for the function of dreaming. *Cognition & Emotion, 22,* 833–861. doi:10.1080/02699930701541591

Vallone, R. P., Ross, L., & Lepper, M. R. (1985). The hostile media phenomenon: Biased perception and perceptions of media bias in coverage of the Beirut massacre. *Journal of Personality and Social Psychology, 49,* 577–585. doi:10.1037/0022-3514.49.3.577

Van Cappellen, P., & Saroglou, V. (2012). Awe activates religious and spiritual feelings and behavioral intentions. *Psychology of Religion and Spirituality, 4,* 223–236. doi:10.1037/a0025986

van der Maas, H. L. J., Dolan, C. V, Grasman, R. P. P. P., Wicherts, J. M., Huizenga, H. M., & Raijmakers, M. E. J. (2006). A dynamical model of general intelligence: The positive manifold of intelligence by mutualism. *Psychological Review, 113,* 842–861. doi:10.1037/0033-295X.113.4.842

Van Dongen, H. P. A, Maislin, G., Mullington, J. M., & Dinges, D. F. (2003). The cumulative cost of additional wakefulness: Dose–response effects on neurobehavioral functions and sleep physiology from chronic sleep restriction and total sleep deprivation. *Sleep, 26,* 117–126. Retrieved from http://www.ncbi.nlm.nih.gov/pubmed/12683469

Van Horn, J. D., Irimia, A., Torgerson, C.M., Chambers, M.C., Kikinis, R. et al. (2012). Mapping connectivity damage in the case of Phineas Gage. *PLoS ONE 7*(5): e37454.

van IJzendoorn, M. H., & Kroonenberg, P. M. (1988). Cross-cultural patterns of attachment: A meta-analysis of the strange situation. *Child Development, 59,* 147–156. doi:10.1111/j.1467-8624.1988.tb03202.x

Van Noppen, B. (2010). *Obsessive compulsive personality disorder (OCPD).* Boston, MA: International OCD Foundation. Retrieved from http://www.ocfoundation.org/uploadedfiles/maincontent/find_help/ocpd%20fact%20sheet.pdf

Van Overwalle, F. (2009). Social cognition and the brain: A meta-analysis. *Human Brain Mapping, 30,* 829–858. doi:10.1002/hbm.20547

van Ree, J. M., Gerrits, M. A., & Vanderschuren, L. J. (1999). Opioids, reward and addiction: An encounter of biology, psychology, and medicine. *Pharmacological Reviews, 51,* 341–396.

Vance, David, Webb, Nicole M., Marceaux, Janice C., Viamonte, Sarah M., Foote, Anne W., & Ball, Karlene K. (2008, January 1). Mental stimulation, neural plasticity, and aging: Directions for nursing research and practice. *Journal of Neuroscience Nursing,* Fig. 2.

Vanhaudenhuyse, A., Boly, M., Balteau, E., Schnakers, C., Moonen, G., Luxen, A., . . . & Faymonville, M. E. (2009). Pain and non-pain processing during hypnosis: A thulium-YAG event-related fMRI study. *NeuroImage, 47,* 1047–1054. doi:10.1016/j.neuroimage.2009.05.031

Vartanian, A. (1973). Man–machine from the Greeks to the computer. *Dictionary of the History of Ideas, 3,* 131–146.

Vaughn, P. W., Rogers, E. M., Singhal, A., & Swalehe, R. M. (2000). Entertainment-education and HIV/AIDS prevention: A field study in Tanzania. *Journal of Health Communication, 5* (Supplement 1), 81–200. doi:10.1080/10810730050019573

Vedantam, S. (2012, April 6). Indian engineers build a stronger society with school lunch program. *NPR, the salt.* Retrieved from http://www.npr.org/blogs/thesalt/2012/04/06/149867092/indian-engineers-build-a-stronger-society-with-school-lunch-program

Veltkamp, M., Aarts, H., & Custers, R. (2008). Perception in the service of goal pursuit: Motivation to attain goals enhances the perceived size of goal-instrumental objects. *Social Cognition, 26,* 720–736. doi:10.1521/soco.2008.26.6.720

Venetsanou, F., & Kambas, A. (2010). Environmental factors affecting preschoolers' motor development. *Early Childhood Education Journal, 37,* 319–327. doi:10.1007/s10643-009-0350-z

Verduyn, P., Van Mechelen, I., & Tuerlinckx, F. (2011). The relation between event processing and the duration of emotional experience. *Emotion, 11,* 20–28. doi:10.1037/a0021239

Virk, G., Reeves, G., Rosenthal, N. E., Sher, L., & Postolache, T. T. (2009). Short exposure to light treatment improves depression scores in patients with seasonal affective disorder: A brief report. *International Journal on Disability and Human Development, 8,* 283–286. doi:10.1515/IJDHD.2009.8.3.283

Vogel, F., & Motulsky, A. G. (1997). *Human genetics: Problems and approaches* (3rd ed.). Berlin, Germany: Springer. doi:10.1007/978-3-662-03356-2

Von Lang, J., & Sibyll, C. (Eds.). (1983). *Eichmann interrogated: Transcripts from the archives of the Israeli police* (R. Manheim, Trans.). New York, NY: Farrar, Straus and Giroux.

Voon, V., Brezing, C., Gallea, C., Ameli, R., Roelofs, K., LaFrance, W. C., & Hallett, M. (2010). Emotional stimuli and motor conversion disorder. *Brain, 133,* 1526–1536. doi:10.1093/brain/awq054

Vygotsky, L.S. (1978). *Mind in society: The development of higher mental processes.* Cambridge, MA: Harvard University Press.

Wagar, B. M., & Dixon, M. (2006). Affective guidance in the Iowa gambling task. *Cognitive, Affective & Behavioral Neuroscience, 6,* 277–290. doi:10.3758/CABN.6.4.277

Wagemans, J., Elder, J. H., Kubovy, M., Palmer, S. E., Peterson, M. A., Singh, M., & von der Heydt, R. (2012). A century of Gestalt psychology in visual perception: I. Perceptual grouping and figure-ground organization. *Psychological Bulletin, 138,* 1172–1217. doi:10.1037/a0029333

Wagenmakers, E.–J., Wetzels, R., Borsboom, D., & van der Maas, H. L. J. (2011). Why psychologists must change the way they analyze their data: The case of psi: Comment on Bem (2011). *Journal of Personality and Social Psychology, 100,* 426–432. doi:10.1037/a0022790

Wahba, A., & Bridgewell, L. (1976) Maslow reconsidered: A review of research on the need hierarchy theory. *Organizational Behavior and Human Performance, 15,* 212–240. doi:10.1016/0030-5073(76)90038-6

Wahl, O. F. (1999). Mental health consumers' experience of stigma. *Schizophrenia Bulletin, 25,* 467–478. doi:10.1093/oxfordjournals.schbul.a033394

Waldinger, R. J. (1987). Intensive psychodynamic therapy with borderline patients: An overview. *American Journal of Psychiatry, 144,* 267–274.

Waller, B. M., Cray, J. J., & Burrows, A. M. (2008). Selection for universal facial emotion. *Emotion, 8,* 435–439. doi:10.1037/1528-3542.8.3.435

Walsh, R., & Shapiro, S. L. (2006). The meeting of meditative disciplines and Western psychology: A mutually enriching dialogue. *The American Psychologist, 61,* 227–239. doi:10.1037/0003-066X.61.3.227

Walster, E., Aronson, V., Abrahams, D., & Rottman, L. (1966). Importance of physical attractiveness in dating behavior. *Journal of Personality and Social Psychology, 4*, 508–516. doi:10.1037/h0021188

Wang, C., Swerdloff, R. S., Iranmanesh, A., Dobs, A., Snyder, P. J., Cunningham, G., . . . & the Testosterone Gel Study Group. (2000). Transdermal testosterone gel improves sexual function, mood, muscle strength, and body composition parameters in hypogonadal men. *Journal of Clinical Endocrinology & Metabolism, 85*, 2839–2853. doi:10.1210/jcem.85.8.6747

Wang, Q. (2004). The emergence of cultural self-constructs: Autobiographical memory and self-description in European American and Chinese children. *Developmental Psychology, 40*, 3–15. doi:10.1037/0012-1649.40.1.3

Wang, Q. (2006). Culture and the development of self-knowledge. *Current Directions in Psychological Science, 15*, 182–187. doi:10.1111/j.1467-8721.2006.00432.x

Ware, N. C., Wyatt, M. A., Geng, E. H., Kaaya, S. F., Agbaji, O. O., Muyindike, W. R., . . . & Agaba, P. A. (2013). Toward an understanding of disengagement from HIV treatment and care in sub-Saharan Africa: A qualitative study. *PLoS Medicine, 10*, e1001369; discussion e1001369. doi:10.1371/journal.pmed.1001369

Wason, P. C. (1960). On the failure to eliminate hypotheses in a conceptual task. *Quarterly Journal of Experimental Psychology, 12*, 129–140. doi:10.1080/17470216008416717

Wasserman, J. D., & Tulsky, D. S. (2005). A history of intelligence assessment. In D. P. Flanagan & P. L. Harrison (Eds.), *Contemporary intellectual assessment: Theories, tests, and issues* (2nd ed., pp. 3–22). New York, NY: Guilford Publications.

Waterhouse, L. (2006). Multiple intelligences, the Mozart effect, and emotional intelligence: A critical review. *Educational Psychologist, 41*, 207–225. doi:10.1207/s15326985ep4104_1

Watkins, M. W., & Smith, L. (2013). Long-term stability of the Wechsler Intelligence Scale for Children—Fourth Edition. *Psychological Assessment, 25*, 477–483. doi:10.1037/a0031653

Watson, D., & Tellegen, A. (1985). Toward a consensual structure of mood. *Psychological Bulletin, 98*, 219–235. doi:10.1037/0033-2909.98.2.219

Watson, J. B. (1913). Psychology as the behaviorist views it. *Psychological Review, 20*, 158–177. (Reprinted in *Psychological Review, 101* (1994), 248–253). doi:10.1037/h0074428

Watson, J. B., & Rayner, R. (1920). Conditioned emotional reactions. *Journal of Experimental Psychology, 3*, 1–14. doi:10.1037/h0069608

Watson, R. I. (1963). *The great psychologists: from Aristotle to Freud.* Oxford, England: Lippincott.

Weaver, I. C. G., Meaney, M. J., & Szyf, M. (2006). Maternal care effects on the hippocampal transcriptome and anxiety-mediated behaviors in the offspring that are reversible in adulthood. *Proceedings of the National Academy of Sciences of the United States of America, 103*, 3480–3485. doi:10.1073/pnas.0507526103

Weber, R., Tamborini, R., Westcott-Baker, A., & Kantor, B. (2009). Theorizing flow and media enjoyment as cognitive synchronization of attentional and reward networks. *Communication Theory, 19*, 397–422. doi:10.1111/j.1468-2885.2009.01352.x

Wechsler, D. (2008). *Wechsler Adult Intelligence Scale–Fourth Edition (WAIS–IV).* San Antonio, TX: NCS Pearson.

Wegner, D. M. (1994). Ironic processes of mental control. *Psychological Review, 101*, 34–52. doi:10.1037/0033-295X.101.1.34

Wegner, D. M., Schneider, D. J., Carter, S. R., & White, T. L. (1987). Paradoxical effects of thought suppression. *Journal of Personality and Social Psychology, 53*, 5–13. doi:10.1037/0022-3514.53.1.5

Weinberger, D. A., Schwartz, G. E., & Davidson, R. J. (1979). Low-anxious, high-anxious, and repressive coping styles: Psychometric patterns and behavioral and physiological responses to stress. *Journal of Abnormal Psychology, 88*, 369–380. doi:10.1037/0021-843X.88.4.369

Weiner, B. (1985). An attributional theory of achievement motivation and emotion. *Psychological Review, 92*, 548–573. doi:10.1037/0033-295X.92.4.548

Weisel, T. N. (1981, December 8). *The postnatal development of the visual cortex and the influence of environment* [Nobel lecture]. Reprinted in *Bioscience Reports, 2* (1982), 351–377. doi:10.1007/BF01119299

Weiss, J. (1971). Effects of coping behavior in different warning-signal conditions on stress pathology in rats. *Journal of Comparative and Physiological Psychology, 77*, 1–13. doi:10.1037/h0031583

Weitzenhoffer, A., & Hilgard, E. (1962). Stanford hypnotic susceptibility scale, form C. Retrieved from http://ist-socrates.berkeley.edu/~kihlstrm/PDFfiles/Hypnotizability/SHSSC Script.pdf

Wellman, H. M., & Gelman, S. A. (1992). Cognitive development: Foundational theories of core domains. *Annual Review of Psychology, 43*, 337–375. doi:10.1146/annurev.ps.43.020192.002005

Wellman, H. M., Cross, D., & Watson, J. (2001). Meta-analysis of theory-of-mind development: The truth about false belief. *Child Development, 72*, 655–684. doi:10.1111/1467-8624.00304

Wellman, K. (1992). *La Mettrie: Medicine, philosophy, and enlightenment.* Durham, NC: Duke.

Werner, E. E. (1993). Risk, resilience, and recovery: Perspectives from the Kauai longitudinal study. *Development and Psychopathology, 5*, 503–515. doi:10.1017/S095457940000612X

Werner, E. E., & Smith, R. S. (1982). *Vulnerable but invincible: A longitudinal study of resilient children and youth.* New York, NY: McGraw-Hill.

Werner, G., & Mitterauer, B. J. (2013). Neuromodulatory systems. *Frontiers in Neural Circuits, 7*, 36. doi:10.3389/fncir.2013.00036

Wertheimer, M. (1970). *A brief history of psychology.* New York, NY: Holt Rinehart & Winston.

Wertsch, J. V. (2007). Mediation. In H. Daniels, M. Cole, & J. V. Wertsch (Eds.), *The Cambridge Companion to Vygotsky* (pp. 178–192). New York, NY: Cambridge University Press. doi:10.1017/CCOL0521831040.008

Wessinger, C. M., Buonocore, M. H., Kussmaul, C. L., & Mangun, G. R. (1997). Tonotopy in human auditory cortex examined with functional magnetic resonance imaging. *Human Brain Mapping, 5*, 18–25. doi:10.1002/(SICI)1097-0193(1997)5:1<18::AID-HBM3>3.0.CO;2-Q

Westen, D. (1999). Scientific status of unconscious processes: Is Freud really dead? *Journal of American Psychoanalytic Association, 47*, 1061–1106. doi:10.1177/000306519904700404

Westen, D. (2007). *The political brain: The role of emotion in deciding the fate of the nation.* New York, NY: Public Affairs.

Wethington, E. (2000). Expecting stress: Americans and the "midlife crisis." *Motivation and Emotion, 24*, 85–103. doi:10.1023/A:1005611230993

Wethington E., Kessler, R. C., & Pixley, J. E. (2004). Turning points in adulthood. In O. G. Brim, C. D. Ryff, & R. C. Kessler (Eds.), *How Healthy Are We? A National Study of Well-Being at Midlife* (pp. 585–613). Chicago, IL: The University of Chicago Press.

Wexler, M., & van Boxtel, J. J. A. (2005). Depth perception by the active observer. *Trends in Cognitive Sciences, 9*, 431–438. doi:10.1016/j.tics.2005.06.018

Wheeler, V. (2008, April 21). Gillian is terrified of buttons: Student Gillian Linkins suffers one of the world's most bizarre phobias—A fear of buttons. *The Sun.* Retrieved from http://www.thesun.co.uk/sol/homepage/news/1066163/Student-is-terrified-of-buttons.html

White, R. W. (1959). Motivation reconsidered: The concept of competence. *Psychological Review, 66*, 297–333. doi:10.1037/h0040934

Whiteman, S. D., McHale, S. M., & Crouter, A. C. (2003). What parents learn from experience: The first child as a first draft? *Journal of Marriage and Family, 65*, 608–621. doi:10.1111/j.1741-3737.2003.00608.x

Who Concert Tragedy Task Force. (1980, July 8). *Crowd management: Report of the Task Force on Crowd Control and Safety* (Report). Cincinnati, OH. Retrieved from http://www.crowdsafe.com/taskrpt/

Whorf, B. L. (1956). *Language, thought and reality*. Cambridge, MA: MIT Press.

Wierzbicka, A. (1999). *Emotions across languages and cultures: Diversity and universals*. Cambridge, UK: Cambridge University Press. doi:10.1017/CBO9780511521256

Wilgus, J., & Wilgus, B. (2009). Face to Face with Phineas Gage. *Journal of the History of the Neurosciences, 18*, 340–345.doi:10.1080/09647040903018402

Williams, C. (2011, August 25). Crittervision: What a dog's nose knows. *NewScientist, 2826*. Available from http://www.newscientist.com/article/mg21128262.000-crittervision-what-a-dogs-nose-knows.html

Williams, J. M. G., & Wells, J. (1989). Suicidal patients. In J. Scott, J. M. G. Williams, & A. T. Beck (Eds.), *Cognitive Therapy in Clinical Practice* (pp. 118–128). London, England: Routledge. doi:10.4324/9780203359365_chapter_nine

Williams, L. E., & Bargh, J. A. (2008). Experiencing physical warmth promotes interpersonal warmth. *Science, 322*, 606–607. doi:10.1126/science.1162548

Williams, S. J., Seale, C., Boden, S., Lowe, P., & Steinberg, D. L. (2008). Waking up to sleepiness: Modafinil, the media and the pharmaceuticalisation of everyday/night life. *Sociology of Health & Illness, 30*, 839–855. doi:10.1111/j.1467-9566.2008.01084.x

Williams, S. L., & Zane, G. (1997). Guided mastery treatment of phobias. *The Clinical Psychologist, 50*, 13–15.

Wilmoth, J. R. (2000). Demography of longevity: Past, present, and future trends. *Experimental Gerontology, 35*, 1111–1129. doi:10.1016/S0531-5565(00)00194-7

Wilson, E. (1922, July 5). A review of James Joyce's *Ulysses. New Republic*. Retrieved from http://www.newrepublic.com/book/review/ulysses

Wilson, M. (2002). Six views of embodied cognition. *Psychonomic Bulletin & Review, 9*, 625–636. doi:10.3758/BF03196322

Wilson, T. D., & Dunn, E. W. (2004). Self-knowledge: Its limits, value, and potential for improvement. *Annual Review of Psychology, 55*, 493–518. doi:10.1146/annurev.psych.55.090902.141954

Wilson, T. D., & Gilbert, D. T. (2003). Affective forecasting. *Advances in Experimental Social Psychology, 35*, 345–411. doi:10.1016/S0065-2601(03)01006-2

Wilson, T. D., & Linville, P. W. (1985). Improving the performance of college freshmen with attributional techniques. *Journal of Personality and Social Psychology, 49*, 287–293. doi:10.1037//0022-3514.49.1.287

Wilson, T. D., Wheatley, T., Meyers, J. M., Gilbert, D. T., & Axsom, D. (2000). Focalism: A source of durability bias in affective forecasting. *Journal of Personality and Social Psychology, 78*, 821–836. doi:10.1037/0022-3514.78.5.821

Wimmer, H., & Perner, J. (1983). Beliefs about beliefs: Representation and constraining function of wrong beliefs in young children's understanding of deception. *Cognition, 13*, 103–128. doi:10.1016/0010-0277(83)90004-5

Wingfield, N. (2007, July 25). Hide the button: Steve Jobs has his finger on it: Apple CEO never liked the physical doodads, not even on his shirts. *The Wall Street Journal*. Retrieved from http://online.wsj.com/news/articles/SB118532502435077009

Winkielman, P., Halberstadt, J., Fazendeiro, T., & Catty, S. (2006). Prototypes are attractive because they are easy on the mind. *Psychological Science, 17*, 799–806. doi:10.1111/j.1467-9280.2006.01785.x

Winkler, S. (2013). Characteristics of human vision. In R. Lukac (Ed.), *Perceptual digital imaging: Methods and applications* (pp. 1–36). Boca Raton, FL: CRC Press.

Wirth, W. (1908). *Die experimentelle analyse der bewußtseinphänomene* (Experimental analysis of the phenomena of consciousness). Braunschweig: Friedrich Vieweg.

Wise, R. A. (1998). Drug-activation of brain reward pathways. *Drug and Alcohol Dependence, 51*, 13–22. doi:10.1016/S0376-8716(98)00063-5

Wise, R. A. (2004). Dopamine, learning and motivation. *Nature Reviews Neuroscience, 5*, 483–494. doi:10.1038/nrn1406

Wise, R. A., Spindler, J., DeWit, H., & Gerber, G. J. (1978). Neuroleptic-induced "anhedonia" in rats: Pimozide blocks reward quality of food. *Science, 201*, 262–264. doi:10.1126/science.566469

Witelson, S. F., Kigar, D., & Harvey, T. 1999. The exceptional brain of Albert Einstein. *Lancet, 353*, 2149–2153. doi:10.1016/S0140-6736(98)10327-6

Withagen, R., & Michaels, C. F. (2005). On ecological conceptualizations of perceptual systems and action systems. *Theory & Psychology, 15*, 603–620. doi:10.1177/0959354305057265

Wittchen, H. U., Gloster, A. T., Beesdo-Baum, K., Fava, G. A., & Craske, M. G. (2010). Agoraphobia: A review of the diagnostic classificatory position and criteria. *Depression and Anxiety, 27*, 113–133. doi:10.1002/da.20646

Wittchen, H. U., & Hoyer, J. (2001). Generalized anxiety disorder: Nature and course. *Journal of Clinical Psychiatry, 62*(s11), 15–19.

Wittgenstein, L. (1953). *Philosophical investigations*. New York, NY: Macmillan.

Wittgenstein, L. (1967). *Zettel* (G. E. M. Anscombe & G. H. von Wright, Eds., G. E. M. Anscombe, Trans.). Berkeley, CA: University of California Press.

Wolpe, J. (1958). *Psychotherapy by reciprocal inhibition*. Stanford, CA: Stanford University Press.

Wong, F., & Halgin, R. (2006). The "model minority": Bane or blessing for Asian Americans? *Journal of Multicultural Counseling and Development, 34*, 38–49. doi:10.1002/j.2161-1912.2006.tb00025.x

Wood, J. N., & Grafman, J. (2003). Human prefrontal cortex: Processing and representational perspectives. *Nature Reviews Neuroscience, 4*, 139–147. doi:10.1038/nrn1033

Wood, R. L., & Williams, C. (2008). Inability to empathize following traumatic brain injury. *Journal of the International Neuropsychological Society, 14*, 289–296. doi:10.1017/S1355617708080326

Woods, D. L., & Alain, C. (2009). Functional imaging of human auditory cortex. *Current Opinion in Otolaryngology & Head and Neck Surgery, 17*, 407–411. doi:10.1097/MOO.0b013e3283303330

Woods, S., Schwartz, M., Baskin, D., & Seeley, R. (2000). Food intake and the regulation of body weight. *Annual Review of Psychology, 51*, 255–277. doi:10.1146/annurev.psych.51.1.255

Woodward, J. (2003). *Making things happen: A theory of causal explanation*. New York, NY: Oxford University Press.

Woollett, K., & Maguire, E. A. (2011). Acquiring "the knowledge" of London's layout drives structural brain changes. *Current Biology, 21*, 2109–2114. doi:10.1016/j.cub.2011.11.018

Woollett, K., Spiers, H. J., & Maguire, E. A. (2009). Talent in the taxi: A model system for exploring expertise. *Philosophical Transactions of the Royal Society of London. Series B, Biological Sciences, 364*, 1407–1416. doi:10.1098/rstb.2008.0288

World Health Organization. (2004). *Neuroscience of psychoactive substance use and dependence.* Geneva, Switzerland: World Health Organization. Retrieved from http://www.who.int/substance_abuse/publications/en/Neuroscience.pdf

World Health Organization. (n.d.). Poverty and health. In *Health and development programmes.* Retrieved from http://www.who.int/hdp/poverty/en/

World-Elephants (based on ancient Hindu myth), http://www.native-science.net/Turtle_Elephant_Myth.htm

Worth, R., & Annese, J. (2012). Brain Observatory and the continuing study of H. M.: Interview with Jacopo Annese. *Europe's Journal of Psychology, 8,* 222–230. doi:10.5964/ejop.v8i2.475

Wright, J. C., & Mischel, W. (1987). A conditional approach to dispositional constructs: The local predictability of social behavior. *Journal of Personality and Social Psychology, 53,* 1159–1177. doi:10.1037/0022-3514.53.6.1159

Wright, R. (for TIME). (2004, April 26). The 2004 TIME 100: Steven Pinker. *TIME,* Vol. 163, No. 17. Retrieved from http://www.time.com/time/specials/packages/article/0,28804,1970858_1970909_1971671,00.html

Wright, S. (1978). The relation of livestock breeding to theories of evolution. *Journal of Animal Science, 46,* 1192–1200. Retrieved from http://www.animal-science.org/content/46/5/1192.short

Wu, C. C., Sacchet, M. D., & Knutson, B. (2012). Toward an affective neuroscience account of financial risk taking. *Frontiers in Neuroscience, 6,* 159–168. doi:10.3389/fnins.2012.00159

Wu, E. Q., Birnbaum, H. G., Shi, L., Ball, D. E., Kessler, R. C., Moulis, M., & Aggarwal, J. (2005). The economic burden of schizophrenia in the United States in 2002. *Journal of Clinical Psychiatry, 66,* 1122–1129. doi:10.4088/JCP.v66n0906

Wyatt, T. D. (2009). Fifty years of pheromones. *Nature, 457,* 262–263. doi:10.1038/457262a

Xie, L., Kang, H., Xu, Q., Chen, M. J., Liao, Y., Thiyagarajan, M., . . . & Nedergaard, M. (2013). Sleep drives metabolite clearance from the adult brain. *Science, 342,* 373–377. doi:10.1126/science.1241224

Xinyan, X. (2013). Chinese dialectical thinking—The yin yang model. *Philosophy Compass 8/5,* 438–446. doi:10.1111/phc3.12035

Xu, C., Aragam, N., Li, X., Villla, E. C., Wang, L., Briones, D., . . . & Wang, K. (2013). BCL9 and C9orf5 are associated with negative symptoms in schizophrenia: Meta-analysis of two genome-wide association studies. *PloS ONE, 8,* e51674. doi:10.1371/journal.pone.0051674

Xu, M. Q., Sun, W. S., Liu, B. X., Feng, G. Y., Yu, L., Yang, L., . . . & He, L. (2009). Prenatal malnutrition and adult schizophrenia: Further evidence from the 1959–1961 Chinese famine. *Schizophrenia Bulletin, 35,* 568–576. doi:10.1093/schbul/sbn168

Yalom, I. D. (1970). *The theory and practice of group psychotherapy.* New York, NY: Basic Books.

Yang, C. (2013). Ontogeny and phylogeny of language. *Proceedings of the National Academy of Sciences, 110,* 6324–6327. doi:10.1073/pnas.1216803110

Younger, J., Aron, A., Parke, S., Chatterjee, N., & Mackey, S. (2010). Viewing pictures of a romantic partner reduces experimental pain: Involvement of neural reward systems. *PLoS One, 5,* e13309. doi:10.1371/journal.pone.0013309

Zajonc, R. B. (1965). Social facilitation. *Science, 149,* 269–274. doi:10.1126/science.149.3681.269

Zajonc, R. B. (1980). Feeling and thinking: Preferences need no inferences. *American Psychologist, 35,* 151–175. doi:10.1037/0003-066X.35.2.151

Zajonc, R. B. (2001). Mere exposure: A gateway to the subliminal. *Current Directions in Psychological Science, 10,* 224–228. doi:10.1111/1467-8721.00154

Zanarini, M. C., Frankenburg, F. R., DeLuca, C. J., Hennen, J., Khera, G. S., & Gunderson, J. G. (1998). The pain of being borderline: Dysphoric states specific to borderline personality disorder. *Harvard Review of Psychiatry, 6,* 201–207. doi:10.3109/10673229809000330

Zatorre, R., Belin, P., & Penhune, V. (2002). Structure and function of auditory cortex: Music and speech. *Trends in Cognitive Sciences, 6,* 37–46. doi:10.1016/S1364-6613(00)01816-7

Zatorre, R., Fields, R., & Johansen-Berg, H. (2013). Plasticity in gray and white: Neuroimaging changes in brain structure during learning. *Nature Neuroscience, 15,* 528–536. doi:10.1038/nn.3045

Zentner, M., & Bates, J. E. (2008). Child temperament: An integrative review of concepts, research programs, and measures. *International Journal of Developmental Science, 2,* 7–37. doi:10.3233/DEV-2008-21203

Zentner, M., & Renaud, O. (2007). Origins of adolescents' ideal self: An intergenerational perspective. *Journal of Personality and Social Psychology, 92,* 557–574. doi:10.1037/0022-3514.92.3.557

Zhang, F., Wang, G., Shugart, Y. Y., Xu, Y., Liu, C., Wang, L., . . . & Zhang, D. (2014). Association analysis of a functional variant in ATXN2 with schizophrenia. *Neuroscience Letters, 562,* 24–27. doi:10.1016/j.neulet.2013.12.001

Zhang, L. I., & Poo, M. M. (2001). Electrical activity and development of neural circuits. *Nature Neuroscience, 4,* 1207–1214. doi:10.1038/nn753

Zhu, G., Evans, D. M., Duffy, D. L., Montgomery, G. W., Medland, S. E., Gillespie, N. A, . . . & Martin, N. G. (2004). A genome scan for eye color in 502 twin families: Most variation is due to a QTL on chromosome 15q. *Twin Research, 7,* 197–210. doi:10.1375/13690520432301 6186

Zimbardo, P. G. (1970). A social-psychological analysis of vandalism: Making sense out of senseless violence. (No. ONR-TR-Z-05). Technical report, Stanford University, Department of Psychology.

Zimbardo, P. G. (1970). The human choice: Individuality, reason, and order versus deindividuation, impulse, and chaos. In W. J. Arnold & D. Levine (Eds.), *Nebraska Symposium on Motivation.* Lincoln, NE: University of Nebraska Press.

Zimbardo, P. G. (1977). *Shyness: What it is, what to do about it.* Reading, MA: Addison-Wesley.

Zimbardo, P. G. (2007). *The lucifer effect: Understanding how good people turn evil.* New York, NY: Random House.

Zimmerman, M. E., Pan, J. W., Hetherington, H. P., Katz, M. J., Verghese, J., Buschke, H., . . . & Lipton, R. B. (2008). Hippocampal neurochemistry, neuromorphometry, and verbal memory in nondemented older adults. *Neurology, 70,* 1594–1600. doi:10.1212/01.wnl.0000306314.77311.be

Zitzmann, M., & Nieschlag, E. (2001). Testosterone levels in healthy men and the relation to behavioural and physical characteristics: Facts and constructs. *European Journal of Endocrinology, 144,* 183–197. doi:10.1530/eje.0.1440183

Zoch, P. A. (1998). *Ancient Rome: An introductory history.* Norman, OK: Oklahoma University Press.

Name Index

Subject Index